UNITED ★ STATES

POSTAGE STAMPS

CATALOG & PRICE GUIDE

GENERAL & COMMEMORATIVE
POSTAL STATIONERY

91ST EDITION

REVENUE STAMPS • AIR POST
U.S. POSSESSIONS

2026 UNITED STATES POSTAGE STAMP CATALOG

At just 14 years old, Henry Ellis Harris placed a free ad in the *Washington Post* in June 1916 offering a risk-free deal—a packet of 10 postage stamps at a $2.00 catalog value for 50 cents—and steadily grew his customer base from there. By 1931, "Harris" had become the most prominent name in stamp collecting, with advertisements in popular magazines like *Boys' Life*, *Popular Mechanics*, and *King Comics*, and even on matchbook covers. In 1935, Harris published the first 64-page Harris US/BNA Catalog, covering United States and British North American stamps. This catalog has since won seven international awards, and it continues to be published today as America's best-selling stamp price guide.

Now, over 100 years after that first free ad, H.E. Harris remains dedicated to providing quality postage stamps, beautifully crafted stamp albums, and the renowned Harris *Postage Stamp Catalog and Price Guide* to collectors.

ISBN: 0794854559

4001 Helton Drive • Building A • Florence, Alabama 35630
Designed in U.S.A. / Printed in China

ABOUT OUR CATALOG PRICES

The prices quoted in this catalog are the prices for which H.E. Harris offers stamps for retail sale at the time of publication. (*Harris no longer offers first day covers for sale.*)

These prices are based on current market values as researched by our staff, but, more importantly, on our day-to-day buying and selling activities in the stamp market.

Although you may certainly use this catalog as a guide to current market prices, you must keep in mind the fact that prices can change in response to varying levels of collector demand, or dealer promotions, and/or special purchases. We are not responsible for typographical errors.

You should also remember that condition is always the key factor in determining the value and price of a given stamp or set of stamps. Unlike some other stamp catalogs, we price U.S. stamps issued up to 1935 in three different condition grades for unused and used examples. For these earlier issues, we have also shown the percentage premium that would apply to Never Hinged Mint examples.

Our illustrated definitions of condition grades are presented on pages XII-XIII.

We have not found it possible to keep every stamp in stock that is listed in this catalog, and we cannot guarantee that we can supply all of the stamps in all conditions that are listed.

However, we will search for any stamp in any condition that a customer may want if that stamp is not in our stock at the time the customer places an order for it.

CONTENTS

UNITED STATES STAMPS

UNITED STATES POSSESSIONS

ADDITIONAL FEATURES

A GUIDE FOR COLLECTORS

In this section we will attempt to define and explain some of the terms commonly used by stamp collectors. Instead of listing the terms in an alphabetical dictionary or glossary format, we have integrated them. In this way, you can see how an individual term fits within the total picture.

PRODUCTION

The manufacture of stamps involves a number of procedures. We will discuss the major steps here, with emphasis on their implications for stamp collectors. Although we present them separately, modern printing presses may combine one or more operations so that the steps tend to blend together. There also are steps in the process that we do not cover here. While they may be important to the production process, their direct implications for most collectors are minimal.

PLATE MAKING

Before anything can be printed, a printing plate must be made. Using the intaglio printing process (which is explained under **printing**) as an example, the steps involved in plate production are as follows:

- A **master die** is made. The design is recess engraved in a reverse mirror-image. Most master dies consist of only one impression of the design.
- The next step is to prepare a **transfer roll**. The soft steel of the transfer roll is rocked back and forth under pressure against the hardened master die and a series of multiple impressions, called **reliefs**, are created in the transfer roll. Note that the impression on the transfer roll will be raised above the surface, since the roll was pressed into the recesses of the master die.
- Once the transfer roll has been made and hardened, it is used to impress designs in to the soft steel of a **printing plate** that can fit up to 400 impressions of small, definitive-sized stamps or 200 impressions of large, commemorative-sized stamps. This time, the raised design on the transfer roll impresses a recessed design into the plate.

The process is much more complex than this, but these are the basics. Once the printing plate is hardened, it is almost ready to be used to create printed sheets of stamps. Depending on the printing equipment to be used, the printing plate will be shaped to fit around a cylinder for rotary press printing or remain flat for flat-bed press printing. In either form, the plate is then hardened and is ready for use in printing.

DESIGN VARIETIES

The complexity of the platemaking process can result in major or minor flaws. The inspection process will catch most of these flaws, but those that escape detection will result in **plate varieties**.

The early United States Classic issues have been examined in minute detail over the decades. Through **plating** studies, minor differences in individual stamps have been used to identify the position on the printing plate of each design variety. Sometimes called **"flyspeck philately"** because it involves the detection of minute "flyspeck" differences, such plating work has resulted in the identification of some of our greatest rarities. Compare the prices for the one cent blue issues of 1851 and 1857 (#s 5-9 and 18-24) and you will see the tremendous dollar difference that can result from minute design variations. (The Harris Stamp Identifier in this catalog explains the design differences.)

During the plate making or subsequent printing process, plate flaws that are detected will be corrected, sometimes incompletely or incorrectly. Corrections or revisions in an individual die impression or in all plate impressions include the following:

- **Retouching**—minor corrections made in a plate to repair damage or wear.
- **Recutting or re-engraving**—similar to, but more extensive than, retouching. Recutting usually applies to changes made before a plate has been hardened, while re-engraving is performed on a plate that has had to be tempered (softened) after hardening.
- **Redrawing**—the intentional creation of a slightly different design. The insertion of secret marks on the National Bank Notes plates when they were turned over to the Continental Bank Note Company in 1873 can be considered redrawings.
- **Reentry**—the reapplication of a design from a transfer roll to the plate, usually to improve a worn plate. If the reentry is not done completely, or if it is not done precisely on top of the previous design, a double transfer will result. Such double transfers will show on the printed stamp as an extra line at one or more points on the stamp.

Other design varieties may result from undetected plate flaws. A **plate crack** (caused by the hardened plate cracking under wear or pressure) or a **plate scratch** (caused by an object cutting into the plate) will show as an ink line on the printed stamp.

One other group that can be covered here to avoid possible confusion includes **reissues, reprints, special printings and reproductions**. None of these are design varieties that result from plate flaws, corrections or revisions. In fact, reissues, reprints and special printings are made from the same, unchanged plates as the originals. They show no differences in design and usually can be identified only by variations in paper, color or gum. Reproductions (such as U.S. #3 and #4), on the other hand, are made from entirely new plates and, therefore, can be expected to show some variation from the originals.

ERRORS, FREAKS, ODDITIES

"EFOs", as they are called, are printed varieties that result from abnormalities in the production process. They are design varieties, but of a special nature because the result looks different from the norm. When you see them, you know something went wrong. Basically, freaks and oddities can be loosely defined as minor errors. They include the following:

• **Misperforations**, that is, the placement of the perforations within the design rather than at the margins.
• **Foldovers**, caused by a sheet being turned, usually at a corner, before printing and/or perforating. The result is part of a design printed on the reverse of the sheet or placement of perforations at odd angles. Such freaks and oddities may be of relatively minor value, but they do make attractive additions to a collection. Truly major errors, on the other hand, can be of tremendous value. It would not be overstating the case to argue that many collectors are initially drawn to the hobby by the publicity surrounding discoveries of valuable errors and the hope that they might someday do the same. Major errors include the following:
• **Inverts.** These are the most dramatic and most valuable of all major errors and almost always result from printing processes that require more than one pass of a sheet through the presses. If the sheet inadvertently gets "flipped" between passes, the portion printed on the second pass will emerge inverted.
Two definitions we should introduce here are **"frame" and "vignette"**. The vignette is the central design of the stamp; the frame encloses the vignette and, at its outer edges, marks the end of the printed stamp design. Oftentimes, stamps described as inverted centers (vignettes) actually are inverted frames. The center was properly printed in the first pass and the frame was inverted in the second pass.
• **Color errors.** The most noticeable color errors usually involve one or more omitted colors. The sheet may not have made it through the second pass in a two-step printing process. In the past such errors were extremely rare because they were obvious enough to be noticed by inspectors. In modern multi-color printings, the chances of such errors escaping detection have increased. Nonetheless, they still qualify as major errors and carry a significant premium. *Other color errors involve the use of an incorrect color. They may not seem as dramatic as missing colors, but the early issues of many countries include some very rare and valuable examples of these color errors. Although technically not a color error, we can include here one of the most unusual of all errors, the United States 1917 5-cent stamps that are supposed to be blue, but are found in the carmine or rose color of the 2-cent stamps. The error was not caused by a sheet of the 5-centers being printed in the wrong color, as you might expect. Rather, because a few impressions on a 2-cent plate needed reentry, they were removed. But an error was made and the 5-cent design was entered. Thus it is a reentry error, but is described in most catalogs as a color error because that is the apparent result. Whatever the description, the 5-cent denomination surrounded by 2-cent stamps is a real showpiece.
• **Imperfs.** A distinction should be drawn here between imperforate errors and intentionally imperforate stamps. When the latter carry a premium value over their perforated counterparts, it is because they were printed in smaller quantities for specialized usages. They might have been intended, for example, for sale to vending machine manufacturers who would privately perforate the imperforate sheets.
On the other hand, errors in which there is absolutely no trace of a perforation between two stamps that were supposed to be perforated carry a premium based on the rarity of the error. Some modern United States coil imperforate errors have been found in such large quantities that they carry little premium value. But imperforate errors found in small quantities represent tremendous rarities.
Be they intentional or errors, imperforate stamps are commonly collected in pairs or larger multiples because it can be extremely difficult—often impossible, to distinguish them from stamps that have had their perforations trimmed away in an attempt to pass them off as more valuable imperfs. Margin singles that show the stamp and a wide, imperforate selvage at one of the edges of the sheet are another collecting option.

PRINTING

There are three basic printing methods:

1. Intaglio, also known as **recess** printing. Line engraved below the surface of the printing plate (that is, in recess) accept the ink and apply it to damp paper that is forced into the recesses of the plate. Intaglio methods include **engraved** and **photogravure (or rotogravure)**. Photogravure is regarded by some as separate from intaglio because the engraving is done by chemical etching and the finished product can be distinguished from hand or machine engraving.
2. Typography. This is similar to intaglio in that it involves engraving, but the action is in reverse with the design left at the surface of the plate and the portions to be unprinted cut away. Ink is then applied to the surface design, which is imprinted onto paper. **Typeset** letterpress printing is the most common form of typography.
3. Lithography. This method differs from the previous two in that it involves **surface printing**, rather than engraving. Based on the principle that oil and water do not mix, the design to be printed is applied with a greasy ink onto a plate that is then wet with a watery fluid. Printing ink run across the plate is accepted only at the greased (oiled) points. The ink applies the design to paper that is brought in contact with the plate. **Offset** printing, a modern lithographic method, involves a similar approach, but uses a rubber blanket to transfer the inked design to paper.

PRINTING, CONTINUED

The printing method that was used to produce a given stamp can be determined by close inspection of that stamp.

1. Because the paper is pressed into the grooves of an intaglio plate, when viewed from the surface the design appears to be slightly raised. Running a fingernail lightly across the surface also will reveal this raised effect. When viewed from the back, the design will appear to be recessed (or pressed out toward the surface). Photogravure stamps have a similar appearance and feel, but when viewed under a magnifier, they reveal a series of dots, rather than line engravings.

2. Because the raised design on a plate is pressed into the paper when the typograph process is used, when viewed from the surface, the printing on the stamp does not have the raised effect of an intaglio product. On the other hand, when viewed from the reverse, a raised impression will be evident where the design was imprinted. Overprints often are applied by typography and usually show the raised effect on the back of the stamp.

3. Unlike either of the previous two methods, lithographed stamps look and feel flat. This dull, flat effect can be noticed on any of the United States 1918-20 offset printings, #525-536.

WATERMARKS

This actually is one of the first steps in the stamp production process because it is part of paper manufacturing. A watermark is a slight thinning of the paper pulp, usually in the form of a relevant design. It is applied by devices attached to the rolls on papermaking machines. Without getting involved in the technical aspects, the result is a watermark that can sometimes be seen when held to the light, but more often requires watermark detector fluid.

A word of caution here. Such detector fluids may contain substances that can be harmful when inhaled. This is particularly true of lighter fluids that often are used by collectors in lieu of specially made stamp watermark detector fluids.

Watermarks are used to help detect counterfeits. Although it is possible to reproduce the appearance of a watermark, it is extremely difficult. The authorities have at times been able to identify a counterfeit by the lack of a watermark that should be present or by the presence of an incorrect watermark.

On the other hand, there are occasions when the incorrect or absent watermark did not indicate a counterfeit, but a printing error. The wrong paper may have been used or the paper may have been inserted incorrectly (resulting in an inverted or sideways watermark). The United States 30 cent orange red that is listed among the 1914-17 issues on unwatermarked paper (#467A) is an example of a printing error. It was produced on watermarked paper as part of the 1914-15 series, but a few sheets were discovered without watermarks.

Unfortunately, the difficulty encountered in detecting watermarks on light shades, such as orange or yellow, makes experts very reluctant to identify single copies of #476A. Although not visible, the watermark just might be there.

Because an examination of a full sheet allows the expert to examine the unprinted selvage and all stamps on that sheet at one time, positive identification is possible and most of the stamps that come down to us today as #476A trace back to such full sheets.

GUMMING

Gumming once was almost always applied after printing and before perforating and cutting of sheets into panes. Today, pregummed paper may be used, so the placement of this step in the process cannot be assured—nor is it the sequence of much significance.

The subject of gum will be treated more fully in the **Condition** section of this catalog. At this point, we will only note that certain stamps can be identified by their gum characteristics. Examples include the identification of rotary press stamps by the presence of gum breaker ridges or lines and the detection of the presence of original gum on certain stamps that indicates they can not be a rarer issue that was issued without gum, such as #40-47. Others, such as #102-111, can be identified in part by their distinctive white, crackly original gum.

PERFORATING

We have already discussed the absence of perforations in the **Errors** section. Here we will concentrate on the perforating process itself.

All perforating machines use devices to punch holes into the printed stamp paper. The holes usually are round and are known as perforations. When two adjacent stamps are separated, the semicircular cutouts are the **perforations**; the remaining paper between the perforations forms **perf tips**, or **"teeth"**.

Most perforations are applied by perforators that contain a full row of punches that are driven through the paper as it is fed through the perforating equipment. **Line Perforators** drive the punches up and down; **rotary perforators** are mounted on cylinders that revolve. There are other techniques, but these are the most common.

To clear up one point of confusion, the **perforation size** (for example, "perf 11") is not the size of the hole or the number of perforations on the side of a given stamp. Rather, it describes the number of perforations that could be fit within two centimeters.

A perf 8 stamp will have visibly fewer perforations than a perf 12 stamp, but it is much harder to distinguish between perf 11 and perf 10½. **Perforation gauges** enable collectors to make these distinctions with relative ease.

TAGGING

Modern, high-speed, mechanical processing of mail has created the need for "tagging" stamps by coating them with a luminescent substance that could be detected under ultraviolet (UV) light or by printing them on paper that included such substances. When passed under a machine capable of detecting these substances, an envelope can be positioned and the stamp automatically cancelled, thereby eliminating time-consuming and tedious manual operations. The tagged varieties of certain predominantly untagged stamps, such as #1036 and #C67, do carry modest premiums. There also are technical differences between phosphorescent and fluorescent types of luminescent substances. But these details are primarily of interest to specialists and will not be discussed in this general work.

PAPER

The fact that we have not devoted more attention to paper should not be an indication of any lack of interest or significance. Books have been written on this one subject alone, and a lack of at least a rudimentary knowledge of the subject can lead to misidentification of important varieties and result in financial loss.

The three most common categories of paper on which stamps are printed are **wove, laid, and India.** The most frequently used is machine-made **wove paper**, similar to that used for most books. The semiliquid pulp for wove paper is fed onto a fine wire screen and is processed much the same as cloth would be woven. Almost all United States postage stamps are printed on wove paper.

Laid paper is formed in a process that uses parallel wires rather than a uniform screen. As a result, the paper will be thinner where the pulp was in contact with the wires. When held to the light, alternating light and dark lines can be seen. Laid paper varieties have been found on some early United States stamps.

India paper is very thin and tough, without any visible texture. It is, therefore, more suited to obtaining the sharp impressions that are needed for printers' pre-production proofs, rather than to the high-volume printing of stamps.

Other varieties include **bluish** paper, so described because of the tone created by certain substances added to the paper, and silk paper, which contains threads or fibers of silk that usually can be seen on the back of the stamp. Many United States revenue stamps were printed on silk paper.

COLLECTING FORMATS

Whatever the production method, stamps reach the collector in a variety of forms. The most common is in sheet, or more correctly, pane form.

Sheets are the full, uncut units as they come from a press. Before distribution to post offices, these sheets are cut into **panes**. For United States stamps, most regular issues are printed in sheets of 400 and cut into panes of 100; most commemoratives are printed in sheets of 200 and cut into panes of 50. There are numerous exceptions to this general rule, and they are indicated in the mint sheet listings in this catalog. Sheets also are cut in **booklet panes** for only a few stamps—usually four to ten stamps per pane. These panes are assembled in complete booklets that might contain one to five panes, usually stapled together between two covers. An intact booklet is described as **unexploded**; when broken apart it is described as exploded.

Coils are another basic form in which stamps reach post offices. Such stamps are wound into continuous coil rolls, usually containing from 100 to 5,000 stamps, the size depending on the volume needs of the expected customer. Almost all coils are produced with perforations on two opposite sides and straight edges on the remaining two sides. Some serious collectors prefer collecting coils in pairs or strips—two or more adjacent stamps—as further assurance of genuineness. It is much easier to fake a coil single that shows only portions of each perforation hole than a larger unit that shows the complete perf hole.

A variation on this theme is the **coil line pair**—adjacent stamps that show a printed vertical line between. On rotary press stamps the line appears where the two ends of a printing plate meet on a rotary press cylinder. The joint is not complete, so ink falls between the plate ends and is transferred onto the printed coil. On flat plate stamps the guideline is the same as that created for sheet stamps, as described below. **Paste-up** coil pairs are not as popular as line pairs. They were a necessary by-product of flat plate printings in which the coil strips cut from separate sheets had to be pasted together for continuous winding into roll form.

The modern collecting counterpart to coil line pairs is the **plate number strip**—three or five adjacent coil stamps with the plate number displayed on the middle stamp. Transportation coil plate strips have become particularly sought after. On most early coil rolls, the plate numbers were supposed to be trimmed off. Freaks in which the number remains are interesting, but do not carry large premiums since they are regarded as examples of miscut oddities rather than printing errors.

Miniature sheets and souvenir sheets are variations on one theme—small units that may contain only one or at most a much smaller quantity of stamps than would be found on the standard postal panes. Stamps may be issued in miniature sheet format for purposes of expedience, as for example the Bret Harte $5 issue (#2196), which was released in panes of 20 to accommodate the proportionately large demand by collectors for plate blocks rather than single stamps. As the name implies, a souvenir sheet is a miniature sheet that was released as a souvenir to be saved, rather than postally used—although such sheets or the stamps cut out from them can be used as postage. **Note: souvenir cards** are created strictly for promotional and souvenir purposes. They contain stamp reproductions that may vary in size, color or design from the originals and are not valid for postal use.

Often, a common design may be produced in sheet, coil and booklet pane form. The common design is designated by collectors as one **type**, even though it may be assigned many different catalog numbers because of variations in color, size, perforations, printing method, denomination, etc. On the other hand, even minor changes in a basic design represent a new type.

Sheet stamps offer the greatest opportunity for format variation and collecting specialization. Using the following illustration for reference, the varieties that can be derived include the following:

Block (a)—this may be any unit of four stamps or more in at least 2 by 2 format. Unless designated as a different size, blocks are assumed to be blocks of four.

Specialized forms of blocks include:

Arrow block (b)—adjacent stamps at the margin of a sheet, showing the arrow printed in the margin for registration in the printing process, as, for example, in two-color printings. When the arrow designates the point at which a sheet is cut into panes, the result will appear as one leg of the arrow, or V, on each pane. **Guideline block (c)**—similar to arrow block, except that it can be any block that shows the registration line between two rows of two stamps each. **Gutter block**—similar to guideline block, except that an uncolored gutter is used instead of a printed line. The best known United States gutter blocks are those cut from full-sheet "Farley printings". Pairs of stamps from adjacent panes on each side of the gutter form the gutter block. **Imprint, or inscription blocks (d)**—include **copyright, mail early, and ZIP (e) blocks**. On most modern United States sheets, the **selvage (f)**, that is, the margin that borders the outer rows of stamps (f), includes one or more inscriptions in addition to the plate numbers. It may be a copyright protection notice or an inscription that encourages mail users to post their mail early or to use the ZIP code on their mail. Because the inscription appears along the margin, rather than in one of the corners, it is customary to collect copyright blocks and mail early blocks in two rows of three stamps each, with the inscription centered in the margin. The ZIP inscription appears in one of the corners of each pane, so it is collected in corner margin blocks of four. **Plate number block (g)**—this is by far the most popular form of block collecting. On each sheet of stamps, a plate number (or numbers) is printed to identify the printing plate(s) used. Should a damage be discovered, the plate can easily be identified. On flat plate sheets, where the plate number appeared along the margin, the format usually is in plate blocks of six, with the plate number centered in the margin. On rotary press and other sheets where a single plate number appears in one of the four corners of the margin, the customary collecting format is a **corner margin block of four (h)**. This also is true for plate blocks with two plate numbers in two adjacent corner stamps and for modern plates where single digits are used to designate each plate number and the complete series (containing one digit for each printing color) appears in the corner. Before single digits were adopted for modern multi-color printings, the five-digit numbers assigned to each plate might run down a substantial portion of the sheet margin. **Plate strips (i)** are collected in such instances. Their size is two rows times as many stamps as are attached to the margin area that shows all plate numbers. Because a sheet of stamps is cut into separate panes, printing plates include plate numbers that can be seen on each of the cut panes. On modern sheets the plate numbers would be located in each of the four corners of the uncut sheet. Once cut, each of the four panes would show the same plate number in one of its corners. The position of the plate number, which matches the position of the pane on the uncut sheet, is designated as upper left or right and lower left or right. Some specialists seek matched sets. A **matched set** is one of each of the four positions for a given plate number. A **complete matched set** is all positions of all plate numbers for a given issue.

***This diagram is for placement purposes only, and is not an exact reproduction of margin markings.*

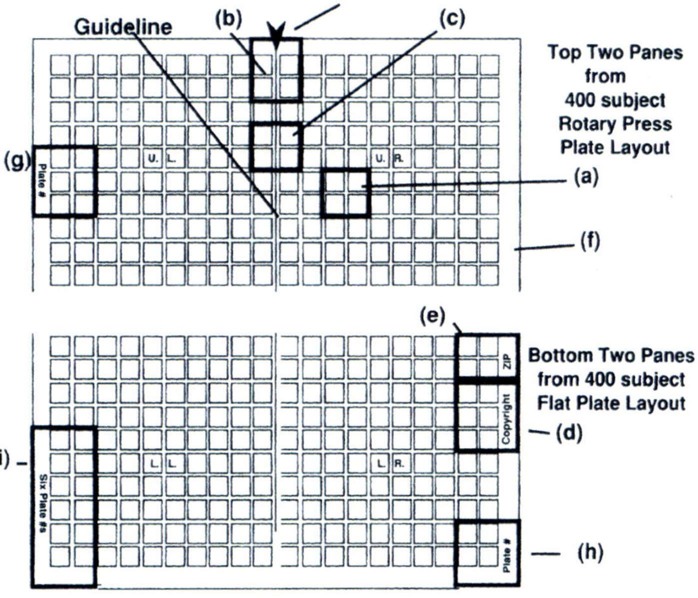

Other definitions that relate in one way or another to the format in which stamps are produced include:

Se-tenant—from the French, meaning joined together. A pair, block, or larger multiple that contains different designs. The 1967 Space Twins issue is an example of a se-tenant pair in which the two different stamps are part of an integral design. The 1968 Historic Flags se-tenant strip contains ten separate designs, each of which can stand alone.

Tete-beche pair—from the French, meaning head-to-tail. Such pairs show adjacent stamps, one of which is upside down in relation to the other.

Proof—any trial impression used in the evaluation of prospective or final designs. Final die proofs—that is, those made from a completed die preparatory to its being used in the production of printing plates—are the standard proof collecting form.

Essay—a partial or complete illustration of a proposed design. In the strict philatelic sense, essays are printed in proof form.

Color trials—a preliminary proof of a stamp design in one or more colors. Trial color proofs are used to select the color in which the stamp will be printed.

Grill—a pattern of embossed cuts that break the stamp paper. See the information at the head of the 1861-67 Issue listings and the section of grills in the Harris Stamp Identifier.

POSTAL MARKINGS

The extensive subject of cancellations and postal markings on stamps and covers is too specialized to present in detail here. Volumes have been written on individual categories of markings—straight line markings, ship cancels, foreign mail cancels, flight covers, etc. In this section we will limit ourselves to the basic definitions related to the stamp and the manner in which it is cancelled, rather than the specialized usage of the envelope to which the stamp is affixed.

- **Manuscript,** or **pen cancels** were the earliest form of "killing" a stamp—that is, marking it to indicate it had been postally used.
- **Handstamps** were created shortly after the first stamps were issued. The early devices might only show a pattern such as a grid and often were carved from cork.
- **Fancy cancels** were an extension of the handstamp. Local postmasters carved cork cancelers that depicted bees, kicking mules, flowers, and hundreds of other figures. Stamps with clear strikes of such fancy cancels usually carry hefty premiums over those with standard cancels.
- **Machine cancels** are applied by mechanical rather than manual means.
- A stamp is **tied** to a cover (or piece) when the cancellation, whatever its form, extends beyond the margins of the stamp onto the cover. Such a tie is one indication of the authenticity of the cover.

Specialized cancellations include the following:

- **Cut cancel**—as the name implies, a cancel that actually cuts the stamp, usually in the form of a thin, straight incision. The most common usage of cut cancels on United States stamps is on Revenue issues.
- **Perfin, or perforated initial**—usually not a cancellation as such, but rather a privately administered punching into the stamp of one or more initials. Most often, the initials were those of a large firm that wished to prevent personal use of their stamps by employees.
- **Precancel**—a cancellation printed on stamps in advance of their sale. The primary purpose of precancels is for sale to large volume mailers, whose mail is delivered to post offices and processed in bulk without necessarily receiving further cancellation.
- **Non-contemporary cancel**—a cancellation applied to a stamp long after the normal period of use for that stamp. A stamp that is worth more used than unused or a damaged unused stamp that would be worth more on cover are examples of candidates for non-contemporary markings.
- **Cancel-to-order, or C.T.O.**—a cancel that is printed on a stamp by an issuing country to give it the appearance of having been used, or to render it invalid for postage in that country. Special fancy cancels or "favor cancels" have been applied at various times in the countries for philatelic reasons.

CATEGORIES

The number of specialized categories into which stamps can be slotted is limited only by the imagination of the individual collector. Some collectors have attempted to collect one of each and every stamp ever issued by every nation that ever existed. Other collectors have concentrated on all the possible varieties and usages of only one stamp. Between these two extremes, stamps can be divided into certain generally accepted categories, whether or not they are used as boundaries for a collection. These categories are as follows:

- **Definitives, or regulars**—stamps that are issued for normal, everyday postage needs. In the United States, they are put on sale for a period limited only by changing rate needs or infrequent issuance of a new definitive series. Post offices can requisition additional stocks of definitives as needed.
- **Commemoratives**—stamps issued to honor a specific event, anniversary, individual or group. They are printed in a predetermined quantity and are intended for sale during a limited period. Although they can be used indefinitely, once stocks are sold out at a local post office, commemoratives usually are not replenished unless the issue has local significance.
- **Pictorials**—stamps that depict a design other than the portrait of an individual or a static design such as a coat of arms or a flag. While some collectors think of these strictly as commemoratives (because most commemoratives are pictorials), some definitives also can be pictorials. Any number of definitives that depict the White House are examples.
- **Airmails, or air posts**—stamps issued specifically for airmail use. Although they do not have to bear a legend, such as "airmail", they usually do. Airmail stamps usually can be used to pay other postage fees. When air flights were a novelty, airmail stamp collecting was an extremely popular specialty. Part of this popularity also can be ascribed to the fact that the first airmail stamps usually were given special attention by issuing postal administrations. Produced using relatively modern technology, they often were among the most attractive of a nation's issues.
- **Zeppelin stamps**—although these do not rate as a major category, they deserve special mention. Zeppelin issues were primarily released for specific use on Zeppelin flights during the 1920s and 1930s. They carried high face values and were issued during the Great Depression period, when most collectors could not afford to purchase them. As a result, most Zeppelin issues are scarce and command substantial premiums. United States "Zepps" are the Graf Zeppelins (C13-C15) and the Century of Progress issue (C18).
- **Back-of-the-book**—specialized stamps that are identified as "back-of-the-book" because of their position in catalogs following the listings of regular and commemorative postal issues. Catalogs identified them with a prefix letter.

Some collectors include airmail stamps in this category, in part because they carry a prefix letter (C) and are listed separately. Most collectors treat the airmails as part of a standard collection and begin the back-of-the-book section with semi-postals (B) or, for the United States, special deliveries (E). Other frequently used "b-o-b" categories include postage dues (J), offices in China, or Shanghais (K), officials (O), parcel posts (Q), newspapers (PR), and revenues (R), the latter including "Duck" hunting permit stamps (RW).

CATEGORIES, CONTINUED

Postal stationery and postal cards are the major non-stamp back-of-the-book categories. A complete envelope or card is called an **entire**; the cutout corner from such a piece, showing the embossed or otherwise printed design, is described as a **cut square**.

Some collecting categories do not relate to the intended use of the stamps. Examples include **topicals** (stamps collected by the theme of the design, such as sports, dance, paintings, space, etc.) and **first day covers**. Modern first day covers show a stamp or stamps postmarked in a designated first day city on the official first day of issue. The cancel design will relate to the issue and the cover may bear a privately-printed cachet that further describes and honors the subject of the stamp.

One of the oddities of the hobby is that **stampless covers** are an accepted form of "stamp" collecting. Such covers display a usage without a stamp, usually during the period before stamps were required for the payment of postage. They bear manuscript or handstamps markings such as "due 5," "PAID," etc. to indicate the manner in which postage was paid.

Although they do not constitute a postal marking, we can include **bisects** here for want of a better place. A bisect is a stamp cut in half and used to pay postage in the amount of one-half of the stamp's denomination. The 1847 ten cent stamp (#2) cut in half and used to pay the five cent rate is an example.

Bisects should be collected only on cover and properly tied. They also should reflect an authorized usage, for example, from a post office that was known to lack the proper denomination, and should pay an amount called for by the usage shown on the cover.

Not discussed in detail here is the vast subject of **covers**, or postal history. Envelopes, usually but not necessarily showing a postal use, are described by collectors as covers. Early "covers" actually were single letter sheets with a message on one side and folded into the form of an enclosing wrapper when viewed from the outside. The modern aerogramme, or air letter, is similar in design to these early folded letters.

USED STAMPS

For used stamps, the presence of gum would be the exception, since it would have been removed when the stamp was washed from the envelope, so gum is not a factor on used stamps. The centering definitions, on the other hand, would be the same as for unused issues. In addition, the cancellation would be a factor. We should point out here that we are not referring to the type of cancellation, such as a fancy cancel that might add considerably to the value of a stamp, or a manuscript cancel that reduces its value. Rather, we are referring to the degree to which the cancellation covers the stamp. A **lightly cancelled** used stamp, with all of the main design elements showing and the usage evidenced by an unobtrusive cancel, is the premier condition sought by collectors of used stamps. On the other hand, a stamp whose design has been substantially obliterated by a **heavy cancel** is at best a space filler that should be replaced by a moderate to lightly cancelled example.

PERFORATIONS

The condition of a stamp's perforations can be determined easily by visual examination. While not necessarily perfect, all perforations should have full teeth and clean perforation holes. A **blunt perf** is one that is shorter than it should be, while a **pulled perf** actually shows a portion of the margin or design having been pulled away. **Blind perfs** are the opposite: paper remains where the perforation hole should have been punched out. One irony of the demand for perforation is that **straight edges**, that is, the normal sheet margin straight edge that was produced when flat-plate sheets were cut into panes, are not acceptable to many collectors. In fact, many collectors will prefer a reperforated stamp to a straight edge. (Technically, **"re"perforated** can only apply to a stamp that is being perforated again, as when a damaged or excessive margin has been cut away and new perforations are applied, but we will follow the common practice of including the perforation of normal straight edges in this category). As a result of this preference, many straight edges no longer exist as such. When one considers that they were in the minority to start with (a pane of 100 flat plate stamps would include 19 straight edges) and that even fewer come down to us today, an argument could be made that they may someday be rarities...although it is hard to conceive of anyone paying a premium for straight edges.

FAKES, FAULTS, AND EXPERTIZING

Below the first quality level—stamps free of defects—a range of stamps can be found from attractive **"seconds"** that have barely noticeable flaws to **space fillers** that may have a piece missing and which ought to be replaced by a better copy—unless we are talking about great rarities which would otherwise be beyond the budget of most collectors. The more common flaws include **thins, tears, creases, stains, pulled perfs, pinholes** (some dealers and collectors used to display their stamps pinned to boards), **face scuffs** or erasures, and **fading**. Stamps with faults sometimes are **repaired**, either to protect them from further damage or to deceive collectors.

While the terms that are applied to stamps that are not genuine often are used interchangeably, they do have specific meaning, as follows:

- **fakes** (in French, faux; in German, falsch)—stamps that appear to be valuable varieties, but which were made from cheaper genuine stamps. Trimming away the perforations to create an imperforate is a common example of a fake.
- **bogus stamps, phantoms, labels**—outright fantasies, usually the product of someone's imagination, produced for amusement rather than deception.

While most stamps are genuine, and the average collector need not be concerned about the possibility of repairs, **expertizing** services do exist for collectors who are willing to pay a fee to obtain an independent opinion on their more valuable stamps.

H.E. Harris Pictorial Guide to Centering

Cat #	Very Fine	Fine	Average
1 to 293 1847 to 1898	Perfs clear of design on all four sides. Margins may not be even.	Perfs well clear of design on at least three sides. But may almost touch design on one side.	Perfs cut into design on at least one side.
294 to 749 1901 to 1934	Perfs clear of design. Margins relatively even on all four sides.	Perfs clear of design. Margins not even on all four sides.	Perfs touch design on at least one side.
750 to Date 1935 to Present	Perfs clear of design. Centered with margins even on all four sides.	Perfs clear of design. Margins may be uneven.	Perfs may touch design on at least one side.

Note: Margins are the area from the edges of stamp to the design. Perfs are the serrations between stamps that aid in separating them.

CENTERING

One major factor in the determination of a stamp's fair value is its **centering**, the relative balance of the stamp design within its margins. Whether the stamp has perforations or is imperforate, its centering can be judged. Because the stamp trade does not have an established system for grading or measuring centering, "eyeballing" has become the standard practice. As a result, one collector's definition may vary from another's. This can create some confusion, but the system seems to work, so it has remained in force. Centering can range from poor to superb, as follows:

- **Poor**—so far off center that a significant portion of the design is lost because of bad centering. On a poorly centered perforated stamp, the perforations cut in so badly that even the perf tips may penetrate the design.
- **Average**—a stamp whose frame or design is cut slightly by the lack of margins on one or two sides. On a perforated stamp, the perf holes might penetrate the stamp, but some margin white space will show on the teeth. Average stamps are accepted by the majority of collectors for 19th century stamps and early 20th century stamps, as well as for the more difficult later issues.
- **Fine**—the perforations are clear of the design, except for those issues that are known to be extremely poorly centered, but the margins on opposite sides will not be balanced, that is, equal to each other. (Note: a stamp whose top and bottom margins are perfectly balanced may still be called fine if the left and right margins differ substantially from each other.)
- **Very fine**—the opposite margins may still appear to differ somewhat, but the stamp is closer to being perfectly centered than it is to being fine centered. Very fine stamps are sought by collectors who are particularly interested in high quality and who are willing to pay the premiums such stamps command.
- **Superb**— perfect centering. They are so scarce that no comprehensive price list could attempt to include a superb category. Superb stamps, when they are available, command very high premiums.
- **"Jumbo"**—an abnormal condition, in which the stamp's margins are oversized compared to those of the average stamp in a given issue. Such jumbos can occur in the plate making process when a design is cut into the printing plate and excessive space is allowed between that design and the adjacent stamps.

Note: Some collectors also define a "fine to very fine" condition, in which the margin balance falls into a mid-range between fine and very fine. In theory it may be an attractive compromise, but in practice the range between fine and very fine is too narrow to warrant a separate intermediate category.

Quality and Condition Definitions

In determining the value of a given stamp, a number of factors have to be taken into consideration. For mint stamps, the condition of the gum, whether or not it has been hinged, and the centering are all major factors that determine their value. For used stamps, the factors to consider are cancellation and centering. The following H.E. Harris guidelines will enable you to determine the quality standards you may choose from in acquiring stamps for your collection.

Mint Stamp Gum

Unused—A stamp that is not cancelled (used), yet has had all the original gum removed. On early U.S. issues this is the condition that the majority of mint stamps exist in, as early collectors often soaked the gum off their stamps to avoid the possibility of the gum drying and splitting.

Original Gum (OG)—A stamp that still retains the adhesive applied when the stamp was made, yet has been hinged or has had some of the gum removed. Mint stamps from #215 to date can be supplied in this condition.

Never Hinged (NH)—A stamp that is in "post office" condition with full gum that has never been hinged. For U.S. #215 to #715 (1935), separate pricing columns or percentages are provided for "Never Hinged" quality. From #772 (1935) to date, all stamps are priced as Never Hinged.

Cancellations

The cancellations on used stamps range from light to heavy. A lightly cancelled stamp has the main design of the stamp clearly showing through the cancel, while a heavy cancel usually substantially obliterates the design elements of the stamp. In general, it should be assumed that Very fine quality stamps will have lighter cancels than average cancellation stamps.

Heavy Cancel

Light Cancel

GUM

The impact of the condition of the back of an unused stamp (i.e. the **gum**) upon that stamp's value in today's market needs careful consideration. The prices for 19th century stamps vary widely based on this element of condition. Some traditional collectors feel that modern collectors pay too much attention to gum condition. Around the turn of the century, some collectors washed the gum off the stamps to prevent it from cracking and damaging the stamp themselves. But that generation has passed and the practice not only is no longer popular, it is almost unheard of. To some extent the washing of gum is no longer necessary, since modern gums are not as susceptible to cracking. A more important development, however, has been the advent of various mounts that allow the collector to place a stamp in an album without the use of a hinge. With that development, "never hinged" became a premium condition that could be obtained on stamps issued from the 1930s to date. As a result, gum took on added significance, and its absence on 20th century stamps became unacceptable.

The standard definitions that pertain to gum condition are as follows:

- **Original gum, or o.g.**—the gum that was applied when the stamp was produced. There are gradations, from "full" original gum through "partial" original gum, down to "traces". For all intents and purposes, however, a stamp must have most of its original gum to be described as "o.g."
- **Regummed**— the stamp has gum, but it is not that which would have been applied when the stamp was produced. Many collectors will avoid regummed stamps because the gum may hide some repair work. At best, regumming may give the stamp an appearance of completeness, but a premium should not be paid for a stamp that lacks its original gum.
- **Unused**—while many collectors think of this as any stamp that is not used, the narrow philatelic definition indicates a stamp that has no gum or is regummed.
- **Unhinged**—as with "unused", the term has a specific meaning to collectors: a regumming that shows no traces of a hinge mark. Unfortunately, in their confusion some collectors purchase stamps described as "unused" and "unhinged" as if they bore original gum.
- **No gum**—the stamp lacks its gum, either because it was intentionally produced without gum (also described as **ungummed**) or had the gum removed at a later date. It is customary to find 19th century stamps without gum, and the condition is acceptable to all but the most fastidious collectors. On 20th century stamps, original gum is to be expected.
- **Hinged**—the gum shows traces of having been mounted with a hinge. This can range from **lightly hinged** (the gum shows traces, but none of the hinge remains) to **heavily hinged** (a substantial portion of one or more hinge remnants is stuck to the stamp, or a significant portion of the gum has been lost in the removal of a hinge).
- **Thinned**— not only has the gum been removed, but a portion of the stamp paper has been pulled away. A thin usually will show when the stamp is held to a light. One of the faults that may be covered over on regummed stamps is a thin that has been filled in.
- **Never hinged**—as the name implies, the stamp has its original gum in post office condition and has never been hinged. Although some collectors think of **"mint"** stamps as any form of unused, o.g. stamps, the more accepted "mint" definition is never hinged.

UNITED STATES **STAMP IDENTIFIER**

Shows you how to distinguish between the rare and common U.S. stamps that look alike.

Types of 1¢ Franklin Design of 1851-60

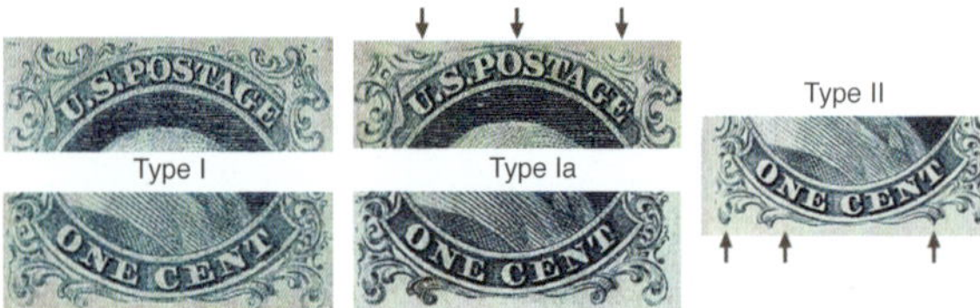

TYPE I has the most complete design of the various types of stamps. At top and bottom there is an unbroken curved line running outside the bands reading "U.S. POSTAGE" and "ONE CENT". The scrolls at bottom are turned under, forming curls. The scrolls and outer line at top are complete.

TYPE Ia is like Type I at bottom but ornaments and curved line at top are partly cut away.

TYPE Ib (not illustrated) is like Type I at top but little curls at bottom are not quite so complete nor clear and scroll work is partly cut away.

TYPE II has the outside bottom line complete, but the little curls of the bottom scrolls and the lower part of the plume ornament are missing. Side ornaments are complete.

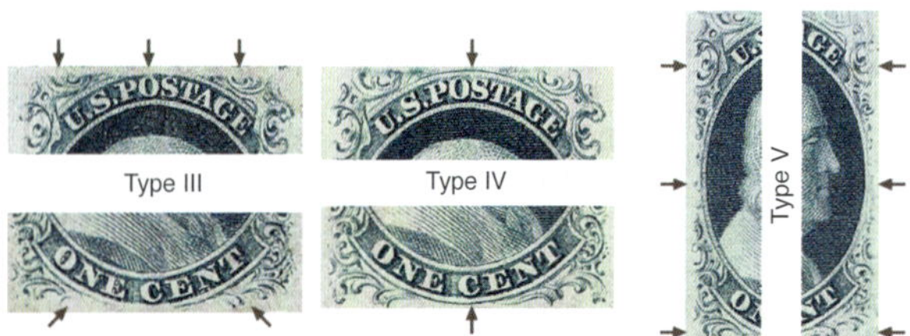

TYPE III has the outside lines at both top and bottom partly cut away in the middle. The side ornaments are complete.

TYPE IIIa (not illustrated) is similar to Type III with the outer line cut away at top or bottom, but not both.

TYPE IV is similar to Type II but the curved lines at top or bottom (or both) have been recut in several different ways, and usually appear thicker than Type IIs.

TYPE V is similar to Type III but has the side ornaments partly cut away. Type V occurs only on perforated stamps.

Types of 3¢ Washington & 5¢ Jefferson Designs of 1851-60

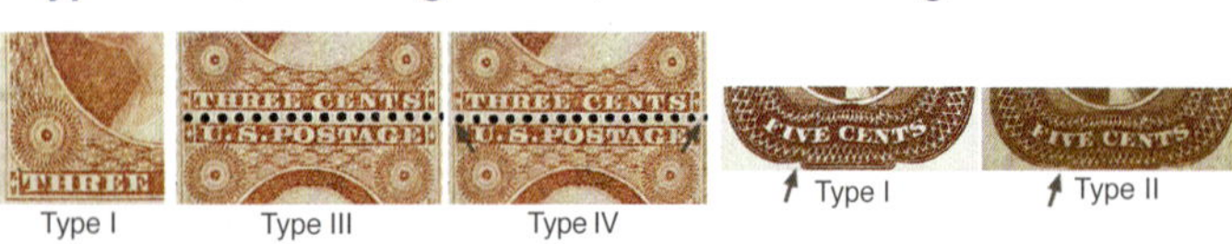

3¢ WASHINGTON

TYPE I has a frame line around the top, bottom and sides.

TYPE III has the frame line removed at top and bottom, while the side frame lines are continuous from the top to bottom of the plate.

TYPE IV is similar to Type III, but the side frame lines were recut individually, and therefore are broken between stamps.

5¢ JEFFERSON

TYPE I is a complete design with projections (arrow) at the top and bottom as well as at the sides.

TYPE II has the projections at the top or bottom partly or completely cut away.

Types of the 10¢ Washington Design of 1851-60

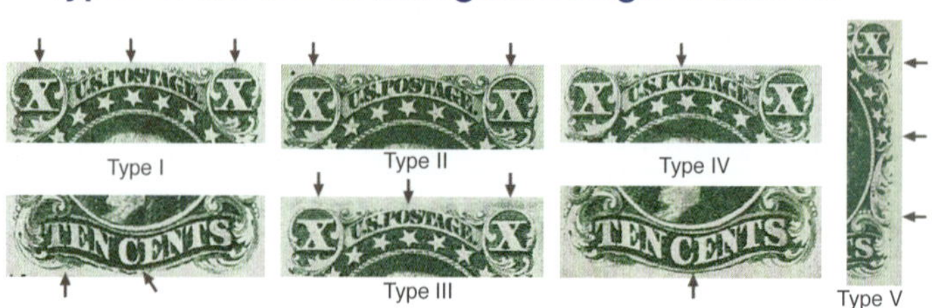

TYPE I has the "shells" at the lower corners practically complete, while the outer line below "TEN CENTS" is very nearly complete. At the top, the outer lines above "U.S. POSTAGE" above the "X" in each corner are broken.

TYPE II has the design complete at the top, but the outer line at the bottom is broken in the middle and the "shells" are partially cut away.

TYPE III has both top and bottom outer lines cut away; similar to Type I at the top and Type II at the bottom.

TYPE IV has the outer lines at the top or bottom of the stamp, or at both place, recut to show more strongly and heavily.

Types I, II, III and IV have complete ornaments at the sides and three small circles or pearls (arrow) at the outer edges of the bottom panel.

TYPE V has the side ornaments, including one or two of the small "pearls" partly cut away. Also, the outside line, over the "X" at the right top, has been partly cut away.

Types of the 12¢ Washington issues of 1851-60

PLATE 1 has stronger, more complete outer frame lines than does Plate 3. Comes imperforate (#17 or perf #36).

PLATE 3 has uneven or broken outer frame lines that are particularly noticeable in the corners. The stamps are perf 15. (#36b)

The 1875 REPRINT plate is similar to plate 1, but the Reprint stamps are greenish black and slightly taller than plate 1 stamps (25mm from top to bottom frame lines versus 24.5 mm) The paper is whiter and the perforations are 12 gauge.

UNITED STATES STAMP IDENTIFIER

Shows you how to distinguish between the rare and common U.S. stamps that look alike.

Types of the 1861 Issue, Grills & Re-Issues

Shortly after the outbreak of the Civil War in 1861, the Post Office demonetized all stamps issued up to that time in order to prevent their use by the Confederacy. Two new sets of designs, consisting of six stamps shown below plus 24¢ and 30¢ demonetized, were prepared by the American Bank Note Company. The first designs, except for the 10¢ and 24¢ values, were not regularly issued and are extremely rare and valuable. The second designs became the regular issue of 1861. The illustrations in the left column show the first (or unissued) designs, which were all printed on thin, semi- transparent paper. The second (or regular) designs are shown at right.

Types of the 1861 Issues

1st

SECOND DESIGN shows a small dash (arrow) under the tip of the ornaments at the right of the figure "1" in the upper left-hand corner of the stamp.

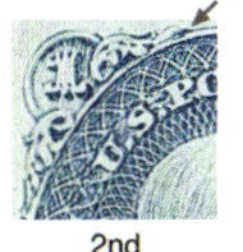

2nd

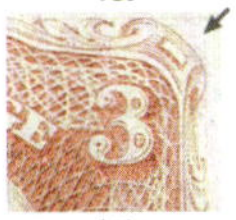

1st

SECOND DESIGN, 3¢ value, shows a small ball (arrow) at each corner of the design. Also, the ornaments at the corners are larger than in the first design.

2nd

1st

SECOND DESIGN, 5¢ value has a leaflet (arrow) projecting from the scrolled ornaments at each corner of the stamp.

2nd

1st

FIRST DESIGN has no curved line below the row of stars and there is only one outer line of the ornaments above them.
SECOND DESIGN has a heavy curved line below the row of stars (arrow); ornaments above the stars have double outer line.

2nd

1st

FIRST DESIGN has rounded corners. **SECOND DESIGN** has a oval and a scroll (arrow) in each corner of the design

2nd

Types of the 15¢ "Landing of Columbus" Design of 1869

Type I

Type II

TYPE I has the central picture without the frame line shown in Type II.
TYPE II has a frame line (arrows) around the central picture; also a diamond shaped ornament appears below the "T" of "Postage".
TYPE III (not illustrated) is like Type I except that the fringe of brown shading lines which appears around the sides and bottom of the picture on Types I and II has been removed.

IDENTIFIER CHART
1861-1867 Bank Notes

Description and Identifying Features				1¢	2¢	3¢	5¢	10¢	12¢	15¢	24¢	30¢	90¢
1861. National. First designs. Thin, semi-transparent paper. No grill.				55		56	57	58[1], 62B	59		60	61	62
1861-62. National. Modified designs[3]. Thicker, opaque paper. No grill.				63		64[2], 65[2], 66[2]	67	68	69		70[2]	71	72
1861-66. National. Thicker, opaque paper. No grill. a. New designs.					73					77			
b. Same designs, new shades.						74[2]	75[2], 76[2]				78[2]		
1867. National. Grills. All on thick, opaque paper.													
Grills	Pts. as seen from stamp face	Area of covered Horiz. x Vert.	# of rows of Pts.										
A	Up	All over	—			79	80					81	
B	Up	18 x 15 mm	22 x 18			82							
C	Up	c. 13 x 16 mm	16-17 x 18-21			83							
D	Down	c. 12 x 14 mm	15 x 17-18		84	85							
Z	Down	c. 11 x 14 mm	13-14 x 17-18	85A	85B	85C		85D	85E	85F			
E	Down	c. 11 x 13 mm	14 x 15-17	86	87	88		89	90	91			
F	Down	c. 9 x 13 mm	11-12 x 15-17	92	93	94	95	96	97	98	99	100	101
1875. National. Re-issues. Hard, white paper. White crackly gum. No grill.				102	103	104	105	106	107	108	109	110	111

FOOTNOTES:
1. #58 does not exist used. Unused, it cannot be distinguished from #62B.
2. Different from corresponding 1861-66 issues only in color.
3. See diagrams for design modification.

UNITED STATES STAMP IDENTIFIER

Shows you how to distinguish between the rare and common U.S. stamps that look alike.

Types of the 1870-71 Through 1887 Bank Notes

The stamps of the 1870-71 issue were printed by the National Bank Note Company. The similar issue of 1873 was printed by the Continental Bank Note Company. When Continental took over the plates previously used by National, they applied the so-called "secret marks" to the designs of the 1¢ through 15¢ denominations by which the two issues can be distinguished as shown below. The illustrations at the left show the original designs of 1870-71; those at the right show secret marks applied to the issue of 1873.

1¢ Secret mark is a small curved mark in the pearl at the left of the figure "1".

2¢ 1870-71 are red brown. The 1873 issue is brown and in some copies has a small diagonal line under the scroll at the left of the "U.S." (arrow).

3¢ Secret mark is the heavily shaded ribbon under the letters "RE".

6¢ Secret mark shows the first four vertical lines of shading in the lower part of the left ribbon greatly strengthened.

7¢ Secret mark is two tiny semicircles drawn around the end of the lines which outline the ball in the lower right-hand corner.

10¢ Secret mark is a small semicircle in the scroll at the right-hand side of the central design.

12¢ Secret mark shows the "balls" at the top and bottom on the figure "2" crescent-shaped (right) instead of nearly round as at the left.

15¢ Secret mark shows as strengthened lines (arrow) in the triangle in the upper left-hand corner, forming a "V".

IDENTIFIER CHART
1870-1887 Bank Notes

Description and Identifying Features	1¢	2¢	3¢	5¢	6¢	7¢	10¢	12¢	15¢	21¢	30¢	90¢
1870-71. National. No secret marks. White wove paper, thin to medium thick. With grills.	134	135	136		137	138	139	140	141	142	143	144
1870-71. National. As above, except without grills.	145	146	147		148	149	150	151	152	153	154[2]	155[2]
1873. Continental. White wove paper, thin to thick. No grills.												
a. With secret marks.	156	157	158		159	160	161	162	163			
b. No secret marks.											165[2]	166[2]
1875. Continental. Special Printing. Same designs as 1873 Continental. Hard, white wove paper. No gum.	167	168	169		170	171	172	173	174	175	176	177
1875. Continenal. New color or denomination. Hard yellowish, wove paper.		178		179								
1875. Continental. Special printing. Same designs as 1875 Continental. Hard, white wove paper. No gum.		180		181								
1879. American. Same designs as 1873-75. Continental. Soft, porous paper.	182	183[3]	184[3]	185	186[3]		188		189[3]		190[3]	191[3]
a. Without secret mark.							187[3]					
1880. American. Special printing. Same as 1879 issue. Soft, porous paper. No gum.	192	193, 203[3]	194[3]	204	195[3]	196	197[3]	198	199[3]	200	201[3]	202[3]
1881-82. American. Designs of 1873. Re-engraved[4]. Soft, porous paper.	206		207[5]		208		209					
1887. American. Same designs as 1881-82. New colors.		214[5]									217	218

FOOTNOTES:
1. See diagrams for secret marks.
2. Corresponding denominations differ from each other only in color.
3. Corresponding denominations differ from each other only in color and gum. The special printings are slightly deeper and richer. The lack of gum is not positive identifier because it can be washed from the 1879 issues.
4. See diagrams for re-engravings.
5. Corresponding denominations differ from each other in color.

UNITED STATES STAMP IDENTIFIER

Shows you how to distinguish between the rare and common U.S. stamps that look alike.

Re-Engraved Designs 1881-82

1¢ has strengthened vertical shading lines in the upper part of the stamp, making the background appear almost solid. Lines of shading have also been added to the curving ornaments in the upper corners.

3¢ has a solid shading line at the sides of the central oval (arrow) that is only about half the previous width. Also a short horizontal line has been cut below the "TS" of "CENTS".

6¢ has only three vertical lines between the edge of the panel and the outside left margin of the stamp. (In the preceding issues, there were four such lines.)

10¢ has only four vertical lines between the left side of the oval and the edge of the shield. (In the preceding issues there were five such lines.) Also, the lines in the background have been made much heavier so that these stamps appear more heavily linked than previous issues.

2¢ Washington Design of 1894-98

TYPE I has horizontal lines of the same thickness within and without the triangle.

TYPE II has horizontal lines which cross the triangle but are thinner within it than without.

YPE III has thin lines inside the triangle and these do not cross the double frame line of the triangle.

2¢ Columbian "Broken Hat" Variety of 1893

As a result of a plate defect, some stamps of the 2¢ Columbian design show a noticeable white notch or gash in the hat worn by the third figure to the left of Columbus. This "broken hat" variety is somewhat less common than the regular 2¢ design.

231

Broken Hat variety, 231c

4¢ Columbian Blue Error

Collectors often mistake the many shades of the normal 4¢ ultramarine for the rare and valuable blue error. Actually, the "error" is not ultramarine at all, but a deep blue, similar to the deeper blue shades of the 1¢ Columbian.

$1 Perry Design of 1894-95

TYPE I shows circles around the "$1" are broken at point where they meet the curved line below "ONE DOLLAR" (arrows).

TYPE II shows these circles complete.

10¢ Webster design of 1898

TYPE I has an unbroken white curved line below the words "TEN CENTS".

TYPE II shows white line is broken by ornaments at a point just below the "E" in "TEN" and the "T" in "CENTS" (arrows).

2¢ Washington Issue of 1903

Die I
319, 319g, 320

The rounded inner frame line below and to the left "T" in "TWO" has a dark patch of color that narrows, but remains strong across the bottom.

Die II
319f, 320a

2¢ "cap of 2" Variety of 1890

Cap on left "2"

Plate defects in the printing of the 2¢ "Washington" stamp of 1890 accounts for the "Cap of left 2" and "Cap on both 2s" varieties illustrated.

Cap on right "2"

UNITED STATES STAMP IDENTIFIER

Shows you how to distinguish between the rare and common U.S. stamps that look alike.

FRANKLIN AND WASHINGTON ISSUES OF 1908-22

Perforation	Watermark	Other Identifying Features		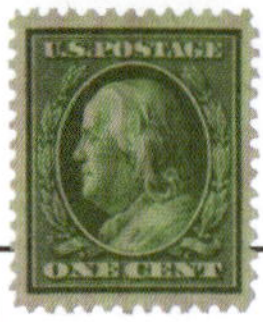	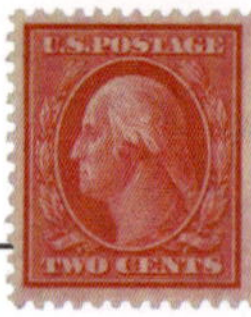		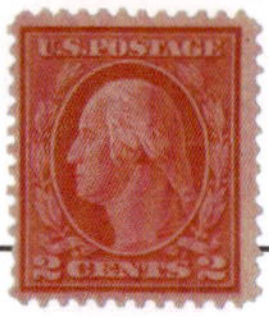	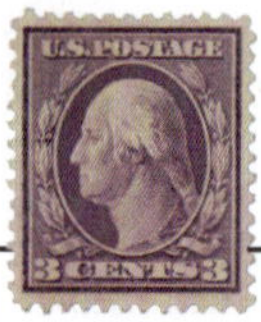 3¢ thru $1 denominations	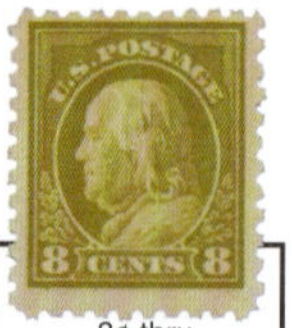 8¢ thru $1 denominations
PERF. 12	**USPS**	White paper		331	332			333-42	422-23
		Bluish gray paper		357	358			359-66	
	USPS	White paper		374	375	405	406	376-82, 407	414-21
COIL 12	**USPS**	Perf. Horizontal		348	349			350-51	
		Perf. Vertical		352	353			354-56	
	USPS	Perf. Horizontal		385	386				
		Perf. Vertical		387	388			389	
IMPERF.	**USPS**			343	344			345-47	
	USPS	Flat Plate		383	384	408	409		
		Rotary Press					459		
	Unwmkd.	Flat Plate				481	482-82A	483-85	
		Offset				531	532-34B	535	
COIL 8-1/2	USPS	Perf. Horizontal		390	391	410	411		
		Perf. Vertical		392	393	412	413	394-96	
PERF. 10	**USPS**								460
	USPS					424	425	426-30	431-40
	Unwmkd.	Flat Plate				462	463	464-69	470-78
		Rotary Press				543			
COIL 10	USPS	Perf. Horizontal	Flat			441	442		
			Rotary			448	449-50		
		Perf. Vertical	Flat			443	444	445-47	
			Rotary			452	453-55	456-58	
	Unwmkd.	Perf. Horizontal				486	487-88	489	
		Perf. Vertical				490	491-92	493-96	497
PERF. 11	**USPS**				519				
	USPS						461		
	Unwmkd.	Flat Plate				498	499-500	501-07	508-18
		Rotary Press				*544-45	546		
		Offset				525	526-28B	529-30	
Perf. 12-1/2	Unwkmd.	Offset				536			
11 x 10	Unwkmd.	Rotary				538	539-40	541	
10 x 11	Unwkmd.	Rotary				542			

* Design of #544 is 19 mm wide x 22-1/2 mm high. #545 is 19-1/2 to 20 mm wide x 22 mm high.

Size of Flat Plate Design

22mm

18-1/2 to 19mm

Stamps printed by rotary press are always slightly wider or taller on issues prior to 1954. Measurements do not apply to booklet singles.

HOW TO USE THIS IDENTIFICATION CHART

Numbers referred to herein are from Scott's Standard Postage Stamp Catalog. To identify any stamp in this series, first check the type by comparing it with the illustrations at the top of the chart. Then check the perforations, and whether the stamp is single or double line watermarked or unwatermarked. With this information you can quickly find out the Standard Catalog number by checking down and across the chart. For example, a 1¢ Franklin, perf. 12, single line watermark, must be Scott's #374.

UNITED STATES STAMP IDENTIFIER

Shows you how to distinguish between the rare and common U.S. stamps that look alike.

Types of The 2¢ Washington Design of 1912-20

Type I

Type I where the ribbon at left above the figure "2" has one shading line in the first curve, while the ribbon at the right has one shading line in the second curve. Bottom of toga has a faint outline. Top line of toga, from bottom to front of throat, is very faint. Shading lines of the face, terminating in front of the ear, are not joined. Type I occurs on both flat and rotary press printings.

Type Ia is similar to Type I except that all of the lines are stronger. Lines of the Toga button are heavy. Occurs only on flat press printings.

Type Ia

Type II

Type II has ribbons shaded as in Type I. Toga button and shading lines to left of it are heavy. Shading lines in front of ear are joined and end in a strong vertically curved line (arrow). Occurs only on rotary press printings.

Type III where ribbons are shaded with two lines instead of one; otherwise similar to Type II. Occurs on rotary press printings only.

Type III

Type IV

Type IV where top line of toga is broken. Shading lines inside the toga bottom read "Did". The Line of color in the left "2" is very thin and usually broken. Occurs on offset printings only.

Type V in which top line of toga is complete. Toga button has five vertical shaded lines. Line of color in the left "2" is very thin and usually broken. Nose shaded as shown in illustration. Occurs on offset printings only.

Type V

Type Va

Type Va is same as Type V except in shading dots of nose. Third row of dots from bottom has four dots instead of six. Also, the Overall height of Type Va is 1/3 millimeter less than Type V. Occurs on offset printings only.

Type VI is same as Type V except that the line of color in left "2" is very heavy (arrow). Occurs in offset printings only.

Type VI

Type VII

Type VII in which line of color in left "2" is clear and continuous and heavier than Types V or Va, but not as heavy as in Type VI. There are three rows of vertical dots (instead of two) in the shading of the upper lip, and additional dots have been added to hair at top of the head. Occurs on offset printings only.

Types of The 3¢ Washington Design of 1908-20

Type I

TYPE I in which the top line of the toga is weak, as are the top parts of the shading lines that join the toga line. The fifth shading line from the left (arrow) is partly cut away at the top. Also the line between the lips is thin. Occurs on flat and rotary press printings.

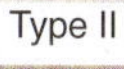
Type II

TYPE II where top line of toga is strong and the shading lines that join it are heavy and complete. The line between the lips is heavy. Occurs on flat and rotary press printings.

Type III

TYPE III in which top line of toga is strong, but the fifth shading line from the left (arrow) is missing. The center line of the toga button consists of two short vertical lines with a dot between them. The "P" and "O" of "POSTAGE" are separated by a small line of color. Occurs on offset printings only.

Type IV

TYPE IV in which the shading lines of the toga are complete. The center line of the toga button consists of a single unbroken vertical line running through the dot in the center. The "P" and the "O" of "POSTAGE" are joined. Type IV occurs only in offset printings.

Types of 5¢ Franklin, 10¢ Washington 1847-1947

In the original 5¢ design, the top edge of Franklin's shirt touches the circular frame about at a level with the top of the "F" of "FIVE", while in the 1875 reproduction it is on a level with the top of the figure "5".

In the original 10¢ design, the left edge of Washington's coat points to the "T" of "TEN", and the right edge points between the "T" and "S" of "CENTS". In the reproductions, the left and right outlines of the coat point to the right edge of "X" and to the center of the "S" of "CENTS" respectively. Also, on the 1875 reprints, the eyes have a sleepy look and the line of the mouth is straighter.

The 1947 "Cipex" Souvenir Sheet, issued on the hundredth anniversary of United States stamps, features reproductions of the two original designs. Stamps cut out of souvenir sheet are, of course, valid postage. However, no difficulty in identification should be encountered since the 1947 reproductions are light blue (5¢) instead of the original red brown, and brownish orange (10¢) instead of the original black.

Commemorative Identifier

The following handy identifier is a list of commemoratives organized alphabetically by key words on the stamp, which are the most prominent after "U.S. Postage," and matches the stamp with its corresponding Scott number.

A

- Aaron, Henry "Hank" ... 5908
- Abbey, Edwin Austin ... 3502k
- Abbott & Costello ... 2566
- Abby Cadabby ... 5394h
- Abstract Expressionists ... 4444
- Abyssinian Cat ... 2373
- Acadia National Park ... 746, 762, 5080d, C138, UX601
- Acheson, Dean ... 2755
- Acoma Pot ... 1709, 3873g
- Acorn Barnacle ... 5802g
- Acuff, Roy ... 3812
- Adams
  - Abigail ... 2146
  - Ansel ... 3649p, 5854
  - John ... 806, 841, 850, 1687a, 2201, 2216b
  - John Quincy ... 811, 846, 2201, 2216f
- Addams, Jane ... 878
- Admiralty Head Lighthouse (WA) ... 2470, 2474
- Adopt a Shelter Pet ... 4451-4460
- Adopting a Child ... 3398
- Adriatic, S.S. ... 117, 128
- Adventures of Huckleberry Finn, The ... 2787
- African
  - Agave Cactus ... 1943
  - Daisy ... 5680
  - Elephant Herd ... 1388
  - Violet ... 2486
- Aging Together ... 2011
- AIDS Awareness ... 2806
- Ailey, Alvin ... 3841
- Air Force
  - Cross ... 5067
  - One ... 4144
  - US ... 1013, 3167, C49
- Air Mail
  - 50th Anniversary ... C74
  - 100th Anniversary ... 5281-5282
- Air Service Emblem ... C5
- Airborne Units Spearhead Attacks ... 2838d
- Aircraft, Classic American ... 3142
- Airlift $1 ... 1341
- Airplane ... 649, 650, 934, 947, 1185, 1511, 1574, 1684, 1710, 2433, 2436, 2438c, 2468, C1, C2-C9, C10-C11, C20-C22, C25-C33, C35-C41, C44-C47, C68, C74, C89-C90, C91-C96, C99, C100, C113-C115, C118-C119, C128-C129
- Alabama ... 1953, 3561, 3696
  - Flag ... 1654, 4274
  - Statehood ... 1375, 5360
- Aladdin & Genie ... 4195
- Alamo, The ... 776, 778, 1043
- Alaska ... 1954, 3562, 3697
  - Flag ... 1681, 4275
  - Highway ... 2635
  - Purchase ... C70
  - Statehood/Territory ... 800, 2066, 4374, C53
  - -Yukon Pacific Exposition ... 370-371
- Alaskan Brown Bear ... 2310
- Alaskan Malamute ... 2100
- Albania (Flag) ... 918
- Alcoholism, You Can Beat It ... 1927
- Alcott, Louisa May ... 862
- Aleutian Islands, Japanese Invasion of the ... 2697e
- Alexandria, VA ... C40
- Alfred B. Maclay Gardens, Florida ... 5468
- Alfred Hitchcock Presents ... 4414o, UX567
- Alger, Horatio ... 2010
- Alice in Wonderland ... 3913
- All Aboard ... 3333-3337
- All in the Family, TV Series ... 3189b
- Allegiance, Pledge of ... 2594
- Allen,
  - Ethan ... 1071
  - Gracie ... 4414p, UX568
  - Richard ... 5056
  - Steve ... 4414r, UX584
- Alley Oop ... 3000n
- Alliance for Progress ... 1234
- Allied Nations ... 907
- Alligator ... 1428, 2950, 4033
- Allison, Fran ... 4414k, UX576
- Allosaurus ... 1390, 3136g
- Aloha Shirts ... 4592-4601, 4682-4686
- Alpha Airplane ... 3142e
- Alpine Buttercup ... 5673, 5678
- Alpine Skiing ... 3180
- Alpine Tundra ... 4198
- Alta, California, 1st Civil Settlement ... 1725
- Alyssum ... 4758
- Alzheimer's Awareness ... 4358, B6
- Amateur Radio ... 1260
- Amaryllis ... 4864
- Amber Alert ... 4031
- Ambulance ... 2128, 2231
- AMC Javelin SST ... 5719
- America
  - Beautification of ... 1318, 1365-1368, 4716a-e
  - Smiles ... 3189m
  - Survives the Depression ... 3185m
- America PUAS ... 2426, 2512, C121, C127
- America/PUASP ... C131
- American
  - Art ... 1484-1487, 1553-1555, 3236
  - Automobile Association ... 1007
  - Bald Eagle ... 1387, 2309
  - Bankers Association, Jan. 3 ... 987
  - Bar Association ... 1022
  - Bicentennial ... 1456-1459, 1476-1479, 1480-1483, 1543-1546, 1559-1568, 1629-1631, 1633-1682, 1686-1689, 1690-94, 1704, 1716-1720, 1722, 1726, 1728, 1753, 1789, 1937-1938, 2052
  - Chemical Society ... 1002, 1685
  - Credo ... 1139-1144
  - Crocodile ... 3105d
  - Dance ... 1749-1752
  - Dogs ... 2098-2101
  - Elk ... 2328
  - Flag ... 1623, 2116 (See *pg. XXVI*)
  - Folklore ... 1317, 1330, 1357, 1370, 1470, 1548
  - Foxhound ... 2101
  - Gardens ... 5461-5470
  - Goldfinch ... 1982, 1999, 4890
  - Illustrators ... 3502
  - Indian ... 565, 695, 1364
  - Indian Dances ... 3072-3076, 5978, 5981
  - Institute of Architects ... 1089
  - Kestrel ... 2476-2477, 3031-3031A, 3044
  - Legion ... 1369
  - Lobster ... 2304
  - Lotus ... 4046
  - Militia ... 1568
  - Music ... 1252
  - Music, Legends of (Series) ... 2721-2723, 2724-2737, 2767-2770, 2771-2778, 2849-2853, 2854-2861, 2982, 2983-2992, 3096-3099, 3100-3103, 3154-3157, 3158-3165, 3212-3215, 3216-3219, 3339-3344, 3345-3350
  - Philatelic Society ... 730-731, 750, 766, 770
  - Realism (Art) ... 3184n
  - Red Cross ... 702, 967, 1910
  - Revolution ... 551, 645, 651, 653, 657, 689, 690, 727, 734, 752, 1010, 1432, 1729, 1851, 1937-1938
  - Revolution Battles ... 617-619, 629-630, 643-644, 646, 688, 1003, 1361, 1563-1564, 1686, 1722, 1728, 1826, 5977
  - Samoa ... 3389, 4276
  - Shoals Lighthouse, Florida ... 2473
  - Treasures ... 3524-3527, 3650, 3804-3807, 3872, 3926-3929, 4089-4098, 4165, 4346, 4473, 4653
  - Wildlife ... 2286-2335
  - Woman ... 1152
- Americana Issue ... 1581-1585, 1590, 1590A, 1591-1599, 1603-1606, 1608, 1610-1619
- Americans, African ... 873, 902, 953, 1085, 1233, 1290, 1361, 1372, 1486, 1490-1491, 1493, 1495, 1554, 1560, 1772, 1790, 1791, 1860, 1865, 2027, 2043, 2051, 2083-2084, 2097, 2164, 2211, 2223, 2275, 2420, 2496, 2746, 2766, 2816, 2851-2852, 2854-2861, 2869g, 2870g, 2956, 2975h, 2982-2992, 3058, 3096, 3121, 3181, 3182l, 3186c, 3188a, 3190j, 3212, 3214-3219, 3273, 3371, 3408a, 3408j, 3408p, 3408r, 3422, 3436, 3501, 3557, 3746, 3834, 3841, 3871, 3896, 3936-3937, 3996, 4020, 4080, C97, C102, C103, C105
- America's Libraries ... 2015
- AMERIPEX '86 ... 2145, 2216-2219
- Amethyst ... 1540
- Amish
  - Horse & Buggy ... C150
  - Quilts ... 3524-3527
- Amendment, 19th ... 3184e
- Amphipod ... 3442
- Anadarko, Oklahoma Post Office Mural ... 5375
- Anderson,
  - C. Alfred "Chief" ... 4879
  - Marian ... 3896
- Anemone ... 3029
- Angelou, Maya ... 4979
- Angels ... 1268, 1276, 1363, 1471, 3012, 3018, 4477
- Angus and Longhorn Cattle ... 1504
- Animal (Muppet) ... 3944g
- Animal Rescue ... 4451-4460
- Annapolis Tercentenary, May 23 ... 984
- Antarctic
  - Expedition, Byrd ... 733, 735, 753, 768
  - Explorers ... 2386-2389
  - Treaty ... 1431, C130
- Anthony, Susan B. ... 784, 1051
- Anti-Aircraft Gun, 90mm ... 900
- Antibiotics Save Lives ... 3186b
- Antillean Euphonia ... 3222
- Antioch Dunes Evening Primrose ... 1786
- Anti-Pollution ... 1410-1413
- Apgar, Virginia ... 2179
- Apollo 8 ... 1371, 2633, 2634
- Apollo-Soyuz ... 1569-1570
- Appalachian Trail ... 5960
- Appalachians ... 4045
- Appaloosa Horse ... 2158
- Apple Blossom ... 1956, 1974
- Apples ... 3491, 3493, 4727-4734, 5037
- Appleseed, Johnny ... 1317
- Appomattox, Civil War Centennial ... 1182, 4981
- Apprenticeship ... 1201
- Apte Tarpon Fishing Fly ... 2547
- Aquaman ... 4084h, 4084r
- Arbor Day ... 717
- Arc de Triomphe ... 934
- Arches National Park ... 5080h
- Architects, Institute of American ... 1089
- Architecture, American ... 1779-1782, 1800-1802, 1838-1841, 1928-1931, 2019-2022, 3910
- Archives, National ... 227, 2081
- Arctic
  - Animals ... 3288-3292
  - Explorations ... 1128
  - Fox ... 3289
  - Hare ... 3288
  - Tundra ... 3802
- Arizona ... 1955, 3563, 3698
  - Flag ... 1680, 4277
  - National Park (Grand Canyon) ... 741, 757, 2512
  - Statehood ... 1192, 4627
  - USS Memorial ... 4873
- Arkansas ... 1657, 1956, 3564, 3699
  - Flag ... 1657, 4278
  - River Navigation ... 1358
  - Statehood ... 782, 2167
- Arlen, Harold ... 3100
- Arlington Amphitheater ... 570, 701
- Arlington Green Bridge ... 4738, U679
- Armadillo, Nine-banded ... 2296
- Armed Forces ... 929, 934-936, 939, 1026
  - Reserve ... 1067
- Armstrong,
  - Edwin ... 2056
  - Louis ... 2982, 2984
  - Neil ... C76
- Army ... 785-789, 934, 985, 998, 1013, 1067, 6003
  - Continental ... 1565
  - Medal of Honor ... 4823, 4823a
  - and Navy ... 900
  - Issue, Salvation ... 1267
- Arnaz, Desi ... 3187l
- Arnold, Gen. H.H. "Hap" ... 2191
- Arranged Diatoms ... 5802e
- Arrigoni Bridge ... 5811
- Arrows ... E22-E23
- Arsenal of Democracy ... 2559e
- Art
  - American Indian ... 3873
  - Deco Style (Chrysler Building) ... 3184j
  - Direction ... 3772f
  - Glass ... 3325-3328
  - Hudson River School Paintings ... 4917-4920
  - of Magic, The ... 5301-5306
  - of the Skateboard ... 5763-5766
- Arthur, Chester A. ... 826, 2218c
- Articles of Confederation ... 1726
- Asawa, Ruth, Art of ... 5504-5513
- Ashe, Arthur ... 3936
- Asia ... C131
- Aspen Leaf ... 5966, 5973
- Assassin Bug ... 3351g
- Assateague Island National Seashore ... 5080f
- Assiniboine Headdress ... 2501
- Aster ... 2993, 4762
- Astronauts ... 1331, 1434-1435, 1912, 2419, 2632, C76
- Atlantic Cable Centenary ... 1112
- Atlantic Cod ... 2206
- Atomic Energy Act ... 1200
- Atoms for Peace ... 1070
- Audubon, John James ... 874, 1241, 1863, 3236e, 3650, C71
- Aurora Australis ... 4123b, 4204
- Aurora Borealis ... 4123a, 4203
- Austin, Stephen F. ... 776, 778
- Australia Bicentennial ... 2370
- Australian Shepherd ... 4458
- Austria (Flag) ... 919
- Authors ... 859-863, 980, 1250, 1281, 1294, 1327, 1487, 1733, 1832, 1848, 1856-1857, 2010, 2047, 2073, 2094, 2168, 2196-2197, 2350, 2418, 2538, 3134, 3221, 3308, 3433-3434, 3444, 3557, 3904

D

I

J

K

GENERAL ISSUES

1847 – THE FIRST ISSUE
Imperforate

"For every single letter in manuscript or paper of any kind by or upon which information shall be asked or communicated in writing or by marks or signs conveyed in the mail, for any distance under three hundred miles, five cents; and for any distance over three hundred miles, ten cents...and every letter or parcel not exceeding half an ounce in weight shall be deemed a single letter, and every additional weight of half ounce, shall be charged with an additional single postage."

With these words, the Act of March 3, 1845, authorized, but not required, the prepayment of postage effective July 1, 1847, and created a need for the first United States postage stamps. Benjamin Franklin, as the first Postmaster General of the United States and the man generally regarded as the "father" of the postal system, was selected for the 5-cent stamp. As the first President of the United States, George Washington was designated for the 10¢ issue.

The 1847 stamps were released July 1, 1847, but were available only in the New York City post office on that date. The earliest known usages are July 7 for the 5-cent stamps and July 2 for the 10-cent stamps.

The best estimates are that 4,400,000 of the 5-cent and 1,050,000 of the 10-cent stamps reached the public. The remaining stocks were destroyed when the stamps were demonetized and could no longer be used for postage as of July 1, 1851.

Like most 19th century United States stamps, the first Issue is much more difficult to find unused than used. Stamps canceled by "handstamp" marking devices—usually carved from cork—are scarcer than those with manuscript, or "pen", cancels.

Issued without gum, the Reproductions of the 1847 issue were printed from entirely new dies for display at the 1876 Centennial Exposition and were not valid for postal use. The issue also was reproduced on a souvenir sheet issued in 1947 to celebrate the centenary of the First Issue. Differences between the 1847 issue, 1875 Reproductions and 1948 stamps are described in the Stamp Identifier at the front of this catalog. (Page XIX)

1, 3
Franklin

2, 4
Washington

SCOTT NO.	DESCRIPTION	UNUSED VF	UNUSED F	UNUSED AVG	USED VF	USED F	USED AVG
	1847 Imperforate (OG + 100%)						
1	5¢ red brown	3500.00	2000.00	1200.00	600.00	475.00	300.00
1	— Pen cancel	....	....	....	475.00	300.00	200.00
2	10¢ black . . .	20000.00	13000.00	7000.00	1200.00	900.00	700.00
2	— Pen cancel	....	....	....	800.00	700.00	600.00
	1875 Reprints of 1847 Issues, without gum						
3	5¢ red brown	1400.00	950.00	750.00	....	....	....
4	10¢ black	1700.00	1200.00	900.00	....	....	....

1851-61 – THE CLASSIC ISSUES

An act of Congress approved March 3, 1851, enacted new, reduced postage rates, introduced additional rates and made the prepayment of additional postage compulsory. Although the use of postage stamps was not required, the 1851 Act stimulated their use and paved the way for their required usage from July 1, 1855 on.

Under the Act of 1851, the basic prepaid single letter rate (defined as one-half ounce or less) was set at 3 cents. As this would be the most commonly used value, it was decided that a likeness of George Washington should grace the 3 cent stamp. Benjamin Franklin was assigned to the 1 cent stamp, which, among other usages, met the newspaper and circular rates.

Washington also appears on the 10, 12, 24 and 90 cent stamps and Franklin on the 30 cent value. Thomas Jefferson was selected for the new 5 cent stamp that was issued in 1856.

By 1857, improved production techniques and the increasing usage of stamps led to the introduction of perforated stamps that could be more easily separated. The result was the 1857-61 series whose designs are virtually identical to the 1851 set. The 1857-61 perforated stamps were set in the printing plates with very little space between each stamp. As a result, insufficient space was allowed to accommodate the perforations, which often cut into the design on these stamps. In fact, stamps with complete designs and wide margins on all four sides are the exception and command very substantial premiums.

The most fascinating—and most challenging—feature of the 1851-61 stamps is the identification of many major and minor types. An extremely slight design variation can mean a difference of thousands of dollars and collectors even today can apply their knowledge to discover rare, misidentified types.

The various "Types", identified below by Roman numerals in parentheses, resulted from minor changes in the printing plates caused by wear or plate retouching. The 1851-57 one-cent blue stamp may be the most studied of all the United States issues and is found in seven major catalog-listed Types (14, if we count imperforate and perforated stamps separately), plus countless minor listed and unlisted varieties. A thorough explanation of the differences in the major types for all denominations of the 1857-61 series is contained in the Harris Stamp Identifier in this catalog.

Shortly after the outbreak of the Civil War, the 1851-61 stamps were demonetized to prevent Southern post offices from selling the stamps in the North to raise cash for the Confederate States. After the war, large supplies of unused 1857-61 stamps were located in Southern post offices and purchased by stamp dealers and collectors. This explains the relatively large supply of unused 1857-61 issues that still exist today. The short life and limited use of 90 cent high value, which was issued in 1860, and the 5 cent orange brown, released May 8, 1861, explains why those stamps sell for more used than unused.

5-9, 18-24, 40
Franklin

10, 11, 25, 26, 41
Washington

12, 27-30A, 42
Jefferson

13-16, 31-35, 43
Washington

17, 36, 44
Washington

SCOTT NO.	DESCRIPTION	UNUSED VF	UNUSED F	UNUSED AVG	USED VF	USED F	USED AVG
	1851-57 Imperforate (OG + 100%)						
5	1¢ blue (I).	....	....	....	....	55000.00	....
5A	1¢ blue (Ib).	13000.00	10750.00	8900.00	9500.00	6425.00	4475.00
6	1¢ dark blue (Ia).	22000.00	16700.00	12250.00	11000.00	8000.00	5275.00
7	1¢ blue (II)	500.00	375.00	250.00	250.00	175.00	100.00
8	1¢ blue (III).	9500.00	6000.00	4200.00	2500.00	1500.00	1000.00
8A	1¢ blue (IIIa).	5000.00	3400.00	2100.00	1725.00	1100.00	800.00
9	1¢ blue (IV).	350.00	270.00	175.00	200.00	125.00	85.00
10	3¢ orange brown (I) . .	2000.00	1200.00	800.00	225.00	180.00	140.00
11	3¢ deep claret (I)	200.00	185.00	75.00	30.00	17.25	15.00
12	5¢ red brown (I)	13650.00	10250.00	6750.00	1100.00	600.00	450.00
13	10¢ green (I).	11050.00	8500.00	6000.00	1175.00	650.00	475.00
14	10¢ green (II)	2300.00	1750.00	1350.00	300.00	200.00	180.00
15	10¢ green (III).	2500.00	1800.00	1300.00	300.00	200.00	180.00
16	10¢ green (IV)	18900.00	12500.00	10000.00	2000.00	1500.00	1150.00
17	12¢ black	3250.00	2500.00	1750.00	300.00	200.00	150.00

***NOTE:** For further details on the various types of similar appearing stamps please refer to our U.S. Stamp Identifier.*

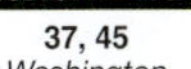

37, 45
Washington

38, 46
Franklin

39, 47
Washington

1857-61 Same design as preceding Issue, Perf. 15½ (†) (OG + 75%)

SCOTT NO.	DESCRIPTION	UNUSED VF	UNUSED F	UNUSED AVG	USED VF	USED F	USED AVG
18	1¢ blue (I)	1500.00	950.00	700.00	1000.00	550.00	300.00
19	1¢ blue (Ia)	22000.00	12500.00	9125.00	9000.00	5900.00	3790.00
20	1¢ blue (II)	750.00	525.00	400.00	400.00	290.00	160.00
21	1¢ blue (III)	8150.00	5500.00	4200.00	3000.00	1700.00	1200.00
22	1¢ blue (IIIa)	1350.00	950.00	650.00	795.00	425.00	300.00
23	1¢ blue (IV)	4900.00	3400.00	2400.00	1500.00	925.00	600.00
24	1¢ blue (V)	95.00	60.00	35.00	70.00	40.00	30.00
25	3¢ rose (I)	1750.00	1300.00	1000.00	230.00	153.50	97.25
26	3¢ dull red (III)	45.00	25.00	15.00	20.00	7.50	5.00
26a	3¢ dull red (IV)	350.00	265.00	185.00	170.00	120.00	85.00
27	5¢ brick red (I)	22000.00	15750.00	10750.00	2250.00	1685.00	900.00
28	5¢ red brown (I)	20000.00	13000.00	8500.00	2000.00	1350.00	825.00
28A	5¢ Indian red (I)	40000.00	20000.00	13000.00	3600.00	2800.00	2000.00
29	5¢ brown (I)	1800.00	975.00	725.00	590.00	325.00	200.00
30	5¢ orange brown (II)	925.00	650.00	500.00	2100.00	1400.00	800.00
30A	5¢ brown (II)	1250.00	975.00	650.00	475.00	275.00	180.00
31	10¢ green (I)	12000.00	9500.00	6000.00	1500.00	1100.00	650.00
32	10¢ green (II)	3200.00	2200.00	1650.00	450.00	220.00	150.00
33	10¢ green (III)	3200.00	2200.00	1650.00	375.00	295.00	190.00
34	10¢ green (IV)	22500.00	15750.00	12500.00	2600.00	2100.00	1650.00
35	10¢ green (V)	180.00	75.00	50.00	120.00	65.00	45.00
36	12¢ black, Plate I	1100.00	800.00	600.00	550.00	375.00	200.00
36b	12¢ black, Plate III	550.00	380.00	250.00	400.00	275.00	185.00
37	24¢ gray lilac	800.00	500.00	300.00	500.00	400.00	200.00
38	30¢ orange	1250.00	700.00	500.00	700.00	400.00	275.00
39	90¢ blue	1700.00	1100.00	600.00	10000.00	7750.00	5750.00

1875 Reprints of 1857-61 Issue. Perf. 12 Without Gum

SCOTT NO.	DESCRIPTION	UNUSED VF	UNUSED F	UNUSED AVG	USED VF	USED F	USED AVG
40	1¢ bright blue	700.00	550.00	300.00	....	....	....
41	3¢ scarlet	5000.00	3200.00	2800.00	....	....	....
42	5¢ orange brown	3000.00	1700.00	1200.00	....	....	....
43	10¢ blue green	4300.00	3200.00	2200.00	....	....	....
44	12¢ greenish black	4500.00	3500.00	2000.00	....	....	....
45	24¢ blackish violet	5600.00	3800.00	2200.00	....	....	....
46	30¢ yellow orange	5400.00	3800.00	2200.00	....	....	....
47	90¢ deep blue	4500.00	3500.00	2000.00	....	....	....

THE 1861-67 ISSUE

The 1861-66 Issue and its 1867 Grilled varieties are among the most interesting and controversial of all stamps. Born out of the need to demonetize previously-issued stamps in the possession of Southern post offices, they were rushed into service shortly after the outbreak of the Civil War.

The controversy begins with the "August Issues", catalog numbers 55-62B. It is now generally accepted that all but the 10 and 24 cent values never were issued for use as postage. The set is more aptly described as "First Designs", because they were printed by the National Bank Note Company and submitted to the Post Office Department as fully gummed and perforated sample designs.

63, 85A, 86, 92, 102
Franklin

64-65, 79, 82, 83, 85, 85C, 88, 94, 104
Washington

67, 75, 76, 80, 95, 105
Jefferson

62B, 68, 85D, 89, 96, 106
Washington

69, 85E, 90, 97, 107
Washington

70, 78, 99, 109
Washington

71, 81, 100, 110
Franklin

72, 101, 111
Washington

(†) means Issue is actually very poorly centered. Perforations may touch the design on "Fine" quality.

73, 84, 85B, 87, 93, 103
Jackson

77, 85F, 91, 98, 108
Lincoln

1861 First Design (†) Perf. 12 (OG + 75%)

SCOTT NO.	DESCRIPTION	UNUSED VF	UNUSED F	UNUSED AVG	USED VF	USED F	USED AVG
62B	10¢ dark green	3600.00	2200.00	1325.00	1900.00	1325.00	875.00

1861-62 Second Design (†) Perf. 12 (OG + 75%)

SCOTT NO.	DESCRIPTION	UNUSED VF	UNUSED F	UNUSED AVG	USED VF	USED F	USED AVG
63	1¢ blue	160.00	85.00	60.00	55.00	40.00	25.00
64	3¢ pink	5500.00	3900.00	2800.00	750.00	575.00	400.00
64b	3¢ rose pink	325.00	250.00	190.00	165.00	115.00	90.00
65	3¢ rose	60.00	40.00	28.00	4.50	3.00	2.00
66	3¢ lake	2850.00	2100.00	1500.00	....	....	....
67	5¢ buff	11550.00	7250.00	5500.00	975.00	700.00	550.00
68	10¢ yellow green	500.00	300.00	220.00	85.00	50.00	38.00
69	12¢ black	825.00	600.00	380.00	125.00	80.00	50.00
70	24¢ red lilac	1400.00	800.00	500.00	400.00	200.00	135.00
71	30¢ orange	1280.00	775.00	500.00	250.00	180.00	100.00
72	90¢ blue	1600.00	900.00	600.00	650.00	480.00	325.00

1861-66 (†) (OG + 75%)

SCOTT NO.	DESCRIPTION	UNUSED VF	UNUSED F	UNUSED AVG	USED VF	USED F	USED AVG
73	2¢ black	200.00	120.00	75.00	115.00	75.00	45.00
75	5¢ red brown	2800.00	2200.00	1450.00	600.00	475.00	300.00
76	5¢ brown	700.00	450.00	275.00	170.00	120.00	70.00
77	15¢ black	2000.00	1325.00	850.00	220.00	185.00	115.00
78	24¢ lilac	1200.00	725.00	450.00	350.00	175.00	120.00

From 1867 to 1870, grills were embossed into the stamp paper to break the fiber and prevent the eradication of cancellations. The first "A" grilled issues were grilled all over. When postal clerks found that the stamps were as likely to separate along the grill as on the perforations, the Post Office abandoned the "A" grill and tried other configurations, none of which proved to be effective. The Grilled Issues include some of our greatest rarities. The most notable is the 1 cent "Z", only two of which are known to exist. One realized $4,400,000 in a 2024 auction, making it the most valuable United States stamp. The grills are fully explained and identified in the Harris Stamp Identifiers.

1867 Grill with Points Up
A. Grill Covering Entire Stamp (†) (OG + 75%)

SCOTT NO.	DESCRIPTION	UNUSED VF	UNUSED F	UNUSED AVG	USED VF	USED F	USED AVG
79	3¢ rose	....	5000.00	3500.00	....	1400.00	975.00
80	5¢ brown	....	....	....	....	350000.00	....
81	30¢ orange	....	....	....	....	....	250000.00

B. Grill about 18 x 15 mm. (OG + 75%)

SCOTT NO.	DESCRIPTION	UNUSED VF	UNUSED F	UNUSED AVG	USED VF	USED F	USED AVG
82	3¢ rose	....	....	....	....	950000.00	....

C. Grill About 13 x 16 mm. (†) (OG + 75%)

SCOTT NO.	DESCRIPTION	UNUSED VF	UNUSED F	UNUSED AVG	USED VF	USED F	USED AVG
83	3¢ rose	2500.00	1400.00	1000.00	1200.00	800.00	500.00

1867 Grill with Points Down
D. Grill About 12 x 14 mm. (†) (OG + 75%)

SCOTT NO.	DESCRIPTION	UNUSED VF	UNUSED F	UNUSED AVG	USED VF	USED F	USED AVG
84	2¢ black	10000.00	8000.00	6000.00	8000.00	5000.00	3000.00
85	3¢ rose	3200.00	1800.00	1200.00	1200.00	800.00	500.00

Z. Grill About 11 x 14 mm. (†) (OG + 75%)

SCOTT NO.	DESCRIPTION	UNUSED VF	UNUSED F	UNUSED AVG	USED VF	USED F	USED AVG
85A	1¢ blue	....	....	....	....	....	....
85B	2¢ black	7000.00	5000.00	3000.00	1350.00	1050.00	700.00
85C	3¢ rose	9500.00	6750.00	4800.00	3500.00	3050.00	2075.00
85D	10¢ green	....	....	....	750000.00	675000.00	....
85E	12¢ black	8400.00	6250.00	4700.00	2500.00	1900.00	1500.00
85F	15¢ black	....	....	....	2000000.00	....	....

E. Grill About 11 x 13 mm. (†) (OG + 75%)

SCOTT NO.	DESCRIPTION	UNUSED VF	UNUSED F	UNUSED AVG	USED VF	USED F	USED AVG
86	1¢ blue	1600.00	1100.00	650.00	775.00	400.00	200.00
87	2¢ black	800.00	615.00	450.00	325.00	190.00	130.00
88	3¢ rose	495.00	375.00	250.00	45.00	30.75	20.50
89	10¢ green	2400.00	1500.00	900.00	375.00	220.00	150.00
90	12¢ black	2200.00	1200.00	850.00	500.00	250.00	160.00
91	15¢ black	5200.00	3000.00	2000.00	750.00	550.00	325.00

Showgard® MOUNTS

All showgard mounts are only available with black backgrounds.

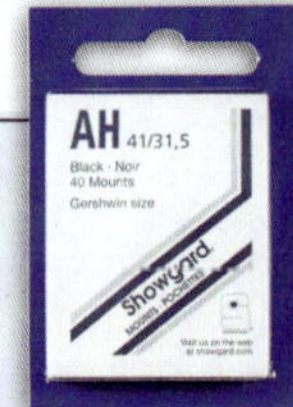

Cut Style

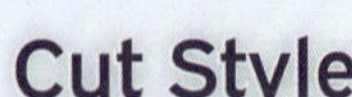

Stock No. Showgard	Stock No. Harris	Pieces/ Pack	Description	Retail
AH41/31	9SGD10	40	U.S. Semi Jumbo Gershwin, etc.	$4.95
AV31/41	9SGD3184	40	Legends of the West	$4.95
C50/31	9SGD1	40	U.S. Jumbo Singles Horizontal	$4.95
CV31/50	9SGD2	40	U.S. Jumbo Singles Vertical	$4.95
DH52/36	9SGD3081	30	U.S. Duck Stamps	$4.95
E22/25	9SGD5	40	U.S. Regular Issues	$4.95
EH25/22	9SGD6	40	U.S. Regular Issues Horizontal	$4.95
J40/25	9SGD3	40	U.S. Comm. Horizontal	$4.95
JV25/40	9SGD4	40	U.S. Comm. Vertical	$4.95
N40/27	9SGD9	40	United Nations	$4.95
S31/31	9SGD3329	40	Celebrate the Century	$4.95
T25/27	9SGD7	40	U.S. Famous Americans	$4.95
U33/27	9SGD8	40	U.N. and Germany	$4.95

Plate Blocks & Covers

Stock No. Showgard	Stock No. Harris	Pieces/ Pack	Description	Retail
57/55	9SGD13	25	Regular issue U.S. Plate Blocks	$9.95
67/25	9SGD2341	40	U.S. Coil Strips of three	$9.95
105/57	9SGD15	20	U.S. Giori Press. Modern. Plate Block	$9.95
106/55	9SGD14	20	U.S. 3¢, 4¢ Comm. Plate Block	$9.95
127/70	9SGD16	10	U.S. Jumbo Issues Plate Block	$9.95
140/89	9SGD2342	10	Postcards	$9.95
165/94	9SGD17	10	First Day Covers	$9.95

Strips 215mm Long

Stock No. Showgard	Stock No. Harris	Pieces/ Pack	Description	Retail
20	9SGD18	22	Mini Stamps U.S., etc.	$11.95
22	9SGD19	22	Narrow U.S. Airs	$11.95
24	9SGD20	22	U.K. and Canada Early U.S.	$11.95
25	9SGD21	22	U.S. Comm. and Regular Issue	$11.95
27	9SGD22	22	U.S. Famous Americans and U.N.	$11.95
28	9SGD23	22	Switzerland, Liechtenstein	$11.95
30	9SGD24	22	U.S. Jamestown, Foreign	$11.95
31	9SGD25	22	U.S. Squares and Semi-Jumbo	$11.95
33	9SGD26	22	GB Issues, Misc. Foreign	$11.95
36	9SGD27	15	Duck Stamps, Misc. Foreign	$11.95
39	9SGD28	15	U.S. Magsaysay, Misc. Foreign	$11.95
41	9SGD29	15	U.S. Vertical Comm. Israel Tabs	$11.95
44	9SGD30	15	U.S. Hatteras Block of four	$11.95
48	9SGD31	15	Canada Reg. Issue and Comm. Blks.	$11.95
50	9SGD32	15	U.S. Plain Blocks of four	$11.95
52	9SGD33	15	France Paintings	$11.95
57	9SGD34	15	U.S. Comm. Plate Blocks (4)	$11.95
61	9SGD35	15	Souvenir Sheets, Tab Singles	$11.95

Strips 240mm Long

Stock No. Showgard	Stock No. Harris	Pieces/ Pack	Description	Retail
63	9SGD36	10	U.S. Squares, Plain Blocks (4)	$16.50
66	9SGD37	10	Israel Plate Blocks, etc.	$16.50
68	9SGD38	10	Can. Plate Blocks, $1 Fundy, etc.	$16.50
74	9SGD39	10	U.N. Inscription Blocks (4)	$16.50
80	9SGD40	10	U.S. Comm. Plain Blocks (4)	$16.50
82	9SGD41	10	U.N. Chagall SS, Canada Plate Blks	$16.50
84	9SGD42	10	Israel, Tab Blocks, etc.	$16.50
89	9SGD43	10	U.N. Inscription Blocks (6)	$16.50
100	9SGD44	7	U.S. Squares - Plate Blocks	$16.50
120	9SGD45	7	Miniature Sheets	$16.50

Strips 264mm Long

Stock No. Showgard	Stock No. Harris	Pieces/ Pack	Description	Retail
70	9SGD46	10	U.S. Jumbo Plate Blocks	$18.95
91	9SGD47	10	GB Souvenir Sheets	$18.95
105	9SGD48	10	GB Blocks, Covers, Cards	$18.95
107	9SGD49	10	U.S. Plate No. Strip (20)	$18.95
111	9SGD54	5	U.S. Floating No. Plate Strips (20)	$18.95
127	9SGD55	5	U.S. UPU and LBJ Plate Blocks (15)	$18.95
137	9SGD56	5	GB Coronations, U.N., SS	$18.95
158	9SGD57	5	Souvenir Sheets, Apollo Soyuz, Plate Block	$18.95
175	9SGD2471	5	U.S. Sheets Love, Christmas	$18.95
188	9SGD2892	5	Marilyn Monroe Miniature Sheets	$18.95
198	9SGD2893	5	Legends of the West Miniature Sheets	$18.95

Assortments & Mount Accessories

Stock No. Showgard	Stock No. Harris	Pieces/ Pack	Description	Retail
Group AB	9SGD52	11	Souvenir Sheets	$11.95
265/231	9SGD53	5	Full Sheets and Souvenir Cards	$23.50
Group 94	9SGD2650	5	1994 Souvenir Sheets-Clear	$10.25
MPK	9SGD50	12	Assortment #22-41	$8.95
MPK II	9SGD51	15	Assortment #76-171	$37.95
US3	9SGD12	75	Indexed Tray and Strip Set Assortment (#22-52)	$49.95
507	9SGD2112	1	Desert Magic II Drying Book 8.5" x 11"	$13.50

Blocks

Stock No. Showgard	Stock No. Harris	Pieces/ Pack	Description	Retail
111/91	9SGD2756	6	Columbian Souvenir Sheets	$9.25
120/207	9SGD2113	4	Ameripex Presidential Sheets	$10.95
187/144	9SGD61	10	U.N. Flags Sheetlets	$25.95
191/229	9SGD3330	5	Celebrate the Century Sheets (5)	$15.95
192/201	9SGD3071	5	Legends of the West Sheet	$15.75
204/153	9SGD62	5	U.S. Bicentennial and W. Plains SS	$15.95
229/131	9SGD2713	5	WWII Souvenir Sheets	$17.25
260/25	9SGD2382	25	U.S. Coil Strips (up to 11 stamps)	$14.25
260/40	9SGD58	10	U.S. Postal People Full Strip	$11.25
260/46	9SGD3277	10	U.S. Vending Booklets	$12.50
260/55	9SGD59	10	U.S. 13¢ Eagle Full Strip	$12.50
260/59	9SGD60	10	U.S. Double Press Regular Issue Strip (20)	$14.50
Group Pac 97	9SGD3274	7	Pacific 97 Issues	$5.75
Trans-Miss	9SGD3341	11	Trans-Miss. Reissues	$5.75
Space	9SGD4122	5	Space Exploration	$7.25

Accommodation Range Mount

Stock No. Showgard	Stock No. Harris	Description	Retail
76	9SGD4119	Bright Eyes (Top), Challenger Shuttle Plate Blocks	$13.25
96	9SGD3010	Flowering Trees, Christmas Plate Blocks	$13.25
109	9SGD3122	109 Strip	$13.25
115	9SGD3012	115 Strip	$19.00
117	9SGD4111	117 Strip	$19.00
121	9SGD4112	121 Strip	$19.00
131	9SGD2746	131 Strip	$19.00
135	9SGD4113	135 Strip	$19.00
139	9SGD4114	139 Strip	$19.00
143	9SGD4115	143 Strip	$19.00
147	9SGD3123	Cinco De Mayo, Miniature Sheet	$19.00
151	9SGD4116	Automobiles, Hanukkah, Miniature Sheets	$19.00
163	9SGD3011	Kwanzaa Miniature Sheet	$19.00
167	9SGD4117	IA, TN, Bright Eyes, Miniature Sheets	$19.00
181	9SGD4120	All Aboard	$19.00
201	9SGD3230	World of Dinosaurs, Miniature Sheet	$19.00
215	9SGD4121	Arctic Animals	$19.00
171	9SGD4118	Helping Children	$19.00

Stamp Tongs

Stock No. Showgard	Stock No. Harris	Pieces/ Pack	Description	Retail
904	9SGD2570	1	Professional Round Tip	$11.95
905	9SGD2571	1	Beginner Round Tip	$5.95
907	9SGD95	1	Professional Angled Tip	$11.95

H.E. Harris Call to order 1·800·546·2995
Or shop at heharris.com

SCOTT NO.	DESCRIPTION	UNUSED VF	UNUSED F	UNUSED AVG	USED VF	USED F	USED AVG
	F. Grill About 9 x 13 mm. (†) (OG + 75%)						
92	1¢ blue	1250.00	775.00	500.00	600.00	375.00	200.00
93	2¢ black	375.00	180.00	140.00	100.00	60.00	40.00
94	3¢ red	220.00	150.00	90.00	15.00	10.00	6.00
95	5¢ brown	1800.00	1400.00	950.00	1125.00	775.00	475.00
96	10¢ yellow green	1300.00	700.00	400.00	350.00	240.00	135.00
97	12¢ black	1600.00	1000.00	580.00	320.00	275.00	160.00
98	15¢ black	2100.00	1300.00	800.00	400.00	300.00	190.00
99	24¢ gray lilac	4300.00	2500.00	1900.00	2000.00	1200.00	750.00
100	30¢ orange	4500.00	2600.00	2000.00	1000.00	800.00	500.00
101	90¢ blue	7000.00	4000.00	3000.00	3000.00	2000.00	1200.00

The Re-Issues of the 1861-66 Issue were issued with gum and, while scarce, are found used. They can be distinguished by their bright colors, sharp printing impressions, hard paper and white, crackly original gum.

SCOTT NO.	DESCRIPTION	UNUSED VF	UNUSED F	UNUSED AVG	USED VF	USED F	USED AVG
	1875. Re-Issue of 1861-66 Issue. Hard White Paper (OG + 75%)						
102	1¢ blue	450.00	325.00	225.00	1600.00	1225.00	850.00
103	2¢ black	2000.00	1200.00	875.00	13000.00	9500.00	7000.00
104	3¢ brown red	2200.00	1500.00	1000.00	17000.00	14785.00	10000.00
105	5¢ brown	1400.00	900.00	650.00	7200.00	5000.00	3000.00
106	10¢ green	1800.00	1400.00	950.00	125000.00	95000.00	77250.00
107	12¢ black	2200.00	1500.00	1100.00	15000.00	12000.00	9250.00
108	15¢ black	2300.00	1800.00	1175.00	35000.00	28000.00	22000.00
109	24¢ deep violet	3200.00	2200.00	1400.00	20000.00	16000.00	13000.00
110	30¢ brownish orange	3400.00	2600.00	1500.00	25000.00	20000.00	16875.00
111	90¢ blue	4200.00	2400.00	1700.00	225000.00	....	130000.00

THE 1869 PICTORIALS

As the first United States series to include pictorial designs, the 1869 issue is one of the most popular today. They were so unpopular that they were removed from sale less than a year after issue. Most protests were directed toward their odd size and the tradition-breaking pictorial designs.

The 1869 issue broke important new ground in the use of two color designs. Not only does this add to their attractiveness; it also is the source for the first United States "Inverted Centers". These inverted errors appear on the bicolored 15, 24 and 30 cent values. The printing technology of the time required a separate printing pass for each color. On the first pass, the central designs, or vignettes, were printed. The second pass applied the frames.

In a very few instances, the sheets with their central designs already printed were passed upside down through the printing press. As a result, the frames were printed upside down. So the description "inverted center" for the 15 and 24 cent errors is technically incorrect, but the form in which these errors are photographed and displayed is with the center, rather than the frame, inverted.

Used copies of the 1869 Pictorials are not as scarce as might be expected. Any of the stamps above the 3 cent denomination were used on mail to Europe and were saved by collectors overseas. When stamp collecting became popular in the United States and Americans were able to purchase stamps abroad at relatively low prices, many of these used 1869 Pictorials found their way back to this country. On the other hand, because of the short life of the issue in post offices and their sudden withdrawal, unused stamps—particularly the high values—are quite rare.

All values of the 1869 Pictorials are found with the "G" grill. Ungrilled varieties are known on all values except the 6, 10, 12 and type II 15 cent stamps. (The Harris Stamp Identifier describes the difference in the three 15 cent types.)

The 1869 Pictorials were re-issued in 1875 in anticipation of the 1876 Centennial Exposition. Most collectors who had missed the original 1869 issue were delighted to have a second chance to purchase the stamps, which explains why the high value re-issues carry lower prices today than do the original 1869 pictorials. At the time, most collectors did not realize they were buying entirely different stamps. The same designs were used, but the re-issues were issued on a distinctive hard, white paper without grills.

The 1 cent stamp was re-issued a second time, in 1880. This re-issue can be distinguished by the lack of a grill and by the soft, porous paper used by the American Bank Note Company.

112, 123, 133,133a
Franklin

113, 124
Pony Express Rider

114, 125
Locomotive

115, 126
Washington

116, 127
Shield & Eagle

117, 128
S.S. Adriatic

118, 119, 129
Landing of Columbus

120, 130
Signing of Declaration

121, 131
Shield, Eagle & Flags

122, 132
Lincoln

SCOTT NO.	DESCRIPTION	UNUSED VF	UNUSED F	UNUSED AVG	USED VF	USED F	USED AVG
	1869 G. Grill measuring 9½ x 9½ mm. (†) (OG + 75%)						
112	1¢ buff	375.00	190.00	120.00	200.00	150.00	90.00
113	2¢ brown	320.00	195.00	115.00	115.00	90.00	60.00
114	3¢ ultramarine	150.00	80.00	50.00	25.00	18.00	12.00
115	6¢ ultramarine	1300.00	900.00	500.00	220.00	175.00	100.00
116	10¢ yellow	1200.00	750.00	400.00	150.00	120.00	80.00
117	12¢ green	1200.00	750.00	400.00	150.00	120.00	80.00
118	15¢ brown & blue (I)	4600.00	3000.00	2500.00	950.00	650.00	400.00
119	15¢ brown & blue (II)	1700.00	1000.00	650.00	275.00	190.00	120.00
120	24¢ green & violet	4000.00	2200.00	1500.00	700.00	490.00	320.00
121	30¢ blue & carmine	2000.00	1400.00	1000.00	550.00	350.00	250.00
122	90¢ carmine & black	4500.00	3500.00	2000.00	2400.00	1800.00	1200.00
	1875 Re-Issue of 1869 Issue. Hard White Paper. Without Grill (OG + 75%)						
123	1¢ buff	390.00	275.00	175.00	450.00	325.00	230.00
124	2¢ brown	390.00	275.00	175.00	900.00	650.00	450.00
125	3¢ blue	3000.00	1800.00	1200.00	....	25000.00	....
126	6¢ blue	900.00	550.00	450.00	3500.00	2200.00	1200.00
127	10¢ yellow	950.00	650.00	450.00	2400.00	2000.00	1300.00
128	12¢ green	1600.00	850.00	550.00	3500.00	2400.00	1350.00
129	15¢ brown & blue (III)	950.00	600.00	400.00	1300.00	900.00	600.00
130	24¢ green & violet	1300.00	850.00	600.00	1900.00	1200.00	900.00
131	30¢ blue & carmine	1400.00	900.00	675.00	3200.00	2300.00	1500.00
132	90¢ carmine & black	2000.00	1550.00	1250.00	6500.00	4800.00	3600.00
	1880 Re-Issue. Soft Porous Paper, Issued Without Grill (†) (#133 OG +50%)						
133	1¢ buff	200.00	150.00	95.00	550.00	450.00	300.00
133a	1¢ brown orange (issued w/o gum)	425.00	350.00	225.00	650.00	500.00	320.00

(†) means Issue is actually very poorly centered. Perforations may touch the design on "Fine" quality.

THE 1870-88 BANK NOTE ISSUES

The "Bank Notes" are stamps that were issued between 1870 and 1888 by the National, Continental and American Bank Note Companies.

The myriad of varieties, secret marks, papers, grills, re-engravings and special printings produced by the three companies resulted in no less than 87 major catalog listings for what basically amounts to 16 different designs. For collectors, what seems to be the very difficult task of properly identifying all these varieties can be eased by following these guidelines:

1. The chronological order in which the three Bank Note companies produced stamps is their reverse alphabetical order: National, Continental, American.

2. "3, 6, 9" identifies the number of years each of the companies printed stamps within the 18-year Bank Note period. Starting in 1870, National continued its work for 3 more years, until 1873, when the Continental Company began printing stamps. That company served for the next 6 years, until 1879, when American took over the Continental company. Although American printed some later issues, the "Bank Note" period ended 9 years later, in 1888.

3. The first Bank Note issue, the Nationals of 1870-71, continued the practice of grilling stamps. Although some specialists contend there are grilled Continental stamps, for all intents and purposes, if a Bank Note stamp bears a genuine grill, it must be from the 1870-71 National issue.

4. The secret marks on values through the 12 cent, and possibly the 15 cent value, were added when the Continental Company took over. They enabled the government to distinguish between National's work and that of its successor. If a Bank Note stamp did not show a secret mark, the Post Office could identify it as the work of the National Bank Note Company. You can do the same.

5. The paper used by the National and Continental companies is similar, but that of the American Bank Note company is noticeably different from the first two. When held to the light, the thick, soft American paper shows its coarse, uneven texture, while that of its two predecessors is more even and translucent. The American Bank Note paper also reveals a yellowish hue when held to the light, whereas the National and Continental papers are whiter.

6. Experienced collectors also apply a "snap test" to identify American Bank Note paper by gently flexing a Bank Note stamp at one of its corners. The American Bank Note paper will not "snap" back into place. The National and Continental stamps, on the other hand, often give off a noticeable sound when the flex is released.

7. By purchasing one Bank Note design put into use after 1882 (which can only be an American) and one early Bank Note stamp without the secret mark, (which can only be a National), the collector has a reference point against which to compare any other Bank Note stamp. If it is a soft paper, it is an American Bank Note issue; if a harder paper, it is either a National or a Continental—and these two can be classified by the absence (National) or presence (Continental) of the secret marks or other distinguishing features or colors. The Harris Stamp Identifier in this catalog provides illustrations of the secret marks and further information on the distinguishing features of the various Bank Notes. With two reference stamps, some practice and the use of the information in this catalog, collectors can turn the "job" of understanding the Bank Notes into a pleasant adventure.

134, 145, 156, 167, 182, 192, 206
Franklin

135, 146, 157, 168, 178, 180, 183, 193, 203
Jackson

136, 147, 158, 169, 184, 194, 207, 214
Washington

NOTE: For further details on the various types of similar appearing stamps please refer to our U.S. Stamp Identifier.

(†) means Issue is actually very poorly centered. Perforations may touch the design on "Fine" quality.

137, 148, 159, 170, 186, 195, 208
Lincoln

138, 149, 160, 171, 196
Stanton

139, 150, 161, 172, 187, 188, 197, 209
Jefferson

140, 151, 162, 173, 198
Clay

141, 152, 163, 174, 189, 199
Webster

142, 153, 164, 175, 200
Scott

143, 154, 165, 176, 190, 201, 217
Hamilton

144, 155, 166, 177, 191, 202, 218
Perry

SCOTT NO.	DESCRIPTION	UNUSED VF	UNUSED F	UNUSED AVG	USED VF	USED F	USED AVG
	1870 National Bank Note Co., without Secret Marks. With H Grill about (10 x 12 mm. or 8½ x 10 mm.) Perf 12. (†) (OG +75%)						
134	1¢ ultramarine	850.00	650.00	500.00	300.00	200.00	110.00
135	2¢ red brown	450.00	360.00	275.00	110.00	85.00	50.00
136	3¢ green	300.00	200.00	150.00	45.00	30.00	15.00
137	6¢ carmine	2000.00	1700.00	1000.00	600.00	450.00	250.00
138	7¢ vermillion	1800.00	1250.00	900.00	650.00	450.00	300.00
139	10¢ brown	3000.00	2500.00	1750.00	1300.00	800.00	525.00
140	12¢ dull violet	16800.00	11500.00	6500.00	3800.00	2800.00	1800.00
141	15¢ orange	4750.00	2700.00	1850.00	1500.00	1100.00	650.00
142	24¢ purple	....	....	....	7500.00	6000.00	4300.00
143	30¢ black	10000.00	6750.00	4800.00	4000.00	2800.00	1800.00
144	90¢ carmine	12100.00	7250.00	4500.00	2600.00	1800.00	1200.00
	1870-71. National Bank Note Co., without Secret Marks. Without Grill. Perf 12. (†) (OG +75%)						
145	1¢ ultramarine	400.00	275.00	150.00	30.00	20.00	15.00
146	2¢ red brown	250.00	155.00	100.00	25.00	16.00	10.50
147	3¢ green	275.00	170.00	112.00	4.00	2.75	1.60
148	6¢ carmine	675.00	400.00	225.00	50.00	31.00	19.00
149	7¢ vermillion	700.00	450.00	250.00	165.00	92.00	56.00
150	10¢ brown	850.00	600.00	395.00	63.00	43.00	27.00
151	12¢ dull violet	1500.00	1000.00	600.00	325.00	215.00	135.00
152	15¢ bright orange	1500.00	1000.00	600.00	350.00	235.00	150.00
153	24¢ purple	1250.00	800.00	550.00	300.00	180.00	120.00
154	30¢ black	4000.00	2800.00	1600.00	450.00	300.00	175.00
155	90¢ carmine	3000.00	2000.00	1150.00	500.00	350.00	200.00
	1873. Continental Bank Note Co. Same designs as 1870-71, with Secret Marks, on thin hard grayish white paper. Perf 12 (†) (OG + 75%)						
156	1¢ ultramarine	110.00	90.00	65.00	5.00	3.75	2.25
157	2¢ brown	150.00	125.00	75.00	30.00	21.00	12.00
158	3¢ green	75.00	40.00	25.00	1.25	.75	.50
159	6¢ dull pink	150.00	125.00	85.00	35.00	20.00	14.00
160	7¢ orange vermillion	400.00	325.00	250.00	150.00	105.00	68.00
161	10¢ brown	500.00	250.00	195.00	40.00	28.00	17.00
162	12¢ black violet	800.00	600.00	400.00	200.00	130.00	86.00
163	15¢ yellow orange	800.00	600.00	400.00	225.00	150.00	90.00
165	30¢ gray black	1450.00	1250.00	700.00	200.00	130.00	83.00
166	90¢ rose carmine	1000.00	850.00	500.00	475.00	300.00	175.00
	1875 Special Printing–On Hard White Wove Paper–Without Gum Perf. 12						
167	1¢ ultramarine	20000.00	13250.00	7500.00	....	....	....
168	2¢ dark brown	10000.00	6500.00	4400.00	....	....	....
169	3¢ blue green	25000.00	16750.00	11250.00	....	....	....
170	6¢ dull rose	25000.00	16750.00	11250.00	....	....	....
171	7¢ reddish vermillion	6500.00	4300.00	3000.00	....	....	....
172	10¢ pale brown	23500.00	15750.00	10500.00	....	....	....
173	12¢ dark violet	8000.00	5250.00	3800.00	....	....	....
174	15¢ bright orange	23000.00	15500.00	10250.00	....	....	....
175	24¢ dull purple	5750.00	3800.00	2600.00	....	....	....
176	30¢ greenish black	20000.00	13500.00	9250.00	....	....	....
177	90¢ violet carmine	32500.00	21500.00	15000.00	....	....	....

179, 181, 185, 204
Taylor

205, 205C, 216
Garfield

SCOTT NO.	DESCRIPTION	UNUSED VF	UNUSED F	UNUSED AVG	USED VF	USED F	USED AVG
	1875 Continental Bank Note Co. Hard yellowish paper, Perf 12. (†) (OG + 50%)						
178	2¢ vermillion	145.00	100.00	75.00	20.00	14.00	9.50
179	5¢ blue	350.00	225.00	150.00	45.00	28.00	15.00
	1875 Continental Bank Note Co., Special Printings. Same as 1875, on hard white paper, without gum. Perf 12.						
180	2¢ carmine vermillion	80000.00	60000.00	36500.00	....	....	....
181	5¢ bright blue	500000.00	375000.00	235000.00	....	....	....
	1879 American Bank Note Co. Same designs as 1870-71 Issue (with Secret Marks) and 1875 Issue on soft, porous, coarse, yellowish paper. Perf 12. (†) (OG + 60%)						
182	1¢ dark ultramarine	150.00	100.00	80.00	8.00	5.00	3.00
183	2¢ vermilion	60.00	40.00	25.00	5.50	4.00	3.00
184	3¢ green	45.00	35.00	27.00	1.00	.70	.50
185	5¢ blue	185.00	130.00	100.00	26.00	18.00	12.00
186	6¢ pink	350.00	275.00	195.00	45.00	32.50	19.50
187	10¢ brown (no secret mark)	1500.00	1000.00	600.00	70.00	50.00	30.00
188	10¢ brown (secret mark)	900.00	600.00	450.00	50.00	36.50	21.95
189	15¢ red orange	100.00	85.00	50.00	40.00	30.00	17.25
190	30¢ full black	400.00	350.00	200.00	150.00	100.00	67.00
191	90¢ carmine	900.00	700.00	525.00	500.00	320.00	230.00
	1880 American Bank Note Co., Special Printings. Same as 1879 Issue, on soft, porous paper, without gum. Perf 12.						
192	1¢ dark ultramarine	75000.00	47000.00	28000.00	....	....	....
193	2¢ black brown	28000.00	19750.00	12750.00	....	....	....
194	3¢ blue green	120000.00	75000.00	48000.00	....	....	....
195	6¢ dull rose	90000.00	55000.00	34000.00	....	....	....
196	7¢ scarlet vermillion	9000.00	6250.00	4200.00	....	....	....
197	10¢ deep brown	55000.00	35500.00	21000.00	....	....	....
198	12¢ black purple	15000.00	10500.00	7000.00	....	....	....
199	15¢ orange	35000.00	25000.00	18000.00	....	....	....
200	24¢ dark violet	15000.00	10500.00	7000.00	....	....	....
201	30¢ greenish black	25000.00	18000.00	12000.00	....	....	....
202	90¢ dull carmine	35000.00	26000.00	18000.00	....	....	....
203	2¢ scarlet vermillion	120000.00	90000.00	60000.00	....	....	....
204	5¢ deep blue	260000.00	200000.00	145000.00	....	....	....
	1882 American Bank Note Company Perf 12. (OG + 60%)						
205	5¢ yellow brown	110.00	85.00	65.00	15.00	11.00	7.00
	1882 American Bank Note Co., Special Printing. Same as in 1882 Issue, on soft, porous Paper. Perf 12.						
205C	5¢ gray brown	....	45000.00	....	....	....	....

210, 211B, 213
Washington

211, 211D, 215
Jackson

212
Franklin

SCOTT NO.	DESCRIPTION	UNUSED VF	UNUSED F	UNUSED AVG	USED VF	USED F	USED AVG
	1881-83 American Bank Note Co. Same designs as 1873, Re-Engraved. On soft, porous paper. Perf 12. (†) (OG + 100%)						
206	1¢ gray blue	45.00	30.00	25.00	1.50	.95	.70
207	3¢ blue green	35.00	25.00	18.00	1.25	.75	.55
208	6¢ rose	250.00	170.00	100.00	130.00	100.00	70.00
208a	6¢ brown red	175.00	150.00	120.00	175.00	130.00	87.50
209	10¢ brown	75.00	65.00	50.00	10.00	7.50	4.50
209b	10¢ black brown	1100.00	950.00	600.00	350.00	250.00	150.00
210	2¢ red brown	25.00	17.00	12.00	.75	.45	.35
211	4¢ blue green	100.00	80.00	60.00	32.50	23.00	17.00

SCOTT NO.	DESCRIPTION	UNUSED VF	UNUSED F	UNUSED AVG	USED VF	USED F	USED AVG
	1883 American Bank Note Co. Special Printing. Same design as 1883 Issue, on soft porous paper. Perf 12.						
211B	2¢ pale red brown	175.00	100.00	80.00	....	....	....
211D	4¢ deep blue green	50000.00	....	....	....	....	....
	1887 American Bank Note Co. New designs or colors. Perf 12. (OG + 60%)						
212	1¢ ultramarine	50.00	40.00	30.00	3.00	2.15	1.25
213	2¢ green	30.00	18.00	10.00	.60	.40	.30
214	3¢ vermillion	60.00	40.00	25.00	100.00	64.00	40.00

SCOTT NO.	DESCRIPTION	UNUSED O.G. VF	UNUSED O.G. F	UNUSED O.G. AVG	USED VF	USED F	USED AVG
	1888 American Bank Note Company. New Colors Perf 12. (NH + 100%)						
215	4¢ carmine	290.00	187.50	125.00	35.00	25.00	15.00
216	5¢ indigo	300.00	195.00	130.00	22.50	16.00	3.75
217	30¢ orange brown	400.00	200.00	150.00	125.00	100.00	55.00
218	90¢ purple	1000.00	500.00	300.00	345.00	250.00	150.00

THE 1890-93 SMALL BANK NOTE ISSUES

Unlike the complex Large Bank Notes, the 1890-93 series is the simplest of the 19th century definitive issues. They were printed by the American Bank Note Company and what few printing varieties there are can easily be determined by using the Harris Stamp Identifier.

The two major printing varieties are the 2 cent carmine with a "cap" on the left 2 (#219a) or both 2s (#219c).

The "cap" appears to be just that—a small flat hat just to the right of center on top of the denomination numeral 2. It was caused by a breakdown in the metal of the transfer roll that went undetected while it was being used to enter the designs into a few printing plates.

219
Franklin

219D, 220
Washington

221
Jackson

222
Lincoln

223
Grant

224
Garfield

225
Sherman

226
Webster

227
Clay

228
Jefferson

229
Perry

SCOTT NO.	DESCRIPTION	UNUSED O.G. VF	UNUSED O.G. F	UNUSED O.G. AVG	USED VF	USED F	USED AVG
	(NH +100%)						
219	1¢ dull blue	45.00	25.00	20.50	.60	.45	.35
219D	2¢ lake	250.00	180.00	110.00	5.00	3.50	1.85
220	2¢ carmine	35.00	19.00	14.00	.55	.40	.30
220a	Cap on left "2"	250.00	140.00	90.00	....	....	....
220c	Cap on both "2"s	750.00	400.00	275.00	40.00	25.00	18.50
221	3¢ purple	95.00	60.00	45.00	13.50	8.00	6.00
222	4¢ dark brown	135.00	80.00	60.00	6.50	4.95	3.50
223	5¢ chocolate	120.00	78.00	54.00	6.50	4.90	3.25
224	6¢ brown red	110.00	70.00	50.00	34.00	23.00	16.00
225	8¢ lilac	95.00	65.00	47.50	20.00	13.00	9.00
226	10¢ green	250.00	160.00	110.00	5.75	3.75	2.25
227	15¢ indigo	350.00	210.00	150.00	42.00	30.00	19.00
228	30¢ black	550.00	350.00	245.00	58.00	38.00	23.00
229	90¢ orange	700.00	425.00	300.00	175.00	100.00	70.00

230 *In Sight of Land*
231 *Landing of Columbus*
232 *Flagship*
233 *Fleet of Columbus*
234 *Soliciting Aid*
235 *At Barcelona*
236 *Restored To Favor*
237 *Presenting Natives*
238 *Discovery*
239 *At La Rábida*
240 *Recall of Columbus*
241 *Pledging Jewels*
242 *Columbus in Chains*
243 *Describing Third Voyage*
244 *Isabella & Columbus*
245 *Portrait of Columbus*

THE COLUMBIANS

Perhaps the most glamorous of all United States issues is the 1893 Columbians set. Consisting of 16 denominations, the set was issued to celebrate the 1893 World's Columbian Exposition.

Even then, the Post Office Department was aware that stamps could be useful for more than just the prepayment of postage. We quote from an internal Post Office Department report of November 20, 1892:

"During the past summer the determination was reached by the Department to issue, during the progress of the Columbian Exposition at Chicago, a special series of adhesive postage stamps of such a character as would help to signalize the four hundredth anniversary of the discovery of America by Columbus. This course was in accordance with the practice of other great postal administrations on occasions of national rejoicing.

The collecting of stamps is deserving of encouragement, for it tends to the cultivation of artistic tastes and the study of history and geography, especially on the part of the young. The new stamps will be purchased in large quantities simply for the use of collections, without ever being presented in payment of postage; and the stamps sold in this way will, of course, prove a clear gain to the department."

As it turned out, the Columbians issue did sell well, being purchased in large quantities not only by collectors, but by speculators hoping to capitalize on the expected demand for the stamps and the fact that they were supposed to be on sale for only one year, from January 2 to December 31, 1893. (The 8 cent stamp was issued March 3,1893 to meet the new, reduced Registration fee.)

Although sales of the stamps were brisk at the Exposition site in Chicago, speculation proved less than rewarding. The hordes that showed up on the first day of sale in Chicago (January 3rd) and purchased large quantities of the issue ended up taking losses on most of the stamps.

The set was the most expensive postal issue produced to date by the Post Office. The lower denominations matched those of the previous, "Small" Bank Note issue and the 50 cent Columbian replaced the 90 cent Bank Note denomination. But the $1 through $5 denominations were unheard of at that time. The reason for their release was explained in the November 20, 1892 report: "...such high denominations having heretofore been called for by some of the principal post offices".

The Columbians were an instant success. Businesses did not like the wide size, but they usually could obtain the smaller Bank Note issue. Collectors enjoyed the new stamps, although at least one complained that some of the high values purchased by him had straight edges—and was quickly authorized to exchange "the imperfect stamps" for perfect ones.

The one major variety in this set is the 4 cent blue error of color. It is similar to, but richer in color than, the 1 cent Columbian and commands a larger premium over the normal 4 cent ultramarine color.

The imperforates that are known to exist for all values are proofs which were distributed as gifts and are not listed as postage stamps. The only exception, the 2 cent imperforate, is believed to be printers' waste that was saved from destruction.

SCOTT NO.	DESCRIPTION	UNUSED O.G. VF	F	AVG	USED VF	F	AVG
	1893 COLUMBIAN ISSUE (NH + 100%)						
230	1¢ deep blue	25.00	15.00	12.75	.70	.50	.30
231	2¢ brown violet. . .	25.00	18.00	12.75	.30	.25	.20
231C	2¢ "broken hat". . .	70.00	50.00	40.00	3.50	2.50	1.50
232	3¢ green.	70.00	50.00	40.00	25.00	15.00	10.00
233	4¢ ultramarine . . .	90.00	60.00	35.00	11.00	7.50	4.50
234	5¢ chocolate.	90.00	60.00	35.00	11.00	7.50	4.75
235	6¢ purple	90.00	60.00	35.00	45.00	25.00	12.00
236	8¢ magenta	80.00	50.00	40.00	25.00	14.00	10.00
237	10¢ black brown. .	160.00	100.00	80.00	13.00	8.50	5.50
238	15¢ dark green. . .	350.00	250.00	150.00	115.00	70.00	50.00
239	30¢ orange brown	350.00	250.00	150.00	115.00	70.00	50.00
240	50¢ slate blue. . . .	700.00	450.00	350.00	220.00	180.00	140.00
241	$1 salmon.	1450.00	925.00	725.00	700.00	500.00	400.00
242	$2 brown red	1475.00	975.00	775.00	700.00	500.00	400.00
243	$3 yellow green . .	2200.00	1350.00	900.00	900.00	700.00	500.00
244	$4 crimson lake . .	3000.00	1800.00	1500.00	1375.00	1000.00	725.00
245	$5 black	3400.00	2200.00	1700.00	1400.00	1100.00	750.00

(†) means Issue is actually very poorly centered. Perforations may touch the design on "Fine" quality.

246, 247, 264, 279 *Franklin* · 248-252, 265-267, 279B *Washington* · 253, 268 *Jackson* · 254, 269, 280 *Lincoln* · 255, 270, 281 *Grant*

256, 271, 282 *Garfield* · 257, 272 *Sherman* · 258, 273, 282C, 283 *Webster* · 259, 274, 284 *Clay* · 260, 275 *Jefferson*

261, 261A, 276, 276A *Perry* · 262, 277 *Madison* · 263, 278 *Marshall*

1894-98 THE FIRST BUREAU ISSUES

In 1894, the United States Bureau of Engraving and Printing replaced the American Bank Note Company as the contractor for all United States postage stamps. The "First" Bureau issues, as they are commonly known, actually consist of three series, as follows:

The 1894 Series. In order to expedite the transfer of production to the Bureau, the plates then being used by the American Bank Note Company for the 1890-93 Small Bank Notes were modified, small triangles being added in the upper corners. The 1 cent through 15 cent stamps are otherwise essentially the same as the 1890-93 issue although minor variations have been noted on some values. The 30 cent and 90 cent 1890-93 denominations were changed to 50 cents and $1, respectively, and new $2 and $5 denominations were added.

The 1895 Series. To protect against counterfeiting of United Sates stamps, the Bureau adopted the use of watermarked paper. (A scheme for counterfeiting 2 cent stamps had been uncovered around the same time the watermarked paper was being adopted. Some of these counterfeits are known postally used.) This series is almost exactly the same as the 1984 series except for the presence of watermarks. The watermarks can be difficult t detect on this series, particularly on the light-colored stamps, such as the 50 cent, and on used stamps. Since the 1894 unwatermarked stamps (with the exception of the 2 cent carmine type I) are worth more than the 1895 watermarked stamps, collectors will want to examine their 1894 stamps carefully. (Some collectors feel they can recognize the 1894 stamps by their ragged perforations, caused by difficulties the Bureau encountered when it first took over the production of postage stamps. This is not a reliable method.)

The 1898 "Color Changes." With the adoption of a Universal Postal Union code that recommended standard colors for international mail, the United States changed the colors for the lower values in the 1895 Series. The stamps were printed on the same watermarked paper as that used for the 1895 Series. Except for the 2 cent,which was changed from carmine to red, the colors of the 1898 Series are easily differentiated from the 1895 set. The 2 cent value is the most complicated of the First Bureau Issues. In addition to the color changes that took place, three different triangle types are known. The differences are attributed to the possibility that the work of engraving the triangles into the American Bank Note plates was performed by several Bureau engravers.

The 10 cent and $1 types I and II can be distinguished by the circles surrounding the numeral denominations. The Type IIs are identical to the circles of the 1890-93 Small Bank Notes.

All stamps in these series are perf. 12. The Harris Stamp Identifier at the front of this catalog provides additional information on the major types and watermarks of all three series.

SCOTT NO.	DESCRIPTION	UNUSED O.G. VF	F	AVG	USED VF	F	AVG
	1894 Unwatermarked (†) (NH + 100%)						
246	1¢ ultramarine . . .	50.00	32.75	23.75	10.50	6.75	4.25
247	1¢ blue	90.00	53.00	37.00	4.00	2.50	1.75
248	2¢ pink (I)	35.00	22.00	16.00	12.50	8.00	5.00
249	2¢ carmine lake (I)	275.00	160.00	110.00	10.00	6.75	4.00
250	2¢ carmine (I)	50.00	32.75	23.00	2.00	1.00	.75
251	2¢ carmine (II) . . .	400.00	250.00	150.00	18.00	12.75	8.00
252	2¢ carmine (III) . . .	165.00	90.00	60.00	20.00	14.50	9.00
253	3¢ purple	145.00	85.00	60.00	17.50	9.75	6.50
254	4¢ dark brown . . .	195.00	110.00	80.00	16.00	9.75	6.25
255	5¢ chocolate	160.00	90.00	70.00	14.00	8.50	5.50
256	6¢ dull brown	210.00	125.00	85.00	39.00	28.00	19.00
257	8¢ violet brown . . .	200.00	130.00	94.00	35.00	21.25	16.95
258	10¢ dark green . . .	375.00	240.00	160.00	20.00	10.00	7.00
259	15¢ dark blue	385.00	240.00	180.00	96.00	58.00	38.00
260	50¢ orange	725.00	425.00	315.00	185.00	115.00	70.00
261	$1 black (I)	1300.00	800.00	550.00	625.00	375.00	260.00
261A	$1 black (II)	2700.00	1750.00	1200.00	1000.00	675.00	450.00
262	$2 bright blue	3600.00	2300.00	1850.00	1500.00	1100.00	725.00
263	$5 dark green	5050.00	3700.00	2900.00	3000.00	2100.00	1500.00
	1895 Double Line Watermark "USPS" (†) (NH + 75%)						
264	1¢ blue	8.50	5.50	3.75	.50	.35	.25
265	2¢ carmine (I)	55.00	35.00	25.00	4.00	2.65	1.75
266	2¢ carmine (II) . . .	60.00	38.50	25.00	6.00	4.20	2.75
267	2¢ carmine (III) . . .	6.50	4.00	3.00	.35	.30	.25
268	3¢ purple	50.00	31.25	22.25	3.00	1.90	1.25
269	4¢ dark brown . . .	65.00	38.00	26.00	4.25	2.85	1.50
270	5¢ chocolate	52.50	36.00	22.00	4.25	2.75	1.75
271	6¢ dull brown	165.00	90.00	65.00	9.00	6.00	4.50
272	8¢ violet brown . . .	85.00	50.00	35.00	3.50	2.00	1.25
273	10¢ dark green . . .	125.00	70.00	50.00	2.75	1.75	1.00
274	15¢ dark blue	300.00	170.00	110.00	27.50	18.00	12.25
275	50¢ orange	375.00	225.00	160.00	75.00	52.50	32.00
276	$1 black (I)	775.00	450.00	310.00	155.00	100.00	64.00
276A	$1 black (II)	1500.00	1000.00	700.00	275.00	195.00	135.00
277	$2 bright blue	1100.00	825.00	625.00	625.00	450.00	305.00
278	$5 dark green	2500.00	1800.00	1050.00	925.00	600.00	425.00
	1898 New Colors (NH + 75%)						
279	1¢ deep green . . .	15.00	9.00	6.50	.50	.35	.25
279B	2¢ red (IV)	13.00	7.50	5.00	.50	.30	.25
279Bc	2¢ rose carmine (IV)	325.00	195.00	120.00	200.00	125.00	95.00
279Bd	2¢ orange red (IV)	17.50	10.00	7.00	2.00	1.50	1.00
280	4¢ rose brown . . .	55.00	37.25	24.75	4.00	2.65	1.75
281	5¢ dark blue	48.00	29.00	18.00	2.75	1.85	1.00
282	6¢ lake	80.00	52.50	40.00	8.00	5.50	3.25
282C	10¢ brown (I)	265.00	180.00	125.00	7.00	4.65	3.00
283	10¢ orange brown (II)	210.00	125.00	78.00	9.00	5.75	3.50
284	15¢ olive green. . .	190.00	115.00	80.00	20.00	12.50	8.75

1898 THE TRANS-MISSISSIPPI ISSUE

Issued for the Trans-Mississippi Exposition in Omaha, Nebraska, the "Omahas", as they also are known, did not receive the same welcome from collectors as that accorded the first commemorative set, the 1893 Columbians. Although the uproar was ascribed to the fact that collectors felt put upon by another set with $1 and $2 values, had the $1 to $5 values in the Columbian series appreciated in value, no doubt the protests would have been muted.

On the other hand, the public at large enjoyed the new issue. The Trans-Mississippi issues depict various works of art and are among the most beautiful stamps ever issued by the United States. The 8 and 10 cent values reproduce works by Frederic Remington and the $1 "Western Cattle in Storm", based on a work by J.A. MacWhirter, is regarded as one of our finest examples of the engraver's art.

As appealing as these stamps are in single colors, the set might have been even more beautiful. The original intent was to print each stamp with the vignette, or central design, in black and the frame in a distinctive second color that would be different for each denomination. That plan had to be dropped when the Bureau was called upon to produce large quantities of revenue stamps at the outbreak of the Spanish-American War.

285
Marquette on the Mississippi

286
Farming in the West

287
Indian Hunting Buffalo

288
Fremont on the Rocky Mountains

289
Troops Guarding Train

290
Hardships of Emigration

291
Western Mining Prospector

292
Western Cattle in Storm

293
Eads Bridge over Mississippi River

SCOTT NO.	DESCRIPTION	UNUSED O.G. VF	F	AVG	USED VF	F	AVG
	1898 Trans-Mississippi Exposition Issue (†) (NH + 100%)						
285	1¢ dark yellow green	55.00	36.75	25.75	10.00	6.50	4.00
286	2¢ copper red............	35.00	23.00	17.50	3.00	2.00	1.25
287	4¢ orange..................	225.00	135.00	95.00	59.00	35.00	22.00
288	5¢ dull blue................	240.00	135.00	92.00	32.00	20.00	11.00
289	8¢ violet brown..........	310.00	200.00	125.00	85.00	55.00	32.00
290	10¢ gray violet...........	260.00	165.00	100.00	56.00	33.00	19.00
291	50¢ sage green.........	950.00	575.00	475.00	250.00	180.00	140.00
292	$1 black.....................	2000.00	1150.00	850.00	990.00	775.00	600.00
293	$2 orange brown.......	2500.00	1600.00	1000.00	1200.00	950.00	700.00

1901 THE PAN-AMERICAN ISSUE

Issued to commemorate the Pan-American Exposition in Buffalo, N.Y., this set depicts important engineering and manufacturing achievements. The beautiful engraving is showcased by the bicolored printing.

294, 294a
Fast Lake Navigation

295, 295a
Fast Express

296, 296a
Automobile

297
Bridge at Niagara Falls

298
Canal at Sault Ste. Marie

299
Fast Ocean Navigation

SCOTT NO.	DESCRIPTION	UNUSED O.G. VF	F	AVG	USED VF	F	AVG
	1901 Pan-American Issue (NH + 75%)						
294-99	**1¢-10¢ (6 varieties, complete) .....**	**530.00**	**370.00**	**300.00**	**190.00**	**125.00**	**80.00**
294	1¢ green & black.........	25.00	16.00	12.00	3.00	2.20	1.50
294a	same, center inverted	...	10000.00	...	...	16000.00	...
295	2¢ carmine & black.....	22.00	14.00	11.00	1.30	.90	.40
295a	same, center inverted	...	45000.00	...	...	40000.00	...
296	4¢ deep red brown & black...	90.00	70.00	60.00	24.00	14.00	11.00
296a	same, center inverted	...	50000.00	...	...	...	...
296aS	same, center inverted (Specimen)......	...	7500.00	...	...	...	...
297	5¢ ultramarine & black	90.00	70.00	60.00	24.00	14.00	11.00
298	8¢ brown violet & black	150.00	90.00	70.00	95.00	60.00	40.00
299	10¢ yellow brown & black.	175.00	130.00	90.00	45.00	35.00	20.00

	UNUSED PLATE BLOCKS OF 6 NH F	NH AVG	OG F	OG AVG	UNUSED ARROW BLOCKS NH F	NH AVG	OG F	OG AVG
294	475.00	340.00	285.00	215.00	165.00	105.00	72.50	57.50
295	475.00	340.00	280.00	215.00	160.00	100.00	65.00	50.00
296	3750.00	2750.00	2100.00	1650.00	825.00	575.00	375.00	315.00
297	4200.00	3250.00	2600.00	2000.00	825.00	550.00	400.00	325.00
298	7500.00	5500.00	4000.00	3200.00	1050.00	700.00	500.00	375.00
299	10500.00	8000.00	6000.00	4800.00	1500.00	900.00	695.00	500.00

(†) means Issue is actually very poorly centered. Perforations may touch the design on "Fine" quality.

THE 1902-03 SERIES

The Series of 1902-03 was the first regular issue designed and produced by the United States Bureau of Engraving and Printing, most of the work on the 1894-98 series having been performed by the American Bank Note Company. (When the Bureau was awarded the contract to produce the 1894 series, they added triangles in the upper corners of the American Bank Note designs.)

The new series filled a number of gaps and was the first United States issue to feature a woman—in this case Martha Washington, on the 8-cent value.

Modern collectors consider the 1902-03 issue one of the finest regular series ever produced by the Bureau.

The intricate frame designs take us back to a period when such work still was affordable. In its time, however, the 1902-03 set was looked upon with disdain. The 2-cent Washington, with its ornate frame design and unflattering likeness of George Washington, came in for particular scorn. Yielding to the clamor, in 1903, less than one year after its release, the Post Office recalled the much criticized 2-cent stamp and replaced it with an attractive, less ornate design that cleaned up Washington's appearance, particularly in the area of the nose, and used a shield design that was less ornate.

The issue marked the first time United States stamps were issued in booklet form, the 1-cent and 2-cent values being printed in panes of six stamps each. Also for the first time since perforating was adopted in 1857, United States stamps were once again deliberately issued in imperforate form for postal use. The intent was to have such stamps available in sheet and coil form for use in vending machines. The manufacturers of such machines could purchase the imperforate stamps and perforate them to fit their equipment. One of these imperforate issues, the 4-cent brown of 1908 (#314A), ranks as one of the great rarities of 20th century philately. It is found only with the private perforations of the Schermack Mailing Machine Company.

Coil stamps intended for use in stamp affixing and vending machines also made their inaugural appearance with this issue. Their availability was not widely publicized and few collectors obtained copies of these coils. All genuine coils from this series are very rare and extremely valuable. We emphasize the word "genuine" because most coils that are seen actually have been faked by trimming the perforated stamps or fraudulently perforating the imperfs.

The only major design types are found on the 1903 2-cent, catalog numbers 319 and 320. Identified as Die I and Die II, the differences are described in the Harris Stamp Identifier.

300, 314, 316, 318
Franklin

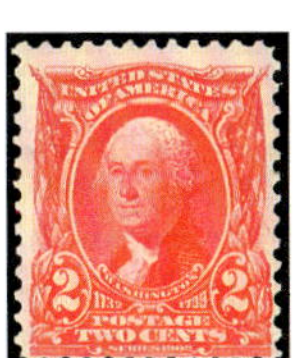
301
Washington

302
Jackson

303, 314A
Grant

304, 315, 317
Lincoln

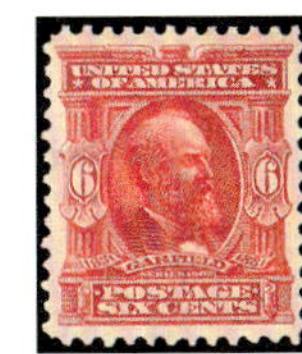
305
Garfield

306
Martha Washington

307
Webster

308
Harrison

309
Clay

310
Jefferson

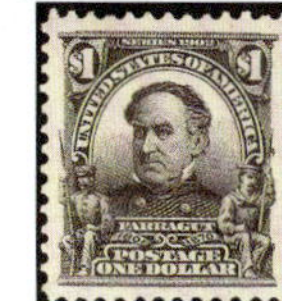
311
Farragut

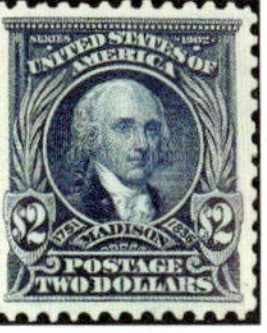
312, 479
Madison

313, 480
Marshall

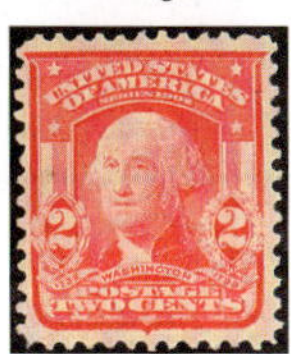
319-22
Washington

SCOTT NO.	DESCRIPTION	UNUSED O.G. VF	F	AVG	USED VF	F	AVG
	1902-03 Perf. 12 (†) (NH + 75%)						
300	1¢ blue green	16.00	9.00	6.00	.35	.25	.20
300b	1¢ booklet pane of 6	....	550.00	375.00	....	....	....
301	2¢ carmine	19.50	13.00	8.00	.35	.25	.20
301c	2¢ booklet pane of 6	....	475.00	335.00	....	....	....
302	3¢ brown violet . . .	75.00	43.00	30.00	6.00	3.95	2.25
303	4¢ brown	75.00	43.00	30.00	2.50	1.50	1.00
304	5¢ blue	82.50	50.00	35.00	3.50	1.75	.90
305	6¢ claret	90.00	50.00	35.00	9.00	5.00	3.00
306	8¢ violet black . . .	65.00	35.00	27.00	5.00	2.75	1.75
307	10¢ pale red brown	85.00	50.00	36.00	4.00	2.25	1.50
308	13¢ purple black . .	60.00	35.00	25.00	17.00	11.00	6.50
309	15¢ olive green. . .	225.00	140.00	98.00	17.00	11.00	7.00
310	50¢ orange	625.00	375.00	260.00	52.00	33.00	23.00
311	$1 black	800.00	525.00	360.00	120.00	73.00	46.00
312	$2 dark blue	1000.00	900.00	550.00	325.00	250.00	180.00
313	$5 dark green	2500.00	2000.00	1500.00	1000.00	750.00	525.00
	1906-08 Imperforate (NH + 75%)						
	This and all subsequent imperforate issues can usually be priced as unused pairs at double the single price.						
314	1¢ blue green	20.00	15.00	10.00	35.00	20.00	15.00
314A	4¢ brown	....	160000.00	....	....	50000.00	....
315	5¢ blue	600.00	400.00	300.00	1500.00	900.00	650.00
	1908 Coil Stamps. Perf 12 Horizontally						
316	1¢ blue green, pair	....	....	....	....	....	....
317	5¢ blue, pair	....	6000.00	....	....	....	....
	1908 Coil Stamps. Perf 12 Vertically						
318	1¢ blue green, pair	....	5500.00	....	....	....	....
	1903. Perf. 12 (†) (NH + 60%)						
319	2¢ carmine, Die I .	10.00	6.00	4.75	.50	.30	.20
319f	2¢ lake, Die II	17.50	11.00	7.50	1.00	.70	.50
319g	2¢ carmine, Die I, booklet pane of 6 .	....	160.00	....	....	....	....
	1906 Imperforate (NH + 75%)						
320	2¢ carmine, Die I .	55.00	40.00	28.00	79.00	45.00	31.00
320a	2¢ lake, Die I	80.00	65.00	45.00	58.00	40.00	28.00
	1908 Coil Stamps. Perf 12 Horizontally						
321	2¢ carmine, pair . .	....	....	....	....	....	....
	1908 Coil Stamps. Perf 12 Vertically						
322	2¢ carmine, pair . .	....	7500.00	....	....	....	....

SCOTT NO.	UNUSED NH F	AVG	UNUSED OG F	AVG	SCOTT NO.	UNUSED NH F	AVG	UNUSED OG F	AVG
	PLATE BLOCKS OF 6					**CENTER LINE BLOCKS**			
300	350.00	200.00	215.00	137.50	314	300.00	200.00	180.00	145.00
301	425.00	220.00	235.00	155.00	320	335.00	235.00	200.00	175.00
314	425.00	315.00	290.00	215.00		**ARROW BLOCKS**			
319	295.00	200.00	160.00	115.00	314	235.00	185.00	140.00	110.00
320	415.00	290.00	225.00	175.00	320	250.00	200.00	135.00	100.00

1904 THE LOUISIANA PURCHASE ISSUE

Issued to commemorate the Louisiana Purchase Exposition held in St. Louis in 1904, these stamps were not well received. Collectors at the time did not purchase large quantities of the stamps, and the series was on sale for only seven months. As a result, well centered unused stamps are extremely difficult to locate.

323
Robert R. Livingston

324
Jefferson

325
Monroe

326
McKinley

327
Map of Louisiana Purchase

SCOTT NO.	DESCRIPTION	UNUSED O.G. VF	F	AVG	USED VF	F	AVG
	1904 Louisiana Purchase Issue (NH + 75%)						
323-27	**1¢-10¢ (5 varieties, complete)**	**460.00**	**325.00**	**185.00**	**120.00**	**70.00**	**52.00**
323	1¢ green	45.00	25.00	20.00	8.00	6.00	3.00
324	2¢ carmine	30.00	22.00	16.00	2.75	2.25	1.25
325	3¢ violet	120.00	80.00	50.00	40.00	20.00	15.00
326	5¢ dark blue	120.00	80.00	50.00	30.00	20.00	15.00
327	10¢ red brown	150.00	120.00	100.00	40.00	25.00	20.00

1907 THE JAMESTOWN EXPOSITION ISSUE

This set may be the most difficult United States 20th century issue to find well centered. Issued in April, 1907 for the Jamestown Exposition at Hampton Roads, Virginia, the set was removed from sale when the Exposition closed on November 30th of that year. Very fine copies carry hefty premiums.

328
Capt. John Smith

329
Founding of Jamestown

330
Pocahontas

SCOTT NO.	DESCRIPTION	UNUSED O.G. VF	F	AVG	USED VF	F	AVG
	1907 Jamestown Exposition Issue (NH + 75%)						
328-30	**1¢-5¢ (3 varieties, complete)**	**220.00**	**155.00**	**100.00**	**50.00**	**35.00**	**22.00**
328	1¢ green	35.00	20.00	15.00	6.00	4.00	3.00
329	2¢ carmine	40.00	20.00	14.00	6.00	4.00	2.00
330	5¢ blue	150.00	120.00	80.00	40.00	30.00	20.00

SCOTT NO.	UNUSED PLATE BLOCKS OF 6 NH F	NH AVG	OG F	OG AVG	UNUSED ARROW BLOCKS NH F	NH AVG	OG F	OG AVG
323	550.00	415.00	275.00	220.00	200.00	120.00	130.00	85.00
324	550.00	412.50	290.00	220.00	160.00	100.00	95.00	65.00
325	1750.00	1325.00	1120.00	840.00	550.00	355.00	400.00	265.00
326	1750.00	1150.00	965.00	845.00	675.00	380.00	375.00	250.00
327	3000.00	1950.00	1500.00	1150.00	1100.00	715.00	650.00	530.00
328	700.00	490.00	400.00	300.00	150.00	95.00	100.00	75.00
329	700.00	475.00	415.00	285.00	195.00	110.00	120.00	95.00
330	5000.00	3000.00	2750.00	1950.00	800.00	475.00	400.00	300.00

THE WASHINGTON-FRANKLIN HEADS

The Washington-Franklin Heads—so called because all stamps in the regular series featured the busts of George Washington and Benjamin Franklin—dominated the postal scene for almost two decades. Using a variety of papers, denominations, perforation sizes and formats, watermarks, design modifications and printing processes, almost 200 different major catalog listings were created from two basic designs.

The series started modestly, with the issuance of 12 stamps (#331-342) between November 1908 and January 1909. The modest designs on the new set replaced the ornate 1902-03 series. Their relative simplicity might have relegated the set to a secondary position in 20th century United States philately had it not been for the complexity of the varieties and the years of study the Washington-Franklin Heads now present to collectors.

The first varieties came almost immediately, in the form of imperforate stamps (#343-347) and coils, the latter being offered with horizontal (#348-351) or vertical (#352-356) perforations. The imperfs were intended for the fading vending machine technology that required private perforations while the coils were useful in standardized dispensers that were just coming into their own.

Then, in 1909, the Post Office began its experimentation. In this instance, it was the paper. As noted in our introduction to the 1909 Bluish Papers which follows, the Post Office Department and the Bureau of Engraving and Printing hoped that the new paper would reduce losses due to uneven shrinkage of the white wove paper used at the time. The experimental Washington-Franklin Bluish Papers (#357-66) are now among the most valuable in the series and the 8-cent Bluish Paper (#363) is the highest priced of the major listed items.

Attention was next directed to the double line watermark as the cause of the uneven shrinkage, as well as for weakness and thinning in the paper. As a result, a narrower, single line watermark was adopted for sheet stamps (#374-82), imperforates (#383-84), and coils with horizontal perfs (#385-86) and vertical perfs (#387-89).

Even as these experiments were being conducted, the perforation size was being examined to determine if a change was in order. Up until now, the perf 12 gauge had been used on all Washington-Franklin Heads.

The first perforation change was necessitated by the development of new coil manufacturing equipment. Under the increased pressure of the new equipment, the coil strips with the closely-spaced perf 12 gauge were splitting while being rolled into coils. To add paper between the holes, a perf 8½ gauge was adopted for coil stamps and two new major varieties were created: with horizontal perfs (#390-91) and vertical perfs (#392-396).

Necessity was the driving force behind still more changes in 1912, when stamps with numeral denominations were issued to replace the "ONE CENT" and "TWO CENTS" stamps. This responded to the need for numeral denominations on foreign mail and created new sheets (#410-11) and vertically perforated (#412-13) coils. At the same time, a 7-cent value (#407) was issued to meet changing rate requirements.

In conjunction with the introduction of numerals on the 1-cent and 2-cent stamps, the design of the 1-cent was changed, with the bust of Washington replacing that of Franklin. Meanwhile, the bust of Franklin, which had been used only on the 1-cent stamp, was placed on all values from 8 cents to the $1 (#414-21) and a ribbon was added across their top to make the high value stamp even more noticeable to postal clerks.

As if to add just a little more variety while all the other changes were being made—but in actuality to use up a supply of old double-line watermark paper—50 cent and $1 issues with double-line watermarks (#422-23) were introduced.

The work with perforation changes on coil stamps carried over to sheet stamps in 1914 with the release of a perf 10 series (#424-40). The perf 10 size was then adapted to coils perforated horizontally (#441-42) and vertically (#443-47).

The transition to Rotary Press printing created new coils perforated 10 horizontally (#448-50) and vertically (#452-58). An imperforate Rotary coil (#459) for vending machine manufacturers also was produced.

A perf 10 double-line watermark $1 (#460) and a perf 11 two-cent sheet stamp (#461) added only slightly to the variety, but were followed by completely new runs on unwatermarked paper: perf 10 sheet stamps (#462-478) and imperforates (#481-84) were produced on the flat plate presses, while the Rotary press was used for coils perforated horizontally (#486-489) and vertically (#490-97).

While all this was taking place, the amazing 5-cent carmine error of color (#485) appeared on certain imperf 2-cent sheets. That same error (in rose, #505) was found when perf 11 sheet stamps (#498-518) were issued. The stamps turned out to be too hard to separate. Another strange issue, a 2-cent stamp on double-line watermark paper but perforated 11 (#519), came about when a small supply of old imperfs (#344) were discovered and put into the postal stream.

New $2 and $5 Franklins (#523-24), the former using an erroneous color, were released. To compensate for plate damage being caused by poor quality offset printings, perf 11 (#525-530) and imperforate (#531-535) were tried—and quickly resulted in a whole new series of "types" that had collectors spending more time with their magnifying glasses than with their families.

Odd perf sizes and printings (#538/546) came about as the Bureau cleaned out old paper stock. Then, in one final change, the Bureau corrected the color of the $2 from orange red and black to carmine and black. Almost 200 different stamps, all from two basic designs!

1909 THE BLUISH PAPERS

The Bluish Paper varieties are found on the 1 through 15 cent Washington-Franklin series of 1908-09 and on the 1909 Commemoratives. According to Post Office notices of the period, the experimental paper was a 30% rag stock that was intended to reduce paper waste. After being wet, a preliminary operation in the printing process, the standard white wove paper often would shrink so much that the perforators would cut into the designs. The rag paper did not solve the problem, the experiment was quickly abandoned and the 1909 Bluish Papers became major rarities.

The Harris Stamp Identifier provides further information on identifying the Washington-Franklin Heads.

331, 343, 348, 352, 357, 374, 383, 385, 387, 390, 392
Franklin

332, 344, 349, 353, 358, 375, 384, 386, 388, 391, 393
Washington

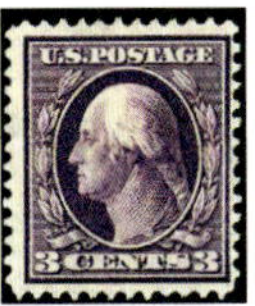

333, 345, 359, 376, 389, 394
Washington

334, 346, 350, 354, 360, 377, 395
Washington

335, 347, 351, 355, 361, 378, 396
Washington

336, 362, 379
Washington

337, 363, 380
Washington

338, 356, 364, 381
Washington

339, 365
Washington

340, 366, 382
Washington

341
Washington

342
Washington

***NOTE:** For further details on the various types of similar appearing stamps please refer to our U.S. Stamp Identifier.*

SCOTT NO.	DESCRIPTION	UNUSED O.G. VF	F	AVG	USED VF	F	AVG
	1908-09 Double Line Watermark "USPS" Perf. 12 (NH + 75%)						
331-42	**1¢-$1 (12 varieties, complete) ......**	**1600.00**	**960.00**	**620.00**	**300.00**	**200.00**	**115.00**
331	1¢ green........	11.25	6.50	4.00	1.00	.70	.60
331a	1¢ booklet pane of 6	200.00	145.00	95.00	......	......	......
332	2¢ carmine......	11.25	7.00	4.25	.75	.50	.40
332a	2¢ booklet pane of 6	185.00	120.00	85.00	......	......	......
333	3¢ deep violet (I) .	52.50	29.00	18.00	6.50	4.25	2.50
334	4¢ orange brown .	55.00	34.00	22.00	2.00	1.25	.80
335	5¢ blue.........	72.00	40.00	24.00	3.75	2.60	1.75
336	6¢ red orange....	80.00	50.00	30.00	8.50	5.00	3.25
337	8¢ olive green....	60.00	38.00	24.00	5.50	3.25	2.25
338	10¢ yellow	85.00	58.00	43.00	4.75	2.50	1.50
339	13¢ blue green...	60.00	34.00	23.00	80.00	50.00	29.00
340	15¢ pale ultramarine	82.00	50.00	35.00	12.00	8.00	5.00
341	50¢ violet.......	400.00	235.00	145.00	45.00	30.00	18.00
342	$1 violet brown...	675.00	400.00	260.00	145.00	100.00	63.00
	1908-09 Imperforate (NH + 75%)						
343-47	**1¢-5¢ (5 varieties, complete) ......**	**90.00**	**65.00**	**50.00**	**100.00**	**75.00**	**50.00**
343	1¢ green........	6.00	4.00	3.00	5.75	4.50	2.75
344	2¢ carmine......	6.50	4.50	4.00	5.00	4.00	2.75
345	3¢ deep violet (I) .	16.00	14.00	12.00	28.00	19.00	11.00
346	4¢ orange brown .	18.00	15.00	10.00	28.00	20.00	18.00
347	5¢ blue.........	45.00	30.00	24.00	42.00	30.00	20.00
	1908-10 Coil Stamps Perf. 12 Horizontally (NH + 75%)						
348	1¢ green........	48.00	30.00	28.00	55.00	35.00	25.00
349	2¢ carmine......	115.00	80.00	55.00	160.00	80.00	70.00
350	4¢ orange brown .	175.00	100.00	85.00	250.00	160.00	140.00
351	5¢ blue.........	175.00	100.00	85.00	300.00	220.00	160.00

NOTE: **Counterfeits are common on #348-56 and #385-89**

SCOTT NO.	DESCRIPTION	UNUSED O.G. VF	F	AVG	USED VF	F	AVG
	1909 Coil Stamps Perf. 12 Vertically (NH + 75%)						
352	1¢ green........	140.00	80.00	70.00	250.00	175.00	90.00
353	2¢ carmine......	175.00	125.00	82.50	240.00	150.00	70.00
354	4¢ orange brown .	275.00	170.00	110.00	290.00	175.00	110.00
355	5¢ blue.........	300.00	180.00	120.00	350.00	250.00	175.00
356	10¢ yellow	3500.00	2500.00	2000.00	6000.00	4000.00	3000.00

SCOTT NO.	UNUSED NH F	AVG	UNUSED OG F	AVG	SCOTT NO.	UNUSED NH F	AVG	UNUSED OG F	AVG
PLATE BLOCKS OF 6					**CENTER LINE BLOCKS**				
331	140.00	110.00	100.00	70.00	343	80.00	60.00	60.00	45.00
332	140.00	110.00	100.00	70.00	344	105.00	90.00	87.50	55.00
333	450.00	325.00	290.00	210.00	345	250.00	185.00	190.00	155.00
334	635.00	415.00	400.00	280.00	346	325.00	285.00	275.00	200.00
335	950.00	700.00	600.00	475.00	347	450.00	315.00	325.00	230.00
336	1250.00	900.00	700.00	495.00					
337	700.00	495.00	375.00	275.00					
338	1000.00	790.00	735.00	475.00	**ARROW BLOCKS**				
339	750.00	615.00	430.00	320.00					
343	125.00	115.00	80.00	60.00	343	57.50	52.00	52.00	37.50
344	175.00	140.00	152.50	110.00	344	100.00	87.50	85.00	55.00
345	330.00	250.00	320.00	240.00	345	240.00	180.00	185.00	150.00
346	600.00	450.00	465.00	390.00	346	295.00	260.00	250.00	175.00
347	650.00	525.00	555.00	400.00	347	390.00	300.00	320.00	210.00

(NH + 75%)

	COIL LINE PAIRS UNUSED OG VF	F	AVG	COIL PAIRS UNUSED OG VF	F	AVG
348	365.00	235.00	160.00	180.00	125.00	80.00
349	675.00	450.00	310.00	300.00	215.00	130.00
350	1300.00	1000.00	725.00	650.00	420.00	310.00
351	2250.00	1675.00	1225.00	600.00	400.00	270.00
352	1050.00	765.00	540.00	350.00	250.00	175.00
353	700.00	500.00	350.00	330.00	230.00	165.00
354	1650.00	1100.00	775.00	800.00	570.00	395.00
355	1650.00	1100.00	775.00	800.00	625.00	445.00
356	17500.00	12000.00	9000.00	10000.00	6800.00	4500.00

SCOTT NO.	DESCRIPTION	UNUSED O.G. VF	F	AVG	USED VF	F	AVG
	1909 Bluish Gray paper Perf. 12 (NH + 75%)						
357	1¢ green........	105.00	80.00	55.00	175.00	140.00	100.00
358	2¢ carmine......	100.00	75.00	50.00	175.00	140.00	100.00
359	3¢ deep violet (I) .	2400.00	1800.00	1300.00	9800.00	7000.00	6000.00
360	4¢ orange brown .	......	27000.00	18000.00	......	......	......
361	5¢ blue.........	7000.00	3900.00	2800.00	20000.00	15000.00	11500.00
362	6¢ red orange....	2000.00	1200.00	800.00	22500.00	15500.00	11350.00
363	8¢ olive green....	......	30000.00	20000.00	......	......	......
364	10¢ yellow	2500.00	1500.00	1100.00	12000.00	9000.00	8000.00
365	13¢ blue green...	3500.00	2200.00	1500.00	4000.00	2700.00	1850.00
366	15¢ pale ultramarine	1900.00	1400.00	1100.00	13000.00	10000.00	7000.00

THE 1909 COMMEMORATIVES

After the 16-value Columbian commemorative set, the Post Office Department began gradually reducing the number of stamps in subsequent series. The 1909 commemoratives were the first to use the single-stamp commemorative approach that is now the common practice.

The Lincoln Memorial issue was released on the 100th anniversary of the birth of America's 16th President. The Alaska-Yukon was issued for the Alaska-Yukon Exposition held in Seattle to publicize the development of the Alaska territory. The Hudson-Fulton stamp commemorated Henry Hudson's 1609 discovery of the river that bears his name, the 1809 voyage of Robert Fulton's "Clermont" steamboat and the 1909 celebration of those two events.

As noted earlier, the 1909 Commemoratives were issued on experimental "bluish" paper in addition to the white wove standard. The stamps on white wove paper also were issued in imperforate form for private perforation by vending and stamp-affixing machine manufacturers.

367-369
Lincoln

370, 371
William H. Seward

372, 373
S.S. Clermont

SCOTT NO.	DESCRIPTION	UNUSED O.G. VF	F	AVG	USED VF	F	AVG
	1909 LINCOLN MEMORIAL ISSUE (NH + 50%)						
367	2¢ carmine, perf. .	8.00	5.50	3.50	2.00	1.50	1.00
368	2¢ carmine, imperf.	25.00	15.00	12.00	28.00	18.00	15.00
369	2¢ carmine (bluish paper)	200.00	165.00	115.00	270.00	180.00	140.00
	1909 ALASKA-YUKON ISSUE						
370	2¢ carmine, perf. .	11.00	8.00	5.50	3.00	2.20	1.40
371	2¢ carmine, imperf.	20.00	12.00	10.00	25.00	16.00	10.00
	1909 HUDSON-FULTON ISSUE						
372	2¢ carmine, perf. .	12.50	8.00	6.00	5.00	3.20	2.00
373	2¢ carmine, imperf	22.00	15.00	11.00	30.00	18.00	13.00
	1910-11 Single Line Watermark "USPS" Perf. 12 (NH + 50%)						
374-82	**1¢-15¢ (9 varieties, complete) . . . . . .**	**700.00**	**495.00**	**398.00**	**60.00**	**40.00**	**28.00**
374	1¢ green.	15.00	9.50	6.00	.30	.30	.20
374a	1¢ booklet pane of 6	225.00	145.00	100.00	......	......	......
375	2¢ carmine	14.50	9.00	6.00	.30	.30	.20
375a	2¢ booklet pane of 6	150.00	105.00	66.00	......	......	......
376	3¢ deep violet (I) .	32.50	18.00	12.00	4.25	2.50	1.50
377	4¢ brown	47.50	28.50	21.50	1.25	.85	.55
378	5¢ blue	40.00	24.00	18.00	1.50	1.10	.75
379	6¢ red orange. . . .	60.00	36.00	23.00	2.25	1.25	.85
380	8¢ olive green. . . .	115.00	90.00	70.00	22.00	15.00	11.00
381	10¢ yellow	125.00	95.00	75.00	7.00	5.50	3.75
382	15¢ pale ultramarine	255.00	190.00	170.00	25.00	16.00	11.00
	1911 Imperforate						
383	1¢ green.	3.25	2.70	1.50	2.75	1.75	1.10
384	2¢ carmine	4.20	3.25	2.10	3.00	2.20	1.80

SCOTT NO.	UNUSED NH F	AVG	UNUSED OG F	AVG
	PLATE BLOCKS OF 6			
367	225.00	155.00	160.00	110.00
368	385.00	270.00	300.00	220.00
370	320.00	220.00	220.00	150.00
371	475.00	330.00	345.00	235.00
372	400.00	250.00	290.00	200.00
373	475.00	330.00	345.00	235.00
374	150.00	90.00	85.00	60.00
375	150.00	85.00	95.00	70.00
376	350.00	230.00	245.00	220.00
377	390.00	250.00	285.00	185.00
378	325.00	245.00	245.00	185.00
383	100.00	68.75	62.50	45.00
384	210.00	150.00	140.00	95.00

SCOTT NO.	UNUSED NH F	AVG	UNUSED OG F	AVG
	CENTER LINE BLOCKS			
368	225.00	165.00	165.00	125.00
371	300.00	200.00	200.00	150.00
373	365.00	265.00	265.00	200.00
383	45.00	30.00	30.00	25.00
384	90.00	55.00	65.00	40.00
	ARROW BLOCKS			
368	180.00	130.00	120.00	110.00
371	235.00	190.00	180.00	135.00
373	265.00	200.00	200.00	160.00
383	42.00	30.00	30.00	20.00
384	50.00	45.00	45.00	36.00

Very Fine Plate Blocks from this period command premiums.

SCOTT NO.	DESCRIPTION	UNUSED O.G. VF	F	AVG	USED VF	F	AVG
	COIL STAMPS 1910 Perf. 12 Horizontally (NH + 75%)						
385	1¢ green.	60.00	45.00	30.00	48.00	30.00	20.00
386	2¢ carmine	165.00	100.00	70.00	100.00	70.00	55.00
	1910-11 Perf. 12 Vertically (†)						
387	1¢ green.	240.00	180.00	130.00	145.00	110.00	70.00
388	2¢ carmine	1650.00	1200.00	875.00	2500.00	1600.00	1100.00
389	3¢ deep violet (I) .	......	110000.00	......	......	12500.00	......
	1910 Perf. 8½ Horizontally						
390	1¢ green.	7.00	4.00	3.00	15.00	11.00	8.00
391	2¢ carmine	65.00	38.00	22.00	60.00	42.00	28.00
	1910-13 Perf. 8½ Vertically						
392	1¢ green.	35.00	24.00	15.00	60.00	39.00	25.00
393	2¢ carmine	55.00	38.00	22.00	50.00	30.00	20.00
394	3¢ deep violet (I) .	75.00	55.00	45.00	70.00	45.00	30.00
395	4¢ brown	75.00	55.00	45.00	80.00	75.00	52.00
396	5¢ blue	70.00	50.00	40.00	98.00	68.00	45.00

(NH + 75%)

SCOTT NO.	COIL LINE PAIRS UNUSED OG VF	F	AVG	COIL PAIRS UNUSED OG VF	F	AVG
385	450.00	300.00	195.00	200.00	125.00	87.50
386	1300.00	800.00	550.00	330.00	225.00	130.00
387	1200.00	825.00	585.00	700.00	460.00	310.00
390	50.00	35.00	22.50	25.00	16.50	9.00
391	330.00	235.00	140.00	150.00	100.00	60.00
392	225.00	140.00	95.00	120.00	82.00	48.00
393	325.00	210.00	150.00	155.00	100.00	60.00
394	600.00	395.00	265.00	200.00	135.00	85.00
395	475.00	315.00	225.00	220.00	150.00	95.00
396	450.00	295.00	200.00	210.00	136.00	90.00

THE PANAMA-PACIFIC ISSUE

The Panama-Pacific stamps were issued to commemorate the discovery of the Pacific Ocean in 1513 and the opening of the 1915 Panama-Pacific Exposition that celebrated the completion of the Panama Canal. Released in perf 12 form in 1913, the set of four denominations was changed to perf 10 in 1914. Before the perf change, the 10 cent orange yellow shade was determined to be too light. It was changed to the deeper orange color that is found both perf 12 and perf 10.

Because many collectors ignored the perf 10 stamps when they were issued, these stamps are scarcer than their perf 12 predecessors. In fact, #404 is the rarest 20th century commemorative issue.

397, 401
Balboa

398, 402
Panama Canal

399, 403
Golden Gate

400, 400A, 404
Discovery of San Francisco Bay

SCOTT NO.	DESCRIPTION	UNUSED O.G. VF	F	AVG	USED VF	F	AVG
	1913 Perf. 12 (NH + 75%)						
397-400A	**1¢-10¢ (5 varieties, complete) . . . .**	**510.00**	**380.00**	**260.00**	**70.00**	**48.50**	**34.00**
397	1¢ green.	25.00	14.00	10.00	2.50	1.70	1.00
398	2¢ carmine	28.00	16.00	12.00	1.75	.90	.75
399	5¢ blue	85.00	65.00	45.00	12.00	8.00	6.00
400	10¢ orange yellow	140.00	114.00	80.00	30.00	22.00	16.00
400A	10¢ orange. . . .	240.00	180.00	118.00	25.00	18.00	12.00
	1914-15 Perf. 10 (NH + 75%)						
401-04	**1¢-10¢ (4 varieties, complete) . . . .**	**1240.00**	**995.00**	**745.00**	**115.00**	**72.00**	**55.00**
401	1¢ green.	35.00	25.00	18.00	9.00	7.00	5.00
402	2¢ carmine	90.00	65.00	52.00	4.50	2.75	1.75
403	5¢ blue	220.00	170.00	120.00	24.00	15.00	10.00
404	10¢ orange. . . .	900.00	740.00	560.00	80.00	50.00	40.00

405/545
Washington

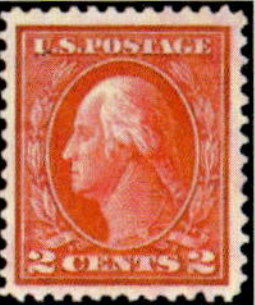
406/546
Washington

426/541
Washington

427, 446, 457, 465, 495, 503
Washington

428, 447, 458, 466, 467, 496, 504, 505
Washington

429, 468, 506
Washington

407, 430, 469, 507
Washington

414, 431, 470, 508
Franklin

415, 432, 471, 509
Franklin

416, 433, 472, 497, 510
Franklin

434, 473, 511
Franklin

417, 435, 474 512
Franklin

513
Franklin

418, 437, 475, 514
Franklin

419, 438, 476, 515
Franklin

420, 439, 476A, 516
Franklin

421, 422, 440, 477, 517
Franklin

423, 478, 518, 460
Franklin

SCOTT NO.	DESCRIPTION	UNUSED O.G. VF	F	AVG	USED VF	F	AVG
	1912-14 Single Line Watermark Perf. 12 (NH + 60%)						
405	1¢ green.	16.50	9.50	5.50	1.00	.80	.65
405b	1¢ booklet pane of 6	95.00	65.00	45.00	......	......	......
406	2¢ carmine (I). .	11.00	7.00	4.25	.75	.65	.50
406a	2¢ booklet pane of 6	95.00	65.00	45.00	......	......	......
407	7¢ black	125.00	75.00	50.00	25.00	16.00	10.50
	1912 Imperforate						
408	1¢ green.	2.75	2.00	1.50	1.50	.95	.65
409	2¢ carmine (I). .	3.95	3.00	2.00	1.50	1.15	.85

SCOTT NO.	UNUSED NH F	AVG	UNUSED OG F	AVG
	PLATE BLOCKS OF 6			
397	350.00	237.50	260.00	167.50
398	450.00	350.00	290.00	200.00
401	425.00	250.00	275.00	195.00
405	160.00	120.00	100.00	70.00
406	160.00	120.00	100.00	70.00
408	32.00	24.00	19.00	14.00
409	56.00	40.00	35.00	25.00

SCOTT NO.	UNUSED NH F	AVG	UNUSED OG F	AVG
	CENTER LINE BLOCKS			
408	15.50	11.00	11.00	8.50
409	17.00	11.95	14.50	9.50
	ARROW BLOCKS			
408	10.00	9.00	7.50	6.00
409	12.00	10.00	10.00	8.00

SCOTT NO.	DESCRIPTION	UNUSED O.G. VF	F	AVG	USED VF	F	AVG
	COIL STAMPS 1912 Perf. 8½ Horizontally (NH + 60%)						
410	1¢ green.	8.95	5.50	3.75	17.50	10.00	5.75
411	2¢ carmine (I). .	14.00	8.50	5.50	14.00	9.00	5.50
	1912 Perf. 8½ Vertically						
412	1¢ green.	32.00	22.00	15.00	40.00	30.00	24.00
413	2¢ carmine (I). .	75.00	43.00	28.00	50.00	40.00	30.00

(NH + 60%)

SCOTT NO.	COIL LINE PAIRS UNUSED OG VF	F	AVG	COIL PAIRS UNUSED OG VF	F	AVG
410	48.00	29.00	18.00	19.00	12.50	8.00
411	70.00	45.00	30.00	30.00	20.00	12.50
412	150.00	100.00	65.00	80.00	60.00	40.00
413	375.00	250.00	170.00	150.00	100.00	65.00

SCOTT NO.	DESCRIPTION	UNUSED O.G. VF	F	AVG	USED VF	F	AVG
	1912-14 Perf. 12 Single Line Watermark (NH + 60%)						
414	8¢ pale olive green	70.00	45.75	30.00	3.50	2.00	1.50
415	9¢ salmon red .	80.00	51.00	30.00	20.00	15.00	10.00
416	10¢ orange yellow	70.00	38.00	24.00	.75	.50	.35
417	12¢ claret brown	70.00	46.00	30.00	7.50	5.00	3.25
418	15¢ gray.	140.00	77.00	50.00	7.00	4.25	3.00
419	20¢ ultramarine	275.00	185.00	115.00	20.00	15.00	10.00
420	30¢ orange red.	160.00	105.00	65.00	20.00	15.00	10.00
421	50¢ violet	575.00	340.00	225.00	30.00	20.00	10.00
	1912 Double Line Watermark "USPS" Perf 12						
422	50¢ violet	350.00	225.00	150.00	30.00	25.00	15.00
423	$1 violet black .	675.00	425.00	250.00	100.00	85.00	60.00
	1914-15 Single Line Watermark, "USPS" Perf. 10 (NH + 60%)						
424-40	**1¢-50¢ (16 varieties, complete) . . . .**	**2220.00**	**1375.00**	**925.00**	**125.00**	**80.00**	**60.00**
424	1¢ green.	6.50	4.00	2.50	.25	.20	.15
424d	1¢ booklet pane of 6	8.00	4.00	3.00	....	....	....
425	2¢ rose red. . . .	5.00	2.50	1.75	.25	.20	.15
425e	2¢ booklet pane of 6	30.00	23.00	16.00	....	....	....
426	3¢ deep violet (I)	32.50	20.00	13.00	2.00	1.50	1.00
427	4¢ brown	55.00	34.00	24.00	1.25	.75	.50
428	5¢ blue	55.00	39.00	28.00	1.25	.75	.50
429	6¢ red orange. .	70.00	45.00	30.00	3.25	1.75	1.00
430	7¢ black	135.00	79.00	59.00	5.00	3.50	2.25
431	8¢ pale olive green	75.00	48.75	30.00	4.50	3.25	2.25
432	9¢ salmon red .	77.50	42.00	27.00	12.00	7.00	5.00
433	10¢ orange yellow	72.50	43.00	29.00	1.75	1.25	1.00
434	11¢ dark green.	42.50	28.00	20.00	12.00	7.00	5.00
435	12¢ claret brown	40.00	26.00	18.00	8.00	6.00	4.00
437	15¢ gray.	170.00	105.00	80.00	12.00	7.00	5.00
438	20¢ ultramarine	275.00	165.00	115.00	10.00	6.25	4.25
439	30¢ orange red.	400.00	220.00	170.00	28.00	18.00	15.00
440	50¢ violet	800.00	500.00	325.00	28.00	18.00	15.00

UNUSED PLATE BLOCKS OF 6

SCOTT NO.	NH F	AVG	OG F	AVG	SCOTT NO.	NH F	AVG	OG F	AVG
414	600.00	400.00	450.00	285.00	429	525.00	315.00	340.00	200.00
415	875.00	612.50	600.00	437.50	430	1350.00	950.00	900.00	615.00
416	700.00	450.00	430.00	300.00	431	650.00	500.00	500.00	360.00
417	875.00	595.00	562.50	375.00	432	875.00	630.00	650.00	465.00
418	900.00	650.00	600.00	450.00	433	800.00	575.00	600.00	425.00
424 (6)	75.00	55.00	40.00	27.25	434	400.00	260.00	290.00	165.00
424 (10)	225.00	140.00	155.00	95.00	435	400.00	225.00	270.00	170.00
425 (6)	75.00	40.00	37.50	30.00	437	1200.00	850.00	850.00	625.00
425 (10)	225.00	150.00	145.00	100.00	438	3850.00	2950.00	2500.00	1950.00
426	350.00	275.00	250.00	150.00	439	6000.00	4275.00	3700.00	2850.00
427	600.00	415.00	445.00	315.00	440	20000.00	13500.00	14500.00	10500.00
428	500.00	315.00	350.00	210.00					

SCOTT NO.	DESCRIPTION	UNUSED O.G. VF	F	AVG	USED VF	F	AVG
	COIL STAMPS 1914 Perf. 10 Horizontally (NH + 60%)						
441	1¢ green.	2.75	1.50	1.00	2.50	1.90	1.25
442	2¢ carmine (I). .	17.50	11.00	7.00	50.00	40.00	25.00
	1914 Perf. 10 Vertically (NH + 60%)						
443	1¢ green.	50.00	33.00	21.00	40.00	24.00	14.00
444	2¢ carmine (I). .	75.00	44.00	27.00	30.00	21.75	13.50
445	3¢ violet (I)	400.00	255.00	180.00	315.00	200.00	125.00
446	4¢ brown	300.00	200.00	150.00	150.00	90.00	65.00
447	5¢ blue	72.50	47.00	33.00	120.00	80.00	50.00

SCOTT NO.	DESCRIPTION	UNUSED O.G. VF	F	AVG	USED VF	F	AVG
	ROTARY PRESS COIL STAMPS 1915-16 Perf. 10 Horizontally (NH + 60%)						
448	1¢ green.	9.50	7.00	4.00	20.00	13.50	8.50
449	2¢ red (I)	3500.00	2100.00	1450.00	725.00	550.00	335.00
450	2¢ carmine (III).	27.50	20.00	14.00	25.00	16.50	8.25
	1914-16 Perf. 10 Vertically (NH + 60%)						
452	1¢ green.	22.50	16.00	12.00	25.00	17.75	12.50
453	2¢ carmine rose (I)	200.00	137.50	93.75	45.00	35.00	25.00
454	2¢ red (II)	145.00	100.00	65.00	25.00	14.25	10.00
455	2¢ carmine (III).	14.00	10.00	6.50	4.50	3.35	1.70
456	3¢ violet (I)	450.00	300.00	190.00	185.00	160.00	140.00
457	4¢ brown	60.00	31.00	22.00	56.00	35.00	21.00
458	5¢ blue.	45.00	30.00	20.00	40.00	38.00	23.00
	1914 Imperforate Coil (NH + 60%)						
459	2¢ carmine (I). .	475.00	375.00	250.00	1400.00	1000.00	....
	1915 Flat Plate Printing Double Line Watermark Perf. 10 (NH + 60%)						
460	$1 violet black .	950.00	550.00	425.00	150.00	125.00	100.00
	1915 Single Line Watermark "USPS" Perf. 11 (NH + 60%)						
461	2¢ pale carmine red (I)	250.00	130.00	73.00	350.00	250.00	170.00
	1916-17 Unwatermarked Perf. 10 (NH + 60%)						
462	1¢ green.	17.50	12.00	8.00	.50	.30	.20
462a	1¢ booklet pane of 6	25.00	16.00	9.50	....	....	....
463	2¢ carmine (I). .	7.95	5.50	3.50	.50	.30	.20
463a	2¢ booklet pane of 6	110.00	80.00	55.00	....	....	....
464	3¢ violet (I)	130.00	70.00	52.00	20.00	15.00	10.00
465	4¢ orange brown	80.00	50.00	30.00	3.25	2.25	1.25
466	5¢ blue	120.00	65.00	40.00	5.00	3.50	2.00
467	5¢ carmine (error)	800.00	500.00	350.00	3000.00	2000.00	1500.00
468	6¢ red orange. .	155.00	83.00	50.00	12.00	9.00	7.50
469	7¢ black	210.00	115.00	80.00	15.00	10.00	8.00
470	8¢ olive green .	135.00	75.00	50.00	10.00	8.50	6.00
471	9¢ salmon red .	150.00	83.00	53.00	22.00	15.00	10.00
472	10¢ orange yellow	180.00	94.00	69.00	5.50	3.00	2.00
473	11¢ dark green.	85.00	54.00	31.50	25.00	18.00	15.00
474	12¢ claret brown	140.00	90.00	65.00	10.00	8.00	5.00
475	15¢ gray.	325.00	225.00	130.00	20.00	15.00	10.00
476	20¢ light ultramarine	400.00	220.00	160.00	22.00	15.00	10.00
476A	30¢ orange red.	....	4800.00	....	....	....	....
477	50¢ light violet .	1600.00	950.00	625.00	100.00	80.00	62.00
478	$1 violet black. .	1200.00	690.00	510.00	38.00	23.00	19.00
	Design of 1902-03						
479	$2 dark blue . . .	485.00	335.00	245.00	50.00	40.00	35.00
480	$5 light green . .	425.00	270.00	160.00	55.00	45.00	35.00
	1916-17 Imperforate (NH + 60%)						
481	1¢ green.	2.50	1.75	.75	1.50	1.00	.50
482	2¢ carmine (I). .	2.50	2.00	1.00	1.75	1.25	1.00
483	3¢ violet (I)	35.00	25.00	17.00	18.00	13.00	10.00
484	3¢ violet (II) . . .	22.50	19.00	13.00	14.00	10.00	8.00

(NH + 60%)

SCOTT NO.	COIL LINE PAIRS UNUSED OG VF	F	AVG	COIL PAIRS UNUSED OG VF	F	AVG
441	12.50	8.75	5.00	5.75	3.75	2.50
442	90.00	48.00	30.00	40.00	25.00	16.00
443	180.00	120.00	75.00	100.00	66.00	42.00
444	425.00	300.00	185.00	150.00	88.00	54.00
445	1600.00	900.00	600.00	750.00	495.00	350.00
446	900.00	500.00	350.00	550.00	370.00	275.00
447	325.00	185.00	125.00	175.00	110.00	75.00
448	62.00	39.00	25.00	32.00	18.00	12.00
450	90.00	65.00	40.00	58.00	40.00	28.00
452	115.00	65.00	40.00	47.50	35.00	24.00
453	850.00	500.00	350.00	400.00	250.00	174.00
454	750.00	425.00	325.00	350.00	200.00	140.00
455	90.00	50.00	35.00	32.00	20.00	13.00
456	1350.00	900.00	550.00	900.00	625.00	380.00
457	240.00	130.00	90.00	120.00	80.00	52.00
458	250.00	145.00	95.00	115.00	85.00	50.00
459	1800.00	1250.00	900.00	1350.00	1150.00	900.00

***NOTE:** For further details on the various types of similar appearing stamps please refer to our U.S. Stamp Identifier.*

UNUSED PLATE BLOCKS OF 6

SCOTT NO.	NH F	NH AVG	OG F	OG AVG	SCOTT NO.	NH F	NH AVG	OG F	OG AVG
462	195.00	125.00	125.00	80.00	472	2000.00	1500.00	1500.00	1000.00
463	175.00	110.00	110.00	67.50	473	550.00	400.00	375.00	275.00
464	1500.00	1100.00	1150.00	825.00	474	950.00	600.00	600.00	400.00
465	800.00	500.00	600.00	425.00	481	35.00	25.00	25.00	16.50
466	1100.00	850.00	950.00	565.00	482	35.00	22.00	22.50	17.00
470	750.00	550.00	600.00	350.00	483	200.00	160.00	160.00	110.00
471	850.00	675.00	595.00	400.00	484	150.00	95.00	125.00	85.00
	CENTER LINE BLOCKS					**ARROW BLOCKS**			
481	10.00	6.00	5.00	4.00	481	8.00	5.00	4.00	3.00
482	13.50	8.00	8.50	5.50	482	11.00	7.00	7.75	4.75
483	130.00	95.00	97.50	72.50	483	125.00	90.00	95.00	70.00
484	80.00	55.00	70.00	55.00	484	75.00	50.00	65.00	50.00

SCOTT NO.	DESCRIPTION	UNUSED O.G. VF	F	AVG	USED VF	F	AVG
	ROTARY PRESS COIL STAMPS 1916-19 Perf. 10 Horizontally (NH + 60%)						
486	1¢ green.	1.75	1.00	.50	1.00	.75	.50
487	2¢ carmine (II) .	32.50	19.00	12.00	20.00	12.00	10.00
488	2¢ carmine (III).	5.95	3.75	2.50	5.00	3.50	2.00
489	3¢ violet (I)	7.00	4.50	3.00	2.75	1.95	1.00
	1916-22 Perf. 10 Vertically (NH + 60%)						
490	1¢ green.	1.00	.50	.50	1.00	.50	.50
491	2¢ carmine (II) .	2750.00	1950.00	1300.00	800.00	550.00	375.00
492	2¢ carmine (III).	16.00	9.00	6.00	1.00	.50	.50
493	3¢ violet (I)	37.50	21.00	16.00	7.00	4.25	2.75
494	3¢ violet (II) . . .	22.50	13.00	8.50	2.50	1.50	1.00
495	4¢ orange brown	27.50	15.75	11.00	10.50	6.00	4.00
496	5¢ blue	7.00	4.00	3.00	2.60	1.75	1.00
497	10¢ orange yellow	35.00	20.00	15.00	25.00	16.50	9.25

(NH + 60%)

SCOTT NO.	COIL LINE PAIRS UNUSED OG VF	F	AVG	COIL PAIRS UNUSED OG VF	F	AVG
486	6.50	4.50	3.50	3.50	2.00	1.25
487	160.00	105.00	75.00	67.50	42.00	25.00
488	28.00	18.00	12.00	12.50	9.00	5.75
489	40.00	30.00	24.00	16.00	10.00	7.00
490	6.00	3.75	1.90	2.50	1.50	1.00
491	......	10000.00	6000.00	6450.00	4500.00	3000.00
492	70.00	50.00	35.00	36.00	20.00	14.00
493	160.00	100.00	70.00	78.75	60.00	35.00
494	90.00	60.00	48.00	47.00	35.00	19.50
495	100.00	75.00	55.00	55.00	35.00	22.00
496	40.00	28.00	19.50	15.00	9.00	7.00
497	160.00	115.00	75.00	75.00	45.00	35.00

1917-19 Flat Plate Printing Perf. 11 (NH + 60%)

SCOTT NO.	DESCRIPTION	UNUSED O.G. VF	F	AVG	USED VF	F	AVG
498/518	**(498-99, 501-04, 506-18) 19 varieties**	**680.00**	**410.00**	**270.00**	**45.00**	**25.00**	**19.00**
498	1¢ green.	.90	.50	.50	.35	.25	.20
498e	1¢ booklet pane of 6	7.50	4.50	3.25	....	....	....
498f	1¢ booklet pane of 30.	1300.00	800.00	550.00	....	....	....
499	2¢ rose (I).	.90	.50	.25	.35	.25	.20
499e	2¢ booklet pane of 6	7.00	4.50	3.50	....	....	....
500	2¢ deep rose (Ia)	400.00	225.00	165.00	300.00	200.00	125.00
501	3¢ light violet (I)	25.00	15.00	10.00	1.00	.70	.50
501b	3¢ booklet pane of 6	95.00	65.00	45.00	....	....	....
502	3¢ dark violet (II)	26.00	15.00	10.00	2.25	1.50	.95
502b	3¢ booklet pane of 6	100.00	56.00	38.00	....	....	....
503	4¢ brown	17.00	10.00	6.00	1.25	.85	.50
504	5¢ blue	15.00	8.50	5.50	1.00	.75	.45
505	5¢ rose (error) .	500.00	325.00	260.00	700.00	475.00	300.00
506	6¢ red orange. .	22.00	13.00	8.00	.75	.50	.35
507	7¢ black	42.00	25.00	17.00	2.75	2.00	1.10
508	8¢ olive bistre. .	25.00	15.00	9.00	1.50	1.20	.80
509	9¢ salmon red .	24.00	14.00	9.00	4.75	2.95	2.00
510	10¢ orange yellow	30.00	17.00	10.50	.30	.25	.20
511	11¢ light green .	22.50	13.00	8.00	7.50	4.75	3.25
512	12¢ claret brown	22.50	13.00	8.00	1.25	.75	.60
513	13¢ apple green	25.00	14.00	10.00	17.00	10.00	9.00
514	15¢ gray.	64.00	38.00	26.00	2.50	1.50	1.25
515	20¢ light ultramarine	85.00	46.00	34.00	.75	.50	.35
516	30¢ orange red.	70.00	40.00	30.00	2.50	1.50	1.25
517	50¢ red violet . .	100.00	75.00	50.00	1.50	.80	.75
518	$1 violet black .	110.00	75.00	50.00	4.25	2.75	1.75
	1917 Design of 1908-09 Double Line Watermark Perf. 11						
519	2¢ carmine	550.00	385.00	255.00	1800.00	1400.00	1100.00

SCOTT NO.	NH F	NH AVG	OG F	OG AVG	SCOTT NO.	NH F	NH AVG	OG F	OG AVG
				UNUSED PLATE BLOCKS OF 6					
498	25.00	18.75	17.95	15.50	511	225.00	125.00	165.00	100.00
499	25.00	18.75	17.95	15.50	512	220.00	125.00	155.00	100.00
501	200.00	150.00	165.00	115.00	513	220.00	150.00	145.00	90.00
502	225.00	200.00	195.00	150.00	514	835.00	465.00	595.00	385.00
503	215.00	165.00	150.00	130.00	515	975.00	565.00	675.00	425.00
504	165.00	100.00	135.00	80.00	516	800.00	475.00	640.00	375.00
506	275.00	200.00	195.00	135.00	517	2000.00	1350.00	1300.00	900.00
507	375.00	285.00	265.00	225.00	518	1750.00	1080.00	1225.00	800.00
508	375.00	255.00	300.00	200.00	519	5000.00	2785.00	3575.00	2150.00
509	220.00	150.00	175.00	120.00			ARROW BLOCK		
510	325.00	270.00	200.00	155.00	518	450.00	280.00	300.00	225.00

523, 547
Franklin

524
Franklin

SCOTT NO.	DESCRIPTION	UNUSED O.G. VF	F	AVG	USED VF	F	AVG
	1918 Unwatermarked (NH + 60%)						
523	$2 orange red & black	500.00	325.00	250.00	350.00	200.00	125.00
524	$5 deep green & black	250.00	150.00	100.00	60.00	40.00	20.00
	1918-20 Offset Printing Perf. 11 (NH + 60%)						
525	1¢ gray green. .	6.00	4.00	2.50	1.25	.85	.50
526	2¢ carmine (IV)	42.50	30.00	16.00	7.00	5.00	3.25
527	2¢ carmine (V) .	35.00	23.00	14.00	2.25	1.50	.85
528	2¢ carmine (Va)	17.00	11.00	8.00	1.00	.75	.55
528A	2¢ carmine (VI)	72.50	55.00	36.00	2.00	1.50	1.00
528B	2¢ carmine (VII)	38.50	25.00	18.00	.60	.50	.35
529	3¢ violet (III) . . .	7.50	5.50	4.50	.50	.35	.25
530	3¢ purple (IV) . .	2.50	1.75	1.25	.50	.30	.20
	1918-20 Offset Printing Imperforate						
531	1¢ gray green. .	22.50	14.00	10.50	18.00	12.00	10.00
532	2¢ carmine rose (IV)	100.00	71.00	54.00	60.00	50.00	40.00
533	2¢ carmine (V) .	225.00	120.00	135.00	210.00	150.00	110.00
534	2¢ carmine (Va)	42.50	33.00	19.00	27.00	20.00	15.00
534A	2¢ carmine (VI)	130.00	73.00	53.00	44.00	29.00	22.00
534B	2¢ carmine (VII)	2500.00	1800.00	1350.00	1550.00	1275.00	770.00
535	3¢ violet (IV). . .	18.50	13.00	9.00	12.00	10.00	8.50
	1919 Offset Printing Perf. 12½						
536	1¢ gray green. .	40.00	28.00	18.00	45.00	30.00	20.00

537
"Victory" and Flags

SCOTT NO.	DESCRIPTION	UNUSED O.G. VF	F	AVG	USED VF	F	AVG
	1919 VICTORY ISSUE (NH + 50%)						
537	3¢ violet	18.50	10.50	6.50	5.00	3.50	2.50
	1919-21 Rotary Press Printings—Perf. 11 x 10 (†) (NH + 50%)						
538	1¢ green.	25.00	14.00	9.50	12.00	10.00	8.00
538a	Same, imperf. horizontally. . . .	80.00	50.00	36.00	....	....	....
539	2¢ carmine rose (II)	5300.00	3000.00	2600.00	....	22000.00	....
540	2¢ carmine rose (III)	17.50	10.00	6.00	15.00	12.00	10.50
540a	Same, imperf. horizontally. . . .	85.00	48.00	38.00	....	....	....
541	3¢ violet (II) . . .	80.00	48.00	37.00	45.00	40.00	30.00
	Perf. 10 x 11						
542	1¢ green.	17.00	11.00	7.00	2.25	1.35	1.00
	Perf. 10						
543	1¢ green.	1.35	.75	.50	.75	.40	.20

SCOTT NO.	DESCRIPTION	UNUSED O.G. VF	F	AVG	USED VF	F	AVG
	Perf. 11						
544	1¢ green (19 x 22½mm) .	....	20000.00	17000.00	....	4000.00	....
545	1¢ green (19½ x 22mm) .	300.00	200.00	130.00	300.00	185.00	125.00
546	2¢ carmine rose (III)	165.00	110.00	68.25	300.00	185.00	125.00
	1920 Flat Plate Printing Perf. 11						
547	$2 carmine & black	200.00	150.00	100.00	59.00	40.00	30.00

SCOTT NO.	NH F	NH AVG	OG F	OG AVG	SCOTT NO.	NH F	NH AVG	OG F	OG AVG
		UNUSED PLATE BLOCKS OF 6					UNUSED PLATE BLOCKS OF (—)		
525 (6)	45.00	30.00	25.00	20.00	535 (6)	105.00	85.00	85.00	65.00
526 (6)	400.00	275.00	250.00	200.00	536 (6)	250.00	175.00	175.00	135.00
527 (6)	300.00	200.00	180.00	150.00	537 (6)	250.00	175.00	165.00	125.00
528 (6)	150.00	100.00	95.00	60.00	538 (4)	135.00	97.50	90.00	60.00
528A (6)	700.00	450.00	490.00	315.00	540 (4)	130.00	80.00	80.00	50.00
528B (6)	300.00	200.00	195.00	145.00	541 (4)	500.00	350.00	330.00	225.00
529 (6)	100.00	67.50	65.00	45.00	542 (6)	195.00	135.00	135.00	90.00
530 (6)	40.00	26.50	25.00	17.00	543 (4)	35.00	20.00	15.00	10.00
531 (6)	150.00	112.50	110.00	85.00	543 (6)	55.00	32.00	30.00	20.00
532 (6)	650.00	500.00	485.00	375.00	545 (4)	1200.00	800.00	950.00	675.00
533 (6)	2100.00	1800.00	1575.00	1175.00	546 (4)	1000.00	700.00	700.00	475.00
534 (6)	275.00	200.00	435.00	150.00	547 (8)	6000.00	4575.00	4350.00	3150.00
534A (6)	800.00	550.00	525.00	415.00	548 (6)	100.00	65.00	67.50	50.00
					549 (6)	110.00	70.00	75.00	55.00
					550 (6)	725.00	525.00	475.00	330.00
		CENTER LINE					ARROW BLOCKS		
531	80.00	50.00	55.00	35.00	531	60.00	45.00	50.00	40.00
532	325.00	200.00	225.00	145.00	532	275.00	170.00	195.00	120.00
533	2000.00	1250.00	1000.00	650.00	533	1000.00	700.00	700.00	500.00
534	95.00	55.00	70.00	50.00	534	90.00	55.00	60.00	45.00
534A	275.00	200.00	185.00	125.00	534A	220.00	160.00	160.00	120.00
535	90.00	65.00	55.00	40.00	535	85.00	60.00	52.50	37.50
547	1400.00	975.00	1175.00	835.00	547	1275.00	900.00	1100.00	825.00

548
The "Mayflower"

549
Landing of the Pilgrims

550
Signing of the Compact

SCOTT NO.	DESCRIPTION	UNUSED O.G. VF	F	AVG	USED VF	F	AVG
	1920 PILGRIM TERCENTENARY ISSUE (NH + 50%)						
548-50	**1¢-5¢ (3 varieties, complete) . . . .**	**75.00**	**48.00**	**37.00**	**42.00**	**21.00**	**18.50**
548	1¢ green.	9.50	6.50	4.75	7.00	3.75	2.50
549	2¢ carmine rose	12.00	7.50	4.25	4.50	2.50	2.00
550	5¢ deep blue . .	70.00	40.00	32.00	37.00	20.00	18.00

For Your Convenience in Ordering, Complete Sets are Listed Before Single Stamp Listings!

551, 653
Nathan Hale

552, 575, 578, 581, 594, 596, 597, 604, 632
Franklin

553, 576, 582, 598, 605, 631, 633
Harding

554, 577, 579, 583, 595, 599-99A, 606, 634-34A
Washington

555, 584, 600, 635
Lincoln

556, 585, 601, 636
Martha Washington

557, 586, 602, 637
Roosevelt

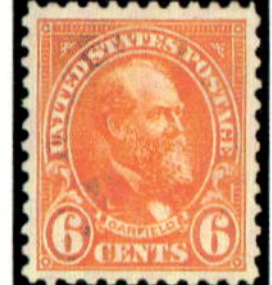
558, 587, 638, 723
Garfield

559, 588, 639
McKinley

560, 589, 640
Grant

561, 590, 641
Jefferson

562, 591, 603, 642
Monroe

563, 692
Hayes

564, 693
Cleveland

565, 695
American Indian

566, 696
Statue of Liberty

567, 698
Golden Gate

568, 699
Niagara Falls

569,700
Bison

570, 701
Arlington Amphitheater

571
Lincoln Memorial

572
U.S. Capitol

573
"America"

SCOTT NO.	DESCRIPTION	UNUSED O.G. VF	UNUSED O.G. F	UNUSED O.G. AVG	USED VF	USED F	USED AVG
	THE 1922-25 ISSUE **Flat Plate Printings** **Perf. 11 (NH + 60%)**						
551-73	**½¢-$5 (23 varieties, complete) . . . .**	**1145.00**	**760.00**	**555.00**	**74.00**	**40.00**	**28.00**
551	½¢ olive brown (1925)	.60	.50	.25	.25	.20	.15
552	1¢ deep green (1923)	4.25	3.00	2.25	1.00	.80	.60
552a	1¢ booklet pane of 6	17.50	13.00	9.00	....	....	....
553	1½¢ yellow brown (1925).	5.25	3.25	2.50	2.00	1.35	.95
554	2¢ carmine (1923)	4.50	3.00	2.00	1.00	.80	.60
554c	2¢ booklet pane of 6	12.00	9.00	5.50	....	....	......
555	3¢ violet (1923)	32.50	23.00	15.00	2.00	1.50	1.00
556	4¢ yellow brown (1923).	33.50	24.00	15.00	1.00	.65	.50
557	5¢ dark blue . . .	33.50	24.00	15.00	1.00	.65	.50
558	6¢ red orange. .	60.00	38.00	28.00	2.75	1.75	1.25
559	7¢ black (1923)	17.50	12.00	9.00	2.25	1.25	.90
560	8¢ olive green (1923)	65.00	44.00	31.00	2.00	1.25	.95
561	9¢ rose (1923) .	30.00	18.00	12.00	4.00	2.25	1.50
562	10¢ orange (1923)	35.00	23.00	15.00	.30	.20	.15
563	11¢ light blue . .	4.25	3.00	2.00	.75	.50	.30
564	12¢ brown violet (1923).	15.00	8.00	5.00	.75	.50	.40
565	14¢ blue (1923)	9.00	5.00	3.00	2.50	2.00	1.25
566	15¢ gray.	40.00	23.00	18.00	.25	.20	.15
567	20¢ carmine rose (1923).	40.00	25.00	20.00	.25	.20	.15
568	25¢ yellow green	33.50	21.00	15.00	2.25	1.50	1.25
569	30¢ olive brown (1923).	60.00	39.00	28.00	1.00	.60	.40
570	50¢ lilac	95.00	56.00	45.00	.50	.25	.20
571	$1 violet black (1923)	72.50	48.00	37.00	2.00	1.25	.75
572	$2 deep blue (1923)	165.00	105.00	88.00	18.00	11.00	6.50
573	$5 carmine & blue (1923).	300.00	220.00	160.00	29.00	18.00	12.00
	1923-25 Imperforate						
575	1¢ green.	16.50	12.00	9.00	14.00	8.00	5.50
576	1½¢ yellow brown (1925).	3.25	2.00	1.25	4.75	2.50	2.00
577	2¢ carmine	3.25	2.25	1.25	4.25	2.50	1.75
	Rotary Press Printings 1923 Perf. 11 x 10 (†) **(NH + 60%)**						
578	1¢ green	100.00	85.00	60.00	250.00	180.00	130.00
579	2¢ carmine . . .	150.00	87.00	62.50	225.00	140.00	100.00
	1923-26 Perf. 10 (†)						
581-91	**1¢-10¢ (11 varieties, complete) . . . .**	**285.00**	**175.00**	**125.00**	**49.00**	**29.00**	**18.00**
581	1¢ green.	18.25	12.00	7.50	1.25	.85	.60
582	1½¢ brown (1925)	6.00	4.00	3.00	1.25	.90	.65
583	2¢ carmine (1924)	4.00	2.00	1.25	.25	.20	.15
583a	2¢ booklet pane of 6 (1924).	110.00	70.00	50.00	....	....	....
584	3¢ violet (1925)	40.00	24.00	17.00	5.00	3.50	2.00
585	4¢ yellow brown (1925).	24.00	16.00	11.00	1.50	1.15	.75
586	5¢ blue (1925) .	24.00	16.00	11.00	1.00	0.50	0.30
587	6¢ red orange (1925)	18.50	10.00	6.50	1.50	.90	.60
588	7¢ black (1926)	25.00	16.00	10.50	18.00	12.00	8.00
589	8¢ olive green (1926)	40.00	24.00	15.00	13.00	8.50	5.00
590	9¢ rose (1926) .	8.00	4.00	3.00	10.00	5.00	3.25
591	10¢ orange (1925)	90.00	55.00	42.00	.55	.45	.35
	Perf. 11 (†)						
594	1¢ green.	....	65000.00	....	....	11000.00	8800.00
595	2¢ carmine	275.00	225.00	170.00	550.00	350.00	225.00
	Perf. 11						
596	1¢ green.	....	....	....	....	200000.00	....

SCOTT NO.		PLATE BLOCKS (6) UNUSED NH VF	F	AVG.	UNUSED OG VF	F	AVG.
551	½¢ olive brown (1923)	25.00	20.00	15.00	15.00	12.00	9.00
552	1¢ deep green (1923)	52.00	30.00	25.00	32.50	20.00	14.00
553	1½¢ yellow brown (1923)	95.00	80.00	65.00	65.00	55.00	35.00
554	2¢ carmine (1923)	50.00	30.00	22.50	32.50	21.50	15.00
555	3¢ violet (1923)	350.00	225.00	180.00	195.00	150.00	110.00
556	4¢ yellow brown (1923)	365.00	235.00	185.00	205.00	150.00	110.00
557	5¢ dark blue	375.00	240.00	200.00	210.00	160.00	125.00
558	6¢ red orange	750.00	450.00	400.00	500.00	350.00	250.00
559	7¢ black (1923)	150.00	100.00	70.00	100.00	65.00	45.00
560	8¢ olive green (1923)	1100.00	740.00	650.00	750.00	500.00	375.00
561	9¢ rose (1923)	340.00	225.00	160.00	195.00	160.00	130.00
562	10¢ orange (1923)	400.00	290.00	200.00	300.00	200.00	160.00
563	11¢ light blue	55.00	38.00	32.00	45.00	28.00	18.50
564	12¢ brown violet (1923)	250.00	145.00	100.00	175.00	100.00	80.00
565	14¢ blue (1923)	120.00	80.00	57.50	85.00	52.50	42.50
566	15¢ grey	500.00	350.00	240.00	350.00	225.00	175.00
567	20¢ carmine rose (1923)	475.00	320.00	240.00	400.00	220.00	190.00
568	25¢ yellow green	420.00	260.00	200.00	325.00	190.00	125.00
569	30¢ olive brown (1923)	550.00	375.00	295.00	325.00	225.00	160.00
570	50¢ lilac	1350.00	1000.00	750.00	850.00	600.00	450.00
571	$1 violet black (1923)	800.00	520.00	400.00	550.00	400.00	300.00
572	$2 deep blue (1923)	1750.00	1300.00	1000.00	1100.00	850.00	650.00
573(8)	$5 carmine + blue (1923)	3000.00	2000.00	1500.00	2000.00	1800.00	1200.00

SCOTT NO.		CENTER LINE BLOCKS F/NH	F/OG	AVG/OG	ARROW BLOCKS F/NH	F/OG	AVG/OG
571	$1 violet black	....	....	....	310.00	210.00	140.00
572	$2 deep blue	....	....	....	650.00	450.00	360.00
573	$5 carmine & blue	1100.00	925.00	775.00	1050.00	900.00	750.00
575	1¢ imperforate	58.00	50.00	40.00	55.00	47.50	38.00
576	1½¢ imperforate	19.50	15.00	10.50	11.00	8.00	5.00
577	2¢ imperforate	22.50	17.50	12.00	12.00	9.00	7.00

SCOTT NO.		PLATE BLOCKS UNUSED NH VF	F	AVG.	UNUSED OG VF	F	AVG.
575 (6)	1¢ green	160.00	110.00	75.00	110.00	70.00	50.00
576 (6)	1½¢ yellow brown (1925)	50.00	33.00	25.00	35.00	22.00	16.00
577 (6)	2¢ carmine	50.00	34.00	25.00	42.00	25.00	18.00
578	1¢ green	2100.00	1200.00	950.00	1300.00	900.00	675.00
579	2¢ carmine	1100.00	700.00	525.00	695.00	450.00	350.00
581	1¢ green	225.00	140.00	100.00	160.00	100.00	70.00
582	1½¢ brown (1925)	85.00	55.00	35.00	60.00	38.00	25.00
583	2¢ carmine (1923)	75.00	45.00	28.50	55.00	33.00	20.00
584	3¢ violet (1925)	400.00	260.00	190.00	260.00	190.00	150.00
585	4¢ yellow green (1925)	300.00	200.00	157.50	220.00	160.00	115.00
586	5¢ blue (1925)	375.00	240.00	170.00	275.00	170.00	120.00
587	6¢ red orange (1925)	225.00	145.00	95.00	150.00	95.00	65.00
588	7¢ black (1926)	250.00	155.00	100.00	175.00	110.00	70.00
589	8¢ olive green (1926)	400.00	260.00	190.00	275.00	190.00	125.00
590	9¢ rose (1926)	115.00	70.00	45.00	80.00	50.00	30.00
591	10¢ orange (1925)	1050.00	700.00	500.00	650.00	475.00	380.00

SCOTT NO.	DESCRIPTION	UNUSED VF	F	AVG	USED VF	F	AVG
	1923-29 Rotary Press Coil Stamps (NH + 50%)						
597/606	**597-99, 600-06 (10 varieties)**	**34.25**	**23.50**	**15.50**	**3.50**	**2.45**	**1.65**
	Perf. 10 Vertically						
597	1¢ green	.60	.25	.25	1.00	.80	.60
598	1½¢ deep brown (1925)	1.35	1.00	.75	1.00	.65	.50
599	2¢ carmine (I) (1923)	.60	.50	.25	1.00	.80	.60
599A	2¢ carmine (II) (1929)	210.00	115.00	73.50	25.00	15.25	9.75
600	3¢ violet (1924)	13.75	9.00	5.50	1.00	.70	.45
601	4¢ yellow brown	8.25	5.50	4.25	1.50	.75	.45
602	5¢ dark blue (1924)	2.95	1.75	1.25	1.00	.75	.50
603	10¢ orange (1924)	7.25	5.00	3.50	1.00	.75	.50
	Perf. 10 Horizontally						
604	1¢ yellow green (1924)	.60	.50	.25	1.00	.75	.50
605	1½¢ yellow brown (1925)	.75	.50	.25	1.00	.75	.50
606	2¢ carmine	.65	.50	.25	1.00	.75	.50

NOTE: For further details on the various types of similar appearing stamps please refer to our U. S. Stamp Identifier.

SCOTT NO.		UNUSED OG (NH + 40%) COIL LINE PAIRS VF	F	AVG.	COIL PAIRS VF	F	AVG.
597	1¢ green	2.55	1.95	1.40	1.20	.65	.50
598	1½¢ brown (1925)	6.75	5.25	4.00	2.70	2.00	1.50
599	2¢ carmine (I)	2.15	1.65	1.20	1.25	1.00	.55
599A	2¢ carmine (II) (1929)	825.00	557.50	375.00	450.00	247.50	157.50
600	3¢ deep violet (1924)	40.00	30.00	23.75	28.00	18.00	11.50
601	4¢ yellow brown	35.75	27.50	22.00	16.50	12.00	8.50
602	5¢ dark blue (1924)	11.75	9.00	6.00	6.25	4.25	2.75
603	10¢ orange (1924)	35.00	27.00	20.00	15.00	10.00	7.00
604	1¢ green (1924)	3.40	2.60	1.65	1.25	1.00	.50
605	1½¢ yellow brown (1925)	4.25	3.00	2.00	1.50	1.00	.75
606	2¢ carmine	2.75	2.00	1.35	1.30	1.00	.50

610-613
Harding

SCOTT NO.	DESCRIPTION	UNUSED VF	F	AVG	USED VF	F	AVG
	1923 HARDING MEMORIAL ISSUE (NH + 50%)						
610	2¢ black, perf 11 flat	1.50	1.00	.75	1.00	.75	.50
611	2¢ black, imperf	17.50	10.50	8.00	15.00	10.00	8.00
612	2¢ black, perf 10 rotary	27.00	14.00	12.00	6.00	3.50	2.50
613	2¢ black perf 11 rotary	......	......	......	......	45000.00	36500.00

614
Ship "New Netherlands"

615
Landing at Fort Orange

616
Monument at Mayport, Fla.

1924 HUGUENOT-WALLOON ISSUE (NH + 40%)

SCOTT NO.	DESCRIPTION	UNUSED VF	F	AVG	USED VF	F	AVG
614-16	**1¢-5¢ (3 varieties, complete)**	**39.00**	**24.00**	**18.00**	**28.00**	**12.50**	**8.00**
614	1¢ dark green	5.00	2.50	1.50	5.00	2.00	1.50
615	2¢ carmine rose	6.00	3.25	2.00	4.75	2.00	1.00
616	5¢ dark blue	30.00	20.00	15.00	20.00	10.00	6.00

617
Washington at Cambridge

618
Birth of Liberty

619
The Minute Man

1925 LEXINGTON-CONCORD SESQUICENTENNIAL (NH + 40%)

SCOTT NO.	DESCRIPTION	UNUSED VF	F	AVG	USED VF	F	AVG
617-19	**1¢-5¢ (3 varieties, complete)**	**40.00**	**24.00**	**18.00**	**25.00**	**15.00**	**10.00**
617	1¢ deep green	5.00	3.00	2.00	5.00	3.00	2.00
618	2¢ carmine rose	6.00	4.00	2.50	6.00	4.00	2.50
619	5¢ dark blue	30.00	18.00	15.00	15.00	10.00	7.00

SCOTT NO.	DESCRIPTION	UNUSED O.G. VF	F	AVG	USED VF	F	AVG

620
Sloop "Restaurationen"

621
Viking Ship

1925 NORSE-AMERICAN ISSUE (NH + 40%)

SCOTT NO.	DESCRIPTION	UNUSED O.G. VF	F	AVG	USED VF	F	AVG
620-21	**2¢-5¢ (2 varieties, complete) . . . .**	**30.00**	**13.00**	**8.00**	**19.00**	**10.00**	**6.00**
620	2¢ carmine & black	6.00	3.50	2.50	5.00	2.50	1.50
621	5¢ dark blue & black	25.00	10.00	6.00	15.00	8.00	5.00

622, 694
Harrison

623, 697
Wilson

1925-26 Flat Plate Printings, Perf. 11

SCOTT NO.	DESCRIPTION	UNUSED O.G. VF	F	AVG	USED VF	F	AVG
622	13¢ green (1926)	25.00	16.00	11.00	1.25	.75	.60
623	17¢ black	31.50	19.00	15.00	.75	.50	.40

SCOTT NO.	PLATE BLOCKS	UNUSED NH VF	F	AVG.	UNUSED OG VF	F	AVG.
610 (6)	2¢ black perf 11 flat	45.00	30.00	22.00	33.00	23.00	18.00
611 (6)	2¢ black imperf.	210.00	140.00	90.00	160.00	105.00	80.00
611 (4)	2¢ black center line block	110.00	85.00	60.00	77.50	60.00	45.00
611 (4)	2¢ black arrow block	58.00	45.00	32.50	45.00	35.00	25.00
612 (4)	2¢ black perf 10 rotary	500.00	370.00	300.00	390.00	275.00	210.00
614 (6)	1¢ dark green	80.00	54.00	40.00	60.00	39.00	25.00
615 (6)	2¢ carmine rose	150.00	90.00	65.00	110.00	75.00	55.00
616 (6)	5¢ dark blue	620.00	450.00	350.00	510.00	325.00	250.00
617 (6)	1¢ deep green	90.00	50.00	40.00	65.00	40.00	30.00
618 (6)	2¢ carmine rose	160.00	95.00	75.00	115.00	72.00	55.00
619 (6)	5¢ dark blue	510.00	395.00	300.00	410.00	315.00	220.00
620 (8)	2¢ carmine black	325.00	250.00	175.00	235.00	180.00	125.00
621 (8)	5¢ dark blue+black	1050.00	800.00	550.00	815.00	625.00	435.00
622 (6)	13¢ green (1926)	280.00	215.00	150.00	190.00	145.00	105.00
623 (6)	17¢ black	325.00	250.00	175.00	255.00	195.00	136.50

627
Liberty Bell

628
John Ericsson Statue

629, 630
Hamilton's Battery

1926-27 COMMEMORATIVES (NH + 40%)

SCOTT NO.	DESCRIPTION	UNUSED O.G. VF	F	AVG	USED VF	F	AVG
627/644	**627-29, 643-44 (5 varieties, complete) . . . . . .**	**32.00**	**25.00**	**17.00**	**17.00**	**12.00**	**7.50**

1926 COMMEMORATIVES

SCOTT NO.	DESCRIPTION	UNUSED O.G. VF	F	AVG	USED VF	F	AVG
627	2¢ Sesquicentennial	5.75	4.25	3.25	1.00	.80	.55
628	5¢ Ericsson Memorial	16.25	13.00	9.00	7.00	5.00	3.50
629	2¢ White Plains	3.75	2.75	2.00	3.25	2.50	1.50
630	White Plains Sheet of 25.	425.00	300.00	250.00	550.00	425.00	300.00
630V	2¢ Dot over "S" variety.	450.00	350.00	300.00	600.00	475.00	350.00

Rotary Press Printings Designs of 1922-25 1926 Imperforate

SCOTT NO.	DESCRIPTION	UNUSED O.G. VF	F	AVG	USED VF	F	AVG
631	1½¢ yellow brown	4.95	3.75	2.75	6.00	4.25	3.00
631	1½¢ center line block	26.00	20.00	13.50	....	....	....
631	1½¢ arrow block	12.25	9.50	6.50	....	....	....

1926-28 Perf. 11 x 10½

SCOTT NO.	DESCRIPTION	UNUSED O.G. VF	F	AVG	USED VF	F	AVG
632/42	**1¢-10¢ (632-34, 635-42 11 varieties) . . .**	**41.00**	**33.00**	**25.00**	**2.60**	**2.10**	**1.55**
632	1¢ green (1927)	.50	.25	.25	.25	.20	.15
632a	1¢ booklet pane of 6	7.00	5.00	3.50	....	....	....
633	1½¢ yellow brown (1927).	3.75	2.75	2.00	.25	.20	.15
634	2¢ carmine (I). .	.40	.25	.25	.25	.20	.15
634	Electric Eye Plate	5.50	4.25	2.75	....	....	....
634d	2¢ booklet pane of 6	2.15	1.75	1.25	....	....	....
634A	2¢ carmine (II) (1928).	550.00	395.00	255.00	25.00	17.00	11.00
635	3¢ violet (1927)	1.00	.75	.50	.25	.20	.15
636	4¢ yellow brown (1927)	4.25	3.25	2.75	.50	.30	.25
637	5¢ dark blue (1927)	3.95	3.00	2.25	25	.20	.15
638	6¢ red orange (1927)	6.25	4.75	3.50	25	.20	.15
639	7¢ black (1927)	6.00	4.50	3.25	25	.20	.15
640	8¢ olive green (1927)	6.00	4.50	3.25	25	.20	.15
641	9¢ orange red (1931)	4.50	3.50	2.50	25	.20	.15
642	10¢ orange (1927)	6.75	5.50	4.00	.25	.20	.15

643

644

1927 COMMEMORATIVES

SCOTT NO.	DESCRIPTION	UNUSED O.G. VF	F	AVG	USED VF	F	AVG
643	2¢ Vermont. . . .	3.25	2.50	1.75	2.75	2.15	1.50
644	2¢ Burgoyne. . .	6.95	5.50	3.75	5.00	3.95	2.50

645

646

647

648

649

650

1928 COMMEMORATIVES (NH + 40%)

SCOTT NO.	DESCRIPTION	UNUSED O.G. VF	F	AVG	USED VF	F	AVG
645-50	**6 varieties, complete**	**61.00**	**42.00**	**30.00**	**52.00**	**34.00**	**25.00**
645	2¢ Valley Forge	2.50	2.00	1.50	1.50	1.10	.80
646	2¢ Molly Pitcher	2.35	2.00	1.50	2.75	2.25	1.50
647	2¢ Hawaii	7.75	5.00	3.25	7.50	6.00	3.50
648	5¢ Hawaii	32.50	23.00	16.75	33.00	25.00	17.00
649	2¢ Aeronautics .	4.00	2.50	2.00	4.00	2.25	1.50
650	5¢ Aeronautics .	13.50	9.00	7.00	9.00	5.00	3.75

651

654-656

657

1929 COMMEMORATIVES (NH + 40%)

SCOTT NO.	DESCRIPTION	UNUSED O.G. VF	F	AVG	USED VF	F	AVG
651/81	**651, 654-55, 657, 680-81 (6 varieties) . . .**	**10.25**	**8.25**	**5.25**	**5.00**	**3.70**	**2.75**
651	2¢ George R. Clark	2.25	1.25	1.25	1.75	1.10	.90
	Same, arrow block of 4	4.50	3.35	2.35	....	....	....

1929 Design of 1922-25 Rotary Press Printing Perf. 11 x 10½

SCOTT NO.	DESCRIPTION	UNUSED O.G. VF	F	AVG	USED VF	F	AVG
653	½¢ olive brown.	.60	.50	.50	.25	.20	.15

SCOTT NO.	DESCRIPTION	UNUSED O.G. VF	F	AVG	USED VF	F	AVG
	1929 COMMEMORATIVES						
654	2¢ Edison, Flat, Perf 11	2.15	1.75	1.25	1.75	1.40	1.00
655	2¢ Edison, Rotary, 11 x 10½	1.50	1.25	1.00	.50	.45	.35
656	2¢ Edison, Rotary Press Coil, Perf. 10 Vertically	28.50	22.00	15.00	3.00	2.35	1.50
657	2¢ Sullivan Expedition	1.60	1.25	1.00	1.75	1.40	1.10
	1929. 632-42 Overprinted Kansas (NH + 50%)						
658-68	**1¢-10¢ (11 varieties, complete) ....**	**250.00**	**200.00**	**165.00**	**200.00**	**160.00**	**110.00**
658	1¢ green......	3.00	1.75	1.25	2.10	1.60	1.20
659	1½¢ brown....	4.25	3.25	2.25	3.25	2.00	1.40
660	2¢ carmine....	4.25	3.00	2.00	1.75	1.25	.75
661	3¢ violet......	20.00	16.00	14.00	20.00	15.00	12.00
662	4¢ yellow brown	22.00	17.00	12.00	15.00	10.00	7.00
663	5¢ deep blue ..	15.00	12.00	9.00	12.00	9.00	6.00
664	6¢ red orange. .	30.00	25.00	20.00	22.00	18.00	12.00
665	7¢ black......	30.00	25.00	20.00	28.00	22.00	18.00
666	8¢ olive green .	80.00	70.00	60.00	70.00	62.00	40.00
667	9¢ light rose . . .	18.00	12.50	10.00	13.00	11.00	7.00
668	10¢ orange yellow	28.00	22.00	18.00	14.00	12.00	10.00
	1929. 632-42 Overprinted Nebraska (NH + 50%)						
669-79	**1¢-10¢, 11 varieties, complete.....**	**330.00**	**240.00**	**185.00**	**210.00**	**164.00**	**120.00**
669	1¢ green......	3.75	3.00	2.20	3.10	2.20	1.60
670	1½¢ brown....	4.00	2.50	2.00	3.20	2.50	1.80
671	2¢ carmine....	4.00	2.50	2.00	2.00	1.50	1.00
672	3¢ violet......	12.00	10.50	8.00	17.50	12.00	8.00
673	4¢ yellow brown	22.00	15.00	12.00	18.00	15.50	11.00
674	5¢ deep blue ..	20.00	14.00	11.00	18.00	15.50	11.00
675	6¢ red orange. .	38.00	26.00	22.00	30.00	22.00	16.00
676	7¢ black......	28.00	21.00	16.00	22.00	18.00	14.00
677	8¢ olive green .	35.00	26.00	18.00	35.00	24.00	18.00
678	9¢ light rose . . .	40.00	35.00	25.00	38.00	30.00	25.00
679	10¢ orange yellow	125.00	88.00	77.00	32.00	22.00	15.00

PLATE BLOCKS

SCOTT NO.		UNUSED NH VF	F	AVG.	UNUSED OG VF	F	AVG.
627 (6)	Sesquicentennial................	65.00	50.00	35.00	49.50	38.00	26.00
628 (6)	5¢ Ericsson Memorial.........	145.00	110.00	77.50	110.00	85.00	60.00
629 (6)	2¢ White Plains	67.50	52.00	35.00	52.00	40.00	30.00
631	1½¢ yellow brown	93.00	71.50	50.00	70.00	55.00	40.00
632	1¢ green............................	3.25	2.50	1.75	2.60	2.00	1.40
633	1½¢ yellow brown (1927)...	120.00	92.50	65.00	90.00	70.00	48.00
634	2¢ carmine (1)....................	2.60	1.95	1.40	2.10	1.70	1.25
635	3¢ violet.............................	15.00	12.50	9.00	10.50	7.50	4.50
636	4¢ yellow brown (1927)......	130.00	95.00	70.00	105.00	80.00	55.00
637	5¢ dark blue (1927)............	29.50	22.50	15.75	22.75	17.50	12.75
638	6¢ red orange (1927)	29.50	22.50	15.75	22.75	17.50	12.75
639	7¢ black (1927).................	29.50	22.50	15.75	22.75	17.50	12.75
640	8¢ olive green (1927)	29.50	22.50	15.75	22.75	17.50	12.75
641	9¢ orange red (1931)	30.00	23.00	16.00	23.00	18.00	13.00
642	10¢ orange (1927)..............	43.50	33.50	23.00	34.00	26.00	18.25
643 (6)	2¢ Vermont........................	65.00	50.00	35.00	58.00	42.00	28.00
644 (6)	2¢ Burgoyne......................	80.00	57.00	42.00	60.00	45.00	30.00
645 (6)	2¢ Valley Forge	58.00	40.00	28.00	41.00	30.00	19.50
646	2¢ Molly Pitcher..................	60.00	42.50	32.00	42.00	33.00	25.00
647	2¢ Hawaii	205.00	140.00	110.00	145.00	110.00	77.00
648	5¢ Hawaii	425.00	315.00	225.00	335.00	260.00	185.00
649 (6)	2¢ Aeronautics	24.00	18.00	12.00	19.50	14.00	10.00
650 (6)	5¢ Aeronautics	115.00	90.00	65.00	85.00	65.00	47.50
651 (6)	2¢ George R. Clark	19.50	15.00	10.00	14.50	11.00	7.50
653	½¢ olive brown....................	2.75	2.00	1.25	1.95	1.50	.95
654 (6)	2¢ Edison	51.00	39.50	28.00	40.00	31.50	22.50
655	2¢ Edison	70.00	55.00	40.00	58.00	45.00	30.50
657 (6)	2¢ Sullivan Expedition........	45.00	35.00	26.50	39.50	30.00	22.50
	LINE PAIR						
656	2¢ Edison, coil....................	125.00	95.00	65.00	80.00	62.50	45.00

PLATE BLOCKS

SCOTT NO.		UNUSED NH VF	F	AVG.	UNUSED OG VF	F	AVG.
658	1¢ green............................	65.00	40.00	30.00	45.00	30.00	20.00
659	1½¢ brown	80.00	50.00	35.00	60.00	38.00	25.00
660	2¢ carmine	80.00	50.00	35.00	60.00	38.00	25.00
661	3¢ violet.............................	425.00	265.00	200.00	275.00	200.00	225.00
662	4¢ yellow brown	375.00	225.00	150.00	250.00	165.00	115.00
663	5¢ deep blue	275.00	165.00	125.00	185.00	120.00	90.00
664	6¢ red orange......................	850.00	550.00	400.00	525.00	325.00	225.00
665	7¢ black.............................	850.00	550.00	400.00	525.00	325.00	225.00
666	8¢ olive green.....................	1500.00	900.00	750.00	1000.00	625.00	475.00
667	9¢ light rose........................	450.00	300.00	200.00	295.00	200.00	125.00
668	10¢ orange yellow...............	650.00	425.00	295.00	425.00	285.00	195.00
669	1¢ green............................	85.00	50.00	40.00	55.00	35.00	25.00
670	1½¢ brown	100.00	60.00	40.00	60.00	35.00	25.00
671	2¢ carmine	80.00	50.00	35.00	55.00	35.00	25.00
672	3¢ violet.............................	350.00	200.00	140.00	225.00	135.00	95.00
673	4¢ yellow brown	475.00	300.00	200.00	325.00	200.00	140.00
674	5¢ deep blue	500.00	300.00	200.00	350.00	210.00	150.00
675	6¢ red orange......................	1000.00	550.00	450.00	650.00	375.00	265.00
676	7¢ black.............................	550.00	325.00	225.00	335.00	215.00	155.00
677	8¢ olive green.....................	750.00	450.00	315.00	475.00	350.00	250.00
678	9¢ light rose........................	1000.00	550.00	400.00	600.00	375.00	265.00
679	10¢ orange yellow...............	2000.00	1200.00	850.00	1200.00	750.00	550.00

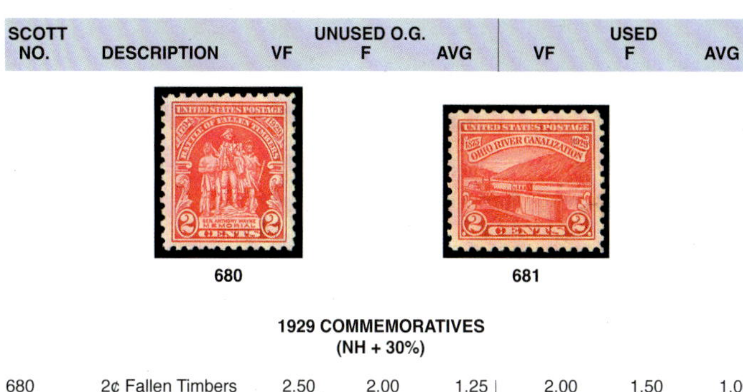

680 681

SCOTT NO.	DESCRIPTION	UNUSED O.G. VF	F	AVG	USED VF	F	AVG
	1929 COMMEMORATIVES (NH + 30%)						
680	2¢ Fallen Timbers	2.50	2.00	1.25	2.00	1.50	1.00
681	2¢ Ohio River Canal	1.50	1.25	1.00	1.25	1.00	.75

682

683

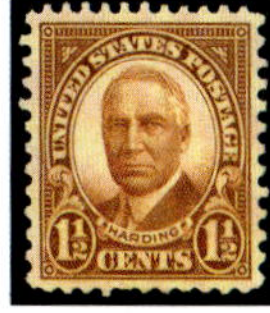

684, 686

685, 687

1930-31 COMMEMORATIVES

SCOTT NO.	DESCRIPTION	UNUSED O.G. VF	F	AVG	USED VF	F	AVG
682/703	**(682-83, 688-90, 702-03) 7 varieties, complete**	**5.50**	**4.10**	**3.10**	**5.35**	**4.15**	**2.85**
	1930 COMMEMORATIVES						
682	2¢ Massachusetts Bay	1.50	1.25	1.00	1.25	1.00	.65
683	2¢ Carolina-Charleston	2.50	2.00	1.50	3.25	2.50	1.75
	1930 Rotary Press Printing Perf. 11 x 10½ (NH + 30%)						
684	1½¢ Harding ..	.75	.50	.50	.25	.20	.15
685	4¢ Taft	1.50	1.25	.75	.25	.20	.15
	1930 Rotary Press Coil Stamps Perf. 10 Vertically						
686	1½¢ Harding ..	2.95	2.25	1.50	.25	.20	.15
687	4¢ Taft	4.75	3.75	2.50	1.00	.75	.50

688

689

690

SCOTT NO.	DESCRIPTION	UNUSED O.G. VF	F	AVG	USED VF	F	AVG
	1930 COMMEMORATIVES						
688	2¢ Braddock's Field	1.95	1.50	1.00	2.50	1.80	1.25
689	2¢ von Steuben	1.10	1.00	.75	1.25	.90	.65
	1931 COMMEMORATIVES						
690	2¢ Pulaski	.75	.50	.50	.50	.40	.30

SCOTT NO.		PLATE BLOCKS UNUSED NH VF	F	AVG.	UNUSED OG VF	F	AVG.
680 (6)	2¢ Fallen Timbers..............	48.00	35.00	22.50	36.00	27.50	21.00
681 (6)	2¢ Ohio River Canal...........	33.75	25.00	15.75	26.00	20.00	12.00
682 (6)	2¢ Massachusetts Bay.......	58.50	40.00	27.00	39.00	30.00	18.00
683 (6)	2¢ Carolina-Charleston	85.00	60.00	40.00	64.50	49.50	36.00
684	1½¢ Harding.......................	3.65	2.50	1.70	2.90	2.25	1.65
685	4¢ Taft................................	17.00	12.00	9.00	13.00	10.00	6.00
686	....	15.00	10.75	7.50	10.00	8.00	6.00
687	....	30.00	22.50	15.00	20.00	15.00	10.00
688 (6)	3¢ Braddock's Field...........	71.50	47.50	33.00	52.00	40.00	24.00
689 (6)	2¢ Von Steuben..................	40.00	31.50	18.00	32.50	25.00	15.00
690 (6)	2¢ Pulaski..........................	23.50	17.00	10.75	10.25	14.00	8.50

SCOTT NO.	DESCRIPTION	UNUSED VF	F	AVG	USED VF	F	AVG
	1931 Designs of 1922-26. Rotary Press Printing. (NH + 35%)						
692-701	**11¢ to 50¢ (10 varieties, complete) . . . .**	**184.00**	**140.00**	**105.00**	**3.25**	**2.75**	**2.25**
	Perf. 11 x 10½						
692	11¢ light blue . .	5.50	4.25	3.50	.25	.20	.15
693	12¢ brown violet	10.50	8.00	5.50	.25	.25	.20
694	13¢ yellow green	4.00	3.00	2.25	1.00	.75	.50
695	14¢ dark blue . .	10.50	8.00	5.50	3.00	2.50	1.90
696	15¢ gray.	16.00	12.00	9.00	.25	.20	.15
	Perf. 10½ x 11						
697	17¢ black	12.50	9.50	6.50	.50	.40	.30
698	20¢ carmine rose	16.50	13.00	9.00	.25	.20	.15
699	25¢ blue green.	16.00	12.00	9.00	.25	.20	.15
700	30¢ brown	36.50	28.00	21.00	.25	.20	.15
701	50¢ lilac	65.00	50.00	41.00	.25	.20	.15

702

703

1931 COMMEMORATIVES (NH + 30%)

SCOTT NO.	DESCRIPTION	UNUSED VF	F	AVG	USED VF	F	AVG
702	2¢ Red Cross . .	.50	.25	.25	.25	.25	.20
702	2¢ arrow block .	1.50	1.00	.65	....	....	....
703	2¢ Yorktown . . .	.60	.50	.50	.75	.50	.40
703	2¢ center line block	3.00	2.15	1.75	....	....	....
703	2¢ arrow block .	2.75	1.95	1.45	....	....	....

1932 WASHINGTON BICENTENNIAL ISSUE

Planning for this set, which celebrated the 200th anniversary of the birth of George Washington, began more than eight years before its release. Despite many suggestions that a pictorial series be created, the final set depicted 12 portraits of Washington at various stages of his life. For reasons of economy, the stamps were produced in single colors and in the same size as regular issues. Nevertheless, the set was an instant success and it was reported that more than a million covers were mailed from Washington, D.C. on January 1, 1932, the first day of issue.

704

705

706

707

708

709

710

711

712

713

714

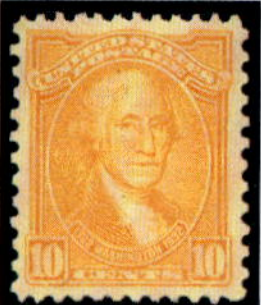
715

SCOTT NO.	DESCRIPTION	UNUSED VF	F	AVG	USED VF	F	AVG
	(NH + 40%)						
704-15	**½¢ to 10¢ (12 varieties, complete) . . . .**	**32.00**	**21.00**	**16.00**	**4.50**	**3.40**	**2.50**
704	½¢ olive brown.	.35	.25	.25	.25	.20	.15
705	1¢ green.	.40	.25	.25	.25	.20	.15
706	1½¢ brown	.75	.50	.25	.25	.25	.20
707	2¢ carmine rose	.40	.25	.25	.25	.20	.15
708	3¢ deep violet. .	.90	.70	.40	.25	.20	.15
709	4¢ light brown. .	.75	.50	.50	.25	.25	.20
710	5¢ blue	2.20	1.70	1.20	.50	.25	.20
711	6¢ red orange. .	5.00	3.00	2.00	.25	.20	.15
712	7¢ black	.95	.75	.50	.50	.30	.20
713	8¢ olive bistre. .	5.00	2.50	2.00	1.50	1.00	.75
714	9¢ pale red. . . .	3.00	2.00	1.20	.30	.25	.20
715	10¢ orange yellow	15.00	10.00	8.00	.25	.20	.15

716

717

718

719

1932 COMMEMORATIVES (NH + 30%)

SCOTT NO.	DESCRIPTION	UNUSED VF	F	AVG	USED VF	F	AVG
716/25	**(716-19, 724-25) 6 varieties . . . .**	**12.75**	**9.50**	**7.50**	**2.10**	**1.55**	**1.25**
716	2¢ Winter Olympics	.95	.75	.50	.50	.40	.35
717	2¢ Arbor Day . .	.40	.25	.25	.25	.20	.15
718	3¢ Summer Olympics	4.00	3.00	2.50	.25	.20	.15
719	5¢ Summer Olympics	6.00	4.50	3.50	.75	.50	.40

720-722

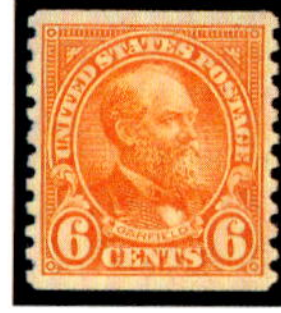

723

724

725

726

SCOTT NO.	DESCRIPTION	UNUSED VF	F	AVG	USED VF	F	AVG
	1932 Rotary Press						
720	3¢ deep violet. .	.50	.25	.25	.25	.20	.15
720b	3¢ booklet pane of 6	60.00	40.00	28.00	....	....	....
721	3¢ deep violet coil perf 10 vertically	3.95	3.00	2.00	.25	.20	.15
722	3¢ deep violet coil perf 10 horizontally	2.95	2.25	1.50	1.00	.80	.65
723	6¢ Garfield, coil perf 10 vertically	17.50	13.00	9.00	.75	.75	.65
	1932 COMMEMORATIVES						
724	3¢ Penn	1.10	.75	.50	.50	.30	.25
725	3¢ Webster. . . .	1.30	.75	.50	.55	.40	.30

SCOTT NO.		UNUSED OG (NH + 30%) COIL LINE PAIRS VF	F	AVG.	COIL PAIRS VF	F	AVG.
686	1½¢ Harding.......................	10.00	8.00	5.50	5.90	4.50	3.00
687	4¢ Taft................................	20.00	15.00	10.00	9.50	7.50	5.00
721	3¢ deep violet perf 10 vertically.................	10.75	8.25	5.50	7.90	6.00	4.00
722	3¢ deep violet perf 10 horizontally............	7.75	6.00	4.15	5.90	4.50	3.00
723	6¢ Garfield perf 10 vertically................	71.50	55.00	33.00	35.00	26.00	18.00

727, 752 728, 730, 766 729, 731, 767

1933 COMMEMORATIVES (NH + 30%)

SCOTT NO.	DESCRIPTION	UNUSED VF	UNUSED F	UNUSED AVG	USED VF	USED F	USED AVG
726/34	(726-29, 732-34) 7 varieties	3.40	2.65	2.00	2.40	1.90	1.40
726	3¢ Oglethorpe .	1.30	.75	.75	.30	.30	.20
727	3¢ Washington's Headquarters . .	.50	.50	.25	.25	.20	.15
728	1¢ Fort Dearborn	.60	.50	.25	.25	.20	.15
729	3¢ Federal Building	.80	.75	.50	.25	.20	.15

Special Printing for A.P.S. Convention
Imperforate: Without Gum

SCOTT NO.	DESCRIPTION	UNUSED VF	UNUSED F	UNUSED AVG	USED VF	USED F	USED AVG
730	1¢ yellow green, sheet of 25	....	42.50	....	....	43.00	....
730a	1¢ yellow green single	1.25	1.00	.75	.75	1.00	.65
731	3¢ violet, sheet of 25	....	33.50	....	....	34.00	....
731a	3¢ violet, single	1.25	1.25	.75	.60	1.25	.90

732

733, 735, 753, 768

734

736

SCOTT NO.	DESCRIPTION	UNUSED VF	UNUSED F	UNUSED AVG	USED VF	USED F	USED AVG
732	3¢ N.R.A.	.40	.25	.25	.25	.20	.15
733	3¢ Byrd.	1.50	1.25	1.00	1.75	1.25	.95
734	5¢ Kosciuszko .	1.50	1.25	1.00	1.50	1.25	.90

1934 NATIONAL PHILATELIC EXHIBITION
Imperforate Without Gum

SCOTT NO.	DESCRIPTION	UNUSED VF	UNUSED F	UNUSED AVG	USED VF	USED F	USED AVG
735	3¢ dark blue, sheet of 6	....	21.50	....	....	17.00	....
735a	3¢ dark blue, single	4.50	4.25	....	2.75	2.50	....

737, 738, 754

739, 755

1934 COMMEMORATIVES (NH + 30%)

SCOTT NO.	DESCRIPTION	UNUSED VF	UNUSED F	UNUSED AVG	USED VF	USED F	USED AVG
736-39	4 varieties	1.95	1.45	.85	1.15	.90	.75
736	3¢ Maryland . . .	.55	.50	.25	.30	.30	.25
737	3¢ Mother's Day, rotary, perf 11 x 10½ . .	.50	.25	.25	.30	.25	.20
738	3¢ Mother's Day, flat, perf 11	.60	.50	.25	.50	.35	.30
739	3¢ Wisconsin . .	.60	.50	.25	.30	.25	.20

For Your Convenience in Ordering, Complete Sets are Listed Before Single Stamp Listings!

740, 751, 756, 769

742, 750, 758, 770

744, 760

746, 762

748, 764

741, 757

743, 759

745, 761

747, 763

749, 765

1934 NATIONAL PARKS ISSUE (NH + 30%)

SCOTT NO.	DESCRIPTION	UNUSED VF	UNUSED F	UNUSED AVG	USED VF	USED F	USED AVG
740-49	1¢-10¢ (10 varieties, complete)	22.25	16.00	12.75	9.25	7.95	5.35
740	1¢ Yosemite . . .	.30	.25	.25	.25	.20	.15
741	2¢ Grand Canyon	.30	.25	.25	.25	.20	.15
742	3¢ Mt. Rainier. .	.50	.25	.25	.25	.20	.15
743	4¢ Mesa Verde.	1.60	1.25	1.00	.75	.65	.45
744	5¢ Yellowstone.	2.00	1.50	1.25	1.75	1.35	.95
745	6¢ Crater Lake.	3.35	2.25	1.75	2.50	1.95	1.25
746	7¢ Acadia	1.75	1.25	1.00	2.00	1.65	1.10
747	8¢ Zion.	4.50	3.50	2.50	4.75	3.65	2.50
748	9¢ Glacier.	4.25	3.00	2.50	1.75	1.30	.90
749	10¢ Great Smoky Mountains	6.50	5.00	4.00	2.50	2.00	1.25

Special Printing for the A.P.S. Convention & Exhibition of Atlantic City
Imperforate Souvenir Sheet
(NH + 30%)

SCOTT NO.	DESCRIPTION	UNUSED VF	UNUSED F	UNUSED AVG	USED VF	USED F	USED AVG
750	3¢ deep violet, sheet of 6	....	45.00	....	....	43.00	....
750a	3¢ deep violet, single	7.25	6.50	....	6.00	5.00	....

Special Printing for Trans-Mississippi Philatelic Exposition and Convention at Omaha
Imperforate Souvenir Sheet
(NH + 30%)

SCOTT NO.	DESCRIPTION	UNUSED VF	UNUSED F	UNUSED AVG	USED VF	USED F	USED AVG
751	1¢ green, sheet of 6	....	16.50	....	....	17.00	....
751a	1¢ green, single	3.25	2.75	....	2.75	2.25	....

SCOTT NO.		PLATE BLOCKS UNUSED NH VF	F	AVG.	UNUSED OG VF	F	AVG.
692	11¢ light blue	22.50	16.50	10.00	16.50	12.75	9.50
693	12¢ brown violet	47.50	32.50	20.00	33.00	25.00	19.75
694	13¢ yellow green	21.50	16.50	10.00	16.50	12.75	9.50
695	14¢ dark blue	50.00	33.50	26.50	37.50	25.00	23.50
696	15¢ grey	65.00	50.00	35.00	49.75	36.00	27.00
697	17¢ black	65.00	47.50	30.00	40.00	30.00	20.00
698	20¢ carmine rose	75.00	55.00	40.00	55.00	43.00	30.00
699	25¢ blue green	75.00	60.00	40.00	55.00	45.00	30.00
700	30¢ brown	145.00	100.00	75.00	105.00	75.00	55.00
701	50¢ lilac	350.00	275.00	155.00	250.00	195.00	115.00
702	2¢ Red Cross	4.00	3.00	2.00	3.00	2.50	1.75
703	2¢ Yorktown (4)	5.75	4.00	2.70	4.25	3.35	2.65
704-15	Washington Bicentennial	590.00	435.00	290.00	445.00	335.00	248.50
704	½¢ olive brown	7.50	5.00	3.50	5.50	4.00	3.00
705	1¢ green	7.50	5.00	3.50	5.75	4.50	3.25
706	1½¢ brown	34.50	23.50	17.00	25.00	18.00	13.25
707	2¢ carmine rose	3.00	2.00	1.25	2.25	1.60	1.10
708	3¢ deep violet	25.00	18.50	12.50	21.00	15.00	10.50
709	4¢ light brown	11.50	8.00	6.00	8.50	6.00	4.50
710	5¢ blue	30.00	20.00	16.00	23.50	18.00	14.00
711	6¢ red orange	105.00	80.00	49.50	78.00	60.00	46.50
712	7¢ black	12.00	8.50	6.00	9.00	7.00	5.50
713	8¢ olive bistre	105.00	80.00	49.50	78.00	60.00	40.00
714	9¢ pale red	80.00	55.00	40.00	57.50	42.50	30.00
715	10¢ orange yellow	200.00	150.00	100.00	155.00	115.00	90.00
716 (6)	2¢ Winter Olympics	22.00	16.00	11.00	16.95	13.00	9.50
717	2¢ Arbor Day	14.00	10.50	6.50	10.75	8.25	6.00
718	3¢ Summer Olympics	30.00	22.50	15.00	21.00	15.00	11.00
719	5¢ Summer Olympics	45.00	35.00	25.00	35.00	28.00	20.00
720	3¢ deep violet	2.95	2.00	1.40	2.15	1.65	1.10
724 (6)	3¢ Penn	20.00	14.00	9.50	14.00	11.00	9.00
725 (6)	3¢ Daniel Webster	35.75	26.00	14.00	28.00	22.00	16.00
726 (6)	3¢ Oglethorpe	23.50	16.50	11.00	18.00	14.00	10.00
727	3¢ Washington Hdqrs	10.00	7.00	4.50	7.95	6.00	4.50
728	1¢ Fort Dearborn	3.55	2.75	1.65	2.95	2.25	1.65
729	3¢ Federal Building	6.00	4.00	2.75	4.25	3.35	2.25
732	3¢ N.R.A.	2.95	2.00	1.40	2.55	1.95	1.40
733 (6)	3¢ Byrd	27.50	20.00	13.00	21.00	16.00	13.00
734 (6)	5¢ Kosciuszko	60.00	45.00	28.00	42.95	33.00	25.00
736 (6)	3¢ Maryland	17.50	12.50	8.25	13.00	10.00	8.25
737	3¢ Mother's Day, rotary perf. 11 x 10½	2.95	2.00	1.30	2.40	1.75	1.40
738 (6)	3¢ Mother's Day, flat, perf. 11	8.50	6.50	3.95	6.50	5.00	3.85
739 (6)	3¢ Wisconsin	9.50	7.50	5.00	7.00	5.50	4.00
740-49	10 varieties complete	210.00	160.00	96.50	160.00	125.00	94.00
740 (6)	1¢ Yosemite	3.75	2.65	1.70	2.85	2.00	1.60
741 (6)	2¢ Grand Canyon	4.50	3.25	2.00	3.35	2.50	1.90
742 (6)	3¢ Mt. Rainier	3.50	2.75	1.65	3.00	2.30	1.55
743 (6)	4¢ Mesa Verde	15.50	12.00	7.25	13.00	10.00	7.00
744 (6)	5¢ Yellowstone	19.50	15.00	9.00	14.00	11.00	8.25
745 (6)	6¢ Crater Lake	33.50	26.00	15.50	26.50	20.50	15.50
746 (6)	7¢ Acadia	21.50	16.50	10.00	17.25	13.25	10.00
747 (6)	8¢ Zion	33.50	26.00	15.50	26.50	20.50	15.50
748 (6)	9¢ Glacier	33.50	26.00	15.50	26.50	20.50	15.50
749 (6)	10¢ Great Smoky Mountains	53.50	41.25	24.75	39.00	30.00	23.50

SELECTED U.S. COMMEMORATIVE MINT SHEETS

SCOTT NO.	F/NH SHEET	SCOTT NO.	F/NH SHEET
610 (100)	175.00	709 (100)	72.50
614 (50)	350.00	710 (100)	400.00
615 (50)	500.00	711 (100)	800.00
617 (50)	400.00	712 (100)	90.00
618 (50)	650.00	713 (100)	925.00
620 (100)	1175.00	714 (100)	675.00
627 (50)	275.00	715 (100)	2450.00
628 (50)	775.00	716 (100)	90.00
629 (100)	350.00	717 (100)	45.00
643 (100)	335.00	718 (100)	365.00
644 (50)	325.00	719 (100)	600.00
645 (100)	275.00	724 (100)	100.00
646 (100)	265.00	725 (100)	125.00
647 (100)	895.00	726 (100)	115.00
648 (100)	3895.00	727 (100)	50.00
649 (50)	175.00	728 (100)	55.00
650 (50)	650.00	729 (100)	72.50
651 (50)	95.00	732 (100)	35.00
654 (100)	225.00	733 (50)	135.00
655 (100)	200.00	734 (100)	155.00
657 (100)	175.00	736 (100)	55.00
680 (100)	250.00	737 (50)	22.50
681 (100)	130.00	738 (50)	26.50
682 (100)	145.00	739 (50)	30.00
683 (100)	275.00	740-49 set	925.00
688 (100)	225.00	740 (50)	12.00
689 (100)	110.00	741 (50)	12.00
690 (100)	70.00	742 (50)	20.00
702 (100)	42.50	743 (50)	65.00
703 (50)	28.00	744 (50)	80.00
704-15 set	4975.00	745 (50)	140.00
704 (100)	35.00	746 (50)	75.00
705 (100)	30.00	747 (50)	175.00
706 (100)	95.00	748 (50)	170.00
707 (100)	37.50	749 (50)	300.00
708 (100)	125.00		

THE FARLEY PERIOD

The 1933-35 period was one of great excitement for the hobby. With a stamp collector in the White House, in the person of President Franklin Delano Roosevelt, it was a period during which special Souvenir Sheets were issued for the A.P.S. Convention in 1933 (catalog #730) and the National Philatelic Exhibition in 1934 (#735). Collectors gloried in the limelight.

But there was a darker side, in the form of rare imperforate sheets that were being released to then Postmaster General James A. Farley, President Roosevelt himself, and a few other prominent personages. The protests against the practice grew to unmanageable proportions when word got around that one of the imperforate sheets of the 1934 Mother's Day issue had been offered to a stamp dealer for $20,000. Adding insult to injury, it was learned shortly thereafter that not only were there individual sheets floating around, but full, uncut sheets also had been presented as gifts to a fortunate few.

The outcry that followed could not be stifled. Congress had become involved in the affair and the demands were mounting that the gift sheets be recalled and destroyed. This being deemed impractical or undesirable, another solution was found—one that comes down to us today in the form of "The Farleys".

The solution was to let everyone "share the wealth", so to speak. Instead of recalling the few sheets in existence, additional quantities of the imperforates were issued in the same full sheet form as the gift sheets. Naturally, this step substantially reduced the value of the original, very limited edition, but it satisfied most collectors and left as its legacy "The Farley Issues".

The Farleys were issued March 15, 1935, and consisted of reprints of 20 issues. They remained on sale for three months, a relatively short time by most standards, but more than enough time for collectors who really cared. Although purists felt then—and some still do now—that President Roosevelt would have saved collectors a considerable sum by having the first few sheets destroyed, the issue has provided us with a wondrous selection of Gutters and Lines, arrow blocks, single sheets and full panes.

The collector on a limited budget can fill the spaces in an album with single imperforates. But the Farleys are such an interesting study that owning and displaying at least one of each variety of any one issue is a must. We illustrate here one of the full sheets of the 1 cent Century of Progress Farley Issue. The full sheets consisted of nine panes of 25 stamps each. The individual panes were separated by wide horizontal **(A)** or vertical **(B)** gutters and the gutters of four adjacent sheets formed a cross gutter **(C)**.

NOTE: For #753-765 and #771, lines separated the individual panes. The lines ended in arrows at the top, bottom and side margins.

1935 "FARLEY SPECIAL PRINTINGS"
Designs of 1933-34 Imperforate (#752, 753 Perf.) Without Gum

SCOTT NO.		PLATE BLOCK	CENTER LINE BLOCK	ARROW BLOCK T OR B	ARROW BLOCK L OR R	PAIR WITH V. LINE	PAIR WITH H. LINE	FINE UNUSED	FINE USED
752-71	**20 varieties, complete . .**	**.......**	**470.00**	**.......**	**.......**	**135.00**	**91.50**	**35.00**	**29.75**
752	3¢ Newburgh	27.00	50.00	16.50	9.50	8.50	5.00	.45	.40
753	3¢ Byrd	(6)19.00	95.00	90.00	4.00	42.50	1.80	.75	.75
754	3¢ Mother's Day.	(6)19.00	9.50	4.00	4.25	1.80	2.00	.75	.65
755	3¢ Wisconsin	(6)19.00	9.50	4.00	4.25	2.00	2.25	.75	.65
756-65	**1¢-10¢ Parks (10 varieties, complete). .**	**295.00**	**150.00**	**140.00**	**140.00**	**42.25**	**43.50**	**19.50**	**17.00**
756	1¢ Yosemite	(6) 5.00	4.00	1.40	1.10	.60	.50	.30	.25
757	2¢ Grand Canyon	(6) 6.50	5.50	1.55	1.45	.65	.85	.40	.30
758	3¢ Mt. Rainier	(6)16.50	6.50	3.60	4.00	1.55	1.75	.75	.65
759	4¢ Mesa Verde	(6)22.00	11.00	6.00	7.00	2.50	3.10	1.50	1.35
760	5¢ Yellowstone	(6)27.50	16.50	12.00	10.50	5.25	4.75	2.50	2.00
761	6¢ Crater Lake	(6)45.00	22.00	15.00	16.50	6.50	7.50	3.00	2.75
762	7¢ Acadia . .	(6)36.00	18.00	10.50	12.25	4.50	5.50	2.25	2.00
763	8¢ Zion	(6)45.00	20.00	14.50	12.00	7.00	5.50	2.75	2.25
764	9¢ Glacier . .	(6)50.00	22.00	13.00	5.75	5.75	6.50	3.00	2.50
765	10¢ Great Smoky Mountains . .	(6)57.50	33.00	25.00	22.00	11.00	10.00	5.00	4.25
766a-70a	**5 varieties, complete . .**	**.......**	**95.00**	**.......**	**.......**	**40.00**	**35.50**	**9.45**	**7.75**
766a	1¢ Fort Dearborn	....	20.00	....	....	9.00	6.50	.85	.65
767a	3¢ Federal Building. . . .	....	21.50	....	....	9.00	6.50	.75	.65
768a	3¢ Byrd	....	19.00	....	....	8.25	7.25	3.00	2.75
769a	1¢ Yosemite	....	12.00	....	....	7.75	5.50	1.85	1.60
770a	3¢ Mt. Rainier	....	28.00	....	....	11.50	13.00	3.60	3.05
771	16¢ Air Post Special Delivery. . . .	(6)80.00	82.50	15.00	16.50	6.75	8.25	3.50	3.20

U.S. FARLEY ISSUE COMPLETE MINT SHEETS

SCOTT NO.	F/NH SHEET	SCOTT NO.	F/NH SHEET
752-71 set	7500.00	761 (200)	650.00
752 (400)	440.00	762 (200)	500.00
753 (200)	635.00	763 (200)	550.00
754 (200)	190.00	764 (200)	600.00
755 (200)	190.00	765 (200)	950.00
756-65 set	4100.00	766 (225)	400.00
756 (200)	75.00	767 (225)	400.00
757 (200)	90.00	768 (150)	550.00
758 (200)	160.00	769 (120)	275.00
759 (200)	280.00	770 (120)	600.00
760 (200)	450.00	771 (200)	600.00

772, 778a

773, 778b

774

775, 778c

1935-36 COMMEMORATIVES

SCOTT NO.	DESCRIPTION	FIRST DAY COVERS SING	FIRST DAY COVERS PL. BLK.	MINT SHEET	PLATE BLOCK F/NH	UNUSED F/NH	USED F
772/84	**(772-77, 782-84) 9 varieties.......**		**.......**	**.......**	**.......**	**3.60**	**1.75**
772	3¢ Connecticut.	12.00	19.50	18.50 (50)	2.25	.40	.25
773	3¢ San Diego.	12.00	19.50	18.50 (50)	1.85	.40	.25
774	3¢ Boulder Dam.	12.00	19.50	25.00 (50)	(6)3.50	.50	.25
775	3¢ Michigan	12.00	19.50	22.00 (50)	3.00	.50	.25

776, 778d

777

1936 COMMEMORATIVE

SCOTT NO.	DESCRIPTION	FIRST DAY COVERS SING	FIRST DAY COVERS PL. BLK.	MINT SHEET	PLATE BLOCK F/NH	UNUSED F/NH	USED F
776	3¢ Texas	15.00	25.00	22.00 (50)	2.55	.50	.25
777	3¢ Rhode Island	12.00	19.50	24.00 (50)	3.00	.50	.25

778

782

783

784

1936 THIRD INTERNATIONAL PHILATELIC EXHIBITION
"TIPEX" Imperforate Souvenir Sheet
Designs of 772, 773, 775, 776

SCOTT NO.	DESCRIPTION	FIRST DAY COVERS SING	FIRST DAY COVERS PL. BLK.	MINT SHEET	PLATE BLOCK F/NH	UNUSED F/NH	USED F
778	red violet, sheet of 4	16.50	....	....	....	3.50	3.00
778a	3¢ Connecticut.	....	....	....	....	1.00	.75
778b	3¢ San Diego.	....	....	....	....	1.00	.75
778c	3¢ Michigan	....	....	....	....	1.00	.75
778d	3¢ Texas	....	....	....	....	1.00	.75
782	3¢ Arkansas Statehood . .	12.00	19.50	24.00 (50)	3.00	.55	.25
783	3¢ Oregon Territory	12.00	19.50	22.00 (50)	1.85	.45	.25
784	3¢ Suffrage for Women . .	12.00	19.50	31.00 (100)	1.75	.40	.25

FIRST DAY COVERS:

First Day Covers are envelopes cancelled on the "First Day of Issue" of the stamp used on an envelope. Usually they also contain a picture (cachet) on the left side designed to go with the theme of the stamp. From 1935 to 1949, prices listed are for cacheted, addressed covers. From 1950 to date, prices are for cacheted, unaddressed covers. ***While we list values for these, H.E. Harris no longer sells them.***

785

786

787

788

789

1936-37 ARMY AND NAVY ISSUE

SCOTT NO.	DESCRIPTION	FIRST DAY COVERS SING	FIRST DAY COVERS PL. BLK.	MINT SHEET	PLATE BLOCK F/NH	UNUSED F/NH	USED F
785-94	**10 varieties, complete**	**57.50**	**......**	**......**	**59.00**	**5.50**	**2.30**

ARMY COMMEMORATIVES

SCOTT NO.	DESCRIPTION	FIRST DAY COVERS SING	FIRST DAY COVERS PL. BLK.	MINT SHEET	PLATE BLOCK F/NH	UNUSED F/NH	USED F
785	1¢ green	6.00	12.00	15.00 (50)	1.60	.40	.25
786	2¢ carmine	6.00	12.00	17.00 (50)	1.75	.40	.25
787	3¢ purple	6.00	12.00	24.00 (50)	3.00	.60	.25
788	4¢ gray	6.00	14.50	40.00 (50)	12.00	.60	.30
789	5¢ ultramarine	7.00	14.50	43.00 (50)	13.50	.75	.35

790

791

792

793

794

NAVY COMMEMORATIVES

SCOTT NO.	DESCRIPTION	FIRST DAY COVERS SING	FIRST DAY COVERS PL. BLK.	MINT SHEET	PLATE BLOCK F/NH	UNUSED F/NH	USED F
790	1¢ green	6.00	12.00	14.00 (50)	1.75	.30	.25
791	2¢ carmine	6.00	12.00	14.00 (50)	1.85	.35	.25
792	3¢ purple	6.00	12.00	22.00 (50)	2.50	.50	.25
793	4¢ gray	6.00	14.50	42.00 (50)	12.25	.75	.30
794	5¢ ultramarine	7.00	14.50	50.00 (50)	13.25	1.25	.35

795

796

1937 COMMEMORATIVES

SCOTT NO.	DESCRIPTION	FIRST DAY COVERS SING	FIRST DAY COVERS PL. BLK.	MINT SHEET	PLATE BLOCK F/NH	UNUSED F/NH	USED F
795/802	**(795-96, 798-802) 7 varieties**	**.......**	**.......**	**.......**	**.......**	**3.25**	**2.10**
795	3¢ Northwest Ordinance	8.50	16.00	19.00 (50)	2.00	.45	.25
796	5¢ Virginia Dare	8.50	16.00	25.00 (48)	8.50(6)	.45	.30

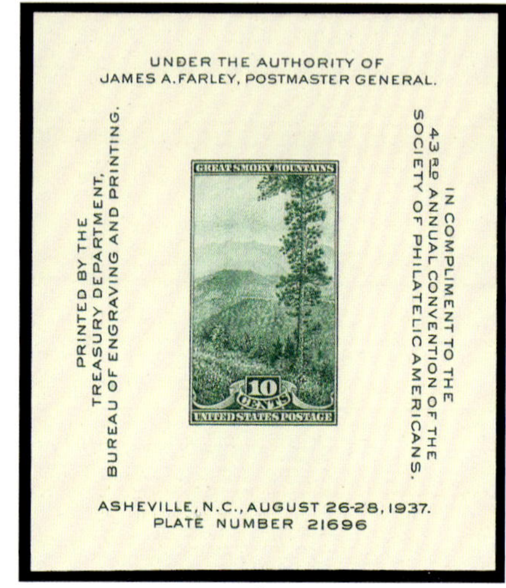

797

1937 S.P.A. CONVENTION ISSUE
Design of 749 Imperforate Souvenir Sheet

SCOTT NO.	DESCRIPTION	FIRST DAY COVERS SING	FIRST DAY COVERS PL. BLK.	MINT SHEET	PLATE BLOCK F/NH	UNUSED F/NH	USED F
797	10¢ blue green	8.50	....	....	....	1.00	.80

798

799

800

801

802

SCOTT NO.	DESCRIPTION	FIRST DAY COVERS SING	FIRST DAY COVERS PL. BLK.	MINT SHEET	PLATE BLOCK F/NH	UNUSED F/NH	USED F
798	3¢ Constitution	10.00	16.00	34.00 (50)	4.00	.75	.25
799	3¢ Hawaii	10.00	16.00	26.00 (50)	2.75	.50	.25
800	3¢ Alaska	10.00	16.00	23.00 (50)	2.75	.50	.25
801	3¢ Puerto Rico	10.00	16.00	29.00 (50)	3.00	.55	.25
802	3¢ Virgin Islands	10.00	16.00	29.00 (50)	3.00	.55	.25

1938 PRESIDENTIAL SERIES

In 1938, a new set of definitive stamps was issued honoring the first 29 presidents, Benjamin Franklin, Martha Washington, and the White House. These were regular issues that effectively replaced the previous definitive issues of the 1922-25 series.

The "Presidential Series" contained 32 denominations ranging from ½¢-$5. It is an interesting series because various printing methods were employed. The ½¢-50¢ values were printed in single colors on rotary presses using both normal and "electric eye" plates. The $1 to $5 values were printed in two colors on flat plate presses.

The $1 value was reprinted twice, once in 1951 on revenue paper watermarked "USIR" (#832b) and again in 1954. The 1954 issue was "dry printed" on thick white paper, with an experimental colorless gum (832c).

This series in regular and coil form was used for 16 years until it was replaced by the new definitive issues of 1954.

803 | 804, 839, 848 | 805, 840, 849 | 806, 841, 850 | 807, 842, 851 | 808, 843 | 809, 844 | 810, 845 | 811, 846 | 812 | 813 | 814 | 815, 847 | 816 | 817 | 818 | 819 | 820 | 821 | 822

823 | 824 | 825 | 826 | 827 | 828 | 829 | 830 | 831 | 832 | 833 | 834

SCOTT NO.	DESCRIPTION	FIRST DAY COVERS SING	FIRST DAY COVERS PL. BLK.	MINT SHEET	PLATE BLOCK F/NH	UNUSED F/NH	USED F
	1938 PRESIDENTIAL SERIES						
803-34	**½¢-$5, 32 varieties, complete**	**520.00**	....	....	**900.00**	**200.00**	**17.50**
803-31	**½¢-50¢, 29 varieties.**	**110.00**	....	....	**225.00**	**50.00**	**6.50**
803	½¢ Franklin	2.50	5.50	17.00(100)	1.00	.25	.25
804	1¢ G. Washington	2.50	5.50	22.00(100)	1.15	.25	.25
804b	1¢ booklet pane of 6	14.00	....	....	....	2.25	....
805	1½¢ M. Washington	2.50	5.50	23.00(100)	1.15	.25	.25
806	2¢ J. Adams	2.50	5.50	32.00(100)	1.50	.30	.25
806	E.E. Plate Block of 10	....	....	....	7.00	....	....
806b	2¢ booklet pane of 6	14.00	....	....	....	6.25	....
807	3¢ Jefferson	2.50	5.50	30.00(100)	1.50	.30	.25
807	E.E. Plate Block of 10	....	....	....	125.00	....	....
807a	3¢ booklet pane of 6	14.00	....	....	....	9.25	....
808	4¢ Madison	2.50	5.50	90.00(100)	5.25	1.00	.25
809	4½¢ White House	2.50	5.50	43.00(100)	2.00	.50	.25
810	5¢ J. Monroe	2.50	5.50	52.00(100)	2.50	.50	.25
811	6¢ J.Q. Adams	2.50	5.50	75.00(100)	3.50	.75	.25
812	7¢ A. Jackson	2.50	5.50	56.00(100)	3.00	.60	.25
813	8¢ Van Buren	2.50	5.50	75.00(100)	3.75	.80	.25
814	9¢ Harrison	2.50	5.50	66.00(100)	4.00	.75	.25
815	10¢ Tyler	2.50	5.50	58.00(100)	3.00	.60	.25
816	11¢ Polk	3.75	6.75	94.00(100)	5.00	1.00	.25
817	12¢ Taylor	3.75	6.75	130.00(100)	7.00	1.75	.25
818	13¢ Fillmore	3.75	6.75	158.00(100)	8.50	1.75	.25
819	14¢ Pierce	3.75	6.75	143.00(100)	7.00	1.75	.25
820	15¢ Buchanan	3.75	6.75	124.00(100)	5.00	1.35	.25
821	16¢ Lincoln	4.50	8.25	194.00(100)	8.75	2.00	.55
822	17¢ Johnson	4.50	8.25	158.00(100)	7.75	2.00	.25
823	18¢ Grant	4.50	8.25	325.00(100)	17.00	4.00	.25
824	19¢ Hayes	4.50	8.25	214.00(100)	9.00	2.00	.75
825	20¢ Garfield	4.75	11.25	228.00(100)	9.75	2.25	.25
826	21¢ Arthur	5.25	11.25	215.00(100)	12.00	2.75	.25
827	22¢ Cleveland	5.25	11.25	196.00(100)	12.00	2.00	.75
828	24¢ B. Harrison	6.25	11.25	440.00(100)	20.00	4.00	.30
829	25¢ McKinley	6.25	13.75	173.00(100)	9.50	1.75	.25
830	30¢ T. Roosevelt	8.50	13.75	670.00(100)	26.00	6.50	.25
831	50¢ Taft	15.00	30.00	895.00(100)	36.00	8.00	.25
	Flat Plate Printing Perf. 11						
832	$1 Wilson	70.00	150.00	1225.00(100)	55.00	12.00	.25
832	$1 center line block	....	....	....	55.00	....	....
832	$1 arrow block	....	....	....	50.00	....	....
832b	$1 Watermarked "USIR"	....	....	....	....	300.00	70.00
832c	$1 dry print thick paper (1954)	35.00	75.00	1100.00(100)	40.00	8.50	.25
833	$2 Harding	135.00	275.00	....	140.00	25.00	5.50
833	$2 center line block	....	....	....	130.00	....	....
833	$2 arrow block	....	....	....	130.00	....	....
834	$5 Coolidge	225.00	400.00	....	600.00	125.00	5.25
834	$5 center line block	....	....	....	600.00	....	....
834	$5 arrow block	....	....	....	625.00	....	....

835

836

837

838

1938-39 COMMEMORATIVES

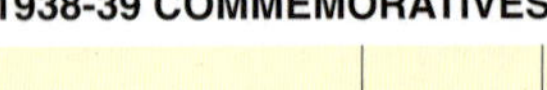

SCOTT NO.	DESCRIPTION	FIRST DAY COVERS SING	FIRST DAY COVERS PL. BLK.	MINT SHEET	PLATE BLOCK F/NH	UNUSED F/NH	USED F
835/58	(835-38, 852-58) 11 varieties, complete	....	....	....	....	7.00	2.15
835	3¢ Ratification	10.00	14.00	35.00(50)	6.00	.70	.25
836	3¢ Swedes-Finns. . . .	10.00	14.00	20.00(48)	(6)4.00	.40	.25
837	3¢ Northwest Territory	10.00	14.00	40.00(100)	9.00	.40	.25
838	3¢ Iowa Territory	10.00	14.00	40.00(50)	8.50	.70	.25

1939 PRESIDENTIALS ROTARY PRESS COIL

SCOTT NO.	DESCRIPTION	FIRST DAY COVERS SING	LINE PAIR	MINT SHEET	LINE PAIR	UNUSED F/NH	USED F
839-51	13 varieties, complete	67.50	120.00	....	148.50	36.75	5.30
	Perforated 10 Vertically						
839	1¢ G. Washington . . .	5.00	8.50	....	1.75	.40	.25
840	1½¢ M. Washington. .	5.00	8.50	....	1.75	.40	.25
841	2¢ J. Adams.	5.00	8.50	....	1.85	.45	.25
842	3¢ T. Jefferson.	5.00	8.50	....	2.00	.70	.25
843	4¢ J. Madison	5.75	10.50	....	35.00	8.00	.70
844	4½¢ White House . . .	5.75	10.50	....	6.25	.75	.50
845	5¢ J. Monroe	5.75	11.00	....	32.00	5.75	.50
846	6¢ J.Q. Adams.	5.75	11.00	....	8.25	1.50	.40
847	10¢ J. Tyler	8.50	16.00	....	56.00	12.00	1.00
	Perforated 10 Horizontally						
848	1¢ G. Washington . . .	5.00	8.50	....	3.25	1.10	.30
849	1½¢ M. Washington. .	5.00	8.50	....	5.00	1.50	.70
850	2¢ J. Adams.	5.00	8.50	....	9.00	3.00	.80
851	3¢ T. Jefferson.	5.00	8.50	....	8.75	3.00	.80

852

853

854

855

856

1939 COMMEMORATIVES

SCOTT NO.	DESCRIPTION	FIRST DAY COVERS SING	FIRST DAY COVERS PL. BLK.	MINT SHEET	PLATE BLOCK F/NH	UNUSED F/NH	USED F
852	3¢ Golden Gate	12.00	19.50	20.00(50)	2.00	.40	.25
853	3¢ World's Fair	12.00	19.50	20.00(50)	2.50	.40	.25
854	3¢ Inauguration	12.00	19.50	40.00(50)	(6)7.00	.75	.25
855	3¢ Baseball	37.50	60.00	110.00(50)	12.00	2.00	.30
856	3¢ Panama Canal . . .	17.50	25.00	25.00(50)	(6)5.00	.60	.25

857

858

1939 COMMEMORATIVES

SCOTT NO.	DESCRIPTION	FIRST DAY COVERS SING	FIRST DAY COVERS PL. BLK.	MINT SHEET	PLATE BLOCK F/NH	UNUSED F/NH	USED F
857	3¢ Printing	12.00	19.50	20.00(50)	2.35	.40	.25
858	3¢ Four States.	10.00	14.50	30.00(50)	3.75	.75	.25

859

860

861

862

863

1940 FAMOUS AMERICANS ISSUES

SCOTT NO.	DESCRIPTION	FIRST DAY COVERS SING	FIRST DAY COVERS PL. BLK.	MINT SHEET	PLATE BLOCK F/NH	UNUSED F/NH	USED F
859-93	35 varieties, complete	130.00	....	....	475.00	43.00	19.95
	American Authors						
859	1¢ Washington Irving.	3.00	4.00	20.00(70)	1.75	.35	.25
860	2¢ James F. Cooper .	3.00	4.00	25.00(70)	2.00	.35	.25
861	3¢ Ralph W. Emerson	3.00	4.00	24.00(70)	2.00	.35	.25
862	5¢ Louisa May Alcott .	4.00	6.00	45.00(70)	13.00	.60	.35
863	10¢ Samuel L. Clemens	7.50	13.50	180.00(70)	49.50	2.25	1.75

864

865

866

867

868

American Poets

SCOTT NO.	DESCRIPTION	FIRST DAY COVERS SING	FIRST DAY COVERS PL. BLK.	MINT SHEET	PLATE BLOCK F/NH	UNUSED F/NH	USED F
864	1¢ Henry W. Longfellow	3.00	4.00	26.00(70)	3.50	.35	.25
865	2¢ John Whittier.	3.00	4.00	24.00(70)	3.50	.35	.25
866	3¢ James Lowell	3.00	4.00	29.00(70)	4.25	.35	.25
867	5¢ Walt Whitman	4.00	6.00	60.00(70)	15.00	.80	.35
868	10¢ James Riley	7.50	11.50	195.00(70)	42.00	2.75	1.75

SCOTT NO.	DESCRIPTION	FIRST DAY COVERS SING	FIRST DAY COVERS PL. BLK.	MINT SHEET	PLATE BLOCK F/NH	UNUSED F/NH	USED F

869 870 871

872 873

American Educators

SCOTT NO.	DESCRIPTION	FDC SING	FDC PL. BLK.	MINT SHEET	PLATE BLOCK F/NH	UNUSED F/NH	USED F
869	1¢ Horace Mann	3.00	4.00	23.00(70)	3.25	.35	.25
870	2¢ Mark Hopkins	3.00	4.00	23.00(70)	2.50	.35	.25
871	3¢ Charles W. Eliot . .	3.00	4.00	24.00(70)	4.00	.40	.25
872	5¢ Frances Willard. . .	4.00	6.00	65.00(70)	15.00	.80	.35
873	10¢ Booker T. Washington	9.50	13.50	295.00(70)	44.00	3.50	1.75

874

875

876

877

878

American Scientists

SCOTT NO.	DESCRIPTION	FDC SING	FDC PL. BLK.	MINT SHEET	PLATE BLOCK F/NH	UNUSED F/NH	USED F
874	1¢ John J. Audubon. .	3.00	4.00	22.00(70)	1.75	.35	.25
875	2¢ Dr. Crawford Long	3.00	4.00	22.00(70)	1.75	[illegible]	.25
876	3¢ Luther Burbank. . .	3.00	4.00	29.00(70)	1.85	.40	.25
877	5¢ Dr. Walter Reed . .	4.00	6.00	49.00(70)	11.00	.55	.35
878	10¢ Jane Addams . . .	6.00	11.50	145.00(70)	28.00	2.25	1.60

879

880

881

882

883

American Composers

SCOTT NO.	DESCRIPTION	FDC SING	FDC PL. BLK.	MINT SHEET	PLATE BLOCK F/NH	UNUSED F/NH	USED F
879	1¢ Stephen Foster. . .	3.00	4.00	22.00(70)	1.75	.35	.25
880	2¢ John Philip Sousa.	3.00	4.00	22.00(70)	1.75	.35	.25
881	3¢ Victor Herbert	3.00	4.00	26.00(70)	1.85	.40	.25
882	5¢ Edward A. MacDowell	4.00	6.00	70.00(70)	14.00	.75	.35
883	10¢ Ethelbert Nevin. .	6.00	11.50	360.00(70)	50.00	5.50	2.00

884

885

886

887

888

American Artists

SCOTT NO.	DESCRIPTION	FDC SING	FDC PL. BLK.	MINT SHEET	PLATE BLOCK F/NH	UNUSED F/NH	USED F
884	1¢ Gilbert Stuart	3.00	4.00	25.00(70)	1.75	.40	.25
885	2¢ James Whistler. . .	3.00	4.00	21.00(70)	1.75	.35	.25
886	3¢ A. Saint-Gaudens .	3.00	4.00	30.00(70)	2.45	.40	.25
887	5¢ Daniel C. French. .	4.00	6.00	55.00(70)	12.50	.85	.35
888	10¢ Frederic Remington	6.00	11.50	185.00(70)	36.00	2.75	1.75

889

890

891

892

893

American Inventors

SCOTT NO.	DESCRIPTION	FDC SING	FDC PL. BLK.	MINT SHEET	PLATE BLOCK F/NH	UNUSED F/NH	USED F
889	1¢ Eli Whitney	3.00	4.00	30.00(70)	3.25	.40	.25
890	2¢ Samuel Morse . . .	3.00	4.00	42.00(70)	3.35	.70	.25
891	3¢ Cyrus McCormick .	3.00	4.00	[illegible]	2.75	.55	.25
892	5¢ Elias Howe	4.00	6.00	100.00(70)	10.00	1.50	.45
893	10¢ Alexander G. Bell	8.00	20.00	850.00(70)	85.00	14.00	3.50

894

895

1940 COMMEMORATIVES

SCOTT NO.	DESCRIPTION	FDC SING	FDC PL. BLK.	MINT SHEET	PLATE BLOCK F/NH	UNUSED F/NH	USED F
894-902	**9 varieties, complete**	....	....	....	....	**3.80**	**1.80**
894	3¢ Pony Express	7.00	11.00	30.00(50)	4.75	.70	.25
895	3¢ Pan Am Union. . . .	5.00	11.00	22.00(50)	4.50	.45	.25

MINT SHEETS: From 1935 to date, we list prices for standard size Mint Sheets in Fine, Never Hinged condition. The number of stamps in each sheet is noted in ( ).

FAMOUS AMERICANS: Later additions to the Famous American series include #945 Edison, #953 Carver, #960 White, #965 Stone, #975 Rogers, #980 Harris, #986 Poe, and #988 Gompers.

896

897

898

1940 COMMEMORATIVES

SCOTT NO.	DESCRIPTION	FIRST DAY COVERS SING	FIRST DAY COVERS PL. BLK.	MINT SHEET	PLATE BLOCK F/NH	UNUSED F/NH	USED F
896	3¢ Idaho Statehood . .	6.00	11.00	29.00(50)	3.50	.60	.25
897	3¢ Wyoming Statehood	6.00	11.00	28.00(50)	3.25	.60	.25
898	3¢ Coronado Expedition	6.00	11.00	32.00(52)	3.75	.75	.25

899

900

901

902

NATIONAL DEFENSE ISSUE

SCOTT NO.	DESCRIPTION	FIRST DAY COVERS SING	FIRST DAY COVERS PL. BLK.	MINT SHEET	PLATE BLOCK F/NH	UNUSED F/NH	USED F
899	1¢ Liberty.	4.00	7.00	20.00(100)	1.25	.30	.25
900	2¢ Gun.	4.00	7.00	20.00(100)	1.25	.30	.25
901	3¢ Torch.	4.00	7.00	24.00(100)	1.50	.30	.25
902	3¢ Emancipation	9.00	11.00	27.50(50)	4.75	.60	.35

903

1941-43 COMMEMORATIVES

SCOTT NO.	DESCRIPTION	FIRST DAY COVERS SING	FIRST DAY COVERS PL. BLK.	MINT SHEET	PLATE BLOCK F/NH	UNUSED F/NH	USED F
903-08	**3¢-5¢ 6 varieties. . . .**	....	....	....	....	**4.75**	**1.00**

1941 COMMEMORATIVES

SCOTT NO.	DESCRIPTION	FIRST DAY COVERS SING	FIRST DAY COVERS PL. BLK.	MINT SHEET	PLATE BLOCK F/NH	UNUSED F/NH	USED F
903	3¢ Vermont	7.00	10.75	30.00(50)	3.00	.55	.25

904

905

906

1942 COMMEMORATIVES

SCOTT NO.	DESCRIPTION	FIRST DAY COVERS SING	FIRST DAY COVERS PL. BLK.	MINT SHEET	PLATE BLOCK F/NH	UNUSED F/NH	USED F
904	3¢ Kentucky.	5.00	10.75	22.00(50)	2.50	.50	.25
905	3¢ Win The War.	4.50	7.50	52.00(100)	2.25	.55	.25
906	5¢ China Resistance .	12.00	20.00	400.00(50)	36.00	3.50	.45

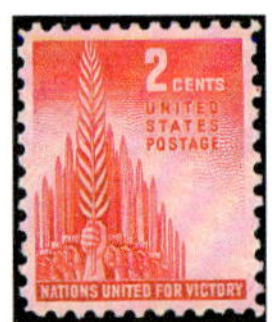

907

908

1943 COMMEMORATIVES

SCOTT NO.	DESCRIPTION	FIRST DAY COVERS SING	FIRST DAY COVERS PL. BLK.	MINT SHEET	PLATE BLOCK F/NH	UNUSED F/NH	USED F
907	2¢ Allied Nations	6.00	7.50	16.00(100)	1.25	.30	.25
908	1¢ Four Freedoms. . .	6.00	10.50	15.00(100)	1.25	.30	.25

909

910

911

912

913

914

915

916

917

918

919

920

921

1943-44 OVERRUN COUNTRIES SERIES

SCOTT NO.	DESCRIPTION	FIRST DAY COVERS SING	FIRST DAY COVERS PL. BLK.	MINT SHEET	PLATE BLOCK F/NH	UNUSED F/NH	USED F
909-21	**13 varieties, complete**	**50.00**	....	....	**75.00**	**6.50**	**3.50**
909	5¢ Poland	5.00	10.00	24.00(50)	9.00	.40	.25
910	5¢ Czechoslovakia . .	5.00	10.00	20.00(50)	4.00	.40	.25
911	5¢ Norway	5.00	10.00	19.00(50)	2.75	.40	.25
912	5¢ Luxembourg	5.00	10.00	18.00(50)	2.00	.40	.25
913	5¢ Netherlands	5.00	10.00	18.00(50)	2.00	.40	.25
914	5¢ Belgium.	5.00	10.00	18.00(50)	2.00	.40	.25
915	5¢ France	5.00	10.00	20.00(50)	2.00	.75	.25
916	5¢ Greece	5.00	10.00	47.00(50)	16.00	.75	.40
917	5¢ Yugoslavia	5.00	10.00	27.50(50)	8.00	.60	.30
918	5¢ Albania	5.00	10.00	25.00(50)	8.00	.60	.30
919	5¢ Austria.	5.00	10.00	24.00(50)	6.00	.60	.30
920	5¢ Denmark.	5.00	10.00	34.00(50)	8.00	.75	.30
921	5¢ Korea (1944).	5.00	10.00	30.00(50)	8.55	.60	.30

922 923

924 925

926 927

1944 COMMEMORATIVES

SCOTT NO.	DESCRIPTION	FIRST DAY COVERS SING	FIRST DAY COVERS PL. BLK.	MINT SHEET	PLATE BLOCK F/NH	UNUSED F/NH	USED F
922-26	5 varieties.	....	....	....	....	1.90	1.00
922	3¢ Railroad	9.00	12.00	32.00(50)	3.50	.55	.25
923	3¢ Steamship.	9.00	12.00	20.00(50)	2.50	.40	.25
924	3¢ Telegraph	9.00	12.00	18.00(50)	2.25	.40	.25
925	3¢ Corregidor.	9.00	12.00	17.50(50)	2.50	.40	.25
926	3¢ Motion Picture. . . .	9.00	12.00	15.00(50)	2.00	.40	.25

928

929

1945-46 COMMEMORATIVES

SCOTT NO.	DESCRIPTION	FIRST DAY COVERS SING	FIRST DAY COVERS PL. BLK.	MINT SHEET	PLATE BLOCK F/NH	UNUSED F/NH	USED F
927-38	1¢-5¢ (12 varieties, complete)	....	....	....	....	4.00	2.50
927	3¢ Florida.	10.00	15.00	17.00(50)	2.00	.40	.25
928	5¢ Peace Conference	10.00	15.00	16.00(50)	1.75	.35	.25
929	3¢ Iwo Jima	17.00	20.00	29.00(50)	3.50	.60	.25

930

931

932

933

SCOTT NO.	DESCRIPTION	FIRST DAY COVERS SING	FIRST DAY COVERS PL. BLK.	MINT SHEET	PLATE BLOCK F/NH	UNUSED F/NH	USED F
930	1¢ FDR & Hyde Park	4.00	6.00	7.50(50)	1.10	.30	.25
931	2¢ FDR & "Little White House". .	4.00	6.00	8.50(50)	1.10	.30	.25
932	3¢ FDR & White House	4.00	6.00	13.00(50)	1.50	.30	.25
933	5¢ FDR & Globe (1946)	4.00	6.00	17.00(50)	1.75	.35	.25

934 935

936 937 938

SCOTT NO.	DESCRIPTION	FIRST DAY COVERS SING	FIRST DAY COVERS PL. BLK.	MINT SHEET	PLATE BLOCK F/NH	UNUSED F/NH	USED F
934	3¢ Army	10.00	14.00	18.50(50)	2.00	.35	.25
935	3¢ Navy	10.00	14.00	18.50(50)	2.00	.35	.25
936	3¢ Coast Guard	10.00	14.00	14.00(50)	1.75	.35	.25
937	3¢ Al Smith	10.00	14.00	27.00(100)	1.75	.35	.25
938	3¢ Texas Statehood. .	10.00	14.00	18.00(50)	2.25	.50	.25

939 940

941 942

943 944

1946-47 COMMEMORATIVES

SCOTT NO.	DESCRIPTION	FIRST DAY COVERS SING	FIRST DAY COVERS PL. BLK.	MINT SHEET	PLATE BLOCK F/NH	UNUSED F/NH	USED F
939/52	(939-47, 949-52) 13 varieties.	....	....	....	....	4.50	2.50
939	3¢ Merchant Marine. .	10.00	12.00	15.00(50)	1.50	.35	.25
940	3¢ Honorable Discharge	10.00	12.00	26.00(100)	1.50	.35	.25
941	3¢ Tennessee Statehood	3.00	5.00	15.00(50)	1.50	.35	.25
942	3¢ Iowa Statehood. . .	3.00	5.00	15.00(50)	1.50	.40	.25
943	3¢ Smithsonian Institute	3.00	5.00	15.00(50)	1.50	.40	.25
944	3¢ Kearny Expedition	3.00	5.00	15.00(50)	1.50	.40	.25

945

946

947

1947 COMMEMORATIVES

SCOTT NO.	DESCRIPTION	FIRST DAY COVERS SING	FIRST DAY COVERS PL. BLK.	MINT SHEET	PLATE BLOCK F/NH	UNUSED F/NH	USED F
945	3¢ Thomas A. Edison	3.00	5.00	19.00(70)	1.40	.30	.25
946	3¢ Joseph Pulitzer. . .	3.00	5.00	14.00(50)	1.40	.30	.25
947	3¢ Stamp Centenary .	3.00	5.00	15.00(50)	1.50	.30	.25

NEVER HINGED: From 1888 to 1935, Unused OG or Unused prices are for stamps with original gum that have been hinged. If you desire Never Hinged stamps, refer to the NH listings.

"CIPEX" SOUVENIR SHEET

SCOTT NO.	DESCRIPTION	FIRST DAY COVERS SING	FIRST DAY COVERS PL. BLK.	MINT SHEET	PLATE BLOCK F/NH	UNUSED F/NH	USED F
948	5¢ & 10¢ Sheet of 2. .	4.00	....	....	....	1.25	1.00
948a	5¢ blue, single stamp	....	....	....	....	.65	.50
948b	10¢ brown orange, single stamp	....	....	....	....	.65	.50

949

950

951

952

953

SCOTT NO.	DESCRIPTION	FIRST DAY COVERS SING	FIRST DAY COVERS PL. BLK.	MINT SHEET	PLATE BLOCK F/NH	UNUSED F/NH	USED F
949	3¢ Doctors	8.00	12.00	15.50(50)	1.50	.35	.25
950	3¢ Utah Centennial . .	3.00	5.00	18.00(50)	1.85	.50	.25
951	3¢ "Constitution"	8.00	12.00	13.50(50)	1.50	.40	.25
952	3¢ Everglades National Park.	4.00	6.00	15.50(50)	1.85	.45	.25

954

955

956

957

1948 COMMEMORATIVES

SCOTT NO.	DESCRIPTION	FIRST DAY COVERS SING	FIRST DAY COVERS PL. BLK.	MINT SHEET	PLATE BLOCK F/NH	UNUSED F/NH	USED F
953-80	**3¢-5¢ (28 varieties, complete)**	....	....	....	....	**9.25**	**5.50**
953	3¢ George Washington Carver	6.00	10.00	19.00(70)	1.60	.35	.25
954	3¢ Gold Rush.	2.40	5.00	16.00(50)	1.60	.35	.25
955	3¢ Mississippi Territory	2.40	5.00	16.00(50)	1.60	.35	.25
956	3¢ Chaplains	3.00	5.00	16.00(50)	1.60	.35	.25
957	3¢ Wisconsin Statehood	2.40	5.00	16.00(50)	1.75	.45	.25

958

959

960

961

962

963

SCOTT NO.	DESCRIPTION	FIRST DAY COVERS SING	FIRST DAY COVERS PL. BLK.	MINT SHEET	PLATE BLOCK F/NH	UNUSED F/NH	USED F
958	5¢ Swedish Pioneer. .	2.40	5.00	16.00(50)	1.80	.35	.25
959	3¢ Women's Progress	2.40	5.00	15.00(50)	1.25	.40	.25
960	3¢ William White	2.40	5.00	18.00(70)	1.50	.35	.25
961	3¢ U.S.-Canada Friendship	2.40	5.00	13.00(50)	1.50	.35	.25
962	3¢ Francis S. Key . . .	2.40	5.00	13.00(50)	1.50	.35	.25
963	3¢ Salute to Youth . . .	2.40	5.00	13.00(50)	1.50	.35	.25

964

965

966

967

968

969

970

SCOTT NO.	DESCRIPTION	FIRST DAY COVERS SING	FIRST DAY COVERS PL. BLK.	MINT SHEET	PLATE BLOCK F/NH	UNUSED F/NH	USED F
964	3¢ Oregon Territory . .	2.40	5.00	18.00(50)	2.00	.50	.25
965	3¢ Harlan Stone.	2.40	5.00	18.00(70)	1.50	.35	.25
966	3¢ Mt. Palomar	3.00	5.00	19.00(70)	1.75	.35	.25
967	3¢ Clara Barton	3.00	5.00	13.00(50)	1.60	.35	.25
968	3¢ Poultry	2.40	5.00	16.00(50)	1.75	.35	.25
969	3¢ Gold Star Mothers	2.40	5.00	12.50(50)	1.60	.35	.25
970	3¢ Fort Kearny.	2.40	5.00	17.00(50)	2.00	.45	.25

PLATE BLOCKS are portions of a sheet of stamps adjacent to the number(s) indicating the printing plate number used to produce that sheet. Flat plate issues are usually collected in plate blocks of six (number opposite middle stamp) while rotary issues are normally corner blocks of four.

971

972

973

974

SCOTT NO.	DESCRIPTION	FIRST DAY COVERS SING	FIRST DAY COVERS PL. BLK.	MINT SHEET	PLATE BLOCK F/NH	UNUSED F/NH	USED F
971	3¢ Volunteer Firemen	5.00	7.00	14.00(50)	1.50	.35	.25
972	3¢ Indian Centennial .	2.40	5.00	14.00(50)	1.50	.35	.25
973	3¢ Rough Riders	2.40	5.00	16.00(50)	1.50	.35	.25
974	3¢ Juliette Low.	7.00	10.00	14.00(50)	1.70	.35	.25

975

976

977

978

979

980

SCOTT NO.	DESCRIPTION	FIRST DAY COVERS SING	FIRST DAY COVERS PL. BLK.	MINT SHEET	PLATE BLOCK F/NH	UNUSED F/NH	USED F
975	3¢ Will Rogers	2.40	5.00	20.00(50)	1.70	.40	.25
976	3¢ Fort Bliss.	2.40	5.00	22.00(50)	1.70	.40	.25
977	3¢ Moina Michael . . .	2.40	5.00	13.00(50)	1.50	.35	.25
978	3¢ Gettysburg Address	3.00	5.00	16.00(50)	1.75	.35	.25
979	3¢ American Turners .	2.40	5.00	13.00(50)	1.40	.35	.25
980	3¢ Joel C. Harris	2.40	5.00	19.00(70)	1.40	.35	.25

981

982

983

984

1949-50 COMMEMORATIVES

SCOTT NO.	DESCRIPTION	FIRST DAY COVERS SING	FIRST DAY COVERS PL. BLK.	MINT SHEET	PLATE BLOCK F/NH	UNUSED F/NH	USED F
981-97	**17 varieties, complete**	....	....	....	....	**5.70**	**3.40**
981	3¢ Minnesota Territory	2.40	4.25	17.00(50)	1.60	.40	.25
982	3¢ Washington & Lee University.	2.40	4.25	12.50(50)	1.35	.35	.25
983	3¢ Puerto Rico.	3.00	4.25	18.00(50)	2.00	.45	.25
984	3¢ Annapolis	3.00	4.25	12.50(50)	1.40	.35	.25

985

986

SCOTT NO.	DESCRIPTION	FIRST DAY COVERS SING	FIRST DAY COVERS PL. BLK.	MINT SHEET	PLATE BLOCK F/NH	UNUSED F/NH	USED F
985	3¢ G.A.R.	3.00	4.25	18.00(50)	1.65	.35	.25
986	3¢ Edgar A. Poe	3.00	4.25	20.00(70)	1.85	.45	.25

987

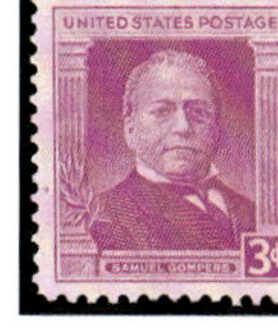

988

989

1950 COMMEMORATIVES

SCOTT NO.	DESCRIPTION	FIRST DAY COVERS SING	FIRST DAY COVERS PL. BLK.	MINT SHEET	PLATE BLOCK F/NH	UNUSED F/NH	USED F
987	3¢ Bankers Association	2.40	4.25	14.00(50)	1.50	.35	.25
988	3¢ Samuel Gompers .	2.40	4.25	18.00(70)	1.50	.35	.25
989	3¢ Statue of Freedom	2.40	4.25	15.00(50)	1.50	.35	.25

990

991

992

993

994

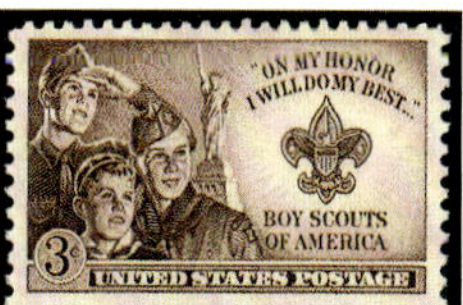

995

996

997

SCOTT NO.	DESCRIPTION	FIRST DAY COVERS SING	FIRST DAY COVERS PL. BLK.	MINT SHEET	PLATE BLOCK F/NH	UNUSED F/NH	USED F
990	3¢ Executive Mansion	2.40	4.25	18.00(50)	1.75	.50	.25
991	3¢ Supreme Court . . .	2.40	4.25	16.00(50)	1.75	.35	.25
992	3¢ United States Capitol	2.40	4.25	16.00(50)	1.75	.35	.25
993	3¢ Railroad	4.00	5.25	16.00(50)	1.75	.35	.25
994	3¢ Kansas City	2.40	4.25	16.00(50)	1.60	.35	.25
995	3¢ Boy Scouts	7.00	10.00	16.00(50)	1.60	.35	.25
996	3¢ Indiana Territory . .	2.40	4.25	18.00(50)	2.00	.50	.25
997	3¢ California Statehood	2.40	4.25	18.00(50)	2.00	.50	.25

998

999

1000

1001

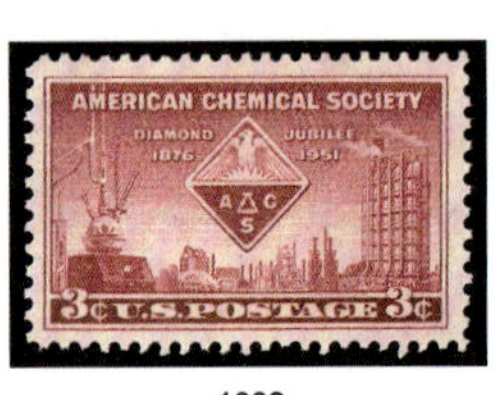

1002

1003

1951-52 COMMEMORATIVES

SCOTT NO.	DESCRIPTION	FIRST DAY COVERS SING	PL. BLK.	MINT SHEET	PLATE BLOCK F/NH	UNUSED F/NH	USED F
998-1016	19 varieties, complete	....	....	....	....	6.40	3.95
998	3¢ Confederate Veterans	3.00	4.25	21.00(50)	2.25	.40	.25
999	3¢ Nevada Settlement	2.00	4.25	15.00(50)	1.75	.35	.25
1000	3¢ Landing of Cadillac	2.00	4.25	15.00(50)	1.50	.35	.25
1001	3¢ Colorado Statehood	2.00	4.25	17.00(50)	1.50	.35	.25
1002	3¢ Chemical Society .	2.00	4.25	16.00(50)	1.50	.35	.25
1003	3¢ Battle of Brooklyn .	2.00	4.25	12.50(50)	1.50	.35	.25

1004

1005

1006

1007

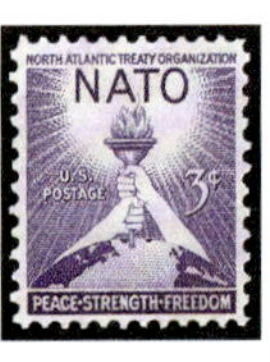

1008

1009

1010

1952 COMMEMORATIVES

SCOTT NO.	DESCRIPTION	FIRST DAY COVERS SING	PL. BLK.	MINT SHEET	PLATE BLOCK F/NH	UNUSED F/NH	USED F
1004	3¢ Betsy Ross	2.50	5.50	13.50(50)	1.40	.40	.25
1005	3¢ 4-H Club	6.00	10.00	14.00(50)	1.40	.40	.25
1006	3¢ B. & O. Railroad . .	4.00	6.50	17.50(50)	2.25	.40	.25
1007	3¢ AAA.	2.00	4.25	14.00(50)	1.60	.40	.25
1008	3¢ NATO	2.00	4.25	24.00(100)	1.60	.40	.25
1009	3¢ Grand Coulee Dam	2.00	4.25	18.00(50)	1.75	.40	.25
1010	3¢ Lafayette.	2.00	4.25	13.50(50)	1.40	.40	.25

1011

1012

1013

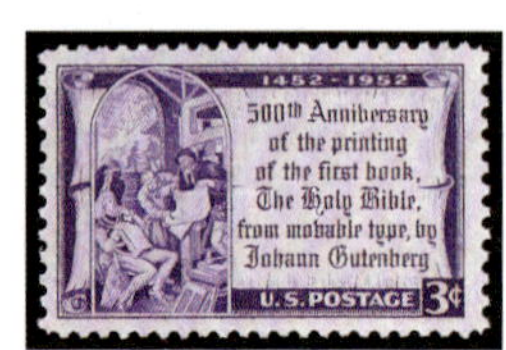

1014

1015

1016

SCOTT NO.	DESCRIPTION	FIRST DAY COVERS SING	PL. BLK.	MINT SHEET	PLATE BLOCK F/NH	UNUSED F/NH	USED F
1011	3¢ Mt. Rushmore. . . .	2.00	4.25	19.00(50)	2.25	.50	.25
1012	3¢ Civil Engineers . . .	2.00	4.25	12.50(50)	1.40	.35	.25
1013	3¢ Service Women . . .	2.25	4.25	13.50(50)	1.40	.35	.25
1014	3¢ Gutenburg Press .	2.00	4.25	13.50(50)	1.40	.35	.25
1015	3¢ Newspaper Boys .	2.00	4.25	12.50(50)	1.40	.35	.25
1016	3¢ Red Cross	3.00	6.25	12.50(50)	1.40	.35	.25

1017

1018

1019

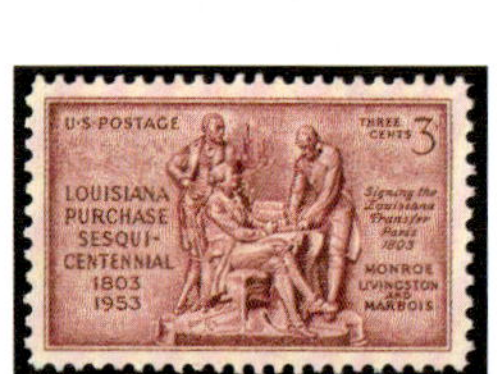

1020

1021

1022

1953-54 COMMEMORATIVES

SCOTT NO.	DESCRIPTION	FIRST DAY COVERS SING	PL. BLK.	MINT SHEET	PLATE BLOCK F/NH	UNUSED F/NH	USED F
1017/63	(1017-29, 1060-63) 17 varieties, complete	....	....	....	....	5.55	3.55
1017	3¢ National Guard . . .	2.00	4.25	12.50(50)	1.40	.35	.25
1018	3¢ Ohio Statehood. . .	2.00	4.25	17.50(70)	1.40	.35	.25
1019	3¢ Washington Territory	2.00	4.25	18.00(50)	2.25	.50	.25
1020	3¢ Louisiana Purchase	4.00	6.00	13.50(50)	1.85	.40	.25
1021	5¢ Opening of Japan .	3.00	4.25	14.00(50)	1.50	.40	.25
1022	3¢ American Bar Association	5.00	6.25	14.00(50)	1.50	.40	.25

1023 1024

1025 1026

1027 1028

SCOTT NO.	DESCRIPTION	FIRST DAY COVERS SING	FIRST DAY COVERS PL. BLK.	MINT SHEET	PLATE BLOCK F/NH	UNUSED F/NH	USED F
1023	3¢ Sagamore Hill. . . .	2.00	4.25	12.50(50)	1.40	.35	.25
1024	3¢ Future Farmers. . .	2.00	4.25	12.50(50)	1.40	.35	.25
1025	3¢ Trucking Industry .	2.50	4.50	12.50(50)	1.40	.35	.25
1026	3¢ Gen. George S. Patton	3.00	4.75	12.50(50)	1.40	.35	.25
1027	3¢ New York City. . . .	2.00	4.25	12.50(50)	1.40	.35	.25
1028	3¢ Gadsden Purchase	2.00	4.25	15.00(50)	1.60	.35	.25

1029

1954 COMMEMORATIVES

SCOTT NO.	DESCRIPTION	FIRST DAY COVERS SING	FIRST DAY COVERS PL. BLK.	MINT SHEET	PLATE BLOCK F/NH	UNUSED F/NH	USED F
1029	3¢ Columbia University	2.00	4.25	12.50(50)	1.40	.35	.20

1030 1031, 1054 1031A, 1054A 1032

1033, 1055 1034, 1056 1035, 1057, 1075a 1036, 1058

1037, 1059 1038 1039 1040

1041, 1075b, 1041b 1042 1043

1044 1044A 1045 1046

1047 1048, 1059A 1049 1050

1051 1052 1053

1954-68 LIBERTY SERIES

SCOTT NO.	DESCRIPTION	FIRST DAY COVERS SING	FIRST DAY COVERS PL. BLK.	MINT SHEET	PLATE BLOCK F/NH	UNUSED F/NH	USED F
1030-53	**½¢-$5, 27 varieties, complete. . . . .**	**110.00**	**235.00**	**. . . . . . .**	**385.00**	**100.00**	**12.50**
1030-51	**½¢-50¢, 25 varieties.**	**55.00**	**115.00**	**. . . . . . .**	**85.00**	**19.00**	**5.50**
1030	½¢ Benjamin Franklin (1955)	2.00	4.25	13.00(100)	1.00	.25	.25
1031	1¢ George Washington	2.00	4.25	20.00(100)	1.25	.25	.25
1031A	1-1/4¢ Palace of Governors (1960) . . .	2.00	4.25	16.00(100)	1.25	.25	.25
1032	1½¢ Mount Vernon . .	2.00	4.25	20.00(100)	2.50	.25	.25
1033	2¢ Thomas Jefferson.	2.00	4.25	19.00(100)	1.25	.25	.25
1034	2½¢ Bunker Hill (1959)	2.00	4.25	18.00(100)	1.25	.25	.25
1035	3¢ Statue of Liberty . .	2.00	4.25	23.00(100)	1.25	.35	.25
1035a	3¢ booklet pane of 6 .	3.50	. . . .	. . . .	. . . .	6.00	. . . .
1036	4¢ Abraham Lincoln. .	2.00	4.25	25.00(100)	1.50	.25	.25
1036a	4¢ booklet pane of 6 .	3.00	. . . .	. . . .	. . . .	3.75	. . . .
1037	4½¢ Hermitage (1959)	2.00	4.25	30.00(100)	2.00	.40	.25
1038	5¢ James Monroe . . .	2.00	4.25	30.00(100)	2.00	.40	.25
1039	6¢ T. Roosevelt (1955)	2.00	4.25	40.00(100)	2.25	.60	.25
1040	7¢ Woodrow Wilson (1956)	2.00	4.25	48.00(100)	2.75	.55	.25
1041	8¢ Statue of Liberty (flat plate).	2.00	4.25	30.00(100)	2.50	.40	.25
1041B	8¢ Statue of Liberty . .	2.00	4.25	120.00(100)	6.00	.70	.25
1042	8¢ Liberty re-engraved (1958)	2.00	4.25	35.00(100)	2.00	.45	.25
1043	9¢ Alamo (1956)	2.25	5.00	52.00(100)	3.00	.65	.25
1044	10¢ Independence Hall (1956)	2.25	5.00	52.00(100)	3.00	.60	.25
1044A	11¢ Statue of Liberty (1961)	2.25	5.00	52.00(100)	3.50	.75	.25
1045	12¢ Benjamin Harrison (1959)	2.25	5.00	88.00(100)	4.00	.85	.25
1046	15¢ John Jay (1958) .	2.50	5.25	90.00(100)	5.50	1.25	.25
1047	20¢ Monticello (1956)	2.50	5.25	125.00(100)	6.50	1.30	.25
1048	25¢ Paul Revere (1958)	2.50	5.25	200.00(100)	10.00	2.50	.25
1049	30¢ Robert E. Lee (1955)	3.75	6.00	243.00(100)	17.00	3.00	.25
1050	40¢ John Marshall (1955)	3.75	7.00	280.00(100)	16.00	3.50	.25
1051	50¢ Susan B. Anthony (1955)	5.50	8.50	280.00(100)	15.00	3.00	.25
1052	$1 Patrick Henry (1955)	9.25	17.50	615.00(100)	35.50	7.00	.25
1053	$5 Alexander Hamilton (1956)	50.00	110.00	. . . .	350.00	85.00	10.00

1954-65 COIL STAMPS
Perf. 10 Vertically or Horizontally

SCOTT NO.	DESCRIPTION	FIRST DAY COVERS SING	LINE PAIR	MINT SHEET	LINE PAIR	UNUSED F/NH	USED F
1054-59A	**1¢-25¢ (8 varieties, complete). . . . .**	**16.00**	**29.75**	**. . . . . . .**	**32.00**	**4.65**	**2.75**
1054	1¢ George Washington	2.00	3.75	. . . .	1.25	.30	.25
1054A	1-1/4¢ Palace of Governors(1960)	2.00	3.75	. . . .	3.00	.30	.25
1055	2¢ Thomas Jefferson(1957)	2.00	3.75	. . . .	2.75	.50	.25
1056	2½¢ Bunker Hill Mon. (1959)	2.00	3.75	. . . .	5.00	.45	.30
1057	3¢ Statue of Liberty(1956)	2.00	3.75	. . . .	.85	.25	.25
1058	4¢ Abraham Lincoln (1958)	2.00	3.75	. . . .	1.00	.35	.25
1059	4½¢ Hermitage (1959)	2.00	3.75	. . . .	19.00	2.00	2.00
1059A	25¢ Paul Revere (1965)	2.50	5.00	. . . .	3.50	1.25	.25

NOTE: **Pairs of the above can be priced at two times the single price.**

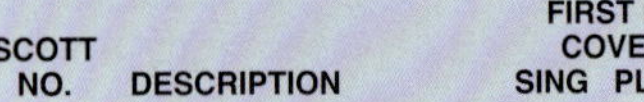

1060

1061

1062

1063

1954 COMMEMORATIVES

SCOTT NO.	DESCRIPTION	FIRST DAY COVERS SING	FIRST DAY COVERS PL. BLK.	MINT SHEET	PLATE BLOCK F/NH	UNUSED F/NH	USED F
1060	3¢ Nebraska Territory	2.00	4.25	13.00(50)	1.50	.35	.25
1061	3¢ Kansas Territory . .	2.00	4.25	14.00(50)	1.50	.50	.25
1062	3¢ George Eastman .	2.00	4.25	17.00(70)	1.50	.35	.25
1063	3¢ Lewis & Clark	4.00	6.00	16.00(50)	2.25	.65	.25

1064

1065

1066

1067

1069

1068

1955 COMMEMORATIVES

SCOTT NO.	DESCRIPTION	FIRST DAY COVERS SING	FIRST DAY COVERS PL. BLK.	MINT SHEET	PLATE BLOCK F/NH	UNUSED F/NH	USED F
1064-72	3¢-8¢ (9 varieties, complete)	....	....	....	....	2.95	1.95
1064	3¢ Pennsylvania Academy	2.00	4.25	16.00(50)	1.50	.40	.25
1065	3¢ Land Grant Colleges	2.50	4.50	17.00(50)	1.85	.50	.25
1066	8¢ Rotary International	5.00	7.00	20.00(50)	2.00	.55	.25
1067	3¢ Armed Forces Reserve	2.00	4.25	13.00(50)	1.55	.35	.25
1068	3¢ Great Stone Face .	2.00	4.25	19.00(50)	1.75	.45	.25
1069	3¢ Soo Locks.	2.00	4.25	13.00(50)	1.35	.50	.25

1070

1071

1072

SCOTT NO.	DESCRIPTION	FIRST DAY COVERS SING	FIRST DAY COVERS PL. BLK.	MINT SHEET	PLATE BLOCK F/NH	UNUSED F/NH	USED F
1070	3¢ Atoms for Peace . .	2.00	4.25	12.50(50)	1.35	.35	.25
1071	3¢ Fort Ticonderoga .	2.00	4.25	14.00(50)	1.50	.40	.25
1072	3¢ Andrew Mellon . . .	2.00	4.25	19.00(70)	1.75	.40	.25

1073

1074

1075

1956 COMMEMORATIVES

SCOTT NO.	DESCRIPTION	FIRST DAY COVERS SING	FIRST DAY COVERS PL. BLK.	MINT SHEET	PLATE BLOCK F/NH	UNUSED F/NH	USED F
1073/85	(1073-74, 1076-85) 12 varieties.	....	....	....	....	4.00	2.00
1073	3¢ Benjamin Franklin.	2.00	4.25	14.00(50)	1.40	.35	.25
1074	3¢ Booker T. Washington	3.50	5.50	14.00(50)	1.40	.35	.25
1075	3¢ & 8¢ FIPEX Sheet of 2	6.00	....	....	....	3.25	3.25
1075a	3¢ deep violet, single.	....	....	....	....	1.25	1.05
1075b	8¢ violet blue & carmine, single	....	....	....	....	1.75	1.25

1076

1077

1078

1079

SCOTT NO.	DESCRIPTION	FIRST DAY COVERS SING	FIRST DAY COVERS PL. BLK.	MINT SHEET	PLATE BLOCK F/NH	UNUSED F/NH	USED F
1076	3¢ FIPEX	2.00	4.25	12.50(50)	1.30	.35	.25
1077	3¢ Wild Turkey.	2.75	4.50	14.00(50)	1.55	.35	.25
1078	3¢ Antelope	2.75	4.50	14.00(50)	1.55	.35	.25
1079	3¢ Salmon	2.75	4.50	14.00(50)	1.55	.35	.25

PLATE BLOCKS are portions of a sheet of stamps adjacent to the number(s) indicating the printing plate number used to produce that sheet. Flat plate issues are usually collected in plate blocks of six (number opposite middle stamp) while rotary issues are normally corner blocks of four.

1080

1081

1082

SCOTT NO.	DESCRIPTION	FIRST DAY COVERS SING	FIRST DAY COVERS PL. BLK.	MINT SHEET	PLATE BLOCK F/NH	UNUSED F/NH	USED F
1080	3¢ Pure Food & Drug Act	2.00	4.25	13.50(50)	1.35	.35	.25
1081	3¢ "Wheatland"	2.00	4.25	13.50(50)	1.35	.35	.25
1082	3¢ Labor Day.	2.00	4.25	13.50(50)	1.35	.35	.25

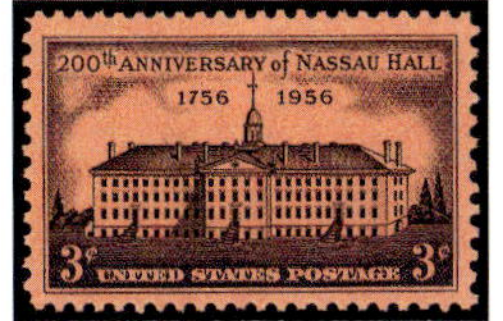

1083

1084

1085

SCOTT NO.	DESCRIPTION	FIRST DAY COVERS SING	FIRST DAY COVERS PL. BLK.	MINT SHEET	PLATE BLOCK F/NH	UNUSED F/NH	USED F
1083	3¢ Nassau Hall	2.00	4.25	13.50(50)	1.35	.35	.25
1084	3¢ Devil's Tower	2.00	4.25	16.00(50)	1.75	.50	.25
1085	3¢ Children of the World	2.00	4.25	13.00(50)	1.50	.35	.25

1086

1087

1088

1089

1090

1092

1093

1094

1095

1096

1097

SCOTT NO.	DESCRIPTION	FIRST DAY COVERS SING	FIRST DAY COVERS PL. BLK.	MINT SHEET	PLATE BLOCK F/NH	UNUSED F/NH	USED F
1092	3¢ Oklahoma Statehood	2.00	4.25	15.00(50)	2.00	.50	.25
1093	3¢ School Teachers. .	2.25	4.50	12.50(50)	1.35	.45	.25
1094	4¢ 48-Star Flag	2.00	4.25	12.50(50)	1.35	.35	.25
1095	3¢ Shipbuilding Anniversary	2.00	4.25	17.00(70)	1.50	.35	.25
1096	8¢ Ramon Magsaysay	2.50	4.25	17.00(48)	1.75	.40	.25
1097	3¢ Birth of Lafayette .	2.00	4.25	12.50(50)	1.35	.35	.25

1098

1099

1100

SCOTT NO.	DESCRIPTION	FIRST DAY COVERS SING	FIRST DAY COVERS PL. BLK.	MINT SHEET	PLATE BLOCK F/NH	UNUSED F/NH	USED F
1098	3¢ Whooping Cranes.	2.25	4.50	12.50(50)	1.35	.35	.25
1099	3¢ Religious Freedom	2.00	4.25	12.50(50)	1.35	.35	.25

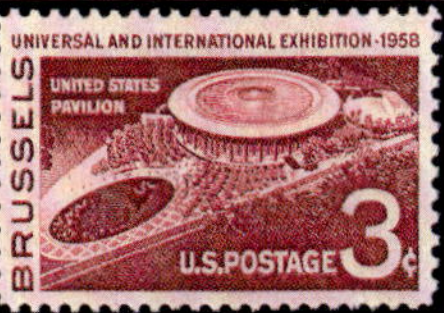

1104

1105

1106

1107

1957 COMMEMORATIVES

SCOTT NO.	DESCRIPTION	FIRST DAY COVERS SING	FIRST DAY COVERS PL. BLK.	MINT SHEET	PLATE BLOCK F/NH	UNUSED F/NH	USED F
1086-99	**14 varieties, complete**	....	....	....	....	**4.35**	**3.00**
1086	3¢ Alexander Hamilton	2.00	4.25	17.00(50)	1.85	.45	.25
1087	3¢ Polio	2.25	4.50	13.00(50)	1.35	.35	.25
1088	3¢ Coast & Geodetic Survey	2.00	4.25	13.00(50)	1.35	.35	.25
1089	3¢ Architects	2.00	4.25	13.00(50)	1.35	.35	.25
1090	3¢ Steel Industry	2.00	4.25	13.00(50)	1.35	.35	.25
1091	3¢ International Naval Review.	2.00	4.25	13.00(50)	1.35	.35	.25

1958 COMMEMORATIVES

SCOTT NO.	DESCRIPTION	FIRST DAY COVERS SING	FIRST DAY COVERS PL. BLK.	MINT SHEET	PLATE BLOCK F/NH	UNUSED F/NH	USED F
1100-23	**21 varieties, complete**	....	....	....	....	**7.00**	**4.40**
1100	3¢ Gardening & Horticulture.	2.00	4.25	12.50(50)	1.35	.35	.25
1104	3¢ Brussels Exhibition	2.00	4.25	12.50(50)	1.35	.35	.25
1105	3¢ James Monroe . . .	2.00	4.25	25.00(70)	2.00	.35	.25
1106	3¢ Minnesota Statehood	2.00	4.25	14.00(50)	1.75	.40	.25
1107	3¢ Int'l. Geophysical Year	2.00	4.25	12.50(50)	1.35	.35	.25

1108

1109

1110, 1111

1112

SCOTT NO.	DESCRIPTION	FIRST DAY COVERS SING	FIRST DAY COVERS PL. BLK.	MINT SHEET	PLATE BLOCK F/NH	UNUSED F/NH	USED F
1108	3¢ Gunston Hall.	2.00	4.25	12.50(50)	1.30	.35	.25
1109	3¢ Mackinac Bridge . .	2.00	4.25	13.00(50)	1.30	.40	.25
1110	4¢ Simon Bolivar	2.00	4.25	17.00(70)	1.30	.35	.25
1111	8¢ Simon Bolivar	2.00	4.50	28.00(72)	2.50	.40	.25
1112	4¢ Atlantic Cable Centenary	2.00	4.25	14.00(50)	1.30	.35	.25

1113

1114

1115

1116

SCOTT NO.	DESCRIPTION	FIRST DAY COVERS SING	FIRST DAY COVERS PL. BLK.	MINT SHEET	PLATE BLOCK F/NH	UNUSED F/NH	USED F
1113	1¢ Abraham Lincoln (1959)	2.00	4.25	8.00(50)	1.00	.30	.25
1114	3¢ Bust of Lincoln (1959)	2.00	4.25	13.50(50)	1.75	.40	.25
1115	4¢ Lincoln-Douglas Debates	2.00	4.25	15.00(50)	1.75	.40	.25
1116	4¢ Statue of Lincoln (1959)	2.00	4.25	19.00(50)	2.15	.45	.25

1117, 1118

1119

1120

SCOTT NO.	DESCRIPTION	FIRST DAY COVERS SING	FIRST DAY COVERS PL. BLK.	MINT SHEET	PLATE BLOCK F/NH	UNUSED F/NH	USED F
1117	4¢ Lajos Kossuth. . . .	2.00	4.25	18.00(70)	1.35	.35	.25
1118	8¢ Lajos Kossuth. . . .	2.00	4.50	20.00(72)	1.75	.35	.25
1119	4¢ Freedom of Press.	2.00	4.25	12.50(50)	1.35	.35	.25
1120	4¢ Overland Mail	2.00	4.25	12.50(50)	1.35	.35	.25

Plate blocks will be blocks of 4 stamps unless otherwise noted.

1121

1122

1123

SCOTT NO.	DESCRIPTION	FIRST DAY COVERS SING	FIRST DAY COVERS PL. BLK.	MINT SHEET	PLATE BLOCK F/NH	UNUSED F/NH	USED F
1121	4¢ Noah Webster. . . .	2.00	4.25	17.00(70)	1.25	.35	.25
1122	4¢ Forest Conservation	2.00	4.25	14.00(50)	1.50	.35	.25
1123	4¢ Fort Duquesne . . .	2.00	4.25	12.50(50)	1.25	.35	.25

1124

1125, 1126

1127

1128

1129

1959 COMMEMORATIVES

SCOTT NO.	DESCRIPTION	FIRST DAY COVERS SING	FIRST DAY COVERS PL. BLK.	MINT SHEET	PLATE BLOCK F/NH	UNUSED F/NH	USED F
1124-38	**4¢-8¢, 15 varieties . .**	......	....	....	....	**4.95**	**3.25**
1124	4¢ Oregon Statehood	2.00	4.25	17.00(50)	1.70	.35	.25
1125	4¢ José de San Martin	2.00	4.25	17.00(70)	1.40	.35	.25
1126	8¢ José de San Martin	2.00	4.25	19.50(72)	1.75	.35	.25
1127	4¢ NATO	2.00	4.25	17.00(70)	1.40	.35	.25
1128	4¢ Arctic Exploration .	2.00	4.25	12.50(50)	1.40	.35	.25
1129	8¢ World Peace & Trade	2.00	4.25	19.00(50)	1.95	.40	.25

1130

1131

1132

1133

1134

1135

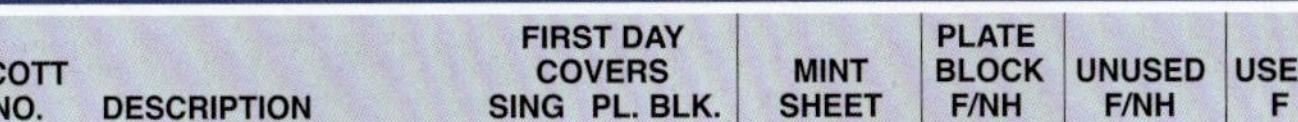

1136, 1137

1138

SCOTT NO.	DESCRIPTION	FIRST DAY COVERS SING	FIRST DAY COVERS PL. BLK.	MINT SHEET	PLATE BLOCK F/NH	UNUSED F/NH	USED F
1130	4¢ Silver Centennial .	2.00	4.25	19.00(50)	1.95	.50	.25
1131	4¢ St. Lawrence Seaway	2.00	4.25	12.50(50)	1.35	.35	.25
1132	4¢ 49-Star Flag	2.00	4.25	12.50(50)	1.35	.35	.25
1133	4¢ Soil Conservation .	2.00	4.25	13.00(50)	1.40	.35	.25
1134	4¢ Petroleum	2.00	4.25	15.00(50)	1.40	.40	.25
1135	4¢ Dental Health	5.00	7.00	15.00(50)	1.40	.40	.25
1136	4¢ Ernst Reuter	2.00	4.25	17.00(70)	1.40	.35	.25
1137	8¢ Ernst Reuter	2.00	4.25	20.00(72)	1.75	.35	.25
1138	4¢ Dr. Ephraim McDowell	2.00	4.25	18.00(70)	1.50	.35	.25

1139

1140

1141

1142

1143

1144

1960-61 CREDO OF AMERICA SERIES

SCOTT NO.	DESCRIPTION	FIRST DAY COVERS SING	FIRST DAY COVERS PL. BLK.	MINT SHEET	PLATE BLOCK F/NH	UNUSED F/NH	USED F
1139-44	**6 varieties, complete**	....	....	....	....	**1.85**	**1.15**
1139	4¢ Credo—Washington	2.00	4.25	14.00(50)	1.35	.50	.25
1140	4¢ Credo—Franklin . .	2.00	4.25	12.50(50)	1.35	.35	.25
1141	4¢ Credo—Jefferson	2.00	[illegible]	[illegible]	[illegible]	.50	.25
1142	4¢ Credo—Key	[illegible]	[illegible]	[illegible]	[illegible]	[illegible]	[illegible]
1143	4¢ Credo—Lincoln. . .	2.00	4.25	12.50(50)	1.35	.35	.25
1144	4¢ Credo—Henry (1961)	2.00	4.25	15.00(50)	1.50	.35	.25

1145

1146

1147, 1148

1149

1150

1151

1152

1153

1960 COMMEMORATIVES

SCOTT NO.	DESCRIPTION	FIRST DAY COVERS SING	FIRST DAY COVERS PL. BLK.	MINT SHEET	PLATE BLOCK F/NH	UNUSED F/NH	USED F
1145-73	**4¢-8¢, 29 varieties . .**	....	....	....	....	**8.85**	**5.25**
1145	4¢ Boy Scouts	8.50	10.50	14.00(50)	1.75	.40	.25
1146	4¢ Winter Olympics . .	2.00	4.25	12.50(50)	1.35	.35	.25
1147	4¢ Thomas Masaryk .	2.00	4.25	17.00(70)	1.35	.35	.25
1148	8¢ Thomas Masaryk .	2.00	4.25	21.00(72)	1.75	.40	.25
1149	4¢ World Refugee Year	2.00	4.25	12.50(50)	1.35	.35	.25
1150	4¢ Water Conservation	2.00	4.25	12.50(50)	1.35	.35	.25
1151	4¢ SEATO	2.00	4.25	17.00(70)	1.50	.35	.25
1152	4¢ American Women .	2.00	4.25	12.50(50)	1.35	.35	.25
1153	4¢ 50-Star Flag	2.00	4.25	15.00(50)	1.50	.35	.25

1154

1155

1156

1157

1158

1159, 1160

1161

1162

1163

SCOTT NO.	DESCRIPTION	FIRST DAY COVERS SING	FIRST DAY COVERS PL. BLK.	MINT SHEET	PLATE BLOCK F/NH	UNUSED F/NH	USED F
1154	4¢ Pony Express	2.00	4.25	15.00(50)	1.70	.45	.25
1155	4¢ Employ the Handicapped	2.00	4.25	12.00(50)	1.35	.35	.25
1156	4¢ World Forestry Congress	2.00	4.25	15.00(50)	1.50	.40	.25
1157	4¢ Mexican Independence	2.00	4.25	12.00(50)	1.35	.35	.25
1158	4¢ U.S.-Japan Treaty	2.00	4.25	17.00(50)	1.70	.35	.25
1159	4¢ Ignacy Paderewski	2.00	4.25	17.00(70)	1.75	.35	.25
1160	8¢ Ignacy Paderewski	2.00	4.25	20.00(72)	1.75	.35	.25
1161	4¢ Robert A. Taft	2.00	4.25	19.00(70)	1.75	.35	.25
1162	4¢ Wheels of Freedom	2.00	4.25	15.00(50)	1.50	.35	.25
1163	4¢ Boys' Club of America	2.25	4.25	12.00(50)	1.40	.35	.25

1164

1165, 1166

1167

1168, 1169

1170

1171

1172

1173

SCOTT NO.	DESCRIPTION	FIRST DAY COVERS SING	PL. BLK.	MINT SHEET	PLATE BLOCK F/NH	UNUSED F/NH	USED F
1164	4¢ Automated Post Office	2.00	4.25	16.00(50)	1.50	.45	.25
1165	4¢ Gustaf Mannerheim	2.00	4.25	17.00(70)	1.40	.30	.25
1166	8¢ Gustaf Mannerheim	2.00	4.25	19.50(72)	1.60	.35	.25
1167	4¢ Camp Fire Girls	5.00	7.25	17.00(50)	1.40	.60	.25
1168	4¢ Giuseppe Garibaldi	2.00	4.25	17.00(70)	1.40	.30	.25
1169	8¢ Giuseppe Garibaldi	2.00	4.25	19.50(72)	1.50	.35	.25
1170	4¢ Walter George	2.00	4.25	20.00(70)	1.50	.50	.25
1171	4¢ Andrew Carnegie	2.00	4.25	17.50(70)	1.25	.35	.25
1172	4¢ John Foster Dulles	2.00	4.25	17.50(70)	1.25	.35	.25
1173	4¢ "ECHO I" Satellite	3.00	6.50	17.00(50)	1.40	.70	.25

1174, 1175

1176

1177

1961 COMMEMORATIVES

SCOTT NO.	DESCRIPTION	FIRST DAY COVERS SING	PL. BLK.	MINT SHEET	PLATE BLOCK F/NH	UNUSED F/NH	USED F
1174/90	**(1174-77, 1183-90) 12 varieties . . . .**	....	....	....	....	**5.75**	**2.55**
1174	4¢ Mahatma Gandhi .	2.00	4.25	20.00(70)	1.35	.50	.25
1175	8¢ Mahatma Gandhi .	2.00	4.25	20.00(72)	1.75	.50	.25
1176	4¢ Range Conservation	2.00	4.25	17.00(50)	1.75	.50	.25
1177	4¢ Horace Greeley . .	2.00	4.25	20.00(70)	1.75	.50	.25

1178

1179

1180

1181

1182

1183

1961-65 CIVIL WAR CENTENNIAL SERIES

SCOTT NO.	DESCRIPTION	FIRST DAY COVERS SING	PL. BLK.	MINT SHEET	PLATE BLOCK F/NH	UNUSED F/NH	USED F
1178-82	**4¢-5¢, 5 varieties, complete . . . .**	....	....	....	....	**2.75**	**1.05**
1178	4¢ Fort Sumter.	7.50	10.00	20.00(50)	2.00	.60	.25
1179	4¢ Shiloh (1962)	7.50	10.00	22.00(50)	1.75	.40	.25
1180	5¢ Gettysburg (1963).	7.50	10.00	22.00(50)	2.25	.60	.25
1181	5¢ Wilderness (1964)	7.50	10.00	22.00(50)	1.75	.55	.25
1181	Zip Code Block	....	....	....	1.40	....	....
1182	5¢ Appomattox (1965)	7.50	10.00	25.00(50)	3.00	.75	.25
1182	Zip Code Block	....	....	....	3.50	....	....

1184

1185

1186

1187

1188

1189

1190

1961 COMMEMORATIVES

SCOTT NO.	DESCRIPTION	FIRST DAY COVERS SING	PL. BLK.	MINT SHEET	PLATE BLOCK F/NH	UNUSED F/NH	USED F
1183	4¢ Kansas Statehood	2.00	4.25	17.00(50)	1.50	.60	.25
1184	4¢ George W. Norris .	2.00	4.25	12.00(50)	1.30	.35	.25
1185	4¢ Naval Aviation. . . .	2.00	4.25	14.00(50)	1.30	.35	.25
1186	4¢ Workmen's Compensation	2.00	4.25	13.00(50)	1.30	.35	.25
1187	4¢ Frederic Remington	2.00	4.25	15.00(50)	1.30	.35	.25
1188	4¢ Sun Yat-sen	6.00	10.00	34.00(50)	3.75	.85	.25
1189	4¢ Basketball.	9.00	12.00	17.00(50)	1.30	.65	.25
1190	4¢ Nursing	13.50	20.00	17.00(50)	1.30	.65	.25

NOTE: **To determine the VF price on stamps issued from 1941 to date, add 20% to the F/NH or F (used) price (minimum .03 per item). All VF unused stamps from 1941 date priced as NH.**

1191

1192

1193

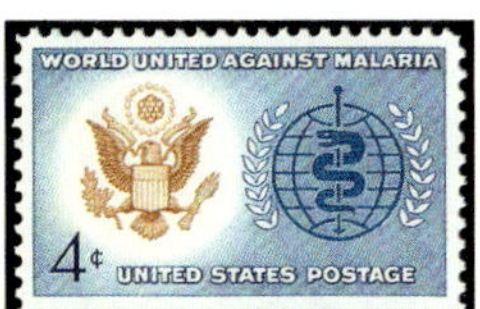

1194

1962 COMMEMORATIVES

SCOTT NO.	DESCRIPTION	FIRST DAY COVERS SING	FIRST DAY COVERS PL. BLK.	MINT SHEET	PLATE BLOCK F/NH	UNUSED F/NH	USED F
1191-1207	17 varieties	....	....	....	....	5.40	3.40
1191	4¢ New Mexico Statehood	1.75	4.00	15.00(50)	1.50	.40	.25
1192	4¢ Arizona Statehood	1.75	4.00	15.00(50)	1.50	.35	.25
1193	4¢ Project Mercury	5.00	7.50	14.00(50)	1.40	.35	.25
1194	4¢ Malaria Eradication	1.75	4.00	14.00(50)	1.40	.35	.25

1195

1196

1197

SCOTT NO.	DESCRIPTION	FIRST DAY COVERS SING	FIRST DAY COVERS PL. BLK.	MINT SHEET	PLATE BLOCK F/NH	UNUSED F/NH	USED F
1195	4¢ Charles Evans Hughes	2.00	4.00	13.00(50)	1.40	.35	.25
1196	4¢ Seattle World's Fair	2.00	4.00	15.00(50)	2.00	.35	.25
1197	4¢ Louisiana Statehood	2.00	4.00	15.00(50)	1.50	.40	.25

1198

1199

1200

1201

1202

1203

Christmas 1962
1205

1206

1207

SCOTT NO.	DESCRIPTION	FIRST DAY COVERS SING	FIRST DAY COVERS PL. BLK.	MINT SHEET	PLATE BLOCK F/NH	UNUSED F/NH	USED F
1198	4¢ Homestead Act.	2.00	4.00	14.00(50)	1.40	.35	.25
1199	4¢ Girl Scouts	7.00	10.00	14.00(50)	1.40	.35	.25
1200	4¢ Brien McMahon	2.00	4.00	14.00(50)	1.50	.35	.25
1201	4¢ Apprenticeship .	2.00	4.00	14.00(50)	1.40	.35	.25
1202	4¢ Sam Rayburn . .	2.00	4.00	17.00(50)	1.50	.35	.25
1203	4¢ Dag Hammarskjold	2.00	4.00	12.00(50)	1.40	.35	.25
1204	same, yellow inverted	5.00	10.25	12.00(50)	1.50	.35	.25
1205	4¢ Christmas 1962	2.00	4.00	23.00(50)	2.00	.35	.25
1206	4¢ Higher Education	2.00	4.00	12.00(50)	1.40	.35	.25
1207	4¢ Winslow Homer	2.00	4.00	12.50(50)	1.40	.35	.25

1208

1209, 1225

1213, 1229

1214

1962-66 REGULAR ISSUE

SCOTT NO.	DESCRIPTION	FIRST DAY COVERS SING	FIRST DAY COVERS PL. BLK.	MINT SHEET	PLATE BLOCK F/NH	UNUSED F/NH	USED F
1208	5¢ Flag & White House (1963)	2.00	4.25	22.00(100)	1.35	.30	.25
1209	1¢ Andrew Jackson (1963)	2.00	4.00	20.00(100)	2.00	.30	.25
1213	5¢ Washington . . .	2.00	4.00	27.50(100)	1.50	.30	.25
1213a	5¢ b. pane of 5—Slog. I	2.50	....	....	....	6.50	....
1213a	5¢ b. pane of 5—Slog. II (1963)	....	....	....	....	20.00	....
1213a	5¢ b. pane of 5—Slog. III (1964)	....	....	....	....	3.50	....
1213c	5¢ Tagged pane of 5 Slogan II (1963). . .	....	....	....	....	105.00	....
1213c	5¢ b. p. of 5—Slog. III (1963)	....	....	....	....	2.50	....
1214	8¢ John J. Pershing (1961)	2.25	5.00	40.00(100)	2.95	.65	.25

Slogan I—Your Mailman Deserves Your Help · Keep Harmful Objects Out of...
Slogan II—Add Zip to Your Mail · Use Zone Numbers for Zip Code.
Slogan III—Add Zip to Your Mail · Always Use Zip Code.

1962-66 COIL STAMPS Perf. 10 Vertically

SCOTT NO.	DESCRIPTION	FIRST DAY COVERS SING	LINE PAIRS	MINT SHEET	LINE PAIRS	UNUSED F/NH	USED F
1225	1¢ Andrew Jackson (1963)	2.00	3.00	....	3.00	.50	.25
1229	5¢ Washington ([illegible])	2.00	[illegible]	....	4.00	1.25	.25

1230

1231

1232

1233

1963 COMMEMORATIVES

SCOTT NO.	DESCRIPTION	FIRST DAY COVERS SING	FIRST DAY COVERS PL. BLK.	MINT SHEET	PLATE BLOCK F/NH	UNUSED F/NH	USED F
1230-41	12 varieties.	....	....	....	....	3.85	2.00
1230	5¢ Carolina Charter	2.00	4.00	14.00(50)	1.50	.40	.25
1231	5¢ Food for Peace	2.00	4.00	12.00(50)	1.40	.35	.25
1232	5¢ West Virginia Statehood	2.00	4.00	15.00(50)	1.70	.50	.25
1233	5¢ Emancipation Proclamation	4.00	6.00	12.50(50)	1.70	.35	.25

1234

1235

1236

1237

1238

1239

1240

1241

1242

1243

1963 COMMEMORATIVES

SCOTT NO.	DESCRIPTION	FIRST DAY COVERS SING	FIRST DAY COVERS PL. BLK.	MINT SHEET	PLATE BLOCK F/NH	UNUSED F/NH	USED F
1234	5¢ Alliance for Progress	2.00	4.00	12.00(50)	1.30	.30	.25
1235	5¢ Cordell Hull. . . .	2.00	4.00	12.00(50)	1.75	.40	.25
1236	5¢ Eleanor Roosevelt	2.00	4.00	12.50(50)	1.30	.35	.25
1237	5¢ The Sciences . .	2.00	4.00	12.00(50)	1.30	.30	.25
1238	5¢ City Mail Delivery	2.00	4.00	12.00(50)	1.30	.30	.25
1239	5¢ International Red Cross.	2.00	4.00	12.00(50)	1.30	.30	.25
1240	5¢ Christmas 1963	2.00	4.00	25.00(100)	1.50	.35	.25
1241	5¢ John J. Audubon	2.00	4.00	12.00(50)	1.30	.30	.25

1244

1245

1964 COMMEMORATIVES

SCOTT NO.	DESCRIPTION	FIRST DAY COVERS SING	FIRST DAY COVERS PL. BLK.	MINT SHEET	PLATE BLOCK	UNUSED F/NH	USED
1242-60	**19 varieties. . . . .**	....	....	....	....	**6.95**	**3.90**
1242	5¢ Sam Houston	4.00	6.00	17.50(50)	1.75	.70	.25
1243	5¢ Charles M. Russell	2.00	4.00	15.00(50)	1.75	.35	.25
1244	5¢ New York World's Fair	2.00	4.00	12.50(50)	1.30	.35	.25
1245	5¢ John Muir	2.00	4.00	18.00(50)	2.00	.50	.25

1246

1247

SCOTT NO.	DESCRIPTION	FIRST DAY COVERS SING	FIRST DAY COVERS PL. BLK.	MINT SHEET	PLATE BLOCK F/NH	UNUSED F/NH	USED F
1246	5¢ John F. Kennedy. .	2.50	5.00	17.00(50)	1.75	.50	.25
1247	5¢ New Jersey Tercentenary	1.75	4.00	12.00(50)	1.35	.35	.25

1248

1249

1250

1251

1252

SCOTT NO.	DESCRIPTION	FIRST DAY COVERS SING	FIRST DAY COVERS PL. BLK.	MINT SHEET	PLATE BLOCK F/NH	UNUSED F/NH	USED F
1248	5¢ Nevada Statehood	2.00	4.00	16.00(50)	1.50	.35	.25
1249	5¢ Register and Vote.	2.00	4.00	14.00(50)	1.50	.30	.25
1250	5¢ Shakespeare	2.00	4.00	12.00(50)	1.35	.30	.25
1251	5¢ Mayo Brothers . . .	5.00	7.00	14.00(50)	1.50	.60	.25
1252	5¢ American Music . .	2.00	4.00	12.00(50)	1.35	.30	.25

1253

1254

1255

1256

1257

SCOTT NO.	DESCRIPTION	FIRST DAY COVERS SING	FIRST DAY COVERS PL. BLK.	MINT SHEET	PLATE BLOCK F/NH	UNUSED F/NH	USED F
1253	5¢ Homemakers	2.00	4.00	15.00(50)	1.50	.30	.25
1254-57	5¢ Christmas, 4 varieties, attached .	5.25	7.50	42.00(100)	2.50	2.00	1.50
1254	5¢ Holly	2.75	....	....	....	.40	.25
1255	5¢ Mistletoe	2.75	....	....	....	.40	.25
1256	5¢ Poinsettia	2.75	....	....	....	.40	.25
1257	5¢ Pine Cone.	2.75	....	....	....	.40	.25

COMMEMORATIVES: Commemorative stamps are special issues released to honor or recognize persons, organizations, historical events or landmarks. They are usually issued in the current first class denomination to supplement regular issues.

1258

1259

1260

SCOTT NO.	DESCRIPTION	FIRST DAY COVERS SING	FIRST DAY COVERS PL. BLK.	MINT SHEET	PLATE BLOCK F/NH	UNUSED F/NH	USED
1258	5¢ Verrazano-Narrows. Bridge	2.00	4.00	12.50(50)	1.30	.35	.25
1259	5¢ Modern Art	2.00	4.00	12.00(50)	1.30	.35	.25
1260	5¢ Radio Amateurs . . .	8.00	10.00	23.50(50)	2.50	.60	.25

1261

1262

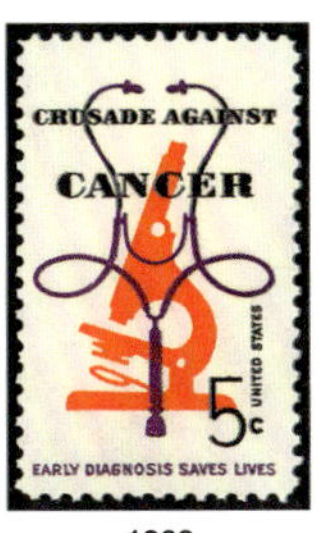

1263

1264

1265

1965 COMMEMORATIVES

SCOTT NO.	DESCRIPTION	FIRST DAY COVERS SING	FIRST DAY COVERS PL. BLK.	MINT SHEET	PLATE BLOCK F/NH	UNUSED F/NH	USED
1261-76	**5¢-11¢, 16 varieties . .**	....	....	....	....	**5.15**	**3.30**
1261	5¢ Battle of New Orleans	2.00	4.00	14.00(50)	1.75	.40	.25
1262	5¢ Physical Fitness . . .	2.00	4.00	14.00(50)	1.35	.30	.25
1263	5¢ Crusade Against Cancer	4.00	6.00	13.00(50)	[illegible]	[illegible]	[illegible]
1264	5¢ Winston Churchill	2.00	4.00	13.00(50)	[illegible]	[illegible]	[illegible]
1265	5¢ Magna Carta.	2.00	4.00	12.00(50)	1.35	.30	.25

1266

1267

1268

1269

1270

1271

1272

1273

SCOTT NO.	DESCRIPTION	FIRST DAY COVERS SING	FIRST DAY COVERS PL. BLK.	MINT SHEET	PLATE BLOCK F/NH	UNUSED F/NH	USED
1266	5¢ International Cooperation Year.	2.00	4.00	12.50(50)	1.25	.30	.25
1267	5¢ Salvation Army	3.00	4.00	12.50(50)	1.25	.30	.25
1268	5¢ Dante Alighieri	2.00	4.00	12.50(50)	1.25	.30	.25
1269	5¢ Herbert Hoover	2.00	4.00	14.00(50)	1.75	.50	.25
1270	5¢ Robert Fulton	2.00	4.00	14.00(50)	1.20	.45	.25
1271	5¢ Florida Settlement .	2.00	4.00	14.00(50)	1.75	.40	.25
1272	5¢ Traffic Safety.	2.00	4.00	14.00(50)	1.75	.40	.25
1273	5¢ John S. Copley	2.00	4.00	12.00(50)	1.20	.30	.25

1274

1275

1276

SCOTT NO.	DESCRIPTION	FIRST DAY COVERS SING	FIRST DAY COVERS PL. BLK.	MINT SHEET	PLATE BLOCK F/NH	UNUSED F/NH	USED
1274	11¢ Telecom-munication	2.00	4.00	30.00(50)	5.00	.75	.40
1275	5¢ Adlai Stevenson . . .	2.00	4.00	12.00(50)	1.20	.30	.25
1276	5¢ Christmas 1965 . . .	2.00	4.00	28.00(100)	2.00	.30	.25

STAMP HISTORY

THATCHER FERRY BRIDGE

In 1962, during the regular course of business, H.E. Harris purchases, at their 4 cent face value, a pane of 50 stamps honoring the Canal Zone's Thatcher Ferry Bridge. Due to a printing error, the silver bridge has been omitted. Harris discovers that his is the only pane from the sheet of 200 printed that has reached the public. Because a recent error in a Dag Hammerskjold stamp prompted the U.S. Postal Service to reprint thousands in order to make the error worthless, Harris questions how the Canal Zone will handle the bridge error. Flooding the market, he insists, would blunt the fun and excitement of stamp collecting. When the Canal Zone says it will reprint the error, Harris sues. March 25, 1965, The Federal District Court in Washington rules in Harris' favor, stopping the Canal Zone authorities from reprinting the stamp error. Viewed as a precedent-setting event in philately, the effort won Harris the respect and awards of his fellow collectors.

1278, 1299

1279

1280

1281, 1297

1282, 1303

1283, 1304

1283B, 1304C

1284, 1298

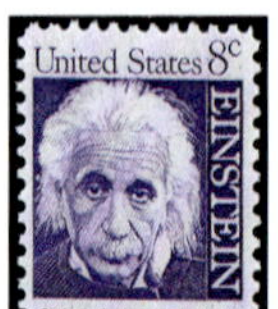
1285

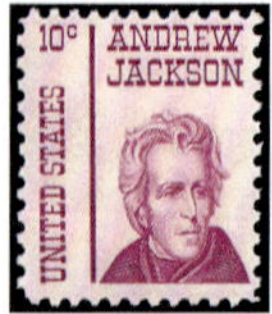
1286

1286A

1287

1288, 1288B, 1288d, 1305E, 1305Ei

1289

1290

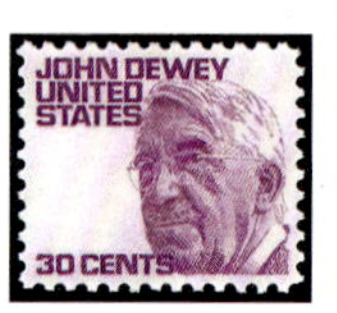
1291

1292

1293

1294, 1305C

1295

1305

1965-78 PROMINENT AMERICAN SERIES

SCOTT NO.	DESCRIPTION	FIRST DAY COVERS SING	FIRST DAY COVERS PL. BLK.	MINT SHEET	PLATE BLOCK F/NH	UNUSED F/NH	USED
1278-95	1¢-$5, 20 varieties, complete (No #1288B or 1288d)...........	91.50	....	....	150.00	32.50	7.75
1278	1¢ T. Jefferson (1968) .	1.75	4.00	12.00(100)	1.00	.25	.25
1278a	1¢ bklt.pane of 8	2.50	....	....	....	1.55	....
1278ae	1¢ test gum	90.00	....	....	....	2.00	....
1278b	1¢ bklt pane of 4 (1971)	18.00	....	....	....	1.00	....
1279	1¼¢ A. Gallatin (1967)	1.75	4.00	18.00(100)	12.00	.25	.25
1280	2¢ F.L. Wright (1966). .	1.75	4.00	15.00(100)	.90	.25	.25
1280a	2¢ bklt pane of 5 (1968)	2.50	....	....	....	1.00	....
1280c	2¢ bklt pane of 6 (1971)	18.00	....	....	....	1.00	....
1280ce	2¢ test gum	125.00	....	....	....	1.00	....
1281	3¢ F. Parkman (1967) .	1.75	4.00	14.00(100)	1.15	.25	.25
1282	4¢ A. Lincoln	1.75	4.00	22.00(100)	1.15	.25	.25
1283	5¢ G. Washington (1966)	1.75	4.00	23.00(100)	1.15	.25	.25
1283B	5¢ Washington, ... redrawn (1967)	1.75	4.00	21.00(100)	1.25	.30	.25
1284	6¢ F. D. Roosevelt(1966)	1.75	4.00	24.00(100)	1.35	.35	.25
1284b	6¢ bklt pane of 8 (1967)	3.00	....	....	....	1.75	....
1284c	6¢ bklt pane of 5 (1968)	150.00	....	....	....	1.60	....
1285	8¢ A. Einstein (1966) . .	4.00	6.00	40.00(100)	2.25	.50	.25
1286	10¢ A. Jackson (1967).	2.00	4.25	48.00(100)	2.25	.50	.25
1286A	12¢ H. Ford (1968) . . .	2.00	4.25	46.00(100)	2.25	.50	.25
1287	13¢ J.F. Kennedy (1967)	2.50	4.50	52.00(100)	3.50	.70	.25
1288	15¢ O.W. Holmes, die I (1968)	2.25	4.50	48.00(100)	2.25	.60	.25
1288d	15¢ Holmes, die II (1979)	....	....	90.00(100)	14.00	1.10	.45

SCOTT NO.	DESCRIPTION	FIRST DAY COVERS SING	FIRST DAY COVERS PL. BLK.	MINT SHEET	PLATE BLOCK F/NH	UNUSED F/NH	USED
1288B	same, from bklt pane (1978)........	2.25	....	....	....	.60	.25
1288Bc	15¢ bklt pane of 8 . . .	3.75	....	....	....	4.75	....
1289	20¢ G.C. Marshall (1967)	2.25	4.50	65.00(100)	5.00	.70	.25
1290	25¢ F. Douglass (1967)	5.00	6.00	96.00(100)	5.50	1.20	.25
1291	30¢ J. Dewey (1968) .	2.50	5.00	130.00(100)	7.00	1.25	.25
1292	40¢ T. Paine (1968) . .	2.50	5.00	155.00(100)	6.50	1.50	.25
1293	50¢ L. Stone (1968) . .	3.75	7.25	210.00(100)	8.00	2.00	.25
1294	$1 E. O'Neil (1967) . .	6.00	12.50	395.00(100)	18.00	5.00	.25
1295	$5 J. B. Moore (1966)	50.00	115.00	....	70.00	16.00	3.50

BOOKLET PANE SLOGANS

Slogan IV: Mail Early in the Day.
Slogan V: Use Zip Code.

#1278b–Slogans IV and V
#1280a, 1284c–Slogans IV or V

1966-81 COIL STAMPS

SCOTT NO.	DESCRIPTION	FIRST DAY COVERS SING	LINE PAIR	MINT SHEET	LINE PAIR	UNUSED F/NH	USED
1297/1305C	1¢-$1, 9 varieties, (No #1305Ei).....	....	....	....	15.00	6.80	2.75
	Perf. 10 Horizontally						
1297	3¢ F. Parkman (1975) .	1.75	2.75	....	.70	.25	.25
1298	6¢ F.D. Roosevelt (1967)	1.75	2.75	....	1.70	.40	.25
	Perf. 10 Vertically						
1299	1¢ T. Jefferson (1968) .	1.75	2.75	....	.65	.35	.25
1303	4¢ A. Lincoln	1.75	2.75	....	1.00	.35	.25
1304	5¢ G. Washington	1.75	2.75	....	1.00	1.00	.25
1304C	5¢ Washington, redrawn (1981)	1.75	2.75	....	2.75	.30	.25
1305	6¢ F.D. Roosevelt (1968)	1.75	2.75	....	.85	.50	.25
1305E	15¢ O.W. Holmes, die I (1978)	2.00	3.25	....	1.40	.50	.25
1305Ei	15¢ O.W. Holmes, die II (1979).........	....	....	....	4.50	1.25	.30
1305C	$1 E. O'Neil (1973) . . .	5.00	9.50	....	10.00	3.95	1.50

1306

1307

1308

1309

1310

1312

1313

1314

1966 COMMEMORATIVES

SCOTT NO.	DESCRIPTION	FIRST DAY COVERS SING	FIRST DAY COVERS PL. BLK.	MINT SHEET	PLATE BLOCK F/NH	UNUSED F/NH	USED
1306/22	(1306-10, 1312-22) 16 varieties.........	....	....	....	....	5.10	3.35
1306	5¢ Migratory Bird Treaty	2.00	4.25	17.00(50)	1.50	.35	.25
1307	5¢ A.S.P.C.A.........	2.00	4.00	14.00(50)	1.50	.35	.25
1308	5¢ Indiana Statehood .	2.00	4.00	14.00(50)	1.95	.35	.25
1309	5¢ American Circus . . .	3.00	4.25	14.00(50)	1.60	.35	.25
1310	5¢ SIPEX (single)	2.00	4.00	12.50(50)	1.25	.35	.25
1311	5¢ SIPEX, Imperf Souvenir Sheet	2.00	....	....	....	.35	.25
1312	5¢ Bill of Rights	2.25	4.00	15.00(50)	1.60	.35	.25
1313	5¢ Polish Millennium . .	2.00	4.00	12.50(50)	1.25	.35	.25
1314	5¢ National Park Service	2.00	4.00	22.00(50)	2.40	.55	.25

1315 1316 1317

1318

1319

1320

SCOTT NO.	DESCRIPTION	FIRST DAY COVERS SING	FIRST DAY COVERS PL. BLK.	MINT SHEET	PLATE BLOCK F/NH	UNUSED F/NH	USED
1315	5¢ Marine Corps Reserve	2.00	4.00	18.00(50)	2.00	.30	.25
1316	5¢ Women's Clubs. . .	2.00	4.00	12.50(50)	1.25	.30	.25
1317	5¢ Johnny Appleseed	2.00	4.00	22.00(50)	1.50	.40	.25
1318	5¢ Beautification	2.00	4.00	15.00(50)	1.50	.55	.25
1319	5¢ Great River Road .	2.00	4.00	15.00(50)	1.50	.40	.25
1320	5¢ Servicemen–Bonds.	2.00	4.00	12.50(50)	1.20	.30	.25

1321

1322

1323

SCOTT NO.	DESCRIPTION	FIRST DAY COVERS SING	FIRST DAY COVERS PL. BLK.	MINT SHEET	PLATE BLOCK F/NH	UNUSED F/NH	USED
1321	5¢ Christmas 1966 . .	1.75	4.00	24.00(100)	1.50	.35	.25
1322	5¢ Mary Cassatt	1.75	4.00	12.00(50)	1.20	.30	.25

1324

1325

1326 1327

1967 COMMEMORATIVES

SCOTT NO.	DESCRIPTION	FIRST DAY COVERS SING	FIRST DAY COVERS PL. BLK.	MINT SHEET	PLATE BLOCK F/NH	UNUSED F/NH	USED
1323-37	**15 varieties, complete. . . . .**	....	....	....	....	**7.50**	**3.25**
1323	5¢ National Grange . . .	2.00	4.00	12.00(50)	1.25	.35	.25
1324	5¢ Canada Centennial.	2.00	4.00	12.00(50)	1.25	.30	.25
1325	5¢ Erie Canal.	2.00	4.00	14.00(50)	1.50	.40	.25
1326	5¢ Search for Peace . .	2.00	4.00	12.00(50)	1.25	.30	.25
1327	5¢ Henry D. Thoreau . .	2.00	4.00	14.00(50)	1.75	.40	.25

1328

1329

1330

SCOTT NO.	DESCRIPTION	FIRST DAY COVERS SING	FIRST DAY COVERS PL. BLK.	MINT SHEET	PLATE BLOCK F/NH	UNUSED F/NH	USED
1328	5¢ Nebraska Statehood	2.00	4.00	20.00(50)	2.00	.30	.25
1329	5¢ Voice of America. . .	4.00	6.00	12.00(50)	1.25	.30	.25
1330	5¢ Davy Crockett.	2.50	4.25	12.00(50)	1.25	.30	.25

1331 1332

SCOTT NO.	DESCRIPTION	FIRST DAY COVERS SING	FIRST DAY COVERS PL. BLK.	MINT SHEET	PLATE BLOCK F/NH	UNUSED F/NH	USED
1331-32	5¢ Space, attached, 2 varieties	12.50	25.00	30.00(50)	3.50	1.75	1.20
1331	5¢ Astronaut	4.00	....	....	....	1.50	.40
1332	5¢ Gemini 4 Capsule. .	4.00	....	....	....	1.50	.40

1333

1334

SCOTT NO.	DESCRIPTION	FIRST DAY COVERS SING	FIRST DAY COVERS PL. BLK.	MINT SHEET	PLATE BLOCK F/NH	UNUSED F/NH	USED
1333	5¢ Urban Planning. . . .	2.00	4.00	12.00(50)	1.20	.30	.25
1334	5¢ Finland Independence	2.00	4.00	12.00(50)	1.20	.30	.25

1335

1336

1337

SCOTT NO.	DESCRIPTION	FIRST DAY COVERS SING	FIRST DAY COVERS PL. BLK.	MINT SHEET	PLATE BLOCK F/NH	UNUSED F/NH	USED
1335	5¢ Thomas Eakins . . .	2.00	4.00	12.00(50)	1.20	.30	.25
1336	5¢ Christmas 1967 . . .	2.00	4.00	12.00(50)	1.20	.30	.25
1337	5¢ Mississippi Statehood	2.00	4.00	17.00(50)	1.75	.45	.25

For Your Convenience in Ordering, Complete Sets are Listed Before Single Stamp Listings!

1338, 1338A, 1338D

1338F, 1338G

SCOTT NO.	DESCRIPTION	FIRST DAY COVERS SING	FIRST DAY COVERS PL. BLK.	MINT SHEET	PLATE BLOCK	UNUSED F/NH	USED
	GIORI PRESS 1968 Design size: 18½ x 22 mm Perf. 11						
1338	6¢ Flag & White House	1.75	4.00	24.00(100)	1.20	.30	.25
	HUCK PRESS Design size: 18 x 21 mm 1969 Coil Stamp Perf. 10 Vertically						
1338A	6¢ Flag & White House	1.75	....	....	5.75	.30	.25
	1970 Perf. 11 x 10½						
1338D	6¢ Flag & White House	2.00	4.25	23.00(100)	5.25(20)	.30	.25
	1971 Perf. 11 x 10½						
1338F	8¢ Flag & White House	2.00	4.25	33.00(100)	8.00(20)	.45	.25
	Coil Stamp Perf. 10 Vertically						
1338G	8¢ Flag & White House	2.00	....	....	....	.45	.25

1339

1340

1968 COMMEMORATIVES

SCOTT NO.	DESCRIPTION	FIRST DAY COVERS SING	FIRST DAY COVERS PL. BLK.	MINT SHEET	PLATE BLOCK	UNUSED F/NH	USED
1339/64	**(1339-40, 1342-64) 25 varieties.........**	....	....	....	....	**11.75**	**5.95**
1339	6¢ Illinois Statehood . .	2.00	4.00	15.00(50)	1.50	.50	.25
1340	6¢ Hemisfair '68.	2.00	4.00	12.00(50)	1.25	.30	.25

1341

SCOTT NO.	DESCRIPTION	FIRST DAY COVERS SING	FIRST DAY COVERS PL. BLK.	MINT SHEET	PLATE BLOCK	UNUSED F/NH	USED
1341	$1 Airlift to Servicemen	8.50	17.50	165.00(50)	15.00	3.95	2.75

1342

1343

1344

SCOTT NO.	DESCRIPTION	FIRST DAY COVERS SING	FIRST DAY COVERS PL. BLK.	MINT SHEET	PLATE BLOCK	UNUSED F/NH	USED
1342	6¢ Support our Youth. .	2.00	4.00	12.00(50)	1.25	.30	.25
1343	6¢ Law and Order	4.00	6.00	19.00(50)	1.95	.45	.25
1344	6¢ Register and Vote. .	2.00	4.00	12.00(50)	1.25	.30	.25

1345

1346

1347

1348

1349

1350

1351

1352

1353

1354

1968 HISTORIC AMERICAN FLAGS

SCOTT NO.	DESCRIPTION	FIRST DAY COVERS SING	FIRST DAY COVERS PL. BLK.	MINT SHEET	PLATE BLOCK	UNUSED F/NH	USED
1345-54	**10 varieties, complete, attached ....**	**10.00**	....	**20.00(50)**	**10.00**	**5.25**	....
1345-54	**Same, set of singles .**	**57.50**	....	....	....	**4.25**	**3.25**
1345	6¢ Fort Moultrie Flag . .	6.00	....	....	....	.55	.45
1346	6¢ Fort McHenry Flag .	6.00	....	....	....	.55	.45
1347	6¢ Washington's Cruisers	6.00	....	....	....	.55	.45
1348	6¢ Bennington Flag . . .	6.00	....	....	....	.55	.45
1349	6¢ Rhode Island Flag .	6.00	....	....	....	.55	.45
1350	6¢ First Stars & Stripes	6.00	....	....	....	.55	.45
1351	6¢ Bunker Hill Flag . . .	6.00	....	....	....	.55	.45
1352	6¢ Grand Union Flag . .	6.00	....	....	....	.55	.45
1353	6¢ Philadelphia Light Horse	6.00	....	....	....	.55	.45
1354	6¢ First Navy Jack. . . .	6.00	....	....	....	.55	.45

NOTE: All ten varieties of 1345-54 were printed on the same sheet; therefore, plate and regular blocks are not available for each variety separately. Plate blocks of four will contain two each of #1346, with number adjacent to #1345 only; Zip blocks will contain two each of #1353 and #1354, with inscription adjacent to #1354 only; Mail Early blocks will contain two each of #1347-49 with inscription adjacent to #1348 only. A plate strip of 20 stamps, with two of each variety will be required to have all stamps in plate block form and will contain all marginal inscription.

1355

1356

1357

1358

1359

1360

1361

1968 COMMEMORATIVES

SCOTT NO.	DESCRIPTION	FIRST DAY COVERS SING	FIRST DAY COVERS PL. BLK.	MINT SHEET	PLATE BLOCK	UNUSED F/NH	USED
1355	6¢ Walt Disney.	40.00	50.00	40.00(50)	4.75	1.25	.30
1356	6¢ Father Marquette .	2.00	4.00	15.00(50)	2.25	.50	.25
1357	6¢ Daniel Boone	2.00	4.00	15.00(50)	1.50	.50	.25
1358	6¢ Arkansas River . . .	2.00	4.00	15.00(50)	1.75	.50	.25
1359	6¢ Leif Erikson.	2.00	4.00	12.00(50)	1.25	.50	.25
1360	6¢ Cherokee Strip . . .	2.00	4.00	25.00(50)	2.50	.70	.25
1361	6¢ Trumbull Art	4.00	6.00	14.00(50)	1.30	.40	.25

1362

1363

1364

SCOTT NO.	DESCRIPTION	FIRST DAY COVERS SING	FIRST DAY COVERS PL. BLK.	MINT SHEET	PLATE BLOCK	UNUSED F/NH	USED
1362	6¢ Waterfowl Conservation	2.00	4.00	15.00(50)	1.70	.40	.25
1363	6¢ Christmas 1968 . . .	2.00	....	12.00(50)	3.25(10)	.30	.25
1364	6¢ Chief Joseph.	2.00	4.00	17.00(50)	1.70	.40	.25

1365 1366

1367 1368

1969 COMMEMORATIVES

SCOTT NO.	DESCRIPTION	FIRST DAY COVERS SING	FIRST DAY COVERS PL. BLK.	MINT SHEET	PLATE BLOCK	UNUSED F/NH	USED
1365-86	**22 varieties, complete**	....	....	....	....	**10.25**	**5.00**
1365-68	Beautification, 4 varieties, attached.	6.00	8.50	20.00(50)	3.00	2.50	2.00
1365	6¢ Azaleas & Tulips . .	3.00	....	....	....	1.00	.25
1366	6¢ Daffodils	3.00	....	....	....	1.00	.25
1367	6¢ Poppies.	3.00	....	....	....	1.00	.25
1368	6¢ Crabapple Trees. .	3.00	....	....	....	1.00	.25

1369 1370 1371

SCOTT NO.	DESCRIPTION	FIRST DAY COVERS SING	FIRST DAY COVERS PL. BLK.	MINT SHEET	PLATE BLOCK	UNUSED F/NH	USED
1369	6¢ American Legion. . .	2.00	4.00	12.00(50)	1.40	.30	.25
1370	6¢ Grandma Moses. . .	2.00	4.00	12.00(50)	1.40	.30	.25
1371	6¢ Apollo 8 Moon Orbit	2.50	5.00	22.00(50)	2.40	.50	.25

1372

1373

1374

1375

SCOTT NO.	DESCRIPTION	FIRST DAY COVERS SING	FIRST DAY COVERS PL. BLK.	MINT SHEET	PLATE BLOCK	UNUSED F/NH	USED
1372	6¢ W.C. Handy–Musician	3.50	5.00	13.00(50)	1.50	.40	.25
1373	6¢ California Settlement	2.00	4.00	13.00(50)	1.50	.40	.25
1374	6¢ Major J.W. Powell. .	2.00	4.00	13.00(50)	1.50	.40	.25
1375	6¢ Alabama Statehood	2.00	4.00	13.00(50)	1.50	.40	.25

1376 1377

1378 1379

SCOTT NO.	DESCRIPTION	FIRST DAY COVERS SING	FIRST DAY COVERS PL. BLK.	MINT SHEET	PLATE BLOCK	UNUSED F/NH	USED
1376-79	Botanical Congress, 4 varieties, attached . .	7.00	9.50	24.00(50)	3.75	2.50	2.25
1376	6¢ Douglas Fir	3.00	....	....	....	1.00	.25
1377	6¢ Lady's-slipper	3.00	....	....	....	1.00	.25
1378	6¢ Ocotillo	3.00	....	....	....	1.00	.25
1379	6¢ Franklinia	3.00	....	....	....	1.00	.25

AVERAGE QUALITY: From 1935 to date, deduct 20% from the Fine price to determine the price for an Average quality stamp.

MINT SHEETS: From 1935 to date, we list prices for standard size Mint Sheets in Fine, Never Hinged condition. The number of stamps in each sheet is noted in ( ).

1380

1381

1383

1382

SCOTT NO.	DESCRIPTION	FIRST DAY COVERS SING	FIRST DAY COVERS PL. BLK.	MINT SHEET	PLATE BLOCK	UNUSED F/NH	USED
1380	6¢ Dartmouth College .	2.00	4.00	12.00(50)	1.50	.40	.25
1381	6¢ Professional Baseball	16.00	25.00	30.00(50)	3.00	.60	.30
1382	6¢ College Football . . .	7.00	13.50	20.00(50)	2.00	.40	.25
1383	6¢ Eisenhower.	2.00	4.00	12.00(32)	1.75	.40	.25

1384

1385

1386

SCOTT NO.	DESCRIPTION	FIRST DAY COVERS SING	FIRST DAY COVERS PL. BLK.	MINT SHEET	PLATE BLOCK	UNUSED F/NH	USED
1384	6¢ Christmas 1969 . . .	2.00	....	14.00(50)	3.50(10)	.30	.25
1384a	6¢ precancelled set of 4 cities	....	....	280.00(50)	150.00(10)	4.50	....
1385	6¢ Rehabilitation	2.00	4.00	12.00(50)	1.20	.30	.25
1386	6¢ William M. Harnett .	2.00	4.00	8.00(32)	1.20	.30	.25

1387

1388

1389

1390

1391

1392

1970 COMMEMORATIVES

SCOTT NO.	DESCRIPTION	FIRST DAY COVERS SING	FIRST DAY COVERS PL. BLK.	MINT SHEET	PLATE BLOCK	UNUSED F/NH	USED
1387/1422	**(1387-92, 1405-22) 24 varieties, (No precancels). . . .**	....	....	....	....	**11.85**	**5.75**
1387-90	Natural History, 4 varieties, attached . .	5.00	7.00	12.00(32)	2.25	1.95	1.50
1387	6¢ Bald Eagle	2.50	....	....	....	.50	.25
1388	6¢ Elephant Herd.	2.50	....	....	....	.50	.25
1389	6¢ Haida Canoe.	2.50	....	....	....	.50	.25
1390	6¢ Reptiles.	2.50	....	....	....	.50	.25
1391	6¢ Maine Statehood . .	2.00	4.00	14.00(50)	1.75	.40	.25
1392	6¢ Wildlife–Buffalo. . . .	2.00	4.00	17.00(50)	2.00	.40	.25

1393, 1401

1393D

1394

1395, 1402

1396

1397

1398

1399

1400

1970-74 REGULAR ISSUE

SCOTT NO.	DESCRIPTION	FIRST DAY COVERS SING	FIRST DAY COVERS PL. BLK.	MINT SHEET	PLATE BLOCK	UNUSED F/NH	USED
1393/1400	**6¢-21¢, 8 varieties, complete (No #1395)**	....	....	....	....	**3.85**	**1.30**
1393	6¢ D. Eisenhower	1.75	4.00	23.00(100)	1.50	.30	.25
1393a	6¢ bklt pane of 8	2.75	....	....	....	1.95	....
1393ae	6¢ test gum	90.00	....	....	....	1.90	....
1393b	6¢ bklt pane of 5– Slogan IV or V	3.75	....	....	....	1.75	....
1393D	7¢ B. Franklin (1972). .	1.75	4.00	28.00(100)	1.75	.35	.25
1394	8¢ Ike–black, blue, red (1971)	1.75	4.00	32.00(100)	1.60	.30	.25
1395	same, deep claret bklt single (1971)	2.50	....	....	....	.45	.25
1395a	8¢ bklt pane of 8	2.50	....	....	....	2.40	....
1395b	8¢ bklt pane of 6	2.25	....	....	....	1.90	....
1395c	8¢ bklt pane of 4, VI & VII (1972).	2.00	....	....	....	1.95	....
1395d	8¢ bklt pane of 7 II or V (1972)	2.50	....	....	....	3.75	....
1396	8¢ Postal Service Emblem (1971)	1.75	4.00	24.00(100)	3.75(12)	.35	.25
1397	14¢ F. LaGuardia (1972)	1.75	4.00	50.00(100)	3.50	.75	.25
1398	16¢ E. Pyle (1971). . . .	2.50	4.50	60.00(100)	3.75	.85	.25
1399	18¢ E. Blackwell (1974)	2.00	4.25	60.00(100)	3.50	.75	.25
1400	21¢ A.P. Giannini (1973)	2.50	4.50	70.00(100)	3.75	.75	.30

1970-71 COIL STAMPS–Perf. 10 Vertically

SCOTT NO.	DESCRIPTION	FIRST DAY COVERS SING	LINE PAIR	MINT SHEET	LINE PAIR	UNUSED F/NH	USED
1401	6¢ D. Eisenhower	1.75	2.75	....	.90	.30	.25
1402	8¢ Eisenhower, claret (1971)	1.75	2.75	....	1.00	.35	.25

1405

1406

1407

1408

1409

1970 COMMEMORATIVES

SCOTT NO.	DESCRIPTION	FIRST DAY COVERS SING	FIRST DAY COVERS PL. BLK.	MINT SHEET	PLATE BLOCK	UNUSED F/NH	USED
1405	6¢ E.L. Masters–Poet .	2.00	4.00	13.00(50)	1.50	.40	.25
1406	6¢ Woman Suffrage. . .	2.00	4.00	14.00(50)	1.75	.70	.25
1407	6¢ South Carolina Tercentenary	2.00	4.00	12.50(50)	1.50	.50	.25
1408	6¢ Stone Mountain Memorial	2.00	4.00	14.00(50)	1.75	.50	.25
1409	6¢ Fort Snelling	2.00	4.00	19.50(50)	2.00	.50	.25

1412 1413

1410 1411

SCOTT NO.	DESCRIPTION	FIRST DAY COVERS SING	FIRST DAY COVERS PL. BLK.	MINT SHEET	PLATE BLOCK	UNUSED F/NH	USED
1410-13	Anti-Pollution, 4 varieties, attached . .	5.00	7.00	15.00(50)	4.00(10)	2.00	1.75
1410	6¢ Globe & Wheat	2.50				.40	.25
1411	6¢ Globe & City	2.50	....	....	....	.40	.25
1412	6¢ Globe & Bluegill . . .	2.50	....	....	....	.40	.25
1413	6¢ Globe & Seagull . . .	2.50	....	....	....	.40	.25

1414

SCOTT NO.	DESCRIPTION	FIRST DAY COVERS SING	FIRST DAY COVERS PL. BLK.	MINT SHEET	PLATE BLOCK	UNUSED F/NH	USED
1414	6¢ Nativity	1.75	....	12.00(50)	2.75(8)	.30	.25

FIRST DAY COVERS: First Day Covers are envelopes cancelled on the "First Day of Issue" of the stamp used on the envelope. Usually they also contain a picture (cachet) on the left side designed to go with the theme of the stamp. From 1935 to 1949, prices listed are for cacheted, addressed covers. From 1950 to date, prices are for cacheted, unaddressed covers.

1415 1416

1417 1418

SCOTT NO.	DESCRIPTION	FIRST DAY COVERS SING	FIRST DAY COVERS PL. BLK.	MINT SHEET	PLATE BLOCK	UNUSED F/NH	USED
1415-18	Christmas Toys, 4 varieties, attached . .	5.50	....	20.00(50)	5.50(8)	3.75	2.25
1415	6¢ Locomotive	3.00	....	....	....	1.00	.30
1416	6¢ Horse	3.00	....	....	....	1.00	.30
1417	6¢ Tricycle	3.00	....	....	....	1.00	.30
1418	6¢ Doll Carriage.	3.00	....	....	....	1.00	.30
	Precancelled						
1414a	6¢ Nativity (precancelled)	4.00	....	14.00(50)	2.75(8)	.30	.25
1415a-18a	6¢ Christmas Toys, precancelled, 4 varieties attached . . .	45.00	....	40.00(50)	8.50(8)	4.25	3.75
1415a	6¢ Locomotive	7.00	....	....	....	1.50	.25
1416a	6¢ Horse	7.00	....	....	....	1.50	.25
1417a	6¢ Tricycle	7.00	....	....	....	1.50	.25
1418a	6¢ Doll Carriage.	7.00	....	....	....	1.50	.25

NOTE: Unused precancels are with original gum, while used are without gum.

1419

1420

SCOTT NO.	DESCRIPTION	FIRST DAY COVERS SING	FIRST DAY COVERS PL. BLK.	MINT SHEET	PLATE BLOCK	UNUSED F/NH	USED
1419	6¢ U.N. 25th Anniversary	2.00	4.00	18.00(50)	1.95	.45	.25
1420	6¢ Pilgrim Landing. . . .	2.00	4.00	12.00(50)	1.35	.35	.25

1421 1422

SCOTT NO.	DESCRIPTION	FIRST DAY COVERS SING	FIRST DAY COVERS PL. BLK.	MINT SHEET	PLATE BLOCK	UNUSED F/NH	USED
1421-22	D.A.V. Servicemen, 2 varieties, attached . .	3.00	5.00	15.00(50)	2.25	.75	.60
1421	6¢ Disabled Veterans .	2.00	....	....	....	.35	.30
1422	6¢ Prisoners of War. . .	2.00	....	....	....	.35	.30

SE-TENANTS: Beginning with the 1964 Christmas issue (#1254-57), the United States has issued numerous Se-Tenant stamps covering a wide variety of subjects. Se-Tenants are issues where two or more different stamp designs are produced on the same sheet in pair, strip or block form. Mint stamps are usually collected in attached blocks, etc.; used stamps are generally saved as single stamps.

1423

1424

1425

1426

1971 COMMEMORATIVES

SCOTT NO.	DESCRIPTION	FIRST DAY COVERS SING	FIRST DAY COVERS PL. BLK.	MINT SHEET	PLATE BLOCK	UNUSED F/NH	USED
1423-45	**6¢-8¢, 23 varieties complete**	....	....	....	....	**9.75**	**4.95**
1423	6¢ Sheep	1.75	4.00	14.00(50)	1.60	.50	.25
1424	6¢ General D. MacArthur	1.75	4.00	14.00(50)	1.60	.50	.25
1425	6¢ Blood Donors	1.75	4.00	12.00(50)	1.35	.30	.25
1426	8¢ Missouri Statehood	1.75	4.00	17.00(50)	5.50(12)	.50	.25

1427 1428

1429 1430

SCOTT NO.	DESCRIPTION	FIRST DAY COVERS SING	FIRST DAY COVERS PL. BLK.	MINT SHEET	PLATE BLOCK	UNUSED F/NH	USED
1427-30	Wildlife Conservation, 4 varieties, attached	5.00	9.00	12.50(32)	2.50	2.00	1.50
1427	8¢ Trout	2.50	....	....	....	.40	.25
1428	8¢ Alligator	2.50	....	....	....	.40	.25
1429	8¢ Polar Bear	2.50	....	....	....	.40	.25
1430	8¢ Condor	2.50	....	....	....	.40	.25

1431

1432

1433

SCOTT NO.	DESCRIPTION	FIRST DAY COVERS SING	FIRST DAY COVERS PL. BLK.	MINT SHEET	PLATE BLOCK	UNUSED F/NH	USED
1431	8¢ Antarctic Treaty	2.00	4.00	14.00(50)	1.75	.40	.25
1432	8¢ American Revolution	2.00	4.00	12.00(50)	1.50	.40	.25
1433	8¢ John Sloan–Artist	2.00	4.00	12.00(50)	1.50	.35	.25

1434 1435

SCOTT NO.	DESCRIPTION	FIRST DAY COVERS SING	FIRST DAY COVERS PL. BLK.	MINT SHEET	PLATE BLOCK	UNUSED F/NH	USED
1434-35	Space Achievements, 2 varieties, attached	3.50	4.50	13.50(50)	1.75	.75	.55
1434	8¢ Moon, Earth, Sun & Landing Craft	2.00	....	....	....	.45	.30
1435	8¢ Lunar Rover	2.00	....	....	....	.45	.30

1436

1437

1438

1439

SCOTT NO.	DESCRIPTION	FIRST DAY COVERS SING	FIRST DAY COVERS PL. BLK.	MINT SHEET	PLATE BLOCK	UNUSED F/NH	USED
1436	8¢ Emily Dickinson	2.00	4.00	14.00(50)	1.70	.40	.25
1437	8¢ San Juan	2.00	4.00	28.00(50)	2.50	.65	.25
1438	8¢ Drug Addiction	2.00	4.00	13.00(50)	2.25(6)	.35	.25
1439	8¢ CARE	2.00	4.00	14.00(50)	2.70(8)	.45	.25

1440 1441

1442 1443

SCOTT NO.	DESCRIPTION	FIRST DAY COVERS SING	FIRST DAY COVERS PL. BLK.	MINT SHEET	PLATE BLOCK	UNUSED F/NH	USED
1440-43	Historic Preservation 4 varieties, attached	5.00	6.00	12.50(32)	2.00	1.75	1.00
1440	8¢ Decatur House	2.50	....	....	....	.40	.25
1441	8¢ Whaling Ship	2.50	....	....	....	.40	.25
1442	8¢ Cable Car	2.50	....	....	....	.40	.25
1443	8¢ Mission	2.50	....	....	....	.40	.25

1444

1445

SCOTT NO.	DESCRIPTION	FIRST DAY COVERS SING	FIRST DAY COVERS PL. BLK.	MINT SHEET	PLATE BLOCK	UNUSED F/NH	USED
1444	8¢ Christmas Nativity. .	2.00	4.00	12.00(50)	4.25(12)	.35	.25
1445	8¢ Christmas Partridge	2.00	4.00	12.00(50)	4.25(12)	.35	.25

1446

1447

1972 COMMEMORATIVES

SCOTT NO.	DESCRIPTION	FIRST DAY COVERS SING	FIRST DAY COVERS PL. BLK.	MINT SHEET	PLATE BLOCK	UNUSED F/NH	USED
1446/74	**29 varieties, complete. . . . .**	....	....	....	....	**10.15**	**6.00**
1446	8¢ Sidney Lanier–Poet	2.00	4.00	14.00(50)	1.75	.50	.25
1447	8¢ Peace Corps.	2.00	4.00	12.50(50)	2.25(6)	.40	.25

1448 1449

1450 1451

1452

1454

1453

1972 NATIONAL PARKS CENTENNIAL

SCOTT NO.	DESCRIPTION	FIRST DAY COVERS SING	FIRST DAY COVERS PL. BLK.	MINT SHEET	PLATE BLOCK	UNUSED F/NH	USED
1448-54	**2¢-15¢, 7 varieties, complete . . . .**	....	....	....	....	**2.50**	**1.50**
1448-51	Cape Hatteras, 4 varieties, attached.	6.00	7.00	13.00(100)	1.15	1.00	.65
1448	2¢ Ship's Hull.	....	....	....	....	.25	.25
1449	2¢ Lighthouse	....	....	....	....	.25	.25
1450	2¢ Three Seagulls	....	....	....	....	.25	.25
1451	2¢ Two Seagulls	....	....	....	....	.25	.25
1452	6¢ Wolf Trap Farm Park	2.00	4.00	13.00(50)	1.75	.50	.25
1453	8¢ Yellowstone Park . .	2.00	4.00	16.00(32)	2.75	.50	.25
1454	15¢ Mount McKinley . .	2.00	4.00	24.00(50)	2.75	.60	.35

1455

1972 COMMEMORATIVES

SCOTT NO.	DESCRIPTION	FIRST DAY COVERS SING	FIRST DAY COVERS PL. BLK.	MINT SHEET	PLATE BLOCK	UNUSED F/NH	USED
1455	8¢ Family Planning . . .	2.00	4.00	14.00(50)	1.50	.35	.25

1456 1457

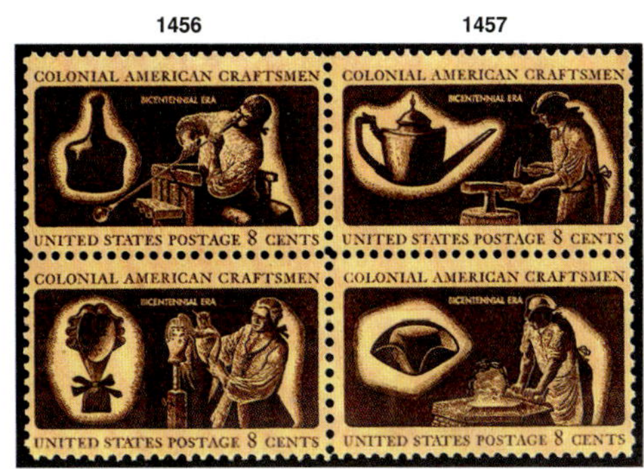

1458 1459

SCOTT NO.	DESCRIPTION	FIRST DAY COVERS SING	FIRST DAY COVERS PL. BLK.	MINT SHEET	PLATE BLOCK	UNUSED F/NH	USED
1456-59	Colonial Craftsmen, 4 varieties, attached . .	3.75	4.75	15.00(50)	1.75	1.50	1.20
1456	8¢ Glassmaker	2.25	....	....	....	.45	.25
1457	8¢ Silversmith	2.25	....	....	....	.45	.25
1458	8¢ Wigmaker	2.25	....	....	....	.45	.25
1459	8¢ Hatter	2.25	....	....	....	.45	.25

1460

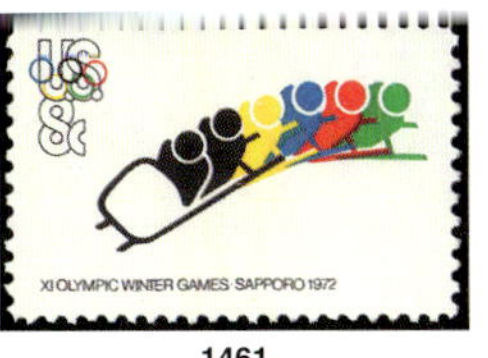

1461

1462

SCOTT NO.	DESCRIPTION	FIRST DAY COVERS SING	FIRST DAY COVERS PL. BLK.	MINT SHEET	PLATE BLOCK	UNUSED F/NH	USED
1460	6¢ Olympics–Cycling. .	2.10	4.25	12.00(50)	3.25(10)	.30	.25
1461	8¢ Olympics–Bob Sled Racing.	2.10	4.25	12.25(50)	3.25(10)	.35	.25
1462	15¢ Olympics–Foot Racing.	2.10	4.25	22.00(50)	6.00(10)	.50	.45

1463

SCOTT NO.	DESCRIPTION	FIRST DAY COVERS SING	FIRST DAY COVERS PL. BLK.	MINT SHEET	PLATE BLOCK	UNUSED F/NH	USED
1463	8¢ Parent Teacher Association	2.00	4.00	14.00(50)	1.50	.40	.25
1463a	Same, Reversed Plate Number	2.00	4.00	15.00(50)	1.75	....	....

SCOTT NO.	DESCRIPTION	FIRST DAY COVERS SING	FIRST DAY COVERS PL. BLK.	MINT SHEET	PLATE BLOCK	UNUSED F/NH	USED

1464 1465 1466 1467

SCOTT NO.	DESCRIPTION	FIRST DAY COVERS SING	FIRST DAY COVERS PL. BLK.	MINT SHEET	PLATE BLOCK	UNUSED F/NH	USED
1464-67	Wildlife Conservation, 4 varieties, attached . .	4.00	6.00	17.00(32)	3.25	2.00	1.50
1464	8¢ Fur Seal	2.00	....	....	....	.50	.25
1465	8¢ Cardinal	2.00	....	....	....	.50	.25
1466	8¢ Brown Pelican.	2.00	....	....	....	.50	.25
1467	8¢ Bighorn Sheep	2.00	....	....	....	.50	.25

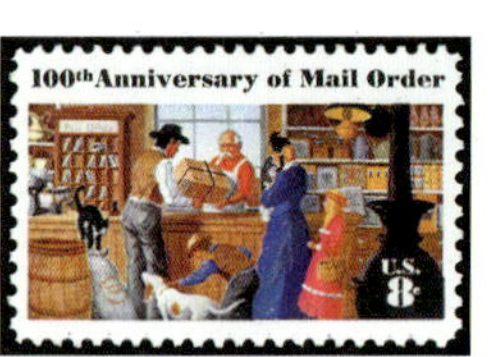

1468

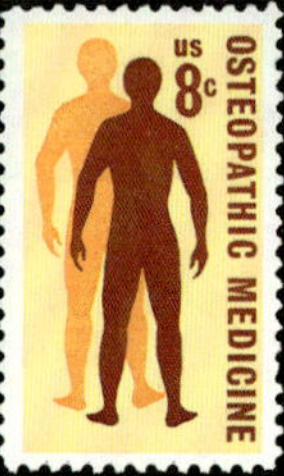

1469

Tom Sawyer United States 8c

1470

SCOTT NO.	DESCRIPTION	FIRST DAY COVERS SING	FIRST DAY COVERS PL. BLK.	MINT SHEET	PLATE BLOCK	UNUSED F/NH	USED
1468	8¢ Mail Order Business	2.00	4.00	13.00(50)	4.25(12)	.35	.25
1469	8¢ Osteopathic Medicine	2.00	4.25	15.00(50)	2.75(6)	.45	.25
1470	Tom Sawyer–Folklore .	2.00	4.00	14.00(50)	2.25	.35	.25

1471

1472

PHARMACY 8c UNITED STATES POSTAGE

1473

SCOTT NO.	DESCRIPTION	FIRST DAY COVERS SING	FIRST DAY COVERS PL. BLK.	MINT SHEET	PLATE BLOCK	UNUSED F/NH	USED
1471	8¢ Christmas–Virgin Mother.	1.75	4.00	13.00(50)	4.50(12)	.35	.25
1472	8¢ Christmas–Santa . . Claus	1.75	4.00	13.00(50)	4.50(12)	.35	.25
1473	8¢ Pharmacy	8.00	10.00	13.00(50)	1.75(4)	.35	.25

1474

1475

SCOTT NO.	DESCRIPTION	FIRST DAY COVERS SING	FIRST DAY COVERS PL. BLK.	MINT SHEET	PLATE BLOCK	UNUSED F/NH	USED
1474	8¢ Stamp Collecting . .	2.00	4.25	10.00(40)	1.50(4)	.35	.25

1476

1477

1478

1479

1973 COMMEMORATIVES

SCOTT NO.	DESCRIPTION	FIRST DAY COVERS SING	FIRST DAY COVERS PL. BLK.	MINT SHEET	PLATE BLOCK	UNUSED F/NH	USED
1475-1508	**34 varieties, complete**	....	....	....	....	**12.00**	**7.60**
1475	8¢ "Love"	2.25	5.00	12.50(50)	2.25(6)	.35	.25

COLONIAL COMMUNICATIONS

SCOTT NO.	DESCRIPTION	FIRST DAY COVERS SING	FIRST DAY COVERS PL. BLK.	MINT SHEET	PLATE BLOCK	UNUSED F/NH	USED
1476	8¢ Pamphlet Printing . .	2.00	4.00	12.50(50)	1.50	.35	.25
1477	8¢ Posting Broadside .	2.00	4.00	12.50(50)	1.50	.35	.25
1478	8¢ Colonial Post Rider.	2.00	4.00	12.50(50)	1.50	.35	.25
1479	8¢ Drummer & Soldiers	2.00	4.00	12.50(50)	1.50	.35	.25

1480 1481

1482 1483

SCOTT NO.	DESCRIPTION	FIRST DAY COVERS SING	FIRST DAY COVERS PL. BLK.	MINT SHEET	PLATE BLOCK	UNUSED F/NH	USED
1480-83	Boston Tea Party, 4 varieties, attached . .	4.50	6.50	16.00(50)	1.85	1.60	1.25
1480	8¢ Throwing Tea	2.25	....	....	....	.45	.25
1481	8¢ Ship	2.25	....	....	....	.45	.25
1482	8¢ Rowboats	2.25	....	....	....	.45	.25
1483	8¢ Rowboat & Dock. . .	2.25	....	....	....	.45	.25

1484

1485

Copernicus 1473-1973 8¢US

1488

1486

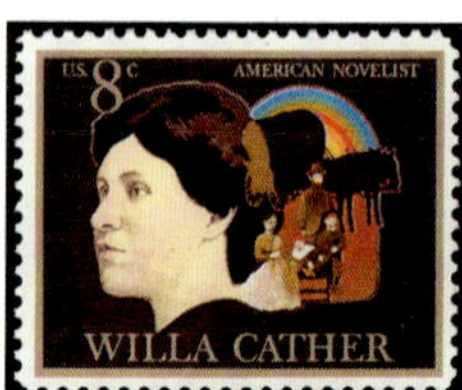

1487

SCOTT NO.	DESCRIPTION	FIRST DAY COVERS SING	FIRST DAY COVERS PL. BLK.	MINT SHEET	PLATE BLOCK	UNUSED F/NH	USED
	AMERICAN ARTS						
1484	8¢ George Gershwin–Composer	2.00	4.00	10.25(40)	4.00(12)	.35	.25
1485	8¢ Robinson Jeffers–Poet.	2.00	4.00	10.25(40)	4.25(12)	.35	.25
1486	8¢ Henry O. Tanner–Artist	5.00	6.00	10.25(40)	4.00(12)	.35	.25
1487	8¢ Willa Cather–Novelist	2.00	4.00	14.00(40)	7.00(12)	.60	.25
1488	8¢ Nicolaus Copernicus	2.00	4.00	12.25(40)	1.50	.35	.25

1489

1490

1491

1492

1493

1494

1495

1496

1497

1498

1973 POSTAL SERVICE EMPLOYEES

SCOTT NO.	DESCRIPTION	FIRST DAY COVERS SING	FIRST DAY COVERS PL. BLK.	MINT SHEET	PLATE BLOCK	UNUSED F/NH	USED
1489-98	**10 varieties, complete, attached . .**	**6.50**	**........**	**18.00(50)**	**9.00(20)**	**4.50**	**3.60**
1489-98	**Set of singles, complete**	**22.00**	**........**	**........**	**........**	**4.25**	**3.25**
1489	8¢ Window Clerk	2.25	....	....	....	.45	.35
1490	8¢ Mail Pickup	2.25	....	....	....	.45	.35
1491	8¢ Conveyor Belt.	2.25	....	....	....	.45	.35
1492	8¢ Sacking Parcels . . .	2.25	....	....	....	.45	.35
1493	8¢ Mail Cancelling	2.25	....	....	....	.45	.35
1494	8¢ Manual Sorting	2.25	....	....	....	.45	.35
1495	8¢ Machine Sorting . . .	2.25	....	....	....	.45	.35
1496	8¢ Loading Truck	2.25	....	....	....	.45	.35
1497	8¢ Letter Carrier	2.25	....	....	....	.45	.35
1498	8¢ Rural Delivery	2.25	....	....	....	.45	.35

1499

1500

1501

1502

1503

1973 COMMEMORATIVES

SCOTT NO.	DESCRIPTION	FIRST DAY COVERS SING	FIRST DAY COVERS PL. BLK.	MINT SHEET	PLATE BLOCK	UNUSED F/NH	USED
1499	8¢ Harry S. Truman . . .	2.00	4.00	12.00(32)	2.25	.50	.25
1500	6¢ Electronics	2.00	4.00	12.00(50)	1.50	.35	.25
1501	8¢ Electronics	2.00	4.00	14.00(50)	1.75	.35	.25
1502	15¢ Electronics	2.00	4.00	25.00(50)	2.50	.60	.40
1503	8¢ Lyndon B. Johnson.	2.00	4.00	12.00(32)	5.50(12)	.50	.25

1504

1505

1506

1973-74 RURAL AMERICA

SCOTT NO.	DESCRIPTION	FIRST DAY COVERS SING	FIRST DAY COVERS PL. BLK.	MINT SHEET	PLATE BLOCK	UNUSED F/NH	USED
1504	8¢ Angus Cattle	2.00	4.00	16.50(50)	1.85	.45	.25
1505	10¢ Chautauqua (1974)	2.00	4.00	16.50(50)	1.85	.45	.25
1506	10¢ Winter Wheat (1974)	2.00	4.00	14.00(50)	1.85	.45	.25

1507

1508

1973 CHRISTMAS

SCOTT NO.	DESCRIPTION	FIRST DAY COVERS SING	FIRST DAY COVERS PL. BLK.	MINT SHEET	PLATE BLOCK	UNUSED F/NH	USED
1507	8¢ Madonna.	2.25	3.25	13.00(50)	4.25(12)	.40	.25
1508	8¢ Christmas Tree	2.25	3.25	13.00(50)	4.25(12)	.40	.25

1509, 1519

1510, 1520

1511

1518

1973-74 REGULAR ISSUES

SCOTT NO.	DESCRIPTION	FIRST DAY COVERS SING	FIRST DAY COVERS PL. BLK.	MINT SHEET	PLATE BLOCK	UNUSED F/NH	USED
1509	10¢ Crossed Flags . . .	2.25	4.00	32.00(100)	7.75(20)	.40	.25
1510	10¢ Jefferson Memorial	2.25	4.00	34.00(100)	2.50	.50	.25
1510b	10¢ bklt pane of 5–Slogan VIII.	2.25	....	....	....	1.85	....
1510c	10¢ bklt pane of 8	2.25	....	....	....	3.00	....
1510d	10¢ bklt pane of 6 (1974)	2.25	....	....	....	6.50	....
1511	10¢ Zip Code Theme (1974)	2.25	4.00	29.50(100)	2.75(8)	.35	.25

BOOKLET PANE SLOGANS

VI–Stamps in This Book.... VII– This Book Contains 25.... VIII–Paying Bills....

COIL STAMPS Perf.10 Vertically

SCOTT NO.	DESCRIPTION	FIRST DAY COVERS SING	LINE PAIR	MINT SHEET	LINE PAIR	UNUSED F/NH	USED
1518	6.3¢ Liberty Bell.	2.25	2.75	....	.90	.40	.25
1519	10¢ Crossed Flags . . .	2.25	....	....	....	.50	.25
1520	10¢ Jefferson Memorial	2.25	2.75	....	1.25	.40	.25

1525

1526

1527

HORSE RACING
U.S. postage 10 cents
1528

1529

1974 COMMEMORATIVES

SCOTT NO.	DESCRIPTION	FIRST DAY COVERS SING	FIRST DAY COVERS PL. BLK.	MINT SHEET	PLATE BLOCK	UNUSED F/NH	USED
1525-52	**28 varieties, complete. . . . .**	....	....	....	....	**11.00**	**6.00**
1525	10¢ Veterans of Foreign Wars	2.25	4.00	14.00(50)	1.50	.40	.25
1526	10¢ Robert Frost	2.25	4.00	16.50(50)	1.85	.40	.25
1527	10¢ Environment–EXPO '74.	2.25	4.00	16.00(40)	6.00(12)	.40	.25
1528	10¢ Horse Racing	2.25	4.00	19.50(50)	6.00(12)	.40	.25
1529	10¢ Skylab Project. . . .	2.25	4.00	14.25(50)	1.75	.40	.25

1530

1531

1532

1533

1534

1535

1536

1537

1974 UNIVERSAL POSTAL UNION

SCOTT NO.	DESCRIPTION	FIRST DAY COVERS SING	FIRST DAY COVERS PL. BLK.	MINT SHEET	PLATE BLOCK	UNUSED F/NH	USED
1530-37	**8 varieties, attached .**	**6.00**	....	**13.00(32)**	**7.50(16)**	**3.50(8)**	**2.95**
1530-37	**Set of singles, complete**	**17.50**	....	....	....	**3.25**	**2.25**
1530	10¢ Raphael	2.75	....	....	....	.50	.35
1531	10¢ Hokusai.	2.75	....	....	....	.50	.35
1532	10¢ J.F. Peto	2.75	....	....	....	.50	.35
1533	10¢ J.E. Liotard	2.75	....	....	....	.50	.35
1534	10¢ G. Terborch.	2.75	....	....	....	.50	.35
1535	10¢ J.B.S. Chardin . . .	2.75	....	....	....	.50	.35
1536	10¢ T. Gainsborough . .	2.75	....	....	....	.50	.35
1537	10¢ F. de Goya	2.75	....	....	....	.50	.35

1538

1540 1539

1541

1974 COMMEMORATIVES

SCOTT NO.	DESCRIPTION	FIRST DAY COVERS SING	FIRST DAY COVERS PL. BLK.	MINT SHEET	PLATE BLOCK	UNUSED F/NH	USED
1538-41	Mineral Heritage, 4 varieties, attached . .	3.50	5.00	18.00(48)	2.25	1.75	1.25
1538	10¢ Petrified Wood . . .	2.25	....	....	....	.50	.25
1539	10¢ Tourmaline	2.25	....	....	....	.50	.25
1540	10¢ Amethyst.	2.25	....	....	....	.50	.25
1541	10¢ Rhodochrosite . . .	2.25	....	....	....	.50	.25

1542

SCOTT NO.	DESCRIPTION	FIRST DAY COVERS SING	FIRST DAY COVERS PL. BLK.	MINT SHEET	PLATE BLOCK	UNUSED F/NH	USED
1542	10¢ Fort Harrod Bicentennial.	2.25	4.00	15.00(50)	1.75	.40	.25

1543 1544

1545 1546

SCOTT NO.	DESCRIPTION	FIRST DAY COVERS SING	FIRST DAY COVERS PL. BLK.	MINT SHEET	PLATE BLOCK	UNUSED F/NH	USED
1543-46	Continental Congress, 4 varieties, attached . .	4.50	6.00	17.00(50)	2.25	1.75	1.25
1543	10¢ Carpenter's Hall . .	2.25	....	....	....	.40	.25
1544	10¢ Quote–First Congress	2.25	....	....	....	.40	.25
1545	10¢ Quote–Declaration– of Independence	2.25	....	....	....	.40	.25
1546	10¢ Independence Hall	2.25	....	....	....	.40	.25

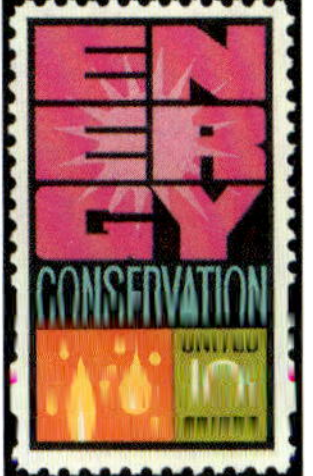

1547

1548

1549

SCOTT NO.	DESCRIPTION	FIRST DAY COVERS SING	FIRST DAY COVERS PL. BLK.	MINT SHEET	PLATE BLOCK	UNUSED F/NH	USED
1547	10¢ Energy Conservation	2.25	4.00	19.00(50)	1.90	.45	.25
1548	10¢ Sleepy Hollow. . . .	2.25	4.00	20.00(50)	1.75	.40	.25
1549	10¢ Retarded Children	2.25	4.00	19.00(50)	1.90	.40	.25

1550

1551

1552

SCOTT NO.	DESCRIPTION	FIRST DAY COVERS SING	FIRST DAY COVERS PL. BLK.	MINT SHEET	PLATE BLOCK	UNUSED F/NH	USED
1550	10¢ Christmas–Angel .	2.25	4.00	14.00(50)	4.50(10)	.35	.25
1551	10¢ Christmas–Currier & Ives.	2.25	4.00	14.00(50)	5.00(12)	.35	.25
1552	10¢ Christmas– Dove of Peace.	2.25	4.00	18.00(50)	9.50(20)	.40	.25
1552	same	....	....	....	5.50(12)	....	....

1553

1554

1555

1975 COMMEMORATIVES

SCOTT NO.	DESCRIPTION	FIRST DAY COVERS SING	FIRST DAY COVERS PL. BLK.	MINT SHEET	PLATE BLOCK	UNUSED F/NH	USED
1553-80	**8¢-10¢, 28 varieties, complete. . . . .**	....	....	....	....	**12.00**	**6.25**
1553	10¢ Benjamin West– Arts	2.25	4.00	16.00(50)	5.00(10)	.45	.25
1554	10¢ Paul Dunbar–Arts .	2.25	4.00	18.00(50)	5.00(10)	.45	.25
1555	10¢ D.W. Griffith–Arts .	2.25	4.00	17.00(50)	2.00	.45	.25

1556

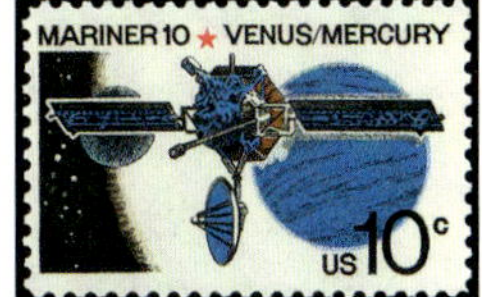

1557

1558

SCOTT NO.	DESCRIPTION	FIRST DAY COVERS SING	FIRST DAY COVERS PL. BLK.	MINT SHEET	PLATE BLOCK	UNUSED F/NH	USED
1556	10¢ Pioneer 10	2.25	4.00	16.00(50)	2.00	.45	.25
1557	10¢ Mariner 10	2.25	4.00	16.00(50)	2.00	.45	.25
1558	10¢ Collective Bargaining	2.25	4.00	16.00(50)	3.25(8)	.40	.25

1559

1560

1561

1562

SCOTT NO.	DESCRIPTION	FIRST DAY COVERS SING	FIRST DAY COVERS PL. BLK.	MINT SHEET	PLATE BLOCK	UNUSED F/NH	USED
1559	8¢ Sybil Ludington. . . .	2.25	4.00	14.00(50)	4.00(10)	.35	.25
1560	10¢ Salem Poor.	2.25	4.00	16.00(50)	5.00(10)	.45	.25
1561	10¢ Haym Salomon. . .	2.25	4.00	16.00(50)	5.00(10)	.45	.25
1562	18¢ Peter Francisco . .	2.25	4.00	27.50(50)	8.00(10)	.70	.40

1563

1564

SCOTT NO.	DESCRIPTION	FIRST DAY COVERS SING	FIRST DAY COVERS PL. BLK.	MINT SHEET	PLATE BLOCK	UNUSED F/NH	USED
1563	10¢ Lexington-Concord	2.25	4.00	15.00(40)	5.75(12)	.45	.25
1564	10¢ Battle of Bunker Hill	2.25	4.00	16.00(40)	5.50(12)	.45	.25

1565

1566

1567

1568

SCOTT NO.	DESCRIPTION	FIRST DAY COVERS SING	FIRST DAY COVERS PL. BLK.	MINT SHEET	PLATE BLOCK	UNUSED F/NH	USED
1565-68	Military Uniforms, 4 varieties, attached . .	4.00	6.00	17.00(50)	5.75(12)	1.75	1.30
1565	10¢ Continental Army .	2.25	....	....	....	.50	.25
1566	10¢ Continental Navy .	2.25	....	....	....	.50	.25
1567	10¢ Continental Marines	2.25	....	....	....	.50	.25
1568	10¢ American Militia . .	2.25	....	....	....	.50	.25

1569

1570

SCOTT NO.	DESCRIPTION	FIRST DAY COVERS SING	FIRST DAY COVERS PL. BLK.	MINT SHEET	PLATE BLOCK	UNUSED F/NH	USED
1569-70	Apollo-Soyuz Mission,. 2 varieties, attached . .	3.00	4.50	11.00(24)	5.75(12)	.95	.65
1569	10¢ Docked	2.25	....	....	....	.50	.30
1570	10¢ Docking.	2.25	....	....	....	.50	.30

1571

SCOTT NO.	DESCRIPTION	FIRST DAY COVERS SING	FIRST DAY COVERS PL. BLK.	MINT SHEET	PLATE BLOCK	UNUSED F/NH	USED
1571	10¢ International Women's Year	2.25	4.00	14.00(50)	2.40(6)	.35	.25

1572 1573

1574 1575

SCOTT NO.	DESCRIPTION	FIRST DAY COVERS SING	FIRST DAY COVERS PL. BLK.	MINT SHEET	PLATE BLOCK	UNUSED F/NH	USED
1572-75	Postal Service Bicentennial, 4 varieties, attached . .	4.00	5.00	19.00(50)	5.50(12)	1.85	1.50
1572	10¢ Stagecoach & Trailer	2.25	....	....	....	.50	.25
1573	10¢ Locomotives	2.25	....	....	....	.50	.25
1574	10¢ Airplanes.	2.25	....	....	....	.50	.25
1575	10¢ Satellite.	2.25	....	....	....	.50	.25

1576

1577 1578

SCOTT NO.	DESCRIPTION	FIRST DAY COVERS SING	FIRST DAY COVERS PL. BLK.	MINT SHEET	PLATE BLOCK	UNUSED F/NH	USED
1576	10¢ World Peace through Law	2.25	4.00	15.00(50)	2.00	.45	.25
1577-78	Banking & Commerce, 2 varieties, attached . .	2.50	3.75	15.00(40)	2.25	1.00	.70
1577	10¢ Banking.	2.25	....	....	....	.60	.25
1578	10¢ Commerce	2.25	....	....	....	.60	.25

1579

1580

SCOTT NO.	DESCRIPTION	FIRST DAY COVERS SING	FIRST DAY COVERS PL. BLK.	MINT SHEET	PLATE BLOCK	UNUSED F/NH	USED
1579	(10¢) Madonna	2.25	4.00	15.00(50)	5.00(12)	.45	.25
1580	(10¢) Christmas Card .	2.25	4.00	15.00(50)	5.00(12)	.45	.25
1580b	(10¢) Christmas Card, perf. 10½ x 11	....	....	66.00(50)	19.00(12)	1.40	.80

1581, 1811

1582

1584

1585

1590, 1591, 1616

1592, 1617

1593

1594, 1816

1595, 1618

1596

1597, 1598, 1618C

1599, 1619

1603

1604

1605

1606

1608 1610 1611 1612

1975-81 AMERICANA ISSUE

SCOTT NO.	DESCRIPTION	FIRST DAY COVERS SING	FIRST DAY COVERS PL. BLK.	MINT SHEET	PLATE BLOCK	UNUSED F/NH	USED
1581/1612	1¢-$5, (No #1590, 1590a, 1595, or 1598) 19 varieties, complete	51.50	....	....	155.00	33.50	6.95
1581	1¢ Inkwell & Quill (1977)	2.25	4.00	10.00(100)	1.25	.35	.25
1582	2¢ Speaker's Stand (1977)	2.25	4.00	10.00(100)	2.00	.25	.25
1584	3¢ Ballot Box (1977) . .	2.25	4.00	17.00(100)	2.00	.30	.25
1585	4¢ Books & Eyeglasses (1977)	2.25	4.00	18.00(100)	2.00	.30	.25
1590	9¢ Capitol, from bklt pane (1977)	15.00	....	....	....	1.25	1.00
1590a	same, perf 10 (1977) . .	....	....	....	....	33.00	....
1590,1623	Attached pair, from bklt pane	....	....	....	....	1.75	....
1590a, 1623b	Attached pair, perf. 10 .	....	....	....	....	35.00	....
1591	9¢ Capitol, grey paper .	2.25	4.00	30.00(100)	1.75	.40	.25
1592	10¢ Justice (1977)	2.25	4.00	32.00(100)	1.75	.40	.25
1593	11¢ Printing Press	2.25	4.00	36.00(100)	2.25	.50	.25
1594	12¢ Torch (1981)	2.25	4.00	38.50(100)	2.50	.50	.25
1595	13¢ Liberty Bell from bklt pane	2.25	....	....	....	.50	.25
1595a	13¢ bklt pane of 6	2.25	....	....	....	3.25	....
1595b	13¢ bklt pane of 7– Slogan VIII	2.50	....	....	....	3.50	....
1595c	13¢ bklt pane of 8	2.50	....	....	....	3.75	....
1595d	13¢ bklt pane of 5– Slogan IX (1976)	2.25	....	....	....	3.50	....

VIII–Paying Bills... IX–Collect Stamps...

SCOTT NO.	DESCRIPTION	FIRST DAY COVERS SING	FIRST DAY COVERS PL. BLK.	MINT SHEET	PLATE BLOCK	UNUSED F/NH	USED
1596	13¢ Eagle & Shield . . .	2.25	4.00	40.00(100)	7.00(12)	.50	.25
1597	15¢ Fort McHenry Flag (1978)	2.25	4.00	43.00(100)	12.00(20)	.50	.25
1598	same, from bklt pane . . (1978)	2.25	....	....	....	.90	.25
1598a	15¢ bklt pane of 8	3.00	....	....	....	8.50	....
1599	16¢ Statue of Liberty (1978)	2.25	4.00	52.00(100)	3.00	.60	.30
1603	24¢ Old North Church .	2.25	4.00	72.00(100)	4.50	.95	.25
1604	28¢ Fort Nisqually (1978)	2.25	4.00	92.00(100)	5.75	1.10	.35
1605	29¢ Lighthouse (1978)	2.25	4.00	100.00(100)	5.75	1.20	.50
1606	30¢ School House (1979)	2.25	4.00	100.00(100)	6.00	1.20	.30
1608	50¢ "Betty" Lamp (1979)	2.50	5.25	150.00(100)	9.00	2.00	.30
1610	$1 Rush Lamp (1979) .	3.50	17.50	305.00(100)	16.00	3.50	.30
1610c	Same, candle flame inverted......		....	....	....	14500.00	....
1611	$2 Kerosene Lamp (1978)	7.00	14.50	600.00(100)	32.50	7.25	.85
1612	$5 Conductor's Lantern (1979)	15.00	31.50	1375.00(100)	74.00	16.00	3.00

1613 1614 1615 1615C

1975-79 COIL STAMPS Perforated Vertically

SCOTT NO.	DESCRIPTION	FIRST DAY COVERS SING	FIRST DAY COVERS PL. BLK.	MINT SHEET	LINE PR.	UNUSED F/NH	USED
1613-19	3.1¢-16¢, 9 varieties, . complete	....	....	....	12.50	3.75	1.80
1613	3.1¢ Guitar (1979)	2.25	2.75	....	1.20	.45	.25
1614	7.7¢ Saxhorns (1976) .	2.25	2.75	....	1.50	.60	.40
1615	7.9¢ Drum (1976)	2.25	2.75	....	1.40	.60	.40
1615C	8.4¢ Piano (1978)	2.25	2.75	....	5.00	.60	.40
1616	9¢ Capitol (1976)	2.25	2.75	....	1.30	.60	.40
1617	10¢ Justice (1977)	2.25	2.75	....	1.25	.50	.25
1618	13¢ Liberty Bell	2.25	2.75	....	1.50	.60	.30
1618C	15¢ Fort McHenry Flag (1978)	2.25	....	....	....	.85	.25
1619	16¢ Statue of Liberty (1978)	2.25	2.75	....	2.50	.75	.60

COIL LINE PAIRS: are two connected coil stamps with a line the same color as the stamps printed between the two stamps. This line usually appears every 20 to 30 stamps on a roll depending on the issue.

1622, 1625 1623, 1623b

1975-77 REGULAR ISSUES

SCOTT NO.	DESCRIPTION	FIRST DAY COVERS SING	FIRST DAY COVERS PL. BLK.	MINT SHEET	PLATE BLOCK	UNUSED F/NH	USED
1622	13¢ Flag & Independence Hall, 11 x 10½	2.25	4.00	40.00(100)	12.00(20)	.55	.25
1622c	same, perf. 11 (1981) .	....	....	150.00(100)	90.00(20)	1.20	....
1623	13¢ Flag & Capitol from bklt pane, perf 11 x 10½ (1977)	3.00	....	....	....	.50	.50
1623a	bklt pane of 8 (one–1590, seven–1623)	30.00	....	....	....	4.00	3.75
1623b	13¢ Flag & Capitol from bklt pane, perf. 10	2.25	....	....	....	.90	.75
1623c	bklt pane of 8 (one–1590a, seven–1623b)	17.00	....	....	....	30.00	....

1975 COIL STAMP

SCOTT NO.	DESCRIPTION	FIRST DAY COVERS SING	FIRST DAY COVERS PL. BLK.	MINT SHEET	PLATE BLOCK	UNUSED F/NH	USED
1625	13¢ Flag & Independence Hall	2.25	....	....	3.75	.55	.25

1629 1630 1631

1632

1976 COMMEMORATIVES

SCOTT NO.	DESCRIPTION	FIRST DAY COVERS SING	FIRST DAY COVERS PL. BLK.	MINT SHEET	PLATE BLOCK	UNUSED F/NH	USED
1629/1703	(1629-32, 1683-85, 1690-1703) 21 varieties	....	....	....	....	12.80	3.50
1629-31	Spirit of '76, 3 varieties, attached	[illegible]	[illegible]	22.00(50)	7.25(12)	1.75	1.25
1629	13¢ Boy Drummer	2.00	....	....	....	.60	.25
1630	13¢ Older Drummer . . .	2.00	....	....	....	.60	.25
1631	13¢ Fifer	2.00	....	....	....	.60	.25
1632	13¢ Interphil	2.25	4.00	19.00(50)	2.25	.50	.25

1633 1682

1976 BICENTENNIAL STATE FLAGS
Complete Set Printed in One Sheet of 50 Stamps

1633 *Delaware*
1634 *Pennsylvania*
1635 *New Jersey*
1636 *Georgia*
1637 *Connecticut*
1638 *Massachusetts*
1639 *Maryland*
1640 *South Carolina*
1641 *New Hampshire*
1642 *Virginia*
1643 *New York*
1644 *North Carolina*
1645 *Rhode Island*
1646 *Vermont*
1647 *Kentucky*
1648 *Tennessee*
1649 *Ohio*
1650 *Louisiana*
1651 *Indiana*
1652 *Mississippi*
1653 *Illinois*
1654 *Alabama*
1655 *Maine*
1656 *Missouri*
1657 *Arkansas*
1658 *Michigan*
1659 *Florida*
1660 *Texas*
1661 *Iowa*
1662 *Wisconsin*
1663 *California*
1664 *Minnesota*
1665 *Oregon*
1666 *Kansas*
1667 *West Virginia*
1668 *Nevada*
1669 *Nebraska*
1670 *Colorado*
1671 *North Dakota*
1672 *South Dakota*
1673 *Montana*
1674 *Washington*
1675 *Idaho*
1676 *Wyoming*
1677 *Utah*
1678 *Oklahoma*
1679 *New Mexico*
1680 *Arizona*
1681 *Alaska*
1682 *Hawaii*

1976 BICENTENNIAL STATE FLAGS
Complete Set Printed in One Sheet of 50 Stamps
Continued

SCOTT NO.	DESCRIPTION	FIRST DAY COVERS SING	PL. BLK.	MINT SHEET	PLATE BLOCK	UNUSED F/NH	USED
1633-82	13¢ State Flags, 50 varieties, attached............	....	....	29.00(50)	....	29.00	....
	Set of 50 singles	95.00	....	....	....	....	18.75
	Singles of above	2.50	....	....	....	1.00	.50

1683

1684

1685

SCOTT NO.	DESCRIPTION	FIRST DAY COVERS SING	PL. BLK.	MINT SHEET	PLATE BLOCK	UNUSED F/NH	USED
1683	13¢ Telephone.......	2.25	4.00	28.00(50)	2.75	.60	.25
1684	13¢ Aviation.........	2.25	4.00	20.00(50)	8.50(10)	.75	.25
1685	13¢ Chemistry.......	2.25	4.00	25.00(50)	7.50(12)	.60	.25

1686

1687

1976 BICENTENNIAL SOUVENIR SHEETS

SCOTT NO.	DESCRIPTION	FIRST DAY COVERS SING	PL. BLK.	MINT SHEET	PLATE BLOCK	UNUSED F/NH	USED
1686-89	4 varieties, complete ..	32.50	....	....	....	30.00	27.00
1686	13¢ Cornwallis Surrender	6.00	....	....	....	5.00	4.75
1686a-e	13¢ singles, each.....	3.50	....	....	....	1.20	1.10
1687	18¢ Independence....	7.50	....	....	....	7.00	6.50
1687a-e	18¢ singles, each....	3.75	....	....	....	1.60	1.50
1688	24¢ Washington Crossing Delaware	9.50	....	....	....	9.00	8.25
1688a-e	24¢ singles, each.....	4.25	....	....	....	1.90	1.80
1689	31¢ Washington at Valley Forge..............	11.50	....	....	....	12.00	10.50
1689a-e	31¢ singles, each.....	5.25	....	....	....	2.40	2.30

1690

1691 1692 1693 1694

SCOTT NO.	DESCRIPTION	FIRST DAY COVERS SING	PL. BLK.	MINT SHEET	PLATE BLOCK	UNUSED F/NH	USED
1690	13¢ Benjamin Franklin.	2.25	4.00	21.00(50)	2.25	.50	.25
1691-94	Declaration of Independence, 4 varieties, attached ..	5.00	10.00	26.00(50)	12.00(16)	3.50	3.00
1691	13¢ Delegation members	2.25	....	....	....	1.10	.25
1692	13¢ Adams, etc.......	2.25	....	....	....	1.10	.25
1693	13¢ Jefferson, Franklin, etc.	2.25	....	....	....	1.10	.25
1694	13¢ Hancock, Thomson, etc.	2.25	....	....	....	1.10	.25

1695

1696

1697

1698

SCOTT NO.	DESCRIPTION	FIRST DAY COVERS SING	PL. BLK.	MINT SHEET	PLATE BLOCK	UNUSED F/NH	USED
1695-98	Olympic Games, 4 varieties, attached ..	4.00	6.00	24.00(50)	7.50(12)	2.40	1.95
1695	13¢ Diving	2.25	....	....	....	.75	.25
1696	13¢ Skiing	2.25	....	....	....	.75	.25
1697	13¢ Running	2.25	....	....	....	.75	.25
1698	13¢ Skating	2.25	....	....	....	.75	.25

1699

1700

SCOTT NO.	DESCRIPTION	FIRST DAY COVERS SING	PL. BLK.	MINT SHEET	PLATE BLOCK	UNUSED F/NH	USED
1699	13¢ Clara Maass.....	2.25	4.00	17.00(40)	7.00(12)	.60	.25
1700	13¢ Adolph S. Ochs...	2.25	4.00	16.00(32)	2.50	.60	.25

1701

1702, 1703

SCOTT NO.	DESCRIPTION	FIRST DAY COVERS SING	PL. BLK.	MINT SHEET	PLATE BLOCK	UNUSED F/NH	USED
1701	13¢ Nativity	2.25	....	20.00(50)	6.50(12)	.55	.25
1702	13¢ "Winter Pastime" (Andreotti)	2.25	....	20.00(50)	5.50(10)	.55	.25
1703	13¢ "Winter Pastime" (Gravure Int.)........	2.25	....	22.00(50)	13.00(20)	.55	.25

1704

1705

1977 COMMEMORATIVES

SCOTT NO.	DESCRIPTION	FIRST DAY COVERS SING	PL. BLK.	MINT SHEET	PLATE BLOCK	UNUSED F/NH	USED
1704-30	**27 varieties, complete**	....	....	....	....	**13.00**	**5.00**
1704	13¢ Princeton	2.25	4.00	16.00(40)	5.50(10)	.60	.25
1705	13¢ Sound Recording .	2.25	4.00	20.00(50)	2.25	.60	.25

1708 1709

1706 1707

SCOTT NO.	DESCRIPTION	FIRST DAY COVERS SING	PL. BLK.	MINT SHEET	PLATE BLOCK	UNUSED F/NH	USED
1706-09	Pueblo Art, 4 varieties, attached ..	4.00	....	19.00(40)	6.50(10)	3.00	2.50
1706	13¢ Zia.	2.25	....	....	....	.75	.25
1707	13¢ San Ildefonso	2.25	....	....	....	.75	.25
1708	13¢ Hopi	2.25	....	....	....	.75	.25
1709	13¢ Acoma	2.25				.75	.25

1710

1711

SCOTT NO.	DESCRIPTION	FIRST DAY COVERS SING	PL. BLK.	MINT SHEET	PLATE BLOCK	UNUSED F/NH	USED
1710	13¢ Transatlantic Flight	3.00	5.00	22.00(50)	7.50(12)	.50	.25
1711	13¢ Colorado Statehood	2.25	4.00	22.00(50)	7.50(12)	.50	.25

1712 1713

Mint Sheets: From 1935 to date, we list prices for standard size Mint Sheets Fine, Never Hinged condition. The number of stamps in each sheet is noted in ( ).

1714

1715

1716

SCOTT NO.	DESCRIPTION	FIRST DAY COVERS SING	PL. BLK.	MINT SHEET	PLATE BLOCK	UNUSED F/NH	USED
1712-15	Butterflies, 4 varieties, attached ..	4.00	6.00	22.00(50)	7.50(12)	3.00	2.50
1712	13¢ Swallowtail	2.25	....	....	....	.60	.25
1713	13¢ Checkerspot	2.25	....	....	....	.60	.25
1714	13¢ Dogface	2.25	....	....	....	.60	.25
1715	13¢ Orange-Tip	2.25	....	....	....	.60	.25
1716	13¢ Lafayette........	2.25	6.00	17.00(40)	2.25	.50	.25

1717 1718

1719 1720

SCOTT NO.	DESCRIPTION	FIRST DAY COVERS SING	PL. BLK.	MINT SHEET	PLATE BLOCK	UNUSED F/NH	USED
1717-20	Skilled Hands, 4 varieties, attached ..	4.00	....	22.00(50)	7.25(12)	2.50	2.00
1717	13¢ Seamstress	2.25				[illegible]	[illegible]
1718	13¢ Blacksmith	2.25		....	....	.60	.25
1719	13¢ Wheelwright	2.25			....	.60	.25
1720	[illegible]	[illegible]	....			[illegible]	[illegible]

1721

1722

1723

1724

SCOTT NO.	DESCRIPTION	FIRST DAY COVERS SING	PL. BLK.	MINT SHEET	PLATE BLOCK	UNUSED F/NH	USED
1721	13¢ Peace Bridge	2.25	4.00	21.00(50)	3.00	.50	.25
1722	13¢ Herkimer at Oriskany	2.25	4.00	17.50(40)	5.25(10)	.50	.25
1723-24	Energy, 2 varieties, attached ..	2.50	....	18.00(40)	7.25(12)	1.10	.85
1723	13¢ Conservation	2.25	....	....	....	.60	.25
1724	13¢ Development	2.25	....	....	....	.60	.25

1725 1726

1727 1728

1729 1730

SCOTT NO.	DESCRIPTION	FIRST DAY COVERS SING	FIRST DAY COVERS PL. BLK.	MINT SHEET	PLATE BLOCK	UNUSED F/NH	USED
1725	13¢ Alta California	2.25	4.00	20.00(50)	2.25	.45	.25
1726	13¢ Articles of Confederation	2.25	4.00	20.00(50)	2.25	.45	.25
1727	13¢ Talking Pictures . .	2.25	4.00	20.00(50)	2.25	.45	.25
1728	13¢ Surrender at Saratoga	2.25	....	17.50(40)	5.25(10)	.45	.25
1729	13¢ Washington, Christmas	2.50	....	48.00(100)	13.00(20)	.60	.25
1730	13¢ Rural Mailbox, Christmas	2.50	....	39.00(100)	5.25(10)	.50	.25

1731 1732 1733

1978 COMMEMORATIVES

SCOTT NO.	DESCRIPTION	FIRST DAY COVERS SING	FIRST DAY COVERS PL. BLK.	MINT SHEET	PLATE BLOCK	UNUSED F/NH	USED
1731/69	**(1731-33, 1744-56, 1758-69) 28 varieties .**	....	....	....	....	**19.50**	**7.00**
1731	13¢ Carl Sandburg . . .	2.25	4.00	22.00(50)	2.50	.50	.25
1732-33	Captain Cook, 2 varieties, attached . .	2.00	....	24.00(50)	12.00(20)	1.50	1.20
1732	13¢ Captain Cook (Alaska)	2.25	4.00	....	2.50	.55	.25
1733	13¢ "Resolution" (Hawaii)	2.25	4.00	....	2.50	.55	.25

NOTE: The Plate Block set includes #1732 & 1733 Plate Blocks of four.

1734 1735, 1736, 1743 1737

1978-80 DEFINITIVES

SCOTT NO.	DESCRIPTION	FIRST DAY COVERS SING	FIRST DAY COVERS PL. BLK.	MINT SHEET	PLATE BLOCK	UNUSED F/NH	USED
1734	13¢ Indian Head Penny	2.25	4.00	58.00(150)	2.50	.60	.25
1735	(15¢) "A" Defintive (Gravure)	2.25	4.00	45.00(100)	2.50	.60	.25
1736	same (Intaglio), from bklt pane	2.25	....	....	....	.60	.25
1736a	15¢ "A" bklt pane of 8 .	3.50	....	....	....	4.50	....
1737	15¢ Roses	2.25	....	....	....	.60	.25
1737a	same, bklt pane of 8 . .	4.00	....	....	....	4.50	....

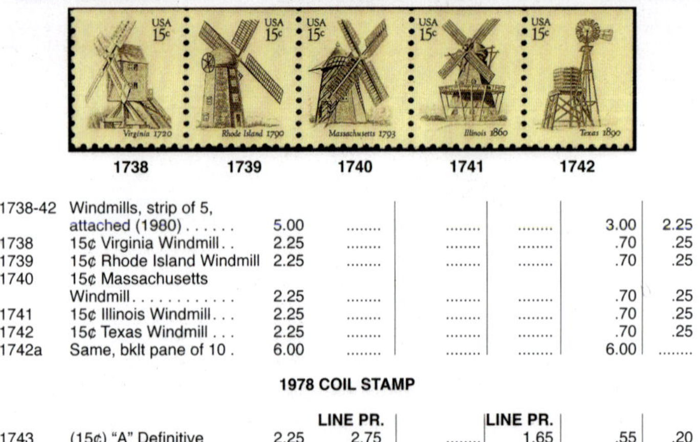

1738 1739 1740 1741 1742

SCOTT NO.	DESCRIPTION	FIRST DAY COVERS SING	FIRST DAY COVERS PL. BLK.	MINT SHEET	PLATE BLOCK	UNUSED F/NH	USED
1738-42	Windmills, strip of 5, attached (1980)	5.00	....	....	....	3.00	2.25
1738	15¢ Virginia Windmill . .	2.25	....	....	....	.70	.25
1739	15¢ Rhode Island Windmill	2.25	....	....	....	.70	.25
1740	15¢ Massachusetts Windmill	2.25	....	....	....	.70	.25
1741	15¢ Illinois Windmill . . .	2.25	....	....	....	.70	.25
1742	15¢ Texas Windmill . . .	2.25	....	....	....	.70	.25
1742a	Same, bklt pane of 10 .	6.00	....	....	....	6.00	....

1978 COIL STAMP

SCOTT NO.	DESCRIPTION	FIRST DAY COVERS SING	LINE PR.	MINT SHEET	LINE PR.	UNUSED F/NH	USED
1743	(15¢) "A" Definitive	2.25	2.75	....	1.65	.55	.20

1745

1744

1746

1747

1748

SCOTT NO.	DESCRIPTION	FIRST DAY COVERS SING	FIRST DAY COVERS PL. BLK.	MINT SHEET	PLATE BLOCK	UNUSED F/NH	USED
1744	13¢ Harriet Tubman. . .	5.00	7.00	29.00(50)	9.50(12)	.65	.25
1745-48	Quilts, 4 varieties, attached	3.50	....	30.00(48)	12.00(12)	3.00	2.00
1745	13¢ Flowers	2.25	....	....	....	.75	.25
1746	13¢ Stars	2.25	....	....	....	.75	.25
1747	13¢ Stripes	2.25	....	....	....	.75	.25
1748	13¢ Plaid	2.25	....	....	....	.75	.25

1750

1749 1752

1751

SCOTT NO.	DESCRIPTION	FIRST DAY COVERS SING	FIRST DAY COVERS PL. BLK.	MINT SHEET	PLATE BLOCK	UNUSED F/NH	USED
1749-52	American Dance, 4 varieties, attached . .	5.00	....	22.00(48)	7.75(12)	3.00	2.00
1749	13¢ Ballet.	2.25	....	....	....	.75	.25
1750	13¢ Theater	2.25	....	....	....	.75	.25
1751	13¢ Folk.	2.25	....	....	....	.75	.25
1752	13¢ Modern	2.25	....	....	....	.75	.25

1753

1754

1755

1756

SCOTT NO.	DESCRIPTION	FIRST DAY COVERS SING	FIRST DAY COVERS PL. BLK.	MINT SHEET	PLATE BLOCK	UNUSED F/NH	USED
1753	13¢ French Alliance . . .	2.25	4.00	16.00(40)	2.25	.50	.25
1754	13¢ Dr. Papanicolaou .	2.25	4.00	20.00(50)	2.25	.60	.25
1755	13¢ Jimmie Rodgers . .	2.25	4.00	23.00(50)	8.00(12)	.75	.25
1756	15¢ George M. Cohan .	2.25	4.00	23.00(50)	8.00(12)	.75	.25

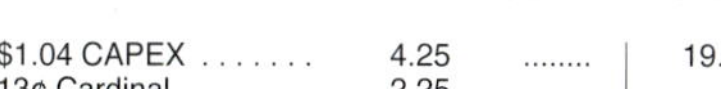

1757

1978 CAPEX SOUVENIR SHEET

SCOTT NO.	DESCRIPTION	FIRST DAY COVERS SING	FIRST DAY COVERS PL. BLK.	MINT SHEET	PLATE BLOCK	UNUSED F/NH	USED
1757	$1.04 CAPEX	4.25	....	19.00(6)	4.00	3.50	3.00
1757a	13¢ Cardinal	2.25	....	....	....	.45	.40
1757b	13¢ Mallard	2.25	....	....	....	.45	.40
1757c	13¢ Canada Goose . . .	2.25	....	....	....	.45	.40
1757d	13¢ Blue Jay	2.25	....	....	....	.45	.40
1757e	13¢ Moose.	2.25	....	....	....	.45	.40
1757f	13¢ Chipmunk	2.25	....	....	....	.45	.40
1757g	13¢ Red Fox	2.25	....	....	....	.45	.40
1757h	13¢ Raccoon	2.25	....	....	....	.45	.40

1758

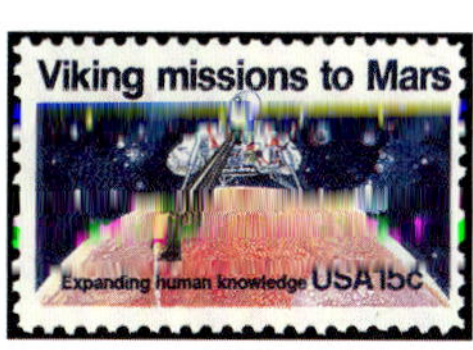

1759

SCOTT NO.	DESCRIPTION	FIRST DAY COVERS SING	FIRST DAY COVERS PL. BLK.	MINT SHEET	PLATE BLOCK	UNUSED F/NH	USED
1758	15¢ Photography	2.25	4.00	17.00(40)	7.25(12)	.60	.25
1759	15¢ Viking Mission. . . .	2.25	4.00	23.00(50)	3.00	.60	.25

1760

1761

1762

1763

SCOTT NO.	DESCRIPTION	FIRST DAY COVERS SING	FIRST DAY COVERS PL. BLK.	MINT SHEET	PLATE BLOCK	UNUSED F/NH	USED
1760-63	American Owls, 4 varieties, attached.	5.00	6.00	30.00(50)	3.50	3.00	2.00
1760	15¢ Great Gray	2.25	....	....	....	.70	.25
1761	15¢ Saw-Whet.	2.25	....	....	....	.70	.25
1762	15¢ Barred Owl	2.25	....	....	....	.70	.25
1763	15¢ Great Horned	2.25	....	....	....	.70	.25

1764 1765

1766 1767

SCOTT NO.	DESCRIPTION	FIRST DAY COVERS SING	FIRST DAY COVERS PL. BLK.	MINT SHEET	PLATE BLOCK	UNUSED F/NH	USED
1764-67	Trees, 4 varieties, attached.	5.00	....	28.00(40)	12.00(12)	3.25	2.00
1764	15¢ Giant Sequoia. . . .	2.25	....	....	....	.70	.25
1765	15¢ Pine	2.25	....	....	....	.70	.25
1766	15¢ Oak.	2.25	....	....	....	.70	.25
1767	15¢ Birch	2.25	....	....	....	.70	.25

1768

1769

SCOTT NO.	DESCRIPTION	FIRST DAY COVERS SING	FIRST DAY COVERS PL. BLK.	MINT SHEET	PLATE BLOCK	UNUSED F/NH	USED
1768	15¢ Madonna, Christmas	2.25	4.00	44.00(100)	7.25(12)	.60	.25
1769	15¢ Hobby Horse, Christmas	2.25	4.00	44.00(100)	8.25(12)	.60	.25

1770

1771

1979 COMMEMORATIVES

SCOTT NO.	DESCRIPTION	FIRST DAY COVERS SING	FIRST DAY COVERS PL. BLK.	MINT SHEET	PLATE BLOCK	UNUSED F/NH	USED
1770/1802	**(1770-94, 1799-1802) 29 varieties, complete**	....	....	....	....	**17.50**	**6.00**
1770	15¢ Robert F. Kennedy	2.25	4.00	25.00(48)	2.75	.65	.25
1771	15¢ Martin L. King, Jr. .	3.00	5.00	25.00(50)	8.50(12)	.75	.25

1772

1773

1774

SCOTT NO.	DESCRIPTION	FIRST DAY COVERS SING	FIRST DAY COVERS PL. BLK.	MINT SHEET	PLATE BLOCK	UNUSED F/NH	USED
1772	15¢ International Year of the Child	2.25	4.00	23.50(50)	2.75	.65	.25
1773	15¢ John Steinbeck. . .	2.25	4.00	25.00(50)	2.75	.65	.25
1774	15¢ Albert Einstein. . . .	3.00	5.00	25.00(50)	3.25	.75	.25

U.S. BICENTENNIAL: The USPS issued stamps commemorating the 200th anniversary of the struggle for independence from 1775 through 1783. These include numbers: 1432, 1476-83, 1543-46, 1559-68, 1629-31, 1633-82, 1686-89, 1691-94, 1704, 1716-20, 1722, 1726, 1728-29, 1753, 1789, 1826, 1937-38, 1941, 2052 and C98.

1775 1776

1777 1778

1779 1780

1781 1782

SCOTT NO.	DESCRIPTION	FIRST DAY COVERS SING	FIRST DAY COVERS PL. BLK.	MINT SHEET	PLATE BLOCK	UNUSED F/NH	USED
1775-78	Pennsylvania Toleware, 4 varieties, attached . .	5.00	....	20.00(40)	6.75(10)	2.50	2.00
1775	15¢ Coffee Pot.	2.25	....	....	....	.75	.25
1776	15¢ Tea Caddy	2.25	....	....	....	.75	.25
1777	15¢ Sugar Bowl	2.25	....	....	....	.75	.25
1778	15¢ Coffee Pot.	2.25	....	....	....	.75	.25
1779-82	Architecture, 4 varieties, attached.	5.00	6.00	27.00(48)	4.00	3.50	2.75
1779	15¢ Virginia Rotunda . .	2.25	....	....	....	1.00	.25
1780	15¢ Baltimore Cathedral	2.25	....	....	....	1.00	.25
1781	15¢ Boston State House	2.25	....	....	....	1.00	.25
1782	15¢ Philadelphia Exchange	2.25	....	....	....	1.00	.25

1783 1784 1785 1786

SCOTT NO.	DESCRIPTION	FIRST DAY COVERS SING	FIRST DAY COVERS PL. BLK.	MINT SHEET	PLATE BLOCK	UNUSED F/NH	USED
1783-86	Endangered Flora, 4 varieties, attached . .	5.00	....	25.00(50)	8.25(12)	2.75	2.25
1783	15¢ Trillium	2.25	....	....	....	.75	.25
1784	15¢ Broadbean	2.25	....	....	....	.75	.25
1785	15¢ Wallflower	2.25	....	....	....	.75	.25
1786	15¢ Primrose	2.25	....	....	....	.75	.25

1787 1788 1789, 1789a 1790

SCOTT NO.	DESCRIPTION	FIRST DAY COVERS SING	FIRST DAY COVERS PL. BLK.	MINT SHEET	PLATE BLOCK	UNUSED F/NH	USED
1787	15¢ Guide Dog	2.25	....	24.00(50)	12.00(20)	.70	.25
1788	15¢ Special Olympics .	2.25	....	24.00(50)	6.00(10)	.65	.25
1789	15¢ John Paul Jones perf. 11 x 12.	2.25	....	24.00(50)	6.00(10)	.65	.25
1789a	same, perf. 11	2.25	....	35.00(50)	9.00(10)	1.00	.30

NOTE: #1789a may be included in year date sets and special offers and not 1789.

SCOTT NO.	DESCRIPTION	FIRST DAY COVERS SING	FIRST DAY COVERS PL. BLK.	MINT SHEET	PLATE BLOCK	UNUSED F/NH	USED
1790	10¢ Summer Olympics, Javelin Thrower	2.25	4.00	15.00(50)	5.25(12)	.40	.25

1791 1792

1793 1794

SCOTT NO.	DESCRIPTION	FIRST DAY COVERS SING	FIRST DAY COVERS PL. BLK.	MINT SHEET	PLATE BLOCK	UNUSED F/NH	USED
1791-94	Summer Olympics, 4 varieties, attached . .	5.00	....	24.00(50)	8.25(12)	2.50	2.00
1791	15¢ Runners	2.25	....	....	....	.70	.25
1792	15¢ Swimmers.	2.25	....	....	....	.70	.25
1793	15¢ Rowers	2.25	....	....	....	.70	.25
1794	15¢ Equestrian	2.25	....	....	....	.70	.25

1795 1796

1797 1798

1980

SCOTT NO.	DESCRIPTION	FIRST DAY COVERS SING	FIRST DAY COVERS PL. BLK.	MINT SHEET	PLATE BLOCK	UNUSED F/NH	USED
1795-98	Winter Olympics, 4 varieties, attached . .	5.00	....	25.00(50)	8.25(12)	2.75	2.00
1795	15¢ Skater	2.25	....	....	....	.70	.25
1796	15¢ Downhill Skier. . . .	2.25	....	....	....	.70	.25
1797	15¢ Ski Jumper	2.25	....	....	....	.70	.25
1798	15¢ Hockey	2.25	....	....	....	.70	.25
1795a-98a	same, perf. 11, attached	....	....	45.00(50)	15.00(12)	4.50	3.50
1795a	15¢ Skater	....	....	....	....	1.20	.75
1796a	15¢ Downhill Skier. . . .	....	....	....	....	1.20	.75
1797a	15¢ Ski Jumper	....	....	....	....	1.20	.75
1798a	15¢ Hockey	....	....	....	....	1.20	.75

1799

1800

1979 COMMEMORATIVES

SCOTT NO.	DESCRIPTION	FIRST DAY COVERS SING	FIRST DAY COVERS PL. BLK.	MINT SHEET	PLATE BLOCK	UNUSED F/NH	USED
1799	15¢ Christmas–Madonna	2.25	....	44.00(100)	7.25(12)	.60	.25
1800	15¢ Christmas–Santa Claus	2.25	....	49.00(100)	8.00(12)	.70	.25

1801

1802

SCOTT NO.	DESCRIPTION	FIRST DAY COVERS SING	FIRST DAY COVERS PL. BLK.	MINT SHEET	PLATE BLOCK	UNUSED F/NH	USED
1801	15¢ Will Rogers	3.00	....	25.00(50)	8.00(12)	.70	.25
1802	15¢ Vietnam Veterans	3.00	5.25	27.00(50)	8.00(10)	.70	.25

1803

1804

1980 COMMEMORATIVES

SCOTT NO.	DESCRIPTION	FIRST DAY COVERS SING	FIRST DAY COVERS PL. BLK.	MINT SHEET	PLATE BLOCK	UNUSED F/NH	USED
1795/1843	**(1795-98, 1803-10, 1821-43) 35 varieties, complete**	....	....	....	....	**23.00**	**7.50**
1803	15¢ W.C. Fields	2.25	4.00	24.00(50)	7.25(12)	.60	.25
1804	15¢ Benjamin Banneker	2.25	4.00	27.00(50)	8.75(12)	.70	.25

1805

1806, 1808, 1810

1807

1809

SCOTT NO.	DESCRIPTION	FIRST DAY COVERS SING	FIRST DAY COVERS PL. BLK.	MINT SHEET	PLATE BLOCK	UNUSED F/NH	USED
1805-10	6 varieties, attached	4.50	....	32.00(60)	24.00(36)	4.25	2.75
1805-06	2 varieties, attached	2.50	....	....	....	....	....
1807-08	2 varieties, attached	2.50	....	....	....	....	....
1809-10	2 varieties, attached	2.50	....	....	....	....	....
1805	15¢ "Letters Preserve Memories"	2.25	....	....	....	.75	.35
1806	15¢ claret & multicolor	2.25	....	....	....	.75	.35
1807	15¢ "Letters Lift Spirits"	2.25	....	....	....	.75	.35
1808	15¢ green & multicolor	2.25	....	....	....	.75	.35
1809	15¢ "Letters Shape Opinions"	2.25	....	....	....	.75	.35
1810	15¢ red, white & blue	2.25	....	....	....	.75	.35

1813

1818, 1819, 1820

1980-81 Coil Stamps, Perf. 10 Vertically

SCOTT NO.	DESCRIPTION	FIRST DAY COVERS SING	FIRST DAY COVERS PL. BLK.	MINT SHEET	PLATE BLOCK	UNUSED F/NH	USED
			LINE PR.		LINE PR.		
1811	1¢ Inkwell & Quill	2.25	2.75	....	.60	.20	.25
1813	3.5¢ Two Violins	2.25	2.75	....	1.40	.30	.25
1816	12¢ Torch (1981)	2.25	2.75	....	2.25	.50	.40
1818	(18¢) "B" definitive	2.50	3.50	55.00(100)	3.25	.70	.25
1819	(18¢) "B" definitive, from bklt pane	2.25	....	....	....	.70	.25
1819a	(18¢) "B" bklt pane of 8	4.00	....	....	....	5.25	....

1981 Coil Stamp Perf. Vertically

SCOTT NO.	DESCRIPTION	FIRST DAY COVERS SING	FIRST DAY COVERS PL. BLK.	MINT SHEET	PLATE BLOCK	UNUSED F/NH	USED
1820	(18¢) "B" definitive	2.25	2.75	....	2.00	.75	.25

1821

1822

1823

1824

1825

1826

SCOTT NO.	DESCRIPTION	FIRST DAY COVERS SING	FIRST DAY COVERS PL. BLK.	MINT SHEET	PLATE BLOCK	UNUSED F/NH	USED
1821	15¢ Frances Perkins	2.25	4.00	23.00(50)	2.50	.55	.25
1822	15¢ Dolley Madison	2.25	4.00	72.00(150)	2.75	.60	.25
1823	15¢ Emily Bissell	2.25	4.00	23.00(50)	2.50	.60	.25
1824	15¢ Helen Keller & Anne Sullivan	2.25	4.00	27.00(50)	3.00	.60	.25
1825	15¢ Veterans Administration	2.25	4.00	25.00(50)	2.50	.60	.25
1826	15¢ General Bernardo. de Galvez	2.25	4.00	25.00(50)	3.50	.60	.25

1827

1828

1829

1830

SCOTT NO.	DESCRIPTION	FIRST DAY COVERS SING	FIRST DAY COVERS PL. BLK.	MINT SHEET	PLATE BLOCK	UNUSED F/NH	USED
1827-30	Coral Reefs, 4 varieties, attached	5.00	....	40.00(50)	13.00(12)	4.00	2.75
1827	15¢ Brain Coral, Virgin Is.	2.25	....	....	....	1.00	.30
1828	15¢ Elkhorn Coral, Florida	2.25	....	....	....	1.00	.30
1829	15¢ Chalice Coral, American Samoa	2.25	....	....	....	1.00	.30
1830	15¢ Finger Coral, Hawaii	2.25	....	....	....	1.00	.30

1831

Edith Wharton — USA 15c
1832

Learning never ends — USA 15c
1833

SCOTT NO.	DESCRIPTION	FIRST DAY COVERS SING	FIRST DAY COVERS PL. BLK.	MINT SHEET	PLATE BLOCK	UNUSED F/NH	USED
1831	15¢ Organized Labor	2.25	4.00	29.00(50)	10.00(12)	.65	.25
1832	15¢ Edith Wharton	2.25	4.00	25.00(50)	2.75	.65	.25
1833	15¢ Education	2.25	4.00	25.00(50)	3.75(6)	.65	.25

SCOTT NO.	DESCRIPTION	FIRST DAY COVERS SING	FIRST DAY COVERS PL. BLK.	MINT SHEET	PLATE BLOCK	UNUSED F/NH	USED

1834 1835

1836 1837

SCOTT NO.	DESCRIPTION	FIRST DAY COVERS SING	FIRST DAY COVERS PL. BLK.	MINT SHEET	PLATE BLOCK	UNUSED F/NH	USED
1834-37	American Folk Art, 4 varieties, attached . .	5.00	....	24.00(40)	9.00(10)	3.25	2.00
1834	15¢ Bella Bella Tribe . .	2.25	....	....	....	1.00	.25
1835	15¢ Chilkat Tlingit Tribe	2.25	....	....	....	1.00	.25
1836	15¢ Tlingit Tribe.	2.25	....	....	....	1.00	.25
1837	15¢ Bella Coola Tribe .	2.25	....	....	....	1.00	.25

1838 1839

1840 1841

SCOTT NO.	DESCRIPTION	FIRST DAY COVERS SING	FIRST DAY COVERS PL. BLK.	MINT SHEET	PLATE BLOCK	UNUSED F/NH	USED
1838-41	American Architecture, 4 varieties, attached . .	4.00	5.00	25.00(40)	3.50	3.00	2.00
1838	15¢ Smithsonian	2.25	....	....	....	1.00	.25
1839	15¢ Trinity Church	2.25	....	....	....	1.00	.25
1840	15¢ Penn Academy . . .	2.25	....	....	....	1.00	.25
1841	15¢ Lyndhurst	2.25	....	....	....	1.00	.25

1842

1843

SCOTT NO.	DESCRIPTION	FIRST DAY COVERS SING	FIRST DAY COVERS PL. BLK.	MINT SHEET	PLATE BLOCK	UNUSED F/NH	USED
1842	15¢ Madonna.	2.25	4.00	22.50(50)	7.00(12)	.55	.25
1843	15¢ Christmas Wreath & Toy.	2.25	4.00	23.50(50)	12.00(20)	.55	.25

SE-TENANTS: Beginning with the 1964 Christmas issue (#1254-57), the United States has issued numerous Se-Tenant stamps covering a wide variety of subjects. Se-Tenants are issues where two or more different stamp designs are produced on the same sheet in pair, strip or block form. Mint stamps are usually collected in attached blocks, etc.; used are generally saved as single stamps.

SCOTT NO.	DESCRIPTION	FIRST DAY COVERS SING	FIRST DAY COVERS PL. BLK.	MINT SHEET	PLATE BLOCK	UNUSED F/NH	USED

1844 1845 1846 1847

1848 1849 1850 1851

1852 1853 1854 1855

1856 1857 1858 1859

1860 1861 1862 1863

1864 1865 1866 1867

1868

1869

1980-85 GREAT AMERICANS

SCOTT NO.	DESCRIPTION	FIRST DAY COVERS SING	FIRST DAY COVERS PL. BLK.	MINT SHEET	PLATE BLOCK	UNUSED F/NH	USED
1844-69	**1¢-50¢, 26 varieties, complete. . . . .**	....	....	....	....	**17.50**	**6.40**
1844	1¢ Dorothea Dix, 11.2, (1983)	2.25	4.00	13.00(100)	5.00(20)	.25	.25
1844c	1¢ Dorothea Dix, 10.9, small block tagging . . .	....	....	16.00(100)	5.00(20)	.25	.25
1844d	1¢ Dorothea Dix, 10.95 large block tagging . . .	....	....	17.00(100)	7.00(20)	.85	.45
1845	2¢ Igor Stravinsky (1982)	2.25	4.00	13.00(100)	1.25	.25	.25
1846	3¢ Henry Clay (1983) .	2.25	4.00	21.00(100)	2.25	.25	.25
1847	4¢ Carl Schurz (1983) .	2.25	4.00	22.00(100)	1.35	.25	.25
1848	5¢ Pearl Buck (1983). .	2.25	4.00	38.00(100)	3.00	.70	.25
1849	6¢ Walter Lippmann (1985)	2.25	4.00	23.00(100)	6.25(20)	.40	.25
1850	7¢ Abraham Baldwin (1985)	2.25	4.00	33.00(100)	7.75(20)	.60	.25
1851	8¢ Henry Knox (1985) .	2.25	4.00	29.00(100)	1.75	.30	.25
1852	9¢ Sylvanus Thayer (1985)	2.25	4.00	33.00(100)	8.00(20)	.40	.25
1853	10¢ Richard Russell (1984)	2.25	4.00	53.00(100)	15.00(20)	.60	.25
1854	11¢ Partridge (1985) . .	2.25	4.00	64.00(100)	4.00	.65	.25
1855	13¢ Crazy Horse (1982)	2.25	4.00	49.00(100)	3.00	.50	.40
1856	14¢ Sinclair Lewis (1985)	2.25	4.00	66.00(100)	17.00(20)	.80	.25
1857	17¢ Rachel Carson (1981)	2.25	4.00	53.00(100)	3.25	.60	.25
1858	18¢ George Mason (1981)	2.25	4.00	58.00(100)	3.75	.60	.25
1859	19¢ Sequoyah	2.25	4.00	65.00(100)	3.75	.75	.40
1860	20¢ Ralph Bunche (1982)	2.25	4.00	79.00(100)	4.00	.80	.25
1861	20¢ T. H. Gallaudet (1983)	2.25	4.00	80.00(100)	4.75	1.00	.25

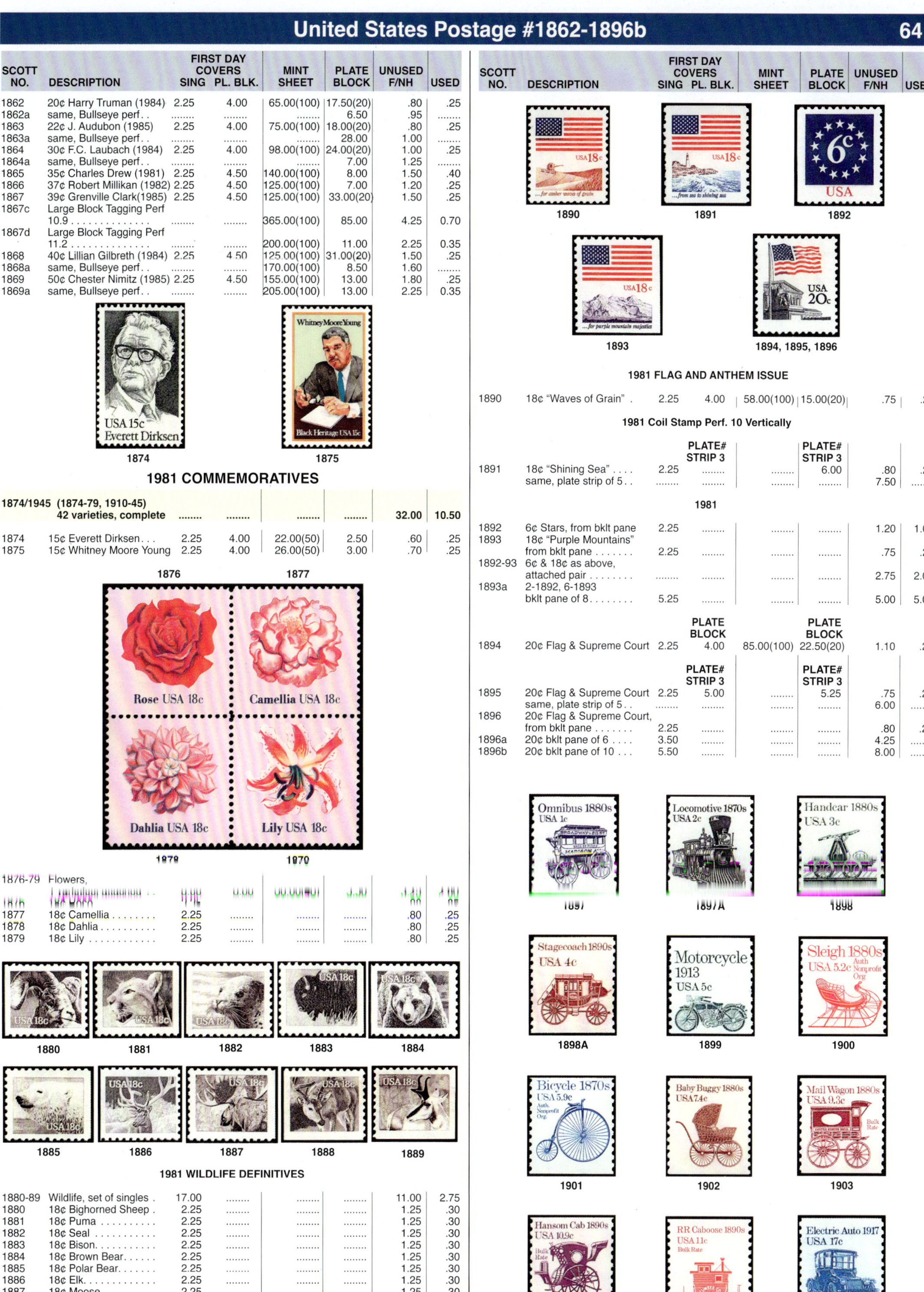

SCOTT NO.	DESCRIPTION	FIRST DAY COVERS SING	FIRST DAY COVERS PL. BLK.	MINT SHEET	PLATE BLOCK	UNUSED F/NH	USED
1862	20¢ Harry Truman (1984)	2.25	4.00	65.00(100)	17.50(20)	.80	.25
1862a	same, Bullseye perf. .	....	....	....	6.50	.95	....
1863	22¢ J. Audubon (1985)	2.25	4.00	75.00(100)	18.00(20)	.80	.25
1863a	same, Bullseye perf. .	....	....	....	28.00	1.00	....
1864	30¢ F.C. Laubach (1984)	2.25	4.00	98.00(100)	24.00(20)	1.00	.25
1864a	same, Bullseye perf. .	....	....	....	7.00	1.25	....
1865	35¢ Charles Drew (1981)	2.25	4.50	140.00(100)	8.00	1.50	.40
1866	37¢ Robert Millikan (1982)	2.25	4.50	125.00(100)	7.00	1.20	.25
1867	39¢ Grenville Clark(1985)	2.25	4.50	125.00(100)	33.00(20)	1.50	.25
1867c	Large Block Tagging Perf 10.9	....	....	365.00(100)	85.00	4.25	0.70
1867d	Large Block Tagging Perf 11.2	....	....	200.00(100)	11.00	2.25	0.35
1868	40¢ Lillian Gilbreth (1984)	2.25	4.50	125.00(100)	31.00(20)	1.50	.25
1868a	same, Bullseye perf. .	....	....	170.00(100)	8.50	1.60	....
1869	50¢ Chester Nimitz (1985)	2.25	4.50	155.00(100)	13.00	1.80	.25
1869a	same, Bullseye perf. .	....	....	205.00(100)	13.00	2.25	0.35

1874 1875

1981 COMMEMORATIVES

SCOTT NO.	DESCRIPTION	FIRST DAY COVERS SING	FIRST DAY COVERS PL. BLK.	MINT SHEET	PLATE BLOCK	UNUSED F/NH	USED
1874/1945	(1874-79, 1910-45) 42 varieties, complete	....	....	....	....	32.00	10.50
1874	15¢ Everett Dirksen. . .	2.25	4.00	22.00(50)	2.50	.60	.25
1875	15¢ Whitney Moore Young	2.25	4.00	26.00(50)	3.00	.70	.25

1876 1877

1878 1879

SCOTT NO.	DESCRIPTION	FIRST DAY COVERS SING	FIRST DAY COVERS PL. BLK.	MINT SHEET	PLATE BLOCK	UNUSED F/NH	USED
1876-79	Flowers, [illegible]	[illegible]	[illegible]	[illegible]	[illegible]	[illegible]	[illegible]
1876	[illegible]	[illegible]				[illegible]	[illegible]
1877	18¢ Camellia	2.25	....	....	....	.80	.25
1878	18¢ Dahlia	2.25	....	....	....	.80	.25
1879	18¢ Lily	2.25	....	....	....	.80	.25

1880 1881 1882 1883 1884

1885 1886 1887 1888 1889

1981 WILDLIFE DEFINITIVES

SCOTT NO.	DESCRIPTION	FIRST DAY COVERS SING	FIRST DAY COVERS PL. BLK.	MINT SHEET	PLATE BLOCK	UNUSED F/NH	USED
1880-89	Wildlife, set of singles .	17.00	....	....	....	11.00	2.75
1880	18¢ Bighorned Sheep .	2.25	....	....	....	1.25	.30
1881	18¢ Puma	2.25	....	....	....	1.25	.30
1882	18¢ Seal	2.25	....	....	....	1.25	.30
1883	18¢ Bison.	2.25	....	....	....	1.25	.30
1884	18¢ Brown Bear.	2.25	....	....	....	1.25	.30
1885	18¢ Polar Bear.	2.25	....	....	....	1.25	.30
1886	18¢ Elk.	2.25	....	....	....	1.25	.30
1887	18¢ Moose.	2.25	....	....	....	1.25	.30
1888	18¢ White-tailed Deer .	2.25	....	....	....	1.25	.30
1889	18¢ Pronghorned Antelope	2.25	....	....	....	1.25	.30
1889a	Wildlife, bklt pane of 10	6.50	....	....	....	12.00	....

1890 1891 1892

1893 1894, 1895, 1896

1981 FLAG AND ANTHEM ISSUE

SCOTT NO.	DESCRIPTION	FIRST DAY COVERS SING	FIRST DAY COVERS PL. BLK.	MINT SHEET	PLATE BLOCK	UNUSED F/NH	USED
1890	18¢ "Waves of Grain" .	2.25	4.00	58.00(100)	15.00(20)	.75	.25
	1981 Coil Stamp Perf. 10 Vertically						
			PLATE# STRIP 3		PLATE# STRIP 3		
1891	18¢ "Shining Sea"	2.25	....	....	6.00	.80	.25
	same, plate strip of 5 . .	....	....	....	....	7.50	....
	1981						
1892	6¢ Stars, from bklt pane	2.25	....	....	....	1.20	1.00
1893	18¢ "Purple Mountains" from bklt pane	2.25	....	....	....	.75	.25
1892-93	6¢ & 18¢ as above, attached pair	....	....	....	....	2.75	2.00
1893a	2-1892, 6-1893 bklt pane of 8.	5.25	....	....	....	5.00	5.00
			PLATE BLOCK		PLATE BLOCK		
1894	20¢ Flag & Supreme Court	2.25	4.00	85.00(100)	22.50(20)	1.10	.25
			PLATE# STRIP 3		PLATE# STRIP 3		
1895	20¢ Flag & Supreme Court	2.25	5.00	....	5.25	.75	.25
	same, plate strip of 5 . .	....	....	....	....	6.00	....
1896	20¢ Flag & Supreme Court, from bklt pane	2.25	....	....	....	.80	.25
1896a	20¢ bklt pane of 6	3.50	....	....	....	4.25	....
1896b	20¢ bklt pane of 10 . . .	5.50	....	....	....	8.00	....

1897 1897A 1898

1898A 1899 1900

1901 1902 1903

1904 1905 1906

SCOTT NO.	DESCRIPTION	FIRST DAY COVERS SING	FIRST DAY COVERS PL. BLK.	MINT SHEET	PLATE BLOCK	UNUSED F/NH	USED

1907

1908

NOTE: #1898A—"Stagecoach 1890s" is 19½ mm long.

1981-84 Perf. 10 Vertically TRANSPORTATION COILS

SCOTT NO.	DESCRIPTION	SING	PLATE# STRIP 3	MINT SHEET	PLATE# STRIP 3	UNUSED F/NH	USED
1897-1908	1¢-20¢, 14 varieties, complete	29.50	....	....	....	4.50	3.10
1897	1¢ Omnibus (1983) . . .	2.25	17.50	....	.70	.25	.25
1897A	2¢ Locomotive (1982) .	2.25	25.00	....	.75	.25	.25
1898	3¢ Handcar (1983). . . .	2.25	25.00	....	1.05	.25	.25
1898A	4¢ Stagecoach (1982) .	2.25	22.50	....	1.80	.25	.25
1899	5¢ Motorcycle (1983). .	2.25	25.00	....	1.25	.25	.25
1900	5.2¢ Sleigh (1983)	2.25	37.50	....	5.00	.35	.25
1901	5.9¢ Bicycle (1982) . . .	2.25	37.50	....	5.00	.50	.40
1902	7.4¢ Baby Buggy (1984)	2.25	25.00	....	5.00	.50	.40
1903	9.3¢ Mail Wagon	2.25	42.50	....	4.00	.50	.25
1904	10.9¢ Hansom Cab (1982)	2.25	40.00	....	8.00	.50	.40
1905	11¢ Caboose (1984) . .	2.25	40.00	....	4.00	.50	.25
1906	17¢ Electric Car.	2.25	37.50	....	3.75	.70	.25
1907	18¢ Surrey.	2.25	55.00	....	4.00	.75	.25
1908	20¢ Fire Pumper	2.25	55.00	....	3.75	.75	.25

PRECANCELLED COILS

The following are for precancelled, unused, never hinged stamps. Stamps without gum sell for less.

SCOTT NO.		PL# STRIP 3	UNUSED
1895b	20¢ Supreme Court	45.00	1.00
1898Ab	4¢ Stagecoach	5.00	.35
1900a	5.2¢ Sleigh	6.00	.30
1901a	5.9¢ Bicycle	18.00	.45
1902a	7.4¢ Baby Buggy	6.00	.40
1903a	9.3¢ Mail Wagon	4.50	.40
1904a	10.9¢ Hansom Cab	18.00	.50
1905a	11¢ Caboose	4.50	.45
1906a	17¢ Electric Car	5.00	.55

PLATE NUMBER STRIPS OF 5

SCOTT NO.	UNUSED F/NH	SCOTT NO.	UNUSED F/NH	SCOTT NO.	UNUSED F/NH
1897	.95	1903	9.00	1901A	25.00
1897A	.85	1904	10.00	1902A	8.00
1898	1.20	1905	5.50	1903A	5.25
1898A	2.00	1906	4.00	1904A	30.00
1899	1.60	1907	5.25	1905A	5.25
1900	9.00	1908	5.00	1906A	7.00
1901	9.00	1898Ab	8.00		
1902	8.00	1900A	8.00		

1909

1983 EXPRESS MAIL BOOKLET SINGLE

SCOTT NO.	DESCRIPTION	SING	PL. BLK.	MINT SHEET	PLATE BLOCK	UNUSED F/NH	USED
1909	$9.35 Eagle & Moon . .	75.00	....	....	....	35.00	22.50
1909a	$9.35 bklt pane of 3. . .	200.00	....	....	....	105.00	....

1910

1911

1981 COMMEMORATIVES (Continued)

SCOTT NO.	DESCRIPTION	SING	PL. BLK.	MINT SHEET	PLATE BLOCK	UNUSED F/NH	USED
1910	18¢ American Red Cross	2.25	4.00	27.75(50)	3.25	.60	.25
1911	18¢ Savings & Loans Assoc.	2.25	4.00	25.75(50)	3.00	.60	.25

1912

1913

1914

1915

1916

1917

1918

1919

SCOTT NO.	DESCRIPTION	SING	PL. BLK.	MINT SHEET	PLATE BLOCK	UNUSED F/NH	USED
1912-19	Space Achievement, 8 varieties, attached . .	6.00	9.00	32.00(48)	7.25(8)	5.75	5.50
1912-19	same, set of singles. . .	15.50	....	....	....	....	2.50
1912	18¢ Exploring the Moon	2.00	....	....	....	1.00	.35
1913	18¢ Releasing Boosters	2.00	....	....	....	.80	.35
1914	18¢ Cooling Electric Systems.	2.00	....	....	....	.80	.35
1915	18¢ Understanding the Sun	2.00	....	....	....	.80	.35
1916	18¢ Probing the Planets	2.00	....	....	....	.80	.35
1917	18¢ Shuttle and Rockets	2.00	....	....	....	.80	.35
1918	18¢ Landing.	2.00	....	....	....	.80	.35
1919	18¢ Comprehending the Universe	2.00	....	....	....	.80	.35

1920

SCOTT NO.	DESCRIPTION	SING	PL. BLK.	MINT SHEET	PLATE BLOCK	UNUSED F/NH	USED
1920	18¢ Professional Management	2.25	4.00	26.50(50)	3.25	.65	.25

1921

1922

1923

1924

SCOTT NO.	DESCRIPTION	SING	PL. BLK.	MINT SHEET	PLATE BLOCK	UNUSED F/NH	USED
1921-24	Wildlife Habitats, 4 varieties, attached . .	5.00	6.00	38.00(50)	5.00	4.00	3.00
1921	18¢ Blue Heron	2.25	....	....	....	.90	.25
1922	18¢ Badger	2.25	....	....	....	.90	.25
1923	18¢ Grizzly Bear	2.25	....	....	....	.90	.25
1924	18¢ Ruffled Grouse . . .	2.25	....	....	....	.90	.25

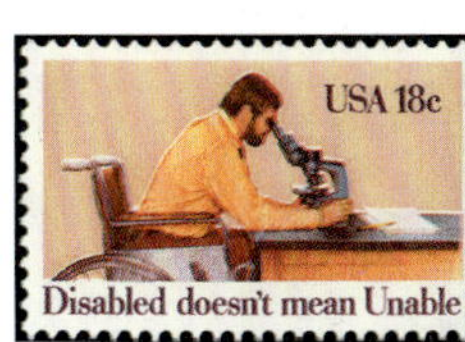

1925

1926

1927

SCOTT NO.	DESCRIPTION	FIRST DAY COVERS SING	FIRST DAY COVERS PL. BLK.	MINT SHEET	PLATE BLOCK	UNUSED F/NH	USED
1925	18¢ Disabled Persons .	2.25	4.00	26.00(50)	3.25	.75	.25
1926	18¢ Edna St. Vincent Millay	2.25	4.00	26.00(50)	3.25	.75	.25
1927	18¢ Alcoholism	4.50	7.00	60.00(50)	47.50(20)	.75	.25

1928 1929

1930 1931

SCOTT NO.	DESCRIPTION	FIRST DAY COVERS SING	FIRST DAY COVERS PL. BLK.	MINT SHEET	PLATE BLOCK	UNUSED F/NH	USED
1928-31	American Architecture, 4 varieties, attached . .	5.00	6.00	26.00(40)	4.25	3.75	3.00
1928	18¢ New York Univ. Library	2.25	....	....	....	1.00	.25
1929	18¢ Biltmore House. . .	2.25	....	....	....	1.00	.25
1930	18¢ Palace of the Arts .	2.25	....	....	....	1.00	.25
1931	18¢ National Farmers Bank	2.25	....	....	....	1.00	.25

1932

1933

SCOTT NO.	DESCRIPTION	FIRST DAY COVERS SING	FIRST DAY COVERS PL. BLK.	MINT SHEET	PLATE BLOCK	UNUSED F/NH	USED
1932	18¢ Babe Zaharias . . .	12.00	15.00	30.00(50)	4.50	.90	.30
1933	18¢ Bobby Jones.	15.00	18.00	39.00(50)	6.00	1.20	.30

1934

1935

1936

1937 1938

SCOTT NO.	DESCRIPTION	FIRST DAY COVERS SING	FIRST DAY COVERS PL. BLK.	MINT SHEET	PLATE BLOCK	UNUSED F/NH	USED
1934	18¢ Coming Through the Rye	2.25	4.50	32.00(50)	3.75	.80	.25
1935	18¢ James Hoban	2.25	4.00	29.00(50)	3.25	.70	.25
1936	20¢ James Hoban	2.25	4.00	33.00(50)	3.25	.70	.30
1937-38	Yorktown/Virginia Capes, 2 varieties, attached . .	2.00	4.00	34.00(50)	3.50	1.75	1.25
1937	18¢ Yorktown.	2.25	....	....	....	1.00	.30
1938	18¢ Virginia Capes . . .	2.25	....	....	....	1.00	.30

1939

1940

1941

SCOTT NO.	DESCRIPTION	FIRST DAY COVERS SING	FIRST DAY COVERS PL. BLK.	MINT SHEET	PLATE BLOCK	UNUSED F/NH	USED
1939	(20¢) Madonna & Child	2.25	4.00	51.00(100)	3.25	.75	.25
1940	(20¢) Christmas Toy . .	2.25	4.00	28.00(50)	3.25	.75	.25
1941	20¢ John Hanson	2.25	4.00	29.50(50)	3.25	.75	.25

1943

1942 1944 1945

SCOTT NO.	DESCRIPTION	FIRST DAY COVERS SING	FIRST DAY COVERS PL. BLK.	MINT SHEET	PLATE BLOCK	UNUSED F/NH	USED
1942-45	Desert Plants, 4 varieties, attached . .	5.00	6.00	29.00(40)	4.00	3.75	3.00
1942	20¢ Barrel Cactus	2.25	....	....	....	1.00	.25
1943	20¢ Agave	2.25	....	....	....	1.00	.25
1944	20¢ Beavertail Cactus .	2.25	....	....	....	1.00	.25
1945	20¢ Saguaro	2.25	....	....	....	1.00	.25

1946, 1947, 1948

1949

1981-1982 Regular Issues

SCOTT NO.	DESCRIPTION	FIRST DAY COVERS SING	FIRST DAY COVERS PL. BLK.	MINT SHEET	PLATE BLOCK	UNUSED F/NH	USED
1946	(20¢) "C" Eagle, 11x10½	2.25	4.00	65.00(100)	3.75	.75	.25
			LINE PAIR		LINE PAIR		
1947	(20¢) "C" Eagle, coil. . .	2.25	2.75	....	2.75	.95	.25
1948	(20¢) "C" Eagle, from pane	2.25	....	....	....	.95	.25
1948a	same, bklt pane of 10 .	6.00	....	....	....	8.00	....
1949	20¢ Bighorned Sheep, blue, from bklt pane (1982) .	2.25	....	....	....	.95	.25
1949a	same, bklt pane of 10 .	6.00	....	....	....	8.50	....
1949c	Type II, from bklt pane.	....	....	....	....	2.25	.40
1949d	same, bklt pane of 10 .	....	....	....	....	20.00	....

1950

1951

1952

1982 COMMEMORATIVES

SCOTT NO.	DESCRIPTION	FIRST DAY COVERS SING	FIRST DAY COVERS PL. BLK.	MINT SHEET	PLATE BLOCK	UNUSED F/NH	USED
1950/2030	(1950-52, 2003-04, 2006-30) 30 varieties	....	....	....	....	26.00	7.00
1950	20¢ Franklin D. Roosevelt	2.25	4.00	31.00(48)	3.25	.80	.25
1951	20¢ LOVE, perf. 11 . . .	1.85	4.25	31.00(50)	3.25	.65	.25
1951a	same, perf. 11 x 10½ . .	....	....	48.00(50)	5.50	1.10	.75

NOTE: **Perforations will be mixed on Used #1951.**

SCOTT NO.	DESCRIPTION	FIRST DAY COVERS SING	FIRST DAY COVERS PL. BLK.	MINT SHEET	PLATE BLOCK	UNUSED F/NH	USED
1952	20¢ George Washington	2.25	4.00	30.00(50)	3.75	.80	.25

1982 STATE BIRDS AND FLOWERS

1953

1973

1953 *Alabama*
1954 *Alaska*
1955 *Arizona*
1956 *Arkansas*
1957 *California*
1958 *Colorado*
1959 *Connecticut*
1960 *Delaware*
1961 *Florida*
1962 *Georgia*
1963 *Hawaii*
1964 *Idaho*
1965 *Illinois*
1966 *Indiana*
1967 *Iowa*
1968 *Kansas*
1969 *Kentucky*
1970 *Louisiana*
1971 *Maine*
1972 *Maryland*
1973 *Massachusetts*
1974 *Michigan*
1975 *Minnesota*
1976 *Mississippi*
1977 *Missouri*
1978 *Montana*
1979 *Nebraska*
1980 *Nevada*
1981 *New Hampshire*
1982 *New Jersey*
1983 *New Mexico*
1984 *New York*
1985 *North Carolina*
1986 *North Dakota*
1987 *Ohio*
1988 *Oklahoma*
1989 *Oregon*
1990 *Pennsylvania*
1991 *Rhode Island*
1992 *South Carolina*
1993 *South Dakota*
1994 *Tennessee*
1995 *Texas*
1996 *Utah*
1997 *Vermont*
1998 *Virginia*
1999 *Washington*
2000 *West Virginia*
2001 *Wisconsin*
2002 *Wyoming*

1966

2002

Perf. 10½ x 11

SCOTT NO.	DESCRIPTION	FIRST DAY COVERS SING	FIRST DAY COVERS PL. BLK.	MINT SHEET	PLATE BLOCK	UNUSED F/NH	USED
1953-2002	20¢, 50 varieties, attached.......		....	38.00(50)	....	38.00	....
	set of singles.	86.00	....	....	....	40.00	25.00
	singles of above	2.00	....	....	....	1.25	.65
1953a-2002a	same, perf. 11.	....	....	48.00(50)	....	48.00	....
	singles of above	....	....	....	....	50.00	

NOTE: **Used singles will not be sorted by perf. sizes.**

2003

2004

2005

SCOTT NO.	DESCRIPTION	FIRST DAY COVERS SING	FIRST DAY COVERS PL. BLK.	MINT SHEET	PLATE BLOCK	UNUSED F/NH	USED
2003	20¢ USA/Netherlands .	2.25	4.00	32.00(50)	17.00(20)	.70	.25
2004	20¢ Library of Congress	2.25	4.00	49.00(50)	5.00	1.25	.25
			PLATE# STRIP 3		PLATE# STRIP 3		
2005	20¢ Consumer Education, Coil	2.25	60.00	....	18.00	1.20	.25
	same, plate strips of 5 .	....	....	....	....	50.00	....

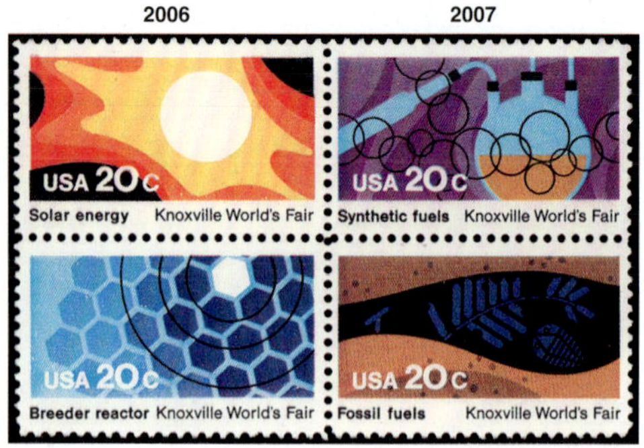

2006 2007 2008 2009

SCOTT NO.	DESCRIPTION	FIRST DAY COVERS SING	FIRST DAY COVERS PL. BLK.	MINT SHEET	PLATE BLOCK	UNUSED F/NH	USED
2006-09	World's Fair, 4 varieties, attached . .	5.00	6.00	36.00(50)	4.50	4.00	2.00
2006	20¢ Solar Energy.	2.25	....	....	....	1.00	.25
2007	20¢ Synthetic Fuels . .	2.25	....	....	....	1.00	.25
2008	20¢ Breeder Reactor . .	2.25	....	....	....	1.00	.25
2009	20¢ Fossil Fuels	2.25	....	....	....	1.00	.25

2010

2011

2012

SCOTT NO.	DESCRIPTION	FIRST DAY COVERS SING	FIRST DAY COVERS PL. BLK.	MINT SHEET	PLATE BLOCK	UNUSED F/NH	USED
2010	20¢ Horatio Alger.	2.25	4.00	29.00(50)	3.25	.70	.25
2011	20¢ Aging Together . . .	2.25	4.00	29.00(50)	3.25	.70	.25
2012	20¢ Barrymores.	2.25	4.00	30.00(50)	3.25	.70	.25

2013

2014

2015

SCOTT NO.	DESCRIPTION	FIRST DAY COVERS SING	FIRST DAY COVERS PL. BLK.	MINT SHEET	PLATE BLOCK	UNUSED F/NH	USED
2013	20¢ Dr. Mary Walker . .	2.25	4.00	29.50(50)	3.25	.70	.25
2014	20¢ Peace Garden . . .	2.25	4.00	48.00(50)	6.00	1.20	.25
2015	20¢ America's Libraries	2.25	4.00	29.00(50)	3.25	.60	.25

2016

2017

2018

SCOTT NO.	DESCRIPTION	FIRST DAY COVERS SING	FIRST DAY COVERS PL. BLK.	MINT SHEET	PLATE BLOCK	UNUSED F/NH	USED
2016	20¢ Jackie Robinson . .	7.00	13.50	90.00(50)	11.00	2.50	.25
2017	20¢ Touro Synagogue .	3.00	4.00	40.00(50)	18.00(20)	.85	.25
2018	20¢ Wolf Trap Farm. . .	2.25	4.00	29.00(50)	3.25	.75	.25

PLATE BLOCKS are portions of a sheet of stamps adjacent to the number(s) indicating the printing plate number used to produce that sheet. Flat plate issues are usually collected in plate blocks of six (number opposite middle stamp) while rotary issues are normally corner blocks of four.

2019 2020

2021 2022

SCOTT NO.	DESCRIPTION	FIRST DAY COVERS SING	FIRST DAY COVERS PL. BLK.	MINT SHEET	PLATE BLOCK	UNUSED F/NH	USED
2019-22	American Architecture, 4 varieties, attached . .	5.00	6.00	32.00(40)	4.50	4.00	3.25
2019	20¢ Fallingwater Mill Run	2.25	....	....	....	1.25	.25
2020	20¢ Illinois Inst. Tech . .	2.25	....	....	....	1.25	.25
2021	20¢ Gropius House . . .	2.25	....	....	....	1.25	.25
2022	20¢ Dulles Airport	2.25	....	....	....	1.25	.25

2023

2024

2025

2026

SCOTT NO.	DESCRIPTION	FIRST DAY COVERS SING	FIRST DAY COVERS PL. BLK.	MINT SHEET	PLATE BLOCK	UNUSED F/NH	USED
2023	20¢ St. Francis of Assisi	[illegible]	4.00	30.00(50)	3.25	.75	.25
2024	20¢ Ponce de Leon . . .	2.25	4.00	39.00(50)	20.00(20)	1.00	.25
2025	13¢ Kitten & Puppy, Christmas	2.25	4.00	25.00(50)	2.50	.60	.25
2026	20¢ Madonna & Child, Christmas	2.25	4.00	30.00(50)	17.00(20)	.75	.25

2027 2028

2029 2030

SCOTT NO.	DESCRIPTION	FIRST DAY COVERS SING	FIRST DAY COVERS PL. BLK.	MINT SHEET	PLATE BLOCK	UNUSED F/NH	USED
2027-30	Winter Scenes, Christmas, 4 varieties, attached . .	4.00	5.00	38.00(50)	5.00	4.25	3.50
2027	20¢ Sledding	2.25	....	....	....	1.25	.25
2028	20¢ Snowman	2.25	....	....	....	1.25	.25
2029	20¢ Skating	2.25	....	....	....	1.25	.25
2030	20¢ Decorating	2.25	....	....	....	1.25	.25

2031

1983 COMMEMORATIVES

SCOTT NO.	DESCRIPTION	FIRST DAY COVERS SING	FIRST DAY COVERS PL. BLK.	MINT SHEET	PLATE BLOCK	UNUSED F/NH	USED
2031-65	**13¢-20¢, 35 varieties, complete. . . . .**	....	....	....	....	**28.40**	**7.70**
2031	20¢ Science & Industry	2.25	4.00	29.00(50)	3.25	.75	.25

2033

2032 2034 2035

SCOTT NO.	DESCRIPTION	FIRST DAY COVERS SING	FIRST DAY COVERS PL. BLK.	MINT SHEET	PLATE BLOCK	UNUSED F/NH	USED
2032-35	20¢ Ballooning, 4 varieties, attached . .	5.00	6.00	33.00(40)	4.00	3.55	2.50
2032	20¢ Intrepid	2.25	....	....	....	1.10	.25
2033	20¢ Red, white, & blue balloon.	2.25	....	....	....	1.10	.25
2034	20¢ Yellow, gold & green balloon.	2.25	....	....	....	1.10	.25
2035	20¢ Explorer II	2.25	....	....	....	1.10	.25

2036

2037

2038

SCOTT NO.	DESCRIPTION	FIRST DAY COVERS SING	FIRST DAY COVERS PL. BLK.	MINT SHEET	PLATE BLOCK	UNUSED F/NH	USED
2036	20¢ USA/Sweden	2.25	4.00	29.00(50)	3.25	.70	.25
2037	20¢ Civilian Conservation Corps.	2.25	4.00	29.00(50)	3.25	.70	.25
2038	20¢ Joseph Priestley . .	2.25	4.00	29.00(50)	3.25	.70	.25

2039

2040

2041

SCOTT NO.	DESCRIPTION	FIRST DAY COVERS SING	FIRST DAY COVERS PL. BLK.	MINT SHEET	PLATE BLOCK	UNUSED F/NH	USED
2039	20¢ Volunteerism.	2.25	4.00	34.50(50)	18.00(20)	.70	.25
2040	20¢ German Immigrants	2.25	4.00	29.00(50)	3.00	.70	.25
2041	20¢ Brooklyn Bridge . .	3.00	5.00	30.00(50)	3.00	.70	.25

SCOTT NO.	DESCRIPTION	FIRST DAY COVERS SING	PL. BLK.	MINT SHEET	PLATE BLOCK	UNUSED F/NH	USED

2042

2043

2044

SCOTT NO.	DESCRIPTION	FIRST DAY COVERS SING	PL. BLK.	MINT SHEET	PLATE BLOCK	UNUSED F/NH	USED
2042	20¢ Tennessee Valley Authority	2.25	4.00	30.00(50)	16.00(20)	.70	.25
2043	20¢ Physical Fitness . .	2.25	4.00	30.00(50)	16.00(20)	.70	.25
2044	20¢ Scott Joplin.	2.25	4.00	35.00(50)	4.00	.75	.25

2045

2046

2047

SCOTT NO.	DESCRIPTION	FIRST DAY COVERS SING	PL. BLK.	MINT SHEET	PLATE BLOCK	UNUSED F/NH	USED
2045	20¢ Medal of Honor. . .	6.00	8.00	35.00(40)	4.50	1.00	.25
2046	20¢ Babe Ruth.	8.00	16.00	75.00(50)	10.00	2.00	.25
2047	20¢ Nathaniel Hawthorne	2.25	4.00	32.50(50)	4.00	.75	.25

2048 2049

2050 2051

SCOTT NO.	DESCRIPTION	FIRST DAY COVERS SING	PL. BLK.	MINT SHEET	PLATE BLOCK	UNUSED F/NH	USED
2048-51	Olympics, 4 varieties, attached . .	5.00	6.00	29.00(50)	3.50	3.00	2.75
2048	13¢ Discus.	2.25	....	....	....	1.00	.30
2049	13¢ High Jump	2.25	....	....	....	1.00	.30
2050	13¢ Archery	2.25	....	....	....	1.00	.30
2051	13¢ Boxing.	2.25	....	....	....	1.00	.30

2052

2053

2054

SCOTT NO.	DESCRIPTION	FIRST DAY COVERS SING	PL. BLK.	MINT SHEET	PLATE BLOCK	UNUSED F/NH	USED
2052	20¢ Treaty of Paris . . .	2.25	4.00	24.00(40)	3.25	.75	.25
2053	20¢ Civil Service	2.25	4.00	32.00(50)	18.00(20)	.75	.25
2054	20¢ Metropolitan Opera	2.25	4.00	30.00(50)	3.25	.75	.25

MINT SHEETS: From 1935 to date, we list prices for standard size Mint Sheets in Fine, Never Hinged condition. The number of stamps in each sheet is noted in ( ).

SCOTT NO.	DESCRIPTION	FIRST DAY COVERS SING	PL. BLK.	MINT SHEET	PLATE BLOCK	UNUSED F/NH	USED

2055 2056

2057 2058

SCOTT NO.	DESCRIPTION	FIRST DAY COVERS SING	PL. BLK.	MINT SHEET	PLATE BLOCK	UNUSED F/NH	USED
2055-58	Inventors, 4 varieties, attached . .	5.00	6.00	38.00(50)	4.50	4.00	3.00
2055	20¢ Charles Steinmetz	2.25	....	....	....	1.35	.25
2056	20¢ Edwin Armstrong .	2.25	....	....	....	1.35	.25
2057	20¢ Nikola Tesla	2.25	....	....	....	1.35	.25
2058	20¢ Philo T. Farnsworth	2.25	....	....	....	1.35	.25

2059 2060

2061 2062

SCOTT NO.	DESCRIPTION	FIRST DAY COVERS SING	PL. BLK.	MINT SHEET	PLATE BLOCK	UNUSED F/NH	USED
2059-62	Streetcars, 4 varieties, attached . .	5.00	6.00	40.00(50)	4.50	4.00	3.00
2059	20¢ First Streetcar. . . .	2.25	....	....	....	1.25	.25
2060	20¢ Electric Trolley . . .	2.25	....	....	....	1.25	.25
2061	20¢ "Bobtail"	2.25	....	....	....	1.25	.25
2062	20¢ St. Charles Streetcar	2.25	....	....	....	1.25	.25

2063

2064

SCOTT NO.	DESCRIPTION	FIRST DAY COVERS SING	PL. BLK.	MINT SHEET	PLATE BLOCK	UNUSED F/NH	USED
2063	20¢ Madonna.	2.25	4.00	32.00(50)	3.75	.75	.25
2064	20¢ Santa Claus	2.25	4.00	32.00(50)	16.00(20)	.85	.25

2065

SCOTT NO.	DESCRIPTION	FIRST DAY COVERS SING	PL. BLK.	MINT SHEET	PLATE BLOCK	UNUSED F/NH	USED
2065	20¢ Martin Luther	2.25	4.00	33.00(50)	3.75	.85	.25

2066

1984 COMMEMORATIVES

SCOTT NO.	DESCRIPTION	FIRST DAY COVERS SING	FIRST DAY COVERS PL. BLK.	MINT SHEET	PLATE BLOCK	UNUSED F/NH	USED
2066-2109	44 varieties, complete	....	....	....	....	37.50	9.30
2066	20¢ Alaska Statehood .	2.25	4.00	32.00(50)	3.25	.70	.25

2067

2068

2069

2070

SCOTT NO.	DESCRIPTION	FIRST DAY COVERS SING	FIRST DAY COVERS PL. BLK.	MINT SHEET	PLATE BLOCK	UNUSED F/NH	USED
2067-70	Winter Olympics, 4 varieties, attached . .	5.00	6.00	36.00(50)	4.50	3.50	3.00
2067	20¢ Ice Dancing.	2.25	....	....	....	1.10	.30
2068	20¢ Downhill Skiing . . .	2.25	....	....	....	1.10	.30
2069	20¢ Cross Country Skiing	2.25	....	....	....	1.10	.30
2070	20¢ Hockey	2.25	....	....	....	1.10	.30

2071

2072

2073

2074

SCOTT NO.	DESCRIPTION	FIRST DAY COVERS SING	FIRST DAY COVERS PL. BLK.	MINT SHEET	PLATE BLOCK	UNUSED F/NH	USED
2071	20¢ Federal Deposit Insurance Corporation	[illegible]	[illegible]	[illegible](50)	[illegible]	.75	.25
[illegible]	[illegible]	[illegible]	[illegible]	[illegible]	10.50(20)	.75	.25
2073	20¢ Carter G. Woodson	[illegible]	4.00	[illegible](50)	3.50	[illegible]	[illegible]
2074	20¢ Conservation	2.25	4.00	29.00(50)	3.25	.75	.25

2076

2075

2077

2078

2079

SCOTT NO.	DESCRIPTION	FIRST DAY COVERS SING	FIRST DAY COVERS PL. BLK.	MINT SHEET	PLATE BLOCK	UNUSED F/NH	USED
2075	20¢ Credit Union	1.95	4.50	29.00(50)	3.25	.70	.25
2076-79	Orchids, 4 varieties, attd.	4.00	5.00	34.00(48)	3.75	3.25	2.75
2076	20¢ Wild Pink.	2.25	....	....	....	.95	.25
2077	20¢ Yellow Lady's-slipper	2.25	....	....	....	.95	.25
2078	20¢ Spreading Pogonia	2.25	....	....	....	.95	.25
2079	20¢ Pacific Calypso . . .	2.25	....	....	....	.95	.25

2080

2081

SCOTT NO.	DESCRIPTION	FIRST DAY COVERS SING	FIRST DAY COVERS PL. BLK.	MINT SHEET	PLATE BLOCK	UNUSED F/NH	USED
2080	20¢ Hawaii Statehood .	2.25	4.00	32.00(50)	3.50	.75	.25
2081	20¢ National Archives .	2.25	4.00	34.00(50)	3.75	.85	.25

2082

2083

2084

2085

SCOTT NO.	DESCRIPTION	FIRST DAY COVERS SING	FIRST DAY COVERS PL. BLK.	MINT SHEET	PLATE BLOCK	UNUSED F/NH	USED
2082-85	Olympics, 4 varieties, attached.	5.00	6.00	37.00(50)	5.00	4.50	4.00
2082	20¢ Men's Diving	2.25	....	....	....	1.20	.25
2083	20¢ Long Jump	2.25	....	....	....	1.20	.25
2084	20¢ Wrestling.	2.25	....	....	....	1.20	.25
2085	20¢ Women's Kayak . .	2.25	....	....	....	1.20	.25

2086

2087

2088

SCOTT NO.	DESCRIPTION	FIRST DAY COVERS SING	FIRST DAY COVERS PL. BLK.	MINT SHEET	PLATE BLOCK	UNUSED F/NH	USED
2086	20¢ Louisiana Exposition	[illegible]	[illegible]	[illegible](40)	4.50	[illegible]	[illegible]
[illegible]	20¢ Health Research	[illegible]	4.00	[illegible](50)	[illegible]	.70	.25
2088	20¢ Douglas Fairbanks	[illegible]	4.00	[illegible](50)	[illegible](30)	[illegible]	[illegible]

2089

2090

2091

SCOTT NO.	DESCRIPTION	FIRST DAY COVERS SING	FIRST DAY COVERS PL. BLK.	MINT SHEET	PLATE BLOCK	UNUSED F/NH	USED
2089	20¢ Jim Thorpe	4.50	8.00	66.00(50)	8.50	2.00	.30
2090	20¢ John McCormack .	3.00	4.00	30.00(50)	3.25	.65	.25
2091	20¢ St. Lawrence Seaway	3.00	4.00	30.00(50)	3.25	.65	.25

SE-TENANTS: Beginning with the 1964 Christmas issue (#1254-57), the United States has issued numerous Se-Tenant stamps covering a wide variety of subjects. Se-Tenants are issues where two or more different stamp designs are produced on the same sheet in pair, strip or block form. Mint stamps are usually collected in attached blocks, etc.—Used are generally saved as single stamps. Our Se-Tenant prices follow in this collecting pattern.

2092 2093 2105 2106 2107

SCOTT NO.	DESCRIPTION	FIRST DAY COVERS SING	FIRST DAY COVERS PL. BLK.	MINT SHEET	PLATE BLOCK	UNUSED F/NH	USED
2092	Preserving Wetlands . .	1.95	4.00	34.00(50)	3.50	.80	.25
2093	Roanoke Voyages	2.25	4.00	34.00(50)	3.50	.80	.25

2094 2095 2096 2097

SCOTT NO.	DESCRIPTION	FIRST DAY COVERS SING	FIRST DAY COVERS PL. BLK.	MINT SHEET	PLATE BLOCK	UNUSED F/NH	USED
2094	20¢ Herman Melville .	2.25	4.00	29.00(50)	3.25	.70	.25
2095	20¢ Horace Moses . .	2.25	4.00	31.00(50)	19.00(20)	.90	.25
2096	20¢ Smokey Bear . . .	2.25	4.00	34.00(50)	3.50	.90	.25
2097	20¢ Roberto Clemente	12.00	20.00	95.00(50)	10.00	2.00	.50

2098 2099

2100 2101

SCOTT NO.	DESCRIPTION	FIRST DAY COVERS SING	FIRST DAY COVERS PL. BLK.	MINT SHEET	PLATE BLOCK	UNUSED F/NH	USED
2098-2101	American Dogs, 4 varieties, attached .	5.00	6.00	32.50(40)	4.75	4.25	3.75
2098	20¢ Beagle, Boston Terrier	2.25	....	....	....	1.25	.25
2099	20¢ Chesapeake Bay Retriever, Cocker Spaniel	2.25	....	....	....	1.25	.25
2100	20¢ Alaskan Malamute, Collie	2.25	....	....	....	1.25	.25
2101	20¢ Black & Tan Coonhound, American Foxhound . .	2.25	....	....	....	1.25	.25

2102 2103 2104

SCOTT NO.	DESCRIPTION	FIRST DAY COVERS SING	FIRST DAY COVERS PL. BLK.	MINT SHEET	PLATE BLOCK	UNUSED F/NH	USED
2102	20¢ Crime Prevention .	2.25	4.00	29.00(50)	3.25	.60	.25
2103	20¢ Hispanic Americans	3.00	4.00	28.00(40)	4.00	.60	.25
2104	20¢ Family Unity	2.25	4.00	36.00(50)	20.00(20)	1.00	.25

SCOTT NO.	DESCRIPTION	FIRST DAY COVERS SING	FIRST DAY COVERS PL. BLK.	MINT SHEET	PLATE BLOCK	UNUSED F/NH	USED
2105	20¢ Eleanor Roosevelt	2.25	4.00	28.00(40)	3.25	.70	.25
2106	20¢ Nation of Readers	2.25	4.00	33.00(50)	4.00	1.10	.30
2107	20¢ Madonna & Child .	2.25	4.00	29.00(50)	3.25	.60	.25

2108 2109

SCOTT NO.	DESCRIPTION	FIRST DAY COVERS SING	FIRST DAY COVERS PL. BLK.	MINT SHEET	PLATE BLOCK	UNUSED F/NH	USED
2108	20¢ Santa Claus	1.35	4.00	30.00(50)	3.25	.60	.30
2109	20¢ Vietnam Veterans .	5.00	4.00	32.00(40)	4.65	1.00	.30

2110

1985 COMMEMORATIVES

SCOTT NO.	DESCRIPTION	FIRST DAY COVERS SING	FIRST DAY COVERS PL. BLK.	MINT SHEET	PLATE BLOCK	UNUSED F/NH	USED
2110/2166	**(2110, 2137-47, 2152-66) 27 varieties . . . .**	....	....	....	....	**33.50**	**7.50**
2110	22¢ Jerome Kern	2.25	4.00	32.00(50)	3.25	.70	.25

2111-2113 2114, 2115 2116

1985 REGULAR ISSUES

SCOTT NO.	DESCRIPTION	FIRST DAY COVERS SING	FIRST DAY COVERS PL. BLK.	MINT SHEET	PLATE BLOCK	UNUSED F/NH	USED
2111	(22¢) "D" Eagle	2.25	4.00	72.00(100)	25.00(20)	.90	.25
			PLATE# STRIP 3		PLATE# STRIP 3		
2112	(22¢) "D" Eagle, coil. . .	2.25	21.00	....	6.75	.75	.25
	same, plate strip of 5 . . .	....	....	....	....	10.00	....
2113	(22¢) "D" Eagle from bklt pane	2.25	....	....	....	1.25	.25
2113a	same, bklt pane of 10 .	7.50	....	....	....	10.00	....
			PLATE BLOCK		PLATE BLOCK		
2114	22¢ Flag over Capitol	2.25	4.00	75.00(100)	4.00	.80	.25
			PLATE# STRIP 3		PLATE# STRIP 3		
2115	22¢ Flag over Capitol, coil	2.25	27.50	....	3.75	.85	.25
	same, plate strip of 5 . . .	....	....	....	....	5.50	....
2115a	same, narrow block tagging	....	....	....	4.50	.85	.25
	same, plate strip of 5 . . .	....	....	....	....	5.50	....
2115b	same, wide & tall block tagging	....	....	....	65.00	2.00	....
	same, plate strip of 5 . . .	....	....	....	....	85.00	....
2115c	22¢ Flag over Capitol "T" Coil (1985-87)	2.90	....	....	4.50	.90	.75
	same, plate strip of 5 . . .	....	....	....	....	6.00	....
2116	22¢ Flag over Capitol from booklet pane	2.25	....	....	....	1.00	.25
2116a	same, bklt pane of 5 . . .	2.90	....	....	....	5.00	....

2117

2118

2119

2120

2121

1985 SEASHELLS FROM BOOKLET PANE

SCOTT NO.	DESCRIPTION	FIRST DAY COVERS SING	FIRST DAY COVERS PL. BLK.	MINT SHEET	PLATE BLOCK	UNUSED F/NH	USED
2117-21	Shells, strip of 5, attached	3.00	....	....	....	4.25	4.00
2117	22¢ Frilled Dogwinkle .	2.25	....	....	....	.90	.25
2118	22¢ Reticulated Helmet	2.25	....	....	....	.90	.25
2119	22¢ New England Neptune	2.25	....	....	....	.90	.25
2120	22¢ Calico Scallop. . . .	2.25	....	....	....	.90	.25
2121	22¢ Lightning Whelk . .	2.25	....	....	....	.90	.25
2121a	22¢ Seashells, bklt pane of 10.	7.50	....	....	....	8.00	6.50

2122

1985 EXPRESS MAIL STAMP FROM BOOKLET PANE

SCOTT NO.	DESCRIPTION	FIRST DAY COVERS SING	FIRST DAY COVERS PL. BLK.	MINT SHEET	PLATE BLOCK	UNUSED F/NH	USED
2122	$10.75 Eagle & Moon .	65.00	....	....	....	40.00	15.00
2122a	same, bklt pane of 3 . .	160.00	....	....	....	115.00	....
2122b	Type II, from bklt pane.	....	....	....	....	45.00	20.00
2122c	same, bklt pane of 3 . .	....	....	....	....	135.00	....

2123

2124

2125

2126

2127

2128

2129

2130

2131

2132

2133

2134

2135

2136

TRANSPORTATION COILS 1985-87 PERF. 10

SCOTT NO.	DESCRIPTION	FIRST DAY COVERS SING	FIRST DAY COVERS PLATE# STRIP 3	MINT SHEET	PLATE# STRIP 3	UNUSED F/NH	USED
2123	3.4¢ School Bus	2.00	11.50	....	1.50	.35	.30
2124	4.9¢ Buckboard	2.00	14.00	....	1.25	.35	.30
2125	5.5¢ Star Route Truck (1986)	2.00	15.00	....	2.50	.35	.30
2126	6¢ Tricycle	2.00	14.00	....	3.25	.35	.30
2127	7.1¢ Tractor (1987) . .	2.00	15.00	....	3.15	.35	.30
2128	8.3¢ Ambulance.	2.00	14.00	....	1.95	.35	.30
2129	8.5¢ Tow Truck (1987)	2.00	12.50	....	4.00	.35	.30
2130	10.1¢ Oil Wagon	2.00	12.50	....	8.00	1.00	.30
2131	11¢ Stutz Bearcat . . .	2.00	18.00	....	2.75	.40	.30
2132	12¢ Stanley Steamer.	2.00	15.00	....	3.00	.60	.30
2133	12.5¢ Pushcart	2.00	15.00	....	4.75	.40	.30
2134	14¢ Iceboat	2.00	15.00	....	2.50	.40	.30
2135	17¢ Dog Sled (1986) .	2.00	12.50	....	5.75	.70	.30
2136	25¢ Bread Wagon (1986)	2.00	15.00	....	4.00	.80	.25

PRECANCELLED COILS

The following are for precancelled, unused, never hinged stamps. Stamps without gum sell for less.

SCOTT NO.		PL# STRIP 3	UNUSED
2123a	3.4¢ School Bus.	7.50	.35
2124a	4.9¢ Buckboard	2.35	.35
2125a	5.5¢ Star Route Truck	2.50	.35
2126a	6¢ Tricycle	2.75	.35
2127a	7.1¢ Tractor	4.00	.35
2127b	7.1¢ Tractor, precancel (1989).	3.25	.35
2128a	8.3¢ Ambulance	2.50	.35
2129a	8.5¢ Tow Truck.	4.25	.35
2130a	10.1¢ Oil Wagon	3.75	.35
2130b	10.1¢ Oil Wagon, red precancel (1988).	4.00	.35
2132a	12¢ Stanley Steamer	4.00	.60
2132b	12¢ Stanley Steamer "B" Press	18.00	1.85
2133a	12.5¢ Pushcart.	4.00	.40

PLATE NUMBER STRIPS OF 5

SCOTT NO.	UNUSED F/NH	SCOTT NO.	UNUSED F/NH	SCOTT NO.	UNUSED F/NH
2123	2.00	2132	4.50	2127A	4.50
2124	1.80	2133	4.75	2127Av	3.25
2125	2.75	2134	3.50	2128A	3.00
2126	2.40	2135	6.00	2129A	4.50
2127	3.50	2136	6.50	2130A	3.50
2128	2.75	2123A	7.00	2130Av	3.25
2129	5.00	2124A	2.50	2132A	4.50
2130	8.50	2125A	3.50	2132B	25.00
2131	3.00	2126A	3.00	2133A	4.50

2137

1985 COMMEMORATIVES (continued)

SCOTT NO.	DESCRIPTION	FIRST DAY COVERS SING	FIRST DAY COVERS PL. BLK.	MINT SHEET	PLATE BLOCK	UNUSED F/NH	USED
2137	22¢ Mary Bethune	2.25	4.00	40.00(50)	5.00	1.00	.25

2138 2139

2140 2141

SCOTT NO.	DESCRIPTION	FIRST DAY COVERS SING	FIRST DAY COVERS PL. BLK.	MINT SHEET	PLATE BLOCK	UNUSED F/NH	USED
2138-41	Duck Decoys, 4 varieties, attached . .	5.00	6.00	65.00(50)	7.00	6.00	5.00
2138	22¢ Broadbill	2.25	....	....	....	1.75	.40
2139	22¢ Mallard	2.25	....	....	....	1.75	.40
2140	22¢ Canvasback	2.25	....	....	....	1.75	.40
2141	22¢ Redhead	2.25	....	....	....	1.75	.40

2143

2142

2144

2145

SCOTT NO.	DESCRIPTION	FIRST DAY COVERS SING	FIRST DAY COVERS PL. BLK.	MINT SHEET	PLATE BLOCK	UNUSED F/NH	USED
2142	22¢ Winter Special Olympics	2.25	4.00	49.00(40)	7.00	1.70	.25
2143	22¢ "LOVE"	1.95	4.00	34.00(50)	3.50	.70	.25
2144	22¢ Rural Electricity	2.25	....	46.00(50)	28.00(20)	1.50	.25
2145	22¢ Ameripex '86	2.25	4.00	34.00(48)	3.75	1.00	.25

2146

2147

SCOTT NO.	DESCRIPTION	FIRST DAY COVERS SING	FIRST DAY COVERS PL. BLK.	MINT SHEET	PLATE BLOCK	UNUSED F/NH	USED
2146	22¢ Abigail Adams	2.25	4.00	33.00(50)	3.75	.85	.25
2147	22¢ Frederic Bartholdi	2.25	4.00	34.00(50)	4.00	1.00	.25

2149

2150

1985 REGULAR ISSUE COILS

SCOTT NO.	DESCRIPTION	FIRST DAY COVERS SING	PLATE# STRIP 3	MINT SHEET	PLATE# STRIP 3	UNUSED F/NH	USED
2149	18¢ George Washington	2.25	50.00	....	3.50	.85	.30
	same, plate strip of 5	....	....	....	....	4.50	....
2149a	18¢ George Washington, precancel	....	....	....	3.25	.70	.40
	same, plate strip of 5	....	....	....	....	4.00	....
2150	21.1¢ Envelope	2.25	32.50	....	3.75	.90	.60
	same, plate strip of 5	....	....	....	....	5.50	....
2150a	21.1¢ Envelope, precancel	....	....	....	3.85	.75	.50
	same, plate strip of 5	....	....	....	....	5.25	....

2152

2153

2154

SCOTT NO.	DESCRIPTION	FIRST DAY COVERS SING	FIRST DAY COVERS PL. BLK.	MINT SHEET	PLATE BLOCK	UNUSED F/NH	USED
2152	22¢ Korean War Veterans	3.00	4.00	41.50(50)	5.00	1.00	.25
2153	22¢ Social Security	2.25	4.00	32.00(50)	3.50	1.00	.25
2154	22¢ World War I Veterans	3.00	4.00	58.00(50)	5.00	1.00	.25

2155 2156

2157 2158

SCOTT NO.	DESCRIPTION	FIRST DAY COVERS SING	FIRST DAY COVERS PL. BLK.	MINT SHEET	PLATE BLOCK	UNUSED F/NH	USED
2155-58	American Horses, 4 varieties, attached	5.00	6.00	68.00(40)	10.00	8.00	5.00
2155	22¢ Quarter Horse	2.25	....	....	....	2.25	.50
2156	22¢ Morgan	2.25	....	....	....	2.25	.50
2157	22¢ Saddlebred	2.25	....	....	....	2.25	.50
2158	22¢ Appaloosa	2.25	....	....	....	2.25	.50

2160

2159

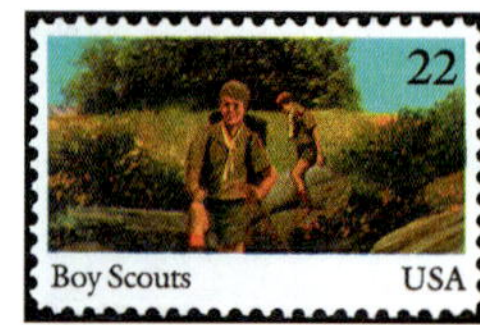

2161

2162

2163

SCOTT NO.	DESCRIPTION	FIRST DAY COVERS SING	FIRST DAY COVERS PL. BLK.	MINT SHEET	PLATE BLOCK	UNUSED F/NH	USED
2159	22¢ Public Education	2.25	4.00	50.00(50)	5.00	1.20	.25
2160-63	Youth Year, 4 varieties, attached	5.00	6.00	61.00(50)	8.00	6.00	4.50
2160	22¢ YMCA	2.25	....	....	....	1.75	.40
2161	22¢ Boy Scouts	2.25	....	....	....	1.75	.40
2162	22¢ Big Brothers & Big Sisters	2.25	....	....	....	1.75	.40
2163	22¢ Camp Fire	2.25	....	....	....	1.75	.40

2164

2165

2166

2167

SCOTT NO.	DESCRIPTION	FIRST DAY COVERS SING	FIRST DAY COVERS PL. BLK.	MINT SHEET	PLATE BLOCK	UNUSED F/NH	USED
2164	22¢ Help End Hunger	2.25	4.00	32.75(50)	3.25	.70	.25
2165	22¢ Madonna & Child	2.25	4.00	32.00(50)	3.25	.60	.25
2166	22¢ Poinsettia	2.25	4.00	38.00(50)	3.25	.60	.25
2167	22¢ Arkansas Statehood	2.25	4.00	39.00(50)	5.00	1.00	.25

2168 2169 2170 2171

2172 2173 2175 2176

2177 2178 2179 2180

2181 2182, 2197 2183 2184

2185 2186 2187 2188

2189 2190 2191 2192

2193 2194 2195 2196

1986-93 GREAT AMERICANS

SCOTT NO.	DESCRIPTION	FIRST DAY COVERS SING	FIRST DAY COVERS PL. BLK.	MINT SHEET	PLATE BLOCK	UNUSED F/NH	USED
2168-96	**(28 varieties) . . . .**		**........**	**........**	**225.00**	**45.00**	**12.50**
2168	1¢ Margaret Mitchell . .	5.00	6.00	11.00(100)	1.15	.30	.25
2169	2¢ Mary Lyon (1987) . .	2.25	4.00	11.00(100)	1.15	.30	.25
2170	3¢ Dr. Paul D. White . .	2.25	4.00	14.00(100)	1.00	.30	.25
2171	4¢ Father Flanagan . . .	2.25	4.00	20.00(100)	1.00	.30	.25
2172	5¢ Hugo L. Black	2.25	4.00	35.00(100)	2.00	.50	.25
2173	5¢ Luis Muñoz Marin (1990)	2.25	4.00	38.00(100)	2.25	.30	.25
2175	10¢ Red Cloud (1987) .	2.25	4.00	45.00(100)	2.50	.40	.25
2176	14¢ Julia Ward Howe (1987)	2.25	4.00	60.00(100)	2.75	1.00	.25
2177	15¢ Buffalo Bill Cody (1988)	2.25	4.00	90.00(100)	12.00	1.00	.25
2178	17¢ Belva Ann Lockwood	2.25	4.00	60.00(100)	3.25	1.00	.25
2179	20¢ Virginia Apgar (1994)	2.25	4.00	62.00(100)	3.75	1.00	.25
2180	21¢ Chester Carlson (1988)	2.25	4.00	68.00(100)	3.75	1.00	.50
2181	23¢ Mary Cassatt (1988)	2.25	4.00	73.00(100)	4.00	1.00	.25
2182	25¢ Jack London (1988)	2.25	4.00	73.00(100)	4.25	1.00	.25
2182a	as above bklt pane of 10	8.00	....	....		7.75	....
2183	28¢ Sitting Bull (1989) .	2.25	....	125.00(100)	7.00	1.30	.50
2184	29¢ Earl Warren (1992)	2.25	4.00	110.00(100)	6.00	1.00	.25
2185	29¢ Thomas Jefferson (1993)	2.25	4.75	110.00(100)	6.00(4)	1.00	.25
2185b	same, Plate Block of 8 .	....	....	....	8.75(8)	....	....
2186	35¢ Dennis Chavez (1991)	2.25	4.00	107.00(100)	6.00	1.20	.50
2187	40¢ Claire Lee Chennault (1990)	3.00	5.00	120.00(100)	7.00	1.35	.25
2188	45¢ Dr. Harvey Cushing (1988)	1.85	4.25	142.00(100)	9.00	1.50	.25

SCOTT NO.	DESCRIPTION	FIRST DAY COVERS SING	FIRST DAY COVERS PL. BLK.	MINT SHEET	PLATE BLOCK	UNUSED F/NH	USED
2189	52¢ Hubert Humphrey (1991)	2.00	4.50	160.00(100)	9.00	1.75	.25
2190	56¢ John Harvard	3.00	4.50	167.00(100)	10.00	1.75	.25
2191	65¢ H.H. Arnold (1988)	3.00	4.25	195.00(100)	11.00	2.25	.25
2192	75¢ Wendell Willkie (1992)	2.75	5.50	238.00(100)	13.00	2.75	.25
2193	$1 Dr. Bernard Revel . .	5.00	10.00	375.00(100)	20.00	4.00	.50
2194	$1 John Hopkins (1989)	5.00	10.00	60.00(20)	15.00	3.75	.50
2195	$2 William Jennings Bryan	8.00	10.00	595.00(100)	29.00	6.75	1.00
2196	$5 Bret Harte (1987) . .	17.50	28.50	290.00(20)	73.00	17.00	3.50
2197	25¢ Jack London, bklt single (1988)	2.25	....	....	....	.90	.25
2197a	as above bklt pane (6), perf. 10	5.00	....	....	....	5.25	....

2198

2199

2200

2201

1986 COMMEMORATIVES

SCOTT NO.	DESCRIPTION	FIRST DAY COVERS SING	FIRST DAY COVERS PL. BLK.	MINT SHEET	PLATE BLOCK	UNUSED F/NH	USED
2167/2245	**(2167, 2202-04, 2210-11, 2220-24, 2235-45) 22 varieties . . . .**		**........**	**........**	**........**	**24.00**	**5.95**
2198	22¢ Cover & Handstamp	2.25	....	....	....	.90	.55
2199	22¢ Collector with Album	2.25	....	....	....	.90	.55
2200	22¢ No. 836 under magnifier	2.25	....			.90	.55
2201	22¢ President sheet. . .	2.25	....	....	....	[illegible]	[illegible]
2201a	Stamp Collecting bklt pane, 4 varieties, attached	6.00				3.50	2.80

2202

2203

2204

SCOTT NO.	DESCRIPTION	FIRST DAY COVERS SING	FIRST DAY COVERS PL. BLK.	MINT SHEET	PLATE BLOCK	UNUSED F/NH	USED
2202	22¢ LOVE	1.95	4.25	39.00(50)	4.00	1.00	.25
2203	22¢ Sojourner Truth. . .	3.00	4.00	41.00(50)	4.50	1.00	.25
2204	22¢ Texas Republic . . .	3.00	4.00	44.00(50)	6.00	1.25	.25

BOOKLET PANE SINGLES: Traditionally, booklet panes have been collected only as intact panes since, other than the straight edged sides, they were identical to sheet stamps. However, starting with the 1971 8¢ Eisenhower stamp, many issues differ from the comparative sheet stamp or may even be totally different issues (e.g. #1738-42 Windmills). These newer issues are now collected as booklet singles or panes—both methods being acceptable.

2205

2206

2207

2208

2209

SCOTT NO.	DESCRIPTION	FIRST DAY COVERS SING	PL. BLK.	MINT SHEET	PLATE BLOCK	UNUSED F/NH	USED
2205	22¢ Muskellunge	2.25	....	....	....	1.85	.35
2206	22¢ Atlantic Cod	2.25	....	....	....	1.85	.35
2207	22¢ Largemouth Bass .	2.25	....	....	....	1.85	.35
2208	22¢ Bluefin Tuna	2.25	....	....	....	1.85	.35
2209	22¢ Catfish	2.25	....	....	....	1.85	.35
2209a	Fish, bklt pane, 5 varieties, attached.	6.50	....	....	....	8.50	6.00

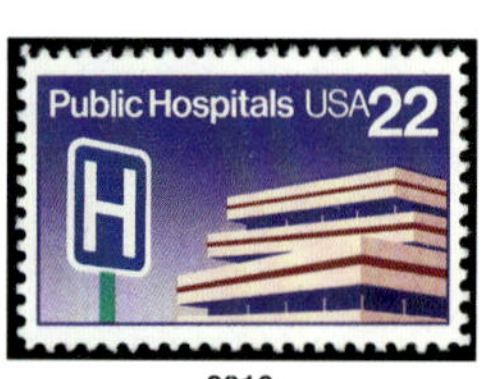

2210

2211

SCOTT NO.	DESCRIPTION	FIRST DAY COVERS SING	PL. BLK.	MINT SHEET	PLATE BLOCK	UNUSED F/NH	USED
2210	22¢ Public Hospitals . .	2.25	4.00	34.00(50)	3.75	.75	.25
2211	22¢ Duke Ellington . . .	4.00	6.00	38.00(50)	4.50	1.00	.25

1986 PRESIDENTS MINIATURE SETS

Complete set printed on 4 miniature sheets of 9 stamps each.

2216a *Washington*
2216b *Adams*
2216c *Jefferson*
2216d *Madison*
2216e *Monroe*
2216f *J.Q. Adams*
2216g *Jackson*
2216h *Van Buren*
2216i *W.H. Harrison*
2217a *Tyler*
2217b *Polk*
2217c *Taylor*
2217d *Fillmore*
2217e *Pierce*
2217f *Buchanan*
2217g *Lincoln*
2217h *A. Johnson*
2217i *Grant*
2218a *Hayes*
2218b *Garfield*
2218c *Arthur*
2218d *Cleveland*
2218e *B. Harrison*
2218f *McKinley*
2218g *T. Roosevelt*
2218h *Taft*
2218i *Wilson*
2219a *Harding*
2219b *Coolidge*
2219c *Hoover*
2219d *F.D. Roosevelt*
2219e *White House*
2219f *Truman*
2219g *Eisenhower*
2219h *Kennedy*
2219i *L.B. Johnson*

2216

1986 AMERIPEX '86 MINIATURE SHEETS

SCOTT NO.	DESCRIPTION	FIRST DAY COVERS SING	PL. BLK.	MINT SHEET	PLATE BLOCK	UNUSED F/NH	USED
2216-19	22¢ 36 varieties complete in 4 miniature sheets	29.95	....	....	....	35.00	30.00
2216a-19i	set of 36 singles.	70.00	....	....	....	40.00	22.50

2220 2221

2222 2223

1986 COMMEMORATIVES

SCOTT NO.	DESCRIPTION	FIRST DAY COVERS SING	PL. BLK.	MINT SHEET	PLATE BLOCK	UNUSED F/NH	USED
2220-23	Explorers, 4 varieties, attached . .	6.00	7.00	50.00(50)	6.00	5.00	4.50
2220	22¢ Elisha Kent Kane .	2.50	....	....	....	1.40	.40
2221	22¢ Adolphus W. Greely	2.50	....	....	....	1.40	.40
2222	22¢ Vilhjalmur Stefansson	2.50	....	....	....	1.40	.40
2223	22¢ R.E. Peary, M. Henson	2.50	....	....	....	1.40	.40

2224

SCOTT NO.	DESCRIPTION	FIRST DAY COVERS SING	PL. BLK.	MINT SHEET	PLATE BLOCK	UNUSED F/NH	USED
2224	22¢ Statue of Liberty . .	4.00	6.00	38.00(50)	4.00	.80	.25

2225

2226

2228

1986-91 TRANSPORTATION COILS–"B" Press
Perf. 10 Vertically

SCOTT NO.	DESCRIPTION	FIRST DAY COVERS SING	PLATE# STRIP 3	MINT SHEET	PLATE# STRIP 3	UNUSED F/NH	USED
2225	1¢ Omnibus	2.25	6.50	....	.85	.25	.25
	same, plate strip of 5 . .	....	....	....	....	1.20	....
2225a	1¢ Omnibus, untagged (1991)	....	....	....	1.50	.25	.25
	same, plate strip of 5 . .	....	....	....	....	2.00	....
2226	2¢ Locomotive (1987) .	2.25	6.50	....	1.00	.25	.20
	same, plate strip of 5 . .	....	....	....	....	1.20	....
2226a	plate strip of 5	....	....	....	....	2.50	....
2226b	2¢ Locomotive, untagged (1994)	....	....	....	1.25	.25	.25
2228	4¢ Stagecoach.	....	....	....	2.50	.30	.25
	same, plate strip of 5 . .	....	....	....	....	2.00	....
2228a	same, overall tagging (1990)	....	....	....	7.00	.60	.30
	same, plate strip of 5 . .	....	....	....	....	10.00	....
2231	8.3¢ Ambulance precancelled (1986). . .	....	....	....	7.00	2.00	.60
	same, plate strip of 5 . .	....	....	....	....	8.00	....

#2225—"¢" sign eliminated. #1897 has "1¢".
#2226—inscribed "2 USA". #1897A inscribed "USA 2¢".
#2228—"Stagecoach 1890s" is 17 mm long.

2235 2236 2237 2238

1986 COMMEMORATIVES (continued)

SCOTT NO.	DESCRIPTION	FIRST DAY COVERS SING	PL. BLK.	MINT SHEET	PLATE BLOCK	UNUSED F/NH	USED
2235-38	Navajo Art, 4 varieties, attached . .	4.00	5.00	51.00(50)	6.50	6.00	3.50
2235	22¢ Navajo Art.	2.25	....	....	....	1.75	.25
2236	22¢ Navajo Art.	2.25	....	....	....	1.75	.25
2237	22¢ Navajo Art.	2.25	....	....	....	1.75	.25
2238	22¢ Navajo Art.	2.25	....	....	....	1.75	.25

2239

SCOTT NO.	DESCRIPTION	FIRST DAY COVERS SING	PL. BLK.	MINT SHEET	PLATE BLOCK	UNUSED F/NH	USED
2239	22¢ T.S. Eliot	2.25	4.00	38.00(50)	4.00	1.00	.25

2240 2241 2242 2243

SCOTT NO.	DESCRIPTION	FIRST DAY COVERS SING	PL. BLK.	MINT SHEET	PLATE BLOCK	UNUSED F/NH	USED
2240-43	Woodcarved Figurines, 4 varieties, attached . .	4.00	5.00	39.00(50)	4.50	4.25	3.00
2240	[illegible]	[illegible]	....			1.10	.30
2241	22¢ Ship Figurehead . .	2.25	....	....	....	1.10	.30
2242	22¢ Nautical Figure . . .	2.25				1.10	.30
2243	22¢ Cigar Store Figure	2.25	....	....	....	1.10	.30

2244

2245

SCOTT NO.	DESCRIPTION	FIRST DAY COVERS SING	PL. BLK.	MINT SHEET	PLATE BLOCK	UNUSED F/NH	USED
2244	22¢ Madonna.	2.25	4.00	66.00(100)	4.00	.75	.25
2245	22¢ Village Scene	2.25	4.00	66.00(100)	4.00	.75	.25

2246

2247

2248

2249

2250

2251

1987 COMMEMORATIVES

SCOTT NO.	DESCRIPTION	FIRST DAY COVERS SING	PL. BLK.	MINT SHEET	PLATE BLOCK	UNUSED F/NH	USED
2246/2368	(2246-51, 2275, 2336-38, 2349-54, 2360-61, 2367-68) 20 varieties	....	....	....	....	18.50	5.25
2246	22¢ Michigan Statehood	2.25	4.00	39.00(50)	4.50	1.00	.25
2247	22¢ Pan American Games	2.25	4.00	38.00(50)	4.00	.95	.25
2248	22¢ LOVE	3.00	4.50	68.00(100)	4.00	.95	.25
2249	22¢ Jean Baptiste Pointe du Sable	2.25	4.00	36.00(50)	4.00	.95	.25
2250	22¢ Enrico Caruso. . . .	2.25	4.00	36.00(50)	4.00	.95	.25
2251	22¢ Girls Scouts	2.25	4.00	36.00(50)	4.00	.95	.25

2252

2253

2254

2255

2256

2257

2258

2259

2260

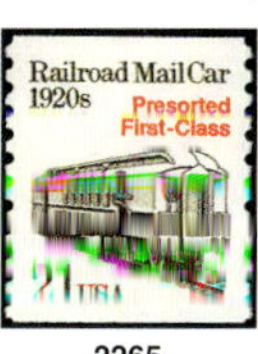
2261

2262

2263

2264 2265 2266

1987-93 TRANSPORTATION COILS

SCOTT NO.	DESCRIPTION	FIRST DAY COVERS SING	PLATE# STRIP 3	MINT SHEET	PLATE# STRIP 3	UNUSED F/NH	USED
2252	3¢ Conestoga Wagon (1988)	2.25	9.00	....	1.25	.25	.25
2252a	same, untagged (1992)	....	9.00	....	2.50	.25	.25
2253	5¢ Milk Wagon	2.25	9.00	....	1.90	.25	.25
2254	5.3¢ Elevator,precancel ('88)	2.25	9.00	....	1.90	.40	.25
2255	7.6¢ Carreta, precancel ('88)	2.25	9.00	....	3.25	.40	.25
2256	8.4¢ Wheel Chair, precancel (1988)	2.25	9.00	....	3.50	.40	.25
2257	10¢ Canal Boat	2.25	9.00	....	3.50	.40	.25
2257a	same, overall tagging (1993)		9.00	....	12.00	3.00	.25
2258	13¢ Police Wagon, precancel (1988)	2.25	9.00	....	6.00	.90	.25
2259	13.2¢ Railroad Coal Car, precancel (1988)	2.25	9.00	....	3.50	.40	.25
2260	15¢ Tugboat (1988) . . .	2.25	9.00	....	4.00	.50	.25
2260a	same, overall tagging (1990)		9.00	....	6.00	.75	.25
2261	16.7¢ Popcorn Wagon, precancel (1988)	2.25	9.00	....	4.00	.60	.25
2262	17.5¢ Racing Car.	2.25	9.00	....	5.25	1.25	.35
2262a	17.5¢ Racing Car, precancel (1988)	2.25	9.00	....	5.25	.90	.55
2263	20¢ Cable Car (1988) .	2.25	9.00	....	4.50	.70	.25
2263b	same, overall tagging (1990)		9.00	....	11.00	1.85	.40
2264	20.5¢ Fire Engine, precancel (1988)	2.25	9.00	....	8.00	1.50	.55
2265	21¢ Railroad Mail Car, precancel (1988)	2.25	9.00	....	4.00	.80	.45
2266	24.1¢ Tandem Bicycle, precancel (1988)	2.25	9.00	....	6.00	1.20	.90

PLATE NUMBER STRIPS OF 5

SCOTT NO.	UNUSED F/NH	SCOTT NO.	UNUSED F/NH	SCOTT NO.	UNUSED F/NH
2252	1.40	2257a	18.00	2262a	8.00
2252a	3.50	2258	7.50	2263	7.00
2253	2.50	2259	5.00	2263b	14.00
2254	2.50	2260	6.25	2264	10.00
2255	3.50	2260a	8.00	2265	6.00
2256	3.50	2261	4.75	2266	7.00
2257	4.50	2262	7.00		

2267

2268

2269

2270

2271

2272

2273

2274

1987 SPECIAL OCCASIONS BOOKLET PANE

SCOTT NO.	DESCRIPTION	FIRST DAY COVERS SING	FIRST DAY COVERS PL. BLK.	MINT SHEET	PLATE BLOCK	UNUSED F/NH	USED
2267	22¢ Congratulations! . .	2.25	....	....	....	2.00	.55
2268	22¢ Get Well!.	2.25	....	....	....	2.00	.55
2269	22¢ Thank You!	2.25	....	....	....	2.00	.55
2270	22¢ Love You, Dad! . . .	2.25	....	....	....	2.00	.55
2271	22¢ Best Wishes!.	2.25	....	....	....	2.00	.55
2272	22¢ Happy Birthday! . .	2.25	....	....	....	2.00	.55
2273	22¢ Love You, Mother!	2.25	....	....	....	2.00	.55
2274	22¢ Keep in Touch! . . .	2.25	....	....	....	2.00	.55
2274a	Special Occasions bklt pane of 10, attached . .	17.00	....	....	....	15.00	....

NOTE: **#2274a contains 1 each of #2268-71, 2273-74 and 2 each of #2267 and 2272.**

2275

1987 COMMEMORATIVES (continued)

SCOTT NO.	DESCRIPTION	FIRST DAY COVERS SING	FIRST DAY COVERS PL. BLK.	MINT SHEET	PLATE BLOCK	UNUSED F/NH	USED
2275	22¢ United Way	2.25	4.00	34.00(50)	3.50	1.00	.25

2276

2277, 2279, 2282, 2282a

2278, 2285A, 2285Ac

1987-88 REGULAR ISSUE

SCOTT NO.	DESCRIPTION	FIRST DAY COVERS SING	FIRST DAY COVERS PL. BLK.	MINT SHEET	PLATE BLOCK	UNUSED F/NH	USED
2276	22¢ Flag & Fireworks. .	2.25	4.00	68.00(100)	4.00	1.00	.25
2276a	bklt pane of 20	12.50	....	....	....	13.50	....
2277	(25¢) "E" Earth (1988) .	2.25	4.00	72.00(100)	4.50	.95	.25
2278	25¢ Flag with Clouds (1988)	2.25	4.00	72.00(100)	5.00	1.00	.25

2280

2281

2283, 2283a

2284

2285, 2285b

SCOTT NO.	DESCRIPTION	FIRST DAY COVERS SING	PLATE # STRIP 3	MINT SHEET	PLATE# STRIP 3	UNUSED F/NH	USED
2279	(25¢) "E" Earth coil (1988)	2.25	7.50	....	4.50	.80	.25
	same, plate strip of 5 . .	....	....	....	....	5.00	....
2280	25¢ Flag over Yosemite, coil (1988)	2.25	7.50	....	4.50	.90	.25
	same, plate strip of 5 . .	....	....	....	....	6.00	....
2280a	25¢ Flag over Yosemite, phosphor (1989)	2.25	....	....	5.00	.95	.25
	same, plate strip of 5 . .	....	....	....	....	6.50	....
2281	25¢ Honey Bee, coil (1988)	2.25	7.50	....	5.00	.85	.25
	same, plate strip of 5 . .	....	....	....	....	6.50	....
2282	(25¢) "E" Earth, bklt single (1988)	2.25	....	....	....	.85	.25
2282a	(25¢) "E" Earth, bklt pane of 10.	7.25	....	....	....	9.75	....
2283	25¢ Pheasant bklt single (1988)	2.25	....	....	....	1.50	.25
2283a	25¢ Pheasant, bklt pane of 10.	7.25	....	....	....	10.00	....
2283b	25¢ Pheasant, (red omitted) bklt single.	....	....	....	....	11.00	....
2283c	25¢ Pheasant, (red omitted) bklt pane of 10.	....	....	....	....	105.00	....
2284	25¢ Grosbeak, bklt single (1988)	2.25	....	....	....	1.00	.25
2285	25¢ Owl bklt single . . .	2.25	....	....	....	1.00	.25
2285b	25¢ Owl/Grosbeck, bklt pane of 10.	7.25	....	....	....	8.75	....
2285A	25¢ Flag with Clouds, bklt single.	2.25	....	....	....	.95	.25
2285Ac	as above, bklt pane of 6 (1988).	4.00	....	....	....	5.75	....

2286

2310

2335

1987 AMERICAN WILDLIFE

- 2286 *Barn Swallow*
- 2287 *Monarch Butterfly*
- 2288 *Bighorn Sheep*
- 2289 *Broad-tailed Hummingbird*
- 2290 *Cottontail*
- 2291 *Osprey*
- 2292 *Mountain Lion*
- 2293 *Luna Moth*
- 2294 *Mule Deer*
- 2295 *Gray Squirrel*
- 2296 *Armadillo*
- 2297 *Eastern Chipmunk*
- 2298 *Moose*
- 2299 *Black Bear*
- 2300 *Tiger Swallowtail*
- 2301 *Bobwhite*
- 2302 *Ringtail*
- 2303 *Red-winged Blackbird*
- 2304 *American Lobster*
- 2305 *Black-tailed Jack Rabbit*
- 2306 *Scarlet Tanager*
- 2307 *Woodchuck*
- 2308 *Roseate Spoonbill*
- 2309 *Bald Eagle*
- 2310 *Alaskan Brown Bear*
- 2311 *Iiwi*
- 2312 *Badger*
- 2313 *Pronghorn*
- 2314 *River Otter*
- 2315 *Ladybug*
- 2316 *Beaver*
- 2317 *White-tailed Deer*
- 2318 *Blue Jay*
- 2319 *Pika*
- 2320 *Bison*
- 2321 *Snowy Egret*
- 2322 *Gray Wolf*
- 2323 *Mountain Goat*
- 2324 *Deer Mouse*
- 2325 *Black-tailed Prairie Dog*
- 2326 *Box Turtle*
- 2327 *Wolverine*
- 2328 *American Elk*
- 2329 *California Sea Lion*
- 2330 *Mockingbird*
- 2331 *Raccoon*
- 2332 *Bobcat*
- 2333 *Black-footed Ferret*
- 2334 *Canada Goose*
- 2335 *Red Fox*

SCOTT NO.	DESCRIPTION	FIRST DAY COVERS SING	FIRST DAY COVERS PL. BLK.	MINT SHEET	PLATE BLOCK	UNUSED F/NH	USED
2286-2335	22¢, 50 varieties, attached.	70.00	....	45.00(50)	....	45.00	....
	set of singles	86.00	....	....	....	50.00	30.00
	singles of above, each	2.00	....	....	....	1.50	.75

2336

2337

2338

2339

SCOTT NO.	DESCRIPTION	FIRST DAY COVERS SING	FIRST DAY COVERS PL. BLK.	MINT SHEET	PLATE BLOCK	UNUSED F/NH	USED

2340

2341

2342

2343

2344

2345

2346

2347

2348

1987-90 COMMEMORATIVES

SCOTT NO.	DESCRIPTION	FIRST DAY COVERS SING	FIRST DAY COVERS PL. BLK.	MINT SHEET	PLATE BLOCK	UNUSED F/NH	USED
2336	22¢ Delaware Statehood	2.25	4.00	40.00(50)	4.00	1.00	.25
2337	22¢ Pennsylvania Statehood	2.25	4.00	40.00(50)	4.00	1.00	.25
2338	22¢ New Jersey Statehood	2.25	4.00	40.00(50)	4.00	1.00	.25
2339	22¢ Georgia Statehood (1988)	2.25	4.00	40.00(50)	4.00	1.00	.35
2340	22¢ Connecticut Statehood (1988)	2.25	4.00	40.00(50)	4.00	1.00	.25
2341	22¢ Massachusetts Statehood (1988).	2.25	4.00	40.00(50)	4.00	1.00	.40
2342	22¢ Maryland Statehood (1988)	2.25	4.00	40.00(50)	4.00	1.00	.40
2343	25¢ South Carolina Statehood (1988).	2.25	4.00	40.00(50)	4.00	1.00	.25
2344	25¢ New Hampshire Statehood (1988).	2.25	4.00	40.00(50)	4.00	1.00	.25
2345	25¢ Virginia Statehood (1988)	2.25	4.00	40.00(50)	4.00	1.00	.25
2346	25¢ New York Statehood (1988)	2.25	4.00	40.00(50)	4.00	1.00	.25
2347	25¢ North Carolina Statehood (1989).	2.25	4.00	45.00(50)	5.50	1.50	.25
2348	25¢ Rhode Island Statehood (1990)	2.25	9.00	45.00(50)	5.50	1.50	.25

2349

2350

SCOTT NO.	DESCRIPTION	FIRST DAY COVERS SING	FIRST DAY COVERS PL. BLK.	MINT SHEET	PLATE BLOCK	UNUSED F/NH	USED
2349	22¢ Morocco	2.25	4.00	35.00(50)	3.75	.80	.25
2350	22¢ William Faulkner. .	2.25	4.00	37.00(50)	4.75	1.25	.25

2351 2352

2353 2354

SCOTT NO.	DESCRIPTION	FIRST DAY COVERS SING	FIRST DAY COVERS PL. BLK.	MINT SHEET	PLATE BLOCK	UNUSED F/NH	USED
2351-54	Lacemaking, 4 varieties, attached.	4.00	5.00	38.00(40)	5.00	4.50	3.50
2351	22¢ Lace, Ruth Maxwell	2.25	....	....	....	1.25	.30
2352	22¢ Lace, Mary McPeek	2.25	....	....	....	1.25	.30
2353	22¢ Lace, Leslie K. Saari	2.25	....	....	....	1.25	.30
2354	22¢ Lace, Trenna Ruffner	2.25	....	....	....	1.25	.30

2355

2356

2357

2358

2359

SCOTT NO.	DESCRIPTION	FIRST DAY COVERS SING	FIRST DAY COVERS PL. BLK.	MINT SHEET	PLATE BLOCK	UNUSED F/NH	USED
2355	22¢ "The Bicentennial"	2.25	....	....	....	1.50	.30
2356	22¢ "We the people" . .	2.25	....	....	....	1.50	.30
2357	22¢ "Establish justice" .	2.25	....	....	....	1.50	.30
2358	22¢ "And secure".	2.25	....	....	....	1.50	.30
2359	22¢ "Do ordain"	2.25	....	....	....	1.50	.30
2359a	Drafting of Constitution bklt pane, 5 varieties, attached.	4.60	....	....	....	6.75	6.50

2360

2361

SCOTT NO.	DESCRIPTION	FIRST DAY COVERS SING	FIRST DAY COVERS PL. BLK.	MINT SHEET	PLATE BLOCK	UNUSED F/NH	USED
2360	22¢ Signing of U.S. Constitution	2.25	4.00	45.00(50)	4.50	1.00	.25
2361	22¢ Certified Public Accountants.	12.00	15.00	75.00(50)	7.50	1.75	.25

2362

2363

2364

2365

2366

LOCOMOTIVES ISSUE

SCOTT NO.	DESCRIPTION	FIRST DAY COVERS SING	FIRST DAY COVERS PL. BLK.	MINT SHEET	PLATE BLOCK	UNUSED F/NH	USED
2362	22¢ "Stourbridge Lion, 1829"	2.25	....	....	....	1.25	.25
2363	22¢ "Best Friend of Charleston, 1830"	2.25	....	....	....	1.25	.25
2364	22¢ "John Bull, 1831"	2.25	....	....	....	1.25	.25
2365	22¢ "Brother Jonathan, 1832"	2.25	....	....	....	1.25	.25
2366	22¢ "Gowan + Marx, 1839"	2.25	....	....	....	1.25	.25
2366a	Locomotives, bklt pane, 5 varieties, attached	4.60	....	....	....	5.00	4.75

2367

2368

SCOTT NO.	DESCRIPTION	FIRST DAY COVERS SING	FIRST DAY COVERS PL. BLK.	MINT SHEET	PLATE BLOCK	UNUSED F/NH	USED
2367	22¢ Madonna	2.25	4.00	68.00(100)	4.00	.90	.25
2368	22¢ Ornament	2.25	4.00	68.00(100)	4.00	.90	.25

2369

2370

2371

2372 2373

2374 2375

2376

2377

2378

1988 COMMEMORATIVES

SCOTT NO.	DESCRIPTION	FIRST DAY COVERS SING	FIRST DAY COVERS PL. BLK.	MINT SHEET	PLATE BLOCK	UNUSED F/NH	USED
2339/2400	(2339-46, 2369-80, 2386-93, 2399-2400) 30 varieties	....	....	....	....	29.00	9.00
2369	22¢ Winter Olympics	2.25	4.00	47.00(50)	7.00	1.50	.25
2370	22¢ Australia Bicentennial	2.25	4.00	28.00(50)	3.50	.75	.25
2371	22¢ James Weldon Johnson	2.25	4.00	44.00(50)	5.00	1.00	.30
2372-75	Cats, 4 varieties, attached	8.00	12.00	40.00(40)	6.50	5.00	4.00
2372	22¢ Siamese, Exotic Shorthair	2.25	....	....	....	1.50	.75
2373	22¢ Abyssinian, Himalayan	2.25	....	....	....	1.50	.75
2374	22¢ Maine Coon, Burmese	2.25	....	....	....	1.50	.75
2375	22¢ American Shorthair, Persian	2.25	....	....	....	1.50	.75
2376	22¢ Knute Rockne	4.00	6.00	45.00(50)	4.75	1.20	.50
2377	25¢ Francis Ouimet	8.00	10.00	48.00(50)	7.00	1.25	.30
2378	25¢ LOVE	2.25	4.00	72.00(100)	4.00	.85	.25

2379

2380

SCOTT NO.	DESCRIPTION	FIRST DAY COVERS SING	FIRST DAY COVERS PL. BLK.	MINT SHEET	PLATE BLOCK	UNUSED F/NH	USED
2379	45¢ LOVE	2.25	4.00	67.50(50)	7.00	1.50	.25
2380	25¢ Summer Olympics	2.25	4.00	46.00(50)	4.75	1.00	.25

2381

2382

2383

2384

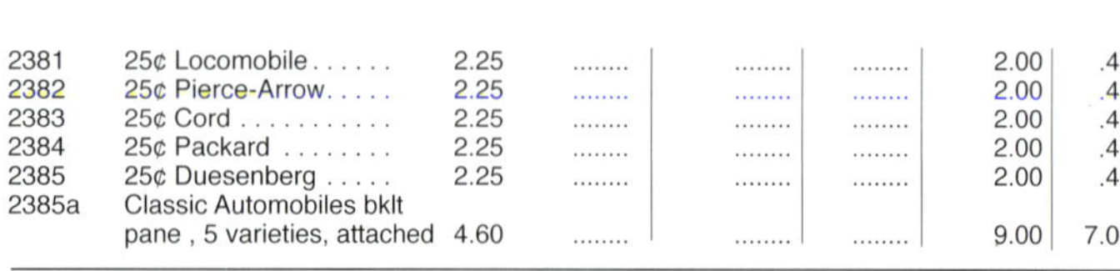

2385

SCOTT NO.	DESCRIPTION	FIRST DAY COVERS SING	FIRST DAY COVERS PL. BLK.	MINT SHEET	PLATE BLOCK	UNUSED F/NH	USED
2381	25¢ Locomobile	2.25	....	....	....	2.00	.40
2382	25¢ Pierce-Arrow	2.25	....	....	....	2.00	.40
2383	25¢ Cord	2.25	....	....	....	2.00	.40
2384	25¢ Packard	2.25	....	....	....	2.00	.40
2385	25¢ Duesenberg	2.25	....	....	....	2.00	.40
2385a	Classic Automobiles bklt pane , 5 varieties, attached	4.60	....	....	....	9.00	7.00

BOOKLET PANE SINGLES: Traditionally, booklet panes have been collected only as intact panes since, other than the straight edged sides, they were identical to sheet stamps. However, starting with the 1971 8¢ Eisenhower stamp, many issues differ from the comparative sheet stamp or may even be totally different issues (e.g. #1738-42 Windmills). These newer issues are now collected as booklet singles or panes—both methods being acceptable.

2386 2387

2388 2389

SCOTT NO.	DESCRIPTION	FIRST DAY COVERS SING	FIRST DAY COVERS PL. BLK.	MINT SHEET	PLATE BLOCK	UNUSED F/NH	USED
2386-89	Antarctic Explorers, 4 varieties, attached . .	4.00	5.00	48.00(50)	6.00	5.75	4.00
2386	25¢ Nathaniel Palmer .	2.25	....	....	....	1.50	.45
2387	25¢ Lt. Charles Wilkes.	2.25	....	....	....	1.50	.45
2388	25¢ Richard E. Byrd . .	2.25	....	....	....	1.50	.45
2389	25¢ Lincoln Ellsworth. .	2.25	....	....	....	1.50	.45

2390

2391

2392

2393

SCOTT NO.	DESCRIPTION	FIRST DAY COVERS SING	FIRST DAY COVERS PL. BLK.	MINT SHEET	PLATE BLOCK	UNUSED F/NH	USED
2390-93	Carousel Animals, 4 varieties, attached . .	4.00	5.00	52.50(50)	6.75	6.00	4.00
2390	25¢ Deer	2.25	....	....	....	1.60	.30
2391	25¢ Horse	2.25	....	....	....	1.60	.30
2392	25¢ Camel	2.25	....	....	....	1.60	.30
2393	25¢ Goat	2.25	....	....	....	1.60	.30

2394

SCOTT NO.	DESCRIPTION	FIRST DAY COVERS SING	FIRST DAY COVERS PL. BLK.	MINT SHEET	PLATE BLOCK	UNUSED F/NH	USED
2394	$8.75 Express Mail . . .	32.00	70.00	535.00(20)	125.00	30.00	10.00

2395

2396

2397

2398

SCOTT NO.	DESCRIPTION	FIRST DAY COVERS SING	FIRST DAY COVERS PL. BLK.	MINT SHEET	PLATE BLOCK	UNUSED F/NH	USED
2395-2398	Special Occasions, bklt singles.	7.00	....	....	....	4.50	1.85
2396a	Bklt pane (6) with gutter 3–#2395 + 3–#2396 . .	4.60	....	....	....	6.00	5.00
2398a	Bklt pane (6) with gutter 3–#2397 + 3–#2398 . .	4.60	....	....	....	6.00	5.00

2399

2400

SCOTT NO.	DESCRIPTION	FIRST DAY COVERS SING	FIRST DAY COVERS PL. BLK.	MINT SHEET	PLATE BLOCK	UNUSED F/NH	USED
2399	25¢ Madonna and Child	2.25	4.00	36.00(50)	3.75	1.00	.25
2400	25¢ One Horse Sleigh .	2.25	4.00	36.00(50)	3.75	1.00	.25

2401

2402

1989 COMMEMORATIVES

SCOTT NO.	DESCRIPTION	FIRST DAY COVERS SING	FIRST DAY COVERS PL. BLK.	MINT SHEET	PLATE BLOCK	UNUSED F/NH	USED
2347/2437	**(2347, 2401-04, 2410-14, 2416-18, 2420-28, 2434-37) 26 varieties . . . .**	....	....	....	....	**27.75**	**6.25**
2401	25¢ Montana Statehood	2.25	4.00	60.00(50)	7.00	1.50	.25
2402	25¢ A.P. Randolph	3.00	4.00	55.00(50)	5.00	1.20	.25

2403

2404

SCOTT NO.	DESCRIPTION	FIRST DAY COVERS SING	FIRST DAY COVERS PL. BLK.	MINT SHEET	PLATE BLOCK	UNUSED F/NH	USED
2403	25¢ North Dakota Statehood	2.25	4.00	65.00(50)	7.00	1.50	.25
2404	25¢ Washington Statehood	2.25	4.00	60.00(50)	7.00	1.50	.25

2405

2406

2407

2408

2409

SCOTT NO.	DESCRIPTION	FIRST DAY COVERS SING	FIRST DAY COVERS PL. BLK.	MINT SHEET	PLATE BLOCK	UNUSED F/NH	USED
2405	25¢ "Experiment,1788-90"	2.25	....	....	....	1.40	.35
2406	25¢ "Phoenix, 1809" . .	2.25	....	....	....	1.40	.35
2407	25¢ "New Orleans, 1812"	2.25	....	....	....	1.40	.35
2408	25¢ "Washington, 1816"	2.25	....	....	....	1.40	.35
2409	25¢ "Walk in the Water,1818"	2.25	....	....	....	1.40	.35
2409a	Steamboat, bklt pane, 5 varieties, attached . .	6.00	....	....	....	6.50	4.00
2409av	same, bklt pane, unfolded	....	....	....	....	12.00	....

2410  2411

SCOTT NO.	DESCRIPTION	FIRST DAY COVERS SING	FIRST DAY COVERS PL. BLK.	MINT SHEET	PLATE BLOCK	UNUSED F/NH	USED
2410	25¢ World Stamp Expo '89	2.25	4.00	36.00(50)	3.75	1.00	.25
2411	25¢ Arturo Toscanini . .	2.25	4.00	38.00(50)	3.75	1.00	.25

2412  2413  2414  2415

SCOTT NO.	DESCRIPTION	FIRST DAY COVERS SING	FIRST DAY COVERS PL. BLK.	MINT SHEET	PLATE BLOCK	UNUSED F/NH	USED
2412	25¢ U.S. House of Representatives.	2.25	4.00	45.00(50)	4.50	1.00	.25
2413	25¢ U.S. Senate	2.25	4.00	58.00(50)	5.25	1.15	.25
2414	25¢ Executive Branch .	2.25	4.00	40.00(50)	4.00	1.00	.25
2415	25¢ U.S. Supreme Court (1990)	2.25	4.00	40.00(50)	4.00	1.00	.25

2416

SCOTT NO.	DESCRIPTION	FIRST DAY COVERS SING	FIRST DAY COVERS PL. BLK.	MINT SHEET	PLATE BLOCK	UNUSED F/NH	USED
2416	25¢ South Dakota Statehood	2.25	4.00	55.00(50)	6.00	1.50	.25

2417  2418

SCOTT NO.	DESCRIPTION	FIRST DAY COVERS SING	FIRST DAY COVERS PL. BLK.	MINT SHEET	PLATE BLOCK	UNUSED F/NH	USED
2417	25¢ Lou Gehrig	5.00	8.00	55.00(50)	6.00	1.20	.30
2418	25¢ Ernest Hemingway	2.25	4.00	42.50(50)	4.50	1.00	.25

2419

SCOTT NO.	DESCRIPTION	FIRST DAY COVERS SING	FIRST DAY COVERS PL. BLK.	MINT SHEET	PLATE BLOCK	UNUSED F/NH	USED
2419	$2.40 Moon Landing . .	7.50	15.75	165.00(20)	40.00	10.00	5.00

2420 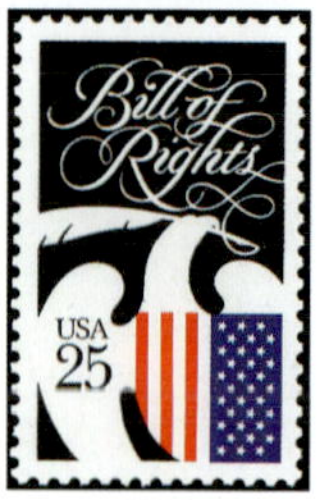 2421

SCOTT NO.	DESCRIPTION	FIRST DAY COVERS SING	FIRST DAY COVERS PL. BLK.	MINT SHEET	PLATE BLOCK	UNUSED F/NH	USED
2420	25¢ Letter Carriers. . . .	2.25	4.00	29.00(50)	4.00	1.00	.25
2421	25¢ Bill of Rights	2.25	4.00	43.00(50)	5.00	1.25	.25
2422-25	Prehistoric Animals, 4 attached	5.00	7.00	38.00(40)	5.50	5.00	3.75
2422	25¢ Tyrannosaurus Rex	2.50	....	....	....	1.40	.25
2423	25¢ Pteranodon.	2.50	....	....	....	1.40	.25
2424	25¢ Stegosaurus	2.50	....	....	....	1.40	.25
2425	25¢ Brontosaurus	2.50	....	....	....	1.40	.25
2426	25¢ Kachina Doll	2.25	4.00	38.00(50)	4.00	1.00	.25
2427	25¢ Madonna & Child .	1.75	4.00	40.00(50)	4.00	1.00	.25
2427a	same, bklt pane of 10 .	7.25	....	....	....	9.00	....
2427av	same, bklt pane, unfolded	....	....	....	....	15.00	....
2428	25¢ Sleigh full of Presents	2.25	4.00	40.00(50)	4.00	.85	.25
2429	25¢ Sleigh full of Presents, bklt single.	2.25	....	....	....	.90	.25
2429a	same, bklt pane of 10 .	7.25	....	....	....	9.00	....
2429av	same, bklt pane, unfolded	....	....	....	....	19.00	....
2431	25¢ Eagle & Shield, self-adhesive	1.95	....	....	....	1.25	.75
2431a	same, bklt pane of 18 .	32.00	....	....	....	18.00	....
2431	same, coil	....	....	....	3.00(3)	1.25	....

2422 2423 2424 2425

2426

2427 2428, 2429 2431

2433

SCOTT NO.	DESCRIPTION	FIRST DAY COVERS SING	FIRST DAY COVERS PL. BLK.	MINT SHEET	PLATE BLOCK	UNUSED F/NH	USED
2433	$3.60 World Stamp Expo, Imperf. Souvenir Sheet	15.00	....	....	....	22.00	18.00

2434 2435

2436 2437

SCOTT NO.	DESCRIPTION	FIRST DAY COVERS SING	FIRST DAY COVERS PL. BLK.	MINT SHEET	PLATE BLOCK	UNUSED F/NH	USED
2434-37	Classic Mail Delivery, 4 attached	5.00	7.00	40.00(40)	5.75	5.00	4.00
2434	25¢ Stagecoach.	2.25	....	....	....	1.50	.40
2435	25¢ Paddlewheel Steamer	2.25	....	....	....	1.50	.40
2436	25¢ Biplane	2.25	....	....	....	1.50	.40
2437	25¢ Automobile	2.25	....	....	....	1.50	.40
2438	$1.00 Classic Mail Delivery Imperf. Souvenir Sheet	4.50	....	....	....	8.00	6.50

2439

2440, 2441

2442

1990 COMMEMORATIVES

SCOTT NO.	DESCRIPTION	FIRST DAY COVERS SING	FIRST DAY COVERS PL. BLK.	MINT SHEET	PLATE BLOCK	UNUSED F/NH	USED
2348/2515	(2348, 2415, 2439-40, 2442, 2444-49, 2496-2500, 2506-15, 26 varieties	....	....	....	....	32.00	6.25
2439	25¢ Idaho Statehood . .	2.25	4.00	60.00(50)	5.00	1.50	.25
2440	25¢ LOVE	2.25	4.00	44.00(50)	4.00	1.50	.25
2441	25¢ LOVE, bklt single .	2.25	....	....	....	1.25	.25
2441a	25¢ LOVE bklt pane of 10	8.65	....	....	....	10.00	....
2441av	same, bklt pane, unfolded	....	....	....	....	50.00	....
2442	25¢ Ida B. Wells	3.00	4.00	60.00(50)	5.00	1.50	.25

2443

2444

2445

2446

2449

2447

2448

SCOTT NO.	DESCRIPTION	FIRST DAY COVERS SING	FIRST DAY COVERS PL. BLK.	MINT SHEET	PLATE BLOCK	UNUSED F/NH	USED
2443	15¢ Umbrella, bklt single	2.25	....	....	....	.60	.25
2443a	15¢ Umbrella, bklt pane of 10.	5.75	....	....	....	5.00	3.40
2443av	same, bklt pane, unfolded	....	....	....	....	10.00	....
2444	25¢ Wyoming Statehood	8.00	10.00	60.00(50)	6.00	1.75	.25
2445-48	Classic Films, 4 varieties, attached . .	8.00	7.00	65.00(40)	8.00	7.50	5.00
2445	25¢ Wizard of OZ	4.00	....	....	....	2.25	.35
2446	25¢ Gone with the Wind	4.00	....	....	....	2.25	.35
2447	25¢ Beau Geste.	4.00	....	....	....	2.25	.35
2448	25¢ Stagecoach.	4.00	....	....	....	2.25	.35
2449	25¢ Marianne Craig Moore	2.25	4.00	48.00(50)	5.00	1.50	.20

2451

2452, 2452B, 2452D

2453, 2454

2457, 2458

2463 2464 2466 2468

1990-95 TRANSPORTATION COILS

SCOTT NO.	DESCRIPTION	FIRST DAY COVERS SING	PLATE# STRIP 3	MINT SHEET	PLATE# STRIP 3	UNUSED F/NH	USED
2451	4¢ Steam Carriage (1991)	2.25	6.50	....	1.50	.25	.25
	same, plate strip of 5	....	....	....	....	1.60	....
2451b	4¢ Steam Carriage, untagged	......	....	....	1.50	.25	.25
	same, plate strip of 5	....	....	....	....	1.60	....
2452	5¢ Circus Wagon	2.25	6.50	....	1.50	.25	.25
	same, plate strip of 5	....	....	....	....	2.00	....
2452a	5¢ Circus Wagon, untagged	....	....	....	3.50	.25	.25
	same, plate strip of 5	....	....	....	....	4.00	....
2452B	5¢ Circus Wagon, Gravure (1992)	2.25	6.50	....	1.50	.35	.25
	same, plate strip of 5 . .	....	....	....	....	2.50	....
2452D	5¢ Circus Wagon, coil (Reissue, 1995 added)	3.00	10.00	....	2.00	.35	.25
	same, plate strip of 5 . .	....	....	....	....	3.00	....
2453	5¢ Canoe, precancel, brown (1991)	2.25	6.50	....	2.00	.35	.25
	same, plate strip of 5 . .	....	....	....	....	2.75	....
2454	5¢ Canoe, precancel, red (1991)	2.25	6.50	....	2.50	.35	.25
	same, plate strip of 5 . .	....	....	....	....	3.00	....
2457	10¢ Tractor Trailer (1991)	2.25	6.50	....	3.00	.45	.25
	same, plate strip of 5 . .	....	....	....	....	4.25	....
2458	10¢ Tractor Trailer, Gravure (1994)	2.25	6.50	....	6.00	.70	.50
	same, plate strip of 5 . .	....	....	....	....	8.00	....
2463	20¢ Cog Railway Car, coil	1.95	10.00	....	4.00	.70	.25
	same, plate strip of 5 . .	....	....	....	....	6.00	....
2464	23¢ Lunch Wagon (1991)	2.25	6.50	....	5.00	.85	.25
	same, plate strip of 5 . .	....	....	....	....	7.00	....
2466	32¢ Ferryboat, coil. . . .	1.95	10.00	....	6.75	1.25	.25
	same, plate strip of 5 . .	....	....	....	....	8.75.	....
2468	$1 Seaplane, coil.	3.00	10.00	....	15.00	4.00	1.00
	same, plate strip of 5 . .	....	....	....	....	21.50	....

2470

2471

2472

2473

2474

SCOTT NO.	DESCRIPTION	FIRST DAY COVERS SING	FIRST DAY COVERS PL. BLK.	MINT SHEET	PLATE BLOCK	UNUSED F/NH	USED
2470	25¢ Admiralty Head Lighthouse..........	2.25	....	....	....	2.25	.25
2471	25¢ Cape Hatteras Lighthouse..........	2.25	....	....	....	2.25	.25
2472	25¢ West Quoddy Head Lighthouse.....	2.25	....	....	....	2.25	.25
2473	25¢ American Shoals Lighthouse..........	2.25	....	....	....	2.25	.25
2474	25¢ Sandy Hook Lighthouse..........	2.25	....	....	....	2.25	.25
2474a	Lighthouse, bklt pane, 5 varieties	4.60	....	....	....	12.00	6.50
2474av	Same, bklt pane, unfolded	....	....	....	....	18.00	....

2475

SCOTT NO.	DESCRIPTION	FIRST DAY COVERS SING	FIRST DAY COVERS PL. BLK.	MINT SHEET	PLATE BLOCK	UNUSED F/NH	USED
2475	25¢ ATM Plastic Stamp, single........	2.25	....	....	....	1.75	1.25
2475a	Same, pane of 12	20.00	....	....	....	13.00	....

2476

2477

2478

2479

2480

2481

2482

2483

1990-95 REGULAR ISSUE

SCOTT NO.	DESCRIPTION	FIRST DAY COVERS SING	FIRST DAY COVERS PL. BLK.	MINT SHEET	PLATE BLOCK	UNUSED F/NH	USED
2476	1¢ Kestrel (1991).....	2.25	4.00	10.00(100)	.90	.25	.25
2477	1¢ Kestrel (redesign 1¢, 1995)	2.25	4.00	10.00(100)	.90	.25	.25
2478	3¢ Bluebird (1993)....	2.25	4.00	15.00(100)	1.50	.25	.25
2479	19¢ Fawn (1993).....	2.25	4.00	58.00(100)	5.00	.75	.25
2480	30¢ Cardinal (1993)...	2.25	4.00	85.00(100)	5.25	1.10	.80
2481	45¢ Pumpkinseed Sunfish (1992).......	2.00	4.50	135.00(100)	7.75	1.50	.75
2482	$2 Bobcat	6.00	14.00	110.00(20)	28.00	6.50	1.15
2483	20¢ Blue Jay, bklt single (1995)	1.95	....	....	....	.85	.30
2483a	same, bklt pane of 10 .	9.00	....	....	....	9.00	....
2483av	same, bklt pane, unfolded	....	....	....	....	11.00	....

2484, 2485

2486

2487, 2493, 2495

2488, 2494, 2495A

2489

2490

2491

2492

SCOTT NO.	DESCRIPTION	FIRST DAY COVERS SING	FIRST DAY COVERS PL. BLK.	MINT SHEET	PLATE BLOCK	UNUSED F/NH	USED
2484	29¢ Wood Duck, bklt single (BEP) (1991)	2.25	....	....	....	.95	.25
2484a	same, bklt pane of 10 (BEP)..............	9.00	....	....	....	9.50	....
2484av	same, bklt pane, unfolded	....	....	....	....	13.00	....
2485	29¢ Wood Duck, bklt single (KCS) (1991)........	2.25	....	....	....	1.20	.25
2485a	same, bklt pane of 10 (KCS).............	9.00	....	....	....	10.50	....
2485av	same, bklt pane, unfolded	....	....	....	....	14.00	....
2486	29¢ African Violet, bklt single..........	2.25	....	....	....	1.10	.25
2486a	same, bklt pane of 10 .	9.00	....	....	....	12.00	....
2486av	same, bklt pane, unfolded	....	....	....	....	14.00	....
2487	32¢ Peach, bklt single .	1.95	....	....	....	1.25	.25
2488	32¢ Pear, bklt single . .	1.95	....	....	....	1.25	.25
2488a	32¢ Peach & Pear, bklt pane of 10.......	7.25	....	....	....	12.00	....
2488av	same, bklt pane, unfolded	....	....	....	....	15.00	....
2489	29¢ Red Squirrel, self-adhesive (1993) . .	2.25	....	....	....	1.10	.45
2489a	same, bklt pane of 18 .	13.50	....	....	....	20.00	....
2489v	same, coil	....	....	....	3.00(3)	1.10	....
2490	29¢ Rose, self-adhesive (1993)	2.25	....	....	....	1.10	.40
2490a	same, bklt pane of 18 .	13.50	....	....	....	20.00	....
2491	29¢ Pine Cone, self-adhesive........	2.25	....	....	....	1.10	.40
2491a	same, bklt pane of 18 .	13.50	....	....	....	19.00	....
2492	32¢ Pink Rose, self-adhesive........	1.95	....	....	....	1.10	.30
2492a	same, bklt pane of 20 .	14.50	....	....	....	20.00	....
2492b	same, bklt pane of 15 .	11.50	....	....	....	18.00	....
2493	32¢ Peach, self-adhesive........	1.95	....	....	....	1.10	.30
2494	32¢ Pear, self-adhesive	1.95	....	....	....	1.10	.30
2494a	32¢ Peach & Pear, self-adhesive, bklt pane of 20.......	14.50	....	....	....	22.00	....
2495	32¢ Peach, self-adhesive coil (1993)	1.95	....	....	15.00(3)	3.50	....
2495A	32¢ Pear, self-adhesive coil	1.95	....	....	....	3.50	....
2495Ab	plate strip of 5	....	....	....	....	20.00	....

2496

2497

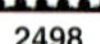
2498

2499

2500

SCOTT NO.	DESCRIPTION	FIRST DAY COVERS SING	FIRST DAY COVERS PL. BLK.	MINT SHEET	PLATE BLOCK	UNUSED F/NH	USED
2496-2500	Olympians, strip of 5, attached..........	7.50	10.00	35.00(35)	12.00(10)	7.00	5.00
2496	25¢ Jesse Owens....	2.40	....	....	....	1.75	.50
2497	25¢ Ray Ewry	2.40	....	....	....	1.75	.50
2498	25¢ Hazel Wightman . .	2.40	....	....	....	1.75	.50
2499	25¢ Eddie Eagan.....	2.40	....	....	....	1.75	.50
2500	25¢ Helene Madison . .	2.40	....	....	....	1.75	.50

2501

2502

2503

2504

2505

SCOTT NO.	DESCRIPTION	FIRST DAY COVERS SING	FIRST DAY COVERS PL. BLK.	MINT SHEET	PLATE BLOCK	UNUSED F/NH	USED
2501-05	25¢ Headdresses strip of 5					9.00	
2501	25¢ Assiniboine	2.40	....	....	....	2.00	.40
2502	25¢ Cheyenne	2.40	....	....	....	2.00	.40
2503	25¢ Comanche	2.40	....	....	....	2.00	.40
2504	25¢ Flathead	2.40	....	....	....	2.00	.40
2505	25¢ Shoshone	2.40	....	....	....	2.00	.40
2505a	25¢ bklt pane of 10 . . .	7.85	....	....	....	18.00	....
2505av	same, bklt pane, unfolded	....	....	....	....	25.00	....

2506 2507

SCOTT NO.	DESCRIPTION	FIRST DAY COVERS SING	FIRST DAY COVERS PL. BLK.	MINT SHEET	PLATE BLOCK	UNUSED F/NH	USED
2506-07	Micronesia + Marshall Islands 2 varieties, attached . .	5.00	6.00	48.00(50)	5.00	2.00	1.30
2506	25¢ Micronesia	2.50	....	....	....	1.00	.25
2507	25¢ Marshall Islands . .	2.50	....	....	....	1.00	.25

2508 2509

2510 2511

1990 REGULAR ISSUES

SCOTT NO.	DESCRIPTION	FIRST DAY COVERS SING	FIRST DAY COVERS PL. BLK.	MINT SHEET	PLATE BLOCK	UNUSED F/NH	USED
2508-11	Sea Creatures, ... 4 varieties, attached . .	5.00	6.00	37.00(40)	6.00	5.50	3.50
2508	25¢ Killer Whales.	2.50	....	....	....	1.40	.40
2509	25¢ Northern Sea Lions	2.50	....	....	....	1.40	.40
2510	25¢ Sea Otter	2.50	....	....	....	1.40	.40
2511	25¢ Common Dolphin .	2.50	....	....	....	1.40	.40

2512

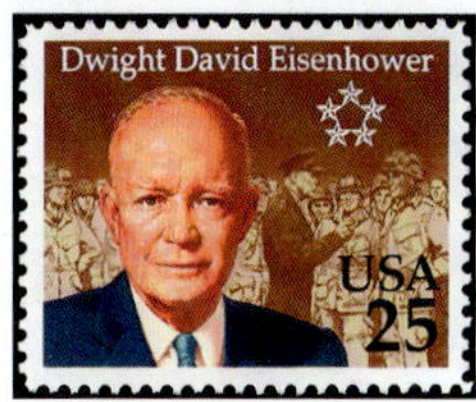

2513

2514

2515, 2516

SCOTT NO.	DESCRIPTION	FIRST DAY COVERS SING	FIRST DAY COVERS PL. BLK.	MINT SHEET	PLATE BLOCK	UNUSED F/NH	USED
2512	25¢ Americas Issue (Grand Canyon).	2.25	4.00	42.00(50)	5.00	1.25	.25
2513	25¢ Dwight D. Eisenhower	2.25	4.00	38.00(40)	5.00	1.25	.25
2514	25¢ Madonna & Child–Antonello	2.25	4.00	38.00(50)	3.50	.95	.25
2514a	same, bklt pane of 10 .	6.50	....	....	....	10.00	....
2514av	same, bklt pane, unfolded	....	....	....	....	15.00	....
2515	25¢ Christmas Tree . . .	2.25	4.00	38.00(50)	4.00	.75	.25
2516	25¢ Christmas Tree bklt single.	2.25	....	....	....	1.50	.25
2516a	same, bklt pane of 10 .	6.00	....	....	....	12.00	....
2516av	same, bklt pane, unfolded	....	....	....	....	19.50	....

2517- 2519, 2520

1991 REGULAR ISSUES

SCOTT NO.	DESCRIPTION	FIRST DAY COVERS SING	FIRST DAY COVERS PL. BLK.	MINT SHEET	PLATE BLOCK	UNUSED F/NH	USED
2517	(29¢) 'F" Flower	2.25	4.25	90.00(100)	4.25	.95	.25
			PLATE # STRIP 3		PLATE# STRIP 3		
2518	(29¢) "F" Flower, coil . .	2.25	10.00	....	4.00	.95	.25
	same, plate strip of 5 . .	....	....	....	....	6.00	....
2519	(29¢) "F" Flower, bklt single (BEP).	2.25	....	....	....	1.00	.25
2519a	same, bklt pane of 10 (BEP)	6.50	....	....	....	11.00	....
2520	(29¢) "F" Flower, bklt single (KCS).	3.00	....	....	....	3.50	.70
2520a	same, bklt pane of 10 (KCS)	6.50	....	....	....	30.00	

2521

2522

SCOTT NO.	DESCRIPTION	FIRST DAY COVERS SING	FIRST DAY COVERS PL. BLK.	MINT SHEET	PLATE BLOCK	UNUSED F/NH	USED
2521	(4¢) "F" Make-up Rate.	2.25	4.25	17.00(100)	1.00	.20	.25
2522	(29¢) "F" ATM Plastic Stamp, single.	2.25	....	....	....	1.00	.50
2522a	same, pane of 12.	9.00	....	....	....	16.00	....

2523, 2523A

SCOTT NO.	DESCRIPTION	FIRST DAY COVERS SING	FIRST DAY COVERS PL. BLK.	MINT SHEET	PLATE BLOCK	UNUSED F/NH	USED
			PLATE# STRIP 3		PLATE# STRIP 3		
2523	29¢ Flag over Mt. Rushmore, coil	2.25	10.00	....	5.00	1.50	.25
	same, plate strip of 5 .	....	....	....	....	7.00	....
2523A	29¢ Flag over Mt. Rushmore, photogravure coil	2.25	10.00	....	5.00	1.50	1.00
	same, plate strip of 5 .	....	....	....	....	7.50	....

2524-27

SCOTT NO.	DESCRIPTION	FIRST DAY COVERS SING	FIRST DAY COVERS PL. BLK.	MINT SHEET	PLATE BLOCK	UNUSED F/NH	USED
2524	29¢ Flower..........	2.25	4.25	90.00(100)	5.00	1.00	.25
2524A	29¢ Flower, perf. 13...	....	....	155.00(100)	55.00	1.40	.50
			PLATE# STRIP 3		PLATE# STRIP 3		
2525	29¢ Flower, coil rouletted	2.25	10.00	....	5.00	1.20	.25
	same, plate strip of 5..	....	....	....	....	7.00	....
2526	29¢ Flower, coil, perf (1992)	2.25	10.00	....	5.50	1.30	.25
	same, plate strip of 5..	....	....	....	....	8.00	....
2527	29¢ Flower, bklt single	2.25	....	....	....	1.20	.25
2527a	same, bklt pane of 10 .	6.50	....	....	....	9.50	....
2527av	same, bklt pane, unfolded	....	....	....	....	12.00	....

2528

2529, 2529C

2530

2531

2531A

SCOTT NO.	DESCRIPTION	FIRST DAY COVERS SING	FIRST DAY COVERS PL. BLK.	MINT SHEET	PLATE BLOCK	UNUSED F/NH	USED
			PLATE# STRIP 3		PLATE# STRIP3		
2528	29¢ Flag with Olympic Rings, bklt single...........	2.25	....	....	....	1.10	.25
2528a	same, bklt pane of 10 .	6.50	....	....	....	10.00	....
2528av	same, bklt pane, unfolded	....	....	....	....	12.00	....
2529	19¢ Fishing Boat Type I	2.25	10.00	....	4.00	.75	.25
	same, plate strip of 5..	....	....	....	....	5.00	....
2529a	same, Type II (1993) ..	....	....	....	4.50	.75	.40
	same, plate strip of 5..	....	....	....	....	5.50	....
2529C	19¢ Fishing Boat (re-engraved)........	2.25	10.00	....	9.00	1.25	.60
	same, plate strip of 5..	....	....	....	....	11.50	....
2530	19¢ Hot-Air Balloon bklt single..........	2.25	....	....	....	.70	.25
2530a	same, bklt pane of 10 .	10.00	....	....	....	6.75	.25
2530av	same, bklt pane, unfolded	....	....	....	....	8.00	....
2531	29¢ Flags on Parade ..	2.25	4.25	95.00(100)	5.00	1.25	.25
2531A	29¢ Liberty Torch ATM Stamp	2.25	....	....	....	1.25	.30
2531Ab	same, pane of 18.....	15.00	....	....	....	18.00	....

2532

1991 COMMEMORATIVES

SCOTT NO.	DESCRIPTION	FIRST DAY COVERS SING	FIRST DAY COVERS PL. BLK.	MINT SHEET	PLATE BLOCK	UNUSED F/NH	USED
2532/2579	**(2532-35, 2537-38, 2550-51, 2553-61, 2567, 2578-79) 29 varieties ....**	....	....	....	....	**32.00**	**11.50**
2532	50¢ Switzerland.....	2.25	5.00	58.00(40)	7.00	1.75	.40

2533

2534

2535, 2536

2537

2538

2539

SCOTT NO.	DESCRIPTION	FIRST DAY COVERS SING	FIRST DAY COVERS PL. BLK.	MINT SHEET	PLATE BLOCK	UNUSED F/NH	USED
2533	29¢ Vermont Statehood	2.25	4.25	56.00(50)	6.00	1.50	.25
2534	29¢ Savings Bonds ...	2.25	4.25	45.00(50)	4.75	1.00	.25
2535	29¢ Love	2.25	4.25	43.00(50)	4.75	1.00	.25
2535a	29¢ Love, perf 11.....	2.25	4.25	65.00(50)	8.50	1.50	.25
2536	29¢ Love, bklt single..	2.25	....	....	....	1.00	.25
2536a	same, bklt pane of 10 .	6.50	....	....	....	10.00	....
2536av	same, bklt pane, unfolded	....	....	....	....	13.00	....
2537	52¢ Love	2.25	5.00	80.00(50)	8.50	1.75	.35
2538	29¢ William Saroyan ..	2.25	4.25	45.00(50)	5.00	1.00	.25
2539	$1 USPS/Olympic Rings	3.00	6.50	58.00(20)	15.00	3.50	1.50

2540

SCOTT NO.	DESCRIPTION	FIRST DAY COVERS SING	FIRST DAY COVERS PL. BLK.	MINT SHEET	PLATE BLOCK	UNUSED F/NH	USED
2540	$2.90 Eagle and Olympic Rings	10.00	16.50	210.00(20)	55.00	13.00	5.50

2541

2542

SCOTT NO.	DESCRIPTION	FIRST DAY COVERS SING	FIRST DAY COVERS PL. BLK.	MINT SHEET	PLATE BLOCK	UNUSED F/NH	USED
2541	$9.95 Express Mail ...	27.00	50.00	600.00(20)	150.00	33.00	11.00
2542	$14.00 Express Mail ..	35.00	67.50	825.00(20)	200.00	45.00	23.00

2543

2544

2544A

SCOTT NO.	DESCRIPTION	FIRST DAY COVERS SING	FIRST DAY COVERS PL. BLK.	MINT SHEET	PLATE BLOCK	UNUSED F/NH	USED
2543	$2.90 Space Vehicle, Priority Mail	8.00	17.50	375.00(40)	45.00	10.00	2.75
2544	$3 Challenger Shuttle, Priority Mail (1995) ...	8.00	17.50	170.00(20)	42.00	9.00	3.00
2544A	$10.75 Endeavour Shuttle, Express Mail (1995)...	27.50	57.50	625.00(20)	155.00	30.00	10.00
2544b	Challenger Shuttle, Priority Mail (1996).....	....	....	180.00(20)	42.00	10.00	3.50

SCOTT NO.	DESCRIPTION	FIRST DAY COVERS SING	FIRST DAY COVERS PL. BLK.	MINT SHEET	PLATE BLOCK	UNUSED F/NH	USED

2545

2546

2547

2548

2549

SCOTT NO.	DESCRIPTION	FIRST DAY COVERS SING	FIRST DAY COVERS PL. BLK.	MINT SHEET	PLATE BLOCK	UNUSED F/NH	USED
2545	29¢ "Royal Wulff".	2.25	....	....	....	2.00	.25
2546	29¢ "Jock Scott".	2.25	....	....	....	2.00	.25
2547	29¢ "Apte Tarpon"	2.25	....	....	....	2.00	.25
2548	29¢ "Lefty's Deceiver" .	2.25	....	....	....	2.00	.25
2549	29¢ "Muddler Minnow".	2.25	....	....	....	2.00	.25
0C10a	Fishing Flies, bklt pane, 5 varieties, attached . .	4.50	....	....	....	12.00	9.00
2549av	same, bklt pane, unfolded	....	....	....	....	18.00	....

2550

2551, 2552

SCOTT NO.	DESCRIPTION	FIRST DAY COVERS SING	FIRST DAY COVERS PL. BLK.	MINT SHEET	PLATE BLOCK	UNUSED F/NH	USED
2550	29¢ Cole Porter	2.25	4.25	50.00(50)	5.00	1.10	.25
2551	29¢ Desert Storm	2.25	4.25	50.00(50)	4.75	1.10	.25
2552	29¢ Desert Storm, bklt single.	2.25	....	....	....	2.50	.25
2552a	same, bklt pane of 5 . .	4.75	....	....	....	5.50	....
2552av	same, bklt pane, unfolded	....	....	....	....	7.50	

2553

2554

2555

2556

2557

2558

SCOTT NO.	DESCRIPTION	FIRST DAY COVERS SING	FIRST DAY COVERS PL. BLK.	MINT SHEET	PLATE BLOCK	UNUSED F/NH	USED
2553-57	Summer Olympics, 5 varieties, attached . .	4.50	....	38.00(40)	12.00(10)	5.25	4.50
2553	29¢ Pole Vault	2.25	....	....	....	1.10	.60
2554	29¢ Discus.	2.25	....	....	....	1.10	.60
2555	29¢ Sprinters	2.25	....	....	....	1.10	.60
2556	29¢ Javelin	2.25	....	....	....	1.10	.60
2557	29¢ Hurdles	2.25	....	....	....	1.10	.60
2558	29¢ Numismatics.	2.25	4.25	60.00(50)	6.00	1.30	.60

2559

SCOTT NO.	DESCRIPTION	FIRST DAY COVERS SING	FIRST DAY COVERS PL. BLK.	MINT SHEET	PLATE BLOCK	UNUSED F/NH	USED
2559	$2.90 World War II, 1941, souvenir sheet of 10 . .	14.00	....	22.00(20)	....	14.00	11.00
2559a	29¢ Burma Road	3.00	....	....	....	1.35	.75
2559b	29¢ Peacetime Draft . .	3.00	....	....	....	1.35	.75
2559c	29¢ Lend-Lease Act. . .	3.00	....	....	....	1.35	.75
2559d	29¢ Atlantic Charter. . .	3.00	....	....	....	1.35	.75
2559e	29¢ "Arsenal of Democracy"	3.00	....	....	....	1.35	.75
2559f	29¢ Destroyer "Reuben James".	3.00	....	....	....	1.35	.75
2559g	29¢ Civil Defense	3.00	....	....	....	1.35	.75
2559h	29¢ Liberty Ship.	3.00	....	....	....	1.35	.75
[illegible]	[illegible] Pearl Harbor	[illegible]	....	....	....	1.35	.75
[illegible]	[illegible] Declaration of War on Japan	3.00				1.35	.75

2560

SCOTT NO.	DESCRIPTION	FIRST DAY COVERS SING	FIRST DAY COVERS PL. BLK.	MINT SHEET	PLATE BLOCK	UNUSED F/NH	USED
2560	29¢ Basketball.	3.00	4.50	65.00(50)	6.50	1.50	.25

2561

SCOTT NO.	DESCRIPTION	FIRST DAY COVERS SING	FIRST DAY COVERS PL. BLK.	MINT SHEET	PLATE BLOCK	UNUSED F/NH	USED
2561	29¢ District of Columbia	2.25	4.25	45.00(50)	4.50	1.30	.25

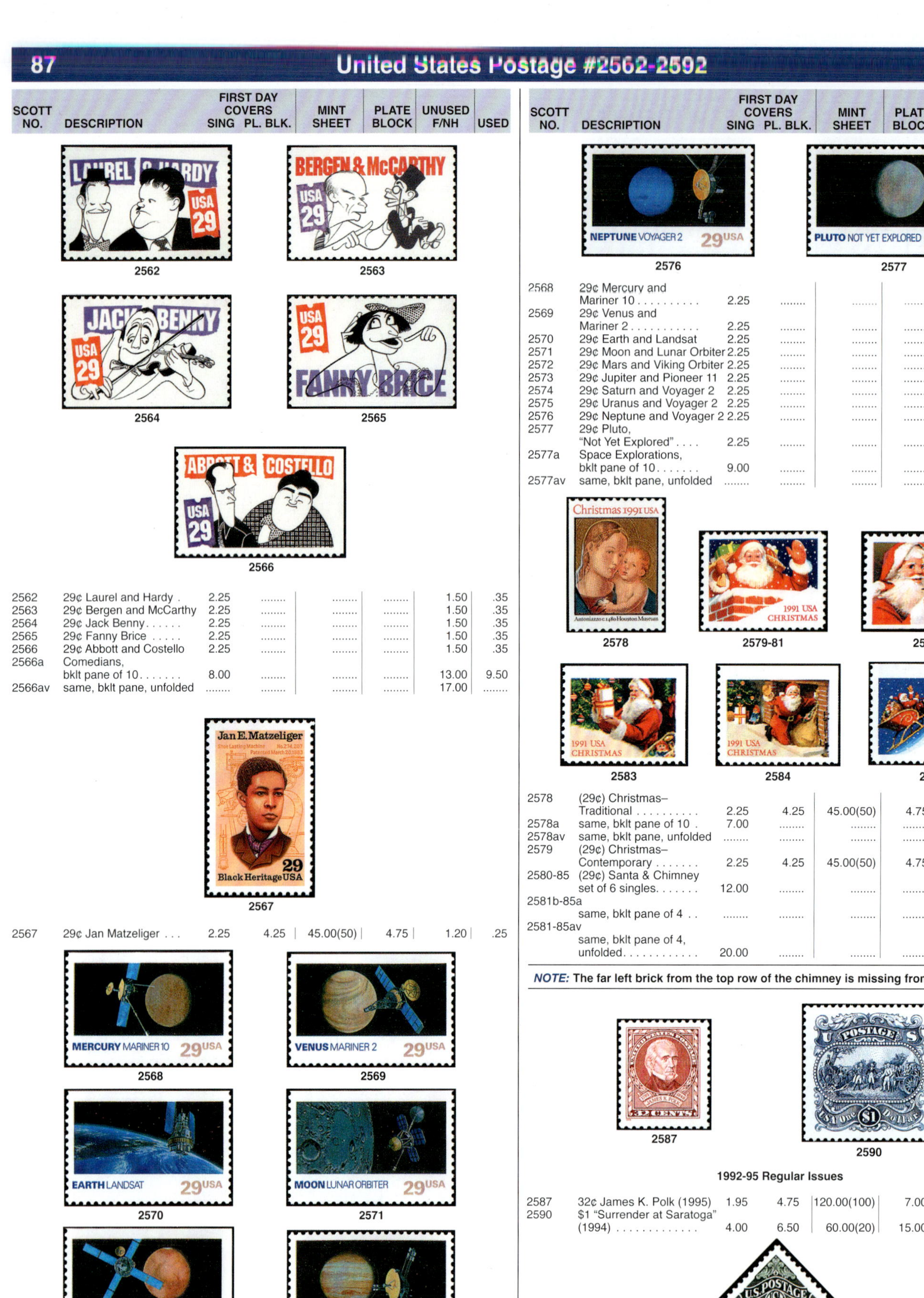

SCOTT NO.	DESCRIPTION	FIRST DAY COVERS SING	FIRST DAY COVERS PL. BLK.	MINT SHEET	PLATE BLOCK	UNUSED F/NH	USED
2562	29¢ Laurel and Hardy .	2.25	....	....	....	1.50	.35
2563	29¢ Bergen and McCarthy	2.25	....	....	....	1.50	.35
2564	29¢ Jack Benny.	2.25	....	....	....	1.50	.35
2565	29¢ Fanny Brice	2.25	....	....	....	1.50	.35
2566	29¢ Abbott and Costello	2.25	....	....	....	1.50	.35
2566a	Comedians, bklt pane of 10.	8.00	....	....	....	13.00	9.50
2566av	same, bklt pane, unfolded	....	....	....	....	17.00	....

SCOTT NO.	DESCRIPTION	FIRST DAY COVERS SING	FIRST DAY COVERS PL. BLK.	MINT SHEET	PLATE BLOCK	UNUSED F/NH	USED
2567	29¢ Jan Matzeliger . . .	2.25	4.25	45.00(50)	4.75	1.20	.25

SCOTT NO.	DESCRIPTION	FIRST DAY COVERS SING	FIRST DAY COVERS PL. BLK.	MINT SHEET	PLATE BLOCK	UNUSED F/NH	USED
2568	29¢ Mercury and Mariner 10	2.25	....	....	....	1.50	.40
2569	29¢ Venus and Mariner 2	2.25	....	....	....	1.50	.40
2570	29¢ Earth and Landsat	2.25	....	....	....	1.50	.40
2571	29¢ Moon and Lunar Orbiter	2.25	....	....	....	1.50	.40
2572	29¢ Mars and Viking Orbiter	2.25	....	....	....	1.50	.40
2573	29¢ Jupiter and Pioneer 11	2.25	....	....	....	1.50	.40
2574	29¢ Saturn and Voyager 2	2.25	....	....	....	1.50	.40
2575	29¢ Uranus and Voyager 2	2.25	....	....	....	1.50	.40
2576	29¢ Neptune and Voyager 2	2.25	....	....	....	1.50	.40
2577	29¢ Pluto, "Not Yet Explored"	2.25	....	....	....	1.50	.40
2577a	Space Explorations, bklt pane of 10.	9.00	....	....	....	14.00	12.00
2577av	same, bklt pane, unfolded	....	....	....	....	20.00	....

SCOTT NO.	DESCRIPTION	FIRST DAY COVERS SING	FIRST DAY COVERS PL. BLK.	MINT SHEET	PLATE BLOCK	UNUSED F/NH	USED
2578	(29¢) Christmas–Traditional	2.25	4.25	45.00(50)	4.75	1.00	.25
2578a	same, bklt pane of 10 .	7.00	....	....	....	10.00	....
2578av	same, bklt pane, unfolded	....	....	....	....	15.00	....
2579	(29¢) Christmas–Contemporary	2.25	4.25	45.00(50)	4.75	.95	.25
2580-85	(29¢) Santa & Chimney set of 6 singles.	12.00	....	....	....	13.50	3.50
2581b-85a	same, bklt pane of 4 . .	....	....	....	....	28.00	....
2581-85av	same, bklt pane of 4, unfolded.	20.00	....	....	....	32.50	....

NOTE: **The far left brick from the top row of the chimney is missing from Type II, No. 2581**

1992-95 Regular Issues

SCOTT NO.	DESCRIPTION	FIRST DAY COVERS SING	FIRST DAY COVERS PL. BLK.	MINT SHEET	PLATE BLOCK	UNUSED F/NH	USED
2587	32¢ James K. Polk (1995)	1.95	4.75	120.00(100)	7.00	1.75	.25
2590	$1 "Surrender at Saratoga" (1994)	4.00	6.50	60.00(20)	15.00	3.50	1.00
2592	$5 Washington & Jackson (1994)	22.00	30.00	300.00(20)	68.00	16.50	3.00

2593, 2594

SCOTT NO.	DESCRIPTION	FIRST DAY COVERS SING	FIRST DAY COVERS PL. BLK.	MINT SHEET	PLATE BLOCK	UNUSED F/NH	USED
2593	29¢ Pledge of Allegiance (black) bklt single.	2.25	....	....	....	1.00	.25
2593a	same, bklt pane of 10 .	7.00	....	....	....	10.00	....
2593av	same, bklt pane, unfolded	....	....	....	....	14.00	....
2594	29¢ Pledge of Allegiance (red) bklt single (1993).	2.25	....	....	....	1.50	.25
2594a	same, bklt pane of 10 .	7.00	....	....	....	11.00	....
2594av	same, bklt pane, unfolded	....	....	....	....	14.00	....

2595-97

2598

2599

1992-94 Self-Adhesive Stamps

SCOTT NO.	DESCRIPTION	FIRST DAY COVERS SING	FIRST DAY COVERS PL. BLK.	MINT SHEET	PLATE BLOCK	UNUSED F/NH	USED
2595	29¢ Eagle & Shield (brown) bklt single	2.25	....	....	....	1.20	.30
2595a	same, bklt pane of 17 .	12.00	....	....	....	18.00	....
2595v	same, coil	2.50	....	....	....	1.20	.30
2596	29¢ Eagle & Shield (green) bklt single	1.75	....	....	....	1.20	.30
2596a	same, bklt pane of 17 .	12.00	....	....	....	18.00	....
2596v	same, coil	2.50	....	....	....	1.20	.30
2597	29¢ Eagle & Shield (red) bklt single	2.25	....	....	....	1.20	.30
2597a	same, bklt pane of 17 .	12.00	....	....	....	18.00	....
2597v	same, coil	2.50	....	....	....	1.20	.30
2598	29¢ Eagle (1994)	2.25	....	....	....	1.20	.30
2598a	same, bklt pane of 18 .	13.50	....	....	....	18.00	....
2598v	29¢ Eagle, coil.	2.50	....	....	10.00(3)	1.20	....
2598b	same, plate strip of 5 . .	....	....	....	....	12.00	....
2599	29¢ Statue of Liberty (1994)	2.25	....	....	....	1.20	.30
2599a	same, bklt pane of 18 .	13.50	....	....	....	18.00	....
2599v	29¢ Statue of Liberty, coil	2.50	....	....	10.00(3)	1.20	....
2599b	same, plate strip of 5 . .	....	....	....	....	12.00	....

2602

2603, 2604

2605

2606-08

2609

1991-93 Regular Issue

SCOTT NO.	DESCRIPTION	FIRST DAY COVERS SING	PLATE# STRIP 3	MINT SHEET	PLATE# STRIP 3	UNUSED F/NH	USED
2602	(10¢) Eagle, Bulk-Rate coil	2.25	10.00	....	3.00	.40	.25
	same, plate strip of 5 . .	....	....	....	....	4.00	....
2603	(10¢) Eagle, Bulk-Rate coil (orange-yellow) (BEP)	2.25	10.00	....	3.00	.40	.25
	same, plate strip of 5 . .	....	....	....	....	4.00	....
2604	(10¢) Eagle, Bulk-Rate coil (Stamp Ventures) (gold) (1993)	2.25	10.00	....	3.00	.40	.25
2605	23¢ Flag, Presort First-Class	2.25	10.00	....	4.00	.75	.30
	same, plate strip of 5 . .	....	....	....	....	5.50	....
2606	23¢ USA, Presort First-Class (ABN) (1992)	2.25	10.00	....	4.50	.75	.30
	same, plate strip of 5 . .	....	....	....	....	7.00	....
2607	23¢ USA, Presort First-Class (BEP) (1992)	2.25	10.00	....	4.50	.75	.30
	same, plate strip of 5 . .	....	....	....	....	7.00	....
2608	23¢ USA, Presort First-Class (Stamp Ventures) (1993)	2.25	10.00	....	7.00	1.40	.30
	same, plate strip of 5 . .	....	....	....	....	10.00	....
2609	29¢ Flag over White House, coil (1992)	2.25	10.00	....	5.00	1.20	.25
	same, plate strip of 5 . .	....	....	....	....	7.00	....

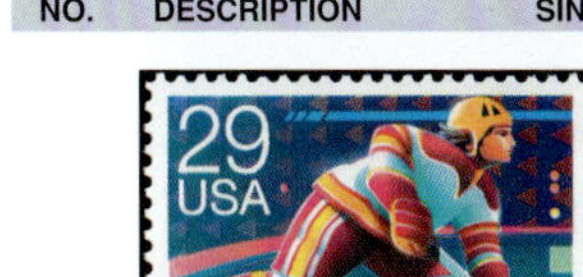

2611

2612

2613

2614

2615

1992 COMMEMORATIVES

SCOTT NO.	DESCRIPTION	FIRST DAY COVERS SING	FIRST DAY COVERS PL. BLK.	MINT SHEET	PLATE BLOCK	UNUSED F/NH	USED
2611/2720	**(2611-23, 2630-41, 2697-2704, 2710-14, 2720) 48 varieties . . . .**	....	....	....	....	**50.00**	**16.50**
2611-15	Winter Olympics, 5 varieties, attached . .	6.00	....	40.00(35)	12.00(10)	5.75	4.50
2611	29¢ Hockey	2.25	....	....	....	1.30	.25
2612	29¢ Figure Skating . . .	2.25	....	....	....	1.30	.25
2613	29¢ Speed Skating . . .	2.25	....	....	....	1.30	.25
2614	29¢ Skiing	2.25	....	....	....	1.30	.25
2615	29¢ Bobsledding	2.25	....	....	....	1.30	.25

2616

2617

SCOTT NO.	DESCRIPTION	FIRST DAY COVERS SING	FIRST DAY COVERS PL. BLK.	MINT SHEET	PLATE BLOCK	UNUSED F/NH	USED
2616	29¢ World Columbian Expo	2.25	4.25	45.00(50)	4.75	1.50	.25
2617	29¢ W.E.B. Du Bois. . .	3.00	4.25	52.00(50)	5.50	1.50	.25

2618

2619

SCOTT NO.	DESCRIPTION	FIRST DAY COVERS SING	FIRST DAY COVERS PL. BLK.	MINT SHEET	PLATE BLOCK	UNUSED F/NH	USED
2618	29¢ Love	2.25	4.25	45.00(50)	4.50	.95	.25
2619	29¢ Olympic Baseball .	3.75	5.50	52.00(50)	6.50	1.25	.25

2620 2621

2622 2623

SCOTT NO.	DESCRIPTION	FIRST DAY COVERS SING	PL. BLK.	MINT SHEET	PLATE BLOCK	UNUSED F/NH	USED
2620-23	First Voyage of Columbus	4.00	5.00	40.00(40)	5.50	4.25	4.00
2620	29¢ Seeking Isabella's Support	2.25	....	....	....	1.25	.35
2621	29¢ Crossing the Atlantic	2.25	....	....	....	1.25	.35
2622	29¢ Approaching Land	2.25	....	....	....	1.25	.35
2623	29¢ Coming Ashore . . .	2.25	....	....	....	1.25	.35

2624

2625

2626

2627

2628

2629

SCOTT NO.	DESCRIPTION	FIRST DAY COVERS SING	PL. BLK.	MINT SHEET	PLATE BLOCK	UNUSED F/NH	USED
2624-29	1¢-$5 Columbian Souvenir Sheets (6). . .	55.00	....	....	....	50.00	40.00
2624a-29a	same, set of 16 singles	105.00	....	....	....	54.00	39.00

2630

SCOTT NO.	DESCRIPTION	FIRST DAY COVERS SING	PL. BLK.	MINT SHEET	PLATE BLOCK	UNUSED F/NH	USED
2630	29¢ NY Stock Exchange	4.00	6.00	35.00(40)	4.75	1.00	.25

2631 2632 2633 2634

SCOTT NO.	DESCRIPTION	FIRST DAY COVERS SING	PL. BLK.	MINT SHEET	PLATE BLOCK	UNUSED F/NH	USED
2631-34	Space, US/Russian Joint Issue	4.00	5.00	48.00(50)	5.50	5.00	3.50
2631	29¢ Cosmonaut & Space Shuttle	2.50	....	....	....	1.30	.40
2632	29¢ Astronaut & Mir Space Station	2.50	....	....	....	1.30	.40
2633	29¢ Apollo Lunar Module & Sputnik	2.50	....	....	....	1.30	.40
2634	29¢ Soyuz, Mercury & Gemini Space Craft . . .	2.50	....	....	....	1.30	.40

2635

2636

SCOTT NO.	DESCRIPTION	FIRST DAY COVERS SING	PL. BLK.	MINT SHEET	PLATE BLOCK	UNUSED F/NH	USED
2635	29¢ Alaska Highway . .	2.25	4.75	45.00(50)	4.75	1.20	.25
2636	29¢ Kentucky Statehood	2.25	4.75	45.00(50)	4.75	1.20	.25

2637

2638

2639

2640

2641

SCOTT NO.	DESCRIPTION	FIRST DAY COVERS SING	FIRST DAY COVERS PL. BLK.	MINT SHEET	PLATE BLOCK	UNUSED F/NH	USED
2637-41	Summer Olympics, 5 varieties, attached . .	5.50	....	39.00(35)	14.00(10)	6.00	5.00
2637	29¢ Soccer	2.25	....	....	....	1.30	.75
2638	29¢ Women's Gymnastics	2.25	....	....	....	1.30	.75
2639	29¢ Volleyball	2.25	....	....	....	1.30	.75
2640	29¢ Boxing.	2.25	....	....	....	1.30	.75
2641	29¢ Swimming.	2.25	....	....	....	1.30	.75

2642

2643

2644

2645

2646

SCOTT NO.	DESCRIPTION	FIRST DAY COVERS SING	FIRST DAY COVERS PL. BLK.	MINT SHEET	PLATE BLOCK	UNUSED F/NH	USED
2642	29¢ Ruby-throated Hummingbird.	2.25	....	....	....	1.30	.60
2643	29¢ Broad-billed Hummingbird.	2.25	....	....	....	1.30	.60
2644	29¢ Costa's Hummingbird	2.25	....	....	....	1.30	.60
2645	29¢ Rufous Hummingbird	2.25	....	....	....	1.30	.60
2646	29¢ Calliope Hummingbird	2.25	....	....	....	1.30	.60
2646a	29¢ Hummingbirds, bklt pane, 5 vareities, attached . .	5.00	....	....	....	5.75	....
2646av	same, bklt pane, unfolded	....	....	....	....	6.50	....

2647

2648

2649

1992 WILDFLOWERS

2647 *Indian Paintbrush*
2648 *Fragrant Water Lily*
2649 *Meadow Beauty*
2650 *Jack-in-the-Pulpit*
2651 *California Poppy*
2652 *Large-Flowered Trillium*
2653 *Tickseed*
2654 *Shooting Star*
2655 *Stream Violet*
2656 *Bluets*
2657 *Herb Robert*
2658 *Marsh Marigold*
2659 *Sweet White Violet*
2660 *Claret Cup Cactus*
2661 *White Mountain Avens*
2662 *Sessile Bellwort*
2663 *Blue Flag*
2664 *Harlequin Lupine*
2665 *Twinflower*
2666 *Common Sunflower*
2667 *Sego Lily*
2668 *Virginia Bluebells*
2669 *Ohi'a Lehua*
2670 *Rosebud Orchid*
2671 *Showy Evening Primrose*
2672 *Fringed Gentian*
2673 *Yellow Lady's Slipper*
2674 *Passionflower*
2675 *Bunchberry*
2676 *Pasqueflower*
2677 *Round-lobed Hepatica*
2678 *Wild Columbine*
2679 *Fireweed*
2680 *Indian Pond Lily*
2681 *Turk's Cap Lily*
2682 *Dutchman's Breeches*
2683 *Trumpet Honeysuckle*
2684 *Jacob's Ladder*
2685 *Plains Prickly Pear*
2686 *Moss Campion*
2687 *Bearberry*
2688 *Mexican Hat*
2689 *Harebell*
2690 *Desert Five Spot*
2691 *Smooth Solomon's Seal*
2692 *Red Maids*
2693 *Yellow Skunk Cabbage*
2694 *Rue Anemone*
2695 *Standing Cypress*
2696 *Wild Flax*

SCOTT NO.	DESCRIPTION	FIRST DAY COVERS SING	FIRST DAY COVERS PL. BLK.	MINT SHEET	PLATE BLOCK	UNUSED F/NH	USED
2647-96	29¢ Wildflowers, 50 varieties, attached .	70.00	....	55.00(50)	....	55.00	....
	set of singles	86.00	....	....	....	....	29.00
	singles of above, each.	1.75	....	....	....	1.50	.85

2697

SCOTT NO.	DESCRIPTION	FIRST DAY COVERS SING	FIRST DAY COVERS PL. BLK.	MINT SHEET	PLATE BLOCK	UNUSED F/NH	USED
2697	$2.90 World War II (1942) Souvenir Sheet of 10. .	12.00	....	22.50(20)	....	14.00	11.00
2697a	29¢ Tokyo Raid	2.50	....	....	....	1.35	.75
2697b	29¢ Commodity Rationing	2.50	....	....	....	1.35	.75
2697c	29¢ Battle of Coral Sea	2.50	....	....	....	1.35	.75
2697d	29¢ Fall of Corregidor .	2.50	....	....	....	1.35	.75
2697e	29¢ Japan Invades Aleutians	2.50	....	....	....	1.35	.75
2697f	29¢ Allies Break Codes	2.50	....	....	....	1.35	.75
2697g	29¢ USS Yorktown Lost	2.50	....	....	....	1.35	.75
2697h	29¢ Women Join War Effort	2.50	....	....	....	1.35	.75
2697i	29¢ Marines on Guadalcanal	2.50	....	....	....	1.35	.75
2697j	29¢ Allies Land in North Africa	2.50	....	....	....	1.35	.75

2698

2699

SCOTT NO.	DESCRIPTION	FIRST DAY COVERS SING	FIRST DAY COVERS PL. BLK.	MINT SHEET	PLATE BLOCK	UNUSED F/NH	USED
2698	29¢ Dorothy Parker . . .	2.25	4.75	45.00(50)	5.00	1.50	.25
2699	29¢ Dr. T. von Kármán.	2.25	4.75	45.00(50)	4.75	1.50	.25

2700

2701

2704

2702

2703

SCOTT NO.	DESCRIPTION	FIRST DAY COVERS SING	FIRST DAY COVERS PL. BLK.	MINT SHEET	PLATE BLOCK	UNUSED F/NH	USED
2700-03	Minerals, 4 varieties, attached . .	5.00	4.00	55.00(40)	7.00	6.50	4.00
2700	29¢ Azurite.	2.25	....	....	....	1.50	.75
2701	29¢ Copper	2.25	....	....	....	1.50	.75
2702	29¢ Variscite	2.25	....	....	....	1.50	.75
2703	29¢ Wulfenite.	2.25	....	....	....	1.50	.75
2704	29¢ Juan Rodriguez Cabrillo	2.25	4.75	49.00(50)	4.75	1.00	.25

2705

2706

2707

2708

2709

SCOTT NO.	DESCRIPTION	FIRST DAY COVERS SING	FIRST DAY COVERS PL. BLK.	MINT SHEET	PLATE BLOCK	UNUSED F/NH	USED
2705	29¢ Giraffe.	2.25	....	....	....	1.25	.40
2706	29¢ Giant Panda	2.25	....	....	....	1.25	.40
2707	29¢ Flamingo.	2.25	....	....	....	1.25	.40
2708	29¢ King Penguins . . .	2.25	....	....	....	1.25	.40
2709	29¢ White Bengal Tiger	2.25	....	....	....	1.25	.40
2709a	29¢ Wild Animals, bklt pane of 5.	5.00	....	....	....	6.00	4.50
2709av	same, bklt pane , unfolded	....	....	....	....	7.75	....

2710

SCOTT NO.	DESCRIPTION	FIRST DAY COVERS SING	FIRST DAY COVERS PL. BLK.	MINT SHEET	PLATE BLOCK	UNUSED F/NH	USED
2710	29¢ Christmas–Traditional	2.25	4.75	45.00(50)	5.00	1.00	.25
2710a	same, bklt pane of 10 .	9.00	....	....	....	9.00	....
2710av	same, bklt pane, unfolded	....	....	....	....	12.00	....

2711, 2715   2712, 2716, 2719

2713, 2717   2714, 2718

SCOTT NO.	DESCRIPTION	FIRST DAY COVERS SING	FIRST DAY COVERS PL. BLK.	MINT SHEET	PLATE BLOCK	UNUSED F/NH	USED
2711-14	Christmas Toys, 4 varieties, attached . .	4.00	5.00	52.00(50)	6.00	5.50	4.50
2711	29¢ Hobby Horse.	2.25	....	....	....	1.50	.30
2712	29¢ Locomotive	2.25	....	....	....	1.50	.30
2713	29¢ Fire Engine	2.25	....	....	....	1.50	.30
2714	29¢ Steamboat	2.25	....	....	....	1.50	.30
2715	29¢ Hobby Horse (gravure) bklt single.	2.25	....	....	....	1.50	.30
2716	29¢ Locomotive (gravure) bklt single.	2.25	....	....	....	1.50	.30
2717	29¢ Fire Engine (gravure) bklt single.	2.25	....	....	....	1.50	.30
2718	29¢ Steamboat (gravure) bklt single.	2.25	....	....	....	1.50	.30
2718a	29¢ Christmas Toys (gravure) bklt pane of 4.	9.00	....	....	....	7.00	5.50
2718av	same, bklt pane, unfolded	....	....	....	....	9.00	....
2719	29¢ Locomotive ATM, self-adhesive	2.25	....	....	....	1.20	.75
2719a	same, bklt pane of 18 .	13.50	....	....	....	18.00	....

2720

SCOTT NO.	DESCRIPTION	FIRST DAY COVERS SING	FIRST DAY COVERS PL. BLK.	MINT SHEET	PLATE BLOCK	UNUSED F/NH	USED
2720	29¢ Happy New Year. .	3.00	4.75	27.00(20)	6.50	1.20	.25

2721   2722

2723

1993 COMMEMORATIVES

SCOTT NO.	DESCRIPTION	FIRST DAY COVERS SING	FIRST DAY COVERS PL. BLK.	MINT SHEET	PLATE BLOCK	UNUSED F/NH	USED
2721/2806	(2721-30, 2746-59, 2765-66, 2771-74, 2779-89, 2791-94, 2804-06) 57 varieties	....	....	....	....	74.00	25.00
2721	29¢ Elvis Presley.	2.00	5.00	35.00(40)	4.50	1.00	.25
2722	29¢ "Oklahoma!"	2.25	4.75	35.00(40)	4.00	1.00	.25
2723	29¢ Hank Williams. . . .	2.25	4.75	75.00(40)	9.00	2.00	.25
2723a	29¢ Hank Williams, perf. 11.2 x 11.4.	....	....	400.00(40)	100.00	15.00	10.00

2724, 2731

2725, 2732

2726, 2733

2727, 2734

2728, 2735

2729, 2736

2730, 2737

SCOTT NO.	DESCRIPTION	FIRST DAY COVERS SING	FIRST DAY COVERS PL. BLK.	MINT SHEET	PLATE BLOCK	UNUSED F/NH	USED
2724-30	Rock & Roll/Rhythm & Blues, 7 varieties, attached . .	12.00	....	50.00(35)	14.00(8)	11.00	9.00
2724-30	same, Top Plate Block of 10	....	....	....	18.00(10)	....	....
2724	29¢ Elvis Presley	3.00	....	....	....	1.50	1.25
2725	29¢ Bill Haley.	3.00	....	....	....	1.50	1.25
2726	29¢ Clyde McPhatter . .	3.00	....	....	....	1.50	1.25
2727	29¢ Ritchie Valens. . . .	3.00	....	....	....	1.50	1.25
2728	29¢ Otis Redding.	3.00	....	....	....	1.50	1.25
2729	29¢ Buddy Holly	3.00	....	....	....	1.50	1.25
2730	29¢ Dinah Washington	3.00	....	....	....	1.50	1.25
2731	29¢ Elvis Presley, bklt single.	3.00	....	....	....	1.25	.50
2732	29¢ Bill Haley, bklt single	3.00	....	....	....	1.25	.50
2733	29¢ Clyde McPhatter, bklt single.	3.00	....	....	....	1.25	.50
2734	29¢ Ritchie Valens, bklt single.	3.00	....	....	....	1.25	.50
2735	29¢ Otis Redding, bklt single.	3.00	....	....	....	1.25	.50
2736	29¢ Buddy Holly, bklt single.	3.00	....	....	....	1.25	.50
2737	29¢ Dinah Washington, bklt single.	3.00	....	....	....	1.25	.50
2737a	same, bklt pane of 8 . .	10.00	....	....	....	12.00	....
2737av	same, bklt pane, unfolded	....	....	....	....	14.00	....
2737b	same, bklt pane of 4 . .	5.00	....	....	....	6.50	....
2737bv	same, bklt pane, unfolded	....	....	....	....	7.50	....

2741

2742

2743

2744

2745

SCOTT NO.	DESCRIPTION	FIRST DAY COVERS SING	FIRST DAY COVERS PL. BLK.	MINT SHEET	PLATE BLOCK	UNUSED F/NH	USED
2741	29¢ Saturn & 3 Rockets	2.25	....	....	....	1.00	.35
2742	29¢ 2 Flying Saucers . .	2.25	....	....	....	1.00	.35
2743	29¢ 3 Rocketeers	2.25	....	....	....	1.00	.35
2744	29¢ Winged Spaceship	2.25	....	....	....	1.00	.35
2745	29¢ 3 Space Ships . . .	2.25	....	....	....	1.00	.35
2745a	29¢ Space Fantasy, bklt pane of 5.	4.50	....	....	....	5.25	4.00
2745av	same, bklt pane, unfolded	....	....	....	....	6.75	....

2746

2747

2748

2749

2750 2751

2752 2753

SCOTT NO.	DESCRIPTION	FIRST DAY COVERS SING	FIRST DAY COVERS PL. BLK.	MINT SHEET	PLATE BLOCK	UNUSED F/NH	USED
2746	29¢ Percy Lavon Julian	3.00	4.75	48.00(50)	5.00	1.20	.25
2747	29¢ Oregon Trail	2.25	4.75	48.00(50)	5.00	1.70	.25
2748	29¢ World University Games	2.25	4.75	45.00(50)	4.75	.95	.25
2749	29¢ Grace Kelly	3.00	4.75	49.00(50)	5.00	.95	.25
2750-53	Circus, 4 varieties, attached	5.00	6.00	45.00(40)	9.00(6)	5.00	4.00
2750	29¢ Clown	2.25	....	....	....	1.35	.30
2751	29¢ Ringmaster	2.25	....	....	....	1.35	.30
2752	29¢ Trapeze Artist	2.25	....	....	....	1.35	.30
2753	29¢ Elephant	2.25	....	....	....	1.35	.30

2754

2755

SCOTT NO.	DESCRIPTION	FIRST DAY COVERS SING	FIRST DAY COVERS PL. BLK.	MINT SHEET	PLATE BLOCK	UNUSED F/NH	USED
2754	29¢ Cherokee Strip	2.25	4.75	30.00(20)	7.00	1.50	.35
2755	29¢ Dean Acheson	2.25	4.75	45.00(50)	5.00	1.00	.25

2756 2757

2758 2759

SCOTT NO.	DESCRIPTION	FIRST DAY COVERS SING	FIRST DAY COVERS PL. BLK.	MINT SHEET	PLATE BLOCK	UNUSED F/NH	USED
2756-59	Sporting Horses, 4 varieties, attached . .	7.50	9.75	45.00(40)	6.00	5.75	4.50
2756	29¢ Steeplechase	3.00	....	....	....	1.25	.75
2757	29¢ Thoroughbred	3.00	....	....	....	1.25	.75
2758	29¢ Harness	3.00	....	....	....	1.25	.75
2759	29¢ Polo	3.00	....	....	....	1.25	.75

2760

2761

2762

2763

2764

SCOTT NO.	DESCRIPTION	FIRST DAY COVERS SING	FIRST DAY COVERS PL. BLK.	MINT SHEET	PLATE BLOCK	UNUSED F/NH	USED
2760	29¢ Hyacinth	2.25	....	....	....	1.15	.30
2761	29¢ Daffodil	2.25	....	....	....	1.15	.30
2762	29¢ Tulip	2.25	....	....	....	1.15	.30
2763	29¢ Iris.	2.25	....	....	....	1.15	.30
2764	29¢ Lilac	2.25	....	....	....	1.15	.30
2764a	Garden Flowers, bklt pane of 5.	4.50	....	....	....	6.50	4.00
2764av	same, bklt pane, unfolded	....	....	....	....	8.50	....

2765

SCOTT NO.	DESCRIPTION	FIRST DAY COVERS SING	FIRST DAY COVERS PL. BLK.	MINT SHEET	PLATE BLOCK	UNUSED F/NH	USED
2765	$2.90 World War II, 1943, Souvenir Sheet of 10. .	12.00	....	22.50(20)	....	14.00	11.00
2765a	29¢ Allies Battle U-boats	2.50	....	....	....	1.35	.75
2765b	29¢ Medics Treat Wounded	2.50	....	....	....	1.35	.75
2765c	29¢ Allies Attack Sicily.	2.50	....	....	....	1.35	.75
2765d	29¢ B-24's Hit Ploesti Refineries	2.50	....	....	....	1.35	.75
2765e	29¢ V-Mail	2.50	....	....	....	1.35	.75
2765f	29¢ Italy Invaded by Allies	2.50	....	....	....	1.35	.75
2765g	29¢ Bonds and Stamps Help	2.50	....	....	....	1.35	.75
2765h	29¢ "Willie and Joe". . .	2.50	....	....	....	1.35	.75
2765i	29¢ Gold Stars.	2.50	....	....	....	1.35	.75
2765j	29¢ Marines Assault Tarawa	2.50	....	....	....	1.35	.75

2766

SCOTT NO.	DESCRIPTION	FIRST DAY COVERS SING	FIRST DAY COVERS PL. BLK.	MINT SHEET	PLATE BLOCK	UNUSED F/NH	USED
2766	29¢ Joe Louis	5.00	6.00	48.00(50)	5.00	1.50	.25

2767

2768

2769

2770

SCOTT NO.	DESCRIPTION	FIRST DAY COVERS SING	FIRST DAY COVERS PL. BLK.	MINT SHEET	PLATE BLOCK	UNUSED F/NH	USED
2767	29¢ "Show Boat"	2.50	....	....	....	1.75	.30
2768	29¢ "Porgy & Bess" . . .	2.50	....	....	....	1.75	.30
2769	29¢ "Oklahoma!"	2.50	....	....	....	1.75	.30
2770	29¢ "My Fair Lady" . . .	2.50	....	....	....	1.75	.30
2770a	Broadway Musicals, bklt pane of 4.	6.00	....	....	....	6.00	....
2770av	same, bklt pane, unfolded	....	....	....	....	8.50	....

2771, 2775

2772, 2777

2773, 2776

2774, 2778

SCOTT NO.	DESCRIPTION	FIRST DAY COVERS SING	FIRST DAY COVERS PL. BLK.	MINT SHEET	PLATE BLOCK	UNUSED F/NH	USED
2771-74	Country Music, 4 varieties, attached . .	6.00	7.00	28.00(20)	7.50	6.50	6.00
2771	29¢ Hank Williams. . . .	2.50	....	....	....	1.50	.65
2772	29¢ Patsy Cline	2.50	....	....	....	1.50	.65
2773	29¢ The Carter Family.	2.50	....	....	....	1.50	.65
2774	29¢ Bob Wills.	2.50	....	....	....	1.50	.65
2775	29¢ Hank Williams, bklt single.	2.50	....	....	....	1.20	.30
2776	29¢ The Carter Family, bklt single.	2.50	....	....	....	1.20	.30
2777	29¢ Patsy Cline, bklt single	2.50	....	....	....	1.20	.30
2778	29¢ Bob Wills, bklt single	2.50	....	....	....	1.20	.30
2778a	Country Music, bklt pane of 4.	5.00	....	....	....	4.75	....
2778av	same, bklt pane, unfolded	....	....	....	....	6.50	....

2779 2780

2781 2782

2783

2784

SCOTT NO.	DESCRIPTION	FIRST DAY COVERS SING	FIRST DAY COVERS PL. BLK.	MINT SHEET	PLATE BLOCK	UNUSED F/NH	USED
2779-82	National Postal Museum, 4 varieties, attached . .	4.00	5.00	27.00(20)	7.75	6.50	5.00
2779	29¢ Ben Franklin	2.25	....	....	....	1.75	1.00
2780	29¢ Soldier & Drum . . .	2.25	....	....	....	1.75	1.00
2781	29¢ Lindbergh	2.25	....	....	....	1.75	1.00
2782	29¢ Stamps & Bar Code	2.25	....	....	....	1.75	1.00
2783-84	American Sign Language/ Deaf Communication, 2 varieties, attached . .	2.50	4.75	22.00(20)	5.50	2.00	1.25
2783	29¢ Mother/Child	2.25	....	....	....	1.10	.35
2784	29¢ Hand Sign.	2.25	....	....	....	1.10	.35

2785 2786

2787 2788

SCOTT NO.	DESCRIPTION	FIRST DAY COVERS SING	FIRST DAY COVERS PL. BLK.	MINT SHEET	PLATE BLOCK	UNUSED F/NH	USED
2785-88	Youth Classics, 4 varieties, attached . .	5.00	6.00	47.00(40)	7.00	6.00	4.50
2785	29¢ Rebecca of Sunnybrook Farm	2.25	....	....	....	1.60	.45
2786	29¢ Little House on the Prairie	2.25	....	....	....	1.60	.45
2787	29¢ Adventures of Huckleberry Finn	2.25	....	....		1.60	.45
2788	29¢ Little Women.	2.25	....		....	1.60	.45

2789, 2790

2791, 2798, 2801

2792, 2797, 2802

2793, 2796, 2799, 2803

2794, 2795, 2800

SCOTT NO.	DESCRIPTION	FIRST DAY COVERS SING	FIRST DAY COVERS PL. BLK.	MINT SHEET	PLATE BLOCK	UNUSED F/NH	USED
2789	29¢ Christmas–Traditional	2.25	4.75	45.00(50)	5.25	1.00	.25
2790	29¢ Christmas–Traditional, bklt single.	2.25	....	....	....	1.00	.25
2790a	same, bklt pane of 4 . .	3.00	....	....	....	4.00	....
2790av	same, bklt pane, unfolded	....	....	....	....	6.00	....
2791-94	Christmas–Contemporary, 4 varieties, attached . .	3.00	4.75	55.00(50)	6.50	5.50	4.00
2791	29¢ Jack-in-the-Box. . .	2.25	....	....	....	1.25	.25
2792	29¢ Red-Nosed Reindeer	2.25	....	....	....	1.25	.25
2793	29¢ Snowman	2.25	....	....	....	1.25	.25
2794	29¢ Toy Soldier Blowing Horn.	2.25	....	....	....	1.25	.25
2795	29¢ Toy Soldier Blowing Horn, bklt single.	2.25	....	....	....	1.40	.25
2796	29¢ Snowman, bklt single	2.25	....	....	....	1.40	.25
2797	29¢ Red-Nosed Reindeer, bklt single.	2.25	....	....	....	1.40	.25
2798	29¢ Jack-in-the-Box, bklt single.	2.25	....	....	....	1.40	.25
2798a	same, bklt pane of 10 .	7.00	....	....	....	12.00	....
2798av	same, bklt pane, unfolded	....	....	....	....	16.00	....
2799-2802v	29¢ Christmas–Contemporary, coil	....	....	....	18.00(8)	7.50(4)	....
2802b	same, plate strip of 5 . .	....	....	....	....	14.00	....
2799	29¢ Snowman, self-adhesive (3 buttons)	2.25	....	....	....	1.25	.80
2800	29¢ Toy Soldier Blowing Horn, self-adhesive . . .	2.25	....	....	....	1.25	.80
2801	29¢ Jack-in-the-Box, self-adhesive	2.25	....	....	....	1.25	.80
2802	29¢ Red-Nosed Reindeer, self-adhesive	2.25	....	....	....	1.25	.80
2802a	same, bklt pane of 12 .	9.00	....	....	....	17.00	....
2803	29¢ Snowman, self-adhesive (2 buttons)	2.25	....	....	....	1.25	.80
2803a	same, bklt pane of 18 .	13.50	....	....	....	18.00	....

2804

2805

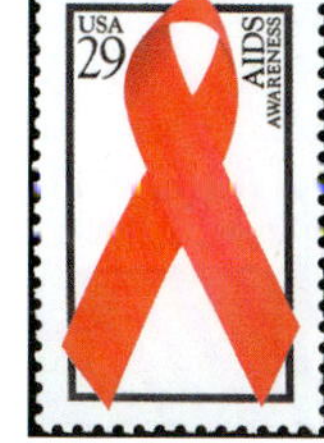

2806

SCOTT NO.	DESCRIPTION	FIRST DAY COVERS SING	FIRST DAY COVERS PL. BLK.	MINT SHEET	PLATE BLOCK	UNUSED F/NH	USED
2804	29¢ Commonwealth of North Mariana Islands .	2.25	4.75	25.00(20)	6.00	1.75	.25
2805	29¢ Columbus Landing in Puerto Rico	2.25	4.75	48.00(50)	4.75	1.20	.25
2806	29¢ AIDS Awareness. .	2.25	4.75	45.00(50)	4.50	1.20	.25
2806a	29¢ AIDS Awareness, bklt single.	2.25	....	....	....	1.10	.25
2806b	same, bklt pane of 5 . .	9.00	....	....	....	4.00	....
2806bv	same, bklt pane, unfolded	....	....	....	....	6.50	....

2807

2808

2809

2810

2811

1994 COMMEMORATIVES

SCOTT NO.	DESCRIPTION	FIRST DAY COVERS SING	FIRST DAY COVERS PL. BLK.	MINT SHEET	PLATE BLOCK	UNUSED F/NH	USED
2807/76	**(2807-12, 2814C-28, 2834-36, 2838-39, 2848-68, ... 2871-72, 2876) 59 varieties........**	....		....	....	**80.00**	**35.50**
2807-11	Winter Olympics, 5 varieties, attached . .	5.00	....	22.00(20)	12.00(10)	7.00	6.00
2807	29¢ Alpine Skiing	2.25	....	....	....	1.50	.50
2808	29¢ Luge	2.25	....	....	....	1.50	.50
2809	29¢ Ice Dancing.	2.25	....	....	....	1.50	.50
2810	29¢ Cross Country Skiing	2.25	....	....	....	1.50	.50
2811	29¢ Ice Hockey	2.25	....	....	....	1.50	.50

2812

2813

2815

2814

1994 COMMEMORATIVES (continued)

SCOTT NO.	DESCRIPTION	FIRST DAY COVERS SING	FIRST DAY COVERS PL. BLK.	MINT SHEET	PLATE BLOCK	UNUSED F/NH	USED
2812	29¢ Edward R. Murrow	2.25	4.75	65.00(50)	8.00	1.75	.25
2813	29¢ Love (sunrise), self-adhesive	2.25	....	....	....	1.25	.30
2813a	same, bklt pane of 18	13.50	....	....	....	18.00	....
2813v	29¢ Love (sunrise), self-adhesive coil	2.50	....	....	7.00(3)	1.40	....
2813b	same, plate strip of 5	....	....	....	....	10.00	....
2814	29¢ Love (dove), bklt single	2.25	....	....	....	1.10	.30
2814a	same, bklt pane of 10	7.00	....	....	....	11.00	....
2814av	same, bklt pane, unfolded	....	....	....	....	12.00	....
2814C	29¢ Love (dove)	2.25	4.75	48.00(50)	5.00	1.20	.25
2815	52¢ Love (dove)	2.00	4.50	75.00(50)	9.00(4)	1.75	.40
....	same, plate block of 10	....	....	....	16.00(10)	....	....

2816

2817

2818

SCOTT NO.	DESCRIPTION	FIRST DAY COVERS SING	FIRST DAY COVERS PL. BLK.	MINT SHEET	PLATE BLOCK	UNUSED F/NH	USED
2816	29¢ Allison Davis	2.25	4.75	30.00(20)	8.00	1.50	.25
2817	29¢ Chinese New Year of the Dog	2.25	4.75	29.00(20)	8.00	1.75	.25
2818	29¢ Buffalo Soldiers	4.00	5.00	20.00(20)	4.75	1.50	.25

2819

2820

2821

2822

2823

2824

2825

2826

2827

2828

SCOTT NO.	DESCRIPTION	FIRST DAY COVERS SING	FIRST DAY COVERS PL. BLK.	MINT SHEET	PLATE BLOCK	UNUSED F/NH	USED
2819	29¢ Rudolph Valentino	2.25	....	....	....	2.00	.95
2920	29¢ Clara Bow	2.25	....	....	....	2.00	.95
2821	29¢ Charlie Chaplin	2.25	....	....	....	2.00	.95
2822	29¢ Lon Chaney	2.25	....	....	....	2.00	.95
2823	29¢ John Gilbert	2.25	....	....	....	2.00	.95
2824	29¢ ZaSu Pitts	2.25	....	....	....	2.00	.95
2825	29¢ Harold Lloyd	2.25	....	....	....	2.00	.95
2826	29¢ Keystone Cops	2.25	....	....	....	2.00	.95
2827	29¢ Theda Bara	2.25	....	....	....	2.00	.95
2828	29¢ Buster Keaton	2.25	....	....	....	2.00	.95
2819-28	Silent Screen Stars, 10 varieties, attached	7.00	....	59.00(40)	22.50(10)	18.00	15.00

2829

2830

2831

2832

2833

SCOTT NO.	DESCRIPTION	FIRST DAY COVERS SING	FIRST DAY COVERS PL. BLK.	MINT SHEET	PLATE BLOCK	UNUSED F/NH	USED
2829	29¢ Lily	2.25	....	....	....	1.25	.30
2830	29¢ Zinnia	2.25	....	....	....	1.25	.30
2831	29¢ Gladiola	2.25	....	....	....	1.25	.30
2832	29¢ Marigold	2.25	....	....	....	1.25	.30
2833	29¢ Rose	2.25	....	....	....	1.25	.30
2833a	Summer Garden Flowers, bklt pane of 5	4.50	....	....	....	6.00	5.00
2833av	same, bklt pane, unfolded	....	....	....	....	7.50	....

2834

2835

2836

2837

SCOTT NO.	DESCRIPTION	FIRST DAY COVERS SING	FIRST DAY COVERS PL. BLK.	MINT SHEET	PLATE BLOCK	UNUSED F/NH	USED
2834	29¢ World Cup Soccer	2.25	4.75	20.00(20)	4.50	1.00	.50
2835	40¢ World Cup Soccer	2.25	4.75	25.00(20)	5.50	1.50	1.00
2836	50¢ World Cup Soccer	2.25	5.50	28.00(20)	6.50	1.75	1.25
2837	29¢-50¢ World Cup Soccer Souvenir Sheet	3.50	....	....	....	7.00	4.00

2838

SCOTT NO.	DESCRIPTION	FIRST DAY COVERS SING	FIRST DAY COVERS PL. BLK.	MINT SHEET	PLATE BLOCK	UNUSED F/NH	USED
2838	$2.90 World War II, 1944, Souvenir Sheet of 10. .	12.00	....	49.50(20)	....	30.00	20.00
2838a	29¢ Allied forces retake New Guinea.	2.50	....	....	....	2.75	1.00
2838b	29¢ P-51s escort B-17s on bombing raids	2.50	....	....	....	2.75	1.00
2838c	29¢ Allies in Normandy, D-Day, June 6	2.50	....	....	....	2.75	1.00
2838d	29¢ Airborne Units Spearhead Attacks	2.50				2.75	1.00
2838e	29¢ Submarines Shorten War in Pacific.	2.50	....	....	....	2.75	1.00
2838f	29¢ Allies Free Rome, June 4; Paris, August 25	2.50	....	....	....	2.75	1.00
2838g	29¢ U.S. Troops Clear Saipan Bunkers	2.50	....	....	....	2.75	1.00
2838h	29¢ Red Ball Express Speeds Vital Supplies .	2.50	....	....	....	2.75	1.00
2838i	29¢ Battle for Leyte Gulf, October, 23-26.	2.50	....	....	....	2.75	1.00
2838j	29¢ Bastogne and Battle of the Bulge, December. .	2.50	....	....	....	2.75	1.00

2839

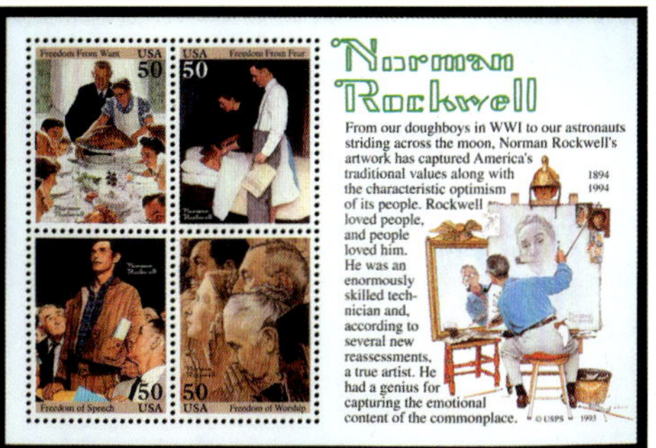

2840

SCOTT NO.	DESCRIPTION	FIRST DAY COVERS SING	FIRST DAY COVERS PL. BLK.	MINT SHEET	PLATE BLOCK	UNUSED F/NH	USED
2839	29¢ Norman Rockwell .	1.75	4.75	48.00(50)	4.50	1.75	.75
2840	50¢ "Four Freedoms" Souvenir Sheets	5.00	....	....	....	9.00	7.00

2841

SCOTT NO.	DESCRIPTION	FIRST DAY COVERS SING	FIRST DAY COVERS PL. BLK.	MINT SHEET	PLATE BLOCK	UNUSED F/NH	USED
2841	29¢ Moon Landing 25th Anniversary, Sheet of 12	12.00	....	....	....	16.00	....
2841a	29¢ Moon Landing 25th Anniversary, single stamp	1.75	....	....	....	1.50	.50

2842

SCOTT NO.	DESCRIPTION	FIRST DAY COVERS SING	FIRST DAY COVERS PL. BLK.	MINT SHEET	PLATE BLOCK	UNUSED F/NH	USED
2842	$9.95 Moon Landing Express Mail Stamp.	27.00	50.00	675.00(20)	150.00	30.00	25.00

2843

2845

2846

2844

2847

SCOTT NO.	DESCRIPTION	FIRST DAY COVERS SING	FIRST DAY COVERS PL. BLK.	MINT SHEET	PLATE BLOCK	UNUSED F/NH	USED
2843	29¢ Hudson's General.	2.25	....	....	....	1.50	.35
2844	29¢ McQueen's Jupiter	2.25	....	....	....	1.50	.35
2845	29¢ Eddy's No. 242 . . .	2.25	....	....	....	1.50	.35
2846	29¢ Ely's No. 10	2.25	....	....	....	1.50	.35
2847	29¢ Buchanan's No. 999	2.25	....	....	....	1.50	.35
2847a	Locomotives, bklt pane of 5.	4.50	....	....	....	6.00	4.25
2847av	same, bklt pane, unfolded	....	....	....	....	8.00	....

2848

SCOTT NO.	DESCRIPTION	FIRST DAY COVERS SING	FIRST DAY COVERS PL. BLK.	MINT SHEET	PLATE BLOCK	UNUSED F/NH	USED
2848	29¢ George Meany . . .	1.75	4.75	45.00(50)	4.50	1.00	.25

SCOTT NO.	DESCRIPTION	FIRST DAY COVERS SING	FIRST DAY COVERS PL. BLK.	MINT SHEET	PLATE BLOCK	UNUSED F/NH	USED

2849

2850

2851

2852

2853

SCOTT NO.	DESCRIPTION	FIRST DAY COVERS SING	FIRST DAY COVERS PL. BLK.	MINT SHEET	PLATE BLOCK	UNUSED F/NH	USED
2849-53	Popular Singers, 5 varieties, attached . .	8.00	....	30.00(20)	15.00(6)	9.50	6.00
2849	29¢ Al Jolson	3.00	....	....	....	1.75	1.00
2850	29¢ Bing Crosby	3.00	....	....	....	1.75	1.00
2851	29¢ Ethel Waters	3.00	....	....	....	1.75	1.00
2852	29¢ Nat "King" Cole . . .	3.00	....	....	....	1.75	1.00
2853	29¢ Ethel Merman	3.00	....	....	....	1.75	1.00
....	same, Plate Block of 12	....	....	....	22.50(12)	....	....

2854

2855

2856

2857

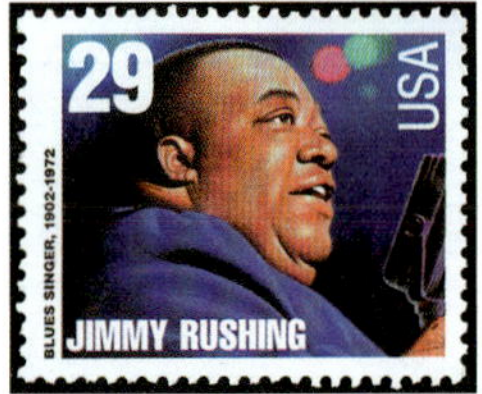

2858

2859

2860

2861

SCOTT NO.	DESCRIPTION	FIRST DAY COVERS SING	FIRST DAY COVERS PL. BLK.	MINT SHEET	PLATE BLOCK	UNUSED F/NH	USED
2854-61	Blues & Jazz Singers, 8 varieties, attached .	12.00	....	58.00(35)	22.00(10)	23.00	12.00
....	same, Horizontal Plate Block of 10 w/Top Label	....	....	....	26.00(10)	....	....
2854	29¢ Bessie Smith	3.00	....	....	....	2.00	1.25
2855	29¢ Muddy Waters . .	3.00	....	....	....	2.00	1.25
2856	29¢ Billie Holiday	3.00	....	....	....	2.00	1.25
2857	29¢ Robert Johnson .	3.00	....	....	....	2.00	1.25
2858	29¢ Jimmy Rushing . .	3.00	....	....	....	2.00	1.25
2859	29¢ "Ma" Rainey	3.00	....	....	....	2.00	1.25
2860	29¢ Mildred Bailey . . .	3.00	....	....	....	2.00	1.25
2861	29¢ Howlin' Wolf	3.00	....	....	....	2.00	1.25

2862

SCOTT NO.	DESCRIPTION	FIRST DAY COVERS SING	FIRST DAY COVERS PL. BLK.	MINT SHEET	PLATE BLOCK	UNUSED F/NH	USED
2862	29¢ James Thurber . . .	1.75	4.75	45.00(50)	4.75	1.00	.25

2863 2864

2865 2866

SCOTT NO.	DESCRIPTION	FIRST DAY COVERS SING	FIRST DAY COVERS PL. BLK.	MINT SHEET	PLATE BLOCK	UNUSED F/NH	USED
2863-66	Wonders of the Sea, 4 varieties, attached . .	5.00	6.00	35.00(24)	7.00	6.50	5.00
2863	29¢ Diver & Motorboat.	2.25	....	....	....	1.75	.55
2864	29¢ Diver & Ship	2.25	....	....	....	1.75	.55
2865	29¢ Diver & Ship's Wheel	2.25	....	....	....	1.75	.55
2866	29¢ Diver & Coral	2.25	....	....	....	1.75	.55

2867 2868

SCOTT NO.	DESCRIPTION	FIRST DAY COVERS SING	FIRST DAY COVERS PL. BLK.	MINT SHEET	PLATE BLOCK	UNUSED F/NH	USED
2867-68	Cranes.	4.00	5.00	19.50(20)	5.00	2.25	1.50
2867	29¢ Black-Necked Crane	3.00	....	....	....	1.15	.30
2868	29¢ Whooping Crane. .	3.00	....	....	....	1.15	.30

2869

Legends of the West

2869a	*Home on the Range*	**2869k**	*Nellie Cashman*
2869b	*Buffalo Bill Cody*	**2869l**	*Charles Goodnight*
2869c	*Jim Bridger*	**2869m**	*Geronimo*
2869d	*Annie Oakley*	**2869n**	*Kit Carson*
2869e	*Native American Culture*	**2869o**	*Wild Bill Hickok*
2869f	*Chief Joseph*	**2869p**	*Western Wildlife*
2869g	*Bill Pickett*	**2869q**	*Jim Beckwourth*
2869h	*Bat Masterson*	**2869r**	*Bill Tilghman*
2869i	*John Fremont*	**2869s**	*Sacagawea*
2869j	*Wyatt Earp*	**2869t**	*Overland Mail*

2869g

2870g

SCOTT NO.	DESCRIPTION	FIRST DAY COVERS SING	FIRST DAY COVERS PL. BLK.	MINT SHEET	PLATE BLOCK	UNUSED F/NH	USED
2869	Legends of the West, 20 varieties, attached .	....	....	30.00(20)	....	30.00	25.00
....	set of singles	31.50	....	....	....	....	17.00
....	singles of above, each.	....	....	....	....	....	1.00
2869v	same as above, uncut sheet of 120 (6 panes)	....	....	100.00(120)	....	100.00	....
....	block of 40 with vertical or horizontal, gutter between (2 panes)	....	....	27.50(40)	....	27.50	....
....	block of 24 with vertical gutter.....		....	20.75(24)	....	20.75	....
....	block of 25 with horizontal gutter	....	....	21.50(25)	....	21.50	....
....	cross gutter block of 20	....	....	....	....	31.00	....
....	cross gutter block of 4 .	....	....	....	....	17.00	....
....	vertical pair with horizontal gutter	....	....	....	....	2.75	....
....	horizontal pair with vertical gutter	....	....	....	....	2.75	....
2870	Legends of the West, (Recalled), 20 varieties, attached.	....	....	200.00(20)	....	200.00	....

2871

2872

2873

2874

SCOTT NO.	DESCRIPTION	FIRST DAY COVERS SING	FIRST DAY COVERS PL. BLK.	MINT SHEET	PLATE BLOCK	UNUSED F/NH	USED
2871	29¢ Christmas–Traditional	2.25	4.75	45.00(50)	5.00	1.25	.25
2871a	29¢ Christmas–Traditional bklt single.	2.25	....	....	....	1.10	.30
2871b	same, bklt pane of 10 .	9.00	....	....	....	10.00	....
2871bv	same, bklt pane, unfolded	....	....	....	....	12.00	....
2872	29¢ Christmas Stocking	2.25	4.75	45.00(50)	5.00	1.25	.25
2872v	29¢ Christmas Stocking, bklt single.	2.25	....	....	....	1.25	.25
2872a	same, bklt pane of 20 .	....	....	....	....	20.00	....
2872av	same, bklt pane, unfolded	....	....	....	....	26.00	....
2873	29¢ Santa Claus, self-adhesive	2.25	....	....	....	1.20	.25
2873a	same, bklt pane of 12 .	9.00	....	....	....	14.00	....
2874	29¢ Cardinal in Snow, self-adhesive	2.25	....	....	....	1.50	1.20
2874a	same, bklt pane of 18 .	13.50	....	....	....	18.00	....

2875

SCOTT NO.	DESCRIPTION	FIRST DAY COVERS SING	FIRST DAY COVERS PL. BLK.	MINT SHEET	PLATE BLOCK	UNUSED F/NH	USED
2875	$2 B.E.P. Souvenir Sheet of 4 (Madison)	25.00	....	....	....	25.00	20.00
2875a	single from above ($2 Madison)	6.00	....	....	....	5.00	3.00

2876

2877, 2878

SCOTT NO.	DESCRIPTION	FIRST DAY COVERS SING	FIRST DAY COVERS PL. BLK.	MINT SHEET	PLATE BLOCK	UNUSED F/NH	USED
2876	29¢ Year of the Boar . .	3.00	4.75	24.00(20)	5.75	1.25	.45
2877	(3¢) "G" Make-up Rate (ABN, bright blue)	2.25	4.75	17.00(100)	1.00	.25	.25
2878	(3¢) "G" Make-up Rate (SVS, dark blue)	2.25	4.75	20.00(100)	1.25	.25	.25

2879, 2880 — 2881-85, 2889-92 — 2886, 2887 — 2888

SCOTT NO.	DESCRIPTION	FIRST DAY COVERS SING	FIRST DAY COVERS PL. BLK.	MINT SHEET	PLATE BLOCK	UNUSED F/NH	USED
2879	(20¢) "G" Old Glory Postcard Rate (BEP, black "G") .	2.25	4.75	80.00(100)	9.50	.75	.25
2880	(20¢) "G" Old Glory Postcard Rate (SVS, red "G") . . .	2.25	4.75	110.00(100)	25.00	1.00	.25
2881	(32¢) "G" Old Glory (BEP, black "G").	2.25	4.75	350.00(100)	80.00	3.00	.50
2882	(32¢) "G" Old Glory (SVS, red "G")	2.25	4.75	96.00(100)	9.00	1.10	.25
2883	(32¢) "G" Old Glory, bklt single (BEP, black "G")	2.25	....	....	....	1.10	.25
2883a	same, bklt pane of 10 .	7.25	....	....	....	10.00	....
2884	(32¢) "G" Old Glory, bklt single (ABN, blue "G") .	2.25	....	....	....	1.25	.25
2884a	same, bklt pane of 10 .	7.25	....	....	....	10.00	....
2885	(32¢) "G" Old Glory, bklt single (KCS, red "G"). .	2.25	....	....	....	1.50	.25
2885a	same, bklt pane of 10 .	7.25	....	....	....	14.00	....
2886	(32¢) "G", self-adhesive	2.25	....	....	....	1.10	.30
2886a	same, bklt pane of 18 .	13.50	....	....	....	16.00	....
2887	(32¢) "G" Old Glory, self-adhesive (blue shading)	2.25	....	....	....	1.25	.85
2887a	same, bklt pane of 18 .	13.50	....	....	....	20.00	....
			PLATE# STRIP 3		PLATE# STRIP 3		
2886b	(32¢) "G" Old Glory, coil	....	....	....	14.00	2.50	......
2888	(25¢) Old Glory First-Class Presort, coil	2.25	10.00	....	6.75	1.50	.65
2889	(32¢) "G" Old Glory, coil (BEP, black "G").	2.25	10.00	....	12.50	3.00	.85
2890	(32¢) "G" Old Glory, coil (ABN, blue "G") . . .	2.25	10.00	....	6.25	1.10	.25
2891	(32¢) "G" Old Glory, coil (SVS, red "G")	2.25	10.00	....	9.00	1.50	.40
2892	(32¢) "G" Old Glory, coil (SVS, red "G") rouletted	2.25	10.00	....	8.00	1.50	.20

2893 — 2897, 2913-16, 2920, 2921 — 2902, 2902B — 2903, 2904, 2904A, 2904B

2905, 2906 — 2907 — 2908-10 — 2911, 2912, 2912A, 2912B

1995-97 Regular Issues

SCOTT NO.	DESCRIPTION	FIRST DAY COVERS SING	FIRST DAY COVERS PL. BLK.	MINT SHEET	PLATE BLOCK	UNUSED F/NH	USED
2893	(5¢) "G" Old Glory, Nonprofit, coil.	1.95	10.00	....	4.50	1.00	.40
2897	32¢ Flag over Porch . .	1.95	4.75	100.00(100)	7.50	1.50	.25

1995-97 Regular Issue Coils

SCOTT NO.	DESCRIPTION	FIRST DAY COVERS SING	PLATE# STRIP 3	MINT SHEET	PLATE# STRIP 3	UNUSED F/NH	USED
2902	(5¢) Butte, Nonprofit, coil	1.95	10.00	....	2.00	.30	.25
2902B	(5¢) Butte, self-adhesive coil	1.95	....	....	2.75	.45	.25
2903	(5¢) Mountain, (BEP, violet 1996)	2.25	10.00	....	2.00	.25	.25
2904	(5¢) Mountain (SVS, blue 1996)	2.25	10.00	....	4.00	.45	.25
2904A	(5¢) Mountain, self-adhesive coil.	2.25	....	....	4.00	.45	.25
2904B	(5¢) Mountain, self-adhesive coil (1997)	2.25	....	....	4.00	.45	.25
2905	(10¢) Automobile, Bulk Rate, coil	2.25	10.00	....	3.75	.45	.35
2905a	(10¢) Automobile, Large, "1995" date (1996). . . .	....	....	....	6.50	.45	.25
2906	(10¢) Automobile, self-adhesive coil.	2.25	....	....	6.00	.65	.25
2907	(10¢) Eagle, bulk-rate, coil (1996)	2.25	....	....	7.50	.80	.35
2908	(15¢) Auto Tail Fin, Presorted First-Class Card, coil (BEP).	2.25	10.00	....	3.50	.50	.45
2909	(15¢) Auto Tail Fin, Presorted First-Class Card, coil (SVS).	2.25	10.00	....	3.50	.50	.45
2910	(15¢) Auto Tail Fin, self-adhesive coil. . . .	2.25	....	....	3.75	.55	.45

SCOTT NO.	DESCRIPTION	FIRST DAY COVERS SING	PLATE# STRIP 3	MINT SHEET	PLATE# STRIP 3	UNUSED F/NH	USED
2911	(25¢) Jukebox, Presorted First-Class, coil (BEP)	2.25	10.00	....	5.75	.80	.45
2912	(25¢) Jukebox, Presorted First-Class, coil (SVS)	2.25	10.00	....	5.75	.85	.45
2912A	(25¢) Jukebox, self-adhesive coil. . . .	2.25	....	....	6.00	1.10	.45
2912B	(25¢) Jukebox, self-adhesive coil (1997)	2.25	....	....	6.00	1.25	.45
2913	32¢ Flag over Porch, coil (BEP, red date)	2.25	10.00	....	6.00	1.10	.25
2914	32¢ Flag over Porch, coil (SVS, blue date)	2.25	10.00	....	7.00	1.10	.70
2915	32¢ Flag over Porch, self-adhesive coil (Die Cut 8.7)	2.25	....	....	14.00	1.60	.80
2915A	32¢ Flag over Porch, self-adhesive coil (1996, Die Cut 9.8)	2.25	....	....	8.00	1.40	.30
2915B	32¢ Flag over Porch, self-adhesive coil (1996, Die Cut 11.5)	2.25	....	....	9.00	1.50	1.00
2915C	32¢ Flag over Porch, self-adhesive coil (1996, Die Cut 10.9)	10.00	....	....	29.00	3.00	2.00
2915D	32¢ Flag over Porch, self adhesive coil (1997)	2.25	....	....	14.00	2.40	1.50

PLATE NUMBER STRIPS OF 5

SCOTT NO.	UNUSED F/NH	SCOTT NO.	UNUSED F/NH	SCOTT NO.	UNUSED F/NH
2886b	20.00	2904	2.95	2912	7.50
2888	10.00	2904A	6.00	2912A	8.75
2889	20.00	2904B	7.50	2912B	9.00
2890	9.50	2905	4.00	2913	8.00
2891	10.00	2906	8.00	2914	10.00
2892	14.00	2907	9.00	2915	15.00
2893	7.00	2908	4.00	2915A	10.00
2902	3.00	2909	4.00	2915B	12.00
2902B	4.00	2910	5.00	2915C	35.00
2903	2.50	2911	7.50	2915D	23.00

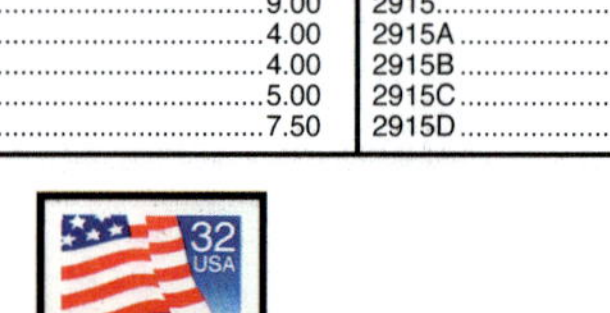

2919

1995-97 Booklet Panes

SCOTT NO.	DESCRIPTION	FIRST DAY COVERS SING	FIRST DAY COVERS PL. BLK.	MINT SHEET	PLATE BLOCK	UNUSED F/NH	USED
2916	32¢ Flag over Porch, bklt single.	2.25	....	....	....	1.10	.25
2916a	same, bklt pane of 10	7.25	....	....	....	10.00	....
2916av	same, bklt pane, unfolded	....	....	....	....	12.00	....
2919	32¢ Flag over Field self-adhesive	2.25	....	....	....	1.25	.65
2919a	same, bklt pane of 18	13.50	....	....	....	20.00	....
2920	32¢ Flag over Porch, self-adhesive (large "1995").	2.25	....	....	....	1.25	.30
2920a	same, bklt pane of 20	14.50	....	....	....	22.00	....
2920b	32¢ Flag over Porch, self-adhesive (small "1995")	10.00	....	....	....	7.00	3.00
2920c	same, bklt pane of 20	50.00	....	....	....	140.00	....
2920D	32¢ Flag over Porch ("1996" date) self-adhesive	2.25	....	....	....	2.00	1.00
2920De	same, Bklt pane of 10	9.00	....	....	....	16.00	....
2920f	same, Bklt pane of 15+ label	.....	....	....	....	17.00	....
2920h	same, Bklt pane of 15	....	....	....	....	120.00	....
2921	32¢ Flag over Porch, self-adhesive (Red 1996, Die Cut 9.8)	2.25	....	....	....	1.35	.60
2921a	same, bklt pane of 10	7.00	....	....	....	14.00	....
2921av	same, bklt pane, unfolded	....	....	....	....	18.00	....
2921b	32¢ Flag over Porch, (Red 1997).	2.25	....	....	....	1.75	.35
2921c	same, bklt pane of 10	6.95	....	....	....	19.00	....
2921d	same, bklt pane of 5 .	5.50	....	....	....	10.00	....

2933

2934

2935

2936

2938

2940

2941

2942

2943

1995-99 GREAT AMERICANS

SCOTT NO.	DESCRIPTION	FIRST DAY COVERS SING	FIRST DAY COVERS PL. BLK.	MINT SHEET	PLATE BLOCK	UNUSED F/NH	USED
2933	32¢ Milton S. Hershey .	2.25	4.75	120.00(100)	7.50	1.40	.55
2934	32¢ Carl Farley (1996).	2.25	4.75	110.00(100)	7.00	1.30	.50
2935	32¢ Henry R. Luce (1998)	2.25	4.75	20.00(20)	5.50	1.15	.80
2936	32¢ Lila & DeWitt Wallace (1998)	2.25	4.75	20.00(20)	5.50	1.10	.90
2938	46¢ Ruth Benedict . . .	2.25	5.00	150.00(100)	8.50	1.75	1.05
2940	55¢ Alice Hamilton. . . .	2.25	5.00	155.00(100)	9.00	1.85	.35
2941	55¢ Justin Morrill (1999)	2.25	5.00	30.00(20)	8.50	1.85	.35
2942	77¢ Mary Breckenridge (1998)	2.25	5.50	48.00(20)	12.00	2.75	1.55
2943	78¢ Alice Paul	2.25	5.50	245.00(100)	14.00	2.75	.50

2948

2949

2950

1995 COMMEMORATIVES

SCOTT NO.	DESCRIPTION	FIRST DAY COVERS SING	FIRST DAY COVERS PL. BLK.	MINT SHEET	PLATE BLOCK	UNUSED F/NH	USED
2948/3023	**(2948, 2950-58, 2961-68, 2974, 2976-92, 2998-99, 3001-07, 3019-23) 50 varieties . . . .**	....	....	....	....	**90.00**	**32.00**
2948	(32¢) Love (Cherub) . .	2.25	4.75	46.00(50)	5.00	1.10	.25
2949	(32¢) Love (Cherub), self-adhesive	2.25	....	....	....	1.25	.25
2949a	same, bklt pane of 20 .	14.50	....	....	....	20.00	....
2950	32¢ Florida Statehood .	2.25	4.75	25.00(20)	7.00	1.60	.25

2951 2952

2953 2954

SCOTT NO.	DESCRIPTION	FIRST DAY COVERS SING	FIRST DAY COVERS PL. BLK.	MINT SHEET	PLATE BLOCK	UNUSED F/NH	USED
2951-54	Kids Care About Environment, 4 varieties, attached.	4.00	4.75	18.00(16)	5.50	4.95	3.50
2951	32¢ Earth in a Bathtub.	2.25	....	....	....	1.20	.35
2952	32¢ Solar Energy.	2.25	....	....	....	1.20	.35
2953	32¢ Tree Planting	2.25	....	....	....	1.20	.35
2954	32¢ Beach Clean-Up . .	2.25	....	....	....	1.20	.35

2955

2956

2957, 2959

2958

2960

SCOTT NO.	DESCRIPTION	FIRST DAY COVERS SING	FIRST DAY COVERS PL. BLK.	MINT SHEET	PLATE BLOCK	UNUSED F/NH	USED
2955	32¢ Richard M. Nixon .	2.25	4.75	65.00(50)	6.00	1.35	.30
2956	32¢ Bessie Coleman . .	2.25	4.75	60.00(50)	7.00	1.50	.30
2957	32¢ Love (Cherub). . . .	2.25	4.75	55.00(50)	6.00	1.25	.25
2958	55¢ Love (Cherub). . . .	2.50	5.00	83.00(50)	8.00	1.85	.60
2959	32¢ Love (Cherub), bklt single.	2.25	....	....	....	1.30	.30
2959a	same, bklt pane of 10 .	7.25	....	....	....	10.00	....
2959av	same, bklt pane, unfolded	....	....	....	....	12.00	....
2960	55¢ Love (Cherub), self-adhesive	2.50	....	....	....	1.85	.70
2960a	same, bklt pane of 20 .	23.50	....	....	....	30.00	9.95

2961

2962

2963

2964

2965

SCOTT NO.	DESCRIPTION	FIRST DAY COVERS SING	FIRST DAY COVERS PL. BLK.	MINT SHEET	PLATE BLOCK	UNUSED F/NH	USED
2961-65	Recreational Sports, 5 varieties, attached . .	7.00	....	22.00(20)	13.00(10)	6.00	4.50
2961	32¢ Volleyball	3.00	....	....	....	1.20	1.00
2962	32¢ Softball	3.00	....	....	....	1.20	1.00
2963	32¢ Bowling	[illegible]	....	....	....	1.20	1.00
2964	32¢ Tennis	3.00	....	....	....	1.20	1.00
2965	32¢ Golf	[illegible]	[illegible]	....	....	1.20	1.00

2966

2967

2968

SCOTT NO.	DESCRIPTION	FIRST DAY COVERS SING	FIRST DAY COVERS PL. BLK.	MINT SHEET	PLATE BLOCK	UNUSED F/NH	USED
2966	32¢ POW & MIA	3.00	4.00	20.00(20)	5.00	1.20	.30
2967	32¢ Marilyn Monroe. . .	4.00	5.00	30.00(20)	6.00	1.75	.35
2967v	same as above, uncut sheet of 120 (6 panes)	....	....	180.00(120)	....	....	....
....	block of 8 with vertical gutter	....	....	....	....	50.00	....
....	cross gutter block of 8 .	....	....	....	....	65.00	....
....	vertical pair with horizontal gutter	....	....	....	....	5.50	....
....	horizontal pair with vertical gutter	....	....	....	....	9.50	....
2968	32¢ Texas Statehood . .	3.00	4.75	28.00(20)	5.50	1.35	.35

2969 2970 2971

2972

2973

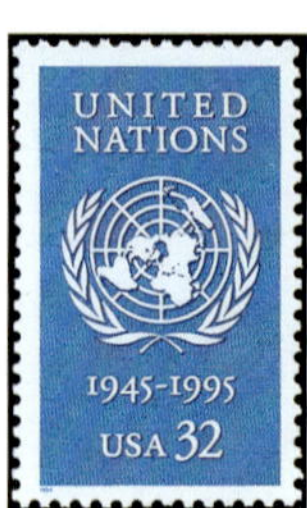
2974

SCOTT NO.	DESCRIPTION	FIRST DAY COVERS SING	FIRST DAY COVERS PL. BLK.	MINT SHEET	PLATE BLOCK	UNUSED F/NH	USED
2969	32¢ Split Rock Lighthouse	2.25	....	....	....	2.00	.40
2970	32¢ St. Joseph Lighthouse	2.25	....	....	....	2.00	.40
2971	32¢ Spectacle Reef Lighthouse.	2.25	....	....	....	2.00	.40
2972	32¢ Marblehead Lighthouse	2.25	....	....	....	2.00	.40
2973	32¢ Thirty Mile Point Lighthouse.	2.25	....	....	....	2.00	.40
2973a	Great Lakes Lighthouses, bklt pane of 5.	5.50	....	....	....	10.00	6.50
2973av	same, bklt pane, unfolded	....	....	....	....	12.00	....
2974	32¢ United Nations . . .	1.75	4.75	19.00(20)	4.75	1.00	.25

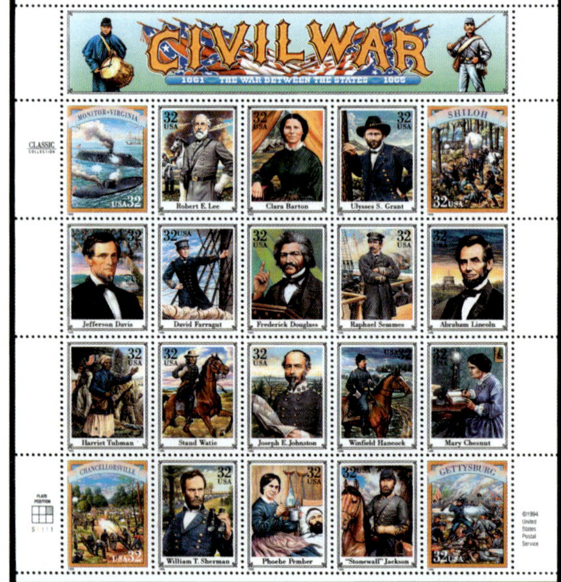

2975

CIVIL WAR

2975a	*Monitor-Virginia*	**2975k**	*Harriet Tubman*
2975b	*Robert E. Lee*	**2975l**	*Stand Watie*
2975c	*Clara Barton*	**2975m**	*Joseph E. Johnston*
2975d	*Ulysses S. Grant*	**2975n**	*Winfield Hancock*
2975e	*Shiloh*	**2975o**	*Mary Chestnut*
2975f	*Jefferson Davis*	**2975p**	*Chancellorsville*
2975g	*David Farragut*	**2975q**	*William T. Sherman*
2975h	*Frederick Douglass*	**2975r**	*Phoebe Pember*
2975i	*Raphael Semmes*	**2975s**	*"Stonewall" Jackson*
2975j	*Abraham Lincoln*	**2975t**	*Gettysburg*

SCOTT NO.	DESCRIPTION	FIRST DAY COVERS SING	FIRST DAY COVERS PL. BLK.	MINT SHEET	PLATE BLOCK	UNUSED F/NH	USED
2975	32¢ Civil War, 20 varieties, attached .	....	....	35.00(20)	....	35.00	30.00
....	set of singles	35.00	....	....	....	....	25.00
....	singles of above, each.	....	....	....	....	....	1.25
2975v	32¢ Civil War, uncut sheet of 120 (6 panes)	....	....	150.00(120)	....	150.00	....
....	cross gutter block of 20	....	....	....	....	55.00	....
....	cross gutter block of 4	....	....	....	....	27.50	....
....	vertical pair with horizontal gutter	....	....	....	....	6.00	....
....	horizontal pair with vertical gutter	....	....	....	....	6.00	....

2976

2977

2978

2979

SCOTT NO.	DESCRIPTION	FIRST DAY COVERS SING	FIRST DAY COVERS PL. BLK.	MINT SHEET	PLATE BLOCK	UNUSED F/NH	USED
2976-79	Carousel Horses, 4 varieties, attached . .	4.00	4.75	23.00(20)	5.75	5.00	3.75
2976	32¢ Palomino.	2.25	....	....	....	1.25	.45
2977	32¢ Pinto Pony	2.25	....	....	....	1.25	.45
2978	32¢ Armored Jumper . .	2.25	....	....	....	1.25	.45
2979	32¢ Brown Jumper . . .	2.25	....	....	....	1.25	.45

2980

SCOTT NO.	DESCRIPTION	FIRST DAY COVERS SING	FIRST DAY COVERS PL. BLK.	MINT SHEET	PLATE BLOCK	UNUSED F/NH	USED
2980	32¢ Women's Suffrage	1.95	4.75	44.00(40)	5.00	1.10	.30

2981

SCOTT NO.	DESCRIPTION	FIRST DAY COVERS SING	FIRST DAY COVERS PL. BLK.	MINT SHEET	PLATE BLOCK	UNUSED F/NH	USED
2981	$3.20 World War II (1945) Souvenir Sheet of 10. .	8.25	....	40.00(20)	....	22.00	15.00
2981a	32¢ Marines Raise Flag on Iwo Jima	2.25	....	....	....	2.50	1.00
2981b	32¢ Fierce Fighting Frees Manila	2.25	....	....	....	2.50	1.00
2981c	32¢ Okinawa, the Last Big Battle.	2.25	....	....	....	2.50	1.00
2981d	32¢ U.S. & Soviets Link Up at Elbe River	2.25	....	....	....	2.50	1.00
2981e	32¢ Allies Liberate Holocaust Survivors	2.25	....	....	....	2.50	1.00
2981f	32¢ Germany Surrenders at Reims	2.25	....	....	....	2.50	1.00
2981g	32¢ By 1945, World War II Has Uprooted Millions .	2.25	....	....	....	2.50	1.00
2981h	32¢ Truman Announces Japan's Surrender	2.25	....	....	....	2.50	1.00
2981i	32¢ News of Victory Hits Home.	2.25	....	....	....	2.50	1.00
2981j	32¢ Hometowns Honor Their Returning Veterans . . .	2.25	....	....	....	2.50	1.00

SCOTT NO.	DESCRIPTION	FIRST DAY COVERS SING	FIRST DAY COVERS PL. BLK.	MINT SHEET	PLATE BLOCK	UNUSED F/NH	USED

2982

2982	32¢ Louis Armstrong . .	1.95	4.75	25.00(20)	5.50	1.50	.50

2983 2984

2985 2986

2987 2988

2989 2990

2991 2992

SCOTT NO.	DESCRIPTION	FIRST DAY COVERS SING	FIRST DAY COVERS PL. BLK.	MINT SHEET	PLATE BLOCK	UNUSED F/NH	USED
2983-92	Jazz Musicians, 10 varieties attached	8.25	....	65.00(20)	35.00(10)	32.00	24.00
2983	32¢ Coleman Hawkins.	2.25	....	....	....	3.00	2.50
2984	32¢ Louis Armstrong . .	2.25	....	....	....	3.00	2.50
2985	32¢ James P. Johnson	2.25	....	....	....	3.00	2.50
2986	32¢ "Jelly Roll" Morton.	2.25	....	....	....	3.00	2.50
2987	32¢ Charlie Parker. . . .	2.25	....	....	....	3.00	2.50
2988	32¢ Eubie Blake	2.25	....	....	....	3.00	2.50
2989	32¢ Charles Mingus. . .	2.25	....	....	....	3.00	2.50
2990	32¢ Thelonious Monk .	2.25	....	....	....	3.00	2.50
2991	32¢ John Coltrane	2.25	....	....	....	3.00	2.50
2992	32¢ Erroll Garner.	2.25	....	....	....	3.00	2.50

SCOTT NO.	DESCRIPTION	FIRST DAY COVERS SING	FIRST DAY COVERS PL. BLK.	MINT SHEET	PLATE BLOCK	UNUSED F/NH	USED

2993 2994 2995 2996

2997

2998

2999

SCOTT NO.	DESCRIPTION	FIRST DAY COVERS SING	FIRST DAY COVERS PL. BLK.	MINT SHEET	PLATE BLOCK	UNUSED F/NH	USED
2993	32¢ Aster	2.25	....		....	1.25	.40
2994	32¢ Chrysanthemum . .	2.25	....	....	....	1.25	.40
2995	32¢ Dahlia	2.25	....	....	....	1.25	.40
2996	32¢ Hydrangea	2.25	....	....	....	1.25	.40
2997	32¢ Rudbeckia.	2.25	....	....	....	1.25	.40
2997a	Fall Garden Flowers, bklt pane of 5.	5.50	....	....	....	6.00	4.00
2997av	same, bklt pane, unfolded	....	....	....	....	9.00	....
2998	60¢ Eddie Rickenbacker	2.25	5.00	100.00(50)	10.00	3.25	.50
2998a	Large, 1995 date (1999)	2.25	5.00	128.00(50)	16.00	2.75	1.00
2999	32¢ Republic of Palau .	2.25	4.75	46.00(50)	5.00	1.20	.25

3000

COMIC STRIPS

3000a	*The Yellow Kid*	**3000k**	*Popeye*
3000b	*Katzenjammer Kids*	**3000l**	*Blondie*
3000c	*Little Nemo*	**3000m**	*Dick Tracy*
3000d	*Bringing Up Father*	**3000n**	*Alley Oop*
3000e	*Krazy Kat*	**3000o**	*Nancy*
3000f	*Rube Goldberg*	**3000p**	*Flash Gordon*
3000g	*Toonerville Folks*	**3000q**	*Li'l Abner*
3000h	*Gasoline Alley*	**3000r**	*Terry and the Pirates*
3000i	*Barney Google*	**3000s**	*Prince Valiant*
3000j	*Little Orphan Annie*	**3000t**	*Brenda Starr*

SCOTT NO.	DESCRIPTION	FIRST DAY COVERS SING	FIRST DAY COVERS PL. BLK.	MINT SHEET	PLATE BLOCK	UNUSED F/NH	USED
3000	32¢ Comic Strips, 20 varieties, attached .	....	....	25.00(20)	....	25.00	20.00
....	set of singles	50.00	....	....	....	12.75	
....	single of above, each. .	....	....	....	....	....	1.00

SCOTT NO.	DESCRIPTION	FIRST DAY COVERS SING	PL. BLK.	MINT SHEET	PLATE BLOCK	UNUSED F/NH	USED
	COMIC STRIPS (continued)						
3000v	32¢ Comic Strips, uncut sheet of 120 (6 panes)	....	....	120.00(120)	....	120.00	....
....	cross gutter block of 20	....	....	....	....	40.00	....
....	cross gutter block of 4	....	....	....	....	18.50	....
....	vertical pair with horizontal gutter.	....	....	....	....	4.50	....
....	horizontal pair with vertical gutter.	....	....	....	....	4.50	....

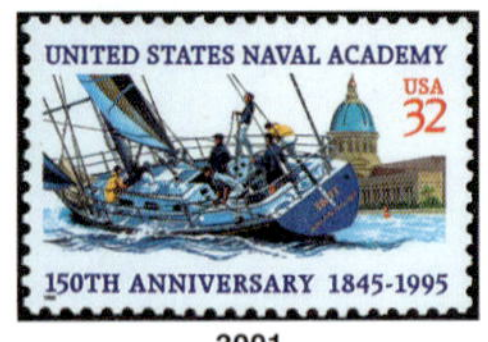

3001

3002

SCOTT NO.	DESCRIPTION	FIRST DAY COVERS SING	PL. BLK.	MINT SHEET	PLATE BLOCK	UNUSED F/NH	USED
3001	32¢ Naval Academy. . .	2.25	4.75	35.00(20)	8.00	1.50	.35
3002	32¢ Tennessee Williams	2.25	4.75	25.00(20)	6.00	1.50	.40

3003

3004, 3010, 3016

3005, 3009, 3015

3006, 3011, 3017

3007, 3008, 3014

3012, 3018

SCOTT NO.	DESCRIPTION	FIRST DAY COVERS SING	PL. BLK.	MINT SHEET	PLATE BLOCK	UNUSED F/NH	USED
3003	32¢ Madonna & Child .	2.25	4.75	47.00(50)	5.00	1.00	.25
3003a	32¢ Madonna & Child, bklt single.	2.25	....	....	....	1.10	.25
3003b	same, bklt pane of 10 .	7.25	....	....	....	10.00	....
3003bv	same, bklt pane, unfolded	....	....	....	....	11.50	....
3004-07	Santa & Children with Toys, 4 varieties, attached . .	4.00	4.75	50.00(50)	6.50	5.00	4.00
3004	32¢ Santa at Chimney.	2.25	....	....	....	1.65	.40
....	same, bklt single	2.25	....	....	....	1.65	.40
3005	32¢ Girl holding Jumping Jack.	2.25	....	....	....	1.65	.40
....	same, bklt single	2.25	....	....	....	1.65	.40
3006	32¢ Boy holding Toy Horse	2.25	....	....	....	1.65	.40
....	same, bklt single	2.25	....	....	....	1.65	.40
3007	32¢ Santa working on Sled	2.25	....	....	....	1.65	.40
....	same, bklt single	2.25	....	....	....	1.65	.40
3007b	32¢ Santa & Children with Toys, bklt pane of 10 (3 each of 3004-05) . . .	7.25	....	....	....	12.50	....
....	same, bklt pane unfolded	....	....	....	....	14.00	....
3007c	32¢ Santa & Children with Toys, bklt pane of 10 (3 each of 3006-07) . . .	7.25	....	....	....	12.50	....
....	same, bklt pane, unfolded	....	....	....	....	14.00	....
3008	32¢ Santa working on Sled, self-adhesive	2.25	....	....	....	1.75	.50
3009	32¢ Girl holding Jumping Jack, self-adhesive . . .	2.25	....	....	....	1.75	.50
3010	32¢ Santa at Chimney, self-adhesive	2.25	....	....	....	1.75	.50
3011	32¢ Boy holding Toy Horse, self-adhesive	2.25	....	....	....	1.75	.50
3011a	32¢ Santa & Children with Toys, self-adhesive, pane of 20	14.50	....	....	....	30.00	....
3012	32¢ Midnight Angel, self-adhesive	2.25	....	....	....	1.25	.45
3012a	same, bklt pane of 20 .	14.50	....	....	....	22.50	....

3013

SCOTT NO.	DESCRIPTION	FIRST DAY COVERS SING	PL. BLK.	MINT SHEET	PLATE BLOCK	UNUSED F/NH	USED
3013	32¢ Children Sledding, self-adhesive	2.25	....	....	....	1.25	.80
3013a	same, bklt pane of 18 .	13.00	....	....	....	20.00	....
3014-17	Santa & Children with Toys, self-adhesive, coil strip of 4	....	....	....	45.00(8)	20.00	....
3017a	same, plate strip of 5 . .	....	....	....	....	35.00	....
3014	32¢ Santa working on Sled, self-adhesive coil	2.25	....	....	....	5.50	1.35
3015	32¢ Girl holding Jumping Jack, self-adhesive coil	2.25	....	....	....	5.50	1.35
3016	32¢ Santa at Chimney, self-adhesive coil.	2.25	....	....	....	5.50	1.35
3017	32¢ Boy holding Toy Horse, self-adhesive coil	2.25	....	....	....	5.50	1.35
3018	32¢ Midnight Angel, self-adhesive coil.	3.00	....	....	17.75(3)	1.75	1.00

3019

3020

3021

3022

3023

SCOTT NO.	DESCRIPTION	FIRST DAY COVERS SING	PL. BLK.	MINT SHEET	PLATE BLOCK	UNUSED F/NH	USED
3019-23	Antique Automobiles, 5 varieties, attached . .	5.50	....	30.00(25)	12.50(10)	7.50	6.50
3019	32¢ 1893 Duryea.	2.25	....	....	....	1.50	.90
3020	32¢ 1894 Haynes	2.25	....	....	....	1.50	.90
3021	32¢ 1898 Columbia . . .	2.25	....	....	....	1.50	.90
3022	32¢ 1899 Winton	2.25	....	....	....	1.50	.90
3023	32¢ 1901 White	2.25	....	....	....	1.50	.90

3024

3025

3026

3027

3028

3029

1996 COMMEMORATIVES

SCOTT NO.	DESCRIPTION	FIRST DAY COVERS SING	FIRST DAY COVERS PL. BLK.	MINT SHEET	PLATE BLOCK	UNUSED F/NH	USED
3024/3118	**(3024, 3030, 3058-67, 3069-70, 3072-88, 3090-3104, 3106-11, 3118) 53 varieties**	....		....	....	**68.00**	**25.50**
3024	32¢ Utah Statehood. . .	2.25	4.75	65.00(50)	7.00	1.85	.40
3025	32¢ Crocus	2.25	....	....	....	1.85	.40
3026	32¢ Winter Aconite . . .	2.25	....	....	....	1.85	.40
3027	32¢ Pansy	2.25	....	....	....	1.85	.40
3028	32¢ Snowdrop	2.25	....	....	....	1.85	.40
3029	32¢ Anemone	2.25	....	....	....	1.85	.40
3029a	Winter Garden Flowers, bklt pane of 5.	5.50	....	....	....	6.50	5.00
3029av	same, bklt pane, unfolded	....	....	....	....	7.75	....

3030

3031, 3031A, 3044

3032, 3045

3033

3036, 3036a

3048, 3053

3049, 3054

3050, 3051, 3055

3052, 3052E

SCOTT NO.	DESCRIPTION	FIRST DAY COVERS SING	FIRST DAY COVERS PL. BLK.	MINT SHEET	PLATE BLOCK	UNUSED F/NH	USED
3030	32¢ Love (Cherub), self-adhesive	2.25	....	....	....	1.25	.25
3030a	same, bklt pane of 20 .	14.50	....	....	....	22.00	9.95
3030b	same, bklt pane of 15 .	11.50	....	....	....	15.00	....
3031	1¢ Kestrel, self-adhesive	2.25	....	10.00(50)	1.15	.25	.25
3031A	1¢ Kestrel, self-adhesive (2000)	1.95	....	12.00(50)	1.15	.25	.25
3032	2¢ Red-headed Woodpecker	2.25	4.75	15.00(100)	1.25	.25	.25
3033	3¢ Eastern Bluebird (redesign 3¢)	2.25	4.75	16.00(100)	1.35	.25	.25
3036	$1 Red Fox, self-adhesive	5.00	10.00	125.00(20)	25.00	8.00	.75
3036a	$1 Red Fox, 11¾ x 11 (2002)	....	....	130.00(20)	30.00	9.00	.85
3044	1¢ Kestrel, coil	2.25	5.00	....	1.00	.25	.25
	same, plate strip of 5 . .	....	....	....	....	1.50	....
3044a	1¢ Kestrel, large date, coil (1999)	2.25	5.00	....	1.00	.25	.25
3045	2¢ Red-headed Wood-pecker, coil.	2.25	....	....	1.00	.25	.25
	same, plate strip of 5 . .	....	....	....	....	1.50	....
3048	20¢ Blue Jay, self-adhesive (1996)	2.25	....	....	....	.75	.30
3048a	same, bklt pane of 10 .	8.00	....	....	....	7.25	....
3049	32¢ Yellow Rose, self-adhesive	2.25	....	....	....	1.10	.25
3049a	same, bklt pane of 20 .	14.50	....	....	....	20.00	....
3049b	same, bklt pane of 4 . .	....	....	....	....	5.50	....
3049c	same, bklt pane of 5 and label		....	....	....	6.75	....
3049d	same, bklt pane of 6 . .	....	....	....	....	6.75	....
3050	20¢ Ring-necked Pheasant, self-adhesive	2.25	....	....	....	.90	.25
3050a	same, bklt pane of 10 .	9.00	....	....	....	9.25	....
3050b	20¢ Pheasant, die cut 11	2.25	....	....	....	5.25	.85
3050c	same, bklt pane of 10 .	5.50	....	....	....	45.00	....
3051	20¢ Ring-necked Pheasant, die cut 10½ x 11, self-adhesive	2.25	....	....	....	1.60	1.00
3051A	same, die cut 10.6 x 10.4	2.25	....	....	....	13.00	6.00
3051b	same, bklt pane of 5, (4 #3051, 1 #3051a) . .	3.50	....	....	....	17.50	....
3052	33¢ Coral Pink Rose, self-adhesive (1999) . .	2.25	....	....	....	1.35	.30
3052a	same, bklt pane of 4 . .	3.00	....	....	....	5.25	....
3052b	same, bklt pane of 5 . .	3.75	....	....	....	6.50	....
3052c	same, bklt pane of 6 . .	4.50	....	....	....	7.50	....
3052d	same, bklt pane of 20 .	14.50	....	....	....	20.00	....
3052E	33¢ Coral Pink Rose, die-cut 10¾ x 10½, self-adhesive (2000) . .	2.25	....	....	....	1.40	.30
3052Ef	same, bklt pane of 20 .	14.50	....	....	....	18.00	....
3053	20¢ Blue Jay, self-adhesive, coil (1996)	2.25	....	....	6.50	1.00	.25
3054	32¢ Yellow Rose, self-adhesive coil (1997)	2.25	....	....	7.00	1.00	.25
	same, plate strip of 5 . .	....	....	....	....	8.00	....
3055	20¢ Ring-necked Pheasant, self-adhesive coil (1998)	2.25	....	....	4.00	.80	.25
	same, plate strip of 5 . .	....	....	....	....	6.00	....

3058

3059

3060

SCOTT NO.	DESCRIPTION	FIRST DAY COVERS SING	FIRST DAY COVERS PL. BLK.	MINT SHEET	PLATE BLOCK	UNUSED F/NH	USED
3058	32¢ Ernest Just	3.00	4.75	22.50(20)	5.00	1.50	.25
3059	32¢ Smithsonian Institution	2.25	4.75	19.50(20)	5.00	1.20	.25
3060	32¢ Year of the Rat . . .	2.25	4.75	25.00(20)	5.50	1.40	.25

3061

3062

3063

3064

SCOTT NO.	DESCRIPTION	FIRST DAY COVERS SING	FIRST DAY COVERS PL. BLK.	MINT SHEET	PLATE BLOCK	UNUSED F/NH	USED
3061-64	Pioneers of Communication, 4 varieties, attached . .	4.00	4.75	22.00(20)	5.50	5.00	3.25
3061	32¢ Eadweard Muybridge	2.25	....	....	....	1.55	.65
3062	32¢ Ottmar Mergenthaler	2.25	....	....	....	1.55	.65
3063	32¢ Frederic E. Ives . .	2.25	....	....	....	1.55	.65
3064	32¢ William Dickson . .	2.25	....	....	....	1.55	.65

3066

3065

3067

SCOTT NO.	DESCRIPTION	FIRST DAY COVERS SING	FIRST DAY COVERS PL. BLK.	MINT SHEET	PLATE BLOCK	UNUSED F/NH	USED
3065	32¢ Fulbright Scholarships	2.25	4.75	70.00(50)	8.00	1.85	.25
3066	50¢ Jacqueline Cochran	2.25	5.00	83.00(50)	8.50	2.00	.60
3067	32¢ Marathon	3.00	4.75	20.00(20)	5.00	1.00	.25

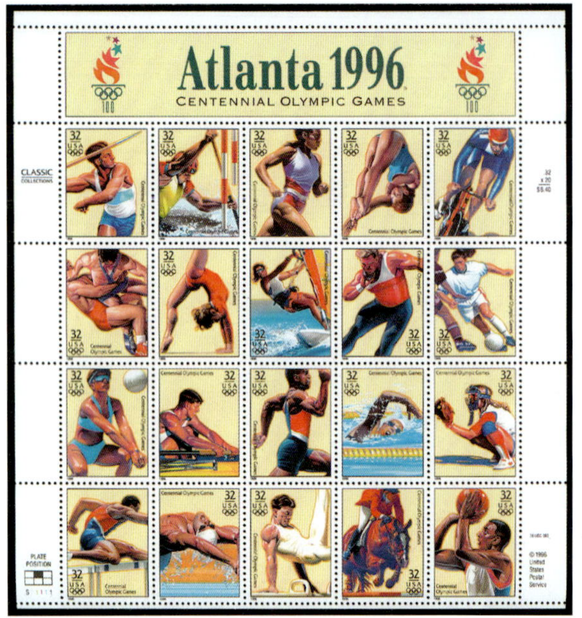

3068

1996 SUMMER OLYMPIC GAMES

3068a	*Decathlon*	**3068k**	*Beach volleyball*
3068b	*Men's canoeing*	**3068l**	*Men's rowing*
3068c	*Women's running*	**3068m**	*Men's sprints*
3068d	*Women's diving*	**3068n**	*Women's swimming*
3068e	*Men's cycling*	**3068o**	*Women's softball*
3068f	*Freestyle wrestling*	**3068p**	*Men's hurdles*
3068g	*Women's gymnastics*	**3068q**	*Men's swimming*
3068h	*Women's sailboarding*	**3068r**	*Men's gymnastics*
3068i	*Men's shot put*	**3068s**	*Equestrian*
3068j	*Women's soccer*	**3068t**	*Men's basketball*

SCOTT NO.	DESCRIPTION	FIRST DAY COVERS SING	FIRST DAY COVERS PL. BLK.	MINT SHEET	PLATE BLOCK	UNUSED F/NH	USED
3068	32¢ Centennial Olympic Games, 20 varieties, attached	....	....	25.00(20)	....	25.00	20.00
....	set of singles	35.00	....	....	....	....	17.00
....	single of above, each	....	....	....	....	....	1.00
3068v	same as above, uncut sheet of 120 (6 panes)	....	....	135.00(120)	....	135.00	....
....	cross gutter block of 20	....	....	....	....	35.00	....
....	cross gutter block of 4	....	....	....	....	19.50	....
....	vertical pair with horizontal gutter	....	....	....	....	4.50	....
....	horizontal pair with vertical gutter	....	....	....	....	4.50	....

3069

3070, 3071

SCOTT NO.	DESCRIPTION	FIRST DAY COVERS SING	FIRST DAY COVERS PL. BLK.	MINT SHEET	PLATE BLOCK	UNUSED F/NH	USED
3069	32¢ Georgia O'Keeffe	2.25	....	23.00(15)	7.50	1.75	.25
3070	32¢ Tennessee Statehood	2.25	4.75	60.00(50)	6.00	1.25	.25
3071	32¢ Tennessee Statehood, self-adhesive	2.25	....	....	....	1.40	.40
3071a	same, bklt pane of 20	14.50	....	....	....	30.00	....

3072

3073

3074

3075 3076

SCOTT NO.	DESCRIPTION	FIRST DAY COVERS SING	FIRST DAY COVERS PL. BLK.	MINT SHEET	PLATE BLOCK	UNUSED F/NH	USED
3072-76	American Indian Dances, 5 varieties, attached	5.50	....	28.00(20)	16.00(10)	8.00	7.00
3072	32¢ Fancy Dance	2.25	....	....	....	1.50	.85
3073	32¢ Butterfly Dance	2.25	....	....	....	1.50	.85
3074	32¢ Traditional Dance	2.25	....	....	....	1.50	.85
3075	32¢ Raven Dance	2.25	....	....	....	1.50	.85
3076	32¢ Hoop Dance	2.25	....	....	....	1.50	.85

3077 3078

3079 3080

SCOTT NO.	DESCRIPTION	FIRST DAY COVERS SING	FIRST DAY COVERS PL. BLK.	MINT SHEET	PLATE BLOCK	UNUSED F/NH	USED
3077-80	Prehistoric Animals, 4 varieties, attached	4.00	4.75	22.00(20)	5.50	5.00	3.50
3077	32¢ Eohippus	2.25	....	....	....	1.25	.40
3078	32¢ Woolly Mammoth	2.25	....	....	....	1.25	.40
3079	32¢ Mastodon	2.25	....	....	....	1.25	.40
3080	32¢ Saber-tooth Cat	2.25	....	....	....	1.25	.40

3081

3082

SCOTT NO.	DESCRIPTION	FIRST DAY COVERS SING	FIRST DAY COVERS PL. BLK.	MINT SHEET	PLATE BLOCK	UNUSED F/NH	USED
3081	32¢ Breast Cancer Awareness	2.25	4.75	20.00(20)	5.00	1.10	.25
3082	32¢ James Dean	3.00	4.75	25.00(20)	6.00	1.50	.25
....	vertical pair with horizontal gutter	....	....	....	....	4.50	....
....	horizontal pair with vertical gutter	....	....	....	....	7.00	....

3083 3084 3085 3086

SCOTT NO.	DESCRIPTION	FIRST DAY COVERS SING	FIRST DAY COVERS PL. BLK.	MINT SHEET	PLATE BLOCK	UNUSED F/NH	USED
3083-86	Folk Heroes, 4 varieties, attached . .	4.00	4.75	25.00(20)	7.00	6.00	4.75
3083	32¢ Mighty Casey	2.25	....	....	....	1.60	1.05
3084	32¢ Paul Bunyan	2.25	....	....	....	1.60	1.05
3085	32¢ John Henry	2.25	....	....	....	1.60	1.05
3086	32¢ Pecos Bill	2.25	....	....	....	1.60	1.05

3087

3088, 3089

SCOTT NO.	DESCRIPTION	FIRST DAY COVERS SING	FIRST DAY COVERS PL. BLK.	MINT SHEET	PLATE BLOCK	UNUSED F/NH	USED
3087	32¢ Olympic Discus Thrower	2.25	4.75	27.50(20)	6.00	1.50	.30
3088	32¢ Iowa Statehood. . .	2.25	4.75	65.00(50)	7.00	1.75	.30
3089	32¢ Iowa Statehood, self-adhesive	2.25	....	....	....	1.25	.35
3089a	same, bklt pane of 20 .	14.50	....	....	....	22.00	....

3090

SCOTT NO.	DESCRIPTION	FIRST DAY COVERS SING	FIRST DAY COVERS PL. BLK.	MINT SHEET	PLATE BLOCK	UNUSED F/NH	USED
3090	32¢ Rural Free Delivery	2.25	4.75	30.00(20)	7.00	1.50	.30

3091

3092

3093

3094

3095

SCOTT NO.	DESCRIPTION	FIRST DAY COVERS SING	FIRST DAY COVERS PL. BLK.	MINT SHEET	PLATE BLOCK	UNUSED F/NH	USED
3091-95	Riverboats, 5 varieties, attached . .	6.50	....	25.00(20)	14.00(10)	7.00	5.00
3091	32¢ Robt. E. Lee	2.25	....	....	....	1.50	.40
3092	32¢ Sylvan Dell	2.25	....	....	....	1.50	.40
3093	32¢ Far West	2.25	....	....	....	1.50	.40
3094	32¢ Rebecca Everingham	2.25	....	....	....	1.50	.40
3095	32¢ Bailey Gatzert	2.25	....	....	....	1.50	.40
3091-95b	32¢ Riverboats, special die cutting, 5 attached		....	....	210.00(10)	97.00	....
3095b	same, as above, pane of 20		....	325.00(20)	....	325.00	....

3098 3099

3096 3097

SCOTT NO.	DESCRIPTION	FIRST DAY COVERS SING	FIRST DAY COVERS PL. BLK.	MINT SHEET	PLATE BLOCK	UNUSED F/NH	USED
3096-99	Big Band Leaders, 4 varieties, attached . .	6.00	7.00	25.00(20)	6.50	6.00	4.50
3096	32¢ Count Basie	2.25	....	....	....	1.60	.85
3097	32¢ Tommy & Jimmy Dorsey	2.25	....	....	....	1.60	.85
3098	32¢ Glenn Miller	2.25	....	....	....	1.60	.85
3099	32¢ Benny Goodman. .	2.25	....	....	....	1.60	.85

3102 3103

3100 3101

SCOTT NO.	DESCRIPTION	FIRST DAY COVERS SING	FIRST DAY COVERS PL. BLK.	MINT SHEET	PLATE BLOCK	UNUSED F/NH	USED
3100-03	Songwriters, 4 varieties, attached . .	[illegible]	7.00	[illegible]	[illegible]	[illegible]	[illegible]
3100	32¢ Harold Arlen	2.25	....	....	....	1.50	.75
3101	32¢ Johnny Mercer . . .	2.25	....	....	....	1.50	.75
3102	32¢ Dorothy Fields . . .	2.25	....	....	....	1.50	.75
3103	32¢ Hoagy Carmichael	2.25	....	....	....	1.50	.75

3104

SCOTT NO.	DESCRIPTION	FIRST DAY COVERS SING	FIRST DAY COVERS PL. BLK.	MINT SHEET	PLATE BLOCK	UNUSED F/NH	USED
3104	23¢ F. Scott Fitzgerald	2.25	4.75	45.00(50)	5.00	1.20	.25

SE-TENANTS: Beginning with the 1964 Christmas issue (#1254-57), the United States has issued numerous Se-Tenant stamps covering a wide variety of subjects. Se-Tenants are issues where two or more different stamp designs are produced on the same sheet in pair, strip or block form. Mint stamps are usually collected in attached blocks, etc.—Used are generally saved as single stamps. Our Se-Tenant prices follow in this collecting pattern.

3105

ENDANGERED SPECIES

- **3105a** *Black-footed ferret*
- **3105b** *Thick-billed parrot*
- **3105c** *Hawaiian monk seal*
- **3105d** *American crocodile*
- **3105e** *Ocelot*
- **3105f** *Schaus swallowtail butterfly*
- **3105g** *Wyoming toad*
- **3105h** *Brown pelican*
- **3105i** *California condor*
- **3105j** *Gila trout*
- **3105k** *San Francisco garter snake*
- **3105l** *Woodland caribou*
- **3105m** *Florida panther*
- **3105n** *Piping plover*
- **3105o** *Florida manatee*

SCOTT NO.	DESCRIPTION	FIRST DAY COVERS SING	FIRST DAY COVERS PL. BLK.	MINT SHEET	PLATE BLOCK	UNUSED F/NH	USED
3105	32¢ Endangered Species, 15 varieties, attached .	15.00	....	22.00(15)	....	22.00	17.00
....	set of singles	27.50	....	....	....	....	12.00
....	singles of above, each.	....	....	....	....	....	1.25

3106

3107, 3112

SCOTT NO.	DESCRIPTION	FIRST DAY COVERS SING	FIRST DAY COVERS PL. BLK.	MINT SHEET	PLATE BLOCK	UNUSED F/NH	USED
3106	32¢ Computer Technology	2.25	4.75	40.00(40)	5.00	1.00	.25
3107	32¢ Madonna & Child	2.25	4.75	47.00(50)	5.00	1.00	.25

3108, 3113 — 3109, 3114 — 3110, 3115 — 3111, 3116

SCOTT NO.	DESCRIPTION	FIRST DAY COVERS SING	FIRST DAY COVERS PL. BLK.	MINT SHEET	PLATE BLOCK	UNUSED F/NH	USED
3108-11	Christmas Family Scenes, 4 varieties, attached .	4.00	4.75	55.00(50)	6.00	5.50	4.00
3108	32¢ Family at Fireplace	2.25	....	....	....	1.25	.35
3109	32¢ Decorating Tree .	2.25	....	....	....	1.25	.35
3110	32¢ Dreaming of Santa Claus	2.25	....	....	....	1.25	.35
3111	32¢ Holiday Shopping	2.25	....	....	....	1.25	.35
3112	32¢ Madonna & Child, self-adhesive	2.25	....	....	....	1.25	.30
3112a	same, bklt pane of 20	14.50	....	....	....	21.00	....
3113	32¢ Family at Fireplace, self-adhesive	2.25	....	....	....	1.25	.35
3114	32¢ Decorating Tree, self-adhesive	2.25	....	....	....	1.25	.35
3115	32¢ Dreaming of Santa Claus, self-adhesive	2.25	....	....	....	1.25	.35
3116	32¢ Holiday Shopping, self-adhesive	2.25	....	....	....	1.25	.35
3116a	Christmas Family Scenes, self-adhesive, bklt pane of 20	14.50	....	....	....	20.00	....

3117

3118

SCOTT NO.	DESCRIPTION	FIRST DAY COVERS SING	FIRST DAY COVERS PL. BLK.	MINT SHEET	PLATE BLOCK	UNUSED F/NH	USED
3117	32¢ Skaters, self-adhesive	2.25	....	....	....	1.70	1.00
3117a	same, bklt pane of 18	13.00	....	....	....	19.00	....
3118	32¢ Hanukkah, self-adhesive	2.25	....	22.00(20)	4.50	1.00	.25

3119

SCOTT NO.	DESCRIPTION	FIRST DAY COVERS SING	FIRST DAY COVERS PL. BLK.	MINT SHEET	PLATE BLOCK	UNUSED F/NH	USED
3119	50¢ Cycling, sheet of 2	4.00	....	....	....	4.50	4.00
3119a-b	same, set of 2 singles	5.00	....	....	....	5.00	3.00

3120

3121

1997 COMMEMORATIVES

SCOTT NO.	DESCRIPTION	FIRST DAY COVERS SING	FIRST DAY COVERS PL. BLK.	MINT SHEET	PLATE BLOCK	UNUSED F/NH	USED
3120/75	**(3120-21, 3125, 3130-31, 3134-35, 3141, 3143-50, 3152-75) 40 varieties .**	....	....	....	....	**50.00**	**26.00**
3120	32¢ Year of the Ox. . . .	3.00	....	24.00(20)	5.50	1.25	.25
3121	32¢ Benjamin O. Davis, Sr.	3.00	4.75	30.00(20)	5.50	1.50	.50

3122

SCOTT NO.	DESCRIPTION	FIRST DAY COVERS SING	FIRST DAY COVERS PL. BLK.	MINT SHEET	PLATE BLOCK	UNUSED F/NH	USED
3122	32¢ Statue of Liberty, self-adhesive (1997) .	2.25	....	....	....	1.45	.25
3122a	same, bklt pane of 20	14.50	....	....	....	22.00	....
3122b	same, bklt pane of 4 .	4.75	....	....	....	5.00	....
3122c	same, bklt pane of 5 .	5.00	....	....	....	6.00	....
3122d	same, bklt pane of 6 .	5.75	....	....	....	12.00	....
3122E	32¢ Statue of Liberty, die cut 11.5 x 11.8 . . .	....	....	....	....	2.75	1.00
3122Ef	same, bklt pane of 20	....	....	....	....	40.00	....
3122Eg	same, bklt pane of 6 .	....	....	....	....	15.00	....

3123

3124

SCOTT NO.	DESCRIPTION	FIRST DAY COVERS SING	FIRST DAY COVERS PL. BLK.	MINT SHEET	PLATE BLOCK	UNUSED F/NH	USED
3123	32¢ Swans, self-adhesive	2.25	....	....	....	1.25	.35
3123a	same, bklt pane of 20	14.50	....	....	....	20.00	....
3124	55¢ Swans, self-adhesive	2.50	....	....	....	2.00	.60
3124a	same, bklt pane of 20	19.75	....	....	....	30.00	....

3125

SCOTT NO.	DESCRIPTION	FIRST DAY COVERS SING	FIRST DAY COVERS PL. BLK.	MINT SHEET	PLATE BLOCK	UNUSED F/NH	USED
3125	32¢ Helping Children Learn	2.25	4.75	19.50(20)	5.00	1.10	.30

3126, 3128 3127, 3129

SCOTT NO.	DESCRIPTION	FIRST DAY COVERS SING	FIRST DAY COVERS PL. BLK.	MINT SHEET	PLATE BLOCK	UNUSED F/NH	USED
3126	32¢ Citron, Moth, Larvae, Pupa, Beetle, self-adhesive (Die Cut 10.9 x 10.2) . .	2.25	....	....	....	1.15	.35
3127	32¢ Flowering Pineapple, Cockroaches, self-adhesive (Die Cut 10.9 x 10.2) . .	2.25	....	....		1.15	.35
3127a	same, bklt pane of 20 (10–#3126, 10–#3127)	14.50	....	....	....	20.00	....
3128	32¢ Citron, Moth, Larvae, Pupa, Beetle, self-adhesive (Die Cut 11.2 x 10.8) . .	2.25	....	....	....	1.95	1.30
3128a	same, stamp sideways	2.25	....	....	....	6.00	3.50
3128b	same, bklt pane of 5 (2–#3128 & #3129, 1–#3128a)	5.50	....	....	....	13.00	....
3129	32¢ Flowering Pineapple, Cockroaches, self-adhesive (Die Cut 11.2 x 10.8) . .	2.25	....	....	....	1.95	1.30
3129a	same, stamp sideways	2.25	....	....	....	12.00	4.00
3129b	same, bklt pane of 5 (2–#3128 & #3129, 1–#3129a)	5.50	....	....	....	19.00	....

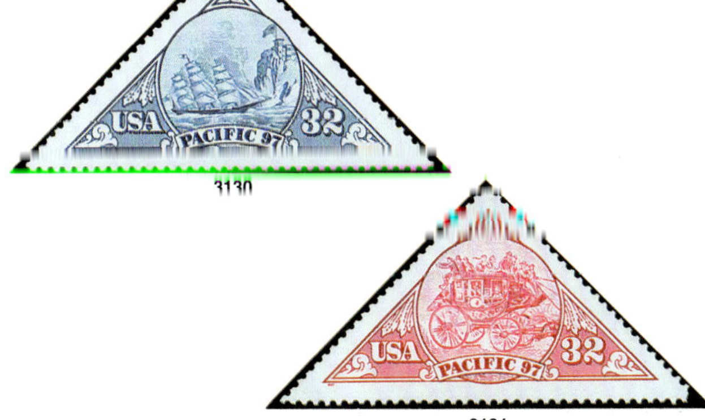

3130

3131

SCOTT NO.	DESCRIPTION	FIRST DAY COVERS SING	FIRST DAY COVERS PL. BLK.	MINT SHEET	PLATE BLOCK	UNUSED F/NH	USED
3130-31	32¢ Stagecoach & Ship, (Pacific '97) 2 varieties, attached.	3.00	4.75	19.00(16)	6.00	2.75	2.00
3130	32¢ Ship	2.25	....	....	....	1.40	.35
3131	32¢ Stagecoach.	2.25	....	....	....	1.40	.35
3130-31v	same, as above, uncut sheet of 96 (6 panes)	....	....	110.00(96)	....	110.00	....
....	block of 32 with vertical or horizontal gutter between (2 panes)	....	....	37.50(32)	....	37.50	....
....	cross gutter block of 16	....	....	....	....	30.00	....
....	vertical pairs with horizontal gutter	....	....	....	....	10.00	....
....	horizontal pairs with vertical gutter	....	....	....	....	8.00	....

3132

SCOTT NO.	DESCRIPTION	FIRST DAY COVERS SING	FIRST DAY COVERS PL. BLK.	MINT SHEET	PLATE BLOCK	UNUSED F/NH	USED
3132	(25¢) Jukebox, self-adhesive linerless coil.	2.25	....	....	10.00(3)	2.35	1.25
	same, plate strip of 5 . .	....	....	....	....	15.00	....
3133	32¢ Flag Over Porch, self-adhesive, linerless coil	2.25	....	....	11.00(3)	2.00	1.10
	same, plate strip of 5 . .	....	....	....	....	15.00	....

3134

3135

SCOTT NO.	DESCRIPTION	FIRST DAY COVERS SING	FIRST DAY COVERS PL. BLK.	MINT SHEET	PLATE BLOCK	UNUSED F/NH	USED
3134	32¢ Thornton Wilder . .	2.25	4.75	20.00(20)	5.25	1.10	.30
3135	32¢ Raoul Wallenberg .	3.00	4.75	20.00(20)	5.25	1.10	.30

3136

DINOSAURS

3136a	*Ceratosaurus*	3136f	*Stegosaurus*	3136k	*Daspletosaurus*
[illegible]	[illegible]	[illegible]	[illegible]	[illegible]	[illegible]
[illegible]	[illegible]	3136h	*Opisthias*	3136m	*Corythosaurus*
3136d	*Brachiosaurus*	3136i	*Edmontonia*	3136n	*Ornithomimus*
3136e	*Goniopholis*	3136j	*Einiosaurus*	3136o	*Parasaurolophus*

SCOTT NO.	DESCRIPTION	FIRST DAY COVERS SING	FIRST DAY COVERS PL. BLK.	MINT SHEET	PLATE BLOCK	UNUSED F/NH	USED
3136	32¢ Dinosaurs, 15 varieties, attached	11.50	....	....	....	20.00	18.00
....	set of singles	26.50	....	....	....	....	12.00
....	singles of above, each	....	....	....	....	....	1.00

3137, 3138

SCOTT NO.	DESCRIPTION	FIRST DAY COVERS SING	FIRST DAY COVERS PL. BLK.	MINT SHEET	PLATE BLOCK	UNUSED F/NH	USED
3137	32¢ Bugs Bunny, self-adhesive, pane of 10	9.50	....	....	....	13.00	....
3137a	same, single from pane	2.50	....	....	....	1.25	.35
3137b	same, pane of 9 (#3137a)	....	....	....	....	10.00	....
3137c	same, pane of 1 (#3137a)	....	....	....	....	2.50	....
3137v	same, top press sheet (6 panes) ...		....	350.00	....	350.00	....
3137v	same, bottom press w/ plate# (6 panes)		....	800.00	....	800.00	....
....	pane of 10 from press sheet		....	95.00	....	95.00	....
....	pane of 10 from press sheet w/ plate#		....	500.00	....	500.00	....

1997 COMMEMORATIVES (continued)

SCOTT NO.	DESCRIPTION	FIRST DAY COVERS SING	FIRST DAY COVERS PL. BLK.	MINT SHEET	PLATE BLOCK	UNUSED F/NH	USED
3138	32¢ Bugs Bunny, self-adhesive, Die Cut, pane of 10 . . .	....	....	....	....	130.00	....
3138a	same, single from pane	....	....	....	....	....	....
3138b	same, pane of 9 (#3138a)	....	....	....	....	....	....
3138c	same, pane of 1 (#3138a)	....	....	....	....	....	....

3139

3140

SCOTT NO.	DESCRIPTION	FIRST DAY COVERS SING	FIRST DAY COVERS PL. BLK.	MINT SHEET	PLATE BLOCK	UNUSED F/NH	USED
3139	50¢ Benjamin Franklin, Souvenir Sheet of 12 (Pacific '97)	25.00	....	....	....	22.00	20.00
3139a	same, single from sheet	5.00	....	....	....	1.90	1.50
3140	60¢ George Washington, Souvenir Sheet of 12 (Pacific '97)	25.00	....	....	....	25.00	24.00
3140a	same, single from sheet	5.00	....	....	....	2.00	1.50

3141

SCOTT NO.	DESCRIPTION	FIRST DAY COVERS SING	FIRST DAY COVERS PL. BLK.	MINT SHEET	PLATE BLOCK	UNUSED F/NH	USED
3141	32¢ Marshall Plan	1.95	4.75	20.00(20)	5.00	1.00	.30

3142

CLASSIC AMERICAN AIRCRAFT

3142a	*Mustang*	**3142k**	*Flying Fortress*
3142b	*Model B*	**3142l**	*Stearman*
3142c	*Cub*	**3142m**	*Constellation*
3142d	*Vega*	**3142n**	*Lightning*
3142e	*Alpha*	**3142o**	*Peashooter*
3142f	*B-10*	**3142p**	*Tri-Motor*
3142g	*Corsair*	**3142q**	*DC-3*
3142h	*Stratojet*	**3142r**	*314 Clipper*
3142i	*GeeBee*	**3142s**	*Jenny*
3142j	*Staggerwing*	**3142t**	*Wildcat*

SCOTT NO.	DESCRIPTION	FIRST DAY COVERS SING	FIRST DAY COVERS PL. BLK.	MINT SHEET	PLATE BLOCK	UNUSED F/NH	USED
3142	32¢ Classic American Aircraft, 20 varieties, attached . .	....	....	25.00(20)	....	25.00	20.00
....	set of singles	35.00	....	....	....	....	14.00
....	singles of above, each.	....	....	....	....	....	1.00
3142v	same as above, uncut sheet of 120 (6 panes)	....	....	125.00(120)	....	125.00	....
....	cross gutter block of 20	....	....	....	....	28.00	....
....	cross gutter block of 4 .	....	....	....	....	18.50	....
....	vertical pair with horizontal gutter	....	....	....	....	3.50	....
....	horizontal pair with vertical gutter	....	....	....	....	3.50	....

3143, 3148 — 3144, 3149

3145, 3147 — 3146, 3150

SCOTT NO.	DESCRIPTION	FIRST DAY COVERS SING	FIRST DAY COVERS PL. BLK.	MINT SHEET	PLATE BLOCK	UNUSED F/NH	USED
3143-46	Legendary Football Coaches, 4 varieties, attached . .	4.00	4.75	25.00(20)	5.50	5.25	4.00
3143	32¢ Paul "Bear" Bryant	2.25	....	....	....	1.30	1.30
3144	32¢ Glenn "Pop" Warner	2.25	....	....	....	1.30	1.30
3145	32¢ Vince Lombardi. . .	2.25	....	....	....	1.30	1.30
3146	32¢ George Halas	2.25	....	....	....	1.30	1.30
3147	32¢ Vince Lombardi. . .	2.25	4.75	24.00(20)	5.50	1.30	1.30
3148	32¢ Paul "Bear" Bryant	2.25	4.75	24.00(20)	5.50	1.30	1.30
3149	32¢ Glenn "Pop" Warner	2.25	4.75	24.00(20)	5.50	1.30	1.30
3150	32¢ George Halas	2.25	4.75	24.00(20)	5.50	1.30	1.30

3151

CLASSIC AMERICAN DOLLS

3151a *"Alabama Baby," and doll by Martha Chase*
3151b *"Columbian Doll"*
3151c *Johnny Gruelle's "Raggedy Ann"*
3151d *Doll by Martha Chase*
3151e *"American Child"*
3151f *"Baby Coos"*
3151g *Plains Indian*
3151h *Doll by Izannah Walker*
3151i *"Babyland Rag"*
3151j *"Scootles"*
3151k *Doll by Ludwig Greiner*
3151l *"Betsy McCall"*
3151m *Percy Crosby's "Skippy"*
3151n *"Maggie Mix-up"*
3151o *Dolls by Albert Schoenhut*

SCOTT NO.	DESCRIPTION	FIRST DAY COVERS SING	FIRST DAY COVERS PL. BLK.	MINT SHEET	PLATE BLOCK	UNUSED F/NH	USED
3151	32¢ Classic American Dolls, 15 varieties, attached	....	....	22.50(15)	....	22.50	18.00
....	set of singles	30.00	....	....	....	....	14.00
....	singles of above, each	....	....	....	....	....	1.00

3152

SCOTT NO.	DESCRIPTION	FIRST DAY COVERS SING	FIRST DAY COVERS PL. BLK.	MINT SHEET	PLATE BLOCK	UNUSED F/NH	USED
3152	32¢ Humphrey Bogart	3.00		37.00(20)	6.00	1.50	.35
3152v	same, as above, uncut sheet of 120 (6 panes)	....	....	125.00(120)	....	125.00	....
....	block of 8 with vertical gutter	....	....	....	....	18.00	....
....	cross gutter block of 8	....	....	....	....	21.00	....
....	vertical pair with horizontal gutter	....	....	....	....	3.50	....
....	horizontal pair with vertical gutter	....	....	....	....	5.00	....

3153

SCOTT NO.	DESCRIPTION	FIRST DAY COVERS SING	FIRST DAY COVERS PL. BLK.	MINT SHEET	PLATE BLOCK	UNUSED F/NH	USED
3153	32¢ "The Stars & Stripes Forever"	2.25	4.75	47.00(50)	5.00	1.00	.30

3154

3155

3156

3157

SCOTT NO.	DESCRIPTION	FIRST DAY COVERS SING	FIRST DAY COVERS PL. BLK.	MINT SHEET	PLATE BLOCK	UNUSED F/NH	USED
3154-57	Opera Singers, 4 varieties, attached	4.00	4.75	22.00(20)	5.50	4.75	4.00
3154	32¢ Lily Pons	2.25	....	....	....	1.25	1.00
3155	32¢ Richard Tucker	2.25	....	....	....	1.25	1.00
3156	32¢ Lawrence Tibbett	2.25	....	....	....	1.25	1.00
3157	32¢ Rosa Ponselle	2.25	....	....	....	1.25	1.00

3158

3159

3160

3161

3162

3163

3164

3165

SCOTT NO.	DESCRIPTION	FIRST DAY COVERS SING	FIRST DAY COVERS PL. BLK.	MINT SHEET	PLATE BLOCK	UNUSED F/NH	USED
3158-65	Composers and Conductors, 8 varieties, attached	7.00	....	39.00(20)	20.00(8)	17.00	10.00
3158	32¢ Leopold Stokowski	2.25	....	....	....	2.00	1.00
3159	32¢ Arthur Fiedler	2.25	....	....	....	2.00	1.00
3160	32¢ George Szell	2.25	....	....	....	2.00	1.00
3161	32¢ Eugene Ormandy	2.25	....	....	....	2.00	1.00
3162	32¢ Samuel Barber	2.25	....	....	....	2.00	1.00
3163	32¢ Ferde Grofé	2.25	....	....	....	2.00	1.00
3164	32¢ Charles Ives	2.25	....	....	....	2.00	1.00
3165	32¢ Louis Moreau Gottschalk	2.25	....	....	....	2.00	1.00

3166

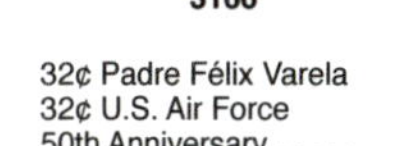

3167

SCOTT NO.	DESCRIPTION	FIRST DAY COVERS SING	FIRST DAY COVERS PL. BLK.	MINT SHEET	PLATE BLOCK	UNUSED F/NH	USED
3166	32¢ Padre Félix Varela	2.25	4.75	19.00(20)	4.75	1.00	.50
3167	32¢ U.S. Air Force 50th Anniversary	4.00	6.00	19.00(20)	4.75	1.25	.30

3168

3169

3170

3171

3172

SCOTT NO.	DESCRIPTION	FIRST DAY COVERS SING	PL. BLK.	MINT SHEET	PLATE BLOCK	UNUSED F/NH	USED
3168-72	Movie Monster, 5 varieties, attached . .	10.00	....	27.50(20)	15.00(10)	7.00	5.00
3168	32¢ Lon Chaney as The Phantom of the Opera .	2.25	....	....	....	1.50	1.00
3169	32¢ Bela Lugosi as Dracula	2.25	....	....	....	1.50	1.00
3170	32¢ Boris Karloff as Frankenstein's Monster	2.25	....	....	....	1.50	1.00
3171	32¢ Boris Karloff as The Mummy	2.25	....	....	....	1.50	1.00
3172	32¢ Lon Chaney, Jr. as The Wolfman	2.25	....	....	....	1.50	1.00
3168-72v	same as above, uncut sheet of 180 (9 panes)	....	....	225.00(180)	....	225.00	....
....	block of 8 with vertical gutter	....	....	....	....	14.00	....
....	block of 10 with horizontal gutter	....	....	....	....	17.50	....
....	cross gutter block of 8 .	....	....	....	....	22.50	....
....	vertical pair with horizontal gutter	....	....	....	....	4.00	....
....	horizontal pair with vertical gutter	....	....	....	....	4.00	....

3173

SCOTT NO.	DESCRIPTION	FIRST DAY COVERS SING	PL. BLK.	MINT SHEET	PLATE BLOCK	UNUSED F/NH	USED
3173	32¢ First Supersonic Flight, 50th Anniversary	3.00	4.75	20.00(20)	5.00	1.00	.30

3174

SCOTT NO.	DESCRIPTION	FIRST DAY COVERS SING	PL. BLK.	MINT SHEET	PLATE BLOCK	UNUSED F/NH	USED
3174	32¢ Women in Military Service.	3.00	4.75	24.00(20)	6.25	1.35	.35

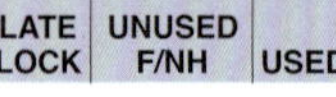

3175

SCOTT NO.	DESCRIPTION	FIRST DAY COVERS SING	PL. BLK.	MINT SHEET	PLATE BLOCK	UNUSED F/NH	USED
3175	32¢ Kwanzaa.	3.00	4.75	47.00(50)	5.00	1.00	.30
....	same, as above, uncut sheet of 250 (5 panes)	....	....	725.00(250)	....	....	....

3176

3177

SCOTT NO.	DESCRIPTION	FIRST DAY COVERS SING	PL. BLK.	MINT SHEET	PLATE BLOCK	UNUSED F/NH	USED
3176	32¢ Madonna & Child, self-adhesive	2.25	....	....	....	1.00	.25
3176a	same, bklt pane of 20 .	14.50	....	....	....	19.00	....
3177	32¢ American Holly, self-adhesive	2.25	....	....	....	1.00	.25
3177a	same, bklt pane of 20 .	14.50	....	....	....	19.00	....
3177b	same, bklt pane of 4 . .	3.00	....	....	....	5.50	....
3177c	same, bklt pane of 5 . .	3.75	....	....	....	6.75	....
3177d	same, bklt pane of 6 . .	4.50	....	....	....	7.25	....

3178

SCOTT NO.	DESCRIPTION	FIRST DAY COVERS SING	PL. BLK.	MINT SHEET	PLATE BLOCK	UNUSED F/NH	USED
3178	$3 Mars Rover Sojourner, Souvenir Sheet	14.00	....	....	....	9.50	5.00
....	same, as above, uncut sheet of 18 souvenir sheets .	....	....	175.00(18)	....	175.00	....
3178v	single souvenir sheet from uncut sheet of 18.	....	....	....	....	10.50	....

3179

1998 COMMEMORATIVES

SCOTT NO.	DESCRIPTION	FIRST DAY COVERS SING	PL. BLK.	MINT SHEET	PLATE BLOCK	UNUSED F/NH	USED
3179/3252	**(3179-81, 3192-3203, 3206, 3211-27, 3230-35, 3237-43, 3249-52) 50 varieties**	....	....	....	....	**72.00**	**27.00**
3179	32¢ Year of the Tiger . .	3.00	4.75	22.50(20)	5.50	1.20	.30

3180

3181

SCOTT NO.	DESCRIPTION	FIRST DAY COVERS SING	PL. BLK.	MINT SHEET	PLATE BLOCK	UNUSED F/NH	USED
3180	32¢ Alpine Skiing.	2.25	4.75	25.00(20)	6.00	1.75	.30
3181	32¢ Madam C.J. Walker	3.00	4.75	22.50(20)	5.50	1.50	.35

3182

CELEBRATE THE CENTURY 1900s

- **3182a** *Model T Ford*
- **3182b** *Theodore Roosevelt*
- **3182c** *"The Great Train Robbery" 1903*
- **3182d** *Crayola Crayons, introduced, 1903*
- **3182e** *St. Louis World's Fair, 1904*
- **3182f** *Pure Food & Drug Act, 1906*
- **3182g** *Wright Brothers first flight, 1903*
- **3182h** *Boxing match in painting*
- **3182i** *Immigrants arrive.*
- **3182j** *John Muir, preservationist*
- **3182k** *"Teddy" bear created*
- **3182l** *W.E.B. DuBois, social activist*
- **3182m** *Gibson Girl*
- **3182n** *First baseball World Series, 1903*
- **3182o** *Robie House, Chicago*

SCOTT NO.	DESCRIPTION	FIRST DAY COVERS SING	FIRST DAY COVERS PL. BLK.	MINT SHEET	PLATE BLOCK	UNUSED F/NH	USED
3182	32¢ Celebrate the Century 1900's, 15 varieties, attached.	17.50	....	18.00(15)	....	18.00	14.00
....	set of singles	32.00	....	....	....	....	12.00
....	singles of above, each.	....	....	....	....	....	1.00
3182v	same as above, uncut sheet of 60 (4 panes)	....	....	70.00(4)	....	70.00	....

3183

CELEBRATE THE CENTURY 1910s

- **3183a** *Charlie Chaplin as the Little Tramp*
- **3183b** *Federal Reserve system created, 1913*
- **3183c** *George Washington Carver*
- **3183d** *Avant-garde art, 1913*
- **3183e** *First-Transcontinental telephone line, 1914*
- **3183f** *Panama Canal opens, 1914*
- **3183g** *Jim Thorpe wins decathlon, 1912*
- **3183h** *Grand Canyon National Park, 1913*
- **3183i** *United States enters WWI*
- **3183j** *Boy Scouts, 1910*
- **3183k** *Woodrow Wilson*
- **3183l** *First crossword puzzle, pub., 1913*
- **3183m** *Jack Dempsey wins title, 1919*
- **3183n** *Construction toys*
- **3183o** *Child labor reform*

SCOTT NO.	DESCRIPTION	FIRST DAY COVERS SING	FIRST DAY COVERS PL. BLK.	MINT SHEET	PLATE BLOCK	UNUSED F/NH	USED
3183	32¢ Celebrate the Century 1910's, 15 varieties, attached.	17.50	....	18.00(15)	....	18.00	14.00
....	set of singles	32.00	....	....	....	....	12.00
....	singles of above, each.	....	....	....	....	....	1.00
3183v	same as above, uncut sheet of 60 (4 panes)	....	....	70.00(4)	....	70.00	....

3184

CELEBRATE THE CENTURY 1920s

- **3184a** *Babe Ruth*
- **3184b** *The Gatsby style*
- **3184c** *Prohibition enforced*
- **3184d** *Electric toy trains*
- **3184e** *19th Amendment*
- **3184f** *Emily Post's Etiquette*
- **3184g** *Margaret Mead, anthropologist*
- **3184h** *Flappers do the Charleston*
- **3184i** *Radio entertains America*
- **3184j** *Art Deco style (Chrysler Building)*
- **3184k** *Jazz flourishes*
- **3184l** *Four Horsemen of Notre Dame*
- **3184m** *Lindbergh flies the Atlantic*
- **3184n** *American realism*
- **3184o** *Stock Market crash, 1929*

SCOTT NO.	DESCRIPTION	FIRST DAY COVERS SING	FIRST DAY COVERS PL. BLK.	MINT SHEET	PLATE BLOCK	UNUSED F/NH	USED
3184	32¢ Celebrate the Century 1920's, 15 varieties, attached.	17.50	....	18.00(15)	....	18.00	14.00
....	set of singles	32.00	....	....	....	....	12.00
....	singles of above, each.	....	....	....	....	....	1.00
3184v	same, as above, uncut sheet of 60 (4 panes)	....	....	70.00(4)	....	70.00	....

3185

CELEBRATE THE CENTURY 1930s

- **3185a** *Franklin D. Roosevelt*
- **3185b** *Empire State Building*
- **3185c** *1st Issue of Life Magazine*
- **3185d** *Eleanor Roosevelt*
- **3185e** *FDR's New Deal*
- **3185f** *Superman arrives*
- **3185g** *Household conveniences*
- **3185h** *"Snow White and the Seven Dwarfs"*
- **3185i** *"Gone with the Wind"*
- **3185j** *Jesse Owens*
- **3185k** *Streamline design*
- **3185l** *Golden Gate Bridge*
- **3185m** *America survives the Depression*
- **3185n** *Bobby Jones wins Grand Slam*
- **3185o** *The Monopoly Game*

SCOTT NO.	DESCRIPTION	FIRST DAY COVERS SING	FIRST DAY COVERS PL. BLK.	MINT SHEET	PLATE BLOCK	UNUSED F/NH	USED
3185	32¢ Celebrate the Century 1930's, 15 varieties, attached.	17.50	....	18.00(15)	....	18.00	14.00
....	set of singles	32.00	....	....	....	....	12.00
....	singles of above, each.	....	....	....	....	....	1.00
3185v	same as above, uncut sheet of 60 (4 panes)	....	....	70.00(4)	....	70.00	....

3186

CELEBRATE THE CENTURY 1940s

3186a	*World War II*	**3186i**	*GI Bill, 1944*
3186b	*Antibiotics save lives*	**3186j**	*Big Band Sounds*
3186c	*Jackie Robinson*	**3186k**	*Intl. Style of Architecture*
3186d	*Harry S. Truman*	**3186l**	*Postwar Baby Boom*
3186e	*Women support war effort*	**3186m**	*Slinky, 1945*
3186f	*TV entertains America*	**3186n**	*"A Streetcar Named Desire" 1947*
3186g	*Jitterbug sweeps nation*	**3186o**	*Orson Welles' "Citizen Kane"*
3186h	*Jackson Pollock, Abstract Expressionism*		

SCOTT NO.	DESCRIPTION	FIRST DAY COVERS SING	FIRST DAY COVERS PL. BLK.	MINT SHEET	PLATE BLOCK	UNUSED F/NH	USED
3186	33¢ Celebrate the Century 1940's, 15 varieties, attached.	17.50	....	22.00(15)	....	22.00	15.00
....	set of singles	32.00	....	....	....	....	14.00
....	singles of above, each.	....	....	....	....	....	.85
3186v	same as above, uncut sheet of 60 (4 panes)	....	....	70.00(4)	....	70.00	1.00

3187

CELEBRATE THE CENTURY 1950s

3187a	*Polio vaccine developed*	**3187i**	*Drive-in movies*
3187b	*teen fashions*	**3187j**	*World series rivals*
3187c	*The "Shot Heard Round the World"*	**3187k**	*Rocky Marciano, undefeated*
3187d	*US launches satellites*	**3187l**	*"I Love Lucy"*
3187e	*Korean War*	**3187m**	*Rock 'n Roll*
3187f	*Desegregation public schools*	**3187n**	*Stock car racing*
3187g	*Tail fins, chrome*	**3187o**	*Movies go 3-D*
3187h	*Dr. Seuss "The Cat in the Hat"*		

SCOTT NO.	DESCRIPTION	FIRST DAY COVERS SING	FIRST DAY COVERS PL. BLK.	MINT SHEET	PLATE BLOCK	UNUSED F/NH	USED
3187	33¢ Celebrate the Century 1950's, 15 varieties, attached.	17.50	....	22.00(15)	....	22.00	15.00
....	set of singles	32.00	....	....	....	....	14.00
....	singles of above, each.	....	....	....	....	....	1.00
3187v	same as above, uncut sheet of 60 (4 panes)	....	....	70.00(4)	....	70.00	....

3188

CELEBRATE THE CENTURY 1960s

3188a	*"I Have a Dream" Martin Luther King*	**3188i**	*Barbie Doll*
3188b	*Woodstock*	**3188j**	*The Integrated Circuit*
3188c	*Man Walks on the Moon*	**3188k**	*Lasers*
3188d	*Green Bay Packers*	**3188l**	*Super Bowl I*
3188e	*Star Trek*	**3188m**	*Peace Symbol*
3188f	*The Peace Corps*	**3188n**	*Roger Maris, 61 in '61*
3188g	*The Vietnam War*	**3188o**	*The Beatles "Yellow Submarine"*
3188h	*Ford Mustang*		

SCOTT NO.	DESCRIPTION	FIRST DAY COVERS SING	FIRST DAY COVERS PL. BLK.	MINT SHEET	PLATE BLOCK	UNUSED F/NH	USED
3188	33¢ Celebrate the Century 1960's, 15 varieties, attached.	17.50	....	22.00(15)	....	22.00	15.00
....	set of singles	32.00	....	....	....	....	14.00
....	singles of above, each.	....	....	....	....	....	1.00
3188v	same as above, uncut sheet of 60 (4 panes)	....	....	70.00(4)	....	70.00	....

3189

CELEBRATE THE CENTURY 1970s

3189a	*Earth Day Celebrated*	**3189i**	*Pioneer 10*
3189b	*"All in the Family", TV Series*	**3189j**	*Women's Rights Movement*
3189c	*Sesame Street*	**3189k**	*1970's Fashion*
3189d	*Disco Music*	**3189l**	*Monday Night Football*
3189e	*Steelers Win Four Super Bowls*	**3189m**	*America Smiles*
3189f	*U.S. Celebrates 200th Birthday*	**3189n**	*Jumbo Jets*
3189g	*Secretariat Wins Triple Crown*	**3189o**	*Medical Imaging*
3189h	*VCR's Transform Entertainment*		

SCOTT NO.	DESCRIPTION	FIRST DAY COVERS SING	FIRST DAY COVERS PL. BLK.	MINT SHEET	PLATE BLOCK	UNUSED F/NH	USED
3189	33¢ Celebrate the Century 1970's, 15 varieties, attached.	17.50	....	22.00(15)	....	22.00	15.00
....	set of singles	32.00	....	....	....	....	14.00
....	singles of above, each.	....	....	....	....	....	1.00
3189v	same as above, uncut sheet of 60 (4 panes)	....	....	70.00(4)	....	70.00	....

3190

CELEBRATE THE CENTURY 1980s

3190a *Space Shuttle program*
3190b *Cats, Musical Smash*
3190c *San Francisco 49ers*
3190d *Hostages Come Home*
3190e *Figure Skating*
3190f *Cable TV*
3190g *Vietnam Veterans Memorial*
3190h *Compact Discs*
3190i *Cabbage Patch Kids*
3190j *"The Cosby Show", Hit Comedy*
3190k *Fall of the Berlin Wall*
3190l *Video Games*
3190m *"E.T. The Extra-Terrestrial"*
3190n *Personal Computers*
3190o *Hip-hop Culture*

SCOTT NO.	DESCRIPTION	FIRST DAY COVERS SING	PL. BLK.	MINT SHEET	PLATE BLOCK	UNUSED F/NH	USED
3190	33¢ Celebrate the Century 1980's, 15 varieties, attached.	17.50	....	22.00(15)	....	22.00	15.00
....	set of singles	32.00	....	....	....	....	14.00
....	singles of above, each.	....	....	....	....	....	1.00
3190v	same as above, uncut sheet of 60 (4 panes)	....	....	70.00(4)	....	70.00	....

3191

CELEBRATE THE CENTURY 1990s

3191a *New Baseball Records*
3191b *Gulf War*
3191c *"Seinfeld" Sitcom Sensation*
3191d *Extreme Sports*
3191e *Improving Education*
3191f *Computer Art and Graphics*
3191g *Recovering Species*
3191h *Return to Space*
3191i *Special Olympics*
3191j *Virtual Reality*
3191k *"Jurassic Park"*
3191l *"Titanic" Blockbuster Film*
3191m *Sport Utility Vehicles*
3191n *World Wide Web*
3191o *Cellular Phones*

SCOTT NO.	DESCRIPTION	FIRST DAY COVERS SING	PL. BLK.	MINT SHEET	PLATE BLOCK	UNUSED F/NH	USED
3191	33¢ Celebrate the Century 1990's, 15 varieties, attached.	17.50	....	22.00(15)	....	22.00	15.00
....	set of singles	32.00	....	....	....	....	14.00
....	singles of above, each.	....	....	....	....	....	1.00
3191v	same as above, uncut sheet of 60 (4 panes)	....	....	70.00(4)	....	70.00	....

3192

SCOTT NO.	DESCRIPTION	FIRST DAY COVERS SING	PL. BLK.	MINT SHEET	PLATE BLOCK	UNUSED F/NH	USED
3192	32¢ "Remember the Maine"	3.00	4.75	27.00(20)	6.75	1.50	.30

3193

3194

3195

3196

3197

SCOTT NO.	DESCRIPTION	FIRST DAY COVERS SING	PL. BLK.	MINT SHEET	PLATE BLOCK	UNUSED F/NH	USED
3193-97	Flowering Trees, self-adhesive, 5 varieties, attached.	5.75	....	26.00(20)	15.00(10)	7.00	5.00
3193	32¢ Southern Magnolia	2.25	....	....	....	1.10	.40
3194	32¢ Blue Paloverde . .	2.25	....	....	....	1.10	.40
3195	32¢ Yellow Poplar . . .	2.25	....	....	....	1.10	.40
3196	32¢ Prairie Crab Apple	2.25	....	....	....	1.10	.40
3197	32¢ Pacific Dogwood.	2.25	....	....	....	1.10	.40

3198

3199

3200

3201

3202

SCOTT NO.	DESCRIPTION	FIRST DAY COVERS SING	PL. BLK.	MINT SHEET	PLATE BLOCK	UNUSED F/NH	USED
3198-3202	Alexander Calder, 5 varieties, attached.	5.75	....	27.00(20)	16.00(10)	7.50	5.50
3198	32¢ Black Cascade, 13 Verticals, 1959 . . .	1.95	....	....	....	1.50	1.00
3199	32¢ Untitled, 1965 . . .	1.95	....	....	....	1.50	1.00
3200	32¢ Rearing Stallion, 1928	1.95	....	....	....	1.50	1.00
3201	32¢ Portrait of a Young Man, c. 1945.	1.95	....	....	....	1.50	1.00
3202	32¢ Un Effet du Japonais, 1945.	1.95	....	....	....	1.50	1.00
3198-3202v	same, as above, uncut sheet of 120 (6 panes)	....	....	140.00(120)	....	....	....

3203

SCOTT NO.	DESCRIPTION	FIRST DAY COVERS SING	FIRST DAY COVERS PL. BLK.	MINT SHEET	PLATE BLOCK	UNUSED F/NH	USED
3203	32¢ Cinco De Mayo, self-adhesive	2.25	4.75	22.00(20)	5.75	1.10	.30
3203v	same as above, uncut sheet of 180 (9 panes)	....	....	180.00(180)	....	180.00	....
....	cross gutter block of 4 .	....	....	....	....	16.00	....
....	vertical pair with horizontal gutter	....	....	....	....	3.00	....
....	horizontal pair with vertical gutter	....	....	....	....	3.00	....

3204, 3205

SCOTT NO.	DESCRIPTION	FIRST DAY COVERS SING	FIRST DAY COVERS PL. BLK.	MINT SHEET	PLATE BLOCK	UNUSED F/NH	USED
3204	32¢ Sylvester & Tweety, self-adhesive, pane of 10	12.00	....	....	....	12.00	....
3204a	same, single from pane	2.25	....	....	....	1.35	.35
3204b	same, pane of 9 (#3204a)	....	....	....	....	9.75	....
3204c	same, pane of 1 (#3204a)	7.00	....	....	....	2.75	....
....	same, top press sheet of 60 (6 panes)	....	....	100.00(60)	....	100.00	....
....	same, bottom press sheet of 60 (6 panes)	....	....	175.00(60)	....	175.00	....
....	same, pane of 10 from press sheet	....	....	....	....	17.50	....
....	same, pane of 10 from press sheet w/ plate # .	....	....	....	....	80.00	....
....	vert. pair with horiz. gutter	....	....	....	....	10.00	....
....	horiz pair with vert. gutter	....	....	....	....	20.00	....
3205	32¢ Sylvester & Tweety, self-adhesive, Die-Cut, pane of 10	20.00	....	....	....	22.00	....
3205a	same, single from pane	....	....	....	....	1.75	....
3205b	same, pane of 9 (#3205a)	....	....	....	....	14.00	....
3205c	same, pane of 1, imperf.	12.00	....	....	....	6.00	....

3206

SCOTT NO.	DESCRIPTION	FIRST DAY COVERS SING	FIRST DAY COVERS PL. BLK.	MINT SHEET	PLATE BLOCK	UNUSED F/NH	USED
3206	32¢ Wisconsin, self-adhesive	1.95	4.75	20.00(20)	5.00	1.20	.30

3207, 3207a

3208, 3208a

SCOTT NO.	DESCRIPTION	FIRST DAY COVERS SING	PLATE# STRIP 3	MINT SHEET	PLATE# STRIP 3	UNUSED F/NH	USED
3207	(5¢) Wetlands, Nonprofit, coil	2.25	10.00	....	1.85	.25	.25
	same, plate strip of 5 . .	....	....	....	....	2.00	....
3207A	same, self-adhesive coil	2.25	....	....	1.85	.25	.25
	same, plate strip of 5 . .	....	....	....	....	2.00	....
3207Ab	same, self-adhesive coil, large date.	....	....	....	3.75	.40	.25
....	same, plate strip of 5 . .	....	....	....	....	4.50	....
3208	(25¢) Diner, Presorted First-Class, coil	1.95	10.00	....	5.00	1.00	.50
3208a	same, self-adhesive coil, die cut 9.7	1.95	....	....	6.00	1.00	.50
....	same, plate strip of 5 . .	....	....	....	....	7.00	....

3209

SCOTT NO.	DESCRIPTION	FIRST DAY COVERS SING	FIRST DAY COVERS PL. BLK.	MINT SHEET	PLATE BLOCK	UNUSED F/NH	USED
3209	1¢-$2 Trans-Mississippi, Souvenir Sheet of 9. . .	12.00	....	....	....	18.00	13.00
....	same, set of 9 singles .	18.00	....	....	....	16.00	12.00
3209v	block of 9 with horiz. gutter	....	....	....	....	60.00	....
3209v	vert. pair with horiz. gutter	....	....	....	....	12.50	....

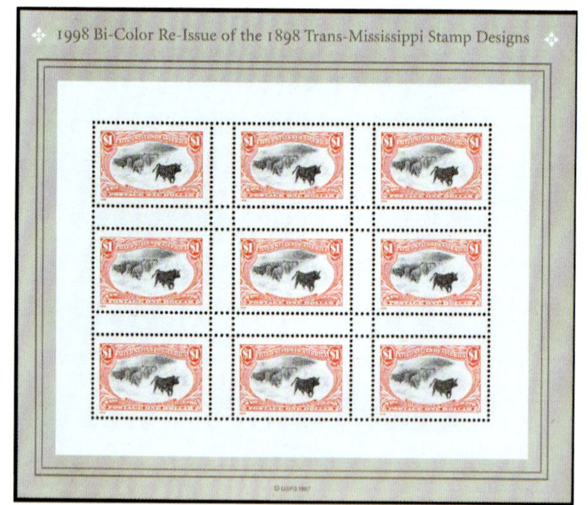

3210

SCOTT NO.	DESCRIPTION	FIRST DAY COVERS SING	FIRST DAY COVERS PL. BLK.	MINT SHEET	PLATE BLOCK	UNUSED F/NH	USED
3210	$1 Cattle in Storm, Souvenir Sheet of 9. . .	17.50	....	....	....	32.00	22.00
....	same, single stamp . . .	....	....	....	....	3.75	2.50
3209-10	same, press sheet of 54 (6 panes, 3–#3209 & 3–#3210).	....	....	175.00(54)	....	175.00	....
3210v	cross gutter block of 12	....	....	....	....	85.00	....
3210v	vert. pair with horiz. gutter	....	....	....	....	12.50	....
3210v	horiz. pair with vert. gutter	....	....	....	....	12.50	....

3211

SCOTT NO.	DESCRIPTION	FIRST DAY COVERS SING	FIRST DAY COVERS PL. BLK.	MINT SHEET	PLATE BLOCK	UNUSED F/NH	USED
3211	32¢ Berlin Airlift, 50th Anniversary	1.95	4.75	25.00(20)	6.00	1.35	.30

3212 3213

3215 3214

SCOTT NO.	DESCRIPTION	FIRST DAY COVERS SING	FIRST DAY COVERS PL. BLK.	MINT SHEET	PLATE BLOCK	UNUSED F/NH	USED
3212-15	Folk Musicians, 4 varieties, attached . .	12.00	14.00	32.00(20)	8.00	7.00	5.00
	Same, Top plate block of 8		....	....	15.00(8)	....	....
3212	32¢ Huddie "Leadbelly" Ledbetter	3.00	....	....	....	1.75	1.00
3213	32¢ Woody Guthrie . . .	3.00	....	....	....	1.75	1.00
3214	32¢ Sonny Terry	3.00	....	....	....	1.75	1.00
3215	32¢ Josh White	3.00	....	....	....	1.75	1.00

3216 3217

3218 3219

SCOTT NO.	DESCRIPTION	FIRST DAY COVERS SING	FIRST DAY COVERS PL. BLK.	MINT SHEET	PLATE BLOCK	UNUSED F/NH	USED
3216-19	Gospel Singers, 4 varieties, attached . .	12.00	14.00	36.00(20)	8.00	7.00	4.00
	Same, Top plate block of 8		....	....	16.00(8)	....	....
3216	32¢ Mahalia Jackson. .	3.00	....	....	....	1.75	1.00
3217	32¢ Roberta Martin . . .	3.00	....	....	....	1.75	1.00
3218	32¢ Clara Ward	3.00	....	....	....	1.75	1.00
3219	32¢ Sister Rosetta Tharpe	3.00	....	....	....	1.75	1.00

3220

3221

SCOTT NO.	DESCRIPTION	FIRST DAY COVERS SING	FIRST DAY COVERS PL. BLK.	MINT SHEET	PLATE BLOCK	UNUSED F/NH	USED
3220	32¢ Spanish Settlement of the Southwest	2.25	4.75	19.50(20)	4.75	1.20	.25
3221	32¢ Stephen Vincent Bénét	2.25	4.75	19.50(20)	4.75	1.20	.35

3222 3223

3224 3225

SCOTT NO.	DESCRIPTION	FIRST DAY COVERS SING	FIRST DAY COVERS PL. BLK.	MINT SHEET	PLATE BLOCK	UNUSED F/NH	USED
3222-25	Tropical Birds, 4 varieties, attached . .	5.00	6.00	22.00(20)	6.50	6.00	4.00
3222	32¢ Antillean Euphonia	2.25	....	....	....	1.25	.75
3223	32¢ Green-throated Carib	2.25	....	....	....	1.25	.75
3224	32¢ Crested Honeycreeper	2.25	....	....	....	1.25	.75
3225	32¢ Cardinal Honeyeater	2.25	....	....	....	1.25	.75

3226

SCOTT NO.	DESCRIPTION	FIRST DAY COVERS SING	FIRST DAY COVERS PL. BLK.	MINT SHEET	PLATE BLOCK	UNUSED F/NH	USED
3226	32¢ Alfred Hitchcock .	2.25	....	26.00(20)	6.00	1.50	.35
3226v	same as above, uncut sheet of 120 (6 panes)	....	....	120.00(120)	....	120.00	....
....	block of 8 with vertical gutter	....	....	....	....	18.00	....
....	cross gutter block of 8	....	....	....	....	25.00	....
....	vertical pair with horizontal gutter	....	....	....	....	4.50	....
....	horizontal pair with vertical gutter	....	....	....	....	6.00	....

3227

3228, 3229

SCOTT NO.	DESCRIPTION	FIRST DAY COVERS SING	FIRST DAY COVERS PL. BLK.	MINT SHEET	PLATE BLOCK	UNUSED F/NH	USED
3227	32¢ Organ & Tissue Donation, self-adhesive	2.25	....	22.00(20)	5.50	1.20	.25
3228	(10¢) Modern Bicycle, self-adhesive coil, die cut 9.8	2.25	....	....	3.00(3)	.40	.25
	same, plate strip of 5 .	....	....	....	....	4.00	....
3228a	large "1998" date	....	....	....	3.50(3)	.75	.50
....	same, plate strip of 5 .	....	....	....	....	4.50	....
3229	(10¢) Modern Bicycle, coil	2.25	10.00	....	3.00(3)	.40	.25
	same, plate strip of 5 .	....	....	....	....	3.75	....

3230

3231

3232

3233

SCOTT NO.	DESCRIPTION	FIRST DAY COVERS SING	FIRST DAY COVERS PL. BLK.	MINT SHEET	PLATE BLOCK	UNUSED F/NH	USED

1998 COMMEMORATIVES (continued)

3231

SCOTT NO.	DESCRIPTION	FIRST DAY COVERS SING	FIRST DAY COVERS PL. BLK.	MINT SHEET	PLATE BLOCK	UNUSED F/NH	USED
3230-34	Bright Eyes, self-adhesive, 5 varieties, attached .	12.00	....	28.00(20)	15.00(10)	7.00	6.00
3230	32¢ Bright Eyes Dog .	3.00	....	....	....	1.50	.45
3231	32¢ Bright Eyes Fish .	3.00	....	....	....	1.50	.45
3232	32¢ Bright Eyes Cat. .	3.00	....	....	....	1.50	.45
3233	32¢ Bright Eyes Parakeet	3.00	....	....	....	1.50	.45
3234	32¢ Bright Eyes Hamster	3.00	....	....	....	1.50	.45

3235

SCOTT NO.	DESCRIPTION	FIRST DAY COVERS SING	FIRST DAY COVERS PL. BLK.	MINT SHEET	PLATE BLOCK	UNUSED F/NH	USED
3235	32¢ Klondike Gold Rush	2.25	....	22.00(20)	6.00	1.20	.25

3236

AMERICAN ART

3236a *"Portrait of Richard Mather," by John Foster*
3236b *"Mrs. Elizabeth Freake and Baby Mary," by The Freake Limner*
3236c *"Girl in Red Dress with Cat and Dog," by Ammi Phillips*
3236d *"Rubens Peale with Geranium," by Rembrandt Peale*
3236e *"Long-billed Curlew, Numenius Longrostris," by John James Audubon*
3236f *"Boatmen on the Missouri," by George Caleb Bingham*
3236g *"Kindred Spirits," by Asher B. Durand*
3236h *"The Westwood Children," by Joshua Johnson*
3236i *"Music and Literature," by William Harnett*
3236j *"The Fog Warning," by Winslow Homer*
3236k *"The White Cloud, Head Chief of the Iowas," by George Catlin*
3236l *"Cliffs of Green River," by Thomas Moran*
3236m *"The Last of the Buffalo," by Alfred Bierstadt*
3236n *"Niagara," by Frederic Edwin Church*
3236o *"Breakfast in Bed," by Mary Cassatt*
3236p *"Nighthawks," by Edward Hopper*
3236q *"American Gothic," by Grant Wood*
3236r *"Two Against the White," by Charles Sheeler*
3236s *"Mahoning," by Franz Kline*
3236t *"No. 12," by Mark Rothko*

SCOTT NO.	DESCRIPTION	FIRST DAY COVERS SING	FIRST DAY COVERS PL. BLK.	MINT SHEET	PLATE BLOCK	UNUSED F/NH	USED
3236	32¢ American Art, 20 varieties, attached	....	....	30.00(20)	....	30.00	25.00
....	set of singles	35.00	....	....	....	....	19.00
....	same as above, uncut sheet of 120 (6 panes)	....	....	175.00(120)	....	175.00	....
....	block of 24 with vert. gutter........		....	....	....	27.50	....
....	block of 25 with horiz. gutter......		....	....	....	32.50	....
....	cross gutter block of 20	....	....	....	....	40.00	....
....	vert. pair with horiz. gutter		....	....	....	7.00	....

AMERICAN ART (continued)

SCOTT NO.	DESCRIPTION	FIRST DAY COVERS SING	FIRST DAY COVERS PL. BLK.	MINT SHEET	PLATE BLOCK	UNUSED F/NH	USED
....	horiz. pair with vert. gutter		....	....	....	9.00	....
....	horiz. blk of 8 with vert. gutter		....	....	....	....	....
....	vert. blk of 10 with horiz. gutter		....	....	....	....	....

3237

3243

SCOTT NO.	DESCRIPTION	FIRST DAY COVERS SING	FIRST DAY COVERS PL. BLK.	MINT SHEET	PLATE BLOCK	UNUSED F/NH	USED
3237	32¢ Ballet.	1.95	....	23.00(20)	6.00	1.50	.35
....	same,uncut sheet of 120 (6 panes)	....	....	115.00(120)	....	115.00	....
....	cross gutter blk of 4 . .	....	....	....	....	13.00	....
....	vert. pair with horiz. gutter		....	....	....	3.00	....
....	horiz. pair with vert. gutter		....	....	....	3.00	....

3238

3239

3240

3241

3244

3242

SCOTT NO.	DESCRIPTION	FIRST DAY COVERS SING	FIRST DAY COVERS PL. BLK.	MINT SHEET	PLATE BLOCK	UNUSED F/NH	USED
3238-42	Space Discovery, 5 varieties, attached .	5.75	11.00	24.00(20)	15.00(10)	7.50	6.50
3238	32¢ Space City	2.25	....	....	....	1.50	1.00
3239	32¢ Space ship landing	2.25	....	....	....	1.50	1.00
3240	32¢ Person in space suit	2.25	....	....	....	1.50	1.00
3241	32¢ Space Ship taking off	2.25	....	....	....	1.50	1.00
3242	32¢ Large domed structure	2.25	....	....	....	1.50	1.00
3238-42v	same, uncut sheet of 180 (9 panes)	....	....	185.00(180)	....	185.00	....
....	cross gutter blk of 10 .	....	....	....	....	27.50	....
....	vert. blk of 10 with horiz. gutter	....	....	....	....	20.00	....
....	horiz. pair with vert. gutter	....	....	....	....	3.50	....
....	vert. pair with horiz. gutter		....	....	....	3.50	....

3245, 3249

3246, 3250

3247, 3251

3248, 3252

SCOTT NO.	DESCRIPTION	FIRST DAY COVERS SING	FIRST DAY COVERS PL. BLK.	MINT SHEET	PLATE BLOCK	UNUSED F/NH	USED
3243	32¢ Giving and Sharing, self-adhesive	2.25	4.75	22.00(20)	5.50	1.20	.30
3244	32¢ Madonna & Child, self-adhesive	2.25	....	....	....	1.50	.25
3244a	same, booklet pane of 20	14.50	....	....	....	20.00	....
3245	32¢ Evergreen Wreath, self-adhesive	2.25	....	....	....	4.00	1.00
3246	32¢ Victorian Wreath, self-adhesive	2.25	....	....	....	4.00	1.00
3247	32¢ Chili Pepper Wreath, self-adhesive	2.25	....	....	....	4.00	1.00
3248	32¢ Tropical Wreath self-adhesive	2.25	....	....	....	4.00	1.00

SCOTT NO.	DESCRIPTION	FIRST DAY COVERS SING	PL. BLK.	MINT SHEET	PLATE BLOCK	UNUSED F/NH	USED
3248a	32¢ Christmas Wreaths, self-adhesive, bklt pane of 4	4.00	....	....	....	20.00	....
3248b	same, bklt pane of 5 .	5.00	....	....	....	25.00	....
3248c	same, bklt pane of 6 .	5.50	....	....	....	30.00	....
3249-52	32¢ Christmas Wreaths, self-adhesive, 4 varieties, attached.	4.00	4.75	60.00(20)	15.00	13.00	....
3249-52a	die cut 11.7 x 11.6 . . .	....	....	....	....	19.00	....
3249	32¢ Evergreen Wreath, self-adhesive	2.25	....	....	....	2.50	.75
3249a	32¢ Evergreen Wreath, self-adhesive, die-cut 11.7 x 11.6	2.25	....	....	....	2.75	1.00
3250	32¢ Victorian Wreath, self-adhesive	2.25	....	....	....	2.50	.75
3250a	32¢ Victorian Wreath, self-adhesive, die-cut 11.7 x 11.6	2.25	....	....	....	2.75	1.00
3251	32¢ Chili Pepper Wreath, self-adhesive	2.25	....	....	....	2.50	.75
3251a	32¢ Chili Pepper Wreath, self-adhesive, die-cut 11.7 x 11.6	2.25	....	....	....	2.75	1.00
3252	32¢ Tropical Wreath, self-adhesive	2.25	....	....	....	2.50	.75
3252a	32¢ Tropical Wreath, self-adhesive, die-cut 11.7 x 11.6	2.25	....	....	....	2.75	1.00
3252c	same, bklt pane of 20	14.50	....	....	....	55.00	....
3252e	bklt pane of 20, 5 each of 3249a-52a + label . . .	14.50	....	....	....	60.00	....

3257, 3258

3259, 3263

3260, 3264, 3265, 3266, 3267, 3268, 3269

SCOTT NO.	DESCRIPTION	FIRST DAY COVERS SING	PL. BLK.	MINT SHEET	PLATE BLOCK	UNUSED F/NH	USED
3257	(1¢) Weather Vane (white USA)	2.25	3.50	11.00(50)	1.10	.25	.25
3258	(1¢) Weather Vane (pale blue USA)	2.25	3.50	11.00(50)	1.10	.25	.25
3259	22¢ Uncle Sam, self-adhesive	2.25	4.75	14.00(20)	3.75	.75	.35
3259a	22¢ Uncle Sam, die cut 10.8	....	....	30.00(20)	12.00	3.50	1.35
3260	(33¢) Uncle Sam's Hat	2.25	4.75	50.00(50)	7.00	1.25	.35

3261

3262

SCOTT NO.	DESCRIPTION	FIRST DAY COVERS SING	PL. BLK.	MINT SHEET	PLATE BLOCK	UNUSED F/NH	USED
3261	$3.20 Space Shuttle Landing, self-adhesive	7.50	26.50	200.00(20)	46.00	11.00	5.00
3262	$11.75 Piggyback Space Shuttle, self-adhesive	28.50	95.00	695.00(20)	150.00	38.00	22.00
3263	22¢ Uncle Sam, self adhesive coil	2.25	....	....	5.75	.85	.35
....	same, plate strip of 5 .	....	....	....	....	6.50	....
3264	(33¢) Uncle Sam's Hat, coil	2.25	10.00	....	8.00	1.20	.65
....	same, plate strip of 5 .	....	....	....	....	9.50	....
3265	(33¢) Uncle Sam's Hat, self-adhesive coil, die cut 9.9	2.25	....	....	11.00	1.25	.30
....	same, plate strip of 5 .	....	....	....	....	12.00	....
3266	(33¢) Uncle Sam's Hat, self-adhesive coil, die cut 9.7	2.25	....	....	20.00(3)	3.00	1.65
....	same, plate strip of 5 .	....	....	....	....	24.00	....
3267	(33¢) Uncle Sam's Hat, self-adhesive, die cut 9.9	2.25	....	....	....	1.25	.30
3267a	same, bklt pane of 10	7.25	....	....	....	10.00	....
3268	(33¢) Uncle Sam's Hat, self-adhesive, die cut 11.2 x 11.1	2.25	....	....	....	1.25	.30
3268a	same, bklt pane of 10	7.25	....	....	....	10.00	....
3268b	(33¢) Uncle Sam's Hat, d/c 11	....	....	....	....	1.25	.50
3268c	same, bklt pane of 20	14.50	....	....	....	23.00	....
3269	(33¢) Uncle Sam's Hat, self-adhesive, die cut 8	2.25	....	....	....	1.30	.75
3269a	same, bklt pane of 18	13.50	....	....	....	20.00	....

SCOTT NO.	DESCRIPTION	FIRST DAY COVERS SING	PL. BLK.	MINT SHEET	PLATE BLOCK	UNUSED F/NH	USED
3270	(10¢) Eagle, Presorted Std. coil, d/c 9.8, small date	2.25	....	....	3.00(3)	.40	.25
3270a	same, large date	....	....	....	10.00(3)	.85	.50
	plate strip of 5	....	....	....	....	12.00	....
3271	(10¢) Eagle, Presorted Std., self-adhesive coil d/c 9.9	2.25	....	....	4.00	.40	.25
....	same, plate strip of 5 .	....	....	....	4.50	....	....
3271a	same, large date	....	....	....	12.00(5)	1.25	.30

3270, 3271

3272

3273

1999 COMMEMORATIVES

SCOTT NO.	DESCRIPTION	FIRST DAY COVERS SING	PL. BLK.	MINT SHEET	PLATE BLOCK	UNUSED F/NH	USED
3272/3369	**(3272-73, 3276, 3286-92, 3308-09, 3314-3350, 3352, 3354, 3356-59, 3368-69) 56 varieties . . . .**	....	....	....	....	**84.00**	**28.00**
3272	33¢ Year of the Rabbit .	2.25	4.75	22.00(20)	5.00	1.25	.25
3273	33¢ Malcolm X, Civil Rights, self-adhesive	2.25	4.75	24.00(20)	6.00	1.50	.25

3274

3275

SCOTT NO.	DESCRIPTION	FIRST DAY COVERS SING	PL. BLK.	MINT SHEET	PLATE BLOCK	UNUSED F/NH	USED
3274	33¢ Love, self-adhesive	2.25	....	....	....	1.25	.25
3274a	same, bklt pane of 20	14.50	....	....	....	20.00	....
3275	55¢ Love, self-adhesive	2.50	....	30.00(20)	7.50	1.70	.50

3276

3277, 3278, 3279, 3280, 3281, 3282

3282

SCOTT NO.	DESCRIPTION	FIRST DAY COVERS SING	PL. BLK.	MINT SHEET	PLATE BLOCK	UNUSED F/NH	USED
3276	33¢ Hospice Care, self-adhesive	2.25	4.75	20.00(20)	5.00	1.00	.25
3277	33¢ Flag and City . . .	2.25	4.75	250.00(100)	48.00	2.50	.75
3278	33¢ Flag and City, self-adhesive, die cut 11.1	1.95	4.75	25.00(20)	6.00	1.10	.25
3278a	same, bklt pane of 4 .	4.00	....	....	....	5.25	....
3278b	same, bklt pane of 5 .	5.00	....	....	....	6.75	....
3278c	same, bklt pane of 6 .	5.50	....	....	....	8.00	....
3278d	same, bklt pane of 10	7.25	....	....	....	18.00	....
3278e	same, bklt pane of 20	14.50	....	....	....	21.00	....
3278F	33¢ Flag and City, self-adhesive, die cut 11½ x 11¾	2.25	....	....	....	1.95	.50
3278Fg	same, bklt pane of 20	14.50	....	....	....	36.00	....
3278i	Flag and City, die cut 11¼	2.25	....	....	....	5.00	2.50
3278j	same, bklt pane of 10	7.25	....	....	....	45.00	....
3279	33¢ Flag and City, self-adhesive, die cut 9.8	2.25	....	....	....	1.25	.30
3279a	same, bklt pane of 10	7.25	....	....	....	13.00	....
3280	33¢ Flag and City, coil d/c 9.9	2.25	....	....	6.00	1.15	.25
....	same, plate strip of 5 .	....	....	....	....	7.75	....
3280a	33¢ Flag and City coil, large date.	....	....	....	....	2.50	1.15
....	same, plate strip of 5 .	....	....	....	....	14.00	....
3281	33¢ Flag and City, self-adhesive coil (square corners) large date	2.25	....	....	7.00	1.25	.25
....	same, plate strip of 5 .	....	....	....	....	8.50	....
3281c	same, small date, type II	2.25	....	....	10.00(3)	2.00	.25
....	same, plate strip of 5 .	....	....	....	....	12.00	....
3281d	same, small date, type I	....	....	....	....	7.00	....
....	plate and strip of 5 . . .	....	....	....	....	50.00	....

SCOTT NO.	DESCRIPTION	FIRST DAY COVERS SING	FIRST DAY COVERS PL. BLK.	MINT SHEET	PLATE BLOCK	UNUSED F/NH	USED
3282	33¢ Flag and City, self-adhesive coil (round corners)	2.25	....	....	6.00(3)	1.50	.60
....	same, plate strip of 5 .	....	....	....	....	10.00	....
3283	33¢ Flag and Chalkboard, self-adhesive	2.25	....	....	....	1.25	.50
3283a	same, bklt pane of 18	13.50	....	....	....	20.00	....

3286

3287

SCOTT NO.	DESCRIPTION	FIRST DAY COVERS SING	FIRST DAY COVERS PL. BLK.	MINT SHEET	PLATE BLOCK	UNUSED F/NH	USED
3286	33¢ Irish Immigration .	2.25	4.75	22.00(20)	5.50	1.20	.25
3287	33¢ Alfred Lunt & Lynn Fontanne, Actors	2.25	4.75	20.00(20)	4.75	1.20	.25

3288

3289

3290

3291

3292

SCOTT NO.	DESCRIPTION	FIRST DAY COVERS SING	FIRST DAY COVERS PL. BLK.	MINT SHEET	PLATE BLOCK	UNUSED F/NH	USED
3288-92	Arctic Animals, 5 varieties, attached .	12.00	....	20.00(15)	15.00(10)	7.50	5.00
3288	33¢ Arctic Hare	2.25	....	....	....	1.50	.75
3289	33¢ Arctic Fox	2.25	....	....	....	1.50	.75
3290	33¢ Snowy Owl	2.25	....	....	....	1.50	.75
3291	33¢ Polar Bear.	2.25	....	....	....	1.50	.75
3292	33¢ Gray Wolf	2.25	....	....	....	1.50	.75

3293
SONORAN DESERT

3293a *Cactus wren, brittlebush, teddy bear cholla*
3293b *Desert tortoise*
3293c *White-winged dove, prickly pear*
3293d *Gambel quail*
3293e *Saguaro cactus*
3293f *Desert mule deer*
3293g *Desert cottontail, hedgehog cactus*
3293h *Gila monster*
3293i *Western diamondback rattlesnake, cactus mouse*
3293j *Gila woodpecker*

SCOTT NO.	DESCRIPTION	FIRST DAY COVERS SING	FIRST DAY COVERS PL. BLK.	MINT SHEET	PLATE BLOCK	UNUSED F/NH	USED
3293	33¢ Sonoran Desert, 10 varieties, attached, self-adhesive	....	....	16.00(10)	....	16.00	....
....	set of singles	18.50	....	....	....	....	9.00
3293v	same, uncut sheet of 60 (6 panes)	....	....	80.00(60)	....	80.00	....

3294, 3298, 3302 — 3295, 3299, 3303 — 3296, 3300, 3304 — 3297, 3301, 3305

SCOTT NO.	DESCRIPTION	FIRST DAY COVERS SING	FIRST DAY COVERS PL. BLK.	MINT SHEET	PLATE BLOCK	UNUSED F/NH	USED
3294	33¢ Blueberries, self-adhesive, die cut 11.2 x 11.7	2.25	....	....	....	1.30	.30
3294a	same, dated "2000" . .	2.25	....	....	....	1.75	.30
3295	33¢ Raspberries, self-adhesive, die cut 11.2 x 11.7	2.25	....	....	....	1.50	.30
3295a	same, dated "2000" . .	2.25	....	....	....	1.75	.30
3296	33¢ Strawberries, self-adhesive, die cut 11.2 x 11.7	2.25	....	....	....	1.50	.30
3296a	same, dated "2000" . .	2.25	....	....	....	1.75	.30
3297	33¢ Blackberries, self-adhesive, die cut 11.2 x 11.7	2.25	....	....	....	1.50	.30
3297b	same, bklt pane of 20 (3294-97 x 5 of each)	14.50	....	....	....	27.00	....
3297a	same, dated "2000" . .	2.25	....	....	....	1.75	.30
3297d	same, bklt pane of 20	14.50	....	....	....	34.00	....
3297e	same, block of 4, (#3294a-96a, 3297c) .	4.00	....	....	....	8.50	....
3298	33¢ Blueberries, self-adhesive, die cut 9½ x 10	2.25	....	....	....	1.75	.55
3299	33¢ Strawberries, self-adhesive, die cut 9½ x 10	2.25	....	....	....	1.75	.55
3300	33¢ Raspberries, self-adhesive, die cut 9½ x 10	2.25	....	....	....	1.75	.55
3301	33¢ Blackberries, self-adhesive, die cut 9½ x 10	2.25	....	....	....	1.75	.55
3301a	same, bklt pane of 4 (3298-3301 x 1)	4.00	....	....	....	8.00	....
3301b	same, bklt pane of 5, (3298, 3299, 3301, 3300 x 2)	5.00	....	....	....	10.00	....
3301c	same, bklt pane of 6, (3300, 3301, 3298 x 2, 3299)	6.00	....	....	....	12.00	....
3302-05	33¢ Berries, self-adhesive coil, strip of 4, attached	4.00	....	....	....	10.00	....
3302	33¢ Blueberries, self-adhesive coil	2.25	....	....	....	2.00	.50
3303	33¢ Raspberries, self-adhesive coil	2.25	....	....	....	2.00	.50
3304	33¢ Blackberries, self-adhesive coil	2.25	....	....	....	2.00	.50
3305	33¢ Strawberries, self-adhesive coil	2.25	....	....	....	2.00	.50
3302-05	33¢ Berries, self-adhesive coil, pl# strip of 5 (3302 x 2, 3303-05 x 1)	10.00	....	....	....	16.00(5)	....

3306, 3307

3308

SCOTT NO.	DESCRIPTION	FIRST DAY COVERS SING	FIRST DAY COVERS PL. BLK.	MINT SHEET	PLATE BLOCK	UNUSED F/NH	USED
3306	33¢ Daffy Duck, self-adhesive, pane of 10	12.00	....	....	....	12.50	....
3306a	same, single from pane	2.25	....	....	....	1.25	.45
3306b	same, pane of 9 (3306a)	....	....	....	....	9.50	....
3306c	same, pane of 1 (3306a)	7.00	....	....	....	2.50	....
3306v	same, top press sheet of 60 (6 panes)	....	....	80.00(60)	....	80.00	....
....	same, bottom press sheet of 60 w/ plate # (6 panes)	....	....	110.00(60)	....	110.00	....
....	same, pane of 10 from press sheet	....	....	....	....	15.00	....
....	same, pane of 10 from press sheet with plate #	....	....	....	....	85.00	....
....	vert. pair with horiz. gutter	....	....	....	....	5.00	....
....	horiz. pair with vert. gutter	....	....	....	....	10.00	....
3307	33¢ Daffy Duck, self-adhesive, die cut, pane of 10	15.00	....	....	....	23.00	....
3307a	same, single from pane	....	....	....	....	2.00	....
3307b	same, pane of 9 (3307a)	....	....	....	....	16.00	....
3307c	same, pane of 1, imperf.	12.00	....	....	....	6.00	....
3308	33¢ Ayn Rand	2.25	4.75	20.00(20)	5.00	1.10	.35

3309

SCOTT NO.	DESCRIPTION	FIRST DAY COVERS SING	FIRST DAY COVERS PL. BLK.	MINT SHEET	PLATE BLOCK	UNUSED F/NH	USED
3309	33¢ Cinco de Mayo, self-adhesive	2.25	4.75	20.00(20)	5.00	1.10	.30

3310

3311

3312

3313

SCOTT NO.	DESCRIPTION	FIRST DAY COVERS SING	FIRST DAY COVERS PL. BLK.	MINT SHEET	PLATE BLOCK	UNUSED F/NH	USED
3310-13	33¢ Tropical Flowers, self-adhesive, 4 varieties, attached.	8.00	....	....	....	5.00	5.00
3310	33¢ Bird of Paradise, self-adhesive	2.25	....	....	....	1.25	.35
3311	33¢ Royal Poinciana, self-adhesive	2.25	....	....	....	1.25	.35
3312	33¢ Gloriosa Lily, self-adhesive	2.25	....	....	....	1.25	.35
3313	33¢ Chinese Hibiscus, self-adhesive	2.25	....	....	....	1.25	.35
3313a	same, bklt pane of 20 (3310-13 x 5)	....	....	....	....	22.00	....

3314

3315

3316

SCOTT NO.	DESCRIPTION	FIRST DAY COVERS SING	FIRST DAY COVERS PL. BLK.	MINT SHEET	PLATE BLOCK	UNUSED F/NH	USED
3314	33¢ John & William Bartram, Botanists	2.25	4.75	20.00(20)	5.00	1.10	.30
3315	33¢ Prostate Cancer Awareness.	2.25	4.75	20.00(20)	5.00	1.10	.30
3316	33¢ California Gold Rush	2.25	4.75	20.00(20)	5.00	1.10	.30

3317

3318

3319

3320

SCOTT NO.	DESCRIPTION	FIRST DAY COVERS SING	FIRST DAY COVERS PL. BLK.	MINT SHEET	PLATE BLOCK	UNUSED F/NH	USED
3317-20	Aquarium Fish, self-adhesive, 4 varieties, attached.	8.00	....	25.00(20)	11.00(8)	6.50	6.00
3317	33¢ Yellow fish, red fish, cleaner shrimp	2.25	....	....	....	1.40	.35
3318	33¢ Fish, thermometer	2.25	....	....	....	1.40	.35
3319	33¢ Red fish, blue fish	2.25	....	....	....	1.40	.35
3320	33¢ Fish, heater.	2.25	....	....	....	1.40	.35

3321

3322

3323

3324

SCOTT NO.	DESCRIPTION	FIRST DAY COVERS SING	FIRST DAY COVERS PL. BLK.	MINT SHEET	PLATE BLOCK	UNUSED F/NH	USED
3321-24	X-treme Sports, self-adhesive, 4 varieties, attached.	8.00	....	22.00(20)	5.00	4.50	4.00
3321	33¢ Skateboarding . .	2.25	....	....	....	1.25	.45
3322	33¢ BMX biking	2.25	....	....	....	1.25	.45
3323	33¢ Snowboarding. . .	2.25	....	....	....	1.25	.45
3324	33¢ In-line skating . . .	2.25	....	....	....	1.25	.45

3325

3326

3327

3328

SCOTT NO.	DESCRIPTION	FIRST DAY COVERS SING	FIRST DAY COVERS PL. BLK.	MINT SHEET	PLATE BLOCK	UNUSED F/NH	USED
3325-28	American Glass, 4 varieties, attached .	10.00	....	30.00(15)	....	10.00	5.00
3325	33¢ Free-blown glass	3.00	....	....	....	2.25	.45
3326	33¢ Mold-blown glass	3.00	....	....	....	2.25	.45
3327	33¢ Pressed glass. . .	3.00	....	....	....	2.25	.45
3328	33¢ Art glass	3.00	....	....	....	2.25	.45

3329

SCOTT NO.	DESCRIPTION	FIRST DAY COVERS SING	FIRST DAY COVERS PL. BLK.	MINT SHEET	PLATE BLOCK	UNUSED F/NH	USED
3329	33¢ James Cagney . .	1.95	4.75	28.00(20)	7.00	1.50	.35

3330

3331

3332

SCOTT NO.	DESCRIPTION	FIRST DAY COVERS SING	FIRST DAY COVERS PL. BLK.	MINT SHEET	PLATE BLOCK	UNUSED F/NH	USED
3330	55¢ General William "Billy" Mitchell, self-adhesive	2.50	....	32.00(20)	7.75	1.75	.75
3331	33¢ Honoring Those Who Served, self-adhesive	2.25	....	25.00(20)	5.50	1.50	.30
3332	45¢ Universal Postal Union	2.25	5.00	27.00(20)	6.50	1.60	1.00

3333 3334 3335 3336 3337

SCOTT NO.	DESCRIPTION	FIRST DAY COVERS SING	FIRST DAY COVERS PL. BLK.	MINT SHEET	PLATE BLOCK	UNUSED F/NH	USED
3333-37	33¢ Famous Trains, 5 varieties, attached .	10.00	15.00	25.00(20)	14.00(8)	7.00	7.00
3333	33¢ Daylight.	3.00	....	....	....	1.40	.45
3334	33¢ Congressional. . .	3.00	....	....	....	1.40	.45
3335	33¢ 20th Century Limited	3.00	....	....	....	1.40	.45
3336	33¢ Hiawatha.	3.00	....	....	....	1.40	.45
3337	33¢ Super Chief.	3.00	....	....	....	1.40	.45
3333-37v	same, uncut sheet of 120 (6 panes)	....	....	175.00(120)	....	175.00	....
....	block of 8 with horiz. gutter	....	....	....	....	22.50	....
....	block of 10 with vert. gutter	....	....	....	....	23.50	....
....	cross gutter block of 8	....	....	....	....	25.00	....
....	horiz. pair with vert. gutter		....	....	....	4.00	....
....	vert. pair with horiz. gutter		....	....	....	4.00	....

3338

SCOTT NO.	DESCRIPTION	FIRST DAY COVERS SING	FIRST DAY COVERS PL. BLK.	MINT SHEET	PLATE BLOCK	UNUSED F/NH	USED
3338	33¢ Frederick Law Olmsted, Landscape Architect .	1.95	4.75	19.50(20)	5.00	1.10	.30

3339 3340 3341 3342 3343 3344

SCOTT NO.	DESCRIPTION	FIRST DAY COVERS SING	FIRST DAY COVERS PL. BLK.	MINT SHEET	PLATE BLOCK	UNUSED F/NH	USED
3339-44	33¢ Hollywood Composers, 6 varieties, attached .	12.00	17.00	30.00(20)	14.00(6)	12.00	8.00
....	same, plate block of 8	....	....	....	18.00	....	....
3339	33¢ Max Steiner	3.00	....	....	....	1.75	.95
3340	33¢ Dimitri Tiomkin . .	3.00	....	....	....	1.75	.95
3341	33¢ Bernard Herrmann	3.00	....	....	....	1.75	.95
3342	33¢ Franz Waxman . .	3.00	....	....	....	1.75	.95
3343	33¢ Alfred Newman . .	3.00	....	....	....	1.75	.95
3344	33¢ Erich Wolfgang Korngold	3.00	....	....	....	1.75	.95

3345 3346 3347 3348 3349 3350

SCOTT NO.	DESCRIPTION	FIRST DAY COVERS SING	FIRST DAY COVERS PL. BLK.	MINT SHEET	PLATE BLOCK	UNUSED F/NH	USED
3345-50	33¢ Broadway Songwriters, 6 varieties, attached .	12.00	17.00	30.00(20)	14.00(6)	12.00	7.75
....	same, plate block of 8	....	....	18.00	....	....	
3345	33¢ Ira & George Gershwin	3.00	....	....	....	1.75	1.00
3346	33¢ Lerner & Loewe .	3.00	....	....	....	1.75	1.00
3347	33¢ Lorenz Hart.	3.00	....	....	....	1.75	1.00
3348	33¢ Rodgers & Hammerstein	3.00	....	....	....	1.75	1.00
3349	33¢ Meredith Willson .	3.00	....	....	....	1.75	1.00
3350	33¢ Frank Loesser. . .	3.00	....	....	....	1.75	1.00

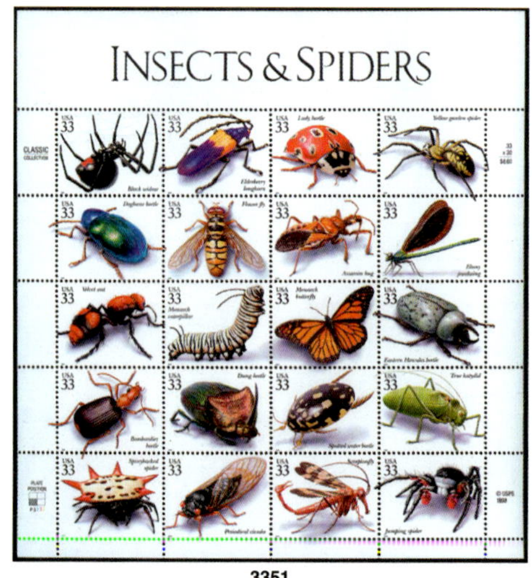

3351

INSECTS & SPIDERS

3351a	*Black Widow*	**3351k**	*Monarch butterfly*
3351b	*Elderberry longhorn*	**3351l**	*Eastern Hercules beetle*
3351c	*Lady beetle*	**3351m**	*Bombardier beetle*
3351d	*Yellow garden spider*	**3351n**	*Dung beetle*
3351e	*Dogbane beetle*	**3351o**	*Spotted water beetle*
3351f	*Flower fly*	**3351p**	*True katydid*
3351g	*Assassin bug*	**3351q**	*Spinybacked spider*
3351h	*Ebony jewelwing*	**3351r**	*Periodical cicada*
3351i	*Velvet ant*	**3351s**	*Scorpionfly*
3351j	*Monarch caterpillar*	**3351t**	*Jumping spider*

SCOTT NO.	DESCRIPTION	FIRST DAY COVERS SING	FIRST DAY COVERS PL. BLK.	MINT SHEET	PLATE BLOCK	UNUSED F/NH	USED
	INSECTS & SPIDERS (continued)						
3351	33¢ Insects & Spiders, 20 varieties, attached .	....	....	25.00(20)	....	25.00	18.00
....	set of singles	37.50	....	....	....	....	14.00
....	same, uncut sheet of 80 (4 panes)	....	....	100.00(80)	....	100.00	....
....	same, block of 10 with vert. gutter	....	....	....	....	25.00	....
....	same, block of 8 with horiz. gutter	....	....	....	....	25.00	....
....	same, cross gutter block of 20.	....	....	....	....	35.00	....
....	same, vert. pair with horiz. gutter	....	....	....	....	3.00	....
....	same, horiz. pair with vert. gutter	....	....	....	....	3.00	....

3352

SCOTT NO.	DESCRIPTION	FIRST DAY COVERS SING	FIRST DAY COVERS PL. BLK.	MINT SHEET	PLATE BLOCK	UNUSED F/NH	USED
3352	33¢ Hanukkah, self-adhesive	2.25	4.75	20.00(20)	5.00	1.10	.30

3353

SCOTT NO.	DESCRIPTION	FIRST DAY COVERS SING	FIRST DAY COVERS PL. BLK.	MINT SHEET	PLATE BLOCK	UNUSED F/NH	USED
3353	22¢ Uncle Sam, coil. .	1.95	....	....	5.00	.75	.50
....	same, plate strip of 5 .	....	....	....	....	6.00	....

3354 3355

SCOTT NO.	DESCRIPTION	FIRST DAY COVERS SING	FIRST DAY COVERS PL. BLK.	MINT SHEET	PLATE BLOCK	UNUSED F/NH	USED
3354	33¢ NATO, 50th Anniv.	2.25	4.75	20.00(20)	5.00	1.10	.35
3355	33¢ Madonna & Child, self-adhesive	2.25	....	....	....	1.20	.25
3355a	same, bklt pane of 20	14.50	....	....	....	22.00	....

3356, 3360, 3364 3357, 3361, 3365 3358, 3362, 3366 3359, 3363, 3367

SCOTT NO.	DESCRIPTION	FIRST DAY COVERS SING	FIRST DAY COVERS PL. BLK.	MINT SHEET	PLATE BLOCK	UNUSED F/NH	USED
3356-59	33¢ Christmas Deer, self-adhesive	4.00	....	49.00(20)	12.50	11.00	....
3356	33¢ Christmas Deer, gold & red, self-adhesive	2.25	....	....	....	2.75	.85
3357	33¢ Christmas Deer, gold & blue, self-adhesive	2.25	....	....	....	2.75	.85
3358	33¢ Christmas Deer, gold & purple, self-adhesive	2.25	....	....	....	2.75	.85
3359	33¢ Christmas Deer, gold & green, self-adhesive	2.25	....	....	....	2.75	.85
3360	33¢ Christmas Deer, gold & red, bklt single, self-adhesive	2.25	....	....	....	1.75	.45
3361	33¢ Christmas Deer, gold & blue, bklt single, self-adhesive	2.25	....	....	....	1.75	.45
3362	33¢ Christmas Deer, gold & purple, bklt single, self-adhesive	2.25	....	....	....	1.75	.45
3363	33¢ Christmas Deer, gold & green, bklt single, self-adhesive	2.25	....	....	....	1.75	.45
3363a	same, bklt pane of 20	14.50	....	....	....	38.00	....
3364	33¢ Christmas Deer, gold & red, bklt single, (21x19mm), self-adhesive	2.25	....	....	....	2.25	.65
3365	33¢ Christmas Deer, gold & blue, bklt single, (21x19mm), self-adhesive	2.25	....	....	....	2.25	.65
3366	33¢ Christmas Deer, gold & purple, bklt single (21x19mm), self-adhesive	2.25	....	....	....	2.25	.65
3367	33¢ Christmas Deer, gold & green, bklt single, (21x19mm), self-adhesive	2.25	....	....	....	2.25	.65
3367a	same, bklt pane of 4 (3364-67 x 1)	4.00	....	....	....	10.00	....
3367b	same, bklt pane of 5 (3364, 3366, 3367, 3365 x 2)	5.00	....	....	....	12.00	....
3367c	same, bklt pane of 6 (3365, 3367, 3364 x 2, 3366)	6.00	....	....	....	15.00	....

3368 3369

SCOTT NO.	DESCRIPTION	FIRST DAY COVERS SING	FIRST DAY COVERS PL. BLK.	MINT SHEET	PLATE BLOCK	UNUSED F/NH	USED
3368	33¢ Kwanzaa, self-adhesive	2.25	....	20.00(20)	5.00	1.10	.35
3369	33¢ Baby New Year, self-adhesive	2.25	....	20.00(20)	5.00	1.10	.35

3370 3371 3372

2000 COMMEMORATIVES

SCOTT NO.	DESCRIPTION	FIRST DAY COVERS SING	FIRST DAY COVERS PL. BLK.	MINT SHEET	PLATE BLOCK	UNUSED F/NH	USED
3370/3446	**(3370-72, 3379-90, 3393-3402 3414-17, 3438-46) 38 varieties. . . . . . .**	**........**	**........**	**........**	**........**	**46.00**	**20.00**
3370	33¢ Year of the Dragon	2.25	4.75	23.00(20)	5.50	1.20	.35
3371	33¢ Patricia Roberts Harris, self-adhesive	2.25	....	24.00(20)	6.00	1.50	.35
3372	33¢ Los Angeles Class Submarine (microprint USPS)	2.25	4.75	23.00(20)	5.50	1.20	.35

3373 3374

3375 3376

3377

SCOTT NO.	DESCRIPTION	FIRST DAY COVERS SING	FIRST DAY COVERS PL. BLK.	MINT SHEET	PLATE BLOCK	UNUSED F/NH	USED
3373	22¢ S Class Submarine	2.25	....	....	....	1.50	2.00
3374	33¢ Los Angeles Class Submarine (no microprint)	2.25	....	....	....	2.00	2.50
3375	55¢ Ohio Class Submarine	2.50	....	....	....	2.50	3.75
3376	60¢ USS Holland Submarine	2.50	....	....	....	3.00	3.50
3377	$3.20 Gato Class Submarine	7.50	....	....	....	12.00	9.00
3377a	same, bklt pane of 5, (#3373-77).	12.00	....	....	....	18.00	....
....	same, complete booklet of 2 panes	....	....	....	....	32.00	....

3378

PACIFIC COAST RAIN FOREST

3378a *Harlequin duck*
3378b *Dwarf Oregon grape, snail-eating ground beetle*
3378c *American dipper*
3378d *Cutthroat trout*
3378e *Roosevelt elk*
3378f *Winter wren*
3378g *Pacific giant salamander, Rough-skinned newt*
3378h *Western tiger swallowtail*
3378i *Douglas squirrel, foliose lichen*
3378j *Foliose lichen, banana slug*

SCOTT NO.	DESCRIPTION	FIRST DAY COVERS SING	FIRST DAY COVERS PL. BLK.	MINT SHEET	PLATE BLOCK	UNUSED F/NH	USED
3378	33¢ Pacific Coast Rain Forest, 10 varieties, attached, self-adhesive	....	....	14.00(10)	....	14.00	....
....	set of singles	25.00	....	....	....	....	6.00
3378v	same, uncut sheet of 60 (6 panes)	....	....	60.00(60)	....	60.00	....

3379

3380

3381

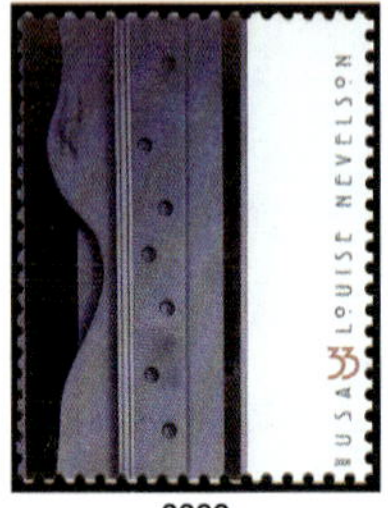

3382

3383

SCOTT NO.	DESCRIPTION	FIRST DAY COVERS SING	FIRST DAY COVERS PL. BLK.	MINT SHEET	PLATE BLOCK	UNUSED F/NH	USED
3379-83	33¢ Louise Nevelson, (1899-1988), Sculptor, 5 varieties, attached .	10.00	15.00	20.00(20)	12.00(10)	6.00	4.50
3379	33¢ Silent Music I . . .	2.25	....	....	....	1.40	.90
3380	33¢ Royal Tide I.	2.25	....	....	....	1.40	.90
3381	33¢ Black Chord	2.25	....	....	....	1.40	.90
3382	33¢ Nightsphere-Light	2.25	....	....	....	1.40	.90
3383	33¢ Dawn's Wedding Chapel I.	2.25	....	....	....	1.40	.75

3384

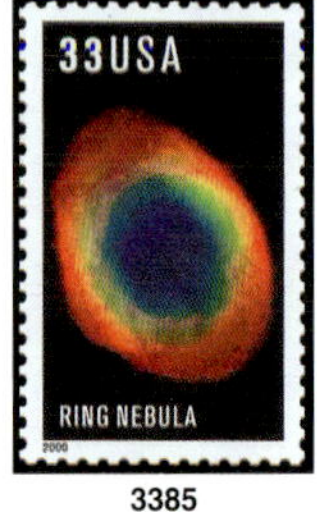

3385

3386

3387

3388

SCOTT NO.	DESCRIPTION	FIRST DAY COVERS SING	FIRST DAY COVERS PL. BLK.	MINT SHEET	PLATE BLOCK	UNUSED F/NH	USED
3384-88	33¢ Hubble Space Telescope Images, 5 varieties, attached.	10.00	15.00	23.00(20)	12.00(10)	6.00	4.55
3384	33¢ Eagle Nebula . . .	3.00	....	....	....	1.40	.55
3385	33¢ Ring Nebula	3.00	....	....	....	1.40	.55
3386	33¢ Lagoon Nebula . .	3.00	....	....	....	1.40	.55
3387	33¢ Egg Nebula.	3.00	....	....	....	1.40	.55
3388	33¢ Galaxy NGC 1316	3.00	....	....	....	1.40	.55

3389

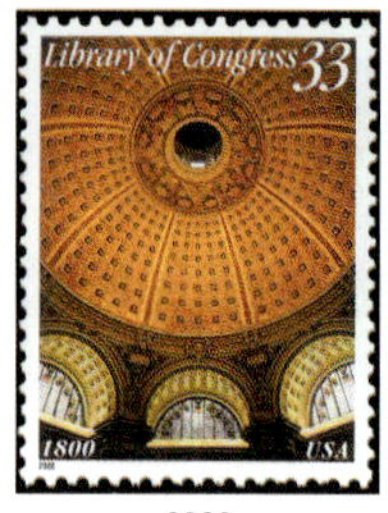

3390

SCOTT NO.	DESCRIPTION	FIRST DAY COVERS SING	FIRST DAY COVERS PL. BLK.	MINT SHEET	PLATE BLOCK	UNUSED F/NH	USED
3389	33¢ American Samoa	2.25	4.75	30.00(20)	8.00	1.85	1.00
3390	33¢ Library of Congress	2.25	4.75	20.00(20)	5.00	1.10	.35

3391, 3392

SCOTT NO.	DESCRIPTION	FIRST DAY COVERS SING	FIRST DAY COVERS PL. BLK.	MINT SHEET	PLATE BLOCK	UNUSED F/NH	USED
3391	33¢ Road Runner & Wile E. Coyote, self-adhesive, pane of 10	12.00	....	....	....	14.00	....
3391a	same, single from pane	2.25	....	....	....	1.50	.35
3391b	same, pane of 9 (3391a)	....	....	....	....	11.00	....
3391c	same, pane of 1 (3391a)	7.00	....	....	....	3.50	....
....	same, top press sheet of 60 (6 panes) w/ plate #	....	....	80.00(60)	....	80.00	....
....	same, bottom press sheet of 60 (6 panes) w/ plate #	....	....	95.00(60)	....	95.00	....
....	same, pane of 10 from press sheet	....	....	....	....	15.00	....
....	same, pane of 10 with plate # on front . .	....	....	....	....	65.00	....
....	vert. pair with horiz. gutter	....	....	....	....	4.00	....
....	horiz. pair with vert. gutter	....	....	....	....	8.00	....
3392	33¢ Road Runner & Wile E. Coyote, self-adhesive, die cut, pane of 10. . .	15.00	....	....	....	50.00	....
3392a	same, single from pane	....	....	....	....	4.00	....
3392b	same, pane of 9 (3392a)	....	....	....	....	42.00	....
3392c	same, pane of 1, imperf.	12.00	....	....	....	11.00	....

3393 3394

3395 3396

SCOTT NO.	DESCRIPTION	FIRST DAY COVERS SING	PL. BLK.	MINT SHEET	PLATE BLOCK	UNUSED F/NH	USED
3393-96	33¢ Distinguished Soldiers, 4 varieties, attached .	8.00	12.00	29.00(20)	7.00	5.75	5.00
3393	33¢ Major General John L. Hines (1868-1968). . .	2.25	....	....	....	1.50	.45
3394	33¢ General Omar N. Bradley (1893-1981) .	2.25	....	....	....	1.50	.45
3395	33¢ Sergeant Alvin C. York (1887-1964). . . .	2.25	....	....	....	1.50	.45
3396	33¢ Second Lieutenant Audie L. Murphy (1924-71)	2.25	....	....	....	1.50	.45

3397

3398

SCOTT NO.	DESCRIPTION	FIRST DAY COVERS SING	PL. BLK.	MINT SHEET	PLATE BLOCK	UNUSED F/NH	USED
3397	33¢ Summer Sports. .	2.25	4.75	20.00(20)	4.75	1.10	.30
3398	33¢ Adoption, self-adhesive	2.25	....	20.00(20)	4.75	1.10	.30

3399 3400

3401 3402

SCOTT NO.	DESCRIPTION	FIRST DAY COVERS SING	PL. BLK.	MINT SHEET	PLATE BLOCK	UNUSED F/NH	USED
3399-3402	33¢ Youth Team Sports, 4 varieties, attached .	8.00	12.00	20.00(20)	5.00	4.75	4.00
3399	33¢ Basketball.	3.00	....	....	....	1.40	.85
3400	33¢ Football.	3.00	....	....	....	1.40	.85
3401	33¢ Soccer	3.00	....	....	....	1.40	.85
3402	33¢ Baseball	3.00	....	....	....	1.40	.85

3403

THE STARS AND STRIPES

3403a	*Sons of Liberty Flag, 1775*	3403k	*Star-Spangled Banner, 1814*
3403b	*New England, 1775*	3403l	*Bennington Flag, c.1820*
3403c	*Forster Flag, 1775*	3403m	*Great Star Flag, 1837*
3403d	*Continental Colors, 1776*	3403n	*29-Star Flag, 1847*
3403e	*Francis Hopkinson Flag, 1777*	3403o	*Fort Sumter Flag, 1861*
3403f	*Brandywine Flag, 1777*	3403p	*Centennial Flag, 1876*
3403g	*John Paul Jones Flag, 1779*	3403q	*38-Star Flag*
3403h	*Pierre L'Enfant Flag, 1783*	3403r	*Peace Flag, 1891*
3403i	*Indian Peace Flag, 1803*	3403s	*48-Star Flag, 1912*
3403j	*Easton Flag, 1814*	3403t	*50-Star Flag, 1960*

SCOTT NO.	DESCRIPTION	FIRST DAY COVERS SING	PL. BLK.	MINT SHEET	PLATE BLOCK	UNUSED F/NH	USED
3403	33¢ The Stars & Stripes, 20 varieties, attached, self-adhesive	....	....	25.00(20)	....	25.00	....
....	set of singles	37.50	....	....	....	....	15.00
3403v	same, uncut sheet of 120 (6 panes)	....	....	150.00(120)	....	150.00	....
....	same, block of 8 with horiz. gutter	....	....	....	....	18.00	....
....	same, block of 10 with vert. gutter	....	....	....	....	20.00	....
....	same, cross gutter block of 20	....	....	....	....	40.00	....
....	vert. pair with horiz. gutter	....	....	....	....	4.50	....
....	horiz. pair with vert. gutter	....	....	....	....	4.50	....

3404

3405

3406

3407

SCOTT NO.	DESCRIPTION	FIRST DAY COVERS SING	PL. BLK.	MINT SHEET	PLATE BLOCK	UNUSED F/NH	USED
3404	33¢ Blueberries, self-adhesive linerless coil	2.25	....	....	....	3.50	1.50
3405	33¢ Strawberries, self-adhesive linerless coil	2.25	....	....	....	3.50	1.50
3406	33¢ Blackberries, self-adhesive linerless coil	2.25	....	....	....	3.50	1.50
3407	33¢ Raspberries, self-adhesive linerless coil	2.25	....	....	....	3.50	1.50
3404-07	33¢ Berries, self-adhesive linerless coil, strip of 4	5.00	....	....	....	15.00	....
....	same, pl# strip of 5 . .	....	....	....	....	22.00	....

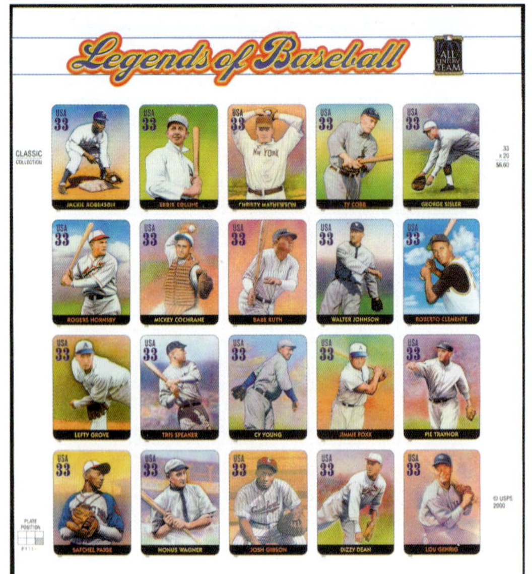

3408

LEGENDS OF BASEBALL

3408a	*Jackie Robinson*	**3408k**	*Lefty Grove*
3408b	*Eddie Collins*	**3408l**	*Tris Speaker*
3408c	*Christy Mathewson*	**3408m**	*Cy Young*
3408d	*Ty Cobb*	**3408n**	*Jimmie Foxx*
3408e	*George Sisler*	**3408o**	*Pie Traynor*
3408f	*Rogers Hornsby*	**3408p**	*Satchel Paige*
3408g	*Mickey Cochrane*	**3408q**	*Honus Wagner*
3408h	*Babe Ruth*	**3408r**	*Josh Gibson*
3408i	*Walter Johnson*	**3408s**	*Dizzy Dean*
3408j	*Roberto Clemente*	**3408t**	*Lou Gehrig*

SCOTT NO.	DESCRIPTION	FIRST DAY COVERS SING	FIRST DAY COVERS PL. BLK.	MINT SHEET	PLATE BLOCK	UNUSED F/NH	USED
3408	33¢ Legends of Baseball, 20 varieties, attached, self-adhesive	....	....	25.00(20)	....	25.00	....
....	set of singles	37.50	....	....	....	....	15.00
3408v	same, uncut sheet of 120 (6 panes)	....	....	135.00(120)	....	135.00	....
....	cross gutter block of 20	....	....	....	....	40.00	....
....	block of 8 with vert. gutter	....	....	....	....	22.50	....
....	block of 10 with horiz. gutter	....	....	....	....	22.50	....
....	vert. pair with horiz. gutter	....	....	....	....	3.50	....
....	horiz. pair with vert. gutter	....	....	....	....	4.50	....

3409

SCOTT NO.	DESCRIPTION	FIRST DAY COVERS SING	FIRST DAY COVERS PL. BLK.	MINT SHEET	PLATE BLOCK	UNUSED F/NH	USED
3409	60¢ Probing the Vastness of Space, souvenir sheet of six	15.00	....	....	....	23.00	....
3409a	60¢ Hubble Space Telescope	3.00	....	....	....	4.00	3.00
3409b	60¢ National Radio Astronomy Observatory	3.00	....	....	....	4.00	3.00
3409c	60¢ Keck Observatory	3.00	....	....	....	4.00	3.00
3409d	60¢ Cerro Tololo Inter-American Observatory	3.00	....	....	....	4.00	3.00
3409e	60¢ Mt. Wilson Observatory	3.00	....	....	....	4.00	3.00
3409f	60¢ Arecibo Observatory	3.00	....	....	....	4.00	....

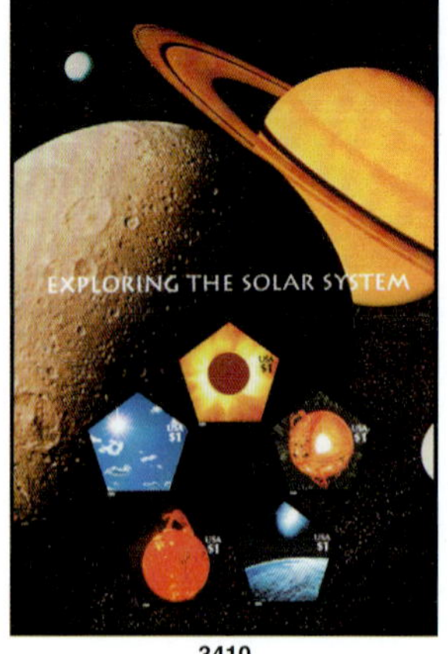

3410

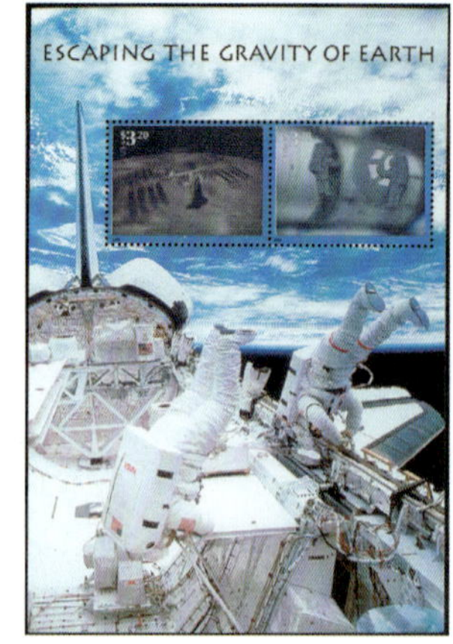

3411

SCOTT NO.	DESCRIPTION	FIRST DAY COVERS SING	FIRST DAY COVERS PL. BLK.	MINT SHEET	PLATE BLOCK	UNUSED F/NH	USED
3410	$1 Exploring the Solar System, souvenir sheet of five.	13.50	....	....	....	28.00	....
3410a	$1 Solar eclipse.	3.50	....	....	....	5.50	3.00
3410b	$1 Cross-section of sun	3.50	....	....	....	5.50	3.00
3410c	$1 Sun and Earth. . . .	3.50	....	....	....	5.50	3.00
3410d	$1 Sun & solar flare. .	3.50	....	....	....	5.50	3.00
3410e	$1 Sun with clouds . .	3.50	....	....	....	5.50	3.00
3411	$3.20 Escaping the Gravity of Earth hologram, souvenir sheet of two.	16.50	....	....	....	35.00	....
3411a	$3.20 International Space Station hologram, from souvenir sheet. .	7.50	....	....	....	18.00	13.00
3411b	$3.20 Astronauts Working hologram, from souvenir sheet	7.50	....	....	....	18.00	13.00

3412

SCOTT NO.	DESCRIPTION	FIRST DAY COVERS SING	FIRST DAY COVERS PL. BLK.	MINT SHEET	PLATE BLOCK	UNUSED F/NH	USED
3412	$11.75 Space Achievement and Exploration hologram, souvenir sheet of one	27.50	....	....	....	47.50	....

3413

SCOTT NO.	DESCRIPTION	FIRST DAY COVERS SING	FIRST DAY COVERS PL. BLK.	MINT SHEET	PLATE BLOCK	UNUSED F/NH	USED
3413	$11.75 Landing on the Moon hologram, souvenir sheet of one.	27.50	....	....	....	47.50	....

3414 3415

3416 3417

SCOTT NO.	DESCRIPTION	FIRST DAY COVERS SING	FIRST DAY COVERS PL. BLK.	MINT SHEET	PLATE BLOCK	UNUSED F/NH	USED
3414-17	33¢ Stampin' the Future, 4 varieties, attached .	8.00	10.00	20.00(20)	10.00(8)	5.50	4.00
3414	33¢ Designed by Zachary Canter	2.25	....	....	....	1.40	.50
3415	33¢ Designed by Sarah Lipsey	2.25	....	....	....	1.40	.50
3416	33¢ Designed by Morgan Hill	2.25	....	....	....	1.40	.50
3417	33¢ Designed by Ashley Young	2.25	....	....	....	1.40	.50

3420 3422, 3436 3426 3427

3427A 3428 3430 3431, 3432

3432A 3432B 3433, 3434 3435

2000-2009 DISTINGUISHED AMERICANS

SCOTT NO.	DESCRIPTION	FIRST DAY COVERS SING	FIRST DAY COVERS PL. BLK.	MINT SHEET	PLATE BLOCK	UNUSED F/NH	USED
3420	10¢ Joseph W. Stilwell	2.25	4.00	7.00(20)	1.75	.40	.25
3422	23¢ Wilma Rudolph, self-adhesive, die cut 11¼ x 10¾ . . .	2.25	4.75	15.00(20)	3.50	.85	.40
3426	33¢ Claude Pepper . .	2.25	4.75	20.00(20)	5.00	1.10	.55
3427	58¢ Margaret Chase Smith, self-adhesive (2007) .	2.25	5.50	32.00(20)	8.50	1.75	.65
3427a	59¢ James A. Michener	2.25	5.50	32.00(20)	8.50	1.75	.70
3428	63¢ Dr. Jonas Salk (2006)	2.25	6.00	34.00(20)	9.25	1.85	.70
3430	75¢ Harriet Beecher Stowe, self-adhesive (2007) .	2.95	6.00	38.00(20)	10.50	2.25	.95
3431	76¢ Hattie W. Caraway, die cut 11	2.95	5.50	54.00(20)	16.00	3.00	.60
3432	76¢ Hattie W. Caraway, die cut 11½ x 11.	....	....	135.00(20)	36.00	8.00	4.00
3432a	76¢ Edward Trudeau .	2.95	5.75	37.00(20)	9.50	2.50	.95
3432b	78¢ Mary Lasker (2009)	3.75	....	34.00(20)	9.50	2.25	.75
3433	83¢ Edna Ferber, die cut 11 x 11½.	2.95	5.50	52.00(20)	14.00	3.00	.95
3434	83¢ Edna Ferber, die cut 11¼ (2003). . .	2.95	5.50	48.00(20)	13.00	2.75	.90
3435	87¢ Dr. Albert Sabin (2006)	2.95	5.50	46.00(20)	12.00	2.75	.95
3436	23¢ Wilma Rudolph, self-adhesive, die cut 11¼ x 10¾ . . .	2.25	....	....	....	.85	.50
3436a	same, bklt pane of 4 .	3.00	....	....	....	3.25	....
3436b	same, bklt pane of 6 .	4.00	....	....	....	4.75	....
3436c	same, bklt pane of 10	6.75	....	....	....	7.50	....

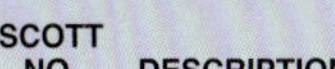

3438

SCOTT NO.	DESCRIPTION	FIRST DAY COVERS SING	FIRST DAY COVERS PL. BLK.	MINT SHEET	PLATE BLOCK	UNUSED F/NH	USED
3438	33¢ California Statehood, self-adhesive	2.25	....	22.00(20)	6.00	1.50	.40

3439 3440

3441

3442 [illegible]

SCOTT NO.	DESCRIPTION	FIRST DAY COVERS SING	FIRST DAY COVERS PL. BLK.	MINT SHEET	PLATE BLOCK	UNUSED F/NH	USED
3439-43	33¢ Deep Sea Creatures, [illegible]	[illegible]	11.00	20.00(15)	....	7.00	4.75
3439	33¢ Fanfin Anglerfish.	2.25	....	....	....	1.40	.85
3440	33¢ Sea Cucumber . .	2.25	....	....	....	1.40	.85
3441	33¢ Fangtooth	2.25	....	....	....	1.40	.85
3442	33¢ Amphipod	2.25	....	....	....	1.40	.85
3443	33¢ Medusa.	2.25	....	....	....	1.40	.85

3444 3445 3446

SCOTT NO.	DESCRIPTION	FIRST DAY COVERS SING	FIRST DAY COVERS PL. BLK.	MINT SHEET	PLATE BLOCK	UNUSED F/NH	USED
3444	33¢ Thomas Wolfe . .	2.25	4.75	20.00(20)	4.75	1.10	.30
3445	33¢ White House. . . .	2.25	4.75	35.00(20)	9.00	2.00	.35
3446	33¢ Edward G. Robinson	2.25	4.75	49.00(20)	12.00	3.00	2.00
....	same, uncut sheet of 120 (6 panes)	....	....	175.00(120)	....	240.00	....
....	cross gutter block of 8	....	....	....	....	35.00	....
....	block of 8 with vert. gutter	....	....	....	....	24.00	....
....	horiz. pair with vert. gutter	....	....	....	....	6.00	....
....	vert. pair with horiz. gutter	....	....	....	....	4.50	....

3447 | 3448, 3449, 3450, | 3451, 3452, 3453

SCOTT NO.	DESCRIPTION	FIRST DAY COVERS SING	FIRST DAY COVERS PL. BLK.	MINT SHEET	PLATE BLOCK	UNUSED F/NH	USED
3447	10¢ New York Public Library Lion, coil	2.25	....	....	4.00	.50	.25
....	same, pl# strip of 5	....	....	....	....	5.00	....
3447a	10¢ New York Public Library, self-adhesive, coil, die cut 11.5	2.25	....	....	....	.75	.60
....	same, pl# strip of 5	....	....	....	....	5.00	....
3448	(34¢) Flag over Farm	2.25	4.75	45.00(20)	12.00	1.50	.75
3449	(34¢) Flag over Farm self-adhesive	2.25	4.75	30.00(20)	6.00	1.30	.30
3450	(34¢) Flag over Farm, self-adhesive	2.25	....	....	....	1.60	.75
3450a	same, bklt pane of 18	14.00	....	....	....	29.00	....
3451	(34¢) Statue of Liberty, self-adhesive	2.25	....	....	....	1.20	.35
3451a	same, bklt pane of 20	14.50	....	....	....	24.00	....
3451b	same, bklt pane of 4	4.00	....	....	....	7.00	....
3451c	same, bklt pane of 6	5.50	....	....	....	10.50	....
3452	(34¢) Statue of Liberty, coil	2.25	....	....	7.00	1.25	.25
....	same, pl# strip of 5	....	....	....	....	9.00	....
3453	(34¢) Statue of Liberty, self-adhesive coil	1.95	....	....	10.00	1.25	.25
....	same, pl# strip of 5	....	....	....	....	12.00	....
3453b	same, large date	....	....	....	15.00(3)	1.80	.30

3454, 3458, 3465 | 3455, 3459, 3464 | 3456, 3460, 3463 | 3457, 3461, 3462

SCOTT NO.	DESCRIPTION	FIRST DAY COVERS SING	FIRST DAY COVERS PL. BLK.	MINT SHEET	PLATE BLOCK	UNUSED F/NH	USED
3454-57	(34¢) Flowers, self-adhesive, 4 varieties attached	4.25	....	....	....	7.50	....
3454	(34¢) Freesia, self-adhesive, die cut 10¼ x 10¾	2.25	....	....	....	2.50	.40
3455	(34¢) Cymbidium Orchid, self-adhesive, die cut 10¼ x 10¾	2.25	....	....	....	2.50	.40
3456	(34¢) Longiflorum Lily, self-adhesive, die cut 10¼ x 10¾	2.25	....	....	....	2.50	.40
3457	(34¢) Asian Hybrid Lily, self-adhesive, die cut 10¼ x 10¾	2.25	....	....	....	2.50	.40
3457b	same, bklt pane of 4 (3454-57)	4.00	....	....	....	8.50	....
3457c	same, bklt pane of 6 (3456, 3457, 3454 x 2 3455 x 2)	5.50	....	....	....	14.00	....
3457d	same, bklt pane of 6 (3454, 3455, 3456 x 2 3457 x 2)	5.50	....	....	....	14.00	....
3457e	(34¢) Flowers, bklt pane of 20, self-adhesive (5 each 3457a + label)	14.50	....	....	....	36.00	....
3458-61	(34¢) Flowers, self-adhesive, 4 varieties attached	4.25	....	....	....	18.00	....
3458	(34¢) Freesia, bklt single, self-adhesive, die cut 11½ x 11¾	2.25	....	....	....	5.50	1.00
3459	(34¢) Cymbidium Orchid, bklt single, self-adhesive, die cut 11½ x 11¾	2.25	....	....	....	5.50	1.00
3460	(34¢) Longiflorum Lily, bklt single, self-adhesive, die cut 11½ x 11¾	2.25	....	....	....	5.50	1.00
3461	(34¢) Asian Hybrid Lily, bklt single, self-adhesive, die cut 11½ x 11¾	2.25	....	....	....	5.50	1.00
3461b	same, bklt pane of 20, self-adhesive (2 each 3461a, 3 each 3457a)	14.50	....	....	....	70.00	....
3461c	same, bklt pane of 20, self-adhesive (2 each 3457a, 3 each 3461a)	14.50	....	....	....	90.00	....
3462	(34¢) Longiflorum Lily, self-adhesive coil	2.25	....	....	....	5.00	.60
3463	(34¢) Asian Hybrid Lily, self-adhesive coil	2.25	....	....	....	5.00	60
3464	(34¢) Cymbidium Orchid, self-adhesive coil	2.25	....	....	....	5.00	.60
3465	(34¢) Freesia, self-adhesive coil	2.25	....	....	....	5.00	.60
3462-65	(34¢) Flowers, self-adhesive coil, strip of 4	4.25	....	....	....	20.00	....
....	same, pl# strip of 5	....	....	....	....	28.00	....

3466, 3476, 3477, 3485 | 3467, 3468, 3475, 3484, 3484A | 3468A, 3475A | 3469, 3470

3471 | 3471A

2001 REGULAR ISSUES

SCOTT NO.	DESCRIPTION	FIRST DAY COVERS SING	FIRST DAY COVERS PL. BLK.	MINT SHEET	PLATE BLOCK	UNUSED F/NH	USED
3466	34¢ Statue of Liberty, self-adhesive coil, die cut 9¾ (round corners)	2.25	....	....	8.50	1.30	.50
....	same, pl# strip of 5	....	....	....	11.00	....	....
3467	21¢ Buffalo	2.25	4.75	100.00(100)	30.00	1.50	.75
3468	21¢ Buffalo. self-adhesive	2.25	4.75	16.00(20)	4.50	.90	.75
3468A	23¢ George Washington, self-adhesive	2.25	4.75	15.00(20)	4.00	.90	.75
3469	34¢ Flag over Farm	2.25	4.75	170.00(100)	38.00	1.50	.90
3470	34¢ Flag over Farm, self-adhesive	2.25	4.75	28.00(20)	8.00	2.00	.50
3471	55¢ Eagle, self-adhesive	2.50	5.00	45.00(20)	11.00	2.25	.80
3471A	57¢ Eagle, self-adhesive	2.50	5.00	41.00(20)	11.00	2.50	80

3472 | 3473

SCOTT NO.	DESCRIPTION	FIRST DAY COVERS SING	FIRST DAY COVERS PL. BLK.	MINT SHEET	PLATE BLOCK	UNUSED F/NH	USED
3472	$3.50 Capitol Dome, self-adhesive	8.00	30.00	210.00(20)	48.00	12.00	5.00
3473	$12.25 Washington Monument, self-adhesive	30.00	98.50	700.00(20)	155.00	40.00	12.00
3475	21¢ Buffalo, self-adhesive coil	2.25	....	....	5.00	.75	.35
....	same, pl# strip of 5	....	....	....	....	6.00	....
3475A	23¢ George Washington, self-adhesive coil	2.25	....	....	....	1.20	.30
....	same, pl# strip of 5	....	....	....	....	9.00	....
3476	34¢ Statue of Liberty, coil	2.25	....	....	7.00	1.50	.40
....	same, pl# strip of 5	....	....	....	....	9.00	....
3477	34¢ Statue of Liberty, self-adhesive coil die cut 9¾ (square corners)	2.25	....	....	7.75	1.50	.25
....	same, pl# strip of 5	....	....	....	....	10.00	....

3478, 3489 | 3479, 3490 | 3480, 3488 | 3481, 3487

SCOTT NO.	DESCRIPTION	FIRST DAY COVERS SING	FIRST DAY COVERS PL. BLK.	MINT SHEET	PLATE BLOCK	UNUSED F/NH	USED
3478	34¢ Longiflorum Lily, self-adhesive coil	2.25	....	....	....	2.50	.50
3479	34¢ Asian Hybrid Lily, self-adhesive coil	2.25	....	....	....	2.50	50
3480	34¢ Cymbidium Orchid, self-adhesive coil	2.25	....	....	....	2.50	.50
3481	34¢ Freesia, self-adhesive coil	2.25	....	....	....	2.50	.50
3478-81	34¢ Flowers, self-adhesive, coil, strip of 4	4.25	....	....	....	9.00	....
....	same, pl# strip of 5	....	....	....	....	14.00	....

3482, 3483 | 3491, 3493 | 3492, 3494 | 3495

SCOTT NO.	DESCRIPTION	FIRST DAY COVERS SING	FIRST DAY COVERS PL. BLK.	MINT SHEET	PLATE BLOCK	UNUSED F/NH	USED
3482	20¢ George Washington, self-adhesive, die cut 11¼	2.25	....	....	....	1.00	.50
3482a	same, bklt pane of 10	5.50	....	....	....	9.50	....
3482b	same, bklt pane of 4, die cut 11¼ x 11.	3.00	....	....	....	6.50	....
3482c	same, bklt pane of 6, die cut 11¼ x 11.	4.00	....	....	....	5.00	....
3483	20¢ George Washington, self-adhesive, die cut 10½ x 11¼.	2.25	....	....	....	7.00	1.80
3483a	same, bklt pane of 4 (2 each 3482-3483) . .	3.00	....	....	....	22.00	....
3483b	same, bklt pane of 6 (3 each 3482-3483) . .	4.00	....	....	....	33.00	....
3483c	same, bklt pane of 10, die cut 10½ x 11 (3482 x 5 at L, 3483 x 5 at R) . .	5.50	....	....	....	38.00	....
3483d	same, bklt pane of 4 (2 each 3482-3483), die cut 11¼ x 11.	....	....	....	....	20.00	....
3483e	same, bklt pane of 6 (2 each 3482-3483), die cut 11¼ x 11.	....	....	....	....	34.00	....
3483f	same, bklt pane of 10 (5 each 3482-3483), die cut 11¼ x 11.	....	....	....	....	38.00	....
3483g	pair, 3482 at left, 3483 at right.	....	....	....	....	8.50	
3483h	pair 3483 at left, 3482 at right.	....	....	....	....	8.50	....
3484	21¢ Buffalo, self-adhesive, die cut 11¼	2.25	....	....	....	1.00	.50
3484b	same, bklt pane of 4 .	3.00	....	....	....	4.00	....
3484c	same, bklt pane of 6 .	4.00	....	....	....	5.00	....
3484d	same, bklt pane of 10	5.50	....	....	....	9.50	....
3484A	21¢ Buffalo, self-adhesive, die cut 10½ X 11¼. . .	2.25	....	....	....	7.00	2.50
3484Ae	same, bklt pane of 4 (3484 x 2 at L, 3484A x 2 at R)		....	....	....	22.00	....
3484Af	same, bklt pane of 6 (3484 x 3 at L, 3484A x 3 at R)		....	....	....	34.00	....
3484Ag	same, bklt pane of 10 (3484 x 5 at L, 3484A x 5 at R)		....	....	....	38.00	....
3484Ah	same, bklt pane of 4 (3484A x 2 at L, 3484 x 2 at R)		....	....	....	23.00	....
3484Ai	same, bklt pane of 6 (3484A x 3 at L, 3484 x 3 at R)		....	....	....	34.00	....
3484Aj	same, bklt pane of 10 (3484A x 5 at L, 3484 x 5 at R)		....	....	....	38.00	....
3484Ak	same, pair (3484 at L, 3484A at R)		....	....	....	7.50	....
3484Al	same, pair (3484A at L, 3484 at R)........		....	....	....	8.00	....
3485	34¢ Statue of Liberty, self-adhesive	2.25	....			1.45	.25
3485a	same, bklt pane of 10	[illegible]		....	....	11.00	....
3485b	same, bklt pane of 20	14.50	....	....	....	28.00	....
[illegible]	[illegible]	[illegible]				[illegible]	
3485d	same, bklt pane of 6	5.50		....	....	[illegible]	
[illegible]	[illegible] 4 varieties attached	4.25	....	....	....	6.00	3.50
3487	34¢ Freesia, self-adhesive, die cut 10¼ x 10¾ . . .	2.25	....	....	....	1.75	.35
3488	34¢ Cymbidium Orchid, self-adhesive, die cut 10¼ x 10¾.	2.25	....	....	....	1.75	.35
3489	34¢ Longiflorum Lily, self-adhesive, die cut 10¼ x 10¾.	2.25	....	....	....	1.75	.35
3490	34¢ Asian Hybrid Lily, self-adhesive, die cut 10¼ x 10¾.	2.25	....	....	....	1.75	.35
3490b	same, bklt pane of 4 (3487-90 x 1)	4.00	....	....	....	6.50	....
3490c	same, bklt pane of 6 (3489-3490, 3487 x 2, 3488 x 2)	5.50	....	....	....	8.50	....
3490d	same, bklt pane of 6 (3487-3488, 3498 x 2 3490 x 2)	5.50	....	....	....	8.50	....
3490e	same, bklt pane of 20 (3487-90 x 5 + label) .	14.50	....	....	....	28.00	....
3491	34¢ Apple, self-adhesive	2.25	....	....	....	1.75	.25
3492	34¢ Orange, self-adhesive	2.25	....	....	....	1.75	.25
3491-92	34¢ Apple & Orange, Pair	2.50	....	....	....	3.50	....
3492b	34¢ Apple & Orange, bklt pane of 20, self-adhesive	14.50	....	....	....	26.00	....
3493	34¢ Apple, self-adhesive, die cut 11½ x 10¾ . . .	2.25	....	....	....	2.50	.65
3494	34¢ Orange, self-adhesive, die cut 11½ x 10¾ . . .	2.25	....	....	....	2.50	.65
3493-94	34¢ Apple & Orange, Pair	2.50	....	....	....	5.00	....
3494b	same, bklt pane of 4 (3493 x 2, 3494 x 2) . .	4.00	....	....	....	10.00	....

SCOTT NO.	DESCRIPTION	FIRST DAY COVERS SING	FIRST DAY COVERS PL. BLK.	MINT SHEET	PLATE BLOCK	UNUSED F/NH	USED
3494c	same, bklt pane of 6 (3493 x 3, 3494 x 3) (3493 at UL).	5.50	....	....	....	15.00	....
3494d	same, bklt pane of 6 (3493 x 3, 3494 x 3) (3494 at UL).	5.50	....	....	....	15.00	....
3495	34¢ Flag over Farm, self-adhesive	1.95	....	....	....	2.00	.50
3495a	same, ATM bklt pane of 18	14.00	....	....	....	37.00	....

3496 | 3497, 3498 | 3499

SCOTT NO.	DESCRIPTION	FIRST DAY COVERS SING	FIRST DAY COVERS PL. BLK.	MINT SHEET	PLATE BLOCK	UNUSED F/NH	USED
3496	(34¢) LOVE, self-adhesive, die cut 11¾	2.25	....	....	....	1.50	.30
3496a	same, bklt pane of 20	14.50	....	....	....	30.00	....
3497	34¢ LOVE, self-adhesive, die cut 11¼	2.25	....	....	....	1.50	.30
3497a	same, bklt pane of 20	14.50	....	....	....	30.00	....
3498	34¢ LOVE, self-adhesive, die cut 11½ x 10¾ . . .	2.25	....	....	....	2.50	.30
3498a	same, bklt pane of 4 .	4.00	....	....	....	9.00	....
3498b	same, bklt pane of 6 .	5.50	....	....	....	12.00	....
3499	55¢ LOVE, self-adhesive	2.50	5.00	35.00(20)	8.50	1.85	.65

3500

3501

2001 COMMEMORATIVES

SCOTT NO.	DESCRIPTION	FIRST DAY COVERS SING	FIRST DAY COVERS PL. BLK.	MINT SHEET	PLATE BLOCK	UNUSED F/NH	USED
3500/3548	**(3500-01, 3503-04, 3507-19, 3521, 3523-33, 3536-40, 3545-48) 38 varieties. . . . . . .**	....	....	....	....	**49.00**	**13.50**
3500	34¢ Year of the Snake	2.25	4.75	25.00(20)	6.00	1.50	.35
3501	34¢ Roy Wilkins, self-adhesive	2.25	4.75	27.00(20)	6.50	1.50	.30

3502

AMERICAN ILLUSTRATORS

3502a *Marine Corps poster*
3502b *"Interlude (The Lute Players)"*
3502c *Advertisement for Arrow Collars and Shirts*
3502d *Advertisement for Carrier Corp. Refrigeration*
3502e *Advertisement for Luxite Hosiery*
3502f *Illustration for correspondence school lesson*
3502g *"Br'er Rabbit"*
3502h *"An Attack on a Galleon"*
3502i *Kewpie and Kewpie Doodle Dog*
3502j *Illustration for cover of True Magazine*
3502k *"Galahad's Departure"*
3502l *"The First Lesson"*
3502m *Illustration for cover of McCall's*
3502n *"Back Home for Keeps"*
3502o *"Something for Supper"*
3502p *"A Dash for the Timber"*
3502q *Illustration for "Moby Dick"*
3502r *"Captain Bill Bones"*
3502s *Illustration for The Saturday Evening Post*
3502t *"The Girl He Left Behind"*

SCOTT NO.	DESCRIPTION	FIRST DAY COVERS SING	FIRST DAY COVERS PL. BLK.	MINT SHEET	PLATE BLOCK	UNUSED F/NH	USED
	AMERICAN ILLUSTRATORS (Continued)						
3502	34¢ American Illustrators, 20 varieties, attached, self-adhesive	....	....	25.00(20)	....	25.00	....
....	set of singles	37.50	....	....	....	....	15.00
3502v	same, uncut sheet of 80 (4 panes)	....	....	120.00(80)	....	120.00	....
....	cross gutter block of 20	....	....	....	....	60.00	....
....	block of 8 with horiz. gutter	....	....	....	....	40.00	....
....	block of 10 with vert. gutter	....	....	....	....	40.00	....
....	vert. pair with horiz. gutter	....	....	....	....	7.00	....
....	horiz. pair with vert. gutter	....	....	....	....	7.00	....

3503

3504

SCOTT NO.	DESCRIPTION	FIRST DAY COVERS SING	FIRST DAY COVERS PL. BLK.	MINT SHEET	PLATE BLOCK	UNUSED F/NH	USED
3503	34¢ Diabetes Awareness	2.25	4.75	22.00(20)	5.75	1.25	.30
3504	34¢ Nobel Prize Centenary	2.25	4.75	22.00(20)	5.75	1.25	.30

3505

SCOTT NO.	DESCRIPTION	FIRST DAY COVERS SING	FIRST DAY COVERS PL. BLK.	MINT SHEET	PLATE BLOCK	UNUSED F/NH	USED
3505	1¢-80¢ Pan-American Expo. Invert Souvenir Sheet of 7	10.00	....	....	....	12.00	8.00
....	same, uncut sheet of 28 (4 panes)	....	....	....	....	60.00	....

3506

GREAT PLAINS PRAIRIE

3506a *Pronghorns, Canada geese*
3506b *Burrowing owls, American buffalo*
3506c *American buffalo, Black-tailed prairie dogs, wild alfalfa*
3506d *Black-tailed prairie dogs, American buffalo*
3506e *Painted lady butterfly, American buffalo, prairie coneflowers, prairie wild roses*
3506f *Western Meadowlark, camel cricket, prairie coneflowers, prairie wild roses*
3506g *Badger, harvester ants*
3506h *Eastern short-horned lizard, plains pocket gopher*
3506i *Plains spadefoot, dung beetle, prairie wild roses*
3506j *Two-striped grasshopper, Ord's kangaroo rat*

SCOTT NO.	DESCRIPTION	FIRST DAY COVERS SING	FIRST DAY COVERS PL. BLK.	MINT SHEET	PLATE BLOCK	UNUSED F/NH	USED
3506	34¢ Great Plains Prairie, 10 varieties, attached, self-adhesive	....	....	15.00(10)	....	15.00	....
....	set of singles	19.50	....	....	....	....	7.00
3506v	same, uncut sheet of 60 (6 panes)	....	....	60.00(60)	....	60.00	....

3509

3507

3508

SCOTT NO.	DESCRIPTION	FIRST DAY COVERS SING	FIRST DAY COVERS PL. BLK.	MINT SHEET	PLATE BLOCK	UNUSED F/NH	USED
3507	34¢ Peanuts, self-adhesive	2.25	4.75	25.00(20)	6.50	1.50	.35
3508	34¢ US Veterans, self-adhesive	2.25	4.75	34.00(20)	7.00	1.85	.35
3509	34¢ Frida Kahlo	2.25	4.75	22.00(20)	5.50	1.25	.30

3510 3511

3512 3513 3514 3515 3516 3517 3518 3519

BASEBALL'S LEGENDARY PLAYING FIELDS

3510 *Ebbets Field*
3511 *Tiger Stadium*
3512 *Crosley Field*
3513 *Yankee Stadium*
3514 *Polo Grounds*
3515 *Forbes Field*
3516 *Fenway Park*
3517 *Comiskey Park*
3518 *Shibe Park*
3519 *Wrigley Field*

SCOTT NO.	DESCRIPTION	FIRST DAY COVERS SING	FIRST DAY COVERS PL. BLK.	MINT SHEET	PLATE BLOCK	UNUSED F/NH	USED
3510-19	34¢ Baseball's Legendary Playing Fields, 10 varieties, self-adhesive	7.25	....	25.00(20)	15.00(10)	14.00	12.00
....	set of singles	25.00	....	....	....	....	6.00
3510-19v	same, uncut sheet of 160 (8 panes)	....	....	160.00(160)	....	160.00	....
....	cross gutter block of 12	....	....	....	....	25.00	....
....	block of 10 with vert. gutter	....	....	....	....	15.00	....
....	block of 4 with horiz. gutter	....	....	....	....	7.50	....
....	vert. pair with horiz. gutter	....	....	....	....	3.50	....
....	horiz. pair with vert. gutter	....	....	....	....	3.50	....

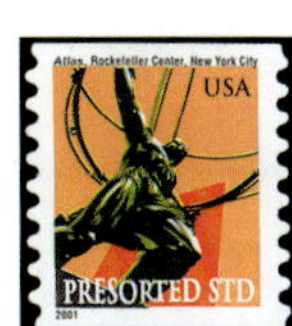

3520

3521

3522

SCOTT NO.	DESCRIPTION	FIRST DAY COVERS SING	FIRST DAY COVERS PL. BLK.	MINT SHEET	PLATE BLOCK	UNUSED F/NH	USED
3520	10¢ Atlas Statue, coil. self-adhesive, die cut 8½	2.25	....	....	4.00	.35	.25
....	same, pl# strip of 5 . .	....	....	....	....	4.50	....
3521	34¢ Leonard Bernstein	2.25	4.75	20.00(20)	5.00	1.10	.40
3522	15¢ Woody Wagon, self-adhesive coil	2.25	....	....	4.00	.50	.40
....	same, pl# strip of 5 . .	....	....	....	....	5.00	....

3523

SCOTT NO.	DESCRIPTION	FIRST DAY COVERS SING	FIRST DAY COVERS PL. BLK.	MINT SHEET	PLATE BLOCK	UNUSED F/NH	USED
3523	34¢ Lucille Ball, self-adhesive	2.25	4.75	28.00(20)	6.50	1.50	.35
3523v	same, uncut sheet of 180 (9 panes)	....	....	185.00(180)	....	185.00	....
....	cross gutter block of 8	....	....	....	....	30.00	....
....	block of 8 with vert. gutter	....	....	....	....	22.50	....
....	vert. pair with horiz. gutter	....	....	....	....	3.00	....
....	horiz. pair with vert. gutter	....	....	....	....	4.00	....

3524 3525

3526 3527

SCOTT NO.	DESCRIPTION	FIRST DAY COVERS SING	FIRST DAY COVERS PL. BLK.	MINT SHEET	PLATE BLOCK	UNUSED F/NH	USED
3524-27	34¢ Amish Quilts, 4 varieties attached . .	4.25	5.25	22.00(20)	5.50	5.00	4.00
3524	34¢ Diamond in the Square	2.25	....	....	....	1.30	.50
3525	34¢ Lone Star	2.25	....	....	....	1.30	.50
3526	34¢ Sunshine and Shadow	2.25	....	....	....	1.30	.50
3527	34¢ Double Ninepatch Variation	2.25	....	....	....	1.30	.50

3528

3529

3530

3531

SCOTT NO.	DESCRIPTION	FIRST DAY COVERS SING	FIRST DAY COVERS PL. BLK.	MINT SHEET	PLATE BLOCK	UNUSED F/NH	USED
3528-31	34¢ Carnivorous Plants, 4 varieties attached . .	4.25	5.25	23.00(20)	5.25	5.00	4.00
3528	34¢ Venus Flytrap . . .	2.25	....	....	....	1.30	.40
3529	34¢ Yellow Trumpet . .	2.25	....	....	....	1.30	.40
3530	34¢ Cobra	2.25	....	....	....	1.30	.40
3531	34¢ English Sundew .	2.25	....	....	....	1.30	.40

3532

3533

3534, 3535

SCOTT NO.	DESCRIPTION	FIRST DAY COVERS SING	FIRST DAY COVERS PL. BLK.	MINT SHEET	PLATE BLOCK	UNUSED F/NH	USED
3532	34¢ "Eid Mubarak", self-adhesive	2.25	4.75	21.00(20)	5.50	1.25	.30
3533	34¢ Enrico Fermi, self-adhesive	2.25	4.75	22.00(20)	5.50	1.25	.30
3534	34¢ That's All Folks, self-adhesive, pane of 10	12.50	....	....	....	18.00	....
3534a	same, single from pane	2.50	....	....	....	1.50	.30
3534b	same, pane of 9 (3534a)	....	....	....	....	12.00	....
3534c	same, pane of 1 (3534a)	7.25	....	....	....	3.25	....
....	same, top press sheet of 60 (6 panes) w/ pl# . .	....	....	80.00(60)	....	80.00	....
....	same, bottom press sheet of 60 (6 panes) w/ pl#	....	....	95.00(60)	....	95.00	....
....	same, pane of 10 from press sheet	....	....	....	....	15.00	....
....	same, pane of 10 w/ pl# on front.	....	....	....	....	70.00	....
....	vert. pair with horiz. gutter	....	....	....	....	4.00	....
....	horiz. pair with vert. gutter	....	....	....	....	7.50	....
3535	34¢ That's All Folks, die cut, self-adhesive, pane of 10	15.00	....	....	....	85.00	....
3535a	same, single form pane	....	....	....	....	8.00	....
3535b	same, pane of 9 (3435a)	....	....	....	....	65.00	....
3535c	same, pane of 1, imperf.	12.50	....	....	....	25.00	

3536

SCOTT NO.	DESCRIPTION	FIRST DAY COVERS SING	FIRST DAY COVERS PL. BLK.	MINT SHEET	PLATE BLOCK	UNUSED F/NH	USED
3536	34¢ Madonna and Child, self-adhesive	2.25	....	....	....	1.30	.25
3536a	same, bklt pane of 20	14.50	....	....	....	25.00	....

3537, 3537a, 3541

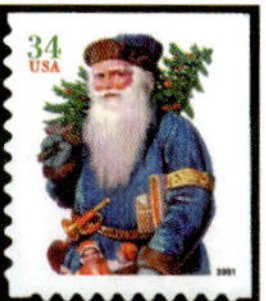

3538, 3538a, 3542

3539, 3539a, 3543

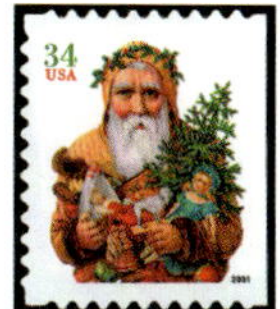

3540, 3540a, 3544

SCOTT NO.	DESCRIPTION	FIRST DAY COVERS SING	FIRST DAY COVERS PL. BLK.	MINT SHEET	PLATE BLOCK	UNUSED F/NH	USED
3537-40	34¢ Santas, self-adhesive, 4 varieties attach, large date	4.25	5.25	30.00(20)	6.50	5.75	....
3537	34¢ Santa w/ horse, large date	2.25	....	....	....	1.40	.50
3538	34¢ Santa w/ horn, large date	2.25	....	....	....	1.40	.50
3539	34¢ Santa w/ drum, large date	2.25	....	....	....	1.40	.50
3540	34¢ Santa w/ dog, large date	2.25	....	....	....	1.40	.50

SCOTT NO.	DESCRIPTION	FIRST DAY COVERS SING	FIRST DAY COVERS PL. BLK.	MINT SHEET	PLATE BLOCK	UNUSED F/NH	USED
3537a-40a	34¢ Santas, self-adhesive, 4 varieties attach, small date	4.25	5.25	....	....	5.75	4.50
3537a	34¢ Santa w/ horse, small date	2.25	....	....	....	1.30	.60
3538a	34¢ Santa w/ horn, small date	2.25	....	....	....	1.30	.60
3539a	34¢ Santa w/ drum, small date	2.25	....	....	....	1.30	.60
3540a	34¢ Santa w/ dog, small date	2.25	....	....	....	1.30	.60
3540d	same, bklt pane of 20, 3537a-40a x 5 + label	14.50	....	....	....	28.00	....
3537b-40e	34¢ Santas, self-adhesive, 4 varieties attach, large date	4.25	5.25	....	....	15.00	11.00
3537b	34¢ Santa w/ horse, large date	2.25	....	....	....	4.00	.75
3538b	34¢ Santa w/ horn, large date	2.25	....	....	....	4.00	.75
3539b	34¢ Santa w/ drum, large date	2.25	....	....	....	4.00	.75
3540e	34¢ Santa w/ dog, large date	2.25	....	....	....	4.00	.75
3540g	same, bklt pane of 20, 3537b-40e x 5 + label	14.50	....	....	....	65.00	....
3541-44	34¢ Santas, self-adhesive, 4 varieties attach, green denom.	4.25	....	....	....	7.50	....
3541	34¢ Santa w/ horse, green denom	2.25	....	....	....	1.85	.50
3542	34¢ Santa w/ horn, green denom	2.25	....	....	....	1.85	.50
3543	34¢ Santa w/ drum, green denom.	2.25	....	....	....	1.85	.50
3544	34¢ Santa w/ dog, green denom	2.25	....	....	....	1.85	.50
3544b	same, bklt pane of 4 (3541-3544).	4.00	....	....	....	8.00	....
3544c	same, bklt pane of 6 (3543-44, 3541-42 x 2)	5.50	....	....	....	12.00	....
3544d	same, bklt pane of 6 (3541-42, 3543-44 x 2)	5.50	....	....	....	12.00	....

3545

SCOTT NO.	DESCRIPTION	FIRST DAY COVERS SING	FIRST DAY COVERS PL. BLK.	MINT SHEET	PLATE BLOCK	UNUSED F/NH	USED
3545	34¢ James Madison .	2.25	4.75	25.00(20)	6.00	1.25	.30
3545v	same, uncut sheet of 120 (6 panes)	....	....	150.00(120)	....	150.00	....
....	cross gutter block of 4	....	....	....	....	11.00	....
....	horiz. pair with vert. gutter	....	....	....	....	4.50	....
....	vert. pair with horiz. gutter	....	....	....	....	3.50	....

3546

3547 3548

SCOTT NO.	DESCRIPTION	FIRST DAY COVERS SING	FIRST DAY COVERS PL. BLK.	MINT SHEET	PLATE BLOCK	UNUSED F/NH	USED
3546	34¢ We Give Thanks, self-adhesive	2.25	4.75	20.00(20)	5.00	1.10	.35
3547	34¢ Hanukkah, self-adhesive	2.25	4.75	22.00(20)	5.50	1.25	.30
3548	34¢ Kwanzaa, self-adhesive	2.25	4.75	22.00(20)	5.50	1.25	.30

3549, 3549B, 3550, 3550A

3551

SCOTT NO.	DESCRIPTION	FIRST DAY COVERS SING	FIRST DAY COVERS PL. BLK.	MINT SHEET	PLATE BLOCK	UNUSED F/NH	USED
3549	34¢ United We Stand, self-adhesive	2.25	....	....	....	1.75	.30
3549a	same, bklt pane of 20	14.50	....	....	....	36.00	....
3549B	34¢ United We Stand, die cut 10½ x 10¾ on 2 or 3 sides	2.25	....	....	....	1.90	.30
3549Bc	same, bklt pane of 4 .	4.00	....	....	....	7.50	....
3549Bd	same, bklt pane of 6 .	5.50	....	....	....	11.00	....
3549Be	same, bklt pane of 20 (double-sided)	....	....	....	....	38.00	....
3550	34¢ United We Stand, self-adhesive coil (square corners)	2.25	....	....	....	1.40	.30
....	same, pl# strip of 5 . .	....	....	....	....	12.00	....
3550A	34¢ United We Stand, self-adhesive coil, (round corners)	2.25	....	....	....	1.40	.40
....	same, pl# strip of 5 . .	....	....	....	....	12.00	....
3551	57¢ Love, self-adhesive	2.50	5.00	32.00(20)	8.00	1.75	.50

3554 3555

3552 3553

2002 COMMEMORATIVES

SCOTT NO.	DESCRIPTION	FIRST DAY COVERS SING	FIRST DAY COVERS PL. BLK.	MINT SHEET	PLATE BLOCK	UNUSED F/NH	USED
3552/3695	**(3552-60, 3650-56, 3659-74, 3676-79, 3692, 3695) 38 varieties**	....	....	....	....	**55.00**	**12.50**
3552-55	34¢ Winter Olympics, self-adhesive, 4 varieties attached.	4.25	5.25	28.00(20)	7.00	6.00	4.00
3552	34¢ Ski Jumping	2.25	....	....	....	1.60	.40
3553	34¢ Snowboarding. . .	2.25	....	....	....	1.60	.40
3554	34¢ Ice Hockey	2.25	....	....	....	1.60	.40
3555	34¢ Figure Skating . .	2.25	....	....	....	1.60	.40
3552-55v	same, uncut sheet of 180 (9 panes)	....	....	185.00(180)	....	185.00	....
....	cross gutter block of 8	....	....	....	....	25.00	....
....	block of 4 with vert. gutter	....	....	....	....	8.00	....
....	block of 8 with horiz. gutter	....	....	....	....	11.50	....
....	vert. pair with horiz. gutter	....	....	....	....	3.00	....
....	horiz. pair with vert. gutter	....	....	....	....	2.00	....

3556

3557

SCOTT NO.	DESCRIPTION	FIRST DAY COVERS SING	FIRST DAY COVERS PL. BLK.	MINT SHEET	PLATE BLOCK	UNUSED F/NH	USED
3556	34¢ Mentoring a Child, self-adhesive	2.25	4.75	22.00(20)	5.50	1.20	.30
3557	34¢ Langston Hughes, self-adhesive	2.25	4.75	25.00(20)	6.50	1.50	.30

3558

SCOTT NO.	DESCRIPTION	FIRST DAY COVERS SING	FIRST DAY COVERS PL. BLK.	MINT SHEET	PLATE BLOCK	UNUSED F/NH	USED
3558	34¢ Happy Birthday, self-adhesive	2.25	4.75	20.00(20)	5.00	1.20	.30

3559

3560

SCOTT NO.	DESCRIPTION	FIRST DAY COVERS SING	FIRST DAY COVERS PL. BLK.	MINT SHEET	PLATE BLOCK	UNUSED F/NH	USED
3559	34¢ Year of the Horse, self-adhesive	2.25	4.75	27.00(20)	7.00	1.50	.30
3560	34¢ Military Academy Bicentennial, self-adhesive	2.25	4.75	20.00(20)	5.00	1.00	.30

3561

3610

GREETINGS FROM AMERICA

3561	*Alabama*	**3578**	*Louisiana*	**3595**	*Ohio*
3562	*Alaska*	**3579**	*Maine*	**3596**	*Oklahoma*
3563	*Arizona*	**3580**	*Maryland*	**3597**	*Oregon*
3564	*Arkansas*	**3581**	*Massachusetts*	**3598**	*Pennsylvania*
3565	*California*	**3582**	*Michigan*	**3599**	*Rhode Island*
3566	*Colorado*	**3583**	*Minnesota*	**3600**	*South Carolina*
3567	*Connecticut*	**3584**	*Mississippi*	**3601**	*South Dakota*
3568	*Delaware*	**3585**	*Missouri*	**3602**	*Tennessee*
3569	*Florida*	**3586**	*Montana*	**3603**	*Texas*
3570	*Georgia*	**3587**	*Nebraska*	**3604**	*Utah*
3571	*Hawaii*	**3588**	*Nevada*	**3605**	*Vermont*
3572	*Idaho*	**3589**	*New Hampshire*	**3606**	*Virginia*
3573	*Illinois*	**3590**	*New Jersey*	**3607**	*Washington*
3574	*Indiana*	**3591**	*New Mexico*	**3608**	*West Virginia*
3575	*Iowa*	**3592**	*New York*	**3609**	*Wisconsin*
3576	*Kansas*	**3593**	*North Carolina*	**3610**	*Wyoming*
3577	*Kentucky*	**3594**	*North Dakota*		

SCOTT NO.	DESCRIPTION	FIRST DAY COVERS SING	FIRST DAY COVERS PL. BLK.	MINT SHEET	PLATE BLOCK	UNUSED F/NH	USED
3561-3610	34¢ Greetings from America, self-adhesive, 50 varieties attached. .	....	....	50.00(50)	....	50.00	....
....	set of singles.	120.00	....	....	....	....	40.00
	singles each			....	....	....	1.00

3611

LONGLEAF PINE FOREST

3611a	*Bachman's sparrow*	**3611g**	*Gray fox, gopher tortoise*
3611b	*Northern bobwhite, yellow pitcher plants*	**3611h**	*Blind click beetle, sweetbay, pine woods treefrog*
3611c	*Fox squirrel, red-bellied [illegible]*	**3611i**	*[illegible] orchid, pipeworts, southern toad, yellow pitcher plants*
3611d	*Brown-headed nuthatch*	**3611j**	*Grass-pink orchid, yellow-sided skimmer, pipeworts*
3611e	*Broadhead skink, yellow pitcher plants, pipeworts*		
3611f	*Eastern towhee, yellow pitcher plants, meadow beauties, toothache grass*		

SCOTT NO.	DESCRIPTION	FIRST DAY COVERS SING	FIRST DAY COVERS PL. BLK.	MINT SHEET	PLATE BLOCK	UNUSED F/NH	USED
3611	34¢ Longleaf Pine Forest, 10 varieties, attached, self-adhesive	....	....	25.00(10)	....	25.00	....
....	set of singles	25.00	....	....	....	....	10.00
3611v	same, uncut sheet of 90 (9 panes)	....	....	100.00(90)	....	100.00	....

3612

3613, 3614, 3615

3616, 3617, 3618, 3619

3620, 3621, 3622, 3623, 3624, 3625

SCOTT NO.	DESCRIPTION	FIRST DAY COVERS SING	FIRST DAY COVERS PL. BLK.	MINT SHEET	PLATE BLOCK	UNUSED F/NH	USED
3612	5¢ Toleware coffee pot, coil	2.25	....	....	....	.25	.25
....	same, pl# strip of 5 . .	....	....	....	....	2.50	....
3613	3¢ Lithographed Star (year at LL)	2.25	4.75	6.00(50)	1.20	.25	.25
3614	3¢ Photogravure Star (year at LR)	2.25	4.75	6.00(50)	1.20	.25	.25
3615	3¢ Star, coil	2.25	....	....	....	.25	.25
....	same, pl# strip of 5 . .	....	....	....	....	2.00	....
3616	23¢ George Washington	2.25	4.75	150.00(100)	38.00	1.10	.45

SCOTT NO.	DESCRIPTION	FIRST DAY COVERS SING	FIRST DAY COVERS PL. BLK.	MINT SHEET	PLATE BLOCK	UNUSED F/NH	USED
3617	23¢ George Washington, self-adhesive coil. . . .	2.25	....	....	....	.75	.40
....	same pl# strip of 5. . .	....	....	....	....	5.50	....
3618	23¢ George Washington, self-adhesive die cut 11¼	2.25	....	....	....	.95	.45
3618a	same, bklt pane of 4 .	3.00	....	....	....	4.00	....
3618b	same, bklt pane of 6 .	4.00	....	....	....	6.00	....
3618c	same, bklt pane of 10	6.75	....	....	....	8.00	....
3619	23¢ George Washington, self-adhesive, die cut 10½ x 11¼	1.95	....	....	....	6.00	2.75
3619a	same, bklt pane of 4 (3619 x 2 at L, 3618 x 2 at R)........		....	....	....	13.00	....
3619b	same, bklt pane of 6 (3619 x 3 at L, 3618 x 3 at R)........		....	....	....	21.00	....
3619c	same, bklt pane of 4 (3618 x 2 at L, 3619 x 2 at R)........		....	....	....	14.00	....
3619d	same, bklt pane of 6 (3618 x 3 at L, 3619 x 3 at R)		....	....	....	21.00	....
3619e	same, bklt pane of 10 (3619 x 5 at L, 3618 x 5 at R)........		....	....	....	30.00	....
3619f	same, bklt pane of 10 (3618 x 5 at L, 3619 at R)	....	....	....	....	30.00	....
3619g	same, pair (3619 at L, 3618 at R)	....	....	....	....	6.50	....
3619h	same, pair (3618 at L, 3619 at R)	....	....	....	....	6.50	....
3620	(37¢) Flag	2.25	4.75	155.00(100)	23.00	1.40	1.00
3621	(37¢) Flag, self-adhesive	2.25	4.75	30.00(20)	8.00	1.55	.35
3622	(37¢) Flag, self-adhesive coil	2.25	....	....	....	1.50	.25
....	same, pl# strip of 5 . .	....	....	....	....	11.00	....
3623	(37¢) Flag, self-adhesive, die cut 11¼	2.25	....	....	....	1.25	.25
3623a	same, bklt pane of 20	....	....	....	....	24.00	....
3624	(37¢) Flag, self-adhesive, die cut 10½ x 10¾ . . .	2.25	....	....	....	1.75	.65
3624a	same, bklt pane of 4 .	4.00	....	....	....	5.75	....
3624b	same, bklt pane of 6 .	5.50	....	....		8.50	....
[illegible]	same, bklt pane of 20	15.00	....	....	....	33.00	
3625	(37¢) Flag, self-adhesive, die cut 8.	2.25	....	....	....	1.60	.45
3625a	same, ATM bklt pane of 18	15.00	....	....	....	32.00	....

3626, 3639, 3642

3627, 3638, 3643

3628, 3641, 3644

3629, 3640, 3645

SCOTT NO.	DESCRIPTION	FIRST DAY COVERS SING	FIRST DAY COVERS PL. BLK.	MINT SHEET	PLATE BLOCK	UNUSED F/NH	USED
3626	(37¢) Toy mail wagon, self-adhesive	2.25	....	....	....	1.40	.40
3627	(37¢) Toy locomotive, self-adhesive	2.25	....	....	....	1.40	.40
3628	(37¢) Toy taxicab, self-adhesive	2.25	....	....	....	1.40	.40
3629	(37¢) Toy fire pumper, self-adhesive	2.25	....	....	....	1.40	.40
3626-29	(37¢) Antique Toys, self-adhesive, 4 varieties attached . .	4.25	....	....	....	6.00	4.50
3629b	same, bklt pane of 4 (3626-29 x 1)	4.25	....	....	....	6.00	....
3629c	same, bklt pane of 6 [illegible]	5.50	....	....	....	[illegible]	....
3629d	same, bklt pane of 6 . (3626, 3628, 3627 x 2, 3629 x 2)	5.50	....	....	....	9.50	....
3629e	same, bklt pane of 20	15.00	....	....	....	25.00	....
3629F	37¢ Flag.	2.25	4.75	135.00(100)	26.00	1.50	1.00

3629F, 3630, 3631, 3632, 3632A, 3632C, 3633, 3633A, 3633B, 3635, 3636, 3636D, 3637

SCOTT NO.	DESCRIPTION	FIRST DAY COVERS SING	FIRST DAY COVERS PL. BLK.	MINT SHEET	PLATE BLOCK	UNUSED F/NH	USED
3630	37¢ Flag, self-adhesive	2.25	4.75	24.00(20)	8.00	1.20	.30
3631	37¢ Flag, coil	2.25	....	....	....	1.50	.30
....	same, pl# strip of 5 . .	....	....	....	....	12.00	....
3632	37¢ Flag, self-adhesive coil, die cut 10 vert.	2.25	....	....	....	1.25	.30
....	same, pl# strip of 5 . .	....	....	....	....	10.00	....
3632A	37¢ Flag coil, die cut 10, flag lacking star point.	2.25	....	....	....	1.25	.55
....	same, pl# strip of 5 . .	....	....	....	....	10.00	....
3632C	37¢ Flag, self-adhesive coil, die cut 11¾ (2004). . .	2.25	....	....	....	1.25	.80
....	same, pl# strip of 5 . .	....	....	....	....	10.00	....
3633	37¢ Flag, self-adhesive coil, die cut 8½ vert.	2.25	....	....	....	1.25	.60
....	same, pl# strip of 5 . .	....	....	....	....	10.00	....

SCOTT NO.	DESCRIPTION	FIRST DAY COVERS SING	FIRST DAY COVERS PL. BLK.	MINT SHEET	PLATE BLOCK	UNUSED F/NH	USED
3633A	37¢ Flag coil, die cut 8½, right angel corners . . .	1.95	....	....	....	3.00	1.00
....	same, pl# strip of 5 . .	....	....	....	....	20.00	....
3633B	37¢ Flag coil, die cut 9½ (dated 2005)	2.25	....	....	....	10.00	.75
....	same, plt. strip of 5 . .	....	....	....	....	53.00	....
3634	37¢ Flag, self-adhesive, die cut 11	2.25	....	....	....	1.50	1.20
3634a	same, bklt pane of 10	....	....	....	....	16.00	....
3634b	same, self-adhesive, bklt single, dated 2003 . . .	2.25	....	....	....	1.60	1.20
3634c	same, bklt pane of 4 (3634b)	4.25	....	....	....	6.00	....
3634d	same, bklt pane of 6 (3634b)	5.50	....	....	....	9.00	....
3634e	same, die cut 11.3 . . .	....	....	....	....	1.35	.35
3634f	same, bklt pane of 10 of 3634e.	....	....	....	....	9.00	....
3635	37¢ Flag, self-adhesive, die cut 11¼	2.25	....	....	....	1.25	.50
3635a	same, bklt pane of 20	....	....	....	....	25.00	....
3636	37¢ Flag, self-adhesive, die cut 10½ x 10¾ . . .	2.25	....	....	....	3.00	.60
3636a	same, bklt pane of 4 .	....	....	....	....	4.00	....
3636b	same, bklt pan of 6 . .	....	....	....	....	5.00	....
3636c	same, bklt pane of 20	....	....	....	....	28.00	....
3636D	37¢ Flag, die cut 11¼ x 11, self-adhesive	2.25	....	....	....	1.85	.85
3636De	same, bklt pane of 20	....	....	....	....	37.00	....
3637	37¢ Flag, self-adhesive, die cut 8	2.25	....	....	....	1.50	.85
3637a	same, ATM bklt pane of 18	15.00	....	....	....	28.00	....
3638	37¢ Toy locomotive, self-adhesive coil, die cut 8½ horiz.	2.25	....			1.75	.50
3639	37¢ Toy mail wagon, self-adhesive coil, die cut 8½ horiz.	2.25	....			1.75	.50
3640	37¢ Toy fire pumper, self-adhesive coil, die cut 8½ horiz.	2.25	....			1.75	.50
3641	37¢ Toy taxicab, self-adhesive coil, die cut 8½ horiz.	2.25	....			1.75	.50
3638-41	37¢ Antique Toys, self-adhesive coil, strip of 4.	4.25	....	....	....	6.50	5.00
....	same, pl# strip of 5 . .	....	....	....	....	15.50	....
3642	37¢ Toy mail wagon, self-adhesive, die cut 11	2.25	....	....	....	1.50	.50
3642a	same, die cut 11 x 11¼, 2003	2.25	....	....	....	1.50	.50
3643	37¢ Toy locomotive, self-adhesive, die cut 11	2.25	....	....	....	1.50	.50
3643a	same, die cut 11 x 11¼, 2003	2.25	....	....	....	1.50	.50
3644	37¢ Toy taxicab, self-adhesive, die cut 11	2.25	....	....	....	1.50	.50
3644a	same, die cut 11 x 11¼, 2003	2.25	....	....	....	1.50	.50
3645	37¢ Toy fire pumper, self-adhesive, die cut 11	2.25	....	....	....	1.50	.50
3645f	same, die cut 11 x 11¼, 2003	2.25	....	....	....	1.50	.50
3642-45	37¢ Antique Toys, self-adhesive, 4 varieties attach.	4.25	....	....	....	6.00	4.00
3645b	same, bklt pane of 4 (3642-45 x 1)	4.25	....	....	....	9.00	....
3645c	same, bklt pane of 6 (3643, 3645, 3642 x 2, 3644 x 2)	5.50	....	....	....	8.00	....
3645d	same, bklt pane of 6 (3642, 3644, 3642 x 2, 3645 x 2)	5.50	....	....	....	8.00	....
3645e	same, bklt pane of 20	15.00	....	....	....	26.00	....
3645g	37¢ Antique Toys, self-adhesive, blk of 4 (3642a, 3643a, 3644a, 3645f)	4.25	....	....	....	6.00	....
3645h	same, bklt pane of 20	15.00	....	....	....	32.00	....

3646

SCOTT NO.	DESCRIPTION	FIRST DAY COVERS SING	FIRST DAY COVERS PL. BLK.	MINT SHEET	PLATE BLOCK	UNUSED F/NH	USED
3646	60¢ Coverlet Eagle, self-adhesive	2.75	5.50	35.00(20)	8.00	2.00	.50

3648

3647

SCOTT NO.	DESCRIPTION	FIRST DAY COVERS SING	FIRST DAY COVERS PL. BLK.	MINT SHEET	PLATE BLOCK	UNUSED F/NH	USED
3647	$3.85 Jefferson Memorial, self-adhesive	8.75	35.00	230.00(20)	52.00	13.00	7.75
3647A	same, die cut 11 x 10¾, dated 2003.	8.75	35.00	235.00(20)	54.00	14.00	8.75
3648	$13.65 Capitol Dome, self-adhesive	35.00	105.00	775.00(20)	175.00	44.00	12.00

3649

MASTERS OF AMERICAN PHOTOGRAPHY

3649a	*Albert Sands Southworth & Josiah Johnson Hawes*	**3649k**	*James VanDerZee*
3649b	*Timothy H. O'Sullivan*	**3649l**	*Dorothea Lange*
3649c	*Carleton E. Watkins*	**3649m**	*Walker Evans*
3649d	*Gertrude Käsebier*	**3649n**	*Eugene Smith*
3649e	*Lewis W. Hine*	**3649o**	*Paul Strand*
3649f	*Alvin Langdon Coburn*	**3649p**	*Ansel Adams*
3649g	*Edward Steichen*	**3649q**	*Imogen Cunningham*
3649h	*Alfred Stieglitz*	**3649r**	*André Kértész*
3649i	*Man Ray*	**3649s**	*Garry Winogrand*
3649j	*Edward Weston*	**3649t**	*Minor White*

SCOTT NO.	DESCRIPTION	FIRST DAY COVERS SING	FIRST DAY COVERS PL. BLK.	MINT SHEET	PLATE BLOCK	UNUSED F/NH	USED
3649	37¢ Masters of American Photography, self-adhesive, 20 varieties attached .	....	....	30.00(20)	....	30.00	
....	same, set of singles. .	50.00	....	....	....	....	17.00

3650 3652 3651

SCOTT NO.	DESCRIPTION	FIRST DAY COVERS SING	FIRST DAY COVERS PL. BLK.	MINT SHEET	PLATE BLOCK	UNUSED F/NH	USED
3650	37¢ John James Audubon, self-adhesive	2.25	4.75	28.00(20)	6.50	1.75	.30
3651	37¢ Harry Houdini, self-adhesive	2.25	4.75	26.00(20)	6.00	1.50	.30
3652	37¢ Andy Warhol, self-adhesive	2.25	4.75	29.00(20)	7.00	1.50	.30

3653 3654

3655 3656

SCOTT NO.	DESCRIPTION	FIRST DAY COVERS SING	FIRST DAY COVERS PL. BLK.	MINT SHEET	PLATE BLOCK	UNUSED F/NH	USED
3653-56	37¢ Teddy Bears, self-adhesive, 4 varieties attached.	5.00	6.00	30.00(20)	6.75	6.00	5.00
3653	37¢ Bruin Teddy Bear	2.25	....	....	....	1.75	.50
3654	37¢ Stick Teddy Bear.	2.25	....	....	....	1.75	.50
3655	37¢ Gund Teddy Bear	2.25	....	....	....	1.75	.50
3656	37¢ Ideal Teddy Bear.	2.25	....	....	....	1.75	.50

3657

3658

3659

SCOTT NO.	DESCRIPTION	FIRST DAY COVERS SING	FIRST DAY COVERS PL. BLK.	MINT SHEET	PLATE BLOCK	UNUSED F/NH	USED
3657	37¢ Love, self-adhesive	2.25	....	....	....	1.25	.35
....	same, bklt pane of 20	15.00	....	....	....	22.00	....
3658	60¢ Love, self-adhesive	2.75	5.50	35.00(20)	9.00	2.20	.75
3659	37¢ Ogden Nash, self-adhesive	2.25	4.75	22.50(20)	5.50	1.40	.35

3661

3660

3662

3663

3664

SCOTT NO.	DESCRIPTION	FIRST DAY COVERS SING	FIRST DAY COVERS PL. BLK.	MINT SHEET	PLATE BLOCK	UNUSED F/NH	USED
3660	37¢ Duke Kahanamoku, self-adhesive	2.25	4.75	22.00(20)	5.50	1.25	.35
3661-64	37¢ American Bats, self-adhesive, 4 varieties attached.	4.25	4.75	28.50(20)	7.25	7.00	4.00
3661	37¢ Red Bat.	2.25	....	....	....	1.75	.45
3662	37¢ Leaf-nosed Bat . .	2.25	....	....	....	1.75	.45
3663	37¢ Pallid Bat	2.25	....	....	....	1.75	.45
3664	37¢ Spotted Bat.	2.25	....	....	....	1.75	.45

3665 3666

3667 3668

3669

SCOTT NO.	DESCRIPTION	FIRST DAY COVERS SING	FIRST DAY COVERS PL. BLK.	MINT SHEET	PLATE BLOCK	UNUSED F/NH	USED
3665-68	37¢ Women In Journalism, self-adhesive, 4 varieties attached.	6.00	7.00	37.00(20)	9.00	8.00	5.00
3665	37¢ Nellie Bly.	2.25	....	....	....	2.00	.50
3666	37¢ Ida M. Tarbell . . .	2.25	....	....	....	2.00	.50
3667	37¢ Ethel L. Payne . .	2.25	....	....	....	2.00	.50
3668	37¢ Marguerite Higgins	2.25	....	....	....	2.00	.50
3669	37¢ Irving Berlin, self-adhesive	2.25	4.75	25.00(20)	6.00	1.25	.30

3670 3671

SCOTT NO.	DESCRIPTION	FIRST DAY COVERS SING	FIRST DAY COVERS PL. BLK.	MINT SHEET	PLATE BLOCK	UNUSED F/NH	USED
3670-71	37¢ Neuter and Spay, self-adhesive, 2 varieties attached.	4.00	4.75	25.00(20)	6.00	3.50	2.00
3670	37¢ Kitten	2.25	....	....	....	2.00	.40
3671	37¢ Puppy	2.25	....	....	....	2.00	.40

3672

3673

3674

SCOTT NO.	DESCRIPTION	FIRST DAY COVERS SING	FIRST DAY COVERS PL. BLK.	MINT SHEET	PLATE BLOCK	UNUSED F/NH	USED
3672	37¢ Hanukkah, self-adhesive	2.25	4.75	25.00(20)	6.00	1.30	.40
3673	37¢ Kwanzaa, self-adhesive	2.25	4.75	21.00(20)	5.50	1.20	.40
3674	37¢ EID, self-adhesive	2.25	4.75	21.00(20)	5.50	1.20	.40

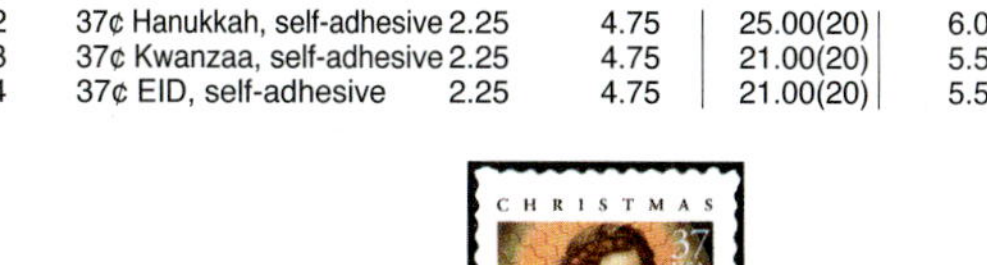

3675

SCOTT NO.	DESCRIPTION	FIRST DAY COVERS SING	FIRST DAY COVERS PL. BLK.	MINT SHEET	PLATE BLOCK	UNUSED F/NH	USED
3675	37¢ Madonna & Child, self-adhesive	2.25	4.75	....	....	1.50	.30
....	same, bklt pane of 20	15.00	....	....	....	27.00	....

3676, 3683, 3684, 3688

3677, 3680, 3685, 3689

3678, 3681, 3686, 3690

3679, 3682, 3687, 3691

SCOTT NO.	DESCRIPTION	FIRST DAY COVERS SING	FIRST DAY COVERS PL. BLK.	MINT SHEET	PLATE BLOCK	UNUSED F/NH	USED
3676-79	37¢ Snowmen, self-adhesive, 4 varieties attached . .	6.00	7.00	32.00(20)	8.50	8.00	4.75
3676	37¢ Snowman with red and green scarf	2.25	....	....	....	2.00	1.25
3677	37¢ Snowman with blue scarf.	2.25	....	....	....	2.00	1.25
3678	37¢ Snowman with pipe	2.25	....	....	....	2.00	1.25
3679	37¢ Snowman with top hat	2.25	....	....	....	2.00	1.25
3680	37¢ Snowman with blue scarf, self-adhesive coil	2.25	....	....	....	2.50	.75
3681	37¢ Snowman with pipe, self-adhesive coil. . . .	2.25	....	....	....	2.50	.75
3682	37¢ Snowman with top hat, self-adhesive coil. . . .	2.25	....	....	....	2.50	.75
3683	37¢ Snowman with red and green scarf, self-adhesive coil	2.25	....	....	....	2.50	.75
3680-83	37¢ Snowmen, self-adhesive coil, strip of 4	4.25				12.00	
....	same, pl# strip of 5 . . .	....	....	....	....	21.00	
3684	37¢ Snowman with red and green scarf, large design	2.25			....	1.75	.50
3685	37¢ Snowman with blue scarf, large design . . .	2.25	....	....	....	1.75	.50
3686	37¢ Snowman with pipe, large design.	2.25	....	....	....	1.75	.50
3687	37¢ Snowman with top hat, large design.	2.25	....	....	....	1.75	.50
3684-87	37¢ Snowman, self-adhesive, 4 varieties attached . .	4.25	....	....	....	7.00	4.75
3687b	same, bklt pane of 20 (3684-87 x 5 + label) .	15.00	....	....	....	36.00	....
3688	37¢ Snowman with red and green scarf, small design	2.25	....	....	....	2.25	.75
3689	37¢ Snowman with blue scarf, small design. . .	2.25	....	....	....	2.25	.75
3690	37¢ Snowman with pipe, small design.	2.25	....	....	....	2.25	.75
3691	37¢ Snowman with top hat, small design.	2.25	....	....	....	2.25	.75
3688-91	37¢ Snowmen , self-adhesive, 4 varieties attached . .	4.25	....	....	....	10.00	6.25
3691b	same, bklt pane of 4, (3688-91).	4.25	....	....	....	10.00	....
3691c	same, bklt pane of 6 (3690-91, 3688-89 x 2)	5.50	....	....	....	15.00	....
3691d	same, bklt pane of 6 (3688-89, 3690-91 x 2)	5.50	....	....	....	15.00	....

3693, 3775, 3785

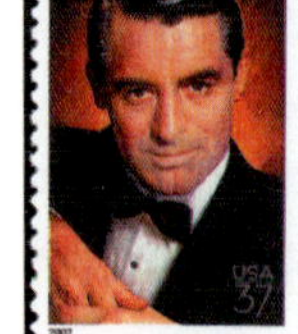

3692

3695

SCOTT NO.	DESCRIPTION	FIRST DAY COVERS SING	FIRST DAY COVERS PL. BLK.	MINT SHEET	PLATE BLOCK	UNUSED F/NH	USED
3692	37¢ Cary Grant, self-adhesive	2.25	4.75	30.00(20)	7.00	1.50	.40
3693	(5¢) Sea Coast coil, self-adhesive	2.25	....	....	....	.25	.20
....	same, pl# strip of 5 . .	....	....	....	....	2.50	....

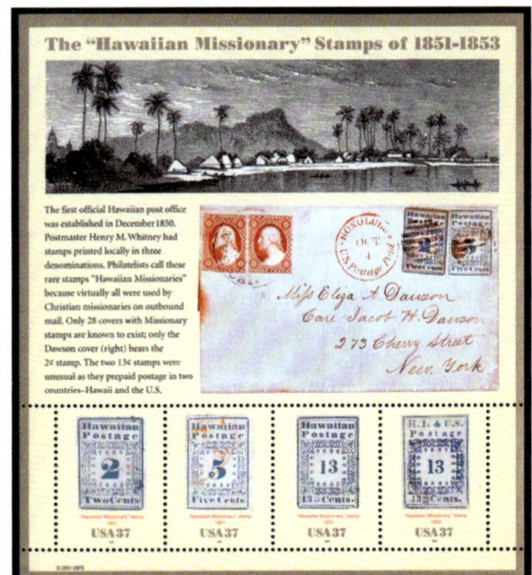
The "Hawaiian Missionary" Stamps of 1851-1853

3694

SCOTT NO.	DESCRIPTION	FIRST DAY COVERS SING	FIRST DAY COVERS PL. BLK.	MINT SHEET	PLATE BLOCK	UNUSED F/NH	USED
3694	37¢ Hawaiian Missionary, souvenir sheet of 4 . .	5.00	....	....	....	8.00	6.00
3694a	37¢ Hawaii 2¢ of 1851	2.25	....	....	....	2.00	1.00
3694b	37¢ Hawaii 5¢ of 1851	2.25	....	....	....	2.00	1.00
3694c	37¢ Hawaii 13¢ of 1851	2.25	....	....	....	2.00	1.00
3694d	37¢ Hawaii 13¢ of 1852	2.25	....	....	....	2.00	1.00
3695	37¢ Happy Birthday, self-adhesive	2.25	4.75	25.00(20)	6.00	1.20	.30

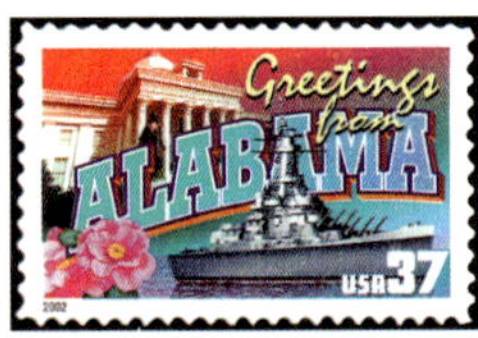

3696

3745

GREETINGS FROM AMERICA

3696	*Alabama*	**3713**	*Louisiana*	**3730**	*Ohio*
3697	*Alaska*	**3714**	*Maine*	**3731**	*Oklahoma*
3698	*Arizona*	**3715**	*Maryland*	**3732**	*Oregon*
3699	*Arkansas*	**3716**	*Massachusetts*	**3733**	*Pennsylvania*
3700	*California*	**3717**	*Michigan*	**3734**	*Rhode Island*
3701	*Colorado*	**3718**	*Minnesota*	**3735**	*South Carolina*
3702	*Connecticut*	**3719**	*Mississippi*	**3736**	*South Dakota*
3703	*Delaware*	**3720**	*Missouri*	**3737**	*Tennessee*
3704	*Florida*	**3721**	*Montana*	**3738**	*Texas*
3705	*Georgia*	**3722**	*Nebraska*	**3739**	*Utah*
3706	*Hawaii*	**3723**	*Nevada*	**3740**	*Vermont*
3707	*Idaho*	**3724**	*New Hampshire*	**3741**	*Virginia*
3708	*Illinois*	**3725**	*New Jersey*	**3742**	*Washington*
3709	*Indiana*	**3726**	*New Mexico*	**3743**	*West Virginia*
3710	*Iowa*	**3727**	*New York*	**3744**	*Wisconsin*
3711	*Kansas*	**3728**	*North Carolina*	**3745**	*Wyoming*
3712	*Kentucky*	**3729**	*North Dakota*		

SCOTT NO.	DESCRIPTION	FIRST DAY COVERS SING	FIRST DAY COVERS PL. BLK.	MINT SHEET	PLATE BLOCK	UNUSED F/NH	USED
3696-3745	37¢ Greetings from America, self-adhesive, 50 varieties attached. .	....	....	50.00(50)	....	50.00	....
....	set of singles.	120.00	....	....	....	....	35.00
	singles each		....	....	....	....	.85

3746

3747

3748

2003 COMMEMORATIVES

SCOTT NO.	DESCRIPTION	FIRST DAY COVERS SING	FIRST DAY COVERS PL. BLK.	MINT SHEET	PLATE BLOCK	UNUSED F/NH	USED
3746/3824	(3746-48, 3771, 3773-74, 3781-82, 3786-91, 3803, 3808-18, 3821-24) 30 varieties.	....	....	....	....	45.00	10.50
3746	37¢ Thurgood Marshall, self-adhesive	2.25	4.75	28.00(20)	7.00	1.50	.30
3747	37¢ Year of the Ram, self-adhesive	2.25	4.75	25.00(20)	6.00	1.50	.30
3748	37¢ Zora Neale Hurston, self-adhesive	2.25	4.75	30.00(20)	7.50	2.00	.30

3749, 3749a, 3758, 3758a

3750, 3751, 3752, 3753, 3758b

3754, 3759

3755, 3761

3756

3757, 3762

AMERICAN DESIGN SERIES

SCOTT NO.	DESCRIPTION	FIRST DAY COVERS SING	FIRST DAY COVERS PL. BLK.	MINT SHEET	PLATE BLOCK	UNUSED F/NH	USED
3749	1¢ Tiffany Lamp, self-adhesive (2007).	2.25	4.75	3.00(20)	.95	.25	.25
3749a	1¢ Tiffany Lamp (2008)	2.95	5.75	4.25(20)	1.00	.25	.25
3750	2¢ Navajo Necklace, self-adhesive ('08) . . .	2.25	4.75	5.00(20)	.90	.25	.25
3751	same, self-adhesive, die cut 11¼ x 11½ ('05)	2.25	4.75	8.00(20)	1.75	.40	.25
3752	same, w/ USPS micro-printing, self-adhesive, die cut 11¼ x 11.	2.25	4.75	7.00(20)	1.75	.30	.25
3753	same, die cut 11½ x 10¾, (2007 date)	2.25	4.75	6.00(20)	1.25	.30	.25
3754	3¢ Silver Coffeepot, self-adhesive (2007).	2.25	4.75	4.50(20)	1.25	.25	.25
3755	4¢ Chippendale Chair, self-adhesive (2004) .	2.25	4.75	5.50(20)	1.20	.25	.25
3756	5¢ Toleware, self-adhesive, (2004)	2.25	4.75	6.00(20)	1.40	.35	.25
3756a	5¢ Toleware, 11¼ x 10¾ (dated 2007)	2.25	4.75	6.00(20)	1.40	.35	.35
3757	10¢ American Clock, self-adhesive	2.25	4.75	7.00(20)	1.50	.35	.25
3758	1¢ Tiffany Lamp, coil (2003)	2.25	....	....	....	.25	.25
....	same, pl# strip of 5 . .	....	....	....	....	2.25	....
3758a	1¢ Tiffany Lamp, coil (2008) perf 10	2.25	....	....	....	.25	.25
....	same, pl# strip of 5 . .	....	....	....	....	2.25	....
3758b	2¢ Navajo Necklace Perf 9.75 vert. (2011)	....	3.75	....	....	.25	....
....	same, plate number strip of 5		....	....	....	2.25	....
3759	3¢ Silver Coffeepot, coil	2.25	....	....	....	.25	.25
....	same, pl# strip of 5 . .	....	....	....	....	8.00	....
3761	4¢ Chippendale Chair, coil (2007)	2.25	....	....	....	.25	.25
....	same, pl# strip of 5 . .	....	....	....	....	3.00	.25
3761A	4¢ Chippendale Chair, Chair Coil (ap) (2013 Date)	2.75	....	....	....	.30	.25
....	Same, Plate # strip of 5	....	....	....	....	1.50	....
3762	10¢ American Clock, coil	2.25	....	....	....	.30	.25
....	same, pl# strip of 5 . .	....	....	....	....	3.00	....
3763	10¢ American Clock (2008)	....	....	....	....	.30	.25
....	same, plate strip of 5.	....	....	....	....	4.00	....
3763A	10¢ American Clock Coil (untagged) (2008 Date)	....	....	....	....	.30	.25
....	Same, Plate # strip of 5	....	....	....	....	4.00	....

3766

3769

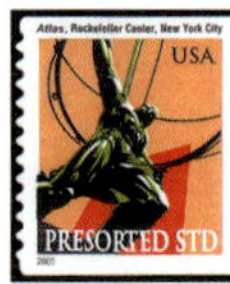

3770

3771

SCOTT NO.	DESCRIPTION	FIRST DAY COVERS SING	FIRST DAY COVERS PL. BLK.	MINT SHEET	PLATE BLOCK	UNUSED F/NH	USED
3766	$1 Wisdom, self-adhesive	3.50	7.50	61.00(20)	14.50	3.25	.70
3766a	$1 Wisdom, (2008) die cut 11¼ x 11	3.50	7.50	60.00(20)	13.50	3.00	.70
3769	(10¢) New York Library Lion, perf. 10 vert. . . .	2.25	....	....	4.00(3)	.30	.20
....	same, pl# strip of 5 . .	....	....	....	....	6.00	....
3770	(10¢) Atlas Statue, self-adhesive coil, die cut 11 dated 2003.	2.25	....	....	....	.30	.25
....	same, pl# strip of 5 . .	....	....	....	....	6.00	....
3771	80¢ Special Olympics, self-adhesive	3.00	7.00	45.00(20)	12.00	2.50	1.00

3772a *Screenwriting*
3772b *Directing*
3772c *Costume design*
3772d *Music*
3772e *Make-up*
3772f *Art Direction*
3772g *Cinematography*
3772h *Film editing*
3772i *Special effects*
3772j *Sound*

3772

AMERICAN FILM MAKING

SCOTT NO.	DESCRIPTION	FIRST DAY COVERS SING	FIRST DAY COVERS PL. BLK.	MINT SHEET	PLATE BLOCK	UNUSED F/NH	USED
3772	37¢ American Film Making, self-adhesive, 10 varieties attached............	....	....	15.00(10)	....	15.00	13.50
....	set of singles	25.00	....	....	....	....	7.00

3773 3774 3781 3782

SCOTT NO.	DESCRIPTION	FIRST DAY COVERS SING	FIRST DAY COVERS PL. BLK.	MINT SHEET	PLATE BLOCK	UNUSED F/NH	USED
3773	37¢ Ohio Statehood, self-adhesive	2.25	4.75	22.00(20)	5.50	1.20	.30
3774	37¢ Pelican Island National Wildlife Refuge, self-adhesive	2.25	4.75	22.00(20)	6.00	1.35	.30
3775	(5¢) Sea Coast coil, perf. 9.75 vert.	2.25	....	....	....	.30	.25
....	same, pl# strip of 5 . .	....	....	....	....	2.75	....

3776 3777 3778 3779

3780 3783 3784, 3784A 3786

SCOTT NO.	DESCRIPTION	FIRST DAY COVERS SING	FIRST DAY COVERS PL. BLK.	MINT SHEET	PLATE BLOCK	UNUSED F/NH	USED
3776	37¢ Uncle Sam on Bicycle	2.25	....	....	....	1.50	1.00
3777	37¢ 1888 Pres. Campaign badge.............	2.25	....	....	....	1.50	1.00
3778	37¢ 1893 Silk bookmark	2.25	....	....	....	1.50	1.00
3779	37¢ Modern hand fan	2.25	....	....	....	1.50	1.00
3780	37¢ Carving of woman with flag & sword	2.25	....	....	....	1.50	1.00
3776-80	37¢ Old Glory, self-adhesive, 5 varieties attached . .	5.00	....	....	....	7.00	....
3780b	same, complete booklet of 2 panes	....	....	....	....	25.00	....
3781	37¢ Cesar E. Chavez, self-adhesive	2.25	4.75	22.00(20)	5.50	1.20	.30
3782	37¢ Louisiana Purchase, self-adhesive	2.25	4.75	34.00(20)	8.00	1.50	.35

SCOTT NO.	DESCRIPTION	FIRST DAY COVERS SING	FIRST DAY COVERS PL. BLK.	MINT SHEET	PLATE BLOCK	UNUSED F/NH	USED
3783	37¢ First Flight of the Wright Brothers, self-adhesive	2.25	....	15.00(10)	....	1.85	.45
3783a	same, bklt pane of 9 .	....	....	....	....	13.00	....
3783b	same, bklt pane of 1 .	7.00	....	....	....	4.50	....
3784	37¢ Purple Heart, self-adhesive	2.25	4.75	22.00(20)	5.50	1.20	.45
3784A	37¢ Purple Heart, self-adhesive, die cut 10¾ x 10¼.........	2.25	4.75	22.00(20)	5.50	1.20	.50
3785	(5¢) Sea Coast coil, four-side die cuts........	2.25	....	....	....	.35	.25
....	same, pl# strip of 5 . .	....	....	....	....	2.50	....
3785A	(5¢) Sea Coast coil, die cut 9¼ x 10	2.25	....	....	....	.35	.25
....	same, pl# strip of 5 . .	....	....	....	....	2.50	....
3786	37¢ Audrey Hepburn, self-adhesive	2.25	4.75	40.00(20)	10.00	2.00	.30

3787 3788 3789

3790

3792–3801, 3792a–3801a

3791

SCOTT NO.	DESCRIPTION	FIRST DAY COVERS SING	FIRST DAY COVERS PL. BLK.	MINT SHEET	PLATE BLOCK	UNUSED F/NH	USED
3787-91	37¢ Southeastern Lighthouses, self-adhesive, 5 varieties attached...........	5.00	....	47.00(20)	28.00(10)	12.00	10.00
3787	37¢ Old Cape Henry, Virginia............	2.25	....	....	....	2.00	.65
3788	37¢ Cape Lookout, North Carolina	2.25	....	....	....	2.00	.65
3788a	same, dropped denomination......		....	....	....	....	....
3789	37¢ Morris Island, South Carolina......	2.25	....	....	....	2.00	.65
3790	37¢ Tybee Island, Georgia	2.25	....	....	....	2.00	.65
3791	37¢ Hillsboro Inlet, Florida	2.25	....	....	....	2.00	.65
3791b	same, strip of 5 (3787, 3788a, 3789-91)	....	....	....	....	....	....
3792	(25¢) Eagle, gray with gold eagle, coil......	2.25	....	....	....	1.00	.60
3792a	same, serpentine die cut 11½ (2005)......	2.25	....	....		1.00	.60
3793	(25¢) Eagle, gold with red eagle, coil	2.25	....	....	....	1.00	.60
3793a	same, serpentine die cut 11½ (2005)......	2.25	....	....	....	1.00	.60
3794	(25¢) Eagle, dull blue with gold eagle, coil . .	2.25	....	....	....	1.00	.60
3794a	same, serpentine die cut 11½ (2005)......	2.25	....	....	....	1.00	.60
3795	(25¢) Eagle, gold with Prussian blue eagle, coil	2.25	....	....	....	1.00	.60
3795a	same, serpentine die cut 11½ (2005)......	2.25	....	....	....	1.00	.60
3796	(25¢) Eagle, green with gold eagle, coil......	2.25	....	....	....	1.00	.60
3796a	same, die cut 11½ (2005)	2.25	....	....	....	1.00	.60
3797	(25¢) Eagle, gold with gray eagle, coil	2.25	....	....	....	1.00	.60
3797a	same, die cut 11½ (2005)	2.25	....	....	....	1.00	.60
3798	(25¢) Eagle, Prussian blue with gold eagle, coil	2.25	....	....	....	1.00	.60
3798a	same, die cut 11½ (2005)	2.25	....	....	....	1.00	.60
3799	(25¢) Eagle, gold with dull blue eagle, coil . .	2.25	....	....	....	1.00	.60
3799a	same, die cut 11½ (2005)	2.25	....	....	....	1.00	.60
3800	(25¢) Eagle, red with gold eagle, coil......	2.25	....	....	....	1.00	.60
3800a	same, die cut 11½ (2005)	2.25	....	....	....	1.00	.60
3801	(25¢) Eagle, gold with green eagle, coil	2.25	....	....	....	1.00	.60
3801a	same, die cut 11½ (2005)	2.25	....	....	....	1.00	.60
3792-3801	(25¢) Eagle, self-adhesive coil, strip of 10	6.00	....	....	....	12.00	....
....	same, pl# strip of 11 .	....	....	....	....	14.00	....
3792a-3801a	same, self-adhesive, coil strip of 10, serpentine die cut 11½ (dated 2005).	6.00	....	....	....	12.00	....
....	same, plt. strip of 11 .	....	....	....	....	14.00	....

SCOTT NO.	DESCRIPTION	FIRST DAY COVERS SING	FIRST DAY COVERS PL. BLK.	MINT SHEET	PLATE BLOCK	UNUSED F/NH	USED

3802

ARCTIC TUNDRA

3802a	*Gyrfalcon*	**3802g**	*Arctic ground squirrel*
3802b	*Gray wolf*	**3802h**	*Willow ptarmigan & bearberry*
3802c	*Common raven*	**3802i**	*Arctic grayling*
3802d	*Musk oxen & caribou*	**3802j**	*Singing vole, thin-legged spider, lingonberry, Labrador tea*
3802e	*Grizzly bears & caribou*		
3802f	*Caribou & willow ptarmigans*		

SCOTT NO.	DESCRIPTION	SING	PL. BLK.	MINT SHEET	PLATE BLOCK	UNUSED F/NH	USED
3802	37¢ Arctic Tundra, 10 varieties, attached, self-adhesive	....	....	15.00(10)	....	15.00	....
....	set of singles	25.00	....	....	....	....	7.00

3803

SCOTT NO.	DESCRIPTION	SING	PL. BLK.	MINT SHEET	PLATE BLOCK	UNUSED F/NH	USED
3803	37¢ Korean War Veterans, Memorial, self-adhesive	2.25	4.75	21.00(20)	5.50	1.20	.30

3804

3805

3806

3807

SCOTT NO.	DESCRIPTION	SING	PL. BLK.	MINT SHEET	PLATE BLOCK	UNUSED F/NH	USED
3804	37¢ Young Mother . . .	2.25	....	....	....	1.50	.40
3805	37¢ Children Playing .	2.25	....	....	....	1.50	.40
3806	37¢ On a Balcony . . .	2.25	....	....	....	1.50	.40
3807	37¢ Child in Straw Hat	2.25	....	....	....	1.50	.40
3804-07	37¢ Mary Cassatt Paintings, self-adhesive, 4 varieties attached.	4.25	....	....	....	6.00	4.00
3807b	same, bklt pane of 20 (3804-07 x 5)	15.00	....	....	....	30.00	....

3808

3809

3810

3811

SCOTT NO.	DESCRIPTION	SING	PL. BLK.	MINT SHEET	PLATE BLOCK	UNUSED F/NH	USED
3808-11	37¢ Early Football Heroes, self-adhesive, 4 varieties attached.	4.25	4.75	25.00(20)	6.50	6.00	5.00
3808	37¢ Bronko Nagurski .	2.25	....	....	....	1.50	.40
3809	37¢ Ernie Nevers. . . .	2.25	....	....	....	1.50	.40
3810	37¢ Walter Camp. . . .	2.25	....	....	....	1.50	.40
3811	37¢ Red Grange	2.25	....	....	....	1.50	.40

3812

3813

SCOTT NO.	DESCRIPTION	SING	PL. BLK.	MINT SHEET	PLATE BLOCK	UNUSED F/NH	USED
3812	37¢ Roy Acuff, self-adhesive	2.25	4.75	24.00(20)	6.00	1.25	.30
3813	37¢ District of Columbia, self-adhesive	2.25	4.75	22.00(16)	6.00	1.50	.40

3814

3815

3816

3817

3819

3818

3820

SCOTT NO.	DESCRIPTION	SING	PL. BLK.	MINT SHEET	PLATE BLOCK	UNUSED F/NH	USED
3814-18	37¢ Reptiles & Amphibians, self-adhesive, 5 varieties attached.	5.00	10.50	28.00(20)	15.00	7.50	5.00
3814	37¢ Scarlet Kingsnake	2.25	....	....	....	1.50	.50
3815	37¢ Blue-spotted Salamander	2.25	....	....	....	1.50	.50
3816	37¢ Reticulate Lizard.	2.25	....	....	....	1.50	.50
3817	37¢ Ornate Chorus Frog	2.25	....	....	....	1.50	.50
3818	37¢ Ornate Box Turtle	2.25	....	....	....	1.50	.50
3819	23¢ George Washington, self-adhesive, die cut 11	2.25	4.75	30.00(20)	12.00	2.00	.75
3820	37¢ Madonna & Child, self-adhesive (2003) .	2.25	....	....	....	1.30	.40
3820a	same, bklt pane of 20	....	....	....	....	24.00	....

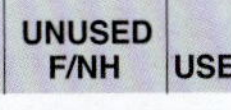

3821, 3825 | 3822, 3826 | 3823, 3827 | 3824, 3828

SCOTT NO.	DESCRIPTION	FIRST DAY COVERS SING	FIRST DAY COVERS PL. BLK.	MINT SHEET	PLATE BLOCK	UNUSED F/NH	USED
3821-24	37¢ Christmas Music Makers, self-adhesive, 4 varieties attached.	4.25	4.75	34.00(20)	7.50	7.00	4.00
3821	37¢ Reindeer with Pipes	2.25	....	....	....	2.00	.75
3822	37¢ Santa Claus with Drum	2.25	....	....	....	2.00	.75
3823	37¢ Santa Claus with Trumpet	2.25	....	....	....	2.00	.75
3824	37¢ Reindeer with Horn	2.25	....	....	....	2.00	.75
3824b	same, bklt pane of 20, (3821-24 x 5 + label) .	15.00	....	....	....	34.00	....
3825	37¢ Reindeer with Pipes, die cut 10½ x 10¾ . . .	2.25	....	....	....	2.00	1.00
3826	37¢ Santa Claus with Drum, die cut 10½ x 10¾ . . .	2.25	....	....	....	2.00	1.00
3827	37¢ Santa Claus with Trumpet die cut 10½ x 10¾ . . .	2.25	....	....	....	2.00	1.00
3828	37¢ Reindeer with Horn die cut 10½ x 10¾ . . .	2.25	....	....	....	2.00	1.00
3825-28	37¢ Christmas Music Makers, self-adhesive, 4 varieties attached, die cut 10½ x 10¾	4.25	....	....	....	7.00	4.00
3828b	same, bklt pane of 4 (3825-28)	4.25	....	....	....	7.00	....
3828c	same, bklt pane of 6 (3827-28, 3825-26 x 2)	5.50	....	....	....	11.00	....
3828d	same, bklt pane of 6 (3825-26, 3827-28 x 2)	5.50	....	....	....	11.00	....

3829, 3829A, 3830, 3830D

SCOTT NO.	DESCRIPTION	FIRST DAY COVERS SING	FIRST DAY COVERS PL. BLK.	MINT SHEET	PLATE BLOCK	UNUSED F/NH	USED
3829	37¢ Snowy Egret, self-adhesive coil, die cut 8½	1.95	....	....	....	1.25	.40
....	same, pl# strip of 5 . .	....	....	....	....	10.00	....
3829A	37¢ Snowy Egret, self-adhesive coil, die cut 9½	1.95	....	....	....	1.25	.35
....	same, pl# strip of 5 . .	....	....	....	....	11.00	....
3830	37¢ Snowy Egret, self adhesive	2.25	....	....	....	1.25	.35
3830a	same, bklt pane of 20	....	....	....	....	26.00	....
3830D	37¢ Snowy Egret, w/ USPS microprinting . .	2.25	....	....	....	10.00	1.50
3830Dc	Booklet Pane of 20 . .	....	....	....	....	170.00	....

3831

PACIFIC CORAL REEF

3831a *Emperor angelfish, blue & mound coral*
3831b *Humphead wrasse, Moorish idol*
3831c *Bumphead parrotfish*
3831d *Black-spotted puffer, threadfin butterflyfish*
3831e *Hawksbill turtle, palette surgeonfish*
3831f *Pink anemonefish, sea anemone*
3831g *Snowflake moray eel, Spanish dancer*
3831h *Lionfish*
3831i *Triton's trumpet*
3831j *Oriental sweetlips, bluestreak cleaner wrasse, mushroom coral*

SCOTT NO.	DESCRIPTION	FIRST DAY COVERS SING	FIRST DAY COVERS PL. BLK.	MINT SHEET	PLATE BLOCK	UNUSED F/NH	USED
3831	37¢ Pacific Coral Reef, 10 varieties, attached, self-adhesive	....	....	15.00(10)	....	15.00	....
....	set of singles	25.00	....	....	....	....	7.00

2004 COMMEMORATIVES

SCOTT NO.	DESCRIPTION	FIRST DAY COVERS SING	FIRST DAY COVERS PL. BLK.	MINT SHEET	PLATE BLOCK	UNUSED F/NH	USED
3832/3886	**(3832, 3834-35, 3837-43 3854, 3857-63, 3865-71, 3876-77, 3880-86) 34 varieties**	....		....	....	**45.00**	**18.00**

3832

3834

3835

SCOTT NO.	DESCRIPTION	FIRST DAY COVERS SING	FIRST DAY COVERS PL. BLK.	MINT SHEET	PLATE BLOCK	UNUSED F/NH	USED
3832	37¢ Year of the Monkey, self-adhesive	2.25	4.75	22.00(20)	5.50	1.20	.40
3833	37¢ Candy Hearts, self-adhesive	2.25	....	....	....	1.20	.30
3833a	same, bklt pane of 20	....	....	....	....	23.00	....
3834	37¢ Paul Robeson, self-adhesive	2.25	4.75	25.00(20)	6.00	1.50	.35
3835	37¢ Theodore Seuss Geisel (Dr. Seuss) self-adhesive	2.25	4.75	22.00(20)	5.00	1.50	.35

3836

3833

3837

SCOTT NO.	DESCRIPTION	FIRST DAY COVERS SING	FIRST DAY COVERS PL. BLK.	MINT SHEET	PLATE BLOCK	UNUSED F/NH	USED
3836	37¢ White Lilacs and Pink Roses, self-adhesive	2.25	....	....	....	1.20	.30
3836a	same, bklt pane of 20	....	....	....	....	23.00	....
3837	60¢ Five varieties of Pink Roses, self-adhesive .	2.75	5.50	42.00(20)	9.50	2.35	1.00

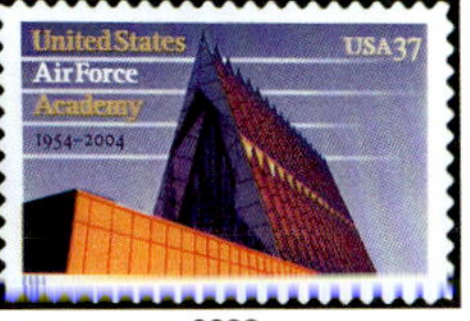

3838

3839

SCOTT NO.	DESCRIPTION	FIRST DAY COVERS SING	FIRST DAY COVERS PL. BLK.	MINT SHEET	PLATE BLOCK	UNUSED F/NH	USED
3838	37¢ United States Air Force Academy, self-adhesive	2.25	4.75	22.00(20)	5.50	1.20	.35
3839	37¢ Henry Mancini, self-adhesive	2.25	4.75	22.00(20)	5.50	1.20	.35

3840

3841

3842

3843

SCOTT NO.	DESCRIPTION	FIRST DAY COVERS SING	FIRST DAY COVERS PL. BLK.	MINT SHEET	PLATE BLOCK	UNUSED F/NH	USED
3840-43	37¢ American Choreographers, self-adhesive, 4 varieties attached.	4.25	4.75	25.00(20)	12.00	6.00	5.00
3840	37¢ Martha Graham .	2.25	....	....	....	1.50	.70
3841	37¢ Alvin Ailey	2.25	....	....	....	1.50	.70
3842	37¢ Agnes de Mille . .	2.25	....	....	....	1.50	.70
3843	37¢ George Balanchine	2.25	....	....	....	1.50	.70

3844, 3845, 3846, 3847, 3848, 3849, 3850, 3851, 3852, 3853

SCOTT NO.	DESCRIPTION	FIRST DAY COVERS SING	FIRST DAY COVERS PL. BLK.	MINT SHEET	PLATE BLOCK	UNUSED F/NH	USED
3844-3853	(25¢) Eagle, water activated coil, strip of 10, perf. 9¾	6.00	....	....	....	20.00	....
....	same, pl# strip of 11 .	....	....	....	....	26.00	....
3844	(25¢) Eagle, gray with gold eagle, coil, perf. 9¾	2.25	....	....	....	2.00	.75
3845	(25¢) Eagle, gold with green eagle, coil, perf. 9¾ . .	2.25	....	....	....	2.00	.75
3846	(25¢) Eagle, red with gold eagle, coil, perf. 9¾ . .	2.25	....	....	....	2.00	.75
3847	(25¢) Eagle, gold with dull blue eagle, coil, perf. 9¾	2.25	....	....	....	2.00	.75
3848	(25¢) Eagle, Prussian blue with gold eagle, coil, perf. 9¾	2.25	....	....	....	2.00	.75
3849	(25¢) Eagle, gold with gray eagle, coil, perf. 9¾	2.25	....	....	....	2.00	.75
3850	(25¢) Eagle, green with gold eagle, coil, perf. 9¾	2.25	....	....	....	2.00	.75
3851	(25¢) Eagle, gold with Prussian blue eagle, coil, perf. 9¾	2.25	....	....	....	2.00	.75
3852	(25¢) Eagle, dull blue with gold eagle, coil, perf. 9¾	2.25	....	....	....	2.00	.75
3853	(25¢) Eagle, gold with red eagle, coil, perf. 9¾	2.25	....	....	....	2.00	.75

3855 3854 3856

SCOTT NO.	DESCRIPTION	FIRST DAY COVERS SING	FIRST DAY COVERS PL. BLK.	MINT SHEET	PLATE BLOCK	UNUSED F/NH	USED
3854	37¢ Lewis & Clark Bicentennial, self-adhesive	2.25	4.75	35.00(20)	9.00	2.00	.40
3855	37¢ Lewis & Clark Bicentennial, Lewis booklet single .	2.25	....	....	....	1.75	1.00
3856	37¢ Lewis & Clark Bicentennial, Clark booklet single . .	2.25	....	....	....	1.75	1.00
3855-56	37¢ Lewis & Clark, pair	5.00	....	....	....	3.75	....
3856b	37¢ Lewis & Clark: The Corps of Discovery, 1804-06, self-adhesive, bklt pane of 10	....	....	....	....	20.00	....
	complete booklet	....	....	....	....	38.00	....

3857

3858

3859 3860

3861

SCOTT NO.	DESCRIPTION	FIRST DAY COVERS SING	FIRST DAY COVERS PL. BLK.	MINT SHEET	PLATE BLOCK	UNUSED F/NH	USED
3857-61	37¢ Isamu Noguchi, self-adhesive, 5 varieties attached.	5.00	9.50	25.00(20)	14.00(10)	7.00	7.00
3857	37¢ Akari 25N	2.25	....	....	....	1.50	1.00
3858	37¢ Margaret La Farge Osborn	2.25	....	....	....	1.50	1.00
3859	37¢ Black Sun	2.25	....	....	....	1.50	1.00
3860	37¢ Mother and Child	2.25	....	....	....	1.50	1.00
3861	37¢ Figure (detail) . . .	2.25	....	....	....	1.50	1.00

3862 3864, 3874, 3874a, 3875 3863

SCOTT NO.	DESCRIPTION	FIRST DAY COVERS SING	FIRST DAY COVERS PL. BLK.	MINT SHEET	PLATE BLOCK	UNUSED F/NH	USED
3862	37¢ National WWII Memorial, self-adhesive	2.25	4.75	25.00(20)	6.00	1.50	.40
3863	37¢ 2004 Olympic Games, Athens, Greece, self-adhesive	2.25	4.75	22.00(20)	5.50	1.25	.30
3864	(5¢) Sea Coast, coil, perf. 9¾ vert.	2.25	....	....	....	.35	.25
....	same, pl # strip of 5 . .	....	....	....	....	2.50	....

3865 3866 3867 3868

SCOTT NO.	DESCRIPTION	FIRST DAY COVERS SING	FIRST DAY COVERS PL. BLK.	MINT SHEET	PLATE BLOCK	UNUSED F/NH	USED
3865-68	37¢ Art of Disney: Friendship, self-adhesive, 4 varieties attached.	4.25	4.75	30.00(20)	7.00	6.50	4.00
3865	37¢ Goofy, Mickey Mouse, Donald Duck .	2.25	....	....	....	1.75	.85
3866	37¢ Bambi, Thumper .	2.25	....	....	....	1.75	.85
3867	37¢ Mufasa, Simba . .	2.25	....	....	....	1.75	.85
3868	37¢ Jiminy Cricket, Pinocchio	2.25	....	....	....	1.75	.85

3869 3870

SCOTT NO.	DESCRIPTION	FIRST DAY COVERS SING	FIRST DAY COVERS PL. BLK.	MINT SHEET	PLATE BLOCK	UNUSED F/NH	USED
3869	37¢ U.S.S. Constellation, self-adhesive	2.25	4.75	24.00(20)	6.00	1.50	.35
3870	37¢ R. Buckminster Fuller, self-adhesive	2.25	4.75	24.00(20)	5.50	1.40	.35

3871 3872

SCOTT NO.	DESCRIPTION	FIRST DAY COVERS SING	FIRST DAY COVERS PL. BLK.	MINT SHEET	PLATE BLOCK	UNUSED F/NH	USED
3871	37¢ James Baldwin, self-adhesive	2.25	4.75	22.00(20)	5.50	1.20	.35
3872	37¢ Giant Magnolias, self-adhesive	2.25	....	....	....	1.20	.40
3872a	same, bklt pane of 20	....	....	....	....	26.00	....

3873

ART OF THE AMERICAN INDIAN

3873a	*Mimbres bowl*	**3873f**	*Mississippian effigy*
3873b	*Kutenai parfleche*	**3873g**	*Acoma pot*
3873c	*Tlingit sculptures*	**3873h**	*Navajo weaving*
3873d	*Ho-Chunk bag*	**3873i**	*Seneca carving*
3873e	*Seminole doll*	**3873j**	*Luiseño basket*

SCOTT NO.	DESCRIPTION	FIRST DAY COVERS SING	FIRST DAY COVERS PL. BLK.	MINT SHEET	PLATE BLOCK	UNUSED F/NH	USED
3873	37¢ Art of the American Indian, 10 varieties attached.	....	....	28.00(10)	....	28.00	....
....	set of singles	25.00	....	....	....	....	8.00
3874	(5¢) Sea Coast, coil, perf. 10 vert., self-adhesive	2.25	....	....	....	.55	.30
....	same, pl# strip of 5 . .	....	....	....	....	4.75	....
3874a	(5¢) Sea Coast with small date, coil, die cut 10 vert., self-adhesive	2.25	....	....	....	.45	.30
....	same, pl# strip of 5 . .	....	....	....	....	3.50	....
3875	(5¢) Sea Coast, coil, perf. 11½ vert., self-adhesive	2.25	....	....	....	.45	.30
....	same, pl# strip of 5 . .	....	....	....	....	3.50	....

3876

TEST EARLY FOR SICKLE CELL
USA 37

3877

SCOTT NO.	DESCRIPTION	FIRST DAY COVERS SING	FIRST DAY COVERS PL. BLK.	MINT SHEET	PLATE BLOCK	UNUSED F/NH	USED
3876	37¢ John Wayne	2.25	4.75	28.00(20)	6.50	1.50	.40
....	same, uncut sheet of 120	....	....	120.00(20)	....	120.00	....
....	cross gutter block of 8	....	....	....	....	21.00	....
....	block of 8 with vert. gutter	....	....	....	....	13.50	....
....	horizontal pair with vertical gutter.	....	....	....	....	4.00	....
....	vertical pair with horizontal gutter.	....	....	....	....	3.00	....
3877	37¢ Sickle Cell Disease Awareness.	2.25	4.75	22.00(20)	5.50	1.20	.40

CLOUDSCAPES

3878

CLOUDSCAPES

3878a	*Cirrus radiatus*	**3878i**	*Altocumulus castellanus*
3878b	*Cirrostratus fibratus*	**3878j**	*Altocumulus lenticularis*
3878c	*Cirrocumulus undulatus*	**3878k**	*Stratocumulus undulatus*
3878d	*Cumulonimbus mammatus*	**3878l**	*Stratus opacus*
3878e	*Cumulonimbus incus*	**3878m**	*Cumulus humilis*
3878f	*Altocumulus stratiformis*	**3878n**	*Cumulus congestus*
3878g	*Altostratus translucidus*	**3878o**	*Cumulonimbus with tornado*
3878h	*Altocumulus undulatus*		

SCOTT NO.	DESCRIPTION	FIRST DAY COVERS SING	FIRST DAY COVERS PL. BLK.	MINT SHEET	PLATE BLOCK	UNUSED F/NH	USED
3878	37¢ Cloudscapes, 15 varieties attached .	35.00	....	24.00(15)	....	24.00	....
....	set of singles	35.00	....	....	....	....	14.00

3879

HANUKKAH
37 USA

3880

SCOTT NO.	DESCRIPTION	FIRST DAY COVERS SING	FIRST DAY COVERS PL. BLK.	MINT SHEET	PLATE BLOCK	UNUSED F/NH	USED
3879	37¢ Madonna & Child, self-adhesive, die cut 10¾ x 11	2.25	....	....	....	1.25	.30
3879a	same, bklt pane of 20	....	....	....	....	26.00	....
3880	37¢ Hanukkah-Dreidel, self-adhesive	2.25	4.75	21.00(20)	5.50	1.25	.30

3881

MOSS HART
37 USA

3882

SCOTT NO.	DESCRIPTION	FIRST DAY COVERS SING	FIRST DAY COVERS PL. BLK.	MINT SHEET	PLATE BLOCK	UNUSED F/NH	USED
3881	37¢ Kwanzaa-People in Robes, self-adhesive	2.25	4.75	21.00(20)	5.50	1.25	.35
3882	37¢ Moss Hart, self-adhesive	2.25	4.75	21.00(20)	5.50	1.25	.40

3883, 3887, 3892

3884, 3888, 3891

3885, 3889, 3894

3886, 3890, 3893

SCOTT NO.	DESCRIPTION	FIRST DAY COVERS SING	FIRST DAY COVERS PL. BLK.	MINT SHEET	PLATE BLOCK	UNUSED F/NH	USED
3883-86	37¢ Santa Christmas Ornaments, self-adhesive, 4 attached	4.25	4.75	27.00(20)	7.00	6.00	4.25
3883	37¢ Purple Santa Ornament	2.25	....	....	....	1.85	.55
3884	37¢ Green Santa Ornament	2.25	....	....	....	1.85	.55
3885	37¢ Blue Santa Ornament	2.25	....	....	....	1.85	.55
3886	37¢ Red Santa Ornament	2.25	....	....	....	1.85	.55
3886b	same, bklt pane of 20	....	....	....	....	32.00	....
3887	37¢ Purple Santa Ornament, die cut 10¼ x 10¾ . . .	2.25	....	....	....	1.85	.55
3888	37¢ Green Santa Ornament, die cut 10¼ x 10¾ . . .	2.25	....	....	....	1.85	.55
3889	37¢ Blue Santa Ornament, die cut 10¼ x 10¾ . . .	2.25	....	....	....	1.85	.55
3890	37¢ Red Santa Ornament, die cut 10¼ x 10¾ . . .	2.25	....	....	....	1.85	.55
3887-90	37¢ Santa Christmas Ornaments, self-adhesive, 4 attached die cut 10¼ x 10¾.	4.25	....	....	....	7.75	3.50
3890b	same, bklt pane of 4 .	4.25	....	....	....	7.75	....
3890c	same, bklt pane of 6 (3889-90, 3887-88 x 2)	5.50	....	....	....	12.00	....
3890d	same, bklt pane of 6 (3887-88, 3889-90 x 2)	5.50	....	....	....	12.00	....
3891	37¢ Green Santa Ornament, die cut 8 . .	2.25	....	....	....	3.00	1.00
3892	37¢ Purple Santa Ornament, die cut 8 . .	2.25	....	....	....	3.00	1.00
3893	37¢ Red Santa Ornament, die cut 8 . .	2.25	....	....	....	3.00	1.00
3894	37¢ Blue Santa Ornament, die cut 8 . .	2.25	....	....	....	3.00	1.00
3891-94	37¢ Christmas Ornaments, self-adhesive, 4 attached, die cut 8.	4.25	....	....	....	14.00	4.00
3894b	same, bklt pane of 18	15.00	....	....	....	52.00	....

3895

CHINESE NEW YEAR TYPES OF 1992-2004

3895a	*Rat*	**3895g**	*Horse*
3895b	*Ox*	**3895h**	*Ram*
3895c	*Tiger*	**3895i**	*Monkey*
3895d	*Rabbit*	**3895j**	*Rooster*
3895e	*Dragon*	**3895k**	*Dog*
3895f	*Snake*	**3895l**	*Boar*

SCOTT NO.	DESCRIPTION	FIRST DAY COVERS SING	FIRST DAY COVERS PL. BLK.	MINT SHEET	PLATE BLOCK	UNUSED F/NH	USED
3895	37¢ Chinese New Year, self-adhesive, 24 varieties attached .	....	....	30.00(24)	....	30.00	....
....	set of singles	23.50	....	....	....	....	13.00

2005 COMMEMORATIVES

SCOTT NO.	DESCRIPTION	FIRST DAY COVERS SING	FIRST DAY COVERS PL. BLK.	MINT SHEET	PLATE BLOCK	UNUSED F/NH	USED
3896/3964	**(3896-97, 3904-3909, 3911-25, 3930, 3936 3938-43, 3945-52 3961-64) 43 varieties**		....	....	....	**56.00**	**27.00**

3896 3897 3898

SCOTT NO.	DESCRIPTION	FIRST DAY COVERS SING	FIRST DAY COVERS PL. BLK.	MINT SHEET	PLATE BLOCK	UNUSED F/NH	USED
3896	37¢ Marian Anderson, self-adhesive	3.00	4.75	27.00(20)	6.25	1.20	.40
3897	37¢ Ronald Reagan, self-adhesive	3.00	4.75	22.00(20)	5.50	1.35	.40
....	same, uncut sheet of 120	....	....	120.00(120)	....	120.00	....
....	cross gutter block of 4	....	....	....	....	9.50	....
....	horiz. pair with vert. gutter	....	....	....	....	4.00	....
....	vert. pair with horiz. gutter	....	....	....	....	3.00	....
3898	37¢ Love-Hand and Flower Bouquet, self-adhesive	3.00	....	....	....	1.20	.30
3898a	same, bklt pane of 20	....	....	....	....	22.00	....

3899

NORTHEAST DECIDUOUS FOREST

3899a	*Eastern buckmoth*	**3899f**	*Long-tailed weasel*
3899b	*Red-shouldered hawk*	**3899g**	*Wild turkey*
3899c	*Eastern red bat*	**3899h**	*Ovenbird*
3899d	*White-tailed deer*	**3899i**	*Red eft*
3899e	*Black bear*	**3899j**	*Eastern chipmunk*

SCOTT NO.	DESCRIPTION	FIRST DAY COVERS SING	FIRST DAY COVERS PL. BLK.	MINT SHEET	PLATE BLOCK	UNUSED F/NH	USED
3899	37¢ Northeast Deciduous Forest, self-adhesive, 10 varieties attached .	....	....	15.00(10)	....	15.00	....
....	set of singles	25.00	....	....	....	....	7.75

3900 3901 3902 3903

SCOTT NO.	DESCRIPTION	FIRST DAY COVERS SING	FIRST DAY COVERS PL. BLK.	MINT SHEET	PLATE BLOCK	UNUSED F/NH	USED
3900	37¢ Hyacinth	3.00	....	....	....	1.75	.45
3901	37¢ Daffodil	3.00	....	....	....	1.75	.45
3902	37¢ Tulip	3.00	....	....	....	1.75	.45
3903	37¢ Iris.	3.00	....	....	....	1.75	.45
3900-03	37¢ Spring Flowers, self-adhesive, 4 varieties attached . .	4.25	....	....	....	7.00	....
3903b	same, bklt pane of 20	....	....	....	....	32.00	....

3904 3905

SCOTT NO.	DESCRIPTION	FIRST DAY COVERS SING	FIRST DAY COVERS PL. BLK.	MINT SHEET	PLATE BLOCK	UNUSED F/NH	USED
3904	37¢ Robert Penn Warren, self-adhesive	3.00	4.75	22.00(20)	5.50	1.50	.35
3905	37¢ Edgar "Yip" Harburg, self-adhesive	3.00	4.75	22.00(20)	5.50	1.50	.35

3906 3907

3908 3909

SCOTT NO.	DESCRIPTION	FIRST DAY COVERS SING	FIRST DAY COVERS PL. BLK.	MINT SHEET	PLATE BLOCK	UNUSED F/NH	USED
3906-09	37¢ American Scientists, self-adhesive, 4 attached	4.25	4.75	27.00(20)	7.00	6.00	3.50
3906	37¢ Barbara McClintock	3.00	....	....	....	1.50	.60
3907	37¢ Josiah Willard Gibbs	3.00	....	....	....	1.50	.60
3908	37¢ John von Neuman	3.00	....	....	....	1.50	.60
3909	37¢ Richard Feynman	3.00	....	....	....	1.50	.60
....	same, plate blk of 8 with Top Label.	....	....	....	10.00(8)	....	....

3910

MODERN AMERICAN ARCHITECTURE

3910a	*Guggenheim Museum*	**3910g**	*National Gallery of Art*
3910b	*Chrysler Building*	**3910h**	*Glass House*
3910c	*Vanna Venturi House*	**3910i**	*Yale Art and Architecture Bldg.*
3910d	*TWA Terminal*	**3910j**	*High Museum of Atlanta*
3910e	*Walt Disney Concert Hall*	**3910k**	*Exeter Academy Library*
3910f	*860-880 Lake Shore Drive*	**3910l**	*Hancock Center*

SCOTT NO.	DESCRIPTION	FIRST DAY COVERS SING	FIRST DAY COVERS PL. BLK.	MINT SHEET	PLATE BLOCK	UNUSED F/NH	USED
3910	37¢ Modern American Architecture, self-adhesive, 12 varieties attached. .	....	....	15.00(12)	....	15.00	....
....	set of singles	....	....	....	....	....	9.00

SCOTT NO.	DESCRIPTION	FIRST DAY COVERS SING	FIRST DAY COVERS PL. BLK.	MINT SHEET	PLATE BLOCK	UNUSED F/NH	USED

3911

SCOTT NO.	DESCRIPTION	FIRST DAY COVERS SING	FIRST DAY COVERS PL. BLK.	MINT SHEET	PLATE BLOCK	UNUSED F/NH	USED
3911	37¢ Henry Fonda, self-adhesive	3.00	4.75	30.00(20)	8.00	1.50	.50
....	same, uncut sheet of 180	....	....	270.00(180)	....	270.00	....

3912 3913

3914 3915

SCOTT NO.	DESCRIPTION	FIRST DAY COVERS SING	FIRST DAY COVERS PL. BLK.	MINT SHEET	PLATE BLOCK	UNUSED F/NH	USED
3912-15	37¢ Disney Characters, self-adhesive, 4 attached	4.25	4.75	24.00(20)	6.50	6.00	3.50
3912	37¢ Pluto, Mickey Mouse	3.00	....	....	....	1.50	.50
3913	37¢ Mad Hatter, Alice	3.00	....	....	....	1.50	.50
3914	37¢ Flounder, Ariel. . .	3.00	....	....	....	1.50	.50
3915	37¢ Snow White, Dopey	3.00	....	....	....	1.50	.50

3916

3917

3918

3919

3920

3921

3922

3923

3924

3925

ADVANCES IN AVIATION

3916	*Boeing 247*	**3921**	*Lockheed P80 Shooting Star*
3917	*Consolidated PBY Catalina*	**3922**	*Consolidated B24 Liberator*
3918	*Grumman F6F*	**3923**	*Boeing B29 Superfortress*
3919	*Republic P47 Thunderbolt*	**3924**	*Beechcraft 35 Bonanza*
3920	*E & R Corp. Ercoupe 415*	**3925**	*Northrop YB-49 Flying Wing*

SCOTT NO.	DESCRIPTION	FIRST DAY COVERS SING	FIRST DAY COVERS PL. BLK.	MINT SHEET	PLATE BLOCK	UNUSED F/NH	USED
3916-25	37¢ Advances in Aviation, self-adhesive, 10 attached	25.00	....	25.00(20)	16.00(10)	15.00	11.00
....	set of singles	....	....	....	....	15.00	9.00

3926

3927

3928

3929

SCOTT NO.	DESCRIPTION	FIRST DAY COVERS SING	FIRST DAY COVERS PL. BLK.	MINT SHEET	PLATE BLOCK	UNUSED F/NH	USED
3926	37¢ Blanket w/ yellow, orange, and red stripes	3.00	....	....	....	1.50	.85
3927	37¢ Blanket w/ black, orange, red, and yellow	3.00	....	....	....	1.50	.85
3928	37¢ Blanket w/ yellow and black diamonds. .	3.00	....	....	....	1.50	.85
3929	37¢ Blanket w/ zigzag diamonds.	3.00	....	....	....	1.50	.85
3926-29	37¢ Rio Grande Blankets, self-adhesive, 4 attached	4.25	....	....	....	6.50	4.00
3929b	same, bklt pane of 20	15.00	....	....	....	29.00	....

3930

3931

3936

3932

3933

3934

3935

SCOTT NO.	DESCRIPTION	FIRST DAY COVERS SING	FIRST DAY COVERS PL. BLK.	MINT SHEET	PLATE BLOCK	UNUSED F/NH	USED
3930	37¢ Presidential Libraries Act, 50th Anniv., self-adhesive	3.00	4.75	22.00(20)	5.50	1.25	.35
3931	37¢ 1953 Studebaker Starliner.	3.00	....	....	....	1.50	.50
3932	37¢ 1954 Kaiser Darrin	3.00	....	....	....	1.50	.50
3933	37¢ 1953 Chevrolet Corvette	3.00	....	....	....	1.50	.50
3934	37¢ 1952 Nash Healey	3.00	....	....	....	1.50	.50
3935	37¢ 1955 Ford Thunderbird	3.00	....	....	....	1.50	.50
3935b	same, bklt pane of 20	15.00	....	....	....	30.00	....
3936	37¢ Arthur Ashe, self-adhesive	3.00	4.75	22.00(20)	5.50	1.20	.40

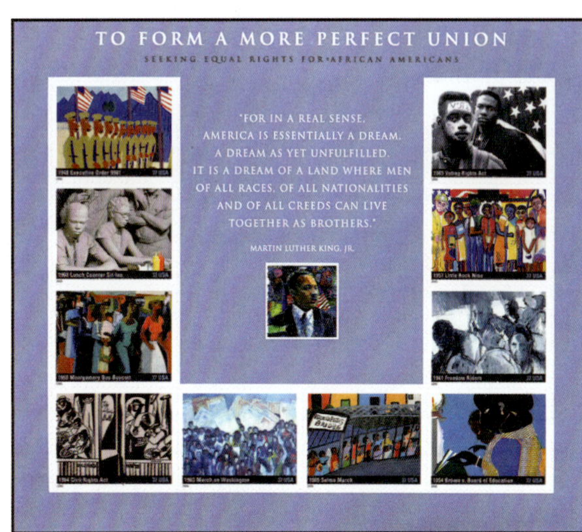

3937

TO FORM A MORE PERFECT UNION

3937a *1948 Executive Order 9981*
3937b *1965 Voting Rights Act*
3937c *1960 Lunch Counter Sit-Ins*
3937d *1957 Little Rock Nine*
3937e *1955 Montgomery Bus Boycott*
3937f *1961 Freedom Riders*
3937g *1964 Civil Rights Act*
3937h *1963 March on Washington*
3937i *1965 Selma March*
3937j *1954 Brown vs. Board of Education*

SCOTT NO.	DESCRIPTION	FIRST DAY COVERS SING	FIRST DAY COVERS PL. BLK.	MINT SHEET	PLATE BLOCK	UNUSED F/NH	USED
3937	37¢ To Form A More Perfect Union, self-adhesive, 10 attached. .	15.00	....	18.00(10)	....	18.00	10.00
....	set of singles	....	....	....	....	18.00	8.75

3938

3939

3943

3940

3941

3942

SCOTT NO.	DESCRIPTION	FIRST DAY COVERS SING	FIRST DAY COVERS PL. BLK.	MINT SHEET	PLATE BLOCK	UNUSED F/NH	USED
3938	37¢ Child Health, self-adhesive	3.00	4.75	24.00(20)	6.00	1.35	.35
3939-42	37¢ Let's Dance, self-adhesive, 4 attached .	4.25	4.75	30.00(20)	14.00	7.50	5.75
3939	37¢ Merengue	3.00	....	....	....	1.75	1.25
3940	37¢ Salsa.	3.00	....	....	....	1.75	1.25
3941	37¢ Cha Cha Cha . . .	3.00	....	....	....	1.75	1.25
3942	37¢ Mambo	3.00	....	....	....	1.75	1.25
3943	37¢ Greta Garbo, self-adhesive	3.00	4.75	22.00(20)	5.50	1.20	1.25

3944

JIM HENSON AND THE MUPPETS

3944a *Kermit the Frog*
3944b *Fozzie Bear*
3944c *Sam the Eagle and flag*
3944d *Miss Piggy*
3944e *Statler and Waldorf*
3944f *The Swedish Chef and fruit*
3944g *Animal*
3944h *Dr. Bunsen Honeydew and Beaker*
3944i *Rowlf the Dog*
3944j *The Great Gonzo and Camilla*
3944k *Jim Henson*

SCOTT NO.	DESCRIPTION	FIRST DAY COVERS SING	FIRST DAY COVERS PL. BLK.	MINT SHEET	PLATE BLOCK	UNUSED F/NH	USED
3944	37¢ Jim Henson and the Muppets, self-adhesive, 11 varieties attached. .	12.00	....	15.00(11)	....	15.00	....
....	set of singles	30.00	....	....	....	15.00	9.00

3945

3946

3947

3948

SCOTT NO.	DESCRIPTION	FIRST DAY COVERS SING	FIRST DAY COVERS PL. BLK.	MINT SHEET	PLATE BLOCK	UNUSED F/NH	USED
3945-48	37¢ Constellations, self-adhesive, 4 attached	4.25	4.75	28.00(20)	6.50	6.00	4.00
3945	37¢ Leo	3.00	....	....	....	1.75	.90
3946	37¢ Orion.	3.00	....	....	....	1.75	.90
3947	37¢ Lyra.	3.00	....	....	....	1.75	.90
3948	37¢ Pegasus	3.00	....	....	....	1.75	.90

3949, 3953, 3957

3950, 3954, 3958

3951, 3955, 3959

3952, 3956, 3960

SCOTT NO.	DESCRIPTION	FIRST DAY COVERS SING	FIRST DAY COVERS PL. BLK.	MINT SHEET	PLATE BLOCK	UNUSED F/NH	USED
3949-52	37¢ Christmas Cookies, self-adhesive, 4 attached	4.25	4.75	28.00(20)	6.75	6.00	4.00
3949	37¢ Santa Claus cookie	3.00	....	....	....	1.50	.55
3950	37¢ Snowmen cookies	3.00	....	....	....	1.50	.55
3951	37¢ Angel cookie	3.00	....	....	....	1.50	.55
3952	37¢ Elves cookies . . .	3.00	....	....	....	1.50	.55
3953	37¢ Santa Claus cookie, die cut 10¾ x 11	3.00	....	....	....	1.75	.60
3954	37¢ Snowmen cookies, die cut 10¾ x 11	3.00	....	....	....	1.75	.60
3955	37¢ Angel cookie, die cut 10¾ x 11	3.00	....	....	....	1.75	.60
3956	37¢ Elves cookies, die cut 10¾ x 11	3.00	....	....	....	1.75	.60
3953-56	37¢ Christmas cookies, self-adhesive, 4 attached, die cut 10¾ x 11	4.25	....	....	....	7.50	4.00
3956b	same, bklt pane of 20	....	....	....	....	38.00	....

SCOTT NO.	DESCRIPTION	FIRST DAY COVERS SING	FIRST DAY COVERS PL. BLK.	MINT SHEET	PLATE BLOCK	UNUSED F/NH	USED
3957	37¢ Santa Claus cookie, die cut 10½ x 10¾ . . .	3.00	....	....	....	2.00	1.00
3958	37¢ Snowmen cookies, die cut 10½ x 10¾ . . .	3.00	....	....	....	2.00	1.00
3959	37¢ Angel cookie, die cut 10½ x 10¾ . . .	3.00	....	....	....	2.00	1.00
3960	37¢ Elves cookies, die cut 10½ x 10¾ . . .	3.00	....	....	....	2.00	1.00
3957-60	37¢ Christmas Cookies, self-adhesvie, 4 attached die cut 10½ x 10¾ . . .	4.25	....	....	....	8.50	5.50
3960b	same, booklet pane of 4	4.25	....	....	....	8.50	....
3960c	same, bklt pane of 6 (3959-60, 3957-58 x2)	5.50	....	....	....	14.00	....
3960d	same, bklt pane of 6 (3957-58, 3959-60 x2)	5.50	....	....	....	14.00	....

3961 3962

3963 3964

SCOTT NO.	DESCRIPTION	FIRST DAY COVERS SING	FIRST DAY COVERS PL. BLK.	MINT SHEET	PLATE BLOCK	UNUSED F/NH	USED
3961-64	37¢ Distinguished Marines, self-adhesive, 4 attached	4.25	4.75	28.00(20)	6.50	6.00	5.00
....	same, plate block of 8	....	....	....	12.00(8)	....	....
3961	37¢ Lt. General John A. Lejeune.	3.00	....	....	....	1.50	1.05
3962	37¢ Lt. General Lewis B. Puller.	3.00	....	....	....	1.50	1.05
3963	37¢ Sgt. John Basilone	3.00	....	....	....	1.50	1.05
3964	37¢ Sgt. Major Daniel J. Daly	3.00	....	....	....	1.50	1.05

3965-3975

3976

3978-3983, 3985

SCOTT NO.	DESCRIPTION	FIRST DAY COVERS SING	FIRST DAY COVERS PL. BLK.	MINT SHEET	PLATE BLOCK	UNUSED F/NH	USED
3965	(39¢) Flag and Statue of Liberty	3.00	4.75	120.00(100)	18.00	1.50	1.00
3966	(39¢) Flag and Statue of Liberty, self-adhesive	3.00	4.75	24.00(20)	7.00	1.50	.40
3966a	same, bklt pane of 20	16.00	....	....	....	30.00	....
3967	(39¢) Flag and Statue of Liberty, coil, die cut 9¾	3.00	....	....	....	1.50	.70
....	same, pl# strip of 5 . .	....	....	....	....	12.00	....
3968	(39¢) Flag and Statue of Liberty, self-adhesive coil, die cut 8½.	3.00	....	....	....	1.50	.35
....	same, pl# strip of 5 . .	....	....	....	....	13.00	....
3969	(39¢) Flag and Statue of Liberty, coil, die cut 10¼	3.00	....	....	....	2.00	.35
....	same, pl# strip of 5 . .	....	....	....	....	14.00	....
3970	(39¢) Flag and Statue of Liberty, self-adhesive coil, die cut 9½.	3.00	....	....	....	3.00	.35
....	same, pl# strip of 5 . .	....	....	....	....	18.00	....
3972	(39¢) Flag and Statue of Liberty, self-adhesive die cut 11¼ x 10¾ . . .	3.00	....	....	....	1.50	.35
3972a	same, bklt pane of 20	16.00	....	....	....	26.00	....
3973	(39¢) Flag and Statue of Liberty, self-adhesive die cut 10¼ x 10¾. . .	3.00	....	....	....	1.50	.25
3973a	same, bklt pane of 20	16.00	....	....	....	26.00	....
3974	(39¢) Flag and Statue of Liberty, self-adhesive die cut 11¼ X 10¾. . .	3.00	....	....	....	1.80	.70
3974a	same, bklt pane of 4. .	4.50	....	....	....	8.00	....
3974b	same, bklt pane of 6 .	6.00	....	....	....	12.00	....

SCOTT NO.	DESCRIPTION	FIRST DAY COVERS SING	FIRST DAY COVERS PL. BLK.	MINT SHEET	PLATE BLOCK	UNUSED F/NH	USED
3975	(39¢) Flag and Statue of Liberty, self-adhesive die cut 8.	3.00	....	....	....	1.55	.35
....	same, bklt pane of 18	16.00	....	....	....	32.00	....
3976	(39¢) Birds	3.00	....	....	....	1.60	.35
3976a	same, bklt pane of 20	30.00	....	....	....	31.00	....
3978	39¢ Flag and Statue of Liberty, self-adhesive die cut 11¼ x 10¾ . . .	3.00	4.75	26.00(20)	6.50	1.50	.35
3978a	same, bklt pane of 10	....	....	....	....	15.00	....
3978b	same, bklt pane of 20	....	....	....	....	32.00	....
3979	39¢ Flag and Statue of Liberty, coil, perf 10	3.00	....	....	....	1.50	.40
....	same, pl# strip of 5	....	....	....	....	9.00	....
3980	same, self-adhesive coil, die cut 11	3.00	....	....	....	1.50	.90
....	same, pl# strip of 5 . .	....	....	....	....	9.50	....
3981	same, self-adhesive coil w/ USPS micro die cut 9½	3.00	....	....	....	2.00	.45
....	same, pl# strip of 5 . .	....	....	....	....	12.00	....
3982	same, self-adhesive coil, die cut 10¼ vertical . .	3.00	....	....	....	1.50	.40
....	same, pl# strip of 5 . .	....	....	....	....	10.00	....
3983	same, self-adhesive coil, die cut 8½	3.00	....	....	....	1.50	.45
....	same, pl# strip of 5 . .	....	....	....	....	10.00	....
3985	39¢ Flag and Statue of Liberty, self-adhesive, die cut 11¼ x 10¾ on 2 or 3 sides. .	3.00	....	....	....	1.50	.50
3985a	same, bklt pane of 20	....	....	....	....	26.00	....
3985b	same, die cut 11.1 on 2 or 3	3.00	....	....	....	1.50	.75
3985c	same, bklt pane of 4 .	....	....	....	....	6.00	....
3985d	same, bklt pane of 6 .	....	....	....	....	8.50	....

2006 COMMEMORATIVES

SCOTT NO.	DESCRIPTION	FIRST DAY COVERS SING	FIRST DAY COVERS PL. BLK.	MINT SHEET	PLATE BLOCK	UNUSED F/NH	USED
3987/4119	**(3987-96, 4020, 4021-28, 4030-32, 4073, 4077-83 4085-88, 4101-04 4117-19) 41 varieties**		....	....	....	**60.00**	**20.00**

3987 3988 3989 3990

3991 3992 3993 3994

FAVORITE CHILDREN'S BOOK ANIMALS

3987	*The Very Hungry Caterpillar*	**3991**	*Wild Thing*
3988	*Wilbur*	**3992**	*Curious George*
3989	*Fox in Socks*	**3993**	*Olivia*
3990	*Maisy*	**3994**	*Frederick*

SCOTT NO.	DESCRIPTION	FIRST DAY COVERS SING	FIRST DAY COVERS PL. BLK.	MINT SHEET	PLATE BLOCK	UNUSED F/NH	USED
3987-94	39¢ Children's Book Animals, self-adhesive 8 attached	10.00	....	25.00(16)	14.00(8)	12.50	10.00
....	set of singles	....	....	....	....	....	5.50
....	same, uncut sheet of 96	....	....	90.00(96)	....	90.00	....
....	cross gutter block of 8	....	....	....	....	17.50	....
....	blk of 8 w/ horiz. gutter	....	....	....	....	10.00	....
....	blk of 8 w/ vert. gutter	....	....	....	....	9.00	....
....	horz. pair w/ vert. gutter	....	....	....	....	2.50	....
....	vert. pair w/ horz. gutter	....	....	....	....	2.50	....

3995

3996

SCOTT NO.	DESCRIPTION	FIRST DAY COVERS SING	FIRST DAY COVERS PL. BLK.	MINT SHEET	PLATE BLOCK	UNUSED F/NH	USED
3995	39¢ 2006 Winter Olympic games, Turin, Italy, self-adhesive	3.00	4.75	24.00(20)	6.00	1.35	.40
3996	39¢ Hattie McDaniel, self-adhesive	3.00	4.75	25.00(20)	6.50	1.60	.40

SCOTT NO.	DESCRIPTION	FIRST DAY COVERS SING	PL. BLK.	MINT SHEET	PLATE BLOCK	UNUSED F/NH	USED

CHINESE NEW YEAR TYPES OF 1992-2004

3997a	*Rat*	**3997g**	*Horse*
3997b	*Ox*	**3997h**	*Ram*
3997c	*Tiger*	**3997i**	*Monkey*
3997d	*Rabbit*	**3997j**	*Rooster*
3997e	*Dragon*	**3997k**	*Dog*
3997f	*Snake*	**3997l**	*Boar*

SCOTT NO.	DESCRIPTION	FIRST DAY COVERS SING	PL. BLK.	MINT SHEET	PLATE BLOCK	UNUSED F/NH	USED
3997	39¢ Chinese New Year self-adhesive, 12 varieties attached . . .	....	....	20.00(12)	....	20.00	....
....	same, set of singles. .	32.00	....	....	....	20.00	10.00

3998 | 4000, 4001, 4002 | 3999

SCOTT NO.	DESCRIPTION	FIRST DAY COVERS SING	PL. BLK.	MINT SHEET	PLATE BLOCK	UNUSED F/NH	USED
3998	39¢ Wedding Doves, Dove Facing Left, self-adhesive	3.00	....	....	....	1.50	.35
3998a	same, bklt pane of 20	16.00	....	....	....	26.00	....
3999	63¢ Wedding Doves, Dove Facing Right, self-adhesive	3.00	....	....	....	3.00	1.80
3999a	same, bklt pane of 40	....	....	....	....	65.00	....
4000	24¢ Common Buckeye butterfly	3.00	4.75	77.00(100)	14.00	.90	.65
4001	24¢ Common Buckeye butterfly self-adhesive, die cut 11	3.00	4.75	15.00(20)	5.00	.90	.35
4001a	same, single from bklt. pane, die cut 10¾ x 11¼	3.00	....	....	....	.85	.35
4001b	same, bklt pane of 10 (4001a)	....	....	....	....	8.50	....
4001c	same, bklt pane of 4 (4001a)	....	....	....	....	3.50	....
4001d	same, bklt pane of 6 (4001a)	....	....	....	....	5.00	....
4002	24¢ Common Buckeye butterfly, self-adhesive, coil, die cut 8½.	3.00	....	....	....	.85	.30
....	same, pl# strip of 5 . .	....	....	....	....	6.00	....

4003, 4012, 4013 | 4004, 4011, 4017 | 4005, 4010, 4016

4006, 4009, 4015 | 4007, 4008, 4014

SCOTT NO.	DESCRIPTION	FIRST DAY COVERS SING	PL. BLK.	MINT SHEET	PLATE BLOCK	UNUSED F/NH	USED
4003	39¢ Chili Peppers, self-adhesive, coil . . .	3.00	....	....	....	2.50	.60
4004	39¢ Beans, self-adhesive, coil	3.00	....	....	....	2.50	.60
4005	39¢ Sunflower and Seeds self-adhesive, coil . . .	3.00	....	....	....	2.50	.60
4006	39¢ Squashes, self-adhesive, coil	3.00	....	....	....	2.50	.60
4007	39¢ Corn, self-adhesive, coil	3.00	....	....	....	2.50	.60
4003-07	39¢ Crops of the Americas, coil, strip of 5	5.00	....	....	....	14.00	3.50
....	same, pl# strip of 5 . .	....	....	....	....	16.00	....
....	same, pl# strip of 11 .	....	....	....	....	30.00	....
4008	39¢ Corn, self-adhesive bklt single, die cut 10¾ x 10½.	3.00	....	....	....	2.25	.40
4009	39¢ Squashes, self-adhesive, bklt single die cut 10¾ x 10½ . . .	3.00	....	....	....	2.25	.40
4010	39¢ Sunflower and Seeds self-adhesive, bklt single, die cut 10¾ x 10½ . . .	3.00	....	....	....	2.25	.40
4011	39¢ Beans, self-adhesive bklt single, die cut 10¾ x 10½.	3.00	....	....	....	2.25	.40
4012	39¢ Chili Peppers, self-adhesive, bklt single, die cut 10¾ x 10½ . . .	3.00	....	....	....	2.25	.40
4012b	same, bklt pane of 20	....	....	....	....	34.00	....
4013	39¢ Chili Peppers, self-adhesive, bklt single, die cut 10¾ x 11¼ . . .	3.00	....	....	....	1.65	.75
4014	39¢ Corn, self-adhesive bklt single, die cut 10¾ x 11¼.	3.00	....	....	....	1.65	.75
4015	39¢ Squashes, self-adhesive, bklt single die cut 10¾ x 11¼ . . .	3.00	....	....	....	1.65	.75
4016	39¢ Sunflower and Seeds self-adhesive, bklt single, die cut 10¾ x 11¼ . . .	3.00	....	....	....	1.65	.75
4016a	same, bklt pane of 4 .	....	....	....	....	6.00	....
4017	39¢ Beans, self-adhesive bklt single, die cut 10¾ x 11¼.	3.00	....	....	....	1.65	.75
4017b	same, bklt pane of 4 .	....	....	....	....	6.00	....
4017c	same, bklt pane of 6 (4013-16, 4017 x2) . .	....	....	....	....	13.00	....
4017d	same, bklt pane of 6 (4013-15, 4017, 4016 x2)	....	....	....	....	13.00	....

4018 | 4020 | 4019

SCOTT NO.	DESCRIPTION	FIRST DAY COVERS SING	PL. BLK.	MINT SHEET	PLATE BLOCK	UNUSED F/NH	USED
4018	$4.05 X-Plane, self-adhesive	9.00	25.00	205.00(20)	50.00	12.00	8.00
4019	$14.40 X-Plane, self-adhesive	30.00	75.00	690.00(20)	180.00	41.00	30.00
4020	39¢ Sugar Ray Robinson, self-adhesive	3.00	4.75	23.00(20)	5.50	1.25	.50

4021 | 4022 | 4023 | 4024

SCOTT NO.	DESCRIPTION	FIRST DAY COVERS SING	PL. BLK.	MINT SHEET	PLATE BLOCK	UNUSED F/NH	USED
4021-24	39¢ Benjamin Franklin (1706-90), self-adhesive 4 attached	4.25	4.75	38.00(20)	10.00	8.50	....
4021	39¢ Benjamin Franklin Statesman	3.00	....	....	....	2.00	1.10
4022	39¢ Benjamin Franklin Scientist.	3.00	....	....	....	2.00	1.10
4023	39¢ Benjamin Franklin Printer	3.00	....	....	....	2.00	1.10
4024	39¢ Benjamin Franklin Postmaster	3.00	....	....	....	2.00	1.10

4025 | 4026 | 4027 | 4028

SCOTT NO.	DESCRIPTION	FIRST DAY COVERS SING	PL. BLK.	MINT SHEET	PLATE BLOCK	UNUSED F/NH	USED
4025-28	39¢ Disney Characters, self-adhesive, 4 attached	4.25	4.75	25.00(20)	6.50	6.00	....

SCOTT NO.	DESCRIPTION	FIRST DAY COVERS SING	FIRST DAY COVERS PL. BLK.	MINT SHEET	PLATE BLOCK	UNUSED F/NH	USED
4025	39¢ Mickey and Minnie Mouse	3.00	....	....	....	1.30	.50
4026	39¢ Cinderella and Prince Charming	3.00	....	....	....	1.30	.50
4027	39¢ Beauty and the Beast	3.00	....	....	....	1.30	.50
4028	39¢ Lady and the Tramp	3.00	....	....	....	1.30	.50

4029

4030

SCOTT NO.	DESCRIPTION	FIRST DAY COVERS SING	FIRST DAY COVERS PL. BLK.	MINT SHEET	PLATE BLOCK	UNUSED F/NH	USED
4029	39¢ Lovebirds, self-adhesive	3.00	....	....	....	1.50	.35
4029a	same, bklt pane of 20	....	....	....	....	32.00	....
4030	39¢ Katherine Anne Porter self-adhesive	3.00	4.75	24.00(20)	5.75	1.50	.35

4031

4032

SCOTT NO.	DESCRIPTION	FIRST DAY COVERS SING	FIRST DAY COVERS PL. BLK.	MINT SHEET	PLATE BLOCK	UNUSED F/NH	USED
4031	39¢ Amber Alert, self-adhesive	3.00	4.75	24.00(20)	5.75	1.50	.40
4032	39¢ Purple Heart, self-adhesive	3.00	4.75	24.00(20)	5.75	1.50	.35

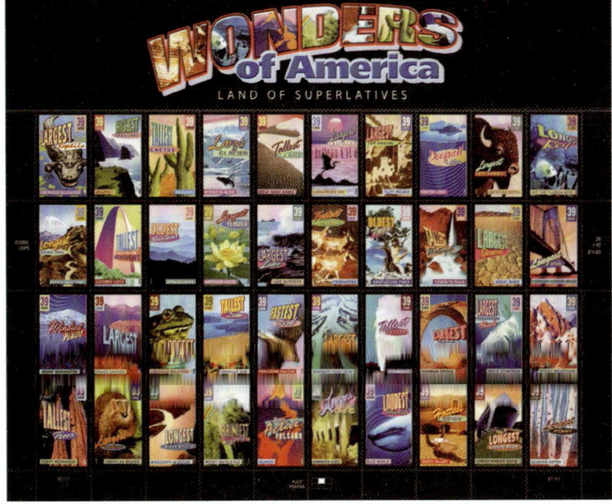

4033-4072

WONDERS OF AMERICA

4033	*American Alligator*	**4053**	*Mount Washington*
4034	*Moloka'i*	**4054**	*Grand Canyon*
4035	*Saguaro*	**4055**	*American Bullfrog*
4036	*Bering Glacier*	**4056**	*Oroville Dam*
4037	*Great Sand Dunes*	**4057**	*Peregrine Falcon*
4038	*Chesapeake Bay*	**4058**	*Mississippi River Delta*
4039	*Cliff Palace*	**4059**	*Steamboat Geyser*
4040	*Crater Lake*	**4060**	*Rainbow Bridge*
4041	*American Bison*	**4061**	*White Sturgeon*
4042	*Off the Florida Keys*	**4062**	*Rocky Mountains*
4043	*Pacific Crest Trail*	**4063**	*Coast Redwoods*
4044	*Gateway Arch*	**4064**	*American Beaver*
4045	*Appalachians*	**4065**	*Mississippi-Missouri*
4046	*American Lotus*	**4066**	*Mount Wai'ale'ale*
4047	*Lake Superior*	**4067**	*Kilauea*
4048	*Pronghorn*	**4068**	*Mammoth Cave*
4049	*Bristlecone Pines*	**4069**	*Blue Whale*
4050	*Yosemite Falls*	**4070**	*Death Valley*
4051	*Great Basin*	**4071**	*Cornish-Windsor Bridge*
4052	*Verrazano-Narrows Bridge*	**4072**	*Quaking Aspen*

SCOTT NO.	DESCRIPTION	FIRST DAY COVERS SING	FIRST DAY COVERS PL. BLK.	MINT SHEET	PLATE BLOCK	UNUSED F/NH	USED
4033-72	39¢ Wonders of America, self-adhesive, 40 attached	....	....	40.00(40)	....	40.00	....
....	same, set of singles. .	....	....	....	....	40.00	34.00

4073, 4074a

SCOTT NO.	DESCRIPTION	FIRST DAY COVERS SING	FIRST DAY COVERS PL. BLK.	MINT SHEET	PLATE BLOCK	UNUSED F/NH	USED
4073	39¢ Samuel de Champlain, self-adhesive	3.00	4.75	24.00(20)	6.00	1.40	.50
4074	39¢ Samuel de Champlain, souvenir sheet of 4 (joint issue,4074a x 2 and Canada 2156a x 2)	....	....	....	....	12.00	....
4074a	same, single from s/s .	....	....	....	....	2.50	1.60

4075

SCOTT NO.	DESCRIPTION	FIRST DAY COVERS SING	FIRST DAY COVERS PL. BLK.	MINT SHEET	PLATE BLOCK	UNUSED F/NH	USED
4075	$1-$5 Washington 2006 World Exhibition, souvenir sheet of 3 . .	....	....	....	....	27.00	....
4075a	$1 Lincoln Memorial .	4.50	....	....	....	4.00	2.00
4075b	$2 U.S. Capitol	7.50	....	....	....	7.00	4.00
4075c	$5 "America"	15.00	....	....	....	17.00	10.00

4076

SCOTT NO.	DESCRIPTION	FIRST DAY COVERS SING	FIRST DAY COVERS PL. BLK.	MINT SHEET	PLATE BLOCK	UNUSED F/NH	USED
4076	39¢ Distinguished American Diplomats, self-adhesive, souvenir sheet of 6 . .	15.00	....	....	....	12.00	....
4076a	39¢ Robert D. Murphy	3.00	....	....	....	2.00	1.25
4076b	39¢ Frances E. Willis.	3.00	....	....	....	2.00	1.25
4076c	39¢ Hiram Bingham IV	3.00	....	....	....	2.00	1.25
4076d	39¢ Philip C. Habib . .	3.00	....	....	....	2.00	1.25
4076e	39¢ Charles E. Bohlen	3.00	....	....	....	2.00	1.25
4076f	39¢ Clifton R. Wharton Sr.	3.00	....	....	....	2.00	1.25

4077

4078

4079

SCOTT NO.	DESCRIPTION	FIRST DAY COVERS SING	FIRST DAY COVERS PL. BLK.	MINT SHEET	PLATE BLOCK	UNUSED F/NH	USED
4077	39¢ Judy Garland, self-adhesive	3.00	4.75	32.00(20)	7.50	1.75	.50
....	same, uncut sheet of 120	....	....	120.00(120)	....	120.00	....
....	block of 8 with vert. gutter	....	....	....	....	10.50	....
....	cross gutter block of 8	....	....	....	....	18.00	....
....	horiz. pair with vert. gutter	....	....	....	....	4.00	....
....	vert. pair with horiz. gutter	....	....	....	....	3.00	....
4078	39¢ Ronald Reagan, self-adhesive	3.00	4.75	30.00(20)	7.00	1.75	.45
4079	39¢ Happy Birthday, Self-adhesive.	3.00	4.75	24.00(20)	6.00	1.50	.50

4080 4081

4082 4083

SCOTT NO.	DESCRIPTION	FIRST DAY COVERS SING	FIRST DAY COVERS PL. BLK.	MINT SHEET	PLATE BLOCK	UNUSED F/NH	USED
4080-83	39¢ Baseball Sluggers, self-adhesive, 4 attached	4.25	4.75	24.00(20)	6.50	6.00	....
4080	39¢ Roy Campanella.	3.00	....	....	....	1.60	.55
4081	39¢ Hank Greenberg.	3.00	....	....	....	1.60	.55
4082	39¢ Mel Ott	3.00	....	....	....	1.60	.55
4083	39¢ Mickey Mantle. . .	3.00	....	....	....	1.60	.55
....	same, uncut sheet of 120	....	....	120.00(120)	....	120.00	....
....	cross gutter blk of 8 . .	....	....	....	....	18.00	....
....	blk of 8 with vert. gutter	....	....	....	....	10.50	....
....	horz. pair with vert. gutter	....	....	....	....	4.00	....
....	vert. pair with horz. gutter	....	....	....	....	4.00	....

4084

D.C. COMICS SUPER HEROES

4084a *Superman*
4084b *Green Lantern*
4084c *Wonder Woman*
4084d *Green Arrow*
4084e *Batman*
4084f *The Flash*
4084g *Plastic Man*
4084h *Aquaman*
4084i *Supergirl*
4084j *Hawkman*
4084k *Superman Cover*
4084l *Green Lantern Cover*
4084m *Wonder Woman Cover*
4084n *Green Arrow Cover*
4084o *Batman Cover*
4084p *The Flash Cover*
4084q *Plastic Man Cover*
4084r *Aquaman Cover*
4084s *Supergirl Cover*
4084t *Hawkman Cover*

SCOTT NO.	DESCRIPTION	FIRST DAY COVERS SING	FIRST DAY COVERS PL. BLK.	MINT SHEET	PLATE BLOCK	UNUSED F/NH	USED
4084	39¢ D.C. Comics Super Heroes, self-adhesive, 20 varieties attached .	....	....	28.00(20)	....	28.00	....
....	same, uncut sheet of 80	....	....	75.00(80)	....	75.00	....
....	cross gutter block of 20	....	....	....	....	25.00	....
....	horz. pair w/ vert. gutter	....	....	....	....	4.00	....
....	vert. pair w/ horz. gutter	....	....	....	....	4.00	....
....	set of singles	....	....	....	....	....	16.00

4085 4086

4087 4088

SCOTT NO.	DESCRIPTION	FIRST DAY COVERS SING	FIRST DAY COVERS PL. BLK.	MINT SHEET	PLATE BLOCK	UNUSED F/NH	USED
4085-88	39¢ Motorcycles, self-adhesive, 4 attached .	4.25	4.75	30.00(20)	7.75	6.50	....
4085	39¢ 1940 Indian Four	3.00	....	....	....	1.75	.60
4086	39¢ 1918 Cleveland. .	3.00	....	....	....	1.75	.60
4087	39¢ 1970 Chopper. . .	3.00	....	....	....	1.75	.60
4088	39¢ 1965 Harley Davidson Electra-Glide	3.00	....	....	....	1.75	.60

4089 4090 4091 4092

4093 4094 4095 4096

4097 4098

SCOTT NO.	DESCRIPTION	FIRST DAY COVERS SING	FIRST DAY COVERS PL. BLK.	MINT SHEET	PLATE BLOCK	UNUSED F/NH	USED
4089-98	39¢ Quilts of Gee's Bend, Alabama, self-adhesive, 10 attached	....	....	....	....	17.00	....
4089	39¢ House Variation by Mary Lee Bendolph . .	3.00	....	....	....	1.75	.85
4090	39¢ Pig in a Pen Medallion by Minnie Sue Coleman	3.00	....	....	....	1.75	.85
4091	39¢ Nine Patch by Ruth P. Mosely.	3.00	....	....	....	1.75	.85
4092	39¢ Housetop Four Block Half Log Cabin by Lottie Mooney	3.00	....	....	....	1.75	.85
4093	39¢ Roman Stripes Variation by Loretta Pettway. . .	3.00	....	....	....	1.75	.85
4094	39¢ Chinese Coins Variation by Arlonzia Pettway . .	3.00	....	....	....	1.75	.85
4095	39¢ Blocks and Stripes by Annie Mae Young . . .	3.00	....	....	....	1.75	.85
4096	39¢ Medallion by Loretta Pettway	3.00	....	....	....	1.75	.85
4097	39¢ Bars and String-pierced Columns by Jessie T. Pettway	3.00	....	....	....	1.75	.85
4098	39¢ Medallion with Checkerboard Center by Patty Ann Williams	3.00	....	....	....	1.75	.85
4098b	same, bklt pane of 20 (4089-4098 x 2)	....	....	....	....	30.00	....

4099

SOUTHERN FLORIDA WETLANDS

4099a *Snail Kite*
4099b *Wood Storks*
4099c *Florida Panther*
4099d *Bald Eagle*
4099e *American Crocodile*
4099f *Roseate Spoonbills*
4099g *Everglades Mink*
4099h *Cape Sable Seaside Sparrow*
4099i *American Alligator*
4099j *White Ibis*

SCOTT NO.	DESCRIPTION	FIRST DAY COVERS SING	FIRST DAY COVERS PL. BLK.	MINT SHEET	PLATE BLOCK	UNUSED F/NH	USED
4099	39¢ Southern Florida Wetlands, self-adhesive, 10 attached	....	....	15.00(10)	....	15.00	....
....	set of singles	20.00	....	....	....	15.00	8.50

SCOTT NO.	DESCRIPTION	FIRST DAY COVERS SING	FIRST DAY COVERS PL. BLK.	MINT SHEET	PLATE BLOCK	UNUSED F/NH	USED

4100

SCOTT NO.	DESCRIPTION	FIRST DAY COVERS SING	FIRST DAY COVERS PL. BLK.	MINT SHEET	PLATE BLOCK	UNUSED F/NH	USED
4100	39¢ Madonna and Child, self-adhesive	3.00	....	....	....	1.50	.40
4100a	same, bklt pane of 20	....	....	....	....	28.00	....

4103, 4107, 4111, 4114

4102, 4106, 4110, 4115

4101, 4105, 4109, 4113

4104, 4108, 4112, 4116

SCOTT NO.	DESCRIPTION	FIRST DAY COVERS SING	FIRST DAY COVERS PL. BLK.	MINT SHEET	PLATE BLOCK	UNUSED F/NH	USED
4101-04	39¢ Snowflakes, self-adhesive, die cut 11¼ x 11, 4 attached	4.25	4.75	30.00(20)	7.50	6.00	....
4101	39¢ Spindly Arms and Branches	3.00	....	....	....	[illegible]	[illegible]
4102	39¢ Leafy Arms	3.00	....	....	....	1.50	.50
4103	39¢ Large Center. . . .	3.00	....	....	....	1.50	.50
4104	39¢ Arms w/ Wide Centers	3.00	....	....	....	1.50	.50
4105-08	39¢ Snowflakes, self-adhesive, die cut 11¼ x 11½, 4 attached	4.25	....	....	....	8.50	....
4105	39¢ Spindly Arms and Branches	3.00	....	....	....	1.75	.50
4106	39¢ Leafy Arms	3.00	....	....	....	1.75	.50
4107	39¢ Large Center. . . .	3.00	....	....	....	1.75	.50
4108	39¢ Arms w/ Wide Centers	3.00	....	....	....	1.75	.50
4108b	same, bklt pane of 20 (4105-08 x 5)	....	....	....	....	32.00	....
4109-12	39¢ Snowflakes, self-adhesive, die cut 11¼ x 10¾, 4 attached	4.25	....	....	....	7.50	....
4109	39¢ Spindly Arms and Branches	3.00	....	....	....	1.75	1.25
4110	39¢ Leafy Arms	3.00	....	....	....	1.75	1.25
4111	39¢ Large Center. . . .	3.00	....	....	....	1.75	1.25
4112	39¢ Arms w/ Wide Centers	3.00	....	....	....	1.75	1.25
4112b	same, bklt pane of 4 (4109-12)........	....	....	....	....	8.00	....
4112c	same, bklt pane of 6 (4111-4112, 4109-4110 x 2).	....	....	....	....	12.00	....
4112d	same, bklt pane of 6 (4109-4110, 4111-4112 x 2). .	....	....	....	....	12.00	....
4113-16	39¢ Snowflakes, die cut 8, self-adhesive, 4 attached	4.25	....	....	....	9.00	....
4113	39¢ Spindly Arms and Branches	3.00			....	[illegible]	[illegible]
4114	39¢ Large Center	3.00	....	....	....	2.00	1.75
[illegible]	[illegible]	[illegible]				[illegible]	[illegible]
4116	39¢ Arms w/ Wide Centers	3.00				2.00	1.75
4116b	same, bklt pane of 18 (4113 x 5, 4114 x 4, 4115 x 5, 4116 x 4)	....	....	....	....	30.00	....

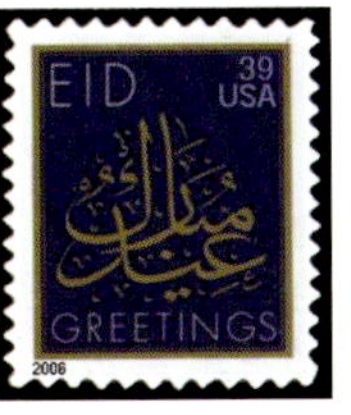

4117

4119

4118

SCOTT NO.	DESCRIPTION	FIRST DAY COVERS SING	FIRST DAY COVERS PL. BLK.	MINT SHEET	PLATE BLOCK	UNUSED F/NH	USED
4117	39¢ EID, self-adhesive	3.00	4.75	22.00(20)	5.50	1.50	.85
4118	39¢ Hanukkah-Dreidel, self-adhesive	3.00	4.75	22.00(20)	5.50	1.50	.40
4119	39¢ Kwanzaa-People self-adhesive	3.00	4.75	22.00(20)	5.50	1.50	.40

2007 COMMEMORATIVES

SCOTT NO.	DESCRIPTION	FIRST DAY COVERS SING	FIRST DAY COVERS PL. BLK.	MINT SHEET	PLATE BLOCK	UNUSED F/NH	USED
4120/4220	(4120, 4121, 4124, 4136, 4146-4150, 4160-4163, 4192-4197, 4199-4205, 4207-4210, 4219, 4220) 32 varieties	....	....	....		44.00	15.00

4120

4121

4122

SCOTT NO.	DESCRIPTION	FIRST DAY COVERS SING	FIRST DAY COVERS PL. BLK.	MINT SHEET	PLATE BLOCK	UNUSED F/NH	USED
4120	39¢ Ella Fitzgerald, self-adhesive	3.00	4.75	22.00(20)	5.50	1.50	.40
4121	39¢ Oklahoma Statehood self-adhesive	3.00	4.75	22.00(20)	5.50	1.50	.40
4122	39¢ Hershey's Kiss, self-adhesive	3.00	4.75	28.00(20)	....	1.50	.40
4122a	same, bklt pane of 20	....	....	....	....	28.00	....

4123

SCOTT NO.	DESCRIPTION	FIRST DAY COVERS SING	FIRST DAY COVERS PL. BLK.	MINT SHEET	PLATE BLOCK	UNUSED F/NH	USED
4123	84¢ International Polar Year, self-adhesive, souvenir sheet of 2 . .	....	....	....	....	8.00	....
4123a	84¢ Aurora Borealis . .	4.00	....	....	....	5.00	2.50
4123b	84¢ Aurora Australis .	4.00	....	....	....	5.00	2.50

4124

4125, 4126, 4127, 4128, 4437

4129, 4130, 4132, 4133, 4134, 4135

SCOTT NO.	DESCRIPTION	FIRST DAY COVERS SING	FIRST DAY COVERS PL. BLK.	MINT SHEET	PLATE BLOCK	UNUSED F/NH	USED
4124	39¢ Henry Wadsworth Longfellow, self-adhesive	3.00	4.75	21.00(20)	5.50	1.50	.40
4125	(41¢) Forever Liberty Bell, self-adhesive, large micro print	3.50	....	....	....	1.50	.35
4125a	same, bklt pane of 20	....	....	....	....	27.00	....
4125b	(42¢) Forever, Liberty Bell, large microprint, bell 16mm wide dated 2008	3.50	....	....	....	1.50	.35
4125c	same, bklt pane of 20	....	....	....	....	27.00	....
4125f	(44¢) Forever, dated 2009, large micro, bell 16mm wide	....	....	....	....	1.50	.45
4125g	same, booklet pane of 20	....	....	....	....	27.00	....
4126	(41¢) Forever, Liberty Bell, self-adhesive, small micro print	3.50	....	....	....	1.50	.35
4126a	same, bklt pane of 20	....	....	....	....	27.00	....
4126b	(42¢) Forever, Liberty Bell, small microprint, bell 16mm wide dated 2008	3.50	....	....	....	1.50	.45
4126c	same, bklt pane of 20	....	....	....	....	27.00	....
4126d	(44¢) Forever, dated 2009, small micro, bell 16mm wide	....	....	....	....	1.50	.45
4126e	same, booklet pane of 20	....	....	....	....	27.00	....
4127	(41¢) Forever Liberty Bell, self-adhesive, medium micro print	3.50	....	....	....	2.00	.35
4127a	same, bklt pane of 20	....	....	....	....	38.00	....
....	solid tagging	....	....	....	....	160.00	....
4127b	same, bklt pane of 4 .	....	....	....	....	5.25	....
4127c	same, bklt pane of 6	....	....	....	....	7.75	....
4127d	(42¢) Forever Liberty Bell, med. microprint, bell 15mm wide, mottled tagging dated 2008	3.50	....	....	....	2.00	.65
4127e	(42¢) Forever Liberty Bell, dbl-sided, bklt pane of 20	....	....	....	....	36.00	....
4127f	(42¢) Forever Liberty Bell, dated 2008, small type, solid tagging	3.50	....	....	....	1.50	....
4127g	(42¢) Forever Liberty Bell, dated 2008, small type, solid tagging, bklt pane of 4	....	....	....	....	5.25	....

SCOTT NO.	DESCRIPTION	FIRST DAY COVERS SING	FIRST DAY COVERS PL. BLK.	MINT SHEET	PLATE BLOCK	UNUSED F/NH	USED
4127h	(42¢) Forever Liberty Bell, (2008), bklt pane of 6	....	....	....	....	7.75	....
	same, vending bklt of 20	....	....	....	....	29.00	....
4127i	(44¢) Forever Liberty Bell, dated 2009 in copper	3.50	....	....	....	1.50	.65
4127j	(44¢) Forever Liberty Bell, double sided pane of 20	....	....	....	....	27.00	....
4128	(41¢) Forever Liberty Bell, self-adhesive, ATM	3.50	....	....	....	1.50	.60
4128a	same, bklt pane of 18	....	....	....	....	28.00	....
4128b	(42¢) Forever, Liberty Bell large micro print, bell 16mm wide dated 2009	3.50	....	....	....	1.50	.65
4128c	same, bklt pane of 18	....	....	....	....	27.00	....
4129	(41¢) American Flag, die cut 11¼	3.50	5.00	127.00(100)	16.00	1.50	1.05
4130	(41¢) American Flag, self-adhesive, 11¼ x 10¾	3.50	5.00	24.00(20)	5.75	1.80	.45
4131	(41¢) American Flag, coil, die cut 9¾	3.50	....	....	....	1.50	.65
	same, pl# strip of 5	....	....	....	....	10.50	....
4132	(41¢) American Flag, coil, self-adhesive, die cut 9½	3.50	....	....	....	1.50	.40
	same, pl# strip of 5	....	....	....	....	10.50	....
4133	(41¢) American Flag, coil, self-adhesive, die cut 11	3.50	....	....	....	1.50	.40
	same, pl# strip of 5	....	....	....	....	10.50	....
4134	(41¢) American Flag, coil, self-adhesive, die cut 8½	3.50	....	....	....	1.50	.40
	same, pl# strip of 5	....	....	....	....	10.00	....
4135	(41¢) American Flag, coil, self-adhesive, rounded corners, die cut 11	3.50	....	....	....	1.70	1.15
	same, pl# strip of 5	....	....	....	....	12.00	....

4136

4137, 4139, 4141, 4142

4138, 4140

SCOTT NO.	DESCRIPTION	FIRST DAY COVERS SING	FIRST DAY COVERS PL. BLK.	MINT SHEET	PLATE BLOCK	UNUSED F/NH	USED
4136	41¢ Settlement of Jamestown, self-adhesive	3.50	5.00	30.00(20)	....	1.50	.50
4137	26¢ Florida Panther, water-activated	3.00	4.75	78.00(100)	13.50	.85	.35
4138	17¢ Big Horn Sheep, self-adhesive	3.00	4.00	13.00(20)	3.50	.75	.35
4139	26¢ Florida Panther, self-adhesive	3.00	4.75	16.00(20)	4.50	.85	.35
4140	17¢ Big Horn Sheep, self-adhesive, coil	3.00	....	....	....	.75	.35
	same, pl# strip of 5	....	....	....	....	6.75	....
4141	26¢ Florida Panther, self-adhesive, coil	3.00	....	....	....	1.00	.35
	same, pl# strip of 5	....	....	....	....	9.00	....
4142	26¢ Florida Panther, self-adhesive	3.00	....	....	....	1.00	.30
4142a	same, bklt pane of 10	....	....	....	....	10.00	....

STAR WARS

4143a *Darth Vader*
4143b *Millennium Falcon*
4143c *Emperor Palpatine*
4143d *Anakin Skywalker and Obi-Wan Kenobi*
4143e *Luke Skywalker*
4143f *Princess Leia & R2-D2*
4143g *C-3PO*
4143h *Queen Padme Amidala*
4143i *Obi-Wan Kenobi*
4143j *Boba Fett*
4143k *Darth Maul*
4143l *Chewbacca and Han Solo*
4143m *X-wing Starfighter*
4143n *Yoda*
4143o *Stormtroopers*

4143

SCOTT NO.	DESCRIPTION	FIRST DAY COVERS SING	FIRST DAY COVERS PL. BLK.	MINT SHEET	PLATE BLOCK	UNUSED F/NH	USED
4143	41¢ Star Wars, self-adhesive, 15 attached	....	....	22.00(15)	....	22.00	....
....	same, set of singles	....	....	....	....	22.00	15.00

4144 4145

SCOTT NO.	DESCRIPTION	FIRST DAY COVERS SING	FIRST DAY COVERS PL. BLK.	MINT SHEET	PLATE BLOCK	UNUSED F/NH	USED
4144	$4.60 Air Force One, self-adhesive	10.00	30.00	230.00(20)	58.00	13.00	10.00
4145	$16.25 Marine One, self-adhesive	35.00	80.00	800.00(20)	200.00	46.00	30.00

4146 4147 4148 4149 4150

SCOTT NO.	DESCRIPTION	FIRST DAY COVERS SING	FIRST DAY COVERS PL. BLK.	MINT SHEET	PLATE BLOCK	UNUSED F/NH	USED
4146-50	41¢ Pacific Lighthouses, self-adhesive, 5 attached	5.50	8.00	30.00(20)	16.00(10)	8.50	....
4146	41¢ Diamond Head	3.50	....	....	....	1.75	.50
4147	41¢ Five Finger	3.50	....	....	....	1.75	.50
4148	41¢ Grays Harbor	3.50	....	....	....	1.75	.50
4149	41¢ Umpqua River	3.50	....	....	....	1.75	.50
4150	41¢ St. George Reef	3.50	....	....	....	1.75	.50

4151 4152

SCOTT NO.	DESCRIPTION	FIRST DAY COVERS SING	FIRST DAY COVERS PL. BLK.	MINT SHEET	PLATE BLOCK	UNUSED F/NH	USED
4151	41¢ Wedding Hearts, self-adhesive	3.50	....	....	....	1.50	.35
4151a	same, bklt pane of 20	....	....	....	....	27.00	....
4152	58¢ Wedding Hearts, self-adhesive	4.00	5.50	33.00(20)	8.00	1.85	.65

4153 4154

4155 4156

SCOTT NO.	DESCRIPTION	FIRST DAY COVERS SING	FIRST DAY COVERS PL. BLK.	MINT SHEET	PLATE BLOCK	UNUSED F/NH	USED
4153-56	41¢ Pollination, self-adhesive, 4 attached	4.50	....	....	....	7.00	....
4153	41¢ Purple Nightshade and Morrison's Bumblebee, type I, straight edge at left	3.50	....	....	....	1.50	.55
4153a	same, type II, straight edge at right	3.50	....	....	....	1.50	.55
4154	41¢ Hummingbird Trumpet and Calliope Hummingbird, type I, straight edge at right	3.50	....	....	....	1.50	.55
4154a	same, type II, straight edge at left	3.50	....	....	....	1.50	.55
4155	41¢ Saguaro and Lesser Long-nosed Bat, type I, straight edge at left	3.50	....	....	....	1.50	.55
4155a	same, type II, straight edge at right	3.50	....	....	....	1.50	.55
4156	41¢ Prairie Ironweed and Southern Dogface Butterfly, type I, straight edge at right	3.50	....	....	....	1.50	.55
4156a	same, type II, straight edge at left	3.50	....	....	....	1.50	.55
4156b	same, blk of 4 (4153-4156)	4.50	....	....	....	6.00	....
4156c	same, blk of 4 (4153a-4156a)	4.50	....	....	....	6.00	....
4156d	same, bklt pane of 20 (4153-4156 x 3, 4153a-4156a x 2)	4.50	....	....	....	28.00	....

SCOTT NO.	DESCRIPTION	FIRST DAY COVERS SING	FIRST DAY COVERS PL. BLK.	MINT SHEET	PLATE BLOCK	UNUSED F/NH	USED
4157	(10¢) Patriotic Banner, self-adhesive, round corners	....	....	....	....	.35	.25
....	same, pl# strip of 5 . .	....	....	....	....	3.50	....
4158	(10¢) Patriotic Banner, self-adhesive, straight corners	....	....	....	....	.35	.25
....	same, pl# strip of 5 . .	....	....	....	....	4.75	....

SUPER HEROES

4159

MARVEL COMICS SUPER HEROES

4159a *Spider-Man*
4159b *The Incredible Hulk*
4159c *Sub-Mariner*
4159d *The Thing*
4159e *Captain America*
4159f *Silver Surfer*
4159g *Spider-Woman*
4159h *Iron Man*
4159i *Elektra*
4159j *Wolverine*
4159k *Spider-Man Cover*
4159l *Incredible Hulk Cover*
4159m *Sub-Mariner Cover*
4159n *Fantastic Four Cover*
4159o *Captain America Cover*
4159p *Silver Surfer Cover*
4159q *Spider-Woman Cover*
4159r *Iron Man Cover*
4159s *Elektra Cover*
4159t *X-Men Cover*

SCOTT NO.	DESCRIPTION	FIRST DAY COVERS SING	FIRST DAY COVERS PL. BLK.	MINT SHEET	PLATE BLOCK	UNUSED F/NH	USED
4159	41¢ Marvel Comics Super Heroes, self-adhesive, 20 varieties attached .	....	....	29.00(20)	....	29.00	....
	same, set of singles. .	....	....	....	....	29.00	20.00

4160 4161 4162 4163

SCOTT NO.	DESCRIPTION	FIRST DAY COVERS SING	FIRST DAY COVERS PL. BLK.	MINT SHEET	PLATE BLOCK	UNUSED F/NH	USED
4160-63	41¢ Vintage Mahogany Speedboats, self-adhesive, 4 attached .	4.50	6.50	18.00(12)	14.00(8)	7.00	....
4160	41¢ 1915 Hutchinson	....	....	....	....	1.75	1.00
4161	41¢ 1945 Chris-Craft	....	....	....	....	1.75	1.00
4162	41¢ 1939 Hacker-Craft	....	....	....	....	1.75	1.00
4163	41¢ 1931 Gar Wood			....	....	1.75	1.00

4157, 4158 4165, 4165a 4164

SCOTT NO.	DESCRIPTION	FIRST DAY COVERS SING	FIRST DAY COVERS PL. BLK.	MINT SHEET	PLATE BLOCK	UNUSED F/NH	USED
4164	41¢ Purple Heart, self-adhesive	3.50	5.00	24.00(20)	5.50	1.50	.40
4165	41¢ Louis Comfort Tiffany, self-adhesive	3.50	....	....	....	1.50	.40
4165a	same, bklt pane of 20	....	....	....	....	28.00	....
4166-75	41¢ Flowers Strip of 10	....	....	....	....	25.00	....
	same, plate strip of 11	....	....	....	....	35.00	....
4166	41¢ Iris S/A coil	$3.75	....	....	....	2.75	.85
4167	41¢ Dahlia S/A coil . .	$3.75	....	....	....	2.75	.85
4168	41¢ Magnolia S/A coil	$3.75	....	....	....	2.75	.85
4169	41¢ Red Gerbera Daisy, S/A coil.	$3.75	....	....	....	2.75	.85
4170	41¢ Coneflower S/A coil	$3.75	....	....	....	2.75	.85
4171	41¢ Tulip S/A coil	$3.75	....	....	....	2.75	.85
4172	41¢ Water Lily S/A coil	$3.75	....	....	....	2.75	.85
4173	41¢ Poppy S/A coil . .	$3.75	....	....	....	2.75	.85
4174	41¢ Chrysanthemum, S/A coil.	$3.75	....	....	....	2.75	.85
4175	41¢ Orange Gerbera Daisy, S/A coil.	$3.75	....	....	....	2.75	.85

4166, 4178 4167, 4179 4168, 4180 4169, 4181

4170, 4184 4171, 4185 4172, 4182

4173, 4183 4174, 4176 4175, 4177

SCOTT NO.	DESCRIPTION	FIRST DAY COVERS SING	FIRST DAY COVERS PL. BLK.	MINT SHEET	PLATE BLOCK	UNUSED F/NH	USED
4176	41¢ Chrysanthemum, booklet single	$3.75	....	....	....	1.50	.60
4177	41¢ Orange Gerbera Daisy, booklet single	$3.75	....	....	....	1.50	.60
4178	41¢ Iris, bklt single. . .	$3.75	....	....	....	1.50	.60
4179	41¢ Dahlia, bklt single	$3.75	....	....	....	1.50	.60
4180	41¢ Magnolia, bklt single	$3.75	....	....	....	1.50	.60
4181	41¢ Red Gerbera Daisy, booklet single	$3.75	....	....	....	1.50	.60
4182	41¢ Water Lily, bklt single	$3.75	....	....	....	1.50	.60
4183	41¢ Poppy, bklt single	$3.75	....	....	....	1.50	.60
4184	41¢ Coneflower, booklet single.	$3.75	....	....	....	1.50	.60
4185	41¢ Tulip, bklt single. .	$3.75	....	....	....	1.50	.60
4185a	41¢ Flowers dbl-sided, booklet pane	....	....	....	....	29.00	....
4186	41¢ Flag S/A coil, die cut 9½, microprint, rt. side of flagpole . . .	3.75	....	....	....	1.50	.35
	same, plate strip of 5 .	....	....	....	....	12.00	....
4187	41¢ Flag S/A coil, die cut 11, microprint, left side of flagpole. . .	3.75	....	....	....	1.50	.35
	same, plate strip of 5 .	....	....	....	....	12.00	....
4188	41¢ Flag S/A coil, 8½ perpendicular corners,	3.75	....	....	....	1.50	.35
	same, plate strip of 5 .	....	....	....	....	12.00	....
4189	41¢ Flag S/A coil, die cut 11 w/round corners,	3.75	....	....	....	1.50	.35
	same, plate strip of 5 .	....	....	....	....	12.00	....
4190	41¢ Flag bklt single, S/A die-cut 11¼ x 10¾, microprint rt. side of pole	3.75	....	....		1.50	.35
4190a	same bklt pane of 10					10.00	
4191	41¢ Flag bklt single, S/A die-cut 11¼ x 10¾, microprint left side of pole	3.75	....	....		1.50	.35
4191a	same bklt pane of 20 .	....	....	....	....	27.00	....

4192 4193 4194 4195

4186-91

4196

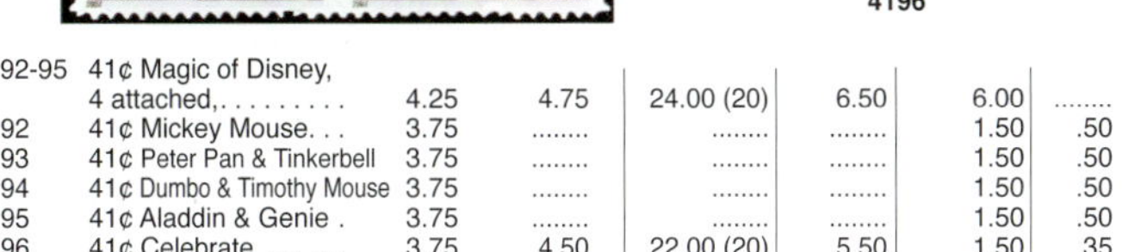

SCOTT NO.	DESCRIPTION	FIRST DAY COVERS SING	FIRST DAY COVERS PL. BLK.	MINT SHEET	PLATE BLOCK	UNUSED F/NH	USED
4192-95	41¢ Magic of Disney, 4 attached,.	4.25	4.75	24.00 (20)	6.50	6.00	....
4192	41¢ Mickey Mouse. . .	3.75	....	....	....	1.50	.50
4193	41¢ Peter Pan & Tinkerbell	3.75	....	....	....	1.50	.50
4194	41¢ Dumbo & Timothy Mouse	3.75	....	....	....	1.50	.50
4195	41¢ Aladdin & Genie .	3.75	....	....	....	1.50	.50
4196	41¢ Celebrate	3.75	4.50	22.00 (20)	5.50	1.50	.35

4197

SCOTT NO.	DESCRIPTION	FIRST DAY COVERS SING	FIRST DAY COVERS PL. BLK.	MINT SHEET	PLATE BLOCK	UNUSED F/NH	USED
4197	41¢ James Stewart . .	3.75	4.50	30.00 (20)	7.50	1.75	.50

4198

ALPINE TUNDRA

4198a	*Elk*	**4198f**	*Magdalena alpine butterfly*
4198b	*Golden eagle*	**4198g**	*Big white-tailed ptarmigan*
4198c	*Yellow-bellied marmot*	**4198h**	*Rocky Mountain parnassian butterfly*
4198d	*American pika*	**4198i**	*Melissa arctic butterfly*
4198e	*Bighorn Sheep*	**4198j**	*Brown-capped rosy-finch*

SCOTT NO.	DESCRIPTION	FIRST DAY COVERS SING	FIRST DAY COVERS PL. BLK.	MINT SHEET	PLATE BLOCK	UNUSED F/NH	USED
4198	41¢ Alpine Tundra,						
	sheet of 10	....	....	15.00 (10)	....	15.00	....
	set of singles	20.00	....	....	....	15.00	9.00

4199 4200 4201

SCOTT NO.	DESCRIPTION	FIRST DAY COVERS SING	FIRST DAY COVERS PL. BLK.	MINT SHEET	PLATE BLOCK	UNUSED F/NH	USED
4199	41¢ Gerald R. Ford . .	3.75	4.50	24.00 (20)	6.00	1.50	.40
4200	41¢ Jury Duty.	3.75	4.50	24.00 (20)	6.00	1.50	.40
4201	41¢ Mendez v. Westminster	3.75	4.50	24.00 (20)	6.00	1.50	.40

4202

SCOTT NO.	DESCRIPTION	FIRST DAY COVERS SING	FIRST DAY COVERS PL. BLK.	MINT SHEET	PLATE BLOCK	UNUSED F/NH	USED
4202	41¢ EID	3.75	4.50	22.00 (20)	5.50	1.40	.35

4203

4204

SCOTT NO.	DESCRIPTION	FIRST DAY COVERS SING	FIRST DAY COVERS PL. BLK.	MINT SHEET	PLATE BLOCK	UNUSED F/NH	USED
4203-04	41¢ Polar Lights	4.25	4.75	32.00 (20)	9.50	3.50	....
4203	41¢ Aurora Borealis. . .	3.75	....	....	....	1.75	.65
4204	41¢ Aurora Australis . .	3.75	....	....	....	1.75	.65

4205 4206

SCOTT NO.	DESCRIPTION	FIRST DAY COVERS SING	FIRST DAY COVERS PL. BLK.	MINT SHEET	PLATE BLOCK	UNUSED F/NH	USED
4205	41¢ Yoda	3.75	4.50	24.00 (20)	6.00	1.50	.40
4206	41¢ Madonna of the Carnation,						
	by Bernardino Luini . .	3.75	....	....	....	1.30	.35
4206a	same, double-sided,						
	booklet pane of 20. . .	....	....	....	....	24.00	....

4207, 4211, 4215 4208, 4212 4216 4209, 4213, 4217 4210, 4214, 4218

SCOTT NO.	DESCRIPTION	FIRST DAY COVERS SING	FIRST DAY COVERS PL. BLK.	MINT SHEET	PLATE BLOCK	UNUSED F/NH	USED
4207-10	41¢ Christmas Knits,						
	S/A, die-cut 10¾	4.75	....	24.00 (20)	6.50	6.00	....
4207	41¢ Knit Reindeer,						
	S/A, die-cut 10¾	3.75	....	....	....	1.25	.50
4208	41¢ Knit Christmas Tree,						
	S/A, die-cut 10¾	3.75	....	....	....	1.25	.50
4209	41¢ Knit Snowman,						
	S/A, die-cut 10¾	3.75	....	....	....	1.25	.50
4210	41¢ Knit Bear,						
	S/A, die-cut 10¾	3.75	....	....	....	1.25	.50
4210b	41¢ Christmas Knits,						
	booklet pane of 20. . .	....	....	....	....	32.00	....
4211-14	41¢ Christmas Knits,						
	S/A, die-cut 11¼ x 11,						
	block of 4 attached . .	4.75	....	....	....	7.50	....
4211	41¢ Knit Reindeer,						
	S/A, die-cut 11¼ x 11 . .	3.75	....	....	....	1.75	.75
4212	41¢ Knit Christmas Tree,						
	S/A, die-cut 11¼ x 11 . .	3.75	....	....	....	1.75	.75
4213	41¢ Knit Snowman,						
	S/A, die-cut 11¼ x 11 . .	3.75	....	....	....	1.75	.75
4214	41¢ Knit Bear,						
	S/A, die-cut 11¼ x 11 .	3.75	....	....	....	1.75	.75
4214b	booklet pane of 4,						
	4211-14	....	....	....	....	7.50	....
4214c	booklet pane of 6,						
	4213-14, 2 ea. 4211-12	....	....	....	....	11.00	....
4214d	booklet pane of 6,						
	4211-12, 2 ea. 4213-14	....	....	....	....	11.00	....
4215-18	41¢ Christmas Knits,						
	S/A, die-cut 8.	4.50	....	....	....	8.00	....
4215	41¢ Knit Reindeer,						
	S/A, die-cut 8.	3.75	....	....	....	2.00	.75
4216	41¢ Knit Christmas Tree,						
	S/A, die-cut 8.	3.75	....	....	....	2.00	.75
4217	41¢ Knit Snowman,						
	S/A, die-cut 8.	3.75	....	....	....	2.00	.75
4218	41¢ Knit Bear,						
	S/A, die-cut 8	3.75	....	....	....	2.00	.75
4218b	booklet pane of 18,						
	4 ea. of 4215, 4218,						
	5 ea. of 4216, 4217. . .	....	....	....	....	34.00	....

4219

4220

SCOTT NO.	DESCRIPTION	FIRST DAY COVERS SING	FIRST DAY COVERS PL. BLK.	MINT SHEET	PLATE BLOCK	UNUSED F/NH	USED
4219	41¢ Hanukkah S/A,						
	die cut 10¾ x 11	3.75	4.50	22.00 (20)	5.50	1.40	.45
4220	41¢ Kwanzaa, S/A,						
	die cut, 11 x 10¾.	3.75	4.50	22.00 (20)	5.50	1.40	.45

2008 COMMEMORATIVES

SCOTT NO.	DESCRIPTION	FIRST DAY COVERS SING	FIRST DAY COVERS PL. BLK.	MINT SHEET	PLATE BLOCK	UNUSED F/NH	USED
4221/4373	(4221-4227, 4248-4252, 4265, 4266, 4334, 4335, 4336-4345, 4349-4351, 4353-4357, 4358, 4372, 4373) 37 varieties	....		....	....	52.00	24.00

4221 4222 4223

SCOTT NO.	DESCRIPTION	FIRST DAY COVERS SING	FIRST DAY COVERS PL. BLK.	MINT SHEET	PLATE BLOCK	UNUSED F/NH	USED
4221	41¢ Year of the Rat, SA. .	3.75	....	17.00 (12)	....	1.50	.45
4222	41¢ Charles W. Chestnutt	3.75	....	24.00 (20)	5.50	1.50	.45
4223	41¢ Marjorie Kinnan Rawlings	3.75	4.50	24.00 (20)	5.50	1.50	.45

4224 4225 4226 4227

SCOTT NO.	DESCRIPTION	FIRST DAY COVERS SING	FIRST DAY COVERS PL. BLK.	MINT SHEET	PLATE BLOCK	UNUSED F/NH	USED
4224-27	41¢ American Scientists. .	4.50	7.50	25.00 (20)	12.00(8)	6.00	....
4224	41¢ Gerty Cori.	3.75	....	....	....	1.50	.90
4225	41¢ Linus Pauling. . . .	3.75	....	....	....	1.50	.90
4226	41¢ Edwin Hubble. . .	3.75	....	....	....	1.50	.90
4227	41¢ John Bardeen. . .	3.75	....	....	....	1.50	.90

4229, 4233, 4237, 4241, 4245 4230, 4234, 4238, 4242, 4246 4231, 4235, 4239, 4243, 4247 4228, 4232, 4236, 4240, 4244

SCOTT NO.	DESCRIPTION	FIRST DAY COVERS SING	FIRST DAY COVERS PL. BLK.	MINT SHEET	PLATE BLOCK	UNUSED F/NH	USED
4228-31	42¢ Flag 24/7, W/A coil.	6.50	....	....	....	9.00	....
	same, plate # strip of 5	....	....	....	....	20.00	....
	same, plate # strip of 9	....	....	....	....	30.00	....
4228	42¢ Flag at Dusk, W/A coil.	3.50	....	....	....	2.50	.85
4229	42¢ Flag at Night, W/A coil.	3.50	....	....	....	2.50	.85
4230	42¢ Flag at Dawn, W/A coil.	3.50	....	....	....	2.50	.85
4231	42¢ Flag at Midday, W/A coil.	3.50	....	....	....	2.50	.85
4232-35	42¢ Flag 24/7, S/A coil 9½ (AP). . . .	6.50	....			7.50	
	same, plate # strip of 5	....	....	....	....	12.00	....
	same, plate # strip of 9	....	....	....	....	10.00	....
4232	42¢ Flag at Dusk, S/A coil 9½ (AP).	3.50	....	....	....	2.50	.60
4233	42¢ Flag at Night, S/A coil 9½ (AP).	3.50	....	....	....	2.50	.60
4234	42¢ Flag at Dawn, S/A coil 9½ (AP)	3.50	....	....	....	2.50	.60
4235	42¢ Flag at Midday, S/A coil 9½ (AP).	3.50	....	....	....	2.50	.60
4236-39	42¢ Flag 24/7, S/A coil, 11 perpend. corners (SSP)	6.50	....	....	....	7.50	....
	same, plate # strip of 5	....	....	....	....	13.00	....
	same, plate # strip of 9	....	....	....	....	19.00	....
4236	42¢ Flag at Dusk, S/A coil, 11 perpend. corners (SSP)	3.50	....	....	....	2.50	.60
4237	42¢ Flag at Night, S/A coil, 11 perpend. corners (SSP)	3.50	....	....	....	2.50	.60
4238	42¢ Flag at Dawn, S/A coil, 11 perpend. corners (SSP)	3.50	....	....	....	2.50	.60
4239	42¢ Flag at Midday, S/A coil, 11 perpend. corners (SSP)	3.50	....	....	....	2.50	.60
4240-43	42¢ Flag 24/7, S/A coil, 8.5 perpend. corners (AV)	6.50	....	....	....	7.50	....
	same, plate # strip of 5	....	....	....	....	13.00	....
	same, plate # strip of 9	....	....	....	....	18.00	....
4240	42¢ Flag at Dusk, S/A coil, 8½ perpend. corners (AV)	3.50	....	....	....	2.50	.60
4241	42¢ Flag at Night, S/A coil, 8½ perpend. corners (AV)	3.50	....	....	....	2.50	.60
4242	42¢ Flag at Dawn, S/A coil, 8½ perpend. corners (AV)	3.50	....	....	....	2.50	.60
4243	42¢ Flag at Midday, S/A coil, 8½ perpend. corners (AV)	3.50	....	....	....	2.50	.60
4244-47	42¢ Flag 24/7, S/A coil, 11 rounded corners (AV)	6.50	....	....	....	7.50	....
	same, plate # strip of 5	....	....	....	....	13.00	....
	same, plate # strip of 9	....	....	....	....	18.00	....
4244	42¢ Flag at Dusk, S/A coil, 11 rounded corners (AV)	3.50	....	....	....	2.50	.60
4245	42¢ Flag at Night, S/A coil, 11 rounded corners (AV)	3.50	....	....	....	2.50	.60
4246	42¢ Flag at Dawn, S/A coil, 11 rounded corners (AV)	3.50	....	....	....	2.50	.60
4247	42¢ Flag at Midday, S/A coil, 11 rounded corners (AV)	3.50	....	....	....	2.50	.60

4248 4249 4250

4251 4252

SCOTT NO.	DESCRIPTION	FIRST DAY COVERS SING	FIRST DAY COVERS PL. BLK.	MINT SHEET	PLATE BLOCK	UNUSED F/NH	USED
4248-52	42¢ American Journalists	4.50	7.50	35.00(20)	18.00(10)	9.00	....
	same	....	....	....	12.00(8)	....	....
4248	42¢ Martha Gellhorn. .	3.75	....	....	....	2.00	1.00
4249	42¢ John Hersey.	3.75				2.00	1.00
4250	42¢ George Polk.. . . .	3.75	....	....	....	2.00	1.00
4251	42¢ Ruben Salazar. . .	3.75	....	....	....	2.00	1.00
4252	42¢ Eric Sevareid. . . .	3.75	....	....	....	2.00	1.00

4253,4258 4254,4259 4255,4260 4256,4261 4257,4262

SCOTT NO.	DESCRIPTION	FIRST DAY COVERS SING	FIRST DAY COVERS PL. BLK.	MINT SHEET	PLATE BLOCK	UNUSED F/NH	USED
4253-57	27¢ Tropical Fruit. . . .	4.75	....	19.00(20)	12.00(10)	6.00	....
4253	27¢ Pomegranate. . . .	2.50	....	....	....	1.25	.50
4254	27¢ Star Fruit.	2.50	....	....	....	1.25	.50
4255	27¢ Kiwi.	2.50	....	....	....	1.25	.50
4256	27¢ Papaya	2.50	....	....	....	1.25	.50
4257	27¢ Guava.	2.50	....	....	....	1.25	.50
4258-62	27¢ Tropical Fruit. . . .	4.75	....	....	....	9.00	....
	same, plate strip of 5 .	....	....	....	....	15.00	....
	same, plate strip of 11	....	....	....		22.00	....
4258	27¢ Pomegranate Coil	2.50	....	....	....	2.00	.50
4259	27¢ Star Fruit Coil	2.50				2.00	.50
4260	27¢ Kiwi Coil.	2.50	....	....	....	2.00	.50
4261	27¢ Papaya Coil	2.50				2.00	.50
4262	27¢ Guava Coil.	2.50	....	....	....	2.00	.50

4263, 4264

SCOTT NO.	DESCRIPTION	FIRST DAY COVERS SING	FIRST DAY COVERS PL. BLK.	MINT SHEET	PLATE BLOCK	UNUSED F/NH	USED
4263	42¢ Purple Heart	3.50	4.75	148.00 (100)	40.00	1.70	.70
4264	42¢ Purple Heart, S/A	3.50	4.75	24.00 (20)	6.00	1.50	.45

4265 4266

SCOTT NO.	DESCRIPTION	FIRST DAY COVERS SING	FIRST DAY COVERS PL. BLK.	MINT SHEET	PLATE BLOCK	UNUSED F/NH	USED
4265	42¢ Frank Sinatra . . .	3.75	4.75	24.00 (20)	6.00	1.50	.40
4266	42¢ Minnesota Statehood	3.75	4.75	22.00 (20)	5.50	1.50	.40

4267 4268 4269

SCOTT NO.	DESCRIPTION	FIRST DAY COVERS SING	FIRST DAY COVERS PL. BLK.	MINT SHEET	PLATE BLOCK	UNUSED F/NH	USED
4267	69¢ Dragonfly	3.75	5.00	55.00 (20)	9.00	3.00	1.25
4268	$4.80 Mount Rushmore	12.00	....	245.00 (20)	65.00	14.00	10.00
4269	$16.50 Hoover Dam . .	35.00	....	800.00 (20)	200.00	45.00	35.00

4270 4271 4272

SCOTT NO.	DESCRIPTION	FIRST DAY COVERS SING	FIRST DAY COVERS PL. BLK.	MINT SHEET	PLATE BLOCK	UNUSED F/NH	USED
4270	42¢ All Heart	3.75	....	....	....	1.40	.40
4270a	42¢ All Heart, pane of 20	....	....	....	....	27.00	....
4271	42¢ Weddings	3.75	....	....	....	1.40	.40
4271a	42¢ Weddings, pane of 20	12.00	....	....	....	27.00	....
4272	59¢ Silver Heart	3.75	....	32.00(20)	9.00	2.00	.75

4273 4332

SCOTT NO.	DESCRIPTION	FIRST DAY COVERS SING	FIRST DAY COVERS PL. BLK.	MINT SHEET	PLATE BLOCK	UNUSED F/NH	USED
4273-82	42¢ Flags of Our Nation, coil strip of 11.	....	....	....	....	14.00	....
	same, plate # strip of 10	....	....	....	....	19.00	....
4273	42¢ American Flag. . .	3.75	....	....	....	1.50	.75
4274	42¢ Alabama Flag . . .	3.75	....	....	....	1.50	.75
4275	42¢ Alaska Flag.	3.75	....	....	....	1.50	.75
4276	42¢ American Samoa Flag	3.75	....	....	....	1.50	.75
4277	42¢ Arizona Flag . . .	3.75	....	....	....	1.50	.75
4278	42¢ Arkansas Flag. . .	3.75	....	....	....	1.50	.75
4279	42¢ California Flag . .	3.75	....	....	....	1.50	.75
4280	42¢ Colorado Flag. . .	3.75	....	....	....	1.50	.75
4281	42¢ Connecticut Flag	3.75	....	....	....	1.50	.75
4282	42¢ Delaware Flag . .	3.75	....	....	....	1.50	.75
4283-92	42¢ Flags of Our Nation	....	....	....	....	14.00	....
	coil strip of 10	....	....	....	....	19.00	....
4283	42¢ District of Columbia Flag	3.75	....	....	....	1.50	.75
4284	42¢ Florida Flag.	3.75	....	....	....	1.50	.75
4285	42¢ Georgia Flag. . . .	3.75	....	....	....	1.50	.75
4286	42¢ Guam Flag	3.75	....	....	....	1.50	.75
4287	42¢ Hawaii Flag.	3.75	....	....	....	1.50	.75
4288	42¢ Idaho Flag.	3.75	....	....	....	1.50	.75
4289	42¢ Illinois Flag	3.75	....	....	....	1.50	.75
4290	42¢ Indiana Flag	3.75	....	....	....	1.50	.75
4291	42¢ Iowa Flag	3.75	....	....	....	1.50	.75
4292	42¢ Kansas Flag	3.75	....	....	....	1.50	.75
4293-4302	44¢ Flags of Our Nation, coil strip of 10	12.00	....	....	....	14.00	....
	same, plate # strip of 11	....	....	....	....	19.00	....
4293	44¢ Kentucky Flag. . .	3.75	....	....	....	1.50	.75
4294	44¢ Louisiana Flag . .	3.75	....	....	....	1.50	.75
4295	44¢ Maine Flag	3.75	....	....	....	1.50	.75
4296	44¢ Maryland Flag. . .	3.75	....	....	....	1.50	.75
4297	44¢ Massachusetts . .	3.75	....	....	....	1.50	.75
4298	44¢ Michigan Flag . . .	3.75	....	....	....	1.50	.75
4299	44¢ Minnesota Flag . .	3.75	....	....	....	1.50	.75
4300	44¢ Mississippi Flag .	3.75	....	....	....	1.50	.75
4301	44¢ Missouri Flag . . .	3.75	....	....	....	1.50	.75
4302	44¢ American Flag & Wheat.	3.75	....	....	....	1.50	.75
4303-12	44¢ Flags of Our Nation coil strip of 10	12.00	....	....	....	14.00	....
	same, plate strip of 11	....	....	....	....	19.00	....
4303	44¢ American Flag and Mountains	3.75	....	....	....	1.50	.75
4304	44¢ Montana Flag . . .	3.75	....	....	....	1.50	.50
4305	44¢ Nebraska Flag . .	3.75	....	....	....	1.50	.50
4306	44¢ Nevada Flag	3.75	....	....	....	1.50	.50
4307	44¢ New Hampshire Flag	3.75	....	....	....	1.50	.50
4308	44¢ New Jersey Flag.	3.75	....	....	....	1.50	.50
4309	44¢ New Mexico Flag	3.75	....	....	....	1.50	.50
4310	44¢ New York Flag . .	3.75	....	....	....	1.50	.50
4311	44¢ North Carolina Flag	3.75	....	....	....	1.50	.50
4312	44¢ North Dakota Flag	3.75	....	....	....	1.50	.50
4313-22	(44¢) Flags of Our Nation	....	....	....	....	14.00	....
	same, plate # strip of 11	....	....	....	....	19.00	....
4313	(44¢) N. Marianas Flag	3.75	....	....	....	1.50	.75
4314	(44¢) Ohio Flag	3.75	....	....	....	1.50	.75
4315	(44¢) Oklahoma Flag.	3.75	....	....	....	1.50	.75
4316	(44¢) Oregon Flag . . .	3.75	....	....	....	1.50	.75
4317	(44¢) Pennsylvania Flag	3.75	....	....	....	1.50	.75
4318	(44¢) Puerto Rico Flag	3.75	....	....	....	1.50	.75
4319	(44¢) Rhode Island Flag	3.75	....	....	....	1.50	.75
4320	(44¢) South Carolina Flag	3.75	....	....	....	1.50	.75
4321	(44¢) South Dakota Flag	3.75	....	....	....	1.50	.75
4322	(44¢) Tennessee Flag	3.75	....	....	....	1.50	.75
4323-32	(45¢) Flags of our Nation	....	....	....	....	40.00	....
	same, plate strip of 11	....	....	....	....	46.00	....
4323	(45¢) Texas Flag	3.75	....	....	....	4.00	1.75
4324	(45¢) Utah Flag	3.75	....	....	....	4.00	1.75
4325	(45¢) Vermont Flag . .	3.75	....	....	....	4.00	1.75
4326	(45¢) Virgin Islands Flag	3.75	....	....	....	4.00	1.75
4327	(45¢) Virginia Flag . . .	3.75	....	....	....	4.00	1.75
4328	(45¢) Washington Flag	3.75	....	....	....	4.00	1.75
4329	(45¢) West Virginia Flag	3.75	....	....	....	4.00	1.75
4330	(45¢) Wisconsin Flag.	3.75	....	....	....	4.00	1.75
4331	(45¢) Wyoming Flag .	3.75	....	....	....	4.00	1.75
4332	(45¢) American Flag and Fruited Plain	3.75	....	....	....	4.00	1.75

4333

CHARLES (1907-78) AND RAY (1912-88) EAMES, DESIGNERS

- **4333a** *Christmas card depicting Charles and Ray Eames*
- **4333b** *"Crosspatch" fabric design*
- **4333c** *Stacking chairs*
- **4333d** *Case Study House #8, Pacific Palisades, CA*
- **4333e** *Wire-base table*
- **4333f** *Lounge chair and ottoman*
- **4333g** *Hang-it-all*
- **4333h** *La Chaise*
- **4333i** *Scene from film, "Tops"*
- **4333j** *Wire mesh chair*
- **4333k** *Cover of May 1943 edition of California Arts & Architecture Magazine*
- **4333l** *House of Cards*
- **4333m** *Molded plywood sculpture*
- **4333n** *Eames Storage Unit*
- **4333o** *Aluminum group chair*
- **4333p** *Molded plywood chair*

SCOTT NO.	DESCRIPTION	FIRST DAY COVERS SING	FIRST DAY COVERS PL. BLK.	MINT SHEET	PLATE BLOCK	UNUSED F/NH	USED
4333	42¢ Charles & Ray Eames	....	....	25.00 (16)	....	25.00	....
4333a	42¢ Charles & Ray Eames	3.75	....	....	....	1.75	.75
4333b	42¢ Crosspatch Fabric Design	3.75	....	....	....	1.75	.75
4333c	42¢ Stacking Chairs .	3.75	....	....	....	1.75	.75
4333d	42¢ Case Study House No. 8	3.75	....	....	....	1.75	.75
4333e	42¢ Wire Base Tables	3.75	....	....	....	1.75	.75
4333f	42¢ Lounge Chair & Ottoman	3.75	....	....	....	1.75	.75
4333g	42¢ Hang-It-All.	3.75	....	....	....	1.75	.75
4333h	42¢ La Chaise	3.75	....	....	....	1.75	.75
4333i	42¢ "Tops".	3.75	....	....	....	1.75	.75
4333j	42¢ Wire Mesh Chair .	3.75	....	....	....	1.75	.75
4333k	42¢ "Arts & Architecture" Cover	3.75	....	....	....	1.75	.75
4333l	42¢ House of Cards .	3.75	....	....	....	1.75	.75
4333m	42¢ Molded Plywood Sculpture	3.75	....	....	....	1.75	.75
4333n	42¢ Eames Storage Unit	3.75	....	....	....	1.75	.75
4333o	42¢ Aluminum Group Chair	3.75	....	....	....	1.75	.75
4333p	42¢ Molded Plywood Chair	3.75	....	....	....	1.75	.75

4334 4335

SCOTT NO.	DESCRIPTION	FIRST DAY COVERS SING	FIRST DAY COVERS PL. BLK.	MINT SHEET	PLATE BLOCK	UNUSED F/NH	USED
4334	Summer Olympics . . .	3.75	4.50	25.00 (20)	6.50	1.60	.40
4335	42¢ Celebrate	3.75	4.50	22.00 (20)	6.00	1.50	.40

4336 4337 4338 4339 4340

SCOTT NO.	DESCRIPTION	FIRST DAY COVERS SING	FIRST DAY COVERS PL. BLK.	MINT SHEET	PLATE BLOCK	UNUSED F/NH	USED
4336-40	42¢ Vintage Black Cinema	....	....	30.00(20)	15.00(10)	8.50	....
4336	42¢ Poster for "Black & Tan"	3.75	....	....	....	1.60	1.50
4337	42¢ Poster for "The Sport of the Gods"	3.75	....	....	....	1.60	1.50
4338	42¢ Poster for "Prinsesse Tam-Tam".	3.75	....	....	....	1.60	1.50
4339	42¢ Poster for "Caledonia"	3.75	....	....	....	1.60	1.50
4340	42¢ Poster for "Hallelujah"	3.75	....	....	....	1.60	1.50

4341

SCOTT NO.	DESCRIPTION	FIRST DAY COVERS SING	FIRST DAY COVERS PL. BLK.	MINT SHEET	PLATE BLOCK	UNUSED F/NH	USED
4341	42¢ Take Me Out to the Ballgame	3.75	4.50	25.00 (20)	6.50	1.50	.40

4342 4343 4344 4345

SCOTT NO.	DESCRIPTION	FIRST DAY COVERS SING	FIRST DAY COVERS PL. BLK.	MINT SHEET	PLATE BLOCK	UNUSED F/NH	USED
4342-45	42¢ Art of Disney. . . .	4.25	4.75	24.00 (20)	7.50	7.00	....
4342	42¢ Lucky & Pongo, from 101 Dalmatians . .	3.75	....	....	....	1.60	.75
4343	42¢ Steamboat Willie .	3.75	....	....	....	1.60	.75
4344	42¢ Sleeping Beauty. .	3.75	....	....	....	1.60	.75
4345	42¢ Mowgli & Baloo, from Jungle Book	3.75	....	....	....	1.60	.75

4346 4347 4348

SCOTT NO.	DESCRIPTION	FIRST DAY COVERS SING	FIRST DAY COVERS PL. BLK.	MINT SHEET	PLATE BLOCK	UNUSED F/NH	USED
4346	42¢ Albert Bierstadt . .	3.75	4.50	....	....	1.50	.45
4346a	42¢ Albert Bierstadt bklt pane of 20.	....	....	....	....	26.00	....
4347	42¢ Sunflower	3.75	....	....	....	1.50	.35
4347a	same, bklt pane of 20	....	....	....	....	26.00	....
4348	5¢ Sea Coast, coil (2008) water-activated	....	....	....	....	.30	.25
	same, plate strip of 5. .	....	....	....	....	3.75	....

4349 4350 4351

SCOTT NO.	DESCRIPTION	FIRST DAY COVERS SING	FIRST DAY COVERS PL. BLK.	MINT SHEET	PLATE BLOCK	UNUSED F/NH	USED
4349	42¢ Latin Jazz	3.75	....	24.00(20)	5.50	1.50	.40
4350	42¢ Bette Davis	3.75	....	36.00(20)	8.00	1.85	.50
4351	42¢ EID, die cut 11 . .	3.75	....	24.00(20)	5.50	1.50	.90

4352

GREAT LAKES DUNES

4352a	*Vesper sparrow*	**4352f**	*Spotted sandpiper*
4352b	*Red fox*	**4352g**	*Tiger beetle*
4352c	*Piping plover*	**4352h**	*White-footed mouse*
4352d	*Eastern hognose snake*	**4352i**	*Piper plover nestings*
4352e	*Common mergansers*	**4352j**	*Red admiral butterfly*

SCOTT NO.	DESCRIPTION	FIRST DAY COVERS SING	FIRST DAY COVERS PL. BLK.	MINT SHEET	PLATE BLOCK	UNUSED F/NH	USED
4352	42¢ Great Lakes Dunes, sheet of 10.	....	....	17.00	....	17.00	....
	set of singles	20.00	....	....	....	....	9.00

4353 4354 4355

4356 4357

SCOTT NO.	DESCRIPTION	FIRST DAY COVERS SING	FIRST DAY COVERS PL. BLK.	MINT SHEET	PLATE BLOCK	UNUSED F/NH	USED
4353-57	42¢ Automobiles of the 1950's	3.75	....	25.00(20)	15.00 (10)	7.50	....
4353	42¢ 1959 Cadillac Eldorado	....	....	....	....	1.50	.85
4354	42¢ 1957 Studebaker Golden Hawk.	....	....	....	....	1.50	.85
4355	42¢ 1957 Pontiac Safari	....	....	....	....	1.50	.85
4356	42¢ 1957 Lincoln Premiere	....	....	....	....	1.50	.85
4357	42¢ 1957 Chrysler 300C	....	....	....	....	1.50	.85

4358 4359

SCOTT NO.	DESCRIPTION	FIRST DAY COVERS SING	FIRST DAY COVERS PL. BLK.	MINT SHEET	PLATE BLOCK	UNUSED F/NH	USED
4358	42¢ Alzheimer's Awareness	....	....	22.00	5.50	1.50	.40
4359	42¢ Virgin and Child, Botticelli	3.75	....	....	....	1.50	.40
4359a	same, bklt pane of 20	....	....	....	....	26.00	....

4360, 4364, 4368 4361, 4365, 4369 4362, 4366, 4370 4363, 4367, 4371

SCOTT NO.	DESCRIPTION	FIRST DAY COVERS SING	FIRST DAY COVERS PL. BLK.	MINT SHEET	PLATE BLOCK	UNUSED F/NH	USED
4360-63	42¢ Nutcrackers, block of 4 die cut 10¾ x 11	....	....	....	....	8.50	....
4360	42¢ Drummer Nutcracker, die cut 10¾ x 11	3.75				1.75	1.00
4361	42¢ Santa Claus Nutcracker, die cut 10¾ x 11	3.75	....	....	....	1.75	1.00
4362	42¢ King Nutcracker, die cut 10¾ x 11	3.75				1.75	1.00
4363	42¢ Soldier Nutcracker, die cut 10¾ x 11	3.75	....	....	....	1.75	1.00
4363b	42¢ Nutcracker, pane of 20	....	....	....	....	34.00	....
4364-67	42¢ Nutcrackers, block of 4 die cut 11¼ x 11.	....	....	....	....	7.50	....
4364	42¢ Drummer Nutcracker, die cut 11¼ x 11.	3.75	....	....	....	2.00	1.25
4365	42¢ Santa Claus Nutcracker, die cut 11¼ x 11.	3.75	....	....	....	2.00	1.25
4366	42¢ King Nutcracker, die cut 11¼ x 11.	3.75	....	....	....	2.00	1.25
4367	42¢ Soldier Nutcracker, die cut 11¼ x 11.	3.75	....	....	....	2.00	1.25
4367b	42¢ Nutcracker, bklt pane of 4.	....	....	....	....	7.50	....
4367c	42¢ Nutcracker, (2 each 4364, 4365) bklt pane of 6.	....	....	....	....	11.00	....
4367d	42¢ Nutcracker, (2 each 4366, 4367) bklt pane of 6.	....	....	....	....	11.00	....
4367bk	42¢ Nutcracker, bklt pane of 20, complete	....	....	....	....	34.00	....
4368-71	42¢ Nutcrackers, block of 4, die cut 8 . .	4.75	....	....	....	9.00	....
4368	42¢ Drummer Nutcracker, die cut 8.	3.75	....	....	....	2.00	1.00
4369	42¢ Santa Claus Nutcracker, die cut 8.	3.75	....	....	....	2.00	1.00
4370	42¢ King Nutcracker, die cut 8.	3.75	....	....	....	2.00	1.00
4371	42¢ Soldier Nutcracker, die cut 8.	3.75	....	....	....	2.00	1.00
4371b	42¢ Nutcracker, bklt pane of 18.	....	....	....	....	34.00	....

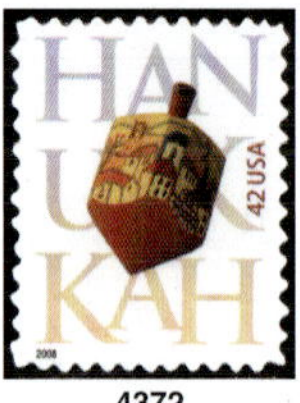

4372

4373

SCOTT NO.	DESCRIPTION	FIRST DAY COVERS SING	FIRST DAY COVERS PL. BLK.	MINT SHEET	PLATE BLOCK	UNUSED F/NH	USED
4372	42¢ Hanukkah	3.75	....	24.00(20)	6.00	1.50	.75
4373	42¢ Kwanzaa.	3.75	....	24.00(20)	6.00	1.50	.75

2009 COMMEMORATIVES

SCOTT NO.	DESCRIPTION	FIRST DAY COVERS SING	FIRST DAY COVERS PL. BLK.	MINT SHEET	PLATE BLOCK	UNUSED F/NH	USED
4374/4434	(4374-4377, 4380-83, 4386, 4406, 4407, 4408, 4409-4413, 4415, 4416, 4417-4420, 4421, 4433, 4434) 26 varieties	......		....	....	43.00	27.50

4374

4375

SCOTT NO.	DESCRIPTION	FIRST DAY COVERS SING	FIRST DAY COVERS PL. BLK.	MINT SHEET	PLATE BLOCK	UNUSED F/NH	USED
4374	42¢ Alaska Statehood	3.75	....	22.00(20)	5.50	1.40	.40
4375	42¢ Year of the Ox. . .	3.75	....	14.00(12)	5.50	1.40	.40

4376

4377

SCOTT NO.	DESCRIPTION	FIRST DAY COVERS SING	FIRST DAY COVERS PL. BLK.	MINT SHEET	PLATE BLOCK	UNUSED F/NH	USED
4376	42¢ Oregon Statehood	3.75	....	22.00(20)	5.50	1.50	.40
4377	42¢ Edgar Allen Poe .	3.75	....	22.00(20)	5.50	1.50	.40

4378

4379

SCOTT NO.	DESCRIPTION	FIRST DAY COVERS SING	FIRST DAY COVERS PL. BLK.	MINT SHEET	PLATE BLOCK	UNUSED F/NH	USED
4378	$4.95 Redwood Forest	12.00	....	245.00(20)	60.00	14.00	10.00
4379	$17.50 Old Faithful . .	35.00	....	840.00(20)	195.00	48.00	30.00

4380

4381

4382

4383

SCOTT NO.	DESCRIPTION	FIRST DAY COVERS SING	FIRST DAY COVERS PL. BLK.	MINT SHEET	PLATE BLOCK	UNUSED F/NH	USED
4380-83	42¢ Lincoln, strip of 4	5.75	....	34.00(20)	16.00(8)	8.50	....
4380	42¢ Lincoln as Rail Splitter	4.75	....	....	....	2.00	.75
4381	42¢ Lincoln as Lawyer	4.75	....	....	....	2.00	.75
4382	42¢ Lincoln as Politician	4.75	....	....	....	2.00	.75
4383	42¢ Lincoln as President	4.75	....	....	....	2.00	.75

4384

SCOTT NO.	DESCRIPTION	FIRST DAY COVERS SING	FIRST DAY COVERS PL. BLK.	MINT SHEET	PLATE BLOCK	UNUSED F/NH	USED
4384	42¢ Civil Rights Pioneers	....	....	....	....	14.00	....
4384a	42¢ Mary Church Terrell & Mary White Ovington	....	....	....	....	2.25	1.50
4384b	42¢ J R Clifford & Joel Elias Spingarn..	....	....	....	....	2.25	1.50
4384c	42¢ Oswald Garrison Villard & Daisy Gatson Bates	....	....	....	....	2.25	1.50
4384d	42¢ Charles Hamilton Houston & Walter White.	....	....	....	....	2.25	1.50
4384e	Medgar Evers & Fannie Lou Hamer..	....	....	....	....	2.25	1.50
4384f	Ella Baker & Ruby Hurley	....	....	....	....	2.25	1.50

4385

4386

SCOTT NO.	DESCRIPTION	FIRST DAY COVERS SING	FIRST DAY COVERS PL. BLK.	MINT SHEET	PLATE BLOCK	UNUSED F/NH	USED
4385	10¢ Patriotic Banner. .	3.75	....	....	....	.50	.30
	same, plate strip of 5..	....	....	....	....	6.00	....
4386	61¢ Richard Wright . .	3.75	....	30.00	8.00	2.00	.85

4387, 4389

4388

4390

SCOTT NO.	DESCRIPTION	FIRST DAY COVERS SING	FIRST DAY COVERS PL. BLK.	MINT SHEET	PLATE BLOCK	UNUSED F/NH	USED
4387	28¢ Polar Bear.	3.75	....	15.00(20)	4.00	.85	.45
4388	64¢ Dolphin	3.75	....	31.00(20)	8.00	1.75	.85
4389	28¢ Polar Bear, coil . .	3.75	....	....	....	.85	.45
	same, plate strip of 5..	....	....	....	....	8.50	....
4390	44¢ Purple Heart	3.75	....	22.50(20)	5.50	1.50	.45
4391	44¢ Flag, water-activated coil . .	3.75	....	....	....	1.50	.80
	same, plate strip of 5 .	....	....	....	....	11.00	....
4392	44¢ Flag, s/a coil die cut 11 w/pointed corners	....	....	....	....	2.50	.45
	same, plate strip of 5 . .	....	....	....	....	13.00	....
4393	44¢ Flag, s/a coil die cut 9½	....	....	....	....	2.00	.45
	same, plate strip of 5 . .	....	....	....	....	12.00	....
4394	44¢ Flag, s/a coil die cut 8½	....	....	....	....	2.00	.45
	same, plate strip of 5 . .	....	....	....	....	12.00	....
4395	44¢ Flag, s/a coil die cut 11 w/rounded corners	3.75	....	....	....	2.00	.55
	same, plate strip of 5 .	....	....	....	....	12.00	....
4396	44¢ American Flag. . .	3.75	....	....	....	1.50	.45
	same, conv. bklt of 10	....	....	....	....	14.00	....

4391-4396

4397

4398

SCOTT NO.	DESCRIPTION	FIRST DAY COVERS SING	FIRST DAY COVERS PL. BLK.	MINT SHEET	PLATE BLOCK	UNUSED F/NH	USED
4397	44¢ Wedding Rings . .	3.75	....	28.00(20)	7.00	1.50	.40
4398	61¢ Wedding Cake . .	3.75	....	40.00(20)	10.00	2.50	.85

4399 4400 4401

4402 4403

SCOTT NO.	DESCRIPTION	FIRST DAY COVERS SING	FIRST DAY COVERS PL. BLK.	MINT SHEET	PLATE BLOCK	UNUSED F/NH	USED
4399	44¢ Homer Simpson .	3.75	....	....	....	1.50	.85
4400	44¢ Marge Simpson .	3.75	....	....	....	1.50	.85
4401	44¢ Bart Simpson . . .	3.75	....	....	....	1.50	.85
4402	44¢ Lisa Simpson . . .	3.75	....	....	....	1.50	.85
4403	44¢ Maggie Simpson.	3.75	....	....	....	1.50	.85
4403a	The Simpsons, bklt pane of 20.	....	....	....	....	30.00	....

4404

4405

SCOTT NO.	DESCRIPTION	FIRST DAY COVERS SING	FIRST DAY COVERS PL. BLK.	MINT SHEET	PLATE BLOCK	UNUSED F/NH	USED
4404	44¢ King of Hearts. . .	3.75	....	....	....	1.50	.50
4405	44¢ Queen of Hearts .	3.75	....	....	....	1.50	.50
4405a	King and Queen of Hearts, conv. bklt of 20.	....	....	....	....	30.00	....

4406

SCOTT NO.	DESCRIPTION	FIRST DAY COVERS SING	FIRST DAY COVERS PL. BLK.	MINT SHEET	PLATE BLOCK	UNUSED F/NH	USED
4406	44¢ Bob Hope	3.75	....	35.00(20)	8.50	1.75	.50

4407

4408

SCOTT NO.	DESCRIPTION	FIRST DAY COVERS SING	FIRST DAY COVERS PL. BLK.	MINT SHEET	PLATE BLOCK	UNUSED F/NH	USED
4407	44¢ Celebrate	3.75	....	22.00(20)	5.50	1.50	.40
4408	44¢ Anna Julia Cooper	3.75	....	24.00(20)	5.50	1.50	.50

4409 4410 4411 4412 4413

SCOTT NO.	DESCRIPTION	FIRST DAY COVERS SING	FIRST DAY COVERS PL. BLK.	MINT SHEET	PLATE BLOCK	UNUSED F/NH	USED
4409-13	44¢ Gulf Coast Lighthouses	6.00	....	28.00(20)	16.00	9.00	....
4409	44¢ Matagorda Island Lighthouse	2.50	....	....	....	1.75	.75
4410	44¢ Sabine Pass Lighthouse	2.50	....	....	....	1.75	.75
4411	44¢ Biloxi Lighthouse. .	2.50	....	....	....	1.75	.75
4412	44¢ Sand Island Lighthouse	2.50	....	....	....	1.75	.75
4413	44¢ Fort Jefferson Lighthouse	2.50	....	....	....	1.75	.75

4414

EARLY TV MEMORIES

4414a	*Milton Berle*	**4414k**	*Kukla, Fran & Ollie*
4414b	*I Love Lucy*	**4414l**	*Phil Silvers Show*
4414c	*The Red Skelton Show*	**4414m**	*The Lone Ranger*
4414d	*Howdy Doody*	**4414n**	*Perry Mason*
4414e	*Dragnet*	**4414o**	*Alfred Hitchcock*
4414f	*Lassie*	**4414p**	*Burns & Allen*
4414g	*Hopalong Cassidy*	**4414q**	*Ozzie & Harriet*
4414h	*Groucho Marx*	**4414r**	*The Tonight Show*
4414i	*The Dinah Shore Show*	**4414s**	*The Twilight Zone*
4414j	*The Ed Sullivan Show*	**4414t**	*The Honeymooners*

SCOTT NO.	DESCRIPTION	FIRST DAY COVERS SING	FIRST DAY COVERS PL. BLK.	MINT SHEET	PLATE BLOCK	UNUSED F/NH	USED
4414	44¢ Early TV Memories	20.00	....	30.00(20)	....	30.00	....
	Set of Singles	....	....	....	....	....	18.00

4415

4416

SCOTT NO.	DESCRIPTION	FIRST DAY COVERS SING	FIRST DAY COVERS PL. BLK.	MINT SHEET	PLATE BLOCK	UNUSED F/NH	USED
4415	44¢ Hawaii Statehood .	2.25	7.50	48.00 (20)	10.00	2.50	.50
4416	44¢ EID	2.25	....	22.00 (20)	6.00	1.50	.50

4417 4418 4419 4420

SCOTT NO.	DESCRIPTION	FIRST DAY COVERS SING	FIRST DAY COVERS PL. BLK.	MINT SHEET	PLATE BLOCK	UNUSED F/NH	USED
4417-20	44¢ Thanksgiving Day Parade	5.25	....	23.00 (20)	12.00 (8)	6.50	......
4417	44¢ Crowd, Street Sign, Bear Balloon	2.25	....	....	....	1.50	.55
4418	44¢ Drum Major, Musicians	2.25	....	....	....	1.50	.55
4419	44¢ Musicians, Balloon, Horse	2.25	....	....	....	1.50	.55
4420	44¢ Cowboy, Turkey Balloon	2.25	....	....	....	1.50	.55

4421

SCOTT NO.	DESCRIPTION	FIRST DAY COVERS SING	FIRST DAY COVERS PL. BLK.	MINT SHEET	PLATE BLOCK	UNUSED F/NH	USED
4421	44¢ Gary Cooper.	2.25	....	35.00 (20)	8.50	1.75	.60

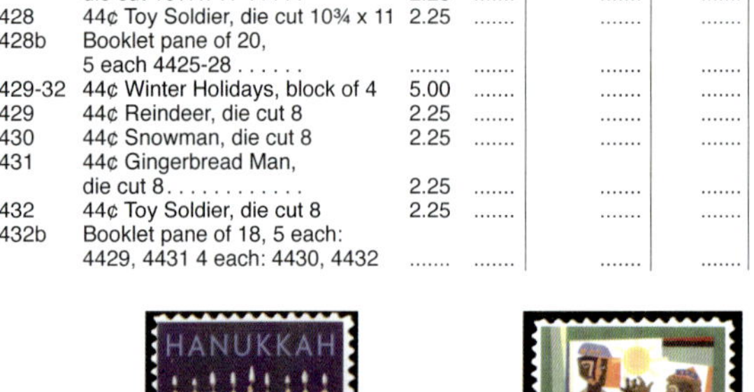

4422

SCOTT NO.	DESCRIPTION	FIRST DAY COVERS SING	FIRST DAY COVERS PL. BLK.	MINT SHEET	PLATE BLOCK	UNUSED F/NH	USED
4422	Supreme Court Justices S/S of 4	4.75	....	....	....	7.00	5.00
4422a	44¢ Felix Frankfurter . .	2.25	....	....	....	1.75	1.00
4422b	44¢ William J. Brennan, Jr.	2.25	....	....	....	1.75	1.00
4422c	44¢ Louis D. Brandeis .	2.25	....	....	....	1.75	1.00
4422d	44¢ Joseph Story.	2.25	....	....	....	1.75	1.00

4423

KELP FOREST

4423a *Brown Pelican*
4423b *Western Gull, Southern Sea Otters, Red Sea Urchin*
4423c *Harbor Seal*
4423d *Lion's Mane Nudibranch*
4423e *Yellow-tail Rockfish, White-spotted Rose Anemone*
4423f *Vermillion Rockfish*
4423g *Copper Rockfish*
4423h *Pacific Rock Crab, Jeweled Top Snail*
4423i *Northern Kelp Crab*
4423j *Treefish, Monterey Turban Snail, Brooding Sea Anemone*

SCOTT NO.	DESCRIPTION	FIRST DAY COVERS SING	FIRST DAY COVERS PL. BLK.	MINT SHEET	PLATE BLOCK	UNUSED F/NH	USED
4423	44¢ Kelp Forest	10.00	....	18.00 (10)	....	18.00	....
	same, set of singles. . .	....		....	....	....	8.00

4424

SCOTT NO.	DESCRIPTION	FIRST DAY COVERS SING	FIRST DAY COVERS PL. BLK.	MINT SHEET	PLATE BLOCK	UNUSED F/NH	USED
4424	44¢ Madonna & Sleeping Child	2.25	....	....	....	1.50	.45
4424a	same, booklet pane of 20	....	....	....	....	28.00	....

4425, 4429 4426, 4430 4427, 4431 4428, 4432

SCOTT NO.	DESCRIPTION	FIRST DAY COVERS SING	FIRST DAY COVERS PL. BLK.	MINT SHEET	PLATE BLOCK	UNUSED F/NH	USED
4425-28	44¢ Winter Holidays, block of 4	5.00	....	....	....	7.50	....
4425	44¢ Reindeer, die cut 10¾ x 11	2.25	....	....	....	1.75	.50
4426	44¢ Snowman, die cut 10¾ x 11	2.25	....	....	....	1.75	.50
4427	44¢ Gingerbread Man, die cut 10¾ x 11	2.25	....	....	....	1.75	.50
4428	44¢ Toy Soldier, die cut 10¾ x 11	2.25	....	....	....	1.75	.50
4428b	Booklet pane of 20, 5 each 4425-28	....	....	....	....	34.00	....
4429-32	44¢ Winter Holidays, block of 4	5.00	....	....	....	7.50	....
4429	44¢ Reindeer, die cut 8	2.25	....	....	....	1.75	.60
4430	44¢ Snowman, die cut 8	2.25	....	....	....	1.75	.60
4431	44¢ Gingerbread Man, die cut 8.	2.25	....	....	....	1.75	.60
4432	44¢ Toy Soldier, die cut 8	2.25	....	....	....	1.75	.60
4432b	Booklet pane of 18, 5 each: 4429, 4431 4 each: 4430, 4432	....	....	....	....	30.00	....

4433 4434

SCOTT NO.	DESCRIPTION	FIRST DAY COVERS SING	FIRST DAY COVERS PL. BLK.	MINT SHEET	PLATE BLOCK	UNUSED F/NH	USED
4433	44¢ Hanukkah	2.25	....	22.00 (20)	5.50	1.50	.50
4434	44¢ Kwanzaa.	2.25	....	22.00 (20)	5.50	1.50	.50

2010 COMMEMORATIVES

SCOTT NO.	DESCRIPTION	FIRST DAY COVERS SING	FIRST DAY COVERS PL. BLK.	MINT SHEET	PLATE BLOCK	UNUSED F/NH	USED
4435/4477	**(4435, 4436, 4440-4443, 4445, 4446-61, 4463-73, 4475, 4476, 4477) 37 varieties**	**.........**		**.........**	**.........**	**55.00**	**18.00**

4435

4436

SCOTT NO.	DESCRIPTION	FIRST DAY COVERS SING	FIRST DAY COVERS PL. BLK.	MINT SHEET	PLATE BLOCK	UNUSED F/NH	USED
4435	44¢ Year of the Tiger . .	2.25	....	15.00 (12)	....	1.75	.55
4436	44¢ 2010 Olympics Snowboarder	2.25	4.75	22.00 (20)	5.50	1.25	.45
4437	44¢ Forever Liberty Bell, dated in copper "2009", medium microprinting, bell 16mm, die-cut 11¼ x 10¾	2.25	....	....	....	1.50	.55
4437a	same, booklet pane of 18	....	....	....	....	26.00	....

4438

4439

SCOTT NO.	DESCRIPTION	FIRST DAY COVERS SING	FIRST DAY COVERS PL. BLK.	MINT SHEET	PLATE BLOCK	UNUSED F/NH	USED
4438	$4.90 Mackinac Bridge.	12.00	....	235.00 (20)	60.00	15.00	10.00
4439	$18.30 Bixby Creek Bridge	39.00	....	875.00 (20)	215.00	55.00	35.00

4440  4441

4442  4443

SCOTT NO.	DESCRIPTION	FIRST DAY COVERS SING	FIRST DAY COVERS PL. BLK.	MINT SHEET	PLATE BLOCK	UNUSED F/NH	USED
4440-43	44¢ Distinguished Sailors, block of 4	5.25	7.50	24.00 (20)	5.50 (4) 10.00 (8)	6.50	....
4440	Admiral William S. Sims	2.25	....	....	....	1.75	1.00
4441	Admiral Arleigh A. Burke	2.25	....	....	....	1.75	1.00
4442	Lt. Commander John McCloy	2.25	....	....	....	1.75	1.00
4443	Petty Officer 3rd Class Doris Miller	2.25	....	....	....	1.75	1.00

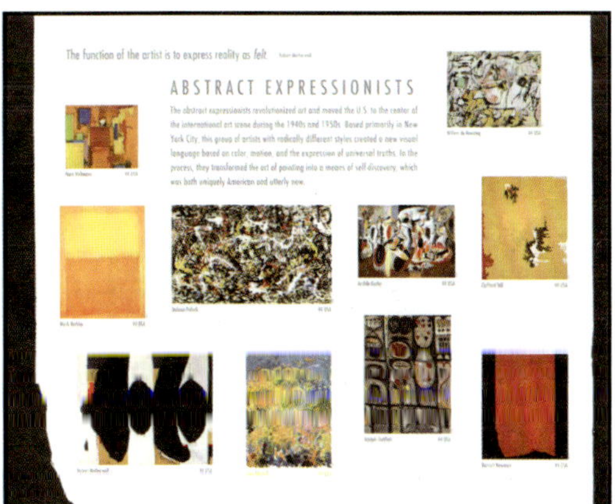
4444

ABSTRACT EXPRESSIONISTS

4444a *The Golden Wall*
4444b *Asheville*
4444c *Orange and Yellow*
4444d *Howdy Doody*
4444e *The Liver is the Cock's Comb*
4444f *1948-C*
4444g *Elegy to the Spanish Republic*
4444h *La Grande Vallée O*
4444i *Romanesque Façade*
4444j *Achilles*

SCOTT NO.	DESCRIPTION	FIRST DAY COVERS SING	FIRST DAY COVERS PL. BLK.	MINT SHEET	PLATE BLOCK	UNUSED F/NH	USED
4444	Abstract Expressionists	....	20.00	....	....	20.00	....
	same, set of singles . . .	....	....	....	....	....	10.00

4445

SCOTT NO.	DESCRIPTION	FIRST DAY COVERS SING	FIRST DAY COVERS PL. BLK.	MINT SHEET	PLATE BLOCK	UNUSED F/NH	USED
4445	44¢ Bill Mauldin	2.25	....	22.00 (20)	5.75	1.50	.45

4446  4447

4448 4449

SCOTT NO.	DESCRIPTION	FIRST DAY COVERS SING	FIRST DAY COVERS PL. BLK.	MINT SHEET	PLATE BLOCK	UNUSED F/NH	USED
4446-49	44¢ Cowboys of the Silver Screen	5.75	....	32.00 (20)	8.00	7.50	....
4446	44¢ Roy Rogers	2.25	....	....	....	2.00	1.00
4447	44¢ Tom Mix	2.25	....	....	....	2.00	1.00
4448	44¢ William S Hart	2.25	....	....	....	2.00	1.00
4449	44¢ Gene Autry.	2.25	....	....	....	2.00	1.00

4450

SCOTT NO.	DESCRIPTION	FIRST DAY COVERS SING	FIRST DAY COVERS PL. BLK.	MINT SHEET	PLATE BLOCK	UNUSED F/NH	USED
4450	44¢ Love: Pansies in a basket	2.25	....	28.00(20)	6.50	1.50	.40

4451

4452

4453

4454 4455

4456

4457

4458

4459

4460

SCOTT NO.	DESCRIPTION	FIRST DAY COVERS SING	FIRST DAY COVERS PL. BLK.	MINT SHEET	PLATE BLOCK	UNUSED F/NH	USED
4451-60	44¢ Adopt a Shelter Pet	11.50	....	32.00(20)	19.00(10)	17.50	....
4451	44¢ Wire-haired Jack Russell Terrier	2.25	....	....	....	1.50	.65
4452	44¢ Maltese cat	2.25	....	....	....	1.50	.65
4453	44¢ Calico cat.	2.25	....	....	....	1.50	.65
4454	44¢ Yellow Labrador Retriever	2.25	....	....	....	1.50	.65
4455	44¢ Golden Retriever . .	2.25	....	....	....	1.50	.65
4456	44¢ Gray, white and tan cat	2.25	....	....	....	1.50	.65
4457	44¢ Black, white and tan cat	2.25	....	....	....	1.50	.65
4458	44¢ Australian Shepherd	2.25	....	....	....	1.50	.65
4459	44¢ Boston Terrier	2.25	....	....	....	1.50	.65
4460	44¢ Orange tabby cat. .	2.25	....	....	....	1.50	.65

4461

4462

SCOTT NO.	DESCRIPTION	FIRST DAY COVERS SING	FIRST DAY COVERS PL. BLK.	MINT SHEET	PLATE BLOCK	UNUSED F/NH	USED
4461	44¢ Katharine Hepburn	2.25	....	24.00(20)	6.00	1.50	.45
4462	64¢ Monarch Butterfly...	2.25	....	31.00(20)	7.50	2.00	1.15

4463

4464

SCOTT NO.	DESCRIPTION	FIRST DAY COVERS SING	FIRST DAY COVERS PL. BLK.	MINT SHEET	PLATE BLOCK	UNUSED F/NH	USED
4463	44¢ Kate Smith.	2.25	....	21.00(20)	5.75	1.50	.45
4464	44¢ Oscar Micheaux. . .	3.75	....	20.00(20)	5.75	1.50	.45

4465 4466

SCOTT NO.	DESCRIPTION	FIRST DAY COVERS SING	FIRST DAY COVERS PL. BLK.	MINT SHEET	PLATE BLOCK	UNUSED F/NH	USED
4465-66	44¢ Negro Leagues Baseball, attached pair.	4.25	7.50	22.00(20)	5.75	3.25	1.25
4465	44¢ Play at Home.	2.50	....	....	....	1.50	.65
4466	44¢ Rube Foster.	2.50	....	....	....	1.50	.65

4467 4468 4469 4470 4471

SCOTT NO.	DESCRIPTION	FIRST DAY COVERS SING	FIRST DAY COVERS PL. BLK.	MINT SHEET	PLATE BLOCK	UNUSED F/NH	USED
4467-71	44¢ Sunday Funnies. . .	4.25	7.50	31.00(20)	18.00(10)	8.00	....
4467	44¢ Beetle Bailey	2.50	....	....	....	1.50	.75
4468	44¢ Calvin and Hobbes	2.50	....	....	....	1.50	.75
4469	44¢ Archie.	2.50	....	....	....	1.50	.75
4470	44¢ Garfield	2.50	....	....	....	1.50	.75
4471	44¢ Dennis the Menace	2.50	....	....	....	1.50	.75

4472

4473

SCOTT NO.	DESCRIPTION	FIRST DAY COVERS SING	FIRST DAY COVERS PL. BLK.	MINT SHEET	PLATE BLOCK	UNUSED F/NH	USED
4472	44¢ Scouting.	2.50	3.75	21.00(20)	5.50	1.50	.45
4473	44¢ Boys in Pasture, Winslow Homer	2.50	3.75	21.00(20)	5.50	1.50	.25

4474

HAWAIIAN RAIN FOREST

4474a	*Hawaii 'amakihi, Hawaii 'elepaio*	**4474f**	*Pulelehua, kolea lau nui, 'ilihia*
4474b	*'Akepa, 'ope'ape'a*	**4474g**	*Koele Mountain damselfly, 'akala*
4474c	*'I'iwi, haha*	**4474h**	*Apapane, Hawaiian Mint*
4474d	*'Oma'o, kanawao, 'ohelo kau la'au*	**4474i**	*Jewel Orchid*
4474e	*'Oha*	**4474j**	*Happyface spider, 'ala'ala wai nui*

SCOTT NO.	DESCRIPTION	FIRST DAY COVERS SING	FIRST DAY COVERS PL. BLK.	MINT SHEET	PLATE BLOCK	UNUSED F/NH	USED
4474	44¢ Hawaiian Rain Forest sheet	10.00		15.00(10)	....	15.00	....
	same, set of singles . . .	....		....	....	....	10.00

4475 4476 4477

SCOTT NO.	DESCRIPTION	FIRST DAY COVERS SING	FIRST DAY COVERS PL. BLK.	MINT SHEET	PLATE BLOCK	UNUSED F/NH	USED
4475	44¢ Mother Teresa	2.50	3.75	22.00(20)	5.50	1.50	.45
4476	44¢ Julia de Burgos . . .	2.50	3.75	21.00(20)	5.50	1.50	.45
4477	44¢ Angel with Lute . . .	2.50	3.75	21.00(20)	5.50	1.50	.45

4478 4479 4480 4481

SCOTT NO.	DESCRIPTION	FIRST DAY COVERS SING	FIRST DAY COVERS PL. BLK.	MINT SHEET	PLATE BLOCK	UNUSED F/NH	USED
4478-81	(44¢) Forever Pine cones, die cut	11.00	5.50	....	....	16.00	....
4478	(44¢) Forever Ponderosa Pine	2.25	....	....	....	4.00	.50
4479	(44¢) Forever Eastern Red Cedar	2.25	....	....	....	4.00	.50
4480	(44¢) Forever Balsam Fir	2.25	....	....	....	4.00	.50
4481	(44¢) Forever Blue Spruce	2.25	....	....	....	4.00	.50
4481b	(44¢) Forever pine cones, die cut 11, bklt pane of 20	....	....	....	....	75.00	....
4482-85	(44¢) Forever pine cones, die cut 11¼ x 10¾	5.50	....	....	....	14.00	....
4482	(44¢) Forever Ponderosa Pine	2.25	....	....	....	2.50	.60
4483	(44¢) Forever Eastern Red Cedar	2.25	....	....	....	4.00	.60
4484	(44¢) Forever Balsam Fir	2.25	....	....	....	2.50	.60
4485	(44¢) Forever Blue Spruce	2.25	....	....	....	4.00	.60
4485b	(44¢) Forever pine cones, die cut 11¼ x 10¾, bklt pane of 18	....	....	....	....	65.00	....

4486, 4488, 4490 — 4487, 4489, 4491

SCOTT NO.	DESCRIPTION	FIRST DAY COVERS SING	FIRST DAY COVERS PL. BLK.	MINT SHEET	PLATE BLOCK	UNUSED F/NH	USED
4486-87	(44¢) Forever Lady Liberty & Flag (AP) die cut 9½ (MICRO forever)		....	....	....	5.00	....
	same, plate strip of 5 . .	....	....	....	16.00	....	....
4486	(44¢) Forever Lady Liberty, (AP) die cut 9½.	2.25	....	....	....	3.00	.45
4487	(44¢) Forever Flag, (AP) die cut 9½.	2.25	....	....	....	3.00	.45
4488-89	(44¢) Forever Lady Liberty & Flag, (SSP) die cut 11 (MICRO forever)		....	....	....	5.00	....
	same, plate strip of 5 . .	....	....	....	16.00	....	....
4488	(44¢) Forever Lady Liberty, (SSP) die cut 11	2.25	....	....	....	3.00	.45
4489	(44¢) Forever Flag	2.25	....	....	....	3.00	.45
4490-91	(44¢) Forever Lady Liberty & Flag, (AV) die cut 8½ (MICRO forever)		....	....	......	5.00	....
	same, plate strip of 5 . .	....	....	....	16.00	....	....
4490	(44¢) Forever Lady Liberty, (AV) die cut 8½.	2.25	....	....	....	3.00	.45
4491	(44¢)Forever Flag.	2.25	....	....	....	3.00	.45

2011 COMMEMORATIVES

SCOTT NO.	DESCRIPTION	FIRST DAY COVERS SING	FIRST DAY COVERS PL. BLK.	MINT SHEET	PLATE BLOCK	UNUSED F/NH	USED
4492/4584	**(4492-4494, 4497-4503, 4522-4523, 4525-4528, 4530, 4541-4545, 4617 4668, 4666 4660, 4583-4584) 41 varieties**		**........**	**.........**	**.........**	**74.00**	**25.00**

4492

4493

SCOTT NO.	DESCRIPTION	FIRST DAY COVERS SING	FIRST DAY COVERS PL. BLK.	MINT SHEET	PLATE BLOCK	UNUSED F/NH	USED
4492	(44¢) Year of the Rabbit	2.25	....	25.00(12)	....	2.25	.45
4493	(44¢) Kansas Statehood	2.25	....	28.00(20)	6.50	1.75	.45

4494

4495

4496

SCOTT NO.	DESCRIPTION	FIRST DAY COVERS SING	FIRST DAY COVERS PL. BLK.	MINT SHEET	PLATE BLOCK	UNUSED F/NH	USED
4494	(44¢) Ronald Reagan . .	2.25	....	35.00(20)	9.00	2.00	.50
4495	(5¢) Art Deco Bird, Non-Profit Coil	2.25		....	....	.25	.25
	same, plate number strip of 5	....		....	....	1.70	....
4496	44¢ Quill and Inkwell Coil	2.25		....	....	1.25	.50
	same, plate number strip of 5	....		....	....	12.00	....

4497-4501

SCOTT NO.	DESCRIPTION	FIRST DAY COVERS SING	FIRST DAY COVERS PL. BLK.	MINT SHEET	PLATE BLOCK	UNUSED F/NH	USED
4497-4501	Latin Music Legends	....	....	35.00(20)	18.00(10)	9.00	....
4497	(44¢) Tito Puente	2.25	....	....	....	2.00	.65
4498	(44¢) Carmen Miranda .	2.25	....	....	....	2.00	.65
4499	(44¢) Selena.	2.25	....	....	....	2.00	.65
4500	(44¢) Carlos Gardel . . .	2.25	....	....	....	2.00	.65
4501	(44¢) Celia Cruz	2.25	....	....	....	2.00	.65

4502

4503

4504

SCOTT NO.	DESCRIPTION	FIRST DAY COVERS SING	FIRST DAY COVERS PL. BLK.	MINT SHEET	PLATE BLOCK	UNUSED F/NH	USED
4502	(44¢) Celebrate.	2.25	....	35.00(20)	7.00	1.80	.45
4503	(44¢) Jazz.	2.25	....	35.00(20)	7.00	1.80	.45
4504	20¢ George Washington	2.25	....	12.00(20)	2.50	.60	.45

4505-09

SCOTT NO.	DESCRIPTION	FIRST DAY COVERS SING	FIRST DAY COVERS PL. BLK.	MINT SHEET	PLATE BLOCK	UNUSED F/NH	USED
4505-09	29¢ Herbs.	....	....	38.00(20)	20.00(10)	10.00	....
4505	29¢ Oregano.	2.25	....	....	....	2.20	.55
4506	29¢ Flax	2.25	....	....	....	2.20	.55
4507	29¢ Foxglove	2.25	....	....	....	2.20	.55
4508	29¢ Lavender	2.25	....	....	....	2.20	.55
4509	29¢ Sage	2.25	....	....	....	2.20	.55

4510

4511

4512

SCOTT NO.	DESCRIPTION	FIRST DAY COVERS SING	FIRST DAY COVERS PL. BLK.	MINT SHEET	PLATE BLOCK	UNUSED F/NH	USED
4510	84¢ Oveta Culp Hobby .	3.75	....	55.00	12.00	3.00	.85
4511	$4.95 New River Gorge Bridge	12.00	....	235.00(20)	55.00	14.00	6.75
4512	20¢ George Washington Coil	2.25	....	....	....	.50	.35
	same, plate # strip of 5 .	....	....	....	7.00	....	....

4513-17

SCOTT NO.	DESCRIPTION	FIRST DAY COVERS SING	FIRST DAY COVERS PL. BLK.	MINT SHEET	PLATE BLOCK	UNUSED F/NH	USED
4513-17	29¢ Herbs Coil	....	....	....	....	12.00	....
	same, plate # strip of 5 .	....	....	....	16.00	....	....
4513	29¢ Oregano Coil	2.25	....	....	....	2.50	.40
4514	29¢ Flax Coil.	2.25	....	....	....	2.50	.40
4515	29¢ Foxglove Coil.	2.25	....	....	....	2.50	.40
4516	29¢ Lavender Coil	2.25	....	....	....	2.50	.40
4517	29¢ Sage Coil.	2.25	....	....	....	2.50	.40

4518-19

SCOTT NO.	DESCRIPTION	FIRST DAY COVERS SING	FIRST DAY COVERS PL. BLK.	MINT SHEET	PLATE BLOCK	UNUSED F/NH	USED
4518-19	(44¢) Lady Liberty and Flag	3.75	....	....	....	3.50	....
4518	(44¢) Lady Liberty.	2.25	....	....	....	1.75	.70
4519	(44¢) Flag.	2.25	....	....	....	1.75	.70
4519b	Booklet pane of 18, (44¢) Lady Liberty & Flag		....	....	....	30.00	....

4520

4521

SCOTT NO.	DESCRIPTION	FIRST DAY COVERS SING	FIRST DAY COVERS PL. BLK.	MINT SHEET	PLATE BLOCK	UNUSED F/NH	USED
4520	(44¢) Wedding Roses. .	2.25	....	125.00(20)	25.00	5.50	.50
4521	64¢ Wedding Cake. . . .	2.75	....	70.00(20)	18.00	4.00	2.00

4522-4523

SCOTT NO.	DESCRIPTION	FIRST DAY COVERS SING	FIRST DAY COVERS PL. BLK.	MINT SHEET	PLATE BLOCK	UNUSED F/NH	USED
4522-23	(44¢) Civil War Sesquicentennial	3.75	....	24.00(12)	....	4.00	....
4522	(44¢) Battle of Fort Sumter	2.25	....	....	....	2.00	.65
4523	(44¢) First Battle of Bull Run	2.25	....	....	....	2.00	.65

4524

GO GREEN

4524a *Buy local produce, reduce bags*
4524b *Fix Water Leaks*
4524c *Share rides*
4524d *Turn off lights when not in use*
4524e *Choose to walk*
4524f *Go green, step by step*
4524g *Compost*
4524h *Let nature do the work*
4524i *Recycle more*
4524j *Ride a bike*
4524k *Plant trees*
4524l *Insulate the home*
4524m *Use public transportation*
4524n *Use efficient light bulbs*
4524o *Adjust the thermostat*
4524p *Maintain tire pressure*

SCOTT NO.	DESCRIPTION	FIRST DAY COVERS SING	FIRST DAY COVERS PL. BLK.	MINT SHEET	PLATE BLOCK	UNUSED F/NH	USED
4524	(44¢) Go Green Pane of 16	....	....	24.00(16)	....	24.00	....
	same, set of singles . . .	....	....	....	....	....	14.00

4525

4526

SCOTT NO.	DESCRIPTION	FIRST DAY COVERS SING	FIRST DAY COVERS PL. BLK.	MINT SHEET	PLATE BLOCK	UNUSED F/NH	USED
4525	(44¢) Helen Hayes	2.25	....	28.00(20)	6.50	1.75	.50
4526	(44¢) Gregory Peck . . .	2.25	....	48.00(20)	11.00	2.50	1.00

4527

4528

SCOTT NO.	DESCRIPTION	FIRST DAY COVERS SING	FIRST DAY COVERS PL. BLK.	MINT SHEET	PLATE BLOCK	UNUSED F/NH	USED
4527-28	(44¢) Space Firsts	3.75	....	28.00(20)	6.50	3.50	1.50
4527	(44¢) Alan B. Shepard, Jr.	2.25	....	....	....	1.75	.65
4528	(44¢) Messenger Mission	2.25	....	....	....	1.75	.65

4529

4530

SCOTT NO.	DESCRIPTION	FIRST DAY COVERS SING	FIRST DAY COVERS PL. BLK.	MINT SHEET	PLATE BLOCK	UNUSED F/NH	USED
4529	(44¢) Purple Heart	2.25	....	28.00(20)	6.50	1.75	.45
4530	(44¢) Indianapolis 500 .	2.25	....	28.00(20)	6.50	1.75	.45

4531-4540

SCOTT NO.	DESCRIPTION	FIRST DAY COVERS SING	FIRST DAY COVERS PL. BLK.	MINT SHEET	PLATE BLOCK	UNUSED F/NH	USED
4531-40	(44¢) Garden of Love . .	12.00	....	75.00(20)	40.00(10)	35.00	....
4531	(44¢) Pink Flower	2.25	....	....	....	3.75	.80
4532	(44¢) Red Flower	2.25	....	....	....	3.75	.80
4533	(44¢) Blue Leaves	2.25	....	....	....	3.75	.80
4534	(44¢) Butterfly.	2.25	....	....	....	3.75	.80
4535	(44¢) Green Vine Leaves	2.25	....	....	....	3.75	.80
4536	(44¢) Blue Flower	2.25	....	....	....	3.75	.80
4537	(44¢) Doves	2.25	....	....	....	3.75	.80
4538	(44¢) Orange Red Flowers	2.25	....	....	....	3.75	.80
4539	(44¢) Strawberry.	2.25	....	....	....	3.75	.80
4540	(44¢) Yellow Orange Flowers	2.25	....	....	....	3.75	.80

4541

4542

4543

4544

SCOTT NO.	DESCRIPTION	FIRST DAY COVERS SING	FIRST DAY COVERS PL. BLK.	MINT SHEET	PLATE BLOCK	UNUSED F/NH	USED
4541-44	(44¢) American Scientists	5.75	....	32.00(20)	15.00(8)	7.00	....
4541	(44¢) Melvin Calvin. . . .	2.75	....	....	....	1.75	.80
4542	(44¢) Asa Gray	2.75	....	....	....	1.75	.80
4543	(44¢) Maria Goeppert Mayer	2.75	....	....	....	1.75	.80
4544	(44¢) Severo Ochoa . . .	2.75	....	....	....	1.75	.80

4545

SCOTT NO.	DESCRIPTION	FIRST DAY COVERS SING	FIRST DAY COVERS PL. BLK.	MINT SHEET	PLATE BLOCK	UNUSED F/NH	USED
4545	(44¢) Mark Twain	2.50	....	30.00(20)	6.50	1.75	.45

4546

PIONEERS OF AMERICAN INDUSTRIAL DESIGN

4546a	*Peter Müller-Munk*	**4546g**	*Norman Bel Geddes*
4546b	*Frederick Hurten Rhead*	**4546h**	*Dave Chapman*
4546c	*Raymond Loewy*	**4546i**	*Greta von Nessen*
4546d	*Donald Deskey*	**4546j**	*Eliot Noyes*
4546e	*Walter Dorwin Teague*	**4546k**	*Russel Wright*
4546f	*Henry Dreyfuss*	**4546l**	*Gilbert Rohde*

SCOTT NO.	DESCRIPTION	FIRST DAY COVERS SING	FIRST DAY COVERS PL. BLK.	MINT SHEET	PLATE BLOCK	UNUSED F/NH	USED
4546	(44¢) Pioneers of American Industrial Design.	15.00	....	22.00(12)	....	22.00	....
	same, set of singles . . .	....	....	....	....	....	15.00

4547

SCOTT NO.	DESCRIPTION	FIRST DAY COVERS SING	FIRST DAY COVERS PL. BLK.	MINT SHEET	PLATE BLOCK	UNUSED F/NH	USED
4547	(44¢) Owney the Postal Dog	2.75	....	38.00(20)	10.00	2.25	.60

4548

4549

4550

4551

SCOTT NO.	DESCRIPTION	FIRST DAY COVERS SING	FIRST DAY COVERS PL. BLK.	MINT SHEET	PLATE BLOCK	UNUSED F/NH	USED
4548-51	(44¢) U.S. Merchant Marine	4.75	....	28.00(20)	8.00	7.00	....
4548	(44¢) Clipper Ship.	2.75	....	....	....	1.75	.75
4549	(44¢) Auxiliary Steamship	2.75	....	....	....	1.75	.75
4550	(44¢) Liberty Ship	2.75	....	....	....	1.75	.75
4551	(44¢) Container Ship . .	2.75	....	....	....	1.75	.75

4552

SCOTT NO.	DESCRIPTION	FIRST DAY COVERS SING	FIRST DAY COVERS PL. BLK.	MINT SHEET	PLATE BLOCK	UNUSED F/NH	USED
4552	(44¢) EID	2.75	.....	28.00(20)	6.50	1.75	.50

4553-57

SCOTT NO.	DESCRIPTION	FIRST DAY COVERS SING	FIRST DAY COVERS PL. BLK.	MINT SHEET	PLATE BLOCK	UNUSED F/NH	USED
4553-57	(44¢) Pixar Films: Send a Hello	5.50	....	32.00(20)	16.00(10)	9.00	....
4553	(44¢) Lightning McQueen & Mater	3.25	....	....	....	1.80	.70
4554	(44¢) Remy the Rat & Linguini	3.25	....	....	....	1.80	.70
4555	(44¢) Buzz Lightyear & Two Aliens	3.25	....	....	....	1.80	.70
4556	(44¢) Carl Fredricksen & Dug	3.25	....	....	....	1.80	.70
4557	(44¢) Wall-E	3.25	....	....	....	1.80	.70

4559, 4561, 4563

4558

4560, 4562, 4564

SCOTT NO.	DESCRIPTION	FIRST DAY COVERS SING	FIRST DAY COVERS PL. BLK.	MINT SHEET	PLATE BLOCK	UNUSED F/NH	USED
4558	(44¢) Edward Hopper . .	2.75	....	45.00(20)	10.00	2.25	.50
4559	(44¢) Lady Liberty (AP)	2.75	....	....	....	2.25	.65
4560	(44¢) American Flag (AP)	2.75	....	....	....	2.25	.65
4560A	Booklet pane of 20	....	....	....	....	45.00	....
4561	(44¢) Lady Liberty (SSP)	2.75	....	....	....	2.25	.65
4562	(44¢) American Flag (SSP)	2.75	....	....	....	2.25	.65
4562A	Booklet pane of 20	....	....	....	....	45.00	....
4563	(44¢) Lady Liberty (AV).	2.75	....	....	....	2.25	.65
4564	(44¢) American Flag (AV)	2.75	....	....	....	2.25	.65
4564B	Booklet pane of 20	....	....	....	....	45.00	....

4565

4566

4567

4570

4568

4569

SCOTT NO.	DESCRIPTION	FIRST DAY COVERS SING	FIRST DAY COVERS PL. BLK.	MINT SHEET	PLATE BLOCK	UNUSED F/NH	USED
4565	(44¢) Barbara Jordan . .	2.75	....	40.00(20)	9.00	2.00	.50
4566-69	(44¢) Romare Bearden.	5.50	....	30.00(16)	14.00(6)	9.00	....
4566	(44¢) Conjunction	2.75	....	....	....	2.00	1.25
4567	(44¢) Odysseus	2.75	....	....	....	2.00	1.25
4568	(44¢) Prevalence of Ritual	2.75	....	....	....	2.00	1.25
4569	(44¢) Falling Star	2.75	....	....	....	2.00	1.25
4570	(44¢) Madonna, Raphael	2.75	....	....	....	1.75	.35
4570a	same, booklet pane of 20	....	....	....	....	30.00	....

4571, 4575, 4579

4572, 4576, 4580

4573, 4577, 4581

4574, 4578, 4582

SCOTT NO.	DESCRIPTION	FIRST DAY COVERS SING	FIRST DAY COVERS PL. BLK.	MINT SHEET	PLATE BLOCK	UNUSED F/NH	USED
4571-74	(44¢)Christmas Ornaments, bklt of 4, 10¾ x 11, microprinted on collar	....	....	....	....	11.00	....
4571	(44¢) Red Ornament. . .	2.75	....	....	....	3.00	.70
4572	(44¢) Blue Ornament, green ribbon	2.75	....	....	....	3.00	.70
4573	(44¢) Blue Ornament, red ribbon	2.75	....	....	....	3.00	.70
4574	(44¢) Green Ornament .	2.75	....	....	....	3.00	.70
4574b	Same, booklet pane of 20	....	....	....	....	55.00	....
4575-78	(44¢) Christmas Ornaments, bklt of 4, 10¾ x 11, . . . microprinted not on collar	2.75	....		....	11.00	....
4575	(44¢) Red Ornament. . .	2.75	....	....	....	3.00	.70
4576	(44¢) Blue Ornament, green ribbon	2.75	....	....	....	3.00	.70
4577	(44¢) Blue Ornament, red ribbon	2.75	....	....	....	3.00	.70
4578	(44¢) Green Ornament .	2.75	....	....	....	3.00	.70
4578b	Same, booklet pane of 20	....	....	....	....	55.00	....
4579-82	(44¢) Christmas Ornament, bklt of 4, 11¼ x 11.	....	....	....	....	15.00	....
4579	(44¢) Red Ornament. . .	2.75	....	....	....	3.75	.70
4580	(44¢) Blue Ornament, green ribbon	2.75	....	....	....	3.75	.70
4581	(44¢) Blue Ornament, red ribbon	2.75	....	....	....	3.75	.70
4582	(44¢) Green Ornament .	2.75	....	....	....	3.75	.70
4582bm	Same, booklet pane of 18	....	....	....	....	60.00	....

4583

4584

SCOTT NO.	DESCRIPTION	FIRST DAY COVERS SING	FIRST DAY COVERS PL. BLK.	MINT SHEET	PLATE BLOCK	UNUSED F/NH	USED
4583	(44¢) Hanukkah	2.75	....	35.00(20)	6.50	1.75	.45
4584	(44¢) Kwanzaa	2.75	....	35.00(20)	6.50	1.75	.45

4585-90

SCOTT NO.	DESCRIPTION	FIRST DAY COVERS SING	FIRST DAY COVERS PL. BLK.	MINT SHEET	PLATE BLOCK	UNUSED F/NH	USED
4585-90	(25¢) Eagles presort, strip of 6	4.75	....	....	....	10.00	....
	same, plate strip of 7 . .	....	....	....	....	18.00	....
4585	(25¢) Eagle, green	2.50	....	....	....	1.70	.60
4586	(25¢) Eagle, blue green	2.50	....	....	....	1.70	.60
4587	(25¢) Eagle, blue	2.50	....	....	....	1.70	.60
4588	(25¢) Eagle, red violet .	2.50	....	....	....	1.70	.60
4589	(25¢) Eagle, brown orange	2.50	....	....	....	1.70	.60
4590	(25¢) Eagle, yellow orange	2.50	....	....	....	1.70	.60

2012 COMMEMORATIVES

SCOTT NO.	DESCRIPTION	FIRST DAY COVERS SING	FIRST DAY COVERS PL. BLK.	MINT SHEET	PLATE BLOCK	UNUSED F/NH	USED
4591/4705	**(4591, 4623-4625, 4627-4628, 4651-4665, 4667-4671, 4677-4681, 4687-4703, 4705) 49 varieties . . . .**	**.......**	**.......**	**.......**	**.......**	**108.00**	**40.00**

4591

SCOTT NO.	DESCRIPTION	FIRST DAY COVERS SING	FIRST DAY COVERS PL. BLK.	MINT SHEET	PLATE BLOCK	UNUSED F/NH	USED
4591	(44¢) New Mexico.	2.75	5.75	30.00(20)	6.50	1.75	.50

4592-96

SCOTT NO.	DESCRIPTION	FIRST DAY COVERS SING	FIRST DAY COVERS PL. BLK.	MINT SHEET	PLATE BLOCK	UNUSED F/NH	USED
4592-96	32¢ Aloha Shirts, strip of 5	5.25	....	44.00(20)	22.00(10)	12.00	....
4592	32¢ Surfers and Palm Trees	2.50	....	....	....	2.25	.55
4593	32¢ Surfers.	2.50	....	....	....	2.25	.55
4594	32¢ Fossil Fish	2.50	....	....	....	2.25	.55
4595	32¢ Shells.	2.50	....	....	....	2.25	.55
4596	32¢ Fish and Starfish . .	2.50	....	....	....	2.25	.55
4597-4601	32¢ Aloha Shirts, coil strip of 5	5.25	....	....	....	10.00	....
4597	32¢ Fish and Starfish . .	2.50	....	....	....	2.00	.55
4598	32¢ Surfers and Palm Trees	2.50	....	....	....	2.00	.55
4599	32¢ Surfers.	2.50	....	....	....	2.00	.55
4600	32¢ Fossil Fish	2.50	....	....	....	2.00	.55
4601	32¢ Shells.	2.50	....	....	....	2.00	.55
	Same, plate # strip of 5	....	....	....	....	16.00	....
	Same, plate # strip of 11	....	....	....	....	30.00	....

4602

4603

4604 4605 4606 4607

SCOTT NO.	DESCRIPTION	FIRST DAY COVERS SING	FIRST DAY COVERS PL. BLK.	MINT SHEET	PLATE BLOCK	UNUSED F/NH	USED
4602	65¢ Wedding Cake	2.75	....	85.00(20)	18.00	4.00	.95
4603	65¢ Baltimore Checkerspot	2.75	....	85.00(20)	22.00	4.50	1.25
4604-07	65¢ Dogs at Work, 4 attached	7.50	....	34.00(20)	10.50	10.00	....
4604	65¢ Seeing Eye Dog. . .	2.75	....	....	....	2.25	1.00
4605	65¢ Therapy Dog	2.75	....	....	....	2.25	1.00
4606	65¢ Military Dog	2.75	....	....	....	2.25	1.00
4607	65¢ Rescue Dog.	2.75	....	....	....	2.25	1.00

4608-4612

SCOTT NO.	DESCRIPTION	FIRST DAY COVERS SING	FIRST DAY COVERS PL. BLK.	MINT SHEET	PLATE BLOCK	UNUSED F/NH	USED
4608-12	85¢ Birds of Prey, strip of 5	10.75	....	75.00(20)	35.00(10)	18.00	....
4608	85¢ Northern Goshawk	3.50	....	....	....	3.75	3.00
4609	85¢ Peregrine Falcon . .	3.50	....	....	....	3.75	3.00
4610	85¢ Golden Eagle.	3.50	....	....	....	3.75	3.00
4611	85¢ Osprey	3.50	....	....	....	3.75	3.00
4612	85¢ Northern Harrier. . .	3.50	....	....	....	3.75	3.00

4613-4617

SCOTT NO.	DESCRIPTION	FIRST DAY COVERS SING	FIRST DAY COVERS PL. BLK.	MINT SHEET	PLATE BLOCK	UNUSED F/NH	USED
4613-17	45¢ Weather Vanes, coil strip of 5	6.75	....	....	....	8.00	....
	Same, plate # strip of 5	....	....	....	....	11.00	....
	Same, plate # strip of 11	....	....	....	....	18.00	....
4613	45¢ Rooster With Perch	2.75	....	....	....	1.75	.60
4614	45¢ Cow	2.75	....	....	....	1.75	.60
4615	45¢ Eagle	2.75	....	....	....	1.75	.60
4616	45¢ Rooster	2.75	....	....	....	1.75	.60
4617	45¢ Centaur	2.75	....	....	....	1.75	.60

4618

4619

4620

4621

4622

SCOTT NO.	DESCRIPTION	FIRST DAY COVERS SING	FIRST DAY COVERS PL. BLK.	MINT SHEET	PLATE BLOCK	UNUSED F/NH	USED
4618-22	(45¢) Bonsai, strip of 5 .	6.75	....	....	....	17.00	....
4618	(45¢) Sierra Juniper . . .	2.50	....	....	....	3.50	.70
4619	(45¢) Black Pine	2.50	....	....	....	3.50	.70
4620	(45¢) Banyan	2.50	....	....	....	3.50	.70
4621	(45¢) Trident Maple . . .	2.50	....	....	....	3.50	.70
4622	(45¢) Azalea	2.50	....	....	....	3.50	.70
4622b	Booklet pane of 20	....	....	....	....	65.00	....

4623

4624

4625

4626

4627

4628

SCOTT NO.	DESCRIPTION	FIRST DAY COVERS SING	FIRST DAY COVERS PL. BLK.	MINT SHEET	PLATE BLOCK	UNUSED F/NH	USED
4623	(45¢) Chinese New Year	2.50	....	24.00(12)	....	2.00	.50
4624	(45¢) John H. Johnson .	2.50	....	30.00(20)	6.50	1.75	.50
4625	(45¢) Heart Health	2.50	....	30.00(20)	6.50	1.75	.50
4626	(45¢) Love Ribbons . . .	2.50	....	30.00(20)	6.50	1.75	.50
4627	(45¢) Arizona Statehood Cent..	2.50	....	30.00(20)	6.50	1.75	.50
4628	(45¢) Danny Thomas . .	2.75	....	30.00(20)	6.50	1.75	.50
4629-32	(45¢) Flag Strip of 4, die cut 8½ vertical.	....	....	....	....	9.00	....
4629	(45¢) Flag & Equality coil, die cut 8½ vertical.	2.50	....	....	....	2.25	.80
4630	(45¢) Flag & Justice coil, die cut 8½ vertical.	2.50	....	....	....	2.25	.80

4629, 4633, 4637, 4643, 4647

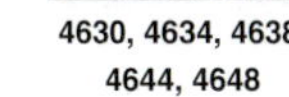
4630, 4634, 4638, 4644, 4648

4631, 4635, 4639, 4641, 4645

4632, 4636, 4640, 4642, 4646

SCOTT NO.	DESCRIPTION	FIRST DAY COVERS SING	FIRST DAY COVERS PL. BLK.	MINT SHEET	PLATE BLOCK	UNUSED F/NH	USED
4631	(45¢) Flag & Freedom coil, die cut 8½ vertical.	2.50	....	....	....	2.25	.80
4632	(45¢) Flag & Liberty coil, die cut 8½ vertical.	2.50	....	....	....	2.25	.80
	Same, plate # strip of 5	....	....	....	....	11.00	....
	Same, plate # strip of 11	....	....	....	....	15.00	....
4633-36	(45¢) Flag strip of 4, die cut 9½ vertical.	....	....	....	....	9.00	....
4633	(45¢) Flag & Equality coil, die cut 9½ vertical	2.50	....	....	....	2.25	.80
4634	(45¢) Flag & Justice coil, die cut 9½ vertical.	2.50	....	....	....	2.25	.80
4635	(45¢) Flag & Freedom coil, die cut 9½ vertical.	2.50	....	....	....	2.25	.80
4636	(45¢) Flag & Liberty coil, die cut 9½ vertical.	2.50	....	....	....	2.25	.80
	Same, plate # strip of 5	....	....	....	....	11.00	....
	Same, plate # strip of 11	....	....	....	....	15.00	....
4637-40	(45¢) Flag strip of 4, die cut 11 vertical	....	....	....	....	9.00	....
4637	(45¢) Flag & Equality coil, die cut 11 vertical	2.50	....	....	....	2.25	.80
4638	(45¢) Flag & Justice coil, die cut 11 vertical	2.50	....	....	....	2.25	.80
4639	(45¢) Flag & Freedom coil, die cut 11 vertical	2.50	....	....	....	2.25	.80
4640	(45¢) Flag & Liberty coil, die cut 11 vertical	2.50	....	....	....	2.25	.80
	Same, plate # strip of 5	....	....	....	....	11.00	....
	Same, plate # strip of 11	....	....	....	....	15.00	....
4641-44	(45¢) Flag block of 4 from bklt, colored dots in stars, 18.5 mm from LL to LR corners of flag	5.50	....	....	....	9.00	....
4641	(45¢) Flag & Freedom bklt Single, colored dots in stars . . .	2.50	....	....	....	2.25	.80
4642	(45¢) Flag & Liberty bklt single, colored dots in stars . . .	2.50	....	....	....	2.25	.80
4643	(45¢) Flag & Equality bklt single, colored dots in stars . . .	2.50	....	....	....	2.25	.80
4644	(45¢) Flag & Justice bklt single, colored dots in stars . . .	2.50	....	....	....	2.25	.80
4644b	Same, bklt pane of 20. .	....	....	....	....	45.00	....
4645-48	(45¢) Flag block of 4 from bklt, dark dots in stars, 19mm from LL to LR corners of flag	5.50	....	....	....	9.00	....
4645	(45¢) Flag & Freedom bklt single, dark dots in stars	2.50	....	....	....	2.25	.80
4646	(45¢) Flag & Liberty bklt single, dark dots in stars	2.50	....	....	....	2.25	.80
4647	(45¢) Flag & Equality bklt single, dark dots in stars	2.50	....	....	....	2.25	.80
4648	(45¢) Flag & Justice bklt single, dark dots in stars	2.50	....	....	....	2.25	.80
4648b	Same, bklt pane of 20. .	....				[illegible]	....

4649

4650

4651-4652

SCOTT NO.	DESCRIPTION	FIRST DAY COVERS SING	FIRST DAY COVERS PL. BLK.	MINT SHEET	PLATE BLOCK	UNUSED F/NH	USED
4649	$5.15 Sunshine Skyway Bridge	12.00	....	235.00(20)	55.00	15.00	12.00
4650	$18.95 Carmel Mission.	39.00	....	425.00(20)	185.00	50.00	40.00
4651-52	(45¢) Cherry Blossom Centennial	3.75	....	40.00(20)	8.00	4.00	....
	Same, plate block of 8 .	....	....	....	9.00(8)	....	....
4651	(45¢) Cherry Blossoms & Washington Monument.	2.50	....	....	....	2.25	.75
4652	(45¢) Cherry Blossoms & Jefferson Memorial	2.50	....	....	....	2.25	.75

4653

SCOTT NO.	DESCRIPTION	FIRST DAY COVERS SING	FIRST DAY COVERS PL. BLK.	MINT SHEET	PLATE BLOCK	UNUSED F/NH	USED
4653	(45¢) Flowers, by William H. Johnson. . . .	2.50	....	38.00(20)	9.00	2.25	.50
	Same	....	....	....	20.00(10)	....	....

4654-63

SCOTT NO.	DESCRIPTION	FIRST DAY COVERS SING	FIRST DAY COVERS PL. BLK.	MINT SHEET	PLATE BLOCK	UNUSED F/NH	USED
4654-63	(45¢) Twentieth Century Poets	10.00	....	80.00(20)	45.00(10)	38.00	....
4654	(45¢) Joseph Brodsky. .	2.50	....	....	....	4.00	2.75
4655	(45¢) Gwendolyn Brooks	2.50	....	....	....	4.00	2.75
4656	(45¢) William Carlos Williams	2.50	....	....	....	4.00	2.75
4657	(45¢) Robert Hayden . .	2.50	....	....	....	4.00	2.75
4658	(45¢) Sylvia Plath	2.50	....	....	....	4.00	2.75
4659	(45¢) Elizabeth Bishop .	2.50	....	....	....	4.00	2.75
4660	(45¢) Wallace Stevens .	2.50	....	....	....	4.00	2.75
4661	(45¢) Denise Levertov .	2.50	....	....	....	4.00	2.75
4662	(45¢) E.E. Cummings . .	2.50	....	....	....	4.00	2.75
4663	(45¢) Theodore Roethke	3.75	....	....	....	4.00	2.75

4664 4665

SCOTT NO.	DESCRIPTION	FIRST DAY COVERS SING	FIRST DAY COVERS PL. BLK.	MINT SHEET	PLATE BLOCK	UNUSED F/NH	USED
4664-65	(45¢) Civil War Sesquicentennial	3.75	....	24.00(12)	....	4.00	....
4664	(45¢) Battle of New Orleans	2.50	....	....	....	2.00	.80
4665	(45¢) Battle of Antietam	2.50	....	....	....	2.00	.80

4666

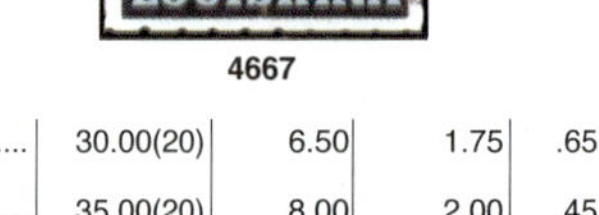

4667

SCOTT NO.	DESCRIPTION	FIRST DAY COVERS SING	FIRST DAY COVERS PL. BLK.	MINT SHEET	PLATE BLOCK	UNUSED F/NH	USED
4666	(45¢) José Ferrer	2.50	....	30.00(20)	6.50	1.75	.65
4667	(45¢) Louisiana Statehood Bicentennial	2.50	....	35.00(20)	8.00	2.00	.45

4668-4671

4672, 4672a

SCOTT NO.	DESCRIPTION	FIRST DAY COVERS SING	FIRST DAY COVERS PL. BLK.	MINT SHEET	PLATE BLOCK	UNUSED F/NH	USED
4668-71	(45¢) Great Film Directors	5.50	....	38.00(20)	10.00	8.00	....
	Same	....	....	....	9.00(8)	....	....
4668	(45¢) John Ford, "The Searchers", John Wayne	2.75	....	....	....	2.25	1.00
4669	(45¢) Frank Capra, "It Happened One Night", Clark Gable and Claudette Colbert	2.75	....	....	....	2.25	1.00
4670	(45¢) Billy Wilder, "Some Like It Hot", Marilyn Monroe.	2.75	....	....	....	2.25	1.00
4671	(45¢) John Huston, "The Maltese Falcon", Humphrey Bogart	2.75	....	....	....	2.25	1.00
4672	1¢ Bobcat	2.25	....	....	....	.25	.25
	Same, plate # strip of 5	....	....	....	.95	....	....
4672a	1¢ Bobcat (dated 2015)	....	....	....	....	.25	.25
	Same, Plate # Strip of 5	....	....	....	1.00	....	....

4673 4674

4675 4676

SCOTT NO.	DESCRIPTION	FIRST DAY COVERS SING	FIRST DAY COVERS PL. BLK.	MINT SHEET	PLATE BLOCK	UNUSED F/NH	USED
4673-76	(45¢) Flags, block or 4 from booklet, colored dots in stars, 19.25 mm from LL to LR corners of flag	5.25	....	....	....	9.00	....
4673	(45¢) Flag & Freedom bklt single, colored dots in stars . . .	2.50	....	....	....	2.25	1.00
4674	(45¢) Flag & Liberty bklt single, colored dots in stars . . .	2.50	....	....	....	2.25	1.00
4675	(45¢) Flag & Equality bklt single, colored dots in stars . . .	2.50	....	....	....	2.25	1.00
4676	(45¢) Flag & Justice bklt single, colored dots in stars . . .	2.50	....	....	....	2.25	1.00
4676b	Same, booklet pane of 10	....	....	....	....	20.00	....

4677-81

SCOTT NO.	DESCRIPTION	FIRST DAY COVERS SING	FIRST DAY COVERS PL. BLK.	MINT SHEET	PLATE BLOCK	UNUSED F/NH	USED
4677-81	(45¢) Pixar Mail a Smile	6.75	....	38.00(20)	20.00(10)	10.00	....
4677	(45¢) Flik & Dot from "A Bug's Life"	2.75	....	....	....	2.00	.65
4678	(45¢) Bob Parr & Dashiell Parr from "The Incredibles"	2.75	....	....	....	2.00	.65
4679	(45¢) Nemo & Squirt from "Finding Nemo".	2.75	....	....	....	2.00	.65
4680	(45¢) Jessie, Woody, & Bullseye from "Toy Story 2".	2.75	....	....	....	2.00	.65
4681	(45¢) Boo, Mike Wazowski & James P. "Sulley" Sullivan from Monsters, Inc.	2.75	....	....	....	2.00	.65

4682-4686

SCOTT NO.	DESCRIPTION	FIRST DAY COVERS SING	FIRST DAY COVERS PL. BLK.	MINT SHEET	PLATE BLOCK	UNUSED F/NH	USED
4682-86	32¢ Aloha shirts, strip of 5 from booklet	5.00	....	....	....	65.00	....
4682	32¢ Surfers & Palm Trees	2.50	....	....	....	13.00	3.00
4683	32¢ Fossil Fish	2.50	....	....	....	13.00	3.00
4684	32¢ Fish & Starfish	2.50	....	....	....	13.00	3.00
4685	32¢ Surfers.	2.50	....	....	....	13.00	3.00
4686	32¢ Shells.	2.50	....	....	....	13.00	3.00
4686b	32¢ Aloha shirts, bklt pane of 10	....	....	....	....	120.00	....

4687-4690

SCOTT NO.	DESCRIPTION	FIRST DAY COVERS SING	FIRST DAY COVERS PL. BLK.	MINT SHEET	PLATE BLOCK	UNUSED F/NH	USED
4687-90	(45¢) Bicycling	5.75	....	30.00(20)	12.00(8)	7.00	....
4687	(45¢) Child on bicycle with Training Wheels	2.50	....	....	....	1.75	.90
4688	(45¢) Commuter on Bicycle with Panniers	2.50	....	....	....	1.75	.90
4689	(45¢) Road Racer.	2.50	....	....	....	1.75	.90
4690	(45¢) BMX Biker.	2.50	....	....	....	1.75	.90

4691

4692 4693

SCOTT NO.	DESCRIPTION	FIRST DAY COVERS SING	FIRST DAY COVERS PL. BLK.	MINT SHEET	PLATE BLOCK	UNUSED F/NH	USED
4691	(45¢) Scouting	2.50	....	35.00(20)	8.00	2.00	.50
4692-93	(45¢) Musicians	3.75	....	30.00(20)	7.50(5)	4.00	....
	same.	....	....	....	18.00(10)	....	....
4692	(45¢) Edith Piaf.	2.50	....	....	....	2.00	1.00
4693	(45¢) Miles Davis	2.50	....	....	....	2.00	1.00

4694 4695

4696 4697

SCOTT NO.	DESCRIPTION	FIRST DAY COVERS SING	FIRST DAY COVERS PL. BLK.	MINT SHEET	PLATE BLOCK	UNUSED F/NH	USED
4694	(45¢) Ted Williams	2.50	....	28.00(20)	6.50(4)	1.75	.70
	. . . .	....	....	....	12.00(8)	....	....
4695	(45¢) Larry Doby.	2.50	....	28.00(20)	6.50(4)	1.75	.70
	. . . .	....	....	....	12.00(8)	....	....
4696	(45¢) Willie Stargell . . .	2.50	....	28.00(20)	6.50(4)	1.75	.70
	. . . .	....	....	....	12.00(8)	....	....
4697	(45¢) Joe DiMaggio . . .	2.50	....	28.00(20)	6.50(4)	1.75	.70
	. . . .	....	....	....	12.00(8)	....	....
4697a	(45¢) Major League Baseball All-Stars	6.50	....	30.00(20)	7.00(4)	7.00	.....
	. . . .	....	....	....	14.00(8)	....	.....

4698

4699

4700

4701

SCOTT NO.	DESCRIPTION	FIRST DAY COVERS SING	FIRST DAY COVERS PL. BLK.	MINT SHEET	PLATE BLOCK	UNUSED F/NH	USED
4698-4701	(45¢) Innovative Choreographers	5.50	....	30.00(20)	14.00(8)	7.00	.....
4698	(45¢) Isadora Duncan. .	2.50	....	....	....	1.75	1.00
4699	(45¢) Jose Limon	2.50	....	....	....	1.75	1.00
4700	(45¢) Katherine Dunham	2.50	....	....	....	1.75	1.00
4701	(45¢) Bob Fosse.	2.50	....	....	....	1.75	1.00

4702 4703

SCOTT NO.	DESCRIPTION	FIRST DAY COVERS SING	FIRST DAY COVERS PL. BLK.	MINT SHEET	PLATE BLOCK	UNUSED F/NH	USED
4702	(45¢) Edgar Rice Burroughs	2.50	....	28.00(20)	6.50(4)	1.75	.50
4703	(45¢) War of 1812 Bicentennial	2.50	....	35.00(20)	....	2.25	.50

4704, 4704b 4705

SCOTT NO.	DESCRIPTION	FIRST DAY COVERS SING	FIRST DAY COVERS PL. BLK.	MINT SHEET	PLATE BLOCK	UNUSED F/NH	USED
4704	(45¢) Purple Heart	2.50	....	28.00(20)	6.50(4)	1.75	.40
4704b	(49¢) Purple Heart (dated 2014)	....	....	28.00	6.50(4)	1.75	.40
4705	(45¢) O. Henry	2.50	....	28.00(20)	6.50(4)	1.75	.45

4706 4707 4708 4709

SCOTT NO.	DESCRIPTION	FIRST DAY COVERS SING	FIRST DAY COVERS PL. BLK.	MINT SHEET	PLATE BLOCK	UNUSED F/NH	USED
4706-09	(45¢) Flags, 11¼ x 10¾ colored dots in stars . . .	....	....	....	....	7.00	......
4706	(45¢) Flag and Freedom	2.50	....	....	....	1.75	1.50
4707	(45¢) Flag and Liberty .	2.50	....	....	....	1.75	1.50
4708	(45¢) Flag and Justice .	2.50	....	....	....	1.75	1.50
4709	(45¢) Flag and Equality	2.50	....	....	....	1.75	1.50
4709b	(45¢) Flags ATM booklet pane of 18.	....	....	....	....	30.00	......

4710

EARTHSCAPES

4710a *Glacier & Icebergs*
4710b *Volcanic Crater*
4710c *Geothermal Spring*
4710d *Butte in Fog*
4710e *Inland Marsh*
4710f *Salt Evaporation Pond*
4710g *Log Rafts*
4710h *Center-Pivot Irrigation*
4710i *Cherry Orchard*
4710j *Cranberry Harvest*
4710k *Residential Subdivision*
4710l *Barge Fleeting*
4710m *Railroad Roundhouse*
4710n *Skyscraper Apartments*
4710o *Highway Interchange*

SCOTT NO.	DESCRIPTION	FIRST DAY COVERS SING	FIRST DAY COVERS PL. BLK.	MINT SHEET	PLATE BLOCK	UNUSED F/NH	USED
4710	(45¢) Earthscapes	2.50	....	38.00	....	38.00	......
	Set of Singles	....	....	....	....	....	25.00

4711

4712 4713

4714 4715

SCOTT NO.	DESCRIPTION	FIRST DAY COVERS SING	FIRST DAY COVERS PL. BLK.	MINT SHEET	PLATE BLOCK	UNUSED F/NH	USED
4711	(45¢) Holy Family & Donkey	2.50	....	....	....	2.00	.45
4711a	same, booklet pane of 20	....	....	....	....	38.00	......
4712-15	(45¢) Christmas Santa & Sleigh	....	....	....	....	9.00	......
4712	(45¢) Reindeer in Flight & Moon	2.50	....	....	....	2.25	.60
4713	(45¢) Santa and Sleigh.	2.50	....	....	....	2.25	.60
4714	(45¢) Reindeer over roof	2.50	....	....	....	2.25	.60
4715	(45¢) Snow-covered buildings	2.50	....	....	....	2.25	.60
4715a	same, booklet pane of 20	....	....	....	....	40.00	......

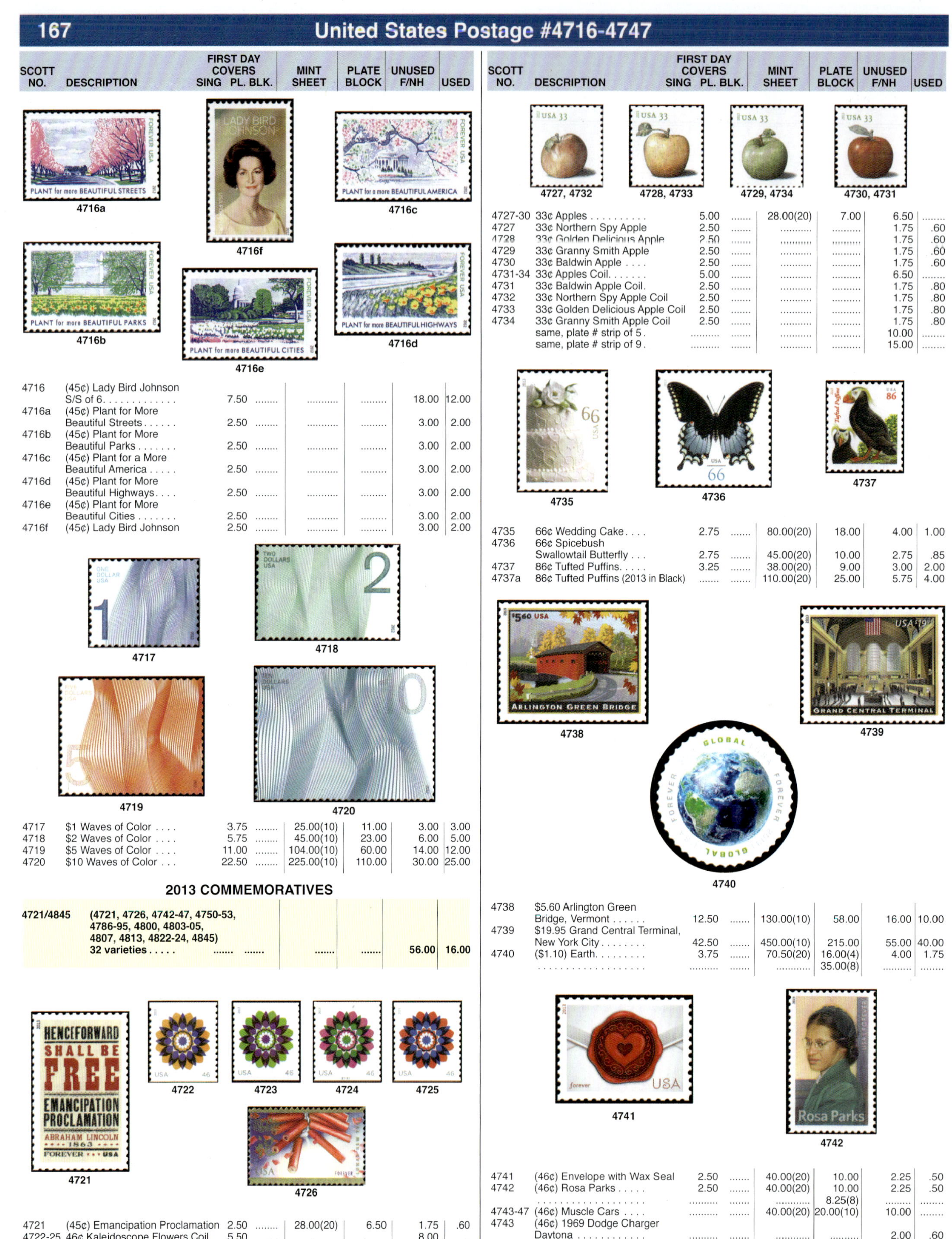
4716a 4716f 4716c 4716b 4716e 4716d 4717 4718 4719 4720 4721 4722 4723 4724 4725 4726 4727, 4732 4728, 4733 4729, 4734 4730, 4731 4735 4736 4737 4738 4739 4740 4741 4742

SCOTT NO.	DESCRIPTION	FIRST DAY COVERS SING	FIRST DAY COVERS PL. BLK.	MINT SHEET	PLATE BLOCK	UNUSED F/NH	USED
4716	(45¢) Lady Bird Johnson S/S of 6	7.50				18.00	12.00
4716a	(45¢) Plant for More Beautiful Streets	2.50				3.00	2.00
4716b	(45¢) Plant for More Beautiful Parks	2.50				3.00	2.00
4716c	(45¢) Plant for a More Beautiful America	2.50				3.00	2.00
4716d	(45¢) Plant for More Beautiful Highways	2.50				3.00	2.00
4716e	(45¢) Plant for More Beautiful Cities	2.50				3.00	2.00
4716f	(45¢) Lady Bird Johnson	2.50				3.00	2.00
4717	$1 Waves of Color	3.75		25.00(10)	11.00	3.00	3.00
4718	$2 Waves of Color	5.75		45.00(10)	23.00	6.00	5.00
4719	$5 Waves of Color	11.00		104.00(10)	60.00	14.00	12.00
4720	$10 Waves of Color	22.50		225.00(10)	110.00	30.00	25.00

2013 COMMEMORATIVES

SCOTT NO.	DESCRIPTION	FIRST DAY COVERS SING	FIRST DAY COVERS PL. BLK.	MINT SHEET	PLATE BLOCK	UNUSED F/NH	USED
4721/4845	**(4721, 4726, 4742-47, 4750-53, 4786-95, 4800, 4803-05, 4807, 4813, 4822-24, 4845) 32 varieties**					**56.00**	**16.00**
4721	(45¢) Emancipation Proclamation	2.50		28.00(20)	6.50	1.75	.60
4722-25	46¢ Kaleidoscope Flowers Coil	5.50				8.00	
4722	46¢ Yellow Orange	2.50				2.00	.75
4723	46¢ Yellow Green	2.50				2.00	.75
4724	46¢ Red Violet	2.50				2.00	.75
4725	46¢ Red	2.50				2.00	.75
	same, plate # strip of 5				12.00		
	same, plate # strip of 9				18.00		
4726	(45¢) Chinese New Year	2.50		24.00(12)		2.00	.55
4727-30	33¢ Apples	5.00		28.00(20)	7.00	6.50	
4727	33¢ Northern Spy Apple	2.50				1.75	.60
4728	33¢ Golden Delicious Apple	2.50				1.75	.60
4729	33¢ Granny Smith Apple	2.50				1.75	.60
4730	33¢ Baldwin Apple	2.50				1.75	.60
4731-34	33¢ Apples Coil	5.00				6.50	
4731	33¢ Baldwin Apple Coil	2.50				1.75	.80
4732	33¢ Northern Spy Apple Coil	2.50				1.75	.80
4733	33¢ Golden Delicious Apple Coil	2.50				1.75	.80
4734	33¢ Granny Smith Apple Coil	2.50				1.75	.80
	same, plate # strip of 5					10.00	
	same, plate # strip of 9					15.00	
4735	66¢ Wedding Cake	2.75		80.00(20)	18.00	4.00	1.00
4736	66¢ Spicebush Swallowtail Butterfly	2.75		45.00(20)	10.00	2.75	.85
4737	86¢ Tufted Puffins	3.25		38.00(20)	9.00	3.00	2.00
4737a	86¢ Tufted Puffins (2013 in Black)			110.00(20)	25.00	5.75	4.00
4738	$5.60 Arlington Green Bridge, Vermont	12.50		130.00(10)	58.00	16.00	10.00
4739	$19.95 Grand Central Terminal, New York City	42.50		450.00(10)	215.00	55.00	40.00
4740	($1.10) Earth	3.75		70.50(20)	16.00(4)	4.00	1.75
					35.00(8)		
4741	(46¢) Envelope with Wax Seal	2.50		40.00(20)	10.00	2.25	.50
4742	(46¢) Rosa Parks	2.50		40.00(20)	10.00	2.25	.50
					8.25(8)		
4743-47	(46¢) Muscle Cars			40.00(20)	20.00(10)	10.00	
4743	(46¢) 1969 Dodge Charger Daytona					2.00	.60
4744	(46¢) 1966 Pontiac GTO					2.00	.60
4745	(46¢) 1967 Ford Mustang Shelby GT					2.00	.60
4746	(46¢) 1970 Chevrolet Chevelle SS					2.00	.60
4747	(46¢) 1970 Plymouth Hemi Barracuda					2.00	.60

4743 4744 4745 4746 4747

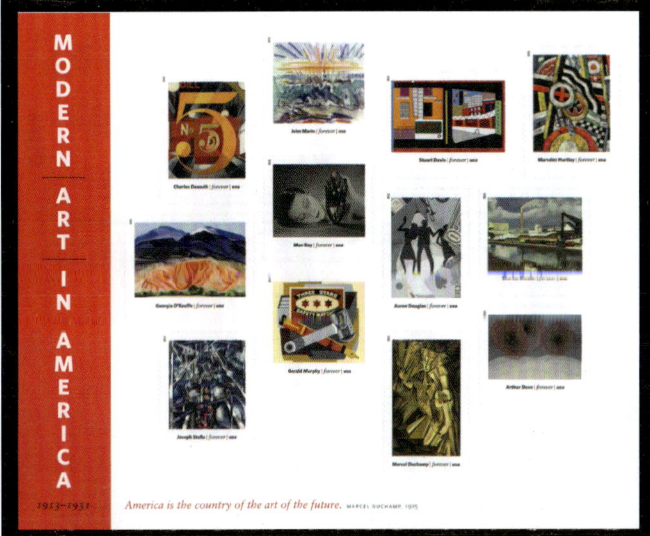

4748

MODERN ART IN AMERICA

4748a *I Saw The Figure 5 (Demuth)*
4748b *Sunset, Main Coast, (Marin)*
4748c *House and Street (Davis)*
4748d *Painting, number 5 (Hartley)*
4748e *Black Mesa Landscape (O'Keeffe)*
4748f *Noire et Blanche (Ray)*
4748g *The Prodigal Son (Douglas)*
4748h *American Landscape (Sheeler)*
4748i *Brooklyn Bridge (Stella)*
4748j *Razor (Murphy)*
4748k *Nude Descending a Staircase (Duchamp)*
4748l *Fog Horns (Dove)*

SCOTT NO.	DESCRIPTION	FIRST DAY COVERS SING	FIRST DAY COVERS PL. BLK.	MINT SHEET	PLATE BLOCK	UNUSED F/NH	USED
4748	(46¢) Modern Art in America	13.00	....	30.00(12)	....	30.00	....
	Set of Singles		....	....	....	....	18.00

4749

4750 4751 4752 4753

SCOTT NO.	DESCRIPTION	FIRST DAY COVERS SING	FIRST DAY COVERS PL. BLK.	MINT SHEET	PLATE BLOCK	UNUSED F/NH	USED
4749	46¢ Patriotic Star Coil. .	2.50	....	....	....	1.75	.40
	same, plate number strip of 5	....	....	....	10.00	....	....
4750-53	(46¢) La Florida	6.25	....	30.00(16)	9.00	8.00	....
4750	(46¢) Red and Pink Hibiscus	2.75	....	....	....	2.00	.75
4751	(46¢) Yellow Cannas. . .	2.75	....	....	....	2.00	.75
4752	(46¢) Red, White and Purple Morning Glories	2.75	....	....	....	2.00	.75
4753	(46¢) White and Purple Passion Flowers.	2.75	....	....	....	2.00	.75

4754 4755 4756 4757

4758 4759 4760

4761 4762 4763

SCOTT NO.	DESCRIPTION	FIRST DAY COVERS SING	FIRST DAY COVERS PL. BLK.	MINT SHEET	PLATE BLOCK	UNUSED F/NH	USED
4754-63	(46¢) Vintage Seed Packets, block of 10	12.50	....	....	....	38.00	....
4754	(46¢) Phlox	2.75	....	....	....	4.00	1.00
4755	(46¢) Calendula	2.75	....	....	....	4.00	1.00
4756	(46¢) Digitalis	2.75	....	....	....	4.00	1.00
4757	(46¢) Linum	2.75	....	....	....	4.00	1.00
4758	(46¢) Alyssum.	2.75	....	....	....	4.00	1.00
4759	(46¢) Zinnias.	2.75	....	....	....	4.00	1.00
4760	(46¢) Pinks	2.75	....	....	....	4.00	1.00
4761	(46¢) Cosmos	2.75	....	....	....	4.00	1.00
4762	(46¢) Aster	2.75	....	....	....	4.00	1.00
4763	(46¢) Primrose	2.75	....	....	....	4.00	1.00
4763b	same, booklet pane of 20	....	....	....	....	80.00	....

4764, 4764a

4765

SCOTT NO.	DESCRIPTION	FIRST DAY COVERS SING	FIRST DAY COVERS PL. BLK.	MINT SHEET	PLATE BLOCK	UNUSED F/NH	USED
4764	(46¢) Where Dreams Blossom flowers	2.75	....	35.00(20)	8.00	2.00	.50
4764a	(49¢) Wedding Flowers [illegible]	[illegible]		[illegible]	[illegible]	[illegible]	[illegible]
4765	66¢ Wedding Flowers and [illegible]	[illegible]		[illegible]	[illegible]	[illegible]	[illegible]

4766, 4770, 4777, 4780, 4784, 4798

4767, 4771, 4774, 4781, 4785, 4799

4768, 4772, 4775, 4778, 4782, 4796

4769, 4773, 4776, 4779, 4783, 4797

SCOTT NO.	DESCRIPTION	FIRST DAY COVERS SING	FIRST DAY COVERS PL. BLK.	MINT SHEET	PLATE BLOCK	UNUSED F/NH	USED
4766-69	(46¢) Flags Forever Coil, die cut 8½ (AD).	5.75	....	....	....	10.00	....
	same, plate # strip of 5 .	....	....	....	....	16.00	....
	same, plate # strip of 9 .	....	....	....	....	25.00	....
4766	(46¢) Flag in Autumn, S/A Coil, 8½ (AD)	2.75	....	....	....	2.25	.40
4767	(46¢) Flag in Winter, S/A Coil, 8½ (AD)	2.75	....	....	....	2.25	.40
4768	(46¢) Flag in Spring, S/A Coil, 8½ (AD)	2.75	....	....	....	2.25	.40
4769	(46¢) Flag in Summer, S/A Coil, 8½ (AD)	2.75	....	....	....	2.25	.40
4770-73	(46¢) Flags Forever Coil, die cut 9½ (AP).	5.75	....	....	....	10.00	....
	same, plate # strip of 5 .	....	....	....	....	16.00	....
	same, plate # strip of 9 .	....	....	....	....	25.00	....
4770	(46¢) Flag in Autumn, S/A Coil, 9½ (AP)	2.75	....	....	....	2.25	.40
4771	(46¢) Flag in Winter, S/A Coil, 9½ (AP)	2.75	....	....	....	2.25	.40
4772	(46¢) Flag in Spring, S/A Coil, 9½ (AP)	2.75	....	....	....	2.25	.40

SCOTT NO.	DESCRIPTION	FIRST DAY COVERS SING	FIRST DAY COVERS PL. BLK.	MINT SHEET	PLATE BLOCK	UNUSED F/NH	USED
4773	(46¢) Flag in Autumn, S/A Coil, 9½ (AP)	2.75	....	....	....	3.00	.40
4774-77	(46¢) Flags Forever Coil, D/C 11 (SSP)	5.75	....	....	....	14.00	....
	same, plate # strip of 5 .	....	....	....	....	20.00	....
	same, plate # strip of 9 .	....	....	....	....	35.00	....
4774	(46¢) Flag in Winter, S/A Coil, 11 (SSP)	2.75	....	....	....	2.00	.40
4775	(46¢) Flag in Spring, S/A Coil, 11 (SSP)	2.75	....	....	....	2.00	.40
4776	(46¢) Flag in Summer, S/A Coil, 11 (SSP)	2.75	....	....	....	2.00	.40
4777	(46¢) Flag in Autumn, S/A Coil, 11 (SSP)	2.75	....	....	....	2.00	.40
4778-81	Flags Forever, booklet stamps, Microprint at Lower Left Corner of Flag (AP)	5.75	....	....	....	8.50	....
4778	(46¢) Flag in Spring, booklet single, Microprint at Lower Left Corner of Flag (AP) . . .	2.75	....	....	....	2.00	.40
4779	(46¢) Flag in Summer, booklet single, Microprint at Lower Left Corner of Flag (AP) . . .	2.75	....	....	....	2.00	.40
4780	(46¢) Flag in Autumn, booklet single, Microprint at Lower Left Corner of Flag (AP) . . .	2.75	....	....	....	2.00	.40
4781	(46¢) Flag in Winter, booklet single, Microprint at Lower Left Corner of Flag (AP) . . .	2.75	....	....	....	2.00	.40
4781	same, booklet pane of 20	....	....	....	....	38.00	....
4782-85	Flags Forever, booklet stamps, microprinted near top of pole or at lower left near rope (SSP)	5.75	....	....	....	7.50	....
4782a 4785a-	Flags Forever, bklt stmps, Microprint near top of pole or lower left near rope (SSP) overall tag	5.75	....	....	....	7.50	....
4782b- 4785b	Flags Forever, bklt stmps, Microprint near top of pole or lower left near rope (SSP) overall tag, 2014 date . .	5.75	....	....	....	7.50	....
4782	(46¢) Flag in Spring, Bk Sng, SSP	2.75	....	....	....	1.75	.40
4782a	(46¢) Flag in Spring, Booklet Single,(SSP) overall tagging	2.75	....	....	....	1.75	.40
4782b	(46¢) Flag in Spring, Booklet Single, (SSP) overall tagging, 2014 date	2.75	....	....	....	1.75	.40
4783	(46¢) Flag in Summer,Bk Sng,SSP	2.75	....			1.75	.40
4783a	(46¢) Flag in Summer,Booklet single, (SSP) overall tagging . .	2.75	....	....	....	1.50	.40
4783b	(46¢) Flag in Summer,Booklet single, (SSP) overall tagging, 2014 date	2.75	....	....	....	1.75	.40
4784	(46¢) Flag in Autumn,Bk.Sng,SSP	2.75				1.75	.40
4784a	(46¢) Flag in Autumn,Booklet Single, (SSP) overall tagging . .	2.75	....	....	....	1.75	.40
4784b	(46¢) Flag in Autumn,Booklet Single, (SSP) overall tagging, 2014 date	2.75	....	....	....	1.75	.40
4785	(46¢) Flag in Winter, Bkl.Sng,SSP	2.75				1.75	.40
4785a	(46¢) Flag in Winter, Booklet Single, (SSP) overall tagging . .	2.75	....	....	....	1.75	.40
4785b	(46¢) Flag in Winter, Booklet Single, (SSP) overall tagging, 2014 date	2.75	....	....	....	1.75	.40
4785d	same, booklet pane of 20 (4782-85)	22	....	....	....	34.00	.40
4785f	same, booklet pane of 10 overall tagging (4782a-85a)	22	....	....	....	20.00	.40
4785h	same, booklet pane of 20, overall tagging, 2014 date(4782b-85b)	22	....	....	....	34.00	.40

4786

SCOTT NO.	DESCRIPTION	FIRST DAY COVERS SING	FIRST DAY COVERS PL. BLK.	MINT SHEET	PLATE BLOCK	UNUSED F/NH	USED
4786	(46¢) Lydia Mendoza . .	2.75	....	25.00(16)	....	1.75	.55

4787

4788

SCOTT NO.	DESCRIPTION	FIRST DAY COVERS SING	FIRST DAY COVERS PL. BLK.	MINT SHEET	PLATE BLOCK	UNUSED F/NH	USED
4787-88	(46¢) Civil War Sesquicentennial	3.75	....	24.00 (12)	....	4.00	....
4787	(46¢) Battle of Vicksburg	2.75	....	....	....	2.00	1.00
4788	(46¢) Battle of Gettysburg	2.75	....	....	....	2.00	1.00

4789

4790

4791-95

4800

SCOTT NO.	DESCRIPTION	FIRST DAY COVERS SING	FIRST DAY COVERS PL. BLK.	MINT SHEET	PLATE BLOCK	UNUSED F/NH	USED
4789	(46¢) Johnny Cash	2.75	....	24.00(16)	....	1.75	.30
4790	(46¢) West Virginia Statehood, 150th Anniversary.	2.75	....	28.00(20)	6.50	1.75	.30
4791-95	(46¢) New England Coastal Lighthouses	7.50	....	40.00(20)	20.00(10)	10.00	....
4791	(46¢) Portland Head Lighthouse, Maine	2.75	....	....	....	2.00	.80
4792	(46¢) Portsmouth Harbor Lighthouse, New Hampshire	2.75	....	....	....	2.00	.80
4793	(46¢) Boston Harbor Lighthouse, Massachusetts	2.75	....	....	....	2.00	.80
4794	(46¢) Point Judith Lighthouse, Rhode Island	2.75	....	....	....	2.00	.80
4795	(46¢) New London Harbor Lighthouse, Connecticut	2.75	....	....	....	2.00	.80
4796-99	(46¢) Flags Forever, die cut 11¼ x 11½.	5.75	....	....	....	12.00	....
4796	(46¢) Flag in Spring, Booklet Single, die cut 11¼ x 11½.	2.75	....	....	....	3.00	....
4797	(46¢) Flag in Summer,Booklet single, die cut 11¼ x 11½.	2.75	....	....	....	3.00	....
4798	(46¢) Flag in Autumn,Booklet Single, die cut 11¼ x 11½.	2.75	....	....	....	3.00	....
4799	(46¢) Flag in Winter, Booklet Single, die cut 11¼ x 11½.	2.75	....	....	....	3.00	....
4799b	Double Sided Booklet pane of 20			....	....	55.00	....
4800	(46¢) EID	2.75	....	28.00(20)	6.50	1.75	1.00

4801
MADE IN AMERICA - BUILDING A NATION

4801a	*Airplane Mechanic (Lewis Hine)*	**4801g**	*Coal Miner (Anonymous)*
4801b	*Derrick Man, Empire State Building (Hine)*	**4801h**	*Riveters, Empire State Building (Hine)*
4801c	*Millinery Apprentice (Hine)*	**4801i**	*Powerhouse Mechanic (Hine)*
4801d	*Man on Hoisting Ball, Empire State Building (Hine)*	**4801j**	*Railroad Track Walker (Hine)*
		4801k	*Textile Worker (Hine)*
4801e	*Linotype Operator (Hine)*	**4801l**	*Man Guiding Beam on Empire State Building (Hine)*
4801f	*Welder On Empire State Building (Hine)*		

SCOTT NO.	DESCRIPTION	FIRST DAY COVERS SING	FIRST DAY COVERS PL. BLK.	MINT SHEET	PLATE BLOCK	UNUSED F/NH	USED
4801	(46¢) Building a Nation .	13.50	....	24.00(12)	....	24.00	....

4802

4803

4804

4805

SCOTT NO.	DESCRIPTION	FIRST DAY COVERS SING	FIRST DAY COVERS PL. BLK.	MINT SHEET	PLATE BLOCK	UNUSED F/NH	USED
4802	1¢ Bobcat coil (SSP) die cut 9¾, (2013)	2.75	....	....	.75	.25	.25
4803	(46¢) Althea Gibson . . .	2.75	....	35.00(20)	8.00	2.00	.50
4804	(46¢) 1963 March on Washington	2.75	....	28.00(20)	6.50	1.75	.50
4805	(46¢) Battle of Lake Erie	2.75	....	28.00(20)	....	1.75	.50

4806a

4807

4808-12

SCOTT NO.	DESCRIPTION	FIRST DAY COVERS SING	FIRST DAY COVERS PL. BLK.	MINT SHEET	PLATE BLOCK	UNUSED F/NH	USED
4806	$2 Inverted Jenny Sheet of 6	27.00	....	....	....	30.00	....
4806a	same, single stamp. . . .	6.50	....		....	6.00	4.00
4807	(46¢) Ray Charles	2.75	....	24.00(16)	....	1.75	.50
4808-12	(10¢) Snowflakes, Presorted	3.75	....	....	....	2.00	....
	same, plate number strip of 11		....	....	....	9.00	....
	same, plate number strip of 5	4.25	....	....	....	4.50	....
4808	(10¢) light blue & multicolored		....	....	....	1.50	.25
4809	(10¢) pale blue & multicolored		....	....	....	1.50	.25
4810	(10¢) light blue & multicolored		....	....	....	1.50	.25
4811	(10¢) pale blue & multicolored		....	....	....	1.50	.25
4812	(10¢) lilac & multicolored		....	....	....	1.50	.25

4813

4814

4815

4816, 4816b, 4816c, 4821

SCOTT NO.	DESCRIPTION	FIRST DAY COVERS SING	FIRST DAY COVERS PL. BLK.	MINT SHEET	PLATE BLOCK	UNUSED F/NH	USED
4813	(46¢) Holy Family & Donkey		....	45.00(20)	10.00	2.25	.25
4814	($1.10) Christmas Wreath		....	45.00(10)	20.00	5.00	1.50
4815	(46¢) Virgin & Child by Jan Gossaert	2.75	....	....	....	2.25	.30
4815a	same, booklet pane of 20		....	....	....	38.00	....
4816	(46¢) Poinsettia	4.25	....	....	....	2.25	.30
4816a	same, booklet pane of 20		....	....	....	38.00	....
4816b	(46¢) Poinsettia, Dated 2014	2.75	....	....	....	2.25	.30
4816c	Same, Booklet Pane of 20 Dated 2014.		....	....	....	38.00	....

4817-4820

4822, 4822a, 4822b

4823, 4823a 4823b

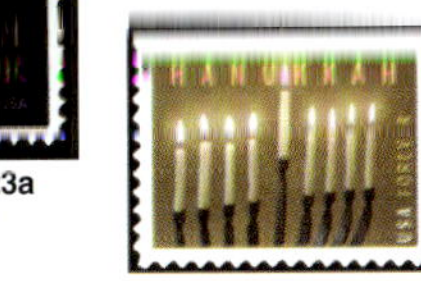

4824

SCOTT NO.	DESCRIPTION	FIRST DAY COVERS SING	FIRST DAY COVERS PL. BLK.	MINT SHEET	PLATE BLOCK	UNUSED F/NH	USED
4817-20	(46¢) Gingerbread Houses		....	....	....	9.00	....
4817	(46¢) Gingerbread House with Red Door	2.75	....	....	....	2.25	.30
4818	(46¢) Gingerbread House with Blue Door	2.75	....	....	....	2.25	.30
4819	(46¢) Gingerbread House with Green Door.	2.75	....	....	....	2.25	.30
4820	(46¢) Gingerbread House with Orange Door.	2.75	....	....	....	2.25	.30
4820b	same, booklet pane of 20		....			40.00	....
4821	(46¢) Poinsettia	2.75	....	....	....	2.25	.30
4821a	same, booklet pane of 18		....	....	....	38.00	....
4822-23	(46¢) Medal of Honor . .	4.50	....	35.00(20)	6.50	4.00	....
4822-23a	(49¢) Medal of Honor, Dated 2014	3.75	....	35.00(20)	6.50	4.00	....
4822	(46¢) Navy Medal of Honor	2.75	....	....	....	2.00	.55
4822a	(49¢) Navy Medal of Honor Dated 2014.	2.50	....	....	....	2.00	.55
4822b	(49¢) Navy Medal of Honor Dated 2015.	2.75	....	....	....	2.00	1.50
4823	(46¢) Army Medal of Honor	2.75	....	....	....	2.00	.55
4823a	(49¢) Army Medal of Honor Dated 2014.	2.50	....	....	....	2.00	.55
4823b	(49¢) Army Medal of Honor Dated 2015.	2.75	....	....	....	2.00	1.50
4824	(46¢) Hanukkah	2.75	....	28.00(20)	6.50	1.75	.55

4825 4826

4827 4828

4829 4830

4831 4832

4833 4834

4835 4836

4837 4838

4839 4840

4841 4842

4843 4844

SCOTT NO.	DESCRIPTION	FIRST DAY COVERS SING	FIRST DAY COVERS PL. BLK.	MINT SHEET	PLATE BLOCK	UNUSED F/NH	USED
4825-44	(46¢) Harry Potter booklet, 5 panes of 4 stamps each	22.00	....	....	....	40.00	....
4825	(46¢) Harry Potter.	2.75	....	....	....	2.50	1.25
4826	(46¢) Harry potter and Ron Weasley	2.75	....	....	....	2.50	1.25
4827	(46¢) Harry Potter, Ron Weasley, Hermione Granger	2.75	....	....	....	2.50	1.25
4828	(46¢) Hermione Granger	2.75	....	....	....	2.50	1.25
4828a	same, booklet pane of 4	....	....	....	....	10.00	
4829	(46¢) Harry Potter and Fawkes the Phoenix	2.75				2.50	1.25
4830	(46¢) Hedwig the Owl. . .	2.75				2.50	1.25
4831	(46¢) Dobby the House Elf	2.75	....	....	....	2.50	1.25
4832	(46¢) Harry Potter and Buckbeak the Hippogriff	2.75	....	....	....	2.50	1.25
4832a	same, booklet pane of 4		....	....	....	10.00	....
4833	(46¢) Headmaster Albus Dumbledore	2.75	....	....	....	2.50	1.25
4834	(46¢) Professor Severus Snape	2.75	....	....	....	2.50	1.25
4835	(46¢) Rubeus Hagrid . .	2.75	....	....	....	2.50	1.25
4836	(46¢) Professor Minerva McGonagall	2.75	....	....	....	2.50	1.25
4836a	same, booklet pane of 4	....	....	....	....	10.00	....
4837	(46¢) Harry Potter, Ron Weasley & Hermione Granger	2.75	....	....	....	2.50	1.25
4838	(46¢) Luna Lovegood . .	2.75	....	....	....	2.50	1.25
4839	(46¢) Fred and George Weasley	2.75	....	....	....	2.50	1.25
4840	(46¢) Ginny Weasley . .	2.75	....	....	....	2.50	1.25
4840a	same, booklet pane of 4		....	....	....	10.00	....
4841	(46¢) Draco Malfoy. . . .	2.75	....	....	....	2.50	1.25
4842	(46¢) Harry Potter.	2.75	....	....	....	2.50	1.25
4843	(46¢) Lord Voldemort . .	2.75	....	....	....	2.50	1.25
4844	(46¢) Bellatrix Lestrange	2.75	....	....	....	2.50	1.25
4844a	same, booklet pane of 4	....	....	....	....	10.00	....

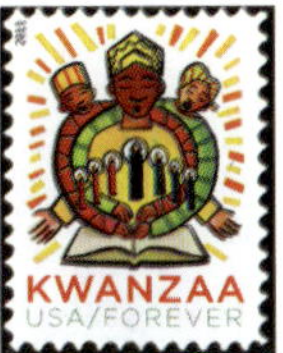

4845

SCOTT NO.	DESCRIPTION	FIRST DAY COVERS SING	FIRST DAY COVERS PL. BLK.	MINT SHEET	PLATE BLOCK	UNUSED F/NH	USED
4845	(46¢) Kwanzaa	2.75	....	28.00(20)	6.50	1.75	1.00

2014 COMMEMORATIVES

SCOTT NO.	DESCRIPTION	FIRST DAY COVERS SING	FIRST DAY COVERS PL. BLK.	MINT SHEET	PLATE BLOCK	UNUSED F/NH	USED
4846/4951	(4846, 4856, 4866, 4880, 4892, 4898-4907, 4910-16, 4921-26, 4928-35, 4950-51) 38 varieties	....	....	....	....	85.00	....

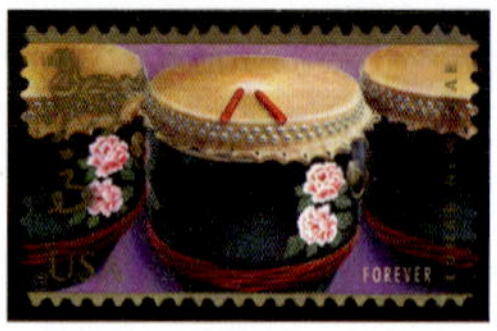

4846

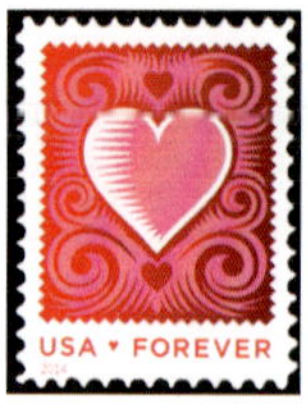

4847

SCOTT NO.	DESCRIPTION	FIRST DAY COVERS SING	FIRST DAY COVERS PL. BLK.	MINT SHEET	PLATE BLOCK	UNUSED F/NH	USED
4846	(46¢) Chinese New Year Year of the Horse	2.75	....	22.00(12)	....	2.00	.60
4847	(46¢) Love	2.75	....	40.00(20)	6.50	2.25	.50

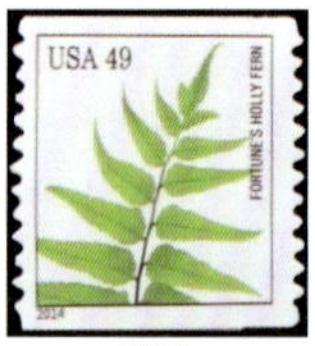

4848

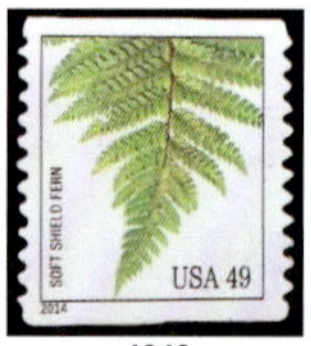

4849

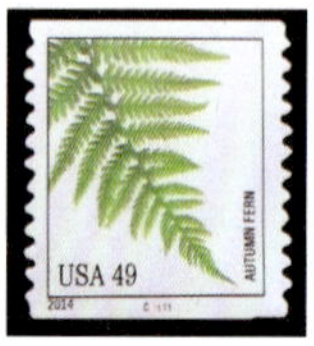

4850

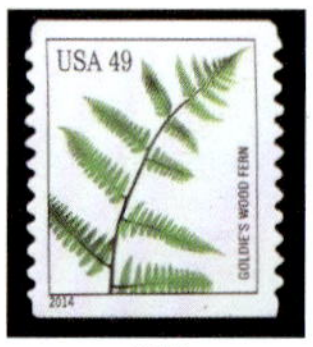

4851

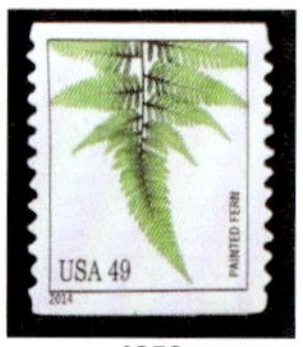

4852

SCOTT NO.	DESCRIPTION	FIRST DAY COVERS SING	FIRST DAY COVERS PL. BLK.	MINT SHEET	PLATE BLOCK	UNUSED F/NH	USED
4848-52	49¢ Ferns Coil	6.75	....	....	....	10.00	....
	same, plate number strip of 5	2.75	....	....	....	12.00	....
4848	49¢ Fortune's Holly Fern	2.75	....	....	....	2.00	.90
4849	49¢ Soft Shield Fern. . .	2.75	....	....	....	2.00	.90
4850	49¢ Autumn Fern	2.75	....	....	....	2.00	.90
4851	49¢ Goldie's Wood Fern	2.75	....	....	....	2.00	.90
4852	49¢ Painted Fern	2.75	....	....	....	2.00	.90

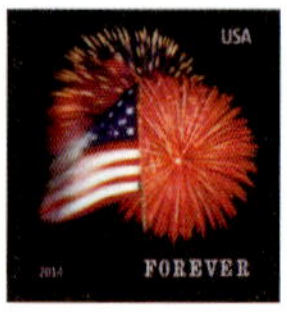

4855,4853, 4868-71

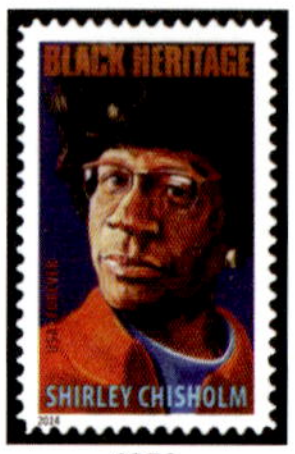

4856

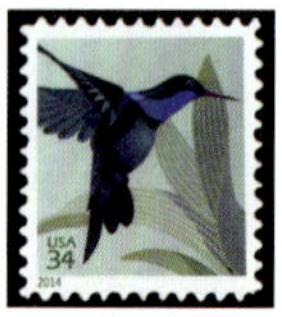

4857, 4858

SCOTT NO.	DESCRIPTION	FIRST DAY COVERS SING	FIRST DAY COVERS PL. BLK.	MINT SHEET	PLATE BLOCK	UNUSED F/NH	USED
4853	(49¢) Ft. McHenry Flag & Fireworks Coil, die cut 8½ (CCL)	2.75	....	....	....	2.25	....
	same, plate number strip of 5		....	....	....	12.00	....
4854	(49¢) Ft. McHenry Flag & Fireworks Coil, die cut 9½ (AP) . .	2.75	....	....	....	2.25	....
	same, plate number strip of 5		....	....	....	12.00	....
4855	(49¢) Ft. McHenry Flag & Fireworks die cut 11¼ x 10¾	2.75	....	....	....	2.25	....
4855a	same, booklet pane of 20	2.75	....	....	....	45.00	....
4856	(49¢) Shirley Chisholm .	2.75	....	38.00(20)	6.50	1.75	.70
4857	34¢ Hummingbird	2.75	....	38.00(20)	6.50	1.75	.30
4858	34¢ Hummingbird coil. .	2.75	....	....	....	1.75	.30
	same, plate number strip of 5		....	....	....	10.00	....

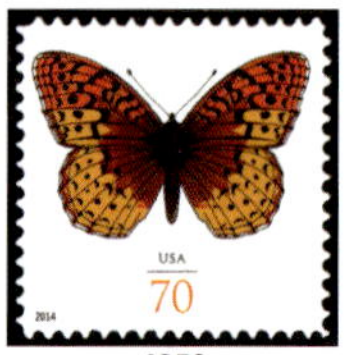

4859

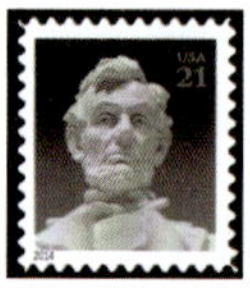

4860

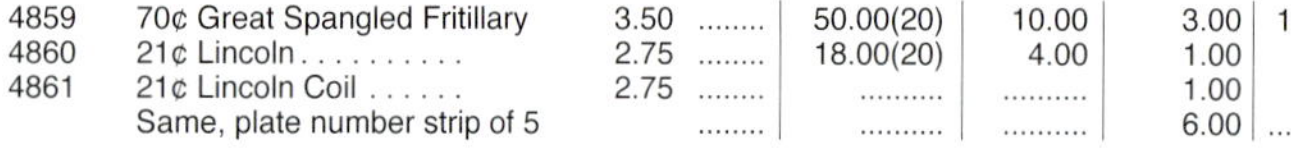

SCOTT NO.	DESCRIPTION	FIRST DAY COVERS SING	FIRST DAY COVERS PL. BLK.	MINT SHEET	PLATE BLOCK	UNUSED F/NH	USED
4859	70¢ Great Spangled Fritillary	3.50	....	50.00(20)	10.00	3.00	1.00
4860	21¢ Lincoln	2.75	....	18.00(20)	4.00	1.00	.30
4861	21¢ Lincoln Coil	2.75	....	....	....	1.00	.30
	Same, plate number strip of 5		....	....	....	6.00	....

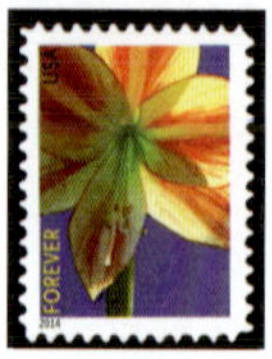

4862

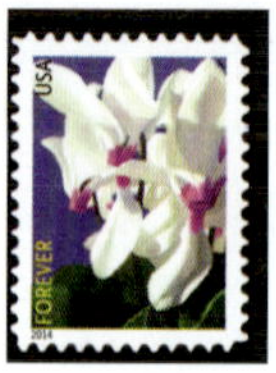

4863

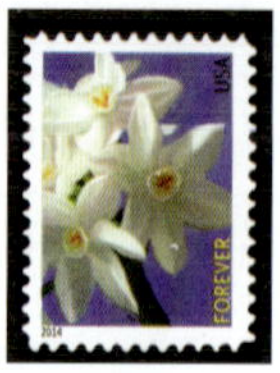

4864

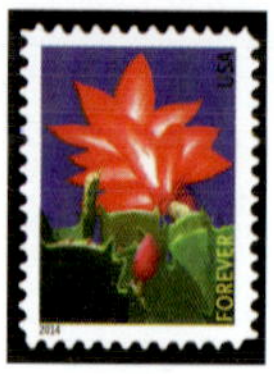

4865

SCOTT NO.	DESCRIPTION	FIRST DAY COVERS SING	FIRST DAY COVERS PL. BLK.	MINT SHEET	PLATE BLOCK	UNUSED F/NH	USED
4862-65	(49¢) Winter Flowers . .	5.75	....	....	....	10.00	....
4862	(49¢) Amaryllis	2.75	....	....	....	2.00	.35
4863	(49¢) Cyclamen	2.75	....	....	....	2.00	.35
4864	(49¢) Paperwhite	2.75	....	....	....	2.00	.35
4865	(49¢) Christmas Cactus	2.75	....	....	....	2.00	.35
4865a	(49¢) Winter Flowers, booklet pane of 20		....	....	....	40.00	....

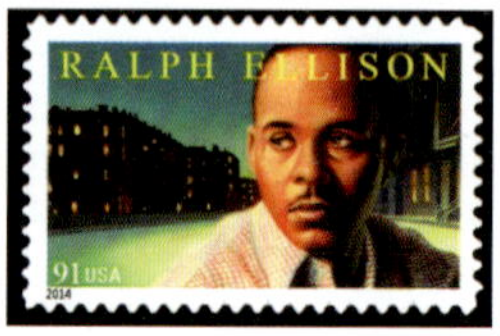

4866

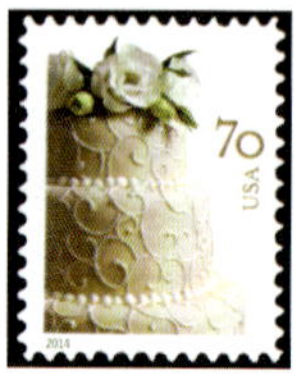

4867

SCOTT NO.	DESCRIPTION	FIRST DAY COVERS SING	FIRST DAY COVERS PL. BLK.	MINT SHEET	PLATE BLOCK	UNUSED F/NH	USED
4866	91¢ Ralph Ellison	3.75	....	58.00(20)	12.00	3.25	1.00
4867	70¢ Wedding Cake	3.50	....	100.00(20)	20.00	5.00	1.50
4868	(49¢) Fort McHenry Flag & Fireworks coil D/C 11 Microprint in Fireworks above flagpole (SSP)	2.75	....	....	....	2.00	.30
	same, plate number strip of 5		....	....	....	12.00	....
4869	(49¢) Fort McHenry Flag & Fireworks die cut 11¼ x 11½ with no Microprint	2.75	....	....	....	2.00	.30
	same, booklet pane of 20		....	....	....	40.00	....
4870	(49¢) Fort McHenry Flag & Fireworks die cut 11¼ x 10¾ with Microprint in fireworks	2.75	....	....	....	2.00	.30
	same, booklet pane of 20			....	....	40.00	....
4871	(49¢) Fort McHenry Flag & Fireworks die cut 11¼ x 11 thin paper	2.75	....	....	....	1.75	.30
	same, booklet pane of 18		....	....	....	35.00	....

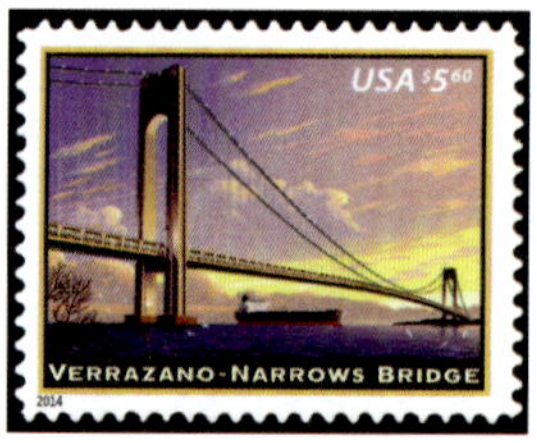

4872

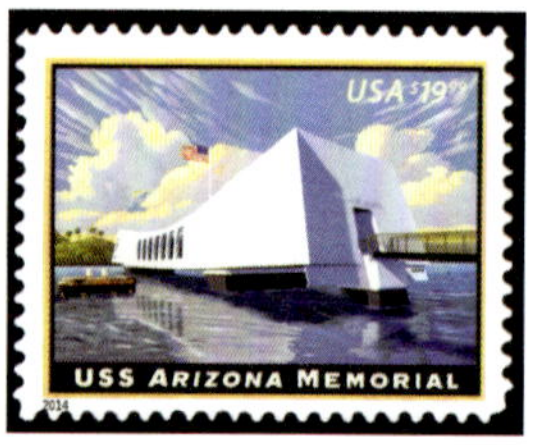

4873

SCOTT NO.	DESCRIPTION	FIRST DAY COVERS SING	FIRST DAY COVERS PL. BLK.	MINT SHEET	PLATE BLOCK	UNUSED F/NH	USED
4872	$5.60 Verrazano-Narrows Bridge	12.50	....	250.00(10)	55.00	15.00	10.00
4873	$19.99 USS Arizona Memorial	45	....	430.00(10)	180.00	50.00	30.00
4874-78	(49¢) Ferns coil.	7.50	....	....	....	18.00	....
	same, plate number strip of 5		....	....	....	22.00	....
	same, Plate Number strip of 11		....	....	....	45.00	....
4874	(49¢) Fortune's Holly Fern	2.75	....	....	....	2.25	1.50
4875	(49¢) Soft Shield Fern .	2.75	....	....	....	2.25	1.50
4876	(49¢) Autumn Fern	2.75	....	....	....	2.25	1.50
4877	(49¢) Goldie's Wood Fern	2.75	....	....	....	2.25	1.50
4878	(49¢) Painted Fern	2.75	....	....	....	2.25	1.50

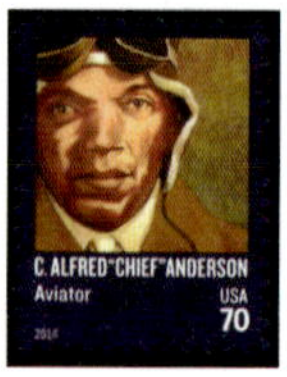

4879

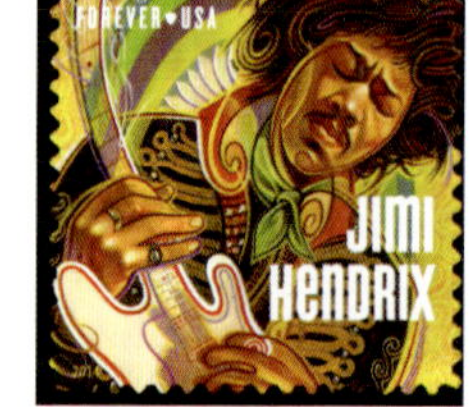

4880

4881

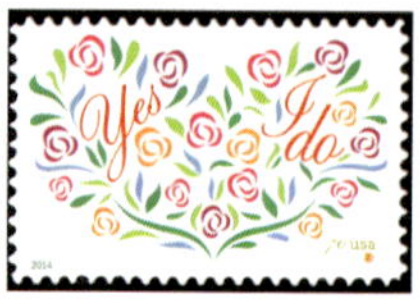

SCOTT NO.	DESCRIPTION	FIRST DAY COVERS SING	FIRST DAY COVERS PL. BLK.	MINT SHEET	PLATE BLOCK	UNUSED F/NH	USED
4879	70¢ C. Alfred "Chief" Anderson	3.25	....	45.00 (20)	9.00	2.50	1.00
4880	(49¢) Jimi Hendrix	2.75	....	28.00(16)	....	2.00	.70
4881	70¢ Yes I Do	3.25	....	75.00(20)	18.00	5.00	3.00

SCOTT NO.	DESCRIPTION	FIRST DAY COVERS SING	FIRST DAY COVERS PL. BLK.	MINT SHEET	PLATE BLOCK	UNUSED F/NH	USED
4882-91	(49¢) Songbirds	11.00	....	....	....	28.00	....
4882	(49¢) Western Meadowlark	2.75	....	....	....	3.00	.70
4883	(49¢) Mountain Bluebird	2.75	....	....	....	3.00	.70
4884	(49¢) Western Tanager.	2.75	....	....	....	3.00	.70
4885	(49¢) Painted Bunting. .	2.75	....	....	....	3.00	.70
4886	(49¢) Baltimore Oriole .	2.75	....	....	....	3.00	.70
4887	(49¢) Evening Grosbeak	2.75	....	....	....	3.00	.70
4888	(49¢) Scarlet Tanager. .	2.75	....	....	....	3.00	.70
4889	(49¢) Rose-breasted Grosbeak	2.75	....	....	....	3.00	.70
4890	(49¢) American Goldfinch	2.75	....	....	....	3.00	.70
4891	(49¢) White-throated Sparrow	2.75	....	....	....	3.00	.70
4891b	Same, booklet pane of 20, 2 each (4882-4891) . . .		....	....	....	55.00	....

SCOTT NO.	DESCRIPTION	FIRST DAY COVERS SING	FIRST DAY COVERS PL. BLK.	MINT SHEET	PLATE BLOCK	UNUSED F/NH	USED
4892	(49¢) Charlton Heston .	2.75	....	30.00(20)	6.50	1.75	.55
4893	($1.15) Map of Sea Surface Temperatures	3.75	....	45.00(10)	18.00	4.50	1.00

SCOTT NO.	DESCRIPTION	FIRST DAY COVERS SING	FIRST DAY COVERS PL. BLK.	MINT SHEET	PLATE BLOCK	UNUSED F/NH	USED
4894-97	(49¢) Flags coil.	6.25	....	....	....	7.00	....
	same, plate number strip of 5		....	....	....	12.00	....
	same, plate number strip of 9		....	....	....	16.00	....
4894	(49¢) Flag with 5 full & 3 partial stars.	2.75	....	....	....	1.75	.30
4895	(49¢) Flag with 3 full stars	2.75	....	....	....	1.75	.30
4896	(49¢) Flag with 4 full & 2 partial stars	2.75	....	....	....	1.75	.30
4897	(49¢) Flag with 2 full and 2 partial stars	2.75	....	....	....	1.75	.30

SCOTT NO.	DESCRIPTION	FIRST DAY COVERS SING	FIRST DAY COVERS PL. BLK.	MINT SHEET	PLATE BLOCK	UNUSED F/NH	USED
4898-4905	(49¢) Circus Posters. . .	10.50	....	35.00(16)	....	18.00	....
4898	(49¢) Barnum and Bailey Circus Poster with Clown.	2.75	....	....	....	2.25	.90
4899	(49¢) Sells-Floto Circus Poster	2.75	....	....	....	2.25	.90
4900	(49¢) Ringling Bros. Barnum & Bailey Circus Poster with Dainty Miss Leitzel	2.75				2.25	.90
4901	(49¢) Al G. Barnes Wild Animal Circus Poster . .	2.75	....	....	....	2.25	.90
4902	(49¢) Ringling Bros. Shows Poster with Hillary Long	2.75	....	....	....	2.25	.90
4903	(49¢) Barnum and Bailey Circus Poster with Tiger	2.75	....	....	....	2.25	.90
4904	(49¢) Ringling Bros. Barnum and Bailey Circus Poster with Elephant	2.75	....	....	....	2.25	.90
4905	(49¢) Carl Hagenbeck-Wallace Circus Poster	2.75	....	....	....	2.25	.90

SCOTT NO.	DESCRIPTION	FIRST DAY COVERS SING	FIRST DAY COVERS PL. BLK.	MINT SHEET	PLATE BLOCK	UNUSED F/NH	USED
4905v	Circus Posters Souvenir Sheet, die cut, from year book.	....	....	....	....	130.00	....
4905c	Circus Posters Souvenir Sheet, imperf, from press sheets	....	....	....	....	20.00	....

4906

4907

SCOTT NO.	DESCRIPTION	FIRST DAY COVERS SING	FIRST DAY COVERS PL. BLK.	MINT SHEET	PLATE BLOCK	UNUSED F/NH	USED
4906	(49¢) Harvey Milk	2.50	....	40.00(20)	8.00	2.00	.70
4907	(49¢) Nevada	2.50	....	30.00(20)	6.50	1.75	.70

4908

4909

SCOTT NO.	DESCRIPTION	FIRST DAY COVERS SING	FIRST DAY COVERS PL. BLK.	MINT SHEET	PLATE BLOCK	UNUSED F/NH	USED
4908-09	(49¢) Hot Rods	3.75	....	....	....	4.00	....
4908	(49¢) Rear of 1932 Ford "Deuce" Roadster.	2.50	....	....	....	2.25	.70
4909	(49¢) Front of 1932 Ford "Deuce" Roadster.	2.50	....	....	....	2.25	.70
4909B	Same, Booklet Pane of 20		....	....	....	40.00	....

4910

4911

SCOTT NO.	DESCRIPTION	FIRST DAY COVERS SING	FIRST DAY COVERS PL. BLK.	MINT SHEET	PLATE BLOCK	UNUSED F/NH	USED
4910-11	(49¢) Civil War	3.75	....	24.00(12)	....	4.00	....
4910	(49¢) Battle of Petersburg	2.50	....	....	....	2.25	1.50
4911	(49¢) Battle of Mobile Bay	2.50	....	....	....	2.25	1.50

4912-4915

SCOTT NO.	DESCRIPTION	FIRST DAY COVERS SING	FIRST DAY COVERS PL. BLK.	MINT SHEET	PLATE BLOCK	UNUSED F/NH	USED
4912-15	(49¢) Farmer's Market .	5.75	....	38.00(20)	16.00(8)	8.00	....
4912	(49¢) Breads.	2.75	....	....	....	2.25	.70
4913	(49¢) Fruits and Vegetables	2.75	....	....	....	2.25	.70
4914	(49¢) Flowers	2.75	....	....	....	2.25	.70
4915	(49¢) Plants	2.75	....	....	....	2.25	.70

4916

4921

SCOTT NO.	DESCRIPTION	FIRST DAY COVERS SING	FIRST DAY COVERS PL. BLK.	MINT SHEET	PLATE BLOCK	UNUSED F/NH	USED
4916	(49¢) Janis Joplin	2.75	....	30.00(16)	....	2.25	.55
4917-20	(49¢) Hudson River School Paintings Block of 4	5.75	....	....	....	9.00	....
4917	(49¢) Grand Canyon by Thomas Moran	2.50	....	....	....	2.25	.70
4918	(49¢) Summer Afternoon by Asher B. Durand.	2.50	....	....	....	2.25	.70
4919	(49¢) Sunset by Frederic Edwin Church	2.50	....	....	....	2.25	.70
4920	(49¢) Distant View of Niagara Falls by Thomas Cole. .	2.50	....	....	....	2.25	.70
4920b	Booklet Pane of 20, Hudson River School Paintings .	....	....	....	....	45.00	....
4921	(49¢) Ft. McHenry, War of 1812	2.50	....	30.00(20)	....	1.75	.70

4917 4918

4919 4920

4922 4923 4924 4925 4926

SCOTT NO.	DESCRIPTION	FIRST DAY COVERS SING	FIRST DAY COVERS PL. BLK.	MINT SHEET	PLATE BLOCK	UNUSED F/NH	USED
4922-26	(49¢) Celebrity Chefs . .	6.75	....	38.00(20)	18.00(10)	10.00	....
4922	(49¢) Edna Lewis	2.50	....	....	....	2.25	1.00
4923	(49¢) Felipe Rojas-Lombardi	2.50	....	....	....	2.25	1.00
4924	(49¢) Joyce Chen	2.50	....	....	....	2.25	1.00
4925	(49¢) James Beard. . . .	2.50	....	....	....	2.25	1.00
4926	(49¢) Julia Child	2.50	....	....	....	2.25	1.00

4927

4936

4928-4935

SCOTT NO.	DESCRIPTION	FIRST DAY COVERS SING	FIRST DAY COVERS PL. BLK.	MINT SHEET	PLATE BLOCK	UNUSED F/NH	USED
4927	$5.75 Glade Creek Grist Mill	12.50	....	130.00(10)	58.00	16.00	10.00
4928-35	(49¢) Batman	9.25	....	45.00(20)	....	24.00	....
4928	(49¢) Bat Signal	2.75	....	....	....	3.50	2.00
4929	(49¢) Bat Signal	2.75	....	....	....	3.50	2.00
4930	(49¢) Bat Signal	2.75	....	....	....	3.50	2.00
4931	(49¢) Bat Signal	2.75	....	....	....	3.50	2.00
4932	(49¢) Batman, Yellow Background	2.75	....	....	....	2.50	1.00
4933	(49¢) Batman and Bat Signal	2.75	....	....	....	2.50	1.00
4934	(49¢) Batman and Rope	2.75	....	....	....	2.50	1.00
4935	(49¢) Batman, Blue Background	2.75	....	....	....	2.50	1.00
4936	($1.15) Silver Bells Wreath	3.75	....	40.00(10)	18.00	5.00	1.00

4937, 4941

4938, 4942

4939, 4943

4940, 4944

SCOTT NO.	DESCRIPTION	FIRST DAY COVERS SING	PL. BLK.	MINT SHEET	PLATE BLOCK	UNUSED F/NH	USED
4937-40	(49¢) Winter Fun.	....	....	....	....	11.00	....
4937	(49¢) Skaters	....	....	....	....	2.75	.35
4938	(49¢) Child Making Snowman	....	....	....	....	2.75	.35
4939	(49¢) Cardinal.	....	....	....	....	2.75	.35
4940	(49¢) Child Making Snow Angel	....	....	....	....	2.75	.35
4940b	Same, Booklet Pane of 20	....	....	....	....	55.00	....
4941-44	(49¢) Winter Fun.	....	....	....	....	16.00	....
4941	(49¢) Skaters	....	....	....	....	4.00	1.75
4942	(49¢) Child Making Snowman	....	....	....	....	4.00	1.75
4943	(49¢) Cardinal.	....	....	....	....	4.00	1.75
4944	(49¢) Child Making Snow Angel	....	....	....	....	4.00	1.75
4944b	Same, ATM Booklet Pane of 18	....	....	....	....	75.00	....

4946

4945

4949

4947

4948

SCOTT NO.	DESCRIPTION	FIRST DAY COVERS SING	PL. BLK.	MINT SHEET	PLATE BLOCK	UNUSED F/NH	USED
4945	(49¢) Magi	2.75	....	....	....	2.25	.30
4945a	Same, Booklet Pane of 20	....	....	....	....	45.00	....
4946-49	(49¢) Rudolph the Red-Nosed Reindeer.	5.75	....	....	....	12.00	....
4946	(49¢) Rudolph the Red-Nosed Reindeer.	2.75	....	....	....	3.00	.35
4947	(49¢) Hermey and Rudolph	....	....	....	....	3.00	.35
4948	(49¢) Santa Claus.	....	....	....	....	3.00	.35
4949	(49¢) Bumble	....	....	....	....	3.00	.35
4949b	Same, Booklet Pane of 20	....	....	....	....	55.00	....

4950-4951

SCOTT NO.	DESCRIPTION	FIRST DAY COVERS SING	PL. BLK.	MINT SHEET	PLATE BLOCK	UNUSED F/NH	USED
4950-51	(49¢) Wilt Chamberlain.	5.75	....	35.00(18)	8.00	4.00	....
4950	(49¢) Wilt Chamberlain in Philadelphia Warriors Uniform	2.75	....	....	....	2.25	.75
4951	(49¢) Wilt Chamberlain in Los Angeles Lakers Uniform	2.75	....	....	....	2.25	.75

2015 COMMEMORATIVES

SCOTT NO.	DESCRIPTION	FIRST DAY COVERS SING	PL. BLK.	MINT SHEET	PLATE BLOCK	UNUSED F/NH	USED
4952/5020	**(4952, 4957-58, 4968-72, 4979-87, 4988a, 5003, 5008-12, 5020) 27 varieties . . . .**	**.......**	**.......**	**.......**	**.......**	**63.00**	**.......**

4952

SCOTT NO.	DESCRIPTION	FIRST DAY COVERS SING	PL. BLK.	MINT SHEET	PLATE BLOCK	UNUSED F/NH	USED
4952	(49¢) Battle of New Orleans	2.75	....	30.00(20)	....	2.00	.30

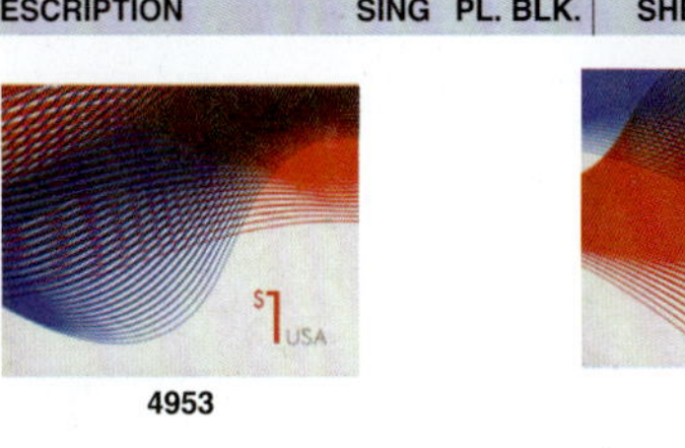
4953

4954

SCOTT NO.	DESCRIPTION	FIRST DAY COVERS SING	PL. BLK.	MINT SHEET	PLATE BLOCK	UNUSED F/NH	USED
4953	$1 Patriotic Waves	3.75	....	22.50(10)	9.00	3.00	1.00
4954	$2 Patriotic Waves	5.75	....	45.00(10)	18.00	5.00	5.00

4955

4956

4957

SCOTT NO.	DESCRIPTION	FIRST DAY COVERS SING	PL. BLK.	MINT SHEET	PLATE BLOCK	UNUSED F/NH	USED
4955-56	(49¢) Love	3.75	....	30.00(20)	8.00	4.00	....
4955	(49¢) Love, Red	2.75	....	....	....	2.25	1.00
4956	(49¢) Love, Red and Gray	2.75	....	....	....	2.25	1.00
4957	(49¢) Chinese New Year	2.75	....	24.00(12)	....	2.25	.90

4959

4958

4960

4961

4962

4963

SCOTT NO.	DESCRIPTION	FIRST DAY COVERS SING	PL. BLK.	MINT SHEET	PLATE BLOCK	UNUSED F/NH	USED
4958	(49¢) Robert Robinson Taylor	2.75		30.00(20)	8.00	2.00	.50
4959	(49¢) Red & Black Rose & Heart	2.75	....	100.00(20)	25.00	5.00	.30
4960	70¢ Black & Red, Tulip & Heart	2.75	....	125.00(20)	30.00	6.00	3.00
4961-63	(10¢) Stars and Stripes	....	....	....	....	1.50	....
	Same, Plate # Strip of 5	....	....	....	....	5.00	....
4961	(10¢) Stripes at Left, Stars at Right		....	....	....	.50	.25
4962	(10¢) Stars & White Stripe		....	....	....	.50	.25
4963	(10¢) Stars at Left, Stripes at Right		....	....	....	.50	.25

4964 4965 4966 4967

SCOTT NO.	DESCRIPTION	FIRST DAY COVERS SING	PL. BLK.	MINT SHEET	PLATE BLOCK	UNUSED F/NH	USED
4964-67	(49¢) Water Lilies	6.50	....	....	....	9.00	....
4964	(49¢) Pale Pink Water Lily	2.75	....	....	....	2.25	.30
4965	(49¢) Red Water Lily. . .	2.75	....	....	....	2.25	.30
4966	(49¢) Purple Water Lily.	2.75	....	....	....	2.25	.30
4967	(49¢) White Water Lily .	2.75	....	....	....	2.25	.30
4967b	Same, Booklet Pane of 20	....	....	....	....	45.00	....

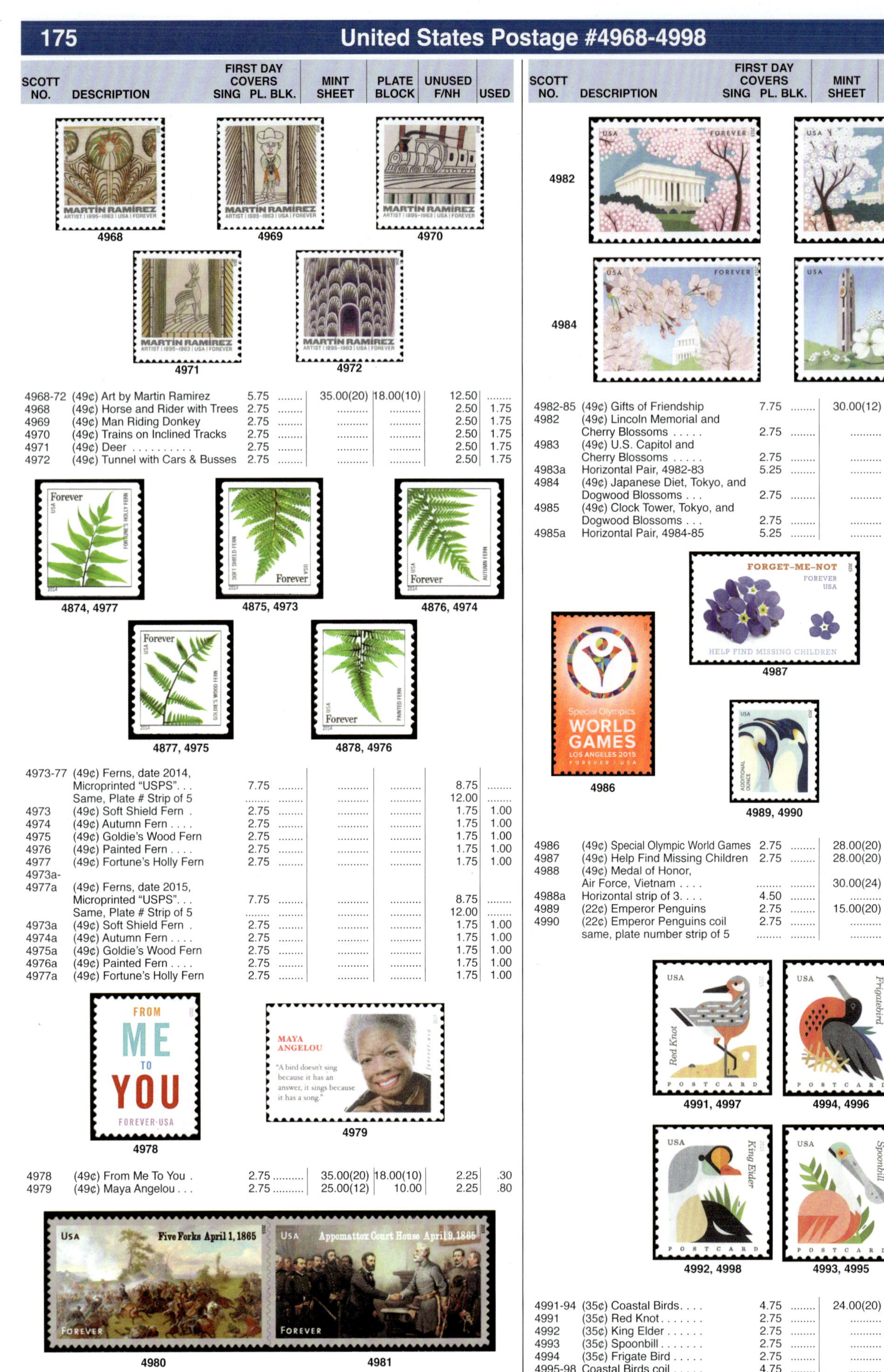

SCOTT NO.	DESCRIPTION	FIRST DAY COVERS SING	FIRST DAY COVERS PL. BLK.	MINT SHEET	PLATE BLOCK	UNUSED F/NH	USED
4968-72	(49¢) Art by Martin Ramirez	5.75		35.00(20)	18.00(10)	12.50	
4968	(49¢) Horse and Rider with Trees	2.75				2.50	1.75
4969	(49¢) Man Riding Donkey	2.75				2.50	1.75
4970	(49¢) Trains on Inclined Tracks	2.75				2.50	1.75
4971	(49¢) Deer	2.75				2.50	1.75
4972	(49¢) Tunnel with Cars & Busses	2.75				2.50	1.75
4973-77	(49¢) Ferns, date 2014, Microprinted "USPS". . .	7.75				8.75	
	Same, Plate # Strip of 5					12.00	
4973	(49¢) Soft Shield Fern	2.75				1.75	1.00
4974	(49¢) Autumn Fern	2.75				1.75	1.00
4975	(49¢) Goldie's Wood Fern	2.75				1.75	1.00
4976	(49¢) Painted Fern	2.75				1.75	1.00
4977	(49¢) Fortune's Holly Fern	2.75				1.75	1.00
4973a-4977a	(49¢) Ferns, date 2015, Microprinted "USPS". . .	7.75				8.75	
	Same, Plate # Strip of 5					12.00	
4973a	(49¢) Soft Shield Fern	2.75				1.75	1.00
4974a	(49¢) Autumn Fern	2.75				1.75	1.00
4975a	(49¢) Goldie's Wood Fern	2.75				1.75	1.00
4976a	(49¢) Painted Fern	2.75				1.75	1.00
4977a	(49¢) Fortune's Holly Fern	2.75				1.75	1.00
4978	(49¢) From Me To You	2.75		35.00(20)	18.00(10)	2.25	.30
4979	(49¢) Maya Angelou	2.75		25.00(12)	10.00	2.25	.80
4980-81	(49¢) Civil War Sheet			24.00(12)		4.00	
4980	(49¢) Battle of Five Forks	2.50				2.25	1.75
4981	(49¢) Surrender at Appomattox Court House	2.50				2.25	1.75
4982-85	(49¢) Gifts of Friendship	7.75		30.00(12)		16.00	
4982	(49¢) Lincoln Memorial and Cherry Blossoms	2.75				4.00	2.00
4983	(49¢) U.S. Capitol and Cherry Blossoms	2.75				4.00	2.00
4983a	Horizontal Pair, 4982-83	5.25				8.00	
4984	(49¢) Japanese Diet, Tokyo, and Dogwood Blossoms	2.75				4.00	2.00
4985	(49¢) Clock Tower, Tokyo, and Dogwood Blossoms	2.75				4.00	2.00
4985a	Horizontal Pair, 4984-85	5.25				8.00	
4986	(49¢) Special Olympic World Games	2.75		28.00(20)	6.50	1.75	.35
4987	(49¢) Help Find Missing Children	2.75		28.00(20)	6.50	1.75	.35
4988	(49¢) Medal of Honor, Air Force, Vietnam			30.00(24)	10.00(6)		
4988a	Horizontal strip of 3	4.50				5.50	
4989	(22¢) Emperor Penguins	2.75		15.00(20)	4.00	1.25	.30
4990	(22¢) Emperor Penguins coil	2.75				1.00	.30
	same, plate number strip of 5					5.00	
4991-94	(35¢) Coastal Birds	4.75		24.00(20)	5.50	5.00	
4991	(35¢) Red Knot	2.75				1.40	1.00
4992	(35¢) King Elder	2.75				1.40	1.00
4993	(35¢) Spoonbill	2.75				1.40	1.00
4994	(35¢) Frigate Bird	2.75				1.40	1.00
4995-98	Coastal Birds coil	4.75				5.00	
	same, plate number strip of 5					8.00	
4995	(35¢) Spoonbill coil	2.75				1.40	.45
4996	(35¢) Frigate Bird coil	2.75				1.40	.45
4997	(35¢) Red Knot coil	2.75				1.40	.45
4998	(35¢) King Elder coil	2.75				1.40	.45

4999

5000

5002

SCOTT NO.	DESCRIPTION	FIRST DAY COVERS SING	FIRST DAY COVERS PL. BLK.	MINT SHEET	PLATE BLOCK	UNUSED F/NH	USED
4999	(71¢) Eastern Tiger Swallowtail Butterfly	3.25	....	55.00(20)	12.00	3.00	1.00
5000	(71¢) Wedding Cake. . .	3.25	....	100.00(20)	20.00	5.00	2.00

5001

5003

SCOTT NO.	DESCRIPTION	FIRST DAY COVERS SING	FIRST DAY COVERS PL. BLK.	MINT SHEET	PLATE BLOCK	UNUSED F/NH	USED
5001	(71¢) Flowers and Yes, I Do	3.25	....	100.00(20)	20.00	5.00	2.00
5002	(71¢) Tulip and Hearts .	3.25		100.00(20)	20.00	5.00	2.00

5004, 5007b

5005, 5007b

5006, 5007b

5007, 5007b

SCOTT NO.	DESCRIPTION	FIRST DAY COVERS SING	FIRST DAY COVERS PL. BLK.	MINT SHEET	PLATE BLOCK	UNUSED F/NH	USED
5003	(93¢) Flannery O'Connor	3.75	....	39.00(20)	8.50	2.50	1.00
5004-07	(49¢) Summer Harvest .	6.50	....	....	....	8.00	....
5004	(49¢) Watermelons	....	....	....	....	2.00	.70
5005	(49¢) Sweet Corn	....	....	....	....	2.00	.70
5006	(49¢) Cantaloupes	....	....	....	....	2.00	.70
5007	(49¢) Tomatoes.	....	....	....	....	2.00	.70
5007b	same, booklet pane of 20	....	....	....	....	40.00	....

5008

5009

SCOTT NO.	DESCRIPTION	FIRST DAY COVERS SING	FIRST DAY COVERS PL. BLK.	MINT SHEET	PLATE BLOCK	UNUSED F/NH	USED
5008	(49¢) Coast Guard	2.75	....	30.00(20)	8.00	2.00	.50
5009	(49¢) Elvis Presley	3.50	....	24.00(20)	....	2.00	.50

5010

5011

5012

SCOTT NO.	DESCRIPTION	FIRST DAY COVERS SING	FIRST DAY COVERS PL. BLK.	MINT SHEET	PLATE BLOCK	UNUSED F/NH	USED
5010-11	(49¢) World Stamp Show	4.25	....	38.00(20)	8.00	5.00	....
5010	(49¢) World Stamp Show, red	2.75	....	....	....	2.25	2.00
5011	(49¢) World Stamp Show, blue	2.75	....	....	....	2.25	2.00
5012	(49¢) Ingrid Bergman . .	2.75	....	40.00(20)	8.00	2.25	.70

5013 5014 5015 5016 5017 5018

SCOTT NO.	DESCRIPTION	FIRST DAY COVERS SING	FIRST DAY COVERS PL. BLK.	MINT SHEET	PLATE BLOCK	UNUSED F/NH	USED
5013-18	(25¢) eagles, strip of 6, D/C 10.25	5.75	....	....	....	15.00	....
	same, plate number strip of 7	....	....	....	....	28.00	....
5013	(25¢) Green	....	....	....	....	2.50	1.25
5014	(25¢) Blue/Green	....	....	....	....	2.50	1.25
5015	(25¢) Blue.	....	....	....	....	2.50	1.25
5016	(25¢) Red/Violet	....	....	....	....	2.50	1.25
5017	(25¢) Brown/Orange. . .	....	....	....	....	2.50	1.25
5018	(25¢) Yellow/Orange. . .	....	....	....	....	2.50	1.25

5019

5020

SCOTT NO.	DESCRIPTION	FIRST DAY COVERS SING	FIRST DAY COVERS PL. BLK.	MINT SHEET	PLATE BLOCK	UNUSED F/NH	USED
5019	(49¢) Celebrate, 2015 date	2.75	....	30.00(20)	8.00	2.25	.40
5020	(49¢) Paul Newman . . .	2.75	....	30.00(20)	8.00	2.25	.70

5021, 5030b

5022, 5030b

5023, 5030b

5024, 5030b

5025, 5030b

5026, 5030b

5027, 5030b

5028, 5030b

5029, 5030b

5030, 5030b

SCOTT NO.	DESCRIPTION	FIRST DAY COVERS SING	FIRST DAY COVERS PL. BLK.	MINT SHEET	PLATE BLOCK	UNUSED F/NH	USED
5021-30	(49¢) Charlie Brown Christmas	12.00	....	....	....	35.00	....
5021	(49¢) Charlie Brown carrying Christmas Tree	....	....	....	....	3.75	1.00
5022	(49¢) Charlie Brown, Pigpen and Dirty Snowman . . .	....	....	....	....	3.75	1.00
5023	(49¢) Snoopy, Lucy, Violet, Sally and Schroeder Skating	....	....	....	....	3.75	1.00
5024	(49¢) Characters, Dog House and Christmas Tree . . .	....	....	....	....	3.75	1.00
5025	(49¢) Linus and Christmas Tree	....	....	....	....	3.75	1.00
5026	(49¢) Charlie Brown looking in Mailbox	....	....	....	....	3.75	1.00
5027	(49¢) Charlie Brown and Linus behind brick wall .	....	....	....	....	3.75	1.00
5028	(49¢) Charlie Brown, Linus and Christmas Tree . . .	....	....	....	....	3.75	1.00
5029	(49¢) Charlie Brown screaming, Snoopy decorating dog house	....	....	....	....	3.75	1.00
5030	(49¢) Charlie Brown hanging ornament on Christmas Tree	....	....	....	....	3.75	1.00
5030b	same, booklet pane of 20	....	....	....	....	70.00	....

5031, 5034b

5035

5032, 5034b

5033, 5034b

5034, 5034b

SCOTT NO.	DESCRIPTION	FIRST DAY COVERS SING	FIRST DAY COVERS PL. BLK.	MINT SHEET	PLATE BLOCK	UNUSED F/NH	USED
5031-34	(49¢) Geometric Snowflakes	5.75	....	....	....	12.00	....
5031	(49¢) Purple and Lilac .	2.75	....	....	....	3.00	.90
5032	(49¢) Dark blue and blue	2.75	....	....	....	3.00	.90
5033	(49¢) Dark green and green	2.75	....	....	....	3.00	.90
5034	(49¢) Crimson and pink	2.75	....	....	....	3.00	.90
5034b	same, booklet pane of 20	....	....	....	....	50.00	....
5035	(49¢) Purple Heart, "USPS" microprinted at left	....	....	30.00(20)	6.50	1.75	.30

2016 COMMEMORATIVES

5036/5153	**(5036, 5056-57, 5059-60, 5062-76, 5091-92, 5100, 5105, 5132-35, 5141-42, 5149-53) 35 varieties**	**.......**	**.......**	**.......**	**.......**	**80.00**	**.......**

5036

5037

5038

5039

SCOTT NO.	DESCRIPTION	FIRST DAY COVERS SING	FIRST DAY COVERS PL. BLK.	MINT SHEET	PLATE BLOCK	UNUSED F/NH	USED
5036	(49¢) Quilled Paper Hearts	2.75	....	45.00(20)	10.00	2.50	.50
5037	1¢ Apples coil	2.75	....	....	....	.20	.20
	same, plate strip of 5 . .	....	....	....	....	1.45	....
5038	5¢ Pinot Noir Grapes coil	2.75	....	....	....	.30	.30
	same, plate number strip of 5	....	....	....	....	1.75	....
5039	10¢ Red Pears coil	2.75	....	....	....	.35	.30
	same, plate number strip of 5	....	....	....	....	2.25	....

5040

5041

SCOTT NO.	DESCRIPTION	FIRST DAY COVERS SING	FIRST DAY COVERS PL. BLK.	MINT SHEET	PLATE BLOCK	UNUSED F/NH	USED
5040	$6.45 La Cueva del Indio, Puerto Rico.	15.00	....	200.00(10)	80.00	25.00	15.00
5041	$22.95 Columbia River Gorge	50.00	....	800.00(10)	350.00	100.00	50.00

5042

5043

5044

5045

5046

5047

5048

5049

5050

5052, 5053, 5054, 5055

5051

SCOTT NO.	DESCRIPTION	FIRST DAY COVERS SING	FIRST DAY COVERS PL. BLK.	MINT SHEET	PLATE BLOCK	UNUSED F/NH	USED
5042-51	(49¢) Botanical Art	11.00	....	....	....	25.00	....
5042	(49¢) Corn Lilies	2.75	....	....	....	2.50	1.00
5043	(49¢) Tulips.	2.75	....	....	....	2.50	1.00
5044	(49¢) Tulips.	2.75	....	....	....	2.50	1.00
5045	(49¢) Dahlias	2.75	....	....	....	2.50	1.00
5046	(49¢) Stocks	2.75	....	....	....	2.50	1.00
5047	(49¢) Roses	2.75	....	....	....	2.50	1.00
5048	(49¢) Japanese Irises. .	2.75	....	....	....	2.50	1.00
5049	(49¢) Tulips.	2.75	....	....	....	2.50	1.00
5050	(49¢) Petunias	2.75	....	....	....	2.50	1.00
5051	(49¢) Jonquils.	2.75	....	....	....	2.50	1.00
5051b	same, booklet pane of 10	....	....	....	....	25.00	....
5051c	same, booklet pane of 20	....	....	....	....	60.00	....
5052	(49¢) Flag, die cut 11, SSP coil	2.75	....	....	....	1.50	.30
	microprinted USPS to right of pole under flag	....	....	....	....	....	....
	same, plate number strip of 5	....	....	....	....	10.00	....
5053	(49¢) Flag, die cut 9½, AP coil	2.75	....	....	....	1.50	.30
	microprinted USPS on second white flag stripe.	....	....	....	....	....	....
	same, plate number strip of 5	....	....	....	....	10.00	....
5054	(49¢) Flag, 11¼ x 10¾, SSP booklet	2.75	....	....	....	1.50	.30
	microprinted USPS to right of pole under the flag	....	....	....	....	....	....
5054a	same, booklet pane of 10	....	....	....	....	15.00	....
5054b	same, booklet pane of 20	....	....	....	....	30.00	....
5055	(49¢) Flag, 11¼ x 10¾, AP booklet	2.75	....	....	....	1.50	.30
	microprinted USPS on second white flag stripe.	....	....	....	....	....	....
5055a	same, booklet pane of 20	....	....	....	....	30.00	....

5056

5057

5058

SCOTT NO.	DESCRIPTION	FIRST DAY COVERS SING	FIRST DAY COVERS PL. BLK.	MINT SHEET	PLATE BLOCK	UNUSED F/NH	USED
5056	(49¢) Richard Allen	2.75	....	30.00(20)	6.50	1.75	.70
5057	(49¢) Chinese New Year Year of the Monkey. . . .	2.75	....	24.00(12)	....	2.25	1.00
5058	($1.20) Moon	4.25	....	55.00(10)	25.00	6.00	1.25

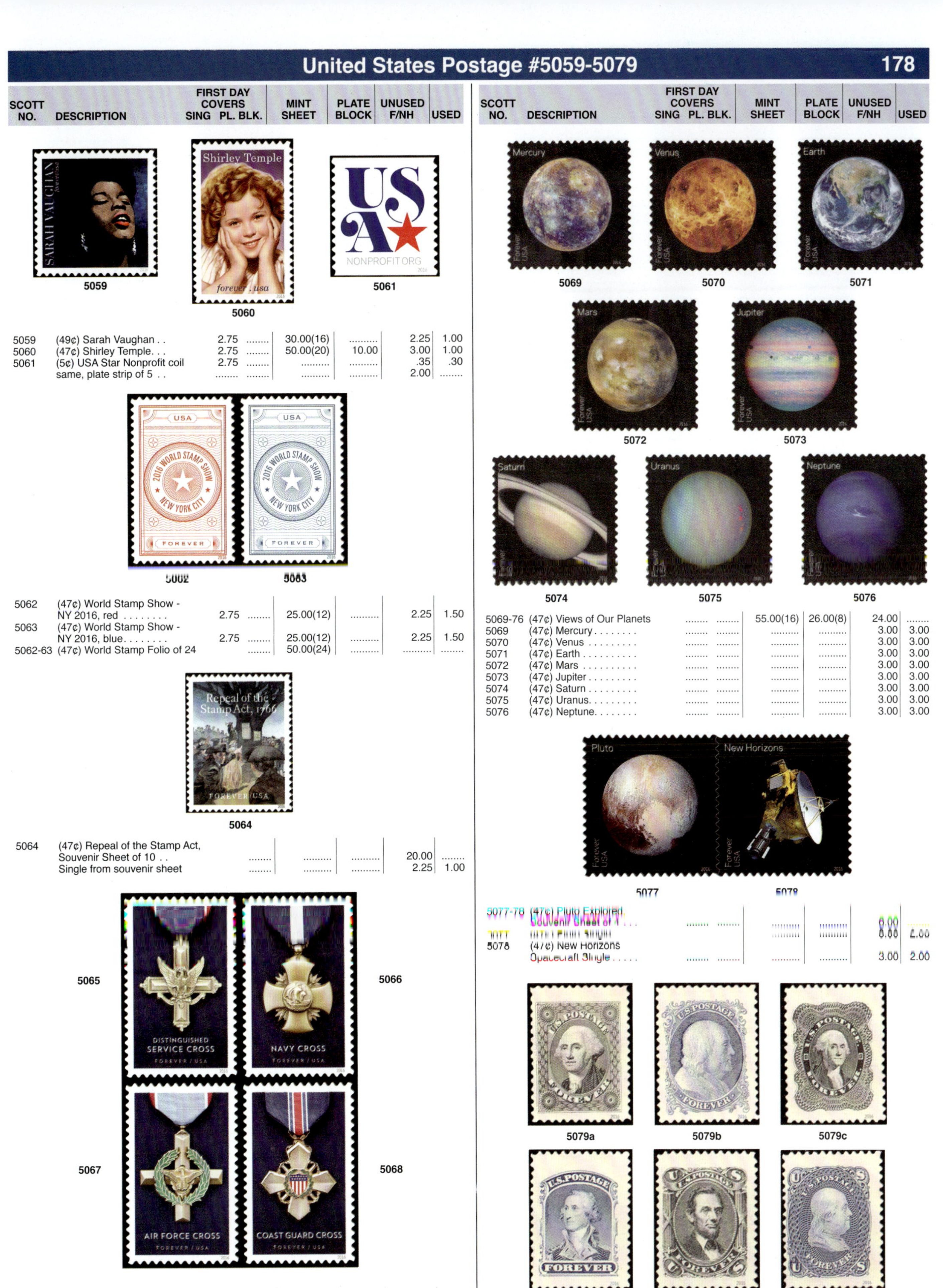

SCOTT NO.	DESCRIPTION	FIRST DAY COVERS SING	FIRST DAY COVERS PL. BLK.	MINT SHEET	PLATE BLOCK	UNUSED F/NH	USED
5059	(49¢) Sarah Vaughan . .	2.75	....	30.00(16)	....	2.25	1.00
5060	(47¢) Shirley Temple. . .	2.75	....	50.00(20)	10.00	3.00	1.00
5061	(5¢) USA Star Nonprofit coil	2.75	....	....	....	.35	.30
	same, plate strip of 5 . .	....	....	....	....	2.00	....
5062	(47¢) World Stamp Show - NY 2016, red	2.75	....	25.00(12)	....	2.25	1.50
5063	(47¢) World Stamp Show - NY 2016, blue.	2.75	....	25.00(12)	....	2.25	1.50
5062-63	(47¢) World Stamp Folio of 24		....	50.00(24)	....	....	....
5064	(47¢) Repeal of the Stamp Act, Souvenir Sheet of 10 . .		....	....	....	20.00	....
	Single from souvenir sheet		....	....	....	2.25	1.00
5065-68	(47¢) Service Cross Medals	6.25	....	24.00(12)	....	8.00	....
5065	(47¢) Distinguished Service Cross	2.75	....	....	....	2.25	1.75
5066	(47¢) Navy Cross	2.75	....	....	....	2.25	1.75
5067	(47¢) Air Force Cross . .	2.75	....	....	....	2.25	1.75
5068	(47¢) Coast Guard Cross	2.75	....	....	....	2.25	1.75
5069-76	(47¢) Views of Our Planets	....	....	55.00(16)	26.00(8)	24.00	....
5069	(47¢) Mercury	....	....	....	....	3.00	3.00
5070	(47¢) Venus	....	....	....	....	3.00	3.00
5071	(47¢) Earth	....	....	....	....	3.00	3.00
5072	(47¢) Mars	....	....	....	....	3.00	3.00
5073	(47¢) Jupiter	....	....	....	....	3.00	3.00
5074	(47¢) Saturn	....	....	....	....	3.00	3.00
5075	(47¢) Uranus.	....	....	....	....	3.00	3.00
5076	(47¢) Neptune.	....	....	....	....	3.00	3.00
5077-78	(47¢) Pluto Explored, Souvenir Sheet of 4 . . .	....	....	....	....	6.00	....
5077	(47¢) Pluto Single			....	....	3.00	2.00
5078	(47¢) New Horizons Spacecraft Single	....	....	....	....	3.00	2.00
5079	(47¢) Classics Forever, pane of 6	7.00	....	14.00	....	....	....
	set of singles.	16.00	....	....	....	14.00	9.00

5080

NATIONAL PARK SERVICE

5080a	*Iceberg in Glacier Bay*	5080i	*Aerial View of Theodore Roosevelt*
5080b	*Mount Rainier*	5080j	*Water Lily at Kenilworth Park*
5080c	*Scenery in the Grand Tetons*	5080k	*Admin Building at Frijoles Canyon*
5080d	*Bass Harbor Head Lighthouse*	5080l	*Everglades*
5080e	*The Grand Canyon of Arizona*	5080m	*Rainbow at Haleakala*
5080f	*Horses at Assateague Island*	5080n	*Bison at Yellowstone*
5080g	*Ship Balclutha*	5080o	*Carlsbad Caverns*
5080h	*Stone Arch*	5080p	*Heron at Gulf Islands*

SCOTT NO.	DESCRIPTION	FIRST DAY COVERS SING	PL. BLK.	MINT SHEET	PLATE BLOCK	UNUSED F/NH	USED
5080	(47¢) National Park Service	38.00(16)	....	40.00(16)	....	....	20.00

5081 5082 5083

5084 5085

5086 5087 5088

5089 5090

SCOTT NO.	DESCRIPTION	FIRST DAY COVERS SING	PL. BLK.	MINT SHEET	PLATE BLOCK	UNUSED F/NH	USED
5081-90	(47¢) Colorful Celebrations	22.00(10)	....	....	....	25.00	....
5081	(47¢) Light Blue Bird & Flowers	....	....	....	....	2.50	1.00
5082	(47¢) Orange Birds & Flowers	....	....	....	....	2.50	1.00
5083	(47¢) Violet Flowers . . .	....	....	....	....	2.50	1.00
5084	(47¢) Rose Pink Flowers	....	....	....	....	2.50	1.00
5085	(47¢) Light Blue Flowers	....	....	....	....	2.50	1.00
5086	(47¢) Orange Flowers. .	....	....	....	....	2.50	1.00
5087	(47¢) Violet Birds and Flowers	....	....	....	....	2.50	1.00
5088	(47¢) Rose Pink Bird & Flowers	....	....	....	....	2.50	1.00
5089	(47¢) Rose Pink Flowers	....	....	....	....	2.50	1.00
5090	(47¢) Violet Birds & Flowers	....	....	....	....	2.50	1.00
5090b	same, double sided convertible booklet of 20.	....	....	....	....	50.00	....

5091

5092

SCOTT NO.	DESCRIPTION	FIRST DAY COVERS SING	PL. BLK.	MINT SHEET	PLATE BLOCK	UNUSED F/NH	USED
5091	(47¢) Indiana Statehood	2.75	....	30.00(20)	8.00	2.00	.70
5092	(47¢) EID Greetings . . .	2.75	....	28.00(20)	6.50	1.75	.70

5093

5095

5094

5096

5097

SCOTT NO.	DESCRIPTION	FIRST DAY COVERS SING	PL. BLK.	MINT SHEET	PLATE BLOCK	UNUSED F/NH	USED
5093-97	(47¢) Soda Fountain Favorites	12.00(5)	....	....	....	10.00	....
5093	(47¢) Ice Cream Cone .	....	....	....	....	2.00	.90
5094	(47¢) Egg Cream	....	....	....	....	2.00	.90
5095	(47¢) Banana Split	....	....	....	....	2.00	.90
5096	(47¢) Root Beer Float. .	....	....	....	....	2.00	.90
5097	(47¢) Hot Fudge Sundae	....	....	....	....	2.00	.90
5097c	same, double sided convertible booklet of 20.	....	....	....	....	40.00	....

5098

5099

5100

SCOTT NO.	DESCRIPTION	FIRST DAY COVERS SING	PL. BLK.	MINT SHEET	PLATE BLOCK	UNUSED F/NH	USED
5098-99	(25¢) Star Quilts coil. . .	2.75	....	....	....	1.90	.70
	same, plate number strip of 5	....	....	....	....	4.25	....
5098	(25¢) Red, White & Blue Center Star	....	....	....	....	1.00	.30
5099	(25¢) Blue & Red Center Star	....	....	....	....	1.00	.30
5100	(47¢) James Escalante.	2.75	....	30.00(20)	8.00	2.00	1.00

5101

5102

5103

5104

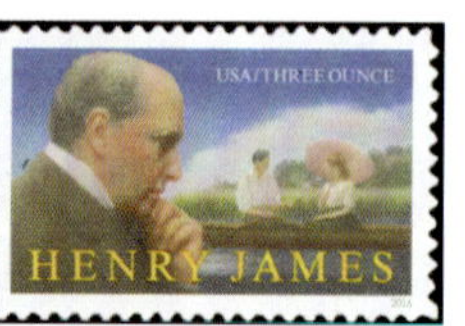

5105

SCOTT NO.	DESCRIPTION	FIRST DAY COVERS SING	PL. BLK.	MINT SHEET	PLATE BLOCK	UNUSED F/NH	USED
5101-04	(47¢) Pick-up Trucks. . .	4.00	....	....	....	9.00	....
5101	(47¢) 1938 International Harvester	....	....	....	....	2.25	.60
5102	(47¢) 1953 Chevy.	....	....	....	....	2.25	.60
5103	(47¢) 1948 Ford F1. . . .	....	....	....	....	2.25	.60
5104	(47¢) 1965 Ford F100. .	....	....	....	....	2.25	.60
5104b	same, convertible bklt of 20	....	....	....	....	45.00	....
5105	(89¢) Henry James. . . .	3.50	....	48.00(20)	12.00	3.00	2.00

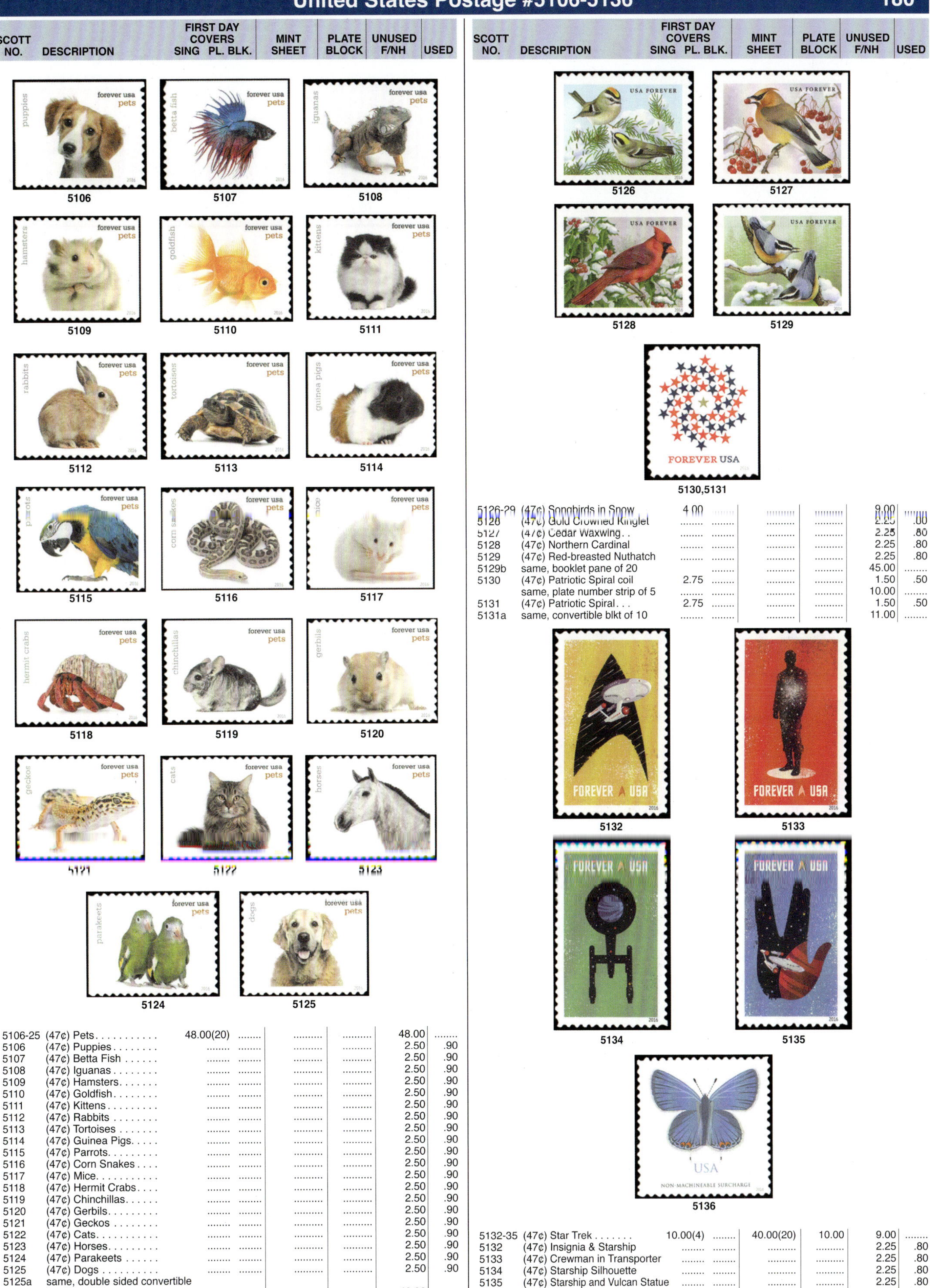

5106 5107 5108 5109 5110 5111 5112 5113 5114 5115 5116 5117 5118 5119 5120 5121 5122 5123 5124 5125

SCOTT NO.	DESCRIPTION	FIRST DAY COVERS SING	FIRST DAY COVERS PL. BLK.	MINT SHEET	PLATE BLOCK	UNUSED F/NH	USED
5106-25	(47¢) Pets.	48.00(20)	....	....	....	48.00	....
5106	(47¢) Puppies	....	....	....	....	2.50	.90
5107	(47¢) Betta Fish	....	....	....	....	2.50	.90
5108	(47¢) Iguanas	....	....	....	....	2.50	.90
5109	(47¢) Hamsters.	....	....	....	....	2.50	.90
5110	(47¢) Goldfish.	....	....	....	....	2.50	.90
5111	(47¢) Kittens	....	....	....	....	2.50	.90
5112	(47¢) Rabbits	....	....	....	....	2.50	.90
5113	(47¢) Tortoises	....	....	....	....	2.50	.90
5114	(47¢) Guinea Pigs.	....	....	....	....	2.50	.90
5115	(47¢) Parrots.	....	....	....	....	2.50	.90
5116	(47¢) Corn Snakes	....	....	....	....	2.50	.90
5117	(47¢) Mice.	....	....	....	....	2.50	.90
5118	(47¢) Hermit Crabs	....	....	....	....	2.50	.90
5119	(47¢) Chinchillas.	....	....	....	....	2.50	.90
5120	(47¢) Gerbils.	....	....	....	....	2.50	.90
5121	(47¢) Geckos	....	....	....	....	2.50	.90
5122	(47¢) Cats.	....	....	....	....	2.50	.90
5123	(47¢) Horses.	....	....	....	....	2.50	.90
5124	(47¢) Parakeets	....	....	....	....	2.50	.90
5125	(47¢) Dogs	....	....	....	....	2.50	.90
5125a	same, double sided convertible booklet of 20.	....	....	....	....	48.00	....

5126 5127 5128 5129

5130,5131

SCOTT NO.	DESCRIPTION	FIRST DAY COVERS SING	FIRST DAY COVERS PL. BLK.	MINT SHEET	PLATE BLOCK	UNUSED F/NH	USED
5126-29	(47¢) Songbirds in Snow	4.00	....	....	....	9.00	....
5126	(47¢) Gold Crowned Kinglet	....	....	....	....	2.25	.80
5127	(47¢) Cedar Waxwing. .	....	....	....	....	2.25	.80
5128	(47¢) Northern Cardinal	....	....	....	....	2.25	.80
5129	(47¢) Red-breasted Nuthatch	....	....	....	....	2.25	.80
5129b	same, booklet pane of 20		....	....	....	45.00	....
5130	(47¢) Patriotic Spiral coil	2.75	....	....	....	1.50	.50
	same, plate number strip of 5	....	....	....	....	10.00	....
5131	(47¢) Patriotic Spiral. . .	2.75	....	....	....	1.50	.50
5131a	same, convertible blkt of 10	....	....	....	....	11.00	....

5132 5133 5134 5135

5136

SCOTT NO.	DESCRIPTION	FIRST DAY COVERS SING	FIRST DAY COVERS PL. BLK.	MINT SHEET	PLATE BLOCK	UNUSED F/NH	USED
5132-35	(47¢) Star Trek	10.00(4)	....	40.00(20)	10.00	9.00	....
5132	(47¢) Insignia & Starship	....	....	....	....	2.25	.80
5133	(47¢) Crewman in Transporter	....	....	....	....	2.25	.80
5134	(47¢) Starship Silhouette	....	....	....	....	2.25	.80
5135	(47¢) Starship and Vulcan Statue	....	....	....	....	2.25	.80
5136	(68¢) Eastern Tailed-Blue Butterfly	3.25	....	75.00(20)	15.00	3.75	1.00

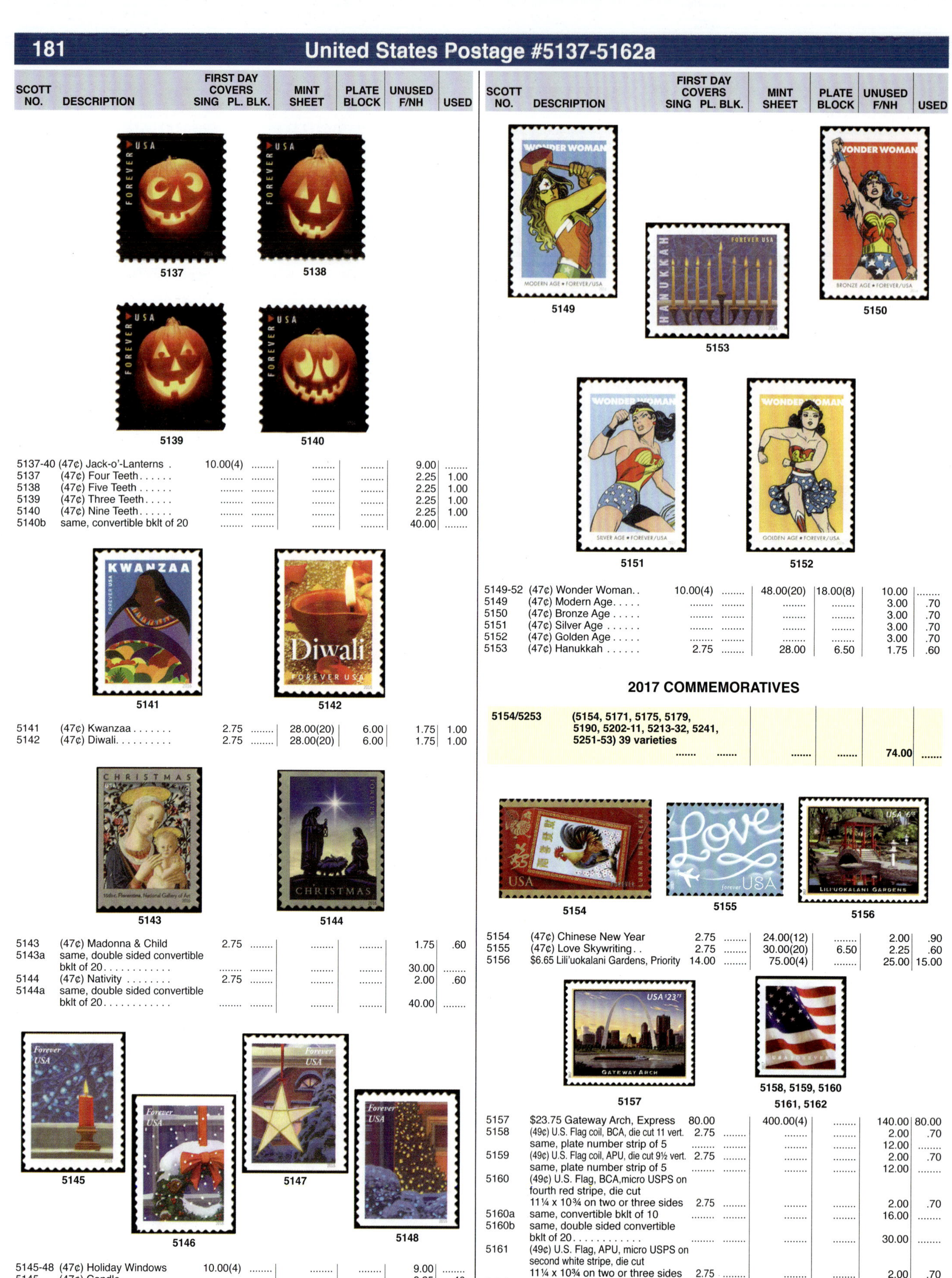

5137 5138

5139 5140

SCOTT NO.	DESCRIPTION	FIRST DAY COVERS SING	FIRST DAY COVERS PL. BLK.	MINT SHEET	PLATE BLOCK	UNUSED F/NH	USED
5137-40	(47¢) Jack-o'-Lanterns .	10.00(4)	....	....	....	9.00	....
5137	(47¢) Four Teeth	....	....	....	....	2.25	1.00
5138	(47¢) Five Teeth	....	....	....	....	2.25	1.00
5139	(47¢) Three Teeth	....	....	....	....	2.25	1.00
5140	(47¢) Nine Teeth	....	....	....	....	2.25	1.00
5140b	same, convertible bklt of 20	....	....	....	....	40.00	....

5141 5142

SCOTT NO.	DESCRIPTION	FIRST DAY COVERS SING	FIRST DAY COVERS PL. BLK.	MINT SHEET	PLATE BLOCK	UNUSED F/NH	USED
5141	(47¢) Kwanzaa	2.75	....	28.00(20)	6.00	1.75	1.00
5142	(47¢) Diwali.	2.75	....	28.00(20)	6.00	1.75	1.00

5143 5144

SCOTT NO.	DESCRIPTION	FIRST DAY COVERS SING	FIRST DAY COVERS PL. BLK.	MINT SHEET	PLATE BLOCK	UNUSED F/NH	USED
5143	(47¢) Madonna & Child	2.75	....	....	....	1.75	.60
5143a	same, double sided convertible bklt of 20.	....	....	....	....	30.00	....
5144	(47¢) Nativity	2.75	....	....	....	2.00	.60
5144a	same, double sided convertible bklt of 20.	....	....	....	....	40.00	....

5145 5146 5147 5148

SCOTT NO.	DESCRIPTION	FIRST DAY COVERS SING	FIRST DAY COVERS PL. BLK.	MINT SHEET	PLATE BLOCK	UNUSED F/NH	USED
5145-48	(47¢) Holiday Windows	10.00(4)	....	....	....	9.00	....
5145	(47¢) Candle.	....	....	....	....	2.25	.40
5146	(47¢) Wreath.	....	....	....	....	2.25	.40
5147	(47¢) Star	....	....	....	....	2.25	.40
5148	(47¢) Tree.	....	....	....	....	2.25	.40
5148b	same, double sided convertible bklt of 20.	....	....	....	....	40.00	....

5149 5153 5150

5151 5152

SCOTT NO.	DESCRIPTION	FIRST DAY COVERS SING	FIRST DAY COVERS PL. BLK.	MINT SHEET	PLATE BLOCK	UNUSED F/NH	USED
5149-52	(47¢) Wonder Woman. .	10.00(4)	....	48.00(20)	18.00(8)	10.00	....
5149	(47¢) Modern Age.	....	....	....	....	3.00	.70
5150	(47¢) Bronze Age	....	....	....	....	3.00	.70
5151	(47¢) Silver Age	....	....	....	....	3.00	.70
5152	(47¢) Golden Age	....	....	....	....	3.00	.70
5153	(47¢) Hanukkah	2.75	....	28.00	6.50	1.75	.60

2017 COMMEMORATIVES

SCOTT NO.	DESCRIPTION	FIRST DAY COVERS SING	FIRST DAY COVERS PL. BLK.	MINT SHEET	PLATE BLOCK	UNUSED F/NH	USED
5154/5253	**(5154, 5171, 5175, 5179, 5190, 5202-11, 5213-32, 5241, 5251-53) 39 varieties**	....	....	....	....	**74.00**	....

5154 5155 5156

SCOTT NO.	DESCRIPTION	FIRST DAY COVERS SING	FIRST DAY COVERS PL. BLK.	MINT SHEET	PLATE BLOCK	UNUSED F/NH	USED
5154	(47¢) Chinese New Year	2.75	....	24.00(12)	....	2.00	.90
5155	(47¢) Love Skywriting. .	2.75	....	30.00(20)	6.50	2.25	.60
5156	$6.65 Lili'uokalani Gardens, Priority	14.00	....	75.00(4)	....	25.00	15.00

5157

5158, 5159, 5160
5161, 5162

SCOTT NO.	DESCRIPTION	FIRST DAY COVERS SING	FIRST DAY COVERS PL. BLK.	MINT SHEET	PLATE BLOCK	UNUSED F/NH	USED
5157	$23.75 Gateway Arch, Express	80.00		400.00(4)	....	140.00	80.00
5158	(49¢) U.S. Flag coil, BCA, die cut 11 vert.	2.75	....	....	....	2.00	.70
	same, plate number strip of 5	....	....	....	....	12.00	....
5159	(49¢) U.S. Flag coil, APU, die cut 9½ vert.	2.75	....	....	....	2.00	.70
	same, plate number strip of 5	....	....	....	....	12.00	....
5160	(49¢) U.S. Flag, BCA,micro USPS on fourth red stripe, die cut 11¼ x 10¾ on two or three sides	2.75	....	....	....	2.00	.70
5160a	same, convertible bklt of 10	....	....	....	....	16.00	....
5160b	same, double sided convertible bklt of 20.	....	....	....	....	30.00	....
5161	(49¢) U.S. Flag, APU, micro USPS on second white stripe, die cut 11¼ x 10¾ on two or three sides	2.75	....	....	....	2.00	.70
5161a	same, double sided convertible bklt of 20.	....	....	....	....	30.00	....
5162	(49¢) U.S. Flag ATM, APU, micro USPS on second stripe near blue field, die cut 11¼ x 10¾	2.75	....	....	....	4.00	1.75
5162a	same, booklet pane of 18	.....	.....	.....	....	68.00	.....

5163, 5169 5164, 5170 5165, 5167 5166, 5168

SCOTT NO.	DESCRIPTION	FIRST DAY COVERS SING	FIRST DAY COVERS PL. BLK.	MINT SHEET	PLATE BLOCK	UNUSED F/NH	USED
5163-66	(34¢) Seashells.	8.00(4)	....	24.00(20)	12.00(8)	5.00	....
5163	(34¢) Queen Conch, die cut 11¼ x 10¾	....	....	....	....	1.25	.60
5164	(34¢) Pacific Calico Scallop, die cut 11¼ x 10¾	....	....	....	....	1.25	.60
5165	(34¢) Alphabet Cone Shell, die cut 11¼ x 10¾	....	....	....	....	1.25	.60
5166	(34¢) Zebra Nerite Shell, die cut 11¼ x 10¾	....	....	....	....	1.25	.60
5167-70	(34¢) Seashells coil . . .	8.00(4)	....	....	....	4.00	....
	same, plate number strip of 5	....	....	....	....	8.00	....
5167	(34¢) Alphabet Cone Shell, die cut 9¾ vertical.	....	....	....	....	1.00	.40
5168	(34¢) Zebra Nerite Shell, die cut 9¾ vertical	....	....	....	....	1.00	.40
5169	(34¢) Queen Conch, die cut 9¾ vertical	....	....	....	....	1.00	.40
5170	(34¢) Pacific Calico Scallop, die cut 9¾ vertical	....	....	....	....	1.00	.40

5171

5172

SCOTT NO.	DESCRIPTION	FIRST DAY COVERS SING	FIRST DAY COVERS PL. BLK.	MINT SHEET	PLATE BLOCK	UNUSED F/NH	USED
5171	(49¢) Dorothy Height . .	2.75	....	30.00(20)	8.00	2.00	.70
5172	(5¢) USA Star Coil	2.75	....	....	....	.30	.30
	same, plate number strip of 5	....	....	....	....	1.75	....

5173

OSCAR DE LA RENTA

5173a	*Photograph of ODLR*	**5173g**	*Blue dress*
5173b	*Bright pink and gray fabric*	**5173h**	*Floral fabric with white*
5173c	*Green dress*	**5173i**	*Yellow dress*
5173d	*Black and white fabric*	**5173j**	*Pink, white and gray floral fabric*
5173e	*Red dress*	**5173k**	*Pink dress*
5173f	*Floral fabric with dull green*		

SCOTT NO.	DESCRIPTION	FIRST DAY COVERS SING	FIRST DAY COVERS PL. BLK.	MINT SHEET	PLATE BLOCK	UNUSED F/NH	USED
5173	(49¢) Oscar de la Renta	....	....	40.00(11)	....	....	....

5174

5175

SCOTT NO.	DESCRIPTION	FIRST DAY COVERS SING	FIRST DAY COVERS PL. BLK.	MINT SHEET	PLATE BLOCK	UNUSED F/NH	USED
5174	(21¢) Uncle Sam's Hat .	2.75	....	16.00(20)	3.50	.95	.30
5175	(49¢) John F. Kennedy .	2.75	....	24.00(12)	8.00	2.25	.70

5177 5178

5179

SCOTT NO.	DESCRIPTION	FIRST DAY COVERS SING	FIRST DAY COVERS PL. BLK.	MINT SHEET	PLATE BLOCK	UNUSED F/NH	USED
5177	5¢ Pinot Noir Grapes . .	2.75	....	3.80(20)	1.50	.30	.30
5178	10¢ Red Pears, die cut 11¼ x 11	2.75	....	5.50(20)	1.50	.35	.30
5179	(49¢) Nebraska Statehood	2.75	....	30.00(20)	6.50	2.00	.70

5180

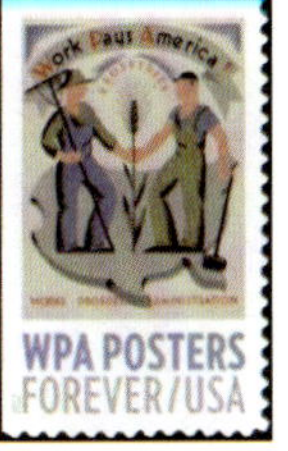

5181

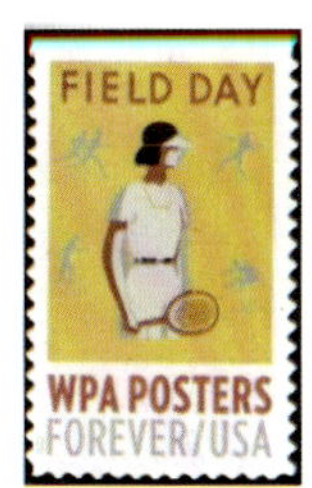

5182

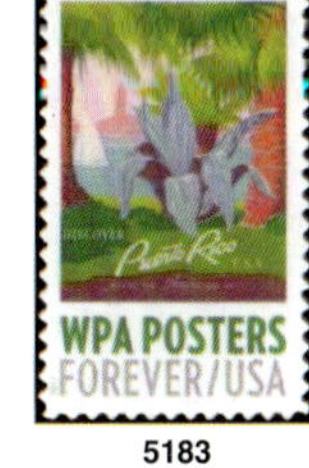

5183

5184

5185

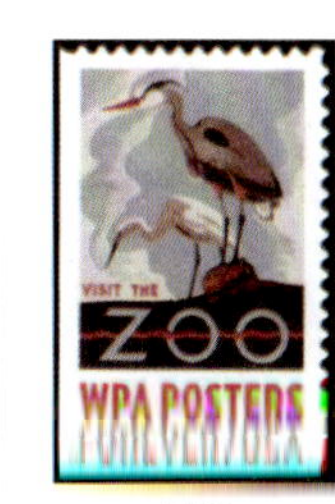

5186

5187

5188

5189

SCOTT NO.	DESCRIPTION	FIRST DAY COVERS SING	FIRST DAY COVERS PL. BLK.	MINT SHEET	PLATE BLOCK	UNUSED F/NH	USED
5180-89	(49¢) WPA Posters	22.00(10)	....	....	....	25.00	....
5180	(49¢) WPA-See America Welcome to Montana . .	....	....	....	....	2.75	.70
5181	(49¢) WPA-Work Pays America	....	....	....	....	2.75	.70
5182	(49¢) WPA-Field Day . .	....	....	....	....	2.75	.70
5183	(49¢) WPA-Discover Puerto Rico	....	....	....	....	2.75	.70
5184	(49¢) WPA-City of NY Municipal Airports	....	....	....	....	2.75	.70
5185	(49¢) WPA-Foreign Trade Zone	....	....	....	....	2.75	.70
5186	(49¢) WPA-Visit the Zoo	....	....	....	....	2.75	.70
5187	(49¢) WPA-Work with Care	....	....	....	....	2.75	.70
5188	(49¢) WPA-National Parks Preserve Wildlife.	....	....	....	....	2.75	.70
5189	(49¢) WPA-Hiking	....	....	....	....	2.75	.70
5189b	same, double sided convertible bklt of 20.	....	....	....	....	48.00	....

5190

5191

SCOTT NO.	DESCRIPTION	FIRST DAY COVERS SING	PL. BLK.	MINT SHEET	PLATE BLOCK	UNUSED F/NH	USED
5190	(49¢) Mississippi Statehood	2.75	....	30.00(20)	6.50	2.00	.70
5191	(70¢) Robert Panara. . .	3.00	....	35.00(20)	8.00	2.25	1.75

5192 5193 5194

5195

5196

5197

SCOTT NO.	DESCRIPTION	FIRST DAY COVERS SING	PL. BLK.	MINT SHEET	PLATE BLOCK	UNUSED F/NH	USED
5192-97	(49¢) Delicioso, Latin American Dishes .	12.00(6)	....	....	....	12.00	....
5192	(49¢) Tamales.	....	....	....	....	2.00	.70
5193	(49¢) Flan	....	....	....	....	2.00	.70
5194	(49¢) Sancocho	....	....	....	....	2.00	.70
5195	(49¢) Empanadas.	....	....	....	....	2.00	.70
5196	(49¢) Chile Relleno. . . .	....	....	....	....	2.00	.70
5197	(49¢) Ceviche	....	....	....	....	2.00	.70
5197b	same, double sided convertible bklt of 20.	....	....	....	....	35.00	....

5198

5199

5200

SCOTT NO.	DESCRIPTION	FIRST DAY COVERS SING	PL. BLK.	MINT SHEET	PLATE BLOCK	UNUSED F/NH	USED
5198	($1.15) Echeveria Plant, Global	4.00	....	35.00(10)	14.00	4.00	.90
5199	(49¢) Boutonniere.	2.75	....	30.00(20)	6.50	2.00	.60
5200	(70¢) Corsage.	2.75	....	35.00(20)	8.00	2.25	.80

5201

5202

SCOTT NO.	DESCRIPTION	FIRST DAY COVERS SING	PL. BLK.	MINT SHEET	PLATE BLOCK	UNUSED F/NH	USED
5201	3¢ Strawberries coil, die cut 10 vertical	2.75	....	....	....	.30	.30
	same, plate number strip of 5	....	....	....	....	1.75	....
5202	(49¢) Henry David Thoreau	2.75	....	30.00(20)	6.50	2.00	.95

5203

5204

5205

5206

5207

5208

5209

5210

SCOTT NO.	DESCRIPTION	FIRST DAY COVERS SING	PL. BLK.	MINT SHEET	PLATE BLOCK	UNUSED F/NH	USED
5203-10	(49¢) Sports Balls.	20.00(8)	.....	28.00(16)	18.50(8)	15.00	.....
5203	(49¢) Football	.....	......	.....	......	2.00	0.70
5204	(49¢) Volleyball.	.....	......	.....	......	2.00	0.70
5205	(49¢) Soccer.	.....	......	.....	......	2.00	0.70
5206	(49¢) Golf	.....	......	.....	......	2.00	0.70
5207	(49¢) Baseball	.....	......	.....	......	2.00	0.70
5208	(49¢) Basketball	.....	......	.....	......	2.00	0.70
5209	(49¢) Tennis	.....	......	.....	......	2.00	0.70
5210	(49¢) Kickball	.....	......	.....	......	2.00	0.70

5211

SCOTT NO.	DESCRIPTION	FIRST DAY COVERS SING	PL. BLK.	MINT SHEET	PLATE BLOCK	UNUSED F/NH	USED
5211	(49¢) Total Eclipse	2.75	....	30.00(16)	6.50	2.00	.70

5212

ANDREW WYETH

5212a	*Wind from the Sea*	**5212g**	*Soaring*
5212b	*Big Room*	**5212h**	*North Light*
5212c	*Christina's World*	**5212i**	*Spring Fed*
5212d	*Alvaro & Christina*	**5212j**	*The Carry*
5212e	*Frostbitten*	**5212k**	*Young Bull*
5212f	*Sailor's Valentine*	**5212l**	*My Studio*

SCOTT NO.	DESCRIPTION	FIRST DAY COVERS SING	PL. BLK.	MINT SHEET	PLATE BLOCK	UNUSED F/NH	USED
5212	(49¢) Andrew Wyeth. . .	25.00(12)	.....	30.00(12)	.....	.....	.....

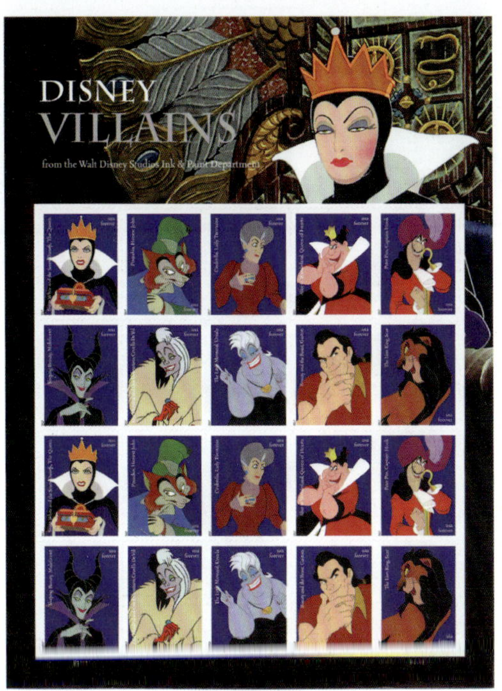

5213-5222

SCOTT NO.	DESCRIPTION	FIRST DAY COVERS SING	FIRST DAY COVERS PL. BLK.	MINT SHEET	PLATE BLOCK	UNUSED F/NH	USED
5213-22	(49¢) Disney Villains. . .	22.00(10)	.....	35.00(20)	25.00(10)	20.00(10)	.....
5213	(49¢) The Queen, Snow White	.....	......	.....	......	2.25	1.00
5214	(49¢) Honest John, Pinocchio	.....	......	.....	......	2.25	1.00
5215	(49¢) Lady Tremaine, Cinderella	.....	......	.....	......	2.25	1.00
5216	(49¢) Queen of Hearts, Alice in Wonderland		......	......	....	2.25	1.00
5217	(49¢) Captain Hook, Peter Pan	.....	......	.....	......	2.25	1.00
5218	(49¢) Maleficent, Sleeping Beauty	.....	......	.....	......	2.25	1.00
5219	(49¢) Cruella De Vil, 101 Dalmatians.....		......	.....	......	2.25	1.00
5220	(49¢) Ursula, Little Mermaid	.....	......	.....	......	2.25	1.00
5221	(49¢) Gaston, Beauty and the Beast.....		......	.....	......	2.25	1.00
5222	(49¢) Scar, The Lion King	.....	......	.....	......	2.25	1.00

5223

WHALE SHARK

5224

5225

5226

5227

SCOTT NO.	DESCRIPTION	FIRST DAY COVERS SING	FIRST DAY COVERS PL. BLK.	MINT SHEET	PLATE BLOCK	UNUSED F/NH	USED
5223-27	(49¢) Sharks.	12.00(5)	.....	30.00(20)	18.00(10)	8.50(5)	.....
5223	(49¢) Mako	.....	......	.....	......	2.00	1.00
5224	(49¢) Whale	.....	......	.....	......	2.00	1.00
5225	(49¢) Thresher	.....	......	.....	......	2.00	1.00
5226	(49¢) Hammerhead . . .	.....	......	.....	......	2.00	1.00
5227	(49¢) Great White.	.....	......	.....	......	2.00	1.00

5228

5229

5230

5231

5232

SCOTT NO.	DESCRIPTION	FIRST DAY COVERS SING	FIRST DAY COVERS PL. BLK.	MINT SHEET	PLATE BLOCK	UNUSED F/NH	USED
5228-32	(49¢) Protect Pollinators	12.00(5)	.....	45.00(20)	24.00(10)	12.00(5)	.....
5228	(49¢) Monarch on Purple Coneflower.....		......	.....	......	2.50	0.95
5229	(49¢) Honeybee on Golden Ragwort					2.50	0.95
5230	(49¢) Monarch on Red Zinnia			.....	......	2.50	0.95
5231	(49¢) Honeybee on Purple Aster			.....	......	2.50	0.95
5232	(49¢) Monarch on Goldenrod	.....	......	.....	......	2.50	0.95

5233, 5237

5236, 5238

5234, 5239

5235, 5240

SCOTT NO.	DESCRIPTION	FIRST DAY COVERS SING	FIRST DAY COVERS PL. BLK.	MINT SHEET	PLATE BLOCK	UNUSED F/NH	USED
5233-36	(49¢) Flowers from the Garden	8.00(4)	.....	.....	.....	9.00	.....
	same, plate number strip of 5	.....	.....	.....	.....	18.00	.....
5233	(49¢) Red Camellias in Yellow Pitcher	.....	.....	.....	.....	2.25	0.95
5234	(49¢) Peonies in Clear Vase	.....	.....	.....	.....	2.25	0.95
5235	(49¢) Hydrangeas in Blue Pot	.....	.....	.....	.....	2.25	0.95
5236	(49¢) Flowers in White Vase	.....	.....	.....	.....	2.25	0.95
5237-40	(49¢) Flowers from the Garden	8.00(4)	.....	.....	.....	9.00	.....
5237	(49¢) Red Camellias in Yellow Pitcher	.....	.....	.....	.....	2.25	0.95
5238	(49¢) Flowers in White Vase	.....	.....	.....	.....	2.25	0.95
5239	(49¢) Peonies in Clear Vase	.....	.....	.....	.....	2.25	0.95
5240	(49¢) Hydrangeas in Blue Pot	.....	.....	.....	.....	2.25	0.95
5240b	same, double-sided bklt pane of 20	.....	.....	.....	.....	45.00	.....

5241, 5242

5243 5244

5245 5246

SCOTT NO.	DESCRIPTION	FIRST DAY COVERS SING	FIRST DAY COVERS PL. BLK.	MINT SHEET	PLATE BLOCK	UNUSED F/NH	USED
5241	(49¢) Father Theodore Hesburgh	2.75	.....	30.00(20)	6.50	2.00	0.60
5242	(49¢) Father Theodore Hesburgh, coil	2.75	.....	.....	.....	2.00	0.95
	same, plate number strip of 5	.....	.....	.....	.....	14.00	.....
5243-46	(49¢) The Snowy Day, Ezra Jack Keats	8.00(4)	.....	.....	.....	8.00	.....
5243	(49¢) Making Snowball.	.....	.....	.....	.....	2.00	0.60
5244	(49¢) Sliding	.....	.....	.....	.....	2.00	0.60
5245	(49¢) Making Snow Angel	.....	.....	.....	.....	2.00	0.60
5246	(49¢) Leaving Footprints	.....	.....	.....	.....	2.00	0.60
5246b	same, double-sided bklt pane of 20	.....	.....	.....	.....	40.00	.....

5247 5248

5249 5250

SCOTT NO.	DESCRIPTION	FIRST DAY COVERS SING	FIRST DAY COVERS PL. BLK.	MINT SHEET	PLATE BLOCK	UNUSED F/NH	USED
5247-50	(49¢) Christmas Carols.	8.00(4)	.....	.....	.....	8.00	.....
5247	(49¢) Deck the Halls . . .	.....	.....	.....	.....	2.00	0.60
5248	(49¢) Silent Night	.....	.....	.....	.....	2.00	0.60
5249	(49¢) Jingle Bells	.....	.....	.....	.....	2.00	0.60
5250	(49¢) Jolly Old St. Nicholas	.....	.....	.....	.....	2.00	0.60
5250b	same, double-sided bklt pane of 20	.....	.....	.....	.....	40.00	.....

5251

SCOTT NO.	DESCRIPTION	FIRST DAY COVERS SING	FIRST DAY COVERS PL. BLK.	MINT SHEET	PLATE BLOCK	UNUSED F/NH	USED
5251	(49¢) National Museum of African American History and Culture	2.75	.....	30.00(20)	6.50	2.00	0.95

5252 5253

SCOTT NO.	DESCRIPTION	FIRST DAY COVERS SING	FIRST DAY COVERS PL. BLK.	MINT SHEET	PLATE BLOCK	UNUSED F/NH	USED
5252-53	(49¢) History of Ice Hockey	5.00(2)	.....	30.00(20)	6.50	4.00	.....
5252	(49¢) Player Wearing Gear	.....	.....	.....	.....	2.00	0.70
5253	(49¢) Player Wearing Hat & Scarf	.....	.....	.....	.....	2.00	0.70
5253c	(49¢) History of Ice Hockey, souvenir sheet of 2.	.....	.....	.....	.....	4.50	.....
5252a	(49¢) Player Wearing Gear	.....	.....	.....	.....	2.25	1.00
5253a	(49¢) Player Wearing Hat & Scarf	.....	.....	.....	.....	2.25	1.00

2018 COMMEMORATIVES

SCOTT NO.	DESCRIPTION	FIRST DAY COVERS SING	FIRST DAY COVERS PL. BLK.	MINT SHEET	PLATE BLOCK	UNUSED F/NH	USED
5254/5338	**(5254, 5259, 5264-79, 5281-84, 5299-5305, 5307-10, 5312-16, 5321-30, 5337-38) 50 varieties**	....	....	....	....	**106.00**	....

5254

5255

5256

SCOTT NO.	DESCRIPTION	FIRST DAY COVERS SING	FIRST DAY COVERS PL. BLK.	MINT SHEET	PLATE BLOCK	UNUSED F/NH	USED
5254	(49¢) Year of the Dog	2.75	.....	20.00(12)	.....	2.00	0.60
5255	(49¢) Love Flourishes	2.75	.....	45.00(20)	8.00	2.50	0.60
5256	2¢ Lemon, coil.	.....	.....	.....	.....	0.30	0.30
	same, plate number strip of 5	.....	.....	.....	.....	1.75	.....

5257 5259 5258

5260, 5261 5262, 5263

SCOTT NO.	DESCRIPTION	FIRST DAY COVERS SING	FIRST DAY COVERS PL. BLK.	MINT SHEET	PLATE BLOCK	UNUSED F/NH	USED
5257	$6.70 Byodo-In-Temple, Priority	20.00	.....	80.00(4)	.....	20.00	20.00
5258	$24.70 Sleeping Bear Dunes, Express	48.00	.....	350.00(4)	.....	95.00	40.00
5259	(50¢) Lena Horne	2.75	.....	30.00(20)	6.50	2.00	0.70
5260	(50¢) U.S. Flag coil, die cut 9.5 vert.	2.75	.....	.....	.....	2.00	0.70
	same, plate number strip of 5	.....	.....	.....	.....	12.00	.....
5261	(50¢) U.S. Flag coil, die cut 11 vert.	2.75	.....	.....	.....	2.00	0.70
	same, plate number strip of 5	.....	.....	.....	.....	12.00	.....
5262	(50¢) U.S. Flag, micro USPS at left of flag	2.75	.....	.....	.....	2.00	0.70
5262a	same, double-sided bklt pane of 20	.....	.....	.....	.....	35.00	.....
5263	(50¢) U.S. Flag, micro USPS at right of flag	2.75	.....	.....	.....	2.00	0.70
5263a	same, double-sided bklt pane of 20	.....	.....	.....	.....	35.00	.....

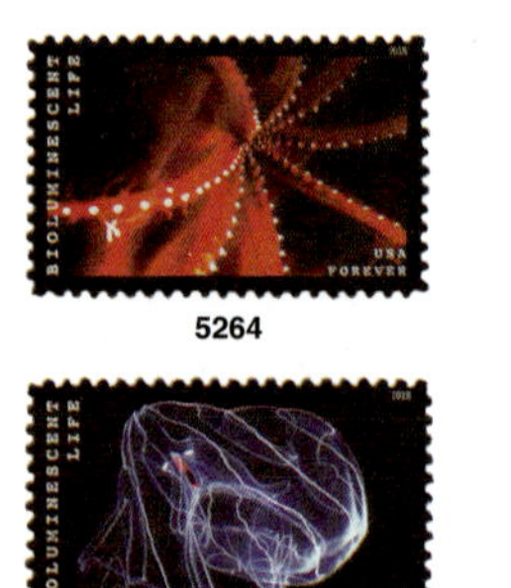

5264

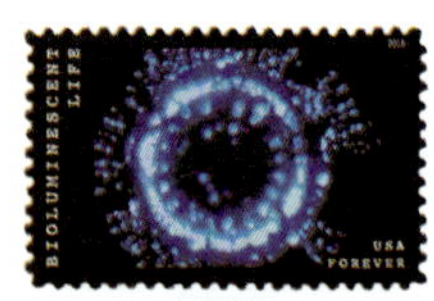

5265

5266

5267

5268

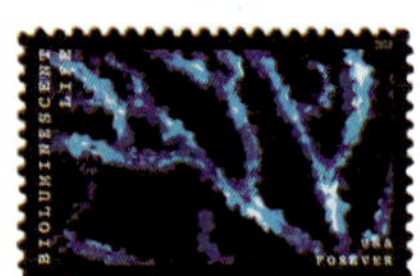

5269

5270

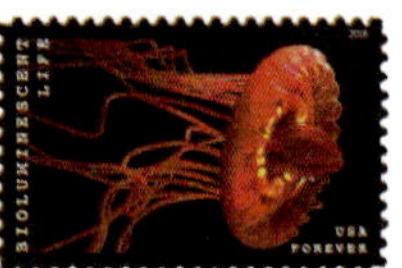

5271

5272 5273

SCOTT NO.	DESCRIPTION	FIRST DAY COVERS SING	FIRST DAY COVERS PL. BLK.	MINT SHEET	PLATE BLOCK	UNUSED F/NH	USED
5264-73	(50¢) Bioluminescent Life .	45.00(20)	.....	58.00(20)	.....	30.00(10)	.....
5264	(50¢) Octopus	.....	.....	.....	.....	3.00	2.25
5265	(50¢) Jellyfish	.....	.....	.....	.....	3.00	2.25
5266	(50¢) Comb Jelly	.....	.....	.....	.....	3.00	2.25
5267	(50¢) Mushrooms	.....	.....	.....	.....	3.00	2.25
5268	(50¢) Firefly.	.....	.....	.....	.....	3.00	2.25
5269	(50¢) Bamboo Coral	.....	.....	.....	.....	3.00	2.25
5270	(50¢) Marine Worm	.....	.....	.....	.....	3.00	2.25
5271	(50¢) Crown Jellyfish.	.....	.....	.....	.....	3.00	2.25
5272	(50¢) Marine Worm	.....	.....	.....	.....	3.00	2.25
5273	(50¢) Sea Pen.	.....	.....	.....	.....	3.00	2.25

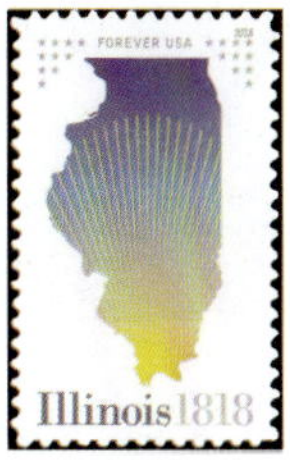

5274

5275

SCOTT NO.	DESCRIPTION	FIRST DAY COVERS SING	FIRST DAY COVERS PL. BLK.	MINT SHEET	PLATE BLOCK	UNUSED F/NH	USED
5274	(50¢) Illinois Statehood	2.75	.....	30.00(20)	6.50	2.00	0.70
5275	(50¢) Mister Rogers	2.75	.....	40.00(20)	10.00	3.00	0.70

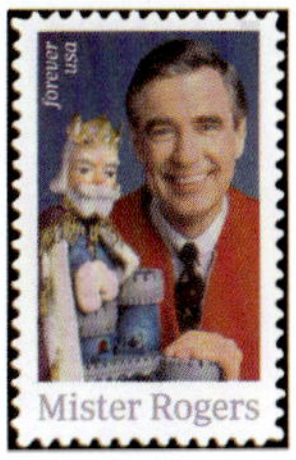

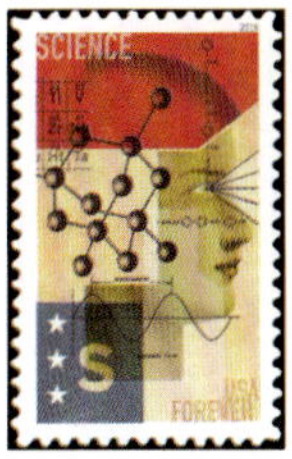

5276

5277

5278

5279

SCOTT NO.	DESCRIPTION	FIRST DAY COVERS SING	FIRST DAY COVERS PL. BLK.	MINT SHEET	PLATE BLOCK	UNUSED F/NH	USED
5276-79	(50¢) STEM Education . . .	15.00(4)	.....	40.00(20)	20.00(8)	8.00	.....
5276	(50¢) Science					2.00	1.00
5277	(50¢) Technology.	.....				2.00	1.00
5278	(50¢) Engineering	.....	.....	.....	.....	2.00	1.00
5279	(50¢) Math.	.....	.....	.....	.....	2.00	1.00

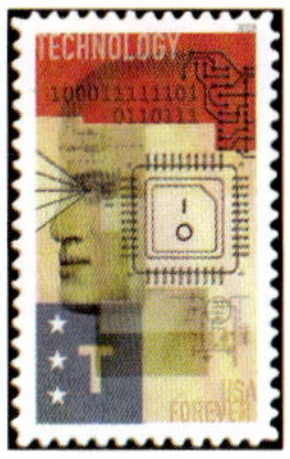

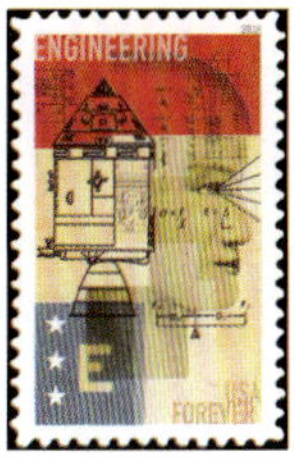

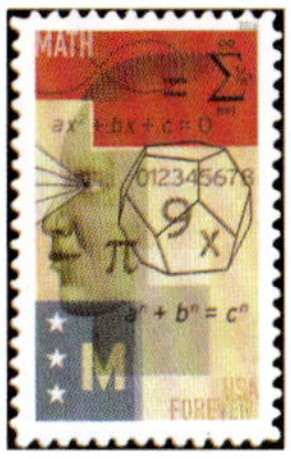

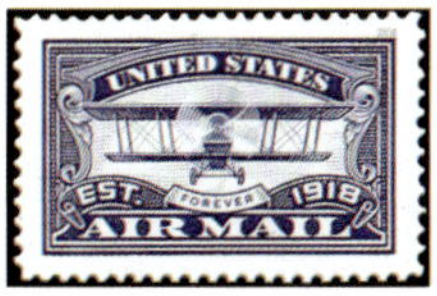

5281

5282

5283

5284

5280

SCOTT NO.	DESCRIPTION	FIRST DAY COVERS SING	FIRST DAY COVERS PL. BLK.	MINT SHEET	PLATE BLOCK	UNUSED F/NH	USED
5280	(50¢) [illegible]	[illegible]	.....	.....	.....	[illegible]	[illegible]
5280a	same, double-sided bklt pane of 20	.....	.....	.....	.....	30.00	.....
5281	(50¢) Air Mail Centenary, blue	[illegible]	.....	[illegible]	[illegible]	[illegible]	[illegible]
5282	(50¢) Air Mail Centenary, red	2.75	.....	30.00(20)	6.50	2.00	0.70
5283	(50¢) Sally Ride	2.75		30.00(20)	6.50	[illegible]	0.70
5284	(50¢) Flag Act of 1818 Bicentennial	2.75	.....	30.00(20)	6.50	2.00	0.70

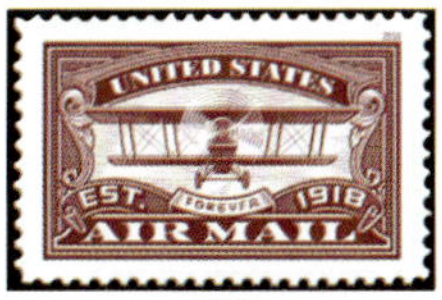

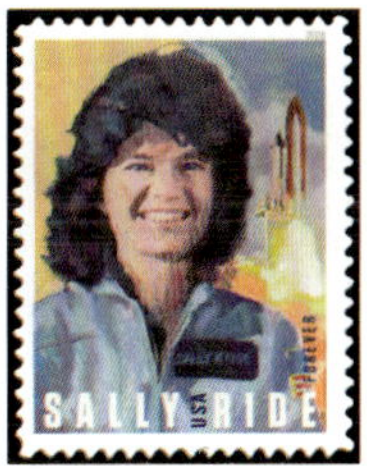

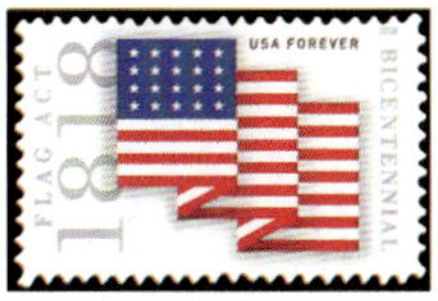

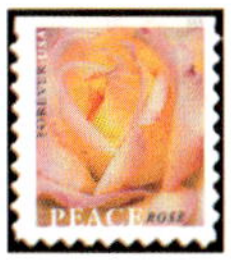

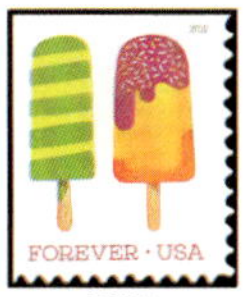

5285

5286

5287

5288

5289

5290

5291

5292

5293

5294

SCOTT NO.	DESCRIPTION	FIRST DAY COVERS SING	FIRST DAY COVERS PL. BLK.	MINT SHEET	PLATE BLOCK	UNUSED F/NH	USED
5285-94	(50¢) Frozen Treats.	22.00(10)	.....	.....	.....	18.00(10)	.....
5285	(50¢) Green striped pop . .	.....	.....	.....	.....	2.00	0.70
5286	(50¢) Watermelon, striped pops	.....	.....	.....	.....	2.00	0.70
5287	(50¢) Twin pop at right. . . .	.....	.....	.....	.....	2.00	0.70
5288	(50¢) Bitten pop at left. . . .	.....	.....	.....	.....	2.00	0.70
5289	(50¢) Sprinkle-topped pops	.....	.....	.....	.....	2.00	0.70
5290	(50¢) Chocolate, vanilla, strawberry pops.	.....	.....	.....	.....	2.00	0.70
5291	(50¢) Bitten pop at right. . .	.....	.....	.....	.....	2.00	0.70
5292	(50¢) Sprinkle-topped pop at left	.....	.....	.....	.....	2.00	0.70
5293	(50¢) Chocolate pop at left	.....	.....	.....	.....	2.00	0.70
5294	(50¢) Sprinkle-topped at right	.....	.....	.....	.....	2.00	0.70
5294b	same, double-sided bklt pane of 20	.....	.....	.....	.....	34.00	.....

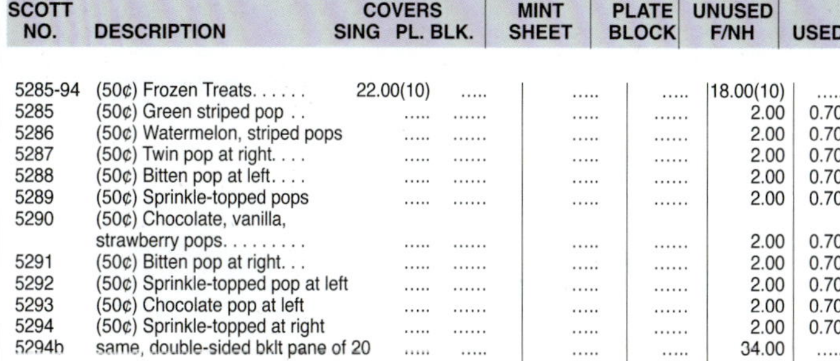

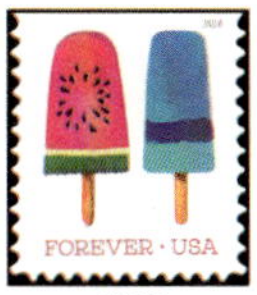

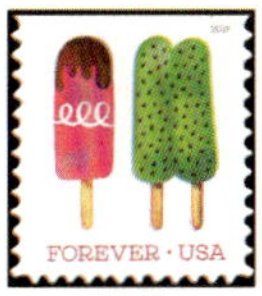

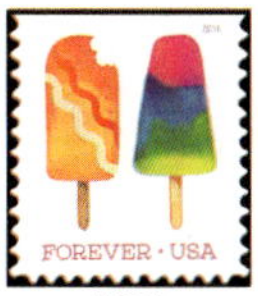

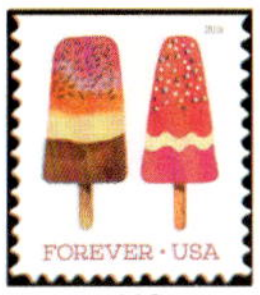

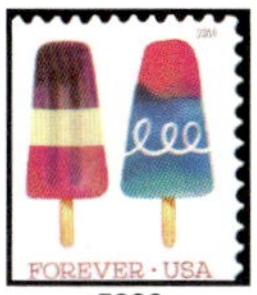

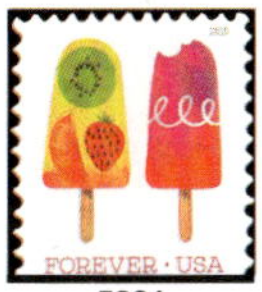

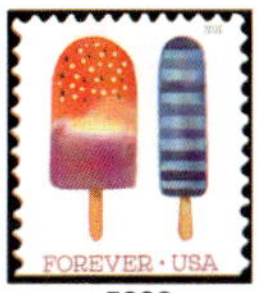

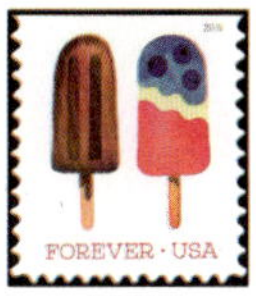

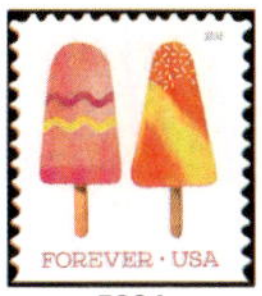

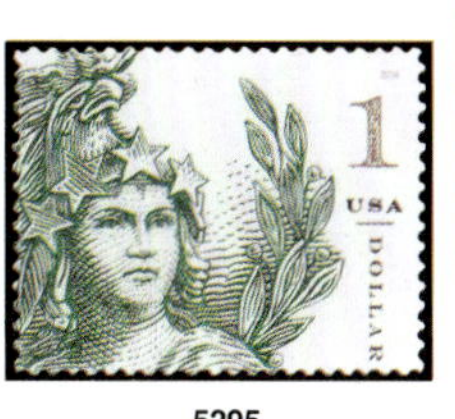

5295

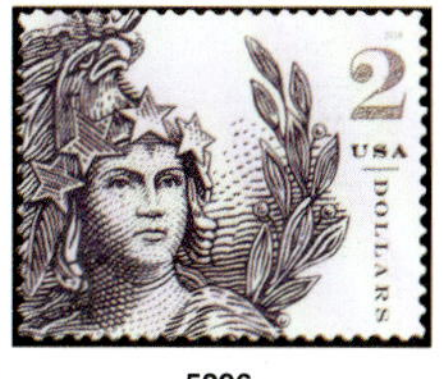

5296

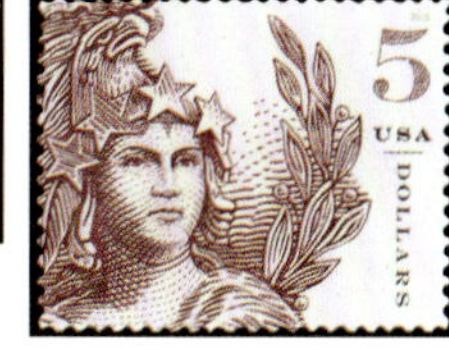

5297

SCOTT NO.	DESCRIPTION	FIRST DAY COVERS SING	FIRST DAY COVERS PL. BLK.	MINT SHEET	PLATE BLOCK	UNUSED F/NH	USED
5295	$1 Statue of Freedom	.....	.....	30.00(10)	12.00	3.50	1.25
5296	$2 Statue of Freedom	.....	.....	55.00(10)	24.00	6.50	3.50
5297	$5 Statue of Freedom	.....	.....	55.00(4)	.....	15.00	8.00

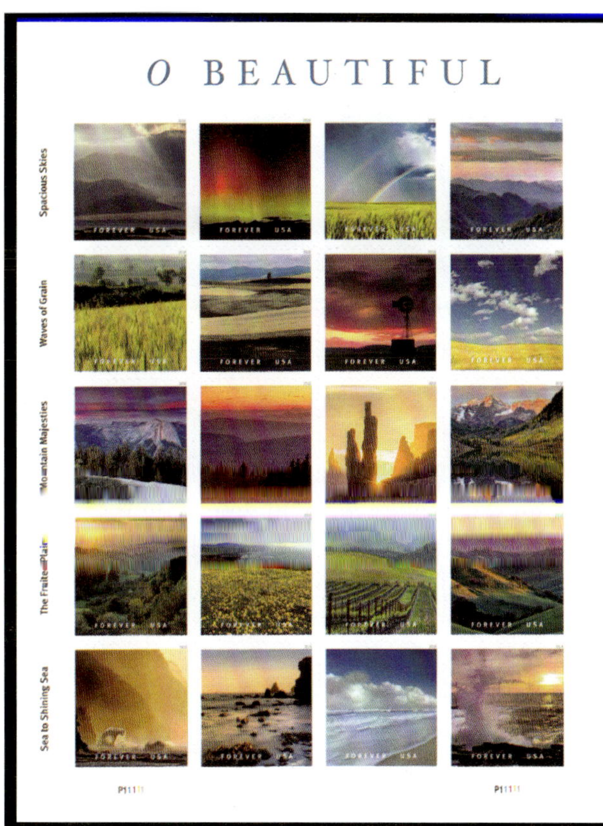

5298

O BEAUTIFUL

5298a	Death Valley National Park	**5298k**	Monument Valley Navajo Tribal Park
5298b	Three Fingers Mountain	**5298l**	Maroon Bells
5298c	Double Rainbow over Kansas Field	**5298m**	Sunrise Near Orinda, California
5298d	Great Smoky Mountains	**5298n**	Pigeon Point
5298e	Field of Wheat, Wisconsin	**5298o**	Edna Valley
5298f	Plowed Wheat Field	**5298p**	Livermore
5298g	Grasslands Wildlife Management Area	**5298q**	Napali Coast State Wilderness Park
5298h	Field of Wheat, Montana	**5298r**	Lone Ranch Beach
5298i	Yosemite National Park	**5298s**	Canaveral National Seashore
5298j	Crater Lake National Park	**5298t**	Bailey Island

SCOTT NO.	DESCRIPTION	FIRST DAY COVERS SING	FIRST DAY COVERS PL. BLK.	MINT SHEET	PLATE BLOCK	UNUSED F/NH	USED
5298	(50¢) O Beautiful	45.00(20)	.....	60.00(20)	.....	.....	18.00

5299 5300

SCOTT NO.	DESCRIPTION	FIRST DAY COVERS SING	FIRST DAY COVERS PL. BLK.	MINT SHEET	PLATE BLOCK	UNUSED F/NH	USED
5299	(50¢) Scooby-Doo.......	2.75	.....	24.00(12)	6.50	2.00	0.70
5300	(50¢) World War I, Turning the Tide	2.75	.....	30.00(20)	6.50	2.00	0.70

5301, 5306a 5302 5303

5304 5305

SCOTT NO.	DESCRIPTION	FIRST DAY COVERS SING	FIRST DAY COVERS PL. BLK.	MINT SHEET	PLATE BLOCK	UNUSED F/NH	USED
5301-05	(50¢) Art of Magic	12.00(5)	.....	38.00(20)	22.00(10)	10.00(5)	.....
5301	(50¢) Rabbit in Hat	.....	.....	.....	.....	2.25	1.50
5302	(50¢) Fortune Teller......	.....	.....	.....	.....	2.25	1.50
5303	(50¢) Woman Hoop......	.....	.....	.....	.....	2.25	1.50
5304	(50¢) Empty Bird Cage ...	.....	.....	.....	.....	2.25	1.50
5305	(50¢) Bird in Flower......	.....	.....	.....	.....	2.25	1.50
5306	(50¢) Art of Magic, souvenir sheet of 3	.....	.....	.....	.....	6.00	.....

5307 5309

5308 5310

SCOTT NO.	DESCRIPTION	FIRST DAY COVERS SING	FIRST DAY COVERS PL. BLK.	MINT SHEET	PLATE BLOCK	UNUSED F/NH	USED
5307-10	(50¢) Dragons	15.00(4)	.....	38.00(16)	10.00(4)	9.00	.....
5307	(50¢) Green Dragon and Castle		.....	.....	.....	2.25	1.50
5308	(50¢) Purple Dragon and Castle		.....	.....	.....	2.25	1.50
5309	(50¢) Dragon and Ship ...	.....	.....	.....	.....	2.25	1.50
5310	(50¢) Dragon and Pagoda.	.....	.....	.....	.....	2.25	1.50

5311

SCOTT NO.	DESCRIPTION	FIRST DAY COVERS SING	FIRST DAY COVERS PL. BLK.	MINT SHEET	PLATE BLOCK	UNUSED F/NH	USED
5311	($1.15) Poinsettia	4.00	.....	30.00(10)	12.00(4)	3.50	1.00

5312 5313

5314 5315

SCOTT NO.	DESCRIPTION	FIRST DAY COVERS SING	FIRST DAY COVERS PL. BLK.	MINT SHEET	PLATE BLOCK	UNUSED F/NH	USED
5312-15	(50¢) John Lennon	15.00(4)	.....	30.00(16)	.....	9.00	.....
5312	(50¢) Red	.....	.....	.....	.....	2.25	0.80
5313	(50¢) Red Lilac	.....	.....	.....	.....	2.25	0.80
5314	(50¢) Violet	.....	.....	.....	.....	2.25	0.80
5315	(50¢) Blue	.....	.....	.....	.....	2.25	0.80

5316

SCOTT NO.	DESCRIPTION	FIRST DAY COVERS SING	FIRST DAY COVERS PL. BLK.	MINT SHEET	PLATE BLOCK	UNUSED F/NH	USED
5316	(50¢) Honoring First Responders.......	2.75	.....	30.00(20)	6.50(4)	2.00	0.70

5317 5318 5319 5320

SCOTT NO.	DESCRIPTION	FIRST DAY COVERS SING	FIRST DAY COVERS PL. BLK.	MINT SHEET	PLATE BLOCK	UNUSED F/NH	USED
5317-20	(50¢) Birds in Winter	15.00(4)	.....	......	.....	9.00	.....
5317	(50¢) Chickadee	.....	.....	.....	.....	2.25	0.80
5318	(50¢) Cardinal	.....	.....	.....	.....	2.25	0.80
5319	(50¢) Woodpecker.......	.....	.....	.....	.....	2.25	0.80
5320	(50¢) Blue Jay..........	.....	.....	.....	.....	2.25	0.80
5320b	same, double-sided bklt pane of 20	.....	.....	.....	.....	35.00	.....

5321

5322

5323

5324

5325

5326

5327

5328

5329

5330

SCOTT NO.	DESCRIPTION	FIRST DAY COVERS SING	FIRST DAY COVERS PL. BLK.	MINT SHEET	PLATE BLOCK	UNUSED F/NH	USED
5321-30	(50¢) Hot Wheels	35.00(10)	.....	30.00(20)	.....	18.00(10)	.....
5321	(50¢) Purple Passion.	.....	.....	.....	.....	2.00	1.50
5322	(50¢) Rocket-Bye-Baby. . .	.....	.....	.....	.....	2.00	1.50
5323	(50¢) Rigor Motor	.....	.....	.....	.....	2.00	1.50
5324	(50¢) Rodger Dodger	.....	.....	.....	.....	2.00	1.50
5325	(50¢) Mach Speeder	.....	.....	.....	.....	2.00	1.50
5326	(50¢) Twin Mill.	.....	.....	.....	.....	2.00	1.50
5327	(50¢) Bone Shaker	.....	.....	.....	.....	2.00	1.50
5328	(50¢) HW40.	.....	.....	.....	.....	2.00	1.50
5329	(50¢) Deora II	.....	.....	.....	.....	2.00	1.50
5330	(50¢) Sharkruiser	.....	.....	.....	.....	2.00	1.50

5332

5333

5334

5335

5336

5331

5337

5338

SCOTT NO.	DESCRIPTION	FIRST DAY COVERS SING	FIRST DAY COVERS PL. BLK.	MINT SHEET	PLATE BLOCK	UNUSED F/NH	USED
5331	(50¢) Madonna and Child .	2.75	.....	.....	.....	2.00	0.95
5331a	same, double-sided bklt pane of 20	.....	.....	.....	.....	30.00	.....
5332-35	(50¢) Sparkling Holiday Santas	8.00(4)	.....	.....	.....	8.00	.....
5332	(50¢) Santa Head	.....	.....	.....	.....	2.00	0.60
5333	(50¢) Santa and Wreath . .	.....	.....	.....	.....	2.00	0.60
5334	(50¢) Santa and Book	.....	.....	.....	.....	2.00	0.60
5335	(50¢) Santa and Card	.....	.....	.....	.....	2.00	0.60
5335b	same, double-sided bklt pane of 20	.....	.....	.....	.....	30.00	.....
5336	(50¢) Sparkling Holiday Santa, souvenir sheet	.....	.....	.....	.....	2.50	.....
5337	(50¢) Kwanzaa	2.75	.....	30.00(20)	6.50(4)	2.00	0.95
5338	(50¢) Hanukkah.	2.75	.....	30.00(20)	6.50(4)	2.00	0.95

2019 COMMEMORATIVES

SCOTT NO.	DESCRIPTION	FIRST DAY COVERS SING	FIRST DAY COVERS PL. BLK.	MINT SHEET	PLATE BLOCK	UNUSED F/NH	USED
5340/5423M	**(5340, 5349, 5360, 5371-80, 5382-93, 5399-5404, 5409-14, 5420-23) 41 varieties**	....	....	....	....	**74.00**	....

5339

5340

SCOTT NO.	DESCRIPTION	FIRST DAY COVERS SING	FIRST DAY COVERS PL. BLK.	MINT SHEET	PLATE BLOCK	UNUSED F/NH	USED
5339	(50¢) Love Hearts	2.75	.....	30.00(20)	8.00(4)	2.00	0.60
5340	(50¢) Year of the Boar. . . .	2.75	.....	24.00(12)	.....	2.00	0.60

5341

5342, 5343

5344, 5345

5346

SCOTT NO.	DESCRIPTION	FIRST DAY COVERS SING	FIRST DAY COVERS PL. BLK.	MINT SHEET	PLATE BLOCK	UNUSED F/NH	USED
5341	(15¢) Uncle Sam Hat, coil.....	.....	.....	.....	.....	0.30	0.30
	same, plate number strip of 5	.....	.....	.....	.....	3.00	.....
5342	(55¢) U.S. Flag coil, die cut 11	2.75	.....	.....	.....	1.50	0.60
	same, plate number strip of 5	.....	.....	.....	.....	10.50	.....
5343	(55¢) U.S. Flag coil, die cut 9.5	2.75	.....	.....	.....	1.50	0.60
	same, plate number strip of 5	.....	.....	.....	.....	10.50	.....
5344	(55¢) U.S. Flag, micro USPS at upper left	2.75	.....	.....	.....	1.50	0.60
5344a	same, double-sided bklt pane of 20	.....	.....	.....	.....	24.50	.....
5345	(55¢) U.S. Flag, micro USPS at right	2.75	.....	.....	.....	1.50	0.60
5345a	same, double-sided bklt pane of 20	.....	.....	.....	.....	24.50	.....
5346	(70¢) California Dogface Butterfly	3.00	.....	30.00(20)	7.50(4)	2.00	0.70

5347

5348

SCOTT NO.	DESCRIPTION	FIRST DAY COVERS SING	FIRST DAY COVERS PL. BLK.	MINT SHEET	PLATE BLOCK	UNUSED F/NH	USED
5347	($7.35) Joshua Tree, Priority Mail	20.00	.....	140.00(4)	.....	40.00	20.00
5348	($25.50) Bethesda Fountain, Express Mail	50.00	.....	600.00(4)	.....	200.00	50.00

5349

SCOTT NO.	DESCRIPTION	FIRST DAY COVERS SING	FIRST DAY COVERS PL. BLK.	MINT SHEET	PLATE BLOCK	UNUSED F/NH	USED
5349	(55¢) Gregory Hines	2.75	.....	38.00(20)	6.50(4)	2.00	0.70

5350  5351  5352

5353  5354  5355  5356

5357  5358  5359

SCOTT NO.	DESCRIPTION	FIRST DAY COVERS SING	FIRST DAY COVERS PL. BLK.	MINT SHEET	PLATE BLOCK	UNUSED F/NH	USED
5350-59	(55¢) Cactus Flowers	30.00(10)	.....	.....	.....	25.00	.....
5350	(55¢) Opuntia Engelmannii	.....	.....	.....	.....	2.50	0.90
5351	(55¢) Rebutia Minuscula.....	.....	.....	.....	.....	2.50	0.90
5352	(55¢) Echinocereus Dasyacanthus	.....	.....	.....	.....	2.50	0.90
5353	(55¢) Echinocereus Poselgeri	.....	.....	.....	.....	2.50	0.90
5354	(55¢) Echinocereus Coccineus	.....	.....	.....	.....	2.50	0.90
5355	(55¢) Pelecyphora Aselliformis	.....	.....	.....	.....	2.50	0.90
5356	(55¢) Parodia Microsperma	.....	.....	.....	.....	2.50	0.90
5357	(55¢) Echinocactus Horizonthalonius	.....	.....	.....	.....	2.50	0.90
5358	(55¢) Thelocactus Heterochromus	.....	.....	.....	.....	2.50	0.90
5359	(55¢) Parodia Scopa	.....	.....	.....	.....	2.50	0.90
5359b	same, double-sided bklt pane of 20	.....	.....	.....	.....	50.00	.....

5360

5361, 5362

SCOTT NO.	DESCRIPTION	FIRST DAY COVERS SING	FIRST DAY COVERS PL. BLK.	MINT SHEET	PLATE BLOCK	UNUSED F/NH	USED
5360	(55¢) Alabama Statehood.............	2.75	.....	30.00(20)	6.50(4)	2.00	0.70
5361	(55¢) Star Ribbon	2.75	.....	30.00(20)	6.50(4)	2.00	0.60
5362	(55¢) Star Ribbon coil.............	2.75	.....	.....	.....	2.00	0.60
	same, plate number strip of 5	.....	.....	.....	.....	12.00	.....

5363, 5369  5364, 5370  5365, 5367  5366, 5368

SCOTT NO.	DESCRIPTION	FIRST DAY COVERS SING	FIRST DAY COVERS PL. BLK.	MINT SHEET	PLATE BLOCK	UNUSED F/NH	USED
5363-66	(35¢) Coral Reefs	6.00(4)	.....	18.00(20)	8.00(8)	4.00	.....
5363	(35¢) French Angelfish . . .	.....	.....	.....	.....	1.00	0.95
5364	(35¢) Spotted Moray Eel . .	.....	.....	.....	.....	1.00	0.95
5365	(35¢) Grouper and Neon Gobies	.....	.....	.....	.....	1.00	0.95
5366	(35¢) Blue-striped Grunts.....	.....	.....	.....	.....	1.00	0.95
5367-70	(35¢) Coral Reefs coil	6.00(4)	.....	.....	.....	4.00	.....
	same, plate number strip of 5	.....	.....	.....	.....	7.00	.....
5367	(35¢) Grouper and Neon Gobies coil	.....	.....	.....	.....	1.00	0.95
5368	(35¢) Blue-striped Grunts coil	.....	.....	.....	.....	1.00	0.95
5369	(35¢) French Angelfish coil	.....	.....	.....	.....	1.00	0.95
5370	(35¢) Spotted Moray Eel coil	.....	.....	.....	.....	1.00	0.95

5371

SCOTT NO.	DESCRIPTION	FIRST DAY COVERS SING	FIRST DAY COVERS PL. BLK.	MINT SHEET	PLATE BLOCK	UNUSED F/NH	USED
5371	(55¢) Marvin Gaye	2.75	.....	28.00(16)	.....	2.00	0.70

5372

5373  5374

5375  5376

SCOTT NO.	DESCRIPTION	FIRST DAY COVERS SING	FIRST DAY COVERS PL. BLK.	MINT SHEET	PLATE BLOCK	UNUSED F/NH	USED
5372-76	(55¢) Post Office Murals...............	15.00(5)	.....	18.00(10)	.....	9.00	.....
5372	(55¢) Piggott, Arkansas...........	.....	.....	.....	.....	2.00	0.80
5373	(55¢) Florence, Colorado...........	.....	.....	.....	.....	2.00	0.80
5374	(55¢) Rockville, Maryland...........	.....	.....	.....	.....	2.00	0.80
5375	(55¢) Anadarko, Oklahoma...........	.....	.....	.....	.....	2.00	0.80
5376	(55¢) Deming, New Mexico...........	.....	.....	.....	.....	2.00	0.80

5377

SCOTT NO.	DESCRIPTION	FIRST DAY COVERS SING	FIRST DAY COVERS PL. BLK.	MINT SHEET	PLATE BLOCK	UNUSED F/NH	USED
5377	(55¢) Maureen Connolly Brinker...	2.75	.....	30.00(20)	6.50(4)	2.00	0.70

5378 5379 5380

SCOTT NO.	DESCRIPTION	FIRST DAY COVERS SING	FIRST DAY COVERS PL. BLK.	MINT SHEET	PLATE BLOCK	UNUSED F/NH	USED
5378-80	Transcontinental Railroad...........	10.00(3)	.....	28.00(18)	10.00(6)	6.00	.....
5378	(55¢) Jupiter Locomotive...........	.....	.....	.....	.....	2.00	0.80
5379	(55¢) Golden Spike	.....	.....	.....	.....	2.00	0.80
5380	(55¢) No. 119 Locomotive...........	.....	.....	.....	.....	2.00	0.80

5381

WILD AND SCENIC RIVERS

5381a	*Merced River*	**5381g**	*Missouri River*
5381b	*Owyhee River*	**5381h**	*Skagit River*
5381c	*Koyukuk River*	**5381i**	*Deschutes River*
5381d	*Niobrara River*	**5381j**	*Tlikakila River*
5381e	*Snake River*	**5381k**	*Ontonagon River*
5381f	*Flathead River*	**5381l**	*Clarion River*

SCOTT NO.	DESCRIPTION	FIRST DAY COVERS SING	FIRST DAY COVERS PL. BLK.	MINT SHEET	PLATE BLOCK	UNUSED F/NH	USED
5381	(55¢) Wild and Scenic Rivers...	10.00(12)	.....	22.00	.....	20.00	

5382 5383 5384 5385 5386

5387 5388 5389 5390 5391

SCOTT NO.	DESCRIPTION	FIRST DAY COVERS SING	FIRST DAY COVERS PL. BLK.	MINT SHEET	PLATE BLOCK	UNUSED F/NH	USED
5382-91	(55¢) Art of Ellsworth Kelly	35.00(10)	.....	30.00(20)	20.00(10)	18.00	.....
5382	(55¢) Yellow White, 1961 .	.....	.....	.....	.....	2.00	1.50
5383	(55¢) Colors for a Large Wall, 1951	.....	.....	.....	.....	2.00	1.50
5384	(55¢) Blue Red Rocker, 1963	.....	.....	.....	.....	2.00	1.50
5385	(55¢) Spectrum I, 1953 . . .	.....	.....	.....	.....	2.00	1.50
5386	(55¢) South Ferry, 1956 . .	.....	.....	.....	.....	2.00	1.50
5387	(55¢) Blue Green, 1962. . .	.....	.....	.....	.....	2.00	1.50
5388	(55¢) Orange Red Relief, 1990	.....	.....	.....	.....	2.00	1.50
5389	(55¢) Meschers, 1951	.....	.....	.....	.....	2.00	1.50
5390	(55¢) Red Blue, 1964	.....	.....	.....	.....	2.00	1.50
5391	(55¢) Gaza, 1956	.....	.....	.....	.....	2.00	1.50

5392 5393

SCOTT NO.	DESCRIPTION	FIRST DAY COVERS SING	FIRST DAY COVERS PL. BLK.	MINT SHEET	PLATE BLOCK	UNUSED F/NH	USED
5392	(55¢) USS Missouri.............	2.75	.....	30.00(20)	6.50(4)	2.00	0.70
5393	(55¢) Pres. George H.W. Bush	2.75	.....	30.00(20)	6.50(4)	2.00	0.60

5394

SESAME STREET

5394a	*Big Bird*	**5394i**	*Herry Monster*
5394b	*Ernie*	**5394j**	*Julia*
5394c	*Bert*	**5394k**	*Guy Smiley*
5394d	*Cookie Monster*	**5394l**	*Snuffleupagus*
5394e	*Rosita*	**5394m**	*Elmo*
5394f	*The Count*	**5394n**	*Telly*
5394g	*Oscar*	**5394o**	*Grover*
5394h	*Abby Cadabby*	**5394p**	*Zoe*

SCOTT NO.	DESCRIPTION	FIRST DAY COVERS SING	FIRST DAY COVERS PL. BLK.	MINT SHEET	PLATE BLOCK	UNUSED F/NH	USED
5394	(55¢) Sesame Street.	[illegible](16)	.....	[illegible] (16)	.....	.....	.....

5395 5396

5397 5398

SCOTT NO.	DESCRIPTION	FIRST DAY COVERS SING	FIRST DAY COVERS PL. BLK.	MINT SHEET	PLATE BLOCK	UNUSED F/NH	USED
5395-98	(55¢) Frogs	15.00(4)	.....	.....	.....	6.50	.....
5395	(55¢) Pacific Tree Frog..............	.....	.....	.....	.....	2.00	0.70
5396	(55¢) Northern Leopard Frog.....	.....	.....	.....	.....	2.00	0.70
5397	(55¢) American Green Tree Frog	.....	.....	.....	.....	2.00	0.70
5398	(55¢) Squirrel Tree Frog.....	.....	.....	.....	.....	2.00	0.70
5398b	same, double-sided bklt pane of 20	.....	.....	.....	.....	30.00	.....

5399 5400

SCOTT NO.	DESCRIPTION	FIRST DAY COVERS SING	FIRST DAY COVERS PL. BLK.	MINT SHEET	PLATE BLOCK	UNUSED F/NH	USED
5399-5400	(55¢) 50th Anniv. First Moon Landing	6.00(2)	.....	30.00(24)	6.50(4)	4.00	.....
5399	(55¢) Edwin E. Aldrin Jr. on Moon	....	.....	.....	.....	2.00	0.70
5400	(55¢) Moon Landing Site.....	.....	.....	.....	.....	2.00	0.70

5401 5402 5403 5404

SCOTT NO.	DESCRIPTION	FIRST DAY COVERS SING	FIRST DAY COVERS PL. BLK.	MINT SHEET	PLATE BLOCK	UNUSED F/NH	USED
5401-04	(55¢) State and County Fairs	18.00(4)	.....	30.00(20)	12.00(8)	6.50	.....
5401	(55¢) Farmers Unloading Fruits	.....	.....	.....	.....	2.00	1.50
5402	(55¢) Girl and Farm Animals	.....	.....	.....	.....	2.00	1.50
5403	(55¢) Parents and Children	.....	.....	.....	.....	2.00	1.50
5404	(55¢) Child and Candy Apple	.....	.....	.....	.....	2.00	1.50

5405

5406

5407

5408

SCOTT NO.	DESCRIPTION	FIRST DAY COVERS SING	FIRST DAY COVERS PL. BLK.	MINT SHEET	PLATE BLOCK	UNUSED F/NH	USED
5405-08	(55¢) Military Working Dogs	15.00(4)	.....	.....	.....	6.50	.....
5405	(55¢) German Shepherd . .	.....	.....	.....	.....	2.00	1.00
5406	(55¢) Labrador Retriever. .	.....	.....	.....	.....	2.00	1.00
5407	(55¢) Belgian Malinois. . . .	.....	.....	.....	.....	2.00	1.00
5408	(55¢) Dutch Shepherd. . . .	.....	.....	.....	.....	2.00	1.00
5408b	same, double-sided bklt pane of 20	.....	.....	.....	.....	30.00	.....

5409

SCOTT NO.	DESCRIPTION	FIRST DAY COVERS SING	FIRST DAY COVERS PL. BLK.	MINT SHEET	PLATE BLOCK	UNUSED F/NH	USED
5409	(55¢) 50th Anniv. Woodstock	2.75	.....	30.00(20)	6.50(4)	2.00	0.70

5410

5411

5412

5413

SCOTT NO.	DESCRIPTION	FIRST DAY COVERS SING	FIRST DAY COVERS PL. BLK.	MINT SHEET	PLATE BLOCK	UNUSED F/NH	USED
5410-13	(55¢) Tyrannosaurus Rex .	15.00(4)	.....	30.00(16)	8.00(4)	7.50	.....
5410	(55¢) Juvenile Tyrannosaurus Rex, Egg, Insect	.....	.....	.....	.....	2.00	1.50
5411	(55¢) Adult Tyrannosaurus Rex	.....	.....	.....	.....	2.00	1.50
5412	(55¢) Young Adult Tyrannosaurus Rex	.....	.....	.....	.....	2.00	1.50
5413	(55¢) Juvenile Tyrannosaurus Rex, Mammal	.....	.....	.....	.....	2.00	1.50

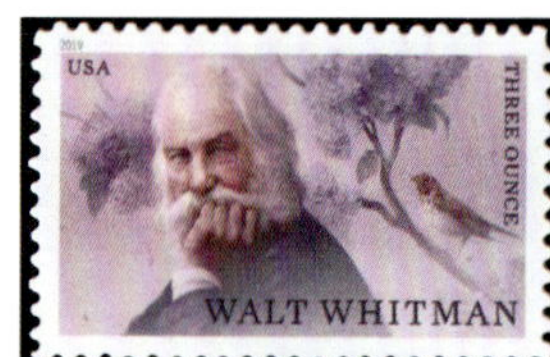

5414

SCOTT NO.	DESCRIPTION	FIRST DAY COVERS SING	FIRST DAY COVERS PL. BLK.	MINT SHEET	PLATE BLOCK	UNUSED F/NH	USED
5414	(85¢) Walt Whitman.	3.20	.....	40.00(20)	10.00(4)	3.00	1.95

5415 5416 5417 5418

SCOTT NO.	DESCRIPTION	FIRST DAY COVERS SING	FIRST DAY COVERS PL. BLK.	MINT SHEET	PLATE BLOCK	UNUSED F/NH	USED
5415-18	(55¢) Winter Berries	15.00(4)	.....	.....	.....	9.00	.....
5415	(55¢) Winterberry	.....	.....	.....	.....	2.25	0.70
5416	(55¢) Juniper Berry	.....	.....	.....	.....	2.25	0.70
5417	(55¢) Beautyberry	.....	.....	.....	.....	2.25	0.70
5418	(55¢) Soapberry	.....	.....	.....	.....	2.25	0.70
5418b	same, double-sided bklt pane of 20	.....	.....	.....	.....	35.00	.....

5419

SCOTT NO.	DESCRIPTION	FIRST DAY COVERS SING	FIRST DAY COVERS PL. BLK.	MINT SHEET	PLATE BLOCK	UNUSED F/NH	USED
5419	(55¢) Purple Heart.	2.75	.....	28.00(20)	6.50(4)	2.00	0.70

5420 5421 5422 5423

SCOTT NO.	DESCRIPTION	FIRST DAY COVERS SING	FIRST DAY COVERS PL. BLK.	MINT SHEET	PLATE BLOCK	UNUSED F/NH	USED
5420-23	(55¢) Spooky Silhouettes .	15.00(4)	.....	35.00(20)	7.00(4)	6.50	.....
5420	(55¢) Cat and Raven.	.....	.....	.....	.....	2.00	1.50
5421	(55¢) Ghosts	.....	.....	.....	.....	2.00	1.50
5422	(55¢) Spider and Web	.....	.....	.....	.....	2.00	1.50
5423	(55¢) Bats	.....	.....	.....	.....	2.00	1.50

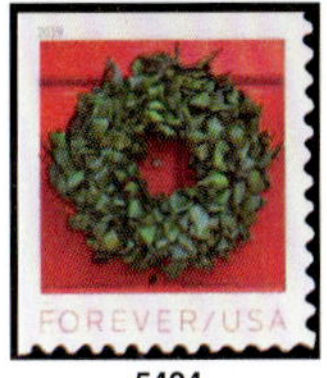
5424

5425

5426

5427

SCOTT NO.	DESCRIPTION	FIRST DAY COVERS SING	FIRST DAY COVERS PL. BLK.	MINT SHEET	PLATE BLOCK	UNUSED F/NH	USED
5424-27	(55¢) Holiday Wreaths. . . .	15.00(4)	.....	.....	.....	6.50	.....
5424	(55¢) Aspidistra Leaf Wreath	.....	.....	.....	.....	2.00	1.50
5425	(55¢) Pine Cone Wreath . .	.....	.....	.....	.....	2.00	1.50
5426	(55¢) Hydrangea, Eucalyptus Wreath	.....	.....	.....	.....	2.00	1.50
5427	(55¢) Woodland Bush Ivy, Red Winterberry Wreath	.....	.....	.....	.....	2.00	1.50
5427b	same, double-sided bklt pane of 20	.....	.....	.....	.....	30.00	....

2020 COMMEMORATIVES

SCOTT NO.	DESCRIPTION	FIRST DAY COVERS SING	FIRST DAY COVERS PL. BLK.	MINT SHEET	PLATE BLOCK	UNUSED F/NH	USED
5428/5542	**(5428, 5432, 5434, 5455, 5456, 5461-70, 5471-74, 5475-79, 5480-83 5494-5503, 5504-13, 5514-18, 5519-22, 5523, 5524, 5530, 5531, 5542) 62 varieties**	**.....**	**.....**	**.....**	**.....**	**105.00**	**.....**

5428

5429

5430

SCOTT NO.	DESCRIPTION	FIRST DAY COVERS SING	FIRST DAY COVERS PL. BLK.	MINT SHEET	PLATE BLOCK	UNUSED F/NH	USED
5428	(55¢) Year of the Rat	2.75	.....	30.00(20)	5.50(4)	2.00	0.70
5429	$7.75 Big Bend National Park, Priority Mail	20.00	.....	80.00(4)	.....	25.00	20.00
5430	$26.35 Grand Island Ice Caves, Express Mail	58.00	.....	250.00(4)	.....	65.00	50.00

5431

5432

5433

SCOTT NO.	DESCRIPTION	FIRST DAY COVERS SING	FIRST DAY COVERS PL. BLK.	MINT SHEET	PLATE BLOCK	UNUSED F/NH	USED
5431	(55¢) Love Hearts	2.75	.....	30.00(20)	6.50(4)	2.00	0.70
5432	(55¢) Gwen Ifill, Journalist.	2.75	.....	30.00(20)	6.50(4)	2.00	1.00
5433	(10¢) Presorted USA Star, coil	.....	.....	.....	.....	0.30	0.30
	same, plate number strip of 5	.....	.....	.....	.....	2.00	....

5434

SCOTT NO.	DESCRIPTION	FIRST DAY COVERS SING	FIRST DAY COVERS PL. BLK.	MINT SHEET	PLATE BLOCK	UNUSED F/NH	USED
5434	Let's Celebrate	2.75	.....	30.00(20)	6.50(4)	2.00	.70

5435, 5452

5436, 5453

5437, 5454

5438, 5449

5439, 5445

5440, 5446

5441, 5447

5442, 5448

5443, 5450

5455

5444, 5451

SCOTT NO.	DESCRIPTION	FIRST DAY COVERS SING	FIRST DAY COVERS PL. BLK.	MINT SHEET	PLATE BLOCK	UNUSED F/NH	USED
5435-44	(55¢) Wild Orchids Coil strip of 10	30.00(10)	.....	.....	.....	18.00	.....
	same, plate number strip of 10	.....	.....	.....	.....	20.00	....
	same, plate number strip of 17, folded	.....	.....	.....	.....	30.00	....
5435	(55¢) Platanthera Grandiflora	.....	.....	.....	.....	2.00	0.90
5436	(55¢) Cyrtopodium Polyphyllum	.....	.....	.....	.....	2.00	0.90
5437	(55¢) Calopogon Tuberosus	.....	.....	.....	.....	2.00	0.90
5438	(55¢) Spiranthes Odorata .	.....	.....	.....	.....	2.00	0.90
5439	(55¢) Triphora Trianthophoros	.....	.....	.....	.....	2.00	0.90
5440	(55¢) Cypripedium Californicum	.....	.....	.....	.....	2.00	0.90
5441	(55¢) Hexalectris Spicata .	.....	.....	.....	.....	2.00	0.90
5442	(55¢) Cypripedium Reginae	.....	.....	.....	.....	2.00	0.90
5443	(55¢) Platanthera Leucophaea	.....	.....	.....	.....	2.00	0.90
5444	(55¢) Triphora Trianthophoros	.....	.....	.....	.....	2.00	0.90
5445-54	(55¢) Wild Orchids, block of 10	30.00(10)	.....	.....	.....	18.00	.....
5445	(55¢) Triphora Trianthophoros	.....	.....	.....	.....	2.00	0.90
5446	(55¢) Cypripedium Californicum	.....	.....	.....	.....	2.00	0.90
5447	(55¢) Hexalectris Spicata .	.....	.....	.....	.....	2.00	0.90
5448	(55¢) Cypripedium Reginae	.....	.....	.....	.....	2.00	0.90
5449	(55¢) Spiranthes Odorata .	.....	.....	.....	.....	2.00	0.90
5450	(55¢) Platanthera Leucophaea	.....	.....	.....	.....	2.00	0.90
5451	(55¢) Triphora Trianthophoros	.....	.....	.....	.....	2.00	0.90
5452	(55¢) Platanthera Grandiflora	.....	.....	.....	.....	2.00	0.90
5453	(55¢) Cyrtopodium Polyphyllum	.....	.....	.....	.....	2.00	0.90
5454	(55¢) Calopogon Tuberosus	.....	.....	.....		[illegible]	[illegible]
5454b	same, double-sided bklt pane of 20	.....	.....	.....		30.00	
5455	(55¢) Arnold Palmer, Golfer	2.75	.....	30.00(20)	6.50(4)	[illegible]	[illegible]

5456

5457

5458

SCOTT NO.	DESCRIPTION	FIRST DAY COVERS SING	FIRST DAY COVERS PL. BLK.	MINT SHEET	PLATE BLOCK	UNUSED F/NH	USED
5456	(55¢) Maine Statehood . . .	2.75	.....	30.00(20)	6.50(4)	2.00	.70
5457	(55¢) Boutonniere	2.75	.....	30.00(20)	6.50(4)	2.00	0.70
5458	(70¢) Corsage	3.75	.....	38.00(20)	8.00(4)	2.50	1.00

5459

5460

SCOTT NO.	DESCRIPTION	FIRST DAY COVERS SING	FIRST DAY COVERS PL. BLK.	MINT SHEET	PLATE BLOCK	UNUSED F/NH	USED
5459	(55¢) Earth Day	2.75	.....	.....	.....	2.00	0.70
5459a	same, double-sided bklt pane of 20	.....	.....	.....	.....	30.00	....
5460	($1.20) Global Chrysanthemum	5.00	.....	30.00(10)	12.00(4)	3.00	1.00

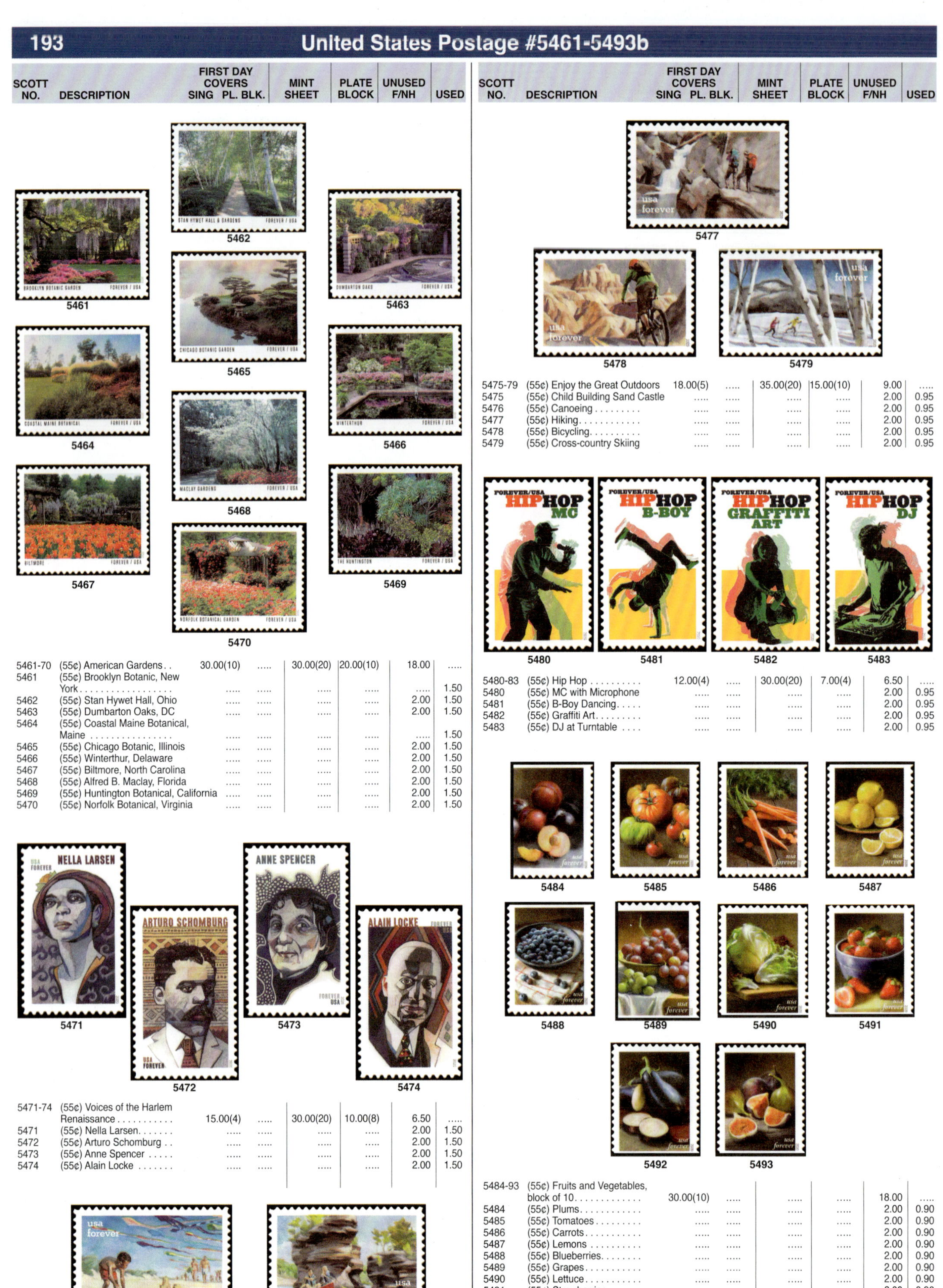

SCOTT NO.	DESCRIPTION	FIRST DAY COVERS SING	PL. BLK.	MINT SHEET	PLATE BLOCK	UNUSED F/NH	USED
5461-70	(55¢) American Gardens. .	30.00(10)	.....	30.00(20)	20.00(10)	18.00	.....
5461	(55¢) Brooklyn Botanic, New York.	.....	.....	.....	.....	.....	1.50
5462	(55¢) Stan Hywet Hall, Ohio	.....	.....	.....	.....	2.00	1.50
5463	(55¢) Dumbarton Oaks, DC	.....	.....	.....	.....	2.00	1.50
5464	(55¢) Coastal Maine Botanical, Maine	.....	.....	.....	.....	.....	1.50
5465	(55¢) Chicago Botanic, Illinois	.....	.....	.....	.....	2.00	1.50
5466	(55¢) Winterthur, Delaware	.....	.....	.....	.....	2.00	1.50
5467	(55¢) Biltmore, North Carolina	.....	.....	.....	.....	2.00	1.50
5468	(55¢) Alfred B. Maclay, Florida	.....	.....	.....	.....	2.00	1.50
5469	(55¢) Huntington Botanical, California	.....	.....	.....	.....	2.00	1.50
5470	(55¢) Norfolk Botanical, Virginia	.....	.....	.....	.....	2.00	1.50

SCOTT NO.	DESCRIPTION	FIRST DAY COVERS SING	PL. BLK.	MINT SHEET	PLATE BLOCK	UNUSED F/NH	USED
5471-74	(55¢) Voices of the Harlem Renaissance.	15.00(4)	.....	30.00(20)	10.00(8)	6.50	.....
5471	(55¢) Nella Larsen.	.....	.....	.....	.....	2.00	1.50
5472	(55¢) Arturo Schomburg . .	.....	.....	.....	.....	2.00	1.50
5473	(55¢) Anne Spencer	.....	.....	.....	.....	2.00	1.50
5474	(55¢) Alain Locke	.....	.....	.....	.....	2.00	1.50

SCOTT NO.	DESCRIPTION	FIRST DAY COVERS SING	PL. BLK.	MINT SHEET	PLATE BLOCK	UNUSED F/NH	USED
5475-79	(55¢) Enjoy the Great Outdoors	18.00(5)	.....	35.00(20)	15.00(10)	9.00	.....
5475	(55¢) Child Building Sand Castle	.....	.....	.....	.....	2.00	0.95
5476	(55¢) Canoeing	.....	.....	.....	.....	2.00	0.95
5477	(55¢) Hiking.	.....	.....	.....	.....	2.00	0.95
5478	(55¢) Bicycling.	.....	.....	.....	.....	2.00	0.95
5479	(55¢) Cross-country Skiing	.....	.....	.....	.....	2.00	0.95

SCOTT NO.	DESCRIPTION	FIRST DAY COVERS SING	PL. BLK.	MINT SHEET	PLATE BLOCK	UNUSED F/NH	USED
5480-83	(55¢) Hip Hop	12.00(4)	.....	30.00(20)	7.00(4)	6.50	.....
5480	(55¢) MC with Microphone	.....	.....	.....	.....	2.00	0.95
5481	(55¢) B-Boy Dancing.	.....	.....	.....	.....	2.00	0.95
5482	(55¢) Graffiti Art.	.....	.....	.....	.....	2.00	0.95
5483	(55¢) DJ at Turntable	.....	.....	.....	.....	2.00	0.95

SCOTT NO.	DESCRIPTION	FIRST DAY COVERS SING	PL. BLK.	MINT SHEET	PLATE BLOCK	UNUSED F/NH	USED
5484-93	(55¢) Fruits and Vegetables, block of 10.	30.00(10)	.....	.....	.....	18.00	.....
5484	(55¢) Plums.	.....	.....	.....	.....	2.00	0.90
5485	(55¢) Tomatoes	.....	.....	.....	.....	2.00	0.90
5486	(55¢) Carrots	.....	.....	.....	.....	2.00	0.90
5487	(55¢) Lemons	.....	.....	.....	.....	2.00	0.90
5488	(55¢) Blueberries.	.....	.....	.....	.....	2.00	0.90
5489	(55¢) Grapes.	.....	.....	.....	.....	2.00	0.90
5490	(55¢) Lettuce.	.....	.....	.....	.....	2.00	0.90
5491	(55¢) Strawberries.	.....	.....	.....	.....	2.00	0.90
5492	(55¢) Eggplant.	.....	.....	.....	.....	2.00	0.90
5493	(55¢) Figs	.....	.....	.....	.....	2.00	0.90
5493b	same, double-sided bklt pane of 20	.....	.....	.....	.....	30.00	.....

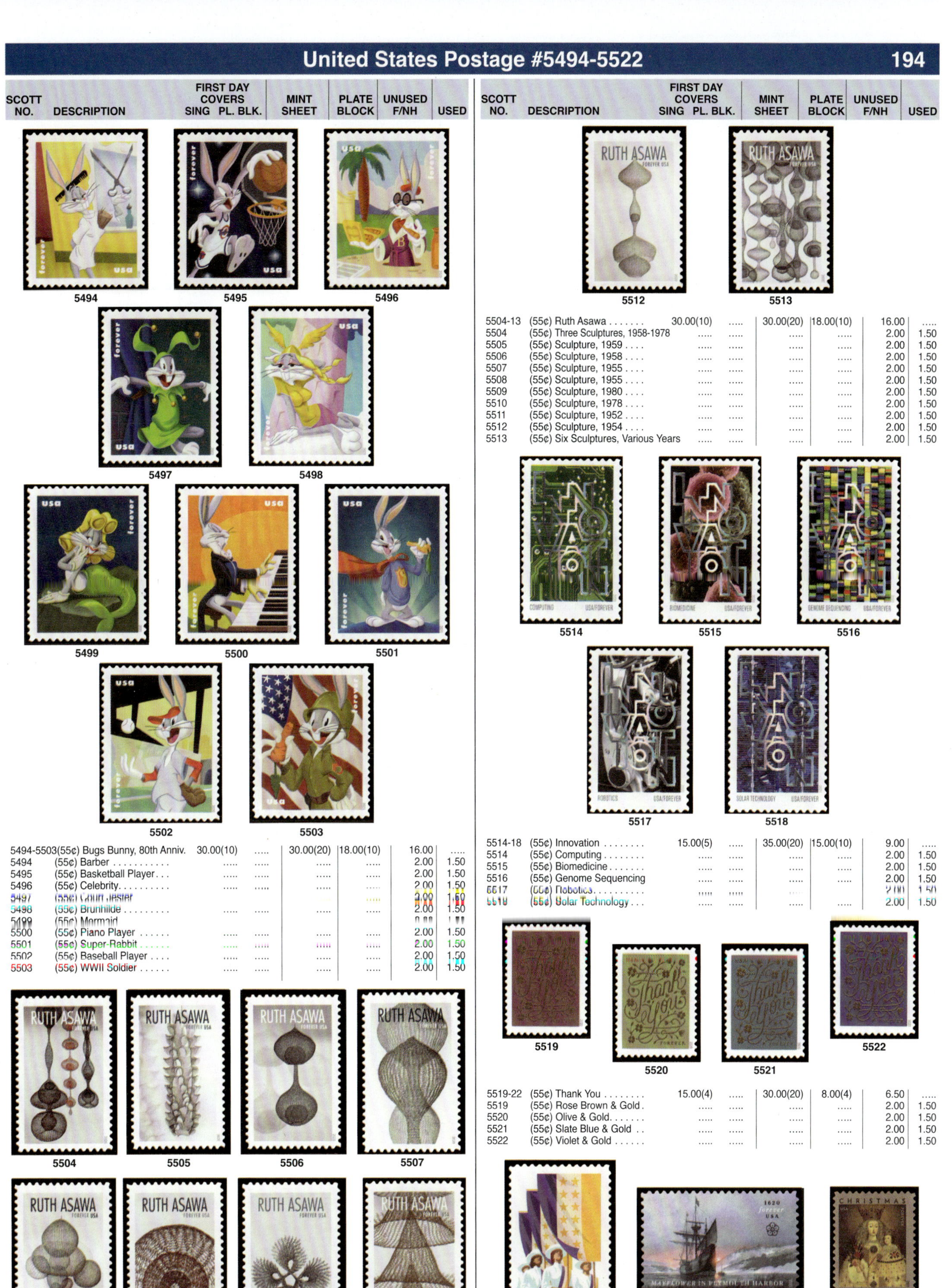

5494 5495 5496 5497 5498 5499 5500 5501 5502 5503

SCOTT NO.	DESCRIPTION	FIRST DAY COVERS SING	FIRST DAY COVERS PL. BLK.	MINT SHEET	PLATE BLOCK	UNUSED F/NH	USED
5494-5503	(55¢) Bugs Bunny, 80th Anniv.	30.00(10)	.....	30.00(20)	18.00(10)	16.00	.....
5494	(55¢) Barber	.....	.....	.....	.....	2.00	1.50
5495	(55¢) Basketball Player . . .	.....	.....	.....	.....	2.00	1.50
5496	(55¢) Celebrity.	.....	.....	.....	.....	2.00	1.50
5497	(55¢) Court Jester				.....	2.00	1.50
5498	(55¢) Brunhilde	.....	.....	.....	.....	2.00	1.50
5499	(55¢) Mermaid					[illegible]	[illegible]
5500	(55¢) Piano Player	.....	.....	.....	.....	2.00	1.50
5501	(55¢) Super-Rabbit	.....	.....	.....	.....	2.00	1.50
5502	(55¢) Baseball Player	.....	.....	.....	.....	2.00	1.50
5503	(55¢) WWII Soldier	.....	.....	.....	.....	2.00	1.50

5504 5505 5506 5507 5508 5509 5510 5511 5512 5513

SCOTT NO.	DESCRIPTION	FIRST DAY COVERS SING	FIRST DAY COVERS PL. BLK.	MINT SHEET	PLATE BLOCK	UNUSED F/NH	USED
5504-13	(55¢) Ruth Asawa	30.00(10)	.....	30.00(20)	18.00(10)	16.00	.....
5504	(55¢) Three Sculptures, 1958-1978	.....	.....	.....	.....	2.00	1.50
5505	(55¢) Sculpture, 1959	.....	.....	.....	.....	2.00	1.50
5506	(55¢) Sculpture, 1958	.....	.....	.....	.....	2.00	1.50
5507	(55¢) Sculpture, 1955	.....	.....	.....	.....	2.00	1.50
5508	(55¢) Sculpture, 1955	.....	.....	.....	.....	2.00	1.50
5509	(55¢) Sculpture, 1980	.....	.....	.....	.....	2.00	1.50
5510	(55¢) Sculpture, 1978	.....	.....	.....	.....	2.00	1.50
5511	(55¢) Sculpture, 1952	.....	.....	.....	.....	2.00	1.50
5512	(55¢) Sculpture, 1954	.....	.....	.....	.....	2.00	1.50
5513	(55¢) Six Sculptures, Various Years	.....	.....	.....	.....	2.00	1.50

5514 5515 5516 5517 5518

SCOTT NO.	DESCRIPTION	FIRST DAY COVERS SING	FIRST DAY COVERS PL. BLK.	MINT SHEET	PLATE BLOCK	UNUSED F/NH	USED
5514-18	(55¢) Innovation	15.00(5)	.....	35.00(20)	15.00(10)	9.00	.....
5514	(55¢) Computing	.....	.....	.....	.....	2.00	1.50
5515	(55¢) Biomedicine	.....	.....	.....	.....	2.00	1.50
5516	(55¢) Genome Sequencing	.....	.....	.....	.....	2.00	1.50
5517	(55¢) Robotics.	.....	.....	.....		2.00	1.50
5518	(55¢) Solar Technology . . .	.....	.....	.....	.....	2.00	1.50

5519 5520 5521 5522

SCOTT NO.	DESCRIPTION	FIRST DAY COVERS SING	FIRST DAY COVERS PL. BLK.	MINT SHEET	PLATE BLOCK	UNUSED F/NH	USED
5519-22	(55¢) Thank You	15.00(4)	.....	30.00(20)	8.00(4)	6.50	.....
5519	(55¢) Rose Brown & Gold .	.....	.....	.....	.....	2.00	1.50
5520	(55¢) Olive & Gold.	.....	.....	.....	.....	2.00	1.50
5521	(55¢) Slate Blue & Gold . .	.....	.....	.....	.....	2.00	1.50
5522	(55¢) Violet & Gold	.....	.....	.....	.....	2.00	1.50

5523 5524, 5524v 5525

SCOTT NO.	DESCRIPTION	FIRST DAY COVERS SING	FIRST DAY COVERS PL. BLK.	MINT SHEET	PLATE BLOCK	UNUSED F/NH	USED
5523	(55¢) Women Suffrage Centenary	2.75	.....	30.00(20)	6.50(4)	2.00	0.70
5524	(55¢) Mayflower, 400th Anniversary	2.75	.....	30.00(20)	6.50(4)	2.00	0.80
5524v	same as above, commemorative book with progressive color proofs, limited 2500	.....	.....	.....	.....	200.00	.....
5525	(55¢) Our Lady of Guápulo	2.75	.....	.....	.....	2.00	0.70
5525a	same, double-sided bklt pane of 20	.....	.....	.....	.....	30.00	.....

5526 5527 5528 5529

SCOTT NO.	DESCRIPTION	FIRST DAY COVERS SING	FIRST DAY COVERS PL. BLK.	MINT SHEET	PLATE BLOCK	UNUSED F/NH	USED
5526-29	(55¢) Holiday Delights. . . .	15.00(4)	.....	.....	.....	6.50	.....
5526	(55¢) Ornament.	.....	.....	.....	.....	2.00	0.70
5527	(55¢) Christmas Tree	.....	.....	.....	.....	2.00	0.70
5528	(55¢) Christmas Stocking .	.....	.....	.....	.....	2.00	0.70
5529	(55¢) Reindeer	.....	.....	.....	.....	2.00	0.70
5529b	same, double-sided bklt pane of 20	.....	.....	.....	.....	30.00	.....

5530 5531

SCOTT NO.	DESCRIPTION	FIRST DAY COVERS SING	FIRST DAY COVERS PL. BLK.	MINT SHEET	PLATE BLOCK	UNUSED F/NH	USED
5530	(55¢) Hanukkah.	2.75	.....	30.00(20)	6.50(4)	2.00	0.70
5531	(55¢) Kwanzaa	2.75	.....	30.00(20)	6.50(4)	2.00	0.70

5532 5533 5534 5535

5536 5537 5538 5539

5540 5541

SCOTT NO.	DESCRIPTION	FIRST DAY COVERS SING	FIRST DAY COVERS PL. BLK.	MINT SHEET	PLATE BLOCK	UNUSED F/NH	USED
5532-41	(55¢) Winter Scenes, block of 10.	30.00(10)	.....	.....	.....	18.00	.....
5532	(55¢) Deer.	.....	.....	.....	.....	2.00	0.90
5533	(55¢) Cardinal	.....	.....	.....	.....	2.00	0.90
5534	(55¢) Snowy Morning	.....	.....	.....	.....	2.00	0.90
5535	(55¢) Red Barn with Wreath	.....	.....	.....	.....	2.00	0.90
5536	(55¢) Barred Owl.	.....	.....	.....	.....	2.00	0.90
5537	(55¢) Blue Jay.	.....	.....	.....	.....	2.00	0.90
5538	(55¢) Mackenzie Barn. . . .	.....	.....	.....	.....	2.00	0.90
5539	(55¢) Rabbit	.....	.....	.....	.....	2.00	0.90
5540	(55¢) After the Snowfall. . .	.....	.....	.....	.....	2.00	0.90
5541	(55¢) Belgian Draft Horses	.....	.....	.....	.....	2.00	0.90
5541b	same, double-sided bklt pane of 20	.....	.....	.....	.....	30.00	.....

5542

SCOTT NO.	DESCRIPTION	FIRST DAY COVERS SING	FIRST DAY COVERS PL. BLK.	MINT SHEET	PLATE BLOCK	UNUSED F/NH	USED
5542	(55¢) Drug Free USA	2.75	.....	30.00(20)	6.50(4)	2.00	0.70

2021 COMMEMORATIVES

SCOTT NO.	DESCRIPTION	FIRST DAY COVERS SING	FIRST DAY COVERS PL. BLK.	MINT SHEET	PLATE BLOCK	UNUSED F/NH	USED
5555/5643	**(5555, 5556, 5557, 5573-82, 5583-92 5593, 5594-97, 5598-5607, 5608, 5609-13, 5614, 5619, 5620, 5621-25 5626, 5627-34, 5636-39, 5640-43) 69 varieties**	.....	.....	.....	.....	**125.00**	.....

5543 5544, 5545

SCOTT NO.	DESCRIPTION	FIRST DAY COVERS SING	FIRST DAY COVERS PL. BLK.	MINT SHEET	PLATE BLOCK	UNUSED F/NH	USED
5543	(55¢) Love.	2.75	.....	30.00(20)	6.50(4)	2.00	0.70
5544	(20¢) Brush Rabbit	2.75	.....	8.00(20)	2.25(4)	0.50	0.30
5545	(20¢) Brush Rabbit, coil. . .	2.75	.....	.....	.....	0.50	0.30
	same, plate number strip of 5	.....	.....	.....	.....	3.00	.....

5546, 5553 5547, 5550

5548, 5552 5549, 5551

SCOTT NO.	DESCRIPTION	FIRST DAY COVERS SING	FIRST DAY COVERS PL. BLK.	MINT SHEET	PLATE BLOCK	UNUSED F/NH	USED
5546-49	(36¢) Barns	15.00(4)	.....	25.00(20)	5.50(4)	5.00	.....
5546	(36¢) Round Barn	.....	.....	.....	.....	1.25	0.60
5547	(36¢) Barn, Windmill	.....	.....	.....	.....	1.25	0.60
5548	(36¢) Forebay Barn.	.....	.....	.....	.....	1.25	0.60
5549	(36¢) Snow-covered Barn .	.....	.....	.....	.....	1.25	0.60
5550-53	(36¢) Barns	15.00(4)	.....	.....	.....	5.00	.....
	same, plate number strip of 5	.....	.....	.....	.....	8.50	.....
5550	(36¢) Barn, Windmill	.....	.....	.....	.....	1.25	0.60
5551	(36¢) Snow-covered Barn .	.....	.....	.....	.....	1.25	0.60
5552	(36¢) Forebay Barn.	.....	.....	.....	.....	1.25	0.60
5553	(36¢) Round Barn	.....	.....	.....	.....	1.25	0.60

5554

5555

SCOTT NO.	DESCRIPTION	FIRST DAY COVERS SING	FIRST DAY COVERS PL. BLK.	MINT SHEET	PLATE BLOCK	UNUSED F/NH	USED
5554	$7.95 Castillo de San Marcos	20.00	.....	75.00(4)	.....	20.00	10.00
5555	(55¢) August Wilson, Playwright	2.75	.....	30.00(20)	6.50(4)	2.00	0.70

5556

5557

SCOTT NO.	DESCRIPTION	FIRST DAY COVERS SING	FIRST DAY COVERS PL. BLK.	MINT SHEET	PLATE BLOCK	UNUSED F/NH	USED
5556	(55¢) Year of the Ox	2.75	.....	30.00(20)	6.50(4)	2.00	0.70
5557	(55¢) Dr. Chien-Shiung Wu, Nuclear Physicist.	2.75	.....	30.00(20)	6.50(4)	2.00	0.70

5558

5559

5560

5561

5562

5563

5564

5565

5566

5567

SCOTT NO.	DESCRIPTION	FIRST DAY COVERS SING	FIRST DAY COVERS PL. BLK.	MINT SHEET	PLATE BLOCK	UNUSED F/NH	USED
5558-67	(55¢) Garden Beauty, block of 10.	30.00(10)	.....	.....	.....	18.00	.....
5558	(55¢) Pink Dogwood	.....	.....	.....	.....	2.00	0.90
5559	(55¢) Orange and Yellow Tulip	.....	.....	.....	.....	2.00	0.90
5560	(55¢) Allium	.....	.....	.....	.....	2.00	0.90
5561	(55¢) Pink Moth Orchid . . .	.....	.....	.....	.....	2.00	0.90
5562	(55¢) Magenta Dahlia	.....	.....	.....	.....	2.00	0.90
5563	(55¢) Yellow Moth Orchid .	.....	.....	.....	.....	2.00	0.90
5564	(55¢) Sacred Lotus	.....	.....	.....	.....	2.00	0.90
5565	(55¢) White Asiatic Lily . . .	.....	.....	.....	.....	2.00	0.90
5566	(55¢) Rose Pink and White Tulip	.....	.....	.....	.....	2.00	0.90
5567	(55¢) Pink American Lotus	.....	.....	.....	.....	2.00	0.90
5567b	same, double-sided bklt pane of 20	.....	.....	.....	.....	35.00	.....

5568

SCOTT NO.	DESCRIPTION	FIRST DAY COVERS SING	FIRST DAY COVERS PL. BLK.	MINT SHEET	PLATE BLOCK	UNUSED F/NH	USED
5568	(75¢) Colorado Hairstreak Butterfly	3.00	.....	50.00(20)	9.00(4)	2.50	1.00

5569

5570

5571

5572

SCOTT NO.	DESCRIPTION	FIRST DAY COVERS SING	FIRST DAY COVERS PL. BLK.	MINT SHEET	PLATE BLOCK	UNUSED F/NH	USED
5569-72	(55¢) Espresso Drinks. . . .	15.00(4)	.....	.....	.....	6.50	.....
5569	(55¢) Caffe Latte	.....	.....	.....	.....	2.00	0.80
5570	(55¢) Espresso Drinks. . . .	.....	.....	.....	.....	2.00	0.80
5571	(55¢) Caffe Mocha.	.....	.....	.....	.....	2.00	0.80
5572	(55¢) Cappuccino	.....	.....	.....	.....	2.00	0.80
5572b	same, double-sided bklt pane of 20	.....	.....	.....	.....	35.00	.....

5573

5574

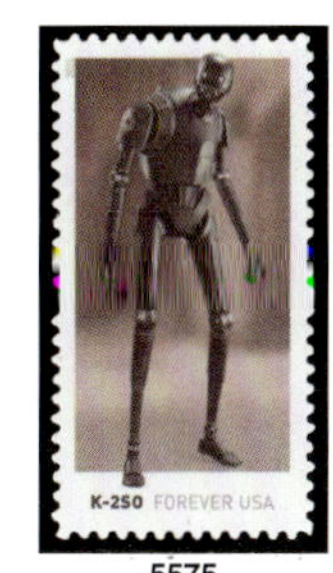
5575

5576

5577

5578

5579

5580

5581

5582

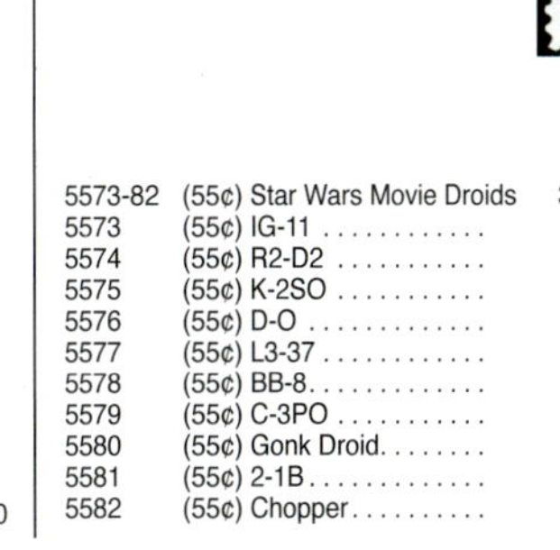

SCOTT NO.	DESCRIPTION	FIRST DAY COVERS SING	FIRST DAY COVERS PL. BLK.	MINT SHEET	PLATE BLOCK	UNUSED F/NH	USED
5573-82	(55¢) Star Wars Movie Droids	30.00(10)	.....	35.00(20)	20.00(10)	18.00	.....
5573	(55¢) IG-11	.....	.....	.....	.....	2.00	1.00
5574	(55¢) R2-D2	.....	.....	.....	.....	2.00	1.00
5575	(55¢) K-2SO	.....	.....	.....	.....	2.00	1.00
5576	(55¢) D-O	.....	.....	.....	.....	2.00	1.00
5577	(55¢) L3-37	.....	.....	.....	.....	2.00	1.00
5578	(55¢) BB-8.	.....	.....	.....	.....	2.00	1.00
5579	(55¢) C-3PO	.....	.....	.....	.....	2.00	1.00
5580	(55¢) Gonk Droid.	.....	.....	.....	.....	2.00	1.00
5581	(55¢) 2-1B.	.....	.....	.....	.....	2.00	1.00
5582	(55¢) Chopper.	.....	.....	.....	.....	2.00	1.00

5584  5585

5583  5586

5588  5589

5587  5590

5591  5592

SCOTT NO.	DESCRIPTION	FIRST DAY COVERS SING	FIRST DAY COVERS PL. BLK.	MINT SHEET	PLATE BLOCK	UNUSED F/NH	USED
5583-92	(55¢) Heritage Breeds. . . .	30.00(10)	.....	35.00(20)	20.00(10)	18.00	.....
5583	(55¢) Mulefoot Hog	.....	.....	.....	.....	2.00	1.00
5584	(55¢) Wyandotte Chicken .	.....	.....	.....	.....	2.00	1.00
5585	(55¢) Milking Devon Cow .	.....	.....	.....	.....	2.00	1.00
5586	(55¢) Narragansett Turkey	.....	.....	.....	.....	2.00	1.00
5587	(55¢) American Mammoth Donkey	.....	.....	.....	.....	2.00	1.00
5588	(55¢) Cotton Patch Goose	.....	.....	.....	.....	2.00	1.00
5589	(55¢) San Clemente Island Goat	.....	.....	.....	.....	2.00	1.00
5590	(55¢) American Cream Draft Horse	.....	.....	.....	.....	2.00	1.00
5591	(55¢) Cayuga Duck	.....	.....	.....	.....	2.00	1.00
5592	(55¢) Barbados Blackbelly Sheep	.....	.....	.....	.....	2.00	1.00

5594

5593

5595

5596

5597

SCOTT NO.	DESCRIPTION	FIRST DAY COVERS SING	FIRST DAY COVERS PL. BLK.	MINT SHEET	PLATE BLOCK	UNUSED F/NH	USED
5593	(55¢) Go For Broke, WWII	2.75	.....	30.00(20)	6.50(4)	2.00	0.80
5594-97	(55¢) Paintings by Emilio Sanchez	15.00(4)	.....	30.00(20)	14.00(8)	7.50	.....
5594	(55¢) Los Toldos, 1973 . . .	.....	.....	.....	.....	2.00	1.00
5595	(55¢) Ty's Place, 1976. . . .	.....	.....	.....	.....	2.00	1.00
5596	(55¢) En el Souk, 1972 . . .	.....	.....	.....	.....	2.00	1.00
5597	(55¢) Untitled, 1981.	.....	.....	.....	.....	2.00	1.00

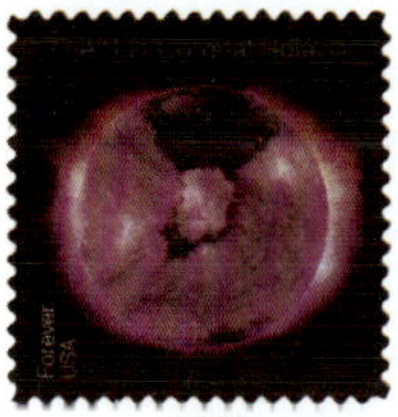

5598 5600

5599

5601  5602

5603 5605

5604

5606  5607

SCOTT NO.	DESCRIPTION	FIRST DAY COVERS SING	FIRST DAY COVERS PL. BLK.	MINT SHEET	PLATE BLOCK	UNUSED F/NH	USED
5598-5607	(55¢) Sun Science.	30.00(10)	.....	35.00(20)	20.00(10)	18.00	.....
5598	(55¢) Coronal Hole, rose. .	.....	.....	.....	.....	2.00	1.00
5599	(55¢) Coronal Loops, orange red	.....	.....	.....	.....	2.00	1.00
5600	(55¢) Solar Flare, blue . . .	.....	.....	.....	.....	2.00	1.00
5601	(55¢) Active Sun	.....	.....	.....	.....	2.00	1.00
5602	(55¢) Plasma Blast	.....	.....	.....	.....	2.00	1.00
5603	(55¢) Coronal Loops	.....	.....	.....	.....	2.00	1.00
5604	(55¢) Sun Sunspots	.....	.....	.....	.....	2.00	1.00
5605	(55¢) Plasma Blast	.....	.....	.....	.....	2.00	1.00
5606	(55¢) Solar Flare, aqua . . .	.....	.....	.....	.....	2.00	1.00
5607	(55¢) Coronal Hole, tan. . .	.....	.....	.....	.....	2.00	1.00

5608

SCOTT NO.	DESCRIPTION	FIRST DAY COVERS SING	FIRST DAY COVERS PL. BLK.	MINT SHEET	PLATE BLOCK	UNUSED F/NH	USED
5608	(55¢) Yogi Berra	2.75	.....	30.00(20)	6.50(4)	2.00	0.80

5609

5610

5611

5612

5613

SCOTT NO.	DESCRIPTION	FIRST DAY COVERS SING	FIRST DAY COVERS PL. BLK.	MINT SHEET	PLATE BLOCK	UNUSED F/NH	USED
5609-13	(55¢) Tap Dance	15.00(5)	.....	35.00(20)	20.00(10)	10.00(5)	.....
5609	(55¢) Max Pollak, bull	.....	.....	.....	.....	2.00	1.00
5610	(55¢) Michela Marino Lerman, rose	.....	.....	.....	.....	2.00	1.00
5611	(55¢) Derick Grant, greenish blue	.....	.....	.....	.....	2.00	1.00
5612	(55¢) Dormeshia Sumbry-Edwards, light blue	.....	.....	.....	.....	2.00	1.00
5613	(55¢) Ayodele Casel, bister	.....	.....	.....	.....	2.00	1.00

5614

SCOTT NO.	DESCRIPTION	FIRST DAY COVERS SING	FIRST DAY COVERS PL. BLK.	MINT SHEET	PLATE BLOCK	UNUSED F/NH	USED
5614	(55¢) Mystery Message. . .	2.75	.....	30.00(20)	6.50(4)	2.00	0.80

5615

5616

5617

5618

SCOTT NO.	DESCRIPTION	FIRST DAY COVERS SING	FIRST DAY COVERS PL. BLK.	MINT SHEET	PLATE BLOCK	UNUSED F/NH	USED
5615-18	(55¢) Western Wear	15.00(4)	.....	.....	.....	7.50	.....
5615	(55¢) Cowboy Hat, Snakes & Roses	.....	.....	.....	.....	2.00	0.80
5616	(55¢) Belt Buckle, Roses, Star & Spurs	.....	.....	.....	.....	2.00	0.80
5617	(55¢) Cowboy Boot, Roses, Cacti & Star.	.....	.....	.....	.....	2.00	0.80
5618	(55¢) Western Shirt, Roses, Cacti & Star.	.....	.....	.....	.....	2.00	0.80
5618b	same, double-sided bklt pane of 20	.....	.....	.....	.....	35.00	.....

5619

5620

SCOTT NO.	DESCRIPTION	FIRST DAY COVERS SING	FIRST DAY COVERS PL. BLK.	MINT SHEET	PLATE BLOCK	UNUSED F/NH	USED
5619	(95¢) Ursula K. Le Guin . .	3.50	.....	50.00(20)	10.50(4)	3.00	1.50
5620	(55¢) Raven Story.	2.75	.....	30.00(20)	6.00(4)	2.00	0.80

5621

5622

5623

5624

5625

SCOTT NO.	DESCRIPTION	FIRST DAY COVERS SING	FIRST DAY COVERS PL. BLK.	MINT SHEET	PLATE BLOCK	UNUSED F/NH	USED
5621-25	(55¢) Mid-Atlantic Lighthouses	15.00(5)	.....	35.00(20)	20.00(10)	10.00	.....
5621	(55¢) Montauk Point	.....	.....	.....	.....	2.00	1.00
5622	(55¢) Navesink Twin	.....	.....	.....	.....	2.00	1.00
5623	(55¢) Erie Harbor					2.00	1.00
5624	(55¢) Harbor of Refuge . . .	.....	.....	.....	.....	2.00	1.00
5625	(55¢) Thomas Point Shoal	.....	.....	.....	.....	2.00	1.00

5626

SCOTT NO.	DESCRIPTION	FIRST DAY COVERS SING	FIRST DAY COVERS PL. BLK.	MINT SHEET	PLATE BLOCK	UNUSED F/NH	USED
5626	(55¢) Missouri Statehood .	2.75	.....	30.00(20)	6.50(4)	2.00	0.80

5627

5628

5629

5630

5631

5632

5633

5634

SCOTT NO.	DESCRIPTION	FIRST DAY COVERS SING	FIRST DAY COVERS PL. BLK.	MINT SHEET	PLATE BLOCK	UNUSED F/NH	USED
5627-34	(55¢) Backyard Games . . .	24.00(8)	.....	30.00(16)	18.00(8)	16.00(8)	.....
5627	(55¢) Horseshoes	.....	.....	.....	.....	2.00	1.00
5628	(55¢) Bocce.	.....	.....	.....	.....	2.00	1.00
5629	(55¢) Flying Disc	.....	.....	.....	.....	2.00	1.00
5630	(55¢) Croquet	.....	.....	.....	.....	2.00	1.00
5631	(55¢) Pick-Up Baseball . . .	.....	.....	.....	.....	2.00	1.00
5632	(55¢) Tetherball	.....	.....	.....	.....	2.00	1.00
5633	(55¢) Badminton	.....	.....	.....	.....	2.00	1.00
5634	(55¢) Cornhole	.....	.....	.....	.....	2.00	1.00

5635

SCOTT NO.	DESCRIPTION	FIRST DAY COVERS SING	FIRST DAY COVERS PL. BLK.	MINT SHEET	PLATE BLOCK	UNUSED F/NH	USED
5635	(58¢) Happy Birthday	2.75	.....	30.00(20)	6.50(4)	2.00	0.80

5636 5637 5638 5639

SCOTT NO.	DESCRIPTION	FIRST DAY COVERS SING	FIRST DAY COVERS PL. BLK.	MINT SHEET	PLATE BLOCK	UNUSED F/NH	USED
5636-39	(58¢) Message Monsters .	15.00(4)	.....	30.00(20)	14.00(8)	7.50	.....
5636	(58¢) Pink & Red Monster.	.....	.....	.....	.....	2.00	1.00
5637	(58¢) Four-Armed Monster	.....	.....	.....	.....	2.00	1.00
5638	(58¢) Tentacled Monster . .	.....	.....	.....	.....	2.00	1.00
5639	(58¢) Red-Headed Monster	.....	.....	.....	.....	2.00	1.00

5640 5641 5642 5643

SCOTT NO.	DESCRIPTION	FIRST DAY COVERS SING	FIRST DAY COVERS PL. BLK.	MINT SHEET	PLATE BLOCK	UNUSED F/NH	USED
5640-43	(58¢) Day of the Dead. . . .	15.00(4)	.....	30.00(20)	14.00(8)	7.50	.....
5640	(58¢) Girl Skull	.....	.....	.....	.....	2.00	1.00
5641	(58¢) Man Skull.	.....	.....	.....	.....	2.00	1.00
5642	(58¢) Woman Skull	.....	.....	.....	.....	2.00	1.00
5643	(58¢) Boy Skull	.....	.....	.....	.....	2.00	1.00

5644 5645 5646 5647

SCOTT NO.	DESCRIPTION	FIRST DAY COVERS SING	FIRST DAY COVERS PL. BLK.	MINT SHEET	PLATE BLOCK	UNUSED F/NH	USED
5644-47	(58¢) Christmas.	15.00(4)	.....	.....	.....	7.50	.....
5644	(58¢) Santa Claus on Roof	.....	.....	.....	.....	2.00	0.80
5645	(58¢) Santa Claus in Fireplace	.....	.....	.....	.....	2.00	0.80
5646	(58¢) Head of Santa Claus	.....	.....	.....	.....	2.00	0.80
5647	(58¢) Santa Claus, Sleigh & Reindeer	.....	.....	.....	.....	2.00	0.80
5647b	same, double-sided bklt pane of 20	.....	.....	.....	.....	35.00	.....

5648 5649 5650 5651

SCOTT NO.	DESCRIPTION	FIRST DAY COVERS SING	FIRST DAY COVERS PL. BLK.	MINT SHEET	PLATE BLOCK	UNUSED F/NH	USED
5648-51	(58¢) Otters in Snow	15.00(4)	.....	.....	.....	7.50	.....
5648	(58¢) Otter in Water.	.....	.....	.....	.....	2.00	0.80
5649	(58¢) Otter, Tail at Right . .	.....	.....	.....	.....	2.00	0.80
5650	(58¢) Otter, Tail at Left. . . .	.....	.....	.....	.....	2.00	0.80
5651	(58¢) Otter in Snow.	.....	.....	.....	.....	2.00	0.80
5651b	same, double-sided bklt pane of 20	.....	.....	.....	.....	35.00	.....

2022 COMMEMORATIVES

SCOTT NO.	DESCRIPTION	FIRST DAY COVERS SING	FIRST DAY COVERS PL. BLK.	MINT SHEET	PLATE BLOCK	UNUSED F/NH	USED
5662/5739	(5662, 5663, 5668-71, 5683, 5688-92, 5693, 5694-97, 5702, 5703-07, 5708, 5709-12, 5715-19, 5720, 5737, 5738, 5739) 37 varieties	.....	.....	.....	.....	57.00	.....

5652, 5653 5654 5655, 5656, 5657 5658, 5659

SCOTT NO.	DESCRIPTION	FIRST DAY COVERS SING	FIRST DAY COVERS PL. BLK.	MINT SHEET	PLATE BLOCK	UNUSED F/NH	USED
5652	4¢ Blueberries, die cut 11¼ x 11	3.00	.....	5.00(20)	1.20(4)	0.30	0.30
5653	4¢ Blueberries, coil, die cut 10¾	3.00	.....	.....	.....	0.30	0.30
	same, plate number strip of 5	.....	.....	.....	.....	1.75	.....
5654	(58¢) Flags, micro above lower connector at left.	3.00	.....	28.00(20)	6.00(4)	1.60	0.70
5655	(58¢) Flags, coil, die cut 10¾	3.00	.....	.....	.....	1.60	0.70
	same, plate number strip of 5	.....	.....	.....	.....	10.50	.....
5656	(58¢) Flags, coil, die cut 11	3.00	.....	.....	.....	1.60	0.70
	same, plate number strip of 5	.....	.....	.....	.....	10.50	.....
5657	(58¢) Flags, coil, die cut 9½, micro above lowest flag. . .	3.00	.....	.....	.....	1.60	0.70
	same, plate number strip of 5	.....	.....	.....	.....	10.50	.....
5658	(58¢) Flags, micro above lower connector at left.	3.00	.....	.....	.....	1.60	0.70
	same, double-sided bklt pane of 20	.....	.....	.....	.....	30.00	.....
5659	(58¢) Flags, micro above lowest flag	3.00	.....	.....	.....	1.60	0.70
	same, double-sided bklt pane of 20	.....	.....	.....	.....	30.00	.....

5660 5661

SCOTT NO.	DESCRIPTION	FIRST DAY COVERS SING	FIRST DAY COVERS PL. BLK.	MINT SHEET	PLATE BLOCK	UNUSED F/NH	USED
5660-61	(58¢) Love.	6.00(2)	.....	28.00(20)	6.00(4)	3.00	.....
5660	(58¢) Blue Gray.	.....	.....	.....	.....	1.60	0.70
5661	(58¢) Pink	.....	.....	.....	.....	1.60	0.70

5662 5663

SCOTT NO.	DESCRIPTION	FIRST DAY COVERS SING	FIRST DAY COVERS PL. BLK.	MINT SHEET	PLATE BLOCK	UNUSED F/NH	USED
5662	(58¢) Year of the Tiger. . . .	3.00	.....	28.00(20)	6.00(4)	1.60	0.80
5663	(58¢) Edmonia Lewis, Sculptor	3.00	.....	28.00(20)	6.00(4)	1.60	0.80

5664 5665

SCOTT NO.	DESCRIPTION	FIRST DAY COVERS SING	FIRST DAY COVERS PL. BLK.	MINT SHEET	PLATE BLOCK	UNUSED F/NH	USED
5664-65	(5¢) Butterfly Garden Flowers, nonprofit	6.00(2)	.....	.....	.....	0.60	.....
5664	(5¢) Cosmos	.....	.....	.....	.....	0.30	0.30
5665	(5¢) Scabiosas	.....	.....	.....	.....	0.30	0.30
	same, plate number strip of 5	.....	.....	.....	.....	2.00	.....

5666

5667

SCOTT NO.	DESCRIPTION	FIRST DAY COVERS SING	FIRST DAY COVERS PL. BLK.	MINT SHEET	PLATE BLOCK	UNUSED F/NH	USED
5666	$8.95 Monument Valley	30.00	.....	75.00(4)	.....	20.00	12.00
5667	$26.95 Palace of Fine Arts	60.00	.....	230.00(4)	.....	60.00	30.00

5668  5669  5670  5671

SCOTT NO.	DESCRIPTION	FIRST DAY COVERS SING	FIRST DAY COVERS PL. BLK.	MINT SHEET	PLATE BLOCK	UNUSED F/NH	USED
5668-71	(58¢) Title IX Civil Rights Law	15.00(4)	.....	28.00(20)	6.00(4)	6.00	.....
5668	(58¢) Runner.	.....	.....	.....	.....	1.60	0.90
5669	(58¢) Swimmer	.....	.....	.....	.....	1.60	0.90
5670	(58¢) Gymnast		.....	.....	.....	1.60	0.90
5671	(58¢) Soccer Player	.....	.....	.....	.....	1.60	0.90

5672  5673  5674  5675

SCOTT NO.	DESCRIPTION	FIRST DAY COVERS SING	FIRST DAY COVERS PL. BLK.	MINT SHEET	PLATE BLOCK	UNUSED F/NH	USED
5672-75	(58¢) Mountain Flora.	15.00(4)	.....	.....	.....	6.00	.....
	same, plate number strip of 7	.....	.....	.....	.....	14.00	.....
5672	(58¢) Wood Lily	.....	.....	.....	.....	1.60	0.80
5673	(58¢) Alpine Buttercup. . . .	.....	.....	.....	.....	1.60	0.80
5674	(58¢) Woods' Rose..	.....	.....	.....	.....	1.60	0.80
5675	(58¢) Pasqueflower		.....	.....	.....	1.60	0.80

5676  5677  5678  5679

SCOTT NO.	DESCRIPTION	FIRST DAY COVERS SING	FIRST DAY COVERS PL. BLK.	MINT SHEET	PLATE BLOCK	UNUSED F/NH	USED
5676-79	(58¢) Mountain Flora.	15.00(4)	.....	.....	.....	6.00	.....
5676	(58¢) Pasqueflower.	.....	.....	.....	.....	1.60	0.80
5677	(58¢) Wood Lily	.....	.....	.....	.....	1.60	0.80
5678	(58¢) Alpine Buttercup. . . .	.....	.....	.....	.....	1.60	0.80
5679	(58¢) Woods's Rose	.....	.....	.....	.....	1.60	0.80
5679b	same, double-sided bklt pane of 20	.....	.....	.....	.....	30.00	.....

5680  5681

5682  5683

SCOTT NO.	DESCRIPTION	FIRST DAY COVERS SING	FIRST DAY COVERS PL. BLK.	MINT SHEET	PLATE BLOCK	UNUSED F/NH	USED
5680	($1.30) African Daisy.	6.00	.....	30.00(10)	12.00(4)	3.00	1.30
5681	(58¢) Tulips	3.00	.....	28.00(20)	6.00(4)	1.60	0.80
5682	(78¢) Sunflower Bouquet .	3.25	.....	32.00(20)	7.00(4)	1.80	0.90
5683	(58¢) Shel Silverstein, Writer	3.00	.....	28.00(20)	6.00(4)	1.60	0.90

5684  5685

5686  5687

SCOTT NO.	DESCRIPTION	FIRST DAY COVERS SING	FIRST DAY COVERS PL. BLK.	MINT SHEET	PLATE BLOCK	UNUSED F/NH	USED
5684-87	(15¢) Flags on Barns, presorted standard	12.00(4)	.....	.....	.....	1.50	.....
5684	(10¢) Flag on Red Barn. . .	.....	.....	.....	.....	0.35	0.30
5685	(10¢) Flag on White Barn in Winter	.....	.....	.....	.....	0.35	0.30
5686	(10¢) Flag on White Barn .	.....	.....	.....	.....	0.35	0.30
5687	(10¢) Flag on Barn Near Windmill...	.....	.....	.....	.....	0.35	0.30
	same, plate number strip of 5	.....	.....	.....	.....	4.00	.....

5688  5689  5690

5691  5692

SCOTT NO.	DESCRIPTION	FIRST DAY COVERS SING	FIRST DAY COVERS PL. BLK.	MINT SHEET	PLATE BLOCK	UNUSED F/NH	USED
5688-92	(58¢) Painting by George Morrison.	18.00(5)	.....	28.00(20)	15.00(10)	8.00(5)	.....
5688	(58¢) Sun and River	.....	.....	.....	.....	1.60	1.00
5689	(58¢) Phenomena Against the Crimson.	.....	.....	.....	.....	1.60	1.00
5690	(58¢) Lake Superior Landscape	.....	.....	.....	.....	1.60	1.00
5691	(58¢) Spirit Path, New Day, Red Rock Variation...	.....	.....	.....	.....	1.60	1.00
5692	(58¢) Untitled, 1995...	.....	.....	.....	.....	1.60	1.00

5693

SCOTT NO.	DESCRIPTION	FIRST DAY COVERS SING	FIRST DAY COVERS PL. BLK.	MINT SHEET	PLATE BLOCK	UNUSED F/NH	USED
5693	(58¢) Eugenie Clark, Ichthyologist	3.00	.....	28.00(20)	6.00(4)	1.60	0.90

5694

5695

5696 5697

SCOTT NO.	DESCRIPTION	FIRST DAY COVERS SING	FIRST DAY COVERS PL. BLK.	MINT SHEET	PLATE BLOCK	UNUSED F/NH	USED
5694-97	(58¢) Women's Rowing . . .	12.00(4)	.....	28.00(20)	13.00(8)	.....	.....
5694-95	(58¢) Women's Rowing in Red, pair	.....	.....	.....	.....	4.00	.....
5696-97	(58¢) Women's Rowing in Blue, pair	.....	.....	.....	.....	4.00	.....
5694	(58¢) Women in Red, No Oar Splash.	.....	.....	.....	.....	1.60	0.90
5695	(58¢) Women in Red, Oar Splash	.....	.....	.....	.....	1.60	0.90
5696	(58¢) Women in Blue, Oar Splash	.....	.....	.....	.....	1.60	0.90
5697	(58¢) Women in Blue, No Oar Splash.	.....	.....	.....	.....	1.60	0.90

5698

MIGHTY MISSISSIPPI

5698a	*Headwater of the Mississippi River*	**5698f**	*Fort Jefferson Hill Park*
5698b	*Great River Road*	**5698g**	*Curved Levee and Farmland*
5698c	*Steamboat American Queen*	**5698h**	*Towboat Pushing Barges*
5698d	*Sailboat and Limestone Cliff*	**5698i**	*Crescent City Connections Bridges*
5698e	*Gateway arch and Skyline*	**5698j**	*Cypress Trees in Bayou*

SCOTT NO.	DESCRIPTION	FIRST DAY COVERS SING	FIRST DAY COVERS PL. BLK.	MINT SHEET	PLATE BLOCK	UNUSED F/NH	USED
5698	(58¢) Mighty Mississippi	32.00(10)	.....	20.00(10)	.....	.....	.....

5700

5699

5701

SCOTT NO.	DESCRIPTION	FIRST DAY COVERS SING	FIRST DAY COVERS PL. BLK.	MINT SHEET	PLATE BLOCK	UNUSED F/NH	USED
5699	(78¢) Katherine Graham, Publisher	3.25	.....	32.00(20)	7.00(4)	1.80	1.00
5700	$2 Floral Geometry	.....	.....	35.00(10)	18.00(4)	5.00	3.00
5701	$5 Floral Geometry	.....	.....	40.00(4)	.....	11.00	8.00

5703

5702

5704

5705

5706

5707

SCOTT NO.	DESCRIPTION	FIRST DAY COVERS SING	FIRST DAY COVERS PL. BLK.	MINT SHEET	PLATE BLOCK	UNUSED F/NH	USED
5702	(58¢) Nancy Reagan, First Lady	3.00	.....	28.00(20)	6.00(4)	1.60	0.80
5703-07	(60¢) Mariachi	18.00(5)	.....	28.00(20)	15.00(10)	8.00(5)	.....
5703	(60¢) Guitarist and Moon .	.....	.....	.....	.....	1.60	1.00
5704	(60¢) Guitarist and Sun . . .	.....	.....	.....	.....	1.60	1.00
5705	(60¢) Violinist and Sun . . .	.....	.....	.....	.....	1.60	1.00
5706	(60¢) Bass Guitarist and Sun	.....	.....	.....	.....	1.60	1.00
5707	(60¢) Trumpet Player and Sun	.....	.....	.....	.....	1.60	1.00

5708

SCOTT NO.	DESCRIPTION	FIRST DAY COVERS SING	FIRST DAY COVERS PL. BLK.	MINT SHEET	PLATE BLOCK	UNUSED F/NH	USED
5708	(60¢) Pete Seeger, Music Icons	3.00	.....	25.00(16)	.....	1.60	0.80

5709

5710

5711

5712

SCOTT NO.	DESCRIPTION	FIRST DAY COVERS SING	FIRST DAY COVERS PL. BLK.	MINT SHEET	PLATE BLOCK	UNUSED F/NH	USED
5709-12	(60¢) Go Beyond, Buzz Lightyear	15.00(4)	.....	28.00(20)	13.00(8)	6.00(4)	.....
5709	(60¢) Head in Profile	.....	.....	.....	.....	1.60	1.00
5710	(60¢) Standing Legs Visible	.....	.....	.....	.....	1.60	1.00
5711	(60¢) Running	.....	.....	.....	.....	1.60	1.00
5712	(60¢) Standing Feet Not Visible	.....	.....	.....	.....	1.60	1.00

SCOTT NO.	DESCRIPTION	FIRST DAY COVERS SING	FIRST DAY COVERS PL. BLK.	MINT SHEET	PLATE BLOCK	UNUSED F/NH	USED

National Marine Sanctuaries

5713

NATIONAL MARINE SANCTUARIES

5713a	[illegible]	5713i	[illegible]
5713b	*Red-footed Boobies*	5713j	*Sea Otter*
5713c	*Humpback Whale*	5713k	*Rockfish Exploring Reef*
5713d	*Sea Stacks*	5713l	*Atlantic Sea Nettle*
5713e	*Mallows Bay*	5713m	*Sea Lions*
5713f	*Farallon Islands*	5713n	*Sand Tiger Shark*
5713g	*Elkhorn Coral*	5713o	*Corals and Fish*
5713h	*Hawaiian Monk Seal*	5713p	*Ice on Shoreline*

SCOTT NO.	DESCRIPTION	FDC SING	FDC PL. BLK.	MINT SHEET	PLATE BLOCK	UNUSED F/NH	USED
5713	(60¢) National Marine Sanctuaries	45.00(16)	.....	25.00(16)	.....	.....	20.00

5714

SCOTT NO.	DESCRIPTION	FDC SING	FDC PL. BLK.	MINT SHEET	PLATE BLOCK	UNUSED F/NH	USED
5714	(60¢) Elephants.	3.00	.....	.....	.....	1.60	0.70
	same, double-sided bklt pane of 20	.....	.....	.....	.....	28.00	.....

5715

5716

5717

5718

5719

SCOTT NO.	DESCRIPTION	FDC SING	FDC PL. BLK.	MINT SHEET	PLATE BLOCK	UNUSED F/NH	USED
5715-19	(60¢) Pony Cars	18.00(5)	.....	28.00(20)	15.00(10)	8.00(5)	.....
5715	(60¢) 1969 Ford Mustang Boss 302	.....	.....	.....	.....	1.60	1.00
5716	(60¢) 1970 Dodge Challenger R/T	.....	.....	.....	.....	1.60	1.00
5717	(60¢) 1969 Chevrolet Camaro Z/28	.....	.....	.....	.....	1.60	1.00
5718	(60¢) 1967 Mercury Cougar XR-7 GT	.....	.....	.....	.....	1.60	1.00
5719	(60¢) 1969 AMC Javelin SST	.....	.....	.....	.....	1.60	1.00

5720

5721

SCOTT NO.	DESCRIPTION	FDC SING	FDC PL. BLK.	MINT SHEET	PLATE BLOCK	UNUSED F/NH	USED
5720	(60¢) James Webb Space Telescope	3.00	.....	28.00(20)	6.00	1.60	0.80
5721	(60¢) Virgin and Child	3.00	.....	.....	.....	1.60	0.80
	same, double-sided bklt pane of 20	.....	.....	.....	.....	28.00	.....

5722 5723

5724

5725

SCOTT NO.	DESCRIPTION	FDC SING	FDC PL. BLK.	MINT SHEET	PLATE BLOCK	UNUSED F/NH	USED
5722-25	(60¢) Holiday Elves	15.00(4)	.....	.....	.....	6.00	.....
5722	(60¢) Elf and Teddy Bear. . .	..	.....	.....	.....	1.60	0.90
5723	(60¢) Elf Tying Ribbon. . . .	.....	.....	.....	.....	1.60	0.90
5724	(60¢) Elf with Toy Car	.....	.....	.....	.....	1.60	0.90
5725	(60¢) Elf with Rocket.	.....	.....	.....		1.60	0.90
[illegible]	same, [illegible] pane of 20	.....	.....	.....	.....	[illegible]	.....

5726a 5726b 5726c

5726d

5726e 5726f

5726g

5726h 5726i

5726j

SCOTT NO.	DESCRIPTION	FDC SING	FDC PL. BLK.	MINT SHEET	PLATE BLOCK	UNUSED F/NH	USED
5726	(60¢) Peanuts, Charles M. Schulz	35.00(10)	.....	30.00(20)	.....	.....	12.00
5726a	(60¢) Charlie Brown	.....	.....	.....	.....	1.60	1.25
5726b	(60¢) Lucy	.....	.....	.....	.....	1.60	1.25
5726c	(60¢) Franklin	.....	.....	.....	.....	1.60	1.25
5726d	(60¢) Sally	.....	.....	.....	.....	1.60	1.25
5726e	(60¢) Pigpen	.....	.....	.....	.....	1.60	1.25
5726f	(60¢) Linus	.....	.....	.....	.....	1.60	1.25
5726g	(60¢) Snoopy and Woodstock	.....	.....	.....	.....	1.60	1.25
5726h	(60¢) Schroeder	.....	.....	.....	.....	1.60	1.25
5726i	(60¢) Peppermint Patty . . .	.....	.....	.....	.....	1.60	1.25
5726j	(60¢) Marcie	.....	.....	.....	.....	1.60	1.25

5727 5728 5729

5730 5731

5732 5733 5734

5735 5736

SCOTT NO.	DESCRIPTION	FIRST DAY COVERS SING	FIRST DAY COVERS PL. BLK.	MINT SHEET	PLATE BLOCK	UNUSED F/NH	USED
5727-36	(60¢) Snowy Beauty	35.00(10)	.....	.....	.....	15.00	.....
5727	(60¢) Camellia.	.....	.....	.....	.....	1.60	1.00
5728	(60¢) Winter Aconite	.....	.....	.....	.....	1.60	1.00
5729	(60¢) Crocuses	.....	.....	.....	.....	1.60	1.00
5730	(60¢) Hellebore	.....	.....	.....	.....	1.60	1.00
5731	(60¢) Winterberry	.....	.....	.....	.....	1.60	1.00
5732	(60¢) Pansies	.....	.....	.....	.....	1.60	1.00
5733	(60¢) Plum Blossoms	.....	.....	.....	.....	1.60	1.00
5734	(60¢) Grape Hyacinths . . .	.....	.....	.....	.....	1.60	1.00
5735	(60¢) Daffodils.	.....	.....	.....	.....	1.60	1.00
5736	(60¢) Ranunculus	.....	.....	.....	.....	1.60	1.00
5736b	same, double-sided bklt pane of 20	.....	.....	.....	.....	30.00	.....

5737

5738

5739

SCOTT NO.	DESCRIPTION	FIRST DAY COVERS SING	FIRST DAY COVERS PL. BLK.	MINT SHEET	PLATE BLOCK	UNUSED F/NH	USED
5737	(60¢) Kwanzaa	3.00	.....	28.00(20)	6.00(4)	1.60	0.80
5738	(60¢) Women Cryptologists of WWII	3.00	.....	28.00(20)	6.00(4)	1.60	0.90
5739	(60¢) Hanukkah.	3.00	.....	28.00(20)	6.00(4)	1.60	0.80

2023 COMMEMORATIVES

SCOTT NO.	DESCRIPTION	FIRST DAY COVERS SING	FIRST DAY COVERS PL. BLK.	MINT SHEET	PLATE BLOCK	UNUSED F/NH	USED
5744/5821	**(5744, 5753, 5754, 5757, 5758-62, 5763-66, 5792-96, 5797, 5798, 5801, 5803-07, 5820, 5821) 28 varieties**	.....	.....	.....	.....	**45.00**	.....

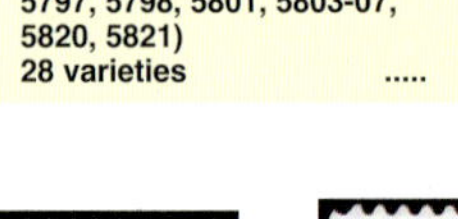

5740, 5741

5742, 5743

5744

SCOTT NO.	DESCRIPTION	FIRST DAY COVERS SING	FIRST DAY COVERS PL. BLK.	MINT SHEET	PLATE BLOCK	UNUSED F/NH	USED
5740	(24¢) School Bus.	3.00	.....	11.00(20)	2.50(4)	0.60	0.30
5741	(24¢) School Bus, coil	3.00	.....	.....	.....	0.60	0.30
	same, plate number strip of 5	.....	.....	.....	.....	5.00	.....
5742	40¢ Red Fox, die cut 11¼ x 11	3.00	.....	22.00(20)	4.25(4)	1.00	0.70
5743	40¢ Red Fox, coil, die cut 11 vert.	3.00	.....	.....	.....	1.00	0.70
	same, plate number strip of 5	.....	.....	.....	.....	7.50	.....
5744	(60¢) Year of the Rabbit . .	3.00	.....	28.00(20)	6.00(4)	1.60	0.90

5745

5746

SCOTT NO.	DESCRIPTION	FIRST DAY COVERS SING	FIRST DAY COVERS PL. BLK.	MINT SHEET	PLATE BLOCK	UNUSED F/NH	USED
5745-46	(60¢) Love, Kitten and Puppy	6.00(2)	.....	28.00(20)	6.00(4)	3.00	0.90
5745	(60¢) Kitten and Heart. . . .	.....	.....	.....	.....	1.60	0.90
5746	(60¢) Puppy and Heart . . .	.....	.....	.....	.....	1.60	0.90

5747, 5750

5748, 5749

SCOTT NO.	DESCRIPTION	FIRST DAY COVERS SING	FIRST DAY COVERS PL. BLK.	MINT SHEET	PLATE BLOCK	UNUSED F/NH	USED
5747-48	(48¢) Sailboats	6.00(2)	.....	22.00(20)	5.00(4)	2.30	....
5747	(48¢) Two Sailboats.	.....	.....	.....	.....	1.20	0.70
5748	(48¢) One Sailboat	.....	.....	.....	.....	1.20	0.70
5749-50	(48¢) Sailboats, coil, die cut 9½ vert.	6.00(2)	.....	.....	.....	2.30	.....
5749	(48¢) One Sailboat	.....	.....	.....	.....	1.20	0.70
5750	(48¢) Two Sailboats.	.....	.....	.....	.....	1.20	0.70
	same, plate number strip of 5	.....	.....	.....	.....	7.50	.....

5751

5752

SCOTT NO.	DESCRIPTION	FIRST DAY COVERS SING	FIRST DAY COVERS PL. BLK.	MINT SHEET	PLATE BLOCK	UNUSED F/NH	USED
5751	$9.65 Florida Everglades .	30.00	.....	80.00(4)	.....	22.00	12.00
5752	$28.75 Great Smoky Mountains	60.00	.....	235.00(4)	.....	65.00	35.00

5753

5754

SCOTT NO.	DESCRIPTION	FIRST DAY COVERS SING	FIRST DAY COVERS PL. BLK.	MINT SHEET	PLATE BLOCK	UNUSED F/NH	USED
5753	(63¢) Ernest J. Gaines, Writer	3.00	.....	28.00(20)	6.00(4)	1.60	0.90
5754	(63¢) Women's Soccer . . .	3.00	.....	28.00(20)	6.00(4)	1.60	0.90

5755

5756, 5756A

5757

SCOTT NO.	DESCRIPTION	FIRST DAY COVERS SING	FIRST DAY COVERS PL. BLK.	MINT SHEET	PLATE BLOCK	UNUSED F/NH	USED
5755	$10 Floral Geometry	.....		80.00(4)	.....	22.00	15.00
5756	(5¢) Stars and Bars, coil, die cut 10¾ vert.	3.00	.....	.....	.....	0.30	0.30
	same, plate number strip of 5	.....	.....	.....	.....	2.00	.....
5756A	(5¢) Stars and Bars, coil, large date,	3.00	.....	.....	.....	0.35	0.30
	DC 10.75 same, plate number strip of 5	.....	.....	.....	.....	2.00	.....
5757	(63¢) Toni Morrison, Writer3.00		.....28.00(20)	6.00(4)	1.60	0.90	

5758  5759 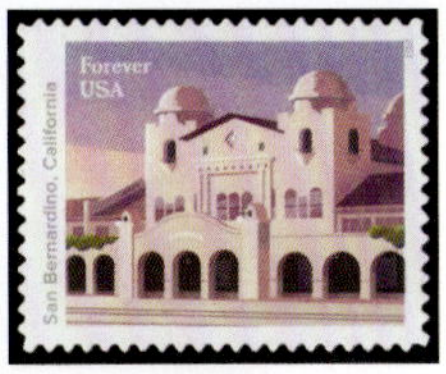 5760

5761  5762

SCOTT NO.	DESCRIPTION	FIRST DAY COVERS SING	FIRST DAY COVERS PL. BLK.	MINT SHEET	PLATE BLOCK	UNUSED F/NH	USED
5758-62	(63¢) Historic Railroad Stations	18.00(5)	.....	28.00(20)	15.00(10)	8.00(5)	.....
5758	(63¢) Point of Rocks Station	.....	.....	.....	.....	1.60	1.00
5759	(63¢) Mail Street Station . .	.....	.....	.....	.....	1.60	1.00
5760	(63¢) Santa Fe Station . . .	.....	.....	.....	.....	1.60	1.00
5761	(63¢) Tamaqua Station . . .	.....	.....	.....	.....	1.60	1.00
5762	(63¢) Union Terminal.	.....	.....	.....	.....	1.60	1.00

5763  5764

5765  5766

SCOTT NO.	DESCRIPTION	FIRST DAY COVERS SING	FIRST DAY COVERS PL. BLK.	MINT SHEET	PLATE BLOCK	UNUSED F/NH	USED
5763-66	(63¢) Art of the Skateboard	15.00(4)	.....	28.00(20)	13.00(8)	6.00(4)	.....
5763	(63¢) Tlingit Athabascan Salmon Design	.....	.....	.....	.....	1.60	1.00
5764	(63¢) Abstract Design	.....	.....	.....	.....	1.60	1.00
5765	(63¢) Navajo Design	.....	.....	.....	.....	1.60	1.00
5766	(63¢) Jaguar Design	.....	.....	.....	.....	1.60	1.00

5773, 5777  5767, 5779 5771, 5778 5774, 5780

5768, 5781  5770, 5782  5769, 5783  5772, 5784

5776, 5785  5775, 5786

SCOTT NO.	DESCRIPTION	FIRST DAY COVERS SING	FIRST DAY COVERS PL. BLK.	MINT SHEET	PLATE BLOCK	UNUSED F/NH	USED
5767-76	(63¢) Tulip Blossoms, coil, die cut 10¾	35.00(10)	.....	.....	.....	15.00(10)	.....
	same, plate number strip of 10	.....	.....	.....	.....	20.00	
5767	(63¢) Pink, Yellowish Base	.....	.....	.....	.....	1.60	1.00
5768	(63¢) Purple, White Base .	.....	.....	.....	.....	1.60	1.00
5769	(63¢) Pink, Orange	.....	.....	.....	.....	1.60	1.00
5770	(63¢) Lilac	.....	.....	.....	.....	1.60	1.00
5771	(63¢) Orange, Red	.....	.....	.....	.....	1.60	1.00
5772	(63¢) Dark Purple	.....	.....	.....	.....	1.60	1.00
5773	(63¢) Brownish, White Base	.....	.....	.....	.....	1.60	1.00
5774	(63¢) Pink, White Base . . .	.....	.....	.....	.....	1.60	1.00
5775	(63¢) Pink, Yellowish Background	.....	.....	.....	.....	1.60	1.00
5776	(63¢) White, Purple Base .	.....	.....	.....	.....	1.60	1.00

SCOTT NO.	DESCRIPTION	FIRST DAY COVERS SING	FIRST DAY COVERS PL. BLK.	MINT SHEET	PLATE BLOCK	UNUSED F/NH	USED
5777-86	(63¢) Tulip Blossoms, die cut 10¾x11	35.00(10)	.....	.....	.....	15.00(10)	.....
5777	(63¢) Brownish, White Base	.....	.....	.....	.....	1.60	1.00
5778	(63¢) Pink, Yellowish Base	.....	.....	.....	.....	1.60	1.00
5779	(63¢) Pink, White Base . . .	.....	.....	.....	.....	1.60	1.00
5780	(63¢) Orange, Red	.....	.....	.....	.....	1.60	1.00
5781	(63¢) Purple, White Base .	.....	.....	.....	.....	1.60	1.00
5782	(63¢) Lilac	.....	.....	.....	.....	1.60	1.00
5783	(63¢) Pink, Orange	.....	.....	.....	.....	1.60	1.00
5784	(63¢) Dark Purple	.....	.....	.....	.....	1.60	1.00
5785	(63¢) White, Purple Base .	.....	.....	.....	.....	1.60	1.00
5786	(63¢) Pink, Yellowish Background	.....	.....	.....	.....	1.60	1.00
5786b	same, double-sided bklt pane of 20	.....	.....	.....	.....	30.00	.....

5787  5788, 5789, 5789A  5790, 5791

SCOTT NO.	DESCRIPTION	FIRST DAY COVERS SING	FIRST DAY COVERS PL. BLK.	MINT SHEET	PLATE BLOCK	UNUSED F/NH	USED
5787	(63¢) Freedom, micro right of lowest stripe	3.00	.....	28.00(20)	6.00(4)	1.60	0.70
5788	(63¢) Freedom, coil, die cut 9½	3.00	.....	.....	.....	1.60	0.70
	same, plate number strip of 5	.....	.....	.....	.....	10.50	.....
5789	(63¢) Freedom, coil, die cut 10¾	3.00	.....	.....	.....	1.60	0.70
	same, plate number strip of 5	.....	.....	.....	.....	10.50	.....
5789A	(63¢) Freedom, coil, die cut 11	3.00	.....	.....	.....	1.60	0.70
	same, plate number strip of 5	.....	.....	.....	.....	10.50	
5790	(63¢) Freedom, micro below left flag field	3.00	.....	.....	.....	1.60	0.70
	same, double sided bklt pane of 20					30.00	
5791	(63¢) Freedom, micro right of lowest stripe	3.00	.....	.....	.....	1.60	0.70
	same, double-sided bklt pane of 20	.....	.....	.....	.....	30.00	.....

5792  5793  5794

5795  5796

SCOTT NO.	DESCRIPTION	FIRST DAY COVERS SING	FIRST DAY COVERS PL. BLK.	MINT SHEET	PLATE BLOCK	UNUSED F/NH	USED
5792-96	(63¢) Roy Liechtenstein . .	18.00(5)	.....	28.00(20)	15.00(10)	8.00(5)	.....
5792	(63¢) Standing Explosion, 1965	.....	.....	.....	.....	1.60	1.00
5793	(63¢) Modern Painting I, 1966	.....	.....	.....	.....	1.60	1.00
5794	(63¢) Still Life Crystal Bowl, 1972	.....	.....	.....	.....	1.60	1.00
5795	(63¢) Still Life Goldfish, 1972	.....	.....	.....	.....	1.60	1.00
5796	(63¢) Woman Portrait, 1979	.....	.....	.....	.....	1.60	1.00

5797

5798

SCOTT NO.	DESCRIPTION	FIRST DAY COVERS SING	FIRST DAY COVERS PL. BLK.	MINT SHEET	PLATE BLOCK	UNUSED F/NH	USED
5797	(63¢) Tomie dePaola, Author	3.00	.....	28.00(20)	6.00(4)	1.60	0.90
5798	(63¢) Chief Standing Bear.	3.00	.....	28.00(20)	6.00(4)	1.60	0.90

SCOTT NO.	DESCRIPTION	FIRST DAY COVERS SING	PL. BLK.	MINT SHEET	PLATE BLOCK	UNUSED F/NH	USED

5799

ENDANGERED SPECIES

5799a	*Laysan Teal*	**5799k**	*Vancouver Island Marmot*
5799b	*Black-footed Ferret*	**5799l**	*Gold-cheeked Warbler*
5799c	*Roanoake Logperch*	**5799m**	*Guam Micronesia Kingfisher*
5799d	*Thick-billed Parrot*	**5799n**	*San Francisco Garter Snake*
5799e	*Candy Darter*	**5799o**	*Mexican Gray Wolf*
5799f	*Florida Panther*	**5799p**	*Attwater's Prairie Chicken*
5799g	*Masked Bobwhite Quail*	**5799q**	*Nashville Crayfish*
5799h	*Key Largo Cotton Mouse*	**5799r**	*Piping Plover*
5799i	*Lower Keys Marsh Rabbit*	**5799s**	*Desert Bighorn Sheep*
5799j	*Wyoming Toad*	**5799t**	*Mississippi Sandhill Crane*

SCOTT NO.	DESCRIPTION	SING	PL. BLK.	MINT SHEET	PLATE BLOCK	UNUSED F/NH	USED
5799	(63¢) Endangered Species	55.00(20)	.....	30.00(20)	.....	.....	22.00

5800

WATERFALLS

5800a	*Deer Creek Falls, AZ*	**5800g**	*Niagara Falls, NY*
5800b	*Nevada Fall, CA*	**5800h**	*Dark Hollow Falls, VA*
5800c	*Harrison Wright Falls, PA*	**5800i**	*Grotto Falls, TN*
5800d	*Lower Falls, Yellow River, WY*	**5800j**	*Sunbeam Falls, WA*
5800e	*Waimoku Falls, HI*	**5800k**	*LaSalle Canyon Waterfall, IL*
5800f	*Stewart Falls, UT*	**5800l**	*Upper Falls, NC*

SCOTT NO.	DESCRIPTION	SING	PL. BLK.	MINT SHEET	PLATE BLOCK	UNUSED F/NH	USED
5800	(63¢) Waterfalls	40.00(12)	.....	22.00(12)	.....	.....	14.00

5801

SCOTT NO.	DESCRIPTION	SING	PL. BLK.	MINT SHEET	PLATE BLOCK	UNUSED F/NH	USED
5801	(66¢) John Lewis, Writer . .	3.00	.....	25.00(15)	6.00(4)	1.60	0.90

5802

LIFE MAGNIFIED

5802a	*Red Blood Cells*	**5802k**	*Starling Bone Tissue*
5802b	*Macaw Parrot Feather*	**5802l**	*Moth Wing Scales*
5802c	*Human Hair*	**5802m**	*Zebrafish*
5802d	*Moss Leaves*	**5802n**	*Mushroom Gills*
5802e	*Arranged Diatoms*	**5802o**	*Freshwater Snail Tongue*
5802f	*Freshwater Protozoans*	**5802p**	*Blue Button Organism*
5802g	*Acorn Barnacle*	**5802q**	*Mold Spores*
5802h	*Moth Antenna*	**5802r**	*Barnacle Legs*
5802i	*Diving Beetle Front Foot*	**5802s**	*Flame Lily Pollen*
5802j	*Mouse Brain Neurons*	**5802t**	*Oak Leaf Surface*

SCOTT NO.	DESCRIPTION	SING	PL. BLK.	MINT SHEET	PLATE BLOCK	UNUSED F/NH	USED
5802	(66¢) Life Magnified . . .	65.00(20)	.....	30.00(20)	.....	.....	25.00

5803

5804

5805

5806

5807

SCOTT NO.	DESCRIPTION	SING	PL. BLK.	MINT SHEET	PLATE BLOCK	UNUSED F/NH	USED
5803-07	(66¢) Thinking of You	18.00(5)	.....	28.00(20)	15.00(10)	8.00(5)	.....
5803	(66¢) Butterfly, Flower, Dog, Cake	.....	.....	.....	.....	1.60	1.00
5804	(66¢) Sun, Flower, Horseshoe, Dandelion	.....	.....	.....	.....	1.60	1.00
5805	(66¢) Leaf, Bouquet, Bandage, Party Hat, Ice Cream.		.....	.....	.....	1.60	1.00
5806	(66¢) Rainbow, Ice Cream, Clover, Cat, Cupcake		.....	.....	.....	1.60	1.00
5807	(66¢) Thumbs Up, Balloons, XOOX, Cup		.....	.....	.....	1.60	1.00

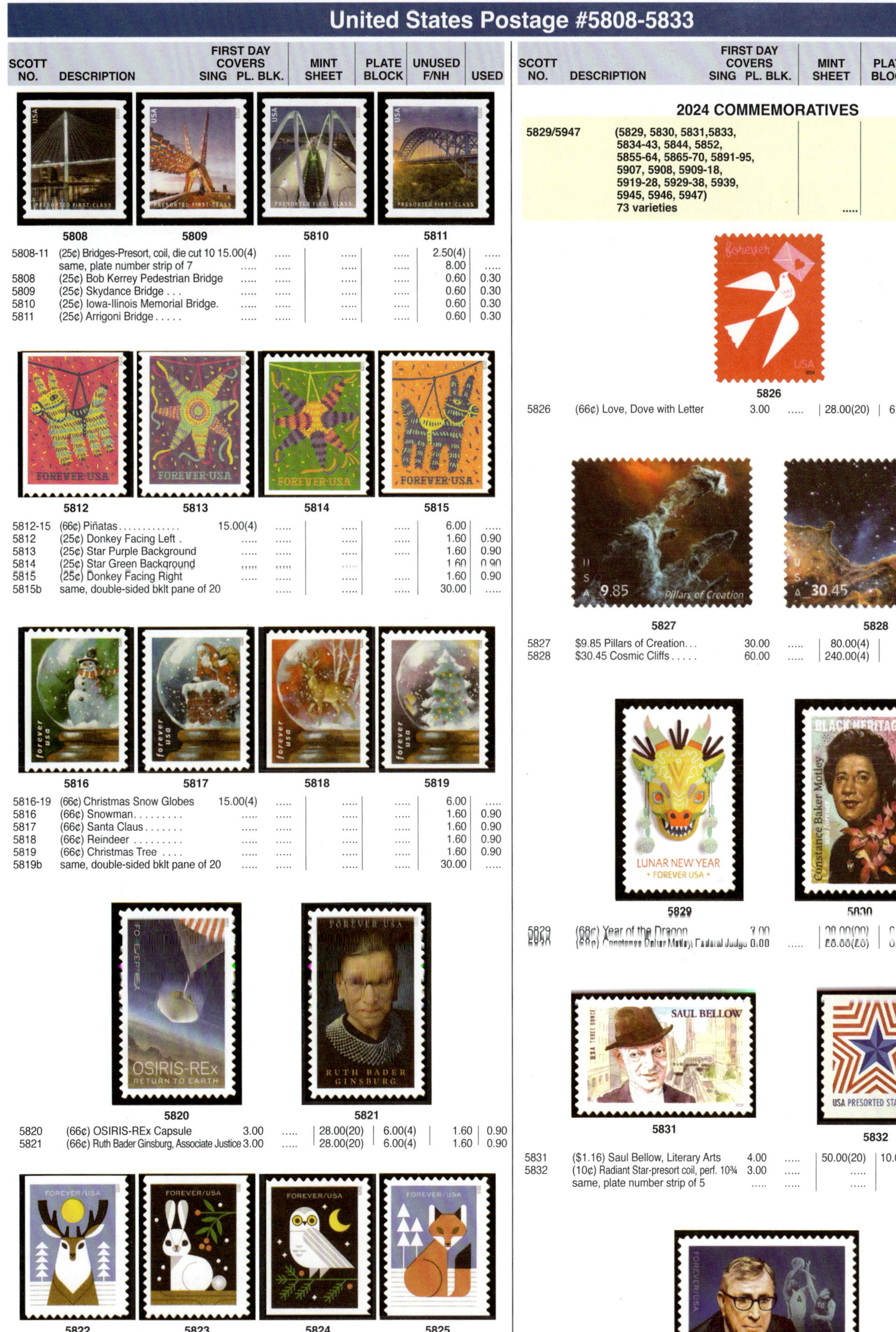

SCOTT NO.	DESCRIPTION	FIRST DAY COVERS SING	FIRST DAY COVERS PL. BLK.	MINT SHEET	PLATE BLOCK	UNUSED F/NH	USED
5808-11	(25¢) Bridges-Presort, coil, die cut 10	15.00(4)	.....	.....	.....	2.50(4)	.....
	same, plate number strip of 7	.....	.....	.....	.....	8.00	.....
5808	(25¢) Bob Kerrey Pedestrian Bridge	.....	.....	.....	.....	0.60	0.30
5809	(25¢) Skydance Bridge . . .	.....	.....	.....	.....	0.60	0.30
5810	(25¢) Iowa-Illinois Memorial Bridge.	.....	.....	.....	.....	0.60	0.30
5811	(25¢) Arrigoni Bridge	.....	.....	.....	.....	0.60	0.30
5812-15	(66¢) Piñatas.	15.00(4)	.....	.....	.....	6.00	.....
5812	(25¢) Donkey Facing Left .	.....	.....	.....	.....	1.60	0.90
5813	(25¢) Star Purple Background	.....	.....	.....	.....	1.60	0.90
5814	(25¢) Star Green Background	.....	.....	.....	.....	1.60	0.90
5815	(25¢) Donkey Facing Right	.....	.....	.....	.....	1.60	0.90
5815b	same, double-sided bklt pane of 20		.....	.....	.....	30.00	.....
5816-19	(66¢) Christmas Snow Globes	15.00(4)	.....	.....	.....	6.00	.....
5816	(66¢) Snowman.	.....	.....	.....	.....	1.60	0.90
5817	(66¢) Santa Claus	.....	.....	.....	.....	1.60	0.90
5818	(66¢) Reindeer	.....	.....	.....	.....	1.60	0.90
5819	(66¢) Christmas Tree	.....	.....	.....	.....	1.60	0.90
5819b	same, double-sided bklt pane of 20	.....	.....	.....	.....	30.00	.....
5820	(66¢) OSIRIS-REx Capsule	3.00	.....	28.00(20)	6.00(4)	1.60	0.90
5821	(66¢) Ruth Bader Ginsburg, Associate Justice	3.00	.....	28.00(20)	6.00(4)	1.60	0.90
5822-25	(66¢) Winter Woodland Animals	15.00(4)	.....	.....	.....	6.00	.....
5822	(66¢) Deer.	.....	.....	.....	.....	1.60	0.90
5823	(66¢) Rabbit	.....	.....	.....	.....	1.60	0.90
5824	(66¢) Owl.	.....	.....	.....	.....	1.60	0.90
5825	(66¢) Fox.	.....	.....	.....	.....	1.60	0.90
5825b	same, double-sided bklt pane of 20	.....	.....	.....	.....	30.00	.....
5826	(66¢) Love, Dove with Letter	3.00	.....	28.00(20)	6.00(4)	1.60	.....
5827	$9.85 Pillars of Creation. . .	30.00	.....	80.00(4)	.....	22.00	.....
5828	$30.45 Cosmic Cliffs	60.00	.....	240.00(4)	.....	70.00	.....

2024 COMMEMORATIVES

SCOTT NO.	DESCRIPTION	FIRST DAY COVERS SING	FIRST DAY COVERS PL. BLK.	MINT SHEET	PLATE BLOCK	UNUSED F/NH	USED
5829/5947	(5829, 5830, 5831,5833, 5834-43, 5844, 5852, 5855-64, 5865-70, 5891-95, 5907, 5908, 5909-18, 5919-28, 5929-38, 5939, 5945, 5946, 5947) 73 varieties			.....	.....	115.00	.....
5829	(68¢) Year of the Dragon	3.00		[illegible]	[illegible]	[illegible]	.....
5830	(68¢) Constance Baker Motley, Federal Judge	3.00	.....	28.00(20)	6.00(4)	1.60	.....
5831	($1.16) Saul Bellow, Literary Arts	4.00	.....	50.00(20)	10.00(4)	2.70	.....
5832	(10¢) Radiant Star-presort coil, perf. 10¾	3.00	.....	.....	.....	0.35	.....
	same, plate number strip of 5	.....	.....	.....	.....	3.00	.....
5833	(68¢) John Wooden.	3.00	.....	30.00(20)	7.00(4)	1.60	.....

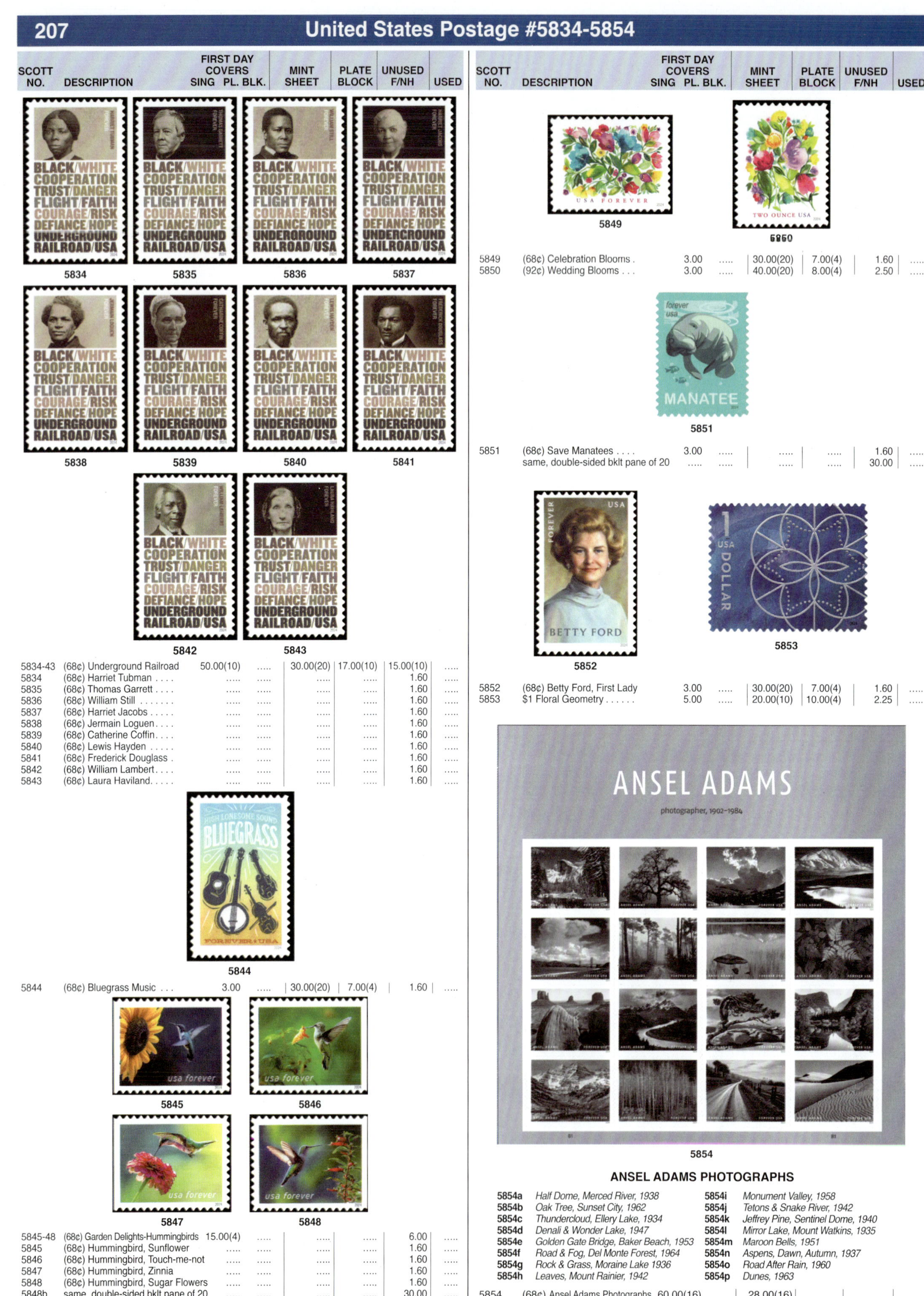

SCOTT NO.	DESCRIPTION	FIRST DAY COVERS SING	FIRST DAY COVERS PL. BLK.	MINT SHEET	PLATE BLOCK	UNUSED F/NH	USED
5834-43	(68¢) Underground Railroad	50.00(10)	.....	30.00(20)	17.00(10)	15.00(10)	.....
5834	(68¢) Harriet Tubman	.....	.....	.....	.....	1.60	.....
5835	(68¢) Thomas Garrett	.....	.....	.....	.....	1.60	.....
5836	(68¢) William Still	.....	.....	.....	.....	1.60	.....
5837	(68¢) Harriet Jacobs	.....	.....	.....	.....	1.60	.....
5838	(68¢) Jermain Loguen	.....	.....	.....	.....	1.60	.....
5839	(68¢) Catherine Coffin. . . .	.....	.....	.....	.....	1.60	.....
5840	(68¢) Lewis Hayden	.....	.....	.....	.....	1.60	.....
5841	(68¢) Frederick Douglass .	.....	.....	.....	.....	1.60	.....
5842	(68¢) William Lambert. . . .	.....	.....	.....	.....	1.60	.....
5843	(68¢) Laura Haviland.	.....	.....	.....	.....	1.60	.....
5844	(68¢) Bluegrass Music . . .	3.00	.....	30.00(20)	7.00(4)	1.60	.....
5845-48	(68¢) Garden Delights-Hummingbirds	15.00(4)	.....	.....	.....	6.00	.....
5845	(68¢) Hummingbird, Sunflower	.....	.....	.....	.....	1.60	.....
5846	(68¢) Hummingbird, Touch-me-not	.....	.....	.....	.....	1.60	.....
5847	(68¢) Hummingbird, Zinnia	.....	.....	.....	.....	1.60	.....
5848	(68¢) Hummingbird, Sugar Flowers	.....	.....	.....	.....	1.60	.....
5848b	same, double-sided bklt pane of 20	.....	.....	.....	.....	30.00	.....

SCOTT NO.	DESCRIPTION	FIRST DAY COVERS SING	FIRST DAY COVERS PL. BLK.	MINT SHEET	PLATE BLOCK	UNUSED F/NH	USED
5849	(68¢) Celebration Blooms .	3.00	.....	30.00(20)	7.00(4)	1.60	.....
5850	(92¢) Wedding Blooms . . .	3.00	.....	40.00(20)	8.00(4)	2.50	.....
5851	(68¢) Save Manatees	3.00	.....	.....	.....	1.60	.....
	same, double-sided bklt pane of 20	.....	.....	.....	.....	30.00	.....
5852	(68¢) Betty Ford, First Lady	3.00	.....	30.00(20)	7.00(4)	1.60	.....
5853	$1 Floral Geometry	5.00	.....	20.00(10)	10.00(4)	2.25	.....

ANSEL ADAMS PHOTOGRAPHS

5854a *Half Dome, Merced River, 1938*
5854b *Oak Tree, Sunset City, 1962*
5854c *Thundercloud, Ellery Lake, 1934*
5854d *Denali & Wonder Lake, 1947*
5854e *Golden Gate Bridge, Baker Beach, 1953*
5854f *Road & Fog, Del Monte Forest, 1964*
5854g *Rock & Grass, Moraine Lake 1936*
5854h *Leaves, Mount Rainier, 1942*
5854i *Monument Valley, 1958*
5854j *Tetons & Snake River, 1942*
5854k *Jeffrey Pine, Sentinel Dome, 1940*
5854l *Mirror Lake, Mount Watkins, 1935*
5854m *Maroon Bells, 1951*
5854n *Aspens, Dawn, Autumn, 1937*
5854o *Road After Rain, 1960*
5854p *Dunes, 1963*

SCOTT NO.	DESCRIPTION	FIRST DAY COVERS SING	FIRST DAY COVERS PL. BLK.	MINT SHEET	PLATE BLOCK	UNUSED F/NH	USED
5854	(68¢) Ansel Adams Photographs	60.00(16)	.....	28.00(16)	.....	.....	.....

5855

5856

5857

5858

5859

5860

5861

5862

5863

5864

SCOTT NO.	DESCRIPTION	FIRST DAY COVERS SING	FIRST DAY COVERS PL. BLK.	MINT SHEET	PLATE BLOCK	UNUSED F/NH	USED
5855-64	(68¢) Carnival Nights	50.00(10)	.....	30.00(20)	17.00(10)	15.00(10)	.....
5855	(68¢) Wave Swinger Ride .	.....	.....	.....	.....	1.60	.....
5856	(68¢) Midway Gondola Wheel & Ring of Fire	.....	.....	.....	.....	1.60	.....
5857	(68¢) Gondola Wheels . . .	.....	.....	.....	.....	1.60	.....
5858	(68¢) Gondola Wheel, Multi Color	.....	.....	.....	.....	1.60	.....
5859	(68¢) Gondola Wheel, Red Orange	.....	.....	.....	.....	1.60	.....
5860	(68¢) Gondola, Wave Swinger & Midway Food	.....	.....	.....	.....	1.60	.....
5861	(68¢) Gondola Wheel, Fireworks	.....	.....	.....	.....	1.60	.....
5862	(68¢) Round-Up Ride	.....	.....	.....	.....	1.60	.....
5863	(68¢) Carousel Horse	.....	.....	.....	.....	1.60	.....
5864	(68¢) Gondola Wheel & Wave Swinger, Fireworks	.....	.....	.....	.....	1.60	.....

5865

5866

5867

5868

5869

5870

SCOTT NO.	DESCRIPTION	FIRST DAY COVERS SING	FIRST DAY COVERS PL. BLK.	MINT SHEET	PLATE BLOCK	UNUSED F/NH	USED
5865-70	(68¢) Protect Sea Turtles .	25.00(6)	.....	28.00(18)	20.00(12)	10.00(6)	.....
5865	(68¢) Kemp's Ridley	.....	.....	.....	.....	1.60	.....
5866	(68¢) Green.	.....	.....	.....	.....	1.60	.....
5867	(68¢) Leatherback	.....	.....	.....	.....	1.60	.....
5868	(68¢) Loggerhead	.....	.....	.....	.....	1.60	.....
5869	(68¢) Hawksbill	.....	.....	.....	.....	1.60	.....
5870	(68¢) Olive Ridley	.....	.....	.....	.....	1.60	.....

5871, 5878, 5879   5872, 5875, 5880   5873, 5776, 5881   5874, 5877, 5882

SCOTT NO.	DESCRIPTION	FIRST DAY COVERS SING	FIRST DAY COVERS PL. BLK.	MINT SHEET	PLATE BLOCK	UNUSED F/NH	USED
5871-74	(68¢) U.S. Flags, coil, die cut 9½	15.00(4)	.....	.....	.....	6.00	.....
	same, plate number strip of 5	.....	.....	.....	.....	18.00	.....
5871	(68¢) Flag, Blue Sky Top, Cloud Bottom	.....	.....	.....	.....	1.60	.....
5872	(68¢) Flag, Dark Clouds . .	.....	.....	.....	.....	1.60	.....
5873	(68¢) Flag, Cloud Top & Bottom	.....	.....	.....	.....	1.60	.....
5874	(68¢) Flag, Blue Sky, Clouds Top	.....	.....	.....	.....	1.60	.....
5875-78	(68¢) U.S. Flags, coil, die cut 11½	15.00(4)	.....	.....	.....	6.00	.....
	same, plate number strip of 5	.....	.....	.....	.....	18.00	.....
5875	(68¢) Flag, Dark Clouds . .	.....	.....	.....	.....	1.60	.....
5876	(68¢) Flag, Cloud Top & Bottom	.....	.....	.....	.....	1.60	.....
5877	(68¢) Flag, Blue Sky, Clouds Top	.....	.....	.....	.....	1.60	.....
5878	(68¢) Flag, Blue Sky Top, Cloud Bottom	.....	.....	.....	.....	1.60	.....
5879-82	(68¢) U.S. Flags, coil, die cut 10	15.00(4)	.....	.....	.....	6.00	.....
	same, plate number strip of 7	.....	.....	.....	.....	18.00	.....
5879	(68¢) Flag, Blue Sky Top, Cloud Bottom	.....	.....	.....	.....	1.60	.....
5880	(68¢) Flag, Dark Clouds . .	.....	.....	.....	.....	1.60	.....
5881	(68¢) Flag, Cloud Top & Bottom	.....	.....	.....	.....	1.60	.....
5882	(68¢) Flag, Blue Sky, Clouds Top	.....	.....	.....	.....	1.60	.....

5883, 5887   5884, 5888   5885, 5889   5886, 5890

SCOTT NO.	DESCRIPTION	FIRST DAY COVERS SING	FIRST DAY COVERS PL. BLK.	MINT SHEET	PLATE BLOCK	UNUSED F/NH	USED
5883-86	(68¢) U.S. Flags						
	18.75 mm x 21.5 mm image	15.00(4)	.....	.....	.....	6.00	.....
5883	(68¢) Flag, Cloud Top & Bottom	.....	.....	.....	.....	1.60	.....
5884	(68¢) Flag, Blue Sky, Clouds Top	.....	.....	.....	.....	1.60	.....
5885	(68¢) Flag, Blue Sky Top, Cloud Bottom	.....	.....	.....	.....	1.60	.....
5886	(68¢) Flag, Dark Clouds . .	.....	.....	.....	.....	1.60	.....
5886b	same, double-sided bklt pane of 20	.....	.....	.....	.....	30.00	.....
5887-90	(68¢) U.S. Flags						
	18.25 mm x 21 mm image	15.00(4)	.....	.....	.....	6.00	.....
5887	(68¢) Flag, Cloud Top & Bottom	.....	.....	.....	.....	1.60	.....
5888	(68¢) Flag, Blue Sky, Clouds Top	.....	.....	.....	.....	1.60	.....
5889	(68¢) Flag, Blue Sky Top, Cloud Bottom	.....	.....	.....	.....	1.60	.....
5890	(68¢) Flag, Dark Clouds . .	.....	.....	.....	.....	1.60	.....
5890b	same, double-sided bklt pane of 20	.....	.....	.....	.....	30.00	.....

5891

5892

5893

5894

5895

SCOTT NO.	DESCRIPTION	FIRST DAY COVERS SING	FIRST DAY COVERS PL. BLK.	MINT SHEET	PLATE BLOCK	UNUSED F/NH	USED
5891-95	(68¢) Horses	18.00(5)	.....	30.00(20)	17.00(10)	8.00(5)	.....
5891	(68¢) Horse, Brown Spots Facing Left	.....	.....	.....	.....	1.60	.....
5892	(68¢) Horse, White Blaze Facing Forward	.....	.....	.....	.....	1.60	.....
5893	(68¢) Horse, Arabian Facing Right	.....	.....	.....	.....	1.60	.....
5894	(68¢) Horse, Brown with Bridle	.....	.....	.....	.....	1.60	.....
5895	(68¢) Horse, Long White Mane	.....	.....	.....	.....	1.60	.....

5896

SHAKER DESIGN

5896a	*Meeting Room*	**5896g**	*Rocking Chair*
5896b	*Tannery*	**5896h**	*Bentwood Box Detail*
5896c	*Spinning Wheel*	**5896i**	*Heater Stove*
5896d	*Staircases*	**5896j**	*Cupboard, Oval Boxes*
5896e	*Dwelling House Hallway*	**5896k**	*Bentwood Boxes, Carriers*
5896f	*Silk Neckerchiefs*	**5896l**	*Cheese Baskets*

SCOTT NO.	DESCRIPTION	FIRST DAY COVERS SING	FIRST DAY COVERS PL. BLK.	MINT SHEET	PLATE BLOCK	UNUSED F/NH	USED
5896	(68¢) Shaker Design. . .	55.00(12)	.....	22.00(12)	.....	.....	.....

5897, 5902 · 5898, 5903 · 5899, 5904

5900, 5905 · 5901, 5906

SCOTT NO.	DESCRIPTION	FIRST DAY COVERS SING	FIRST DAY COVERS PL. BLK.	MINT SHEET	PLATE BLOCK	UNUSED F/NH	USED
5897	1¢ Fringed Tulip	3.00	....	1.00	0.80	0.25	0.25
5898	2¢ Daffodils.	3.00	....	1.25	1.00	0.25	0.25
5899	3¢ Peonies	3.00	....	1.50	1.20	0.30	0.30
5900	5¢ Red Tulips	3.00	....	2.00	1.30	0.30	0.30
5901	10¢ Poppies and Coneflowers	3.00	....	3.00	1.80	0.40	0.30
5902	1¢ Fringed Tulip, coil . .	3.00	....	....	....	0.25	0.25
	same, plate strip of 5 . .	....	....	....	2.00	....	....
5903	2¢ Daffodils, coil	3.00	....	....	....	0.25	0.25
	same, plate strip of 5 . .	....	....	....	2.00	....	....
5904	3¢ Peonies, coil	3.00	....	....	....	0.30	0.30
	same, plate strip of 5 . .	....	....	....	2.00	....	....
5905	5¢ Red Tulips, coil	3.00	....	....	....	0.30	0.30
	same, plate strip of 5 . .	....	....	....	2.50	....	....
5906	10¢ Poppies and Coneflowers, coil	3.00	....	....	....	0.40	0.30
	same, plate strip of 5 . .	....	....	....	3.00	....	....

5907

5908

SCOTT NO.	DESCRIPTION	FIRST DAY COVERS SING	FIRST DAY COVERS PL. BLK.	MINT SHEET	PLATE BLOCK	UNUSED F/NH	USED
5907	(73¢) Alex Trebek, Jeopardy	3.00	....	30.00(20)	7.00(4)	1.60	1.00
5908	(73¢) Hank Aaron	3.00	....	30.00(20)	7.00(4)	1.60	1.00

5909

5910

5911

5912

5913

5914

5915 · 5916 · 5917

5918

SCOTT NO.	DESCRIPTION	FIRST DAY COVERS SING	FIRST DAY COVERS PL. BLK.	MINT SHEET	PLATE BLOCK	UNUSED F/NH	USED
5909-18	(73¢) Dungeons and Dragons Game	55.00(10)	....	30.00(20)	17.00(10)	15.00(10)	....
5909	(73¢) Bronze Dragon and Blue Plesiosaur.	....	....	....	....	1.60	....
5910	(73¢) Five-Headed Tiamat	....	....	....	....	1.60	....
5911	(73¢) Character in Maze	....	....	....	....	1.60	....
5912	(73¢) Character in Blue Robe	....	....	....	....	1.60	....
5913	(73¢) Archlich Acererak Raising Army	....	....	....	....	1.60	....
5914	(73¢) Drizzt Do'Urden Holding Sword	....	....	....	....	1.60	....
5915	(73¢) Warrior Fighting Red Dragon	....	....	....	....	1.60	....
5916	(73¢) Character Holding Container Dragon's Blood	....	....	....	....	1.60	....
5917	(73¢) Death Knight Riding Nightmare	....	....	....	....	1.60	....
5918	(73¢) Purple Worm	....	....	....	....	1.60	....

5919

5920

SCOTT NO.	DESCRIPTION	FIRST DAY COVERS SING	FIRST DAY COVERS PL. BLK.	MINT SHEET	PLATE BLOCK	UNUSED F/NH	USED
5919-28	(73¢) Pinback Buttons .	55.00(10)	....	30.00(20)	17.00(10)	15.00(10)	....
5919	(73¢) Smile Button	....	....	....	....	1.60	....
5920	(73¢) Hello! Button	....	....	....	....	1.60	....

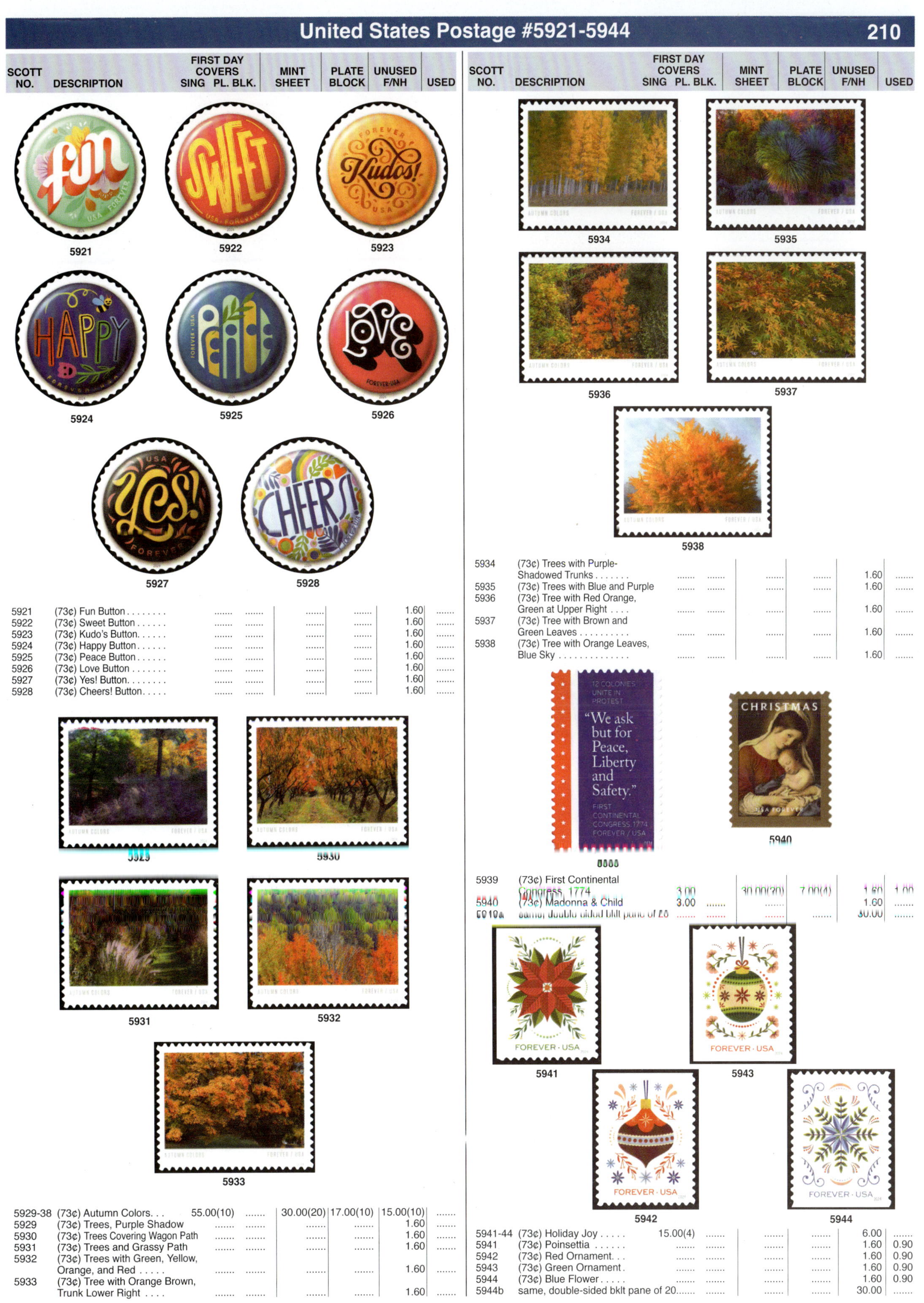

SCOTT NO.	DESCRIPTION	FIRST DAY COVERS SING	FIRST DAY COVERS PL. BLK.	MINT SHEET	PLATE BLOCK	UNUSED F/NH	USED
5921	(73¢) Fun Button	....	....	....	....	1.60	....
5922	(73¢) Sweet Button	....	....	....	....	1.60	....
5923	(73¢) Kudo's Button.	....	....	....	....	1.60	....
5924	(73¢) Happy Button	....	....	....	....	1.60	....
5925	(73¢) Peace Button	....	....	....	....	1.60	....
5926	(73¢) Love Button	....	....	....	....	1.60	....
5927	(73¢) Yes! Button.	....	....	....	....	1.60	....
5928	(73¢) Cheers! Button.	....	....	....	....	1.60	....
5929-38	(73¢) Autumn Colors. . .	55.00(10)	....	30.00(20)	17.00(10)	15.00(10)	....
5929	(73¢) Trees, Purple Shadow	....	....	....	....	1.60	....
5930	(73¢) Trees Covering Wagon Path	....	....	....	....	1.60	....
5931	(73¢) Trees and Grassy Path	....	....	....	....	1.60	....
5932	(73¢) Trees with Green, Yellow, Orange, and Red	....	....	....	....	1.60	....
5933	(73¢) Tree with Orange Brown, Trunk Lower Right	....	....	....	....	1.60	....
5934	(73¢) Trees with Purple-Shadowed Trunks	....	....	....	....	1.60	....
5935	(73¢) Trees with Blue and Purple	....	....	....	....	1.60	....
5936	(73¢) Tree with Red Orange, Green at Upper Right	....	....	....	....	1.60	....
5937	(73¢) Tree with Brown and Green Leaves	....	....	....	....	1.60	....
5938	(73¢) Tree with Orange Leaves, Blue Sky	....	....	....	....	1.60	....
5939	(73¢) First Continental Congress, 1774	3.00		30.00(20)	7.00(4)	1.60	1.00
5940	(73¢) Madonna & Child	3.00	....	....		1.60	....
5940a	same, double-sided bklt pane of 20	....	....	....	....	30.00	....
5941-44	(73¢) Holiday Joy	15.00(4)	....	....	....	6.00	....
5941	(73¢) Poinsettia	....	....	....	....	1.60	0.90
5942	(73¢) Red Ornament. . .	....	....	....	....	1.60	0.90
5943	(73¢) Green Ornament .	....	....	....	....	1.60	0.90
5944	(73¢) Blue Flower	....	....	....	....	1.60	0.90
5944b	same, double-sided bklt pane of 20......	....	....	....	....	30.00	....

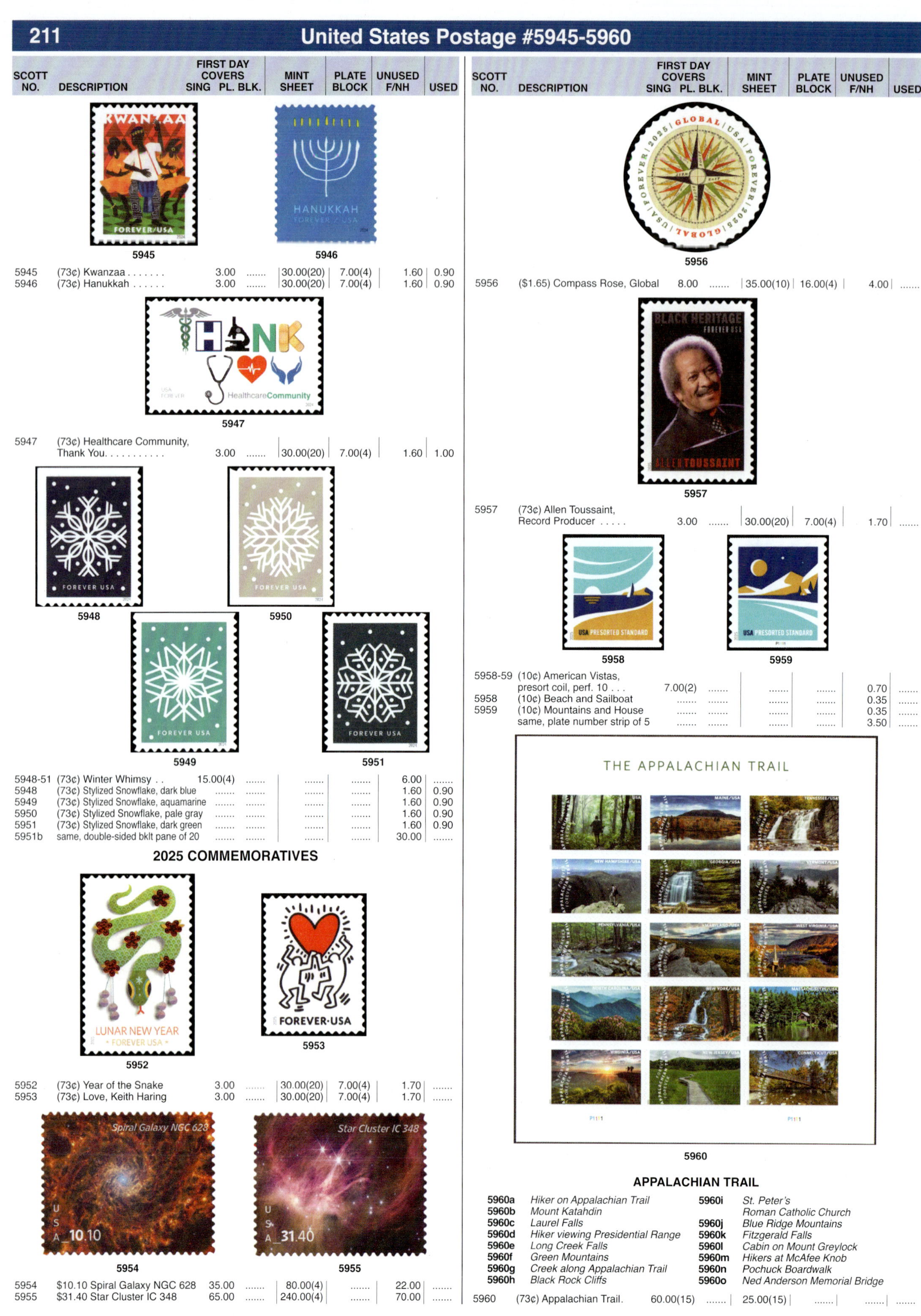

5945

5946

SCOTT NO.	DESCRIPTION	FIRST DAY COVERS SING	FIRST DAY COVERS PL. BLK.	MINT SHEET	PLATE BLOCK	UNUSED F/NH	USED
5945	(73¢) Kwanzaa	3.00	....	30.00(20)	7.00(4)	1.60	0.90
5946	(73¢) Hanukkah	3.00	....	30.00(20)	7.00(4)	1.60	0.90

5947

SCOTT NO.	DESCRIPTION	FIRST DAY COVERS SING	FIRST DAY COVERS PL. BLK.	MINT SHEET	PLATE BLOCK	UNUSED F/NH	USED
5947	(73¢) Healthcare Community, Thank You.	3.00	....	30.00(20)	7.00(4)	1.60	1.00

5948

5950

5949

5951

SCOTT NO.	DESCRIPTION	FIRST DAY COVERS SING	FIRST DAY COVERS PL. BLK.	MINT SHEET	PLATE BLOCK	UNUSED F/NH	USED
5948-51	(73¢) Winter Whimsy . .	15.00(4)	....	....	....	6.00	....
5948	(73¢) Stylized Snowflake, dark blue	....	....	....	....	1.60	0.90
5949	(73¢) Stylized Snowflake, aquamarine	....	....	....	....	1.60	0.90
5950	(73¢) Stylized Snowflake, pale gray	....	....	....	....	1.60	0.90
5951	(73¢) Stylized Snowflake, dark green	....	....	....	....	1.60	0.90
5951b	same, double-sided bklt pane of 20	....	....	....	....	30.00	....

2025 COMMEMORATIVES

5952

5953

SCOTT NO.	DESCRIPTION	FIRST DAY COVERS SING	FIRST DAY COVERS PL. BLK.	MINT SHEET	PLATE BLOCK	UNUSED F/NH	USED
5952	(73¢) Year of the Snake	3.00	....	30.00(20)	7.00(4)	1.70	....
5953	(73¢) Love, Keith Haring	3.00	....	30.00(20)	7.00(4)	1.70	....

5954

5955

SCOTT NO.	DESCRIPTION	FIRST DAY COVERS SING	FIRST DAY COVERS PL. BLK.	MINT SHEET	PLATE BLOCK	UNUSED F/NH	USED
5954	$10.10 Spiral Galaxy NGC 628	35.00	....	80.00(4)	....	22.00	....
5955	$31.40 Star Cluster IC 348	65.00	....	240.00(4)	....	70.00	....

5956

SCOTT NO.	DESCRIPTION	FIRST DAY COVERS SING	FIRST DAY COVERS PL. BLK.	MINT SHEET	PLATE BLOCK	UNUSED F/NH	USED
5956	($1.65) Compass Rose, Global	8.00	....	35.00(10)	16.00(4)	4.00	....

5957

SCOTT NO.	DESCRIPTION	FIRST DAY COVERS SING	FIRST DAY COVERS PL. BLK.	MINT SHEET	PLATE BLOCK	UNUSED F/NH	USED
5957	(73¢) Allen Toussaint, Record Producer	3.00	....	30.00(20)	7.00(4)	1.70	....

5958

5959

SCOTT NO.	DESCRIPTION	FIRST DAY COVERS SING	FIRST DAY COVERS PL. BLK.	MINT SHEET	PLATE BLOCK	UNUSED F/NH	USED
5958-59	(10¢) American Vistas, presort coil, perf. 10 . . .	7.00(2)	....	....	....	0.70	....
5958	(10¢) Beach and Sailboat	....	....	....	....	0.35	....
5959	(10¢) Mountains and House	....	....	....	....	0.35	....
	same, plate number strip of 5	....	....	....	....	3.50	....

5960

APPALACHIAN TRAIL

5960a	*Hiker on Appalachian Trail*	**5960i**	*St. Peter's Roman Catholic Church*
5960b	*Mount Katahdin*	**5960j**	*Blue Ridge Mountains*
5960c	*Laurel Falls*	**5960k**	*Fitzgerald Falls*
5960d	*Hiker viewing Presidential Range*	**5960l**	*Cabin on Mount Greylock*
5960e	*Long Creek Falls*	**5960m**	*Hikers at McAfee Knob*
5960f	*Green Mountains*	**5960n**	*Pochuck Boardwalk*
5960g	*Creek along Appalachian Trail*	**5960o**	*Ned Anderson Memorial Bridge*
5960h	*Black Rock Cliffs*		

SCOTT NO.	DESCRIPTION	FIRST DAY COVERS SING	FIRST DAY COVERS PL. BLK.	MINT SHEET	PLATE BLOCK	UNUSED F/NH	USED
5960	(73¢) Appalachian Trail.	60.00(15)	....	25.00(15)	....	....	....

5961

5962

5963

5964

5965

SCOTT NO.	DESCRIPTION	FIRST DAY COVERS SING	FIRST DAY COVERS PL. BLK.	MINT SHEET	PLATE BLOCK	UNUSED F/NH	USED
5961-65	(73¢) Freshwater Fishing Lures	20.00(5)	....	[illegible]	10.00(10)	[illegible]	....
5961	(73¢) Crankbait Lure. . .	....	....	....	....	1.70	....
5962	(73¢) Popper Lure	....	....	....	....	1.70	....
5963	(73¢) Spoon Lure	....	....	....	....	1.70	....
5964	(73¢) Spinner Lure	....	....	....	....	1.70	....
5965	(73¢) Wakebait Lure . . .	....	....	....	....	1.70	....

5966, 5973

5967, 5974

5968, 5975

5969, 5971

5970, 5972

SCOTT NO.	DESCRIPTION	FIRST DAY COVERS SING	FIRST DAY COVERS PL. BLK.	MINT SHEET	PLATE BLOCK	UNUSED F/NH	USED
5966-70	(56¢) Vibrant Leaves, die cut 11¼ x 11	20.00(5)	....	25.00(20)	14.00(10)	7.00(5)	....
5966	(56¢) Aspen Leaf	....	....	....	....	1.30	....
5967	(56¢) Sassafras Leaf . .	....	....	....	....	1.30	....
5968	(56¢) Oak Leaf	....	....	....	....	1.30	....
5969	(56¢) Maple Leaf	....	....	....	....	1.30	....
5970	(56¢) Sweetgum Leaf . .	....	....	....	....	1.30	....
5971-75	(56¢) Vibrant Leaves, postcard coil, die cut 9½	20.00(5)	....	....	....	7.00(5)	....
	same, plate number strip of 5	....	....	....	....	10.00	....
5971	(56¢) Maple Leaf	....	....	....	....	1.30	....
5972	(56¢) Sweetgum Leaf . .	....	....	....	....	1.30	....
5973	(56¢) Aspen Leaf	....	....	....	....	1.30	....
5974	(56¢) Sassafras Leaf . .	....	....	....	....	1.30	....
5975	(56¢) Oak Leaf	....	....	....	....	1.30	....

5976

SCOTT NO.	DESCRIPTION	FIRST DAY COVERS SING	FIRST DAY COVERS PL. BLK.	MINT SHEET	PLATE BLOCK	UNUSED F/NH	USED
5976	(73¢) Betty White, Actress	4.00	....	30.00(20)	7.00(4)	1.70	....

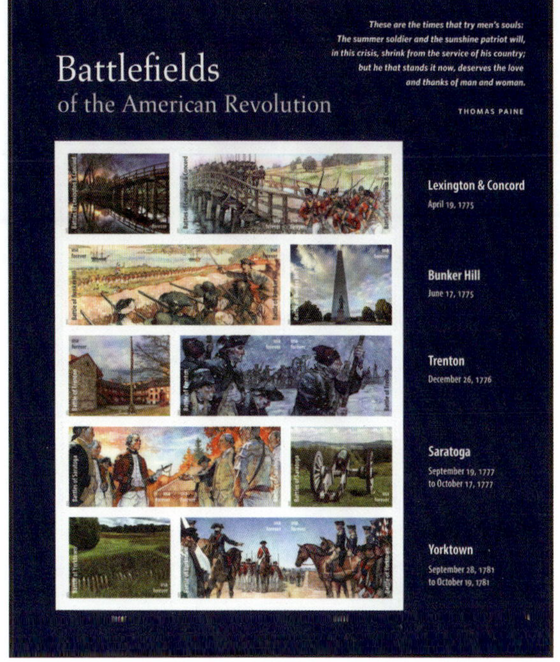

5977

BATTLEFIELDS OF THE AMERICAN REVOLUTION

5977a *Replica of the Old North Bridge*
5977b *American militia members on Old North Bridge*
5977c *British troops withdrawing, Old North Bridge*
5977d *Two ships in harbor, British troops*
5977e *American officer William Prescott with sword*
5977f *Bunker Hill Monument*
5977g *Old Barracks Museum*
5977h *General George Washington, Delaware River*
5977i *Boatmen guiding across the Delaware River*
5977j *British Lieutenant General John Burgoyne*
5977k *American General Horatio Gates*
5977l *Replica of British howitzer*
5977m *Reconstructions of British battlefield redoubts*
5977n *Comte de Rochambeau, British Brigadier General Charles O'Hara*
5977o *Washington, Major General Benjamin Lincoln, Marquis de Lafayette, Major General Friedrich von Steuben*

SCOTT NO.	DESCRIPTION	FIRST DAY COVERS SING	FIRST DAY COVERS PL. BLK.	MINT SHEET	PLATE BLOCK	UNUSED F/NH	USED
5977	(73¢) Battlefields of the American Revolution . .	60.00(15)	....	25.00(15)	....	....	....

5978

5979

5980

5981

SCOTT NO.	DESCRIPTION	FIRST DAY COVERS SING	FIRST DAY COVERS PL. BLK.	MINT SHEET	PLATE BLOCK	UNUSED F/NH	USED
5978-81	(73¢) Powwows	15.00(4)	....	30.00(20)	16.00(8)	7.00	....
5978	(73¢) Crow Hop Dance.	....	....	....	....	1.70	....
5979	(73¢) Women's Traditional Dance	....	....	....	....	1.70	....
5980	(73¢) Women's Fancy Shawl Dance	....	....	....	....	1.70	....
5981	(73¢) Men's Hoop Dance	....	....	....	....	1.70	....

SCOTT NO.	DESCRIPTION	FIRST DAY COVERS SING	PL. BLK.	MINT SHEET	PLATE BLOCK	UNUSED F/NH	USED
5982-91	(73¢) Dahlias, coil, die cut 10	....	....	....	....	16.00(10)	....
	same, plate number strip of 11	....	....	....	....	20.00	....
5982	(73¢) Pale Yellow Dahlia	....	....	....	....	1.60	....
5983	(73¢) Lilac Dahlia	....	....	....	....	1.60	....
5984	(73¢) Red and Yellow Dahlia	....	....	....	....	1.60	....
5985	(73¢) Yellow and Pink Dahlia	....	....	....	....	1.60	....
5986	(73¢) Dark Red Dahlia .	....	....	....	....	1.60	....
5987	(73¢) Lilac Dahlia	....	....	....	....	1.60	....
5988	(73¢) White Dahlia	....	....	....	....	1.60	....
5989	(73¢) White and Lilac Dahlia	....	....	....	....	1.60	....
5990	(73¢) Pink and White Dahlia	....	....	....	....	1.60	....
5991	(73¢) Lilac and White Dahlia	....	....	....	....	1.60	....

SCOTT NO.	DESCRIPTION	FIRST DAY COVERS SING	PL. BLK.	MINT SHEET	PLATE BLOCK	UNUSED F/NH	USED
5992-6001	(73¢) Dahlias, die cut 11 x 10¾	....	....	....	....	16.00(10)	....
5992	(73¢) Pale Yellow Dahlia	....	....	....	....	1.60	....
5993	(73¢) Lilac Dahlia	....	....	....	....	1.60	....
5994	(73¢) Red and Yellow Dahlia	....	....	....	....	1.60	....
5995	(73¢) Yellow and Pink Dahlia	....	....	....	....	1.60	....
5996	(73¢) White and Lilac Dahlia	....	....	....	....	1.60	....
5997	(73¢) Lilac Dahlia	....	....	....	....	1.60	....
5998	(73¢) White Dahlia	....	....	....	....	1.60	....
5999	(73¢) Dark Red Dahlia .	....	....	....	....	1.60	....
6000	(73¢) Pink and White Dahlia	....	....	....	....	1.60	....
6001	(73¢) Lilac and White Dahlia	....	....	....	....	1.60	....
6001b	same, double-sided bklt pane of 20	....	....	....	....	30.00	....

SCOTT NO.	DESCRIPTION	FIRST DAY COVERS SING	PL. BLK.	MINT SHEET	PLATE BLOCK	UNUSED F/NH	USED
6002	(73¢) Goodnight Moon .	30.00(8)	....	25.00(16)	....	....	....
6002a	(73¢) Young Rabbit in Bed	....	....	....	....	1.70	....
6002b	(73¢) Painting of the Three Bears	....	....	....	....	1.70	....
6002c	(73¢) Fireplace	....	....	....	....	1.70	....
6002d	(73¢) Painting of Cow Jumping Over the Moon	....	....	....	....	1.70	....
6002e	(73¢) Table, Lamp, Bowl, Comb, and Brush	....	....	....	....	1.70	....
6002f	(73¢) Dollhouse, Bookshelf, and Toys	....	....	....	....	1.70	....
6002g	(73¢) Rabbit in Rocking Chair	....	....	....	....	1.70	....
6002h	(73¢) Socks and Mittens on Drying Rack, Moon. . . .	....	....	....	....	1.70	....

SCOTT NO.	DESCRIPTION	FIRST DAY COVERS SING	PL. BLK.	MINT SHEET	PLATE BLOCK	UNUSED F/NH	USED
6003	(73¢) U.S. Army, 250th	4.00	....	30.00(20)	7.00(4)	1.70	....
6004	(73¢) U.S. Navy, 250th .	4.00	....	30.00(20)	7.00(4)	1.70	....
6005	(73¢) U.S. Marine Corps, 250th	4.00	....	30.00(20)	7.00(4)	1.70	....

6006 6007 6008

6009 6010

6011 6012 6013

6014 6015

SCOTT NO.	DESCRIPTION	FIRST DAY COVERS SING	FIRST DAY COVERS PL. BLK.	MINT SHEET	PLATE BLOCK	UNUSED F/NH	USED
6006-15	(73¢) Baby Wild Animals	55.00(10)	....	....	....	16.00(10)	....
6006	(73¢) Fox	....	....	....	....	1.70	....
6007	(73¢) Owls	....	....	....	....	1.70	....
6008	(73¢) Deer	....	....	....	....	1.70	....
6009	(73¢) Seal.	....	....	....	....	1.70	....
6010	(73¢) Rabbit	....	....	....	....	1.70	....
6011	(73¢) [illegible]					1.70	
6012	(73¢) Bear.	....	....	....	....	1.70	....
6013	(73¢) Skunk	....	....	....	....	1.70	....
6014	(73¢) Bobcat.	....	....	....	....	1.70	....
6015	(73¢) Chipmunks	[illegible]	....	....	....	1.70	....
6015b	same, double-sided bklt pane of 20	....	....	....	....	30.00	....

6016, 6017

6018, 6020

6019, 6021

SCOTT NO.	DESCRIPTION	FIRST DAY COVERS SING	FIRST DAY COVERS PL. BLK.	MINT SHEET	PLATE BLOCK	UNUSED F/NH	USED
6016	(73¢) U.S. Flag, micro at LR corner of flag field	4.00	....	30.00(20)	7.00(4)	1.70	....
6017	(73¢) U.S. Flag, coil, die cut 9½, micro at LR of flag field.	4.00	....	....	....	1.70	....
	same, plate number strip of 5	....	....	....	....	10.00	....
6018	(73¢) U.S. Flag, coil, die cut 10, on large backing paper.	4.00	....	....	....	1.70	....
	same, plate number strip of 5	....	....	....	....	10.00	....
6019	(73¢) U.S. Flag, coil, die cut 11, micro bottom flag stripe	4.00	....	....	....	1.70	....
	same, plate number strip of 5	....	....	....	....	10.00	....
6020	(73¢) U.S. Flag, micro at LR of flag field.	4.00	....	....	....	1.70	....
	same, double-sided bklt pane of 20	....	....	....	....	30.00	....
6021	(73¢) U.S. Flag, micro bottom flag stripe	4.00	....	....	....	1.70	....
	same, double-sided bklt pane of 20	....	....	....	....	30.00	....

6022

SCOTT NO.	DESCRIPTION	FIRST DAY COVERS SING	FIRST DAY COVERS PL. BLK.	MINT SHEET	PLATE BLOCK	UNUSED F/NH	USED
6022	(73¢) Barbara Bush, First Lady	4.00	....	30.00(20)	7.00(4)	1.70	....

SEMI-POSTAL

B1 (1998 year date)

B2

B3

SCOTT NO.	DESCRIPTION	FIRST DAY COVERS SING	FIRST DAY COVERS PL. BLK.	MINT SHEET	PLATE BLOCK	UNUSED F/NH	USED
	1998						
B1	(32¢ + 8¢) Breast Cancer	2.25	5.50	30.00(20)	5.50	1.50	.50
	2002						
B2	(34¢ + 11¢) Heroes of 2001	2.50	5.50	30.00(20)	5.50	1.50	.50
	2003						
B3	(37¢ + 8¢) Stop Family Violence	2.50	5.50	30.00(20)	5.50	1.50	.50

B4

SCOTT NO.	DESCRIPTION	FIRST DAY COVERS SING	FIRST DAY COVERS PL. BLK.	MINT SHEET	PLATE BLOCK	UNUSED F/NH	USED
	2011						
B4	(44¢ + 11¢) Save Vanishing Species	2.70	....	35.00(20)	7.00	2.00	.65

B5 (2014 year date)

B6

SCOTT NO.	DESCRIPTION	FIRST DAY COVERS SING	FIRST DAY COVERS PL. BLK.	MINT SHEET	PLATE BLOCK	UNUSED F/NH	USED
	2015						
B5	(49¢ + 11¢) Breast Cancer Semi-Postal (2014 date)	2.75	....	35.00(20)	7.00	2.00	.75
	2017						
B6	(49¢ + 11¢) Alzheimer's	2.75	....	35.00(20)	7.00	2.00	.90

B7

SCOTT NO.	DESCRIPTION	FIRST DAY COVERS SING	FIRST DAY COVERS PL. BLK.	MINT SHEET	PLATE BLOCK	UNUSED F/NH	USED
	2019						
B7	(55¢ + 10¢) Healing PTSD	2.75	....	35.00(20)	6.50	1.50	.90

Showgard® MOUNTS

All showgard mounts are only available with black backgrounds.

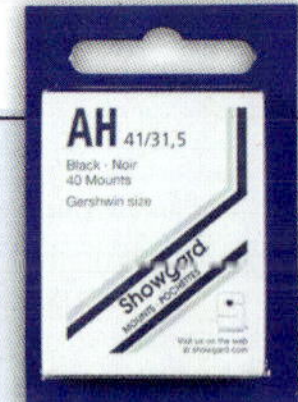

Cut Style

Stock No. Showgard	Stock No. Harris	Pieces/ Pack	Description	Retail
AH41/31	9SGD10	40	U.S. Semi Jumbo Gershwin, etc.	$4.95
AV31/41	9SGD3184	40	Legends of the West	$4.95
C50/31	9SGD1	40	U.S. Jumbo Singles Horizontal	$4.95
CV31/50	9SGD2	40	U.S. Jumbo Singles Vertical	$4.95
DH52/36	9SGD3081	30	U.S. Duck Stamps	$4.95
E22/25	9SGD5	40	U.S. Regular Issues	$4.95
EH25/22	9SGD6	40	U.S. Regular Issues Horizontal	$4.95
J40/25	9SGD3	40	U.S. Comm. Horizontal	$4.95
JV25/40	9SGD4	40	U.S. Comm. Vertical	$4.95
N40/27	9SGD9	40	United Nations	$4.95
S31/31	9SGD3329	40	Celebrate the Century	$4.95
T25/27	9SGD7	40	U.S. Famous Americans	$4.95
U33/27	9SGD8	40	U.N. and Germany	$4.95

Plate Blocks & Covers

Stock No. Showgard	Stock No. Harris	Pieces/ Pack	Description	Retail
57/55	9SGD13	25	Regular issue U.S. Plate Blocks	$9.95
67/25	9SGD2341	40	U.S. Coil Strips of three	$9.95
105/57	9SGD15	20	U.S. Giori Press. Modern. Plate Block	$9.95
106/55	9SGD14	20	U.S. 3¢, 4¢ Comm. Plate Block	$9.95
127/70	9SGD16	10	U.S. Jumbo Issues Plate Block	$9.95
140/89	9SGD2342	10	Postcards	$9.95
165/94	9SGD17	10	First Day Covers	$9.95

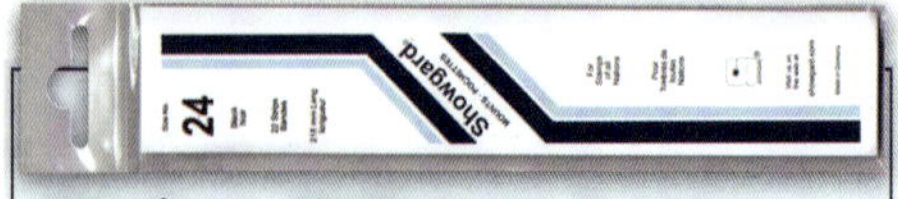

Strips 215mm Long

Stock No. Showgard	Stock No. Harris	Pieces/ Pack	Description	Retail
20	9SGD18	22	Mini Stamps U.S., etc.	$11.95
22	9SGD19	22	Narrow U.S. Airs	$11.95
24	9SGD20	22	U.K. and Canada Early U.S.	$11.95
25	9SGD21	22	U.S. Comm. and Regular Issue	$11.95
27	9SGD22	22	U.S. Famous Americans and U.N.	$11.95
28	9SGD23	22	Switzerland, Liechtenstein	$11.95
30	9SGD24	22	U.S. Jamestown, Foreign	$11.95
31	9SGD25	22	U.S. Squares and Semi-Jumbo	$11.95
33	9SGD26	22	GB Issues, Misc. Foreign	$11.95
36	9SGD27	15	Duck Stamps, Misc. Foreign	$11.95
39	9SGD28	15	U.S. Magsaysay, Misc. Foreign	$11.95
41	9SGD29	15	U.S. Vertical Comm. Israel Tabs	$11.95
44	9SGD30	15	U.S. Hatteras Block of four	$11.95
48	9SGD31	15	Canada Reg. Issue and Comm. Blks.	$11.95
50	9SGD32	15	U.S. Plain Blocks of four	$11.95
52	9SGD33	15	France Paintings	$11.95
57	9SGD34	15	U.S. Comm. Plate Blocks (4)	$11.95
61	9SGD35	15	Souvenir Sheets, Tab Singles	$11.95

Strips 240mm Long

Stock No. Showgard	Stock No. Harris	Pieces/ Pack	Description	Retail
63	9SGD36	10	U.S. Squares, Plain Blocks (4)	$16.50
66	9SGD37	10	Israel Plate Blocks, etc.	$16.50
68	9SGD38	10	Can. Plate Blocks, $1 Fundy, etc.	$16.50
74	9SGD39	10	U.N. Inscription Blocks (4)	$16.50
80	9SGD40	10	U.S. Comm. Plain Blocks (4)	$16.50
82	9SGD41	10	U.N. Chagall SS, Canada Plate Blks	$16.50
84	9SGD42	10	Israel, Tab Blocks, etc.	$16.50
89	9SGD43	10	U.N. Inscription Blocks (6)	$16.50
100	9SGD44	7	U.S. Squares - Plate Blocks	$16.50
120	9SGD45	7	Miniature Sheets	$16.50

Strips 264mm Long

Stock No. Showgard	Stock No. Harris	Pieces/ Pack	Description	Retail
70	9SGD46	10	U.S. Jumbo Plate Blocks	$18.95
91	9SGD47	10	GB Souvenir Sheets	$18.95
105	9SGD48	10	GB Blocks, Covers, Cards	$18.95
107	9SGD49	10	U.S. Plate No. Strip (20)	$18.95
111	9SGD54	5	U.S. Floating No. Plate Strips (20)	$18.95
127	9SGD55	5	U.S. UPU and LBJ Plate Blocks (15)	$18.95
137	9SGD56	5	GB Coronations, U.N., SS	$18.95
158	9SGD57	5	Souvenir Sheets, Apollo Soyuz, Plate Block	$18.95
175	9SGD2471	5	U.S. Sheets Love, Christmas	$18.95
188	9SGD2892	5	Marilyn Monroe Miniature Sheets	$18.95
198	9SGD2893	5	Legends of the West Miniature Sheets	$18.95

Assortments & Mount Accessories

Stock No. Showgard	Stock No. Harris	Pieces/ Pack	Description	Retail
Group AB	9SGD52	11	Souvenir Sheets	$11.95
265/231	9SGD53	5	Full Sheets and Souvenir Cards	$23.50
Group 94	9SGD2650	5	1994 Souvenir Sheets-Clear	$10.25
MPK	9SGD50	12	Assortment #22-41	$8.95
MPK II	9SGD51	15	Assortment #76-171	$37.95
US3	9SGD12	75	Indexed Tray and Strip Set Assortment (#22-52)	$49.95
507	9SGD2112	1	Desert Magic II Drying Book 8.5" x 11"	$13.50

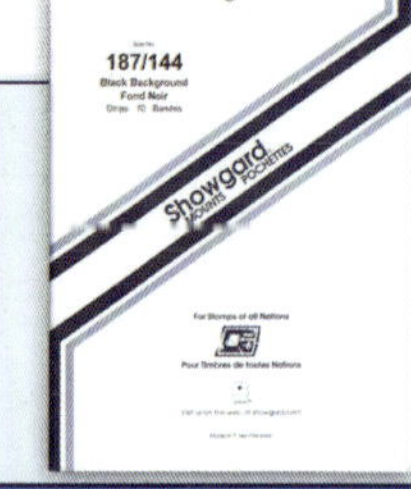

Blocks

Stock No. Showgard	Stock No. Harris	Pieces/ Pack	Description	Retail
111/91	9SGD2756	6	Columbian Souvenir Sheets	$9.25
120/207	9SGD2113	4	Ameripex Presidential Sheets	$10.95
187/144	9SGD61	10	U.N. Flags Sheetlets	$25.95
191/229	9SGD3330	5	Celebrate the Century Sheets (5)	$15.95
192/201	9SGD3071	5	Legends of the West Sheet	$15.75
204/153	9SGD62	5	U.S. Bicentennial and W. Plains SS	$15.95
229/131	9SGD2713	5	WWII Souvenir Sheets	$17.25
260/25	9SGD2382	25	U.S. Coil Strips (up to 11 stamps)	$14.25
260/40	9SGD58	10	U.S. Postal People Full Strip	$11.25
260/46	9SGD3277	10	U.S. Vending Booklets	$12.50
260/55	9SGD59	10	U.S. 13¢ Eagle Full Strip	$12.50
260/59	9SGD60	10	U.S. Double Press Regular Issue Strip (20)	$14.50
Group Pac 97	9SGD3274	7	Pacific 97 Issues	$5.75
Trans-Miss	9SGD3341	11	Trans-Miss. Reissues	$5.75
Space	9SGD4122	5	Space Exploration	$7.25

Accommodation Range Mount

Stock No. Showgard	Stock No. Harris	Description	Retail
76	9SGD4119	Bright Eyes (Top), Challenger Shuttle Plate Blocks	$13.25
96	9SGD3010	Flowering Trees, Christmas Plate Blocks	$13.25
109	9SGD3122	109 Strip	$13.25
115	9SGD3012	115 Strip	$19.00
117	9SGD4111	117 Strip	$19.00
121	9SGD4112	121 Strip	$19.00
131	9SGD2746	131 Strip	$19.00
135	9SGD4113	135 Strip	$19.00
139	9SGD4114	139 Strip	$19.00
143	9SGD4115	143 Strip	$19.00
147	9SGD3123	Cinco De Mayo, Miniature Sheet	$19.00
151	9SGD4116	Automobiles, Hanukkah, Miniature Sheets	$19.00
163	9SGD3011	Kwanzaa Miniature Sheet	$19.00
167	9SGD4117	IA, TN, Bright Eyes, Miniature Sheets	$19.00
181	9SGD4120	All Aboard	$19.00
201	9SGD3230	World of Dinosaurs, Miniature Sheet	$19.00
215	9SGD4121	Arctic Animals	$19.00
171	9SGD4118	Helping Children	$19.00

Stamp Tongs

Stock No. Showgard	Stock No. Harris	Pieces/ Pack	Description	Retail
904	9SGD2570	1	Professional Round Tip	$11.95
905	9SGD2571	1	Beginner Round Tip	$5.95
907	9SGD95	1	Professional Angled Tip	$11.95

H.E. Harris — Call to order 1·800·546·2995 Or shop at heharris.com

In July of 2012, the United States Postal Service released the first self-adhesive imperforate (no die-cuts) press sheets. This section covers the imperforate press sheets, mint sheets or booklet panes, plate blocks or se-tentants, and mint singles from the press sheets.

2012

SCOTT NO.	DESCRIPTION	IMPERF PRESS SHEET	IMPERF MINT SHEET OR BOOKLET	IMPERF PLATE BLOCK	IMPERF UNUSED F/NH
4694	(45¢) Ted Williams	200.00(120)	45.00(20)	19.50(8)	3.00
4695	(45¢) Larry Doby.	200.00(120)	45.00(20)	19.50(8)	3.00
4696	(45¢) Willie Stargell . . .	200.00(120)	45.00(20)	19.50(8)	3.00
4697	(45¢) Joe DiMaggio . . .	200.00(120)	45.00(20)	19.50(8)	3.00
4694-97a	(45¢) Major League Baseball	350.00(120)	70.00 (20)	35.00(8)	15.00
4703	(45¢) War of 1812 Bicentennial	200.00(100)	55.00(20)	9.00(4)	3.00
4704	(45¢) Purple Heart	100.00(60)	50.00(20)	9.00(4)	3.00
4710	(45¢) Earthscapes	750.00(135)	70.00(15)	....	....
4711c	(45¢) Holy Family & Donkey	375.00(200)	45.00(20)	....	2.25
	same, 3 convertible panes of 20	130.00(60)	45.00(20)	....	....
4712-15	(45¢) Christmas Santa & Sleigh	400.00(200)	45.00(20)	....	8.00
	same, 3 convertible panes of 20	130.00(60)	45.00(20)	....	....
4716	(45¢) Lady Bird Johnson	375.00(96)	30.00(6)	....	....

2013

SCOTT NO.	DESCRIPTION	IMPERF PRESS SHEET	IMPERF MINT SHEET OR BOOKLET	IMPERF PLATE BLOCK	IMPERF UNUSED F/NH
4721	(45¢) Emancipation Proclamation	300.00(200)	40.00(20)	9.00(4)	2.25
4726	(45¢) Chinese New Year	150.00(108)	25.00(12)	....	2.25
4727-30	33¢ Apples	250.00(200)	30.00(20)	7.25(4)	7.00
4735	66¢ Wedding Cake. . . .	900.00(200)	90.00(20)	15.00(4)	4.00
4736	66¢ Spicebush Swallowtail	550.00(200)	60.00(20)	9.00(4)	3.25
4737	86¢ Tufted Puffins.	300.00(120)	75.00(20)	15.00(4)	4.25
4740	($1.10) Earth Global . . .	[illegible]	100.00(20)	20.00(4)	6.00
4741	(46¢) Envelope with wax seal	300.00(1[illegible]0)	[illegible]	[illegible](4)	[illegible]
4742	(46¢) Rosa Parks	450.00(200)	55.00(20)	6.75(4)	2.25
4743-47	(46¢) Muscle Cars	500.00(200)	55.00(20)	22.00(10)	10.00
4748	(46¢) Modern Art in America	300.00(60)	80.00(12)	....	....
4750-53	(46¢) La Florida	450.00(160)	65.00(16)	11.00(4)	10.00
4764	(46¢) Where Dreams Blossom	300.00(160)	45.00(20)	9.00(4)	2.75
4765	66¢ Wedding Flowers and "Yes I Do"	400.00(180)	50.00(20)	12.00(4)	3.25
4786	(46¢) Lydia Mendoza . .	175.00(200)	30.00(16)	....	2.25
4787-88	(46¢) Civil War	200.00(72)	45.00(12)	....	6.00
4789	(46¢) Johnny Cash	185.00(128)	30.00(16)	....	2.25
4790	(46¢) West Virginia Statehood	300.00(200)	35.00(20)	9.50(4)	2.25
4791-95	(46¢) New England Lighthouses	350.00(120)	55.00(20)	22.50(10)	11.00
4800	(46¢) EID	275.00(160)	45.00(20)	9.50(4)	2.25
4801	(46¢) Made in America .	350.00(60)	85.00(12)	....	....
4803	(46¢) Althea Gibson . . .	400.00(200)	45.00(20)	9.50(4)	2.25
4804	(46¢) 1963 March on Washington	375.00(200)	35.00(20)	9.50(4)	2.25
4805	(46¢) 1812 Battle of Lake Erie	150.00(120)	30.00(20)	....	2.25
4806	$2 Inverted Jenny.	400.00(36)	80.00(6)	....	14.00
4807	(46¢) Ray Charles	275.00(144)	40.00(16)	....	2.25
4813	(46¢) Holy Family & Donkey	475.00(200)	45.00(20)	9.50(4)	2.25
4814	($1.10) Christmas Wreath	225.00(60)	45.00(20)	15.00(4)	4.25
4815a	(46¢) Virgin & Child, convertible booklet of 20.	350.00(160)	40.00(20)	....	2.25
4816a	(46¢) Poinsettia, convertible booklet of 20.	325.00(160)	50.00(20)	....	2.25
4817-20	(46¢) Gingerbread Houses, convertible booklet of 20	400.00(160)	50.00(20)	....	9.50
4822-23	(46¢) Medal of Honor . .	100.00(60)	50.00(20)	9.50(4)	9.00
4824	(46¢) Hanukkah	[illegible]	[illegible]	[illegible]	[illegible]
4825-44	(46¢) Harry Potter.	400.00(120)	....	....	....
4845	(46¢) Kwanzaa	180.00(160)	35.00(20)	9.50(4)	2.25

2014

SCOTT NO.	DESCRIPTION	IMPERF PRESS SHEET	IMPERF MINT SHEET OR BOOKLET	IMPERF PLATE BLOCK	IMPERF UNUSED F/NH
4822a-4823a	(49¢) Medal of Honor, dated 2014	100.00(60)	45.00(20)	9.50(4)	9.00
4846	(46¢) Chinese New Year	195.00(120)	30.00(12)	....	2.25
4847	(46¢) Love	350.00(120)	50.00(20)	9.50(4)	2.25
4856	(29¢) Shirley Chisholm .	300.00(160)	50.00(20)	9.50(4)	2.25
4859	70¢ Great Spangled Fritillary	580.00(200)	70.00(20)	10.00(4)	3.75
4860	21¢ Abraham Lincoln . .	60.00(60)	30.00(20)	4.50(4)	1.50
4862-65	(49¢) Winter Flowers, convertible booklet of 20	350.00(160)	35.00(20)	....	8.00
4866	91¢ Ralph Ellison	525.00(200)	70.00(20)	15.00(4)	4.00
4873	$19.95 USS Arizona Memorial	1600.00(30)	600.00(10)	220.00(4)	60.00
4879	70¢ Alfred "Chief" Anderson	350.00(160)	50.00(20)	9.50(4)	3.25
4880	(49¢) Jimi Hendrix	300.00(144)	40.00(16)	....	2.25
4882-91	(49¢) Songbirds, convertible booklet of 20	450.00(160)	50.00(20)	....	25.00
4892	(49¢) Charlton Heston .	225.00(180)	35.00(20)	9.50(4)	2.25
4893	($1.15) Map of Sea Surface Temperatures	200.00(50)	50.00(10)	18.00(4)	4.00
4898-4905	(49¢) Circus Posters. . .	250.00(96)	50.00(16)	....	18.00(8)
4906	(49¢) Harvey Milk	525.00(240)	50.00(20)	9.50(4)	2.25
4907	(49¢) Nevada Statehood	380.00(240)	35.00(20)	9.50(4)	2.25
4908-09	(49¢) Hot Rods, convert. bklt of 20	280.00(160)	55.00(20)	....	5.00
4910-11	(49¢) Civil War	150.00(72)	35.00(12)	....	8.00
4912-15	(49¢) Farmer's Market .	200.00(100)	50.00(20)	17.50(8)	11.00
4916	(49¢) Janis Joplin	280.00(144)	50.00(16)	....	2.25
4917-20	(49¢) Hudson River School, convertible booklet of 20	150.00(80)	50.00(20)	....	9.50
4921	(49¢) Ft. McHenry, War of 1812	125.00(100)	35.00(20)	....	2.25

2014, continued

SCOTT NO.	DESCRIPTION	IMPERF PRESS SHEET	IMPERF MINT SHEET OR BOOKLET	IMPERF PLATE BLOCK	IMPERF UNUSED F/NH
4922-26	(49¢) Celebrity Chefs . .	280.00(180)	35.00(20)	25.00(10)	12.00
4927	$5.75 Glade Creek Grist Mill	950.00(60)	180.00(10)	90.00(4)	22.25
4928-35	(49¢) Batman	380.00(180)	55.00(20)	....	30.00(8)
4936	($1.15) Silver Bells Wreath	250.00(60)	55.00(10)	18.00(4)	4.50
4937-40	(49¢) Winter Fun, convert. bklt of 20.	225.00(120)	55.00(20)	....	9.50
4945	(49¢) Magi, convert. bklt of 20	450.00(160)	55.00(20)	....	2.25
4946-49	(49¢) Rudolph, convert. bklt of 20	250.00(120)	55.00(20)	....	9.50
4950-51	(49¢) Wilt Chamberlain.	190.00(144)	40.00(18)	9.50(4)	4.50

2015

SCOTT NO.	DESCRIPTION	IMPERF PRESS SHEET	IMPERF MINT SHEET OR BOOKLET	IMPERF PLATE BLOCK	IMPERF UNUSED F/NH
4952	(49¢) Battle of New Orleans	125.00(100)	35.00(10)	......	2.25
4953	$1 Patriotic Waves	350.00(140)	35.00(10)	16.00(4)	4.00
4954	$2 Patriotic Waves	480.00(100)	60.00(10)	30.00(4)	8.00
4955-56	(49¢) Hearts Forever . .	230.00(60)	35.00(20)	9.50(4)	5.00
4957	(49¢) Chinese New Year	190.00(144)	25.00(12)	....	2.25
4958	(49¢) Robert Robinson Taylor	150.00(120)	45.00(20)	9.50(4)	2.25
4959	(49¢) Rose & Heart . . .	950.00(240)	105.00(20)	9.50(4)	2.25
4960	70¢ Tulip & Heart	1075.00(240)	90.00(20)	10.00(4)	3.75
4964-67	(49¢) Water Lilies, convertible booklet of 20.	580.00(240)	55.00(20)	....	9.50
4968-72	(49¢) Art of Martin Ramirez	400.00(240)	40.00(20)	20.00(10)	12.00
4978	(49¢) From Me To You .	500.00(240)	45.00(20)	20.00(10)	2.25
4979	(49¢) Maya Angelou . . .	225.00(96)	30.00(20)	9.50(4)	2.25
4980-81	(49¢) Civil War	1000.00(72)	235.00(12)	....	35.00
4982-85	(49¢) Gifts of Friendship	180.00(72)	35.00(12)	....	....
4986	(49¢) Special Olympics World Games	100.00(80)	35.00(20)	9.50(4)	2.25
4987	(49¢) Forget-Me-Nots Missing Children.	150.00(120)	35.00(20)	9.50(4)	2.25
4988a	(49¢) Medal of Honor, strip of 3, dated 2015 . .	100.00(72)	50.00(24)	12.00(6)	9.00
4989	(22¢) Emperor Penguins	150.00(200)	15.00(20)	5.00(4)	1.25
4991-94	(35¢) Coastal Birds. . . .	225.00(200)	30.00(20)	5.50(4)	5.00
4999	(71¢) Eastern Tiger Swallowtail	300.00(120)	55.00(20)	12.00(4)	3.00
5003	(93¢) Flannery O'Connor	300.00(120)	60.00(20)	15.00(4)	3.25
5004-07	(49¢) Summer Harvest, convertible bklt of 20. . .	300.00(160)	45.00(20)	....	9.50
5008	(49¢) Coast Guard	225.00(120)	45.00(20)	9.50(4)	2.25
5009	(49¢) Elvis Presley	350.00(144)	35.00(20)	....	2.25
5010-11	(49¢) 2016 World Stamp Show	200.00(120)	50.00(20)	9.50(4)	5.00
5012	(49¢) Ingrid Bergman . .	380.00(180)	45.00(20)	9.50(4)	2.25
5020	(49¢) Paul Newman . . .	160.00(120)	40.00(20)	9.50(4)	2.25
5021-30	(49¢) Charlie Brown, convertible booklet of 20.	470.00(160)	50.00(20)	....	25.00
5031-34	(49¢) Geometric Snowflakes, convertible booklet of 20	250.00(120)	50.00(20)	....	9.50

2016

SCOTT NO.	DESCRIPTION	IMPERF PRESS SHEET	IMPERF MINT SHEET OR BOOKLET	IMPERF PLATE BLOCK	IMPERF UNUSED F/NH
5036	(49¢) Quilled Paper Heart	400.00(200)	45.00(20)	9.50(4)	2.25
5040	$6.45 La Cueva del Indio	950.00(60)	190.00(10)	85.00(4)	20.00
5041	$22.95 Columbia River Gorge	6000.00(30)	2500.00(10)	500.00(4)	225.00
5042-51	(49¢) Botanical Art, convertible bklt of 20.	1500.00(160)	225.00(20)	....	110.00
5056	(49¢) Richard Allen. . . .	320.00(120)	65.00(20)	11.00(4)	3.00
5057	(49¢) Chinese New Year	150.00(72)	30.00(12)	....	2.25

2021

SCOTT NO.	DESCRIPTION	IMPERF PRESS SHEET	IMPERF MINT SHEET OR BOOKLET	IMPERF PLATE BLOCK	IMPERF UNUSED F/NH
5543	(55¢) Love	300.00(160)	45.00(20)	18.00(4)	3.75
5555	(55¢) August Wilson . . .	280.00(120)	65.00(20)	18.00(4)	3.75
5556	(55¢) Year of the Ox . . .	320.00(80)	80.00(20)	18.00(4)	3.75
5557	(55¢) Dr. Chien-Shiung Wu	1020.00(120)	190.00(20)	45.00(4)	14.00
5573-82	(55¢) Star Wars Droids.	1100.00(160)	175.00(20)	90.00(10)	80.00
5583-92	(55¢) Heritage Breeds .	500.00(80)	175.00(20)	90.00(10)	80.00
5593	(55¢) Go for Broke	200.00(120)	45.00(20)	18.00(4)	3.75
5594-97	(55¢) Emilio Sanchez . .	380.00(180)	60.00(20)	30.00(8)	18.00
5598-5607	(55¢) Sun Science	500.00(120)	175.00(20)	90.00(10)	80.00
5608	(55¢) Yogi Berra	280.00(120)	60.00(20)	18.00(4)	3.75
5609-13	(55¢) Tap Dance.	320.00(120)	80.00(20)	35.00(10)	20.00
5614	(55¢) Mystery Message	300.00(160)	60.00(20)	18.00(4)	3.75
5620	(55¢) Raven Story	2000.00(120)	450.00(20)	100.00(4)	28.00
5621-25	(55¢) Mid-Atlantic Lighthouse	220.00(120)	60.00(20)	35.00(10)	20.00
5626	(55¢) Missouri Statehood	200.00(120)	60.00(20)	18.00(4)	3.75
5627-34	(55¢) Backyard Games	280.00(160)	45.00(16)	30.00(8)	25.00
5636-39	(58¢) Message Monsters	120.00(60)	55.00(20)	22.00(8)	10.00
5640-43	(58¢) Day of the Dead .	280.00(160)	55.00(20)	22.00(8)	10.00

SCOTT NO.	DESCRIPTION	IMPERF PRESS SHEET	IMPERF MINT SHEET OR BOOKLET	IMPERF PLATE BLOCK	IMPERF UNUSED F/NH
	2022				
5660-61	(58¢) Love, blue gray & pink	180.00(160)	40.00(20)	9.50(4)	4.75
5662	(58¢) Year of the Tiger .	100.00(80)	40.00(20)	....	2.75
5663	(58¢) Edmonia Lewis . .	100.00(80)	40.00(20)	9.50(4)	2.75
5668-71	(58¢) Title IX Civil Rights Law	220.00(180)	40.00(20)	9.50(4)	9.50
5683	(58¢) The Giving Tree, Shel Silverstein.	180.00(120)	55.00(20)	9.50(4)	2.75
5688-92	(58¢) George Morrison .	220.00(180)	55.00(20)	22.00(10)	12.00
5693	(58¢) Eugenie Clark . . .	180.00(120)	40.00(20)	9.50(4)	2.75
5694-97	(58¢) Womens' Rowing	220.00(180)	40.00(20)	16.00(8)	9.50
5698	(58¢) Mighty Mississippi	100.00(60)	25.00(10)	....	....
5702	(58¢) Nancy Reagan . .	180.00(120)	40.00(20)	9.50(4)	2.75
5703-07	(60¢) Mariachi.	180.00(120)	40.00(20)	20.00(10)	12.00
5708	(60¢) Pete Seeger	200.00(144)	30.00(16)	....	2.75
5709-12	(60¢) Go Beyond, Buzz Lightyear	250.00(180)	40.00(20)	16.00(8)	9.50
5713	(60¢) National Marine Sanctuaries. . . .	120.00 (96)	30.00(16)	....	....
5715-19	(60¢) Pony Cars	180.00(120)	40.00(20)	20.00(10)	12.00(5)
5720	(60¢) James Webb Space Telescope	180.00(120)	40.00(20)	9.50(4)	2.75
5726	(60¢) Peanuts, Charles M. Schulz	180.00(120)	45.00(20)	....	....
5738	(60¢) Women Cryptologists	180.00(120)	40.00(20)	9.50(4)	2.75
	2023				
5744	(60¢) Year of the Rabbit	120.00(80)	40.00(20)	....	2.75
5745-46	(60¢) Love, Puppy and Kitten	200.00(160)	40.00(20)	9.50(4)	4.75
5753	(63¢) Ernest J. Gaines .	220.00(180)	40.00(20)	9.50(4)	2.75
5754	(63¢) Women's Soccer.	180.00(120)	40.00(20)	9.50(4)	2.75
5757	(63¢) Toni Morrison. . . .	180.00(120)	40.00(20)	9.50(4)	2.75
5758-62	(63¢) Historic Railroad Stations	120.00(80)	40.00(20)	20.00(10)	12.00
5763-66	(63¢) Art of the Skateboard	180.00(120)	40.00(20)	16.00(8)	9.50
5792-96	(63¢) Roy Liechtenstein	120.00(80)	40.00(20)	20.00(10)	12.00
5797	(63¢) Tomie dePaola . .	280.00(180)	40.00(20)	9.50(4)	2.75
5798	(63¢) Chief Standing Bear	280.00(180)	40.00(20)	9.50(4)	2.75
5799	(63¢) Endangered Species	380.00(80)	60.00(20)	....	....
5800	(63¢) Waterfalls	200.00(96)	30.00(12)	....	....
5801	(66¢) John Lewis	200.00(135)	30.00(15)	9.50(4)	2.75
5802	(66¢) Life Magnified . . .	220.00(120)	45.00(20)	....	....
5803-07	(66¢) Thinking of You . .	120.00(80)	40.00(20)	20.00(10)	12.00(5)
5808	(66c) OSIRIS-Rex.	280.00(180)	40.00(20)	9.50(4)	2.75
5809	(66c) Ruth Bader Ginsburg	280.00(180)	40.00(20)	9.50(4)	2.75

2024 - 2025 Imperf Issues will be listed in the next edition.

SCOTT NO.	DESCRIPTION	IMPERF PRESS SHEET	IMPERF MINT SHEET OR BOOKLET	IMPERF PLATE BLOCK	IMPERF UNUSED F/NH
	Semi-Postals				
B5	(49¢ + 11¢) Breast Cancer	420.00(240)	45.00(20)	9.50(4)	2.25

AIR POST

C1-C3
Curtiss Jenny Biplane

C4
Airplane Propeller

C5
Badge of Air Service

C6
Airplane

1918 (C1-6 NH + 75%)

SCOTT NO.	DESCRIPTION	UNUSED O.G. VF	F	AVG	USED VF	F	AVG
C1-3	**6¢-24¢, 3 varieties, complete.........**	**250.00**	**200.00**	**176.00**	**115.00**	**95.00**	**80.00**
C1	6¢ orange	75.00	60.00	55.00	35.00	29.00	23.00
C2	16¢ green	85.00	70.00	60.00	38.00	30.00	27.00
C3	24¢ carmine rose & blue	95.00	75.00	65.00	45.00	40.00	35.00
C3a	same, center inverted	....	800000.00	....	....	....	....

SCOTT NO.		CENTER LINE BLOCKS F/NH	F/OG	A/OG	ARROW BLOCKS F/NH	F/OG	A/OG
C1	6¢ orange	800.00	425.00	280.00	550.00	385.00	255.00
C2	16¢ green	625.00	400.00	325.00	550.00	360.00	285.00
C3	24¢ carmine rose & blue	650.00	425.00	330.00	575.00	370.00	275.00

1923

SCOTT NO.	DESCRIPTION	UNUSED O.G. VF	F	AVG	USED VF	F	AVG
C4-6	**8¢-24¢, 3 varieties, complete.........**	**225.00**	**165.00**	**145.00**	**85.00**	**68.00**	**50.00**
C4	8¢ dark green	25.00	20.00	15.00	15.00	12.00	10.00
C5	16¢ dark blue......	95.00	80.00	70.00	35.00	28.00	20.00
C6	24¢ carmine.......	110.00	70.00	65.00	38.00	30.00	22.00

C7-C9
Map of U.S. and Airplanes

1926-30 (C7-12 NH + 50%)

SCOTT NO.	DESCRIPTION	UNUSED O.G. VF	F	AVG	USED VF	F	AVG
C7-9	**10¢-20¢, 3 varieties, complete.........**	**17.50**	**14.50**	**9.50**	**5.95**	**5.00**	**3.45**
C7	10¢ dark blue......	3.75	3.10	2.40	.65	.50	.35
C8	15¢ olive brown....	4.25	3.60	2.75	3.00	2.50	1.75
C9	20¢ yellow green (1927)	11.50	9.00	7.00	2.75	2.25	1.65

C10
Lindbergh's Airplane "Spirit of St. Louis"

1927 LINDBERGH TRIBUTE ISSUE

SCOTT NO.	DESCRIPTION	UNUSED O.G. VF	F	AVG	USED VF	F	AVG
C10	10¢ dark blue......	10.75	8.25	6.00	2.85	2.20	1.75
C10a	same, bklt pane of 3	125.00	95.00	67.50	....	....	....

C11
Beacon and Rocky Mountains

C12, C16, C17, C19
Winged Globe

1928 BEACON

SCOTT NO.	DESCRIPTION	UNUSED O.G. VF	F	AVG	USED VF	F	AVG
C11	5¢ carmine & blue . .	6.50	4.75	3.25	.90	.70	.50

1930 Flat Plate Printing, Perf. 11

SCOTT NO.	DESCRIPTION	UNUSED O.G. VF	F	AVG	USED VF	F	AVG
C12	5¢ violet..........	12.50	9.75	8.50	.85	.65	.50

C13
Graf Zeppelin

C14

C15

1930 GRAF ZEPPELIN ISSUE (NH + 50%)

SCOTT NO.	DESCRIPTION	UNUSED O.G. VF	F	AVG	USED VF	F	AVG
C13-15	**65¢-$2.60, 3 varieties, complete........**	**1620.00**	**1465.00**	**1265.00**	**1500.00**	**1180.00**	**965.00**
C13	65¢ green	300.00	250.00	200.00	275.00	210.00	175.00
C14	$1.30 brown.......	425.00	370.00	320.00	450.00	375.00	295.00
C15	$2.60 blue	900.00	850.00	750.00	800.00	600.00	500.00

1931-32 Rotary Press Printing. Perf. 10½ x 11, Designs as #C12 (C16-C24 NH + 40%)

SCOTT NO.	DESCRIPTION	UNUSED O.G. VF	F	AVG	USED VF	F	AVG
C16	5¢ violet..........	8.00	6.00	5.00	.80	.55	.40
C17	8¢ olive bistre	3.25	2.75	2.15	.55	.40	.35

C18
Graf Zeppelin

1933 CENTURY OF PROGRESS ISSUE

SCOTT NO.	DESCRIPTION	UNUSED O.G. VF	F	AVG	USED VF	F	AVG
C18	50¢ green	100.00	90.00	75.00	80.00	70.00	60.00

1934 DESIGN OF 1930

SCOTT NO.	DESCRIPTION	UNUSED O.G. VF	F	AVG	USED VF	F	AVG
C19	6¢ dull orange	3.75	3.00	2.00	.45	.35	.25

C20-22
China Clipper

1935 TRANS PACIFIC ISSUE

SCOTT NO.	DESCRIPTION	UNUSED O.G. VF	F	AVG	USED VF	F	AVG
C20	25¢ blue...........	[illegible]	[illegible]	1.05	1.10	.90	.80

1937. Type of 1935 Issue, Date Omitted

SCOTT NO.	DESCRIPTION	UNUSED O.G. VF	F	AVG	USED VF	F	AVG
C21	20¢ green	12.00	10.00	7.50	2.00	1.65	1.25
C22	50¢ carmine.......	12.00	10.25	7.75	5.40	4.50	3.75

C23
Eagle

1938

SCOTT NO.	DESCRIPTION	UNUSED O.G. VF	F	AVG	USED VF	F	AVG
C23	6¢ dark blue & carmine	.65	.55	.45	.35	.30	.25

C24
Winged Globe

1939 TRANS-ATLANTIC ISSUE

SCOTT NO.	DESCRIPTION	UNUSED O.G. VF	F	AVG	USED VF	F	AVG
C24	30¢ dull blue	12.50	11.00	10.00	1.70	1.50	1.20

AIR POST PLATE BLOCKS #C1-C24

SCOTT NO.		UNUSED NH VF	F	AVG	UNUSED O.G. VF	F	AVG
C1(6)	6¢ orange.	1550.00	1150.00	925.00	1050.00	875.00	600.00
C2(6)	16¢ green.	2100.00	1975.00	1575.00	1400.00	1100.00	900.00
C3(12)	24¢ carmine rose & blue	2800.00	2000.00	1825.00	1800.00	1700.00	1300.00
C4(6)	8¢ dark green.	610.00	450.00	360.00	350.00	300.00	260.00
C5(6)	16¢ dark blue	3400.00	2700.00	2250.00	2200.00	2000.00	1650.00
C6(6)	24¢ carmine	4300.00	3300.00	2825.00	2800.00	2200.00	1900.00
C7(6)	10¢ dark blue	77.00	55.00	49.00	54.00	41.50	30.00
C8(6)	15¢ olive brown . . .	85.00	66.00	52.75	60.00	50.00	44.00
C9(6)	20¢ yellow green	185.00	155.00	125.00	110.00	90.00	80.00
C10(6)	10¢ dark blue	200.00	188.00	165.00	135.00	115.00	85.00
C11(6)	5¢ carmine & blue .	85.00	65.00	54.00	60.00	46.50	31.50
C12(6)	5¢ violet	285.00	220.00	175.00	215.00	165.00	120.00
C13(6)	65¢ green.	5200.00	3800.00	3000.00	3300.00	2600.00	2100.00
C14(6)	$1.30 brown	12500.00	1100.00	8000.00	8000.00	7000.00	5500.00
C15(6)	$2.60 blue	19000.00	18000.00	13000.00	12000.00	10000.00	8000.00
C16(4)	5¢ violet	150.00	135.00	105.00	110.00	95.00	65.00
C17(4)	8¢ olive bistre.	58.50	45.00	36.00	40.00	30.00	24.00
C18(4)	50¢ green.	1400.00	1150.00	800.00	950.00	795.00	635.00
C19(4)	6¢ dull orange	39.50	33.00	26.00	30.00	25.00	20.00
C20(6)	25¢ blue	33.00	27.50	22.00	26.50	22.00	17.50
C21(6)	20¢ green.	125.00	105.00	90.00	115.00	100.00	85.00
C22(6)	50¢ carmine	125.00	90.00	75.00	90.00	75.00	65.00
C23(4)	6¢ dark blue & carmine	19.00	15.00	12.00	15.00	12.00	9.00
C24(6)	30¢ dull blue.	185.00	155.00	135.00	155.00	130.00	95.00

C25-C31

1941-44 TRANSPORT ISSUE

SCOTT NO.	DESCRIPTION	FIRST DAY COVERS SING	PL. BLK.	MINT SHEET	PLATE BLOCK	UNUSED F/NH	USED
C25-31	**6¢-50¢, 7 varieties, complete. . . . .**	....	....	....	**127.50**	**23.95**	**5.60**
C25	6¢ Transport Plane . . .	7.00	10.00	15.00(50)	1.25	.30	.25
C25a	same, bklt pane of 3 . .	30.00	....	....	....	4.25	....
C26	8¢ Transport Plane . . .	6.00	11.25	16.00(50)	2.20	.30	.25
C27	10¢ Transport Plane . .	8.00	15.00	82.50(50)	9.00	1.65	.25
C28	15¢ Transport Plane . .	8.00	15.00	150.00(50)	13.95	3.25	.40
C29	20¢ Transport Plane . .	10.00	20.00	125.00(50)	14.00	2.75	.40
C30	30¢ Transport Plane . .	20.00	30.00	140.00(50)	14.00	3.00	.40
C31	50¢ Transport Plane . .	28.50	68.75	575.00(50)	65.00	14.00	4.25

C32

1946

SCOTT NO.	DESCRIPTION	FIRST DAY COVERS SING	PL. BLK.	MINT SHEET	PLATE BLOCK	UNUSED F/NH	USED
C32	5¢ DC-4 Skymaster . . .	2.00	4.25	13.00(50)	1.00	.30	.25

C33, C37, C39, C41

C34

C35

C36

SCOTT NO.	DESCRIPTION	FIRST DAY COVERS SING	PL. BLK.	MINT SHEET	PLATE BLOCK	UNUSED F/NH	USED
	1947						
C33-36	**5¢-25¢, 4 varieties, complete. . . . .**	....	....	....	....	**2.10**	**.70**
C33	5¢ DC-4 Skymaster . . .	2.00	4.25	25.00(100)	1.20	.30	.25
C34	10¢ Pan American Bldg.	2.00	4.25	19.00(50)	2.00	.45	.25
C35	15¢ New York Skyline .	2.00	4.25	26.00(50)	2.75	.60	.30
C36	25¢ Plane over Bridge .	2.00	5.00	75.00(50)	7.50	1.60	.30
	1948 Rotary Press Coil–Perf. 10 Horiz.						
			LINE PR.		**LINE PR.**		
C37	5¢ DC-4 Skymaster. . .	2.00	4.25	....	12.00	1.40	1.00

C38

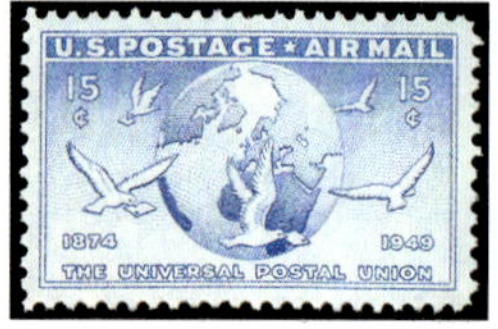

C40

SCOTT NO.	DESCRIPTION	FIRST DAY COVERS SING	PL. BLK.	MINT SHEET	PLATE BLOCK	UNUSED F/NH	USED
C38	5¢ New York Jubliee . .	2.00	4.25	22.00(100)	5.25	.30	.25
	1949						
C39	6¢ DC-4 Skymaster (as #C33).	2.00	4.25	23.00(100)	1.50	.30	.25
C39a	same, bklt pane of 6 . .	10.00	....		....	14.00	....
C40	6¢ Alexandria, Virginia.	2.00	4.25	12.00(50)	1.30	.35	.25
	Rotary Press Coil–Perf. 10 Horiz.						
			LINE PR.		**LINE PR.**		
C41	6¢ DC-4 Skymaster (as#C37)	2.00	4.25	....	22.00	4.25	.25

NOTE: Unused Air Mail coil pairs can be supplied at two times the single price.

C42

C43

C44

1949 U.P.U. ISSUES

SCOTT NO.	DESCRIPTION	FIRST DAY COVERS SING	PL. BLK.	MINT SHEET	PLATE BLOCK	UNUSED F/NH	USED
C42-44	**10¢-25¢, 3 varieties, complete. . . . .**	....	....	....	....	**1.90**	**1.35**
C42	10¢ Post Office	2.00	4.25	17.50(50)	1.85	.40	.30
C43	15¢ Globe & Doves . . .	3.00	5.00	25.00(50)	2.25	.60	.45
C44	25¢ Plane & Globe . . .	4.00	6.25	42.00(50)	7.25	1.10	.75

C45

C46

C47

1949-58

SCOTT NO.	DESCRIPTION	FIRST DAY COVERS SING	PL. BLK.	MINT SHEET	PLATE BLOCK	UNUSED F/NH	USED
C45-51	**7 varieties, complete.**	....	....	....	....	**9.00**	**2.30**
C45	6¢ Wright Brothers (1949)	2.00	4.25	25.00(50)	2.00	.50	.25
C46	80¢ Hawaii (1952). . . .	15.00	35.00	350.00(50)	35.00	8.00	2.00
C47	6¢ Powered Flight (1953)	2.00	4.25	12.00(50)	1.30	.30	.25

C48, C50

1949-58 (continued)

SCOTT NO.	DESCRIPTION	FIRST DAY COVERS SING	FIRST DAY COVERS PL. BLK.	MINT SHEET	PLATE BLOCK	UNUSED F/NH	USED
C48	4¢ Eagle (1954)	2.00	4.25	24.00(100)	1.95	.30	.25

C49

C51, C52, C60, C61

SCOTT NO.	DESCRIPTION	FIRST DAY COVERS SING	FIRST DAY COVERS PL. BLK.	MINT SHEET	PLATE BLOCK	UNUSED F/NH	USED
C49	6¢ Air Force (1957) . .	2.00	4.25	17.00(50)	1.85	.40	.25
C50	5¢ Eagle (1958)	2.00	4.25	19.50(100)	1.90	.30	.25
C51	7¢ Silhouette of Jet, blue (1958)	2.00	4.25	24.00(100)	1.40	.35	.25
C51a	same, bklt pane of 6 .	8.00	....	....	....	14.00	....

Rotary Press Coil–Perf. 10 Horiz.

SCOTT NO.	DESCRIPTION	FIRST DAY COVERS SING	LINE PR.	MINT SHEET	LINE PR.	UNUSED F/NH	USED
C52	7¢ Silhouette of Jet, blue	2.00	3.25	....	24.00	2.75	.25

C53

C54

1959

SCOTT NO.	DESCRIPTION	FIRST DAY COVERS SING	FIRST DAY COVERS PL. BLK.	MINT SHEET	PLATE BLOCK	UNUSED F/NH	USED
C53-56	**4 varieties, complete .**	....	....	....	....	**1.50**	**.85**
C53	7¢ Alaska Statehood . .	2.00	4.25	19.00(50)	1.85	.45	.25
C54	7¢ Balloon Jupiter	2.00	4.25	23.00(50)	2.55	.55	.25

C55

C56

SCOTT NO.	DESCRIPTION	FIRST DAY COVERS SING	FIRST DAY COVERS PL. BLK.	MINT SHEET	PLATE BLOCK	UNUSED F/NH	USED
C55	7¢ Hawaii Statehood .	2.00	4.25	19.00(50)	2.00	.45	.25
C56	10¢ Pan-Am Games .	2.00	4.25	20.00(50)	2.25	.55	.35

C57

C58, C63

C59

C62

1959-66 REGULAR ISSUES

SCOTT NO.	DESCRIPTION	FIRST DAY COVERS SING	FIRST DAY COVERS PL. BLK.	MINT SHEET	PLATE BLOCK	UNUSED F/NH	USED
C57/63	**(C57-60, C62-63) 6 varieties........**	....		....	....	**3.90**	**1.90**

1959-66

SCOTT NO.	DESCRIPTION	FIRST DAY COVERS SING	FIRST DAY COVERS PL. BLK.	MINT SHEET	PLATE BLOCK	UNUSED F/NH	USED
C57	10¢ Liberty Bell (1960)	2.00	4.25	55.00(50)	7.00	1.55	1.00
C58	15¢ Statue of Liberty . .	2.00	4.25	24.00(50)	2.50	.55	.25
C59	25¢ Abraham Lincoln (1960)	2.00	4.25	43.00(50)	4.25	.90	.25

1960. Design of 1958

SCOTT NO.	DESCRIPTION	FIRST DAY COVERS SING	FIRST DAY COVERS PL. BLK.	MINT SHEET	PLATE BLOCK	UNUSED F/NH	USED
C60	7¢ Jet Plane, carmine .	2.00	4.25	22.50(100)	1.50	.35	.25
C60a	same, bklt pane of 6 . .	9.00	....	....	....	17.00	....

Rotary Press Coil–Perf. 10 Horiz.

SCOTT NO.	DESCRIPTION	FIRST DAY COVERS SING	LINE PR.	MINT SHEET	LINE PR.	UNUSED F/NH	USED
C61	7¢ Jet Plane, carmine	2.00	3.25	....	50.00	5.50	.35

1961-67

SCOTT NO.	DESCRIPTION	FIRST DAY COVERS SING	FIRST DAY COVERS PL. BLK.	MINT SHEET	PLATE BLOCK	UNUSED F/NH	USED
C62	13¢ Liberty Bell	2.00	4.25	25.00(50)	2.70	.60	.25
C63	15¢ Statue re-drawn . .	2.00	4.25	25.00(50)	2.60	.60	.25

C64, C65

1962-64

SCOTT NO.	DESCRIPTION	FIRST DAY COVERS SING	FIRST DAY COVERS PL. BLK.	MINT SHEET	PLATE BLOCK	UNUSED F/NH	USED
C64/69	**(C64, C66-69) 5 varieties**	....	....	....	....	**2.00**	**1.25**

1962

SCOTT NO.	DESCRIPTION	FIRST DAY COVERS SING	FIRST DAY COVERS PL. BLK.	MINT SHEET	PLATE BLOCK	UNUSED F/NH	USED
C64	8¢ Plane & Capitol. . . .	2.00	4.25	25.00(100)	1.40	.30	.25
C64b	same, bklt pane of 5, Slogan I	1.95	....	....	....	9.00	....
C64b	bklt pane of 5, Slogan II, (1963)	....	....	....	....	90.00	....
C64b	bklt pane of 5, Slogan III (1964)	....	....	....	....	15.00	....
C64c	bklt pane of 5 tagged, Slogan III (1964)	....	....	....	....	2.25	....

SLOGAN I–Your Mailman Deserves Your Help... **SLOGAN II–Use Zone Numbers..**

SLOGAN III–Always Use Zip Code....

Rotary Press Coil–Perf. 10 Horiz.

SCOTT NO.	DESCRIPTION	FIRST DAY COVERS SING	LINE PR.	MINT SHEET	LINE PR.	UNUSED F/NH	USED
C65	8¢ Plane & Capitol. . . .	2.00	3.25	....	8.00	.65	.30

C66

C67

C68

1963

SCOTT NO.	DESCRIPTION	FIRST DAY COVERS SING	FIRST DAY COVERS PL. BLK.	MINT SHEET	PLATE BLOCK	UNUSED F/NH	USED
C66	15¢ Montgomery Blair .	2.00	4.25	29.00(50)	4.00	.75	.60
C67	6¢ Bald Eagle	2.00	4.25	35.00(100)	2.25	.30	.25
C68	8¢ Amelia Earhart	2.00	4.25	20.00(50)	2.00	.40	.25

C69

1964

SCOTT NO.	DESCRIPTION	FIRST DAY COVERS SING	FIRST DAY COVERS PL. BLK.	MINT SHEET	PLATE BLOCK	UNUSED F/NH	USED
C69	8¢ Dr. Robert H. Goddard	2.00	5.00	20.00(50)	2.25	.50	.25

C70

C71

C72, C73

1967-69

SCOTT NO.	DESCRIPTION	FIRST DAY COVERS SING	FIRST DAY COVERS PL. BLK.	MINT SHEET	PLATE BLOCK	UNUSED F/NH	USED
C70/76	**(C70-72, C74-76) 6 varieties........**	....		....	....	**2.95**	**1.00**

1967-68

SCOTT NO.	DESCRIPTION	FIRST DAY COVERS SING	FIRST DAY COVERS PL. BLK.	MINT SHEET	PLATE BLOCK	UNUSED F/NH	USED
C70	8¢ Alaska Purchase. . .	2.00	4.25	19.00(50)	2.25	.45	.25
C71	20¢ "Columbia Jays" . .	2.00	4.25	44.00(50)	4.50	1.00	.25
C72	10¢ 50-Star (1968) . . .	2.00	4.25	32.50(100)	1.80	.40	.25
C72b	same, bklt pane of 8 . .	3.00	....	....	....	3.25	....
C72c	same, bklt pane of 5, Slogan IV or V	140.00	....	....	....	5.75	....

SLOGAN IV–Mail Early in the Day... **SLOGAN V–Use Zip Code...**

1968 Rotary Press Coil–Perf. 10 Vert.

SCOTT NO.	DESCRIPTION	FIRST DAY COVERS SING	LINE PR.	MINT SHEET	LINE PR.	UNUSED F/NH	USED
C73	10¢ 50-Star	2.00	3.25	....	2.75	.50	.35

C74

C75

SCOTT NO.	DESCRIPTION	FIRST DAY COVERS SING	FIRST DAY COVERS PL. BLK.	MINT SHEET	PLATE BLOCK	UNUSED F/NH	USED
C74	10¢ Air Mail Anniversary	2.00	4.25	15.00(50)	3.10	.40	.25
C75	20¢ "USA" & Plane . . .	2.00	4.25	29.00(50)	3.25	.75	.25

C76

1969

SCOTT NO.	DESCRIPTION	FIRST DAY COVERS SING	FIRST DAY COVERS PL. BLK.	MINT SHEET	PLATE BLOCK	UNUSED F/NH	USED
C76	10¢ Man on the Moon .	6.00	14.50	15.00(32)	2.25	.50	.35

C77

C78, C82

C79, C83

1971-73

SCOTT NO.	DESCRIPTION	FIRST DAY COVERS SING	FIRST DAY COVERS PL. BLK.	MINT SHEET	PLATE BLOCK	UNUSED F/NH	USED
C77-81	**9¢-21¢, 5 varieties, complete. . . . .**	....	....	....	....	**2.25**	**1.25**
C77	9¢ Delta Winged Plane	2.00	4.25	28.00(100)	1.75	.40	.30
C78	11¢ Silhouette of Plane	2.00	4.25	35.00(100)	2.00	.45	.25
C78b	same, precanceled . . .	....	....	....	....	....	.50
C78a	11¢ bklt pane of 4	2.25	....	....	....	1.65	....
C79	13¢ Letter (1973).	2.00	4.25	38.00(100)	2.25	.50	.25
C79b	same, precanceled . . .	....	....	....	....	1.50	1.00
C79a	13¢ bklt pane of 5	2.25	....	....	....	2.50	....

C80

SCOTT NO.	DESCRIPTION	FIRST DAY COVERS SING	FIRST DAY COVERS PL. BLK.	MINT SHEET	PLATE BLOCK	UNUSED F/NH	USED
C80	17¢ Liberty Head	2.00	4.25	27.00(50)	3.00	.65	.25
C81	21¢ "USA" & Plane . . .	2.00	4.25	29.00(50)	3.25	.70	.25

Rotary Press Coils–Perf. 10 Vert.

SCOTT NO.	DESCRIPTION	FIRST DAY COVERS SING	LINE PR.	MINT SHEET	LINE PR.	UNUSED F/NH	USED
C82	11¢ Silhouette of Jet . .	2.00	3.25	....	1.25	.45	.25
C83	13¢ Letter	2.00	3.25	....	1.50	.55	.25

C84

C85

1972-76

SCOTT NO.	DESCRIPTION	FIRST DAY COVERS SING	FIRST DAY COVERS PL. BLK.	MINT SHEET	PLATE BLOCK	UNUSED F/NH	USED
C84-90	**11¢-31¢, 7 varieties, complete. . . . .**	....	....	....	....	**4.70**	**1.50**

1972

SCOTT NO.	DESCRIPTION	FIRST DAY COVERS SING	FIRST DAY COVERS PL. BLK.	MINT SHEET	PLATE BLOCK	UNUSED F/NH	USED
C84	11¢ City of Refuge	2.00	4.25	22.00(50)	2.40	.50	.25
C85	11¢ Olympics	2.00	4.25	18.50(50)	4.50(10)	.45	.35

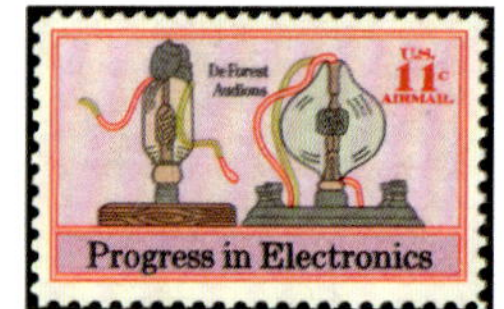

C86

1973

SCOTT NO.	DESCRIPTION	FIRST DAY COVERS SING	FIRST DAY COVERS PL. BLK.	MINT SHEET	PLATE BLOCK	UNUSED F/NH	USED
C86	11¢ Electronics	2.00	4.25	26.50(50)	2.50	.55	.25

C87

C88

1974

SCOTT NO.	DESCRIPTION	FIRST DAY COVERS SING	FIRST DAY COVERS PL. BLK.	MINT SHEET	PLATE BLOCK	UNUSED F/NH	USED
C87	18¢ Statue of Liberty . .	2.00	4.25	27.50(50)	2.75	.65	.50
C88	26¢ Mt. Rushmore	2.00	4.25	50.00(50)	5.00	1.25	.25

C89

C90

1976

SCOTT NO.	DESCRIPTION	FIRST DAY COVERS SING	FIRST DAY COVERS PL. BLK.	MINT SHEET	PLATE BLOCK	UNUSED F/NH	USED
C89	25¢ Plane & Globes. . .	2.00	4.25	37.00 (50)	3.85	.90	.25
C90	31¢ Plane, Flag & Globes	2.00	4.25	47.00 (50)	4.75	1.10	.25

C91 C92

1978-80

SCOTT NO.	DESCRIPTION	FIRST DAY COVERS SING	FIRST DAY COVERS PL. BLK.	MINT SHEET	PLATE BLOCK	UNUSED F/NH	USED
C91-100	**21¢-40¢, 10 varieties, complete**	....	....	....	....	**11.50**	**5.35**
C91-92	Wright Brothers, 2 varieties, attached	2.40	5.00	95.00(100)	5.75	2.25	1.75
C91	31¢ Wright Brothers & Plane	2.00	....	....	....	1.00	.60
C92	31¢ Wright Brothers & Shed	2.00	....	....	....	1.00	.60

C93 C94

1979

SCOTT NO.	DESCRIPTION	FIRST DAY COVERS SING	FIRST DAY COVERS PL. BLK.	MINT SHEET	PLATE BLOCK	UNUSED F/NH	USED
C93-94	Octave Chanute, 2 varieties, attached	2.40	5.00	85.00(100)	5.00	2.10	1.75
C93	21¢ Chanute & Plane	2.00	....	....	....	1.00	.75
C94	21¢ Chanute & 2 Planes	2.00	....	....	....	1.00	.75

C95 C96

SCOTT NO.	DESCRIPTION	FIRST DAY COVERS SING	FIRST DAY COVERS PL. BLK.	MINT SHEET	PLATE BLOCK	UNUSED F/NH	USED
C95-96	Wiley Post, 2 varieties, attached	2.40	5.00	165.00(100)	13.50	3.50	2.75
C95	25¢ Post & Plane	2.00	....	....	....	1.80	1.10
C96	25¢ Plane & Post	2.00	....	....	....	1.80	1.10

C97

SCOTT NO.	DESCRIPTION	FIRST DAY COVERS SING	FIRST DAY COVERS PL. BLK.	MINT SHEET	PLATE BLOCK	UNUSED F/NH	USED
C97	31¢ High Jumper	2.00	4.25	40.00(50)	15.00(12)	1.05	.60

C98

C99

1980

SCOTT NO.	DESCRIPTION	FIRST DAY COVERS SING	FIRST DAY COVERS PL. BLK.	MINT SHEET	PLATE BLOCK	UNUSED F/NH	USED
C98	40¢ Philip Mazzei	2.00	4.25	65.00(50)	18.00 (12)	1.40	.35
C98a	40¢ Philip Mazzei, perf. 10½ x 11¼	2.00	4.25	387.00(50)	140.00 (12)	9.00	2.25
C99	28¢ Blanche S. Scott	2.00	4.25	42.50(50)	14.00 (12)	1.10	.35

C100

SCOTT NO.	DESCRIPTION	FIRST DAY COVERS SING	FIRST DAY COVERS PL. BLK.	MINT SHEET	PLATE BLOCK	UNUSED F/NH	USED
C100	35¢ Glenn Curtiss	2.00	4.25	48.00(50)	15.00(12)	1.20	.35

C101 C102

C103 C104

1983-85

SCOTT NO.	DESCRIPTION	FIRST DAY COVERS SING	FIRST DAY COVERS PL. BLK.	MINT SHEET	PLATE BLOCK	UNUSED F/NH	USED
C101-16	**28¢-44¢, 16 varieties, complete**	....	....	....	....	**21.50**	**11.50**

1983

SCOTT NO.	DESCRIPTION	FIRST DAY COVERS SING	FIRST DAY COVERS PL. BLK.	MINT SHEET	PLATE BLOCK	UNUSED F/NH	USED
C101-04	Summer Olympics, 4 varieties, attached	3.50	4.50	55.00(50)	6.50	5.75	4.50
C101	28¢ Women's Gymnastics	2.00	....	....	....	1.50	.95
C102	28¢ Hurdles	2.00	....	....	....	1.50	.95
C103	28¢ Women's Basketball	2.00	....	....	....	1.50	.95
C104	28¢ Soccer	2.00	....	....	....	1.50	.95

C105 C106

C107 C108

SCOTT NO.	DESCRIPTION	FIRST DAY COVERS SING	FIRST DAY COVERS PL. BLK.	MINT SHEET	PLATE BLOCK	UNUSED F/NH	USED
C105-08	Summer Olympics, 4 varieties, attached	4.50	5.75	60.00(50)	7.25	6.00	4.75
C105	40¢ Shot Put	2.00	....	....	....	1.55	.95
C106	40¢ Men's Gymnastics	2.00	....	....	....	1.55	.95
C107	40¢ Women's Swimming	2.00	....	....	....	1.55	.95
C108	40¢ Weight Lifting	2.00	....	....	....	1.55	.95

C109 C110

C111 C112

SCOTT NO.	DESCRIPTION	FIRST DAY COVERS SING	FIRST DAY COVERS PL. BLK.	MINT SHEET	PLATE BLOCK	UNUSED F/NH	USED
C109-12	Summer Olympics, 4 varieties, attached	4.00	5.00	76.00(50)	10.00	6.75	5.00
C109	35¢ Fencing	2.00	....	....	....	1.75	1.25
C110	35¢ Cycling	2.00	....	....	....	1.75	1.25
C111	35¢ Volleyball	2.00	....	....	....	1.75	1.25
C112	35¢ Pole Vault	2.00	....	....	....	1.75	1.25

C113

C114

C115

C116

1985

SCOTT NO.	DESCRIPTION	FIRST DAY COVERS SING	FIRST DAY COVERS PL. BLK.	MINT SHEET	PLATE BLOCK	UNUSED F/NH	USED
C113	33¢ Alfred Verville . . .	2.00	4.25	48.00(50)	5.25	1.15	.40
C114	39¢ Lawrence and Elmer Sperry	2.00	4.25	59.00(50)	6.75	1.40	.45
C115	44¢ Transpacific	2.00	4.25	63.00(50)	7.25	1.50	.45
C116	44¢ Junipero Serra . .	2.00	4.25	73.00(50)	10.00	1.75	.65

C117

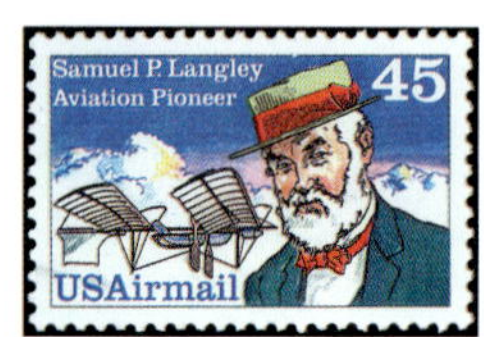

C118

C119

1988

SCOTT NO.	DESCRIPTION	FIRST DAY COVERS SING	FIRST DAY COVERS PL. BLK.	MINT SHEET	PLATE BLOCK	UNUSED F/NH	USED
C117	44¢ New Sweden . . .	2.50	7.50	75.00(50)	10.00	1.65	1.25
C118	45¢ Samuel Langley .	2.00	4.25	67.50(50)	7.00	1.65	.35
C119	36¢ Igor Sikorsky. . . .	2.00	4.25	55.00(50)	6.00	1.40	.60

C120

C121

1989

SCOTT NO.	DESCRIPTION	FIRST DAY COVERS SING	FIRST DAY COVERS PL. BLK.	MINT SHEET	PLATE BLOCK	UNUSED F/NH	USED
C120-25	**6 varieties, complete**	....	....	....	....	**9.00**	**6.00**
C120	45¢ French Revolution	2.00	4.25	39.00(30)	7.00	1.60	1.10
C121	45¢ Americas Issue (Key Marco Cat)	2.00	4.25	87.50(50)	8.00	1.85	1.00

C122 C123

C124 C125

SCOTT NO.	DESCRIPTION	FIRST DAY COVERS SING	FIRST DAY COVERS PL. BLK.	MINT SHEET	PLATE BLOCK	UNUSED F/NH	USED
C122-25	Futuristic Mail Delivery, 4 varieties, attached .	8.00	10.00	65.00(40)	8.50	6.50	5.25
C122	45¢ Spacecraft	2.00	....	....	....	1.75	1.25
C123	45¢ Air Suspended Hover	2.00	....	....	....	1.75	1.25
C124	45¢ Moon Rover	2.00	....	....	....	1.75	1.25
C125	45¢ Space Shuttle . . .	2.00	....	....	....	1.75	1.25
C126	$1.80 Futuristic Mail Imperf. Souvenir Sheet	6.50	....	....	....	9.00	6.75

C127

C128

1990-93

SCOTT NO.	DESCRIPTION	FIRST DAY COVERS SING	FIRST DAY COVERS PL. BLK.	MINT SHEET	PLATE BLOCK	UNUSED F/NH	USED
C127/C132	**1990-93, 6 varieties complete**	....	....	....	....	**12.00**	**4.50**
C127	45¢ Americas Issue (Island Beach)	2.00	4.25	88.00(50)	10.00	2.00	1.00
C128	50¢ Harriet Quimby . .	2.00	4.25	72.50(50)	8.00	1.80	.55
C128b	50¢ Harriet Quimby, reissue, bullseye perf. (1993) .	....	....	85.00(50)	10.00	2.00	1.35

C129, C132

C130

SCOTT NO.	DESCRIPTION	FIRST DAY COVERS SING	FIRST DAY COVERS PL. BLK.	MINT SHEET	PLATE BLOCK	UNUSED F/NH	USED
C129	40¢ William Piper. . . .	2.00	4.25	65.00(50)	7.50	1.35	.50
C130	50¢ Antarctic Treaty. .	2.00	4.25	73.00(50)	8.00	1.50	.80

C131

SCOTT NO.	DESCRIPTION	FIRST DAY COVERS SING	FIRST DAY COVERS PL. BLK.	MINT SHEET	PLATE BLOCK	UNUSED F/NH	USED
C131	50¢ America (Bering Strait) (1991)	2.00	4.25	85.00(50)	8.00	1.75	.80
C132	40¢ William Piper, reissue, bullseye perf. (1993) .	....	....	330.00(50)	83.00	6.00	1.00

C133

C134

C135

C136

C137

1999-2012

SCOTT NO.	DESCRIPTION	FIRST DAY COVERS SING	FIRST DAY COVERS PL. BLK.	MINT SHEET	PLATE BLOCK	UNUSED F/NH	USED
C133-50	**20 varieties complete**	....	....	**225.00**		**50.00**	**20.00**
C133	48¢ Niagara Falls . . .	2.25	5.50	29.00(20)	8.00	1.75	.55
C134	40¢ Rio Grande	2.10	5.00	24.00(20)	6.00	1.40	.75
C135	60¢ Grand Canyon . .	2.25	5.00	36.00(20)	9.00	2.00	.40
C136	70¢ Nine-Mile Prairie, Nebraska	2.50	6.00	42.00(20)	12.00	2.50	.60
C137	80¢ Mt. McKinley	2.75	6.50	48.00(20)	13.00	2.75	.70

C138, C138a, C138b

2001-05

SCOTT NO.	DESCRIPTION	FIRST DAY COVERS SING	FIRST DAY COVERS PL. BLK.	MINT SHEET	PLATE BLOCK	UNUSED F/NH	USED
C138	60¢ Acadia National Park	2.50	5.00	44.00(20)	10.00	2.50	.50
C138a	60¢ Acadia National Park die cut [illegible]	2.75	5.50	50.00(20)	10.00	[illegible]	.55
C138b	same as above, with "2005" date	2.75	5.50	44.00(20)	11.00	2.10	.50

C139

C140

C141

2006

SCOTT NO.	DESCRIPTION	FIRST DAY COVERS SING	FIRST DAY COVERS PL. BLK.	MINT SHEET	PLATE BLOCK	UNUSED F/NH	USED
C139	63¢ Bryce Canyon National Park, self-adhesive . .	2.25	6.00	36.00(20)	9.00	2.00	.70
C140	75¢ Great Smoky Mountains National Park, self-adhesive	2.25	6.00	42.00(20)	11.00	2.50	.80
C141	84¢ Yosemite National Park, self-adhesive	2.50	6.50	47.00(20)	12.00	2.75	.80

C142

C143

2007

SCOTT NO.	DESCRIPTION	FIRST DAY COVERS SING	FIRST DAY COVERS PL. BLK.	MINT SHEET	PLATE BLOCK	UNUSED F/NH	USED
C142	69¢ Okefenokee Swamp, self-adhesive	2.50	6.00	37.00(20)	9.00	2.25	.80
C143	90¢ Hagatña Bay, self-adhesive	2.75	6.50	49.00(20)	12.00	3.00	1.05

C144

C145

2008

SCOTT NO.	DESCRIPTION	FIRST DAY COVERS SING	FIRST DAY COVERS PL. BLK.	MINT SHEET	PLATE BLOCK	UNUSED F/NH	USED
C144	72¢ New Hampshire River Bend	3.75	4.75	34.00(20)	9.00	2.00	1.00
C145	94¢ St. John, US Virgin Islands	3.75	4.75	47.00(20)	12.00	3.00	1.55

C146

C147

2009

SCOTT NO.	DESCRIPTION	FIRST DAY COVERS SING	FIRST DAY COVERS PL. BLK.	MINT SHEET	PLATE BLOCK	UNUSED F/NH	USED
C146	79¢ Zion National Park	3.75	....	48.00(20)	12.00	3.00	2.00
C147	98¢ Grand Teton National Park	3.75	....	48.00(20)	12.00	3.00	1.25

C148

2011

SCOTT NO.	DESCRIPTION	FIRST DAY COVERS SING	FIRST DAY COVERS PL. BLK.	MINT SHEET	PLATE BLOCK	UNUSED F/NH	USED
C148	80¢ Voyagers National Park	3.50	....	60.00(20)	16.00	4.00	3.00

C149

C150

2012

SCOTT NO.	DESCRIPTION	FIRST DAY COVERS SING	FIRST DAY COVERS PL. BLK.	MINT SHEET	PLATE BLOCK	UNUSED F/NH	USED
C149	85¢ Glaciers National Park, Montana.	3.50	....	100.00(20)	24.00	6.00	3.00
C150	$1.05 Amish Horse & Buggy, Lancaster County, Pennsylvania	4.25	....	60.00(20)	12.00	3.00	1.50

AIR POST SPECIAL DELIVERY STAMPS

771, CE1, CE2

SCOTT NO.	DESCRIPTION	PLATE BLOCK F/NH	PLATE BLOCK F	PLATE BLOCK AVG	UNUSED F/NH	UNUSED F	UNUSED AVG	USED F	USED AVG
CE1	16¢ dark blue (1934)	25.00	18.00	14.50	1.10	.80	.60	.70	.55
CE2	16¢ red & blue (1936)	14.00	10.00	8.00	.85	.65	.50	.35	.25
CE2	same, center line block	6.00	4.00	2.00	....	....	....	....	....
CE2	same, arrow block of 4	5.00	3.50	2.75	....	....	....	....	....

SPECIAL DELIVERY STAMPS

E1

E2, E3

E4, E5

(E1-E14 for VF Centering–Fine Price + 35%)

1885 Inscribed "Secures Immediate Delivery at Special Delivery Office" Perf. 12

SCOTT NO.	DESCRIPTION	UNUSED NH F	UNUSED NH AVG	UNUSED OG F	UNUSED OG AVG	USED F	USED AVG
E1	10¢ blue..........	1000.00	650.00	450.00	300.00	60.00	40.00
	1888 Inscribed "Secures Immediate Delivery at any Post Office"						
E2	10¢ blue..........	900.00	680.00	450.00	350.00	38.00	22.00
	1893						
E3	10¢ orange........	580.00	400.00	250.00	175.00	40.00	25.00
	1894 Same type as preceding issue, but with line under "Ten Cents" Unwatermarked						
E4	10¢ blue..........	1900.00	1350.00	750.00	450.00	75.00	50.00
	1895 Double Line Watermark						
E5	10¢ blue..........	400.00	275.00	190.00	120.00	10.00	6.00

E6, E8-11

E7

SCOTT NO.	DESCRIPTION	UNUSED NH F	UNUSED NH AVG	UNUSED OG F	UNUSED OG AVG	USED F	USED AVG
	1902						
E6	10¢ ultramarine	675.00	440.00	350.00	225.00	12.00	8.00
	1908						
E7	10¢ green.........	185.00	120.00	80.00	55.00	50.00	40.00
	1911 Single Line Watermark						
E8	10¢ ultramarine	275.00	175.00	125.00	75.00	12.00	9.00
	1914 Perf. 10						
E9	10¢ ultramarine	500.00	300.00	200.00	130.00	14.00	11.00
	1916 Unwatermarked Perf. 10						
E10	10¢ pale ultra......	775.00	500.00	350.00	220.00	50.00	35.00
	1917 Perf. 11						
E11	10¢ ultramarine	60.00	45.00	30.00	20.00	.95	.70
E11	same, plate block of 6	550.00	400.00	325.00	225.00	....	....

E12, E15

E14, E19

1922-25 Flat Plate Printing Perf. 11

SCOTT NO.	DESCRIPTION	PLATE BLOCK F/NH	PLATE BLOCK F	PLATE BLOCK AVG	UNUSED F/NH	UNUSED F	UNUSED AVG	USED F	USED AVG
E12	10¢ gray violet	(6) 950.00	700.00	550.00	75.00	50.00	30.00	1.50	1.35
E13	15¢ deep orange (1925)	(6) 800.00	650.00	475.00	85.00	60.00	40.00	2.00	1.25
E14	20¢ black (1925)	(6) 80.00	60.00	40.00	4.75	2.75	1.90	2.50	1.75

1927-51 Rotary Press Printing Perf. 11 x 10½

SCOTT NO.	DESCRIPTION	FIRST DAY COVERS SING	FIRST DAY COVERS PL. BLK.	MINT SHEET	PLATE BLOCK	UNUSED F/NH	USED
E15-19	10¢-20¢, 5 varieties .	....	....	....	50.00	9.00	3.25
E15	10¢ gray violet......	....	....	80.00(50)	7.00	1.30	.30
E16	15¢ orange (1931)...	....	....	67.00(50)	6.50	1.30	.30
E17	13¢ blue (1944).....	9.00	20.00	62.00(50)	5.00	1.20	.30
E18	17¢ orange yellow (1944)	12.00	28.00	245.00(50)	28.00	4.00	2.75
E19	20¢ black (1951)....	5.00	12.50	105.00(50)	12.00	1.95	.25

E20

E22

SCOTT NO.	DESCRIPTION	FIRST DAY COVERS SING	FIRST DAY COVERS PL. BLK.	MINT SHEET	PLATE BLOCK	UNUSED F/NH	USED
	1954-57						
E20	20¢ deep blue	2.50	6.25	32.00(50)	3.50	.70	.20
E21	30¢ lake (1957).....	2.50	6.25	43.00(50)	4.50	1.00	.20
	1969-71						
E22	45¢ carmine & violet blue	2.50	6.25	74.00(50)	8.00	1.60	.35
E23	60¢ violet blue & carmine (1971)	2.75	6.75	88.00(50)	9.00	1.85	.20

REGISTRATION STAMP

F1

1911 Registration

SCOTT NO.	DESCRIPTION	UNUSED NH F	UNUSED NH AVG	UNUSED OG F	UNUSED OG AVG	USED F	USED AVG
F1	10¢ ultramarine	200.00	135.00	95.00	60.00	12.00	8.00

U.S. CERTIFIED STAMP

FA1

1955 Certified Mail

SCOTT NO.	DESCRIPTION	FIRST DAY COVERS SING	FIRST DAY COVERS PL. BLK.	MINT SHEET	PLATE BLOCK	UNUSED F/NH	USED
FA1	15¢ red	2.50	6.25	32.00(50)	6.25	.65	.50

J1-J28

J29-J68

SCOTT NO.	DESCRIPTION	UNUSED NH F	UNUSED NH AVG	UNUSED OG F	UNUSED OG AVG	USED F	USED AVG
	1879 Unwatermarked Perf. 12						
J1	1¢ brown	275.00	165.00	95.00	70.00	17.00	11.00
J2	2¢ brown	1200.00	900.00	450.00	450.00	20.00	14.00
J3	3¢ brown	325.00	270.00	120.00	75.00	7.50	6.00
J4	5¢ brown	1900.00	1300.00	750.00	600.00	80.00	38.00
J5	10¢ brown	2700.00	1800.00	1100.00	800.00	80.00	60.00
J6	30¢ brown	1000.00	700.00	500.00	300.00	70.00	55.00
J7	50¢ brown	1900.00	1400.00	700.00	450.00	80.00	60.00
	1884-89						
J15	1¢ red brown	225.00	165.00	85.00	55.00	8.00	6.50
J16	2¢ red brown	275.00	200.00	100.00	70.00	7.00	5.00
J17	3¢ red brown	2900.00	2300.00	1180.00	875.00	350.00	275.00
J18	5¢ red brown	1600.00	1200.00	750.00	475.00	50.00	36.00
J19	10¢ red brown	1600.00	1450.00	750.00	460.00	40.00	30.00
J20	30¢ red brown	385.00	350.00	275.00	185.00	70.00	60.00
J21	50¢ red brown	4400.00	3000.00	2000.00	1450.00	250.00	185.00
	1891						
J22	1¢ bright claret	100.00	75.00	44.00	30.00	2.25	1.25
J23	2¢ bright claret	110.00	85.00	45.00	34.00	2.25	1.25
J24	3¢ bright claret	225.00	160.00	85.00	65.00	18.00	12.00
J25	5¢ bright claret	350.00	225.00	125.00	80.00	18.00	12.00
J26	10¢ bright claret	600.00	450.00	250.00	180.00	35.00	20.00
J27	30¢ bright claret	2000.00	1600.00	800.00	550.00	300.00	175.00
J28	50¢ bright claret	2100.00	1600.00	800.00	600.00	225.00	150.00
	1894 Unwatermarked Perf. 12 (†)						
J29	1¢ pale vermillion ...	6500.00	4200.00	2850.00	2250.00	750.00	600.00
J30	2¢ dark vermillion ...	2250.00	1375.00	900.00	700.00	400.00	255.00
J31	1¢ deep claret	325.00	260.00	90.00	70.00	14.00	12.00
J32	2¢ deep claret	300.00	250.00	75.00	50.00	12.00	9.00
J33	3¢ deep claret	625.00	400.00	225.00	175.00	55.00	40.00
J34	5¢ deep claret	1050.00	825.00	350.00	270.00	60.00	48.00
J35	10¢ deep claret	1200.00	900.00	450.00	300.00	45.00	35.00
J36	30¢ deep claret	1450.00	925.00	650.00	425.00	250.00	150.00
J36b	30¢ pale rose	1300.00	1000.00	600.00	400.00	225.00	125.00
J37	50¢ deep claret	5000.00	3800.00	2250.00	1750.00	850.00	600.00
	1895 Double Line Watermark Perf. 12 (†)						
J38	1¢ deep claret	48.00	40.00	18.00	13.50	1.50	1.00
J39	2¢ deep claret	48.00	40.00	18.00	13.50	1.50	1.00
J40	3¢ deep claret	300.00	250.00	120.00	90.00	4.50	3.00
J41	5¢ deep claret	325.00	275.00	130.00	100.00	4.50	3.00
J42	10¢ deep claret	325.00	275.00	130.00	100.00	7.00	5.50
J43	30¢ deep claret	1900.00	1300.00	800.00	650.00	70.00	60.00
J44	50¢ deep claret	1300.00	900.00	500.00	350.00	55.00	48.00
	1910-12 Single Line Watermark Perf. 12						
J45	1¢ deep claret	135.00	105.00	50.00	40.00	6.00	4.50
J46	2¢ deep claret	125.00	95.00	45.00	35.00	3.00	2.00
[illegible]	[illegible]	[illegible]	[illegible]	[illegible]	[illegible]	[illegible]	[illegible]
J48	5¢ deep claret	350.00	250.00	150.00	115.00	15.00	10.00
J49	10¢ deep claret	375.00	225.00	165.00	125.00	25.00	18.00
J50	50¢ deep claret (1912)	[illegible]	[illegible]	1200.00	[illegible]	195.00	150.00
	1914 Single Line Watermark Perf. 10						
J52	1¢ carmine lake	275.00	150.00	95.00	65.00	16.00	12.00
J53	2¢ carmine lake	225.00	130.00	75.00	55.00	1.25	.80
J54	3¢ carmine lake	3500.00	2500.00	1200.00	900.00	85.00	60.00
J55	5¢ carmine lake	175.00	135.00	60.00	45.00	7.00	5.00
J56	10¢ carmine lake ...	250.00	200.00	95.00	75.00	5.00	3.00
J57	30¢ carmine lake ...	650.00	400.00	300.00	185.00	60.00	40.00
J58	50¢ carmine lake ...	....	....	18500.00	15500.00	1600.00	1300.00
	1916 Unwatermarked Perf. 10						
J59	1¢ rose...........	11000.00	7500.00	5000.00	3500.00	750.00	600.00
J60	2¢ rose...........	800.00	600.00	325.00	250.00	80.00	60.00

SCOTT NO.	DESCRIPTION		PLATE BLOCK (OG) F/NH	PLATE BLOCK (OG) F	PLATE BLOCK (OG) AVG	UNUSED (OG) F/NH	UNUSED (OG) F	UNUSED (OG) AVG	USED F	USED AVG
	1917 Unwatermarked Perf. 11									
J61	1¢ carmine rose ..	(6)	85.00	53.00	35.00	11.00	5.00	3.00	.30	.25
J62	2¢ carmine rose ..	(6)	85.00	53.00	35.00	11.00	5.00	3.00	.30	.25
J63	3¢ carmine rose ..	(6)	170.00	95.00	70.00	45.00	17.00	10.00	.95	.45
J64	5¢ carmine......	(6)	240.00	150.00	95.00	40.00	16.00	8.00	.95	.45
J65	10¢ carmine rose.	(6)	450.00	190.00	145.00	75.00	30.00	18.00	1.25	.85
J66	30¢ carmine rose.		....	....	....	300.00	150.00	95.00	2.50	2.00
J67	50¢ carmine rose.		....	....	....	425.00	100.00	85.00	1.25	.85
	1925									
J68	½¢ dull red......	(6)	20.00	15.00	12.50	2.00	1.25	1.00	.30	.25

J69-J76, J79-J86

J77, J78, J87
1930 Perf. 11

J88-J104

SCOTT NO.	DESCRIPTION		PLATE BLOCK (OG) F/NH	PLATE BLOCK (OG) F	PLATE BLOCK (OG) AVG	UNUSED (OG) F/NH	UNUSED (OG) F	UNUSED (OG) AVG	USED F	USED AVG
J69	½¢ carmine	(6)	70.00	55.00	40.00	11.00	6.00	5.00	2.00	1.50
J70	1¢ carmine	(6)	80.00	60.00	45.00	7.50	3.50	2.50	.40	.30
J71	2¢ carmine	(6)	55.00	60.00	50.00	10.00	6.00	4.00	.40	.25
J72	3¢ carmine	(6)	450.00	300.00	250.00	55.00	35.00	25.00	3.00	2.50
J73	5¢ carmine	(6)	400.00	300.00	230.00	50.00	22.00	17.00	6.00	4.00
J74	10¢ carmine	(6)	675.00	300.00	350.00	100.00	75.00	60.00	2.50	1.85
J75	30¢ carmine		....	....	....	350.00	160.00	125.00	4.50	3.75
J76	50¢ carmine		....	....	....	500.00	325.00	250.00	2.50	1.75
J77	$1 scarlet	(6)	325.00	260.00	210.00	75.00	60.00	40.00	.40	.30
J78	$5 scarlet	(6)	350.00	295.00	220.00	95.00	50.00	38.00	.40	.30
	1931 Rotary Press Printing Perf. 11 x 10½									
J79-86	½¢-50¢, 8 varieties, complete		....	....	....	30.00	24.00	15.00	1.90	1.50
J79	½¢ dull carmine ..		28.00	20.00	18.00	1.75	1.00	.75	.30	.25
J80	1¢ dull carmine...		2.25	1.80	1.25	.35	.30	.25	.30	.25
J81	2¢ dull carmine...		2.25	1.80	1.25	.35	.30	.25	.30	.25
J82	3¢ dull carmine...		3.10	2.50	1.75	.35	.30	.25	.30	.25
J83	5¢ dull carmine...		4.75	3.75	3.00	.40	.35	.25	.30	.25
J84	10¢ dull carmine..		9.75	7.50	5.50	1.90	1.25	.40	.30	.25
J85	30¢ dull carmine..		60.00	45.00	33.00	12.00	8.00	6.00	.30	.25
J86	50¢ dull carmine..		95.00	65.00	50.00	17.00	12.50	10.00	.30	.25
	1956 Rotary Press Printing Perf. 10½ x 11									
J87	$1 scarlet		260.00	210.00	....	50.00	40.00	....	.30	....

SCOTT NO.	DESCRIPTION	MINT SHEET	PLATE BLOCK F/NH	PLATE BLOCK F	UNUSED F/NH	UNUSED F	USED F
	1959						
J88-101	½¢-$5, 14 varieties, complete	....	....	....	20.50	14.50	3.90
J88	½¢ carmine rose & black	400.00(100)	210.00	175.00	1.85	1.50	1.50
J89	1¢ carmine rose & black	9.50(100)	1.25	.75	.30	.25	.25
J90	2¢ carmine rose & black	13.00(100)	1.25	.75	.30	.25	.25
J91	3¢ carmine rose & black	14.00(100)	1.00	.70	.30	.25	.25
J92	4¢ carmine rose & black	20.00(100)	1.25	.85	.30	.25	.25
J93	5¢ carmine rose & black	20.00(100)	1.00	.70	.30	.25	.25
J94	6¢ carmine rose & black	20.00(100)	1.35	.90	.30	.25	.25
J95	7¢ carmine rose & black	32.00(100)	2.25	1.75	.30	.25	.25
J96	8¢ carmine rose & black	32.00(100)	2.25	1.75	.30	.25	.25
J97	10¢ carmine rose & black	32.00(100)	1.80	1.30	.45	.30	.25
J98	30¢ carmine rose & black	97.00(100)	5.25	4.25	1.55	1.00	.25
J99	50¢ carmine rose & black	155.00(100)	7.00	5.75	2.00	1.50	.25
J100	$1 carmine rose & black	310.00(100)	17.00	12.00	3.75	2.75	.25
J101	$5 carmine rose & black	1500.00(100)	72.00	60.00	17.00	13.00	.50
	1978-1985						
J102	11¢ carmine rose & black	37.00(100)	4.00	....	.45	....	.50
J103	13¢ carmine rose & black	42.00(100)	2.95	....	.50	....	.50
J104	17¢ carmine rose & black	116.00(100)	40.00	....	.75	....	.55

OFFICES IN CHINA

SHANGHAI
2¢
CHINA
1919
K1-16: U.S. Postage 498-518 surcharged

SHANGHAI
2 Cts.
CHINA
1922
K17-18: U.S. Postage 498-528B with local surcharge

SCOTT NO.	DESCRIPTION	UNUSED NH F	UNUSED NH AVG	UNUSED OG F	UNUSED OG AVG	USED F	USED AVG
	1919						
K1	2¢ on 1¢ green	75.00	50.00	35.00	25.00	50.00	40.00
K2	4¢ on 2¢ rose	75.00	50.00	35.00	25.00	50.00	40.00
K3	6¢ on 3¢ violet.....	160.00	125.00	75.00	50.00	115.00	85.00
K4	8¢ on 4¢ brown	160.00	135.00	75.00	50.00	115.00	85.00
K5	10¢ on 5¢ blue	180.00	145.00	75.00	50.00	115.00	85.00
K6	12¢ on 6¢ red orange	225.00	185.00	100.00	60.00	165.00	111.00
K7	14¢ on 7¢ black....	230.00	190.00	90.00	60.00	180.00	120.00
K8	16¢ on 8¢ olive bistre	185.00	130.00	75.00	50.00	125.00	90.00
K8a	16¢ on 8¢ olive green	165.00	125.00	75.00	50.00	110.00	95.00
K9	18¢ on 9¢ salmon red	175.00	135.00	70.00	50.00	150.00	100.00
K10	20¢ on 10¢ orange yellow	165.00	125.00	70.00	50.00	125.00	80.00
K11	24¢ on 12¢ brown carmine	225.00	175.00	70.00	50.00	130.00	70.00
K11a	24¢ on 12¢ claret brown	280.00	200.00	115.00	80.00	175.00	110.00
K12	30¢ on 15¢ gray ...	225.00	160.00	100.00	60.00	200.00	160.00
K13	40¢ on 20¢ deep ultra.	325.00	235.00	150.00	90.00	285.00	200.00
K14	60¢ on 30¢ orange red	300.00	200.00	150.00	90.00	240.00	180.00
K15	$1 on 50¢ light violet	1350.00	950.00	600.00	400.00	850.00	600.00
K16	$2 on $1 violet brown	1200.00	[illegible]	[illegible]	400.00	750.00	450.00
	1922 LOCAL ISSUES						
K17	2¢ on 1¢ green	300.00	200.00	140.00	90.00	170.00	125.00
K18	4¢ on 2¢ carmine ..	300.00	200.00	140.00	90.00	150.00	120.00

OFFICIAL STAMPS

O1-O9, O94, O95 — O10-O14 — O15-O24, O96-O103 — O25-O34, O106, O107

Except for the Post Office Department, portraits for the various denominations are the same as on the regular issues of 1870-73

1873 Printed by the Continental Bank Note Co.
Thin hard paper
(OG + 40%)
(O1-O120 for VF Centering–Fine Price + 50%)

SCOTT NO.	DESCRIPTION	UNUSED F	UNUSED AVG	USED F	USED AVG
	DEPARTMENT OF AGRICULTURE				
O1	1¢ yellow	225.00	140.00	175.00	130.00
O2	2¢ yellow	200.00	115.00	80.00	50.00
O3	3¢ yellow	180.00	110.00	18.00	13.00
O4	6¢ yellow	220.00	140.00	65.00	45.00
O5	10¢ yellow	440.00	250.00	175.00	130.00
O6	12¢ yellow	375.00	225.00	220.00	145.00
O7	15¢ yellow	345.00	240.00	200.00	160.00
O8	24¢ yellow	345.00	240.00	190.00	125.00
O9	30¢ yellow	475.00	325.00	250.00	190.00
	EXECUTIVE DEPARTMENT				
O10	1¢ carmine	750.00	500.00	410.00	280.00
O11	2¢ carmine	490.00	410.00	225.00	155.00
O12	3¢ carmine	650.00	475.00	225.00	165.00
O13	6¢ carmine	800.00	675.00	450.00	350.00
O14	10¢ carmine	1100.00	800.00	700.00	500.00
	DEPARTMENT OF THE INTERIOR				
O15	1¢ vermillion	65.00	50.00	11.00	8.50
O16	2¢ vermillion	65.00	50.00	13.00	11.00
O17	3¢ vermillion	70.00	55.00	7.00	5.75
O18	6¢ vermillion	65.00	50.00	11.00	9.00
O19	10¢ vermillion	65.00	50.00	22.00	18.00
O20	12¢ vermillion	80.00	60.00	13.00	10.00
O21	15¢ vermillion	180.00	140.00	26.00	22.00
O22	24¢ vermillion	160.00	130.00	21.00	18.00
O23	30¢ vermillion	240.00	200.00	21.00	17.00
O24	90¢ vermillion	290.00	250.00	48.00	38.00
	DEPARTMENT OF JUSTICE				
O25	1¢ purple	230.00	210.00	100.00	85.00
O26	2¢ purple	280.00	240.00	110.00	95.00
O27	3¢ purple	290.00	240.00	38.00	24.00
O28	6¢ purple	280.00	240.00	45.00	36.00
O29	10¢ purple	290.00	240.00	90.00	70.00
O30	12¢ purple	240.00	195.00	70.00	60.00
O31	15¢ purple	420.00	360.00	185.00	165.00
O32	24¢ purple	1150.00	920.00	400.00	355.00
O33	30¢ purple	1200.00	900.00	340.00	250.00
O34	90¢ purple	1800.00	1400.00	800.00	700.00

O35-O45 — O47-O56, O108 — O57-O67 — O68-O71

NAVY DEPARTMENT
(OG + 30%)

SCOTT NO.	DESCRIPTION	UNUSED F	UNUSED AVG	USED F	USED AVG
O35	1¢ ultramarine	150.00	120.00	55.00	46.00
O36	2¢ ultramarine	155.00	125.00	30.00	26.00
O37	3¢ ultramarine	160.00	130.00	14.00	10.00
O38	6¢ ultramarine	175.00	140.00	23.00	14.00
O39	7¢ ultramarine	600.00	500.00	240.00	185.00
O40	10¢ ultramarine	200.00	160.00	38.00	25.00
O41	12¢ ultramarine	215.00	170.00	38.00	25.00
O42	15¢ ultramarine	350.00	310.00	60.00	35.00
O43	24¢ ultramarine	400.00	350.00	64.00	38.00
O44	30¢ ultramarine	300.00	280.00	45.00	26.00
O45	90¢ ultramarine	900.00	800.00	375.00	320.00

OFFICIAL STAMPS: From 1873 to 1879, Congress authorized the use of Official Stamps to prepay postage on government mail. Separate issues were produced for each department so that mailing costs could be assigned to that department's budget. Penalty envelopes replaced Official Stamps on May 1, 1879.

O72-O82, O109-O113 — O83-O93, O114-O120

SCOTT NO.	DESCRIPTION	UNUSED F	UNUSED AVG	USED F	USED AVG
	POST OFFICE DEPARTMENT				
O47	1¢ black	22.00	17.00	12.00	8.00
O48	2¢ black	25.00	18.00	10.00	7.00
O49	3¢ black	10.00	7.00	2.50	1.00
O50	6¢ black	26.00	20.00	7.00	5.00
O51	10¢ black	120.00	85.00	52.00	40.00
O52	12¢ black	115.00	95.00	12.00	8.00
O53	15¢ black	125.00	90.00	19.00	12.00
O54	24¢ black	175.00	130.00	23.00	15.00
O55	30¢ black	185.00	135.00	24.00	16.00
O56	90¢ black	210.00	130.00	24.00	16.00
	DEPARTMENT OF STATE				
O57	1¢ dark green	240.00	150.00	70.00	55.00
O58	2¢ dark green	280.00	225.00	95.00	75.00
O59	3¢ bright green	195.00	140.00	24.00	18.00
O60	6¢ bright green	195.00	145.00	30.00	20.00
O61	7¢ dark green	300.00	185.00	60.00	45.00
O62	10¢ dark green	210.00	135.00	55.00	40.00
O63	12¢ dark green	270.00	185.00	110.00	75.00
O64	15¢ dark green	285.00	225.00	95.00	78.00
O65	24¢ dark green	485.00	450.00	230.00	175.00
O66	30¢ dark green	450.00	390.00	185.00	145.00
O67	90¢ dark green	900.00	700.00	300.00	250.00
O68	$2 green & black	1450.00	1100.00	2000.00	1400.00
O69	$5 green & black	6400.00	5000.00	10000.00	7000.00
O70	$10 green & black	4450.00	3600.00	6000.00	5500.00
O71	$20 green & black	4800.00	4200.00	4450.00	2900.00
	TREASURY DEPARTMENT (OG + 30%)				
O72	1¢ brown	120.00	90.00	10.00	8.00
O73	2¢ brown	125.00	95.00	8.50	7.00
O74	3¢ brown	110.00	90.00	2.50	1.25
O75	6¢ brown	120.00	90.00	4.50	3.50
O76	7¢ brown	230.00	190.00	37.00	30.00
O77	10¢ brown	230.00	190.00	12.00	8.00
O78	12¢ brown	260.00	200.00	9.00	7.00
O79	15¢ brown	270.00	220.00	12.00	8.00
O80	24¢ brown	575.00	450.00	90.00	70.00
O81	30¢ brown	375.00	275.00	12.00	8.00
O82	90¢ brown	425.00	330.00	15.00	12.00
	WAR DEPARTMENT				
O83	1¢ rose	230.00	180.00	14.00	10.00
O84	2¢ rose	230.00	180.00	14.00	10.00
O85	3¢ rose	230.00	180.00	5.00	3.50
O86	6¢ rose	600.00	475.00	11.00	9.00
O87	7¢ rose	160.00	135.00	85.00	65.00
O88	10¢ rose	140.00	110.00	24.00	18.00
O89	12¢ rose	250.00	220.00	13.00	10.00
O90	15¢ rose	85.00	70.00	16.00	13.00
O91	24¢ rose	85.00	70.00	13.00	11.00
O92	30¢ rose	125.00	110.00	13.00	11.00
O93	90¢ rose	195.00	165.00	55.00	45.00

1879 Printed by American Bank Note Co.
Soft Porous Paper
DEPARTMENT OF AGRICULTURE

SCOTT NO.	DESCRIPTION	UNUSED F	UNUSED AVG	USED F	USED AVG
O94	1¢ yellow	6000.00	4900.00	....	....
O95	3¢ yellow	525.00	450.00	120.00	75.00
	DEPARTMENT OF INTERIOR				
O96	1¢ vermillion	275.00	230.00	320.00	240.00
O97	2¢ vermillion	10.00	8.00	3.50	2.50
O98	3¢ vermillion	9.00	7.00	3.25	2.25
O99	6¢ vermillion	11.00	8.00	13.00	10.00
O100	10¢ vermillion	95.00	80.00	80.00	70.00
O101	12¢ vermillion	225.00	185.00	120.00	100.00
O102	15¢ vermillion	375.00	210.00	400.00	290.00
O103	24¢ vermillion	4200.00	3500.00	6200.00	....
	DEPARTMENT OF JUSTICE				
O106	3¢ bluish purple	175.00	140.00	110.00	85.00
O107	6¢ bluish purple	450.00	385.00	260.00	195.00
	POST OFFICE DEPARTMENT				
O108	3¢ black	32.00	27.00	9.00	6.00
	TREASURY DEPARTMENT				
O109	3¢ brown	80.00	60.00	11.00	8.75
O110	6¢ brown	180.00	130.00	55.00	48.00
O111	10¢ brown	250.00	215.00	75.00	45.00
O112	30¢ brown	2400.00	2000.00	440.00	350.00
O113	90¢ brown	4600.00	3400.00	600.00	375.00

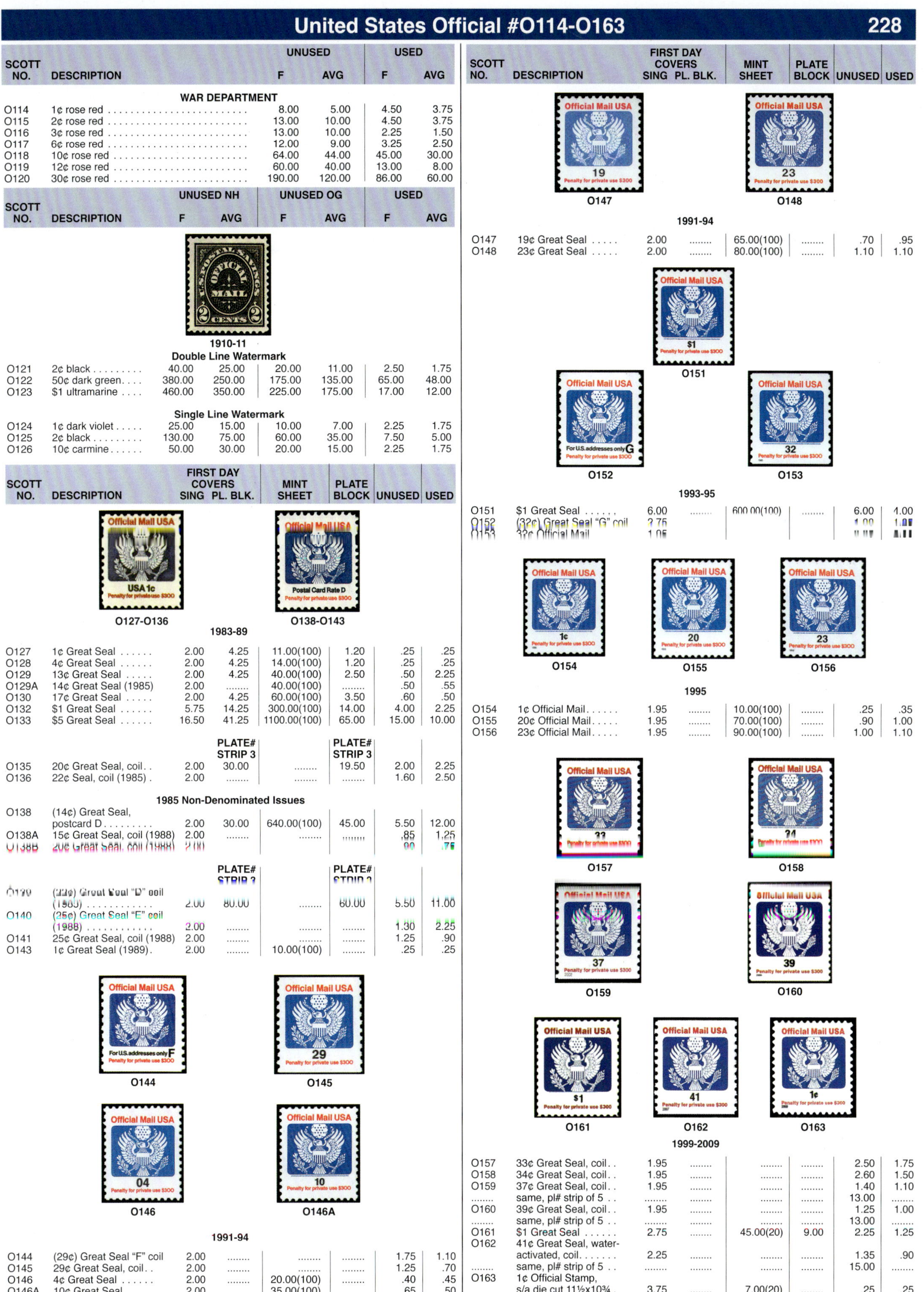

SCOTT NO.	DESCRIPTION	UNUSED F	UNUSED AVG	USED F	USED AVG
	WAR DEPARTMENT				
O114	1¢ rose red	8.00	5.00	4.50	3.75
O115	2¢ rose red	13.00	10.00	4.50	3.75
O116	3¢ rose red	13.00	10.00	2.25	1.50
O117	6¢ rose red	12.00	9.00	3.25	2.50
O118	10¢ rose red	64.00	44.00	45.00	30.00
O119	12¢ rose red	60.00	40.00	13.00	8.00
O120	30¢ rose red	190.00	120.00	86.00	60.00

1910-11

Double Line Watermark

SCOTT NO.	DESCRIPTION	UNUSED NH F	UNUSED NH AVG	UNUSED OG F	UNUSED OG AVG	USED F	USED AVG
O121	2¢ black	40.00	25.00	20.00	11.00	2.50	1.75
O122	50¢ dark green	380.00	250.00	175.00	135.00	65.00	48.00
O123	$1 ultramarine	460.00	350.00	225.00	175.00	17.00	12.00
	Single Line Watermark						
O124	1¢ dark violet	25.00	15.00	10.00	7.00	2.25	1.75
O125	2¢ black	130.00	75.00	60.00	35.00	7.50	5.00
O126	10¢ carmine	50.00	30.00	20.00	15.00	2.25	1.75

USA 1c

O127-O136

Postal Card Rate D

O138-O143

1983-89

SCOTT NO.	DESCRIPTION	FIRST DAY COVERS SING	FIRST DAY COVERS PL. BLK.	MINT SHEET	PLATE BLOCK	UNUSED	USED
O127	1¢ Great Seal	2.00	4.25	11.00(100)	1.20	.25	.25
O128	4¢ Great Seal	2.00	4.25	14.00(100)	1.20	.25	.25
O129	13¢ Great Seal	2.00	4.25	40.00(100)	2.50	.50	2.25
O129A	14¢ Great Seal (1985)	2.00	....	40.00(100)	....	.50	.55
O130	17¢ Great Seal	2.00	4.25	60.00(100)	3.50	.60	.50
O132	$1 Great Seal	5.75	14.25	300.00(100)	14.00	4.00	2.25
O133	$5 Great Seal	16.50	41.25	1100.00(100)	65.00	15.00	10.00
			PLATE# STRIP 3		PLATE# STRIP 3		
O135	20¢ Great Seal, coil	2.00	30.00	....	19.50	2.00	2.25
O136	22¢ Seal, coil (1985)	2.00	....	....	....	1.60	2.50
	1985 Non-Denominated Issues						
O138	(14¢) Great Seal, postcard D	2.00	30.00	640.00(100)	45.00	5.50	12.00
O138A	15¢ Great Seal, coil (1988)	2.00	....	....	....	.85	1.25
O138B	20¢ Great Seal, coil (1988)	2.00				.90	.75
			PLATE# STRIP 3		PLATE# STRIP 3		
O139	(22¢) Great Seal "D" coil (1985)	2.00	80.00	....	60.00	5.50	11.00
O140	(25¢) Great Seal "E" coil (1988)	2.00	....	....	....	1.30	2.25
O141	25¢ Great Seal, coil (1988)	2.00	....	....	....	1.25	.90
O143	1¢ Great Seal (1989)	2.00	....	10.00(100)	....	.25	.25

For U.S. addresses only F

O144

29

O145

04

O146

10

O146A

1991-94

SCOTT NO.	DESCRIPTION	FIRST DAY COVERS SING	FIRST DAY COVERS PL. BLK.	MINT SHEET	PLATE BLOCK	UNUSED	USED
O144	(29¢) Great Seal "F" coil	2.00	....	....	....	1.75	1.10
O145	29¢ Great Seal, coil	2.00	....	....	....	1.25	.70
O146	4¢ Great Seal	2.00	....	20.00(100)	....	.40	.45
O146A	10¢ Great Seal	2.00	....	35.00(100)	....	.65	.50

19

O147

23

O148

1991-94

SCOTT NO.	DESCRIPTION	FIRST DAY COVERS SING	FIRST DAY COVERS PL. BLK.	MINT SHEET	PLATE BLOCK	UNUSED	USED
O147	19¢ Great Seal	2.00	....	65.00(100)	....	.70	.95
O148	23¢ Great Seal	2.00	....	80.00(100)	....	1.10	1.10

$1

O151

For U.S. addresses only G

O152

32

O153

1993-95

SCOTT NO.	DESCRIPTION	FIRST DAY COVERS SING	FIRST DAY COVERS PL. BLK.	MINT SHEET	PLATE BLOCK	UNUSED	USED
O151	$1 Great Seal	6.00	....	600.00(100)	....	6.00	4.00
O152	(32¢) Great Seal "G" coil	2.75				1.00	[illegible]
O153	32¢ Official Mail	1.95				[illegible]	[illegible]

1¢

O154

20

O155

23

O156

1995

SCOTT NO.	DESCRIPTION	FIRST DAY COVERS SING	FIRST DAY COVERS PL. BLK.	MINT SHEET	PLATE BLOCK	UNUSED	USED
O154	1¢ Official Mail	1.95	....	10.00(100)	....	.25	.35
O155	20¢ Official Mail	1.95	....	70.00(100)	....	.90	1.00
O156	23¢ Official Mail	1.95	....	90.00(100)	....	1.00	1.10

33

O157

34

O158

37

O159

39

O160

$1

O161

41

O162

1¢

O163

1999-2009

SCOTT NO.	DESCRIPTION	FIRST DAY COVERS SING	FIRST DAY COVERS PL. BLK.	MINT SHEET	PLATE BLOCK	UNUSED	USED
O157	33¢ Great Seal, coil	1.95	....	....	....	2.50	1.75
O158	34¢ Great Seal, coil	1.95	....	....	....	2.60	1.50
O159	37¢ Great Seal, coil	1.95	....	....	....	1.40	1.10
....	same, pl# strip of 5	....	....	....	....	13.00	....
O160	39¢ Great Seal, coil	1.95	....	....	....	1.25	1.00
....	same, pl# strip of 5	....	....	....	....	13.00	....
O161	$1 Great Seal	2.75	....	45.00(20)	9.00	2.25	1.25
O162	41¢ Great Seal, water-activated, coil	2.25	....	....	....	1.35	.90
....	same, pl# strip of 5	....	....	....	....	15.00	....
O163	1¢ Official Stamp, s/a die cut 11½x10¾	3.75	....	7.00(20)	....	.25	.25

NEWSPAPER AND PERIODICAL STAMPS

In September of the year 1865, stamps specifically designated for newspapers and periodicals were issued and utilized by the USPS. These newly introduced stamps facilitated the prepayment of postage for bulk shipments for the ever-growing demand of newspapers and periodicals. The use of these specialized stamps was ultimately discontinued on July 1, 1898.

SCOTT NO.	DESCRIPTION	UNUSED OG FINE	UNUSED FINE	USED FINE

Values listed are for Fine centering. PR1-PR7 valued with typical faults or straight edges.

PR1 (colored border)
PR4, PR5, PR8 (white border)

PR2, PR6
(colored border)

PR3, PR7
(colored border)

1865 Printed by the National Bank Note Co.
Thin hard paper, without gum
Perf. 12, unwatermarked, colored border

PR1	5¢ dark blue	....	600.00	1500.00
PR2	10¢ blue green	....	250.00	1800.00
PR3	25¢ orange red	....	300.00	2000.00
PR4	5¢ light blue, white border, yellowish paper	....	600.00	2500.00

Reprint of 1865 Issue
1875 Printed by the Continental Bank Note Co.
hard white paper, without gum

PR5	5¢ dull blue, white border	....	200.00	....
PR6	10¢ dark bluish green, colored border	....	220.00	....
PR7	25¢ dark carmine, colored border	....	250.00	....

1881 Printed by the American Bank Note Co.
Soft porous paper, without gum

PR8	5¢ dark blue, white border	....	500.00	....

PR9-15, PR33-39,
PR57-62, PR80-81,
PR90-94

PR16-23, PR40-47,
PR63-70, PR82-89,
PR95-99

PR24, PR48, PR71,

PR25, PR49, PR72, PR100

PR26, PR50, PR73, PR101

PR27, PR51, PR74

SCOTT NO.	DESCRIPTION	UNUSED OG FINE	UNUSED FINE	USED FINE

PR28, PR52, PR75

PR29, PR53, PR76

PR30, PR54, PR77

PR31, PR55, PR78

PR32, PR56, PR79

1875 Printed by the Continental Bank Note Co.
Thin hard paper
Perf. 12, Design size: 24mm x 35mm

PR9	2¢ black	200.00	80.00	40.00
PR10	3¢ black	200.00	80.00	40.00
PR11	4¢ black	200.00	100.00	40.00
PR12	6¢ black	200.00	100.00	40.00
PR13	8¢ black	200.00	100.00	60.00
PR14	9¢ black	350.00	150.00	100.00
PR15	10¢ black	200.00	80.00	60.00
PR16	12¢ rose	500.00	200.00	100.00
PR17	24¢ rose	600.00	200.00	150.00
PR18	36¢ rose	600.00	250.00	200.00
PR19	48¢ rose	850.00	300.00	400.00
PR20	60¢ rose	1100.00	350.00	100.00
PR21	72¢ rose	1200.00	300.00	300.00
PR22	84¢ rose	1200.00	300.00	300.00
PR23	96¢ rose	1400.00	500.00	250.00
PR24	$1.92 dark brown	1400.00	500.00	250.00
PR25	$3 vermillion	1500.00	550.00	500.00
PR26	$6 ultramarine	2500.00	1100.00	700.00
PR27	$9 yellow orange	3000.00	1200.00	2500.00
PR28	$12 blue green	2700.00	1200.00	1400.00
PR29	$24 dark gray violet	3000.00	1200.00	1500.00
PR30	$36 brown rose	3200.00	1500.00	1800.00
PR31	$48 red brown	4700.00	2200.00	2000.00
PR32	$60 violet	4500.00	2000.00	2200.00

Special Printing of 1875 Issue
Printed by the Continental Bank Note Co.
Perf. 12, hard white paper, without gum

PR33	2¢ gray black	....	450.00	....
PR34	3¢ gray black	....	450.00	....
PR35	4¢ gray black	....	420.00	....
PR36	6¢ gray black	....	650.00	....
PR37	8¢ gray black	....	750.00	....
PR38	9¢ gray black	....	800.00	....
PR39	10¢ gray black	....	1000.00	....
PR40	12¢ pale rose	....	1200.00	....
PR41	24¢ pale rose	....	1500.00	....
PR42	36¢ pale rose	....	2000.00	....
PR43	48¢ pale rose	....	3000.00	....
PR44	60¢ pale rose	....	3200.00	....
PR45	72¢ pale rose	....	3000.00	....
PR46	84¢ pale rose	....	4000.00	....
PR47	96¢ pale rose	....	7000.00	....
PR48	$1.92 dark brown	....	....	....
PR49	$3 vermillion	....	....	....
PR50	$6 ultramarine	....	....	....
PR51	$9 yellow orange	....	....	....
PR52	$12 blue green	....	....	....
PR53	$24 dark gray violet	....	....	....
PR54	$36 brown rose	....	....	....
PR55	$48 red brown	....	....	....
PR56	$60 violet	....	....	....

1879 Printed by the American Bank Note Co.
Soft porous paper, unwatermarked

PR57	2¢ black	55.00	20.00	15.00
PR58	3¢ black	55.00	25.00	20.00
PR59	4¢ black	60.00	30.00	25.00
PR60	6¢ black	100.00	35.00	40.00
PR61	8¢ black	100.00	50.00	40.00
PR62	10¢ black	120.00	50.00	40.00
PR63	12¢ red	400.00	150.00	120.00
PR64	24¢ red	400.00	150.00	120.00
PR65	36¢ red	800.00	300.00	350.00
PR66	48¢ red	800.00	300.00	300.00

SCOTT NO.	DESCRIPTION	UNUSED OG FINE	UNUSED FINE	USED FINE
	1879 Printed by the American Bank Note Co. Continued Soft porous paper, unwatermarked			
PR67	60¢ red	900.00	400.00	300.00
PR68	72¢ red	1100.00	500.00	400.00
PR69	84¢ red	900.00	400.00	350.00
PR70	96¢ red	1200.00	500.00	300.00
PR71	$1.92 pale brown	400.00	220.00	200.00
PR72	$3 red vermilion	500.00	220.00	200.00
PR73	$6 blue	700.00	250.00	350.00
PR74	$9 orange	550.00	250.00	300.00
PR75	$12 yellow green	600.00	250.00	300.00
PR76	$24 dark violet	550.00	200.00	350.00
PR77	$36 Indian red	550.00	250.00	400.00
PR78	$48 yellow brown	600.00	250.00	500.00
PR79	$60 purple	600.00	250.00	400.00
	Special Printing of 1879 Issue 1883 Printed by the American Bank Note Co. without gum			
PR80	2¢ intense black	....	1500.00	....
	1885 Regular Issue Printed by the American Bank Note Co. Perf. 12, unwatermarked, with gum			
PR81	1¢ black	60.00	30.00	15.00
PR82	12¢ carmine	150.00	60.00	30.00
PR83	24¢ carmine	200.00	80.00	30.00
PR84	36¢ carmine	250.00	100.00	50.00
PR85	48¢ carmine	300.00	120.00	80.00
PR86	60¢ carmine	500.00	150.00	120.00
PR87	72¢ carmine	500.00	150.00	100.00
PR88	84¢ carmine	600.00	220.00	220.00
PR89	96¢ carmine	550.00	200.00	220.00
	1894 Printed by the Bureau of Engraving and Printing soft woven paper, with pale whitish gum			
PR90	1¢ intense black	300.00	150.00	....
PR91	2¢ intense black	350.00	120.00	....
PR92	4¢ intense black	400.00	150.00	....
PR93	6¢ intense black	3000.00	1400.00	....
PR94	10¢ intense black	1000.00	400.00	....
PR95	12¢ pink	1800.00	800.00	....
PR96	24¢ pink	3000.00	1500.00	....
PR97	36¢ pink	....	....	....
PR98	60¢ pink	....	....	....
PR99	96¢ pink	....	....	....
PR100	$3 scarlet	....	....	....
PR101	$6 pale blue	....	....	....

PR102-105, PR114-117

PR106, PR107, PR118-119

PR108, PR120

PR109, PR121

PR110, PR122

PR111, PR123

PR112, PR124

PR113, PR125

SCOTT NO.	DESCRIPTION	UNUSED OG FINE	UNUSED FINE	USED FINE
	1895 Printed by the Bureau of Engraving and Printing Perf. 12, unwatermarked, with gum			
PR102	1¢ black	150.00	60.00	120.00
PR103	2¢ black	150.00	80.00	100.00
PR104	5¢ black	250.00	100.00	300.00
PR105	10¢ black	500.00	200.00	600.00
PR106	25¢ carmine	500.00	200.00	600.00
PR107	50¢ carmine	1600.00	600.00	1000.00
PR108	$2 scarlet	1500.00	600.00	900.00
PR109	$5 ultra	1600.00	700.00	2000.00
PR110	$10 green	1800.00	800.00	2500.00
PR111	$20 slate	2200.00	1000.00	2500.00
PR112	$50 dull rose	1800.00	1000.00	1200.00
PR113	$100 purple	2500.00	1000.00	....
	1895-97 Printed by the Bureau of Engraving and Printing Perf. 12, double-line watermark, with gum			
PR114	1¢ black	6.00	2.00	20.00
PR115	2¢ black	6.00	2.00	20.00
PR116	5¢ black	10.00	3.00	30.00
PR117	10¢ black	10.00	5.00	20.00
PR118	25¢ carmine	15.00	6.00	50.00
PR119	50¢ carmine	20.00	8.00	60.00
PR120	$2 scarlet	25.00	8.00	85.00
PR121	$5 dark blue	35.00	12.00	100.00
PR122	$10 green	30.00	15.00	100.00
PR123	$20 slate	30.00	15.00	120.00
PR124	$50 dull rose	65.00	20.00	250.00
PR125	$100 purple	65.00	20.00	200.00

PARCEL POST STAMPS

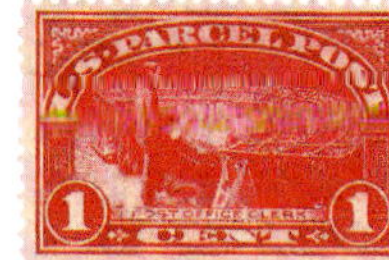
Q1-Q12 Various Designs

SPECIAL HANDLING STAMPS

QE1-QE4

PARCEL POST DUE STAMPS

JQ1-JQ5

SCOTT NO.	DESCRIPTION	UNUSED NH F	UNUSED NH AVG	UNUSED OG F	UNUSED OG AVG	USED F	USED AVG
	(Q1-QE4a for VF Centering–Fine Price + 40%)						
	1912-13 Parcel Post–All Printed in Carmine Rose						
Q1	1¢ Post Office Clerk	15.00	10.00	7.00	5.00	2.00	1.50
Q2	2¢ City Carrier	20.00	12.00	10.00	7.00	1.50	1.20
Q3	3¢ Railway Clerk	45.00	30.00	20.00	15.00	7.00	5.50
Q4	4¢ Rural Carrier	115.00	85.00	50.00	30.00	4.00	2.85
Q5	5¢ Mail Train	100.00	70.00	50.00	40.00	3.00	2.50
Q6	10¢ Steamship	170.00	120.00	80.00	50.00	4.00	3.00
Q7	15¢ Auto Service	185.00	135.00	80.00	55.00	16.00	10.00
Q8	20¢ Airplane	400.00	200.00	[illegible]	125.00	32.00	28.00
Q9	25¢ Manufacturing	300.00	120.00	75.00	55.00	9.00	7.00
Q10	50¢ Dairying	[illegible]	[illegible]	330.00	220.00	52.00	39.00
Q11	75¢ Harvesting	270.00	160.00	120.00	70.00	42.00	36.00
Q12	$1 Fruit Growing	600.00	550.00	250.00	200.00	48.00	38.00
	1913 Parcel Post Due						
JQ1	1¢ dark green	30.00	20.00	12.00	8.00	5.00	4.00
JQ2	2¢ dark green	250.00	150.00	100.00	65.00	18.00	15.00
JQ3	5¢ dark green	45.00	30.00	20.00	12.00	6.00	5.00
JQ4	10¢ dark green	450.00	300.00	200.00	130.00	50.00	44.00
JQ5	25¢ dark green	300.00	200.00	120.00	80.00	6.00	5.00
	1925-29 Special Handling						
QE1	10¢ yellow green	5.00	3.75	3.00	2.50	1.50	1.20
QE2	15¢ yellow green	5.50	40.00	3.50	2.25	2.00	1.20
QE3	20¢ yellow green	8.50	6.00	5.00	4.00	1.95	1.35
QE4	25¢ deep green	50.00	30.00	21.00	16.00	8.00	5.00
QE4a	25¢ yellow green	50.00	40.00	30.00	19.00	18.00	14.00

POSTAL NOTE STAMPS

PN1-P18
All values printed in black

SCOTT NO.	DESCRIPTION	UNUSED F/NH	UNUSED F/OG	USED F
PN1-18	1¢-90¢, 18 varieties, complete	42.00	35.00	5.00

ENVELOPES

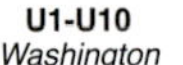

U1-U10
Washington

U19-U24
Franklin

U26, U27
Washington

1853-55

SCOTT NO.	DESCRIPTION	UNUSED ENTIRE	UNUSED CUT SQ.	USED CUT SQ.
U1	3¢ red on white, die 1	1650.00	400.00	38.00
U2	3¢ red on buff, die 1	875.00	95.00	35.00
U3	3¢ red on white, die 2	3800.00	1000.00	52.00
U4	3¢ red on buff, die 2	3275.00	500.00	45.00
U5	3¢ red on white, die 3	26000.00	6000.00	600.00
U6	3¢ red on buff, die 3	....	5200.00	105.00
U7	3¢ red on white, die 4	....	5500.00	160.00
U8	3¢ red on buff, die 4	....	8500.00	485.00
U9	3¢ red on white, die 5	150.00	45.00	45.00
U10	3¢ red on buff, die 5	80.00	25.00	25.00
U11	6¢ red on white	400.00	325.00	100.00
U12	6¢ red on buff	365.00	150.00	100.00
U13	6¢ green on white	600.00	275.00	165.00
U14	6¢ green on buff	400.00	225.00	130.00
U15	10¢ green on white, die 1	750.00	500.00	110.00
U16	10¢ green on buff, die 1	475.00	180.00	100.00
U17	10¢ green on white, die 2	725.00	400.00	150.00
U18	10¢ green on buff, die 2	650.00	375.00	110.00

1860-61

SCOTT NO.	DESCRIPTION	UNUSED ENTIRE	UNUSED CUT SQ.	USED CUT SQ.
U19	1¢ blue on buff, die 1	90.00	35.00	15.50
W20	1¢ blue on buff, die 1	130.00	70.00	55.00
W21	1¢ blue on manila, die 1	135.00	65.00	45.00
W22	1¢ blue on orange, die 1	6500.00	3200.00	....
U23	1¢ blue on orange, die 2	850.00	625.00	350.00
U24	1¢ blue on buff, die 3	725.00	365.00	110.00
U26	3¢ red on white	60.00	30.00	18.00
U27	3¢ red on buff	50.00	25.00	15.00
U28	3¢ & 1¢ red & blue on white	525.00	260.00	240.00
U29	3¢ & 1¢ red & blue on buff	525.00	260.00	260.00
U30	6¢ red on white	3500.00	2200.00	1750.00
U31	6¢ red on buff	5500.00	3700.00	1600.00
U32	10¢ green on white	10000.00	1400.00	460.00
U33	10¢ green on buff	3500.00	1500.00	420.00

U34-U37

U40-U41

Washington

1861

SCOTT NO.	DESCRIPTION	UNUSED ENTIRE	UNUSED CUT SQ.	USED CUT SQ.
U34	3¢ pink on white	65.00	30.00	6.00
U35	3¢ pink on buff	65.00	35.00	6.50
U36	3¢ pink on blue (letter sheet)	250.00	75.00	75.00
U37	3¢ pink on orange	4500.00	3000.00	....
U38	6¢ pink on white	220.00	110.00	85.00
U39	6¢ pink on buff	225.00	65.00	65.00
U40	10¢ yellow green on white	80.00	45.00	35.00
U41	10¢ yellow green on buff	80.00	45.00	35.00
U42	12¢ brown & red on buff	480.00	185.00	185.00
U43	20¢ blue & red on buff	460.00	260.00	225.00
U44	24¢ green & red on buff	640.00	220.00	220.00
U45	40¢ red & black on buff	750.00	325.00	425.00

U46-U49

U50-W57

Jackson

1863-64

SCOTT NO.	DESCRIPTION	UNUSED ENTIRE	UNUSED CUT SQ.	USED CUT SQ.
U46	2¢ black on buff, die 1	85.00	55.00	25.00
W47	2¢ black on dark manila, die 1	125.00	110.00	70.00
U48	2¢ black on buff, die 2	4800.00	2500.00	....
U49	2¢ black on orange, die 2	4200.00	2000.00	....
U50	2¢ black on buff, die 3	45.00	20.00	12.00
W51	2¢ black on buff, die 3	700.00	460.00	280.00
U52	2¢ black on orange, die 3	40.00	23.00	12.00
W53	2¢ black on dark manila, die 3	180.00	50.00	42.00
U54	2¢ black on buff, die 4	40.00	20.00	10.00
W55	2¢ black on buff, die 4	170.00	100.00	70.00
U56	2¢ black on orange, die 4	38.00	25.00	12.00
W57	2¢ black on light manila, die 4	40.00	25.00	15.00

U58-1

U66-U67

Washington

1864-65

SCOTT NO.	DESCRIPTION	UNUSED ENTIRE	UNUSED CUT SQ.	USED CUT SQ.
U58	3¢ pink on white	22.00	12.00	1.80
U59	3¢ pink on buff	22.00	12.00	3.20
U60	3¢ brown on white	140.00	70.00	40.00
U61	3¢ brown on buff	120.00	50.00	30.00
U62	6¢ pink on white	190.00	110.00	30.00
U63	6¢ pink on buff	120.00	48.00	30.00
U64	6¢ purple on white	120.00	58.00	28.00
U65	6¢ purple on buff	75.00	50.00	22.00
U66	9¢ lemon on buff	600.00	400.00	255.00
U67	9¢ orange on buff	220.00	130.00	95.00
U68	12¢ brown on buff	620.00	300.00	280.00
U69	12¢ red brown on buff	185.00	130.00	60.00
U70	18¢ red on buff	185.00	90.00	98.00
U71	24¢ blue on buff	230.00	90.00	98.00
U72	30¢ green on buff	225.00	120.00	85.00
U73	40¢ rose on buff	365.00	110.00	260.00

U74-W77, U108-U121
Franklin

U78-W81, U122-W158
Jackson

U82-U84, U159-U169
Washington

U172-U180
Taylor

U85-U87, U181-U184
Lincoln

U88, U185, U186
Stanton

U89-U92, U187-U194
Jefferson

U93-U95, U195-U197
Clay

U96-U98, U198-U200
Webster

U99-U101, U201-U203
Scott

U102-U104, U204-U210, U336-U341
Hamilton

U105-U107, U211-U217, U342-U347
Perry

NOTE: For details on die or similar appearing varieties of envelopes, please refer to the Scott Specialized Catalogue.

1870-71 REAY ISSUE

SCOTT NO.	DESCRIPTION	UNUSED ENTIRE	UNUSED CUT SQ.	USED CUT SQ.
U74	1¢ blue on white	97.00	60.00	34.00
U74a	1¢ ultramarine on white	150.00	75.00	38.00
U75	1¢ blue on amber	72.00	46.00	30.00
U75a	1¢ ultramarine on amber	105.00	72.00	31.00
U76	1¢ blue on orange	42.00	23.00	16.00
W77	1¢ blue on manila	95.00	53.00	38.00
U78	2¢ brown on white	77.00	48.00	18.00
U79	2¢ brown on amber	46.00	26.00	12.00
U80	2¢ brown on orange	21.00	14.00	7.00
W81	2¢ brown on manila	66.00	32.00	23.00
U82	3¢ green on white	22.00	10.00	1.25
U83	3¢ green on amber	23.00	9.00	2.25
U84	3¢ green on cream	23.00	12.00	5.00
U85	6¢ dark red on white	77.00	42.00	22.00
U86	6¢ dark red on amber	92.00	48.00	22.00
U87	6¢ dark red on cream	96.00	48.00	26.00
U88	7¢ vermillion on amber	96.00	68.00	200.00
U89	10¢ olive black on white	1400.00	1000.00	925.00
U90	10¢ olive black on amber	1400.00	1000.00	925.00
U91	10¢ brown on white	167.00	105.00	74.00
U92	10¢ brown on amber	178.00	115.00	54.00
U93	12¢ plum on white	280.00	142.00	84.00
U94	12¢ plum on amber	263.00	145.00	120.00
U95	12¢ plum on cream	405.00	280.00	260.00
U96	15¢ red orange on white	215.00	92.00	90.00
U97	15¢ red orange on amber	426.00	230.00	310.00
U98	15¢ red orange on cream	455.00	385.00	380.00
U99	24¢ purple on white	225.00	155.00	155.00
U100	24¢ purple on amber	400.00	240.00	350.00
U101	24¢ purple on cream	525.00	330.00	575.00
U102	30¢ black on white	340.00	115.00	120.00
U103	30¢ black on amber	710.00	285.00	500.00
U104	30¢ black on cream	425.00	260.00	525.00
U105	90¢ carmine on white	275.00	185.00	375.00
U106	90¢ carmine on amber	910.00	355.00	975.00
U107	90¢ carmine on cream	625.00	300.00	2550.00

1874-86 PLIMPTON ISSUE

SCOTT NO.	DESCRIPTION	UNUSED ENTIRE	UNUSED CUT SQ.	USED CUT SQ.
U108	1¢ dark blue on white, die 1	320.00	248.00	72.00
U109	1¢ dark blue on amber, die 1	245.00	215.00	78.00
U110	1¢ dark blue on cream, die 1	....	1800.00	....
U111	1¢ dark blue on orange, die 1	46.00	31.00	18.00
U111a	1¢ light blue on orange, die 1	46.00	31.00	18.00
W112	1¢ dark blue on manila, die 1	155.00	87.00	45.00
U113	1¢ light blue on white, die 2	3.25	2.50	1.25
U113a	1¢ dark blue on white, die 2	30.00	10.00	8.00
U114	1¢ light blue on amber, die 2	9.00	5.00	4.50
U115	1¢ blue on cream, die 2	12.50	6.00	5.00
U116	1¢ light blue on orange, die 2	1.40	.85	.50
U116a	1¢ dark blue on orange, die 2	17.00	10.00	2.75
U117	1¢ light blue on blue, die 2	19.00	10.00	5.50
U118	1¢ light blue on fawn, die 2	18.00	10.00	5.50
U119	1¢ light blue on manila, die 2	22.00	10.00	3.60
W120	1¢ light blue on manila, die 2	3.50	2.25	1.20
W120a	1¢ dark blue on manila, die 2	17.00	9.50	8.00
U121	1¢ blue on amber manila, die 2	33.00	22.00	11.00
U122	2¢ brown on white, die 1	200.00	160.00	63.00
U123	2¢ brown on amber, die 1	152.00	82.00	48.00
U124	2¢ brown on cream, die 1	....	1275.00	....
W126	2¢ brown on manila, die 1	330.00	180.00	88.00
W127	2¢ vermillion on manila, die 1	4900.00	3300.00	260.00
U128	2¢ brown on white, die 2	138.00	72.00	40.00
U129	2¢ brown on amber, die 2	[illegible]	[illegible]	48.00
W131	2¢ brown on manila, die 2	38.00	23.00	17.50
U132	2¢ brown on white, die 3	148.00	90.00	30.00
U133	2¢ brown on amber, die 3	655.00	485.00	85.00
U134	2¢ brown on white, die 4	2275.00	1500.00	165.00
U135	2¢ brown on amber, die 4	748.00	550.00	130.00
U136	2¢ brown on orange, die 4	115.00	75.00	[illegible]
W137	2¢ brown on manila, die [illegible]	140.00	90.00	42.00
U139	2¢ brown on white, die 5	102.00	77.00	38.00
U140	2¢ brown on amber, die 5	172.00	115.00	64.00
W141	2¢ brown on manila, die 5	58.00	50.00	28.00
U142	2¢ vermillion on white, die 5	15.00	11.00	5.75
U143	2¢ vermillion on amber, die 5	16.00	11.00	5.75
U144	2¢ vermillion on cream, die 5	32.00	27.00	8.00
U146	2¢ vermillion on blue, die 5	235.00	155.00	42.00
U147	2¢ vermillion on fawn, die 5	18.00	12.00	5.50
W148	2¢ vermillion on manila, die 5	11.00	5.00	4.50
U149	2¢ vermillion on white, die 6	115.00	77.00	35.00
U150	2¢ vermillion on amber, die 6	85.00	52.00	18.00
U151	2¢ vermillion on blue, die 6	22.00	15.00	11.00
U152	2¢ vermillion on fawn, die 6	22.00	16.00	5.00
U153	2¢ vermillion on white, die 7	128.00	92.00	32.00
U154	2¢ vermillion on amber, die 7	475.00	455.00	95.00
W155	2¢ vermillion on manila, die 7	56.00	25.00	12.00
U156	2¢ vermillion on white, die 8	3800.00	1800.00	180.00
W158	2¢ vermillion on manila,die 8	200.00	120.00	65.00
U159	3¢ green on white, die 1	65.00	45.00	12.00
U160	3¢ green on amber, die 1	82.00	45.00	12.00
U161	3¢ green on cream, die 1	85.00	52.00	16.00
U163	3¢ green on white, die 2	5.50	1.75	.40
U164	3¢ green on amber, die 2	5.50	1.75	.75
U165	3¢ green on cream, die 2	22.00	12.00	7.00
U166	3¢ green on blue,die 2	20.00	12.00	7.00
U167	3¢ green on fawn, die 2	11.00	6.00	4.00
U168	3¢ green on white, die 3	5100.00	1600.00	95.00
U169	3¢ green on amber, die 3	870.00	570.00	130.00
U172	5¢ blue on white, die 1	27.00	18.00	12.00
U173	5¢ blue on amber, die 1	27.00	18.00	13.00
U174	5¢ blue on cream, die 1	220.00	148.00	49.00
U175	5¢ blue on blue, die 1	77.00	46.00	20.00
U176	5¢ blue on fawn, die 1	310.00	177.00	72.00
U177	5¢ blue on white, die 2	27.00	15.00	11.00
U178	5¢ blue on amber, die 2	27.00	15.00	11.00
U179	5¢ blue on blue, die 2	66.00	35.00	14.00
U180	5¢ blue on fawn, die 2	250.00	150.00	60.00
U181	6¢ red on white	26.00	16.00	7.00
U182	6¢ red on amber	29.00	16.00	7.00
U183	6¢ red on cream	95.00	60.00	18.00
U184	6¢ red on fawn	37.50	25.00	14.00
U185	7¢ vermillion on white	....	2000.00	....
U186	7¢ vermillion on amber	235.00	185.00	77.00
U187	10¢ brown on white,die 1	74.00	50.00	25.00
U188	10¢ brown on amber, die 1	198.00	100.00	38.00
U189	10¢ chocolate on white, die 2	16.00	9.00	4.50
U190	10¢ chocolate on amber, die 2	18.00	10.00	7.75
U191	10¢ brown on buff, die 2	26.00	21.00	9.00
U192	10¢ brown on blue, die 2	28.00	23.00	9.00
U193	10¢ brown on manila, die 2	31.00	22.00	11.00
U194	10¢ brown/amber manila, die 2	34.00	28.00	10.00
U195	12¢ plum on white	700.00	375.00	110.00
U196	12¢ plum on amber	375.00	300.00	195.00
U197	12¢ plum on cream	950.00	240.00	185.00
U198	15¢ orange on white	115.00	62.00	42.00
U199	15¢ orange on amber	345.00	200.00	120.00
U200	15¢ orange on cream	975.00	675.00	370.00
U201	24¢ purple on white	275.00	215.00	180.00
U202	24¢ purple on amber	275.00	200.00	130.00
U203	24¢ purple on cream	800.00	200.00	130.00
U204	30¢ black on white	95.00	68.00	29.00
U205	30¢ black on amber	165.00	90.00	68.00
U206	30¢ black on cream	825.00	410.00	380.00
U207	30¢ black on oriental buff	200.00	130.00	85.00
U208	30¢ black on blue	200.00	120.00	85.00
U209	30¢ black on manila	200.00	220.00	85.00
U210	30¢ black on amber manila	200.00	205.00	120.00
U211	90¢ carmine on white	185.00	130.00	88.00
U212	90¢ carmine on amber	320.00	230.00	310.00
U213	90¢ carmine on cream	3500.00	1800.00	
U214	90¢ carmine on oriental buff	370.00	220.00	280.00
U215	90¢ carmine on blue	295.00	210.00	260.00
U216	90¢ carmine on manila	280.00	180.00	280.00
U217	90¢ carmine on amber manila	325.00	165.00	220.00

U218-U221, U582
Pony Express Rider and Train

U222-U226
Garfield

Die 1. Single thick line under "POSTAGE" Die 2. Two thin lines under "POSTAGE"

1876 CENTENNIAL ISSUE

SCOTT NO.	DESCRIPTION	UNUSED ENTIRE	UNUSED CUT SQ.	USED CUT SQ.
U218	3¢ red on white, die 1	80.00	55.00	30.00
U219	3¢ green on white, die 1	78.00	50.00	19.00
U221	3¢ green on white, die 2	105.00	58.00	27.00

1882-86

SCOTT NO.	DESCRIPTION	UNUSED ENTIRE	UNUSED CUT SQ.	USED CUT SQ.
U222	5¢ brown on white	14.00	6.00	3.20
U223	5¢ brown on amber	14.00	6.00	3.75
U224	5¢ brown on oriental buff	220.00	150.00	75.00
U225	5¢ brown on blue	148.00	100.00	40.00
U226	5¢ brown on fawn	550.00	410.00	....

U227-U230
Washington

1883 OCTOBER

SCOTT NO.	DESCRIPTION	UNUSED ENTIRE	UNUSED CUT SQ.	USED CUT SQ.
U227	2¢ red on white	12.00	6.00	2.50
U228	2¢ red on amber	14.00	7.00	3.00
U229	2¢ red on blue	16.00	11.00	5.50
U230	2¢ red on fawn	19.00	11.00	5.50

U231-U249, U260-W292
Washington

U250-U259
Jackson

1883 NOVEMBER
Four Wavy Lines in Oval

SCOTT NO.	DESCRIPTION	UNUSED ENTIRE	UNUSED CUT SQ.	USED CUT SQ.
U231	2¢ red on white	13.00	7.00	2.50
U232	2¢ red on amber	14.00	8.00	4.00
U233	2¢ red on blue	20.00	11.00	8.00
U234	2¢ red on fawn	14.00	9.00	5.00
W235	2¢ red on manila	35.00	24.00	6.50

1884 JUNE

SCOTT NO.	DESCRIPTION	UNUSED ENTIRE	UNUSED CUT SQ.	USED CUT SQ.
U236	2¢ red on white	25.00	15.00	4.50
U237	2¢ red on amber	31.00	18.00	11.00
U238	2¢ red on blue	52.00	31.00	13.00
U239	2¢ red on fawn	38.00	27.00	12.00
U240	2¢ red on white (3½ links)	195.00	115.00	50.00
U241	2¢ red on amber (3½ links)	2800.00	1000.00	340.00
U243	2¢ red on white (2 links)	215.00	150.00	90.00
U244	2¢ red on amber (2 links)	560.00	425.00	105.00
U245	2¢ red on blue (2 links)	825.00	500.00	225.00
U246	2¢ red on fawn (2 links)	755.00	475.00	210.00
U247	2¢ red on white (round O)	4600.00	3600.00	775.00
U248	2¢ red on amber	....	5400.00	800.00
U249	2¢ red on fawn (round O)	2200.00	1450.00	800.00

1883-86

SCOTT NO.	DESCRIPTION	UNUSED ENTIRE	UNUSED CUT SQ.	USED CUT SQ.
U250	4¢ green on white, die 1	8.50	5.00	3.75
U251	4¢ green on amber,die 1	9.50	6.50	4.00
U252	4¢ green on buff, die 1	22.00	14.00	10.00
U253	4¢ green on blue, die 1	22.00	14.00	7.00
U254	4¢ green on manila, die 1	24.00	16.00	8.00
U255	4¢ green/amber manila,die 1	40.00	31.00	11.00
U256	4¢ green on white, die 2	23.00	13.00	6.00
U257	4¢ green on amber, die 2	31.00	19.00	8.00
U258	4¢ green on manila, die 2	31.00	16.00	8.00
U259	4¢ green/amber manila,die 2	31.00	16.00	8.00

1884 MAY

SCOTT NO.	DESCRIPTION	UNUSED ENTIRE	UNUSED CUT SQ.	USED CUT SQ.
U260	2¢ brown on white	24.00	20.00	6.00
U261	2¢ brown on amber	24.00	20.00	7.00
U262	2¢ brown on blue	36.00	24.00	11.00
U263	2¢ brown on fawn	25.00	19.00	9.50
W264	2¢ brown on manila	31.00	20.00	12.00

1884 JUNE

SCOTT NO.	DESCRIPTION	UNUSED ENTIRE	UNUSED CUT SQ.	USED CUT SQ.
U265	2¢ brown on white	34.00	20.00	7.00
U266	2¢ brown on amber	91.00	81.00	48.00
U267	2¢ brown on blue	35.00	25.00	10.00
U268	2¢ brown on fawn	28.00	19.00	12.00
W269	2¢ brown on manila	43.00	36.00	16.00
U270	2¢ brown on white (2 links)	205.00	150.00	55.00
U271	2¢ brown on amber (2 links)	655.00	525.00	120.00
U273	2¢ brown on white (round O)	455.00	325.00	120.00
U274	2¢ brown on amber (round O)	455.00	325.00	115.00
U276	2¢ brown on fawn (round O)	1500.00	1000.00	725.00

1884-86
Two Wavy Lines in Oval

SCOTT NO.	DESCRIPTION	UNUSED ENTIRE	UNUSED CUT SQ.	USED CUT SQ.
U277	2¢ brown on white, die 1	.90	.60	.25
U277a	2¢ brown lake on white, die 1	28.00	23.00	22.00
U278	2¢ brown on amber, die 1	1.75	.75	.50
U279	2¢ brown on buff, die 1	10.00	7.00	2.25
U280	2¢ brown on blue, die 1	5.75	3.75	2.25
U281	2¢ brown on fawn, die 1	7.00	4.00	2.50
U282	2¢ brown on manila, die 1	22.00	16.00	4.25
W283	2¢ brown on manila, die 1	12.00	8.75	6.00
U284	2¢ brown/amber manila, die 1	18.00	11.00	6.00
U285	2¢ red on white, die 1	1600.00	775.00	....
U286	2¢ red on blue, die 1	400.00	360.00	....
W287	2¢ red on manila, die 1	235.00	165.00	....
U288	2¢ brown on white, die 2	935.00	400.00	53.00
U289	2¢ brown on amber, die 2	30.00	21.00	14.00
U290	2¢ brown on blue, die 2	2800.00	1950.00	325.00
U291	2¢ brown on fawn, die 2	56.00	38.00	27.00
W292	2¢ brown on manila, die 2	43.00	31.00	20.00

NOTE: For details on die or similar appearing varieties of envelopes, please refer to the Scott Specialized Catalogue.

U293
Grant

1886

SCOTT NO.	DESCRIPTION	UNUSED ENTIRE	UNUSED CUT SQ.	USED CUT SQ.
U293	2¢ green on white Entire letter sheet	.... 45.00	....	.... 23.00

U294-U304, U352-W357
Franklin

U305-U323, U358-U370
Washington

U324-U329
Jackson

U330-U335, U377-U378
Grant

1887-94

SCOTT NO.	DESCRIPTION	UNUSED ENTIRE	UNUSED CUT SQ.	USED CUT SQ.
U294	1¢ blue on white	1.10	.60	.35
U295	1¢ dark blue on white	11.50	8.50	3.00
U296	1¢ blue on amber	7.25	4.00	1.50
U297	1¢ dark blue on amber	77.00	56.00	27.00
U300	1¢ blue on manila	1.40	.75	.40
W301	1¢ blue on manila	1.75	.90	.35
U302	1¢ dark blue on manila	43.00	33.00	13.00
W303	1¢ dark blue on manila	31.00	18.00	12.00
U304	1¢ blue on amber manila	20.00	14.00	5.50
U305	2¢ green on white, die 1	46.00	22.00	11.00
U306	2¢ green on amber, die 1	66.00	51.00	18.00
U307	2¢ green on buff, die 1	150.00	110.00	36.00
U308	2¢ green on blue, die 1	....	22000.00	1300.00
U309	2¢ green on manila, die 1	....	....	800.00
U311	2¢ green on white, die 2	.90	.40	.30
U312	2¢ green on amber, die 2	.95	.55	.30
U313	2¢ green on buff, die 2	1.40	.70	.35
U314	2¢ green on blue, die 2	1.40	.75	.35
U315	2¢ green on manila, die 2	3.60	2.25	.60
W316	2¢ green on manila, die 2	15.50	6.50	3.00
U317	2¢ green/amber manila, die 2	6.95	3.25	2.00
U318	2¢ green on white, die 3	230.00	160.00	15.00
U319	2¢ green on amber, die 3	300.00	220.00	27.00
U320	2¢ green on buff, die 3	287.00	215.00	50.00
U321	2¢ green on blue, die 3	355.00	225.00	71.50
U322	2¢ green on manila, die 3	410.00	330.00	70.00
U323	2¢ green/amber manila, die 3	875.00	500.00	150.00
U324	4¢ carmine on white	7.25	3.50	2.25
U325	4¢ carmine on amber	9.00	4.25	3.75
U326	4¢ carmine on oriental buff	18.50	8.75	4.00
U327	4¢ carmine on blue	16.50	7.75	4.25
U328	4¢ carmine on manila	16.50	10.00	7.50
U329	4¢ carmine on amber/manila	16.50	8.75	4.00
U330	5¢ blue on white, die 1	10.00	5.00	5.00
U331	5¢ blue on amber, die 1	14.00	6.00	3.00
U332	5¢ blue on oriental buff, die 1	22.00	7.00	5.00
U333	5¢ blue on blue, die 1	22.00	12.00	6.50
U334	5¢ blue on white, die 2	55.00	30.00	13.00
U335	5¢ blue on amber, die 2	28.00	18.00	8.00
U336	30¢ red brown on white	87.00	65.00	50.00
U337	30¢ red brown on amber	87.00	65.00	50.00
U338	30¢ red brown/oriental buff	86.00	65.00	50.00
U339	30¢ red brown on blue	86.00	65.00	50.00
U340	30¢ red brown on manila	86.00	65.00	50.00
U341	30¢ red brown/amber manila	86.00	65.00	50.00
U342	90¢ purple on white	120.00	88.00	93.00
U343	90¢ purple on amber	150.00	110.00	93.00
U344	90¢ purple on oriental buff	165.00	115.00	93.00
U345	90¢ purple on blue	175.00	115.00	95.00
U346	90¢ purple on manila	182.00	110.00	95.00
U347	90¢ purple on amber manila	182.00	120.00	95.00

U348-U351
Columbus and Liberty, with Shield and Eagle

1893 COLUMBIAN ISSUE

SCOTT NO.	DESCRIPTION	UNUSED ENTIRE	UNUSED CUT SQ.	USED CUT SQ.
U348	1¢ deep blue on white	4.00	2.50	1.40
U349	2¢ violet on white	4.50	3.00	.75
U350	5¢ chocolate on white	17.00	10.00	9.00
U351	10¢ slate brown on white	78.00	38.00	34.00

U371-U373

U374-W376

Lincoln

1899

SCOTT NO.	DESCRIPTION	UNUSED ENTIRE	UNUSED CUT SQ.	USED CUT SQ.
U352	1¢ green on white	4.00	1.85	.30
U353	1¢ green on amber	12.00	6.50	1.80
U354	1¢ green on oriental buff	24.00	19.00	3.00
U355	1¢ green on blue	24.00	19.00	8.00
U356	1¢ green on manila	7.50	3.00	1.10
W357	1¢ green on manila	12.00	4.00	1.25
U358	2¢ carmine on white, die 1	8.00	3.25	2.00
U359	2¢ carmine on amber, die 1	42.00	27.00	16.00
U360	2¢ carmine on buff, die 1	42.00	27.00	13.00
U361	2¢ carmine on blue, die 1	92.00	77.00	38.00
U362	2¢ carmine on white,die 2	.85	.40	.25
U363	2¢ carmine on amber. die 2	3.75	2.25	.25
U364	2¢ carmine on buff, die 2	3.75	1.55	.25
U365	2¢ carmine on blue, die 2	4.50	2.00	.60
W366	2¢ carmine on manila, die 2	16.00	9.75	3.50
U367	2¢ carmine on white, die 3	14.00	8.00	3.00
U368	2¢ carmine on amber, die 3	18.00	12.00	7.00
U369	2¢ carmine on buff, die 3	44.00	29.00	14.00
U370	2¢ carmine on blue, die 3	34.00	16.00	11.00
U371	4¢ brown on white, die 1	38.00	23.00	14.00
U372	4¢ brown on amber, die 1	40.00	23.00	14.00
U373	4¢ brown on white, die 2	....	....	1300.00
U374	4¢ brown on white, die 3	38.00	18.00	9.00
U375	4¢ brown on amber, die 3	88.00	70.00	26.00
W376	4¢ brown on manila, die 3	30.00	19.00	11.00
U377	5¢ blue on white, die 3	23.00	14.00	11.00
U378	5¢ blue on amber, die 3	31.00	22.00	11.50

U379-W384
Franklin

U385-W389, U395-W399
Washington

U390-W392
Grant

U393, U394
Lincoln

U400-W405, U416, U417
Franklin

U406-W415, U418, U419
Washington

1903

SCOTT NO.	DESCRIPTION	UNUSED ENTIRE	UNUSED CUT SQ.	USED CUT SQ.
U379	1¢ green on white	1.40	.85	.25
U380	1¢ green on amber	26.00	18.00	2.25
U381	1¢ green on oriental buff	31.00	22.00	3.00
U382	1¢ green on blue	38.00	26.00	5.00
U383	1¢ green on manila	6.25	4.75	1.00
W384	1¢ green on manila	5.25	3.50	.50
U385	2¢ carmine on white	1.50	.60	.30
U386	2¢ carmine on amber	4.25	2.75	.55
U387	2¢ carmine on oriental buff	4.00	2.50	.35
U388	2¢ carmine on blue	3.50	2.25	.60
W389	2¢ carmine on manila	32.00	25.00	11.00
U390	4¢ chocolate on white	36.00	28.00	13.00
U391	4¢ chocolate on amber	35.00	25.00	13.00
W392	4¢ chocolate on manila	58.00	32.00	13.00
U393	5¢ blue on white	36.00	25.00	13.00
U394	5¢ blue on amber	36.00	25.00	13.00

1904 RECUT DIE

SCOTT NO.	DESCRIPTION	UNUSED ENTIRE	UNUSED CUT SQ.	USED CUT SQ.
U395	2¢ carmine on white	2.00	1.00	.35
U396	2¢ carmine on amber	15.00	10.00	1.20
U397	2¢ carmine on oriental buff	9.00	7.00	1.50
U398	2¢ carmine on blue	7.00	5.00	1.10
W399	2¢ carmine on manila	36.00	18.00	11.00

1907-16

SCOTT NO.	DESCRIPTION	UNUSED ENTIRE	UNUSED CUT SQ.	USED CUT SQ.
U400	1¢ green on white	.65	.40	.25
U401	1¢ green on amber	4.00	2.25	.50
U402	1¢ green on oriental buff	16.00	11.00	1.50
U403	1¢ green on blue	16.00	11.00	2.00
U404	1¢ green on manila	6.50	3.75	2.10
W405	1¢ green on manila	2.50	1.25	.30
U406	2¢ brown red on white	3.00	1.25	.25
U407	2¢ brown red on amber	9.00	7.00	2.00
U408	2¢ brown red on oriental buff	14.00	10.00	2.00
U409	2¢ brown red on blue	9.25	6.00	2.10
W410	2¢ brown red on manila	66.00	48.00	36.00
U411	2¢ carmine on white	1.25	.35	.25
U412	2¢ carmine on amber	1.25	.65	.25
U413	2¢ carmine on oriental buff	1.50	.75	.25
U414	2¢ carmine on blue	1.50	.75	.25
W415	2¢ carmine on manila	11.00	7.00	2.50
U416	4¢ black on white	14.00	6.50	3.50
U417	4¢ black on amber	17.00	9.50	3.00
U418	5¢ blue on white	16.00	8.00	2.85
U419	5¢ blue on amber	26.00	18.00	13.00

U420-U428, U440-U442
Franklin

U429-U439, U443-U445,
U481-U485, U529-U531
Washington

1916-32

SCOTT NO.	DESCRIPTION	UNUSED ENTIRE	UNUSED CUT SQ.	USED CUT SQ.
U420	1¢ green on white	.40	.35	.25
U421	1¢ green on amber	1.25	.80	.35
U422	1¢ green on oriental buff	3.50	2.50	1.20
U423	1¢ green on blue	1.00	.60	.40
U424	1¢ green on manila	9.50	7.50	4.80
W425	1¢ green on manila	.95	.30	.25
U426	1¢ green on brown (glazed)	66.00	53.00	19.25
W427	1¢ green on brown (glazed)	91.00	78.50	35.00
U428	1¢ green on brown (unglazed)	27.00	18.00	9.00
U429	2¢ carmine on white	.45	.30	.25
U430	2¢ carmine on amber	.50	.30	.25
U431	2¢ carmine on oriental buff	5.75	2.50	.70
U432	2¢ carmine on blue	.65	.40	.25
W433	2¢ carmine on manila	.55	.35	.30
W434	2¢ carmine on brown (glazed)	126.00	100.00	55.00
W435	2¢ carmine/brown (unglazed)	126.00	100.00	55.00
U436	3¢ dark violet on white	.75	.60	.25
U436f	3¢ purple on white (1932)	.75	.55	.25
U436h	3¢ carmine on white (error)	62.00	38.00	33.00
U437	3¢ dark violet on amber	6.00	2.70	1.20
U437a	3¢ purple on amber (1932)	11.00	6.00	1.25
U437g	3¢ carmine on amber (error)	600.00	525.00	360.00
U437h	3¢ black on amber (error)	300.00	200.00	....
U438	3¢ dark violet on buff	38.00	31.00	1.80
U439	3¢ purple on blue (1932)	.80	.35	.25
U439a	3¢ dark violet on blue	18.00	11.00	3.00
U439g	3¢ carmine on blue (error)	500.00	400.00	320.00
U440	4¢ black on white	4.50	2.25	.60
U441	4¢ black on amber	5.50	3.75	.90
U442	4¢ black on blue	6.00	3.75	1.00
U443	5¢ blue on white	7.50	4.00	3.00
U444	5¢ blue on amber	8.00	5.00	2.30
U445	5¢ blue on blue	9.75	4.50	3.50

1920-21 SURCHARGED

Type 1 Type 2

SCOTT NO.	DESCRIPTION	UNUSED ENTIRE	UNUSED CUT SQ.	USED CUT SQ.
U446	2¢ on 3¢ dark violet on white . . . . (U436)	26.00	18.00	11.75

Surcharge on Envelopes of 1916-21 Type 2

SCOTT NO.	DESCRIPTION	UNUSED ENTIRE	UNUSED CUT SQ.	USED CUT SQ.
U447	2¢ on 3¢ dark violet on white, rose . . . . (U436)	18.00	11.00	7.70
U448	2¢ on 3¢ dark violet on white . . . . (U436)	5.00	3.00	2.10
U449	2¢ on 3¢ dark violet on amber . . . . (U437)	12.00	8.00	6.50
U450	2¢ on 3¢ dark violet on oriental buff . . . . (U438)	27.00	21.00	16.00
U451	2¢ on 3¢ dark violet on blue . . . . (U439)	26.00	17.00	11.00

Type 3

Surcharge on Envelopes of 1874-1921
Type 3 bars 2mm apart

SCOTT NO.	DESCRIPTION	UNUSED ENTIRE	UNUSED CUT SQ.	USED CUT SQ.
U454	2¢ on 2¢ carmine on white . . . . (U429)	260.00	175.00	....
U455	2¢ on 2¢ carmine on amber . . . . (U430)	4300.00	2300.00	....
U456	2¢ on 2¢ carmine on oriental buff . . . . (U431)	395.00	300.00	....
U457	2¢ on 2¢ carmine on blue . . . . (U432)	495.00	400.00	....
U458	2¢ on 3¢ dark violet on white . . . . (U436)	1.15	.65	.40
U459	2¢ on 3¢ dark violet on amber . . . . (U437)	7.00	4.00	1.20
U460	2¢ on 3¢ dark violet on oriental buff . . . . (U438)	6.25	4.75	2.25
U461	2¢ on 3¢ dark violet on blue . . . . (U439)	10.00	7.00	1.20
U462	2¢ on 4¢ chocolate on white . . . . (U390)	900.00	650.00	275.00
U463	2¢ on 4¢ chocolate on amber . . . . (U391)	1550.00	1300.00	375.00
U464	2¢ on 5¢ blue on white . . . . (U443)	2050.00	1500.00	....

Type 4 like Type 3, but bars 1½ mm apart

SCOTT NO.	DESCRIPTION	UNUSED ENTIRE	UNUSED CUT SQ.	USED CUT SQ.
U465	2¢ on 1¢ green on white . . . . (U420)	2100.00	1400.00	....
U466A	2¢ on 2¢ carmine on white . . . . (U429)	1500.00	850.00	....
U467	2¢ on 3¢ green on white . . . . (U163)	600.00	450.00	....
U468	2¢ on 3¢ dark violet on white . . . . (U436)	1.20	.85	.50
U469	2¢ on 3¢ dark violet on amber . . . . (U437)	5.50	4.75	2.50
U470	2¢ on 3¢ dark violet on oriental buff . . . . (U438)	12.50	7.25	3.00
U471	2¢ on 3¢ dark violet on blue . . . . (U439)	15.50	8.75	2.00
U472	2¢ on 4¢ chocolate on white . . . . (U390)	34.00	16.00	13.00
U473	2¢ on 4¢ chocolate on amber . . . . (U391)	34.00	19.00	11.00
U474	2¢ on 1¢ on 3¢ dark violet on white . . . . . . (U436)	420.00	325.00	....
U475	2¢ on 1¢ on 3¢ dark violet on amber . . . . . . (U437)	500.00	300.00	....

Type 5 Type 6 Type 7

Surcharge on Envelope of 1916-21 Type 5

SCOTT NO.	DESCRIPTION	UNUSED ENTIRE	UNUSED CUT SQ.	USED CUT SQ.
U476	2¢ on 3¢ dark violet on amber . . . . (U437)	525.00	300.00	....

Surcharge on Envelope of 1916-21 Type 6

SCOTT NO.	DESCRIPTION	UNUSED ENTIRE	UNUSED CUT SQ.	USED CUT SQ.
U477	2¢ on 3¢ dark violet on white . . . . (U436)	215.00	150.00	....
U478	2¢ on 3¢ dark violet on amber . . . . (U437)	500.00	375.00	....

Surcharge on Envelope of 1916-21 Type 7

SCOTT NO.	DESCRIPTION	UNUSED ENTIRE	UNUSED CUT SQ.	USED CUT SQ.
U479	2¢ on 3¢ dark violet on white (black) . . . .(U436)	595.00	475.00	....

1925

SCOTT NO.	DESCRIPTION	UNUSED ENTIRE	UNUSED CUT SQ.	USED CUT SQ.
U481	1½¢ brown on white	.65	.30	.30
U481b	1½¢ purple on white (error)	130.00	105.00	....
U482	1½¢ brown on amber	1.90	1.20	.45
U483	1½¢ brown on blue	2.75	1.80	1.00
U484	1½¢ brown on manila	14.50	8.00	3.75
W485	1½¢ brown on manila	2.00	1.00	.30

Type 8

Surcharge on Envelopes of 1887 Type 8

SCOTT NO.	DESCRIPTION	UNUSED ENTIRE	UNUSED CUT SQ.	USED CUT SQ.
U486	1½¢ on 2¢ green on white . . . . (U311)	1650.00	925.00	....
U487	1½¢ on 2¢ green on amber . . . . (U312)	1800.00	1500.00	....

Surcharge on Envelopes of 1899 Type 8

SCOTT NO.	DESCRIPTION	UNUSED ENTIRE	UNUSED CUT SQ.	USED CUT SQ.
U488	1½¢ on 1¢ green on white . . . . (U352)	1050.00	700.00	....
U489	1½¢ on 1¢ green on amber . . . . (U353)	225.00	138.00	70.00

Surcharge on Envelopes of 1907-10 Type 8

SCOTT NO.	DESCRIPTION	UNUSED ENTIRE	UNUSED CUT SQ.	USED CUT SQ.
U490	1½¢ on 1¢ green on white . . . . (U400)	12.00	7.00	4.20
U491	1½¢ on 1¢ green on amber . . . . (U401)	13.00	12.00	3.00
U492	1½¢ on 1¢ green on oriental buff . . . . (U402a)	750.00	625.00	155.00
U493	1½¢ on 1¢ green on blue . . . . (U403c)	180.00	130.00	70.00
U494	1½¢ on 1¢ green on manila . . . . (U404)	625.00	425.00	110.00

Surcharge on Envelopes of 1916-21 Type 8

SCOTT NO.	DESCRIPTION	UNUSED ENTIRE	UNUSED CUT SQ.	USED CUT SQ.
U495	1½¢ on 1¢ green on white . . . . (U420)	1.25	.85	.30
U496	1½¢ on 1¢ green on amber . . . . (U421)	31.00	22.00	14.00
U497	1½¢ on 1¢ green on oriental buff . . . . (U422)	9.00	5.00	2.50
U498	1½¢ on 1¢ green on blue . . . . (U423)	2.50	1.65	.90
U499	1½¢ on 1¢ green on manila . . . . (U424)	22.00	14.00	8.00
U500	1½¢ on 1¢ green on brown (unglazed) . . . . (U428)	115.00	92.00	40.00
U501	1½¢ on 1¢ green on brown (glazed) . . . . . . (U426)	115.00	92.00	36.00
U502	1½¢ on 2¢ carmine on white . . . . (U429)	525.00	300.00	....
U503	1½¢ on 2¢ carmine on oriental buff . . . . (U431)	540.00	400.00	....
U504	1½¢ on 2¢ carmine on blue . . . . (U432)	570.00	495.00	....

Surcharge on Envelopes of 1925 Type 8

SCOTT NO.	DESCRIPTION	UNUSED ENTIRE	UNUSED CUT SQ.	USED CUT SQ.
U505	1½¢ on 1½¢ brown on white . . . . (U481)	695.00	525.00	....
U506	1½¢ on 1½¢ brown on blue . . . . (U483)	695.00	525.00	....

Type 9

Surcharge on Envelopes of 1899 Type 9

SCOTT NO.	DESCRIPTION	UNUSED ENTIRE	UNUSED CUT SQ.	USED CUT SQ.
U508	1½¢ on 1¢ green on amber . . . . (U353)	105.00	72.00	....

Surcharge on Envelopes of 1903 Type 9

SCOTT NO.	DESCRIPTION	UNUSED ENTIRE	UNUSED CUT SQ.	USED CUT SQ.
U508A	1½¢ on 1¢ green on white . . . . (U379)	7000.00	4800.00	....
U509	1½¢ on 1¢ green on amber . . . . (U380)	34.00	21.00	14.00
U509B	1½¢ on 1¢ green on oriental buff . . . . (U381)	85.00	68.00	50.00

Surcharge on Envelopes of 1907-10 Type 9

SCOTT NO.	DESCRIPTION	UNUSED ENTIRE	UNUSED CUT SQ.	USED CUT SQ.
U510	1½¢ on 1¢ green on white . . . . (U400)	6.00	3.00	1.50
U511	1½¢ on 1¢ green on amber . . . . (U401)	400.00	275.00	105.00
U512	1½¢ on 1¢ green on oriental buff . . . . (U402)	17.00	9.00	4.75
U513	1½¢ on 1¢ green on blue . . . . (U403)	11.00	7.00	5.00
U514	1½¢ on 1¢ green on manila . . . . (U404)	54.00	42.00	12.00
U515	1½¢ on 1¢ green on white . . . . (U420)	.80	.45	.25
U516	1½¢ on 1¢ green on amber . . . . (U421)	76.00	58.00	32.00
U517	1½¢ on 1¢ green on oriental buff . . . . (U422)	12.00	8.00	1.50
U518	1½¢ on 1¢ green on blue . . . . (U423)	12.00	7.00	1.50
U519	1½¢ on 1¢ green on manila . . . . (U424)	52.00	36.00	13.00
U520	1½¢ on 2¢ carmine on white . . . . (U429)	525.00	375.00	....
U521	1½¢ on 1¢ green on white, magenta surcharged . . . . (U420)	7.50	5.00	4.00

U522 U523-U528

U522: Die 1, "E" of "POSTAGE" has center bar shorter than top bar.

U522a: Die 2, "E" of "POSTAGE" has center and top bars same length.

U525: Die 1 "S" of "POSTAGE" even with "T".

U525a: Die 2 "S" of "POSTAGE" higher than "T".

1926 SESQUICENTENNIAL EXPOSITION

SCOTT NO.	DESCRIPTION	UNUSED ENTIRE	UNUSED CUT SQ.	USED CUT SQ.
U522	2¢ carmine on white, die 1	2.50	1.75	.75
U522a	2¢ carmine on white, die 2	12.50	9.00	5.50

1932 WASHINGTON BICENTENNIAL

SCOTT NO.	DESCRIPTION	UNUSED ENTIRE	UNUSED CUT SQ.	USED CUT SQ.
U523	1¢ olive green on white	2.00	1.25	1.00
U524	1½¢ chocolate on white	3.25	2.25	2.00
U525	2¢ carmine on white, die 1	.75	.50	.25
U525a	2¢ carmine on white, die 2	100.00	85.00	22.00
U526	3¢ violet on white	3.00	2.50	.50
U527	4¢ black on white	25.00	22.00	21.00
U528	5¢ dark blue on white	6.00	5.00	21.00

1932 Designs of 1916-32

SCOTT NO.	DESCRIPTION	UNUSED ENTIRE	UNUSED CUT SQ.	USED CUT SQ.
U529	6¢ orange on white	11.00	7.25	5.00
U530	6¢ orange on amber	18.00	13.00	11.00
U531	6¢ orange on blue	18.00	13.00	11.00

U532
Franklin

U533
Washington

U535

1950

SCOTT NO.	DESCRIPTION	FIRST DAY COVER	UNUSED ENTIRE	USED CUT SQ.
U532	1¢ green	2.00	8.75	2.50
U533	2¢ carmine	2.00	1.45	.35
U534	3¢ dark violet	2.00	.75	.30

1952

SCOTT NO.	DESCRIPTION	FIRST DAY COVER	UNUSED ENTIRE	USED CUT SQ.
U535	1½¢ brown	....	7.25	4.00

U537, U538, U552, U556

U539, U540, U545, U553

Surcharge on Envelopes of 1916-32, 1950, 1965, 1971

1958

SCOTT NO.	DESCRIPTION	FIRST DAY COVER	UNUSED ENTIRE	USED CUT SQ.
U536	4¢ red violet	1.75	1.00	.30
U537	2¢ & 2¢ (4¢) carmine (U429)	......	5.25	2.00
U538	2¢ & 2¢ (4¢) carmine (U533)	......	1.25	1.50
U539	3¢ & 1¢ (4¢) purple, die 1 (U436a)	......	18.50	12.00
U539a	3¢ & 1¢ (4¢) purple, die 7 (U436e)	......	15.00	10.00
U539b	3¢ & 1¢ (4¢) purple, die 9 (U436f)	......	36.00	17.00
U540	3¢ & 1¢ (4¢) dark violet (U534)	......	.70	1.25

U541
Franklin

U542
Washington

1960

SCOTT NO.	DESCRIPTION	FIRST DAY COVER	UNUSED ENTIRE	USED CUT SQ.
U541	1¼¢ turquoise	1.75	1.00	.60
U542	2½¢ dull blue	1.75	1.15	.60

U543

SCOTT NO.	DESCRIPTION	FIRST DAY COVER	UNUSED ENTIRE	USED CUT SQ.
U543	4¢ Pony Express	2.00	.80	.40

U544
Lincoln

U546

1962

SCOTT NO.	DESCRIPTION	FIRST DAY COVER	UNUSED ENTIRE	USED CUT SQ.
U544	5¢ dark blue	1.75	1.20	.25

Surcharge on Envelope of 1958

SCOTT NO.	DESCRIPTION	FIRST DAY COVER	UNUSED ENTIRE	USED CUT SQ.
U545	4¢+1¢ red violet (U536)	......	1.80	1.35

1964

SCOTT NO.	DESCRIPTION	FIRST DAY COVER	UNUSED ENTIRE	USED CUT SQ.
U546	5¢ New York World's Fair	1.75	.75	.45

U547, U548, U548A, U566

U549

U550

U551

1965-69

SCOTT NO.	DESCRIPTION	FIRST DAY COVER	UNUSED ENTIRE	USED CUT SQ.
U547	1¼¢ brown	1.75	.95	.55
U548	1 4/10¢ brown (1968)	1.75	1.25	.55
U548A	1 6/10¢ orange (1969)	1.75	1.15	.55
U549	4¢ bright blue	1.75	1.15	.25
U550	5¢ bright purple	1.75	1.00	.25
U551	6¢ light green (1968)	1.75	1.00	.25

U554

1968

1958 Type Surcharges on Envelopes of 1965

SCOTT NO.	DESCRIPTION	FIRST DAY COVER	UNUSED ENTIRE	USED CUT SQ.
U552	4¢ & 2¢ (6¢) blue (U549)	9.00	4.25	2.25
U553	5¢ & 1¢ (6¢) purple (U550)	9.00	4.00	3.00

1970

SCOTT NO.	DESCRIPTION	FIRST DAY COVER	UNUSED ENTIRE	USED CUT SQ.
U554	6¢ Moby Dick	1.75	.65	.25

U555

U557

1971

SCOTT NO.	DESCRIPTION	FIRST DAY COVER	UNUSED ENTIRE	USED CUT SQ.
U555	6¢ Conference on Youth	[illegible]	[illegible]	[illegible]
U556	1 7/10¢ deep lilac	1.75	.40	.25
U557	8¢ ultramarine	1.75	.60	.25

U561 & U562 Surcharge

SCOTT NO.	DESCRIPTION	FIRST DAY COVER	UNUSED ENTIRE	USED CUT SQ.
U561	6¢ & (2¢) (8¢) green (on U551)	4.00	1.25	1.35
U562	6¢ & (2¢) (8¢) blue (on U555)	4.00	3.00	2.75

U563

U564

SCOTT NO.	DESCRIPTION	FIRST DAY COVER	UNUSED ENTIRE	USED CUT SQ.
U563	8¢ Bowling	1.75	.90	.25
U564	8¢ Conference on Aging	1.75	.75	.25

U565

U567

1972

SCOTT NO.	DESCRIPTION	FIRST DAY COVER	UNUSED ENTIRE	USED CUT SQ.
U565	8¢ Transpo '72	1.75	.80	.30

1973

SCOTT NO.	DESCRIPTION	FIRST DAY COVER	UNUSED ENTIRE	USED CUT SQ.
U566	8¢ & 2¢ ultramarine (on U557)	3.00	.65	1.35
U567	10¢ emerald	1.75	.65	.30

U568

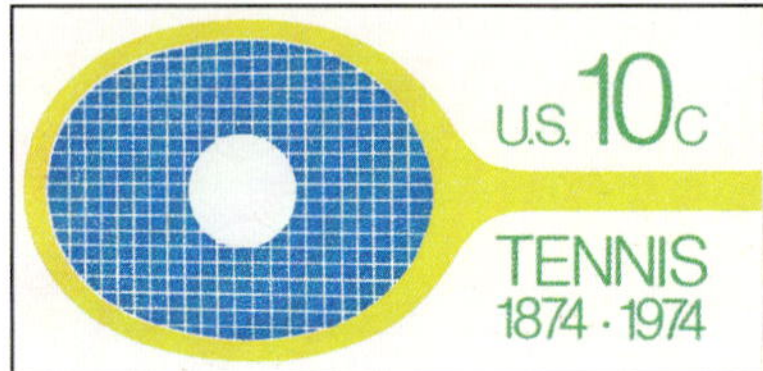

U569

1974

SCOTT NO.	DESCRIPTION	FIRST DAY COVER	UNUSED ENTIRE	USED CUT SQ.
U568	1 8/10¢ blue green	1.75	.85	.30
U569	10¢ Tennis Centenary	2.50	.80	.30

U571

U572

U573

U574

U575

1975-76 BICENTENNIAL ERA

SCOTT NO.	DESCRIPTION	FIRST DAY COVER	UNUSED ENTIRE	USED CUT SQ.
U571	10¢ Seafaring	1.75	.60	.30
U572	13¢ Homemaker (1976)	1.75	.60	.30
U573	13¢ Farmer (1976)	1.75	.60	.30
U574	13¢ Doctor (1976)	1.75	.60	.30
U575	13¢ Craftsman (1976)	1.75	.60	.30

CUT SQUARES: From 1947 to date, Unused Envelope Cut Squares can be supplied at the Unused Entire Price.

U576

1975

SCOTT NO.	DESCRIPTION	FIRST DAY COVER	UNUSED ENTIRE	USED CUT SQ.
U576	13¢ orange brown	1.75	.60	.30

U577

U578

U579

U580

U581

1976-78

SCOTT NO.	DESCRIPTION	FIRST DAY COVER	UNUSED ENTIRE	USED CUT SQ.
U577	2¢ red	1.75	.60	.30
U578	2.1¢ green (1977)	1.75	.70	.30
U579	2.7¢ green (1978)	1.75	.95	.30
U580	(15¢) "A" orange (1978)	1.75	.65	.30
U581	15¢ red & white (1978)	1.75	.65	.30

1976

SCOTT NO.	DESCRIPTION	FIRST DAY COVER	UNUSED ENTIRE	USED CUT SQ.
U582	13¢ Bicentennial (design of U218)	1.75	.55	.30

U583

1977

SCOTT NO.	DESCRIPTION	FIRST DAY COVER	UNUSED ENTIRE	USED CUT SQ.
U583	13¢ Golf	8.00	.80	.35

U584

U585

SCOTT NO.	DESCRIPTION	FIRST DAY COVER	UNUSED ENTIRE	USED CUT SQ.
U584	13¢ Energy Conservation	1.75	.55	.30
U585	13¢ Energy Development	1.75	.55	.30

U586, U588

U586

1978

SCOTT NO.	DESCRIPTION	FIRST DAY COVER	UNUSED ENTIRE	USED CUT SQ.
U586	15¢ on 16¢ blue & white	1.75	.55	.25

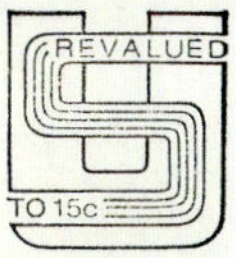

U587

SCOTT NO.	DESCRIPTION	FIRST DAY COVER	UNUSED ENTIRE	USED CUT SQ.
U587	15¢ Auto Racing	2.00	.95	.45
U588	15¢ on 13¢ white, orange brown (U576)	1.75	.55	.25

U589

U590

1979

SCOTT NO.	DESCRIPTION	FIRST DAY COVER	UNUSED ENTIRE	USED CUT SQ.
U589	3.1¢ ultramarine & white	1.75	.55	.60

1980

SCOTT NO.	DESCRIPTION	FIRST DAY COVER	UNUSED ENTIRE	USED CUT SQ.
U590	3.5¢ purple	1.75	.45	.60

U591

U592

U593

U594

1981-82

SCOTT NO.	DESCRIPTION	FIRST DAY COVER	UNUSED ENTIRE	USED CUT SQ.
U591	5.9¢ brown (1982)	1.85	.45	.60
U592	(18¢) "B" violet & white	1.75	.60	.30
U593	18¢ white & dark blue	1.75	.60	.30
U594	(20¢) "C" brown & white	1.75	60	.30

U595

U596

1979

SCOTT NO.	DESCRIPTION	FIRST DAY COVER	UNUSED ENTIRE	USED CUT SQ.
U595	15¢ Veterinarians	1.75	.85	.30
U596	15¢ Moscow Olympics	1.75	.90	.25

U597

U598

U599

1980

SCOTT NO.	DESCRIPTION	FIRST DAY COVER	UNUSED ENTIRE	USED CUT SQ.
U597	15¢ Bicycle	1.75	.65	.25
U598	15¢ America's Cup	1.75	.65	.25
U599	15¢ Honeybee	1.75	.65	.25

U600

U601

1981

SCOTT NO.	DESCRIPTION	FIRST DAY COVER	UNUSED ENTIRE	USED CUT SQ.
U600	18¢ Blinded Veterans	1.75	.65	.25
U601	20¢ deep magenta & white	1.75	.65	.25

U602

U603

1982

SCOTT NO.	DESCRIPTION	FIRST DAY COVER	UNUSED ENTIRE	USED CUT SQ.
U602	20¢ black, blue & magenta	1.75	.65	.60
U603	20¢ Purple Heart	1.75	.95	.25

U604

U605

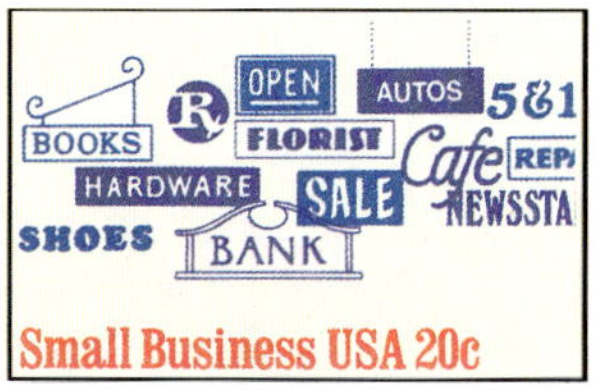

U606

1983

SCOTT NO.	DESCRIPTION	FIRST DAY COVER	UNUSED ENTIRE	USED CUT SQ.
U604	5.2¢ orange & white	1.75	.55	1.40
U605	20¢ Paralyzed Veterans	1.75	.65	.25

1984

SCOTT NO.	DESCRIPTION	FIRST DAY COVER	UNUSED ENTIRE	USED CUT SQ.
U606	20¢ Small Business	2.00	.65	.25

U607

U608

U609

1985

SCOTT NO.	DESCRIPTION	FIRST DAY COVER	UNUSED ENTIRE	USED CUT SQ.
U607	22¢ "D"	1.75	.75	.40
U608	22¢ Bison	1.75	.75	.25
U609	6¢ Old Ironsides	1.75	.45	.40

U610

1986

SCOTT NO.	DESCRIPTION	FIRST DAY COVER	UNUSED ENTIRE	USED CUT SQ.
U610	8.5¢ Mayflower	1.75	.65	.80

U611

U612

U613

1988

SCOTT NO.	DESCRIPTION	FIRST DAY COVER	UNUSED ENTIRE	USED CUT SQ.
U611	25¢ Stars	1.75	.85	.25
U612	8.4¢ Constellation	1.75	.65	.90
U613	25¢ Snowflake	1.75	2.60	25.00

U614

U615

U616

U617, U639

1989

SCOTT NO.	DESCRIPTION	FIRST DAY COVER	UNUSED ENTIRE	USED CUT SQ.
U614	25¢ Stamped Return Envelope	1.75	.80	.30
U615	25¢ "USA" and Stars	1.75	.80	.30
U616	25¢ LOVE	1.75	.80	1.00
U617	25¢ Shuttle Docking Hologram	1.75	1.25	.80

U618

U619

1990-91

SCOTT NO.	DESCRIPTION	FIRST DAY COVER	UNUSED ENTIRE	USED CUT SQ.
U618	25¢ Football Hologram	2.75	1.25	.75
U619	29¢ Star	1.75	.95	.35

U620

SCOTT NO.	DESCRIPTION	FIRST DAY COVER	UNUSED ENTIRE	USED CUT SQ.
U620	11.1¢ Birds on Wire	1.75	.65	1.10

U621

U622

SCOTT NO.	DESCRIPTION	FIRST DAY COVER	UNUSED ENTIRE	USED CUT SQ.
U621	29¢ Love	1.75	.95	.70
U622	29¢ Magazine Industry	1.75	.95	1.05

U623

U624

SCOTT NO.	DESCRIPTION	FIRST DAY COVER	UNUSED ENTIRE	USED CUT SQ.
U623	29¢ Star	1.75	.95	.35
U624	26¢ Country Geese	1.75	.95	.70

U625

U626

1992

SCOTT NO.	DESCRIPTION	FIRST DAY COVER	UNUSED ENTIRE	USED CUT SQ.
U625	29¢ Space Station	1.75	1.25	.60
U626	29¢ Saddle & Blanket	1.75	1.05	1.10

U627

U628

SCOTT NO.	DESCRIPTION	FIRST DAY COVER	UNUSED ENTIRE	USED CUT SQ.
U627	29¢ Protect the Environment	1.75	.95	1.10
U628	19.8¢ Star	1.75	.75	.45

U629, U630

SCOTT NO.	DESCRIPTION	FIRST DAY COVER	UNUSED ENTIRE	USED CUT SQ.
U629	29¢ Americans With Disabilities	1.75	1.10	.40
	1993			
U630	29¢ Kitten	1.75	1.35	1.25

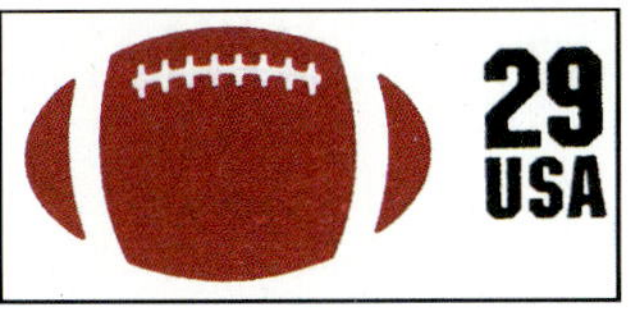

U631

U632, U638

SCOTT NO.	DESCRIPTION	FIRST DAY COVER	UNUSED ENTIRE	USED CUT SQ.
	1994			
U631	29¢ Football	1.75	1.00	1.35

U633, U634

U635

SCOTT NO.	DESCRIPTION	FIRST DAY COVER	UNUSED ENTIRE	USED CUT SQ.
	1995			
U632	32¢ Liberty Bell	1.95	1.10	.35
U633	(32¢) "G" Old Glory (Design size 49x38mm)	1.95	1.85	2.25
U634	(32¢) "G" Old Glory (Design size 53x44mm)	1.95	2.50	2.25
U635	(5¢) Sheep, Nonprofit	1.95	.60	.55

U636

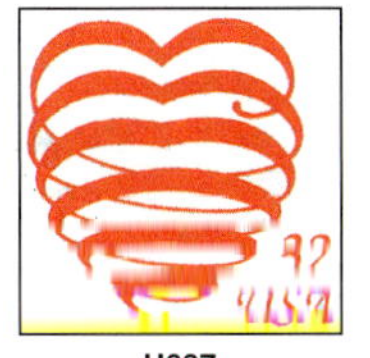

U637

SCOTT NO.	DESCRIPTION	FIRST DAY COVER	UNUSED ENTIRE	USED CUT SQ.
U636	(10¢) Graphic Eagle, Bulk Rate	1.95	.45	1.60
[illegible]	[illegible]	[illegible]	[illegible]	[illegible]
U638	32¢ Liberty Bell, security	1.95	1.10	.35
U639	32¢ Space Station	1.95	1.10	.45

U640

U641

SCOTT NO.	DESCRIPTION	FIRST DAY COVER	UNUSED ENTIRE	USED CUT SQ.
	1996			
U640	32¢ Save our Environment	1.95	1.10	.45
U641	32¢ Paralympic Games	1.95	1.10	.35

U642, U643

U645

U644

SCOTT NO.	DESCRIPTION	FIRST DAY COVER	UNUSED ENTIRE	USED CUT SQ.
	1999-2000			
U642	33¢ Flag, yellow, blue & red	1.95	1.35	.35
U642a	same, tagging bars to right of design	1.95	1.35	.35
U643	33¢ Flag, blue & red	1.95	1.35	.35
U644	33¢ Love	1.95	1.10	.35
U645	33¢ Lincoln, blue & black	1.95	1.10	.35

U646

U647

SCOTT NO.	DESCRIPTION	FIRST DAY COVER	UNUSED ENTIRE	USED CUT SQ.
	2001-03			
U646	34¢ Eagle, blue gray & gray	1.95	1.25	.35
U647	34¢ Lovebirds, rose & dull violet	1.95	1.25	.35

U648

U649

U650

SCOTT NO.	DESCRIPTION	FIRST DAY COVER	UNUSED ENTIRE	USED CUT SQ.
U648	34¢ Community Colleges, dark blue & orange brown	1.95	1.25	.35
U649	37¢ Ribbon Star, red & blue	1.95	1.25	.40
U650	(10¢) Graphic Eagle, Presorted Standard	1.95	1.00	.35

U651

U652

SCOTT NO.	DESCRIPTION	FIRST DAY COVER	UNUSED ENTIRE	USED CUT SQ.
U651	37¢ Nurturing Love	1.95	1.25	.40
U652	$3.85 Jefferson Memorial, pre-paid flat rate	8.75	15.00	8.75

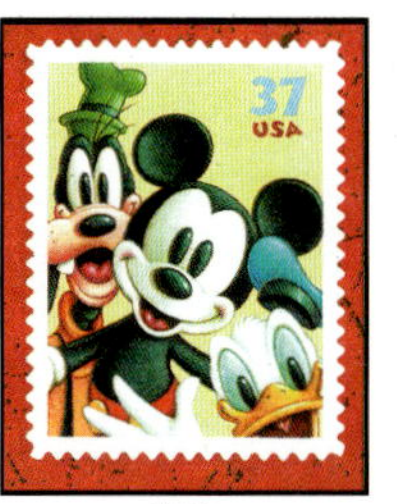

U653

U657

SCOTT NO.	DESCRIPTION	FIRST DAY COVER	UNUSED ENTIRE	USED CUT SQ.
	2004			
U653	37¢ Goofy, Mickey Mouse, Donald Duck	3.00	3.25	2.50
U654	37¢ Bambi, Thumper	3.00	3.25	2.50
U655	37¢ Mufasa, Simba	3.00	3.25	2.50
U656	37¢ Jiminy Cricket, Pinocchio	3.00	3.25	2.50
	2005			
U657	37¢ Wedding Flowers, letter sheet	1.95	3.25	2.75

U658 U659 U660 U661

2006

SCOTT NO.	DESCRIPTION	FIRST DAY COVER	UNUSED ENTIRE	USED CUT SQ.
U658	$4.05 X-Planes, pre-paid flat rate	....	13.00	11.00
U659	39¢ Benjamin Franklin	1.95	1.25	.50

2007

SCOTT NO.	DESCRIPTION	FIRST DAY COVER	UNUSED ENTIRE	USED CUT SQ.
U660	$4.60 Air Force One, priority mail, pre-paid flat rate	....	14.00	9.50
U661	$16.25 Marine One, express mail, pre-paid flat rate	....	48.00	30.00

U662 U663

SCOTT NO.	DESCRIPTION	FIRST DAY COVER	UNUSED ENTIRE	USED CUT SQ.
U662	41¢ Horses	2.00	1.35	.50

2008

SCOTT NO.	DESCRIPTION	FIRST DAY COVER	UNUSED ENTIRE	USED CUT SQ.
U663	42¢ Elk Mint Entire	3.75	1.35	.50
U663b	42¢ Elk, tagging bar 19mm tall, recycling logo at top right side of statement	....	1.35	....

U664 U667 U668

SCOTT NO.	DESCRIPTION	FIRST DAY COVER	UNUSED ENTIRE	USED CUT SQ.
U664	$4.80 Mount Rushmore	11.00	14.00	9.00
U665	42¢ Sunflower	4.75	3.50	3.50

2009

SCOTT NO.	DESCRIPTION	FIRST DAY COVER	UNUSED ENTIRE	USED CUT SQ.
U666	$4.95 Redwood Forest	12.00	14.00	9.50
U667	(44¢) Forever Stamped Envelope	4.75	1.60	.95
U667a	(44¢) Forever Liberty Bell Envelope	2.75	1.60	.95
U668	44¢ Seabiscuit Stamped Envelope	4.75	1.60	.50
U668a	44¢ Seabiscuit Stamped Envelope, typographed	4.75	1.60	.50

U672 U674

SCOTT NO.	DESCRIPTION	FIRST DAY COVER	UNUSED ENTIRE	USED CUT SQ.
U669-73	Gulf Coast Lighthouses	32.50	25.00	....

U675 U676 U677, U678

2010

SCOTT NO.	DESCRIPTION	FIRST DAY COVER	UNUSED ENTIRE	USED CUT SQ.
U674	$4.90 Mackinac Bridge	11.00	13.00	9.50

2011

SCOTT NO.	DESCRIPTION	FIRST DAY COVER	UNUSED ENTIRE	USED CUT SQ.
U675	$4.95 New River Bridge	11.00	13.00	10.00

2012

SCOTT NO.	DESCRIPTION	FIRST DAY COVER	UNUSED ENTIRE	USED CUT SQ.
U676	$5.15 Sunshine Skyway Bridge	12.00	12.50	9.50
U677	(45¢) Purple Martin (design size 33x48mm)	1.50	1.25	0.65
U678	(45¢) Purple Martin (design size 35x50)	1.50	1.25	0.85
U679	$5.60 Arlington Green Bridge	12.00	12.00	8.50
U680	(46¢) Bank Swallowtail (design size 38x35mm)	2.75	1.50	0.75
U681	(46¢) Bank Swallowtail (design size 41x38mm)	2.75	1.50	0.75
U682	(46¢) Eagle, Shield & Flags	2.75	1.75	0.75
U683	$5.60 Verrazano-Narrows Bridge	12.00	....	12.00

U680, U681 U684 U685 U686 U687

2014

SCOTT NO.	DESCRIPTION	FIRST DAY COVER	UNUSED ENTIRE	USED CUT SQ.
U684	(49¢) Poinsettia	2.50	2.25	1.75
U685	(49¢) Snowflake	2.50	2.25	1.75
U686	(49¢) Snowflake	2.50	2.25	1.75
U687	(49¢) Cardinal	2.50	2.25	1.75
U688	(49¢) Child Making Snowman	2.50	2.25	1.75

U688 U689 U690 U691 U692 U693

2015

SCOTT NO.	DESCRIPTION	FIRST DAY COVER	UNUSED ENTIRE	USED CUT SQ.
U689	$5.75 Glade Creek Grist Mill	....	12.50	10.00
U690	(49¢) Pink Water Lily	3.50	2.25	2.25
U691	(49¢) White Water Lily	3.50	2.25	2.25
U692	(49¢) Forget-Me-Not Missing Children	3.50	2.25	2.25

U694 U695 U696 U700

2016-2020

SCOTT NO.	DESCRIPTION	FIRST DAY COVER	UNUSED ENTIRE	USED CUT SQ.
U693	$6.45 La Cueva del Indio Priority Envelope	15.00	15.50	....
U694	(47¢) Northern Cardinal	3.50	2.25	....
U695	$6.65 Lili'uokalani Gardens Priority Envelope	15.00	15.50	....
U696	(49¢) Barn Swallow	3.50	2.25	....
U697	$6.70 Byodo-In Temple, Priority Envelope	15.00	15.50	....
U698	$7.35 Joshua Tree, Priority Envelope	16.00	16.00	....
U699	$7.75 Big Bend, Priority Envelope	16.50	16.50	....
U700	(55¢) Flag and Stars	3.50	2.25	....

U701 U702

2021-2023

SCOTT NO.	DESCRIPTION	FIRST DAY COVER	UNUSED ENTIRE	USED CUT SQ.
U701	$7.95 Castillo de San Marcos, Priority Envelope	16.50	16.50	....
U702	(66¢) Northern Cardinal	4.00	2.50	....

SCOTT NO.	DESCRIPTION	UNUSED ENTIRE	UNUSED CUT SQ.	USED CUT SQ.

UC1

UC2-UC7

Airplane in Circle

Die 1. Vertical rudder not semi-circular, but slopes to the left. Tail projects into "G".
Die 2. Vertical rudder is semi-circular. Tail only touches "G" Die 2a. "6" is 6½mm. wide.
Die 2b. "6" is 6mm. wide.
Die 2c. "6" is 5½mm. wide.
Die 3. Vertical rudder leans forward. "S" closer to "O" than to "T" of "POSTAGE" and "E" has short center bar.

1929-44

SCOTT NO.	DESCRIPTION	UNUSED ENTIRE	UNUSED CUT SQ.	USED CUT SQ.
UC1	5¢ blue, die 1	6.00	4.00	4.00
UC2	5¢ blue, die 2	16.00	12.00	10.00
UC3	6¢ orange, die 2a	2.50	1.75	1.00
UC3n	6¢, die 2a, no border	3.00	1.50	1.00
UC4	6¢, die 2b, with border	72.00	53.00	2.50
UC4n	6¢, die 2b, no border	6.00	4.00	2.50
UC5	6¢, die 2c, no border	1.55	1.00	.50
UC6	6¢ orange on white, die 3	2.25	1.25	.45
UC6n	6¢, die 3, no border	3.00	1.50	.50
UC7	8¢ olive green	21.00	14.50	4.00

REVALUED
5¢
P.O. DEPT.

Envelopes of 1916-32 surcharged

1945

SCOTT NO.	DESCRIPTION	UNUSED ENTIRE	UNUSED CUT SQ.	USED CUT SQ.
UC8	6¢ on 2¢ carmine on white (U429)	1.75	1.55	1.15
UC9	6¢ on 2¢ carmine on white (U525)	120.00	90.00	72.50

1946

SCOTT NO.	DESCRIPTION	UNUSED ENTIRE	UNUSED CUT SQ.	USED CUT SQ.
UC10	5¢ on 6¢, die 2a (UC3n)	6.00	4.50	2.60
UC11	5¢ on 6¢, die 2b (UC4n)	12.00	11.75	8.50
UC12	5¢ on 6¢, die 2c (UC5)	1.50	1.15	.80
UC13	5¢ on 6¢, die 3 (UC6n)	1.15	1.15	.75

UC14: Die 1. Small projection below rudder is rounded.
UC15: Die 2. Small projection below rudder is sharp pointed.

UC14, UC15, UC18, UC26
DC-4 Skymaster

SCOTT NO.	DESCRIPTION	FIRST DAY COVER	UNUSED ENTIRE	USED CUT SQ.
UC14	5¢ carmine, die 1	2.50	1.25	.75
UC15	5¢ carmine, die 2	....	1.25	.75

UC16
DC-4 Skymaster

UC17
Washington and Franklin, Mail-carrying Vehicles

1947

SCOTT NO.	DESCRIPTION	FIRST DAY COVER	UNUSED ENTIRE	USED CUT SQ.
UC16	10¢ red on blue, Entire "Air Letter" on face, 2-line inscription on back	6.00	9.00	10.50
UC16a	Entire, "Air Letter" on face, 4-line inscription on back	....	18.00	15.00
UC16c	Entire "Air Letter" and "Aerogramme" on face, 4-line inscription on back	....	55.00	13.50
UC16d	Entire "Air Letter" and "Aerogramme" on face, 3-line inscription on back	....	9.50	9.00

1947 CIPEX COMMEMORATIVE

SCOTT NO.	DESCRIPTION	FIRST DAY COVER	UNUSED ENTIRE	USED CUT SQ.
UC17	5¢ carmine	3.00	.65	.60

1950 Design of 1946

SCOTT NO.	DESCRIPTION	FIRST DAY COVER	UNUSED ENTIRE	USED CUT SQ.
UC18	6¢ carmine	1.75	.60	.35

1951 (Shaded Numeral)

SCOTT NO.	DESCRIPTION	FIRST DAY COVER	UNUSED ENTIRE	USED CUT SQ.
UC19	6¢ on 5¢, die 1 (UC14)	....	2.40	1.60
UC20	6¢ on 5¢, die 2 (UC15)	....	1.25	1.60

1952 (Solid Numeral)

SCOTT NO.	DESCRIPTION	FIRST DAY COVER	UNUSED ENTIRE	USED CUT SQ.
UC21	6¢ on 5¢, die 1 (UC14)	....	35.00	19.00
UC22	6¢ on 5¢, die 2 (UC15)	....	9.00	2.75
UC23	6¢ on 5¢ (UC17)	....	2100.00	....

SCOTT NO.	DESCRIPTION	FIRST DAY COVER	UNUSED ENTIRE	USED CUT SQ.

ENVELOPE of 1946 Surcharged

ENVELOPE of 1946-47 Surcharged

1956 FIPEX COMMEMORATIVE

SCOTT NO.	DESCRIPTION	FIRST DAY COVER	UNUSED ENTIRE	USED CUT SQ.
UC25	6¢ red	1.75	1.10	.60

1958 Design of 1946

SCOTT NO.	DESCRIPTION	FIRST DAY COVER	UNUSED ENTIRE	USED CUT SQ.
UC26	7¢ blue	1.75	1.10	.60

UC36

UC27-UC31
Surcharge on Envelopes of 1934 to 1956

UC25

1958

SCOTT NO.	DESCRIPTION	FIRST DAY COVER	UNUSED ENTIRE	USED CUT SQ.
UC27	6¢ & 1¢ (7¢) orange, die 2a (UC3n)	....	420.00	....
UC28	6¢ & 1¢ (7¢) orange, die 2b (UC4n)	....	125.00	82.50
UC29	6¢ & 1¢ (7¢) orange, die 2c (UC5)	....	60.00	52.50
UC30	6¢ & 1¢ (7¢) carmine (UC18)	....	1.35	.60
UC31	6¢ & 1¢ (7¢) red (UC25)	....	1.40	.60

UC32

UC33, UC34

UC35

1958-59

SCOTT NO.	DESCRIPTION	FIRST DAY COVER	UNUSED ENTIRE	USED CUT SQ.
UC32	10¢ blue & red Entire letter sheet, 2-line inscription on back (1959)	....	7.00	5.25
UC32a	Entire letter sheet, 3 line inscription on back	2.25	12.00	5.25

1958

SCOTT NO.	DESCRIPTION	FIRST DAY COVER	UNUSED ENTIRE	USED CUT SQ.
UC33	7¢ blue	1.75	.80	.30

1960

SCOTT NO.	DESCRIPTION	FIRST DAY COVER	UNUSED ENTIRE	USED CUT SQ.
UC34	7¢ carmine	1.75	.85	.30

1961

SCOTT NO.	DESCRIPTION	FIRST DAY COVER	UNUSED ENTIRE	USED CUT SQ.
UC35	11¢ red & blue	3.25	3.00	3.75

1962

SCOTT NO.	DESCRIPTION	FIRST DAY COVER	UNUSED ENTIRE	USED CUT SQ.
UC36	8¢ red	1.75	.85	.25

1965

SCOTT NO.	DESCRIPTION	FIRST DAY COVER	UNUSED ENTIRE	USED CUT SQ.
UC37	8¢ red	1.75	.70	.25
UC38	11¢ J.F. Kennedy	1.75	4.00	4.50

UC37

UC38, UC39

UC40

UC41 (surcharge on UC37)

HUMAN RIGHTS YEAR U.S. POSTAGE 13¢

UC42

1967

SCOTT NO.	DESCRIPTION	FIRST DAY COVER	UNUSED ENTIRE	USED CUT SQ.
UC39	13¢ J.F. Kennedy	1.75	3.50	4.50

1968

SCOTT NO.	DESCRIPTION	FIRST DAY COVER	UNUSED ENTIRE	USED CUT SQ.
UC40	10¢ red	1.75	.85	.25
UC41	8¢ & 2¢ (10¢) red	12.00	.95	.25
UC42	13¢ Human Rights Year	1.75	11.00	8.00

UC43

UC44

SCOTT NO.	DESCRIPTION	FIRST DAY COVER	UNUSED ENTIRE	USED CUT SQ.
	1971			
UC43	11¢ red & blue	1.75	.85	1.85
UC44	15¢ gray, red, white and blue Birds in Flight	1.75	2.00	3.50
UC44a	Aerogramme added	1.75	2.00	3.50

UC45 (surcharge on UC40)

UC47

SCOTT NO.	DESCRIPTION	FIRST DAY COVER	UNUSED ENTIRE	USED CUT SQ.
	1971 Revalued			
UC45	10 & (1¢) (11¢) red	6.00	2.50	.25
	1973			
UC46	15¢ Ballooning	1.75	1.25	1.50
UC47	13¢ rose red	1.75	.75	.25

UC48

UC49

SCOTT NO.	DESCRIPTION	FIRST DAY COVER	UNUSED ENTIRE	USED CUT SQ.
	1974			
UC48	18¢ red & blue	1.75	1.50	2.25
UC49	18¢ NATO 25th Anniversary	1.75	1.25	2.25

UC50

UC51

SCOTT NO.	DESCRIPTION	FIRST DAY COVER	UNUSED ENTIRE	USED CUT SQ.
	1976			
UC50	22¢ red, white & blue	1.75	1.55	2.25
	1978			
UC51	22¢ blue	1.75	1.55	2.25

UC52

UC53, UC54

UC55

SCOTT NO.	DESCRIPTION	FIRST DAY COVER	UNUSED ENTIRE	USED CUT SQ.
	1979			
UC52	22¢ Moscow Olympics	1.75	2.25	2.25
	1980-81			
UC53	30¢ red, blue & brown	1.75	1.25	1.75
UC54	30¢ yellow, magenta, blue & black (1981)	1.75	1.25	1.25
	1982			
UC55	30¢ Made in U.S.A.	1.75	1.45	3.00

UC56

UC57

SCOTT NO.	DESCRIPTION	FIRST DAY COVER	UNUSED ENTIRE	USED CUT SQ.
	1983			
UC56	30¢ Communications	1.75	1.25	5.50
UC57	30¢ Olympics	1.75	1.25	5.50

UC58

UC59

SCOTT NO.	DESCRIPTION	FIRST DAY COVER	UNUSED ENTIRE	USED CUT SQ.
	1985			
UC58	36¢ Landsat Satellite	1.75	1.50	5.50
UC59	36¢ Travel	1.75	1.55	3.50
UC60	36¢ Mark Twain, Halley's Comet	1.75	1.75	6.50

UC60

UC61

SCOTT NO.	DESCRIPTION	FIRST DAY COVER	UNUSED ENTIRE	USED CUT SQ.
	1986			
UC61	39¢ Letters	1.75	2.00	6.50
	1989			
UC62	39¢ Blair & Lincoln	1.75	1.75	26.00

UC62

UC63

SCOTT NO.	DESCRIPTION	FIRST DAY COVER	UNUSED ENTIRE	USED CUT SQ.
	1991			
UC63	45¢ Eagle	1.75	1.75	2.50
	1995			
UC64	50¢ Thaddeus Lowe	1.95	1.75	5.50

UC64

UC65

SCOTT NO.	DESCRIPTION	FIRST DAY COVER	UNUSED ENTIRE	USED CUT SQ.
	1999			
UC65	60¢ Voyagers National Park, Minnesota	1.95	2.50	7.75

UO1-UO13 UO14-UO17 UO18-UO69 *Washington*

OFFICIAL ENVELOPES

NOTE: **For details on similar appearing varieties please refer to the Scott Specialized Catalogue**

POST OFFICE DEPARTMENT

1873 SMALL NUMERALS

SCOTT NO.	DESCRIPTION	UNUSED ENTIRE	UNUSED CUT SQ.	USED CUT SQ.
UO1	2¢ black on lemon	40.00	28.00	11.00
UO2	3¢ black on lemon	38.00	21.00	7.00
UO4	6¢ black on lemon	46.00	31.00	17.00

1874-79 LARGE NUMERALS

SCOTT NO.	DESCRIPTION	UNUSED ENTIRE	UNUSED CUT SQ.	USED CUT SQ.
UO5	2¢ black on lemon	19.00	13.00	5.00
UO6	2¢ black on white	255.00	150.00	40.00
UO7	3¢ black on lemon	5.00	4.00	1.00
UO8	3¢ black on white	5800.00	3250.00	2400.00
UO9	3¢ black on amber	180.00	155.00	42.00
UO12	6¢ black on lemon	31.00	18.00	7.00
UO13	6¢ black on white	5800.00	3250.00	....

1877 POSTAL SERVICE

SCOTT NO.	DESCRIPTION	UNUSED ENTIRE	UNUSED CUT SQ.	USED CUT SQ.
UO14	black on white	12.00	8.00	5.00
UO15	black on amber	955.00	250.00	45.00
UO16	blue on amber	955.00	225.00	38.00
UO17	blue on blue	16.00	10.00	7.00

Portraits for the various denominations are the same as on the regular issue of 1870-73

WAR DEPARTMENT

1873 REAY ISSUE

SCOTT NO.	DESCRIPTION	UNUSED ENTIRE	UNUSED CUT SQ.	USED CUT SQ.
UO18	1¢ dark red on white	1150.00	750.00	325.00
UO19	2¢ dark red on white	3250.00	2500.00	475.00
UO20	3¢ dark red on white	110.00	75.00	48.00
UO22	3¢ dark red on cream	1150.00	1050.00	315.00
UO23	6¢ dark red on white	480.00	350.00	95.00
UO24	6¢ dark red on cream	....	8500.00	440.00
UO25	10¢ dark red on white	....	....	2500.00
UO26	12¢ dark red on white	250.00	190.00	65.00
UO27	15¢ dark red on white	225.00	175.00	65.00
UO28	24¢ dark red on white	250.00	200.00	55.00
UO29	30¢ dark red on white	785.00	600.00	165.00
UO30	1¢ vermillion on white	455.00	225.00	....
WO31	1¢ vermillion on manila	42.00	23.00	15.00
UO32	2¢ vermillion on white	....	550.00	....
WO33	2¢ vermillion on manila	750.00	300.00	
UO34	3¢ vermillion on white	225.00	110.00	45.00
UO35	3¢ vermillion on amber	400.00	110.00	....
UO36	3¢ vermillion on cream	45.00	20.00	14.00
UO37	6¢ vermillion on white	200.00	110.00	....
UO38	6¢ vermillion on cream		600.00	....
UO39	10¢ vermillion on white	655.00	375.00	....
UO40	12¢ vermillion on white	[illegible]	105.00	....
UO41	15¢ vermillion on white	3250.00	275.00	....
UO42	24¢ vermillion on white	690.00	475.00	....
UO43	30¢ vermillion on white	680.00	550.00	....

1875 PLIMPTON ISSUE

SCOTT NO.	DESCRIPTION	UNUSED ENTIRE	UNUSED CUT SQ.	USED CUT SQ.
UO44	1¢ red on white	275.00	210.00	95.00
UO45	1¢ red on amber	....	1200.00	....
WO46	1¢ red on manila	10.00	5.25	3.00
UO47	2¢ red on white	225.00	170.00	....
UO48	2¢ red on amber	60.00	40.00	18.00
UO49	2¢ red on orange	85.00	72.00	18.00
WO50	2¢ red on manila	250.00	130.00	60.00
UO51	3¢ red on white	25.00	18.00	11.00
UO52	3¢ red on amber	32.00	26.00	11.00
UO53	3¢ red on cream	10.00	8.00	4.00
UO54	3¢ red on blue	7.00	4.50	3.00
UO55	3¢ red on fawn	12.00	7.00	3.00
UO56	6¢ red on white	125.00	75.00	35.00
UO57	6¢ red on amber	150.00	100.00	50.00
UO58	6¢ red on cream	560.00	250.00	95.00
UO59	10¢ red on white	325.00	275.00	90.00
UO60	10¢ red on amber	1600.00	1320.00	....
UO61	12¢ red on white	200.00	75.00	42.00
UO62	12¢ red on amber	1000.00	850.00	....
UO63	12¢ red on cream	1000.00	800.00	....
UO64	15¢ red on white	325.00	275.00	150.00
UO65	15¢ red on amber	1150.00	1000.00	....
UO66	15¢ red on cream	1000.00	850.00	....
UO67	30¢ red on white	250.00	200.00	150.00
UO68	30¢ red on amber	2500.00	1150.00	....
UO69	30¢ red on cream	1400.00	1100.00	....

UO70-UO72

1911 POSTAL SAVINGS

SCOTT NO.	DESCRIPTION	UNUSED ENTIRE	UNUSED CUT SQ.	USED CUT SQ.
UO70	1¢ green on white	120.00	88.00	27.00
UO71	1¢ green on oriental buff	280.00	255.00	77.00
UO72	2¢ carmine on white	29.00	15.00	4.50

UO73 UO74 UO75

SCOTT NO.	DESCRIPTION	FIRST DAY COVER	UNUSED ENTIRE	USED CUT SQ.
	1983			
UO73	20¢ blue and white	2.50	1.40	40.00
	1985			
UO74	22¢ blue and white	2.00	1.00	35.00
	1987 Design Similar to UO74			
UO75	22¢ Savings Bond	3.25	2.50	35.00

UO76 UO77 UO78

UO81 UO83 UO84

SCOTT NO.	DESCRIPTION	FIRST DAY COVER	UNUSED ENTIRE	USED CUT SQ.
	1989			
UO76	(25¢) "E" black and blue Savings Bonds	2.00	1.65	35.00
UO77	25¢ black and blue	2.00	1.00	25.00
UO78	25¢ black and blue Savings Bonds	2.00	1.45	35.00
	1990			
UO79	45¢ black & blue seal	2.25	1.55	....
UO80	65¢ black & blue seal	3.00	1.95	....
UO81	45¢ Self-sealing Envelope	2.25	1.55	....
UO82	65¢ Self-sealing Envelope	3.00	1.95	....

UO85 UO86, UO87 UO88, UO89, UO90, UO91, UO92, UO93

SCOTT NO.	DESCRIPTION	FIRST DAY COVER	UNUSED ENTIRE	USED CUT SQ.
	1991-92			
UO83	(29¢) "F" black and blue Savings Bond	2.00	1.50	36.00
UO84	29¢ black and blue	2.00	1.00	25.00
UO85	29¢ black and blue Savings Bond	2.00	1.00	25.00
UO86	52¢ Consular Service	2.50	6.00	....
UO87	75¢ Consular Service	3.00	12.50	....
	1995			
UO88	32¢ Great Seal, red and blue	2.00	1.00	25.00
	1999			
UO89	33¢ Great Seal, red and blue	2.00	1.25	25.00
	2001-07			
UO90	34¢ Great Seal, red and blue	2.00	1.25	25.00
UO91	37¢ Great Seal, red and blue	2.00	1.25	....
UO92	39¢ Great Seal, red and blue	2.00	1.25	....
UO93	41¢ Great Seal, red and blue	2.00	1.25	....
UO94	42¢ Great Seal, official stamped envelope	2.50	1.25	....

POSTAL CARDS

Prices Are For Entire Cards

MINT: As Issued, no printing or writing added.
UNUSED: Uncancelled, with printing or writing added.

UX1, UX3, U65

UX4, UX5, UX7
Liberty

UX6, UX13, UX16

SCOTT NO.	DESCRIPTION	MINT	UNUSED	USED
	1873			
UX1	1¢ brown, large watermark	425.00	95.00	27.00
UX3	1¢ brown, small watermark	90.00	26.00	4.00
	1875 Inscribed "Write the Address", etc.			
UX4	1¢ black, watermarked	4100.00	800.00	450.00
UX5	1¢ black, unwatermarked	92.00	9.75	.75
	1879			
UX6	2¢ blue on buff	42.00	15.00	38.50
	1881 Inscribed "Nothing but the Address", etc.			
UX7	1¢ black on buff	85.00	9.00	.50

UX8

UX9

Jefferson

UX10, UX11
Grant

SCOTT NO.	DESCRIPTION	MINT	UNUSED	USED
	1885			
UX8	1¢ brown on buff	60.00	15.00	1.50
	1886			
UX9	1¢ black on buff	31.00	3.00	.65
	1891			
UX10	1¢ black on buff	52.00	11.00	1.75
UX11	1¢ blue on grayish white	26.00	6.00	3.00

UX12

UX14

Jefferson

UX15
John Adams

SCOTT NO.	DESCRIPTION	MINT	UNUSED	USED
	1894			
UX12	1¢ black on buff Small Wreath	57.00	3.50	.75
	1897			
UX13	2¢ blue on cream	250.00	95.00	95.00
UX14	1¢ black on buff Large Wreath	50.00	4.00	.75
	1898			
UX15	1¢ black on buff	58.00	15.00	16.00
UX16	2¢ black on buff	18.00	7.00	20.00

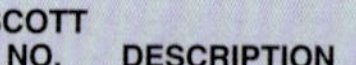

UX18

UX19, UX20
McKinley

UX21

SCOTT NO.	DESCRIPTION	MINT	UNUSED	USED
	1902 Profile Background			
UX18	1¢ black on buff	23.00	3.00	.40
	1907			
UX19	1¢ black on buff	65.00	4.00	.60
	1908 Correspondence Space at Left			
UX20	1¢ black on buff	72.00	12.00	4.50
	1910 Background Shaded			
UX21	1¢ blue on bluish	120.00	25.00	14.00

UX22, UX24
Mckiny

UX23, UX26
Lincoln

UX25
Grant

SCOTT NO.	DESCRIPTION	MINT	UNUSED	USED
	White Portrait Background			
UX22	1¢ blue on bluish	29.00	3.25	.85
	1911			
UX23	1¢ red on cream	12.00	4.00	6.00
UX24	1¢ red on cream	14.00	1.50	.40
UX25	2¢ red on cream	1.75	1.25	22.00
	1913			
UX26	1¢ green on cream	15.00	3.00	9.00

UX27
Jefferson

UX28, UX43
Lincoln

UX29, UX30
Jefferson

1 CENT

UX32, UX33 surcharge

SCOTT NO.	DESCRIPTION	MINT	UNUSED	USED
	1914			
UX27	1¢ green on buff	.45	.35	.40
	1917-18			
UX28	1¢ green on cream	1.00	.40	.40
UX29	2¢ red on buff, die 1	52.00	11.00	4.00
UX30	2¢ red on cream, die 2 (1918)	35.00	7.00	1.80

NOTE: On UX29 end of queue slopes sharply down to right while on UX30 it extends nearly horizontally.

SCOTT NO.	DESCRIPTION	MINT	UNUSED	USED
	1920 UX29 & UX30 Revalued			
UX32	1¢ on 2¢ red, die 1	68.00	22.00	15.00
UX33	1¢ on 2¢ red, die 2	18.00	4.00	3.00

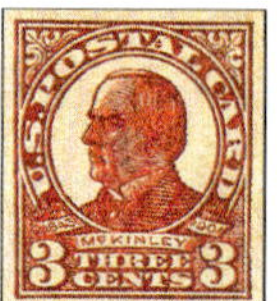

UX37
McKinley

UX38
Franklin

UX39-42 surcharge

SCOTT NO.	DESCRIPTION	MINT	UNUSED	USED
	1926			
UX37	3¢ red on buff	5.50	2.50	17.50

SCOTT NO.	DESCRIPTION	FIRST DAY COVER	MINT	USED
	1951			
UX38	2¢ carmine rose	1.75	.40	.55
	1952 UX27 & UX28 Surcharged by cancelling machine, light green			
UX39	2¢ on 1¢ green	....	.60	.65
UX40	2¢ on 1¢ green	....	.70	.75
	UX27 & UX28 Surcharge Typographed, dark green			
UX41	2¢ on 1¢ green	....	5.75	5.50
UX42	2¢ on 1¢ green	....	6.25	6.00
	1952 Design of 1917			
UX43	2¢ carmine	1.75	.45	1.00

UX44 **UX45, UY16** **UX46, UY17**

SCOTT NO.	DESCRIPTION	FIRST DAY COVER	MINT	USED
	1956 FIPEX COMMEMORATIVE			
UX44	2¢ deep carmine & dark violet	1.75	.45	1.00
	1956 INTERNATIONAL CARD			
UX45	4¢ deep red & ultramarine	1.75	1.95	100.00
	1958			
UX46	3¢ purple	1.75	.65	.25
	As above, but with printed precancel lines			
UX46d	3¢ purple	....	5.00	3.00

ONE CENT ADDITIONAL PAID

UX47 surcharge

UX48, UY18
Lincoln

UX49, UX54, UX59, UY19, UY20

SCOTT NO.	DESCRIPTION	FIRST DAY COVER	MINT	USED
	1958 UX38 Surcharged			
UX47	2¢ & 1¢ carmine rose	....	280.00	685.00
	Mint *UX47 has advertising			
	1962-66			
UX48	4¢ red violet	1.75	.60	.25
UX48a	4¢ luminescent (1966)	3.00	.75	.25
	1963			
UX49	7¢ Tourism	1.75	5.50	75.00

UX50 **UX51**

SCOTT NO.	DESCRIPTION	FIRST DAY COVER	MINT	USED
	1964			
UX50	4¢ Customs Service	1.75	.60	1.00
UX51	4¢ Social Security	1.75	.60	1.00

UX52 **UX53**

SCOTT NO.	DESCRIPTION	FIRST DAY COVER	MINT	USED
	1965			
UX52	4¢ Coast Guard	1.75	.45	1.00
UX53	4¢ Census Bureau	1.75	.45	1.00
	1967 Design of UX49			
UX54	8¢ Tourism	1.75	5.75	75.00

UX55, UY21
Lincoln

UX56

SCOTT NO.	DESCRIPTION	FIRST DAY COVER	MINT	USED
	1968			
UX55	5¢ emerald	1.75	.40	.75
UX56	5¢ Women Marines	1.75	.45	1.00

UX57

SCOTT NO.	DESCRIPTION	FIRST DAY COVER	MINT	USED
	1970			
UX57	5¢ Weather Bureau	1.75	.45	1.00

UX58, UY22

SCOTT NO.	DESCRIPTION	FIRST DAY COVER	MINT	USED
	1971			
UX58	6¢ Paul Revere	1.75	.40	1.00
	Design of UX49			
UX59	10¢ Tourism	1.75	5.75	65.00

UX60

SCOTT NO.	DESCRIPTION	FIRST DAY COVER	MINT	USED
	1971			
UX60	6¢ New York Hospital	1.75	.40	1.00

UX61 **UX62**

UX63

UX64, UY23

SCOTT NO.	DESCRIPTION	FIRST DAY COVER	MINT	USED
	1972			
UX61	6¢ U.S.F. Constellation	1.75	1.00	12.00
UX62	6¢ Monument Valley	1.75	.65	12.00
UX63	6¢ Gloucester, Massachusetts	1.75	.65	7.00
UX64	6¢ John Hanson	1.75	.60	1.00

UX66, UY24

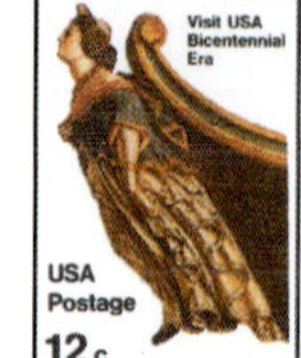

UX67

1973

SCOTT NO.	DESCRIPTION	FIRST DAY COVER	MINT	USED
UX65	6¢ Liberty, magenta, Design of 1873	1.75	.45	1.00
UX66	8¢ Samuel Adams	1.75	.65	1.00

1974

SCOTT NO.	DESCRIPTION	FIRST DAY COVER	MINT	USED
UX67	12¢ Visit USA	1.75	.45	50.00

UX68, UY25

UX69, UY26

UX70, UY27

1975-76

SCOTT NO.	DESCRIPTION	FIRST DAY COVER	MINT	USED
UX68	7¢ Charles Thomson	1.75	.45	12.00
UX69	9¢ J. Witherspoon	1.75	.45	1.00
UX70	9¢ Caesar Rodney	1.75	.45	1.00

UX71

UX72, UY28

1977

SCOTT NO.	DESCRIPTION	FIRST DAY COVER	MINT	USED
UX71	9¢ Federal Court House	1.75	.50	1.00
UX72	9¢ Nathan Hale	1.75	.55	1.00

UX73

UX74, UX75, UY29, UY30

UX76

UX77

1978

SCOTT NO.	DESCRIPTION	FIRST DAY COVER	MINT	USED
UX73	10¢ Music Hall	1.75	.50	1.00
UX74	10¢ John Hancock	1.75	.45	1.00
UX75	10¢ John Hancock	1.75	.50	1.00
UX76	14¢ "Eagle"	1.75	.50	35.00
UX77	10¢ multicolored	1.75	.50	2.00

UX78

UX79

UX80

1979

SCOTT NO.	DESCRIPTION	FIRST DAY COVER	MINT	USED
UX78	10¢ Fort Sackville	1.75	.50	2.00
UX79	10¢ Casimir Pulaski	1.75	.50	2.00
UX80	10¢ Moscow Olympics	1.75	.75	2.00
UX81	10¢ Iolani Palace	1.75	.50	2.00

UX81

UX82

UX83

UX84

UX85

UX86

1980

SCOTT NO.	DESCRIPTION	FIRST DAY COVER	MINT	USED
UX82	14¢ Winter Olympics	1.75	.85	22.00
UX83	10¢ Salt Lake Temple	1.75	.50	2.00
UX84	10¢ Count Rochambeau	1.75	.50	2.00
UX85	10¢ Kings Mountain	1.75	.50	2.00
UX86	19¢ Sir Francis Drake	1.75	1.00	40.00

UX87

UX88, UY31

UX89, UY32

1981

SCOTT NO.	DESCRIPTION	FIRST DAY COVER	MINT	USED
UX87	10¢ Cowpens	1.75	.50	18.50
UX88	"B" 12¢ violet & white	1.75	.45	.75
UX89	12¢ Isaiah Thomas	1.75	.45	.75

SCOTT NO.	DESCRIPTION	FIRST DAY COVER	MINT	USED

UX90 UX91

UX92, UY33 UX93, UY34

SCOTT NO.	DESCRIPTION	FIRST DAY COVER	MINT	USED
UX90	12¢ Eutaw Springs	1.75	.55	17.50
UX91	12¢ Lewis & Clark	1.75	.55	28.00
UX92	13¢ Robert Morris	1.75	.45	.75
UX93	13¢ Robert Morris	1.75	.45	.75

UX94 UX95

UX96

UX97

1982

SCOTT NO.	DESCRIPTION	FIRST DAY COVER	MINT	USED
UX94	13¢ Francis Marion	1.75	.55	1.25
UX95	13¢ La Salle	1.75	.55	1.25
UX96	13¢ Academy of Music	1.75	.55	1.25
UX97	13¢ St. Louis Post Office	1.75	.55	1.25

UX98

UX99

UX100

1983

SCOTT NO.	DESCRIPTION	FIRST DAY COVER	MINT	USED
UX98	13¢ General Oglethorpe	1.75	.55	1.25
UX99	13¢ Washington Post Office	1.75	.55	1.25
UX100	13¢ Olympics	1.75	.55	1.25

UX101

UX102

UX103 UX104

1984

SCOTT NO.	DESCRIPTION	FIRST DAY COVER	MINT	USED
UX101	13¢ "Ark" & "Dove"	1.75	.55	1.25
UX102	13¢ Olympics	1.75	.55	1.50
UX103	13¢ Frederic Baraga	1.75	.55	1.25
UX104	13¢ Historic Preservation	1.75	.55	1.25

UX105, UX106, UY35, UY36

UX107

UX108

1985

SCOTT NO.	DESCRIPTION	FIRST DAY COVER	MINT	USED
UX105	14¢ Charles Carroll	1.75	.50	.75
UX106	14¢ Charles Carroll	1.75	.50	.60
UX107	25¢ Flying Cloud	1.75	.95	25.00
UX108	14¢ George Wythe	1.75	.50	.90

UX109

UX110

UX111

UX112

1986

SCOTT NO.	DESCRIPTION	FIRST DAY COVER	MINT	USED
UX109	14¢ Connecticut	1.75	.55	2.00
UX110	14¢ Stamp Collecting	1.75	.55	1.50
UX111	14¢ Francis Vigo	1.75	.55	1.50
UX112	14¢ Rhode Island	1.75	.55	2.00

UX113

UX114

SCOTT NO.	DESCRIPTION	FIRST DAY COVER	MINT	USED
UX113	14¢ Wisconsin	[illegible]	[illegible]	[illegible]
UX114	14¢ National Guard	1.75	.55	1.50

UX115

UX116

UX117

1987

SCOTT NO.	DESCRIPTION	FIRST DAY COVER	MINT	USED
UX115	14¢ Steel Plow	1.75	.55	1.50
UX116	14¢ Constitution	1.75	.55	1.00
UX117	14¢ Flag	1.75	.55	.75

UX118  UX119

1987 (continued)

SCOTT NO.	DESCRIPTION	FIRST DAY COVER	MINT	USED
UX118	14¢ Take Pride in America	1.75	.55	1.50
UX119	14¢ Timberline Lodge	1.75	.55	1.60

UX120  UX121

1988

SCOTT NO.	DESCRIPTION	FIRST DAY COVER	MINT	USED
UX120	15¢ America the Beautiful	1.75	.55	.75
UX121	15¢ Blair House	1.75	.55	.85

UX122  UX123

SCOTT NO.	DESCRIPTION	FIRST DAY COVER	MINT	USED
UX122	28¢ Yorkshire	1.75	.85	22.50
UX123	15¢ Iowa Territory	1.75	.55	.85

UX124  UX125

SCOTT NO.	DESCRIPTION	FIRST DAY COVER	MINT	USED
UX124	15¢ Northwest Territory	1.75	.55	.85
UX125	15¢ Hearst Castle	1.75	.55	.85

UX126

SCOTT NO.	DESCRIPTION	FIRST DAY COVER	MINT	USED
UX126	15¢ Federalist Papers	1.75	.55	.85

UX127  UX128

1989

SCOTT NO.	DESCRIPTION	FIRST DAY COVER	MINT	USED
UX127	15¢ The Desert	1.75	.55	.85
UX128	15¢ Healy Hall	1.75	.55	.85

UX129  UX130

SCOTT NO.	DESCRIPTION	FIRST DAY COVER	MINT	USED
UX129	15¢ The Wet Lands	1.75	.55	.85
UX130	15¢ Oklahoma Territory	1.75	.55	.85

UX131  UX132

SCOTT NO.	DESCRIPTION	FIRST DAY COVER	MINT	USED
UX131	21¢ The Mountains	1.75	.75	20.00
UX132	15¢ The Seashore	1.75	.55	.85

UX133  UX134

SCOTT NO.	DESCRIPTION	FIRST DAY COVER	MINT	USED
UX133	15¢ The Woodlands	1.75	.55	.85
UX134	15¢ Hull House	1.75	.55	.85

UX135  UX136

SCOTT NO.	DESCRIPTION	FIRST DAY COVER	MINT	USED
UX135	15¢ Philadelphia Cityscape	1.75	.55	.85
UX136	15¢ Baltimore Cityscape	1.75	.55	.85

UX137  UX138

SCOTT NO.	DESCRIPTION	FIRST DAY COVER	MINT	USED
UX137	15¢ New York Cityscape	1.75	.55	.85
UX138	15¢ Washington Cityscape	1.75	.55	.85
UX139-42	15¢ Cityscape sheet of 4 postcards	8.00	18.00	27.50

UX143  UX144

SCOTT NO.	DESCRIPTION	FIRST DAY COVER	MINT	USED
UX143	15¢ White House	1.75	1.85	3.00
UX144	15¢ Jefferson Memorial	1.75	1.85	3.00

UX145  UX146

UX147

UX148

UX150

UX151

UX152

1990

SCOTT NO.	DESCRIPTION	FIRST DAY COVER	MINT	USED
UX145	15¢ Papermaking	1.75	.55	.50
UX146	15¢ Literacy	1.75	.55	.85
UX147	15¢ Bingham	1.75	1.75	3.00
UX148	15¢ Isaac Royall House	1.75	.55	.85
UX150	15¢ Stanford University	1.75	.55	.85
UX151	15¢ DAR Memorial Hall	1.75	1.60	2.50
UX152	15¢ Chicago Orchestra Hall	1.75	.55	.85

UX153

UX154

UX155

1991

SCOTT NO.	DESCRIPTION	FIRST DAY COVER	MINT	USED
UX153	19¢ Flag	1.75	.65	.85
UX154	19¢ Carnegie Hall	1.75	[illegible]	[illegible]
UX155	19¢ Old Red Administration Building	1.75	.65	.50

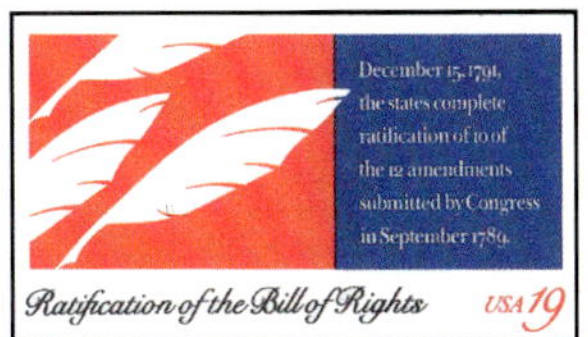
UX156

UX157

SCOTT NO.	DESCRIPTION	FIRST DAY COVER	MINT	USED
UX156	19¢ Bill of Rights	1.75	.65	.85
UX157	19¢ University of Notre Dame, Administration Building	1.75	.65	.85

UX158

UX159

SCOTT NO.	DESCRIPTION	FIRST DAY COVER	MINT	USED
UX158	30¢ Niagara Falls	1.75	.90	10.00
UX159	19¢ Old Mill University of Vermont	1.75	.65	1.00

UX160

UX161

UX162

UX163

UX164

UX165

1992

SCOTT NO.	DESCRIPTION	FIRST DAY COVER	MINT	USED
UX160	19¢ Wadsworth Atheneum	1.75	.65	.85
UX161	19¢ Cobb Hall University of Chicago	1.75	.65	.85
UX162	19¢ Waller Hall	1.75	.65	.85
UX163	19¢ America's Cup	1.75	1.95	4.00
UX164	19¢ Columbia River Gorge	1.75	.65	.85
UX165	19¢ Great Hall, Ellis Island	1.75	.65	.85

UX166

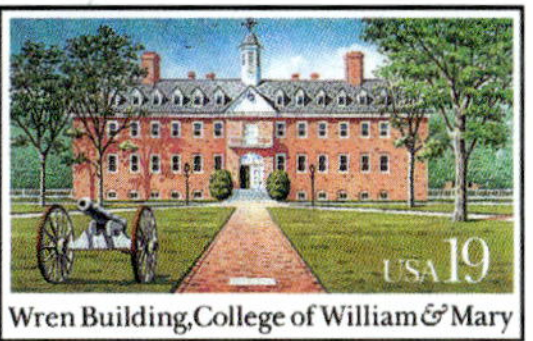
UX167

1993

SCOTT NO.	DESCRIPTION	FIRST DAY COVER	MINT	USED
UX166	19¢ National Cathedral	1.75	.65	.85
UX167	19¢ Wren Building	1.75	.65	[illegible]

UX168

UX169

SCOTT NO.	DESCRIPTION	FIRST DAY COVER	MINT	USED
UX168	19¢ Holocaust Memorial	2.00	1.85	4.00
UX169	19¢ Fort Recovery	1.75	.65	.85

UX170

UX171

SCOTT NO.	DESCRIPTION	FIRST DAY COVER	MINT	USED
UX170	19¢ Playmakers Theatre	1.75	.65	.85
UX171	19¢ O'Kane Hall	1.75	.65	.85

SCOTT NO.	DESCRIPTION	FIRST DAY COVER	MINT	USED

UX172

UX173

1993 (continued)

SCOTT NO.	DESCRIPTION	FIRST DAY COVER	MINT	USED
UX172	19¢ Beecher Hall	1.75	.65	.85
UX173	19¢ Massachusetts Hall	1.75	.65	.85

UX174

UX175

UX176

UX177

1994

SCOTT NO.	DESCRIPTION	FIRST DAY COVER	MINT	USED
UX174	19¢ Abraham Lincoln Home	1.75	.65	.85
UX175	19¢ Myers Hall	1.75	.65	.85
UX176	19¢ Canyon de Chelly	1.75	.65	.85
UX177	19¢ St. Louis Union Station	1.75	.65	.85

UX178

Legends of the West

UX178	*Home on the Range*	**UX188**	*Nellie Cashman*
UX179	*Buffalo Bill*	**UX189**	*Charles Goodnight*
UX180	*Jim Bridger*	**UX190**	*Geronimo*
UX181	*Annie Oakley*	**UX191**	*Kit Carson*
UX182	*Native American Culture*	**UX192**	*Wild Bill Hickok*
UX183	*Chief Joseph*	**UX193**	*Western Wildlife*
UX184	*Bill Pickett*	**UX194**	*Jim Beckwourth*
UX185	*Bat Masterson*	**UX195**	*Bill Tilghman*
UX186	*John Fremont*	**UX196**	*Sacagawea*
UX187	*Wyatt Earp*	**UX197**	*Overland Mail*

SCOTT NO.	DESCRIPTION	FIRST DAY COVER	MINT	USED
UX178-97	19¢ Legends of the West, set of 20	35.00	35.00	65.00

UX198

UX199

UX198

1995

SCOTT NO.	DESCRIPTION	FIRST DAY COVER	MINT	USED
UX198	20¢ Red Barn	1.75	.65	.75
UX199	20¢ "G" Old Glory	1.75	4.25	3.00

UX201

Civil War

UX200	*Monitor-Virginia*	**UX210**	*Tubman*
UX201	*Lee*	**UX211**	*Watie*
UX202	*Barton*	**UX212**	*Johnston*
UX203	*Grant*	**UX213**	*Hancock*
UX204	*Shiloh*	**UX214**	*Chestnut*
UX205	*Davis*	**UX215**	*Chancellorsville*
UX206	*Farragut*	**UX216**	*Sherman*
UX207	*Douglass*	**UX217**	*Pember*
UX208	*Semmes*	**UX218**	*Jackson*
UX209	*Lincoln*	**UX219**	*Gettysburg*

SCOTT NO.	DESCRIPTION	FIRST DAY COVER	MINT	USED
UX200-19	20¢ Civil War, set of 20	35.00	60.00	65.00
UX219a	50¢ Eagle	1.75	1.75	10.00

UX220

UX241

SCOTT NO.	DESCRIPTION	FIRST DAY COVER	MINT	USED
UX220	20¢ American Clipper Ships	1.75	.65	.85

UX221

American Comic Strips

UX221	*Yellow Kid*	**UX231**	*Popeye*
UX222	*Katzenjammer Kids*	**UX232**	*Blondie*
UX223	*Little Nemo*	**UX233**	*Dick Tracy*
UX224	*Bring Up Father*	**UX234**	*Alley Oop*
UX225	*Krazy Kat*	**UX235**	*Nancy*
UX226	*Rube Goldberg*	**UX236**	*Flash Gordon*
UX227	*Toonerville Folks*	**UX237**	*Li'l Abner*
UX228	*Gasoline Alley*	**UX238**	*Terry/Pirates*
UX229	*Barney Google*	**UX239**	*Prince Valiant*
UX230	*Little Orphan Annie*	**UX240**	*Brenda Starr*

SCOTT NO.	DESCRIPTION	FIRST DAY COVER	MINT	USED
UX221-40	20¢ American Comic Strips, set of 20	35.00	68.00	80.00

1996

SCOTT NO.	DESCRIPTION	FIRST DAY COVER	MINT	USED
UX241	20¢ Winter Farm Scene	1.75	.65	.50

UX242

Centennial Olympic Games

UX242	*Men's cycling*	**UX252**	*Women's softball*
UX243	*Women's diving*	**UX253**	*Women's swimming*
UX244	*Women's running*	**UX254**	*Men's sprints*
UX245	*Men's canoeing*	**UX255**	*Men's rowing*
UX246	*Decathlon*	**UX256**	*Beach volleyball*
UX247	*Women's soccer*	**UX257**	*Men's basketball*
UX248	*Men's shot put*	**UX258**	*Equestrian*
UX249	*Women's sailboarding*	**UX259**	*Men's gymnastics*
UX250	*Women's gymnastics*	**UX260**	*Men's swimming*
UX251	*Freestyle wrestling*	**UX261**	*Men's hurdles*

SCOTT NO.	DESCRIPTION	FIRST DAY COVER	MINT	USED
UX242-61	20¢ Centennial Olympic Games, set of 20	35.00	77.00	75.00

UX262

UX263

SCOTT NO.	DESCRIPTION	FIRST DAY COVER	MINT	USED
UX262	20¢ McDowell Hall	1.75	.65	.85
UX263	20¢ Alexander Hall	1.75	.65	.85

Engandered Species

UX264

UX264	*Florida panther*
UX265	*Black-footed ferret*
UX266	*American crocodile*
UX267	*Piping plover*
UX268	*Gila trout*
UX269	*Florida manatee*
UX270	*Schaus swallowtail butterfly*
UX271	*Woodland caribou*
UX272	*Thick-billed parrot*
UX273	*San Francisco garter snake*
UX274	*Ocelot*
UX275	*Wyoming toad*
UX276	*California condor*
UX277	*Hawaiian monk seal*
UX278	*Brown pelican*

SCOTT NO.	DESCRIPTION	FIRST DAY COVER	MINT	USED
UX264-78	20¢ Endangered Species, set of 15	26.50	77.00	70.00

UX279

UX280

1997

SCOTT NO.	DESCRIPTION	FIRST DAY COVER	MINT	USED
UX279	20¢ Swans	2.50	6.00	2.00
UX279a	20¢ Swans, set of 12	20.00(8)	60.00	......
UX280	20¢ Shepard Hall	1.75	.65	1.00

UX281

UX282

SCOTT NO.	DESCRIPTION	FIRST DAY COVER	MINT	USED
UX281	20¢ Bugs Bunny	1.75	1.85	2.50
UX282	20¢ Golden Gate Bridge 1.75	.45	1.00	1.00

UX283

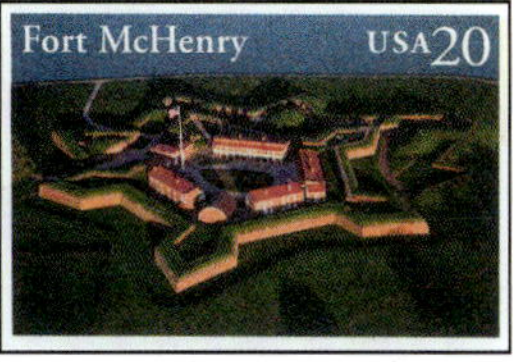
UX284

SCOTT NO.	DESCRIPTION	FIRST DAY COVER	MINT	USED
UX283	50¢ Golden Gate Bridge at Sunset	1.95	1.60	3.00
UX284	20¢ Fort McHenry	1.75	.75	.85

UX285

Classic Movie Monsters

UX285 *Lon Chaney as The Phantom of the Opera*
UX286 *Bela Lugosi as Dracula*
UX287 *Boris Karloff as Frankenstein's Monster*
UX288 *Boris Karloff as The Mummy*
UX289 *Lon Chaney Jr. as The Wolfman*

UX291

SCOTT NO.	DESCRIPTION	FIRST DAY COVER	MINT	USED
UX285	20¢ Classic Movie Monsters, set of 5	8.75	12.00	12.00
UX289a	same, bklt of 20 (4 of each)	....	44.00	....

UX290

UX292

1998

SCOTT NO.	DESCRIPTION	FIRST DAY COVER	MINT	USED
UX290	20¢ University of Mississippi	1.75	.65	.85
UX291	20¢ Sylvester & Tweety	1.75	1.75	3.00
UX291a	same, bklt of 10	....	18.00	....
UX292	20¢ Girard College, Philadelphia, PA	1.75	.65	.85

UX293

UX297

UX298

SCOTT NO.	DESCRIPTION	FIRST DAY COVER	MINT	USED
UX293-96	20¢ Tropical Birds, set of 4	7.00	6.50	7.50
UX296a	same, bklt of 20 (5 of each)	....	32.00	....
UX297	20¢ Ballet	1.75	1.75	1.50
UX297a	same, bklt of 10	....	17.00	....
UX298	20¢ Kerr Hall, Northeastern University	1.75	.65	.85

UX299

UX300

UX301

SCOTT NO.	DESCRIPTION	FIRST DAY COVER	MINT	USED
UX299	20¢ Usen Castle, Brandeis University	1.75	.65	.85

1999

SCOTT NO.	DESCRIPTION	FIRST DAY COVER	MINT	USED
UX300	20¢ Love, Victorian	1.75	1.75	2.50
UX301	20¢ University of Wisconsin-Madison — Bascom Hill	1.75	.65	.75

UX302

UX303

SCOTT NO.	DESCRIPTION	FIRST DAY COVER	MINT	USED
UX302	20¢ Washington and Lee University	1.75	.65	.60
UX303	20¢ Redwood Library & Anthenæum, Newport, RI	1.75	.65	.60

UX304

UX305

SCOTT NO.	DESCRIPTION	FIRST DAY COVER	MINT	USED
UX304	20¢ Daffy Duck	1.75	1.75	1.50
UX304a	same, bklt of 10	....	17.00	....
UX305	20¢ Mount Vernon	1.75	.85	.85

UX306

UX307

Famous Trains

UX307 *Super Chief*
UX308 *Hiawatha*
UX309 *Daylight*
UX310 *Congressional*
UX311 *20th Century Limited*

1999

SCOTT NO.	DESCRIPTION	FIRST DAY COVER	MINT	USED
UX306	20¢ Block Island Lighthouse	1.75	.65	.50
UX307-11	20¢ Famous Trains, set of 5	8.75	9.00	6.00
UX311a	same, bklt of 20 (4 of each)	....	33.00	....

UX312

UX313

UX315

UX316

2000

SCOTT NO.	DESCRIPTION	FIRST DAY COVER	MINT	USED
UX312	20¢ University of Utah	1.75	.65	.70
UX313	20¢ Ryman Auditorium, Nashville, Tennessee	1.75	.65	.70
UX314	20¢ Road Runner & Wile E. Coyote	1.75	1.85	1.50
UX314a	same, bklt of 10	....	18.00	....
UX315	20¢ Adoption	1.75	1.85	1.75
UX315a	same, bklt of 10	....	18.00	....
UX316	20¢ Old Stone Row, Middlebury College, Vermont	1.75	.65	.60

SCOTT NO.	DESCRIPTION	FIRST DAY COVER	MINT	USED

UX336

The Stars and Stripes

UX317 *Sons of Liberty Flag, 1775*
UX318 *New England Flag, 1775*
UX319 *Forster Flag, 1775*
UX320 *Continental Colors, 1776*
UX321 *Francis Hopkinson Flag, 1777*
UX322 *Brandywine Flag, 1777*
UX323 *John Paul Jones Flag, 1779*
UX324 *Pierre L'Enfant Flag, 1783*
UX325 *Indian Peace Flag, 1803*
UX326 *Easton Flag, 1814*
UX327 *Star-Spangled Banner, 1814*
UX328 *Bennington Flag, c. 1820*
UX329 *Great Star Flag, 1837*
UX330 *29-Star Flag, 1847*
UX331 *Fort Sumter Flag, 1861*
UX332 *Centennial Flag, 1876*
UX333 *38-Star Flag*
UX334 *Peace Flag, 1891*
UX335 *48-Star Flag, 1912*
UX336 *50-Star Flag, 1960*

UX317-36	The Stars and Stripes, set of 20	35.00	85.00	58.00

UX337

Legends of Baseball

UX337 *Jackie Robinson*
UX338 *Eddie Collins*
UX339 *Christy Mathewson*
UX340 *Ty Cobb*
UX341 *George Sisler*
UX342 *Rogers Hornsby*
UX343 *Mickey Cochrane*
UX344 *Babe Ruth*
UX345 *Walter Johnson*
UX346 *Roberto Clemente*
UX347 *Lefty Grove*
UX348 *Tris Speaker*
UX349 *Cy Young*
UX350 *Jimmie Foxx*
UX351 *Pie Traynor*
UX352 *Satchel Paige*
UX353 *Honus Wagner*
UX354 *Josh Gibson*
UX355 *Dizzy Dean*
UX356 *Lou Gehrig*

UX337-56	20¢ Legends of Baseball, set of 20	35.00	42.00	40.00

UX357-60

UX361

UX357-60	20¢ Christmas Deer, set of 4	7.00	6.50	5.50

2001

UX361	20¢ Connecticut Hall, Yale University	1.75	.65	.75

UX362

UX363

UX364

UX362	20¢ University of South Carolina	1.75	.65	.85
UX363	20¢ Northwestern University Sesquicentennial 1851-2001	1.75	.65	.85
UX364	20¢ Waldschmidt Hall, The University of Portland	1.75	.65	.75

Legendary Playing Fields

UX365 *Ebbets Field*
UX366 *Tiger Stadium*
UX367 *Crosley Field*
UX368 *Yankee Stadium*
UX369 *Polo Grounds*
UX370 *Forbes Field*
UX371 *Fenway Park*
UX372 *Comiskey Park*
UX373 *Shibe Park*
UX374 *Wrigley Field*

2001

UX365-74	21¢ Legendary Playing Fields, set of 10	35.00	55.00	58.00
UX374a	same, bklt of 10	....	55.00	....

UX375

UX376

UX377

UX375	21¢ White Barn	1.75	.70	.70
UX376	21¢ That's All Folks	2.00	2.00	1.75
UX376a	same, bklt of 10	....	18.00	....
UX377-80	21¢ Santas, set of 4	7.50	8.00	7.00
UX380a	same, complete bklt of 20	....	37.00	....

SCOTT NO.	DESCRIPTION	FIRST DAY COVER	MINT	USED

UX381

UX382

UX386

2002

UX381	23¢ Carlsbad Caverns	1.75	.75	.75
UX382-85	23¢ Teddy Bears, set of 4	7.50	6.00	6.00
UX385a	same, complete bklt of 20	....	29.00	....
UX386-89	23¢ Christmas Snowmen, set of 4	7.50	6.00	6.00
UX389a	same, complete bklt of 20	....	29.00	....

UX390

UX395

UX400

2003

UX390-94	23¢ Old Glory, set of 5	8.75	9.75	9.25
UX394a	same, complete booklet of 20 cards	....	36.00	....
UX395-99	23¢ Southern Lighthouses, set of 5	8.75	7.75	7.75
UX399a	same, complete booklet of 20	....	34.00	....
UX400	23¢ Ohio University, 200th Anniversary	1.75	.75	.75
UX401-04	23¢ Christmas Music Makers, set of 4	7.50	7.00	7.00
UX404a	same, complete bklt of 20	....	34.00	....

UX401

UX405

2004

UX405	23¢ Columbia University, 250th Anniversary	1.75	.75	.75

UX406

UX407

UX406	23¢ Harriton House, 300th Anniversary	1.75	.75	.70
UX407-10	23¢ Art of Disney, set of 4	7.00	7.50	8.50
UX410a	same, complete booklet of 20	....	38.00	....

UX411

UX421

UX411-20	23¢ Art of the American Indian, set of 10	17.50	19.00	19.00
UX420a	same, complete booklet of 20	....	33.00	....
UX421-35	23¢ Cloudscapes, set of 15	26.25	28.00	28.00
UX435a	same, complete booklet of 20	....	35.00	....

SCOTT NO.	DESCRIPTION	FIRST DAY COVER	MINT	USED

UX440

UX449

2005

SCOTT NO.	DESCRIPTION	FIRST DAY COVER	MINT	USED
UX436-39	Disney Characters, set of 4	7.00	7.50	7.50
UX439a	same, complete booklet of 20	....	36.00	....
UX440-44	23¢ Sporty Cars, set of 4	7.00	8.00	8.00
UX444a	same, complete booklet of 20	....	30.00	....
UX445-48	23¢ Let's Dance, set of 4	7.00	65.00	6.50
UX448a	same, complete booklet of 20	....	31.00	....

2006

SCOTT NO.	DESCRIPTION	FIRST DAY COVER	MINT	USED
UX449	24¢ Zebulon Pike Expedition, Bicentennial	1.75	.80	.75

UX450

UX454

SCOTT NO.	DESCRIPTION	FIRST DAY COVER	MINT	USED
UX450-453	24¢ Disney Characters, set of 4	7.00	6.50	6.50
UX453a	same, complete booklet of 20	....	30.00	....
UX454-457	24¢ Baseball Sluggers, set of 4	7.00	6.75	6.75
UX457a	same, complete booklet of 20	....	32.00	....

UX458

D.C. Comics Super Heroes

UX458	*Superman Cover*	**UX468**	*The Flash Cover*
UX459	*Superman*	**UX469**	*The Flash*
UX460	*Batman Cover*	**UX470**	*Plastic Man Cover*
UX461	*Batman*	**UX471**	*Plastic Man*
UX462	*Wonder Woman Cover*	**UX472**	*Aquaman Cover*
UX463	*Wonder Woman*	**UX473**	*Aquaman*
UX464	*Green Lantern Cover*	**UX474**	*Supergirl Cover*
UX465	*Green Lantern*	**UX475**	*Supergirl*
UX466	*Green Arrow Cover*	**UX476**	*Hawkman Cover*
UX467	*Green Arrow*	**UX477**	*Hawkman*

SCOTT NO.	DESCRIPTION	FIRST DAY COVER	MINT	USED
UX458-477	24¢ D.C. Comics Super Heroes, set of 20	40.00	38.00	38.00

Southern Florida Wetlands

UX478	*Snail Kite*	**UX483**	*White Ibis*
UX479	*Cape Sable Seaside Sparrow*	**UX484**	*American Crocodile*
UX480	*Wood Storks*	**UX485**	*Everglades Mink*
UX481	*Florida Panthers*	**UX486**	*Roseate Spoonbills*
UX482	*Bald Eagle*	**UX487**	*American Alligators*

UX483

SCOTT NO.	DESCRIPTION	FIRST DAY COVER	MINT	USED
UX478-87	39¢ Southern Florida Wetlands, set of 10	....	53.00	....

UX488

2007

SCOTT NO.	DESCRIPTION	FIRST DAY COVER	MINT	USED
UX488	26¢ Pineapple	1.95	.95	.95

UX501

Star Wars

UX489	*Darth Vader*	**UX496**	*Obi-Wan Kenobi*
UX490	*Luke Skywalker*	**UX497**	*Boba Fett*
UX491	*C-3PO*	**UX498**	*Darth Maul*
UX492	*Queen Padme Amidala*	**UX499**	*Yoda*
UX493	*Millennium Falcon*	**UX500**	*Princess Leia and R2-D2*
UX494	*Emperor Palpatine*	**UX501**	*Chewbacca and Han Solo*
UX495	*Anakin Skywalker and Obi-Wan Kenobi*	**UX502**	*X-wing Starfighter*
		UX503	*Stormtroopers*

SCOTT NO.	DESCRIPTION	FIRST DAY COVER	MINT	USED
UX489-503	26¢ Star Wars, set of 15	27.50	33.00	33.00

UX505

UX509-28

UX529-32

SCOTT NO.	DESCRIPTION	FIRST DAY COVER	MINT	USED
UX504-508	26¢ Pacific Coast Lighthouses, set of 5	8.00	8.00	8.00
UX508a	same, complete booklet of 20	....	31.00	....
UX509-528	26¢ Marvel Comic Book Heroes, set of 20	40.00	38.00	38.00
UX529-532	26¢ Disney Characters, set of 4	7.50	8.00	8.00
	same, complete booklet of 20	....	38.00	....

UX533

UX534

2008

SCOTT NO.	DESCRIPTION	FIRST DAY COVER	MINT	USED
UX533	27¢ Mount St. Mary's University postal card	2.75	.85	.85
UX534	27¢ Corinthian Column postal card	2.75	.85	.85

UX535

SCOTT NO.	DESCRIPTION	FIRST DAY COVER	MINT	USED
UX535-538	27¢ Art of Disney: Imagination, set of 4	7.00	7.75	7.75
UX538a	same, complete booklet of 20	....	38.00	....

UX539

Great Lakes Dunes

UX539	Vesper Sparrow
UX540	Piping Plover
UX541	Easter Hognose Snake
UX542	Common Mergansers
UX543	Piping Plover Nestlings
UX544	Red Fox
UX545	Tiger Beetle
UX546	White Footed Mouse
UX547	Spotted Sandpiper
UX548	Red Admiral Butterfly

SCOTT NO.	DESCRIPTION	FIRST DAY COVER	MINT	USED
UX539-548	42¢ Great Lakes Dunes postal cards	....	35.00	....

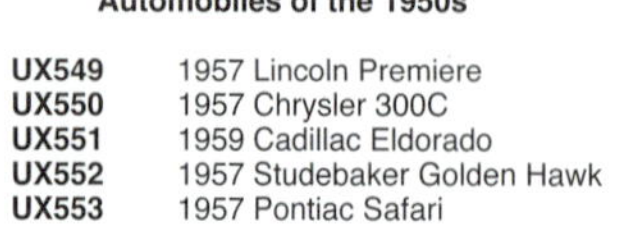

UX549

Automobiles of the 1950s

UX549 1957 Lincoln Premiere
UX550 1957 Chrysler 300C
UX551 1959 Cadillac Eldorado
UX552 1957 Studebaker Golden Hawk
UX553 1957 Pontiac Safari

SCOTT NO.	DESCRIPTION	FIRST DAY COVER	MINT	USED
UX549-53	27¢ Automobiles of the 1950's, set of 5	9.75	9.50	9.50

UX554

UX556

2009

SCOTT NO.	DESCRIPTION	FIRST DAY COVER	MINT	USED
UX554	27¢ Miami University	2.75	.85	.85
UX555	28¢ Koi Fish Postal Card (white fish, orange & white fish)	1.75	.85	.85
UX556	28¢ Koi Fish Postal Card (black fish, red & white fish)	1.75	.85	.85

Simpsons

UX557 Homer
UX558 Marge
UX559 Bart
UX560 Lisa
UX561 Maggie

UX559

UX562

Gulf Coast Lighthouses

UX562 Matagorda Island
UX563 Sabine Pass
UX564 Biloxi
UX565 Sand Island
UX566 Fort Jefferson

SCOTT NO.	DESCRIPTION	FIRST DAY COVER	MINT	USED
UX557-61	28¢ Simpsons Postal Card, set of 5	9.75	9.75	9.75
UX562-66	28¢ Gulf Coast Lighthouses	19.95	9.95	9.95

UX575

Early TV Memories

UX567 Alfred Hitchcock
UX568 Burns & Allen
UX569 Dinah Shore Show
UX570 Dragnet
UX571 Ed Sullivan Show
UX572 The Honeymooners
UX573 Hopalong Cassidy
UX574 Howdy Doody
UX575 I Love Lucy
UX576 Kukla, Fran & Ollie
UX577 Lassie
UX578 The Lone Ranger
UX579 Ozzie & Harriet
UX580 Perry Mason
UX581 Phil Silvers Show
UX582 Red Skelton Show
UX583 Texaco Star Theatre
UX584 The Tonight Show
UX585 The Twilight Zone
UX586 You Bet Your Life

SCOTT NO.	DESCRIPTION	FIRST DAY COVER	MINT	USED
UX567-86	28¢ Early TV Memories, set of 20	60.00	39.00	39.00

UX587

Kelp Forest

UX587 Western Gull
UX588 Lion's Mane Nudibranch
UX589 Northern Kelp Crab
UX590 Vermillion Rockfish
UX591 Yellowtail Rockfish
UX592 Pacific Rock Crab
UX593 Harbor Seal
UX594 Brown Pelican
UX595 Treefish, Monterey Turban Snail
UX596 Copper Rockfish

SCOTT NO.	DESCRIPTION	FIRST DAY COVER	MINT	USED
UX587-96	44¢ Kelp Forest, set of 10 postal cards	32.50	25.00	....

2010

UX597

Cowboys of the Silver Screen

UX597 Roy Rogers
UX598 Tom Mix
UX599 William S. Hart
UX600 Gene Autrey

SCOTT NO.	DESCRIPTION	FIRST DAY COVER	MINT	USED
UX597-600	28¢ Cowboys of the Silver Screen Postal Cards	9.75	8.50	....

UX606

Scenic American Landscapes

UX601 Acadia
UX602 Badlands
UX603 Bryce Canyon
UX604 Grand Canyon
UX605 Great Smokey Mountains
UX606 Mount McKinley
UX607 Mount Rainier
UX608 St. John, U.S. Virgin Islands
UX609 Yosemite
UX610 Zion

SCOTT NO.	DESCRIPTION	FIRST DAY COVER	MINT	USED
UX601-10	28¢ Scenic American Landscapes	29.00	25.00	....

2011

UX614

Hawaiian Rain Forest

UX611 'Apapane, Hawaiian Mint
UX612 Pulelehua butterfly, kolea lau nui, 'ilihia
UX613 Hawaii 'amakihi, Hawaii 'elepaio
UX614 Happyface spider, 'ala'ala wai nui
UX615 'I'wi, haha
UX616 'Akepa, 'ope'ape'a
UX617 Koele Mountain damselfly, 'akala
UX618 Jewel Orchid
UX619 'Oma'o, 'ohelo kau la'au
UX620 'Oha

SCOTT NO.	DESCRIPTION	FIRST DAY COVER	MINT	USED
UX611-20	44¢ Hawaiian Rain Forest Postal Cards, set of 10	29.00	25.00	....

UX621

UX625

Pixar: Send a Hello

UX622 Lightning McQueen & Mater
UX623 Remy the Rat & Linquini
UX624 Buzz Lightyear & Two Aliens
UX625 Carl Fredrickson & Dug
UX626 Wall-E

SCOTT NO.	DESCRIPTION	FIRST DAY COVER	MINT	USED
UX621	29¢ Common Terns	2.75	.75	.75
UX622-26	29¢ Pixar: Send a Hello Postal Cards	15.00	10.00	....

2012

UX627, UX633

UX630

Pixar: Mail a Smile

UX628 Flik and Dot
UX629 Bob & Dashiell Parr
UX630 Nemo & Squirt
UX631 Jessie, Woody and Bullseye
UX632 Boo, Mike Wazowski & Sulley

SCOTT NO.	DESCRIPTION	FIRST DAY COVER	MINT	USED
UX627	32¢ Sailboat Postal Card	2.25	.75	.75
UX628-32	45¢ Pixar: Mail a Smile Postal Cards	15.00	9.50	....
UX633	32¢ Sailboat	2.25	.95	....
	same, sheet of 4	....	4.75	....

UX639

Scenic American Landscapes

UX634 13-Mile Woods
UX635 Glacier National Park
UX636 Grand Teton National Park
UX637 Hagatña Bay
UX638 Lancaster County, PA
UX639 Niagra Falls
UX640 Nine-Mile Prairie
UX641 Okefenokee Swamp
UX642 Rio Grande
UX643 Voyageurs National Park

SCOTT NO.	DESCRIPTION	FIRST DAY COVER	MINT	USED
UX634-43	32¢ Scenic American Landscapes	....	17.50	....

2013

UX644

SCOTT NO.	DESCRIPTION	FIRST DAY COVER	MINT	USED
UX644	33¢ Deer	2.25	.95	.95

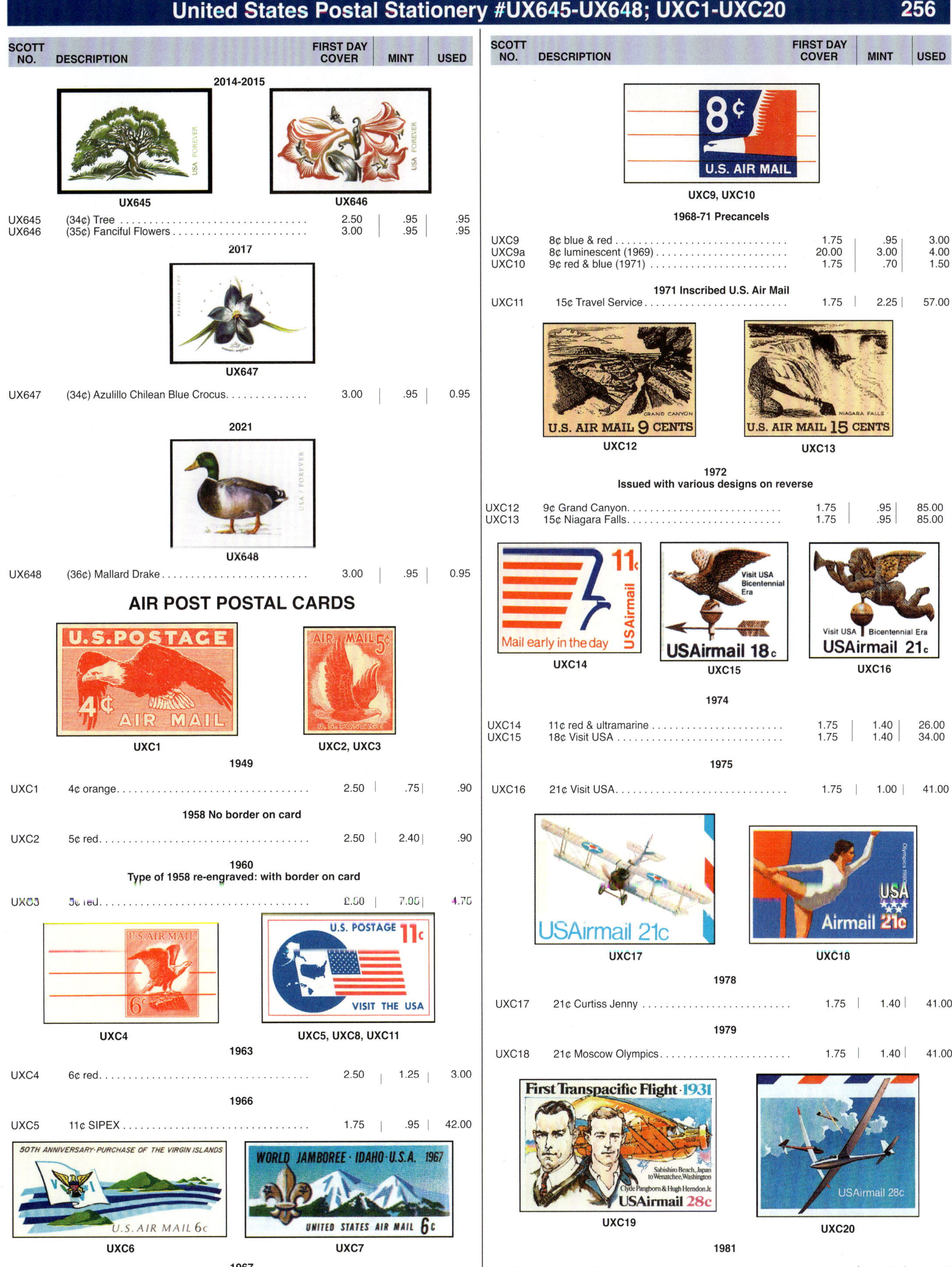

2014-2015

UX645 · UX646

SCOTT NO.	DESCRIPTION	FIRST DAY COVER	MINT	USED
UX645	(34¢) Tree	2.50	.95	.95
UX646	(35¢) Fanciful Flowers	3.00	.95	.95

2017

UX647

SCOTT NO.	DESCRIPTION	FIRST DAY COVER	MINT	USED
UX647	(34¢) Azulillo Chilean Blue Crocus	3.00	.95	0.95

2021

UX648

SCOTT NO.	DESCRIPTION	FIRST DAY COVER	MINT	USED
UX648	(36¢) Mallard Drake	3.00	.95	0.95

AIR POST POSTAL CARDS

UXC1 · UXC2, UXC3

1949

SCOTT NO.	DESCRIPTION	FIRST DAY COVER	MINT	USED
UXC1	4¢ orange	2.50	.75	.90

1958 No border on card

SCOTT NO.	DESCRIPTION	FIRST DAY COVER	MINT	USED
UXC2	5¢ red	2.50	2.40	.90

1960
Type of 1958 re-engraved: with border on card

SCOTT NO.	DESCRIPTION	FIRST DAY COVER	MINT	USED
UXC3	5¢ red	2.50	7.00	4.75

UXC4 · UXC5, UXC8, UXC11

1963

SCOTT NO.	DESCRIPTION	FIRST DAY COVER	MINT	USED
UXC4	6¢ red	2.50	1.25	3.00

1966

SCOTT NO.	DESCRIPTION	FIRST DAY COVER	MINT	USED
UXC5	11¢ SIPEX	1.75	.95	42.00

UXC6 · UXC7

1967

SCOTT NO.	DESCRIPTION	FIRST DAY COVER	MINT	USED
UXC6	6¢ Virgin Islands	1.75	.95	12.50
UXC7	6¢ Boy Scout Jamboree	2.50	.95	18.00
UXC8	13¢ AAM Convention	1.75	1.75	46.00

UXC9, UXC10

1968-71 Precancels

SCOTT NO.	DESCRIPTION	FIRST DAY COVER	MINT	USED
UXC9	8¢ blue & red	1.75	.95	3.00
UXC9a	8¢ luminescent (1969)	20.00	3.00	4.00
UXC10	9¢ red & blue (1971)	1.75	.70	1.50

1971 Inscribed U.S. Air Mail

SCOTT NO.	DESCRIPTION	FIRST DAY COVER	MINT	USED
UXC11	15¢ Travel Service	1.75	2.25	57.00

UXC12 · UXC13

1972
Issued with various designs on reverse

SCOTT NO.	DESCRIPTION	FIRST DAY COVER	MINT	USED
UXC12	9¢ Grand Canyon	1.75	.95	85.00
UXC13	15¢ Niagara Falls	1.75	.95	85.00

UXC14 · UXC15 · UXC16

1974

SCOTT NO.	DESCRIPTION	FIRST DAY COVER	MINT	USED
UXC14	11¢ red & ultramarine	1.75	1.40	26.00
UXC15	18¢ Visit USA	1.75	1.40	34.00

1975

SCOTT NO.	DESCRIPTION	FIRST DAY COVER	MINT	USED
UXC16	21¢ Visit USA	1.75	1.00	41.00

UXC17 · UXC18

1978

SCOTT NO.	DESCRIPTION	FIRST DAY COVER	MINT	USED
UXC17	21¢ Curtiss Jenny	1.75	1.40	41.00

1979

SCOTT NO.	DESCRIPTION	FIRST DAY COVER	MINT	USED
UXC18	21¢ Moscow Olympics	1.75	1.40	41.00

UXC19 · UXC20

1981

SCOTT NO.	DESCRIPTION	FIRST DAY COVER	MINT	USED
UXC19	28¢ Pacific Flight	1.75	1.40	31.00

1982

SCOTT NO.	DESCRIPTION	FIRST DAY COVER	MINT	USED
UXC20	28¢ Gliders	1.75	1.40	36.00

UXC21 UXC22

SCOTT NO.	DESCRIPTION	FIRST DAY COVER	MINT	USED
	1983			
UXC21	28¢ Olympics	1.75	1.80	32.00
	1985			
UXC22	33¢ China Clipper	1.75	1.80	32.00
	1986			
UXC23	33¢ Ameripex '86	1.75	1.35	32.00
	1988			
UXC24	36¢ DC-3	1.75	1.25	32.00
	1991			
UXC25	40¢ Yankee Clipper	1.75	1.35	32.00
	1995			
UXC26	50¢ Soaring Eagle	1.75	1.25	22.50
	1999			
UXC27	55¢ Mount Rainier, Washington	1.75	1.75	32.00
	2001			
UXC28	70¢ Badlands National Park, South Dakota	2.25	2.25	22.50

UXC23 UXC24

UXC25

UXC26

UXC27 UXC28

PAID REPLY POSTAL CARDS

UY1m, UY3m UY2m, UY11m UY4m

UY1r, UY3r UY2r, UY11r UY4r

PAID REPLY CARDS: Consist of two halves—one for your message and one for the other party to use to reply.

SCOTT NO.	DESCRIPTION	MINT	UNUSED	USED
	1892 Card Framed			
UY1	1¢ & 1¢ unsevered	70.00	19.00	9.00
UY1m	1¢ black (Message)	8.00	4.00	2.00
UY1r	1¢ black (Reply)	8.00	4.00	2.00
	1893			
UY2	2¢ & 2¢ unsevered	32.00	18.00	22.00
UY2m	2¢ blue (Message)	7.00	5.00	6.50
UY2r	2¢ blue (Reply)	7.00	5.00	6.50
	1898 Designs of 1892 Card Unframed			
UY3	1¢ & 1¢ unsevered	115.00	18.00	15.00
UY3m	1¢ black (Message)	15.50	7.00	3.00
UY3r	1¢ black (Reply)	15.50	7.00	3.00
	1904			
UY4	1¢ & 1¢ unsevered	75.00	15.00	7.00
UY4m	1¢ black (Message)	12.00	6.00	1.20
UY4r	1¢ black (Reply)	12.00	6.00	1.20
	1910			
UY5	1¢ & 1¢ unsevered	275.00	55.00	26.00
UY5m	1¢ blue (Message)	16.00	10.00	4.00
UY5r	1¢ blue (Reply)	16.00	10.00	4.00
	1911 Double Line Around Instructions			
UY6	1¢ & 1¢ unsevered	270.00	90.00	25.00
UY6m	1¢ green (Message)	32.00	14.00	7.00
UY6r	1¢ green (Reply)	32.00	14.00	7.00
	1915 Single Frame Line Around Instruction			
UY7	1¢ & 1¢ unsevered	1.85	.95	.60
UY7m	1¢ green (Message)	.40	.30	.25
UY7r	1¢ green (Reply)	.40	.30	.25
	1918			
UY8	2¢ & 2¢ unsevered	155.00	42.00	45.00
UY8m	2¢ red (Message)	36.00	12.00	9.00
UY8r	2¢ red (Reply)	36.00	12.00	9.00

UY5m, UY6m, UY7m, UY13m UY8m UY12m

UY5r, UY6r, UY7r, UY13r UY8r UY12r

SCOTT NO.	DESCRIPTION	MINT	UNUSED	USED
	1920 UY8 Surcharged			
UY9	1¢/2¢ & 1¢/2¢ unsevered	34.00	14.00	12.00
UY9m	1¢ on 2¢ red (Message)	8.00	3.00	4.00
UY9r	1¢ on 2¢ red (Reply)	8.00	3.00	4.00
	1924 Designs of 1893			
UY11	2¢ & 2¢ unsevered	3.25	1.75	37.00
UY11m	2¢ red (Message)	1.00	.65	15.00
UY11r	2¢ red (Reply)	1.00	.65	15.00
	1926			
UY12	3¢ & 3¢ unsevered	16.50	8.00	30.00
UY12m	3¢ red (Message)	4.00	1.75	7.00
UY12r	3¢ red (Reply)	4.00	1.75	7.00

SCOTT NO.	DESCRIPTION	FIRST DAY COVER	MINT	USED
	1951 Design of 1910 Single Line Frame			
UY13	2¢ & 2¢ unsevered	2.50	2.50	2.25
UY13m	2¢ carmine (Message)	....	.70	1.00
UY13r	2¢ carmine (Reply)	....	.70	1.00
	1952 **UY7 Surcharged by cancelling machine, light green**			
UY14	2¢/1¢ & 2¢/1¢ unsevered	....	2.50	2.75
UY14m	2¢ on 1¢ green (Message)	....	.50	1.00
UY14r	2¢ on 1¢ green (Reply)	....	.50	1.00
	1952 UY7 Surcharge Typographed, dark green			
UY15	2¢/1¢ & 2¢/1¢ unsevered	....	164.00	50.00
UY15m	2¢ on 1¢ green (Message)	....	20.00	12.00
UY15r	2¢ on 1¢ green (Reply)	....	20.00	12.00
	1956 Design of UX45			
UY16	4¢ & 4¢ unsevered	1.75	1.60	80.00
UY16m	4¢ carmine (Message)	....	.55	40.00
UY16r	4¢ carmine (Reply)	....	.55	40.00
	1958 Design of UX46			
UY17	3¢ & 3¢ purple, unsevered	1.75	6.00	2.50
	1962 Design of UX48			
UY18	4¢ & 4¢ red violet, unsevered	1.75	7.00	2.75
	1963 Design of UX49			
UY19	7¢ & 7¢ unsevered	1.75	5.50	65.00
UY19m	7¢ blue & red (Message)	....	1.75	40.00
UY19r	7¢ blue & red (Reply)	....	1.75	40.00
	1967 Design of UX54			
UY20	8¢ & 8¢ unsevered	1.75	4.50	60.00
UY20m	8¢ blue & red (Message)	[illegible]	[illegible]	[illegible]
UY20r	8¢ blue & red (Reply)		1.75	40.00
	1968 Design of UX55			
UY21	5¢ & 5¢ emerald	1.75	2.50	2.00
	1971 Design of UX58			
UY22	6¢ & 6¢ brown	1.75	1.50	2.00
	1972 Design of UX64			
UY23	6¢ & 6¢ blue	1.75	1.60	2.00
	1973 Design of UX66			
UY24	8¢ & 8¢ orange	1.75	1.35	2.00
	1975			
UY25	7¢ & 7¢ design of UX68	1.75	1.35	9.00
UY26	9¢ & 9¢ design of UX69	1.75	1.35	2.00
	1976			
UY27	9¢ & 9¢ design of UX70	1.75	1.35	2.00
	1977			
UY28	9¢ & 9¢ design of UX72	1.75	1.75	2.00
	1978			
UY29	(10¢ & 10¢) design of UX74	3.00	9.00	10.00
UY30	10¢ & 10¢ design of UX75	1.75	1.75	.40
UY31	(12¢ & 12¢) "B" Eagle, design of UX88	1.75	1.75	2.05
UY32	12¢ & 12¢ light blue, design of UX89	1.75	5.75	2.05
UY33	(13¢ & 13¢) buff, design of UX92	1.75	3.75	2.05
UY34	13¢ & 13¢ buff, design of UX93	1.75	2.00	.25
	1985			
UY35	(14¢ & 14¢) Carroll, design of UX105	1.75	4.75	2.05
UY36	14¢ & 14¢ Carroll, design of UX106	1.75	1.85	2.05
UY37	14¢ & 14¢ Wythe, design of UX108	1.75	1.50	2.05
	1987 -1988			
UY38	14¢ & 14¢ Flag, design of UX117	1.75	1.65	2.25
UY39	15¢ & 15¢ America the Beautiful, design of UX120	1.75	1.50	1.60
	1991			
UY40	19¢ & 19¢ Flag, design of UX153	1.75	1.65	1.50
	1995			
UY41	20¢ & 20¢ Red Barn, design of UX198	1.75	1.65	1.25
	1999			
UY42	20¢ & 20¢ Block Island Lighthouse, design of UX306	1.75	1.65	1.25
	2001-09			
UY43	21¢ & 21¢ White Barn, design of UX375	1.75	1.85	1.50
UY44	23¢ & 23¢ Carlsbad Caverns, design of UX381	1.75	1.85	1.50
UY45	24¢ & 24¢ Zebulon Pike Expedition, design of UX449	1.75	1.85	1.50
UY46	26¢ & 26¢ Pineapple, design of UX488	1.75	1.85	1.50
UY47	27¢ Corinthian Column double-reply postal card	3.75	1.75	1.50
UY48	28¢ Koi Fish reply card	3.50	1.75	1.40
	2011-2012			
UY49	29¢+29¢ Common Terns Postal Reply Card	4.50	1.75	1.75
UY50	32¢+32¢ Sailboat Postal & Reply Card	4.75	1.60	1.75
	2013-2014			
UY51	33¢+33¢ Deer Postal Reply Card	4.75	1.75	1.75
UY52	34¢ + 34¢ tree	4.75	1.75	2.50
	2015			
UY53	35¢ Fanciful Flowers Reply Card	4.75	1.95	2.00
	2017			
UY54	(34¢)+(34¢) Azulillo Chilean Blue Crocus	4.75	1.95	2.00
	2021			
UY55	(36¢)+(36¢) Mallard Drake	4.75	1.95	2.00

OFFICIAL POSTAL CARDS

UZ1 UZ2 UZ3

SCOTT NO.	DESCRIPTION	FIRST DAY COVER	MINT	USED
	1913			
UZ1	1¢ black (Printed Address)	....	755.00	495.00
	1983			
UZ2	13¢ Great Seal	1.75	.95	100.00
	1985			
UZ3	14¢ Great Seal	1.75	.95	90.00

UZ4 UZ5 UZ6

SCOTT NO.	DESCRIPTION	FIRST DAY COVER	MINT	USED
	1988			
UZ4	15¢ Great Seal	1.75	.95	100.00
	1991			
UZ5	19¢ Great Seal	1.75	1.10	100.00
	1995			
UZ6	20¢ Great Seal	1.75	1.10	100.00

1862-71 First Issue

When ordering from this issue be sure to indicate whether the "a", "b" or "c" variety is wanted. Example: R27c. Prices are for used singles.

R1-R4

R5-R15

R16-R42

SCOTT NO.	DESCRIPTION	IMPERFORATE (a) F	AVG	PART PERF. (b) F	AVG	PERFORATED (c) F	AVG
R1	1¢ Express	75.00	58.00	48.00	35.00	1.50	1.15
R2	1¢ Playing Cards	2200.00	1700.00	1600.00	1100.00	195.00	120.00
R3	1¢ Proprietary	1100.00	900.00	275.00	200.00	.60	.40
R4	1¢ Telegraph	600.00	425.00	....	....	18.00	14.00
R5	2¢ Bank Check, blue	1.50	1.15	5.00	2.50	.60	.40
R6	2¢ Bank Check, orange	....	....	60.00	41.25	.30	.20
R7	2¢ Certificate, blue	15.00	11.00	....	....	31.00	22.00
R8	2¢ Certificate, orange	....	....	....	....	43.00	25.00
R9	2¢ Express, blue	15.00	11.00	30.00	28.00	.50	.35
R10	2¢ Express, orange	....	....	1800.00	1200.00	13.00	10.00
R11	2¢ Playing Cards, blue	1500.00	....	270.00	175.00	5.00	3.00
R12	2¢ Playing Cards, orange	....	....	....	....	50.00	38.00
R13	2¢ Proprietary, blue	975.00	610.00	315.00	185.00	.50	.40
R14	2¢ Proprietary, orange	....	....	....	....	60.00	40.00
R15	2¢ U.S. Internal Revenue	....	....	....	....	.40	.35
R16	3¢ Foreign Exchange	....	....	800.00	550.00	5.00	3.25
R17	3¢ Playing Cards	40000.00	....	....	....	165.00	115.00
R18	3¢ Proprietary	....	....	800.00	500.00	8.00	6.50
R19	3¢ Telegraph	85.00	63.00	28.00	19.50	3.00	2.10
R20	4¢ Inland Exchange	....	....	....	....	2.25	1.45
R21	4¢ Playing Cards	....	....	....	....	705.00	430.00
R22	4¢ Proprietary	....	....	525.00	325.00	8.00	6.75
R23	5¢ Agreement	....	....	....	....	.50	.40
R24	5¢ Certificate	3.50	2.25	14.00	9.00	.50	.40
R25	5¢ Express	6.50	3.75	7.00	5.50	.50	.40
R26	5¢ Foreign Exchange	....	....	....	....	.50	.40
R27	5¢ Inland Exchange	8.50	6.50	6.50	4.50	.60	.40
R28	5¢ Playing Cards	....	....	....	....	36.00	26.00
R29	5¢ Proprietary	....	....	....	....	24.00	16.00
R30	6¢ Inland Exchange	....	....	....	....	2.00	1.35
R32	10¢ Bill of Lading	50.00	38.00	400.00	325.00	1.75	1.25
R33	10¢ Certificate	300.00	210.00	815.00	540.00	.35	.25
R34	10¢ Contract, blue	....	....	495.00	295.00	.60	.40
R35	10¢ Foreign Exchange	....	....	....	....	12.00	9.00
R36	10¢ Inland Exchange	395.00	250.00	5.00	3.25	.40	.25
R37	10¢ Power of Attorney	895.00	560.00	28.00	19.00	1.00	.65
R38	10¢ Proprietary	....	....	....	....	18.00	12.00
R39	15¢ Foreign Exchange	....	....	....	....	15.00	12.00
R40	15¢ Inland Exchange	38.00	27.00	13.00	9.00	2.00	1.50
R41	20¢ Foreign Exchange	80.00	55.00	....	....	65.00	48.00
R42	20¢ Inland Exchange	16.00	10.00	21.00	15.00	.50	.35

R43-R53

R54-R65

R66-R76

SCOTT NO.	DESCRIPTION	IMPERFORATE (a) F	AVG	PART PERF. (b) F	AVG	PERFORATED (c) F	AVG
R43	25¢ Bond	245.00	185.00	7.00	5.00	3.75	2.85
R44	25¢ Certificate	11.00	8.00	7.00	5.00	.60	.40
R45	25¢ Entry of Goods	21.00	12.50	235.00	150.00	1.40	1.10
R46	25¢ Insurance	12.00	9.00	15.00	12.00	.35	.25
R47	25¢ Life Insurance	47.00	35.00	800.00	600.00	10.00	7.00
R48	25¢ Power of Attorney	8.00	5.50	35.00	25.00	1.25	.75
R49	25¢ Protest	35.00	25.00	860.00	625.00	8.00	6.00
R50	25¢ Warehouse Receipt	50.00	35.00	850.00	670.00	45.00	35.00
R51	30¢ Foreign Exchange	175.00	95.00	8200.00	5000.00	55.00	39.00
R52	30¢ Inland Exchange	65.00	52.00	75.00	50.00	9.00	7.75
R53	40¢ Inland Exchange	2300.00	1500.00	9.00	6.50	8.00	4.75
R54	50¢ Conveyance, blue	18.00	12.00	3.50	2.75	.40	.30
R55	50¢ Entry of Goods	....	....	15.00	10.00	.50	.35
R56	50¢ Foreign Exchange	60.00	40.00	110.00	80.00	7.00	5.00
R57	50¢ Lease	30.00	21.00	170.00	110.00	10.00	7.00
R58	50¢ Life Insurance	45.00	30.00	155.00	95.00	2.00	1.40
R59	50¢ Mortgage	22.00	16.00	5.00	4.00	.70	.50
R60	50¢ Original Process	6.00	4.00	600.00	400.00	1.10	.90
R61	50¢ Passage Ticket	110.00	85.00	400.00	255.00	2.25	1.55
R62	50¢ Probate of Will	52.00	42.00	200.00	135.00	20.00	13.00
R63	50¢ Surety Bond, blue	275.00	185.00	3.00	2.10	.40	.25
R64	60¢ Inland Exchange	110.00	75.00	95.00	55.00	9.00	7.25
R65	70¢ Foreign Exchange	575.00	450.00	165.00	125.00	13.00	9.00

SCOTT NO.	DESCRIPTION	IMPERFORATE (a) F	AVG	PART PERF. (b) F	AVG	PERFORATED (c) F	AVG
R66	$1 Conveyance	26.00	20.00	2200.00	1350.00	27.50	18.50
R6	$1 Entry of Goods	44.00	32.00	....	....	2.50	2.10
R68	$1 Foreign Exchange	85.00	60.00	....	....	.90	.50
R69	$1 Inland Exchange	16.00	10.00	3200.00	1700.00	.75	.60
R70	$1 Lease	43.00	32.00	....	....	4.00	3.00
R71	$1 Life Insurance	200.00	165.00	....	....	10.00	8.00
R72	$1 Manifest	49.50	33.00	....	....	38.00	26.50
R73	$1 Mortgage	28.00	19.00	....	....	225.00	155.00
R74	$1 Passage Ticket	310.00	210.00	....	....	275.00	210.00
R75	$1 Power of Attorney	85.00	65.00	....	....	3.00	2.00
R76	$1 Probate of Will	85.00	65.00	....	....	55.00	42.50

R77-R80

R81-R87

SCOTT NO.	DESCRIPTION	IMPERFORATE (a) F	AVG	PART PERF. (b) F	AVG	PERFORATED (c) F	AVG
R77	$1.30 Foreign Exchange	8000.00	....	....	....	82.00	59.00
R78	$1.50 Inland Exchange	30.00	21.00	....	....	6.50	5.00
R79	$1.60 Foreign Exchange	1250.00	950.00	....	....	120.00	85.00
R80	$1.90 Foreign Exchange	10000.00	....	....	....	115.00	86.00
R81	$2 Conveyance	195.00	135.00	2100.00	1500.00	4.00	3.00
R82	$2 Mortgage	135.00	95.00	....	....	7.00	5.00
R83	$2 Probate of Will	6000.00	4800.00	....	....	75.00	64.00
R84	$2.50 Inland Exchange	8000.00	6500.00	....	....	22.00	18.00
R85	$3 Charter Party	185.00	125.00	....	....	11.00	9.00
R86	$2 Manifest	165.00	105.00	....	....	52.00	38.00
R87	$3.50 Inland Exchange	7000.00	....	....	....	70.00	53.00

R88-R96

R97-R101

SCOTT NO.	DESCRIPTION	IMPERFORATE (a) F	AVG	PART PERF. (b) F	AVG	PERFORATED (c) F	AVG
R88	$5 Charter Party	300.00	225.00	....	....	10.00	8.00
R89	$5 Conveyance	42.00	35.00	....	....	11.00	8.00
R90	$5 Manifest	185.00	125.00	....	....	90.00	65.00
R91	$5 Mortgage	160.00	135.00	....	....	25.00	17.50
R92	$5 Probate of Will	675.00	550.00	....	....	25.00	17.50
R93	$10 Charter Party	750.00	550.00	....	....	35.00	25.00
R94	$10 Conveyance	125.00	95.00	....	....	75.00	50.00
R95	$10 Mortgage	750.00	550.00	....	....	35.00	25.00
R96	$10 Probate of Will	2100.00	1600.00	....	....	42.00	32.00
R97	$15 Mortgage, blue	2300.00	2100.00	....	....	255.00	180.00
R98	$20 Conveyance	150.00	100.00	....	....	115.00	85.00
R99	$20 Probate of Will	2100.00	1500.00	....	....	2100.00	1500.00
R100	$25 Mortgage	1825.00	1250.00	....	....	185.00	125.00
R101	$50 U.S. Internal Revenue	275.00	195.00	....	....	175.00	150.00

R102

SCOTT NO.	DESCRIPTION	IMPERFORATE (a) F	AVG	PART PERF. (b) F	AVG	PERFORATED (c) F	AVG
R102	$200 U.S. Internal Revenue	2350.00	1850.00	....	....	1000.00	800.00

SCOTT NO.	DESCRIPTION	USED F	AVG

R103, R104, R134, R135, R151

R105-R111, R136-R139

R112-R114

R115-R117, R142-R143

1871 SECOND ISSUE

NOTE: **The individual denominations vary in design from the illustrations shown which are more typical of their relative size.**

SCOTT NO.	DESCRIPTION	USED F	AVG
R103	1¢ blue and black	82.00	72.00
R104	2¢ blue and black	2.50	2.25
R105	3¢ blue and black	52.00	37.00
R106	4¢ blue and black	140.00	90.00
R107	5¢ blue and black	1.75	1.00
R108	6¢ blue and black	205.00	130.00
R109	10¢ blue and black	1.60	1.20
R110	15¢ blue and black	90.00	55.00
R111	20¢ blue and black	10.00	8.00
R112	25¢ blue and black	1.50	.85
R113	30¢ blue and black	130.00	75.00
R114	40¢ blue and black	110.00	70.00
R115	50¢ blue and black	1.35	.85
R116	60¢ blue and black	200.00	155.00
R117	70¢ blue and black	90.00	75.00

R118-R122, R144

R123-R126, R145-R147

SCOTT NO.	DESCRIPTION	USED F	AVG
R118	$1 blue and black	9.25	7.00
R119	$1.30 blue and black	625.00	525.00
R120	$1.50 blue and black	20.00	14.00
R121	$1.60 blue and black	650.00	525.00
R122	$1.90 blue and black	410.00	300.00
R123	$2.00 blue and black	21.00	15.00
R124	$2.50 blue and black	50.00	30.00
R125	$3.00 blue and black	65.00	40.00
R126	$3.50 blue and black	440.00	325.00

R127, R128, R148, R149

R129-R131, R150

SCOTT NO.	DESCRIPTION	USED F	AVG
R127	$5 blue and black	32.50	20.00
R128	$10 blue and black	225.00	155.00
R129	$20 blue and black	875.00	525.00
R130	$25 blue and black	925.00	650.00
R131	$50 blue and black	1050.00	660.00

1871-72 THIRD ISSUE

SCOTT NO.	DESCRIPTION	USED F	AVG
R134	1¢ claret and black	58.00	40.00
R135	2¢ orange and black	.40	.25
R135b	2¢ orange and black (center inverted)	500.00	450.00
R136	4¢ brown and black	77.00	57.00
R137	5¢ orange and black	.40	.25
R138	6¢ orange and black	85.00	64.00
R139	15¢ brown and black	22.00	17.00
R140	30¢ orange and black	32.00	26.00
R141	40¢ brown and black	80.00	65.00
R142	60¢ orange and black	110.00	85.00
R143	70¢ green and black	85.00	60.00
R144	$1 green and black	3.75	2.50
R145	$2 vermillion and black	40.00	30.00
R146	$2.50 claret and black	100.00	70.00
R147	$3 green and black	80.00	65.00
R148	$5 vermillion and black	40.00	30.00
R149	$10 green and black	310.00	185.00
R150	$20 orange and black	800.00	635.00

1874 on greenish paper

SCOTT NO.	DESCRIPTION	USED F	AVG
R151	2¢ orange and black	.40	.25
R151a	2¢ orange and black (center inverted)	650.00	600.00

SCOTT NO.	DESCRIPTION	UNUSED F	UNUSED AVG	USED F	USED AVG

R152
Liberty

I. R.

R153 surcharge

I. R.

R154, R155 surcharge

1875-78

SCOTT NO.	DESCRIPTION	UNUSED F	UNUSED AVG	USED F	USED AVG
R152a	2¢ blue on blue silk paper	....	....	.50	.40
R152b	2¢ watermarked ("USIR") paper	....	....	.40	.30
R152c	2¢ watermarked, rouletted	....	....	35.00	24.00

1898 Postage Stamps 279 & 267 Surcharged

SCOTT NO.	DESCRIPTION	UNUSED F	UNUSED AVG	USED F	USED AVG
R153	1¢ green, small I.R.	5.00	3.50	3.00	2.10
R154	1¢ green, large I.R.	.40	.30	.40	.30
R155	2¢ carmine, large I.R.	.40	.30	.40	.30

DOCUMENTARY STAMPS

Newspaper Stamp PR121 Surcharged

INT. REV.
$5.
DOCUMENTARY.

SCOTT NO.	DESCRIPTION	UNUSED F	UNUSED AVG	USED F	USED AVG
R159	$5 dark blue, red surcharge reading down	475.00	350.00	210.00	175.00
R160	$5 dark blue, red surcharge reading up	150.00	110.00	115.00	95.00

R161-R172

R173-R178, R182, R183

1898 Battleships Inscribed "Documentary"

SCOTT NO.	DESCRIPTION	UNUSED F	UNUSED AVG	USED F	USED AVG
R161	½¢ orange	4.00	3.00	20.00	15.00
R162	½¢ dark gray	.40	.30	.35	.30
R163	1¢ pale blue	.40	.30	.35	.30
R164	2¢ carmine	.40	.30	.45	.35
R165	3¢ dark blue	3.95	2.10	.45	.35
R166	4¢ pale rose	2.00	1.40	.45	.35
R167	5¢ lilac	.65	.45	.40	.45
R168	10¢ dark brown	2.00	1.40	.35	.30
R169	25¢ purple brown	4.35	4.00	.50	.40
R170	40¢ blue lilac (cut cancel .40)	125.00	90.00	1.50	1.00
R171	50¢ slate violet	36.00	18.00	.35	.30
R172	80¢ bistre (cut cancel .25)	110.00	80.00	.40	.30
R173	$1 dark green	22.00	16.00	.30	.25
R174	$3 dark brown (cut cancel .25)	40.00	28.00	1.00	.70
R175	$5 orange red (cut cancel .25)	66.00	48.00	2.00	1.40
R176	$10 black (cut cancel .70)	145.00	90.00	4.00	2.75
R177	$30 red (cut cancel 50.00)	460.00	350.00	160.00	110.00
R178	$50 gray brown (cut cancel 2.50)	260.00	210.00	6.00	3.95

R179, R225, R246, R248

R180, R226, R249

R181, R224, R227, R247, R250

SCOTT NO.	DESCRIPTION	UNUSED F	UNUSED AVG	USED F	USED AVG
	1899 Various Portraits Inscribed "Series of 1898"				
R179	$100 yellow brown & black . . . (cut cancel 25.00)	260.00	200.00	39.00	28.50
R180	$500 carmine lake & black . . (cut cancel 325.00)	1400.00	1100.00	850.00	550.00
R181	$1000 green & black . . . . . . (cut cancel 150.00)	1300.00	675.00	385.00	300.00
	1900				
R182	$1 carmine . . . . (cut cancel .40)	38.00	29.00	.75	.50
R183	$3 lake . . . . (cut cancel 9.00)	300.00	225.00	55.00	42.00

R184-R189 R190-R194

Designs of R173-78 surcharged

SCOTT NO.	DESCRIPTION	UNUSED F	UNUSED AVG	USED F	USED AVG
R184	$1 gray . . . . (cut cancel .25)	31.00	21.00	.40	.25
R185	$2 gray . . . . (cut cancel .25)	31.00	21.00	.40	.25
R186	$3 gray . . . . (cut cancel 5.00)	130.00	85.00	16.00	12.00
R187	$5 gray . . . . (cut cancel 1.50)	75.00	55.00	10.00	7.50
R188	$10 gray . . . . (cut cancel 4.00)	200.00	120.00	22.00	15.00
R189	$50 gray . . . . (cut cancel 130.00)	1875.00	1400.00	550.00	375.00
	1902				
R190	$1 green . . . . (cut cancel .35)	44.00	33.00	4.00	3.00
R191	$2 green . . . . (cut cancel .35)	44.00	33.00	2.00	1.25
R191a	$2 surcharged as R185	125.00	85.00	85.00	60.00
R192	$5 green . . . . (cut cancel 5.00)	200.00	140.00	38.00	29.00
R192a	$5 surcharge omitted	250.00	170.00	....	....
R193	$10 green . . . . (cut cancel 50.00)	450.00	300.00	145.00	95.00
R194	$50 green . . . . (cut cancel 275.00)	2500.00	1900.00	1100.00	795.00

R195-R216

R217-R223

1914 Inscribed "Series of 1914"
Single Line Watermark "USPS"

SCOTT NO.	DESCRIPTION	UNUSED F	UNUSED AVG	USED F	USED AVG
R195	½¢ rose	14.00	10.00	5.00	3.50
R196	1¢ rose	2.50	1.75	.40	.25
R197	2¢ rose	4.00	3.00	.40	.25
R198	3¢ rose	77.00	55.00	35.00	25.00
R199	4¢ rose	23.00	17.00	2.25	1.50
R200	5¢ rose	10.00	7.00	.50	.35
R201	10¢ rose	8.00	6.00	.35	.25
R202	25¢ rose	48.00	34.00	.70	.45
R203	40¢ rose	32.00	24.00	3.00	2.00
R204	50¢ rose	13.00	10.00	.35	.25
R205	80¢ rose	210.00	160.00	15.50	12.00
	1914 Double Line Watermark "USIR"				
R206	½¢ rose	2.00	1.40	.65	.45
R207	1¢ rose	.35	.25	.30	.20
R208	2¢ rose	.40	.25	.30	.25
R209	3¢ rose	2.00	1.40	.35	.25
R210	4¢ rose	4.50	3.00	.60	.40
R211	5¢ rose	2.00	1.40	.40	.25
R212	10¢ rose	.90	.60	.30	.25
R213	25¢ rose	8.00	6.00	1.75	1.20
R214	40¢ rose . . . . (cut cancel .60)	120.00	85.00	15.00	10.00
R215	50¢ rose	26.00	18.00	.35	.25
R216	80¢ rose . . . . (cut cancel 1.25)	175.00	115.00	28.00	21.00
R217	$1 green . . . . (cut cancel .30)	62.00	48.00	.55	.40
R218	$2 carmine . . . . (cut cancel .25)	82.00	58.00	.85	.60
R219	$3 purple. . . . . (cut cancel .60)	110.00	80.00	4.00	2.75
R220	$5 blue . . . . (cut cancel .60)	95.00	70.00	4.00	2.75
R221	$10 orange . . . . (cut cancel 1.00)	210.00	155.00	6.00	4.00
R222	$30 vermillion . . . . (cut cancel 5.50)	675.00	500.00	20.00	14.00
R223	$50 violet . . . . (cut cancel 375.00)	1700.00	1275.00	1100.00	800.00

SCOTT NO.	DESCRIPTION	UNUSED F	UNUSED AVG	USED F	USED AVG
	1914-15 Various Portraits Inscribed "Series of 1914" or "Series of 1915"				
R224	$60 brown. . . . . (cut cancel 70.00)	200.00	140.00	150.00	100.00
R225	$100 green . . . . (cut cancel 17.00)	68.00	50.00	45.00	30.00
R226	$500 blue . . . . (cut cancel 275.00)	....	....	650.00	450.00
R227	$1000 orange . . . . (cut cancel 300.00)	....	....	700.00	400.00

R228-239, R251-256, R260-263

1917 Perf. 11

SCOTT NO.	DESCRIPTION	UNUSED F	UNUSED AVG	USED F	USED AVG
R228	1¢ carmine rose	.40	.30	.25	.20
R229	2¢ carmine rose	.30	.25	.25	.20
R230	3¢ carmine rose	1.85	1.35	.50	.35
R231	4¢ carmine rose	.85	.70	.30	.25
R232	5¢ carmine rose	.40	.35	.25	.20
R233	8¢ carmine rose	2.75	2.00	.40	.25
R234	10¢ carmine rose	2.00	1.60	.40	.30
R235	20¢ carmine rose	.80	.55	.30	.25
R236	25¢ carmine rose	1.50	1.00	.30	.25
R237	40¢ carmine rose	2.50	1.50	.50	.35
R238	50¢ carmine rose	2.75	1.75	.25	.20
R239	80¢ carmine rose	8.00	6.00	.30	.25

R240-245, R257-259

Same design as issue of 1914-15 Without dates.

SCOTT NO.	DESCRIPTION	UNUSED F	UNUSED AVG	USED F	USED AVG
R240	$1 yellow green.	8.50	6.50	.30	.25
R241	$2 rose	14.00	10.00	.25	.20
R242	$3 violet . . . . (cut cancel .30)	55.00	43.00	1.25	.85
R243	$4 yellow brown . . . . (cut cancel .30)	38.00	28.00	2.00	1.40
R244	$5 dark blue . . . . (cut cancel .30)	23.00	17.00	.50	.35
R245	$10 orange . . . . (cut cancel .30)	48.00	38.00	1.50	1.00
	Types of 1899 Various Portraits Perf. 12				
R246	$30 deep orange, Grant . . . . . . (cut cancel 2.50)	50.00	35.00	15.00	10.00
R247	$60 brown, Lincoln . . . . (cut cancel 1.00)	60.00	40.00	8.00	5.50
R248	$100 green, Washington. . . . . . . (cut cancel .45)	40.00	27.00	1.25	.80
R249	$500 blue, Hamilton . . . . (cut cancel 15.00)	325.00	225.00	40.00	28.00
R249a	$500 Numerals in orange	400.00	275.00	60.00	40.00
R250	$1000 orange, Madison (Perf. In. 3.00) . . . . (cut cancel 3.50)	160.00	100.00	13.00	8.00
	1928-29 Perf. 10				
R251	1¢ carmine rose	2.25	1.50	1.80	1.20
R252	2¢ carmine rose	.75	.55	.40	.30
R253	4¢ carmine rose	8.00	5.00	5.00	3.50
R254	5¢ carmine rose	1.80	1.20	.75	.50
R255	10¢ carmine rose	2.75	1.85	1.50	1.00
R256	20¢ carmine rose	7.00	5.00	6.00	4.00
R257	$1 green . . . . (cut cancel 2.00)	175.00	120.00	40.00	27.00
R258	$2 rose	75.00	50.00	3.00	2.00
R259	$10 orange . . . . (cut cancel 7.00)	250.00	175.00	50.00	35.00
	1929-30 Perf. 11 x 10				
R260	2¢ carmine rose	4.00	2.75	3.00	2.00
R261	5¢ carmine rose	3.00	2.00	2.25	1.60
R262	10¢ carmine rose	10.50	7.00	8.00	5.00
R263	20¢ carmine rose	17.00	11.00	9.00	6.00

R733, R734

SCOTT NO.	DESCRIPTION	PLATE BLOCK F/NH	UNUSED F/NH	USED F
	1962 CENTENNIAL INTERNAL REVENUE. Inscribed "Established 1862"			
R733	10¢ violet blue & green.	19.50	1.35	.50
	1964 Without Inscription Date			
R734	10¢ violet blue & green.	34.00	5.00	.75

PROPRIETARY STAMPS

RB1-2 RB3-7

1871-74 Perforated 12

SCOTT NO.	DESCRIPTION	VIOLET PAPER (a) F	AVG	GREEN PAPER (b) F	AVG
RB1	1¢ green & black	7.00	5.00	13.00	8.00
RB2	2¢ green & black	8.00	6.00	28.00	20.00
RB3	3¢ green & black	25.00	17.00	65.00	40.00
RB4	4¢ green & black	15.00	10.00	24.00	16.00
RB5	5¢ green & black	160.00	110.00	195.00	120.00
RB6	6¢ green & black	60.00	40.00	125.00	85.00
RB7	10¢ green & black	240.00	165.00	65.00	45.00
RB8	50¢ green & black (large)	900.00	600.00	750.00	550.00

RB11-12 RB13-19

SCOTT NO.	DESCRIPTION	SILK PAPER (a) F	AVG	WMKD PERF. (b) F	AVG	ROULETTE (c) F	AVG
RB11	1¢ green	2.50	1.90	.50	.35	135.00	100.00
RB12	2¢ brown	2.75	1.85	1.70	1.00	155.00	95.00
RB13	3¢ orange	14.00	10.00	4.50	3.50	130.00	95.00
RB14	4¢ red brown	11.00	8.00	10.00	6.00	....	....
RB15	4¢ red	....	....	7.00	4.00	260.00	200.00
RB16	5¢ black	180.00	140.00	130.00	90.00	....	1800.00
RB17	6¢ violet blue	38.00	29.00	26.00	19.00	495.00	275.00
RB18	6¢ violet	....	....	37.00	28.00	500.00	350.00
RB19	10¢ blue	....	....	350.00	250.00	....	....

RB20-31 RB32-64 RB65-73

SCOTT NO.	DESCRIPTION	UNUSED F	AVG	USED F	AVG
	1898 Battleship Inscribed "Proprietary"				
RB20	7/8¢ yellow green	.35	.25	.35	.25
RB21	¼¢ brown	.35	.25	.25	.20
RB22	3/8¢ deep orange	.30	.25	.50	.40
RB23	5/8¢ deep ultramarine	.30	.25	.30	.25
RB24	1¢ dark green	2.25	1.50	.30	.25
RB25	1¼¢ violet	[illegible]	[illegible]	[illegible]	[illegible]
RB26	17/8¢ dull blue	16.00	12.00	2.25	1.80
RB27	2¢ violet brown	1.50	1.00	.40	.30
RB28	2½¢ lake	4.50	3.15	.30	.25
RB29	3¾¢ olive gray	45.00	30.00	16.00	12.00
RB30	4¢ purple	17.00	12.00	1.60	1.10
RB31	5¢ brown orange	17.00	12.00	1.60	1.10
	1914 Watermarked "USPS"				
RB32	1/8¢ black	.30	.25	.30	.25
RB33	¼¢ black	3.30	2.55	1.60	1.00
RB34	3/8¢ black	.40	.30	.30	.25
RB35	5/8¢ black	6.50	5.00	3.00	2.75
RB36	1¼¢ black	5.00	3.50	2.00	1.25
RB37	17/8¢ black	60.00	48.00	21.00	15.00
RB38	2½¢ black	14.00	10.00	4.00	2.75
RB39	31/8¢ black	130.00	90.00	65.00	45.00
RB40	3¾¢ black	62.00	35.00	26.00	19.00
RB41	4¢ black	77.00	55.00	42.00	32.00
RB43	5¢ black	155.00	115.00	105.00	85.00
	1914 Watermarked "USIR"				
RB44	1/8¢ black	.40	.30	.30	.25
RB45	¼¢ black	.30	.25	.30	.25
RB46	3/8¢ black	.80	.60	.50	.40
RB47	½¢ black	4.00	2.75	3.50	2.50
RB48	5/8¢ black	.30	.25	.30	.25
RB49	1¢ black	6.00	9.50	6.00	4.50
RB50	1¼¢ black	.75	.60	.45	.35
RB51	1½¢ black	4.50	3.50	3.00	2.00
RB52	17/8¢ black	1.40	1.00	1.00	.80
RB53	2¢ black	7.00	5.50	6.00	4.00
RB54	2½¢ black	1.80	1.30	2.00	1.40
RB55	3¢ black	5.50	4.00	4.00	3.00
RB56	3-1/8¢ black	7.00	5.00	5.00	4.00
RB57	3¾¢ black	17.00	11.00	11.00	8.00
RB58	4¢ black	.60	.50	.30	.25
RB59	4-3/8¢ black	19.00	13.00	11.00	8.00
RB60	5¢ black	4.50	3.50	4.00	3.00
RB61	6¢ black	72.00	60.00	48.00	35.00
RB62	8¢ black	26.00	16.00	15.00	11.00
RB63	10¢ black	17.00	13.00	10.00	7.00
RB64	20¢ black	33.00	23.00	22.00	16.00
	1919 Offset Printing				
RB65	1¢ dark blue	.35	.25	.25	.20
RB66	2¢ dark blue	.40	.30	.30	.25
RB67	3¢ dark blue	1.60	1.20	.85	.65
RB68	4¢ dark blue	2.50	2.00	.80	.60
RB69	5¢ dark blue	3.25	2.00	1.40	1.00
RB70	8¢ dark blue	22.00	16.00	14.00	11.00
RB71	10¢ dark blue	10.00	8.00	4.00	2.75
RB72	20¢ dark blue	15.00	12.00	6.00	4.00
RB73	40¢ dark blue	58.00	45.00	15.00	11.00

FUTURE DELIVERY STAMPS

Documentary Stamps of 1917 Overprinted

FUTURE DELIVERY Type I — FUTURE DELIVERY Type II

1918-34 Perforated 11, Type I Overprint Lines 8mm. Apart

SCOTT NO.	DESCRIPTION	UNUSED F	AVG	USED F	AVG
RC1	2¢ carmine rose	8.00	5.00	.30	.25
RC2	3¢ carmine rose (cut cancel 13.50)	42.00	32.00	35.00	29.00
RC3	4¢ carmine rose	13.00	9.00	.30	.25
RC3A	5¢ carmine rose	95.00	60.00	4.00	2.75
RC4	10¢ carmine rose	22.00	15.00	.30	.25
RC5	20¢ carmine rose	35.00	25.00	.30	.25
RC6	25¢ carmine rose (cut cancel .25)	65.00	45.00	.75	.55
RC7	40¢ carmine rose (cut cancel .25)	75.00	50.00	.75	.55
RC8	50¢ carmine rose	16.00	11.00	.30	.25
RC9	80¢ carmine rose (cut cancel 1.00)	145.00	95.00	10.00	7.00
RC10	$1 green (cut cancel .25)	60.00	45.00	.30	.25
RC11	$2 rose (cut cancel .25)	65.00	45.00	.30	.25
RC12	$3 violet (cut cancel .30)	185.00	145.00	4.00	3.25
RC13	$5 dark blue (cut cancel .25)	110.00	90.00	.75	.50
RC14	$10 orange (cut cancel .35)	135.00	95.00	1.50	1.00
RC15	$20 olive bistre (cut cancel .75)	350.00	220.00	8.00	6.00
	Perforated 12				
RC16	$30 vermillion (cut cancel 2.00)	110.00	85.00	7.00	5.00
RC17	$50 olive green (cut cancel 2.00)	90.00	75.00	6.00	5.00
RC18	$60 brown (cut cancel 1.25)	120.00	90.00	9.00	7.00
RC19	$100 yellow green (cut cancel 8.00)	200.00	180.00	40.00	30.00
RC20	$500 blue (cut cancel 6.00)	225.00	130.00	16.00	12.00
RC21	$1000 orange (cut cancel 1.75)	185.00	150.00	8.00	6.00
RC22	1¢ carmine rose (lines 2mm apart)	1.20	.75	.30	.25
RC23	80¢ carmine rose (lines 2mm apart) (cut cancel .40)	190.00	150.00	3.50	2.00
	1925-34 Perforated 11 Type II Overprint				
RC25	$1 green (cut cancel .10)	82.00	60.00	2.00	1.00
RC26	$10 orange (cut cancel 5.75)	220.00	170.00	26.00	22.00

STOCK TRANSFER STAMPS

Documentary Stamps Overprinted

STOCK TRANSFER Type I — STOCK TRANSFER Type II

1918-22 Perforated 11 Type I Overprint

SCOTT NO.	DESCRIPTION	UNUSED F	AVG	USED F	AVG
RD1	1¢ carmine rose	1.00	.70	.30	.25
RD2	2¢ carmine rose	.30	.25	.30	.25
RD3	4¢ carmine rose	.30	.25	.30	.25
RD4	5¢ carmine rose	.35	.30	.30	.25
RD5	10¢ carmine rose	.35	.30	.30	.25
RD6	20¢ carmine rose	.65	.45	.30	.25
RD7	25¢ carmine rose (cut cancel .25)	2.25	1.75	.30	.25
RD8	40¢ carmine rose	2.25	1.15	.30	.25
RD9	50¢ carmine rose	.80	.50	.30	.25
RD10	80¢ carmine rose (cut cancel .25)	9.00	7.00	.50	.35
RD11	$1 green (red overprint) (cut cancel 4.00)	150.00	120.00	28.00	23.00
RD12	$1 green (black overprint)	3.00	2.00	.40	.25
RD13	$2 rose	3.00	2.00	.30	.25
RD14	$3 violet (cut cancel .25)	26.00	19.00	7.00	5.00
RD15	$4 yellow brown (cut cancel .25)	12.00	8.00	.30	.25
RD16	$5 dark blue (cut cancel .25)	8.00	5.00	.30	.25
RD17	$10 orange (cut cancel .25)	27.00	20.00	.50	.45
RD18	$20 olive bistre (cut cancel 3.50)	120.00	95.00	20.00	14.00
	Perforated 12				
RD19	$30 vermillion (cut cancel 1.20)	39.00	33.00	6.00	4.00
RD20	$50 olive green (cut cancel 26.00)	130.00	110.00	65.00	55.00
RD21	$60 brown (cut cancel 10.00)	300.00	230.00	28.00	22.00
RD22	$100 green (cut cancel 3.50)	45.00	35.00	7.00	5.00
RD23	$500 blue (cut cancel 80.00)	500.00	450.00	160.00	120.00
RD24	$1000 orange (cut cancel 33.00)	400.00	350.00	100.00	85.00

SCOTT NO.	DESCRIPTION	UNUSED F	UNUSED AVG	USED F	USED AVG
	1928 Perforated 10 Type I Overprint				
RD25	2¢ carmine rose	5.00	4.00	.40	.35
RD26	4¢ carmine rose	5.00	4.00	.40	.35
RD27	10¢ carmine rose	5.00	4.00	.40	.35
RD28	20¢ carmine rose	6.00	5.00	.40	.35
RD29	50¢ carmine rose	10.00	8.00	.60	.45
RD30	$1 green	40.00	28.00	.40	.30
RD31	$2 carmine rose	40.00	28.00	.35	.30
RD32	$10 orange (cut cancel .25)	40.00	28.00	.50	.35
RD33	2¢ carmine rose	11.00	6.00	1.00	.70
RD34	10¢ carmine rose	3.00	2.00	.40	.35
RD35	20¢ carmine rose	6.00	4.00	.30	.25
RD36	50¢ carmine rose	5.00	4.00	.30	.25
RD37	$1 green (cut cancel .30)	70.00	50.00	13.00	9.00
RD38	$2 rose (cut cancel .30)	90.00	70.00	13.00	9.00
	1920-28 Perforated 10 Type II overprint				
RD39	2¢ carmine rose	11.00	9.00	1.00	.70
RD40	10¢ carmine rose	4.00	2.00	.60	.40
RD41	20¢ carmine rose	6.00	4.00	.30	.25

SILVER TAX STAMPS

Documentary Stamps of 1917 Overprinted
1934-36

SCOTT NO.	DESCRIPTION	UNUSED F	UNUSED AVG	USED F	USED AVG
RG1	1¢ carmine rose	1.70	1.25	1.00	.70
RG2	2¢ carmine rose	2.25	1.50	.75	.50
RG3	3¢ carmine rose	2.40	1.25	.90	.60
RG4	4¢ carmine rose	2.40	1.40	1.75	1.25
RG5	5¢ carmine rose	3.60	2.50	1.50	1.00
RG6	8¢ carmine rose	4.85	3.00	3.50	2.50
RG7	10¢ carmine rose	5.25	3.50	4.00	2.50
RG8	20¢ carmine rose	7.75	5.00	4.00	2.50
RG9	25¢ carmine rose	7.75	5.00	5.00	3.50
RG10	40¢ carmine rose	8.50	6.00	6.50	4.50
RG11	50¢ carmine rose	10.00	7.00	8.00	5.00
RG12	80¢ carmine rose	18.00	12.00	11.00	7.00
RG13	$1 green	42.00	35.00	18.00	13.00
RG14	$2 rose	50.00	45.00	27.00	18.00
RG15	$3 violet	82.00	65.00	40.00	28.00
RG16	$4 yellow brown	80.00	50.00	35.00	17.00
RG17	$5 dark blue	82.00	60.00	33.00	20.00
RG18	$10 orange	115.00	90.00	25.00	17.00
RG19	$30 vermillion (cut cancel 20.00)	245.00	140.00	60.00	40.00
RG20	$60 brown (cut cancel 30.00)	280.00	150.00	85.00	60.00
RG21	$100 green	275.00	185.00	35.00	22.50
RG22	$500 blue (cut cancel 110.00)	600.00	400.00	235.00	160.00
RG23	$1000 orange (cut cancel 70.00)	....	....	120.00	77.50
RG26	$100 green, 11mm spacing	600.00	400.00	85.00	55.00
RG27	$1000 orange, 11mm spacing	....	....	1700.00	1450.00

TOBACCO SALE TAX STAMPS

Documentary Stamps of 1917 Overprinted

1934

SCOTT NO.	DESCRIPTION	UNUSED F	UNUSED AVG	USED F	USED AVG
RJ1	1¢ carmine rose	.40	.35	.25	.20
RJ2	2¢ carmine rose	.45	.30	.25	.20
RJ3	5¢ carmine rose	1.40	.90	.45	.30
RJ4	10¢ carmine rose	1.75	1.15	.45	.30
RJ5	25¢ carmine rose	4.75	3.00	1.85	1.20
RJ6	50¢ carmine rose	4.75	3.00	1.85	1.20
RJ7	$1 green	12.00	8.00	1.85	1.20
RJ8	$2 rose	20.00	14.00	2.15	1.40
RJ9	$5 dark blue	25.00	17.00	4.75	3.00
RJ10	$10 orange	40.00	27.00	12.00	7.75
RJ11	$20 olive bistre	100.00	70.00	15.00	9.75

HUNTING PERMIT

RW1

RW2

RW3

RW4

RW5

1934-1938 Inscribed: DEPARTMENT OF AGRICULTURE (NH + 75%)

SCOTT NO.	DESCRIPTION	UNUSED VF	UNUSED F	UNUSED AVG	USED VF	USED F	USED AVG
RW1	1934 $1 Mallards	650.00	475.00	400.00	160.00	125.00	110.00
RW2	1935 $1 Canvasbacks .	575.00	425.00	375.00	185.00	150.00	125.00
RW3	1936 $1 Canada geese	350.00	250.00	200.00	85.00	70.00	60.00
RW4	1937 $1 Scaup Ducks .	290.00	225.00	160.00	65.00	55.00	40.00
RW5	1938 $1 Pintail Drake . .	450.00	300.00	225.00	65.00	55.00	40.00

RW6

RW7

RW9

RW8

RW10

RW11

SCOTT NO.	DESCRIPTION	UNUSED VF	UNUSED F	UNUSED AVG	USED VF	USED F	USED AVG
RW6	1939 $1 Green-winged teal	200.00	165.00	135.00	55.00	45.00	38.00
RW7	1940 $1 Black Mallards . .	200.00	165.00	135.00	55.00	45.00	38.00
RW8	1941 $1 Ruddy Ducks . . .	200.00	165.00	135.00	55.00	45.00	38.00
RW9	1942 $1 Baldpates	210.00	175.00	140.00	55.00	45.00	35.00
RW10	1943 $1 Wood ducks. . . .	115.00	85.00	77.00	55.00	42.00	30.00
RW11	1944 $1 White-fronted Geese	130.00	90.00	82.00	47.00	37.00	27.00

RW12

RW13

SCOTT NO.	DESCRIPTION	UNUSED VF	UNUSED F	UNUSED AVG	USED VF	USED F	USED AVG
RW12	1945 $1 Shoveller Ducks	95.00	72.00	62.00	36.00	28.00	22.00
RW13	1946 $1 Redhead Ducks.	50.00	35.00	25.00	20.00	15.00	10.00

Note: NH premiums RW6-9 (75%) RW10-16 (50%) RW17-25 (40%)
1939-1958 Inscribed: DEPARTMENT OF INTERIOR

RW14

RW15

SCOTT NO.	DESCRIPTION	UNUSED VF	UNUSED F	UNUSED AVG	USED VF	USED F	USED AVG
RW14	1947 $1 Snow geese	50.00	35.00	25.00	20.00	15.00	10.00
RW15	1948 $1 Buffleheads	50.00	35.00	25.00	20.00	15.00	10.00

RW16

RW17

RW18

RW19

RW20

RW21

SCOTT NO.	DESCRIPTION	UNUSED VF	UNUSED F	UNUSED AVG	USED VF	USED F	USED AVG
RW16	1949 $2 Goldeneye Ducks	60.00	40.00	35.00	18.00	15.00	10.00
RW17	1950 $2 Trumpeter Swans	75.00	55.00	45.00	15.00	12.00	9.00
RW18	1951 $2 Gadwall Ducks . .	75.00	55.00	45.00	15.00	12.00	9.00
RW19	1952 $2 Harlequin Ducks	75.00	55.00	45.00	15.00	12.00	9.00
RW20	1953 $2 Blue-winged teal	80.00	60.00	50.00	15.00	12.00	9.00
RW21	1954 $2 Ring-necked Ducks	85.00	60.00	50.00	13.00	10.00	7.50

RW22

RW23

RW24

RW25

SCOTT NO.	DESCRIPTION	UNUSED VF	UNUSED F	UNUSED AVG	USED VF	USED F	USED AVG
RW22	1955 $2 Blue Geese.	85.00	60.00	50.00	12.00	9.00	7.50
RW23	1956 $2 American Merganser	85.00	60.00	50.00	12.00	9.00	7.50
RW24	1957 $2 American Eiders	85.00	60.00	50.00	12.00	9.00	7.50
RW25	1958 $2 Canada geese . .	85.00	60.00	50.00	12.00	9.00	7.50

PLATE BLOCKS OF 6 RW1-RW25

SCOTT NO.	UNUSED NH F	UNUSED NH AVG	UNUSED OG F	UNUSED OG AVG	SCOTT NO.	UNUSED NH F	UNUSED NH AVG	UNUSED OG F	UNUSED OG AVG
RW1	16000.00	12000.00	13500.00	9500.00	RW14	475.00	375.00	350.00	325.00
RW2	12000.00	9000.00	9500.00	7500.00	RW15	500.00	425.00	425.00	375.00
RW3	5200.00	4300.00	4500.00	3200.00	RW16	575.00	450.00	450.00	400.00
RW4	4600.00	3500.00	4200.00	3300.00	RW17	795.00	650.00	650.00	550.00
RW5	5100.00	4200.00	4400.00	3300.00	RW18	795.00	650.00	650.00	550.00
RW6	4700.00	3800.00	3600.00	2900.00	RW19	795.00	650.00	650.00	550.00
RW7	4700.00	3800.00	3700.00	3100.00	RW20	825.00	675.00	675.00	575.00
RW8	4800.00	3800.00	3700.00	3100.00	RW21	795.00	675.00	675.00	600.00
RW9	4300.00	3600.00	3500.00	2900.00	RW22	795.00	675.00	675.00	600.00
RW10	1075.00	850.00	925.00	775.00	RW23	840.00	725.00	725.00	640.00
RW11	1200.00	875.00	925.00	775.00	RW24	795.00	675.00	650.00	575.00
RW12	900.00	650.00	675.00	550.00	RW25	795.00	675.00	650.00	575.00
RW13	500.00	400.00	350.00	325.00					

Notes on Hunting Permit Stamps

1. Unused stamps without gum (uncancelled) are priced at one-half gummed price.
2. The date printed on the stamp is one year later than the date of issue listed above.
3. #RW1-RW25 and RW31 are plate blocks of 6.

RW26

RW27

RW28

RW29

RW30

RW31

1959-1971 (NH + 40%)

SCOTT NO.	DESCRIPTION	UNUSED VF	UNUSED F	USED VF	USED F
RW26	1959 $3 Labrador Retriever & Mallard	185.00	135.00	12.00	9.00
RW27	1960 $3 Redhead Ducks	135.00	110.00	12.00	9.00
RW28	1961 $3 Mallard Hen & Ducklings	135.00	110.00	12.00	9.00
RW29	1962 $3 Pintail Drakes	150.00	115.00	12.00	9.00
RW30	1963 $3 Brant Ducks Landing	150.00	115.00	12.00	9.00
RW31	1964 $3 Hawaiian Nene Geese	145.00	115.00	12.00	9.00

RW32

RW33

RW34

RW35

SCOTT NO.	DESCRIPTION	UNUSED VF	UNUSED F	USED VF	USED F
RW32	1965 $3 Canvasback Drakes	145.00	115.00	12.00	9.00
RW33	1966 $3 Whistling Swans	145.00	115.00	12.00	9.00
RW34	1967 $3 Oldsquaw Ducks	170.00	125.00	12.00	9.00
RW35	1968 $3 Hooded mergansers	100.00	72.00	12.00	9.00

RW36

RW37

RW38

RW39

Notes on Hunting Permit Stamps

1. Unused stamps without gum (uncancelled) are priced at one-half gummed price.
2. The date printed on the stamp is one year later than the date of issue listed above.
3. #RW1-RW25 and RW31 are plate blocks of 6.

SCOTT NO.	DESCRIPTION	UNUSED VF	UNUSED F	USED VF	USED F
RW36	1969 $3 White-winged Scoters	98.00	72.00	12.00	9.00
RW37	1970 $3 Ross's Geese	98.00	72.00	12.00	9.00
RW38	1971 $3 Three Cinnamon teal	68.00	48.00	12.00	9.00
RW39	1972 $5 Emperor Geese	42.00	32.00	9.00	7.50

RW40

RW41

RW42

RW43

RW44

RW45

1973-1978

SCOTT NO.	DESCRIPTION	UNUSED VF	UNUSED F	USED VF	USED F
RW40	1973 $5 Steller's Eider	32.00	24.00	9.00	7.50
RW41	1974 $5 Wood ducks	32.00	24.00	9.00	7.50
RW42	1975 $5 Canvasbacks & Decoy	29.00	22.00	9.00	7.50
RW43	1976 $5 Canada geese	29.00	22.00	9.00	7.50
RW44	1977 $5 Pair of Ross's Geese	29.00	23.00	9.00	7.50
RW45	1978 $5 Hooded Merganser Drake	29.00	23.00	9.00	7.50

RW46

RW47

RW48

RW49

1979-1986

SCOTT NO.	DESCRIPTION	UNUSED VF	UNUSED F	USED VF	USED F
RW46	1979 $7.50 Green-winged teal	29.00	23.00	10.00	9.00
RW47	1980 $7.50 Mallards	29.00	23.00	10.00	9.00
RW48	1981 $7.50 Ruddy Ducks	29.00	23.00	10.00	9.00
RW49	1982 $7.50 Canvasbacks	29.00	23.00	10.00	9.00

RW50

RW51

SCOTT NO.	DESCRIPTION	UNUSED VF	UNUSED F	USED VF	USED F
RW50	1983 $7.50 Pintails	29.00	23.00	10.00	9.00
RW51	1984 $7.50 Wigeons	29.00	23.00	10.00	9.00

PLATE BLOCKS RW26-RW38					
SCOTT NO.	UNUSED NH F	UNUSED OG F	SCOTT NO.	UNUSED NH F	UNUSED OG F
RW26	740.00	550.00	RW33	750.00	573.00
RW27	700.00	525.00	RW34	750.00	573.00
RW28	700.00	550.00	RW35	395.00	300.00
RW29	750.00	550.00	RW36	395.00	300.00
RW30	725.00	485.00	RW37	270.00	300.00
RW31	2800.00	2400.00	RW38	155.00	220.00
RW32	750.00	573.00			

RW52

RW53

SCOTT NO.	DESCRIPTION	UNUSED NH VF	UNUSED NH F	USED VF	USED F
RW52	1985 $7.50 Cinnamon teal	29.00	23.00	10.00	9.00
RW53	1986 $7.50 Fulvous Whistling	29.00	23.00	10.00	9.00

RW54

RW55

RW56

RW57

1987-1993

SCOTT NO.	DESCRIPTION	UNUSED NH VF	UNUSED NH F	USED VF	USED F
RW54	1987 $10.00 Redhead Ducks	35.00	25.00	13.00	11.00
RW55	1988 $10.00 Snow goose	35.00	27.00	13.00	11.00
RW56	1989 $12.50 Lesser Scaup	35.00	27.00	13.00	11.00
RW57	1990 $12.50 Black-bellied Whistling Duck	35.00	27.00	13.00	11.00

RW58

RW59

RW60

RW61

SCOTT NO.	DESCRIPTION	UNUSED NH VF	UNUSED NH F	USED VF	USED F
RW58	1991 $15.00 King Eiders	55.00	40.00	18.00	15.00
RW59	1992 $15.00 Spectacled Eider	50.00	35.00	17.00	14.00
RW60	1993 $15.00 Canvasbacks	50.00	35.00	17.00	14.00
RW61	1994 $15.00 Red-breasted Merganser	50.00	38.00	17.50	12.50

RW62

RW63

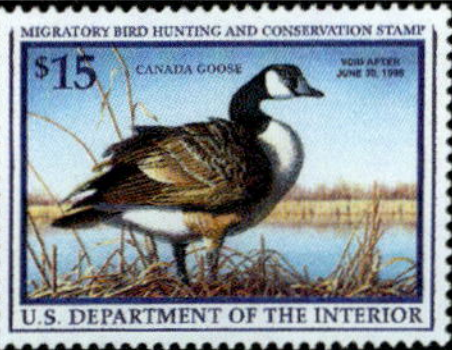
RW64

RW65

RW66

RW67

1992-2000

SCOTT NO.	DESCRIPTION	UNUSED NH VF	UNUSED NH F	USED VF	USED F
RW62	1995 $15.00 Mallards	50.00	38.00	17.50	12.50
RW63	1996 $15.00 Surf Scoters	50.00	38.00	17.50	12.50
RW64	1997 $15.00 Canada goose	50.00	38.00	17.50	12.50
RW65	1998 $15.00 Barrow's Goldeneye	75.00	57.00	32.00	24.00
RW65a	1998 $15.00 Barrow's Goldeneye, self-adhesive, pane of 1	42.00	39.00	18.00	....
RW66	1999 $15.00 Greater Scaup	58.00	47.00	31.00	....
RW66a	1999 $15.00 Greater Scaup, self-adhesive, pane of 1	40.00	34.00	18.00	....
RW67	2000 $15.00 Mottled Duck	40.00	33.00	28.00	....
RW67a	2000 $15.00 Mottled Duck, self-adhesive, pane of 1	37.00	31.00	18.00	....

RW68

RW69

2001-2003

SCOTT NO.	DESCRIPTION	UNUSED NH VF	UNUSED NH F	USED VF	USED F
RW68	2001 $15.00 Northern Pintail	38.00	31.00	26.00	....
RW68a	2001 $15.00 Northern Pintail, self-adhesive, pane of 1	37.00	32.00	18.00	....
RW69	2002 $15.00 Black Scoters	38.00	34.00	26.00	....
RW69a	2002 $15.00 Black Scoters, self-adhesive, pane of 1	37.00	....	18.00	....

RW70

RW71

RW72

RW73

2004-2006

SCOTT NO.	DESCRIPTION	UNUSED NH VF	UNUSED NH F	USED VF	USED F
RW70	2003 $15.00 Snow geese	40.00	32.00	26.00	....
RW70a	2003 $15.00 Snow geese, self-adhesive, pane of 1	37.00	....	18.00	....
RW71	2004 $15.00 Redheads	38.00	32.00	23.00	....
RW71a	2004 $15.00 Redheads, self-adhesive, pane of 1	37.00	....	18.00	....
RW72	2005 $15.00 Hooded mergansers	38.00	32.00	23.00	....
RW72a	2005 $15.00 Hooded mergansers, self-adhesive, pane of 1	37.00	....	20.00	....
RW73	2006 $15.00 Ross's Goose	38.00	32.00	23.00	....
RW73a	2006 $15.00 Ross's Goose, self-adhesive, pane of 1	37.00	....	20.00	....

RW74  RW75

RW76 RW77

2007-2010

SCOTT NO.	DESCRIPTION	UNUSED NH VF	UNUSED NH F	USED VF	USED F
RW74	2007 $15.00 Ring-necked Ducks	38.00	32.00	23.00	....
RW74a	2007 $15.00 Ring-necked Ducks, self-adhesive, pane of 1	37.00	....	22.00	....
RW75	2008 $15 Northern Pintail Ducks	38.00	32.00	26.00	....
RW75a	2008 $15 Northern Pintail Ducks, self-adhesive	37.00	....	22.00	....
RW76	2009 $15 Long-tailed Duck	38.00	32.00	26.00	....
RW76a	2009 $15 Long-tailed Duck, self-adhesive	37.00	....	22.00	....
RW77	2010 $15 American Wigeon	38.00	32.00	26.00	....
RW77a	2010 $15 American Wigeon, self-adhesive	37.00	....	19.00	....

RW78

RW79

RW80

RW81

2011-2014

SCOTT NO.	DESCRIPTION	UNUSED NH VF	UNUSED NH F	USED VF	USED F
RW78	2011 $15 White-fronted Geese	38.00	32.00	26.00	....
RW78a	2011 $15 White-fronted Geese, self-adhesive	35.00	....	19.00	....
RW79	2012 $15 Wood duck	40.00	....	30.00	....
RW79a	2012 $15 Wood duck, self-adhesive	45.00	....	20.00	....
RW80	2013 $15 Common Goldeneye	30.00	....	30.00	....
RW80a	2013 $15 Common Goldeneye, self-adhesive	45.00	....	20.00	....
RW81	2014 $15 Canvasbacks	40.00	....	30.00	....
RW81a	2014 $15 Canvasbacks, self-adhesive	45.00	....	20.00	....

RW82

RW83

RW84

RW85

RW86 RW87

2015-2020

SCOTT NO.	DESCRIPTION	UNUSED NH VF	UNUSED NH F	USED VF	USED F
RW82	2015 $25 Ruddy Ducks	95.00	....	40.00	....
RW82a	2015 $25 Ruddy Ducks, self-adhesive	90.00	....	30.00	....
RW83	2016 $25 Trumpeter Swans	95.00	....	40.00	....
RW83a	2016 $25 Trumpeter Swans, self-adhesive	90.00	....	30.00	....
RW84	2017 $25 Canada geese	50.00	....	40.00	....
RW84a	2017 $25 Canada geese, self-adhesive	50.00	....	40.00	....
RW85	2018 $25 Mallards	60.00	....	40.00	....
RW85a	2018 $25 Mallards, self-adhesive	60.00	....	40.00	....
RW86	2019 $25 Wood duck and Decoy	50.00	....	40.00	....
RW86a	2019 $25 Wood duck and Decoy, self-adhesive.	50.00	....	40.00	....
RW87	2020 $25 Black-bellied Whistling Ducks	50.00	....	40.00	....
RW87a	2020 $25 Black-bellied Whistling Ducks, self adhesive	50.00	....	40.00	....

RW88 RW89

2021-2022

SCOTT NO.	DESCRIPTION	UNUSED NH VF	UNUSED NH F	USED VF	USED F
RW88	$25 Lesser Scaup Drake	50.00	....	40.00	....
RW88a	$25 Lesser Scaup Drake	50.00	....	40.00	....
RW89	$25 Redheads	50.00	....	30.00	....
RW89a	$25 Redheads	50.00	....	30.00	....

RW90

RW91

2023-2024

SCOTT NO.	DESCRIPTION	UNUSED NH VF	UNUSED NH F	USED VF	USED F
RW90	$25 Tundra Swans	50.00	....	30.00	....
RW90A	$25 Tundra Swans	50.00	....	30.00	....
RW91	$25 Northern Pintail	50.00	....	30.00	....
RW91A	$25 Northern Pintail	50.00	....	30.00	....

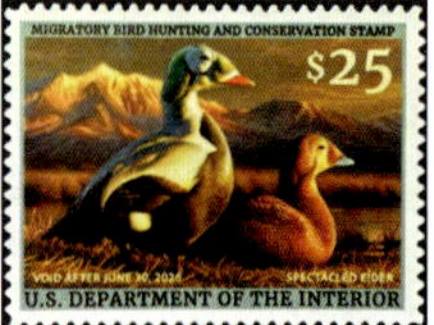

RW92

2025

SCOTT NO.	DESCRIPTION	UNUSED NH VF	UNUSED NH F	USED VF	USED F
RW92	$25 Spectacled Eider	55.00	....	....	....
RW92A	$25 Spectacled Eider	55.00	....	....	....

PLATE BLOCKS RW39-RW92

SCOTT NO.	UNUSED NH F	SCOTT NO.	UNUSED NH F	SCOTT NO.	UNUSED NH F
RW39	125.00	RW58	150.00	RW77	150.00
RW40	115.00	RW59	150.00	RW78	150.00
RW41	100.00	RW60	150.00	RW79	200.00
RW42	90.00	RW61	150.00	RW80	200.00
RW43	90.00	RW62	150.00	RW81	170.00
RW44	90.00	RW63	150.00	RW82	300.00
RW45	90.00	RW64	150.00	RW83	425.00
RW46	90.00	RW65	225.00	RW84	230.00
RW47	90.00	RW66	150.00	RW85	250.00
RW48	90.00	RW67	150.00	RW86	230.00
RW49	90.00	RW68	150.00	RW87	230.00
RW50	90.00	RW69	150.00	RW88	230.00
RW51	90.00	RW70	150.00	RW89	230.00
RW52	90.00	RW71	150.00	RW90	230.00
RW53	90.00	RW72	150.00	RW91	250.00
RW54	110.00	RW73	150.00	RW92	250.00
RW55	110.00	RW74	150.00		
RW56	120.00	RW75	150.00		
RW57	120.00	RW76	150.00		

STATE HUNTING PERMIT

AL7

ALABAMA

NO.	DESCRIPTION	F-VF NH
AL1	'79 $5 Wood ducks	16.00
AL2	'80 $5 Mallards	14.00
AL3	'81 $5 Canada geese	14.00
AL4	'82 $5 Green-winged teal	14.00
AL5	'83 $5 Wigeons	14.00
AL6	'84 $5 Buffleheads	24.00
AL7	'85 $5 Wood ducks	17.00
AL8	'86 $5 Canada geese	17.00
AL9	'87 $5 Pintails	18.00
AL10	'88 $5 Canvasbacks	12.50
AL11	'89 $5 Hooded mergansers	12.50
AL12	'90 $5 Wood ducks	12.50
AL13	'91 $5 Redheads	12.50
AL14	'92 $5 Cinnamon teal	12.50
AL15	'93 $5 Green-winged teal	12.50
AL16	'94 $5 Canvasbacks	13.00
AL17	'95 $5 Canada geese	13.00
AL18	'96 $5 Wood ducks	13.00
AL19	'97 $5 Snow goose	13.00
AL20	'98 $5 Barrow's goldeneye	13.00
AL21	'99 $5 Redheads	13.00
AL22	'00 $5 Buffleheads	13.00
AL23	'01 $5 Ruddy duck	13.00
AL24	'02 $5 Pintail	13.00
AL25	'03 $5 Wood ducks	13.00
AL26	'04 $5 Ring-necked duck	13.00
AL27	'05 $5 Canada geese	13.00
AL28	'06 $5 Canvasback	13.00
AL29	'07 $5 Blue-winged teal	13.00
AL30	'08 $5 Hooded mergansers	13.00
AL31	'09 $5 Wood ducks	13.00
AL32	'10 $5 Pintail	13.00
AL33	'11 $5 Wigeon	11.00
AL34	'12 $6 Ring-necked ducks	11.00
AL35	'13 $5 Canvasbacks	11.00
AL36	'14 $5 Pintails	11.00
AL37	'15 $5 Mallards	11.00
AL38	'16 $10 Wigeons	18.00
AL39	'17 $10 Canada geese	18.00
AL40	'18 $10 Blue-winged teal	18.00
AL41	'19 $10 Wood duck	18.00
AL42	'20 $10 Pintail	18.00

AK1

ALASKA

NO.	DESCRIPTION	F-VF NH
AK1	'85 $5 Emperor geese	14.00
AK2	'86 $5 Steller's eiders	13.00
AK3	'87 $5 Spectacled eiders	15.00
AK4	'88 $5 Trumpeter swans	11.00
AK5	'89 $5 Barrow's goldeneyes	11.00
AK6	'90 $5 Oldsquaws	12.00
AK7	'91 $5 Snow geese	14.00
AK8	'92 $5 Canvasbacks	14.00
AK9	'93 $5 Tule white front geese	14.00
AK10	'94 $5 Harlequin ducks	25.00
AK11	'95 $5 Pacific brant	28.00
AK12	'96 $5 Aleutian Canada geese	30.00
AK13	'97 $5 King eiders	22.00
AK14	'98 $5 Barrow's goldeneye	10.00
AK15	'99 $5 Pintail	18.00
AK16	'00 $5 Common eider	18.00
AK17	'01 $5 American wigeon	15.00
AK18	'02 $5 Black scoter	14.00
AK19	'03 $5 Lesser Canada geese	14.00
AK20	'04 $5 Lesser scaup	14.00
AK21	'05 $5 Hooded merganser	14.00
AK22	'06 $5 Pintails, mallard, Green-winged teal	14.00
AK23	'07 $5 Northern shoveler	14.00
AK24	'08 $5 Northern pintail	14.00
AK25	'09 $5 Mallards	14.00
AK26	'10 $5 Pintails	14.00
AK27	'11 $5 Canada goose	13.00
AK28	'12 $5 Harlequin ducks	11.00
AK29	'13 $5 White-fronted geese	10.00
AK30	'14 $5 White-winged scoter	10.00
AK31	'15 $5 Northern pintail	10.00
AK32	'16 $5 Pacific Brant	10.00
AK33	'17 $10 American Wigeon	18.00
AK34	'18 $10 Bufflehead	18.00
AK35	'19 $10 Emperor goose	18.00
AK36	'20 $10 Gadwall	18.00
AK37	'21 $10 Ring-necked duck	18.00

AZ1

ARIZONA

NO.	DESCRIPTION	F-VF NH
AZ1	'87 $5.50 Pintails	13.00
AZ2	'88 $5.50 Green-winged teal	13.00
AZ3	'89 $5.50 Cinnamon teal	13.00
AZ4	'90 $5.50 Canada geese	15.00
AZ5	'91 $5.50 Blue-winged teal	13.00
AZ6	'92 $5.50 Buffleheads	13.00
AZ7	'93 $5.50 Mexican ducks	15.00
AZ8	'94 $5.50 Mallards	15.00
AZ9	'95 $5.50 Wigeon	15.00
AZ10	'96 $5.50 Canvasback	15.00
AZ11	'97 $5.50 Gadwalls	15.00
AZ12	'98 $5.50 Wood duck	15.00
AZ13	'99 $5.50 Snow goose	15.00
AZ14	'00 $7.50 Ruddy ducks	22.00
AZ15	'01 $7.50 Redheads	18.00
AZ16	'02 $7.50 Ring-necked ducks	18.00
AZ17	'03 $7.50 Northern shovelers	18.00
AZ18	'04 $7.50 Lesser scaup	18.00
AZ19	'05 $7.50 Pintails	18.00
AZ20	'06 $7.50 Canada geese	18.00
AZ21	'07 $8.75 Wood ducks	18.00
AZ22	'08 $8.75 Canvasbacks	18.00
AZ23	'09 $8.75 Hooded mergansers	18.00
AZ24	'10 $8.75 Green-winged teal	18.00
AZ25	'11 $8.75 Bufflehead	18.00
AZ26	'12 $8.75 American wigeons	18.00
AZ27	'13 $8.75 Pintail	18.00

AR5

ARKANSAS

NO.	DESCRIPTION	F-VF NH
AR1	'81 $5.50 Mallards	50.00
AR2	'82 $5.50 Wood ducks	40.00
AR3	'83 $5.50 Green-winged teal	55.00
AR4	'84 $5.50 Pintails	20.00
AR5	'85 $5.50 Mallards	12.00
AR6	'86 $5.50 Black swamp mallards	12.00
AR7	'87 $7 Wood ducks	12.00
AR8	'88 $7 Pintails	12.00
AR9	'89 $7 Mallards	12.00
AR10	'90 $7 Black ducks & mallards	12.00
AR11	'91 $7 Sulphur river wigeons	12.00
AR12	'92 $7 Shirey Bay shovelers	12.00
AR13	'93 $7 Grand prairie mallards	15.00
AR14	'94 $7 Canada goose	19.00
AR15	'95 $7 White River mallards	19.00
AR16	'96 $7 Mallards & black labrador retriever	22.00
AR17	'97 $7 Mallards, labrador retriever	18.00
AR18	'98 $7 Labrador retriever, mallards	18.00
AR19	'99 $7 Wood duck	18.00
AR20	'00 $7 Mallards and golden Retriever	21.00
AR21	'01 $7 Canvasback	18.00
AR22	'02 $7 Mallards	18.00
AR23	'03 $7 Mallards & Chesapeake Bay Retriever	18.00
AR24	'04 $7 Mallards	15.00
AR24a	'04 $20 Mallards	35.00
AR25	'05 $7 Mallards and labrador retriever	16.00
AR25a	'05 $20 Mallards and labrador retriever	35.00
AR26	'06 $7 Mallards	16.00
AR26a	'06 $20 Mallards	35.00
AR27	'07 $7 Mallards, labrador retriever	16.00
AR27a	'07 $20 Mallards, labrador retriever	35.00
AR28	'08 $7 Mallards, labrador retriever	16.00
AR28a	'08 $20 Mallards, labrador retriever	35.00
AR29	'09 $7 Hooded mergansers	16.00
AR29a	'09 $20 Hooded mergansers	35.00
AR30	'10 $7 Mallards and black labrador retriever	16.00
AR30a	'10 $20 Mallards and black labrador retriever	40.00
AR31	'11 $7 Mallards	16.00
AR31a	'11 $20 Mallards	35.00
AR32	'12 $7 Green-winged teal	16.00
AR32a	'12 $20 Green-winged teal	35.00
AR32b	'12 $35.00 Green-winged teal	60.00
AR33	'13 $7 Mallards	16.00
AR33a	'13 $35 Mallards	55.00
AR34	'14 $7 Mallards	16.00
AR34a	'14 $35 Mallards	55.00
AR35	'15 $7 Snow geese	16.00
AR35a	'15 $35 Snow geese	55.00
AR36	'16 $7 Mallards	16.00
AR36a	'16 $35 Mallards	55.00
AR37	'17 $7 Mallards	16.00
AR37a	'17 $35 Mallards	55.00
AR38	'18 $7 Ring-necked ducks	16.00
AR38a	'18 $35 Ring-necked ducks	55.00
AR39	'19 $7 Mallards	16.00
AR39a	'19 $35 Mallards	55.00
AR40	'20 $7 Green-winged teal	16.00
AR40a	'20 $7 Green-winged teal	55.00
AR41	'21 $7 Mallard & black labrador	16.00
AR41a	'21 $35 Mallard & black labrador	55.00

CA16

CALIFORNIA

NO.	DESCRIPTION	F-VF NH
CA1	'71 $1 Pintails	500.00
CA2	'72 $1 Canvasbacks	1400.00
CA3	'73 $1 Mallards	15.00
CA4	'74 $1 White-fronted geese	4.50
CA5	'75 $1 Green-winged teal	150.00
CA6	'76 $1 Wigeons	30.00
CA7	'77 $1 Cinnamon teal	45.00
CA8	'78 $5 Cinnamon teal	13.00
CA9	'78 $5 Hooded mergansers	100.00
CA10	'79 $5 Wood ducks	12.00
CA11	'80 $5 Pintails	12.00
CA12	'81 $5 Canvasbacks	12.00
CA13	'82 $5 Wigeons	12.00
CA14	'83 $5 Green-winged teal	15.00
CA15	'84 $7.50 Mallard decoy	15.00
CA16	'85 $7.50 Ring-necked ducks	15.00
CA17	'86 $7.50 Canada goose	15.00
CA18	'87 $7.50 Redheads	15.00
CA19	'88 $7.50 Mallards	15.00
CA20	'89 $7.50 Cinnamon teal	16.00
CA21	'90 $7.50 Canada goose	19.00
CA22	'91 $7.50 Gadwalls	19.00
CA23	'92 $7.90 White-fronted goose	21.00
CA24	'93 $10.50 Pintails	21.00
CA25	'94 $10.50 Wood duck	23.00
CA26	'95 $10.50 Snow geese	23.00
CA27	'96 $10.50 Mallards	22.00
CA28	'97 $10.50 Pintails	22.00
CA29	'98 $10.50 Green-winged teal (pair)	42.00
CA30	'99 $10.50 Wood duck (pair)	42.00
CA31	'00 $10.50 Canada geese, mallard, wigeon	22.00
CA32	'01 $10.50 Redheads	22.00
CA33	'02 $10.50 Pintails	22.00
CA34	'03 $10.50 Mallards	22.00
CA35	'04 $13.90 Cinnamon teal	22.00
CA36	'05 $14.20 Pintails	22.00
CA37	'06 $14.95 White-fronted goose	24.00
CA38	'07 $16 Pintails	45.00
CA39	'08 $16.80 Mallards	30.00
CA40	'09 $17.50 Shovelers	28.00
CA41	'10 $18.10 Redheads	28.00
CA42	'11 $18.93 Barrow's goldeneyes	95.00
CA43	'12 $19.44 Canada geese	45.00
CA44	'13 $20.01 Wigeons	45.00
CA45	'14 $20.26 Lesser scaup	40.00
CA46	'15 $20.52 Green-winged teal	40.00
CA47	'16 $20.52 Lesser Snow geese	45.00
CA48	'17 $20.52 Ruddy duck	45.00
CA49	'18 $21.09 Black brants	45.00
CA50	'19 $21.86 Pintails	45.00
CA51	'20 $22.42 Pintails	45.00

CO1

COLORADO

NO.	DESCRIPTION	F-VF NH
CO1	'90 $5 Canada geese	17.00
CO2	'91 $5 Mallards	23.00
CO3	'92 $5 Pintails	13.00
CO4	'93 $5 Green-winged teal	13.00
CO5	'94 $5 Wood ducks	13.00
CO6	'95 $5 Buffleheads	13.00
CO7	'96 $5 Cinnamon teal	13.00
CO8	'97 $5 Wigeons	13.00
CO9	'98 $5 Redheads	13.00
CO10	'99 $5 Blue-winged teal	13.00
CO11	'00 $5 Gadwalls	13.00
CO12	'01 $5 Ruddy ducks	13.00
CO13	'02 $5 Common goldeneyes	13.00
CO14	'03 $5 Canvasbacks	13.00
CO15	'04 $5 Snow geese	13.00
CO16	'05 $5 Shovelers	13.00
CO17	'06 $5 Ring-necked ducks	13.00
CO18	'07 $5 Hooded mergansers	13.00
CO19	'08 $5 Lesser scaup	13.00
CO20	'09 $5 Barrow's goldeneye	13.00
CO21	'10 $5 Pintails	13.00
CO22	'11 $5 Green-winged teal	10.00
CO23	'12 $5 Ross's geese	10.00
CO24	'13 $5 Greater scaups	10.00
CO25	'14 $5 Canada geese	10.00
CO26	'15 ($7.50) Wood ducks	13.00
CO27	'16 ($10) Marsh mallards	18.00
CO28	'17 ($10) Redheads	18.00
CO29	'18 ($10) Ring-necked ducks	15.00
CO30	'19 ($10) Northern pintails	15.00
CO31	'20 ($10) Canvasbacks	15.00
CO32	'21 ($10) Canvasbacks	15.00

CT7

CONNECTICUT

NO.	DESCRIPTION	F-VF NH
CT1	'93 $5 Black ducks	15.00
CT2	'94 $5 Canvasbacks	18.00
CT3	'95 $5 Mallards	18.00
CT4	'96 $5 Oldsquaw	23.00
CT5	'97 $5 Green-winged teal	15.00
CT6	'98 $5 Mallards	15.00
CT7	'99 $5 Canada geese	28.00
CT8	'00 $5 Wood duck	15.00
CT9	'01 $5 Buffleheads	15.00
CT10	'02 $5 Greater scaups	18.00
CT11	'03 $5 Black duck	15.00
CT12	'04 $5 Wood duck	15.00
CT13	'05 $10 Mallards	21.00
CT14	'06 $10 Buffleheads	21.00

NO.	DESCRIPTION	F-VF NH
CT15	'07 $10 Black duck decoy	21.00
CT16	'08 $10 Common goldeneyes	21.00
CT17	'09 $10 Black duck	21.00
CT18	'10 $13 Common goldeneyes	23.00
CT19	'12 $13 Pintail	25.00
CT20	'13 $13 Wood ducks	25.00
CT21	'14 $13 Hooded mergansers	25.00
CT22	'15 $13 Canvasbacks	25.00
CT23	'16 $13 Atlantic brant	25.00
CT24	'17 $17 Canvasbacks and lighthouse	28.00
CT25	'18 $17 Black scoter and lighthouse	28.00
CT26	'19 $17 Buffleheads	28.00
CT27	'20 $17 Wood ducks	28.00
CT28	'21 $17 Canada goose	28.00

DE1

DELAWARE

NO.	DESCRIPTION	F-VF NH
DE1	'80 $5 Black ducks	70.00
DE2	'81 $5 Snow geese	55.00
DE3	'82 $5 Canada geese	55.00
DE4	'83 $5 Canvasbacks	40.00
DE5	'84 $5 Mallards	15.00
DE6	'85 $5 Pintail	12.00
DE7	'86 $5 Wigeons	12.00
DE8	'87 $5 Redheads	12.00
DE9	'88 $5 Wood ducks	10.00
DE10	'89 $5 Buffleheads	10.00
DE11	'90 $5 Green-winged teal	10.00
DE12	'91 $5 Hooded merganser	10.00
DE13	'92 $5 Blue-winged teal	10.00
DE14	'93 $5 Goldeneye	10.00
DE15	'94 $5 Blue goose	14.00
DE16	'95 $5 Scaup	14.00
DE17	'96 $6 Gadwall	15.00
DE18	'97 $6 White-winged scoter	15.00
DE19	'98 $6 Blue-winged teal	14.00
DE20	'99 $6 Tundra swan	14.00
DE21	'00 $6 American brant	14.00
DE22	'01 $6 Oldsquaw	15.00
DE23	'02 $6 Ruddy ducks	15.00
DE24	'03 $9 Ring-necked duck	18.00
DE25	'04 $9 Black scoter	20.00
DE26	'05 $9 Common merganser and lighthouse	18.00
DE27	'06 $9 Red-breasted mergansers	18.00
DE28	'07 $9 Surf scoters, lighthouse	18.00
DE29	'08 $9 Greater scaup, lighthouse	18.00
DE30	'09 $9 Black ducks	18.00
DE31	'10 $9 Canvasback	18.00
DE32	'11 $9 Hooded mergansers	18.00
DE33	'12 $9 Lesser scaup	14.00
DE34	'13 $9 Wigeon	14.00
DE35	'14 $9 Blue-winged teal	14.00
DE36	'15 $9 Black duck	14.00
DE37	'16 $9 Green-winged teal	14.00
DE38	'17 $15 Canvasbacks and retriever	25.00
DE39	'18 $15 Pintails and golden retriever	25.00
DE40	'19 $15 Long-tailed duck and retriever	25.00
DE41	'20 $15 Wigeons & labrador	28.00
DE42	'21 $15 Mallard	28.00

FL8

FLORIDA

NO.	DESCRIPTION	F-VF NH
FL1	'79 $3.25 Green-winged teal	160.00
FL2	'80 $3.25 Pintails	18.00
FL3	'81 $3.25 Wigeon	18.00
FL4	'82 $3.25 Ring-necked ducks	18.00
FL5	'83 $3.25 Buffleheads	55.00
FL6	'84 $3.25 Hooded merganser	20.00
FL7	'85 $3.25 Wood ducks	18.00
FL8	'86 $3 Canvasbacks	14.00
FL9	'87 $3.50 Mallards	13.00
FL10	'88 $3.50 Redheads	12.00
FL11	'89 $3.50 Blue-winged teal	12.00
FL12	'90 $3.50 Wood ducks	13.00
FL13	'91 $3.50 Northern Pintails	12.00
FL14	'92 $3.50 Ruddy duck	12.00
FL15	'93 $3.50 American wigeon	12.00
FL16	'94 $3.50 Mottled duck	12.00
FL17	'95 $3.50 Fulvous whistling duck	13.00
FL18	'96 $3.50 Goldeneyes	23.00
FL19	'97 ($3) Hooded mergansers	19.00
FL20	'98 $3 Shoveler	36.00
FL21	'99 $3 Pintail	18.00
FL22	'00 $3 Ring-necked duck	18.00
FL23	'01 $3 Canvasback	18.00
FL24	'02 $3 Mottled duck	66.00
....	'03 $3.50 Green-winged teal	135.00

GA1

GEORGIA

NO.	DESCRIPTION	F-VF NH
GA1	'85 $5.50 Wood ducks	19.00
GA2	'86 $5.50 Mallards	12.00
GA3	'87 $5.50 Canada geese	12.00
GA4	'88 $5.50 Ring-necked ducks	12.00
GA5	'89 $5.50 Duckling & golden retriever puppy	22.00
GA6	'90 $5.50 Wood ducks	12.00
GA7	'91 $5.50 Green-winged teal	12.00
GA8	'92 $5.50 Buffleheads	18.00
GA9	'93 $5.50 Mallards	18.00
GA10	'94 $5.50 Ring-necked ducks	18.00
GA11	'95 $5.50 Wigeons, Labrador retriever	42.00
GA12	'96 $5.50 Black ducks	35.00
GA13	'97 $5.50 Lesser Scaup, Lighthouse	58.00
GA14	'98 $5.50 Black Lab with ring-necked ducks	37.00
GA15	'99 $5.50 Pintails	35.00

HI1

HAWAII

NO.	DESCRIPTION	F-VF NH
HI1	'96 $5 Nene geese	13.00
HI2	'97 $5 Hawaiian duck	13.00
HI3	'98 $5 Wild turkey	15.00
HI4	'99 $5 Ring-necked pheasant	18.00
HI5	'00 $5 Erckel's francolin	15.00
HI6	'01 $5 Japanese green pheasant	15.00
HI7	'02 $10 Chukar partridge	19.00
HI8	'03 $10 Nene geese	19.00
HI9	'04 $10 Nene geese	19.00
HI10	'05 $10 California quail	19.00
HI11	'06 $10 Black francolin	19.00
HI12	'07 $10 Gray francolin	19.00
HI13	'08 $10 Chukar partridge	19.00
HI14	'09 $10 California quail	19.00
HI15	'11 $10 Green pheasant	17.50
HI16	'11 $10 Wild turkey	17.50
HI17	'12 $10 Mouflon sheep	17.50
HI18	'15 $10 Mouflon sheep	17.50
HI19	'16 $10 Axis deer	17.50
HI20	'17 $10 Pheasant and wild sheep	17.50
HI21	'18 $10 Boar	17.50
HI22	'19 $10 Mouflon sheep	17.50
HI23	'20 $10 Black-tailed deer	17.50
HI24	'21 $10 Hybrid sheep	17.50

ID1

IDAHO

NO.	DESCRIPTION	F-VF NH
ID1	'87 $5.50 Cinnamon teal	20.00
ID2	'88 $5.50 Green-winged teal	16.00
ID3	'89 $6 Blue-winged teal	14.00
ID4	'90 $6 Trumpeter swans	28.00
ID6	'91 $6 Wigeons	12.00
ID7	'92 $6 Canada geese	18.00
ID8	'93 $6 Common goldeneye	17.00
ID9	'94 $6 Harlequin ducks	19.00
ID10	'95 $6 Wood ducks	20.00
ID11	'96 $6 Mallard	28.00
ID12	'97 $6.50 Shovelers	20.00
ID13	'98 $6.50 Canada geese	20.00

IL11

ILLINOIS

NO.	DESCRIPTION	F-VF NH
IL1	'75 $5 Mallard	400.00
IL2	'76 $5 Wood ducks	175.00
IL3	'77 $5 Canada goose	125.00
IL4	'78 $5 Canvasbacks	125.00
IL5	'79 $5 Pintail	85.00
IL6	'80 $5 Green-winged teal	85.00
IL7	'81 $5 Wigeons	85.00
IL8	'82 $5 Black ducks	60.00
IL9	'83 $5 Lesser scaup	75.00
IL10	'84 $5 Blue-winged teal	60.00
IL11	'85 $5 Redheads	21.00
IL12	'86 $5 Gadwalls	21.00
IL13	'87 $5 Buffleheads	18.00
IL14	'88 $5 Common goldeneyes	16.00
IL15	'89 $5 Ring-necked ducks	16.00
IL16	'90 $10 Lesser snow geese	21.00
IL17	'91 $10 Labrador retriever & Canada goose	21.00
IL18	'92 $10 Retriever & mallards	35.00
IL19	'93 $10 Pintail decoys & puppy	43.00
IL20	'94 $10 Canvasbacks & retrievers	43.00
IL21	'95 $10 Retriever, green-winged teal, decoys	43.00
IL22	'96 $10 Wood ducks	26.00
IL23	'97 $10 Canvasbacks	25.00
IL24	'98 $10 Canada geese	25.00
IL25	'99 $10 Canada geese, black Labrador retriever	35.00
IL26	'00 $10 Mallards & golden retriever	35.00
IL27	'01 $10 Pintails, yellow Labrador Retriever	35.00
IL28	'02 $10 Canvasbacks, Chesapeake Retriever	35.00
IL29	'03 $10 Chocolate Labrador, green-winged teal	32.00
IL30	'04 $10 Wood ducks	24.00
IL31	'05 $10 Green-winged teal	24.00
IL32	'06 $10 Northern pintails	24.00
IL33	'07 $10 Bufflehead	25.00
IL34	'08 $10 Greater scaup	45.00
IL35	'09 $10 Common goldeneye	85.00
IL36	'10 $15 Blue-winged teal	45.00

IN10

INDIANA

NO.	DESCRIPTION	F-VF NH
IN1	'76 $5 Green-winged teal	13.00
IN2	'77 $5 Pintail	13.00
IN3	'78 $5 Canada geese	13.00
IN4	'79 $5 Canvasbacks	13.00
IN5	'80 $5 Mallard ducklings	13.00
IN6	'81 $5 Hooded mergansers	13.00
IN7	'82 $5 Blue-winged teal	13.00
IN8	'83 $5 Snow geese	13.00
IN9	'84 $5 Redheads	13.00
IN10	'85 $5 Pintail	13.00
IN11	'86 $5 Wood duck	13.00
IN12	'87 $5 Canvasbacks	13.00
IN13	'88 $6.75 Redheads	13.00
IN14	'89 $6.75 Canada goose	13.00
IN15	'90 $6.75 Blue-winged teal	13.00
IN16	'91 $6.75 Mallards	13.00
IN17	'92 $6.75 Green-winged teal	13.00
IN18	'93 $6.75 Wood ducks	13.00
IN19	'94 $6.75 Pintail	13.00
IN20	'95 $6.75 Goldeneyes	13.00
IN21	'96 $6.75 Black ducks	13.00
IN22	'97 $6.75 Canada geese	13.00
IN23	'98 $6.75 Wigeon	13.00
IN24	'99 $6.75 Bluebills	13.00
IN25	'00 $6.75 Ring-necked duck	13.00
IN26	'01 $6.75 Green-winged teal	13.00
IN27	'02 $6.75 Green-winged teal	13.00
IN28	'03 $6.75 Shoveler	13.00
IN29	'04 $6.75 Hooded mergansers	13.00
IN30	'05 $6.75 Buffleheads	13.00
IN31	'06 $6.75 Gadwalls	13.00
IN32	'07 $6.75 Pintails	13.00
IN33	'08 $6.75 Shovelers	13.00
IN34	'09 $6.75 Snow geese	13.00
IN35	'10 $6.75 Black duck	20.00
IN36	'11 $6.75 Wigeon	13.00
IN37	'12 $6.75 Canada geese	20.00
IN38	'13 $6.75 Wood ducks	11.25
IN39	'14 $6.75 Blue-winged teal	11.25

IA14

IOWA

NO.	DESCRIPTION	F-VF NH
IA1	'72 $1 Mallards	125.00
IA2	'73 $1 Pintails	40.50
IA3	'74 $1 Gadwalls	95.00
IA4	'75 $1 Canada geese	100.00
IA5	'76 $1 Canvasbacks	31.00
IA6	'77 $1 Lesser scaup	28.00
IA7	'78 $1 Wood ducks	55.00
IA8	'79 $5 Buffleheads	275.00
IA9	'80 $5 Redheads	30.00
IA10	'81 $5 Green-winged teal	30.00
IA11	'82 $5 Snow geese	22.00
IA12	'83 $5 Wigeons	22.00
IA13	'84 $5 Wood ducks	40.00
IA14	'85 $5 Mallard & mallard Decoy	22.00
IA15	'86 $5 Blue-winged teal	14.00
IA16	'87 $5 Canada goose	14.00
IA17	'88 $5 Pintails	14.00
IA18	'89 $5 Blue-winged teal	14.00
IA19	'90 $5 Canvasbacks	14.00
IA20	'91 $5 Mallards	14.00
IA21	'92 $5 Labrador retriever & ducks	14.00
IA22	'93 $5 Mallards	14.00
IA23	'94 $5 Green-winged teal	14.00
IA24	'95 $5 Canada geese	14.00

NO.	DESCRIPTION	F-VF NH
IA25	'96 $5 Canvasbacks	14.00
IA26	'97 $5 Canada geese	14.00
IA27	'98 $5 Pintails	14.00
IA28	'99 $5 Trumpeter swan	19.00
IA29	'00 $5 Hooded merganser	16.00
IA30	'01 $5 Snow geese	15.00
IA31	'02 $8.50 Northern shoveler	27.00
IA32	'03 $8.50 Ruddy duck	20.00
IA33	'04 $8.50 Wood ducks	18.00
IA34	'05 $8.50 Green-winged teals	18.00
IA35	'06 $8.50 Ring-necked duck	18.00
IA36	'07 $8.50 Wigeon	18.00
IA37	'08 $8.50 Wood duck	18.00
IA38	'09 $10 Pintail	23.00
IA39	'10 $10 Green-winged teal	31.00
IA40	'11 $10 Hooded merganser	22.00
IA41	'12 $10 Blue-winged teal	17.50
IA42	'13 $10 Wood ducks	22.50
IA43	'14 $10 Redhead	17.50
IA44	'15 $10 Canada geese	25.00

KS1

KANSAS

NO.	DESCRIPTION	F-VF NH
KS1	'87 $3 Green-winged teal	15.00
KS2	'88 $3 Canada geese	11.00
KS3	'89 $3 Mallards	11.00
KS4	'90 $3 Wood ducks	11.00
KS5	'91 $3 Pintail	10.00
KS6	'92 $3 Canvasbacks	10.00
KS7	'93 $3 Mallards	12.00
KS8	'94 $3 Blue-winged teal	12.00
KS9	'95 $3 Barrow's goldeneye	12.00
KS10	'96 $3 Wigeon	13.00
KS11	'97 $3 Mallard (blue)	13.00
KS12	'98 $3 Mallard (green)	13.00
KS13	'99 $3 Mallard (red)	13.00
KS14	'00 $3 Mallard (purple)	13.00
KS15	'01 $3 Mallard (orange)	13.00
KS16	'02 $5 Pintail (blue)	13.00
KS17	'03 $5 Pintail (green)	16.00
KS18	'04 $5 Pintail (red)	16.00

KS1

KENTUCKY

NO.	DESCRIPTION	F-VF NH
KY1	'85 $5.25 Mallards	19.00
KY2	'86 $5.25 Wood ducks	13.00
KY3	'87 $5.25 Black ducks	14.00
KY4	'88 $5.25 Canada geese	14.00
KY5	'89 $5.25 Retriever & canvasbacks	19.00
KY6	'90 $5.25 Wigeons	12.00
KY7	'91 $5.25 Pintails	13.00
KY8	'92 $5.25 Green-winged teal	18.00
KY9	'93 $5.25 Canvasbacks & decoy	25.00
KY10	'94 $5.25 Canada goose	21.00
KY11	'95 $7.50 Retriever, decoy, ringnecks	29.00
KY12	'96 $7.50 Blue-winged teal	18.00
KY13	'97 $7.50 Shovelers	18.00
KY14	'98 $7.50 Gadwalls	19.00
KY15	'99 $7.50 Common goldeneyes	19.00
KY16	'00 $7.50 Hooded mergansers	26.00
KY17	'01 $7.50 Mallard	18.00
KY18	'02 $7.50 Pintails	18.00
KY19	'03 $7.50 Snow goose	18.00
KY20	'04 $7.50 Black ducks	19.00
KY21	'05 $7.50 Canada geese	18.00
KY22	'06 $7.50 Mallards	18.00
KY23	'07 $7.50 Green-winged teal	18.00
KY24	'08 $7.50 Pintails	18.00
KY25	'09 $7.50 Snow geese	18.00

LA1

LOUISIANA

NO.	DESCRIPTION	F-VF NH
LA1	'89 $5 Blue-winged teal	15.00
LA1a	'89 $7.50 Blue-winged teal	20.00
LA2	'90 $5 Green-winged teal	12.00
LA2a	'90 $7.50 Green-winged teal	15.00
LA3	'91 $5 Wood ducks	12.00
LA3a	'91 $7.50 Wood ducks	18.00
LA4	'92 $5 Pintails	15.00
LA4a	'92 $7.50 Pintails	18.00
LA5	'93 $5 American wigeon	15.00
LA5a	'93 $7.50 American wigeon	18.00
LA6	'94 $5 Mottled duck	16.00
LA6a	'94 $7.50 Mottled duck	18.00
LA7	'95 $5 Speckle bellied goose	16.00
LA7a	'95 $7.50 Speckle bellied goose	18.00
LA8	'96 $5 Gadwall	15.00
LA8a	'96 $7.50 Gadwall	18.00
LA9	'97 $5.00 Ring-necked duck	16.00
LA9a	'97 $13.50 Ring-necked duck	30.00
LA10	'98 $5.50 Mallards	15.00
LA10a	'98 $13.50 Mallards	30.00
LA11	'99 $5.50 Snow geese	15.00
LA11a	'99 $13.50 Snow geese	30.00
LA12	'00 $5.50 Lesser scaup	15.00
LA12a	'00 $13.50 Lesser scaup	45.00
LA13	'01 $5.50 Northern shoveler	15.00
LA13a	'01 $13.50 Northern shoveler	45.00
LA14	'02 $5.50 Canvasbacks	15.00
LA14a	'02 $25 Canvasbacks	45.00
LA15	'03 $5.50 Redhead	15.00
LA15a	'03 $25.00 Redhead	45.00
LA16	'04 $5.50 Hooded merganser	15.00
LA16a	'04 $25 Hooded merganser	45.00
LA17	'05 $5.50 Pintails and Labrador retriever	15.00
LA17a	'05 $25 Pintails and Labrador retriever	45.00
LA18	'06 $5.50 Mallards, Labrador retriever	15.00
LA18a	'06 $25 Mallards, Labrador retriever	45.00
LA19	'07 $5.50 Mallards, Labrador retriever	15.00
LA19a	'07 $25 Mallards, Labrador retriever	40.00
LA20	'08 $5.50 Wood ducks, golden retriever	15.00
LA20a	'08 $25 Wood ducks, golden retriever	62.50
LA21	'09 $5.50 Ducks, Chesapeake Bay retriever	15.00
LA21a	'09 $25 Ducks, Chesapeake Bay retriever	40.00
LA22	'10 $5.50 Pintails	15.00
LA22a	'10 $25 Pintails	40.00
LA23	'11 $5.50 Wood ducks	20.00
LA23a	'11 $25 Wood ducks	41.00
LA24	'12 $5.50 Wigeons	20.00
LA24a	'12 $25 Wigeons	35.00
LA25	'13 $5.50 Mallards	15.00
LA25a	'13 $25 Mallards	35.00
LA26	'14 $5.50 White-fronted geese	15.00
LA26a	'14 $25 White-fronted geese	35.00
LA27	'15 $5.50 Blue-winged teal	15.00
LA27a	'15 $25 Blue-winged teal	50.00
LA28	'16 $5.50 Gadwalls	35.00
LA28a	'16 $25 Gadwalls	80.00
LA29	'17 $5.50 Green-winged teal	40.00
LA29a	'17 $25 Green-tailed Teal	80.00
LA30	'18 $5.50 Canvasbacks	40.00
LA30a	'18 $25 Canvasbacks	80.00
LA31	'19 $5.50 Shovelers	40.00
LA31a	'19 $25 Shovelers	80.00
LA32	'20 $5.50 Ring-necked ducks	40.00
LA32a	'20 $25 Ring-necked ducks	80.00
LA33	'21 $5.50 Mottled duck	40.00
LA33a	'21 $25 Mottled duck	80.00

ME2

MAINE

NO.	DESCRIPTION	F-VF NH
ME1	'84 $2.50 Black ducks	25.00
ME2	'85 $2.50 Common eiders	45.00
ME3	'86 $2.50 Wood ducks	13.00
ME4	'87 $2.50 Buffleheads	11.00
ME5	'88 $2.50 Green-winged teal	11.00
ME6	'89 $2.50 Common goldeneyes	10.00
ME7	'90 $2.50 Canada geese	10.00
ME8	'91 $2.50 Ring-necked duck	10.00
ME9	'92 $2.50 Oldsquaw	10.00
ME10	'93 $2.50 Hooded merganser	10.00
ME11	'94 $2.50 Mallards	13.00
ME12	'95 $2.50 White-winged scoters	15.00
ME13	'96 $2.50 Blue-winged teal	15.00
ME14	'97 $2.50 Greater scaup	15.00
ME15	'98 $2.50 Surf scoters	15.00
ME16	'99 $2.50 Black duck	12.00
ME17	'00 $2.50 Common eider	10.00
ME18	'01 $2.50 Wood duck	10.00
ME19	'02 $2.50 Bufflehead	10.00
ME20	'03 $5.50 Green-winged teal	18.00
ME21	'04 $8.50 Barrow's goldeneyes	18.00
ME22	'05 $8.50 Canada goose	18.00
ME23	'06 $7.50 Ring-necked ducks	18.00
ME24	'07 $7.50 Long-tailed ducks	18.00
ME25	'08 $7.50 Hooded mergansers	18.00
ME26	'09 $7.50 Mallards	18.00
ME27	'10 $7.50 Harlequin ducks	18.00
ME28	'11 $7.50 Wood ducks	15.00
ME29	'12 $7.50 Ring-necked ducks	15.00
ME30	'13 $7.50 Greater scaup	15.00
ME31	'14 $7.50 Wigeon	15.00
ME32	'15 $7.50 Canvasbacks	15.00
ME33	'16 $7.50 Blue-winged teal	15.00
ME34	'17 $7.50 Common eiders	15.00
ME35	'18 $7.50 Northern pintails	15.00
ME36	'19 $7.50 Canada goose	15.00
ME37	'20 $7.50 Red-breasted mergansers	18.00
ME38	'21 $7.50 Long-tailed ducks	18.00

MD1

MARYLAND

NO.	DESCRIPTION	F-VF NH
MD1	'74 $1.10 Mallards	15.00
MD2	'75 $1.10 Canada geese	15.00
MD3	'76 $1.10 Canvasbacks	15.00
MD4	'77 $1.10 Greater scaup	15.00
MD5	'78 $1.10 Redheads	15.00
MD6	'79 $1.10 Wood ducks	15.00
MD7	'80 $1.10 Pintail decoy	15.00
MD8	'81 $3 Wigeon	12.00
MD9	'82 $3 Canvasback	12.00
MD10	'83 $3 Wood duck	17.00
MD11	'84 $6 Black ducks	18.00
MD12	'85 $6 Canada geese	18.00
MD13	'86 $6 Hooded mergansers	18.00
MD14	'87 $6 Redheads	18.00
MD15	'88 $6 Ruddy ducks	18.00
MD16	'89 $6 Blue-winged teal	18.00
MD17	'90 $6 Lesser scaup	18.00
MD18	'91 $6 Shovelers	18.00
MD19	'92 $6 Bufflehead	18.00
MD20	'93 $6 Canvasbacks	18.00
MD21	'94 $6 Redheads	18.00
MD22	'95 $6 Mallards	40.00
MD23	'96 $6 Canada geese	50.00
MD24	'97 $6 Canvasbacks	18.00
MD25	'98 $6 Pintails	18.00
MD26	'99 $5 Wood ducks	18.00
MD27	'00 $6 Oldsquaws	24.00
MD28	'01 $6 American wigeon	18.00
MD29	'02 $9 Black scoters	24.00
MD30	'03 $9 Lesser scaup	24.00
MD31	'04 $9 Pintails	24.00
MD32	'05 $9 Ruddy duck	24.00
MD33	'06 $9 Canada geese	24.00
MD34	'07 $9 Wood ducks	24.00
MD35	'08 $9 Canvasbacks	18.00
MD36	'09 $9 Blue-winged teal	18.00
MD37	'10 $9 Hooded merganser	18.00
MD38	'11 $9 Canada geese	18.00
MD39	'12 ($9) Wigeons	18.00
MD40	'13 ($9) Lesser scaup	18.00
MD41	'14 ($9) Ring-necked duck	18.00
MD42	'15 ($9) Canvasback	18.00
MD43	'16 ($9) Shovelers	18.00
MD44	'17 ($9) Black ducks	18.00
MD45	'18 ($9) Green-winged teal	18.00
MD46	'19 ($9) Wood ducks	18.00
MD47	'20 ($9) Blue-winged teal	18.00
MD48	'21 ($9) Redheads	18.00

MA12

MASSACHUSETTS

NO.	DESCRIPTION	F-VF NH
MA1	'74 $1.25 Wood duck decoy	19.00
MA2	'75 $1.25 Pintail decoy	16.00
MA3	'76 $1.25 Canada goose decoy	16.00
MA4	'77 $1.25 Goldeneye decoy	16.00
MA5	'78 $1.25 Black duck decoy	18.00
MA6	'79 $1.25 Ruddy turnstone duck decoy	24.00
MA7	'80 $1.25 Oldsquaw decoy	19.00
MA8	'81 $1.25 Red-breasted merganser decoy	19.00
MA9	'82 $1.25 Greater yellowlegs decoy	19.00
MA10	'83 $1.25 Redhead decoy	19.00
MA11	'84 $1.25 White-winged scoter decoy	19.00
MA12	'85 $1.25 Ruddy duck decoy	19.00
MA13	'86 $1.25 Preening bluebill decoy	18.00
MA14	'87 $1.25 American wigeon decoy	18.00
MA15	'88 $1.25 Mallard decoy	18.00
MA16	'89 $1.25 Brant decoy	18.00
MA17	'90 $1.25 Whistler hen decoy	18.00
MA18	'91 $5 Canvasback decoy	15.00
MA19	'92 $5 Black-bellied plover decoy	15.00
MA20	'93 $5 Red-breasted merganser decoy	15.00
MA21	'94 $5 White-winged scoter decoy	15.00
MA22	'95 $5 Female hooded merganser decoy	15.00
MA23	'96 $5 Eider decoy	15.00
MA24	'97 $5 Curlew shorebird decoy	15.00
MA25	'98 $5 Canada goose decoy	15.00
MA26	'99 $5 Oldsquaw decoy	15.00
MA27	'00 $5 Merganser hen decoy	15.00
MA28	'01 $5 Black duck decoy	15.00
MA29	'02 $5 Bufflehead decoy	15.00
MA30	'03 $5 Green-winged teal decoy	14.00
MA31	'04 $5 Wood duck decoy	14.00
MA32	'05 $5 Oldsquaw drake decoy	14.00
MA33	'06 $5 Long-billed curlew decoy	14.00
MA34	'07 $5 Goldeneye decoy	14.00
MA35	'08 $5 Black duck decoy	14.00
MA36	'09 $5 White-winged scoter decoy	14.00

NO.	DESCRIPTION	F-VF NH
MA37	'10 $5 Canada goose decoy	14.00
MA38	'11 $5 Brant decoy	14.00

MI10

MICHIGAN

NO.	DESCRIPTION	F-VF NH
MI1	'76 $2.10 Wood duck	7.00
MI2	'77 $2.10 Canvasbacks	355.00
MI3	'78 $2.10 Mallards	32.00
MI4	'79 $2.10 Canada geese	77.00
MI5	'80 $3.75 Lesser scaup	25.00
MI6	'81 $3.75 Buffleheads	31.00
MI7	'82 $3.75 Redheads	31.00
MI8	'83 $3.75 Wood ducks	31.00
MI9	'84 $3.75 (surcharge on $3.25) Pintails	31.00
MI10	'85 $3.75 Ring-necked ducks	31.00
MI11	'86 $3.75 Common goldeneyes	28.00
MI12	'87 $3.85 Green-winged teal	15.00
MI13	'88 $3.85 Canada geese	12.00
MI14	'89 $3.85 Wigeons	13.00
MI15	'90 $3.85 Wood ducks	13.00
MI16	'91 $3.85 Blue-winged teal	13.00
MI17	'92 $3.85 Red-breasted merganser	11.00
MI18	'93 $3.85 Hooded merganser	11.00
MI19	'94 $3.85 Black duck	11.00
MI20	'95 $4.35 Blue-winged teal	11.00
MI21	'96 $4.35 Canada geese	11.00
MI22	'97 $5 Canvasbacks	30.00
MI23	'98 $5 Pintail	11.00
MI24	'99 $5 Shoveler	13.00
MI25	'00 $5 Mallards	48.00
MI26	'01 $5 Ruddy duck	12.00
MI27	'02 $5 Wigeons	12.00
MI28	'03 $5 Redheads	12.00
MI29	'04 $5 Wood duck	12.00
MI30	'05 $5 Blue-winged teals	12.00
MI31	'06 $5 Wigeon	12.00
MI32	'07 $5 Pintails	12.00
MI33	'08 $5 Wood ducks	12.00
MI34	'09 $5 Canvasbacks	12.00
MI35	'10 $5 Buffleheads	12.00
MI36	'11 $5 Mallard	10.00
MI37	'12 $5 Ring-necked ducks	10.00
MI38	'13 $5 Black duck	10.00
MI39	'14 $5 Long-tailed ducks	10.00
MI40	'15 $6 Common goldeneyes	10.00
MI41	'16 $6 Green-winged teal	10.00
MI42	'17 $6 Shovelers	10.00
MI43	'18 $6 Wigeons and Black Labrador	10.00
MI44	'19 $6 Pintails	10.00
MI45	'20 $6 Canada geese	15.00
MI46	'21 $6 Wood duck	15.00

MN2

MINNESOTA

NO.	DESCRIPTION	F-VF NH
MN1	'77 $3 Mallards	18.00
MN2	'78 $3 Lesser scaup	15.00
MN3	'79 $3 Pintails	15.00
MN4	'80 $3 Canvasbacks	18.00
MN5	'81 $3 Canada geese	18.00
MN6	'82 $3 Redheads	18.00
MN7	'83 $3 Blue geese & snow goose	18.00
MN8	'84 $3 Wood ducks	18.00
MN9	'85 $3 White-fronted geese	12.00
MN10	'86 $5 Lesser Scaup	12.00
MN11	'87 $5 Common goldeneyes	15.00
MN12	'88 $5 Buffleheads	12.00
MN13	'89 $5 Wigeons	12.00
MN14	'90 $5 Hooded mergansers	25.00
MN15	'91 $5 Ross's geese	12.00
MN16	'92 $5 Barrow's goldeneyes	12.00
MN17	'93 $5 Blue-winged teal	12.00
MN18	'94 $5 Ring-necked duck	12.00
MN19	'95 $5 Gadwall	12.00
MN20	'96 $5 Greater scaup	14.00
MN21	'97 $5 Shoveler with decoy	14.00
MN22	'98 $5 Harlequin ducks	14.00
MN23	'99 $5 Green-winged teal	14.00
MN24	'00 $5 Red-breasted merganser	25.00
MN25	'01 $5 Black duck	30.00
MN26	'02 $5 Ruddy duck	18.00
MN27	'03 $5 Long-tailed duck	18.00
MN28	'04 $7.50 Common merganser	18.00
MN29	'05 $7.50 White-winged scoters & lighthouse	18.00
MN30	'06 $7.50 Mallard	18.00
MN31	'07 $7.50 Lesser scaups	18.00
MN32	'08 $7.50 Ross's geese	18.00
MN33	'09 $7.50 Common goldeneyes	18.00
MN34	'10 $7.50 Wood duck	18.00
MN35	'11 $7.50 Red-breasted merganser	18.00
MN36	'12 $7.50 Ruddy duck	18.00
MN37	'13 $7.50 Pintail	20.00
MN38	'14 $7.50 Canada geese	25.00
MN39	'15 $7.50 Harlequin duck	25.00
MN40	'16 $7.50 Wigeon	20.00
MN41	'17 $7.50 Redheads	20.00
MN42	'18 $7.50 White-winged scoters	20.00
MN43	'19 $7.50 Gadwall	20.00
MN44	'20 $7.50 Snow geese	20.00
MN45	'21 $7.50 Greater scaup	20.00

MS10

MISSISSIPPI

NO.	DESCRIPTION	F-VF NH
MS1	'76 $2 Wood duck	27.00
MS2	'77 $2 Mallards	13.00
MS3	'78 $2 Green-winged teal	13.00
MS4	'79 $2 Canvasbacks	12.00
MS5	'80 $2 Pintails	12.00
MS6	'81 $2 Redheads	12.00
MS7	'82 $2 Canada geese	19.00
MS8	'83 $2 Lesser scaup	12.00
MS9	'84 $2 Black ducks	12.00
MS10	'85 $2 Mallards	20.00
MS11	'86 $2 Wigeons	12.00
MS12	'87 $2 Ring-necked ducks	12.00
MS13	'88 $2 Snow geese	12.00
MS14	'89 $2 Wood ducks	9.00
MS15	'90 $2 Snow geese	17.00
MS16	'91 $2 Labrador retriever & canvasbacks	11.00
MS17	'92 $2 Green-winged teal	10.00
MS18	'93 $5 Mallards	11.00
MS19	'94 $5 Canvasbacks	15.00
MS20	'95 $5 Blue-winged teal	17.00
MS21	'96 $5 Hooded merganser	23.00
MS22	'97 $5 Wood duck	30.00
MS23	'98 $5 Pintails	15.00
MS24	'99 $5 Ring-necked duck	15.00
MS24a	'99 $5 Ring-necked duck, S/A, die-cut	15.00
MS25	'00 $5 Mallards	15.00
MS25a	'00 $5 Mallards, S/A, die cut	450.00
MS26	'01 $10 Gadwall	15.00
MS26a	'01 $10 Gadwall, S/A, die cut	15.00
MS27	'02 $10 Wood duck	15.00
MS27a	'02 $10 Wood duck, S/A, die cut	15.00
MS28	'03 $10 Pintail	15.00
MS28a	'03 $10 Pintail, S/A, die cut	15.00
MS29	'04 $10 Wood ducks	15.00
MS29a	'04 $10 Wood ducks, S/A, die cut	15.00
MS30	'05 $10 Blue-winged teal	15.00
MS30a	'05 $10 Blue-winged teal, S/A, die cut	15.00
MS30b	'05 $15 Blue-winged teal, non-resident	24.00
MS31	'06 $10 Labrador retriever	15.00
MS31a	'06 $10 Labrador retriever, S/A, die-cut	15.00
MS31b	'06 $15 Labrador retriever, non-resident	24.00
MS32	'07 $10 Wood ducks	15.00
MS32a	'07 $10 Wood duck, S/A, die-cut	15.00
MS32b	'07 $10 Wood ducks, non-resident	24.00
MS33	'08 $10 Green-winged teal	15.00
MS33a	'08 $10 Green-winged teal, S/A, die-cut	15.00
MS33b	'08 $15 Green-winged teal, non-resident	24.00
MS34	'09 $10 Blue-winged teal	15.00
MS34a	'09 $10 Blue-winged teal, S/A, die-cut	15.00
MS34b	'09 $15 Blue-winged teal, non-resident	24.00
MS35	'10 $10 Mallards	15.00
MS35a	'10 $10 Mallards, S/A, die-cut	15.00
MS35b	'10 $15 Mallards, non-resident	24.00
MS36	'11 $10 Wood duck	15.00
MS36a	'11 $10 Wood duck S/A, die-cut	15.00
MS36b	'11 $15 Wood duck, non-resident	24.00
MS37	'12 $10 Green-winged teal	15.00
MS37a	'12 $10 Green-winged teal, S/A, die-cut	15.00
MS37b	'12 $15 Green-winged teal, non-resident	24.00
MS38	'13 $10 Mallard	15.00
MS38a	'13 $10 Mallard, S/A, die-cut	15.00
MS38b	'13 $15 Mallard, non-resident	24.00
MS39	'14 $10 Wood ducks	17.00
MS39a	'14 $10 Wood ducks, S/A, die-cut	17.00
MS39b	'14 $15 Wood ducks, non-resident	24.00
MS40	'15 $10 Pintail	17.00
MS40a	'15 $10 Pintail, S/A, die-cut	17.00
MS40b	'15 $10 Pintail, non-resident	24.00
MS41	'16 $10 Pintail	20.00
MS41a	'16 $10 Pintail, S/A, die-cut	20.00
MS41b	'16 $10 Pintail, non-resident	30.00
MS42	'17 $10 Gadwall	20.00
MS42a	'17 $10 Gadwall, S/A, die-cut	20.00
MS42b	'17 $15 Gadwall, non-resident	30.00
MS43	'18 $10 Canvasback	20.00
MS43a	'18 $10 Canvasback, S/A, die-cut	20.00
MS43b	'18 $15 Canvasback, non-resident	30.00
MS44	'19 $10 Redheads	20.00
MS44a	'19 $10 Redheads, S/A, die-cut	20.00
MS44b	'19 $15 Redheads, non-resident	30.00
MS45	'20 $10 Black-bellied whistling duck	20.00
MS45a	'20 $10 Black-bellied whistling duck, die-cut	20.00
MS45b	'20 $15 Black-bellied whistling duck, non-resident	30.00
MS46	'21 $10 Black duck	20.00
MS46a	'21 $10 Black duck, die-cut	20.00
MS46b	'21 $15 Black duck, non-resident	30.00

MO9

MISSOURI

NO.	DESCRIPTION	F-VF NH
MO1	'79 $3.40 Canada geese	400.00
MO2	'80 $3.40 Wood ducks	90.00
MO3	'81 $3 Lesser scaup	55.00
MO4	'82 $3 Buffleheads	55.00
MO5	'83 $3 Blue-winged teal	57.00
MO6	'84 $3 Mallards	55.00
MO7	'85 $3 American wigeons	28.00
MO8	'86 $3 Hooded mergansers	18.00
MO9	'87 $3 Pintails	15.00
MO10	'88 $3 Canvasback	14.00
MO11	'89 $3 Ring-necked ducks	11.00
MO12	'90 $5 Redheads	10.00
MO13	'91 $5 Snow geese	10.00
MO14	'92 $5 Gadwalls	10.00
MO15	'93 $5 Green-winged teal	10.00
MO16	'94 $5 White-fronted goose	10.00
MO17	'95 $5 Goldeneyes	12.00
MO18	'96 $5 Black duck	16.00

MT34

MONTANA

NO.	DESCRIPTION	F-VF NH
MT34	'86 $5 Canada geese	15.00
MT35	'87 $5 Redheads	18.00
MT36	'88 $5 Mallards	15.00
MT37	'89 $5 Black Labrador retriever & pintail	15.00
MT38	'90 $5 Blue-winged teal & cinnamon teal	10.00
MT39	'91 $5 Snow geese	10.00
MT40	'92 $5 Wood ducks	10.00
MT41	'93 $5 Harlequin ducks	10.00
MT42	'94 $5 Wigeons	10.00
MT43	'95 $5 Tundra swans	10.00
MT44	'96 $5 Canvasbacks	10.00
MT45	'97 $5 Golden retriever & mallard	10.00
MT46	'98 $5 Gadwalls	10.00
MT47	'99 $5 Barrow's goldeneye	10.00
MT48	'00 $5 Mallard decoy, Chesapeake retriever	10.00
MT49	'01 $5 Canada geese, steamboat	10.00
MT50	'02 ($5) Sandhill crane	10.00
MT51	'03 $5 Mallards	80.00

NE1

NEBRASKA

NO.	DESCRIPTION	F-VF NH
NE1	'91 $6 Canada geese	12.00
NE2	'92 $6 Pintails	12.00
NE3	'93 $6 Canvasbacks	12.00
NE4	'94 $6 Mallards	12.00
NE5	'95 $6 Wood ducks	12.00
NE6	'06 $5 Wood ducks	12.00
NE7	'07 $5 Canvasbacks	12.00
NE8	'08 $5 Trumpeter swans	12.00
NE9	'09 $5 Northern pintail	12.00

NV7

NEVADA

NO.	DESCRIPTION	F-VF NH
NV1	'79 $2 Canvasbacks & decoy	50.00
NV2	'80 $2 Cinnamon teal	10.00
NV3	'81 $2 Whistling swans	12.00
NV4	'82 $2 Shovelers	12.00
NV5	'83 $2 Gadwalls	12.00
NV6	'84 $2 Pintails	12.00
NV7	'85 $2 Canada geese	26.00
NV8	'86 $2 Redheads	26.00
NV9	'87 $2 Buffleheads	23.00
NV10	'88 $2 Canvasbacks	15.00
NV11	'89 $2 Ross's geese	21.00
NV12	'90 $5 Green-winged teal	21.00
NV13	'91 $5 White-faced ibis	15.00
NV14	'92 $5 American wigeon	14.00
NV15	'93 $5 Common goldeneye	14.00
NV16	'94 $5 Mallards	14.00
NV17	'95 $5 Wood duck	14.00
NV18	'96 $5 Ring-necked ducks	24.00
NV19	'97 $5 Ruddy ducks	14.00

NO.	DESCRIPTION	F-VF NH
NV20	'98 $5 Hooded merganser	19.00
NV21	'99 $5 Canvasback decoy	19.00
NV22	'00 $5 Canvasbacks	19.00
NV23	'01 $5 Lesser scaups	19.00
NV24	'02 $5 Cinnamon teal	15.00
NV25	'03 $5 Green-winged teal	15.00
NV26	'04 $10 Redheads	19.00
NV27	'05 $10 Gadwalls	19.00
NV28	'06 $10 Tundra swans	19.00
NV29	'07 $10 Wood ducks	19.00
NV30	'08 $10 Pintail	19.00
NV31	'09 $10 Canada goose	19.00
NV32	'10 $10 Shovelers	19.00
NV33	'11 $10 Green-winged teal	19.00
NV34	'12 $10 Wigeon	18.00
NV35	'13 $10 Snow goose	18.00
NV36	'14 $10 American coots	18.00
NV37	'15 $10 White-footed goose	18.00
NV38	'16 $10 Buffleheads	18.00
NV39	'17 $10 Ruddy duck	18.00

NH2

NEW HAMPSHIRE

NO.	DESCRIPTION	F-VF NH
NH1	'83 $4 Wood ducks	130.00
NH2	'84 $4 Mallards	100.00
NH3	'85 $4 Blue-winged teal	130.00
NH4	'86 $4 Hooded mergansers	25.00
NH5	'87 $4 Canada geese	12.00
NH6	'88 $4 Buffleheads	12.00
NH7	'89 $4 Black ducks	12.00
NH8	'90 $4 Green-winged teal	12.00
NH9	'91 $4 Golden retriever & mallards	16.00
NH10	'92 $4 Ring-necked ducks	12.00
NH11	'93 $4 Hooded mergansers	12.00
NH12	'94 $4 Common goldeneyes	12.00
NH13	'95 $4 Northern pintails	12.00
NH14	'96 $4 Surf scoters	16.00
NH15	'97 $4 Wood ducks	12.00
NH16	'98 $4 Canada geese	12.00
NH17	'99 $4 Mallards	12.00
NH18	'00 $4 Black ducks	12.00
NH19	'01 $4 Blue-winged teal	12.00
NH20	'02 $4 Pintails	12.00
NH21	'03 $4 Wood ducks	12.00
NH22	'04 $4 Wood ducks	12.00
NH23	'05 $4 Oldsquaw and lighthouse	12.00
NH24	'06 $4 Common eiders	12.00
NH25	'07 $4 Black ducks	12.00

NJ1

NEW JERSEY

NO.	DESCRIPTION	F-VF NH
NJ1	'84 $2.50 Canvasbacks	45.00
NJ1a	'84 $5 Canvasbacks	65.00
NJ2	'85 $2.50 Mallards	20.00
NJ2a	'85 $5 Mallards	24.00
NJ3	'86 $2.50 Pintails	23.00
NJ3a	'86 $5 Pintails	16.00
NJ4	'87 $2.50 Canada geese	24.00
NJ4a	'87 $5 Canada geese	22.00
NJ5	'88 $2.50 Green-winged teal	17.00
NJ5a	'88 $5 Green-winged teal	14.00
NJ6	'89 $2.50 Snow geese	16.00
NJ6a	'89 $5 Snow geese	16.00
NJ7	'90 $2.50 Wood ducks	18.00
NJ7a	'90 $5 Wood ducks	12.00
NJ8	'91 $2.50 Atlantic brant	18.00
NJ8a	'91 $5 Atlantic brant	16.00
NJ9	'92 $2.50 Bluebills	16.00
NJ9a	'92 $5 Bluebills	14.00
NJ10	'93 $2.50 Buffleheads	14.00
NJ10a	'93 $5 Buffleheads	14.00
NJ11	'94 $2.50 Black ducks	16.00
NJ11a	'94 $5 Black ducks	16.00
NJ12	'95 $2.50 Wigeons, lighthouse	16.00
NJ12a	'95 $5 Wigeons, lighthouse	16.00
NJ13	'96 $2.50 Goldeneyes	15.00
NJ13a	'96 $5 Goldeneyes	18.00
NJ14	'97 $5 Oldsquaws	16.00
NJ14a	'97 $10 Oldsquaws	22.00
NJ15	'98 $5 Mallards	17.00
NJ15a	'98 $10.00 Mallards	20.00
NJ16	'99 $5 Redheads	17.00
NJ16a	'99 $10 Redheads	20.00
NJ17	'00 $5 Canvasbacks	18.00
NJ17a	'00 $10 Canvasbacks	20.00
NJ18	'01 $5 Tundra swans	16.00
NJ18a	'01 $10 Tundra swans	20.00
NJ19	'02 $5 Wood ducks	16.00
NJ19a	'02 $10 Wood ducks	20.00
NJ20	'03 $5 Pintails & Black Labrador	15.00
NJ20a	'03 $10 Pintails & Black Labrador	20.00
NJ21	'04 $5 Hooded merganser decoy & puppy	13.00
NJ21a	'04 $10 Hooded merganser decoy & puppy	20.00
NJ22	'05 $5 Canvasback decoys and retriever	15.00
NJ22a	'05 $10 Canvasback decoys and retriever	20.00
NJ23	'06 $5 Wood duck decoy, Golden retriever	15.00
NJ23a	'06 $10 Wood duck decoy, Golden retriever	20.00
NJ24	'07 $5 Green-winged teal, Labrador retriever	12.00
NJ24a	'07 $10 Green-winged teal, Labrador retriever	18.00
NJ25	'08 $5 Canvasbacks	12.00
NJ25a	'08 $10 Canvasbacks	18.00

NM1

NEW MEXICO

NO.	DESCRIPTION	F-VF NH
NM1	'91 $7.50 Pintails	18.00
NM2	'92 $7.50 American Wigeon	18.00
NM3	'93 $7.50 Mallard	18.00
NM4	'94 $7.50 Green-winged teal	25.00

NY3

NEW YORK

NO.	DESCRIPTION	F-VF NH
NY1	'85 $5.50 Canada geese	14.00
NY2	'86 $5.50 Mallards	10.00
NY3	'87 $5.50 Wood ducks	10.00
NY4	'88 $5.50 Pintails	10.00
NY5	'89 $5.50 Greater scaup	10.00
NY6	'90 $5.50 Canvasbacks	10.00
NY7	'91 $5.50 Redheads	12.00
NY8	'92 $5.50 Wood ducks	12.00
NY9	'93 $5.50 Blue-winged teal	12.00
NY10	'94 $5.50 Canada geese	12.00
NY11	'95 $5.50 Common goldeneye	12.00
NY12	'96 $5.50 Common loon	12.00
NY13	'97 $5.50 Hooded merganser	12.00
NY14	'98 $5.50 Osprey	12.00
NY15	'99 $5.50 Buffleheads	15.00
NY16	'00 $5.50 Wood ducks	20.00
NY17	'01 $5.50 Pintails	12.00
NY18	'02 $5.50 Canvasbacks	12.00

NC1

NORTH CAROLINA

NO.	DESCRIPTION	F-VF NH
NC1	'83 $5.50 Mallards	60.00
NC2	'84 $5.50 Wood ducks	45.00
NC3	'85 $5.50 Canvasbacks	25.00
NC4	'86 $5.50 Canada geese	25.00
NC5	'87 $5.50 Pintails	18.00
NC6	'88 $5 Green-winged teal	12.00
NC7	'89 $5 Snow geese	18.00
NC8	'90 $5 Redheads	18.00
NC9	'91 $5 Blue-winged teals	10.00
NC10	'92 $5 American wigeons	18.00
NC11	'93 $5 Tundra swans	18.00
NC12	'94 $5 Buffleheads	18.00
NC13	'95 $5 Brant, lighthouse	18.00
NC14	'96 $5 Pintails	18.00
NC15	'97 $5 Wood ducks, perf.	18.00
NC15a	'97 $5 Wood ducks, self-adhesive, die cut	45.00
NC16	'98 $5 Canada geese, perf.	15.00
NC16a	'98 $5 Canada geese, self-adhesive	36.00
NC17	'99 $5 Green-winged teal, perf.	22.00
NC17a	'99 $5 Green-winged teal, self-adhesive	25.00
NC18	'00 $10 Green-winged teal, perf.	24.00
NC18a	'00 $10 Green-winged teal, self-adhesive	36.00
NC19	'01 $10 Black duck, lighthouse, perf.	23.00
NC19a	'01 $10 Black duck, lighthouse, self-adhesive	25.00
NC20	'02 $10 Pintails, hunters, dog, perf.	23.00
NC20a	'02 $10 Pintails, hunters, dog, self-adhesive	35.00
NC21	'03 $10 Ring-necked duck & Brittney Spaniel	20.00
NC21a	'03 $10 Ring-necked duck & Brittney Spaniel, S/A	30.00
NC22	'04 $10 Mallard, perf.	20.00
NC22a	'04 $10 Mallard, self-adhesive	25.00
NC23	'05 $10 Green-winged teals, perf.	24.00
NC23a	'05 $10 Green-winged teals, self-adhesive	25.00
NC24	'06 $10 Lesser scaups, perf.	23.00
NC24a	'06 $10 Lesser scaups, self-adhesive, die-cut	25.00
NC25	'07 $10 Wood ducks	23.00
NC25a	'07 $10 Wood ducks, self-adhesive, die cut	25.00
NC26	'08 $10 Surf scoters, perf.	20.00
NC26a	'08 $10 Surf scoters, self-adhesive, die cut	25.00
NC27	'09 $10 Wigeons, perf.	18.00
NC27a	'09 $10 Wigeons, self-adhesive	24.00
NC28	'10 $10 Snow geese, perf.	19.00
NC28a	'10 $10 Snow geese, self-adhesive, die cut	24.00
NC29	'11 $10 Canada geese, perf.	18.00
NC29a	'11 $10 Canada geese self-adhesive	19.00
NC30	'12 $10 Redheads, perf.	17.00
NC30a	'12 $10 Redheads, self-adehesive	18.00
NC31	'13 $10 Shovelers, perf.	17.00
NC31a	'13 $10 Shovelers, self-adhesive	18.00
NC32	'14 $10 Hooded mergansers, perf.	17.00
NC32a	'14 $10 Hooded mergansers, self-adhesive	18.00
NC33	'15 $10 Black ducks, perf.	17.00
NC33a	'15 $10 Black ducks, self-adhesive, die-cut	20.00
NC34	'16 $13 Atlantic brant and lighthouse, perf.	24.00
NC34a	'16 $13 Atlantic brant and lighthouse, S/A	24.00
NC35	'17 $13 Gadwalls, perf.	24.00
NC35a	'17 $13 Gadwalls, self-adhesive	24.00
NC36	'18 $13 Canvasbacks, perf.	24.00
NC36a	'18 $13 Canvasbacks, self-adhesive	24.00
NC37	'19 $13 Ring-necked ducks, perf.	24.00
NC37a	'19 $13 Ring-necked ducks, self-adhesive	24.00
NC38	'20 $14 Tundra swans, perf.	24.00
NC38a	'20 $14 Tundra swans, self-adhesive	24.00
NC39	'21 $14 Blue-winged teals, perf.	24.00
NC39a	'21 $14 Blue-winged teals, self-adhesive	24.00

ND35

NORTH DAKOTA

NO.	DESCRIPTION	F-VF NH
ND32	'82 $9 Canada geese	120.00
ND35	'83 $9 Mallards	70.00
ND38	'84 $9 Canvasbacks	50.00
ND41	'85 $9 Greater scaup	25.00
ND44	'86 $9 Pintails	25.00
ND47	'87 $9 Snow geese	18.00
ND50	'88 $9 White-winged scoters	16.00
ND53	'89 $6 Redheads	12.00
ND56	'90 $6 Labrador retriever & mallard	12.00
ND59	'91 $6 Green-winged teal	12.00
ND62	'92 $6 Blue-winged teal	12.00
ND65	'93 $6 Wood ducks	12.00
ND67	'94 $6 Canada geese	12.00
ND69	'95 $6 Wigeon	12.00
ND71	'96 $6 Mallards	12.00
ND73	'97 $6 White-fronted geese	12.00
ND75	'98 $6 Blue-winged teal	12.00
ND77	'99 $6 Gadwalls	12.00
ND79	'00 $6 Pintails	12.00
ND81	'01 $6 Canada geese	12.00
ND83	'02 $6 Text, black on green	18.00
ND84	'03 $6 Text, black on green	18.00
ND85	'04 $6 Text, black on green	18.00
ND86	'05 $6 Text, black on green	15.00
ND87	'06 $6 black, green	13.00
ND88	'07 $6 Text, black on green	13.00
ND89	'08 $6 Text, black on green	13.00
ND90	'09 $6 Text, black on green	13.00
ND91	'10 $6 black, green	13.00
ND92	'11 $6 Black	10.00
ND93	'12 $6 Black, green	10.00
ND94	'13 $6 Black, green	10.00
ND95	'14 $10 Black, green	14.00
ND96	'15 $10 Black, green	14.00

OH4

OHIO

NO.	DESCRIPTION	F-VF NH
OH1	'82 $5.75 Wood ducks	60.00
OH2	'83 $5.75 Mallards	40.00
OH3	'84 $5.75 Green-winged teal	40.00
OH4	'85 $5.75 Redheads	35.00
OH5	'86 $5.75 Canvasback	35.00
OH6	'87 $6 Blue-winged teal	15.00
OH7	'88 $6 Common goldeneyes	12.00
OH8	'89 $6 Canada geese	12.00
OH9	'90 $9 Black ducks	18.00
OH10	'91 $9 Lesser scaup	18.00
OH11	'92 $9 Wood duck	18.00
OH12	'93 $9 Buffleheads	18.00
OH13	'94 $11 Mallards	22.00
OH14	'95 $11 Pintails	25.00
OH15	'96 $11 Hooded mergansers	25.00
OH16	'97 $11 Wigeons	22.00
OH17	'98 $11 Gadwall	22.00
OH18	'99 $11 Mallard	20.00
OH19	'00 $11 Buffleheads	20.00
OH20	'01 $11 Canvasback	20.00
OH21	'02 $11 Ring-necked ducks	20.00
OH22	'03 $11 Hooded mergansers	20.00
OH23	'04 $15 Tundra swans	20.00
OH24	'05 $15 Wood duck	20.00
OH25	'06 $15 Pintail	24.00
OH26	'07 $15 Canada goose	45.00
OH27	'08 $15 Green-winged teal	24.00
OH28	'09 $15 Common goldeneye	24.00
OH29	'10 $10 Ruddy ducks	24.00

NO.	DESCRIPTION	F-VF NH
OH30	'11 $15 Red-breasted merganser	40.00
OH31	'12 $15 Mallards	24.00
OH32	'13 $15 Blue-winged teal	24.00
OH33	'14 $15 Pintail	30.00
OH34	'15 $15 Shoveler	30.00
OH35	'16 $15 Wood ducks	30.00
OH36	'17 $15 Wigeons	30.00
OH37	'18 $15 Ring-necked ducks	30.00
OH38	'19 $15 Redheads	30.00
OH39	'20 $15 Black duck	30.00
OH40	'21 $15 Mallard	30.00

OK4

OKLAHOMA

NO.	DESCRIPTION	F-VF NH
OK1	'80 $4 Pintails	50.00
OK2	'81 $4 Canada goose	20.00
OK3	'82 $4 Green-winged teal	12.00
OK4	'83 $4 Wood ducks	12.00
OK5	'84 $4 Ring-necked ducks	12.00
OK6	'85 $4 Mallards	12.00
OK7	'86 $4 Snow geese	12.00
OK8	'87 $4 Canvasbacks	11.00
OK9	'88 $4 Wigeons	10.00
OK10	'89 $4 Redheads	10.00
OK11	'90 $4 Hooded merganser	10.00
OK12	'91 $4 Gadwalls	10.00
OK13	'92 $4 Lesser scaup	10.00
OK14	'93 $4 White-fronted geese	10.00
OK15	'94 $4 Blue-winged teal	10.00
OK16	'95 $4 Ruddy ducks	10.00
OK17	'96 $4 Buffleheads	10.00
OK18	'97 $4 Goldeneyes	10.00
OK19	'98 $4 Shovelers	10.00
OK20	'99 $4 Canvasbacks	10.00
OK21	'00 $4 Pintails	12.00
OK22	'01 $4 Canada goose	12.00
OK23	'02 $4 Green-winged teal	12.00
OK24	'03 $10 Wood duck	18.00
OK25	'04 $10 Mallard	18.00
OK26	'05 $10 Snow geese	18.00
OK27	'06 $10 Wigeons	18.00
OK28	'07 $10 Redheads	18.00
OK29	'08 $10 Mallards, Labrador retriever	18.00
OK30	'09 $10 Gadwalls	18.00
OK31	'10 $10 Ring-necked duck	18.00
OK32	'11 $10 Blue-winged teal	18.00
OK33	'12 $10 White-fronted goose	18.00
OK34	'13 $10 Common goldeneye	18.00
OK35	'14 $10 Canvasback	18.00
OK36	'15 $10 Pintails	18.00
OK37	'16 $10 Mallard	18.00
OK38	'17 $10 Green-winged teal	18.00
OK39	'18 $10 Shovelers	17.00
OK40	'19 $10 Wood duck	17.00
OK41	'20 $10 Canada geese	17.00
OK42	'21 $10 Wigeons	17.00

OR1

OREGON

NO.	DESCRIPTION	F-VF NH
OR1	'84 $5 Canada geese	25.00
OR2	'85 $5 Lesser snow goose	35.00
OR3	'86 $5 Pacific brant	18.00
OR4	'87 $5 White-fronted geese	16.00
OR5	'88 $5 Great Basin Canada geese	16.00
OR7	'89 $5 Black Labrador retriever & pintails	16.00
OR8	'90 $5 Mallards & golden retriever	16.00
OR9	'91 $5 Buffleheads & Chesapeake Bay retriever	16.00
OR10	'92 $5 Green-winged teal	16.00
OR11	'93 $5 Mallards	16.00
OR12	'94 $5 Pintails	16.00
OR14	'95 $5 Wood ducks	16.00
OR16	'96 $5 Mallard, wigeon, and pintail	16.00
OR18	'97 $5 Canvasbacks	16.00
OR20	'98 $5 Pintails	16.00
OR22	'99 $5 Canada geese	16.00
OR24	'00 $7.50 Canada geese, mallard, wigeon	16.00
OR25	'01 $7.50 Canvasbacks	16.00
OR26	'02 $7.50 American wigeon	16.00
OR27	'03 $7.50 Wood duck	16.00
OR28	'04 $7.50 Ross's goose	16.00
OR29	'05 $7.50 Hooded merganser	16.00
OR30	'06 $7.50 Pintail, mallard	16.00
OR31	'07 $7.50 Wood ducks	16.00
OR32	'08 $7.50 Pintails	16.00
OR33	'09 $7.50 Mallards	16.00
OR34	'10 $9.50 Wood duck	18.00
OR35	'11 $9.50 Canvasback	18.00
OR36	'12 $9.50 Mallard	18.00
OR37	'13 $9.50 Wigeons	18.00
OR38	'14 $9.50 Canada geese	18.00
OR39	'15 $9.50 Pintail	18.00
OR40	'16 $10.50 Common mergansers	20.00
OR41	'17 $10.50 Gadwalls	20.00
OR42	'18 $11 Buffleheads	20.00
OR43	'19 $11 White-fronted geese	20.00
OR44	'20 $11.50 Redheads	20.00
OR45	'21 $11.50 Cinnamon teals	20.00

PA1

PENNSYLVANIA

NO.	DESCRIPTION	F-VF NH
PA1	'83 $5.50 Wood ducks	14.00
PA2	'84 $5.50 Canada geese	10.00
PA3	'85 $5.50 Mallards	12.00
PA4	'86 $5.50 Blue-winged teal	12.00
PA5	'87 $5.50 Pintails	12.00
PA6	'88 $5.50 Wood ducks	12.00
PA7	'89 $5.50 Hooded mergansers	10.00
PA8	'90 $5.50 Canvasbacks	10.00
PA9	'91 $5.50 Wigeons	10.00
PA10	'92 $5.50 Canada geese	10.00
PA11	'93 $5.50 Northern shovelers	10.00
PA12	'94 $5.50 Pintails	10.00
PA13	'95 $5.50 Buffleheads	10.00
PA14	'96 $5.50 Black ducks	10.00
PA15	'97 $5.50 Hooded Merganser	10.00
PA16	'98 $5.50 Wood ducks	10.00
PA17	'99 $5.50 Ring-necked ducks	10.00
PA18	'00 $5.50 Green-winged teal	10.00
PA19	'01 ($5.50) Pintails	10.00
PA20	'02 $5.50 Snow geese	10.00
PA21	'03 $5.50 Canvasbacks	10.00
PA22	'04 $5.50 Hooded mergansers	10.00
PA23	'05 $5.50 Red-breasted mergansers	10.00
PA24	'06 $5.50 Pintails	10.00
PA25	'07 $5.50 Wood ducks	10.00
PA26	'08 $5.50 Redheads	10.00
PA27	'09 $5.50 Hooded merganser	10.00
PA28	'10 $5.50 Canvasbacks	10.50
PA29	'11 $5.50 Wigeons	10.50
PA30	'12 $5.50 Ruddy ducks	10.00
PA31	'13 $5.50 Black ducks	10.00
PA32	'14 $5.50 Shoveler	10.00
PA33	'15 $5.50 Green-winged teal	10.00
PA34	'16 $5.50 Pintails	10.00
PA35	'17 $5.50 Buffleheads	9.50
PA36	'18 $5.50 Mallards	9.50
PA37	'19 $5.50 Long-tailed ducks	9.50
PA38	'20 $5.50 Snow geese	9.50
PA39	'21 $5.50 Wood ducks	9.50

RI1

RHODE ISLAND

NO.	DESCRIPTION	F-VF NH
RI1	'89 $7.50 Canvasbacks	15.00
RI2	'90 $7.50 Canada geese	15.00
RI3	'91 $7.50 Wood ducks & Labrador retriever	25.00
RI4	'92 $7.50 Blue-winged teal	18.00
RI5	'93 $7.50 Pintails	18.00
RI6	'94 $7.50 Wood ducks	22.00
RI7	'95 $7.50 Hooded mergansers	18.00
RI8	'96 $7.50 Harlequin	24.00
RI9	'97 $7.50 Greater scaup	18.00
RI10	'98 $7.50 Black ducks	18.00
RI11	'99 $7.50 Common eiders	18.00
RI12	'00 $7.50 Canvasbacks	18.00
RI13	'01 $7.50 Mallard, black duck, lighthouse	18.00
RI14	'02 $7.50 White-winged scoter	17.00
RI15	'03 $7.50 Oldsquaw	15.00
RI16	'04 $7.50 Canvasbacks	15.00
RI17	'05 $7.50 Black ducks and lighthouse	15.00
RI18	'06 $7.50 Canvasbacks, lighthouse	15.00
RI19	'07 $7.50 Harlequin decoy	15.00
RI20	'08 $7.50 Mallard decoys	15.00
RI21	'09 $7.50 Hooded merganser	15.00
RI22	'10 $7.50 Red-breasted merganser	15.00
RI23	'11 $7.50 Barrow's goldeneye	15.00
RI24	'12 $7.50 Mallard	15.50
RI25	'13 $7.50 Canvasback	15.00
RI26	'14 $7.50 Canvasbacks	18.00
RI27	'15 $7.50 Green-winged teal	18.00
RI28	'16 $7.50 Wood duck	18.00
RI29	'17 $7.50 Lesser scaup	18.00
RI30	'18 $7.50 Harlequin, self-adhesive	18.50
RI31	'19 $7.50 Long-tailed duck	20.00
RI32	'20 $7.50 Canada geese	20.00
RI33	'21 $7.50 Mallard	20.00

SC5

SOUTH CAROLINA

NO.	DESCRIPTION	F-VF NH
SC1	'81 $5.50 Wood ducks	65.00
SC2	'82 $5.50 Mallards	100.00
SC3	'83 $5.50 Pintails	100.00
SC4	'84 $5.50 Canada geese	65.00
SC5	'85 $5.50 Green-winged teal	60.00
SC6	'86 $5.50 Canvasbacks	25.00
SC7	'87 $5.50 Black ducks	20.00
SC8	'88 $5.50 Wigeon & spaniel	18.00
SC9	'89 $5.50 Blue-winged teal	12.00
SC10	'90 $5.50 Wood ducks	12.00
SC11	'91 $5.50 Labrador retriever, pintails, & decoy	12.00
SC12	'92 $5.50 Buffleheads	17.00
SC13	'93 $5.50 Lesser scaups	17.00
SC14	'94 $5.50 Canvasbacks	17.00
SC15	'95 $5.50 Shovelers, lighthouse	17.00
SC16	'96 $5.50 Redheads, lighthouse	18.00
SC17	'97 $5.50 Oldsquaws	18.00
SC18	'98 $5.50 Green-winged teals	18.00
SC19	'99 $5.50 Barrow's goldeneyes	18.00
SC20	'00 $5.50 Wood ducks, Boykin spaniel	18.00
SC21	'01 $5.50 Mallard decoy, yellow Labrador	16.00
SC22	'02 $5.50 Wigeons, chocolate Labrador	16.00
SC23	'03 $5.50 Green-winged teal	16.00
SC24	'04 $5.50 Pintails, black Labrador	16.00
SC25	'05 $5.50 Canvasbacks	16.00
SC26	'06 $5.50 Black ducks	16.00
SC27	'07 $5.50 Redheads, Golden retriever	16.00
SC28	'08 $5.50 Blue-winged teal, Labrador retriever	20.00
SC29	'09 $5.50 Ring-necked duck, Labrador retriever	20.00
SC30	'10 $5.50 Wood duck and Boykin spaniel	20.00
SC31	'11 $5.50 Blue-winged teal, Labrador retriever	20.00
SC32	'12 $5.50 Green-winged teal, Golden Retriever	20.00
SC33	'13 $5.50 Black duck and Boykin Spaniel	20.00
SC34	'14 $5.50 Wood ducks	20.00
SC35	'15 $5.50 Hooded mergansers	20.00
SC36	'16 $5.50 Mottled ducks	20.00
SC37	'17 $5.50 Wigeons	20.00
SC38	'18 $5.50 Pintail	20.00
SC39	'19 $5.50 Canvasbacks and Boykin Spaniel	20.00
SC40	'20 $5.50 Wood duck & Labrador retriever	20.00

SD6

SOUTH DAKOTA

NO.	DESCRIPTION	F-VF NH
SD3	'76 $1 Mallards	30.00
SD4	'77 $1 Pintails	75.00
SD5	'78 $1 Canvasbacks	30.00
SD6	'86 $2 Canada geese	15.00
SD7	'87 $2 Blue geese	10.00
SD8	'88 $2 White-fronted geese	10.00
SD9	'89 $2 Mallards	8.00
SD10	'90 $2 Blue-winged teal	8.00
SD11	'91 $2 Pintails	8.00
SD12	'92 $2 Canvasbacks	8.00
SD13	'93 $2 Lesser scaup	8.00
SD14	'94 $2 Redheads	8.00
SD15	'95 $2 Wood ducks	8.00
SD16	'96 $2 Canada geese	8.00
SD17	'97 $2 Wigeons	8.00
SD18	'98 $2 Green-winged teal	8.00
SD19	'99 $3 Tundra swan	10.00
SD20	'00 $3 Buffleheads	10.00
SD21	'01 $3 Mallards	10.00
SD22	'02 $3 Canvasbacks	10.00
SD23	'03 $3 Pintail	10.00
SD24	'04 $3 Text, purple	10.00
SD25	'05 $5 Text, magenta	10.00
SD26	'06 $5 Text, brown orange	10.00
SD27	'07 $5 Text, brown	10.00

TN9

TENNESSEE

NO.	DESCRIPTION	F-VF NH
TN1	'79 $2 Mallards	95.00
TN2	'79 $5 Mallards, non-resident	550.00
TN3	'80 $2 Canvasbacks	55.00
TN4	'80 $5 Canvasbacks, non-resident	185.00
TN5	'81 $2 Wood ducks	50.00

NO.	DESCRIPTION	F-VF NH
TN6	'82 $6 Canada geese	60.00
TN7	'83 $6 Pintails	60.00
TN8	'84 $6 Black ducks	60.00
TN9	'85 $6 Blue-winged teal	25.00
TN10	'86 $6 Mallard	15.00
TN11	'87 $6 Canada geese	15.00
TN12	'88 $6 Canvasbacks	15.00
TN13	'89 $6 Green-winged teal	15.00
TN14	'90 $12 Redheads	15.00
TN15	'91 $12 Mergansers	20.00
TN16	'92 $13 Wood ducks	20.00
TN17	'93 $13 Pintails & decoy	25.00
TN18	'94 $15 Mallard	30.00
TN19	'95 $16 Ring-necked duck	35.00
TN20	'96 $17 Black ducks	45.00
TN21	'99 $10 Mallard	18.00
TN22	'00 $10 Bufflehead	18.00
TN23	'01 $10 Wood ducks	18.00
TN24	'02 $10 Green-winged teal	18.00
TN25	'03 $10 Canada geese	18.00
TN26	'04 $10 Wood ducks	18.00
TN27	'05 $10 Mallards	18.00
TN28	'06 $10 Canada goose	18.00
TN29	'07 $10 Harlequin	18.00
TN30	'08 $10 Wood ducks	18.00
TN31	'09 $10 Mallards	18.00
TN32	'10 $10 Wood ducks	18.00
TN33	'11 $10 Wood ducks	18.00
TN34	'12 $10 Cinnamon teal	18.00
TN35	'13 $10 King eiders	18.00
TN36	'14 $10 Wood ducks	18.00
TN37	'15 $10 Green-winged teal	18.00
TN38	'16 $10 Northern shoveler	18.00
TN39	'17 $10 Cinnamon teal	18.00
TN40	'18 $10 Pintails	19.00
TN41	'19 $10 Shovelers	19.00
TN42	'20 $10 Redheads	19.00
TN43	'21 $10 Hooded merganser	19.00

TX5

TEXAS

NO.	DESCRIPTION	F-VF NH
TX1	'81 $5 Mallards	35.00
TX2	'82 $5 Pintails	25.00
TX3	'83 $5 Wigeons	100.00
TX4	'84 $5 Wood ducks	30.00
TX5	'85 $5 Snow geese	11.00
TX6	'86 $5 Green-winged teal	11.00
TX7	'87 $5 White-fronted geese	11.00
TX8	'88 $5 Pintails	11.00
TX9	'89 $5 Mallards	11.00
TX10	'90 $5 American wigeons	14.00
TX11	'91 $7 Wood duck	14.00
TX12	'92 $7 Canada geese	14.00
TX13	'93 $7 Blue-winged teal	14.00
TX14	'94 $7 Shovelers	14.00
TX15	'95 $7 Buffleheads	14.00
TX16	'96 $3 Gadwalls	75.00
TX17	'97 $3 Cinnamon teal	65.00
TX18	'98 $3 Pintail, Labrador retriever	65.00
TX19	'99 $3 Canvasbacks	42.00
TX20	'00 $3 Hooded merganser	35.00
TX21	'01 $3 Snow geese	25.00
TX22	'02 $3 Redheads	25.00
TX23	'03 $3 Mottled duck	25.00
TX24	'04 $3 American goldeneye	18.00
TX25	'05 $7 Mallards	18.00
TX26	'06 $7 Green-winged teals	21.00
TX27	'07 $7 Wood duck	14.00
TX28	'08 $7 Pintails	14.00
TX29	'09 $7 Blue-winged teal	14.00
TX30	'10 $7 Wigeons	14.00
TX31	'11 $7 White-fronted geese	14.00
TX32	'12 $7 Canada geese	22.00
TX33	'13 $7 Wood ducks	14.00
TX34	'14 $7 Cinnamon teal	14.00
TX35	'15 $7 Ring-necked duck	14.00

UT1

UTAH

NO.	DESCRIPTION	F-VF NH
UT1	'86 $3.30 Whistling swans	12.00
UT2	'87 $3.30 Pintails	10.00
UT3	'88 $3.30 Mallards	10.00
UT4	'89 $3.30 Canada geese	10.00
UT5	'90 $3.30 Canvasbacks	10.00
UT6	'91 $3.30 Tundra swans	13.00
UT7	'92 $3.30 Pintails	13.00
UT8	'93 $3.30 Canvasbacks	13.00
UT9	'94 $3.30 Chesapeake retriever & ducks	100.00
UT10	'95 $3.30 Green-winged teal	13.00
UT11	'96 $7.50 White-fronted goose	18.00
UT12	'97 $7.50 Redheads, pair	95.00

VT1

VERMONT

NO.	DESCRIPTION	F-VF NH
VT1	'86 $5 Wood ducks	14.00
VT2	'87 $5 Common goldeneyes	14.00
VT3	'88 $5 Black ducks	14.00
VT4	'89 $5 Canada geese	14.00
VT5	'90 $5 Green-winged teal	14.00
VT6	'91 $5 Hooded mergansers	14.00
VT7	'92 $5 Snow geese	14.00
VT8	'93 $5 Mallards	14.00
VT9	'94 $5 Ring-necked duck	14.00
VT10	'95 $5 Bufflehead	14.00
VT11	'96 $5 Bluebills	14.00
VT12	'97 $5 Pintail	14.00
VT13	'98 $5 Blue-winged teal	14.00
VT14	'99 $5 Canvasbacks	14.00
VT15	'00 $5 Wigeons	12.00
VT16	'01 $5 Oldsquaw	12.00
VT17	'02 $5 Greater scaups	12.00
VT18	'03 $5 Mallards	12.00
VT19	'04 $5 Pintails	12.00
VT20	'05 $5 Canvasbacks	12.00
VT21	'06 $5 Canada goose	12.00
VT22	'07 $5 Ring-necked duck	12.00
VT23	'08 $7.50 Harlequin	12.00
VT24	'09 $7.50 Harlequin	12.00
VT25	'10 $7.50 Wood duck	12.00
VT26	'11 $7.50 Black and numbered sticker	12.00
VT27	'12 $7.50 Black and numbered sticker	12.00
VT28	'13 $7.50 Black and numbered sticker	12.00

VA1

VIRGINIA

NO.	DESCRIPTION	F-VF NH
VA1	'88 $5 Mallards	15.00
VA2	'89 $5 Canada geese	14.00
VA3	'90 $5 Wood ducks	10.00
VA4	'91 $5 Canvasbacks	10.00
VA5	'92 $5 Buffleheads	10.00
VA6	'93 $5 Black ducks	10.00
VA7	'94 $5 Lesser scaup	10.00
VA8	'95 $5 Snow geese	10.00
VA9	'96 $5 Hooded mergansers	10.00
VA10	'97 ($5) Pintail, Labrador retriever	10.00
VA11	'98 $5 Mallards	14.00
VA12	'99 $5 Green-winged teal	14.00
VA13	'00 $5 Mallards	14.00
VA14	'01 $5 Blue-winged teal	12.00
VA15	'02 $5 Canvasbacks	12.00
VA16	'03 $5 Tundra swan	12.00
VA17	'04 $5 Goldeneyes	12.00
VA18	'05 $9.75 Wood ducks, perf.	10.00
VA18a	'05 $9.75 Wood ducks, rouletted	18.00
VA18b	'05 $9.75 Wood ducks, self-adhesive, die cut	18.00
VA19	'06 $9.75 Black ducks, perf.	18.00
VA19a	'06 $9.75 Black ducks, self-adhesive, die cut	18.00
VA20	'07 $10 Canada geese, perf.	18.00
VA20a	'07 $10 Canada geese, self-adhesive, die cut	18.00
VA21	'08 $10 Wigeons, perf.	18.00
VA21a	'08 $10 Wigeons, self-adhesive, die cut	18.00
VA22	'09 $10 Ring-necked duck, perf.	18.00
VA22a	'09 $10 Ring-necked duck, self-adhesive	18.00
VA23	'10 $10 Green-winged teal, perf.	18.00
VA23a	'10 $10 Green-winged teal, self-adhesive, die cut	18.00
VA24	'11 $10 Redheads, perf.	18.00
VA24a	'11 $10 Redheads, self-adhesive	18.00
VA25	'12 $10 Buffleheads, perf.	18.00
VA25a	'12 $10 Buffleheads, self-adhesive	18.00
VA26	'13 $10 Hooded mergansers, perf.	18.00
VA26a	'13 $10 Hooded mergansers, self-adhesive	18.00
VA27	'14 $10 Canvasbacks, perf.	18.00
VA27a	'14 $10 Canvasbacks, self-adhesive	18.00
VA28	'15 $10 Tundra Swans, perf.	30.00
VA28a	'15 $10 Tundra Swans, self-adhesive, die-cut	25.00
VA29	'16 $10 Pintails, perf.	30.00
VA29a	'16 $10 Pintails, self-adhesive, die-cut	25.00
VA30	'17 $10 Ring-necked ducks, perf.	30.00
VA30a	'17 $10 Ring-necked ducks, self-adhesive, die-cut	25.00
VA31	'18 $10 Canada goose, perf.	30.00
VA31a	'18 $10 Canada goose, self-adhesive, die-cut	25.00
VA32	'19 $10 Shoveler, perf.	30.00
VA32a	'19 $10 Shoveler, self-adhesive, die-cut	25.00
VA33	'20 $10 Canvasbacks, perf.	30.00
VA33a	'20 $10 Canvasbacks, self-adhesive, die-cut	25.00
VA34	'21 $10 Common Goldeneye, perf.	30.00
VA34a	'21 $10 Common Goldeneye, self-adhesive, die-cut	25.00

WA1

WASHINGTON

NO.	DESCRIPTION	F-VF NH
WA1	'86 $5 Mallards	10.00
WA2	'87 $5 Canvasbacks	14.00
WA3	'88 $5 Harlequin	11.00
WA4	'89 $5 American Wigeons	11.00
WA5	'90 $5 Pintails & sour duck	11.00
WA6	'91 $6 Wood duck	13.00
WA8	'92 $6 Labrador puppy & Canada geese	13.00
WA9	'93 $6 Snow geese	13.00
WA10	'94 $6 Black brant	15.00
WA11	'95 $6 Mallards	14.00
WA12	'96 $6 Redheads	24.00
WA13	'97 $6 Canada geese	14.00
WA14	'98 $6 Barrow's goldeneye	18.00
WA15	'99 $6 Bufflehead	18.00
WA16	'00 $6 Canada geese, mallard, wigeon	30.00
WA17	'01 $6 Mallards	22.00
WA18	'02 $10 Green-winged teal	22.00
WA19	'03 $10 Pintails	22.00
WA20	'04 $10 Canada goose	18.00
WA21	'05 $10 Barrow's goldeneyes	18.00
WA22	'06 $10 Wigeons, mallard	18.00
WA23	'07 $10 Ross's goose	18.00
WA24	'08 $10 Wood ducks	18.00
WA25	'09 $11 Canada goose	18.00
WA26	'10 $10 Pintail	40.00
WA27	'11 $10 Ruddy duck	30.00
WA28	'12 $15 Brant	30.00
WA29	'13 $15 Shovelers	30.50
WA30	'14 $15 Redheads	30.00
WA31	'15 $15 Canvasbacks	30.00
WA32	'16 $15 Wooded merganser	30.00
WA33	'17 $15 Cinnamon teal and yellow Labrador	30.00
WA34	'18 $15 Wood ducks	30.00
WA35	'19 $15 Ring-necked duck and brown Labrador	30.00
WA36	'20 $17 Canada geese	30.00
WA37	'21 $17 Mallards & black Labrador retriever	30.00

WV1

WEST VIRGINIA

NO.	DESCRIPTION	F-VF NH
WV1	'87 $5 Canada geese	18.00
WV2	'87 $5 Canada geese, non-resident	18.00
WV3	'88 $5 Wood ducks	12.00
WV4	'88 $5 Wood ducks, non-resident	14.00
WV5	'89 $5 Decoys	14.00
WV6	'89 $5 Decoys, non-resident	20.00
WV7	'90 $5 Labrador Retriever & Decoy	22.00
WV8	'90 $5 Labrador retriever & decoy, non-resident	24.00
WV9	'91 $5 Mallards	14.00
WV10	'91 $5 Mallards, non-resident	14.00
WV11	'92 $5 Canada geese	14.00
WV12	'92 $5 Canada geese, non-resident	14.00
WV13	'93 $5 Pintails	14.00
WV14	'93 $5 Pintails, non-resident	14.00
WV15	'94 $5 Green-winged teal	14.00
WV16	'94 $5 Green-winged teal, non-resident	14.00
WV17	'95 $5 Mallards	14.00
WV18	'95 $5 Mallards, non-resident	14.00
WV19	'96 $5 American Wigeons	14.00
WV20	'96 $5 American Wigeons, non-resident	14.00

WI3

WISCONSIN

NO.	DESCRIPTION	F-VF NH
WI1	'78 $3.25 Wood ducks	80.00
WI2	'79 $3.25 Buffleheads	25.00
WI3	'80 $3.25 Wigeons	12.00
WI4	'81 $3.25 Lesser scaup	12.00
WI5	'82 $3.25 Pintails	11.00
WI6	'83 $3.25 Blue-winged teal	11.00
WI7	'84 $3.25 Hooded merganser	12.00
WI8	'85 $3.25 Lesser scaup	14.00
WI9	'86 $3.25 Canvasbacks	16.00
WI10	'87 $3.25 Canada geese	11.00
WI11	'88 $3.25 Hooded merganser	11.00
WI12	'89 $3.25 Common goldeneye	11.00

NO.	DESCRIPTION	F-VF NH
WI13	'90 $3.25 Redheads	11.00
WI14	'91 $5.25 Green-winged teal	12.00
WI15	'92 $5.25 Tundra swans	12.00
WI16	'93 $5.25 Wood ducks	12.00
WI17	'94 $5.25 Pintails	12.00
WI18	'95 $5.25 Mallards	12.00
WI19	'96 ($5.25) Green-winged teal	12.00
WI20	'97 ($7) Canada geese	18.00
WI21	'98 $7 Snow geese	18.00
WI22	'99 $7 Greater Scaups	14.00
WI23	'00 $7 Canvasbacks	14.00
WI24	'01 $7 Common goldeneyes	16.00
WI25	'02 $7 Shovelers	12.00
WI26	'03 $7 Ring-necked ducks	12.00
WI27	'04 $7 Pintail	12.00
WI28	'05 $7 Wood ducks	14.00
WI29	'06 $7 Green-winged teals	14.00
WI30	'07 $7 Redheads	14.00
WI31	'08 $7 Canvasbacks	14.00
WI32	'09 $7 Wigeons	14.00
WI33	'10 $7 Wood ducks	14.00
WI34	'11 $7 Shovelers	14.00
WI35	'12 $7 Redhead	14.00
WI36	'13 $7 Long-tailed ducks	14.00
WI37	'14 $7 Wood duck	12.00
WI38	'15 $7 Blue-winged teal	14.00
WI39	'16 $7 Ring-necked duck	14.00
WI40	'17 $7 Canvasbacks and Lighthouse	14.00
WI41	'18 $7 Canada geese	13.00
WI42	'19 $7 Redheads	13.00
WI43	'20 $7 Wood ducks	14.00
WI44	'21 $7 Pintails	22.00

WY10

WYOMING

NO.	DESCRIPTION	F-VF NH
WY1	'84 $5 Meadowlark	72.00
WY2	'85 $5 Canada geese	64.00
WY3	'86 $5 Antelope	115.00
WY4	'87 $5 Grouse	115.00
WY5	'88 $5 Trout	120.00
WY6	'89 $5 Mule deer	185.00
WY7	'90 $5 Bear	55.00
WY8	'91 $5 Rams	50.00
WY9	'92 $5 Bald eagle	40.00
WY10	'93 $5 Elk	25.00
WY11	'94 $5 Bobcat	25.00
WY12	'95 $5 Moose	25.00
WY13	'96 $5 Turkey	25.00
WY14	'97 $5 Rocky Mountain goats	25.00
WY15	'98 $5 Trumpeter Swans	25.00
WY16	'99 $5 Brown Trout	25.00
WY17	'00 $5 Buffalo	25.00
WY18	'01 $10 White-tailed Deer	25.00
WY19	'02 $10 River otters	25.00
WY20	'03 $10 Mountain bluebird	25.00
WY21	'04 $10 Cougar	25.00
WY22	'05 $10 Burrowing owls	25.00
WY23	'06 $10.50 Cutthroat trout	25.00
WY24	'07 $10.50 Blue grouses	25.00
WY25	'08 $12.50 Black-footed ferret	25.00
WY26	'09 $12.50 Great gray owl	25.00
WY27	'10 $12.50 Cinnamon teal	25.00
WY28	'11 $12.50 Wolverine	20.00
WY29	'12 $12.50 Black bear	20.00
WY30	'13 $12.50 Greater short-horned lizard	20.00
WY31	'14 $12.50 Ruffled grouse	22.00
WY32	'15 $12.50 Sauger	22.00
WY33	'16 $12.50 Swift fox	22.00
WY34	'17 $12.50 Mallard	22.00
WY35	'18 $12.50 Badger	22.00
WY36	'19 $12.50 Mule deer	24.00
WY37	'20 $20 Cutthroat Trout	35.00
WY38	'21 $20 Osprey	35.00

CANAL ZONE

SCOTT NO.	DESCRIPTION	UNUSED NH F	UNUSED NH AVG	UNUSED OG F	UNUSED OG AVG	USED F	USED AVG

CANAL ZONE

PANAMA

1904
U.S. Stamp 300, 319, 304, 306-07 overprinted

SCOTT NO.	DESCRIPTION	UNUSED NH F	UNUSED NH AVG	UNUSED OG F	UNUSED OG AVG	USED F	USED AVG
4	1¢ blue green	115.00	72.00	50.00	35.00	25.00	20.00
5	2¢ carmine	95.00	65.00	43.00	25.00	25.00	20.00
6	5¢ blue	325.00	200.00	150.00	100.00	65.00	50.00
7	8¢ violet black.	575.00	350.00	270.00	175.00	95.00	75.00
8	10¢ pale red brown. . .	500.00	350.00	270.00	175.00	100.00	80.00

CANAL

ZONE

1924-25
U.S. Stamps 551-54, 557, 562, 564-66, 569-71 overprinted

Type 1 Flat Tops on Letters "A". Perf. 11

SCOTT NO.	DESCRIPTION	UNUSED NH F	UNUSED NH AVG	UNUSED OG F	UNUSED OG AVG	USED F	USED AVG
70	½¢ olive brown	3.50	2.50	1.75	1.40	.75	.65
71	1¢ deep green	3.50	2.50	1.75	1.25	1.10	.70
71e	same, bklt pane of 6 . .	300.00	200.00	170.00	125.00	....	....
72	1½¢ yellow brown. . . .	5.00	3.50	2.50	1.85	1.60	1.35
73	2¢ carmine	20.00	15.00	10.00	7.00	1.75	1.25
73a	same, bklt pane of 6 . .	400.00	315.00	250.00	185.00	....	....
74	5¢ dark blue	50.00	40.00	25.00	20.00	9.00	6.50
75	10¢ orange	110.00	80.00	55.00	40.00	24.00	17.00
76	12¢ brown violet	100.00	75.00	50.00	40.00	27.00	19.50
77	14¢ dark blue	75.00	55.00	40.00	30.00	20.00	16.00
78	15¢ gray	125.00	80.00	65.00	45.00	35.00	30.00
79	30¢ olive brown	100.00	65.00	48.00	35.00	25.00	20.00
80	50¢ lilac	210.00	135.00	100.00	70.00	42.00	35.00
81	$1 violet brown	575.00	395.00	300.00	200.00	100.00	85.00

CANAL

ZONE

1925-28
U.S. Stamps 554-55, 557, 564-66, 623, 567, 569-71, overprinted

Type II Pointed Tops on Letters "A"

SCOTT NO.	DESCRIPTION	UNUSED NH F	UNUSED NH AVG	UNUSED OG F	UNUSED OG AVG	USED F	USED AVG
84	2¢ carmine	80.00	60.00	40.00	30.00	10.00	6.25
84d	same, bklt pane of 6 . .	450.00	350.00	300.00	260.00	....	....
85	3¢ violet	10.00	8.50	5.00	3.75	2.75	1.75
86	5¢ dark blue	10.00	8.50	5.00	3.75	2.75	1.75
87	10¢ orange	92.00	70.00	47.00	35.00	10.00	9.00
88	12¢ brown violet	60.00	50.00	30.00	24.00	14.00	10.00
89	14¢ dark blue	67.00	50.00	36.00	25.00	16.00	13.00
90	15¢ gray	22.00	16.00	11.00	8.00	4.00	2.50
91	17¢ black	11.00	8.00	6.00	4.00	3.00	2.25
92	20¢ carmine rose	20.00	16.00	11.00	8.00	4.00	3.00
93	30¢ olive brown	16.00	12.00	9.00	6.00	4.00	3.00
94	50¢ lilac	635.00	475.00	310.00	250.00	150.00	135.00
95	$1 violet brown	310.00	250.00	180.00	140.00	50.00	45.00

1926
Type II overprint on U.S. Stamp 627

SCOTT NO.	DESCRIPTION	UNUSED NH F	UNUSED NH AVG	UNUSED OG F	UNUSED OG AVG	USED F	USED AVG
96	2¢ carmine rose	10.00	7.00	6.00	4.00	3.75	2.50

1927
Type II overprint on U.S. Stamp 583-84, 591
Rotary Press Printing, Perf. 10

SCOTT NO.	DESCRIPTION	UNUSED NH F	UNUSED NH AVG	UNUSED OG F	UNUSED OG AVG	USED F	USED AVG
97	2¢ carmine	150.00	110.00	80.00	70.00	10.50	8.50
98	3¢ violet	25.00	20.00	12.00	10.00	5.00	4.00
99	10¢ orange	50.00	35.00	30.00	20.00	6.75	5.50

SCOTT NO.	DESCRIPTION	PLATE BLOCK F/NH	PLATE BLOCK F	PLATE BLOCK AVG	UNUSED F/NH	UNUSED F	UNUSED AVG	USED F	USED AVG
100	1¢ green	35.00	25.00	22.00	4.25	2.75	2.00	1.30	1.00
101	2¢ carmine	45.00	30.00	26.00	4.75	3.00	2.00	.90	.80
101a	same, bklt pane of 6	....	....	....	275.00	175.00	150.00	....	....
102	3¢ violet (1931). .	125.00	90.00	80.00	6.50	4.50	3.00	3.50	2.50
103	5¢ dark blue	280.00	200.00	190.00	60.00	40.00	35.00	11.00	9.00
104	10¢ orange (1930)	260.00	180.00	160.00	30.00	23.00	18.00	12.00	10.00

VERY FINE QUALITY: To determine the Very Fine price, add the difference between the Fine and Average prices to the Fine quality price. For example: if the Fine price is $10.00 and the Average price is $6.00, the Very Fine price would be $14.00. From 1935 to date, add 20% to the Fine price to arrive at the Very Fine price.

105,160

106

107

108, 161

109

110

111

112

113

114

1928-40 Builders Issue

SCOTT NO.	DESCRIPTION	PLATE BLOCK F/NH	PLATE BLOCK F	PLATE BLOCK AVG	UNUSED F/NH	UNUSED F	UNUSED AVG	USED F	USED AVG
105-14	**1¢-50¢ complete, 10 varieties . . . .**	....	....	....	**10.40**	**8.05**	**4.95**	**5.70**	**3.45**
105	1¢ Gorgas.	3.75	3.00	2.50	.55	.40	.30	.30	.25
106	2¢ Goethals	4.50(6)	3.25	2.50	.35	.30	.25	.30	.25
106a	same, bklt pane of 6	....	....	....	22.00	20.00	16.00	....	....
107	5¢ Gaillard Cut (1929).	24.00(6)	18.00	16.00	1.65	1.40	1.20	.55	.45
108	10¢ Hodges (1932)	8.00(6)	6.00	4.50	.40	.30	.25	.30	.25
109	12¢ Gaillard (1929)	18.00(6)	15.00	12.00	1.50	1.00	.80	.85	.50
110	14¢ Sibert (1937)	25.00(6)	16.00	14.00	1.40	1.25	.95	1.10	.75
111	15¢ Smith (1932)	15.00(6)	12.00	8.00	.80	.65	.45	.50	.40
112	20¢ Rousseau (1932).	15.00(6)	12.00	8.00	1.25	.75	.65	.30	.25
113	30¢ Williamson (1940).	19.00(6)	15.00	12.00	1.25	1.15	.85	.95	.75
114	50¢ Blackburn (1929).	28.00(6)	17.00	13.50	2.75	1.90	1.50	.85	.70

1933
Type II overprint on U.S. Stamps 720 & 695
Rotary Press Printing, Perf. 11 x 10½

SCOTT NO.	DESCRIPTION	PLATE BLOCK F/NH	PLATE BLOCK F	PLATE BLOCK AVG	UNUSED F/NH	UNUSED F	UNUSED AVG	USED F	USED AVG
115	3¢ Washington . .	56.00	40.00	35.00	4.00	3.50	2.50	.40	.35
116	14¢ Indian.	90.00	70.00	46.00	8.00	6.00	4.00	3.35	2.75

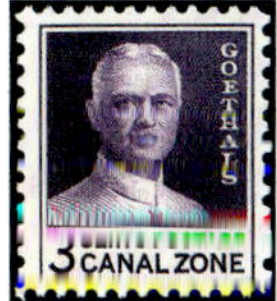

117, 153

1934

SCOTT NO.	DESCRIPTION	PLATE BLOCK F/NH	PLATE BLOCK F	PLATE BLOCK AVG	UNUSED F/NH	UNUSED F	UNUSED AVG	USED F	USED AVG
117	3¢ Goethals	1.75(6)	1.25	1.00	.40	.35	.25	.25	.25
117a	same, bklt pane of 6	....	....	....	100.00	60.00	50.00	....	....

1939 U.S. Stamps 803, 805 overprint

SCOTT NO.	DESCRIPTION	PLATE BLOCK F/NH	PLATE BLOCK F/OG	UNUSED F/NH	UNUSED F/OG	USED F
118	½¢ red orange.	3.75	3.00	.35	.25	.25
119	1½¢ bistre brown	3.25	2.75	.35	.25	.25

FOR YOUR CONVENIENCE, COMPLETE SETS ARE LISTED BEFORE SINGLE STAMP LISTINGS!

120
Balboa—Before

121
Balboa—After

122	*Gaillard Cut—Before*	**123**	*After*
124	*Bas Obispo—Before*	**125**	*After*
126	*Gatun Locks—Before*	**127**	*After*
128	*Canal Channel—Before*	**129**	*After*
130	*Gamboa—Before*	**131**	*After*
132	*Pedro Miguel Locks—Before*	**133**	*After*
134	*Gatun Spillway—Before*	**135**	*After*

1939 25th ANNIVERSARY ISSUE

SCOTT NO.	DESCRIPTION	PLATE BLOCK F/NH	PLATE BLOCK F/OG	UNUSED F/NH	UNUSED F/OG	USED F
120-35	**1¢-50¢ complete, 16 varieties ....**	....	....	**155.00**	**135.00**	**89.50**
120	1¢ yellow green......	20.00(6)	16.00	1.25	.95	.45
121	2¢ rose carmine	20.00(6)	16.00	1.25	.85	.50
122	3¢ purple...........	20.00(6)	16.00	1.25	.85	.25
123	5¢ dark blue	32.00(6)	28.00	2.75	2.00	1.30
124	6¢ red orange	80.00(6)	67.00	5.50	3.75	3.25
125	7¢ black............	80.00(6)	67.00	6.00	4.00	3.25
126	8¢ green	88.00(6)	74.00	7.75	5.50	3.50
127	10¢ ultramarine......	88.00(6)	74.00	7.00	5.00	5.00
128	11¢ blue hreen	180.00(6)	160.00	12.00	9.00	8.00
129	12¢ brown carmine ...	160.00(6)	135.00	12.00	9.00	7.00
130	14¢ dark violet.......	180.00(6)	160.00	12.00	9.00	7.00
131	15¢ olive green	210.00(6)	165.00	16.00	12.00	6.00
132	18¢ rose pink	200.00(6)	160.00	17.00	13.00	8.00
133	20¢ brown..........	240.00(6)	200.00	18.00	14.00	8.00
134	25¢ orange	425.00(6)	350.00	27.00	22.00	18.00
135	50¢ violet brown	475.00(6)	360.00	35.00	27.00	6.00

136

137

138

139

140

1945-49

SCOTT NO.	DESCRIPTION	PLATE BLOCK F/NH	PLATE BLOCK F/OG	UNUSED F/NH	UNUSED F/OG	USED F
136-40	**½¢-25¢ complete 5 varieties ....**	....	....	**3.50**	**2.50**	**1.75**
136	½¢ Major General Davis (1948)	3.50(6)	2.75	.55	.45	.25
137	1½¢ Gov. Magoon (1948)	3.50(6)	2.75	.55	.45	.25
138	2¢ T. Roosevelt (1948)	2.00(6)	1.50	.35	.25	.25
139	5¢ Stevens	3.75(6)	3.00	.50	.40	.25
140	25¢ J.F. Wallace (1948)	12.50(6)	11.00	1.60	1.25	.85

141

1948 CANAL ZONE BIOLOGICAL AREA

SCOTT NO.	DESCRIPTION	PLATE BLOCK F/NH	PLATE BLOCK F/OG	UNUSED F/NH	UNUSED F/OG	USED F
141	10¢ Map & Coatimundi	11.00(6)	8.50	1.95	1.50	1.20

142

143

144

145

1949 CALIFORNIA GOLD RUSH

SCOTT NO.	DESCRIPTION	PLATE BLOCK F/NH	PLATE BLOCK F/OG	UNUSED F/NH	UNUSED F/OG	USED F
142-45	**3¢-18¢ complete 4 varieties ....**	....	....	**5.15**	**4.25**	**3.35**
142	3¢ "Forty Niners".....	7.00(6)	5.00	.70	.55	.35
143	6¢ Journey–Las Cruces	8.25(6)	6.00	.80	.65	.40
144	12¢ Las Cruces–Panama Trail................	23.00(6)	19.00	1.75	1.40	1.10
145	18¢ Departure–San Francisco	28.00(6)	23.00	2.60	2.25	2.75

146

147

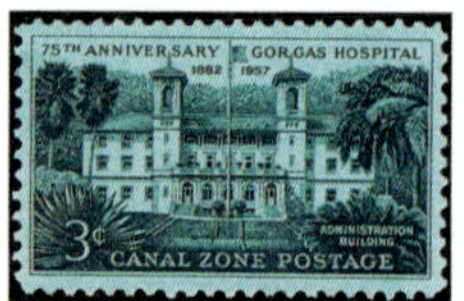

148

149

150

1951-58

SCOTT NO.	DESCRIPTION	PLATE BLOCK F/NH	PLATE BLOCK F/OG	UNUSED F/NH	UNUSED F/OG	USED F
146	10¢ West Indian Labor	28.00(6)	23.00	3.25	2.75	2.25
147	3¢ Panama R.R. (1955)	8.00(6)	7.00	1.10	.80	.80
148	3¢ Gorgas Hospital (1957)	6.00	5.00	.60	.50	.45
149	4¢ S.S. Ancon (1958) .	5.00	4.00	.55	.50	.40
150	4¢ T. Roosevelt (1958)	5.00	4.00	.60	.55	.45

151

152, 154

1960-62

SCOTT NO.	DESCRIPTION	PLATE BLOCK F/NH	PLATE BLOCK F/OG	UNUSED F/NH	UNUSED F/OG	USED F
151	4¢ Boy Scout Badge . .	7.00	5.00	.60	.50	.45
152	4¢ Administration Building	1.75	1.35	.35	.25	.25
	LINE PAIR					
153	3¢ G.W. Goethals, coil	1.40	1.25	.30	.25	.25
154	4¢ Administration Building, coil	1.40	1.25	.30	.25	.25
155	5¢ J.F. Stevens, coil (1962)	1.55	1.25	.40	.30	.25

156

157

SCOTT NO.	DESCRIPTION	PLATE BLOCK F/NH	PLATE BLOCK F/OG	UNUSED F/NH	UNUSED F/OG	USED F
	PLATE BLOCK					
156	4¢ Girl Scout Badge (1962)	4.75	3.50	.45	.40	.35
157	4¢ Thatcher Ferry Bridge (1962)	5.00	4.00	.40	.35	.30
157a	same, silver omitted (bridge)	....	....	8500.00	....	....

158

159

SCOTT NO.	DESCRIPTION	PLATE BLOCK F/NH	PLATE BLOCK F/OG	UNUSED F/NH	UNUSED F/OG	USED F
	1968-78					
158	6¢ Goethals Memorial.	3.50	....	.40	....	.25
159	8¢ Fort San Lorenzo (1971)	3.00	....	.50	....	.25
	LINE PAIR					
160	1¢ W.C. Gorgas, coil (1975)	1.50	....	.35	....	.25
161	10¢ H.F. Hodges, coil (1975)	6.00	....	.90	....	.55
162	25¢ J.F. Wallace, coil (1975)	26.00	....	3.25	....	3.00

163

165

SCOTT NO.	DESCRIPTION	PLATE BLOCK F/NH	PLATE BLOCK F/OG	UNUSED F/NH	UNUSED F/OG	USED F
	PLATE BLOCK					
163	13¢ Cascades Dredge (1976)	2.50	....	.50	....	.30
163a	same, bklt pane of 4 . .	....	....	3.50	....	....
164	5¢ J.F. Stevens (#139) Rotary Press (1977) . .	7.00	....	.90	....	1.00
165	15¢ Locomotive (1978)	2.50	....	.60	....	.40

AIR POST

AIR MAIL

105 & 106 Surcharged

25 CENTS 25

SCOTT NO.	DESCRIPTION	PLATE BLOCK F/NH	PLATE BLOCK F	PLATE BLOCK AVG	UNUSED F/NH	UNUSED F	UNUSED AVG	USED F	USED AVG
	1929-31								
C1	15¢ on 1¢ green, Type I	225.00(6)	150.00	110.00	15.50	12.00	10.00	6.25	4.50
C2	15¢ on 1¢ yellow green, Type II (1931) . . .	....	....	....	120.00	110.00	85.00	75.00	68.00
C3	25¢ on 2¢ carmine	200.00	150.00	140.00	7.00	5.00	4.00	2.50	1.85

AIR MAIL

114 & 106 Surcharged

=10c

SCOTT NO.	DESCRIPTION	PLATE BLOCK F/NH	PLATE BLOCK F	PLATE BLOCK AVG	UNUSED F/NH	UNUSED F	UNUSED AVG	USED F	USED AVG
	1929								
C4	10¢ on 50¢ lilac .	220.00(6)	170.00	150.00	14.00	10.00	8.00	7.00	6.00
C5	20¢ on 2¢ carmine	175.00(6)	135.00	125.00	8.00	7.00	6.00	2.00	1.50

C6-C14

SCOTT NO.	DESCRIPTION	PLATE BLOCK F/NH	PLATE BLOCK F	PLATE BLOCK AVG	UNUSED F/NH	UNUSED F	UNUSED AVG	USED F	USED AVG
	1931-49								
C6-14	**4¢-$1 complete, 9 varieties . . . . .**	....	....	....	**28.00**	**21.00**	**16.00**	**7.60**	**5.00**
C6	4¢ Gaillard Cut, red violet (1949)	11.00(6)	8.00	6.00	1.25	1.00	.75	1.00	.85
C7	5¢ yellow green .	5.50(6)	4.50	2.75	.75	.55	.40	.45	.35
C8	6¢ yellow brown (1946)	9.00(6)	8.00	5.00	1.00	.85	.65	.40	.30
C9	10¢ orange	12.50(6)	9.50	6.00	1.30	1.00	.85	.40	.30
C10	15¢ blue	13.50(6)	10.50	7.00	1.60	1.35	1.00	.40	.30
C11	20¢ red violet . . .	22.00(6)	17.00	13.00	2.85	2.20	1.85	.40	.30
C12	30¢ rose lake (1941)	40.00(6)	36.00	28.00	4.50	3.25	2.75	1.30	.80
C13	40¢ yellow	40.00(6)	30.00	24.00	4.50	3.50	3.00	1.30	1.00
C14	$1 black	105.00(6)	82.50	70.00	12.00	9.00	8.00	2.75	2.25

C15

C16

C17

C18

C19

C20

SCOTT NO.	DESCRIPTION	PLATE BLOCK F/NH	PLATE BLOCK F/OG	UNUSED F/NH	UNUSED F/OG	USED F
	1939 25th ANNIVERSARY ISSUE					
C15-20	**5¢-$1 complete 6 varieties . . . .**	....	....	**95.00**	**75.00**	**52.00**
C15	5¢ Plane over Sosa Hill	50.00(6)	40.00	5.00	4.00	2.75
C16	10¢ Map of Central America.	65.00(6)	50.00	5.00	4.00	3.50
C17	15¢ Scene near Fort Amador	70.00(6)	60.00	7.50	6.00	1.50
C18	25¢ Clipper at Cristobal Harbor.	325.00(6)	250.00	22.00	18.00	9.00
C19	30¢ Clipper over Gaillard Cut	170.00(6)	110.00	21.00	17.00	8.00
C20	$1 Clipper Alighting. . .	600.00(6)	450.00	50.00	42.00	29.00

C21-31, C34

SCOTT NO.	DESCRIPTION	PLATE BLOCK F/NH	PLATE BLOCK F/OG	UNUSED F/NH	UNUSED F/OG	USED F
	1951					
C21-26	**4¢-80¢ complete 6 varieties . . . .**	....	....	**29.25**	**25.50**	**13.00**
C21	4¢ Globe & Wing, red violet	9.00(6)	7.00	1.00	.85	.50
C22	6¢ light brown	8.00(6)	6.00	.85	.60	.40
C23	10¢ light red orange . .	11.00(6)	8.50	1.25	1.10	.50
C24	21¢ light blue.	100.00(6)	85.00	12.00	10.00	5.00
C25	31¢ cerise	100.00(6)	85.00	13.00	11.00	5.00
C26	80¢ Light gray black . .	65.00(6)	48.00	7.75	6.50	2.00
	1958					
C27-31	**5¢-35¢ complete 5 varieties . . . .**		....	**30.75**	**25.00**	**9.70**
C27	5¢ Globe & Wing, yellow green	8.00	6.00	1.20	1.00	.65
C28	7¢ olive	8.00	6.00	1.20	1.00	.60
C29	15¢ brown violet	47.00	39.00	5.50	4.75	3.25
C30	25¢ orange yellow. . . .	120.00	90.00	14.00	12.00	3.25
C31	35¢ dark blue	70.00	65.00	12.00	10.00	3.25

C32

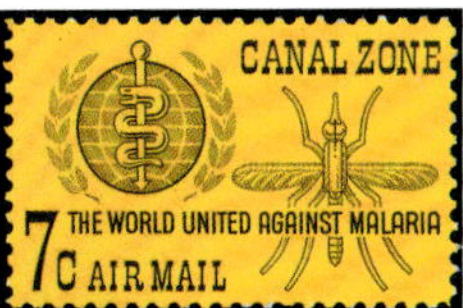

C33

C35

SCOTT NO.	DESCRIPTION	PLATE BLOCK F/NH	PLATE BLOCK F/OG	UNUSED F/NH	UNUSED F/OG	USED F
	1961-63					
C32	15¢ Emblem Caribbean School	16.00	13.00	1.50	1.40	1.00
C33	7¢ Anti-Malaria (1962).	3.50	3.00	.60	.40	.50
C34	8¢ Globe & Wing carmine (1968)	8.00	6.00	.85	.60	.40
C35	15¢ Alliance for Progress (1963)	16.00	13.00	1.60	1.35	1.35

C36 C37 C38 C39 C40 C41

1964 50th ANNIVERSARY ISSUE

SCOTT NO.	DESCRIPTION	PLATE BLOCK F/NH	PLATE BLOCK F/OG	UNUSED F/NH	UNUSED F/OG	USED F
C36-41	**6¢-80¢ complete 6 varieties ....**	....	....	**12.75**	**10.00**	**9.90**
C36	6¢ Cristobal.........	3.85	3.25	.65	.55	.60
C37	8¢ Gatun Locks......	4.25	3.50	.65	.55	.55
C38	15¢ Madden Dam....	9.50	8.00	1.25	1.60	1.60
C39	20¢ Gaillard Cut	12.50	10.00	2.00	1.60	1.20
C40	30¢ Miraflores Locks..	20.00	16.00	3.50	2.50	3.00
C41	80¢ Balboa	28.00	26.00	6.00	5.50	4.50

C42-C53

1965

SCOTT NO.	DESCRIPTION	PLATE BLOCK F/NH	PLATE BLOCK F/OG	UNUSED F/NH	UNUSED F/OG	USED F
C42-47	**6¢-80¢ complete 6 varieties ....**	....	....	**6.40**	....	**2.55**
C42	6¢ Gov. Seal, green & black	3.50	....	.65	....	.40
C43	8¢ rose red & black...	3.50	....	.65	....	.30
C44	15¢ blue & black.....	7.25	....	.85	....	.35
C45	20¢ lilac & black	5.00	....	.85	....	.40
C46	30¢ reddish brown & black	5.25	....	1.25	....	.40
C47	80¢ bistre & black	19.00	....	2.85	....	1.00

1968-76

SCOTT NO.	DESCRIPTION	PLATE BLOCK F/NH	PLATE BLOCK F/OG	UNUSED F/NH	UNUSED F/OG	USED F
C48-53	**10¢-35¢ complete 6 varieties ....**	....	....	**4.60**	....	**5.50**
C48	10¢ Gov. Seal, dull orange& black	3.75	....	.40	....	.25
C48a	same, bklt pane of 4 ..	....	....	4.50	....	....
C49	11¢ Seal, olive & black (1971)	3.75	....	.40	....	.30
C49a	same, bklt pane of 4 ..	....	....	3.50	....	....
C50	13¢ Seal, emerald & black (1974)	5.50	....	1.00	....	.35
C50a	same, bklt pane of 4 ..	....	....	7.00	....	....
C51	22¢ Seal, violet & black (1976)	6.50	....	1.00	....	2.50
C52	25¢ Seal, pale yellow green & black	6.00	....	.90	....	.75
C53	35¢ Seal, salmon & black (1976)	11.00	....	1.35	....	2.20

AIR POST OFFICIAL STAMPS

C7-14 Overprinted
1941-42 Overprint 19 to 20½ mm long

OFFICIAL
PANAMA CANAL

SCOTT NO.	DESCRIPTION	PLATE BLOCK F/NH	PLATE BLOCK F/OG	UNUSED F/NH	UNUSED F/OG	USED F
CO1-7	**5¢-$1 complete 7 varieties ....**	....	....	**132.00**	**93.00**	**40.00**
CO1	5¢ Gaillard Cut, yellow green (C7)..........	....	....	7.50	5.75	2.50
CO2	10¢ orange (C9)	....	....	12.00	9.00	3.00
CO3	15¢ blue (C10)	....	....	15.00	12.00	3.00
CO4	20¢ red violet (C11)...	....	....	23.00	15.00	5.00
CO5	30¢ rose lake (1942) (C12)	....	....	24.00	20.00	7.00
CO6	40¢ yellow (C13).....	....	....	24.00	20.00	10.00
CO7	$1 black (C14).......	....	....	28.00	21.00	14.00

1947 Overprint 19 to 20½mm long

SCOTT NO.	DESCRIPTION	PLATE BLOCK F/NH	PLATE BLOCK F/OG	UNUSED F/NH	UNUSED F/OG	USED F
CO14	6¢ yellow brown (C8) .	....	....	25.00	15.00	6.25

POSTAGE DUE STAMPS

1914
U.S. Postage Due Stamps
J45-46, 49 overprint

CANAL ZONE

SCOTT NO.	DESCRIPTION	UNUSED NH F	UNUSED NH AVG	UNUSED OG F	UNUSED OG AVG	USED F	USED AVG
J1	1¢ rose carmine	155.00	125.00	85.00	70.00	18.00	14.00
J2	2¢ rose carmine	425.00	350.00	225.00	200.00	55.00	45.00
J3	10¢ rose carmine	1700.00	1400.00	925.00	850.00	55.00	45.00

1924
Type I overprint on U.S. Postage Due Stamps J61-62, 65

SCOTT NO.	DESCRIPTION	UNUSED NH F	UNUSED NH AVG	UNUSED OG F	UNUSED OG AVG	USED F	USED AVG
J12	1¢ carmine rose	185.00	145.00	95.00	85.00	30.00	23.00
J13	2¢ deep claret.......	125.00	85.00	60.00	55.00	15.00	12.50
J14	10¢ deep claret......	425.00	350.00	220.00	185.00	55.00	48.00

1925
Canal Zone Stamps
71, 73, 75 overprinted

POSTAGE DUE

SCOTT NO.	DESCRIPTION	UNUSED NH F	UNUSED NH AVG	UNUSED OG F	UNUSED OG AVG	USED F	USED AVG
J15	1¢ deep green	150.00	140.00	85.00	75.00	17.00	14.00
J16	2¢ carmine	45.00	35.00	25.00	20.00	7.50	5.50
J17	10¢ orange.........	85.00	70.00	50.00	40.00	12.50	10.00

1925
Type II overprint on U.S. Postage Due Stamps J61-62, 65

SCOTT NO.	DESCRIPTION	UNUSED NH F	UNUSED NH AVG	UNUSED OG F	UNUSED OG AVG	USED F	USED AVG
J18	1¢ carmine rose	18.00	16.00	8.00	6.50	3.00	2.25
J19	2¢ carmine rose	32.00	27.00	15.00	13.00	5.00	4.00
J20	10¢ carmine rose	350.00	300.00	155.00	140.00	20.00	17.00

1929-39
107 Surcharged

POSTAGE DUE
-1-

SCOTT NO.	DESCRIPTION	UNUSED NH F	UNUSED NH AVG	UNUSED OG F	UNUSED OG AVG	USED F	USED AVG
J21	1¢ on 5¢ blue	10.00	8.00	5.50	4.50	2.20	1.85
J22	2¢ on 5¢ blue	17.00	14.00	9.75	8.00	3.50	2.50
J23	5¢ on 5¢ blue	17.00	14.00	9.75	8.00	4.00	3.00
J24	10¢ on 5¢ blue	17.00	14.00	9.75	8.00	4.00	3.00

J25

1932-41

SCOTT NO.	DESCRIPTION	UNUSED NH F	UNUSED NH AVG	UNUSED OG F	UNUSED OG AVG	USED F	USED AVG
J25-29	**1¢-15¢ complete, 5 varieties ....**	**5.40**	**4.50**	**4.20**	**3.00**	**3.60**	**2.55**
J25	1¢ claret	.50	.40	.40	.30	.30	.25
J26	2¢ claret	.50	.40	.40	.30	.30	.25
J27	5¢ claret	.90	.70	.70	.50	.30	.40
J28	10¢ claret	2.50	1.75	1.75	1.40	1.75	1.40
J29	15¢ claret (1941)	1.95	1.50	1.50	1.00	1.30	.90

OFFICIAL STAMPS

1941
105, 107, 108, 111, 112, 114, 117, 139 overprinted

OFFICIAL
PANAMA
CANAL

"PANAMA" 10mm long

OFFICIAL
PANAMA CANAL

SCOTT NO.	DESCRIPTION	UNUSED F/NH	UNUSED F	USED F
O1/9	**1¢-50¢ (O1-2, O4-7, O9) 7 varieties ....**	**132.50**	**96.75**	**21.25**
O1	1¢ yellow green (105)................	3.50	2.75	.60
O2	3¢ deep violet (117)	7.50	5.50	1.00
O3	5¢ blue (107).......................	......	......	40.00
O4	10¢ orange (108)	12.00	10.00	2.25
O5	15¢ gray black (111)................	20.00	16.00	3.00
O6	20¢ olive brown (112)...............	25.00	18.00	3.50
O7	50¢ lilac (114)......................	60.00	50.00	7.50

1947

SCOTT NO.	DESCRIPTION	UNUSED F/NH	UNUSED F	USED F
O9	5¢ deep blue (139)	15.00	13.00	4.50

SCOTT NO.	DESCRIPTION	MINT ENTIRES

CANAL ZONE MINT POSTAL STATIONERY ENTIRES

U16

ENVELOPES

U16	1934, 3¢ purple	1.50
U17	1958, 4¢ blue	1.65
U18	1969, 4¢ + 1¢ blue	1.65
U19	1969, 4¢ + 2¢ blue	3.25
U20	1971, 8¢ Gaillard Cut	1.00
U21	1974, 8¢ + 2¢ Gaillard Cut	1.35
U22	1976, 13¢ Gaillard Cut	1.00
U23	1978, 13¢ + 2¢ Gaillard Cut	1.00

UC5

AIR POST ENVELOPES

UC3	1949, 6¢ DC-4 Skymaster	4.75
UC4	1958, 7¢ DC-4 Skymaster	5.25
UC5	1963, 3¢ + 5¢ purple	7.25
UC6	1964, 8¢ Tail Assembly	3.00
UC7	1965, 4¢ + 4¢ blue	5.25
UC8	1966, 8¢ Tail Assembly	5.75
UC9	1968, 8¢ + 2¢ Tail Assembly	3.50
UC10	1968, 4¢ + 4¢ + 2¢ Tail Assembly	2.75
UC11	1969, 10¢ Tail Assembly	4.75
UC12	1971, 4¢ + 5¢ + 2¢ blue	4.75
UC13	1971, 10¢ + 1¢ Tail Assembly	4.75
UC14	1971, 11¢ Tail Assembly	1.50
UC15	1974, 11¢ + 2¢ Tail Assembly	2.00
UC16	1975, 8¢ + 2¢ + 3¢ emerald	1.75

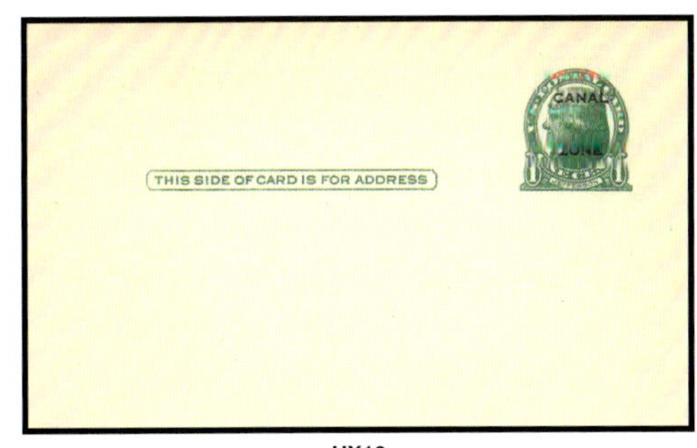

UX10

POSTAL CARDS

UX10	1935, 1¢ overprint on U.S. #UX27	2.25
UX11	1952, 2¢ overprint on U.S. #UX38	2.75
UX12	1958, 3¢ Ship in Lock	2.50
UX13	1963, 3¢ + 1¢ Ship in Lock	4.75
UX14	1964, 4¢ Ship in Canal	4.25
UX15	1965, 4¢ Ship in Lock	1.50
UX16	1968, 4¢ + 1¢ Ship in Lock	1.50
UX17	1969, 5¢ Ship in Lock	1.50
UX18	1971, 5¢ + 1¢ Ship in Lock	1.00
UX19	1974, 8¢ Ship in Lock	1.25
UX20	1976, 8¢ + 1¢ Ship in Lock	1.00
UX21	1978, 8¢ + 2¢ Ship in Lock	1.25

AIR POST POSTAL CARDS

UXC1	1958, 5¢ Plane, Flag & Map	4.25
UXC2	1963, 5¢ + 1¢ Plane, Flag & Map	11.00
UXC3	1965, 4¢ + 2¢ Ship in Lock	4.75
UXC4	1968, 4¢ + 4¢ Ship in Lock	3.50
UXC5	1971, 5¢ + 4¢ Ship in Lock	1.50

CONFEDERATE STATES

1, 4
Jofferson Davis

2, 5
Thomas Jefferson

(Confederate States 1-14 + 40% for VF Centering)

SCOTT NO.	DESCRIPTION	UNUSED OG F	UNUSED OG AVG	UNUSED F	UNUSED AVG	USED F	USED AVG
	1861						
1	5¢ green	325.00	190.00	200.00	140.00	175.00	125.00
2	10¢ blue	325.00	225.00	225.00	150.00	200.00	140.00

3
Andrew Jackson

6, 7
Jefferson Davis
6: Fine Print
7: Coarse Print

SCOTT NO.	DESCRIPTION	UNUSED OG F	UNUSED OG AVG	UNUSED F	UNUSED AVG	USED F	USED AVG
	1862						
3	2¢ green	1150.00	900.00	750.00	550.00	900.00	750.00
4	5¢ blue	275.00	225.00	200.00	125.00	125.00	80.00
5	10¢ rose	1800.00	1200.00	1500.00	1000.00	500.00	450.00
6	5¢ light blue, London Print	45.00	35.00	22.00	18.00	30.00	21.00
7	5¢ blue, Local Print	35.00	25.00	25.00	18.00	21.00	18.00

8
Andrew Jackson

SCOTT NO.	DESCRIPTION	UNUSED OG F	UNUSED OG AVG	UNUSED F	UNUSED AVG	USED F	USED AVG
	1863						
8	2¢ red brown	90.00	70.00	70.00	60.00	400.00	295.00

9

10, 11 (Die A)
Jefferson Davis

12 (Die B)

SCOTT NO.	DESCRIPTION	UNUSED OG F	UNUSED OG AVG	UNUSED F	UNUSED AVG	USED F	USED AVG
9	10¢ blue (TEN)	1200.00	700.00	650.00	500.00	650.00	550.00
10	10¢ blue (with frame line)	....	....	6000.00	4500.00	2500.00	2250.00
11	10¢ blue (no frame)	22.00	15.00	15.00	10.00	25.00	21.00
12	10¢ blue, filled corner	28.00	20.00	20.00	15.00	23.00	19.00

13
George Washington

14
John C. Calhoun

SCOTT NO.	DESCRIPTION	UNUSED OG F	UNUSED OG AVG	UNUSED F	UNUSED AVG	USED F	USED AVG
13	20¢ green	75.00	60.00	60.00	55.00	400.00	350.00
	1862						
14	1¢ orange	160.00	120.00	110.00	80.00	....	....

CUBA

U.S. Administration

1899
U.S. Stamps of 267, 279, 279B, 268, 281, 282C surcharged

CUBA
1 c.
de PESO.

SCOTT NO.	DESCRIPTION	UNUSED NH F	AVG	UNUSED OG F	AVG	USED F	AVG
221	1¢ on 1¢ yellow green	10.00	8.50	5.50	5.00	.65	.55
222	2¢ on 2¢ carmine	19.00	15.00	10.00	8.00	.85	.70
223	2½¢ on 2¢ carmine. . .	12.00	10.00	5.50	5.00	1.00	.75
224	3¢ on 3¢ purple	27.00	19.00	15.00	13.00	2.00	1.50
225	5¢ on 5¢ blue	27.00	19.00	15.00	13.00	2.50	2.00
226	10¢ on 10¢ brown. . . .	65.00	55.00	28.00	23.00	8.00	7.00

227 228 229

230 231

Republic under U.S. Military Rule Watermarked US-C

SCOTT NO.	DESCRIPTION	UNUSED NH F	AVG	UNUSED OG F	AVG	USED F	AVG
227	1¢ Columbus	7.50	5.50	4.00	3.00	.35	.25
228	2¢ Coconut Palms . . .	7.50	5.50	4.00	3.00	.35	.25
229	3¢ Allegory "Cuba" . . .	7.50	5.50	4.00	3.00	.35	.25
230	5¢ Ocean Liner.	9.50	8.00	6.00	4.75	.35	.25
231	10¢ Cane Field.	25.00	17.00	15.00	12.00	.75	.55

SPECIAL DELIVERY

1899
Surcharged of 1899 on U.S. E5

SCOTT NO.	DESCRIPTION	UNUSED NH F	AVG	UNUSED OG F	AVG	USED F	AVG
E1	10¢ on 10¢ blue	270.00	200.00	140.00	95.00	110.00	90.00

E2
Special Delivery Messenger

Republic under U.S. Military Rule
Watermarked US-C Inscribed "Immediate"

SCOTT NO.	DESCRIPTION	UNUSED NH F	AVG	UNUSED OG F	AVG	USED F	AVG
E2	10¢ orange	115.00	85.00	45.00	30.00	18.00	14.00

POSTAGE DUE STAMPS

1899
Surcharge of 1899 on U.S. J38-39, J41-42

SCOTT NO.	DESCRIPTION	UNUSED NH F	AVG	UNUSED OG F	AVG	USED F	AVG
J1	1¢ on 1¢ deep claret. .	90.00	80.00	45.00	40.00	7.00	5.00
J2	2¢ on 2¢ deep claret. .	90.00	80.00	45.00	40.00	7.00	5.00
J3	5¢ on 5¢ deep claret. .	95.00	75.00	45.00	40.00	7.00	5.00
J4	10¢ on 10¢ deep claret	60.00	50.00	25.00	20.00	3.00	2.00

GUAM

1899
U.S. Stamps of 279, 267, 268, 272, 280-82C, 284, 275, 276 overprinted

GUAM

SCOTT NO.	DESCRIPTION	UNUSED NH F	AVG	UNUSED OG F	AVG	USED F	AVG
1	1¢ deep green	40.00	30.00	20.00	13.00	30.00	22.00
2	2¢ red.	38.00	30.00	19.00	13.00	29.00	22.00
3	3¢ purple	250.00	200.00	130.00	90.00	160.00	120.00
4	4¢ lilac brown	220.00	190.00	130.00	90.00	160.00	120.00
5	5¢ blue	60.00	40.00	30.00	20.00	50.00	35.00
6	6¢ lake	220.00	170.00	120.00	90.00	180.00	130.00
7	8¢ violet brown	220.00	170.00	120.00	90.00	180.00	130.00
8	10¢ brown (Type I). . . .	80.00	60.00	40.00	20.00	50.00	30.00
10	15¢ olive green.	250.00	170.00	140.00	100.00	130.00	100.00
11	50¢ orange	650.00	500.00	300.00	200.00	310.00	220.00
12	$1 black (Type I).	650.00	500.00	300.00	200.00	370.00	200.00

SPECIAL DELIVERY

U.S. Stamp E5 overprint

GUAM

SCOTT NO.	DESCRIPTION	UNUSED NH F	AVG	UNUSED OG F	AVG	USED F	AVG
E1	10¢ blue	275.00	200.00	140.00	100.00	200.00	150.00

HAWAII

23, 24 25, 26

1864 Laid Paper

SCOTT NO.	DESCRIPTION	UNUSED NH F	AVG	UNUSED OG F	AVG	USED F	AVG
23	1¢ black	300.00	200.00	230.00	150.00	2000.00	1400.00
24	2¢ black	350.00	220.00	240.00	160.00	920.00	620.00

1865 Wove Paper

SCOTT NO.	DESCRIPTION	UNUSED NH F	AVG	UNUSED OG F	AVG	USED F	AVG
25	1¢ dark blue	375.00	220.00	250.00	170.00	....	....
26	2¢ dark blue	375.00	220.00	250.00	170.00	....	....

27-29, 50-51
King Kamehameha IV

1861-63

SCOTT NO.	DESCRIPTION	UNUSED NH F	AVG	UNUSED OG F	AVG	USED F	AVG
27	2¢ pale rose, horizontal laid paper	400.00	275.00	275.00	185.00	275.00	185.00
28	2¢ pale rose, vertical laid paper	400.00	275.00	275.00	185.00	275.00	185.00

1869 Engraved

SCOTT NO.	DESCRIPTION	UNUSED NH F	AVG	UNUSED OG F	AVG	USED F	AVG
29	2¢ red, thin wove paper	50.00	35.00	40.00	35.00	....	....

30
Princess Kamamalu

31
King Kamehameha IV

32, 39, 52C 33
King Kamehameha V

34
Mataia Kekuanaoa

1864-71 Wove Paper

SCOTT NO.	DESCRIPTION	UNUSED NH F	AVG	UNUSED OG F	AVG	USED F	AVG
30	1¢ purple	12.00	9.00	9.00	7.00	8.50	6.00
31	2¢ rose vermillion	70.00	55.00	52.00	43.00	10.00	7.00
32	5¢ blue	200.00	140.00	150.00	95.00	35.00	25.00
33	6 yellow green	45.00	30.00	30.00	20.00	10.00	7.00
34	18¢ dull rose.	105.00	70.00	80.00	50.00	40.00	28.00

35, 38, 43
King David Kalakaua

36, 46
Prince William Pitt Leleichoku

1875

SCOTT NO.	DESCRIPTION	UNUSED NH F	AVG	UNUSED OG F	AVG	USED F	AVG
35	2¢ brown.	15.00	9.00	6.00	4.00	3.25	2.10
36	12¢ black	110.00	85.00	60.00	38.00	42.00	28.00

37, 42
Princess Likelike

40, 44, 45
King David Kalakaua

41
Queen Kapiolani

47
Statue of King Kamehameha I

48
King William Lunalilo

49
Queen Emma Kaleleonalani

1882

SCOTT NO.	DESCRIPTION	UNUSED NH F	AVG	UNUSED OG F	AVG	USED F	AVG
37	1¢ blue	22.00	11.00	8.00	6.50	7.00	5.00
38	2¢ lilac rose	280.00	110.00	95.00	75.00	45.00	40.00
39	5¢ ultramarine	30.00	14.00	14.00	10.00	4.00	2.75
40	10¢ black	80.00	60.00	40.00	25.00	22.00	18.00
41	15¢ red brown	110.00	75.00	45.00	32.00	26.00	20.00

1883-86

SCOTT NO.	DESCRIPTION	UNUSED NH F	AVG	UNUSED OG F	AVG	USED F	AVG
42	1¢ green	6.00	4.00	3.00	2.00	2.10	1.50
43	2¢ rose	10.00	6.00	3.50	2.50	1.25	.85
44	10¢ red brown	70.00	50.00	25.00	20.00	11.00	7.00
45	10¢ vermillion	75.00	55.00	27.00	22.00	15.00	10.00
46	12¢ red lilac	160.00	85.00	58.00	50.00	35.00	30.00
47	25¢ dark violet	290.00	180.00	120.00	100.00	70.00	55.00
48	50¢ red	300.00	210.00	125.00	100.00	90.00	75.00
49	$1 rose red	500.00	200.00	185.00	155.00	250.00	200.00
50	2¢ Orange Vermillion	150.00	95.00	120.00	90.00	....	....
51	2¢ Carmine	30.00	20.00	25.00	20.00	....	....

52
Queen Liliuokalani

1890-91

SCOTT NO.	DESCRIPTION	UNUSED NH F	AVG	UNUSED OG F	AVG	USED F	AVG
52	2¢ dull violet	12.00	8.00	5.00	3.25	2.00	1.40
52a	6¢ deep indigo	220.00	110.00	77.00	50.00	150.00	100.00

Provisional
GOVT.
1893

1893 Provisional Government
Red Overprint

SCOTT NO.	DESCRIPTION	UNUSED NH F	AVG	UNUSED OG F	AVG	USED F	AVG
53	1¢ purple	14.00	10.00	6.00	4.25	15.00	11.00
54	1¢ blue	14.00	10.00	6.00	4.25	15.00	11.00
55	1¢ green	3.00	2.00	1.50	1.00	4.00	2.75
56	2¢ brown	20.00	14.00	9.00	6.00	25.00	20.00
57	2¢ dull violet	3.00	2.00	1.50	1.00	1.50	1.00
58	5¢ deep indigo	22.00	15.00	11.00	7.00	30.00	22.00
59	5¢ ultramarine	10.00	8.00	6.00	4.00	3.25	1.95
60	6¢ green	26.00	16.00	13.00	9.00	30.00	20.00
61	10¢ black	20.00	17.00	11.00	8.00	17.00	14.00
62	12¢ black	20.00	17.00	9.00	7.00	18.00	14.00
63	12¢ red lilac	300.00	225.00	130.00	95.00	225.00	170.00
64	25¢ dark violet	55.00	35.00	20.00	15.00	50.00	40.00

Black Overprint

SCOTT NO.	DESCRIPTION	UNUSED NH F	AVG	UNUSED OG F	AVG	USED F	AVG
65	2¢ rose vermillion	140.00	80.00	40.00	30.00	85.00	60.00
66	2¢ rose	2.00	1.50	1.20	.80	3.00	2.00
67	10¢ vermillion	38.00	25.00	16.00	10.00	35.00	28.00
68	10¢ red brown	14.00	11.00	7.00	5.00	15.00	10.00
69	12¢ red lilac	510.00	425.00	250.00	175.00	600.00	425.00
70	15¢ red brown	35.00	25.00	17.00	13.00	35.00	25.00
71	18¢ dull rose	55.00	40.00	28.00	22.00	40.00	28.00
72	50¢ red	125.00	90.00	55.00	40.00	100.00	70.00
73	$1 rose red	210.00	170.00	105.00	80.00	190.00	130.00

74, 80
Coat of Arms

75, 81
View of Honolulu

76
Statue of King Kamehameha I

1894

SCOTT NO.	DESCRIPTION	UNUSED NH F	AVG	UNUSED OG F	AVG	USED F	AVG
74	1¢ yellow	4.50	3.25	2.25	1.55	1.40	1.00
75	2¢ brown	4.50	3.25	2.25	1.55	.80	.55
76	5¢ rose lake	10.00	8.50	4.00	2.75	2.00	1.40

77
Star and Palm

78
S.S."Arawa"

79
Pres. S.B. Dole

SCOTT NO.	DESCRIPTION	UNUSED NH F	AVG	UNUSED OG F	AVG	USED F	AVG
77	10¢ yellow green	12.00	9.00	7.00	5.00	6.00	4.00
78	12¢ blue	28.00	23.00	12.00	8.00	18.00	12.00
79	25¢ deep blue	35.00	29.00	15.00	10.00	16.00	11.00

82
Statue of King Kamehameha I

1899

SCOTT NO.	DESCRIPTION	UNUSED NH F	AVG	UNUSED OG F	AVG	USED F	AVG
80	1¢ dark green	3.50	2.00	1.50	1.00	1.50	1.00
81	2¢ rose	3.50	2.00	1.50	1.00	1.50	1.00
82	5¢ blue	13.00	10.00	6.00	4.00	4.00	2.80

O1
Lorrin A. Thurston

1896 OFFICIAL STAMPS

SCOTT NO.	DESCRIPTION	UNUSED NH F	AVG	UNUSED OG F	AVG	USED F	AVG
O1	2¢ green	72.00	50.00	40.00	28.00	20.00	14.00
O2	5¢ black brown	72.00	50.00	40.00	28.00	20.00	14.00
O3	6¢ deep ultramarine	90.00	80.00	40.00	28.00	20.00	14.00
O4	10¢ bright rose	75.00	55.00	40.00	28.00	20.00	14.00
O5	12¢ orange	120.00	90.00	40.00	28.00	20.00	14.00
O6	25¢ gray violet	155.00	110.00	50.00	33.00	20.00	14.00

PHILIPPINES

U.S. Stamps of various issues overprinted

1899
On 260. Unwatermarked

SCOTT NO.	DESCRIPTION	UNUSED NH F	UNUSED NH AVG	UNUSED OG F	UNUSED OG AVG	USED F	USED AVG
212	50¢ orange	975.00	775.00	450.00	325.00	250.00	210.00
	On 279, 279d, 267-68, 281, 282C, 283, 284, 275 Double Line Watermarked						
213	1¢ yellow green	10.50	7.00	14.00	3.00	1.00	.85
214	2¢ orange red	4.00	2.95	1.80	1.25	.85	.60
215	3¢ purple	19.95	14.00	9.75	6.75	1.75	1.30
216	5¢ blue	19.90	14.00	10.00	7.00	1.75	1.25
217	10¢ brown (Type I)	78.00	65.00	35.00	28.00	5.00	3.50
217A	10¢ orange brown (Type II)	350.00	250.00	150.00	125.00	35.00	30.00
218	15¢ olive green	85.00	65.00	45.00	35.00	10.00	8.00
219	50¢ orange	295.00	225.00	150.00	110.00	45.00	39.00
	1901 On 280, 282, 272, 276-78						
220	4¢ orange brown	65.00	48.00	35.00	25.00	6.00	5.00
221	6¢ lake	90.00	70.00	48.00	40.00	7.50	6.00
222	8¢ violet brown	90.00	70.00	48.00	40.00	8.00	6.00
223	$1 black (Type I)	975.00	725.00	550.00	450.00	300.00	255.00
223A	$1 black (Type II)	4800.00	3600.00	3600.00	1800.00	900.00	775.00
224	$2 dark blue	1250.00	900.00	550.00	400.00	400.00	330.00
225	$5 dark green	1600.00	1100.00	950.00	795.00	1000.00	875.00
	1903-04 On 300-313						
226	1¢ blue green	15.00	11.00	8.00	6.50	.50	.40
227	2¢ carmine	18.00	14.00	11.00	8.00	1.35	.95
228	3¢ bright violet	140.00	100.00	85.00	60.00	17.50	11.50
229	4¢ brown	150.00	130.00	100.00	80.00	27.00	18.00
230	5¢ blue	34.00	20.00	19.00	16.00	1.50	.95
231	6¢ brownish lake	175.00	125.00	110.00	75.00	24.50	15.95
232	8¢ violet black	125.00	75.00	70.00	55.00	15.00	11.00
233	10¢ pale red brown	70.00	55.00	35.00	27.00	3.75	2.25
234	13¢ purple black	75.00	50.00	45.00	30.00	20.00	16.00
235	25¢ olive green	135.00	105.00	80.00	65.00	20.00	16.00
236	50¢ orange	250.00	195.00	135.00	105.00	42.50	30.00
237	$1 black	900.00	715.00	550.00	400.00	300.00	250.00
238	$2 dark blue	1800.00	1400.00	1000.00	800.00	900.00	800.00
239	$5 dark green	2100.00	1600.00	1300.00	1050.00	6000.00	5500.00
	On 319						
240	2¢ carmine	15.00	10.00	8.00	6.00	2.75	1.85

SPECIAL DELIVERY STAMPS

1901
U.S. E5 Surcharged

SCOTT NO.	DESCRIPTION	UNUSED NH F	UNUSED NH AVG	UNUSED OG F	UNUSED OG AVG	USED F	USED AVG
E1	10¢ dark blue	250.00	185.00	135.00	95.00	100.00	85.00

POSTAGE DUE STAMPS

1899
U.S. J38-44 overprinted

SCOTT NO.	DESCRIPTION	UNUSED NH F	UNUSED NH AVG	UNUSED OG F	UNUSED OG AVG	USED F	USED AVG
J1	1¢ deep claret	13.00	9.00	8.50	6.00	3.00	2.00
J2	2¢ deep claret	13.00	9.00	8.50	6.00	3.00	2.00
J3	5¢ deep claret	26.00	18.00	17.00	12.00	3.00	2.00
J4	10¢ deep claret	40.00	30.00	25.00	18.00	7.00	5.00
J5	50¢ deep claret	375.00	260.00	230.00	160.00	125.00	85.00
	1901						
J6	3¢ deep claret	30.00	20.00	19.00	13.00	9.00	6.50
J7	30¢ deep claret	475.00	325.00	300.00	200.00	130.00	90.00

PUERTO RICO

1899
U.S. Stamps 279-79B, 281, 272, 282C overprinted

SCOTT NO.	DESCRIPTION	UNUSED NH F	UNUSED NH AVG	UNUSED OG F	UNUSED OG AVG	USED F	USED AVG
210	1¢ yellow green	13.00	9.50	7.50	6.00	1.75	1.15
211	2¢ carmine	10.00	8.00	6.50	4.00	1.65	1.05
212	5¢ blue	26.00	16.00	14.00	10.00	3.00	2.00
213	8¢ violet brown	85.00	60.00	40.00	28.00	26.00	20.00
214	10¢ brown (I)	50.00	38.00	35.00	25.00	7.00	5.00

1900
U.S. 279, 279B overprinted

SCOTT NO.	DESCRIPTION	UNUSED NH F	UNUSED NH AVG	UNUSED OG F	UNUSED OG AVG	USED F	USED AVG
215	1¢ yellow green	17.00	12.00	9.00	5.50	1.75	1.50
216	2¢ carmine	13.00	9.00	7.00	5.00	3.00	2.00

POSTAGE DUE STAMPS

1899
U.S. Postage Due Stamps J38-39, J41 overprinted

SCOTT NO.	DESCRIPTION	UNUSED NH F	UNUSED NH AVG	UNUSED OG F	UNUSED OG AVG	USED F	USED AVG
J1	1¢ deep claret	47.00	36.00	25.00	18.00	8.00	6.60
J2	2¢ deep claret	42.00	34.00	25.00	18.00	7.00	6.00
J3	10¢ deep claret	375.00	300.00	240.00	165.00	75.00	65.00

The Ryukyu Islands were under U.S. administration from April 1, 1945 until May 15, 1972. Prior to the General Issues of 1948, several Provisional Stamps were used.

RYUKYU ISLANDS

1, 1a, 3, 3a

2, 2a, 5, 5a

4, 4a, 6, 6a

7, 7a

1949 Second Printing

White gum & paper, sharp colors; clean perfs.

SCOTT NO.	DESCRIPTION	UNUSED F/NH	F
1-7	**5s to 1y 7 varieties, complete**	**28.75**	**20.50**
1	5s Cycad	3.00	2.75
2	10s Lily	7.00	6.00
3	20s Cycad	4.50	3.75
4	30s Sailing Ship	2.00	1.50
5	40s Lily	2.00	1.50
6	50s Sailing Ship	5.00	4.25
7	1y Farmer	6.75	5.75

1948 First Printing

Thick yellow gum; gray paper; dull colors; rough perfs.

SCOTT NO.	DESCRIPTION	UNUSED F/NH	F
1a-7a	**5s to 1y, 7 varieties, complete**	**525.00**	**425.00**
1a	5s Cycad	3.75	3.75
2a	10s Lily	2.25	2.25
3a	20s Cycad	2.25	2.25
4a	30s Sailing Ship	4.50	3.75
5a	40s Lily	70.00	65.00
6a	50s Sailing Ship	5.00	4.25
7a	1y Farmer	450.00	350.00

8

9

10

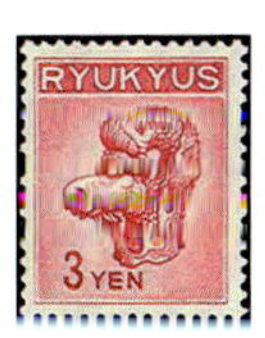

11

12

13

1950

SCOTT NO.	DESCRIPTION	UNUSED F/NH	F
8-13	**50s to 5y, 6 varieties, complete**	**60.00**	**46.00**
8	50s Tile Roof	.30	.25
9	1y Ryukyu Girl	3.50	3.00
10	2y Shuri Castle	10.00	7.00
11	3y Dragon Head	25.00	15.00
12	4y Women at Beach	15.00	15.00
13	5y Seashells	8.00	7.00

NOTE: The 1950 printing of #8 is on toned paper and has yellowish gum. A 1958 printing exhibits white paper and colorless gum.

14

15

1951

SCOTT NO.	DESCRIPTION	UNUSED F/NH	F
14	3y Ryukyu University	55.00	35.00
15	3y Pine Tree	50.00	30.00
16	10y on 50s (no. 8) Type II	10.00	10.00
16a	same, Type I	40.00	40.00
16b	same, Type III	55.00	45.00

18

19

20

21

SCOTT NO.	DESCRIPTION	UNUSED F/NH	F
17	100y on 2y (no. 10)	2150.00	1500.00
18	3y Govt. of Ryukyu	95.00	50.00

Type I—Bars are narrow spaced; "10" normal
Type II—Bars are wide spaced; "10" normal
Type III—Bars are wide spaced; "10" wide spaced

1952-53

SCOTT NO.	DESCRIPTION	UNUSED F/NH	F
19-26	**1y to 100y, 8 varieties, complete**		**50.00**
19	1y Madanbashi Bridge		.35
20	2y Main Hall of Shuri Castle		.40
21	3y Shurei Gate		.50
22	6y Stone Gate, Sogen-ji Temple		3.00
23	10y Benzaiten-do Temple		3.00
24	30y Sonohyan Utaki Altar at Shuri Castle		10.00
25	50y Tamaudun Royal Mausoleum, Shuri		15.00
26	100y Stone Bridge, Hosho Pond, Enkaku Temple		20.00

28

31

29

30

1953

SCOTT NO.	DESCRIPTION	UNUSED F/NH	F
27	3y Reception at Shuri Castle		16.00
28	6y Perry and American Fleet		1.85
29	4y Chofu Ota and Pencil-shaped Matrix		13.00

1954

SCOTT NO.	DESCRIPTION	UNUSED F/NH	F
30	4y Shigo Toma & Pen		15.00

1954-55

SCOTT NO.	DESCRIPTION	UNUSED F/NH	F
31	4y Dachibin Flask (Pottery)		1.25
32	15y Tsuikin Lacquerware (1955)		4.00
33	20y Textile Design (1955)		3.00

SCOTT NO.	DESCRIPTION	UNUSED F/NH

34

35

36

37

38

39

40

1955

34	4y Noguni Shrine & Sweet Potato Plant	15.00

1956

35	4y Stylized Trees	12.00
36	5y Willow Dance	1.25
37	8y Straw Hat Dance	3.00
38	14y Group Dance	5.00
39	4y Dial Telephone	15.00
40	2y Garland, Bamboo & Plum	2.00

41

42

1957

41	4y Map & Pencil Rocket	1.25
42	2y Phoenix	.35

43

44-53

1958

43	4y Ryukyu Stamps	1.00
44-53	**½¢ to $1.00, 10 varieties, complete, ungummed**	**80.00**
44	½¢ Yen, Symbol & Denomination, orange	1.00
45	1¢ same, yellow green	1.60
46	2¢ same, dark blue	2.50
47	3¢ same, deep carmine	1.95
48	4¢ same, bright green	2.75
49	same, orange	5.00
50	10¢ same, aquamarine	6.00
51	25¢ same, bright violet blue	8.00
51a	25¢ same, bright violet blue (with gum)	16.00
52	50¢ same, gray	16.00
52a	50¢ same, gray (with gum)	16.50
53	$1 same, rose lilac	12.00

SCOTT NO.	DESCRIPTION	UNUSED F/NH

54

55

56

57

61, 79

63

54	3¢ Gate of Courtesy	1.50
55	1½¢ Lion Dance	.45

1959

56	3¢ Mountains & Trees	.75
57	3¢ Yonaguni Moth	1.35
58-62	**½¢ to 17¢, 5 varieties, complete**	**44.00**
58	½¢ Hibiscus	.40
59	3¢ Moorish Idol	1.00
60	8¢ Seashell	16.00
61	13¢ Dead Leaf Butterfly	3.25
62	17¢ Jellyfish	28.00
63	1½¢ Toy (Yakaji)	.80

64

65, 81

72

73

74

75

1960

64	3¢ University Badge	1.10

DANCES II

65-68	**1¢-10¢, 4 varieties, complete**	**6.75**
65	1¢ Munjuru	2.25
66	2½¢ Nutwabushi	3.50
67	5¢ Hatomabushi	1.20
68	10¢ Hanafubushi	1.25
72	3¢ Torch & Nago Bay	7.50
73	8¢ Runners at Startling Line	1.25
74	3¢ Egret & Rising Sun	6.00
75	1½¢ Okinawa Bull Fight	2.00

1960-61 REDRAWN INSCRIPTION

76-80	**½¢ to 17¢, 5 varieties, complete**	**19.00**
76	½¢ Hibiscus	.85
77	3¢ Moorish Idol	1.50
78	8¢ Seashell	1.75
79	13¢ Dead Leaf Butterfly	2.00
80	17¢ Jellyfish	14.00

WITH "RYUKYUS" ADDED
1961-64

SCOTT NO.	DESCRIPTION	UNUSED F/NH
81-87	**1¢ to $1.00, 8 varieties, Dancers, complete**	**16.00**
81	1¢ Munjuru	.30
82	2½¢ Nutwabushi (1962)	.30
83	5¢ Hatomabushi (1962)	.45
84	10¢ Hanafubushi (1962)	.65
84A	20¢ Shudun (1964)	4.00
85	25¢ Haodori (1962)	1.50
86	50¢ Nubui Kuduchi	3.00
87	$1 Koteibushi	7.00

88 89 90 91 92

1961

SCOTT NO.	DESCRIPTION	UNUSED F/NH
88	3¢ Pine Tree	1.95
89	3¢ Naha, Steamer & Sailboat	2.50
90	3¢ White Silver Temple	3.00
91	3¢ Books & Bird	1.60
92	1½¢ Eagles & Rising Sun	2.50

93 95 98 105 97 103 104

1962

SCOTT NO.	DESCRIPTION	UNUSED F/NH
93	1½¢ Steps, Trees & Building	.75
94	3¢ GRI Building	1.00
95	3¢ Malaria Eradication	.70
96	8¢ Eradication Emblem	1.10
97	3¢ Children's Day	1.50
98-102	**½¢ to 17¢ varieties, Flowers, complete**	**3.05**
98	½¢ Sea Hibiscus	.50
99	3¢ Indian Coral Tree	.45
100	8¢ Iju	.70
101	13¢ Touch-Me-Not	.90
102	17¢ Shell Flower	1.60
103	3¢ Earthenware	4.00
104	3¢ Japanese Fencing	4.00
105	1½¢ Bingata Cloth	1.25

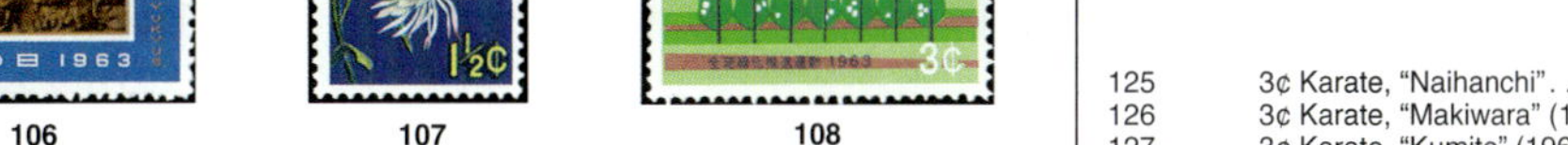
106 107 108

110 109 111

1963

SCOTT NO.	DESCRIPTION	UNUSED F/NH
106	3¢ Stone Relief	1.20
107	1½¢ Gooseneck Cactus	.35
108	3¢ Trees & Hills	1.20
109	3¢ Map of Okinawa	1.50
110	3¢ Hawks & Islands	1.25
111	3¢ Shioya Bridge	1.25

112 113 114 115 116 117

SCOTT NO.	DESCRIPTION	UNUSED F/NH
112	3¢ Tsuikin-wan Lacquerware Bowl	3.25
113	3¢ Map of Far East	1.00
114	15¢ Hamaomoto Plant	2.25
115	3¢ Nakagusuku Castle Site	.95
116	3¢ Human Rights	1.00
117	1½¢ Dragon	.75

118 119 120, 120a 121 122, 122a 123 124

1964

SCOTT NO.	DESCRIPTION	UNUSED F/NH
118	3¢ Mother's Day - Carnation	.50
119	3¢ Agricultural Census - Pineapples & Sugar Cane	.50
120	3¢ Minsah Obi Sash, rose pink	.65
120a	same, deep carmine	.90
121	3¢ Girl Scout & Emblem	.50
122	3¢ Shuri Relay Station	.90
122a	3¢ same, inverted "1"	40.00
123	8¢ Parabolic Antenna & map	1.50
124	3¢ Gate of Courtesy, Olympic Torch, & Emblem	.40

125 126 127

1964-65

SCOTT NO.	DESCRIPTION	UNUSED F/NH
125	3¢ Karate, "Naihanchi"	.70
126	3¢ Karate, "Makiwara" (1965)	.60
127	3¢ Karate, "Kumite" (1965)	.60

SCOTT NO.	DESCRIPTION	UNUSED F/NH

128 129

1964

128	3¢ Miyara Dunchi	.40
129	1½¢ Snake & Iris	.40

130 131 132 133 134 135 136 139

1965

130	3¢ Boy Scouts	.60
131	3¢ Onoyama Stadium	.35
132	3¢ Samisen of King Shoko	.60
133	3¢ Kin Power Plant	.35
134	3¢ ICY and United Nations	.30
135	3¢ Naha City Hall	.30

1965-66

136	3¢ Chinese Box Turtle	.40
137	3¢ Hawksbill Turtle (1966)	.40
138	3¢ Asian Terrapin (1966)	.40

1965

139	1½¢ Horse	.30

140 141 143 146 144 145

1966

140	3¢ Noguchi's Okinawa Woodpecker	.30
141	3¢ Sika Deer	.35
142	3¢ Dugong	.35
143	3¢ Ryukyu Bungalow Swallow	.30
144	3¢ Memorial Day - Lilies & Ruins	.30
145	3¢ University of the Ryukyus	.30
146	3¢ Chunkin Ukuhan Lacquerware	.30

147 148 149 150

147	3¢ UNESCO Emblem & Tile-roofed House	.30
148	3¢ Government Museum & Dragon Statue	.30
149	3¢ Nakasone Toyomiya Genga's Tomb	.30
150	1½¢ Ram in Iris Wreath	.30

SCOTT NO.	DESCRIPTION	UNUSED F/NH

151 156

1966-67

151-55	**5 varieties, Fish, complete**	**1.70**
151	3¢ Clown Fish	.30
152	3¢ Young Boxfish (1967)	.35
153	3¢ Forceps Fish (1967)	.45
154	3¢ Spotted Triggerfish (1967)	.40
155	3¢ Saddleback Butterflyfish (1967)	.40

1966

156	3¢ Tsuboya Urn	.30

157 162 163 164 165 166 167 168

1967-68

157-61	**5 varieties, Seashells, complete**	**1.95**
157	3¢ Episcopal Miter	.30
158	3¢ Venus Comb Murex	.30
159	3¢ Chiragra Spider	.35
160	3¢ Green Turban	.35
161	3¢ Bubble Conch	.75
162	3¢ Red-tiled Roofs & ITY Emblem	.30
163	3¢ Mobile TB Clinic Bus	.30
164	3¢ Hojo Bridge, Enkaku Temple	.30
165	1½¢ Monkey	.30
166	3¢ TV Tower & Map	.35

169 170 171 172 173

1968

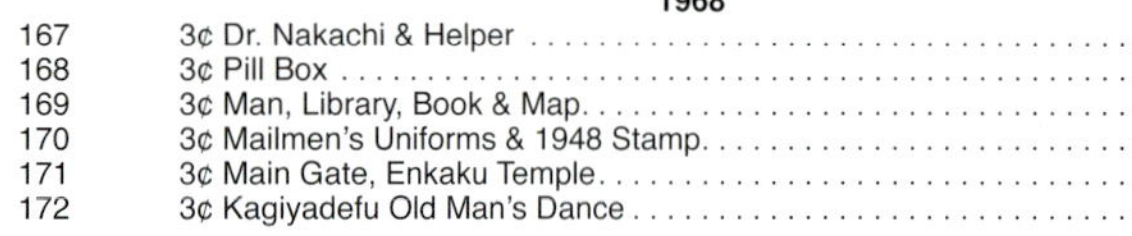

167	3¢ Dr. Nakachi & Helper	.35
168	3¢ Pill Box	.50
169	3¢ Man, Library, Book & Map	.45
170	3¢ Mailmen's Uniforms & 1948 Stamp	.40
171	3¢ Main Gate, Enkaku Temple	.40
172	3¢ Kagiyadefu Old Man's Dance	.40

SCOTT NO.	DESCRIPTION	UNUSED F/NH

1968-69

173-77	**5 varieties, Crabs, complete**	**2.35**
173	3¢ Mictyris Longicarpus	.40
174	3¢ Uca dubia stimpson (1969)	.45
175	3¢ Baptozius vinosus (1969)	.45
176	3¢ Cardisoma carnifex (1969)	.60
177	3¢ Ocypode ceratophthalma pallas (1969)	.60

178

179

180

1968

178	3¢ Saraswati Pavilion	.40
179	3¢ Tennis Player	.40
180	1½¢ Cock & Iris	.30

181

182

183

184

1969

181	3¢ Boxer	.40
182	3¢ Ink Slab Screen	.60
183	3¢ Antennas & Map	.35
184	3¢ Gate of Courtesy & Emblems	.35

185

186

187

188

189

1969-70

185-89	**5 varieties, Folklore, complete**	**2.70**
185	3¢ Tug of War Festival	.45
186	3¢ Hari Boat Race	.45
187	3¢ Izaiho Ceremony, Kudaka Island	.45
188	3¢ Mortar Drum Dance (1970)	.75
189	3¢ Sea God Dance (1970)	.75

SCOTT NO.	DESCRIPTION	UNUSED F/NH

193

191

192

194

改 ½¢

(surcharge)
190

1969

190	½¢ on 3¢ (no. 99) Indian Coral Tree	1.25
191	3¢ Nakamura-ke Farm House	.35
192	3¢ Statue & Maps	.60
193	1½¢ Dog & Flowers	.30
194	3¢ Sake Flask	.35

195

196

197

198

199

200

195-99	**5 varieties, Classic Opera, complete**	**2.85**
195	3¢ "The Bell"	.75
196	3¢ Child & Kidnapper	.75
197	3¢ Robe of Feathers	.75
198	3¢ Vengeance of Two Young Sons	.75
199	3¢ Virgin & the Dragon	.75
195-99a	**5 varieties, complete, sheets of 4**	**26.00**
195a	3¢ sheet of 4	5.75
196a	3¢ sheet of 4	5.75
197a	3¢ sheet of 4	5.75
198a	3¢ sheet of 4	5.75
199a	3¢ sheet of 4	5.75
200	3¢ Underwater Observatory	.40

201

204

205

206

207

1970-71 Portraits

201	3¢ Noboru Jahana	.60
202	3¢ Saion Gushichan Bunjaku	1.00
203	3¢ Choho Giwan (1971)	.65

1970

204	3¢ Map & People	.35
205	3¢ Great Cycad of Une	.35
206	3¢ Japanese Flag, Diet & Map of Ryukyus	1.10
207	1½¢ Boar & Cherry Blossoms	.30

208 210 212

213 214 215

1971

SCOTT NO.	DESCRIPTION	UNUSED F/NH
208-12	**5 varieties, Workers, complete**	**2.10**
208	3¢ Low Hand Loom	.40
209	3¢ Woman Running Filature	.40
210	3¢ Farmer Wearing Palm Bark Raincoat & Kuba Leaf Hat	.45
211	3¢ Woman Hulling Rice	.55
212	3¢ Fisherman's Box & Scoop	.45
213	3¢ Water Carrier	.45
214	3¢ Old & New Naha with City Emblem	.30
215	2¢ Madder (Sandanka)	.30
216	3¢ Ogocho (Caesalpinia pulcherrima)	.30

217 218 220

221 222 223

1971-72 Government Parks

SCOTT NO.	DESCRIPTION	UNUSED F/NH
217	3¢ View from Mabuni Hill	.30
218	3¢ Mt. Arashi from Haneji Sea	.30
219	4¢ Yabuchi Island from Yakena Port (1972)	.35

1971

SCOTT NO.	DESCRIPTION	UNUSED F/NH
220	4¢ Dancer	.30
221	4¢ Deva King	.30
222	2¢ Rat & Chrysanthemums	.30
223	4¢ Student Nurse	.30

224 225

226 227 228

1972

SCOTT NO.	DESCRIPTION	UNUSED F/NH
224	5¢ Birds & Seashore	.55
225	5¢ Coral Reef	.55
226	5¢ Sun Over Islands	.55
227	5¢ Dove & Flags	.95
228	5¢ Antique Sake Pot	.70

C1-3 C4-8

AIR POST STAMPS

1950

SCOTT NO.	DESCRIPTION	UNUSED F/NH
C1	8y Dove & Map, bright blue	140.00
C2	12y same, green	30.00
C3	16y same, rose carmine	10.00

1951-54

SCOTT NO.	DESCRIPTION	UNUSED F/NH
C4-8	**13y to 50y, 5 varieties, complete**	**26.00**
C4	13y Heavenly Maiden, blue	3.00
C5	18y same, green	4.00
C6	30y same, cerise	5.00
C7	40y same, red violet (1954)	7.00
C8	50y same, yellow orange (1954)	8.00

C9-13 C14-18 (surcharge) C19-23

C24 C29 C30

1957

SCOTT NO.	DESCRIPTION	UNUSED F/NH
C9-13	**15y to 60y, 5 varieties, complete**	**70.00**
C9	15y Maiden Playing Flute, blue green	8.00
C10	20y same, rose carmine	12.00
C11	35y same, yellow green	14.00
C12	45y same, reddish brown	18.00
C13	60y same, gray	20.00

1959

SCOTT NO.	DESCRIPTION	UNUSED F/NH
C14-18	**9¢ to 35¢, 5 varieties, complete**	**42.00**
C14	9¢ on 15y (no. C9)	3.00
C15	14¢ on 20y (no. C10)	4.00
C16	19¢ on 35y (no. C11)	8.00
C17	27¢ on 45y (no. C12)	15.00
C18	35¢ on 60y (no. C13)	14.00

1960

SCOTT NO.	DESCRIPTION	UNUSED F/NH
C19-23	**9¢ to 35¢, 5 varieties, complete**	**23.00**
C19	9¢ on 4y (no. 31)	3.00
C20	14¢ on 5y (no. 36)	4.00
C21	19¢ on 15y (no. 32)	3.00
C22	27¢ on 14y (no. 38)	8.00
C23	35¢ on 20y (no. 33)	6.00

1961

SCOTT NO.	DESCRIPTION	UNUSED F/NH
C24-28	**9¢ to 35¢, 5 varieties, complete**	**8.75**
C24	9¢ Heavenly Maiden	.45
C25	14¢ Maiden Playing Flute	.95
C26	19¢ Wind God	1.25
C27	27¢ Wind God, at right	4.00
C28	35¢ Maiden Over Tree Tops	3.00

1963

SCOTT NO.	DESCRIPTION	UNUSED F/NH
C29	5½¢ Jet & Gate of Courtesy	.35
C30	7¢ Jet Plane	.40

E1

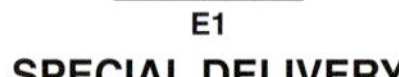

SPECIAL DELIVERY

1950

SCOTT NO.	DESCRIPTION	UNUSED F/NH
E1	5y Dragon & Map of Ryukyus	30.00

HOW TO WRITE YOUR ORDER

PLEASE USE ORDER FORM

1.) Please use black or blue ink (NO PENCIL) and print all requested information (name, address, etc.)
2.) Indicate quantity, country (U.S., UN, Canada or province), catalog number, item description (single, plate block, etc.)
3.) Specify condition (F, VF, NH, etc.) and check whether it is mint or used
4.) Enter price as listed in this catalog
5.) Total all purchases, adding shipping/handling charge from table below. Alabama residents (only) also add sales tax.
6.) Payment may be made by check, money order, or credit card (VISA, Discover, American Express or Mastercard are accepted). ORDERS FROM OUTSIDE THE UNITED STATES MUST BE PAID WITH A CREDIT CARD and all payments must be made in U.S. funds.

SHIPPING AND HANDLING CHARGES*
Safe delivery is guaranteed. We assume all losses.

If ordering STAMPS ONLY Orders under $150.00 .... add $5.95
If order includes supply items and totals
Orders under $50.00 .... add $6.95
Orders from $50.00 to $149.99 .... add $9.95
Orders from $150.00 to $299.99 .... add $12.95
Orders over $300.................................. add $15.95

*The following charges may not fully cover the actual postage or freight, insurance and handling cost for foreign orders, and additional charges may be added.

RETURN POLICY

H.E. Harris offers a 30 day money-back guarantee on every item. The customer has 30 days to examine, grade (at customer's expense) and evaluate every stamp to insure customer satisfaction. If the customer is not completely satisfied with their purchase, they can return it for a full refund or exchange:

- Call 1-800-546-2995, for a Return Authorization Number. You will not receive a credit for the product returned unless you have a Return Authorization Number. The Return Authorization Number must be written on the outside of all boxes returned.
- Please keep a list of the products being sent back.

The credit will be processed after we receive your return. Please allow 4 weeks for the return to show on the account. Sorry, we cannot accept C.O.D. freight or refund the original or return shipping costs. If you have questions about returning a product, please contact our customer service department at 1-800-546-2995 during normal business hours, 8 a.m. to 5 p.m. Central Standard Time.

H.E. HARRIS PERFORMANCE PLEDGE

- All stamps are genuine, exactly as described, and have been inspected by our staff experts.
- H.E. Harris & Co. upholds the standards set forth by the American Philatelic Society and the American Stamp Dealers Association.
- If you have any problem with your order, please call our customer service department at 1-800-546-2995. We will handle it to your complete satisfaction.

NOTES

Worldwide Postage Stamp Packet
33 Different Stamps!

FREE gift for readers of the HARRIS STAMP CATALOG

Complete and mail this card to receive a FREE (1) Worldwide Stamp Packet.

1. What part of the *Harris Catalog* do you like most?
2. Where did you buy your *Harris Catalog*?
3. What year were you born?
4. How long have you been collecting stamps?
5. What is your favorite stamp or era to collect?
6. Are you looking to sell a stamp collection?
   ☐ Yes ☐ No
7. What other things do you collect?

33 different Worldwide Stamps

BONUS WEB OFFER:
Receive a coupon for $10 off at heharris.com

PLEASE PRINT

Name

Address

City

State Zip

Email

Phone

Offer good in contiguous US only. Postcard must be fully completed to receive one (1) Worldwide Stamp Packet. While supplies last. Limit one offer per address. ***Items may be substituted***. You will receive a coupon code by email or by mail for $10 off a purchase of $35.00 or more at heharris.com. Please allow 8-12 weeks for delivery. Offer expires on 12/31/2026. No cash value. Void where prohibited by law.

By providing your email address, you agree to receive email communications from Whitman-CDN Publishing, LLC, including special offers, updates, and news. We respect your privacy. Your information will not be sold or shared. You may unsubscribe from our emails at any time.

View our Privacy Policy at heharris.com/privacy-policy/

A Guide Book of Collectible Postcards

Updated and revised 7th edition!
224 pages, full color, $19.95

How to Collect Stamps, 7th Edition

Every stamp collector benefits from H.E. Harris & Co.'s over 100 years of experience. How to Collect Stamps is a fascinating guide for the beginner and a valuable source of data for the established philatelist.

- Step-by-step guide to stamp collecting
- Philatelic history by country
- Worldwide and U.S. stamp identifier
- Collector's dictionary
- Detailed map with over 400 countries
- Over 600 color images

Modern Liberty Binder

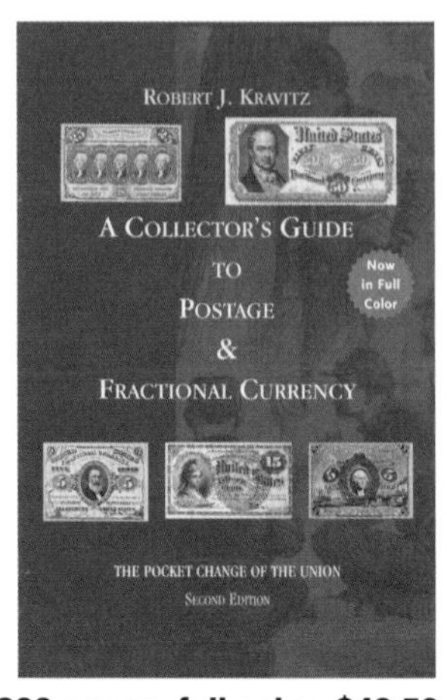

200 pages, full color, $49.50

***A Collector's Guide to Postage & Fractional Currency,* 2nd Edition** by Robert J. Kravitz earned the 2004 Literary Award from the Professional Currency Dealers Association (PCDA) and quickly became a must-have reference for collectors. This updated and expanded edition delivers the latest market trends and pricing for U.S. postage and fractional currency, less-than-one-dollar notes authorized for daily, denomination transactions during the Civil War in response to the hoarding of coins by the general public—plus more than twenty pages of new, in-depth research and never-before-published historical details about this important numismatic chapter in America's history."

Call 1-800-546-2995 to order, or visit heharris.com

Catalog or Stock No.	Qty.	Description	Mint	Used	Unit Price	Total Price
				TOTAL THIS SIDE		

4001 Helton Drive, Bldg. A • Florence, AL 35630
www.heharris.com
You may also order by phone 1-800-546-2995 or Fax 1-256-246-1116

See Page 290 for Return Policy.

Make payment in U.S. dollars by personal check, money order, Visa, Master Card, Discover or American Express. Please do not send cash.

Orders for shipment outside the U.S. must be paid by credit card and shipping charges will be added.

We Thank You For Your Order!

RUSH SHIPMENT TO:

Name ______________________________

Address ______________________________

City/State/Zip ______________________________

Phone *(in case of question about your order)* ______________________________

FAST CREDIT CARD ORDERING

☐ VISA ☐ mastercard ☐ DISCOVER ☐ AMERICAN EXPRESS

Card # ______________________________

Expiration Date ______________ CVV ______________

Signature ______________________________

Catalog or Stock No.	Qty.	Description	Mint	Used	Unit Price	Total Price

Shipping & Handling

If ordering STAMPS ONLY Orders under $150.00..................add $5.95

If order includes supply items and totals

- Orders under $50.00..add $6.95
- Orders from $50.00 to $149.99 ....add $9.95
- Orders from $150.00 to $299.99 ....add $12.95
- Orders over $300..add $15.95

Foreign orders: S&H will be added separately.

Please apply your tax rate if you live in the following states: AL, AR, GA, IL, IN, IA, KS, KY, MI, MN, NE, NV, NJ, NC, ND, NY, OH, OK, PA, RI, SD, TN, UT, VT, VA, WA, WV, WI, WY

TOTAL FRONT	
TOTAL REVERSE	
DISCOUNTS–If applicable	
SUBTOTAL	
SHIPPING CHARGE	
SALES TAX IF APPLICABLE	
TOTAL PURCHASE	

For Office Use Only

2026-PSC

Catalog or Stock No.	Qty.	Description	Mint	Used	Unit Price	Total Price
					TOTAL THIS SIDE	

4001 Helton Drive, Bldg. A • Florence, AL 35630
www.heharris.com
You may also order by phone 1-800-546-2995 or Fax 1-256-246-1116

See Page 290 for Return Policy.

Make payment in U.S. dollars by personal check, money order, Visa, Master Card, Discover or American Express. Please do not send cash.

Orders for shipment outside the U.S. must be paid by credit card and shipping charges will be added.

We Thank You For Your Order!

RUSH SHIPMENT TO:

Name ____________________

Address ____________________

City/State/Zip ____________________

Phone *(in case of question about your order)* ____________________

FAST CREDIT CARD ORDERING

☐ VISA ☐ mastercard ☐ DISCOVER ☐ AMERICAN EXPRESS

Card # ____________________

Expiration Date __________ CVV __________

Signature ____________________

Catalog or Stock No.	Qty.	Description	Mint	Used	Unit Price	Total Price

Shipping & Handling

If ordering STAMPS ONLY Orders under $150.00..................add $5.95
If order includes supply items and totals
- Orders under $50.00..................add $6.95
- Orders from $50.00 to $149.99..................add $9.95
- Orders from $150.00 to $299.99..................add $12.95
- Orders over $300..................add $15.95

Foreign orders: S&H will be added separately.

Please apply your tax rate if you live in the following states:
AL, AR, GA, IL, IN, IA, KS, KY, MI, MN, NE, NV, NJ, NC, ND, NY, OH, OK, PA, RI, SD, TN, UT, VT, VA, WA, WV, WI, WY

TOTAL FRONT	
TOTAL REVERSE	
DISCOUNTS–If applicable	
SUBTOTAL	
SHIPPING CHARGE	
SALES TAX IF APPLICABLE	
TOTAL PURCHASE	

For Office Use Only

2026-PSC

Note: Coupon ONLY valid with order of $50.00 or more from the H.E. Harris 2026 Stamp Catalog. Copies of coupon will not be accepted. Please include this coupon with order and payment. **If placing order by phone, please mention code US**. Coupon expires December 31, 2026.

Note: Coupon ONLY valid with order of $300.00 or more from the H.E. Harris 2026 Stamp Catalog. Copies of coupon will not be accepted. Please include this coupon with order and payment. **If placing order by phone, please mention code US**. Coupon expires December 31, 2026.

Note: Coupon ONLY valid with order of $1000.00 or more from the H.E. Harris 2026 Stamp Catalog. Copies of coupon will not be accepted. Please include this coupon with order and payment. **If placing order by phone, please mention code US**. Coupon expires December 31, 2026.

Note: Coupon ONLY valid with order of $50.00 or more from the H.E. Harris 2026 Stamp Catalog. Copies of coupon will not be accepted. Please include this coupon with order and payment. **If placing order by phone, please mention code US**. Coupon expires December 31, 2026.

Note: Coupon ONLY valid with order of $300.00 or more from the H.E. Harris 2026 Stamp Catalog. Copies of coupon will not be accepted. Please include this coupon with order and payment. **If placing order by phone, please mention code US**. Coupon expires December 31, 2026.

Note: Coupon ONLY valid with order of $1000.00 or more from the H.E. Harris 2026 Stamp Catalog. Copies of coupon will not be accepted. Please include this coupon with order and payment. **If placing order by phone, please mention code US**. Coupon expires December 31, 2026.